# REMEDIES: PUBLIC AND PRIVATE

## Second Edition

By

**David Schoenbrod**
*Professor of Law*
*New York Law School*

**Angus Macbeth**
*Sidley & Austin*
*Washington, D.C.*

**David I. Levine**
*Professor of Law*
*University of California*
*Hastings College of the Law*

**David J. Jung**
*Professor of Law*
*University of California*
*Hastings College of the Law*

AMERICAN CASEBOOK SERIES®

WEST PUBLISHING CO.
ST. PAUL, MINN., 1996

610 Opperman Drive
P.O. Box 64526
St. Paul, MN 55164–0526
1–800–328–9352



**Library of Congress Cataloging-in-Publication Data**

Remedies : public and private / by David Schoenbrod . . . [et al.] — 2nd ed.
p. cm. — (American casebook series)
Includes index.
ISBN 0–314–06778–7
1. Remedies (Law)—United States—Cases. I. Schoenbrod, David. II. Series.
KF9010.A7R46 1996
347.73'7—dc20
[347.3077] 96–372
CIP

**ISBN** 0–314–06778–7

TEXT IS PRINTED ON 10% POST CONSUMER RECYCLED PAPER

Printed with Printwise
Environmentally Advanced Water Washable Ink

*For our families, especially Jan, JoAnn*
*Joanna and Jennifer*
*and in memory of those whose names*
*are blessings to us*

*

# Preface to the Second Edition

Our goals in writing this book are described in the preface to the first edition. They have not changed in preparing the second edition. Above all, we remain committed to providing remedies teachers and students with materials that are coherent, intellectually stimulating, and pedagogically sound. We also remain convinced that studying the way remedies operate in the public law context is critical to a full understanding of the subject.

Overall, the structure and organization of the casebook have changed only slightly since the first edition. To get the course off to a faster start, the first edition's chapter 2, which explored the source and nature of the courts' power to create new remedies, has been streamlined and consolidated with chapter 1. The material on damages has been reorganized to make it more accessible, and the coverage of traditional, private law topics has been expanded somewhat. To recognize the growing scholarly and practical interest in the law of restitution, restitution now has its own chapter.

The past six years have been busy ones for the Supreme Court of the United States in the remedies area, and those developments are well represented in this edition. Some recent developments the second edition includes are decisions on the scope of injunctive relief, the modification and termination of consent decrees, the availability of provisional relief and attorneys' fees, and the constitutional regulation of punitive damages and forfeiture practices. We have avoided, however, change for change's sake, and have introduced new cases only when they represent new developments in the law of remedies, or when experience has proven them to be better teaching tools.

There are many people whom we would like to thank for their contributions to this edition. We are particularly grateful to Russell Pearce for his helpful advice and suggestions. Our student assistants were invaluable; in particular, we would like to acknowledge: Lauren Black, James Fraser, Melanie Goldberg, Karen Kochevar, Noel Lawrence, Jennifer Lehman, James Ponichtera, Kathleen Royle, Cyrus Wadia and Jane Ann Whitchurch. Stephen R. Lothrop and Barbara Topchov at Hastings College of the Law provided invaluable technical assistance in the preparation of the manuscript. Once again, Hastings College of the Law and New York Law School helped us to complete this project on schedule by supporting our research in a number of ways.

DS
AM
DIL
DJJ

April, 1996

*

# Preface to the First Edition

We believe a remedies casebook should meet four needs:

*First, a remedies book should cover the essential topics of remedies law.* Most law schools offer a single remedies course which reviews the damages issues covered piecemeal in first-year courses, such as torts and contracts, and introduces restitution and equitable remedies. Most remedies casebooks cover this material exclusively from the perspective of private law litigation. Our book, as the title suggests, treats remedies in both public and private law cases. Remedies in public law cases are an important topic in practice, important to society, and indeed important to a full understanding of remedies in private law cases. Some existing remedies casebooks do make a bow in the direction of public law remedies, but they usually limit their coverage to the structural injunction, without considering how the full panoply of remedies—damages, injunctions, and restitution—can be applied to public law problems. Moreover, by focusing only on civil rights cases, those books don't do justice to the administrative and regulatory cases that students are far more likely to encounter once they are in practice. Finally, administrative law cases, particularly those enforcing regulatory prohibitions and correcting agency errors, often provide some of the best examples of courts trying to state and apply general remedial principles.

*Second, a remedies book should treat the topic in a coherent way.* In particular, it must be built around a perspective that the teacher can use to make a whole of the many elements that the remedies course combines. The traditional organization of a remedies book subordinates the remedy to the substantive law, classifying the material in whole or in part by cause of action: remedies for damage to chattel, remedies for damage to land, remedies for breach of contract, etc. We believe that there is more to be learned by adopting a transsubstantive approach to remedies. By organizing the material around the remedy, and not the substantive law, our materials allow the professor and the student to explore the concerns that are common to remedial issues in whatever substantive context they arise.

To offer an example, although the remedial problems in, say, a contracts case, a judicial review of administrative action, and a school desegregation case look quite different on the surface, the courts approaching these cases will share common institutional concerns—concerns about their ability to dictate wisely future conduct and the legitimacy of their doing so. Courts in each of these three kinds of cases are therefore inclined to use tactics designed to, in essence, remand the question of future conduct to the defendant. So the contracts remedy is likely to be damages rather than specific performance, the judicial review remedy is likely to be a remand to the agency, and the school desegregation remedy is likely to be a requirement that the school board design a plan to end the violation. Where such approaches result in harm to important interests, the courts become more intrusive, but usually only in graduated increments designed to minimize the impact on judicial capacity.

*Third, a remedies book should offer intellectual stimulation to the students as well as the teacher.* The remedies course can be exciting if it addresses the root questions and deadly dull if it does no more than rehearse doctrine. Our book confronts the root questions frontally and from the outset. Chapter one asks: What does it mean to remedy a wrong? How much discretion should a judge have? How should that discretion be exercised? Chapter two presents some of the rare opinions that openly address these questions. This material raises issues of legitimacy, comity, judicial competence and judicial convenience, which go far to explain judicial conduct in all areas of remedies.

We go on to relate these root questions to the material in the balance of the book, emphasizing material that is not usually covered in other remedies casebooks. For example, we have included a chapter which contrasts civil and criminal penalties, including punitive damages. This juxtaposition raises particularly exciting and sometimes disturbing questions about the use of judicial and legislative power to achieve remedial goals.

*Fourth, a remedies book should teach well.* Our concern with pedagogy is reflected in a number of features of the book.

> —*The book uses text and secondary sources to teach the basics.* The students in the remedies course, having already completed their first year, are entirely familiar with, if not jaded by, the case method and have encountered remedies issues in their first year courses. Using cases to teach them those basics that they can absorb by reading text wastes time better spent on the hard issues.
>
> —*The book uses problems.* We have used one basic fact pattern, styled *Country Lodge v. Miller,* in various problems throughout the casebook. Its recurrence helps to illustrate a variety of issues and encourages a comparison of remedial outcomes in various contexts. We have usually made *Country Lodge* a private law problem to prompt students to find transsubstantive remedial principles in the public law cases that the book frequently features. We have used other fact patterns in problems which did not lend themselves to the *Country Lodge* format, particularly where the problems are based on actual cases.
>
> —*We have resisted the temptation to follow the cases with a profusion of leading questions.* When we have information to convey or an opinion to offer, we make a statement. When we want students to ponder a question, we leave the question unanswered

(except for a citation or two to helpful material). We have limited the number of questions so that students can reasonably be expected to read and consider all of them with care, even though the professor undoubtedly will discuss only some in class.

Although the topic is old and enduring, courts and scholars have far to go in explaining how the law provides remedies. We have enjoyed writing and teaching from these materials because of a sense that we were creating a more coherent way of looking at an important, and all too often jumbled topic. We hope that those who use the book will find that the intellectual stimulation that we have enjoyed will rub off.

---

We have adopted several standard editorial conventions. In editing the judicial opinions and other material, we have eliminated nonessential citations and footnotes without so specifying. Numbered footnotes retain the original numbering. Author-supplied footnotes are lettered rather than numbered. Other omissions are indicated with a series of asterisks.

In the course of the preparation of these materials, we have had the benefit of the suggestions of many professional colleagues, including Philip P. Frickey, Quintin Johnstone, Mary Kay Kane, and John Sexton. We also wish to recognize the intellectual debt we owe to Dan Dobbs, Owen Fiss and Douglas Laycock. Many students who used these materials in earlier forms provided helpful suggestions. Our student assistants provided indispensable help. In particular, we wish to acknowledge Lara Bierman, John Cusker, Andres Diaz, Judy Ganley, James Gregory, David Hays, Stephanie Irey, Carol Johnston, Alice McGill, Eddie Schrock, Lupe Valencia, Seth Watkins, and Jennifer Ways. The technical assistance of Eric Noble and Linda Haumant was invaluable in preparing the manuscript. Hastings and New York Law School helped us to complete this project on schedule by supporting our research in a number of ways.

DS
New York, New York
AM
Washington, D.C.
DIL
DJJ
San Francisco, California

April, 1990

*

# Acknowledgements

The authors wish to acknowledge the following permissions to reprint copyrighted material:

Alexander Bickel, "The Least Dangerous Branch." Copyright © by Yale University Press. Reprinted by permission.

James J. Brown, "Collecting a Judgment," 13 Litigation 31 (1986).

Guido Calabresi & Douglas Melamed, "Property Rules, Liability Rules, and Inalienability: One View of the Cathedral," 85 Harv.L.Rev. 1089 (1972). Copyright © 1972 by the Harvard Law Review Association.

Abram Chayes, "The Role of the Judge in Public Law Litigation," 82 Harv.L.Rev. 1281 (1976). Copyright © 1976 by the Harvard Law Review Association.

Paul Dimond, "*Brown* and the Transformation of the Constitution: Concluding Remarks," 61 Fordham L.Rev. 63, 65–66 (1992).

Dan B. Dobbs, "Contempt of Court: A Survey." Copyright © 1971 by Cornell University and Dan B. Dobbs. All Rights Reserved. This article originally appeared in Volume 56, Number 2 of the Cornell Law Review at page 186.

John F. Dobbyn, "Contempt Power of the Equity Court over Outside Agitators," 8 St.Mary's L.J. 1,7 (1976).

William Drayton, "Economic Law Enforcement," 4 Harv.Envr.L.Rev. 1 (1980). Copied with the permission of the Harvard Environmental Law Review. Copyright © 1980 by the President and Fellows of Harvard College.

Judge Frank A. Easterbrook, "Civil Rights and Remedies," 14 Harv.J.L. & Pub.Pol. 103, 103–104 (1991).

Lisa W. Foderaro, "Threat of Yonkers Layoffs Jolts Foes of Housing Plan." Copyright © 1989 by New York Times Company. Reprinted by permission.

Daniel Friedmann, "Restitution of Benefits Obtained Through the Appropriation of Property or the Commission of a Wrong." Copyright ©1980 by the Directors of the Columbia Law Review Association, Inc. All Rights Reserved. This article originally appeared at 80 Colum.L.Rev. 504 (1980). Reprinted by permission.

Lon Fuller and William Perdue, "The Reliance Interest in Contract Damages." Reprinted by permission of The Yale Law Journal Company and Fred B. Rothman & Company from The Yale Law Journal, Vol. 46, pp. 52–96.

Charles J. Goetz and Robert E. Scott, "Measuring Sellers' Damages: The Lost Profits Puzzle," 31 Stanford L.Rev. 323 (1979). Copyright © 1979 by the Board of Trustees for the Leland Stanford Junior University.

James A. Henderson & Richard A. Pearson, "Implementing Federal Environmental Policies: The Limits of Aspirational Commands." Copyright © 1978 by the Directors of the Columbia Law Review Association, Inc. All Rights Reserved. This article originally appeared at 78 Colum.L.Rev. 1429 (1978). Reprinted by permission.

Timothy S. Jost, "From *Swift* to *Stotts* & Beyond: Modification of Injunctions in the Federal Courts." Published originally in 64 Texas Law Review 1101 (1986). Copyright © 1986 by the Texas Law Review Association. Reprinted by permission.

Douglas Laycock, "Injunctions and the Irreparable Injury Rule." Published originally in 57 Texas Law Review 1065, 1071–72 (1979). Copyright © 1979 by the Texas Law Review Association. Reprinted by permission.

Douglas Laycock, "The Death of the Irreparable Injury Rule," 103 Harv.L.Rev. 687 (1990). Copyright © 1990 by the Harvard Law Review Association.

Douglas Laycock, "The Scope and Significance of Restitution." Published originally in 67 Tex.L.Rev. 1277 (1989). Copyright © 1989 by the Texas Law Review Association. Reprinted by permission.

John Leubsdorf, "The Standard for Preliminary Injunctions," 91 Harv. L.Rev. 525 (1978). Copyright © 1978 by the Harvard Law Review Association.

Murray Levine, Charles P. Ewing & David I. Levine, "The Use of Law for Prevention in the Public Interest," 5 Prevention In Human Services 241 (1987) published by The Haworth Press, Inc., 10 Alice Street, Binghamton, N.Y. 13904.

Michael Lottman, "Enforcement of Judicial Decrees: Now Comes the Hard Part," 1 Mental Disability Law Reporter 69 (1976).

Richard L. Marcus, "*Public Law Litigation* and Legal Scholarship." Reprinted by permission of the University of Michigan Journal of Law Reform from the University of Michigan Journal of Law Reform, Vol. 21, pp. 671–81.

Dale Oesterle, "Deficiencies of the Restitutionary Right to Trace Misappropriated Property in Equity and in UCC § 9–306," 68 Cornell Law Review 172, 198 (1983). Copyright © 1983 by Cornell University; All Rights Reserved.

Richard Posner, *Economic Analysis of Law* (4th ed. 1992). Reprinted with permission of Little, Brown and Company.

David R. Rosenberg, "The Causal Connection in Mass Exposure Cases: A Public Law Vision of the Tort System," 97 Harv.L.Rev. 849 (1984).

David Schoenbrod, "The Measure of an Injunction: A Principle to Replace Balancing the Equities and Tailoring the Remedy," 72 Minn. L.Rev. 627 (1988).

Peter H. Schuck, "The Role of Judges in Settling Complex Cases: The Agent Orange Example." Reprinted by permission of the University of Chicago Law Review from The University of Chicago Law Review, vol. 53, pp. 341–48.

Alan Schwartz, "The Case for Specific Performance." Reprinted by permission of The Yale Law Journal Company and Fred B. Rothman & Company from The Yale Law Journal, Vol. 89, pp. 271–306.

Peter Shane, "Rights, Remedies and Restraint." First printed in 64 Chi. Kent L.Rev. 531 (1988).

Peter Shane, "School Desegregation Remedies and the Fair Governance of School." Reprinted by permission of the University of Pennsylvania Law Review and Fred B. Rothman & Company from 132 U.Pa. L.Rev. 1041, 1065–66 (1984).

Justin Sweet, "Liquidated Damages in California." Copyright © 1972 by California Law Review, Inc. Reprinted from California Law Review, Vol. 60, No. 1, January 1972, pp. 84–146, by permission.

Jack B. Weinstein, "A Trial Judge's First Impression of the Federal Sentencing Guidelines," 52 Albany L.Rev. 1, 10–11 (1987).

Juan Williams, "A Question of Fairness." Atlantic Monthly, February, 1987, at p. 70.

Donald H. Ziegler, "Rights Require Remedies: A New Approach to the Enforcement of Rights in the Federal Courts." Copyright © 1987 Hastings College of Law, reprinted from 38 Hastings L.J. 665 with permission.

"California's Collateral Source Rule and Plaintiffs Receipt of Uninsured Motorist Benefits." Copyright © 1986 Hastings College of Law, reprinted from 37 Hastings L.J. with permission.

"Developments in the Law—Injunctions," 78 Harv.L.Rev. 993 (1965). Copyright © 1965 by the Harvard Law Review Association.

"Interest as Damages in California," 5 UCLA L.Rev. 262 (1958).

"Reestablishing the Federal Judge's Role in Sentencing," Reprinted by permission of The Yale Law Journal Company and Fred B. Rothman & Company from *The Yale Law Journal,* Vol. 101, page 1120.

Restatement of the Law, 2d, Contracts, copyright © 1981 by the American Law Institute; Restatement of the Law, Restitution, copyright © 1937 by the American Law Institute; Restatement of the Law, 2d,

Torts, copyright © 1979 by the American Law Institute. Reprinted with the permission of The American Law Institute.

"Restitution: Concepts and Terms." Copyright © 1986 Hastings College of Law, reprinted from 37 Hastings L.J. 667–695 with permission.

"Special Project—the Remedial Process in Institutional Reform Litigation." Copyright © 1978 by the Directors of the Columbia Law Review Association, Inc. All Rights Reserved. This article originally appeared at 78 Colum.L.Rev. 784 (1978). Reprinted by permission.

# Summary of Contents

# Table of Contents

# Table of Cases

**The principal cases are in bold type. Cases cited or discussed in the text are roman type. References are to pages. Cases cited in principal cases and within other quoted materials are not included.**

# REMEDIES: PUBLIC AND PRIVATE

## Second Edition

*

# Chapter 1

# INTRODUCTION TO THE LAW OF REMEDIES

## A. THE CHOICE OF A REMEDY

Particularly in law school, it is easy to fall into the habit of equating law and liability. Liability—the determination that a defendant is or is not responsible for some past or potential harm to the plaintiff—is, however, only half the story. The other half is the remedy—the action to be taken in response to the harm. The remedy is the more important half, especially for clients, as it is with the remedy that the court acts, for them or against them.

Despite the practical importance of remedies, liability dominates the study of law. The reason perhaps is that it is tempting to think of the appropriate remedy as mechanically derived from the legal harm and therefore obvious. That is what the Babylonian King Hammurabi suggested 4000 years ago by displaying to his subjects a large stone tablet that listed specific remedies for specific wrongs:

> Rule 195. If a son has struck his father, one shall cut off his hands.
>
> Rule 196. If one destroys the eye of a free-born man, his eye one shall destroy. * * *
>
> Rule 198. If the eye of a nobleman he has destroyed, * * * one mina of silver he shall pay.
>
> Rule 199. If he has destroyed the eye of the slave of a free-born man * * *, he shall pay half of [the slave's] price. * * *
>
> Rule 206. If a man has struck another in a quarrel, and has wounded him and that man shall swear, "I did not strike him wittingly," he shall pay the doctor.
>
> Rule 207. If he dies of the blows, he shall swear again, and if it was a free-born man, he shall pay one-half mina of silver.
>
> Rule 208. If it was a freedman, he shall pay one-third a mina of silver.

The Code of Hammurabi, quoted in Howard L. Oleck, Damages to Persons and Property § 2 at 3–4 (1961 rev.ed.).

In practice, however, remedies cannot be carved in stone. A mechanical approach to determining the appropriate remedy is ultimately impractical because no list can include all harms nor take account of the variations in circumstance that would make a given remedy inappropriate. Indeed, Babylonian court records show that courts did not follow the Code of Hammurabi mechanically, but rather took a common law approach to shaping the remedy. The "code" apparently was in fact a systematic presentation of decided cases and related hypotheticals, aimed as much at the public as the judges—a political ad claiming "the rule of law applied here."

The polar opposite of the mechanical approach is to let each judge select whatever remedy does justice in the case at hand. This is what the Ten Commandments seem to do in establishing a law of liability while saying nothing about remedy, as in "Thou shalt not kill." Exodus 20:2–17. But this approach too has its problems. A judge with unfettered discretion over remedy can effectively nullify the prohibitions in constitutions, statutes, and cases. Indeed, Hebrew judges apparently did not have such discretion; the Ten Commandments is followed by "fine print" which speaks to the remedies in terms remarkably similar to the Code of Hammurabi. Exodus 21–22.

Staking out a middle ground between a mechanical and a wholly discretionary approach to remedies requires deciding several issues. Two of the most important in this context are: To what extent should judges in individual cases have discretion or be constrained in formulating a remedy, and, assuming judges must inevitably be left with some discretion, how should the exercise of discretion be controlled?

Whoever gets to craft the remedy must make a series of choices. The first choice is of the remedy's goal. Its goal might be to restore the plaintiff to *plaintiff's rightful position*,[a] that is, to the position that the plaintiff would have occupied if defendant had never violated the law. Or, its goal might be to restore the defendant to the *defendant's rightful position*, that is, the position that the defendant would have occupied absent the violation. Or, its goal might be punishment of the defendant for doing wrong. These three goals usually lead to quite different remedies. What principles might guide the choice between them? See Saul Levmore & William J. Stuntz, Remedies and Incentives in Private and Public Law: A Comparative Essay, 1990 Wis.L.Rev. 483.

The second choice in defining an appropriate remedy is between achieving the remedy's goal in kind (by a *specific* remedy), or in cash (by a *substitutionary* remedy). For example, if the goal of the remedy in a

**a.** Judges use "plaintiff's rightful position" and a variety of different and longer phrases to mean essentially the same thing. Professor Laycock has suggested that "plaintiff's rightful position" be used as a convention to reduce confusion and verbiage and has coined the contrasting term, "defendant's rightful position." Douglas Laycock, Modern American Remedies 16 (2d ed. 1994).

nuisance case is to restore the plaintiff to its rightful position, a specific remedy would order the defendant to stop the nuisance; a substitutionary remedy would order the defendant to compensate the plaintiff in money for the harm to the plaintiff from the nuisance. Again, what principles should guide this choice?

A third choice is how to implement the first two choices by crafting the remedy. If the goal is plaintiff's rightful position, how does the court go about deciding what it is in a particular case? And, if the remedy is to be substitutionary, how does the court decide how much money is an adequate substitute?

The fourth choice is how to enforce the remedy. If the defendant does not cooperate, what should be done?

These questions arise in determining how to make decisions about remedies in any substantive area of the law, whether torts or contracts, admiralty or anti-trust. In that sense, remedies—like civil procedure, administrative law, evidence, or conflicts of law—is "transsubstantive": the problems it addresses arise in all substantive areas of law. Although the substantive law affects how remedies issues are resolved (just as the substantive law affects the outcome of procedural or evidentiary questions), the issues themselves are universal. Thus, after a right is declared, whether by a legislative enactment or judicial decision, these transsubstantive principles can be used to craft the remedy.

Approached from this perspective, remedies is a challenging subject. Although remedies may be touched on in particular substantive courses, the coverage is usually piecemeal: lack of time prevents attention to the transsubstantive principles underlying the decisions. Remedial principles have not been codified as have those in civil procedure (e.g., Federal Rules of Civil Procedure), administrative law (e.g., Administrative Procedure Act, 5 U.S.C. § 551 et seq.), evidence (e.g., Federal Rules of Evidence), or conflicts of law (Restatement (Second) of the Conflict of Laws (1971)).[b] Moreover, the transsubstantive principles of remedies are sometimes not well stated in the case law or recognized in the various research aids that lawyers use. This makes it particularly difficult for lawyers who have not studied remedies or who have done so in a "cookbook" fashion to locate or apply the law that they need to help their clients. They are unable, for instance, to deal with a novel remedies question by drawing appropriate analogies to remedies from other substantive areas of law.

Accordingly, our focus is transsubstantive, and, so, these materials are organized by types of remedies (injunctions, declaratory judgments, punitive damages and other sanctions, compensatory damages, restitution, and attorney's fees), rather than canvassing the remedies for particular harms (remedies for property damage, remedies for breach of

**b.** There is a Restatement of Restitution (1937), but its first concern is with restitution as a source of liability rather than as remedy. The restitution remedy will be considered in chapter 7. At this writing, the American Law Institute is considering whether to commission a Restatement of Remedies.

contract, etc.). By studying each remedy across a variety of cases, from administrative law to breach of contract to civil rights, we hope that, you, unlike Hammurabi, will be able to see remedies not as a list of responses to specific harms, but as a set of principles exemplified in particular cases and extending beyond them.

In this spirit, consider the following problem, which is probably reminiscent of your torts and property courses:

### *Problem: Country Lodge v. Miller*
### *Remedies in a Traditional Private Case*

Miller owns an apple orchard where she recently built a plant to press and bottle apple cider. The cider press produces apple mash as waste. Last fall, her first season of operation, she disposed of the waste by putting it into a pipe that empties into the Rural River. This cost her nothing while the cheapest alternative means of disposal would have cost $20,000 per year. The guests at the nearby, long-established Country Lodge disliked the sight of the apple mash in the water. As a result, Country Lodge lost $10,000 in profits that fall. In a suit that Country Lodge brought against Miller, the judge found Miller's operation to be a nuisance, because her conduct was unreasonable and resulted in substantial harm to Country Lodge.

Consider the remedies that should be available to Country Lodge. Do not be constrained by what you think you know of the applicable precedent. What purpose does each remedy serve? Do you see any problem in achieving that purpose?

---

While the preceding problem involves a dispute between two parties under the common law, much modern litigation is far more complex, thereby complicating the judge's remedial choices, as the following materials suggest.

### *Problem: Country Lodge v. Miller (Reprised)*[c]
### *Remedies in a Public Law Case*

How would your answer in Country Lodge v. Miller change if:

(a) persons other than Country Lodge are hurt by Miller's pollution?

(b) putting the apple mash in the river is not a common law nuisance but does violate a federal environmental statute?

(c) the violator of the statute is not Miller but rather a municipality which puts untreated municipal waste into the river?

c. This problem is the first of many reprises of the Country Lodge v. Miller problem. Each reprise varies the initial fact pattern to illustrate particular aspects of the law of remedies.

(d) the court orders the municipality to build a sewage treatment plant and have it in operation in three years, but the city council does not appropriate the necessary funds?

(e) the city council appropriates the necessary funds, but makes them available on a schedule that would mean that the plant will not be operational for five years?

## ABRAM CHAYES, THE ROLE OF THE JUDGE IN PUBLIC LAW LITIGATION

89 Harv.L.Rev. 1281, 1282–84, 1292–95, 1298 (1976).

* * * We are witnessing the emergence of a new model of civil litigation and, I believe, our traditional conception of adjudication and the assumptions upon which it is based provide an increasingly unhelpful, indeed misleading framework for assessing either the workability or the legitimacy of the roles of judge and court within this model.

In our received tradition, the lawsuit is a vehicle for settling disputes between private parties about private rights. The defining features of this conception of civil adjudication are:

(1) The lawsuit is *bipolar*. Litigation is organized as a contest between two individuals or at least two unitary interests, diametrically opposed, to be decided on a winner-takes-all basis.

(2) Litigation is *retrospective*. The controversy is about an identified set of completed events: whether they occurred, and if so, with what consequences for the legal relations of the parties.

(3) *Right and remedy are interdependent*. The scope of the relief is derived more or less logically from the substantive violation under the general theory that the plaintiff will get compensation measured by the harm caused by the defendant's breach of duty—in contract by giving plaintiff the money he would have had absent the breach; in tort by paying the value of the damage caused.

(4) The lawsuit is a *self-contained* episode. The impact of the judgment is confined to the parties. If plaintiff prevails there is a simple compensatory transfer, usually of money, but occasionally the return of a thing or the performance of a definite act. If defendant prevails, a loss lies where it has fallen. In either case, entry of judgment ends the court's involvement.

(5) The process is *party-initiated* and *party-controlled*. The case is organized and the issues defined by exchanges between the parties. Responsibility for fact development is theirs. The trial judge is a neutral arbiter of their interactions who decides questions of law only if they are put in issue by an appropriate move of a party.

This capsule description of what I have called the traditional conception of adjudication is no doubt overdrawn. It was not often, if ever, expressed so severely; indeed, because it was so thoroughly taken for granted, there was little occasion to do so. Although I do not contend that the traditional conception ever conformed fully to what judges were doing in fact, I believe it has been central to our understanding and our analysis of the legal system.

Whatever its historical validity, the traditional model is clearly invalid as a description of much current civil litigation in the federal district courts. Perhaps the dominating characteristic of modern federal litigation is that lawsuits do not arise out of disputes between private parties about private rights. Instead, the object of litigation is the vindication of constitutional or statutory policies. The shift in the legal basis of the lawsuit explains many, but not all, facets of what is going on "in fact" in federal trial courts. For this reason, although the label is not wholly satisfactory, I shall call the emerging model "public law litigation."

The characteristic features of the public law model are very different from those of the traditional model. The party structure is sprawling and amorphous, subject to change over the course of the litigation. The traditional adversary relationship is suffused and intermixed with negotiating and mediating processes at every point. The judge is the dominant figure in organizing and guiding the case, and he draws for support not only on the parties and their counsel, but on a wide range of outsiders—masters, experts, and oversight personnel. Most important, the trial judge has increasingly become the creator and manager of complex forms of ongoing relief, which have widespread effects on persons not before the court and require the judge's continuing involvement in administration and implementation. School desegregation, employment discrimination, and prisoners' or inmates' rights cases come readily to mind as avatars of this new form of litigation. But it would be mistaken to suppose that it is confined to these areas. Antitrust, securities fraud and other aspects of the conduct of corporate business, bankruptcy and reorganizations, union governance, consumer fraud, housing discrimination, electoral reapportionment, environmental management—cases in all these fields display in varying degrees the features of public law litigation. * * *

One of the most striking procedural developments of this century is the increasing importance of equitable relief. It is perhaps too soon to reverse the traditional maxim to read that money damages will be awarded only when no suitable form of specific relief can be devised. But surely, the old sense of equitable remedies as "extraordinary" has faded.

I am not concerned here with specific performance—the compelled transfer of a piece of land or a unique thing. This remedy is structurally little different from traditional money-damages. It is a one-time, one-way transfer requiring for its enforcement no continuing involvement of the court. Injunctive relief, however, is different in kind, even when it takes the form of a simple negative order. Such an order is a presently operative prohibition, enforceable by contempt, and it is a much greater constraint on activity than the risk of future liability implicit in the damage remedy. Moreover, the injunction is continuing. Over time, the parties may resort to the court for enforcement or modification of the original order in light of changing circumstances. Finally, by issuing the injunction, the court takes public responsibility for any consequences of its decree that may adversely affect strangers to the action.

Beyond these differences, the prospective character of the relief introduces large elements of contingency and prediction into the proceedings. Instead of a dispute retrospectively oriented toward the consequences of a closed set of events, the court has a controversy about future probabilities. Equitable doctrine, naturally enough, given the intrusiveness of the injunction and the contingent nature of the harm, calls for a balancing of the interests of the parties. And if the immediate parties' interests were to be weighed and evaluated, it was not too difficult to proceed to a consideration of other interests that might be affected by the order.

The comparative evaluation of the competing interests of plaintiff and defendant required by the remedial approach of equity often discloses alternatives to a winner-takes-all decision. An arrangement might be fashioned that could safeguard at least partially the interests of both parties, and perhaps even of others as well. And to the extent such an arrangement is possible, equity seems to require it. Negative orders directed to one of the parties—even though pregnant with affirmative implications—are often not adequate to this end. And so the historic power of equity to order affirmative action gradually freed itself from the encrustation of nineteenth century restraints. The result has often been a decree embodying an affirmative regime to govern the range of activities in litigation and having the force of law for those represented before the court.

At this point, right and remedy are pretty thoroughly disconnected. The form of relief does not flow ineluctably from the liability determination, but is fashioned ad hoc. In the process, moreover, right and remedy have been to some extent transmuted. The liability determination is not simply a pronouncement of the legal consequences of past events, but to some extent a prediction of what is likely to be in the future. And relief is not a terminal, compensatory transfer, but an effort to devise a program to contain future consequences in a way that accommodates the range of interests involved. * * * If a mental patient complains that he has been denied a right to treatment, it will not do to order the superintendent to "cease to deny" it. So with segregation in education, discrimination in hiring, apportionment of legislative districts, environmental management. And the list could be extended. * * *

The centerpiece of the emerging public law model is the decree. It differs in almost every relevant characteristic from relief in the traditional model of adjudication, not the least in that it is the centerpiece. The decree seeks to adjust future behavior, not to compensate for past wrong. It is deliberately fashioned rather than logically deduced from the nature of the legal harm suffered. It provides for a complex, on-going regime of performance rather than a simple, one-shot, one-way transfer. Finally, it prolongs and deepens, rather than terminates, the court's involvement with the dispute. * * *

---

## REMEDIES: PUBLIC AND PRIVATE

Professor Chayes views the judge crafting a remedy in a public law case as virtually a legislator in robes. Other observers have used similar terms. E.g., Colin S. Diver, The Judge as Political Powerbroker: Superintending Structural Change in Public Institutions, 65 Va.L.Rev. 43 (1979). It is too early in the course to evaluate this concept, but keep this controversial concept in mind in the chapters to come.

What Professor Chayes terms "public law litigation" is exemplified by Wyatt v. Stickney, 325 F.Supp. 781 (M.D.Ala.1971), enforced 344 F.Supp. 373, 387 (M.D.Ala.1972), modified sub nom. Wyatt v. Aderholt, 503 F.2d 1305 (5th Cir.1974). *Wyatt* began as a class action on behalf of mental patients and employees at a mental hospital against state officials, including the governor, alleging violations of an asserted right of the involuntarily confined to treatment and decent living conditions. The plaintiffs group grew to include mental patients at other hospitals, geriatric patients, and mentally retarded patients. The judge issued orders that imposed detailed guidelines on the operations of the institutions and tried to prompt the state to provide the funds to implement his orders. The judge also involved the United States government and established various entities to oversee implementation of his orders. See, e.g., Note, The *Wyatt* Case: Implementation of a Judicial Decree Ordering Institutional Change, 84 Yale L.J. 1338 (1975). Although older than many law students, the case remains active. E.g., Wyatt v. Poundstone, 892 F.Supp. 1410 (M.D.Ala.1995) (new injunction warranted to correct failure to deal with gang activity, abuse by staff, and use of improper restraints on mentally ill children).

At one point, Professor Chayes appears to say that the difference between "public law litigation" and "private law litigation" lies in the nature of the rights the court is asked to enforce, with public law cases enforcing constitutional or statutory policies concerning important public values and private law cases enforcing private rights. Yet, public policy figures in the contract or tort rules that dispose of many private law cases and constitutional rights are the rights of private persons. At another point, he says the form of relief—a greater tendency to rely on injunctive relief rather than money damages—is what distinguishes public law cases. He later wrote, however, that "further reflection has confirmed me in the view that the nature of the controversy, the sources of the governing law, and consequent extended impact of the decision—rather than the form of relief—are what really differentiate public law from private law adjudication." Abram Chayes, Foreword: Public Law Litigation and the Burger Court, 96 Harv.L.Rev. 4, 58 (1982). Whatever the exact terms of the distinction between private law and public law litigation, they are certainly not totally separate categories but rather poles of a continuum with the public law end of the continuum marked by concern with the case's impact on the public, remedy not so closely linked to rights, prospective orientation, liability founded in authorities with an evident public policy concern, and so on.

In contrast, Professors Theodore Eisenberg and Stephen Yeazell argue that public law litigation is not as new as Professor Chayes suggests; they point to cases long arising in such traditional areas as bankruptcy, probate, and trusts in which the remedy shares many of the characteristics of public law litigation. Theodore Eisenberg & Stephen Yeazell, The Ordinary and the Extraordinary in Institutional Litigation, 93 Harv.L.Rev. 465, 481–86 (1980). Further, Professor Richard Marcus argues that the remedial and procedural changes that Professor Chayes observed in public law cases have spread to a wide range of litigation. Richard L. Marcus, Public Law Litigation and Legal Scholarship, 21 Mich.J.L. Reform 647, 668–82 (1988). This casebook includes many public law cases both because of their intrinsic importance and because they often present, in sharply drawn terms, issues inherent in both private and public law litigation.

## B. "WHERE THERE'S A RIGHT, THERE'S A REMEDY"?

The power of a court to declare a right, whether by interpreting a constitution, applying a statute, or declaring the common law, has often been the subject of controversy, for the exercise of that power invokes concerns about the legitimacy of judicial authority in a democracy. Thus, before it declares a right, a court thinks carefully not simply about the justice of the party's cause, but also about the limits of its own power. Once a right has been established, however, the power of the court to declare a remedy has been much less controversial, and as a result, less scrutinized. Ask where the power to shape a remedy is derived, and the answer is likely to be that it is an inherent power, existing because, "Where there is a right, there must be a remedy."

That rights require remedies is almost definitional; a right without a remedy, some would say, is not a right at all:

> To begin, a right without a remedy is not a legal right; it is merely a hope or a wish. This follows from the definition of a legal right. * * * [By definition], a right entails a correlative duty to act or refrain from acting for the benefit of another person. Unless a duty can be enforced, it is not really a duty; it is only a voluntary obligation that a person can fulfill or not at his whim. In such circumstances, the holder of the correlative "right" can only hope

> that the act or forbearance will occur. Thus, a right without a remedy is simply not a legal right.
>
> To understand why it is important for legal claims to be enforceable to be *rights*—rather than mere requests for favors—it is necessary to explore the purposes of rights. Rights define social relations. They serve as means to very important ends. Rights promote well-being in the broadest sense. They secure the dignity and the integrity of human beings. They enable people to grow, to develop, to fulfill their aspirations, and to accumulate necessary material goods. Rights give people control over their lives and are essential to self-respect. Theories of rights often are considered to conflict with social utility because recognizing rights is sometimes inefficient. Nonetheless, legal rights plainly serve some utilitarian purposes. They assist society in treating people equally. They also promote order and predictability, thus enabling people to act upon reasonable expectations in managing their affairs.
>
> Having described the purposes of rights, it is relatively easy to envision the consequences of their inadequate enforcement. The dignity of the individual is diminished and people are less able to achieve their goals. People feel insecure and lose their self-respect. If the legal system tells a person that it is acceptable for his rights to be violated, the implicit message is that the person lacks worth. And, when the system vindicates another person's rights in similar circumstances, the message is that the other person has greater worth. When denial of rights occurs systematically over time, the result is alienation, isolation, anger, and fear. In extreme cases, the result is totalitarianism or chaos.

Donald H. Zeigler, Rights Require Remedies: A New Approach to the Enforcement of Rights in the Federal Courts, 38 Hastings L.J. 665, 678–79 (1987).

That there must be a remedy for every violation of a right is a powerful idea; Justice Marshall called it "[t]he very essence of civil liberty." Marbury v. Madison, 5 U.S. (1 Cranch) 137, 163, 2 L.Ed. 60 (1803). Yet, if rights "require" remedies, remedies should be an easy subject. As Professor Chayes explains in the excerpt in part A of this chapter, if rights and remedies were so closely linked, judges would be able simply to deduce the proper remedy from the right that was violated. If there were such a close nexus between rights and remedies, there would be no need to look for a source for the courts' remedial power, because deciding on the proper remedy would not be an exercise of power at all, but a formal process of mechanical, logical deduction.

Professor Chayes, however, contends that at least in the context of public law litigation, designing a remedy is far from a mechanical process. Rather, the design of a remedy is an exercise of power independent of the declaration of a right, and so requires its own justification. The remedies course should convince you that public law cases are not unique: Defining the remedy for any particular wrong is an exercise in judgment and discretion—an exercise of power—no different in kind from the decision to declare a right in the first instance.

Thus, if there is one thing to be learned from a course in remedies, it is that "Where there is a right, there is a remedy" is a singularly unhelpful maxim. Providing a complete remedy for every violation of right is an important, well-accepted goal, but it is not the only goal the law serves. Further, in any particular situation, any number of remedies may be available. In that event, who is to decide which remedy is available to whom, and how is that to be decided?

Questions such as these are rarely discussed plainly in the cases. After all, the nature and source of a court's power are abstract concerns, while adjudication is a pragmatic, concrete business. So, despite its being with the declaration of a remedy that the court's power is truly exercised (or perhaps because this is where the power is truly exercised), the nature of a court's remedial authority goes largely undiscussed.

Sometimes, however, courts cannot veil the exercise of judgment in the design of a remedy. For example, where a right unquestionably exists, and the only question is what remedy is appropriate, a court may be forced to explore the whys and wherefores of its remedial power in plain terms. The following case presents such a situation.

## BIVENS v. SIX UNKNOWN NAMED AGENTS OF FEDERAL BUREAU OF NARCOTICS

Supreme Court of the United States, 1971.
403 U.S. 388, 91 S.Ct. 1999, 29 L.Ed.2d 619.

MR. JUSTICE BRENNAN delivered the opinion of the Court.

The Fourth Amendment provides that:

> "The right of the people to be secure in their persons, houses, papers, and effects, against unreasonable searches and seizures, shall not be violated. . . ."

In Bell v. Hood, 327 U.S. 678, 66 S.Ct. 773, 90 L.Ed. 939 (1946), we reserved the question whether violation of that command by a federal agent acting under color of his authority gives rise to a cause of action for damages consequent upon his unconstitutional conduct. Today we hold that it does.

This case has its origin in an arrest and search carried out on the morning of November 26, 1965. Petitioner's complaint alleged that on that day respondents, agents of the Federal Bureau of Narcotics acting under claim of federal authority, entered his apartment and arrested him for alleged narcotics violations. The agents manacled petitioner in front of his wife and children, and threatened to arrest the entire family. They searched the apartment from stem to stern. Thereafter, petitioner was taken to the federal courthouse in Brooklyn, where he was interrogated, booked, and subjected to a visual strip search.

On July 7, 1967, petitioner brought suit in Federal District Court. In addition to the allegations above, his complaint asserted that the arrest and search were effected without a warrant, and that unreasonable force was employed in making the arrest; fairly read, it alleges as well that the arrest was made without probable cause. Petitioner claimed to have suffered great humiliation, embarrassment, and mental suffering as a result of the agents' unlawful conduct, and sought $15,000 damages from each of them. The District Court, on respondents' motion, dismissed the complaint on the ground, *inter alia,* that it failed to state a cause of action. The Court of Appeals, one judge concurring specially, affirmed on that basis. * * * We reverse.

I

Respondents do not argue that petitioner should be entirely without remedy for an unconstitutional invasion of his rights by federal agents. In respondents' view, however, the rights that petitioner asserts—primarily rights of privacy—are creations of state and not of federal law. Accordingly, they argue, petitioner may obtain money damages to redress invasion of these rights only by an action in tort, under state law, in the state courts. In this scheme the Fourth Amendment would serve merely to limit the extent to which the agents could defend the state law tort suit by asserting that their actions were a valid exercise of federal power: if the agents were shown to have violated the Fourth Amendment, such a defense would be lost to them and they would stand before the state law merely as private individuals. * * *

We think that respondents' thesis rests upon an unduly restrictive view of the Fourth Amendment's protection against unreasonable searches and seizures by federal agents, a view that has consistently been rejected by this Court. Respondents seek to treat the relationship between a citizen and a federal agent unconstitutionally exercising his authority as no different from the relationship between two private citizens. In so doing, they ignore the fact that power, once granted, does not disappear like a magic gift when it is wrongfully used. An agent acting—albeit unconstitutionally—in the name of the United States possesses a far greater capacity for harm than an individual trespasser exercising no authority other than his own. Accordingly, as our cases make clear, the Fourth Amendment operates as a limitation upon the exercise of federal power regardless of whether the State in whose jurisdiction that power is exercised would prohibit or penalize the identical act if engaged in by a private citizen. * * *

That damages may be obtained for injuries consequent upon a violation of the Fourth Amendment by federal officials should hardly seem a surprising proposition. Historically, damages have been regarded as the ordinary remedy for an invasion of personal interests in liberty. Of course, the Fourth Amendment does not in so many words provide for its enforcement by an award of money damages for the consequences of its violation. But "it is * * * well settled that where legal rights have been invaded, and a federal statute provides for a general right to sue for such invasion, federal courts may use any available remedy to make good the wrong done." The present case involves no special factors counselling hesitation in the absence of affirmative action by Congress. We are not dealing with a question of "federal fiscal policy," as in United States v. Standard Oil Co., 332 U.S. 301, 311, 67 S.Ct. 1604, 1609–1610, 91 L.Ed. 2067 (1947). In that case we refused to infer from the Government-soldier relationship that the United States could recover damages from one who negligently injured a soldier and thereby caused the Government to pay his medical expenses and lose his services during the course of his hospitalization. Noting that Congress was normally quite solicitous where the federal purse was involved, we pointed out that "the United States [was] the party plaintiff to the suit. And the United States has power at any time to create the liability." Nor are we asked in this case to impose liability upon a congressional employee for actions contrary to no constitutional prohibition, but merely said to be in excess of the authority delegated to him by the Congress. Finally, we cannot accept respondents' formulation of the question as whether the availability of money damages is necessary to enforce the Fourth Amendment. For we have here no explicit congressional declaration that persons injured by a federal officer's violation of the Fourth Amendment may not recover money damages from the agents, but must instead be remitted to another remedy, equally effective in the view of Congress. The question is merely whether petitioner, if he can demonstrate an injury consequent upon the violation by federal agents of his Fourth Amendment rights, is entitled to redress his injury through a particular remedial mechanism normally available in the federal courts. "The very essence of civil liberty certainly consists in the right of every individual to claim the protection of the laws, whenever he receives an injury." Marbury v. Madison, 1 Cranch 137, 163, 2 L.Ed. 60 (1803). Having concluded that petitioner's complaint states a cause of action under the Fourth Amendment, * * * we hold that petitioner is entitled to recover money damages for any injuries he has suffered as a result of the agents' violation of the Amendment.

II

In addition to holding that petitioner's complaint had failed to state facts making out a cause of action, the District Court ruled that in any event respondents were immune from liability by virtue of their official position. This question was not passed upon by the Court of Appeals, and accordingly we do not consider it here. The judgment of the Court of Appeals is reversed and the case is remanded for further proceedings consistent with this opinion.

So ordered.

MR. JUSTICE HARLAN, concurring in the judgment.

* * * For the reasons set forth below, I am of the opinion that federal courts do have the power to award damages for violation of "constitutionally protected interests" and I agree with the Court that a

traditional judicial remedy such as damages is appropriate to the vindication of the personal interests protected by the Fourth Amendment.

I

I turn first to the contention that the constitutional power of federal courts to accord Bivens damages for his claim depends on the passage of a statute creating a "federal cause of action." Although the point is not entirely free of ambiguity, I do not understand either the Government or my dissenting Brothers to maintain that Bivens' contention that he is entitled to be free from the type of official conduct prohibited by the Fourth Amendment depends on a decision by the State in which he resides to accord him a remedy. * * * [T]he interest which Bivens claims—to be free from official conduct in contravention of the Fourth Amendment—is a federally protected interest. Therefore, the question of judicial *power* to grant Bivens damages is not a problem of the "source" of the "right"; instead, the question is whether the power to authorize damages as a judicial remedy for the vindication of a federal constitutional right is placed by the Constitution itself exclusively in Congress' hands.

II

The contention that the federal courts are powerless to accord a litigant damages for a claimed invasion of his federal constitutional rights until Congress explicitly authorizes the remedy cannot rest on the notion that the decision to grant compensatory relief involves a resolution of policy considerations not susceptible of judicial discernment. Thus, in suits for damages based on violations of federal statutes lacking any express authorization of a damage remedy, this Court has authorized such relief where, in its view, damages are necessary to effectuate the congressional policy underpinning the substantive provisions of the statute.

If it is not the nature of the remedy which is thought to render a judgment as to the appropriateness of damages inherently "legislative," then it must be the nature of the legal interest offered as an occasion for invoking otherwise appropriate judicial relief. But I do not think that the fact that the interest is protected by the Constitution rather than statute or common law justifies the assertion that federal courts are powerless to grant damages in the absence of explicit congressional action authorizing the remedy. Initially, I note that it would be at least anomalous to conclude that the federal judiciary—while competent to choose among the range of traditional judicial remedies to implement statutory and common-law policies, and even to generate substantive rules governing primary behavior in furtherance of broadly formulated policies articulated by statute or Constitution—is powerless to accord a damages remedy to vindicate social policies which, by virtue of their inclusion in the Constitution, are aimed predominantly at restraining the Government as an instrument of the popular will.

More importantly, the presumed availability of federal equitable relief against threatened invasions of constitutional interests appears entirely to negate the contention that the status of an interest as constitutionally protected divests federal courts of the power to grant damages absent express congressional authorization. * * *

If explicit congressional authorization is an absolute prerequisite to the power of a federal court to accord compensatory relief regardless of the necessity or appropriateness of damages as a remedy simply because of the status of a legal interest as constitutionally protected, then it seems to me that explicit congressional authorization is similarly prerequisite to the exercise of equitable remedial discretion in favor of constitutionally protected interests. Conversely, if a general grant of jurisdiction to the federal courts by Congress is thought adequate to empower a federal court to grant equitable relief for all areas of subject-matter jurisdiction enumerated therein, see 28 U.S.C. § 1331(a), then it seems to me that the same statute is sufficient to empower a federal court to grant a traditional remedy at law. Of course, the special historical traditions governing the federal equity system might still bear on the comparative appropriateness of granting equitable relief as opposed to money damages. That possibility, however, relates, not to whether the federal courts have the power to afford one type of remedy as opposed to the other, but rather to the criteria which should govern the exercise of our power. To that question, I now pass.

III

The major thrust of the Government's position is that, where Congress has not expressly authorized a particular remedy, a federal court should exercise its power to accord a traditional form of judicial relief at the behest of a litigant, who claims a constitutionally protected interest has been invaded, only where the remedy is "essential," or "indispensable for vindicating constitutional rights." * * * It is argued that historically the Court has rarely exercised the power to accord such relief in the absence of an express congressional authorization and that "[i]f Congress had thought that federal officers should be subject to a law different than state law, it would have had no difficulty in saying so, as it did with respect to state officers * * *" 42 U.S.C. § 1983. Although conceding that the standard of determining whether a damage remedy should be utilized to effectuate statutory policies is one of "necessity" or "appropriateness," the Government contends that questions concerning congressional discretion to modify judicial remedies relating to constitutionally protected interests warrant a more stringent constraint on the exercise of judicial power with respect to this class of legally protected interests.

These arguments for a more stringent test to govern the grant of damages in constitutional cases seem to be adequately answered by the point that the judiciary has a particular responsibility to assure the vindication of constitutional interests such as those embraced by the Fourth Amendment. To be sure, "it must be remembered that legislatures are ultimate guardians of the liberties and welfare of the people in quite as great a degree as the courts." But it must also be recognized that the Bill of Rights is particularly intended to vindicate the interests of the individual in the face of the popular will as expressed in legislative majorities; at the very least, it strikes me as no more appropriate to await express congressional authorization of traditional judicial relief with regard to these legal interests than with respect to interests protected by federal statutes.

The question then, is, as I see it, whether compensatory relief is "necessary" or "appropriate" to the vindication of the interest asserted. In resolving that question, it seems to me that the range of policy considerations we may take into account is at least as broad as the range of those a legislature would consider with respect to an express statutory authorization of a traditional remedy. In this regard I agree with the Court that the appropriateness of according Bivens compensatory relief does not turn simply on the deterrent effect liability will have on federal official conduct. Damages as a traditional form of compensation for invasion of a legally protected interest may be entirely appropriate even if no substantial deterrent effects on future official lawlessness might be thought to result. * * *

And I think it is clear that Bivens advances a claim of the sort that, if proved, would be properly compensable in damages. The personal interests protected by the Fourth Amendment are those we attempt to capture by the notion of "privacy"; while the Court today properly points out that the type of harm which officials can inflict when they invade protected zones of an individual's life are different from the types of harm private citizens inflict on one another, the experience of judges in dealing with private trespass and false imprisonment claims supports the conclusion that courts of law are capable of making the types of judgment concerning causation and magnitude of injury necessary to accord meaningful compensation for invasion of Fourth Amendment rights.

* * * [I]t is apparent that some form of damages is the only possible remedy for someone in Bivens' alleged position. It will be a rare case indeed in which an individual in Bivens' position will be able to obviate the harm by securing injunctive relief from any court. However desirable a direct remedy against the Government might be as a substitute for individual official liability, the sovereign still remains immune to suit. Finally, assuming Bivens' innocence of the crime charged, the "exclusionary rule" is simply irrelevant. For people in Bivens' shoes, it is damages or nothing.

The only substantial policy consideration advanced against recognition of a federal cause of action for violation of Fourth Amendment rights by federal officials is the incremental expenditure of judicial resources that will be necessitated by this class of litigation. * * * I simply cannot agree with my Brother Black that the possibility of "frivolous" claims—if defined simply as claims with no legal merit—

warrants closing the courthouse doors to people in Bivens' situation. There are other ways, short of that, of coping with frivolous lawsuits.

* * * Judicial resources, I am well aware, are increasingly scarce these days. Nonetheless, when we automatically close the courthouse door solely on this basis, we implicitly express a value judgment on the comparative importance of classes of legally protected interests. And current limitations upon the effective functioning of the courts arising from budgetary inadequacies should not be permitted to stand in the way of the recognition of otherwise sound constitutional principles. * * *

[The dissenting opinions of CHIEF JUSTICE BURGER, JUSTICE BLACK, and JUSTICE BLACKMUN have been omitted.]

### *Notes*

1. In a later case based on *Bivens,* Davis v. Passman, 442 U.S. 228, 99 S.Ct. 2264, 60 L.Ed.2d 846 (1979), Justice Brennan took the occasion to define some very basic terms:

> *[J]urisdiction* is a question of whether a federal court has the power, under the constitution or laws of the United States, to hear a case; *standing* is a question of whether a plaintiff is sufficiently adversary to a defendant to create an Art. III case or controversy, or at least to overcome prudential limitations on federal court jurisdiction; *cause of action* is a question of whether a particular plaintiff is a member of the class of litigants that may, as a matter of law, appropriately invoke the power of the court; and *relief* is a question of the various remedies a federal court may make available.

442 U.S. at 239 n.18, 99 S.Ct. at 2274 n.18.

According to Justice Brennan's terminology, did the *Bivens* decision create a cause of action by allowing Bivens to sue for damages, or did it merely declare what relief was available? If the latter, what was the source of Bivens's cause of action?

Frequently, these two possibilities are merged, and *Bivens* is described as "creating a cause of action for damages." The distinction between creating a cause of action, and deciding on the appropriate relief, however, is important. See George D. Brown, Letting Statutory Tails Wag Constitutional Dogs: Have the *Bivens* Dissenters Prevailed?, 64 Ind.L.J. 263, 285 (1989). While a state court's role as the custodian of the common law confers broad authority to create new causes of action, or new remedies for existing actions, federal courts have no general authority to declare common law. See Erie Railroad Co. v. Tompkins, 304 U.S. 64, 58 S.Ct. 817, 82 L.Ed. 1188 (1938).

2. Did the *Bivens* court usurp a power belonging to Congress? Chief Justice Burger, Justice Blackmun, and Justice Black each dissented in *Bivens*. Although each wrote separately, all agreed that creating a remedy for violations of the Fourth Amendment was a power reserved to Congress under the Constitution:

> Although Congress has created such a federal cause of action against *state* officials acting under color of state law [42 U.S.C. § 1983], it has

> never created such a cause of action against federal officials. If it wanted to do so, Congress could, of course, create a remedy against federal officials who violate the Fourth Amendment in the performance of their duties. But the point of this case and the fatal weakness in the Court's judgment is that neither Congress nor the State of New York has enacted legislation creating such a right of action. For us to do so is, in my judgment, an exercise of power that the Constitution does not give us.

403 U.S. at 427–28, 91 S.Ct. at 2020–21 (Black, J. dissenting). See also Carlson v. Green, 446 U.S. 14, 37–38, 100 S.Ct. 1468, 1481–82, 64 L.Ed.2d 15 (1980)(Rehnquist, J. dissenting)(implying a cause of action for damages undermines Congress's authority under article III to determine the jurisdiction of the lower federal courts, and involves the courts in creating federal common law, which is inconsistent with *Erie*).

The dissenters thus argue that the Court cannot provide a remedy for a violation of some constitutional rights unless the remedy is authorized by Congress or by the Constitution itself. The majority seems to say that the Court is free to use any traditional remedy to vindicate the plaintiff's rights, unless Congress has withdrawn that authority. Who has the better of the argument?

As Justice Harlan points out, it has always been presumed that the court has the power to issue an injunction at an individual's behest to stop a federal officer from violating the Constitution, even without an express congressional enactment authorizing that remedy. Would the dissenters deny the court the authority to grant an injunction to prevent a threatened violation of the Constitution? What is the difference between enjoining a future violation and awarding damages for a past violation?

3. Where does the majority locate the authority it is exercising in *Bivens?* Is it conferred by the text of the constitution, perhaps by article III, section 2, which extends the judicial power "to all cases * * * arising under this Constitution"? Or is it by the grant of jurisdiction contained in 28 U.S.C. § 1331(a), which provides, "the district courts shall have original jurisdiction of all civil actions arising under the Constitution, laws, or treaties of the United States"? Sometimes it is suggested that a mandate can be found in the due process clause of the fifth amendment, see Richard H. Fallon, Of Legislative Courts, Administrative Agencies, and Article III, 101 Harv.L.Rev. 916, 955 n.223 (1988), or that the amendments themselves carry "a self-executing force that not only permits but requires the courts to recognize remedies appropriate for their violation." Walter E. Dellinger, Of Rights and Remedies: The Constitution as a Sword, 85 Harv.L.Rev. 1532 (1972); Susan Bandes, Reinventing *Bivens:* The Self–Executing Constitution, 68 S.Cal.L.Rev. 289 (1995). Does the source of the court's authority matter?

4. Once the court has decided that it does not need express congressional authorization to allow Bivens to sue for damages, it still must decide whether damages are appropriate. What is it that convinces the Court that an award of damages is an appropriate remedy for a violation of the fourth amendment? After all, Bivens already had a number of remedies at his disposal. He could have sued to enjoin future violations of his rights. If he

had been arrested, he could have invoked the exclusionary rule to prevent the use of the evidence in a criminal proceeding. He could have sued the federal officers in state court for trespass, battery, false arrest, and intentional infliction of emotional distress. With all of these remedies available, why does the Court allow a suit for damages for violation of Bivens's constitutional rights?

If a damages remedy is appropriate when the fourth amendment is violated, does it necessarily follow that a damages remedy is equally appropriate for all constitutional violations? Justice Harlan's concurrence suggests not. After noting that the personal interests the fourth amendment protects are very closely analogous to such torts as false imprisonment and trespass, providing judges a background of experience for handling compensation claims, Justice Harlan noted "The same, of course, may not be true with respect to other types of constitutionally protected interests, and therefore the appropriateness of money damages may well vary with the nature of the personal interest asserted." 403 U.S. at 409, n.9, 91 S.Ct. at 2011 n.9.

So far, the Court has determined that damages actions may be brought under the due process clause of the fifth amendment, Davis v. Passman, 442 U.S. 228, 99 S.Ct. 2264, 60 L.Ed.2d 846 (1979) and under the eighth amendment's cruel and unusual punishment clause, Carlson v. Green, 446 U.S. 14, 100 S.Ct. 1468, 64 L.Ed.2d 15 (1980).

5. The *Bivens* defendants were sued as individuals, although they acted as agents of the Federal Bureau of Narcotics when they searched Bivens's home. That is to say, were a judgment to be entered in the case, the defendants would pay that judgment out of their own pockets; neither the Bureau nor the United States would be liable. See F.D.I.C. v. Meyer, 510 U.S. ___, 114 S.Ct. 996, 127 L.Ed.2d 308 (1994) (*Bivens* action may not be brought against federal agency).

The plaintiffs sued the agents individually because the United States, as a sovereign government, is immune from suit unless Congress waives the government's sovereign immunity, and there is no general waiver of immunity for actions based on violations of constitutional rights. Further, while government officials may be sued in their official capacities for injunctive relief, damages cannot be recovered from the government without a waiver of immunity. So, the plaintiff who wants damages must generally sue the official individually.

Of course, as a practical matter, governments frequently defend and even indemnify their officers and agents when they have been sued for acts within the scope of their official duties. Also, the doctrine of official immunity sometimes shields government officers from personal liability for damages when they act within the scope of their duties, particularly if their jobs require the exercise of discretion and they did not have reason to know that they were violating the plaintiff's rights.

Plaintiffs who wish to sue state officials for violations of their federal, constitutional rights face some of the same problems. The Eleventh Amendment, which provides that "the Judicial power of the United States shall not be construed to extend to any suit in law or equity, commenced or prosecuted against one of the United States by Citizens of another State or by

Citizens or Subjects of any Foreign State," has been interpreted to embody a general principle of sovereign immunity. Thus, plaintiffs seeking damages for the violation of their constitutional rights by state officials two options. They may sue the officials individually, hoping the officials have assets from which to collect a judgment (assuming, of course, they can overcome the relevant official immunity). Or, they may sue the state in *state* court, where the eleventh amendment is no bar.

There are problems with the latter course, however. Although the eleventh amendment does not apply, sovereign immunity is part of the common law, and the state may not have consented to suit in its own courts, either. But even if the state has consented, or if the doctrine of sovereign immunity has been abrogated entirely, as it has in some jurisdictions, there is a second problem: Where is the plaintiff to find a cause of action?

Where state officials are concerned, Congress has created a cause of action in 42 U.S.C. § 1983 against "every person who, under color of [state law]" violates rights secured by the Constitution and laws of the United States. In Will v. Michigan Department of State Police, 491 U.S. 58, 109 S.Ct. 2304, 105 L.Ed.2d 45 (1989), however, the Court held that neither the State nor a state official sued in his official capacity is a "person" for purposes of section 1983. Therefore, even if the hurdle of sovereign immunity can be overcome, no cause of action for damages exists for the violation of constitutional rights by the state, unless some adventuresome state court would be willing to imply such a cause of action directly from the federal Constitution, by analogy to *Bivens*. For an argument that sound policy favors allowing damage actions for violations of constitutional rights in state court, see Louis E. Wolcher, Sovereign Immunity and the Supremacy Clause: Damages Against States in Their Own Courts for Constitutional Violations, 69 Cal.L.Rev. 189 (1981).

The intricacies of the law of governmental immunity are beyond the scope of the remedies course, for the most part. The law of immunity and the law of remedies do overlap at several points, however. Where necessary, notes explaining relevant aspects of the various immunities are included in the text.

6. State courts have generally held that they, too, have the power to create a cause of action for violations of the state constitution, at least when the state legislature has failed to provide meaningful remedies. See, e.g. Shields v. Gerhart, 658 A.2d 924 (Vt.1995)(reviewing cases from a number of jurisdictions). That is perhaps not surprising; given that state courts generally have exercised broad authority to create new common law causes of action, there is less apparent conflict with the legislature's role. There are, however, exceptions. See, e.g., Smith v. Department of Public Health, 428 Mich. 540, 410 N.W.2d 749 (1987) (declining to infer a right to sue the state for damages for violations of the Michigan constitution).

7. After *Bivens,* what exactly is the relationship between rights and remedies, Congress and the Court? Is it that:

a. The Constitution implicitly requires courts to award damages whenever an individual's constitutional rights are violated?

b. The Court has the authority to ensure that an adequate remedy is available whenever the Constitution is violated?

c. Both the Court and Congress may create remedies for constitutional violations, but if Congress has spoken clearly, the Court must defer to Congress's judgment?

d. The ultimate authority lies with Congress, but the Court will allow a damages action to proceed if it can infer that Congress would agree?

e. The ultimate authority lies with Congress, and Congress must expressly authorize the Court to act?

## SCHWEIKER v. CHILICKY

Supreme Court of the United States, 1988.
487 U.S. 412, 108 S.Ct. 2460, 101 L.Ed.2d 370.

JUSTICE O'CONNOR delivered the opinion of the Court.

This case requires us to decide whether the improper denial of Social Security disability benefits, allegedly resulting from violations of due process by government officials who administered the Federal Social Security program, may give rise to a cause of action for money damages against those officials. We conclude that such a remedy, not having been included in the elaborate remedial scheme devised by Congress, is unavailable.

I

A

[In 1980, Congress passed legislation requiring States to review the disability determinations of persons receiving disability benefits under Title II of the Social Security Act at least every three years. Claimants whose benefits were denied under this continuing disability review (CDR) program could appeal, but the administrative appeals process typically took nine to eighteen months, and during that period claimants received no benefits (although if the termination was later reversed, benefits could be awarded retroactively).] * * *

Finding that benefits were too often being improperly terminated by state agencies, only to be reinstated by a federal administrative law judge (ALJ), Congress enacted [the Social Security Disability Benefits Reform Act of 1984. The 1984 Reform Act required a more careful review before benefits could be terminated, and provided that benefits would continue through the penultimate stage of the appeals process, which was an appeal to a federal ALJ.]

The problems to which Congress responded so emphatically were widespread. One of the cosponsors of the 1984 Reform Act, who had conducted hearings on the administration of CDR, summarized evidence from the General Accounting Office as follows:

> "[T]he message perceived by the State agencies, swamped with cases, was to deny, deny, deny, and, I might add, to process cases faster and faster and faster. In the name of efficiency, we have

scanned our computer terminals, rounded up the disabled workers in the country, pushed the discharge button, and let them go into a free [f]all toward economic chaos." (Sen. Cohen).

* * * The Social Security Administration itself apparently reported that about 200,000 persons were wrongfully terminated, and then reinstated, between March 1981 and April 1984. * * *

Congress was also made aware of the terrible effects on individual lives that CDR had produced. The Chairman of the Senate's Special Committee on Aging pointed out that "[t]he human dimension of this crisis—the unnecessary suffering, anxiety, and turmoil—has been graphically exposed by dozens of congressional hearings and in newspaper articles all across the country." * * *

B

[Respondents James Chilicky, Spencer Harris and Dora Adlerte had their Social Security disability benefits terminated under the CDR program. Harris and Adelerte pursued administrative appeals, and their benefits were reinstated, retroactively. Chilicky filed a new application for benefits, which was granted. He also received a retroactive award.

Chilicky, Harris and Adelerte then sued to recover damages for the harm caused by months-long delay in the restoration of their benefits, including loss of food, shelter, and other necessities, as well as emotional distress. They alleged that state and federal officials had violated their due process rights by adopting illegal policies that terminated their benefits. The District Court dismissed their complaint, but the Court of Appeals reversed and remanded, concluding that respondents and stated a claim under *Bivens*.] * * *

The petition for certiorari presented one question: "Whether a *Bivens* remedy should be implied for alleged due process violations in the denial of social security disability benefits." We granted the petition, and now reverse.

II

A

* * * Our more recent decisions have responded cautiously to suggestions that *Bivens* remedies be extended into new contexts. The absence of statutory relief for a constitutional violation, for example, does not by any means necessarily imply that courts should award money damages against the officers responsible for the violation. Thus, in Chappell v. Wallace, 462 U.S. 296, 103 S.Ct. 2362, 76 L.Ed.2d 586 (1983), we refused—unanimously—to create a *Bivens* action for enlisted military personnel who alleged that they had been injured by the unconstitutional actions of their superior officers and who had no remedy against the Government itself:

> "The special nature of military life—the need for unhesitating and decisive action by military officers and equally disciplined responses by enlisted personnel—would be undermined by a judicially created

> remedy exposing officers to personal liability at the hands of those they are charged to command....
>
> "Also, Congress, the constitutionally authorized source of authority over the military system of justice, has not provided a damages remedy for claims by military personnel that constitutional rights have been violated by superior officers. *Any action to provide a judicial response by way of such a remedy would be plainly inconsistent with Congress' authority in this field.*
>
> "Taken together, the unique disciplinary structure of the Military Establishment and Congress' activity in the field constitute 'special factors' which dictate that it would be inappropriate to provide enlisted military personnel a *Bivens*-type remedy against their superior officers."

* * * Similarly, we refused—again unanimously—to create a *Bivens* remedy for a First Amendment violation "aris[ing] out of an employment relationship that is governed by comprehensive procedural and substantive provisions giving meaningful remedies against the United States." Bush v. Lucas, 462 U.S. 367, 368, 103 S.Ct. 2404, 2406, 76 L.Ed.2d 648 (1983). In that case, a federal employee was demoted, allegedly in violation of the First Amendment, for making public statements critical of the agency for which he worked. He was reinstated through the administrative process, with retroactive seniority and full back pay, but he was not permitted to recover for any loss due to emotional distress or mental anguish, or for attorney's fees. Concluding that the administrative system created by Congress "provides meaningful remedies for employees who may have been unfairly disciplined for making critical comments about their agencies," the Court refused to create a *Bivens* action even though it assumed a First Amendment violation and acknowledged that "existing remedies do not provide complete relief for the plaintiff." The Court stressed that the case involved policy questions in an area that had received careful attention from Congress. Noting that the Legislature is far more competent than the Judiciary to carry out the necessary "balancing [of] governmental efficiency and the rights of employees," we refused to "decide whether or not it would be good policy to permit a federal employee to recover damages from a supervisor who has improperly disciplined him for exercising his First Amendment rights."

In sum, the concept of "special factors counseling hesitation in the absence of affirmative action by Congress" has proved to include an appropriate judicial deference to indications that congressional action has not been inadvertent. When the design of a government program suggests that Congress has provided what it considers adequate remedial mechanisms for constitutional violations that may occur in the course of its administration, we have not created additional *Bivens* remedies.

B

* * * The case before us cannot reasonably be distinguished from *Bush v. Lucas.* Here, exactly as in *Bush,* Congress has failed to provide

for "complete relief": respondents have not been given a remedy in damages for emotional distress or for other hardships suffered because of delays in their receipt of Social Security benefits. The creation of a *Bivens* remedy would obviously offer the prospect of relief for injuries that must now go unredressed. Congress, however, has not failed to provide meaningful safeguards or remedies for the rights of persons situated as respondents were. Indeed, the system for protecting their rights is, if anything, considerably more elaborate than the civil service system considered in *Bush*. The prospect of personal liability for official acts, moreover, would undoubtedly lead to new difficulties and expense in recruiting administrators for the programs Congress has established. Congressional competence at "balancing governmental efficiency and the rights of [individuals]," is no more questionable in the social welfare context than it is in the civil service context.

Congressional attention to problems that have arisen in the administration of CDR (including the very problems that gave rise to this case) has, moreover, been frequent and intense. * * * At each step, Congress chose specific forms and levels of protection for the rights of persons affected by incorrect eligibility determinations under CDR. At no point did Congress choose to extend to any person the kind of remedies that respondents seek in this lawsuit. Thus, congressional unwillingness to provide consequential damages for unconstitutional deprivations of a statutory right is at least as clear in the context of this case as it was in *Bush*.

Respondents nonetheless contend that *Bush* should be confined to its facts, arguing that it applies only in the context of what they call "the special nature of federal employee relations." Noting that the parties to this case did "not share the sort of close, collaborative, continuing juridical relationship found in the federal civil service," respondents suggest that the availability of *Bivens* remedies would create less "inconvenience" to the Social Security system than it would in the context of the civil service. The Solicitor General is less sanguine, arguing that the creation of *Bivens* remedy in this context would lead to "a complete disruption of [a] carefully crafted and constantly monitored congressional scheme."

We need not choose between these competing predictions, which have little bearing on the applicability of *Bush* to this case. The decision in *Bush* did not rest on this Court's belief that *Bivens* actions would be more disruptive of the civil service than they are in other contexts where they have been allowed, such as federal law enforcement agencies (*Bivens* itself) or the federal prisons (Carlson v. Green, 446 U.S. 14, 100 S.Ct. 1468, 64 L.Ed.2d 15 (1980)). Rather, we declined in *Bush* " 'to create a new substantive legal liability ...' because we are convinced that Congress is in a better position to decide whether or not the public interest would be served by creating it." * * *

In the end, respondents' various arguments are rooted in their insistent and vigorous contention that they simply have not been adequately recompensed for their injuries. * * *

We agree that suffering months of delay in receiving the income on which one has depended for the very necessities of life cannot be fully remedied by the "belated restoration of back benefits." The trauma to respondents, and thousands of others like them, must surely have gone beyond what anyone of normal sensibilities would wish to see imposed on innocent disabled citizens. Nor would we care to "trivialize" the nature of the wrongs alleged in this case. Congress, however, has addressed the problems created by state agencies' wrongful termination of disability benefits. Whether or not we believe that its response was the best response, Congress is the body charged with making the inevitable compromises required in the design of a massive and complex welfare benefits program. * * *

JUSTICE STEVENS, concurring in part and concurring in the judgment. [omitted]

JUSTICE BRENNAN, with whom JUSTICE MARSHALL and JUSTICE BLACKMUN join, dissenting. * * *

A

* * * In *Chappell* and *Bush,* we dealt with elaborate administrative systems in which Congress anticipated that federal officials might engage in unconstitutional conduct, and in which it accordingly sought to afford injured persons a form of redress as complete as the Government's institutional concerns would allow. * * *

Here, as the legislative history of the 1984 Reform Act makes abundantly clear, Congress did not attempt to achieve a delicate balance between the constitutional rights of Title II beneficiaries on the one hand, and administrative concerns on the other. * * * Congress confronted a paralyzing breakdown in a vital social program, which it sought to rescue from near-total anarchy. Although the legislative debate surrounding the 1984 Reform Act is littered with references to "arbitrary," "capricious," and "wrongful" terminations of benefits, it is clear that neither Congress nor anyone else identified unconstitutional conduct by state agencies as the cause of this paralysis. Rather, Congress blamed the systemic problems it faced in 1984 on SSA's determination to control the cost of the disability insurance program by accelerating the CDR process and mandating more restrictive reviews. * * *

At no point during the lengthy legislative debate * * * did any Member of Congress so much as hint that the substantive eligibility criteria, notice requirements, and interim payment provisions that would govern *future* disability reviews adequately redressed the harms that beneficiaries may have suffered as a result of the unconstitutional actions of individual state and federal officials in *past* proceedings, or that the constitutional rights of those unjustly deprived of benefits in the past had to be sacrificed in the name of administrative efficiency or any other governmental interest. The Court today identifies no legislative compromise, "inevitable" or otherwise, in which lawmakers expressly declined to afford a remedy for such past wrongs. * * *

The mere fact, that Congress was aware of the prior injustices and failed to provide a form of redress for them, standing alone, is simply not a "special factor counselling hesitation" in the judicial recognition of a remedy. Inaction, we have repeatedly stated, is a notoriously poor indication of congressional intent, all the more so where Congress is legislating in the face of a massive breakdown calling for prompt and sweeping corrective measures. * * *

B

Our decisions in *Chappell* and *Bush* reveal yet another flaw in the "special factors" analysis the Court employs today. In both those cases, we declined to legislate in areas in which Congress enjoys a special expertise that the judiciary clearly lacks. * * *

Ignoring the unique characteristics of the military and civil service contexts that made judicial recognition of a *Bivens* action inappropriate in those cases, the Court today observes that "[c]ongressional competence at 'balancing governmental efficiency and the rights of [individuals]' is no more questionable in the social welfare context than it is in the civil service context." This observation, however, avails the Court nothing, for in *Bush* we declined to create a *Bivens* action for aggrieved federal employees not because Congress is simply competent to legislate in the area of federal employment relations, but because Congress is far more capable of addressing the special problems that arise in those relations than are the courts. * * *

Congress, of course, created the disability insurance program and obviously may legislate with respect to it. But unlike the military setting, where Congress' authority is plenary and entitled to considerable judicial deference, or the federal employment context, where Congress enjoys special expertise, social welfare is hardly an area in which the courts are largely incompetent to act. The disability insurance program is concededly large, but it does not involve necessarily unique relationships like those between enlisted military personnel and their superior officers, or Government workers and their federal employers. Rather, like the federal law enforcement and penal systems that gave rise to the constitutional claims in *Bivens* and *Carlson, supra,* the constitutional issues that surface in the social welfare system turn on the relationship of the Government and those it governs—the relationship that lies at the heart of constitutional adjudication. Moreover, courts do not lack familiarity or expertise in determining what the dictates of the Due Process Clause are. In short, the social welfare context does not give rise to the types of concerns that make it an area where courts should refrain from creating a damages action even in the absence of congressional action. * * *

Because I am convinced that Congress did not intend to preclude judicial recognition of a cause of action for such injuries, and because I believe there are no special factors militating against the creation of such a remedy here, I dissent.

### *Notes*

1. Looking at the majority's rationale for refusing to allow a *Bivens* action, have the *Bivens* dissenters prevailed? See George D. Brown, Letting Statutory Tails Wag Constitutional Dogs—Have the *Bivens* Dissenters Prevailed?, 64 Ind.L.J. 263 (1989). In addition to *Chappell, Bush,* and *Chilicky,* the Court has also refused to allow a *Bivens* action where a serviceman sought to sue civilian doctors involved in an experiment in which he was given LSD without his consent, United States v. Stanley, 483 U.S. 669, 107 S.Ct. 3054, 97 L.Ed.2d 550 (1987).

2. If the violations that plagued the CDR process had continued, could the plaintiffs have sought injunctive relief to prevent further unconstitutional denials of benefits? Despite what appears to be a retreat from *Bivens* so far as damages actions are concerned, no member of the Court has challenged the received wisdom that the federal courts can enjoin continuing violations of the Constitution, even though Congress has never specifically authorized them to do so. Isn't this a fatal inconsistency? If the courts have the authority to enjoin violations, don't they also have the authority to award damages? If the concern in *Chilicky* is with disturbing the operation of Congress's remedial scheme, wouldn't injunctions, which could bring the entire process to a halt, pose a greater threat than isolated damage awards?

3. Could Congress prohibit the federal courts from enjoining ongoing constitutional violations? In Bryant v. Carlucci, 488 U.S. 806, 109 S.Ct. 37, 102 L.Ed.2d 17 (1988), the Supreme Court had granted certiorari to determine whether, under Bush v. Lucas, the remedies provided by the Civil Service Reform Act of 1978 are exclusive, prohibiting even equitable remedies for violations of the first amendment rights of federal employees. The Court vacated the Fourth Circuit's decision holding that the Act deprived the district court of jurisdiction, remanding for reconsideration in light of Webster v. Doe, 486 U.S. 592, 108 S.Ct. 2047, 100 L.Ed.2d 632 (1988).

In *Webster*, a CIA employee alleged that the CIA had violated his constitutional rights by firing him because he was homosexual. The Court held that while his nonconstitutional claims were barred by a statute making the Director's discretion unreviewable, it would not interpret the statute to preclude his claim for an injunction against the violation of his constitutional rights, because "serious constitutional questions would arise if a federal statute were construed to deny any judicial forum for a colorable constitutional claim." Justice Scalia dissented: "[I]t is simply untenable that there must be a judicial remedy for every constitutional violation." 486 U.S. at 613, 108 S.Ct. at 2059.

On remand, the Fourth Circuit avoided the issue, holding that because Bryant could not show that the alleged violation of his constitutional rights might be repeated, he lacked standing to pursue injunctive relief. Bryant v. Cheney, 924 F.2d 525 (4th Cir.1991). The circuit court relied on Los Angeles v. Lyons, 461 U.S. 95, 103 S.Ct. 1660, 75 L.Ed.2d 675 (1983), which is reproduced infra at p. 61. Other circuits have split on this issue. Compare Spagnola v. Mathis, 859 F.2d 223 (D.C.Cir.1988) (equitable remedies not "all together precluded" by CSRA) with Lombardi v. SBA, 889 F.2d 959, 961–962 (10th Cir.1989) (CSRA displaces action for injunctive relief; decided before *Webster*). For a general discussion, see Note, Injunctive

Relief for Constitutional Violations: Does the Civil Service Reform Act Preclude Equitable Remedies?, 90 Mich.L.Rev. 2612 (1992).

4. In Note 7 following *Bivens,* supra p. 20, five possible ways of accommodating the power of the courts and the power of Congress to declare a remedy are suggested. After *Chilicky,* which is correct? Have *Chilicky* and *Bush* made congressional intent dispositive by treating Congress's omission of a private cause of action as a "special factor counselling hesitation"?

## A DIGRESSION: REMEDIAL CHOICE IN THE STATUTORY CONTEXT

Just as the Constitution often confers rights without mentioning remedies, Congress occasionally enacts a statute without expressly indicating whether individuals harmed by a violation of the statute can sue. For example, Congress may pass legislation making conduct a crime, but say nothing about whether those whom the conduct injures may sue for damages, injunctive relief, or any other remedy. In such a case, should the courts recognize a private cause of action if they believe it is "necessary and appropriate" to effectuate the statutory scheme, as Justice Harlan's concurrence in *Bivens* suggests?

The Supreme Court addressed this issue in Cort v. Ash, 422 U.S. 66 , 95 S.Ct. 2080, 45 L.Ed.2d 26 (1975). In *Cort*, Congress had made it a crime, punishable by a fine of $5000, for a corporation to contribute to a Presidential campaign. (The statute was later repealed, although it has been replaced by similar provisions. See 2 U.S.C. § 441b.) Mr. Cort sued on behalf of a corporation in which he held stock, alleging that the corporation's directors had violated the statute, and seeking damages.

Writing for the court, Justice Brennan withdrew considerably from the position that a private cause of action will be made available any time a court views it as "necessary or appropriate" to effectuate the statutory scheme. Rather, to infer that a private cause of action exists, a court must examine four factors:

- Was the statute enacted to benefit a class, of which the plaintiff is a member?
- Did the legislature intend to create a private right of action?
- Is implication of a private right consistent with the legislative scheme?
- Is this an area of law traditionally left to state control?

Applying this test, Justice Brennan concluded that the statute was not intended to protect shareholders from the fiscal consequences of campaign contributions, and that therefore it would be inappropriate to allow shareholders a private cause of action for damages.

Some members of the Court believe that the courts' role in deciding that a private cause of action should exist for statutory violations should be even more limited. According to Justice Scalia, for example, the focus should be exclusively on legislative intent. Thompson v. Thompson, 484 U.S. 174, 188, 108 S.Ct. 513, 521, 98 L.Ed.2d 512 (Scalia, J. concurring). Further, Justice Scalia has argued that Congress should be on notice that it must speak if it wishes to create a remedy, and therefore "a flat rule that private rights of action will not be implied in statutes hereafter enacted ..." should be followed, in order to promote certainty in the law. Id. at 192, 108 S.Ct. at 523. The Court, however, generally remains committed to the *Cort* test. See, e.g., California v. Sierra Club, 451 U.S. 287, 101 S.Ct. 1775, 68 L.Ed.2d 101 (1981); Thompson v. Thompson, 484 U.S. 174, 108 S.Ct. 513, 98 L.Ed.2d 512 (1988).

Which is the better position? Should federal courts be allowed to use any remedy that is effective in pursuing the goals of a law, unless Congress has expressly indicated that the remedial scheme it developed is to be exclusive? Or should courts limit the available remedies to those expressly authorized by Congress, unless evidence exists from which a court can infer that Congress intended other remedies to exist? To the extent that the Court has retreated from its earlier, more expansive view of judicial power, should *Bivens* itself be rethought? Or are constitutional violations different?

Once it has been established that a private cause of action exists, *Davis*'s distinction between "cause of action" and "relief" resurfaces. Thus, in Franklin v. Gwinnett County Public Schools, 503 U.S. 60, 112 S.Ct. 1028, 117 L.Ed.2d 208 (1992), the Court was asked whether a student who had been sexually harassed could recover damages by suing under Title IX, the federal statute that prohibits sex discrimination in schools receiving federal financial assistance. The Court found this an easy question. An earlier case, Cannon v. University of Chicago, 441 U.S. 677, 99 S.Ct. 1946, 60 L.Ed.2d 560 (1979), had established that a private cause of action exists under Title IX, and "if a right of action exists to enforce a federal right and Congress is silent on the question of remedies, a federal court may order any appropriate relief." *Franklin*, 503 U.S. at 69. Damages are appropriate, the Court noted in language reminiscent of *Bivens,* because the limited remedies advocated by the government (back pay and injunctive relief) "would leave petitioner remediless."

In reaching this conclusion, the Court rejected out of hand the notion that awarding damages "unduly expands the federal court's power into a sphere properly reserved to the Executive and Legislative Branches":

> In making this argument, respondents misconceive the difference between a cause of action and a remedy. Unlike the finding of a cause of action, which authorizes a court to hear a case or controversy, the discretion to award appropriate relief involves no such increase in judicial power. Federal courts cannot reach out to award remedies when the Constitution or laws of the United States do not support a cause of action. Indeed, properly understood, respondents' position invites us to abdicate our historic judicial

> authority to award appropriate relief in cases brought in our court system. It is well to recall that such authority historically has been thought necessary to provide an important safeguard against abuses of legislative and executive power, as well as to insure an independent judiciary. Moreover, selective abdication of the sort advocated here would harm separation of powers principles in another way, by giving judges the power to render inutile causes of action authorized by Congress through a decision that no remedy is available.

503 U.S. at 73, 112 S.Ct. at 1037.

Of course, the presumption that a court may order any appropriate relief on behalf of a party who has a cause of action under a statute is subject to the will of Congress, and evidence that Congress intended to limit the available remedies will overcome it. Thus, in Landgraf v. USI Film Products, 511 U.S. ___, 114 S.Ct. 1483, 128 L.Ed.2d 229 (1994)(holding that the compensatory and punitive damage provisions of the Civil Rights Act of 1991 are not retroactive), the Court sounded a cautionary note about *Franklin*:

> Title VII is not a statute to which we would apply the "traditional presumption in favor of all available remedies." That statute did not create a "general right to sue" for employment discrimination, but instead specified a set of "circumscribed remedies." Until the 1991 amendment, the Title VII scheme did not allow for damages. We are not free to fashion remedies that Congress has specifically chosen not to extend.

114 S.Ct. at 1507 n. 38.

Could a plaintiff avoid a court's refusal to infer a cause of action for violation of a federal statute by suing for negligence *per se* in state court? See Sierra–Bay Federal Land Bank Association v. Superior Court, 227 Cal.App.3d 318, 277 Cal.Rptr. 753 (1991) (rejecting such an attempt). How about by pleading a § 1983 claim, if a state actor has violated a federal statute? Not according to Legal Environmental Assistance Foundation, Inc. v. Pegues, 904 F.2d 640 (11th Cir.1990). By couching the violation as a RICO violation? No. Danielsen v. Burnside–Ott Aviation Training Center, 941 F.2d 1220 (D.C.Cir.1991) (Service Contract Act).

---

*"Where there's a right, there's a remedy"*

The idea that there must be a remedy for every violation of right is a powerful one. It has been used, as in *Bivens,* to justify the creation of a cause of action without express constitutional or statutory warrant. It has also been invoked by state courts to check legislative action that limits the remedies available to injured plaintiffs. See, e.g., Kansas Malpractice Victims Coalition v. Bell, 243 Kan. 333, 757 P.2d 251 (1988) (statute limiting recoveries in medical malpractice cases to $1,000,000 violates state constitution's guarantee of a remedy by due course of law);

Lucas v. United States, 757 S.W.2d 687 (Tex.1988)(cap of $500,000 on total damages in personal injury cases violates state constitution's guarantee of open courts for the redress of all wrongs). See also John H. Bauman, Remedies Provisions in State Constitutions and the Proper Role of the State Courts, 26 Wake Forest L.Rev. 237 (1991) (discussing cases interpreting "remedy" or "open courts" guarantees in state constitutions).

Yet, as the materials in this chapter make clear, the commitment to this principle is hardly total. As one scholar has argued, "modern doctrine clearly refutes the notion that there is a constitutional right to a remedy for every constitutional violation." Richard H. Fallon, Jr., Some Confusions About Due Process, Judicial Review, and Constitutional Remedies, 93 Colum.L.Rev. 309 (1993). Even in *Bivens,* after all, Justice Brennan made allowance for "special factors counseling hesitation"—concerns, that is, that are allowed to undercut the goal of a complete remedy. Concerns for federalism, separation of powers, and a proper accommodation of the interests of the plaintiff and the defendant all factor into the search for the proper remedy.

Thus, it is probably more accurate to say that where there's a right, there may be many remedies, or none. The question is, how to choose? Professor Fallon contends that what is constitutionally indispensable is a "scheme of constitutional remedies sufficient to keep government tolerably within the bounds of law." Id. What criteria would you use to determine whether a particular scheme is "sufficient"? Should the range of available remedies be determined by a court, or by a legislature? Whichever body will make the decision, how is it to decide? If more than one remedy is available, how is a lawyer to decide which of the available remedies best serves the client's interests?

These are the questions that occupy the remedies course. Whether it is a legislature, a court, or counsel deciding, the key to choosing among remedies lies in understanding the nature and characteristics of each remedy: how it works, how much it costs, when it works well, and what its limits are. To these issues we now turn.

# Chapter 2

# THE NATURE, AVAILABILITY, AND SCOPE OF INJUNCTIONS

## A. THE NATURE OF AN INJUNCTION

### *Problem: Country Lodge v. Miller (Reprised) The Choice Between an Injunction and Damages*

Country Lodge has requested an injunction (a) requiring Miller to clean up the apple mash that washed ashore on its property last fall and (b) prohibiting Miller from committing future nuisances. Miller urges the court to deny injunctive relief and instead give Country Lodge compensatory damages for both past and future harms. What should the court do?

---

The choice between injunctions and compensatory damages is of real consequence to the parties and court. An injunction, an equitable remedy, is an order that directs a person to act or refrain from acting in a specified way. In contrast, a money judgment, a legal remedy, is not an order and is not directed to a specific person.

> [C]oercive remedies in equity are variants of the injunction. The injunction is a personal order to the defendant. It is not merely a judgment such as the law courts might issue. It did not merely declare the defendant's debt or obligation, but instead commanded the defendant to do or refrain from a specified act. * * * The essence of the remedy in most instances * * * is the *in personam* order, enforced by the distinctive power of contempt. * * *
>
> The old separate law courts did not issue injunctive orders; they rendered judgments instead. The law courts did not seek to enforce their orders by contempt powers, but by seizure of property.

Dan B. Dobbs, The Law of Remedies § 2.1(1)(2d ed.1993).

Violation of an injunction, as an order of the court, is contempt of court and punishable under the courts' contempt power. Chapter 3 treats the contempt power in detail, but it is useful to go over some basics now. If the injunction is violated, the court may award monetary compensation to the plaintiff. This is known as *compensatory civil contempt*. It differs from an ordinary action for compensatory damages in that the contemnor does not have a right to a jury trial and the court generally has authority to award the plaintiff attorney's fees.

If compensatory civil contempt were the only remedy for contempt, an injunction would, in essence, be a substitutionary rather than a specific remedy. In order to enforce their orders specifically, the courts have two other weapons. First, the court may coerce the contemnor into obeying the order by jailing or fining her so long as the disobedience continues. This is known as *coercive civil contempt*. The measure of the duress is what is needed to make the contemnor comply rather than plaintiff's rightful position. Second, if the violation of the injunction is willful, the court may adjudge the contemnor guilty of a crime and impose sentence. This is known as *criminal contempt*.

Both coercive civil contempt and criminal contempt mean that even a defendant willing to pay for any damage done to plaintiff is not free to disregard an injunction. This leads to important differences between injunctive and damage relief, as Judge Guido Calabresi and Mr. Douglas Melamed show in the following excerpt:

> An entitlement [i.e., a right] is protected by a property rule [e.g., an injunction] to the extent that someone who wishes to remove the entitlement from its holder must buy it from him in a voluntary transaction in which the value of the entitlement is agreed upon by the seller. It is the form of entitlement which gives rise to the least amount of state intervention: once the original entitlement is decided upon, the state does not try to decide its value. It lets each of the parties say how much the entitlement is worth to him, and gives the seller a veto if the buyer does not offer enough. Property rules involve a collective decision as to whom is to be given an initial entitlement but not as to the value of the entitlement.
>
> Whenever someone may destroy the initial entitlement if he is willing to pay an objectively determined value for it, an entitlement is protected by a liability rule [e.g., compensatory damages]. This value may be what it is thought the original holder of the entitlement would have sold it for. But the holder's complaint that he would have demanded more will not avail him once the objectively determined value is set. Obviously, liability rules involve an additional stage of state intervention: not only are entitlements protected, but their transfer or destruction is allowed on the basis of a value determined by some organ of the state rather than by the parties themselves.

Guido Calabresi & Douglas Melamed, Property Rules, Liability Rules, and Inalienability: One View of the Cathedral, 85 Harv.L.Rev. 1089, 1092 (1972). The term "property rule" is used because the law tends to protect property entitlements with injunctive relief and/or criminal sanctions, as in cases of trespass or theft.

So, for example, denying Country Lodge an injunction against future nuisances means that Miller may take Country Lodge's entitlement to be free from the nuisance by paying damages. Suppose that the court sets the damages at $10,000 annually, based upon an estimate of lost profits. Miller would obviously prefer this outcome to an injunction because it would cost her $20,000 annually to dispose of the waste without making a nuisance.

There are many reasons why Country Lodge may prefer an injunction. First, and most basically, Miller is taking Country Lodge's entitlement by paying compensation. In contrast, the Constitution's fifth and fourteenth amendments prohibit the taking of private property for *private* purposes, even if compensation is paid. Second, Country Lodge may believe that $10,000 annually underestimates its lost profits. Third, Country Lodge's owners may place a subjective value on a clean river that is not recoverable as damages for lost profits or the decrease in the market value of its property.

Fourth, and finally, if Country Lodge gets an injunction, it might make a deal with Miller to trade the injunction for more than $10,000 annually. Miller would be better off paying any amount up to $20,000 and Country Lodge would be better taking any amount more than the value to it of a clean river. If that amount is less than $20,000, there is room for a deal. If a deal is made, the price that Miller will pay to Country Lodge will depend upon their respective negotiating skills and bargaining positions. Economists call the difference between what a seller (Country Lodge) and a buyer (Miller) places on a right "gains from trade." Relegating Country Lodge to damages gives all of the gains from trade to Miller. Issuing an injunction gives Country Lodge some of these gains, if they make a deal. Country Lodge may think this only fair. On the other hand, Miller may view Country Lodge's demanding more than its subjective loss as extortion.

Miller has other reasons to prefer paying damages to an injunction. First, Miller may fail to get Country Lodge to agree to sell its entitlement. Second, Miller would be the target of what is, in essence, a mini-criminal statute aimed exclusively at her. Third, the court may draft an injunction that is quite broad, prohibiting her from otherwise legal activity. Fourth, should she happen to violate the injunction, Miller will have to pay Country Lodge's attorney's fees and will not have the option to have a jury, as she would in an ordinary civil suit for damages.

The court also has a stake in the choice of remedy. Setting damages and collecting them can be burdensome, but so can be drafting an injunction and enforcing it.

To get an injunction, the plaintiff must establish that it meets a number of prerequisites for injunctive relief. It must show that there is a *threat of harm* from defendant. For instance, Country Lodge could not get an injunction unless Miller seems likely to make a nuisance again.

Plaintiff must also, according to black letter law, show that there is *no adequate remedy at law,* such as compensatory damages. One way to show that the remedy at law is inadequate is to demonstrate that plaintiff could not replace what defendant has taken with compensatory damages—that is, to demonstrate *irreparable injury.* Country Lodge could demonstrate irreparable injury from future nuisances because, apart from Miller, no one can sell it a clean river in front of its property and courts usually treat each piece of real estate as unique. Country Lodge might, however, have a tougher time getting an injunction requiring Miller to clean up the mess from the past nuisance because it could use compensatory damages to hire a contractor to do the job. Indeed, Country Lodge would prefer compensatory damages if it wanted the clean up done before adjudication or the right to choose who did the clean up. But if Country Lodge nonetheless sought an injunction to clean up past wrongs, the court probably would find damages to be an inadequate remedy so that plaintiff would not have to bear the risk that compensatory damages will fall short of the actual costs or suffer the aggravation of correcting defendant's intentional wrongdoing. Douglas Laycock, The Death of the Irreparable Injury Rule, 103 Harv.L.Rev. 688, 710–14 (1990)(the article was republished as a book of the same name in 1991).

A final prerequisite is *practicality of enforcement.* Country Lodge will not get an injunction if the court concludes that enforcing it against Miller is impossible or would unduly burden the court.

These prerequisites are only part of the inquiry. Under the rubric of *balancing the equities,* courts grant injunctions that fall short of plaintiff's rightful position or even deny injunctive relief altogether if an injunction would impose an undue hardship on defendant or otherwise be unfair. If this defense is successful, plaintiff can still get damages for the harm that the injunction fails to prevent. For example, Miller might avoid an injunction prohibiting future nuisances on the ground that this would put her out of business, but she would nonetheless have to pay damages for any future harm.

A court must not aim to give plaintiff more than its rightful position. Nonetheless, it can issue injunctions that achieve more than plaintiff's rightful position when there is no other way of achieving it precisely or when a precise injunction would be difficult to enforce. These are known as *prophylactic injunctions.*

Section B of this chapter considers problems in determining plaintiff's rightful position. Section C considers the prerequisites to injunctive relief—threat of harm, no adequate remedy at law, and practicality of enforcement. Section D considers granting less or more than plaintiff's rightful position—that is, balancing the equities and prophylactic injunctions. Section E considers coercive remedies other than injunctions. These include specific performance of contracts, some judicial orders to correct administrative errors, and administrative orders to enforce regulatory statutes. While these coercive orders do not go by the name "injunction" and are subject to special doctrines, as discussed in section E, they serve a function like that of injunctions and are, in general, controlled by the principles discussed in this chapter. See, e.g., Alfred C. Aman, Jr., Administrative Equity: An Analysis of Exceptions to Administrative Rules, 1982 Duke L.J. 277.

## B. PLAINTIFF'S RIGHTFUL POSITION AS THE MEASURE OF AN INJUNCTION

An injunction's primary mission must be to protect the plaintiff's rightful position. This phrase encompasses preventing future wrongdoing and, if the wrong has already occurred, repairing the harm done to the plaintiff.

In many cases, what an injunction should do to protect the plaintiff's rightful position is evident from the law of liability. When the defendant fails to make deliveries under a contract, an injunction to protect the plaintiff's rightful position would require the defendant to make the deliveries. Or, when the defendant trespasses, an injunction to protect the plaintiff's rightful position would forbid future trespasses.

Sometimes, however, what an injunction should do to protect the plaintiff's rightful position is not so evident.

### *Problem: Country Lodge v. Miller (Reprised)*
### *Defining the Rightful Position*

(a) The court found Miller liable because it is a private nuisance to put enough debris in the river to be visible. Country Lodge has asked for an injunction permanently barring Miller from placing any effluent into the river. Should the court grant such an injunction?

(b) Would your answer change if the basis of liability was, instead of the common law of nuisance, a statute prohibiting placing effluent into a river without a permit?

(c) Can the court also require Miller to attend a two hour course at the local community college on environmental values?

## MT. HEALTHY CITY SCHOOL DISTRICT BOARD OF EDUCATION v. DOYLE

Supreme Court of the United States, 1977.
429 U.S. 274, 97 S.Ct. 568, 50 L.Ed.2d 471.

MR. JUSTICE REHNQUIST delivered the opinion of the Court.

Respondent Doyle sued petitioner Mt. Healthy Board of Education in the United States District Court for the Southern District of Ohio. Doyle claimed that the Board's refusal to renew his contract in 1971 violated his rights under the First and Fourteenth Amendments to the United States Constitution. After a bench trial the District Court held that Doyle was entitled to reinstatement with backpay. The Court of Appeals for the Sixth Circuit affirmed the judgment, and we granted the Board's petition for certiorari * * *.

Doyle was first employed by the Board in 1966. He worked under one-year contracts for the first three years, and under a two-year contract from 1969 to 1971. In 1969 he was elected president of the Teachers' Association * * *. During Doyle's one-year term as president of the Association, and during the succeeding year when he served on its executive committee, there was apparently some tension in relations between the Board and the Association.

Beginning early in 1970, Doyle was involved in several incidents not directly connected with his role in the Teachers' Association. In one instance, he engaged in an argument with another teacher which culminated in the other teacher's slapping him. Doyle subsequently refused to accept an apology and insisted upon some punishment for the other teacher. His persistence in the matter resulted in the suspension of both teachers for one day, which was followed by a walkout by a number of other teachers, which in turn resulted in the lifting of the suspensions.

On other occasions, Doyle got into an argument with employees of the school cafeteria over the amount of spaghetti which had been served him; referred to students, in connection with a disciplinary complaint, as "sons of bitches"; and made an obscene gesture to two girls in connection with their failure to obey commands made in his capacity as cafeteria supervisor. Chronologically the last in the series of incidents which respondent was involved in during his employment by the Board was a telephone call by him to a local radio station. It was the Board's consideration of this incident which the court below found to be a violation of the First and Fourteenth Amendments.

In February 1971, the principal circulated to various teachers a memorandum relating to teacher dress and appearance, which was apparently prompted by the view of some in the administration that there was a relationship between teacher appearance and public support for bond issues. Doyle's response to the receipt of the memorandum on a subject which he apparently understood was to be settled by joint teacher-administration action was to convey the substance of the memorandum to a disc jockey at WSAI, a Cincinnati radio station, who promptly announced the adoption of the dress code as a news item. Doyle subsequently apologized to the principal, conceding that he should have made some prior communication of his criticism to the school administration.

Approximately one month later the superintendent made his customary annual recommendations to the Board as to the rehiring of nontenured teachers. He recommended that Doyle not be rehired. The same recommendation was made with respect to nine other teachers in the district, and in all instances, including Doyle's, the recommendation was adopted by the Board. Shortly after being notified of this decision, respondent requested a statement of reasons for the Board's actions. He received a statement citing "a notable lack of tact in handling professional matters which leaves much doubt as to your sincerity in establishing good school relationships." That general statement was followed by references to the radio station incident and to the obscene-gesture incident.

The District Court found that all of these incidents had in fact occurred. It concluded that respondent Doyle's telephone call to the radio station was "clearly protected by the First Amendment," and that because it had played a "substantial part" in the decision of the Board not to renew Doyle's employment, he was entitled to reinstatement with backpay. * * *

Doyle's claims under the First and Fourteenth Amendments are not defeated by the fact that he did not have tenure. Even though he could have been discharged for no reason whatever, and had no constitutional right to a hearing prior to the decision not to rehire him, he may nonetheless establish a claim to reinstatement if the decision not to rehire him was made by reason of his exercise of constitutionally protected First Amendment freedoms.

* * * We * * * accept the District Court's finding that the communication was protected by the First and Fourteenth Amendments. We are not, however, entirely in agreement with that court's manner of reasoning from this finding to the conclusion that Doyle is entitled to reinstatement with backpay.

The District Court made the following "conclusions" on this aspect of the case:

> "1) If a non-permissible reason, e.g., exercise of First Amendment rights, played a substantial part in the decision not to renew even in the face of other permissible grounds—the decision may not stand (citations omitted).
>
> "2) A non-permissible reason did play a substantial part. That is clear from the letter of the Superintendent immediately following the Board's decision, which stated two reasons—the one, the conversation with the radio station, clearly protected by the First Amendment. A court may not engage in any limitation of First Amendment rights based on 'tact'—that is not to say that the 'tactfulness' is irrelevant to other issues in this case."

At the same time, though, it stated that "(i)n fact, as this Court sees it and finds, both the Board and the Superintendent were faced with a situation in which there did exist in fact reason * * * independent of any First Amendment rights or exercise thereof, to not extend tenure."

Since respondent Doyle had no tenure, and there was therefore not even a state-law requirement of "cause" or "reason" before a decision could be made not to renew his employment, it is not clear what the District Court meant by this latter statement. Clearly the Board legally could have dismissed respondent had the radio station incident never come to its attention. One plausible meaning of the court's statement is that the Board and the Superintendent not only could, but in fact would have reached that decision had not the constitutionally protected incident of the telephone call to the radio station occurred. We are thus brought to the issue whether, even if that were the case, the fact that the protected conduct played a "substantial part" in the actual decision not to renew would necessarily amount to a constitutional violation justifying remedial action. We think that it would not.

A rule of causation which focuses solely on whether protected conduct played a part, "substantial" or otherwise, in a decision not to rehire, could place an employee in a better position as a result of the exercise of constitutionally protected conduct than he would have occupied had he done nothing. The difficulty with the rule enunciated by the District Court is that it would require reinstatement in cases where a dramatic and perhaps abrasive incident is inevitably on the minds of those responsible for the decision to rehire, and does indeed play a part in that decision even if the same decision would have been reached had the incident not occurred. The constitutional principle at stake is sufficiently vindicated if such an employee is placed in no worse a position than if he had not engaged in the conduct. A borderline or marginal candidate should not have the employment question resolved against him because of constitutionally protected conduct. But that same candidate ought not to be able, by engaging in such conduct, to prevent his employer from assessing his performance record and reaching a decision not to rehire on the basis of that record, simply because the protected conduct makes the employer more certain of the correctness of its decision.

This is especially true where, as the District Court observed was the case here, the current decision to rehire will accord "tenure." * * *

Initially, in this case, the burden was properly placed upon respondent to show that his conduct was constitutionally protected, and that this conduct was a "substantial factor" * * * in the Board's decision not to rehire him. Respondent having carried that burden, however, the District Court should have gone on to determine whether the Board had shown by a preponderance of the evidence that it would have reached the same decision as to respondent's reemployment even in the absence of the protected conduct.

We cannot tell from the District Court opinion and conclusions, nor from the opinion of the Court of Appeals affirming the judgment of the District Court, what conclusion those courts would have reached had they applied this test. The judgment of the Court of Appeals is therefore vacated, and the case remanded for further proceedings consistent with this opinion.

### *Notes*

1. *Plaintiff's rightful position is not necessarily what the plaintiff wants.* On remand in *Mt. Healthy,* the district court determined that the

original record established, by a preponderance of the evidence, that Doyle would not have been renewed for reasons quite apart from his constitutionally protected speech, and the Court of Appeals affirmed. Doyle v. Mt. Healthy, 670 F.2d 59 (6th Cir.1982). Should Doyle have gotten his job back anyway?

The Civil Rights Act of 1991 provides a remedy to individuals fired in part because of race, religion, and gender who would have been fired in the absence of an impermissible factor by allowing the court to grant declaratory and injunctive relief against future violations. In addition, the court may grant attorney's fees. 42 U.S.C. §§ 2000e–2(m) & 2000e–5(g).

2. *The court cannot always reproduce the plaintiff's rightful position exactly.* *Mt. Healthy* states that "[t]he constitutional principle at stake is sufficiently vindicated if such an employee is placed in no worse a position than if he had not engaged in the conduct." However, the Court's remedy puts Doyle in a better than rightful position as a practical matter. If Doyle had never contacted the radio station, the school board could have dismissed him without giving any justification; but having violated his rights, the board must reinstate him unless it can convince the district court that there is good reason not to rehire him. Is there any remedy that would put Doyle in the rightful position exactly? When there is no remedy that will achieve the rightful position exactly, the injunction's *terms* may overreach the rightful position so long as the injunction's *aim* is to achieve no more than the rightful position.

3. *Plaintiff's rightful position and questions of causality.* The factual question in *Mt. Healthy* was whether the board would have rehired Doyle but for its reaction to his first amendment activities. Is that a question of remedy or a question of liability? In thinking about this question, suppose that the board rehired Doyle, but gave his call to the radio station as one reason to deny him a pay raise, even though they would have denied him a pay raise even if he had not called the radio station. Could Doyle get an injunction against the board's penalizing his first amendment activities in the future? Even if the board would have fired Doyle anyway, Doyle could recover compensatory damages if he could show that the improper reason given for his firing in fact caused him harm that was foreseeable.

Cause-in-fact can be relevant to liability, as in torts. Price Waterhouse v. Hopkins, 490 U.S. 228, 109 S.Ct. 1775, 104 L.Ed.2d 268 (1989), presents a factual issue similar to that in *Mt. Healthy* in the liability context. Price Waterhouse decided not to promote Ann Hopkins, partly because of her gender and partly because of legitimate reasons. Hopkins sued under Title VII of the Civil Rights Act of 1964, 42 U.S.C. § 2000e et seq., which, inter alia, forbids adverse employment actions "because of" gender. Price Waterhouse claimed that the legitimate reasons were sufficient to block her promotion. All members of the Court agreed that, given the wording of Title VII, liability requires that the impermissible motive must have caused the unfavorable employment decision. At the same time, however, a majority of the court decided that once the employer had purposely taken her gender into account, the burden shifted to it to show that she would not have been promoted for legitimate reasons. On remand in *Price Waterhouse*, the district court held that the firm failed to prove that it would have deferred Hopkins's promotion but for her gender and ordered that she be made a partner. Hopkins v. Price Waterhouse, 737 F.Supp. 1202 (D.D.C.), aff'd, 920 F.2d 967 (D.C.Cir.1990).

4. *The "after-acquired evidence" cases.* In McKennon v. Nashville Banner Publishing Co., 513 U.S. ___, 115 S.Ct. 879, 130 L.Ed.2d 852 (1995), Christine McKennon alleged that the company fired her on account of her age in violation of Age Discrimination Act of 1967. In discovery, she admitted that she had taken home confidential documents, claiming that she wanted them to defend herself should she be illegally fired. Citing *Mt. Healthy,* the lower courts dismissed McKennon's suit on the theory that this evidence acquired after her supposedly illegal firing provided a supervening legal reason to fire her. A unanimous Supreme Court reversed. It distinguished *Mt. Healthy* because there the employer had two motives at the time of firing, one lawful, the other unlawful. But, McKennon "comes to us on the express assumption that an unlawful motive was the sole basis for the firing," the lawful motive for firing coming to light only later. Nonetheless, the after-acquired evidence is relevant to the remedy:

> It would be both inequitable and pointless to order the reinstatement of someone the employer would have terminated, and will terminate, in any event and upon lawful grounds. [As to backpay,] [t]he object of compensation is to restore the employee to the position he or she would have been in absent the discrimination, but that principle is difficult to apply with precision where there is after-acquired evidence of wrongdoing that would have led to termination on legitimate grounds had the employer known about it. * * * The beginning point in the trial court's formulation of a remedy should be calculation of backpay from the date of the unlawful discharge to the date the new information was discovered.

115 S.Ct. at 886. Has the Court put McKennon in her rightful position?

### *Note on Rightful Position as Reconsideration or Remand in Administrative Law*

The most important lesson from *Mt. Healthy* is that plaintiff's rightful position and therefore the aim of the injunction depends upon a clear understanding of plaintiff's right. *The framing of an injunction must begin with a careful definition of the plaintiff's right.* In *Mt. Healthy,* Doyle did not have a right to a government job but rather a right not to be fired for his speech. Given this right, Doyle gets consideration of whether he would have kept his job apart from the violation of his free speech rights rather than the job itself.

*Mt. Healthy* is but one example of a broad range of cases where plaintiff has no absolute right to his ultimate objective but rather a right not to be denied that objective for the wrong reason or in the wrong way. If Doyle had been fired because of accusations to which he was denied an opportunity to respond in violation of due process or in violation of a civil service statute, the injunction would not restore his job but would give him an appropriate hearing to consider the charges. Or, if Doyle was about to lose his job because the school was to be torn down to make way for a highway whose funding was approved without statutorily required environmental analysis, the injunction would not permanently bar the highway but would bar it unless and until the statutorily required analysis was performed to consider whether to approve or disapprove the highway. Or, if Doyle's school received a state or federal grant one of whose conditions was that teachers be paid more, the injunction would not require that Doyle be paid more but that the school not receive the grant unless the teachers were paid more. The school would then have to consider whether to forego the grant or pay more. Rosado v. Wyman, 397 U.S. 397, 420, 90 S.Ct. 1207, 1221–22, 25 L.Ed.2d 442, 460 (1970). See also Note, Injunctive Relief From State Violations of Federal Funding Conditions, 82 Colum.L.Rev. 1236, 1256–59 (1982)(discussing cases that follow and deviate from *Rosado*).

Reconsideration relief is common in the administrative law context. For example, when an administrative agency denies an application for a permit and in so doing considers a factor that is improper under the governing statute, the court sitting in review of the agency will not ordinarily order the agency to grant the permit. To do so may put the applicant in a better than rightful position because the agency might have denied the permit for a statutorily proper reason even if it had not considered the improper factor.

Quite apart from whether the relief shall be reconsideration is the question of *who* should do the reconsidering. In *Mt. Healthy,* the Supreme Court required reconsideration to be by the district court rather than by the school board. Remanding to the board probably would not have been a reliable way to put Doyle in his rightful position because the board might have continued to punish Doyle for his privileged activities while pretending to fire him for some other reason. Transferring the decision whether to reinstate Doyle from the board to the district court is another instance where the aim of putting plaintiff in his rightful position resulted in his ending up in a better position.

In judicial review of agency action, a court's determination that the agency has committed an error is like a judgment of liability in a civil suit. The error may be, for instance, consideration of an improper factor, failing to follow the requisite procedures, or arbitrary reasoning. The agency action may be, for example, the issuance of regulations, the grant of a permit, the issuance of a license, or a decision not to take such actions. What the court does in response to that error is a decision about a remedy. The ordinary remedy is a remand to the agency for a proper reconsideration. SEC v. Chenery Corp., 318 U.S. 80, 63 S.Ct. 454, 87 L.Ed. 626 (1943). But other remedies are possible. If the court is sure that the agency would, for example, have granted the permit that the petitioner had sought, then the court will reverse the agency, ordering it to grant the permit. NLRB v. Wyman–Gordon Co., 394 U.S. 759, 766 n.6, 89 S.Ct. 1426, 1430 n.6, 22 L.Ed.2d 709, 715 n.6 (1969). Or, if the agency had granted the permit and the court is sure that it would not have but for the error, the court could reverse the agency and vacate the permit. However, if the court is sure that agency would have reached the same result even if it had not made the error, the court will say there is no reversible error and will affirm the agency action. NLRB v. American Geri–Care Inc., 697 F.2d 56, 64 (2d Cir.1982), cert. denied, 461 U.S. 906, 103 S.Ct. 1876, 76 L.Ed.2d 807 (1983). But, when in doubt, the court remands.

The remand remedy differs from a simple reversal in two respects. First, as a matter of substance, the successful complainant will not necessarily get what it ultimately wants but rather a reconsideration, theoretically free from error. Second, as a matter of procedure, doubtful cases are to be decided by the governmental entity originally charged with making the decision rather than by the court. Do you see why both these differences are compelled by the rightful position concept?

It may seem bizarre to remand a matter to an agency that has reached a flawed result. However, the defendants in these administrative law cases are coordinate branches of government. Courts generally presume that such coordinate branches will act properly once they have a clear understanding of the law, just as appellate courts usually presume that lower courts will act as instructed when a case is remanded. Should the agency repeat its error on remand, the petitioner can once again get the reviewing court to intervene, if petitioner has the money for legal fees and the time to wait and if the agency has not successfully camouflaged its error with pretexts.

In light of *Mt. Healthy,* it should come as no surprise that Congress, in enacting Title VII, the federal statute forbidding employment discrimination, 42 U.S.C. § 2000e et seq., specified that the remedy should be neither reversal of the employer's decision nor a remand to the employer but rather de novo reconsideration by a court. Under this statute, the Supreme Court has specified in some detail how the district court should try to achieve plaintiff's rightful position by trying to mimic how a fair minded employer would have acted. International Brotherhood of Teamsters v. United States, 431 U.S. 324, 371–72, 97 S.Ct. 1843, 1873, 52 L.Ed.2d 396, 437–38 (1977). When the discriminating employer is a federal agency, the tradition of remand in administrative law could well have resulted in a remand to the agency, but the Supreme Court has read Title VII to require de novo judicial reconsideration even where the defendant is a federal agency. Chandler v. Roudebush, 425 U.S. 840, 862, 96 S.Ct. 1949, 1960, 48 L.Ed.2d 416, 431–32 (1976).

When not constrained by statute, courts sometimes craft creative solutions to problems in taking direct aim at plaintiff's rightful position. In Zorick v. Tynes, 372 So.2d 133 (Fla.App.1979), a public school withdrew an offer to a prospective physical education instructor when it learned he was blind. The court concluded that denying a job on the basis of handicap violated state law and ordered the school board to give the plaintiff a period of trial employment to determine whether he could do the job. That made more sense than holding a judicial hearing, since plaintiff apparently had no work experience to evaluate, or ordering the school to reconsider before the plaintiff went to work, since it would be hard to check whether the board had based its decision on job qualifications or prejudice towards the handicapped.

Courts sometimes remand to legislatures to rewrite invalid laws just as they sometimes remand to agencies to reconsider invalid administrative decisions. So, for example, after holding that the state's educational finance statute failed to comply with the state constitution, the New Jersey Supreme Court requested the legislature to rewrite the statute. Abbott v. Burke, 119 N.J. 287, 575 A.2d 359 (1990).

### *Problem: The Racially Biased Election*

Where plaintiff is a candidate who lost a fraudulently conducted election, a court will ordinarily order a new election be held—in essence remanding the case to the electoral process—rather than ordering the plaintiff be declared the winner. However, if the fraud affected fewer votes than the margin of victory, the court may issue no injunction—in essence affirming the flawed election—because the plaintiff's rightful position is as an electoral loser. See, e.g., Marks v. Stinson, 19 F.3d 873 (3d Cir.1994). Suppose, rather than work-a-day fraud, the problem with the election was unconstitutional exclusion of almost all African–American voters in an election between a white and an African–American candidate and that the margin of victory for the white candidate was several times larger than the number of voters excluded. Would the plaintiffs, the African–American candidate and the excluded voters, be in their rightful position if the election is affirmed? On such facts, Bell v. Southwell, 376 F.2d 659 (5th Cir.1967), ordered a new election on the theory that it cannot be presumed that the African–American candidate would have lost an election untainted by racial discrimination, which may have created a racially charged atmosphere that dissuaded white voters from voting for her. Given southern politics in the 1960's, does this seem realistic? The court offered an additional argument that "state-imposed racial discrimination cannot be tolerated and to eliminate the practice or the temptation toward it, the law must extinguish the judgment wrought by such a procedure." Id. at 663. Is this argument convincing? In connection with another issue in the case, the court stated:

> Mrs. Bell as a former candidate did not seek to be selected over Southwell or any other opponent. What, and all, she and [the other plaintiffs, who were frustrated voters,] sought was an election conducted free of such indefensible, racial distinctions. That being so, it was not the usual case of counting votes and denying relief for want of affirmative proof of a different result.

Id. at 664–65. Does this observation provide a stronger justification for ordering a new election?

## RIZZO v. GOODE

Supreme Court of the United States, 1976.
423 U.S. 362, 96 S.Ct. 598, 46 L.Ed.2d 561.

MR. JUSTICE REHNQUIST delivered the opinion of the Court.

The District Court for the Eastern District of Pennsylvania, after parallel trials of separate actions filed in 1970, entered an order in 1973 requiring petitioners "to submit to [the District] Court for its approval a comprehensive program for improving the handling of citizen complaints alleging police misconduct" in accordance with a comprehensive opinion filed together with the order. The proposed program, negotiated between petitioners and respondents for the purpose of complying with the order, was incorporated six months later into a final judgment. Petitioner City Police Commissioner was thereby required, *inter alia,* to put into force a directive governing the manner by which citizens' complaints against police officers should henceforth be handled by the department. The Court of Appeals for the Third Circuit, upholding the District Court's finding that the existing procedures for handling citizen complaints were "inadequate," affirmed the District Court's choice of equitable relief: "The revisions were . . . ordered because they appeared to have the potential for prevention of future police misconduct." We granted certiorari to consider petitioners' claims that the judgment of the District Court represents an unwarranted intrusion by the federal judiciary into the discretionary authority committed to them by state and local law to perform their official functions. We find ourselves substantially in agreement with these claims, and we therefore reverse the judgment of the Court of Appeals.

I

The central thrust of respondents' efforts in the two trials was to lay a foundation for equitable intervention, in one degree or another, because of an assertedly pervasive pattern of illegal and unconstitutional mistreatment by police officers. This mistreatment was said to have been directed against minority citizens in particular and against all Philadelphia residents in general. The named individual and group respondents were certified to represent these two classes. The principal petitioners here—the Mayor, the City Managing Director, and the Police Commissioner—were charged with conduct ranging from express authorization or encouragement of this mistreatment to failure to act in a manner so as to assure that it would not recur in the future.

Hearing some 250 witnesses during 21 days of hearings, the District Court was faced with a staggering amount of evidence; each of the 40–odd incidents might alone have been the *piece de resistance* of a short, separate trial. * * *

The District Court made a number of conclusions of law, not all of which are relevant to our analysis. It found that the evidence did not establish the existence of any policy on the part of the named petitioners to violate the legal and constitutional rights of the plaintiff classes, but it did find that evidence of departmental procedure indicated a tendency to discourage the filing of civilian complaints and to minimize the consequences of police misconduct. It found that as to the larger plaintiff class, the residents of Philadelphia, only a small percentage of policemen commit violations of their legal and constitutional rights, but that the frequency with which such violations occur is such that "they cannot be dismissed as rare, isolated instances." * * *

The District Court concluded by directing petitioners to draft, for the court's approval, "a comprehensive program for dealing adequately with civilian complaints", to be formulated along * * * "guidelines" suggested by the court * * *.

While noting that the "guidelines" were consistent with "generally recognized minimum standards" and imposed "no substantial burdens" on the police department, the District Court emphasized that respondents had no constitutional *right* to improved police procedures for handling civilian complaints. But given that violations of constitutional rights of citizens occur in "unacceptably" high numbers, and are likely to continue to occur, the court-mandated revision was a "necessary first step" in attempting to prevent future abuses. * * *

II

These actions were brought, and the affirmative equitable relief fashioned, under the Civil Rights Act of 1871, 42 U.S.C. § 1983. It provides that "[e]very person who, under color of [law] subjects, or causes to be subjected, any ... person within the jurisdiction [of the United States] to the deprivation of any rights ... secured by the Constitution and laws, shall be liable to the party injured in an action at law [or] suit in equity...." * * *

The findings of fact made by the District Court at the conclusion of these two parallel trials—in sharp contrast to that which respondents sought to prove with respect to petitioners—disclose a central paradox which permeates that court's legal conclusions. Individual police officers *not named as parties* to the action were found to have violated the constitutional rights of particular individuals, only a few of whom were parties plaintiff. As the facts developed, there was no affirmative link between the occurrence of the various incidents of police misconduct and the adoption of any plan or policy by petitioners—express or otherwise—showing their authorization or approval of such misconduct. Instead, the *sole* causal connection found by the District Court between petitioners and the individual respondents was that in the absence of a change in police disciplinary procedures, the incidents were likely to continue to occur, *not* with respect to them, but as to the members of the classes they represented. In sum, the genesis of this lawsuit—a heated dispute between individual citizens and certain policemen—has evolved into an attempt by the federal judiciary to resolve a "controversy" between the entire citizenry of Philadelphia and the petitioning elected and appointed officials over what steps might, in the Court of Appeals' words, "[appear] to have the potential for prevention of future police misconduct." * * *

B

Nothing in Hague v. CIO, 307 U.S. 496, 59 S.Ct. 954, 83 L.Ed. 1423 (1939), the only decision of this Court cited by the District Court, or any other case from this Court, supports such an open-ended construction of § 1983. In *Hague*, the pattern of police misconduct upon which liability and injunctive relief were grounded was the adoption and enforcement of deliberate policies by the defendants there (including the Mayor and the Chief of Police) of excluding and removing the plaintiff's labor organizers and forbidding peaceful communication of their views to the citizens of Jersey City. These policies were implemented "by force and violence" on the part of individual policemen. There was no mistaking that the defendants proposed to continue their unconstitutional policies against the members of this discrete group. * * *

Respondents stress that the District Court not only found an "unacceptably high" number of incidents but held, as did the Court of Appeals, that "when a *pattern* of frequent police violations of rights is shown, the law is clear that injunctive relief may be granted." However, there was no showing that the behavior of the Philadelphia police was different in kind or degree from that which exists elsewhere; indeed, the District Court found "that the problems disclosed by the record * * * are fairly typical of [those] afflicting police departments in major urban areas." Thus, invocation of the word "pattern" in a case where, unlike *Hague* * * *, the defendants are not causally linked to it, is but a distant echo of the findings in those cases. The focus in *Hague* * * * was not simply on the number of violations which occurred but on the common thread running through them: a "pervasive pattern of intimidation" flowing from a deliberate plan by the *named* defendants to crush the nascent labor organizations. The District Court's unadorned finding of a statistical pattern is quite dissimilar to the factual settings of these two cases.

The theory of liability underlying the District Court's opinion, and urged upon us by respondents, is that even without a showing of direct responsibility for the actions of a small percentage of the police force, petitioners' *failure* to act in the face of a statistical pattern is indistinguishable from the active conduct enjoined in *Hague* * * *. Respondents posit a constitutional "duty" on the part of petitioners (and a corresponding "right" of the citizens of Philadelphia) to "eliminate" future police misconduct; a "default" of that affirmative duty being shown by the statistical pattern, the District Court is empowered to act in petitioners' stead and take whatever preventive measures are necessary, within its discretion, to secure the "right" at issue. Such reasoning, however, blurs accepted usages and meanings in the English language in a way which would be quite inconsistent with the words Congress chose in § 1983. We have never subscribed to these amorphous propositions, and we decline to do so now.

Respondents claim that the theory of liability embodied in the District Court's opinion is supported by desegregation cases such as Swann v. Charlotte–Mecklenburg Board of Education, 402 U.S. 1, 91 S.Ct. 1267, 28 L.Ed.2d 554 (1971). * * *

Respondents, in their effort to bring themselves within the language of *Swann,* ignore a critical factual distinction between their case and the desegregation cases decided by this Court. In the latter, segregation imposed by law had been implemented by state authorities for varying periods of time, whereas in the instant case the District Court found that the responsible authorities had played no affirmative part in depriving any members of the two respondent classes of any constitutional rights. Those against whom injunctive relief was directed in cases such as *Swann* and *Brown* were not administrators and school board members who had in their employ a small number of individuals, which latter on their own deprived Afro–American students of their constitutional rights to a unitary school system. They were administrators and school board members who were found by their *own* conduct in the administration of the school system to have denied those rights. Here, the District Court found that none of the petitioners had deprived the respondent classes of any rights secured under the Constitution. Under the well-established rule that federal "judicial powers may be exercised only on the basis of a constitutional violation," *Swann*, this case presented no occasion for the District Court to grant equitable relief against petitioners.

C

Going beyond considerations concerning the existence of a live controversy and threshold statutory liability, we must address an additional and novel claim advanced by respondent classes. They assert that given the citizenry's "right" to be protected from unconstitutional exercises of police power, and the "need for protection from such abuses," respondents have a right to mandatory equitable relief in some form when those in supervisory positions do not institute steps to reduce the incidence of unconstitutional police misconduct. The scope of federal equity power, it is proposed, should be extended to the fashioning of prophylactic procedures for a state agency designed to minimize this kind of misconduct on the part of a handful of its employees. However, on the facts of this case, not only is this novel claim quite at odds with the settled rule that in federal equity cases "the nature of the violation determines the scope of the remedy,"but important considerations of federalism are additional factors weighing against it. Where, as here, the exercise of authority by state officials is attacked, federal courts must be constantly mindful of the "special delicacy of the adjustment to be preserved between federal equitable power and State administration of its own law." Section 1983 by its terms confers authority to grant equitable relief as well as damages, but its words "allow a suit in equity only when that is the proper proceeding for redress, and they refer to existing standards to determine what is a proper proceeding." * * * When a plaintiff seeks to enjoin the activity of a government agency, even within a unitary court system, his case must contend with "the well-established rule that the Government has traditionally been granted the widest latitude in the 'dispatch of its own internal affairs.' " The District Court's injunctive order here, significantly revising the internal procedures of the Philadelphia police department, was indisputably a sharp limitation on the department's "latitude in the 'dispatch of its own internal affairs'."

When the frame of reference moves from a unitary court system, governed by the principles just stated, to a system of federal courts representing the Nation, subsisting side by side with 50 state judicial, legislative, and executive branches, appropriate consideration must be given to principles of federalism in determining the availability and scope of equitable relief. * * *

Contrary to the District Court's flat pronouncement that a federal court's legal power to "supervise the functioning of the police department ... is firmly established," it is the foregoing cases and principles that must govern consideration of the type of injunctive relief granted here. When it injected itself by injunctive decree into the internal disciplinary affairs of this state agency, the District Court departed from these precepts. * * *

MR. JUSTICE STEVENS took no part in the consideration or decision of this case.

MR. JUSTICE BLACKMUN with whom MR. JUSTICE BRENNAN and MR. JUSTICE MARSHALL join, dissenting.

* * * To be sure, federal-court intervention in the daily operation of a large city's police department, as the Court intimates, is undesirable and to be avoided if at all possible. The Court appropriately observes, however, that what the Federal District Court did here was to engage in a careful and conscientious resolution of often sharply conflicting testimony and to make detailed findings of fact, now accepted by both sides, that attack the problem that is the subject of the respondents' complaint. The remedy was one evolved with the defendant officials' assent, reluctant though that assent may have been, and it was one that the police department concededly could live with. Indeed, the District Court * * * stated that "the resolution of all the disputed items was more nearly in accord with the defendants' position than with the plaintiffs' position," and that the relief * * * "did not go beyond what the defendants had always been willing to accept." No one, not even this Court's majority, disputes the apparent efficacy of the relief or the fact that it effectuated a betterment in the system and should serve to lessen the number of instances of deprival of constitutional rights of members of the respondent classes. What is worrisome to the Court is abstract principle, and, of course, the Court has a right to be concerned with abstract principle that, when extended to the limits of logic, may produce untoward results in other circumstances on a future day.

But the District Court here, with detailed, careful, and sympathetic findings, ascertained the existence of violations of citizens' *constitutional* rights, of a *pattern* of that type of activity, of its likely continuance and recurrence, and of an official indifference as to doing anything about it. * * * There must be federal relief available against persistent deprival of federal constitutional rights even by (or, perhaps I should say, particularly by) constituted authority on the state side. * * *

I would regard what was accomplished in this case as one of those rightly rare but nevertheless justified instances * * * of federal-court "intervention" in a state or municipal executive area. The facts, the deprival of constitutional rights, and the pattern are all proved in sufficient degree. And the remedy is carefully delineated, worked out within the administrative structure rather then superimposed by edict upon it, and essentially, and concededly, "livable." In the City of Brotherly Love—or in any other American city—no less should be expected. It is a matter of regret that the Court sees fit to nullify what so meticulously and thoughtfully has been evolved to satisfy an existing need relating to constitutional rights that we cherish and hold dear. * * *

## *Notes*

1. The majority concludes that plaintiff's rights were violated by individual police officers, but not by the city or its top officials. What sort of a factual showing would have satisfied the majority that the city and its top officials were liable? The majority's reading of the law of liability is controversial, but because our focus is the law of remedies, the important point is that the majority goes on to argue that scope of the remedy is limited to forcing those who violated plaintiff's rights to put them in their rightful position. In other words, where there is no right against a defendant that has been or will be violated by that defendant, there is no remedy against that defendant.

2. Why didn't the plaintiffs side-step the majority's argument by seeking damages from the individual police officers who brutalized them instead of an injunction against the city and its top officials?

3. Plaintiffs, as well as the lower courts, thought that the injunction requiring a civilian complaint review process was the best way to prevent brutality in the future. Although the defendants opposed the review process in concept and participated in its design only under duress, they were able to reach agreement on the specifics. What then does the majority find objectionable about an injunction mandating the complaint review scheme, in these circumstances? After all, Professor Chayes (in the excerpt in chapter 1) sees injunctions in public law litigation as judicial policy making rather than as "logically deduced from the nature of the legal harm suffered."

4. This case was but one aspect of an extended controversy over police brutality in Philadelphia going back to 1952. Phillip J. Cooper, Hard Judicial Choices 297–327 (1988)(detailing background of case). From mid–1976 to mid–1977, 110 lawsuits seeking compensatory and punitive damages for police brutality were filed. Newsweek, Roundhouse Punches, July 4, 1977. After *Rizzo*, a federal investigation brought to light evidence that the City did promote police brutality and an injunction against the chief of police and the mayor was finally granted. United States v. City of Philadelphia,

644 F.2d 187 (3d Cir.1980)(injunction denied); Commonwealth of Pennsylvania v. Porter, 659 F.2d 306 (3d Cir.1981) (injunction granted). While this litigation was pending, Philadelphia voters rejected by a 2 to 1 margin a city charter amendment that would have allowed Mayor Rizzo to seek a third term. Both major party candidates for mayor vowed to reform police practices. All's well that ends well?

## NEWMAN v. ALABAMA

United States Court of Appeals, Fifth Circuit, 1977.
559 F.2d 283, rev'd in part on other grounds, 438 U.S. 781, 98 S.Ct. 3057, 57 L.Ed.2d 1114 (1978).

COLEMAN, CIRCUIT JUDGE.

[The district court had found that conditions in a state prison violated the constitutional prohibitions against cruel and unusual punishment and granted injunctive relief. On appeal, the state challenged the scope of the injunction. The court of appeals begins by observing that a court may not aim to do more than correct defendants' violations, citing *Rizzo v. Goode.*] The remedy must be designed to accomplish that goal, not to exercise judicial power for the attainment of what we as individuals might like to see accomplished in the way of ideal prison conditions. * * *

I

This appeal is concerned with the remedies prescribed by the very able District Court for the eradication of cruel and unusual punishment in the Alabama State Prison System.

The State concedes that the evidence established excessive overcrowding in these prisons, that there were not sufficient guards to reasonably protect the inmates from one another, and that the overcrowding was primarily responsible for and exacerbated all the other ills of the penal system. As detailed in its published opinion, other indefensible conditions were found by the District Court, findings clearly supported by the evidence.

At the outset, then, the case is reduced to a constitutional appraisal of the remedies required of the State. The State contends that in fashioning those remedies the District Court "exceeded its judicial power and abused its discretion".

Our first response is that the determined efforts of the highly dedicated District Judge to put an end to unconstitutional conditions in the Alabama prison system merit high commendation. We cannot believe that the good people of a great state approved the prison situation demonstrated by the evidence in this case. * * *

Our real issue is whether in striving to attain constitutional objectives the District Court in a few respects went impermissibly beyond the requirements of the federal constitution; more specifically, did the Court supersede the duly constituted state authorities in the performance of vital state functions rather than *compelling* those authorities to perform those functions in a constitutional manner? * * * Most assuredly * * * in proper cases a federal court can, and must, compel state officials or employees to perform their official duties in compliance with the Constitution of the United States.

At the outset we hold that the steps taken by the District Court to ensure reasonably adequate food, clothing, shelter, sanitation, necessary medical attention, and personal safety for the prisoners were within its sound discretion and will not be disturbed on appeal. * * *

V

Failure of prison authorities to provide a rehabilitation program, by itself, does not constitute cruel and unusual punishment.

Amicus Curiae, the United States, concedes that there is no constitutional right to rehabilitation for prisoners. It does proceed to argue, however, that "states have a duty to insure that the mental, physical, and emotional status of prisoners in their custody do not deteriorate". On the face of it, this is not a well considered statement. The mental, physical, and emotional status of individuals, whether in or out of custody, do deteriorate and there is no power on earth to prevent it. We think that what the government must have meant is that states may not inflict cruel and unusual punishment that would likely lead to such results. The briefs for the parties plaintiff and for the State of Alabama deal with this idea to considerable length. We decline to enter this uncharted bog. If the State furnishes its prisoners with reasonably adequate food, clothing, shelter, sanitation, medical care, and personal safety, so as to avoid the imposition of cruel and unusual punishment, that ends its obligations under Amendment Eight. The Constitution does not require that prisoners, as individuals or as a group, be provided with any and every amenity which some person may think is needed to avoid mental, physical, and emotional deterioration.[a]

Even so, on the facts of this case, we affirm the actions of the District Court designed to provide Alabama prison inmates with reasonable recreational facilities. We do this simply because such facilities may play an important role in extirpating the effects of the conditions which undisputably prevailed in these prisons at the time the District Court entered its order. * * *

VIII

The District Court directed that each prisoner shall be assigned to a meaningful job on the basis of his or her abilities and interests, and according to institutional needs. While there is no federal constitutional mandate for this proviso, as phrased it should not impose any real burden on the penitentiary authorities, so, in the context of this case we allow it to stand, not, however, to enjoy any precedential status in future cases if they should arise.

**a.** The Fifth Circuit later ruled that the lack of exercise and recreation for prisoners can be cruel and unusual punishment. E.g., Ruiz v. Estelle, 679 F.2d 1115, 1152 (5th Cir.1982), cert. denied, 460 U.S. 1042, 103 S.Ct. 1438, 75 L.Ed.2d 795 (1983).

We interpret those portions of the Order dealing with opportunities to obtain a basic education, to attend vocational school, and to attend a transitional program prior to release as meaning that if the prison authorities operate such programs each prisoner shall have impartially equal access on an objective standard of basic utility to the individual. We would find it difficult to hold, and we do not now hold, that if the state has no such programs it amounts to cruel and unusual punishment within the prohibitions of the Eighth Amendment. As a matter of fact, in the operation of a good prison system, we understand that such programs are fairly standard practices, instituted and operated on the initiative of state prison authorities. * * *

### *Notes*

1. *Preventive v. reparative injunctions.* Professor Owen M. Fiss applies the label "preventive" to injunctions that prevent wrongs, such as future trespasses, and the label "reparative" to injunctions that "seek to eliminate the effects of a past wrong." Owen M. Fiss, The Civil Rights Injunction 10 (1978). An injunction sometimes contains both preventive and reparative orders. In *Newman,* the orders requiring that overcrowding and other unconstitutional conditions be ended are preventive and the order requiring a recreational program is reparative. Does it make any difference that the recreation is justified on a reparative rather than a preventive rationale?

2. Why did the court conclude that the injunction should not require education but could require a recreation program?

3. The court allows the injunction to require jobs, even though it finds no constitutional right to jobs in prison. The court's rationale—that there is no "real burden on the penitentiary authorities"—is in sharp contrast to *Rizzo v. Goode's* insistence that federal courts should interfere with state officials only where necessary to vindicate rights. This passage is illustrative of the broad discretionary powers that courts sometimes claim in providing injunctions. In contrast, a court would never award damages in the absence of the violation of a right because the damages are no "real burden" to a rich defendant. Yet, *Newman* also quotes the passages in *Rizzo* that paint the power to provide injunctive relief as narrow; for example, "an injunction is 'to be used sparingly, and only in a clear and plain case'." Both of these seemingly contradictory themes in *Newman* are prevalent in judicial opinions, although usually not in the same opinions. Yet, what courts say is often quite different from what they do. Courts will, for instance, provide injunctive relief in a case that is not "clear and plain," provided that defendant is liable and the other prerequisites for injunctive relief are met. Moreover, the degree of discretion in the trial court varies with the issue. The trial court in *Newman* had broad discretion in determining what repaired past overcrowding but no discretion to grant relief if defendants were not liable. In reading this book, consider whether the degree of discretion as to various issues follows a pattern, or whether the appellate judges are just making it up as they go along.

4. Suppose that the defendant prison officials created the unconstitutional conditions for malicious reasons. Should that make a difference in the scope of the injunction? It is blackletter law that courts do not have

discretion to use injunctions to punish. Weinberger v. Romero–Barcelo, 456 U.S. 305, 310, 102 S.Ct. 1798, 1802, 72 L.Ed.2d 91, 97 (1982), reproduced infra at page 112. So it is not defendants' culpability but rather plaintiffs' rightful position which is the measure of relief. Nonetheless, do you see why in *Newman* defendants' culpability might affect the scope of the injunction by taking plaintiffs further from their rightful position? Or by changing the likelihood that defendants will obey an injunction to attain it? In regard to the latter question, Professor Fiss also writes of "structural" injunctions, which change how social institutions such as jails or school systems work in order to ensure that preventive or reparative aims are in fact achieved. The Civil Rights Injunction at 9–11. Determining plaintiffs' rightful position and the best way to attain it requires judgment calls on the part of trial judges. Punitive motives sometimes color how judges make these judgment calls and therefore play a latent part in the injunction calculus.

## C. THE PREREQUISITES FOR INJUNCTIVE RELIEF

### 1. THREAT OF HARM

***Problem: Country Lodge v. Miller (Reprised)***
***The Threat of Harm***

Should the court refuse to grant Country Lodge an injunction prohibiting future nuisances if:

(a) Miller was just beginning to build her cider press and has not indicated how she will dispose of the apple mash?

(b) Miller has put mash in the river, was found in violation, and then wrote Country Lodge a letter promising never again to put waste in the river?

(c) Miller wrote such a letter and dismantled her cider press?

(d) Miller made no promises but last fall's discharge of waste would not have caused any harm to Country Lodge except for unusual river conditions—conditions which occur only one year in a hundred?

---

An injunction to prevent future violations will issue only if the plaintiff faces a threat of being harmed by the defendant. For example, a plaintiff will not get an injunction against the defendant entering Blackacre even though defendant's entry would interfere with plaintiff's rightful position as owner of Blackacre unless there is reason to fear that defendant will trespass. To help understand why, even though the defendant has no right to trespass, recall the attributes of an injunction summarized in section A of this chapter, which make it, in essence, a criminal statute applicable only to the persons to whom it is addressed.

The plaintiff can easily show threat of harm if the defendant has made an explicit threat, such as "I'm coming on Blackacre whether you like it or not." If the defendant is not so accommodating, but has trespassed on Blackacre in the past or, clearer still, is engaged in a continuing trespass, the plaintiff can argue that future violations are likely. But past violations are not essential; they are only one kind of evidence of a threat of future harm. For example, in Union Carbide v. UGI Corp., 731 F.2d 1186, 1191–92 (5th Cir.1984), the court enjoined a former Union Carbide employee who knew its trade secrets from working in certain positions at UGI, where the trade secrets would be useful, even in the absence of conclusive proof that the employee had divulged any secrets. The court was influenced by UGI's failure to exclude the employee from situations where disclosure of confidential information would be difficult to avoid.

On the other hand, a court may find no threat of future harm despite past violations.

## HECHT CO. v. BOWLES

Supreme Court of the United States, 1944.
321 U.S. 321, 64 S.Ct. 587, 88 L.Ed. 754.

Mr. Justice Douglas delivered the opinion of the Court.

Sec. 205(a) of the Emergency Price Control Act of 1942 provides:

> "Whenever in the judgment of the Administrator any person has engaged or is about to engage in any acts or practices which constitute or will constitute a violation of any provision of section 4 of this Act, he may make application to the appropriate court for an order enjoining such acts or practices, or for an order enforcing compliance with such provision, and upon a showing by the Administrator that such person has engaged or is about to engage in any such acts or practices a permanent or temporary injunction, restraining order, or other order shall be granted without bond."

The question in this case is whether the Administrator, having established that a defendant has engaged in acts or practices violative of § 4 of the Act is entitled as of right to an injunction restraining the defendant from engaging in such acts or practices or whether the court has some discretion to grant or withhold such relief.

Sec. 4(a) of the Act makes it unlawful for a person to sell or deliver any commodity in violation of specified orders or regulations of the Administrator. A regulation issued under § 2 of the Act and effective in May, 1942 provided that no person should sell or deliver any commodity at a price higher than the authorized maximum price as fixed and determined by the regulation. Since maximum prices were fixed with reference to earlier base periods, the regulation also provided for the preservation and examination of existing records. And provision was likewise made for the keeping of current records reflecting sales made under the regulation and for the filing of maximum prices with the Administrator.

There is no substantial controversy over the facts. Petitioner operates a large department store in Washington, D.C. and did a business of about $20,000,000 in 1942. There are 107 departments in the store and each sells a separate line of merchandise. In the fall of 1942 the Administrator started an investigation to determine whether petitioner was complying with the Act and the regulation. The investigation was a "spot check", confined to seven departments. In each of the seven departments violations were disclosed. As a result of this suit was brought. The complaint charged violations of the maximum price provisions of the regulation and violations of the regulations governing the keeping of records and reporting to the Administrator. The Administrator prayed for an injunction enjoining petitioner from selling, delivering or offering for sale or delivery any commodity in violation of the regulation and from failing to keep complete and accurate records as required by the regulation. In its answer petitioner pleaded among other things that any failure or neglect to comply with the regulation was involuntary and was corrected as soon as discovered.

Numerous violations both as respects prices and records were discovered. Thus in six of the seven departments investigated there had occurred between May and October, 1942 some 3700 sales in excess of the maximum prices with overcharges of some $4600. The statements filed with the Administrator were deficient, some 400 items of merchandise being omitted. And there were over 300 items with respect to which no records were kept showing how the maximum prices had been determined.

There is no doubt, however, of petitioner's good faith and diligence. The District Court found that the manager of the store had offered it as a laboratory in which the Administrator might experiment with any regulation which might be issued. Prior to the promulgation of the regulation the petitioner had created a new section known as the price control office. That office undertook to bring petitioner into compliance with the requirements of the regulation in advance of its effective date. The head of that office together with seven assistants devoted full time to that endeavor. But the store had about 2,000 employees and over one million two hundred thousand articles of merchandise. In the furniture departments alone there were over fifty-four thousand transactions in the first ten months of 1942. Difficulties were encountered in interpreting the regulation, in determining the exact nature of an article and whether it had been previously sold and at what price, etc. The absence of adequate records made it difficult to ascertain prices during the earlier base-period. Misunderstanding of the regulation, confusion on the part of employees not trained in such problems of interpretation and administration, the complexity of the problem, and the fallibility of humans all combined to produce numerous errors. But the District Court concluded that the "mistakes in pricing and listing were all made in good faith and without intent to violate the regulations."

The District Court also found that the mistakes brought to light "were at once corrected, and vigorous steps were taken by The Hecht Company to prevent recurrence of these mistakes or further mistakes in the future." The company increased its price control office to twenty-eight employees. New methods of internal control were instituted early in November, 1942 with the view of avoiding future violations. That new system of control "greatly improved" the situation. Petitioner undertook to make repayment of all overcharges brought to light by the investigation in case of customers who could be identified. It proposed to contribute the remaining amount of such overcharges to some local charity. The District Court concluded that the issuance of an injunction would have "no effect by way of insuring better compliance in the future" and would be "unjust" to petitioner and not "in the public interest". It accordingly dismissed the complaint. On appeal the Court of Appeals for the District of Columbia reversed that judgment * * * [on the basis that § 205(a) mandated the issuance of an injunction or other order once a violation was found].

Respondent insists that the mandatory character of § 205(a) is clear from its language, history and purpose. He argues that "shall be granted" is not permissive, that since the same section provides that the Administrator "may" apply for an injunction and that, if so, the injunction "shall" be granted, "may" and "shall" are each used in the ordinary sense. It is pointed out that when the bill (for which the Act in its final form was substituted) passed the House, § 205(a) provided that "upon a proper showing" an injunction or other order "shall be granted without bond." The words "upon a proper showing" were stricken in the Senate and were replaced by the words "upon a showing by the Administrator that such person has engaged or is about to engage in any such acts or practices." * * *

We agree that the cessation of violations, whether before or after the institution of a suit by the Administrator, is no bar to the issuance of an injunction under § 205(a). But we do not think that under all circumstances the court must issue the injunction or other order which the Administrator seeks.

It seems apparent on the face of § 205(a) that there is some room for the exercise of discretion on the part of the court. For the requirement is that a "permanent or temporary injunction, restraining order, or other order" be granted. Though the Administrator asks for an injunction, some "other order" might be more appropriate, or at least so appear to the court. Thus in the present case one judge in the Court of Appeals felt that the District Court should not have dismissed the complaint but should have entered an order retaining the case on the docket with the right of the Administrator, on notice, to renew his application for injunctive relief if violations recurred. It is indeed not difficult to imagine that in some situations that might be the fairest course to follow and one which would be as practically effective as the issuance of an injunction. Such an order, moreover, would seem to be a type of "other order" which a faithful reading of § 205(a) would permit a court to issue in a compliance proceeding. However that may be, it would seem clear that the court might deem some "other order" more appropriate for the evil at hand than the one which was sought. We cannot say that it lacks the power to make that choice. Thus it seems that § 205(a) falls short of making mandatory the issuance of an injunction merely because the Administrator asks it.

There is, moreover, support in the legislative history of § 205(a) for the view that "shall be granted" is less mandatory than a literal reading might suggest. [The Senate Report states that] "* * * courts are given jurisdiction to issue whatever order to enforce compliance is proper in the circumstances of each particular case." A grant of jurisdiction to issue compliance orders hardly suggests an absolute duty to do so under any and all circumstances. We cannot but think that if Congress had intended to make such a drastic departure from the traditions of equity practice, an unequivocal statement of its purpose would have been made.

We do not stop to compare the provisions of § 205(a) with the requirements of other federal statutes governing administrative agencies which, it is said, make it mandatory that those agencies take action when certain facts are shown to exist. We are dealing here with the requirements of equity practice with a background of several hundred years of history. Only the other day we stated that "An appeal to the equity jurisdiction conferred on federal district courts is an appeal to the sound discretion which guides the determinations of courts of equity." The historic injunctive process was designed to deter, not to punish. The essence of equity jurisdiction has been the power of the Chancellor to do equity and to mould each decree to the necessities of the particular case. Flexibility rather than rigidity has distinguished it. The qualities of mercy and practicality have made equity the instrument for nice adjustment and reconciliation between the public interest and private needs as well as between competing private claims. We do not believe that such a major departure from that long tradition as is here proposed should be lightly implied. We do not think the history or language of § 205(a) compel it. It should be noted, moreover, that § 205(a) governs the procedure in both federal and state courts. For § 205(c) gives the state courts concurrent jurisdiction with federal district courts of civil enforcement proceedings. It is therefore even more compelling to conclude that, if Congress desired to make such an abrupt departure from traditional equity practice as is suggested, it would have made its desire plain. Hence we resolve the ambiguities of § 205(a) in favor of that interpretation which affords a full opportunity for equity courts to treat enforcement proceedings under this emergency legislation in accordance with their traditional practices, as conditioned by the necessities of the public interest which Congress has sought to protect.

We do not mean to imply that courts should administer § 205(a) grudgingly. * * * [T]heir discretion under § 205(a) must be exercised in light of the large objectives of the Act. For the standards of the public interest, not the requirements of private litigation measure the propriety and need for injunctive relief in these cases. That discretion should reflect an acute awareness of the Congressional admonition that "of all the consequences of war, except human slaughter, inflation is the most destructive" and that delay or indifference may be fatal. Whether the District Court abused its discretion in dismissing the complaint is a question which we do not reach. The judgment must be reversed and the cause remanded to the Court of Appeals for that determination. * * *

MR. JUSTICE FRANKFURTER agrees that § 205(a) of the Emergency Price Control Act, apart from dispensing with any requirement for a bond, does not change the historic conditions for the exercise by courts of equity of their power to issue injunctions, according to which the Court of Appeals should now dispose of this cause.

MR. JUSTICE ROBERTS is of opinion that the judgment of the Court of Appeals should be reversed and that of the District Court affirmed.

### *Notes*

1. *Hecht* makes a number of points with import far beyond threat of harm as a prerequisite to injunctive relief. The case is much cited for its statements that courts have great flexibility in framing injunctions, as you will see in section D of this chapter. *Hecht* also states an important canon of statutory construction—that courts should not read statutes to limit traditional equity practices unless the legislature clearly states that it intends to do so. The Court applies this canon in refusing to read the Emergency Price Control Act to transfer from the courts to the administrator the power to determine whether an injunction is warranted.

2. Did *Hecht* hold that there was no threat of future violations? That an injunction would do no good? The majority says that issuing an injunction would not be "just" to Hecht Co. Had not the Hecht Co. earned the disadvantages of an injunction through its violations?

3. Which party should have the burden of showing the probability of a future violation?

### *Note on Mootness and Ripeness*

*Hecht* invoked the doctrine of *equitable discretion* to give effect to its finding that the Hecht Co. posed little threat. Threat of harm finds expression in a variety of overlapping doctrines, another one of which is *mootness,* a constitutional doctrine under which the defendant can get the case dismissed as a matter of right rather than discretion. Suppose that Hecht Co. neither admitted nor denied that its conduct was illegal but stated that it would comply with the regulations. It could not get the case dismissed as moot; United States v. W.T. Grant Co., 345 U.S. 629, 632–33, 73 S.Ct. 894, 897, 97 L.Ed. 1303, 1309 (1953) explains why:

> Both sides agree to the abstract proposition that voluntary cessation of allegedly illegal conduct does not deprive the tribunal of power to hear and determine the case, i.e., does not make the case moot. A controversy may remain to be settled in such circum-

> stances, e.g., a dispute over the legality of the challenged practices. The defendant is free to return to his old ways. This, together with a public interest in having the legality of the practices settled, militates against a mootness conclusion. For to say that the case has become moot means that the defendant is entitled to dismissal as a matter of right. The courts have rightly refused to grant defendants such a powerful weapon against public law enforcement.
>
> The case may nevertheless be moot if the defendant can demonstrate that "there is no reasonable expectation that the wrong will be repeated." The burden is a heavy one. Here the defendants told the court that the [allegedly illegal practices] no longer existed and disclaimed any intention to revive them. Such a profession does not suffice to make a case moot although it is one of the factors to be considered in determining the appropriateness of granting an injunction against the now-discontinued acts.

If Congress repealed the statute that Hecht Co. had violated, the case would certainly be moot because the threat of future violations would have ceased.

*Hecht* dealt with a case in which the issue was whether the violation would recur. It is the small or non-existent probability of *recurrence* that leads to the exercise of equitable discretion or finding of mootness. If, however, no violation had ever taken place and there was no showing a future violation was threatened, a court might say that the threat was not *imminent* or that the case was not *ripe*. The term "imminence" connotes a harm that will take place soon, but, as used by courts, the term refers to how certain illegal injury is rather than when it will take place. A court can find that the threat is not imminent (or the case not ripe) because the plaintiff lacks proof that the defendant will commit a violation.

As a variant on this theme, Professor Gene Shreve notes that "a court may deny a request for an injunction to a plaintiff in imminent danger of being wronged by a defendant because the wrong is not substantial." Gene R. Shreve, Federal Injunctions and the Public Interest, 51 Geo.Wash.L.Rev. 382, 392 (1983). For example, in Fletcher v. Bealey, 28 Ch.D. 688 (1885), the court denied an injunction against defendant's storing chemical wastes on the basis, inter alia, that even if the wastes were released, there was insufficient proof that the wastes would harm plaintiff's business. To be "substantial" a harm does not have to bulk large in monetary terms. For instance, a trespass would be a substantial harm even though plaintiff cannot show that the trespasser will do monetarily significant damage because the law of trespass puts a paramount value on the owner's right to exclude. By contrast, Fletcher v. Bealey arose under nuisance law, which balances the competing interests of neighbors.

Legislatures sometimes borrow the phrase "imminent and substantial," but it sometimes mean something quite different from what it means in traditional equity cases. For example, a federal environmental law empowers courts to order persons responsible for threatened releases of toxic substances to abate the release if "there may be an imminent and substantial endangerment to the public health or welfare or environment," 42 U.S.C. § 9606(a), but Congress intended "imminent and substantial" to mean that injunctions would issue only if there were an emergency with which the Environmental Protection Agency could not cope through ordinary administrative mechanisms in the statute. H.R.Rep. No. 1185, 93d Cong., 2d Sess. 35–36 (1974).

Like recurrence, imminence/ripeness can give rise to the invocation of an equitable, discretionary doctrine (sometimes called *remedial ripeness*) as well as a constitutional, jurisdictional one (sometimes called *constitutional ripeness*) because, when there is no chance of harm, there is no article III "case or controversy." For example, suppose that Hecht Co. had never violated the regulations and was just setting up its business and the government sought an injunction out of concern that the new company would violate the regulations. If the company claimed that the regulations were invalid but that it would not violate them until their invalidity was judicially determined and the government had no proof to the contrary, a court might well decide that the plea for an injunction was not ripe.

The focus so far has been on whether the defendant threatens to violate the law in the future. But even if defendant surely will do so, plaintiff would not satisfy the threat of harm prerequisite unless the court can conclude that the violation will harm the plaintiff. California v. American Stores, 495 U.S. 271, 296, 110 S.Ct. 1853, 1867, 109 L.Ed.2d 240 (1990)("A private litigant [under statute authorizing divestiture as a remedy for anti-competitive mergers] * * * must prove 'threatened loss or damage' to his own interests in order to obtain relief"). Suppose that Bowles was not the public official in charge of enforcing price controls but rather a visitor from Boise, Idaho to Washington, D.C., where the Hecht Company had charged him a higher price than the statute permitted. If the Hecht Company will continue to violate the law, but Bowles has no plans for another visit to our nation's capital, is there an enjoinable threat of harm? See the following case.

## CITY OF LOS ANGELES v. LYONS

Supreme Court of the United States, 1983.
461 U.S. 95, 103 S.Ct. 1660, 75 L.Ed.2d 675.

JUSTICE WHITE delivered the opinion of the Court.

The issue here is whether respondent Lyons satisfied the prerequisites for seeking injunctive relief in the Federal District Court.

### I

This case began on February 7, 1977, when respondent, Adolph Lyons, filed a complaint for damages, injunction, and declaratory relief in the United States District Court for the Central District of California.

The defendants were the City of Los Angeles and four of its police officers. The complaint alleged that on October 6, 1976, at 2 a.m., Lyons was stopped by the defendant officers for a traffic or vehicle code violation and that although Lyons offered no resistance or threat whatsoever, the officers, without provocation or justification, seized Lyons and applied a "chokehold"—either the "bar arm control" hold or the "carotid-artery control" hold or both—rendering him unconscious and causing damage to his larynx. Counts I through IV of the complaint sought damages against the officers and the City. Count V, with which we are principally concerned here, sought a preliminary and permanent injunction against the City barring the use of the control holds. That count alleged that the city's police officers, "pursuant to the authorization, instruction and encouragement of defendant City of Los Angeles, regularly and routinely apply these chokeholds in innumerable situations where they are not threatened by the use of any deadly force whatsoever," that numerous persons have been injured as the result of the application of the chokeholds, that Lyons and others similarly situated are threatened with irreparable injury in the form of bodily injury and loss of life, and that Lyons "justifiably fears that any contact he has with Los Angeles police officers may result in his being choked and strangled to death without provocation, justification or other legal excuse." Lyons alleged the threatened impairment of rights protected by the First, Fourth, Eighth, and Fourteenth Amendments. Injunctive relief was sought against the use of the control holds "except in situations where the proposed victim of said control reasonably appears to be threatening the immediate use of deadly force." Count VI sought declaratory relief against the City, i.e., a judgment that use of the chokeholds absent the threat of immediate use of deadly force is a *per se* violation of various constitutional rights.

The District Court, by order, granted the City's motion for partial judgment on the pleadings and entered judgment for the City on Count V and VI. The Court of Appeals reversed the judgment for the City on Count V and VI, holding over the City's objection that despite our decisions in O'Shea v. Littleton, 414 U.S. 488, 94 S.Ct. 669, 38 L.Ed.2d 674 (1974), and Rizzo v. Goode, 423 U.S. 362, 96 S.Ct. 598, 46 L.Ed.2d 561 (1976), Lyons had standing to seek relief against the application of the chokeholds. The Court of Appeals held that there was a sufficient likelihood that Lyons would again be stopped and subjected to the unlawful use of force to constitute a case or controversy and to warrant the issuance of an injunction, if the injunction was otherwise authorized. We denied certiorari.

On remand, Lyons applied for a preliminary injunction. Lyons pressed only the Count V claim at this point. The motion was heard on affidavits, depositions and government records. The District Court found that Lyons had been stopped for a traffic infringement and that without provocation or legal justification the officers involved had applied a "Department-authorized chokehold which resulted in injuries to the plaintiff." The court further found that the department authorizes the use of the holds in situations where no one is threatened by death or grievous bodily harm, that officers are insufficiently trained, that the use of the holds involves a high risk of injury or death as then employed, and that their continued use in situations where neither death nor serious bodily injury is threatened "is unconscionable in a civilized society." The court concluded that such use violated Lyons' substantive due process rights under the Fourteenth Amendment. A preliminary injunction was entered enjoining "the use of both the carotid-artery and bar arm holds under circumstances which do not threaten death or serious bodily injury." An improved training program and regular reporting and recordkeeping were also ordered. The Court of Appeals affirmed * * *. We granted certiorari and now reverse.

II

Since our grant of certiorari, circumstances pertinent to the case have changed. Originally, Lyons' complaint alleged that at least two deaths had occurred as a result of the application of chokeholds by the police. His first amended complaint alleged that 10 chokehold-related deaths had occurred. By May 1982, there had been five more such deaths. On May 6, 1982, the Chief of Police in Los Angeles prohibited the use of the bar-arm chokehold in any circumstances. A few days later, on May 12, 1982, the Board of Police Commissioners imposed a six-month moratorium on the use of the carotid-artery chokehold except under circumstances where deadly force is authorized.

[Lyons contended that these developments mooted the case because he is no longer subject to a threat of injury so that the preliminary injunction should be vacated.] The City, on the other hand, while acknowledging that subsequent events have significantly changed the posture of this case, again asserts that the case is not moot because the moratorium is not permanent and may be lifted at any time.

We agree with the City that the case is not moot, since the moratorium by its terms is not permanent. * * *

III

It goes without saying that those who seek to invoke the jurisdiction of the federal courts must satisfy the threshold requirement imposed by Art. III of the Constitution by alleging an actual case or controversy. Plaintiffs must demonstrate a "personal stake in the outcome" in order to "assure that concrete adverseness which sharpens the presentation of issues" necessary for the proper resolution of constitutional questions. Baker v. Carr, 369 U.S. 186, 204, 82 S.Ct. 691, 703, 7 L.Ed.2d 663 (1962). Abstract injury is not enough. The plaintiff must show that he "has sustained or is immediately in danger of sustaining some direct injury" as the result of the challenged official conduct and the injury or threat of injury must be both "real and immediate," not "conjectural" or "hypothetical."

In O'Shea v. Littleton, 414 U.S. 488, 94 S.Ct. 669, 38 L.Ed.2d 674 (1974), we dealt with a case brought by a class of plaintiffs claiming that they had been subjected to discriminatory enforcement of the criminal law. Among other things, a county magistrate and judge were accused of discriminatory conduct in various respects, such as sentencing members of plaintiff's class more harshly than other defendants. * * *

Although it was claimed in that case that particular members of the plaintiff class had actually suffered from the alleged unconstitutional practices, we observed that "[p]ast exposure to illegal conduct does not in itself show a present case or controversy regarding injunctive relief * * * if unaccompanied by any continuing, present adverse effects." Past wrongs were evidence bearing on "whether there is a real and immediate threat of repeated injury." But the prospect of future injury rested "on the likelihood that [plaintiffs] will again be arrested for and charged with violations of the criminal law and will again be subjected to bond proceedings, trial, or sentencing before petitioners." The most that could be said for plaintiffs' standing was "that *if* [plaintiffs] proceed to violate an unchallenged law and *if* they are charged, held to answer, and tried in any proceedings before petitioners, they will be subjected to the discriminatory practices that petitioners are alleged to have followed." We could not find a case or controversy in those circumstances: the threat to the plaintiffs was not "sufficiently real and immediate to show an existing controversy simply because they anticipate violating lawful criminal statutes and being tried for their offenses * * *." It was to be assumed "that [plaintiffs] will conduct their activities within the law and so avoid prosecution and conviction as well as exposure to the challenged course of conduct said to be followed by petitioners."

We further observed that case or controversy considerations "obviously shade into those determining whether the complaint states a sound basis for equitable relief," and went on to hold that even if the complaint presented an existing case or controversy, an adequate basis for equitable relief against petitioners had not been demonstrated [because of, inter alia, insufficient threat of harm.]

Another relevant decision for present purposes is *Rizzo v. Goode* [reproduced supra at page 45] * * *. The claim of injury rested upon "what one of a small, unnamed minority of policemen might do to [plaintiffs] in the future because of that unknown policeman's perception of departmental procedures." This hypothesis was "even more attenuated than those allegations of future injury found insufficient in *O'Shea* to warrant [the] invocation of federal jurisdiction."

IV

No extension of *O'Shea* and *Rizzo* is necessary to hold that respondent Lyons has failed to demonstrate a case or controversy with the City that would justify the equitable relief sought.[6] Lyons' standing to seek

6. The City states in its brief that on remand from the Court of Appeals' first judgment "[t]he parties agreed and advised the district court that the respondent's damages claim could be severed from his effort to obtain equitable relief." Respondent does not suggest otherwise. This case, therefore, as it came to us, is on all fours with *O'Shea* and should be judged as such.

the injunction requested depended on whether he was likely to suffer future injury from the use of the chokeholds by police officers. * * * That Lyons may have been illegally choked by the police on October 6, 1976, while presumably affording Lyons standing to claim damages against the individual officers and perhaps against the City, does nothing to establish a real and immediate threat that he would again be stopped for a traffic violation, or for any other offense, by an officer or officers who would illegally choke him into unconsciousness without any provocation or resistance on his part. The additional allegation in the complaint that the police in Los Angeles routinely apply chokeholds in situations where they are not threatened by the use of deadly force falls far short of the allegations that would be necessary to establish a case or controversy between these parties.

In order to establish an actual controversy in this case, Lyons would have had not only to allege that he would have another encounter with the police but also to make the incredible assertion either, (1) that *all* police officers in Los Angeles *always* choke any citizen with whom they happen to have an encounter, whether for the purpose of arrest, issuing a citation or for questioning or, (2) that the City ordered or authorized police officers to act in such manner. Although Count V alleged that the City authorized the use of the control holds in situations where deadly force was not threatened, it did not indicate why Lyons might be realistically threatened by police officers who acted within the strictures of the City's policy. If, for example, chokeholds were authorized to be used only to counter resistance to an arrest by a suspect, or to thwart an effort to escape, any future threat to Lyons from the City's policy or from the conduct of police officers would be no more real than the possibility that he would again have an encounter with the police and that either he would illegally resist arrest or detention or the officers would disobey their instructions and again render him unconscious without any provocation.[7]

**7.** The centerpiece of Justice Marshall's dissent is that Lyons had standing to challenge the City's policy because to recover damages he would have to prove that what allegedly occurred on October 6, 1976, was pursuant to City authorization. We agree completely that for Lyons to succeed in his damages action, it would be necessary to prove that what happened to him—that is, as alleged, he was choked without any provocation or legal excuse whatsoever—was pursuant to a City policy. For several reasons, however, it does not follow that Lyons had standing to seek the injunction prayed for in Count V.

First, [the complaint describes the city's policy] as authorizing the use of chokeholds "in situations where [the officers] are threatened by far less than deadly force." This is not equivalent to the unbelievable assertion that the City either orders or authorizes application of the chokeholds where there is no resistance or other provocation.

Second, even if such an allegation is thought to be contained in the complaint, it is belied by the record made on the application for preliminary injunction.

Third, even if the complaint must be read as containing an allegation that officers are authorized to apply the chokeholds where there is no resistance or other provocation, it does not follow that Lyons has standing to seek an injunction against the application of the restraint holds in situations that he has not experienced, as for example, where the suspect resists arrest or tries to escape but does not threaten the use of deadly force. Yet that is precisely the scope of the injunction that Lyons prayed for in Count V.

Fourth, and in any event, to have a case or controversy with the City that could

Under *O'Shea* and *Rizzo,* these allegations were an insufficient basis to provide a federal court with jurisdiction to entertain Count V of the complaint.[8] * * * For several reasons—each of them infirm, in our view—the Court of Appeals thought reliance on *O'Shea* and *Rizzo* was misplaced and reversed the District Court.

First, the Court of Appeals thought that Lyons was more immediately threatened than the plaintiffs in those cases since, according to the Court of Appeals, Lyons need only be stopped for a minor traffic violation to be subject to the strangleholds. * * * We cannot agree that the "odds" that Lyons would not only again be stopped for a traffic violation but would also be subjected to a chokehold without any provocation whatsoever are sufficient to make out a federal case for equitable relief. We note that five months elapsed between October 6, 1976, and the filing of the complaint, yet there was no allegation of further unfortunate encounters between Lyons and the police.

Of course, it may be that among the countless encounters between the police and the citizens of a great city such as Los Angeles, there will be certain instances in which strangleholds will be illegally applied and injury and death unconstitutionally inflicted on the victim. * * * [I]t is surely no more than speculation to assert either that Lyons himself will again be involved in one of those unfortunate instances, or that he will be arrested in the future and provoke the use of a chokehold by resisting arrest, attempting to escape, or threatening deadly force or serious bodily injury.

Second, the Court of Appeals viewed *O'Shea* and *Rizzo* as cases in which the plaintiffs sought "massive structural" relief against the local law enforcement systems * * *. *O'Shea* and *Rizzo,* however, cannot be so easily confined to their facts. If Lyons has made no showing that he is realistically threatened by a repetition of his experience of October, 1976, then he has not met the requirements for seeking an injunction in a federal court, whether the injunction contemplates intrusive structural relief or the cessation of a discrete practice.

The Court of Appeals also asserted that Lyons "had a live and active claim" against the City "if only for a period of a few seconds" while the stranglehold was being applied to him [so that] the claim had not become moot * * * [T]he issue here is not whether that claim has become moot

sustain Count V, Lyons would have to credibly allege that he faced a realistic threat from the future application of the City's policy. Justice Marshall nowhere confronts this requirement—the necessity that Lyons demonstrate that he, himself, will not only again be stopped by the police but will be choked without any provocation or legal excuse. Justice Marshall plainly does not agree with that requirement, and he was in dissent in *O'Shea v. Littleton.* We are at issue in that respect.

**8.** * * * Lyons alleged that he feared he would be choked in any future encounter with the police. The reasonableness of Lyons' fear is dependent upon the likelihood of a recurrence of the allegedly unlawful conduct. It is the *reality* of the threat of repeated injury that is relevant to the standing inquiry, not the plaintiff's subjective apprehensions. The emotional consequences of a prior act simply are not a sufficient basis for an injunction absent a real and immediate threat of future injury by the defendant. Of course, emotional upset is a relevant consideration in a damages action.

but whether Lyons meets the preconditions for asserting an injunctive claim in a federal forum. The equitable doctrine that cessation of the challenged conduct does not bar an injunction is of little help in this respect, for Lyons' lack of standing does not rest on the termination of the police practice but on the speculative nature of his claim that he will again experience injury as the result of that practice even if continued.

* * * The record and findings made on remand do not improve Lyons' position with respect to standing. * * * The City's policy was described [by the district court] as authorizing the use of the strangleholds "under circumstances where no one is threatened with death or grievous bodily harm." That policy was not further described, but the record before the court contained the department's existing policy * * *.[9] * * * [P]olice officers were instructed to use chokeholds only when lesser degrees of force do not suffice and then only "to gain control of a suspect who is violently resisting the officer or trying to escape."

Our conclusion is that the Court of Appeals failed to heed *O'Shea*, *Rizzo*, and other relevant authority, and that the District Court was quite right in dismissing Count V.

V * * *

Absent a sufficient likelihood that he will again be wronged in a similar way, Lyons is no more entitled to an injunction than any other citizen of Los Angeles; and a federal court may not entertain a claim by any or all citizens who no more than assert that certain practices of law enforcement officers are unconstitutional. This is not to suggest that such undifferentiated claims should not be taken seriously by local authorities. Indeed, the interest of an alert and interested citizen is an essential element of an effective and fair government, whether on the local, state, or national level.[10] A federal court, however, is not the proper forum to press such claims unless the requirements for entry and the prerequisites for injunctive relief are satisfied.

We decline the invitation to slight the preconditions for equitable relief; for as we have held, recognition of the need for a proper balance between state and federal authority counsels restraint in the issuance of injunctions against state officers engaged in the administration of the states' criminal laws in the absence of irreparable injury which is both great and immediate. *O'Shea;* Younger v. Harris, 401 U.S. 37, 46, 91 S.Ct. 746, 751, 27 L.Ed.2d 669 (1971). * * *

**9.** The dissent notes that a LAPD training officer stated that the police are authorized to employ the control holds whenever an officer "feels" that there is about to be a bodily attack. The dissent's emphasis on the word "feels" apparently is intended to suggest that LAPD officers are authorized to apply the holds whenever they "feel" like it. If there is a distinction between permitting the use of the holds when there is a "threat" of serious bodily harm, and when the officer "feels" or believes there is about to be a bodily attack, the dissent has failed to make it clear. * * *

**10.** The City's memorandum suggesting a question of mootness informed the Court that the use of the control holds had become "a major civic controversy" and that in April and May of 1982 "a spirited, vigorous, and at times emotional debate" on the issue took place. The result was the current moratorium on the use of the holds.

As we noted in *O'Shea,* withholding injunctive relief does not mean that the "federal law will exercise no deterrent effect in these circumstances." If Lyons has suffered an injury barred by the Federal Constitution, he has a remedy for damages under § 1983. Furthermore, those who deliberately deprive a citizen of his constitutional rights risk conviction under the federal criminal laws.

Beyond these considerations the state courts need not impose the same standing or remedial requirements that govern federal court proceedings. The individual states may permit their courts to use injunctions to oversee the conduct of law enforcement authorities on a continuing basis. But this is not the role of a federal court absent far more justification than Lyons has proffered in this case. * * *

JUSTICE MARSHALL, with whom JUSTICE BRENNAN, JUSTICE BLACKMUN and JUSTICE STEVENS join, dissenting.

* * * There is plainly a "case or controversy" concerning the constitutionality of the city's chokehold policy. The constitutionality of that policy is directly implicated by Lyons' claim for damages against the city. The complaint clearly alleges that the officer who choked Lyons was carrying out an official policy, and a municipality is liable under 42 U.S.C. § 1983 for the conduct of its employees only if they acted pursuant to such a policy. Monell v. New York City Dept. of Social Services, 436 U.S. 658, 694, 98 S.Ct. 2018, 2037, 56 L.Ed.2d 611 (1978). Lyons therefore has standing to challenge the city's chokehold policy and to obtain whatever relief a court may ultimately deem appropriate. None of our prior decisions suggests that his requests for particular forms of relief raise any additional issues concerning his standing. * * *

II

At the outset it is important to emphasize that Lyons' entitlement to injunctive relief and his entitlement to an award of damages both depend upon whether he can show that the city's chokehold policy violates the Constitution. An indispensable prerequisite of municipal liability under 42 U.S.C. § 1983 is proof that the conduct complained of is attributable to an unconstitutional official policy or custom. * * *

The Court apparently finds Lyons' complaint wanting because, although it alleges that he was choked without provocation and that the officers acted pursuant to an official policy, it fails to allege *in haec verba* that the city's policy authorizes the choking of suspects without provocation. I am aware of no case decided since the abolition of the old common law forms of action, and the Court cites none, that in any way supports this crabbed construction of the complaint. A federal court is capable of concluding for itself that two plus two equals four.

* * * In sum, it's absolutely clear that Lyons' requests for damages and for injunctive relief call into question the constitutionality of the city's policy concerning the use of chokeholds. If he does not show that policy is unconstitutional, he will be no more entitled to damages than to an injunction.

### III

Since Lyons' claim for damages plainly gives him standing, and since the success of that claim depends upon a demonstration that the city's chokehold policy is unconstitutional, it is beyond dispute that Lyons has properly invoked the District Court's authority to adjudicate the constitutionality of the city's chokehold policy. The dispute concerning the constitutionality of that policy plainly presents a "case or controversy" under Art. III. The Court nevertheless holds that a federal court has no power under Art. III to adjudicate Lyons' request, in the same lawsuit, for injunctive relief with respect to that very policy. This anomalous result is not supported either by precedent or by the fundamental concern underlying the standing requirement. Moreover, by fragmenting a single claim into multiple claims for particular types of relief and requiring a separate showing of standing for each form of relief, the decision today departs from this Court's traditional conception of standing and of the remedial powers of the federal courts.

#### A

It is simply disingenuous for the Court to assert that its decision requires "[n]o extension" of *O'Shea* and *Rizzo*. In contrast to this case *O'Shea* and *Rizzo* involved disputes focusing solely on the threat of future injury which the plaintiffs in those cases alleged they faced. * * *

In addition to the risk that he will be subjected to a chokehold in the future, Lyons has suffered past injury.[15] Because he has a live claim for damages, he need not rely solely on the threat of future injury to establish his personal stake in the outcome of the controversy. In the cases relied on by the majority, the Court simply had no occasion to decide whether a plaintiff who has standing to litigate a dispute must clear a separate standing hurdle with respect to each form of relief sought.

#### B

The Court's decision likewise finds no support in the fundamental policy underlying the Art. III standing requirement—the concern that a federal court not decide a legal issue if the plaintiff lacks a sufficient "personal stake in the outcome of the controversy as to assure that concrete adverseness which sharpens the presentation of issues upon which the court so largely depends for illumination of difficult ... questions." Baker v. Carr, 369 U.S. 186, 204, 82 S.Ct. 691, 703, 7 L.Ed.2d 663 (1962). * * *

**15.** In Lankford v. Gelston, 364 F.2d 197 (C.A.4 1966)(en banc), which we cited with approval in Allee v. Medrano, 416 U.S. 802, 816, n. 9, 94 S.Ct. 2191, 2200, n. 9, 40 L.Ed.2d 566 (1974), the Fourth Circuit found standing on facts indistinguishable from this case. In *Lankford*, the Court of Appeals held that four Negro families who had been subjected to an illegal house search were entitled to seek injunctive relief against the Baltimore Police Department's policy of conducting wholesale searches based only on uncorroborated anonymous tips, even though the plaintiffs there did not claim that they were more likely than other Negro residents of the city to be subjected to an illegal search in the future.

Because Lyons has a claim for damages against the city, and because he cannot prevail on that claim unless he demonstrates that the city's chokehold policy violates the Constitution, his personal stake in the outcome of the controversy adequately assures an adversary presentation of his challenge to the constitutionality of the policy. Moreover, the resolution of this challenge will be largely dispositive of his requests for declaratory and injunctive relief. No doubt the requests for injunctive relief may raise additional questions. But these questions involve familiar issues relating to the appropriateness of particular forms of relief, and have never been thought to implicate a litigant's standing to sue. The denial of standing separately to seek injunctive relief therefore cannot be justified by the basic concern underlying the Art. III standing requirement.

C * * *

The Court's fragmentation of the standing inquiry is also inconsistent with the way the federal courts have treated remedial issues since the merger of law and equity. The federal practice has been to reserve consideration of the appropriate relief until after a determination of the merits, not to foreclose certain forms of relief by a ruling on the pleadings. * * *

Rule 54(c) of the Federal Rules of Civil Procedure specifically provides that "every final judgment shall grant the relief to which the party in whose favor it is rendered is entitled, even if the party has not demanded such relief in his pleadings." * * *

VI

The Court's decision removes an entire class of constitutional violations from the equitable powers of a federal court. It immunizes from prospective equitable relief any policy that authorizes persistent deprivations of constitutional rights as long as no individual can establish with substantial certainty that he will be injured, or injured again, in the future. The Chief Justice asked in Bivens v. Six Unknown Fed. Narcotics Agents, 403 U.S. 388, 419, 91 S.Ct. 1999, 2016, 29 L.Ed.2d 619 (1971)(dissenting opinion), "what would be the judicial response to a police order authorizing 'shoot to kill' with respect to every fugitive?" His answer was that it would be "easy to predict our collective wrath and outrage." We now learn that wrath and outrage cannot be translated into an order to cease the unconstitutional practice, but only an award of damages to those who are victimized by the practice and live to sue and to the survivors of those who are not so fortunate. Under the view expressed by the majority today, if the police adopt a policy of "shoot to kill," or a policy of shooting one out of ten suspects, the federal courts will be powerless to enjoin its continuation. The federal judicial power is now limited to levying a toll for such a systematic constitutional violation. * * *

## *Notes*

1. *Lyons* mentions four of the doctrines discussed in the text preceding the case. First, the majority rules that the controversy was not moot.

(Why, by the way, did Lyons argue that the case was moot?) Second, the majority rules that Lyons did not present a case or controversy in his claim for injunctive relief on the theory that there is only a small probability of recurrence. Third, the majority rules that an injunction should be withheld on the basis of equitable discretion on the theory that there is only a small probability of recurrence. (It is over these second and third doctrines that the majority and the dissent clash.) Fourth, the majority mentions that the threatened harm must be substantial, which it undoubtedly would have found it was, if it had reached the question. The majority mentions, in a passage that was deleted, that an injunction will not issue if there is an adequate remedy at law.

If the majority found the harm sufficiently probable, it would undoubtedly find the remedy at law inadequate because damages cannot cure bodily injury or death. However, the dissent chides the majority for in effect relegating Lyons to a damage remedy. The majority retorts that Lyons can seek to prevent injury through the deterrent effect of possible criminal sanctions—which is a remedy at law—as well as other channels, such as the state courts and the political process. The majority invokes these alternatives to injunctive relief to parry Justice Marshall's attack based on the adequacy of the remedy at law rather than as a rationale for the decision on threat of harm.

2. The majority in *Lyons* relies upon the proposition that the plaintiff seeking an injunction must show a significant threat of harm to himself. It discusses this proposition in terms of the threat of harm doctrine and the standing doctrine. How probable is it that Lyons will be subjected in the future to an illegal chokehold? Do you agree with the majority's analysis of that question? The dissent's? If the availability of an injunction depends upon the probability of harm, who should bear the burden on probability?

3. What can a plaintiff in a case like *Lyons* do to satisfy the threat of harm requirement? Consider the following possibilities:

(a) *Bring a class action.* Would it have been easier for Lyons to show a threat of harm if the case were a class action? *Lyons* was never certified as a class action. Lankford v. Gelston, 364 F.2d 197 (4th Cir.1966), which Justice Marshall argues is indistinguishable, was a class action.

(b) *Provide specific statistics showing a threat of harm.* In Adarand Constructors, Inc. v. Pena, ___ U.S. ___, 115 S.Ct. 2097, 132 L.Ed.2d 158 (1995), the Supreme Court found that Adarand showed the imminent threat of harm required to seek injunctive relief. The harm that Adarand alleged was that unjustified race-based preferences, as part of an affirmative action program in federal highway contracting, denied it equal protection of the laws. Adarand showed the likelihood of this harm by proving that the kind of contracts upon which it routinely bid were put out for bid with provisions for race-based preferences at an average rate of one and a half per year for the past seven years and that Adarand usually faced competition from firms eligible for race-based preference.

The plaintiff in a *Lyons*-like case would be well advised to frame the case so that the odds of harm are high. For example, might a court agree that the odds of a young African–American male driver being subject to a chokehold while driving in a rich, white precinct are likely to be much higher than the odds calculated for all drivers in all neighborhoods?

(c) *Allege unequal treatment.* Adarand was not required to show that it would submit the winning bid but for the racial preference because the "injury in cases of this kind is that a 'discriminatory classification prevent[s] the plaintiff from competing on an equal footing.'" *Adarand Constructors,* 115 S.Ct. at 2105 (quoting General Contractors v. Jacksonville, 508 U.S. 656, —, 113 S.Ct. 2297, 2304, 124 L.Ed.2d 589 (1993)). Would Lyons have prevailed if he alleged that the police decided whom to choke partly on the basis of the color of their skin?

4. Justice Marshall argues that the majority is wrong to test standing for each claim for relief rather than testing standing as to the central factual controversy. Is the majority's approach necessary to serve the purposes behind standing or remedial ripeness? From Justice Marshall's perspective, should the plaintiff in *Bivens* be entitled to an injunction against future searches no matter how low the probability of his home being searched again?

5. Would *Lyons* have come out the same way if Los Angeles had left its original chokehold policy in effect?

### *Note on Who Is Protected by an Injunction*

Assuming that Lyons could show sufficient probability of harm to get an injunction, should the injunction limit the use of the chokehold against just him or also against similarly situated persons who are not parties? The question, which arises chiefly in cases against governmental defendants, is answered along two lines: (1) an injunction can protect nonparties where the defendant explicitly or implicitly consents to a decree that protects nonparties, e.g., Catanzano v. Dowling, 847 F.Supp. 1070 (W.D.N.Y.1994), and (2) an injunction can protect only parties, including members of a plaintiff class, but an injunction protecting an individual plaintiff may have the practical effect of protecting others similarly situated, e.g., Kansas Health Care Association, Inc. v. Kansas Dep't of Social & Rehabilitation Services, 31 F.3d 1536 (10th Cir.1994).

For example, if Country Lodge gets an injunction barring Miller from polluting, compliance will protect those situated similarly to Country Lodge. In contrast, Los Angeles could conceivably comply with an injunction against applying the chokehold to Lyons, but apply the chokehold to others similarly situated. When an injunction would have the practical effect of protecting everyone similarly situated, courts following the second approach sometimes decline to certify a class action. Which approach is appropriate? See George Rutherglen, Notice, Scope, and Preclusion in Title VII Class Actions, 69 Va.L.Rev. 11, 17–21 (1983).

An example of the second, and more common approach, is a case brought by a single individual challenging the constitutionality of the military's policy of discharging avowed homosexuals. The district court judge ordered that "[t]he Department of Defense is permanently enjoined from discharging or denying enlistment to *any* person based on sexual orientation in the absence of sexual conduct which interferes with the military mission of the armed forces * * *." Meinhold v. Department of Defense, 808 F.Supp. 1455, 1459 (C.D.Cal.1993)(emphasis added). The Ninth Circuit denied a stay pending appeal because, although it noted a legitimate issue about whether the injunction should protect anyone but Meinhold, it found that the department would not suffer irreparable injury in view of the presidential directive on homosexuals in the military. 61 Empl.Prac.Dec.(CCH) ¶ 42,197 (9th Cir.1993). In a subsequent contempt proceeding brought by Meinhold, the district court amended the injunction, further restraining the Department of Defense from "creating or maintaining files based on sexual orientation and from taking any action against gay or lesbian servicemembers based on their sexual orientation." Meinhold v. Department of Defense, 1993 WL 513209, 62 Empl.Prac.Dec. (CCH) ¶ 42,619 (C.D.Cal.1993). The Supreme Court granted a stay of the amended injunction to the extent that it applied to persons other than Meinhold. ___ U.S. ___, 114 S.Ct. 374, 126 L.Ed.2d 324 (1993). The Ninth Circuit then held that the district court erred in granting an injunction protecting anyone but Meinhold. 34 F.3d 1469 (9th Cir.1994).

### *Note on the Relationship Between Threat of Harm and the Scope of an Injunction*

In Hodgson v. Corning Glass Works, 474 F.2d 226 (2d Cir.1973) aff'd, 417 U.S. 188, 94 S.Ct. 2223, 41 L.Ed.2d 1 (1974), Secretary of Labor James Hodgson brought an action against Corning Glass Works alleging a violation of the Equal Pay Act of 1963. The court found a violation of the act only with respect to one class of employees at the defendant's three plants in Corning, New York and there was no evidence of widespread violations of the act at its 26 branch plants nationwide. The district court had enjoined violations at virtually all of the plants, but the Court of Appeals confined the injunctions, because "absent a showing of a policy of discrimination which extends beyond the plants at issue * * * there is no basis for a nationwide injunction." Id. at 236. What relief if Corning Glass Works dismisses those responsible for the discrimination at its plants in Corning? See Spomer v. Littleton, 414 U.S. 514, 94 S.Ct. 685, 38 L.Ed.2d 694 (1974).

Lujan v. National Wildlife Federation, 497 U.S. 871, 110 S.Ct. 3177, 111 L.Ed.2d 695 (1990), held in a five to four decision that the National Wildlife Federation (NWF) lacked standing to challenge certain government land management practices, but all the justices appeared to agree that the scope of standing can affect the scope of injunctive relief. In the majority's view, NWF lacked standing because the challenged practices were general policies and NWF failed to allege with sufficient specificity that the application of those practices to particular tracts of land injured any of its members. The Court suggested, along the way, that if plaintiff had made sufficient allegations about a particular tract, injunctive relief would be limited to that tract. 497 U.S. at 889–94, 110 S.Ct. at 3189–91, 111 L.Ed.2d at 717–20. On this point, the dissent, by

Justice Blackmun, appeared to agree. 497 U.S. at 913–15, 110 S.Ct. at 3201, 111 L.Ed.2d at 731.

## 2. INADEQUATE REMEDY AT LAW

### *Problem: Country Lodge v. Miller (Reprised)*<br>*The Choice Between Legal and Equitable Remedies*

(a) Is Country Lodge barred from obtaining an injunction to prevent future water pollution because it might instead get a money judgment for compensatory damages?

(b) Is Country Lodge barred from obtaining an injunction to require Miller to clean up the waste because it might get a money judgment for compensatory damages?

(c) If Miller's pollution is a crime, could the prosecutor get an injunction against its repetition? Would it make a difference if the criminal penalty was a $50 or a $50,000 fine?

(d) Country Lodge contracts with Eco-cleaners, Inc., for it to remove the apple mash from the river bank. The contract specifies that Eco-cleaners will reduce the concentration of apple mash on the bank to less than one part per ten thousand. After Eco-cleaners applies the usual clean up techniques that it thought would do the job, the concentration is reduced, but still twice that specified in the contract. Eco-cleaners does not want to take any additional steps because the present concentration is neither visible nor attracts insects and meeting the specifications would result in Eco-cleaners incurring a considerable loss on the contract. Country Lodge wants the contract carried out to the letter. Should Country Lodge's request for specific performance be granted by the court?

---

Your civil procedure course probably covered the development of separate courts of law and equity in England and, subsequently, in the United States. (For a refresher, see William Q. De Funiak, Handbook of Modern Equity 1–10 (1956).) The part of that story relevant here is that the courts of law would hear no suit to prevent an injury to property or to compel performance of a contract. Instead they offered damages after the injury was done. In contrast, the equity courts offered injunctive relief. But, the law courts' jealous protection of their own jurisdiction forced the equity courts to limit access to those who could show that the law courts provided them with no adequate remedy.

The eventual merger of law and equity courts in this country did away with the jealousy between rival judicial systems, but the merged courts continued to insist on the old maxim that equitable remedies are available only if the remedy at law is inadequate. A traditional test of inadequacy is that the remedy at law is not "as practical and as efficient to the ends of justice and its prompt administration, as the remedy in equity." Boyce's Ex'rs v. Grundy, 28 U.S. (3 Pet.) 210, 215, 7 L.Ed. 655, 657 (1830).

Under this test any one of many different considerations can lead to a finding that the remedy at law is inadequate:

1. the defendant is judgment-proof;

2. the defendant is immune from damages, as may be the case with defendants who are officials or governments;

3. damages are difficult to estimate because the size of monetary loss is hard to estimate, as in the case of lost profits from a new business, or because the plaintiff is likely to put a money value on the property higher than the market value, as in the case of an heirloom;

4. damages can not be used to put plaintiff in its rightful position because what is lost is not available in the market place, as in the cases involving a unique item of property, civil rights, or environmental quality;

5. complete recovery would require a multiplicity of suits, as where plaintiff seeks an injunction against an ongoing nuisance and the jurisdiction does not allow the recovery of all future damages in one action; or

6. allowing the injury to take place would be morally repugnant even if it can be repaired, as in the case of intentional injury to plaintiff's property.

See, e.g., Developments in the Law—Injunctions, 78 Harv.L.Rev. 994, 997–1021 (1965). Courts presume that there is no adequate remedy at law when real estate is at stake. This presumption is justified in most but not all cases by sentimental attachments, difficulty in ascertaining the monetary value to plaintiff, or difficulty finding another parcel with exactly the same attributes.

### *Note on the Maxims of Equity*

The inadequate remedy at law rule is one of many so-called "maxims" of equity. Some of the other maxims are closely related to the inadequacy maxim.

One maxim is that equity will not act unless there is "irreparable injury"—meaning that plaintiff would suffer an injury that a legal remedy cannot repair. By this courts mean some or all of the considerations listed above. Commentators take this irreparable injury requirement to be a close relative to the inadequate remedy at law requirement. E.g., Gene R. Shreve, Federal Injunctions and the Public Interest, 51 Geo.Wash.L.Rev. 382, 392–94 (1983).

Another maxim is that "Equity protects property rights, not personal rights." To the extent this maxim means that legal remedies are never an adequate response to trespass, it simply affirms one aspect of the inadequacy doctrine. To the extent that it means legal remedies are always adequate to protect other rights, it erroneously simplifies and generalizes from the traditional tendency to protect contract as opposed to property rights with compensatory damages. The maxim was riddled with exceptions from the beginning and these exceptions grew larger with the growing importance of constitutional rights and statutory rights other than property-related rights and the grant of injunctions to protect them. The maxim is today not a meaningful limitation on the grant of injunctions.

Still another maxim related to the inadequate remedy at law rule is "Equity will not enjoin a crime." Since criminal prosecutions were brought in the courts of law, enjoining a crime deprives defendants of the procedural rights that the criminal law affords, which include not just a jury trial, but also the proof beyond a reasonable doubt standard and more. Nonetheless, the maxim has long been full of exceptions, although there is more left to it than the maxim that equity protects only property rights. Private parties can get injunctions against crimes that are also torts. The government can get an injunction against a crime when it is a public nuisance or creates a national emergency, or a statute specifically grants power to do so. See, e.g., United States v. Bay Mills Indian Community, 692 F.Supp. 777, 779 (W.D.Mich.1988), vacated on joint motion of parties, 727 F.Supp. 1110 (W.D.Mich.1989). Courts will also enjoin crimes where criminal sanctions have failed to stop repetitions of the crime or are unlikely to stop future crimes. State v. Red Owl Stores, Inc., 253 Minn. 236, 92 N.W.2d 103 (1958)(prosecution unlikely to be effective because supermarket chains planned store-by-store defense against prosecution for selling over-the-counter drugs without a pharmacy license and fine for violating statute in question was small); City of Chicago v. Cecola, 75 Ill.2d 423, 27 Ill.Dec. 462, 389 N.E.2d 526 (1979) (prosecution unlikely to be effective because $200 a day fine will not put "massage" parlor out of business). Coercive civil contempt or criminal contempt allows the judge to impose sanctions in excess of the statutory penalty for the crime and to avoid jury nullification. A private plaintiff who would otherwise suffer irreparable injury can get an injunction against a crime when the prosecutor will not bring charges. Is it appropriate for a judge to use the contempt power to impose a sanction harsher than the legislature established for the crime? To circumvent jury nullification?

Maxims of equity provide the illusory comfort of absolute answers. Perhaps that is why there are so many of them. Most are unrelated to the inadequacy of legal remedy rule (such as, "Equality is equity"). A large number of such maxims are collected in P.V. Baker & P.St.J. Langan, Snell's Equity ch. 3 (29th ed.1990), and Howard W. Brill, The Maxims of Equity, 1993 Ark.L.Notes 29 (1993). Like the examples discussed above, these maxims are usually so exception-riddled or vague as to have little meaning. In essence, maxims are a style of discussing equity, and fortunately an increasingly outmoded one.

The maxims' oversimplification and vagueness are understandable because it is hard to write without one or the other. But, maxims unfortunately pack a rhetorical zing that erroneously suggests that they are the end rather than the beginning of proper analysis. Professor Douglas Laycock has neatly punctured the puffery in the inadequate remedy at law maxim:

> [T]he full statement of the traditional rule is as follows:
>
> 1. Equity will not act if there is an adequate remedy at law.
>
> 2. "Adequate remedy" means a remedy as complete, practical, and efficient as the equitable remedy.
>
> This rule could be reformulated as follows:
>
> 1. Plaintiff is entitled in all cases to the most complete, practical, and efficient remedy.
>
> 2. If a legal and an equitable remedy are equally complete, practical, and efficient, the legal remedy shall be used.
>
> Although the two formulations are logically equivalent, they are not rhetorically equivalent, especially if one assumes that under either formulation the broader first rule of the pair will be more widely known than the narrower second rule. The second formulation would make clear that the irreparable injury rule is simply a tie-breaker, and that the plaintiff is not to be disadvantaged because of it. The first formulation suggests a stronger prejudice against equity; it is responsible for judicial statements that injunctions are an extraordinary remedy.

Douglas Laycock, Injunctions and the Irreparable Injury Rule (Book Review), 57 Tex.L.Rev. 1065, 1071–72 (1979).

### *Note on the Declining Importance of the Inadequate Remedy at Law Rule*

The rhetoric of the rule does not fool most modern courts. Rather they weigh the practical merits of equitable and legal relief. As a result, if plaintiff has a good reason for preferring an injunction to damages, that reason is usually good enough to persuade a court to grant injunctive relief, except where there is some special reason for avoiding injunctive relief, such as concern for placing a prior restraint on speech. This does not mean that plaintiffs will always have a good reason, but it does mean that the inadequate remedy at law rule lacks the generalized importance that the maxim suggests.

Professor Laycock has tested this suggestion by systematically surveying modern cases. The Death of the Irreparable Injury Rule, 103 Harv.L.Rev. 687 (1990), published as a book of the same name in 1991. He notes that plaintiffs seek compensatory damages more often than injunctions for a variety of reasons: specific relief may be impossible after the breach; plaintiffs may prefer damages to coerced performance by an unwilling defendant; or compensatory damages may be equivalent to specific performance, as when the promised performance is the payment of money. That plaintiffs seek damages more often than injunctions does not mean that courts usually say "no" to those plaintiffs who do seek injunctions.

Professor Laycock surveyed more than 1400 recent cases in which plaintiffs sought specific relief and the courts discussed the irreparable injury rule or its analogues. In the vast majority of cases, the courts found that the irreparable injury rule was no bar to specific relief for the reasons outlined above. Relatively few cases held the legal remedies adequate. Most of these he attributes to reasons other than a generalized preference for legal remedies, such as, preventing plaintiff from getting an advantage over other creditors of the defendant.

## DOUGLAS LAYCOCK, THE DEATH OF THE IRREPARABLE INJURY RULE

103 Harv.L.Rev. 687, 722–724 (1990).

* * * There are very few cases not subject to at least one of these doctrines for finding legal remedies inadequate or inapplicable. If plaintiff has any plausible need for specific relief, she can describe that need as irreparable injury and find ample precedent to support her claim. Yet there are still some cases denying specific relief and invoking the irreparable injury rule to support their decision. The results in the great bulk of these cases have nothing to do with a preference for legal remedies and can be explained on other grounds. * * *

There remain a handful of cases that can be explained on no ground other than the traditional understanding of the irreparable injury rule. These are cases in which plaintiff seeks some equitable remedy, and is remitted to a legal remedy instead, on the ground that the legal remedy would be adequate. These opinions do not reveal any special difficulty with the equitable remedy or any judicial hostility to the merits of plaintiff's case. There are remarkably few of these cases—fewer than I expected to find when I began this research—but they do occur. These remnants of the irreparable injury rule do not make a persuasive case for retaining the rule.

In a few of these cases, plaintiff is remitted to some legal form of specific relief, such as replevin, that will accomplish exactly what equity could have accomplished. The remedies may differ in means of enforcement, and sometimes these differences are important. But these cases do not present a choice between specific and substitutionary relief—plaintiff gets specific relief either way.

Most of the remaining cases refuse specific performance of contracts to sell goods. In some, it appears that the goods are fungible and the market is orderly; so far as the opinion reveals, plaintiff can easily and immediately exchange money damages for identical goods. Where that is true, the distinction between specific and substitutionary relief disappears. Unless the opinions are omitting critical facts, it is hard to see why plaintiff seeks specific performance in such a case, why defendant resists it, or why we have a rule that encourages the parties to litigate it.

In these cases, the legal remedy really is just as good as the equitable remedy. Either way, plaintiff gets identical goods, and with damages for any difference in price, he gets the goods at the same effective cost. If he measures damages by the difference between the contract price and the cover price, the amount of damages does not even depend on anyone's estimate of value. These cases arise either from bad lawyering or from critical undisclosed facts. If critical facts that drive the litigation are omitted from the opinion, it can only be because the irreparable injury rule has diverted the court's attention from the real issue.

These cases shade into those where the goods are replaceable only with difficulty, or only with similar but not identical goods. Plaintiff argues that cover is difficult or impossible; the court finds that cover is possible and damages are adequate. Where cover is difficult, a majority of cases grant specific relief, but a substantial minority do not. So long as the rule persists that damages are an adequate remedy for breach of a contract to sell goods that are available elsewhere, some cases will fall near the line and some of these cases will be decided each way. We can argue whether this line is worth drawing and litigating over, but for now it survives. It is the principal remnant of the irreparable injury rule.

In the very few cases remaining, damages are plainly not as good for plaintiff as specific relief, but the court fails to recognize the inadequacy or considers it insufficient to satisfy the rule. Plaintiff is worse off for being remitted to damages, and the opinion does not indicate any way in which defendant or the judicial system is better off. Unless there are countervailing considerations that do not appear in the opinions, the irreparable injury rule leads the court to a bad result in these cases. Remarkably, I have found only three modern cases of this sort [out of the sample of 1400 cases]. * * *

---

Justice Holmes wrote that "[t]he duty to keep a contract at common law means a prediction that you must pay damages if you do not keep it,—and nothing else." Oliver W. Holmes, The Path of the Law, 10 Harv.L.Rev. 457, 462 (1897). Is that still true?

### *Note on Whether to Abandon the Inadequacy Requirement*

Professor Laycock views the rule as a source of confusion and litigation costs. Professor Dan Dobbs believes that defendants raise it as a dilatory tactic rather than out of a preference for the legal remedy. Dan B. Dobbs, Law of Remedies § 2.5(3)(2d ed.1993). So why not get rid of it?

With the rule's original purpose vanishing with the merger of law and equity, several additional purposes have been suggested. One purpose is to preserve defendant's option in cases at law to have issues of fact heard by a jury. But, the availability of a jury at law does not so much explain the rule as throw into question the lack of a jury in equity. Moreover, jurisdictions that provide a jury in equity still pay homage to the inadequacy rule. E.g., Duke Power Co. v. City of High Point, 69 N.C.App. 335, 337, 317 S.E.2d 699, 700 (1984). The preference for law makes more sense where the alternative to an injunction is a criminal prosecution with not only a jury trial but also the many other protections of the criminal process. This purpose does not explain the supposed preference for civil remedies at law.

Another explanation of the irreparable injury rule is that injunctions pose problems for the court in both drafting and enforcement. E.g., Doug Rendleman, The Inadequate Remedy at Law Prerequisite to An Injunction, 33 U.Fla.L.Rev. 346, 353–58 (1981). This is sometimes true, as will be seen in chapter 3. But, as the following section will show, there are doctrines that deny injunctive relief where it would unduly burden the court. Moreover, calculating and collecting damages can burden the court, as will be seen in chapters 6 and 8. Whether the equitable or the legal remedy is more burdensome will vary with the case so that burden on the court cannot explain a systematic preference for remedies at law.

Another possible purpose of the rule is to avoid the injunction's intrusion on defendant's liberty. For example, Miller may choose to keep dumping the waste and paying damages to Country Lodge if no injunction issues but, if one does issue, she has lost that choice. On the other hand, preferring the legal remedy takes away Country Lodge's ability to choose between preventing the wrong or collecting damages. So the cost of protecting the wrongdoer's liberty is infringing on the victim's liberty. Conceivably the defendant's liberty interest may be greater, but there is no reason to suppose that it is so in general.

A final explanation for the inadequate remedy at law rule is that it promotes efficient allocation of resources. According to Professor A. Mitchell Polinsky, efficiency is "the relationship between the aggregate benefits of a situation and the aggregate costs of the situation * * *. In other words, efficiency corresponds to the 'size of the pie' [as opposed to] how it is sliced." A. Mitchell Polinsky, An Introduction to Law and Economics 7 (2d ed.1989). For instance, in the Country Lodge problem at the beginning of the chapter, an injunction prohibiting future nuisances might be inefficient because, as discussed, it might impose costs on Miller higher than its benefits to Country Lodge. But, as also seen, courts would regard Country Lodge's damage remedy as inadequate for many reasons. Even in cases where courts find the legal remedy inadequate, concerns about efficiency sometimes lead to denial of injunctive relief under the doctrine of balancing the equities, to be discussed in section D of this chapter. The present question is whether the concept of efficiency can justify the inadequate remedy at law rule where it still holds sway—contracts to deliver goods that are fungible or at least "reasonably" so and cover is easy or at least "reasonably" so.

Suppose that A contracts to deliver a quantity of widgets to B for $18,000, but then C offers A $20,000 for the same widgets. As a naive form of the efficiency argument goes, specific performance would put the widgets into the hands of B who values them less highly than C, while the damage remedy would allow an efficient outcome. This is so, as the argument goes, because A would not breach unless the widgets were worth more to C than B because A would not sell to C unless the price was high enough to cover the cost of delivering the goods to C plus paying damages sufficient to make B whole. However, this argument assumes that damages fully compensate B. Professor Alan Schwartz questions that assumption.

## ALAN SCHWARTZ, THE CASE FOR SPECIFIC PERFORMANCE

89 Yale L.J. 271, 274–278 (1979).

* * * II. CONTRACT REMEDIES AND THE COMPENSATION GOAL

Specific performance is the most accurate method of achieving the compensation goal of contract remedies because it gives the promisee the precise performance that he purchased. The natural question, then, is why specific performance is not routinely available. Three explanations of the law's restrictions on specific performance are possible. First, the law's commitment to the compensation goal may be less than complete; restricting specific performance may reflect an inarticulate reluctance to pursue the compensation goal fully. Second, damages may generally be fully compensatory. In that event, expanding the availability of specific performance would create opportunities for promisees to exploit promisors by threatening to compel, or actually compelling, performance, without furthering the compensation goal. The third explanation is that concerns of efficiency or liberty may justify restricting specific performance, despite its greater accuracy; specific performance might generate higher transaction costs than the damage remedy, or interfere more with the liberty interests of promisors. The first justification is beyond the scope of the analysis here. The second and third explanations will be examined in detail. * * *

It is useful to begin by examining the paradigm case for granting specific performance under current law, the case of unique goods. When a promisor breaches and the promisee can make a transaction that substitutes for the performance the promisor failed to render, the promisee will be fully compensated if he receives the additional amount necessary to purchase the substitute plus the costs of making a second transaction. In some cases, however, such as those involving works of art, courts cannot identify which transactions the promisee would regard as substitutes because that information often is in the exclusive possession of the promisee. Moreover, it is difficult for a court to assess the accuracy of a promisee's claim. For example, if the promisor breaches a contract to sell a rare emerald, the promisee may claim that only the Hope Diamond would give him equal satisfaction, and thus may sue for the price difference between the emerald and the diamond. It would be difficult for a court to know whether this claim is true. If the court seeks to award money damages, it has three choices: granting the price differential, which may overcompensate the promisee; granting the dollar value of the promisee's foregone satisfaction as estimated by the court, which may overcompensate or undercompensate; or granting restitution of any sums paid, which undercompensates the promisee. The promisee is fully compensated without risk of overcompensation or undercompensation if the remedy of specific performance is available to him and its use encouraged by the doctrine that damages must be foreseeable and certain.

If specific performance is the appropriate remedy in such cases, there are three reasons why it should be routinely available. The first reason is that in many cases damages actually are undercompensatory. Although promisees are entitled to incidental damages, such damages are difficult to monetize. They consist primarily of the costs of finding and making a second deal, which generally involve the expenditure of time rather than cash; attaching a dollar value to such opportunity costs is quite difficult. Breach can also cause frustration and anger, especially in a consumer context, but these costs also are not recoverable.

Substitution damages, the court's estimate of the amount the promisee needs to purchase an adequate substitute, also may be inaccurate in many cases less dramatic than the emerald hypothetical discussed above. This is largely because of product differentiation and early obsolescence. As product differentiation becomes more common, the supply of products that will substitute precisely for the promisor's performance is reduced. For example, even during the period when there is an abundant supply of new Datsuns for sale, two-door, two-tone Datsuns with mag wheels, stereo, and air conditioning may be scarce in some local markets. * * * [A] damage award meant to enable a promisee to purchase "another car" could be undercompensatory.

In addition, problems of prediction often make it difficult to put a promisee in the position where he would have been had his promisor performed. If a breach by a contractor would significantly delay or prevent completion of a construction project and the project differs in important respects from other projects—for example, a department store in a different location than previous stores—courts may be reluctant to award "speculative" lost profits attributable to the breach.

Second, promisees have economic incentives to sue for damages when damages are likely to be fully compensatory. A breaching promisor is reluctant to perform and may be hostile. [Especially when the performance is complex and takes place over time, it may well be costly and time consuming if not impossible to hold the promisor to performing satisfactorily.] * * * The very fact that a promisee requests specific performance thus implies that damages are an inadequate remedy.

The third reason why courts should permit promisees to elect routinely the remedy of specific performance is that promisees possess better information than courts as to both the adequacy of damages and the difficulties of coercing performance. Promisees know better than courts whether the damages a court is likely to award would be adequate because promisees are more familiar with the costs that breach imposes on them. In addition, promisees generally know more about their promisors than do courts * * *

In sum, restrictions on the availability of specific performance cannot be justified on the basis that damage awards are usually compensatory. On the contrary, the compensation goal implies that specific performance should be routinely available. This is because damage awards actually are undercompensatory in more cases than is commonly supposed; the fact of a specific performance request is itself good evidence that damages would be inadequate; and courts should delegate to promisees the decision of which remedy best satisfies the compensation goal. Further, expanding the availability of specific performance would not result in greater exploitation of promisors. Promisees would seldom abuse the power to determine when specific performance should be awarded because of the strong incentives that promisees face to seek damages when these would be even approximately compensatory.

III. Specific Performance and Efficiency

[S]uppose that the [compensation] goal rests on * * * an assumption that compensating disappointed promisees fully is less costly than not compensating them fully. If the broader availability of specific performance would generate transaction costs that exceed the costs of undercompensation the equitable remedy would avoid, then current restrictions on specific performance would be justified. On the other hand, if the compensation goal rests on a moral notion that promises should be kept, * * * then specific performance is a preferable remedy to damages even though it might generate higher costs. * * *

Both possible bases of the compensation goal thus would support the routine availability of specific performance unless specific performance is a more costly remedy than damages. * * *

### *Notes*

1. How successful is Professor Schwartz in dealing with the contention that promisees will exploit specific performance to get payments that go beyond compensation? Would that be extortion? If A had stolen the goods from B rather than failed to deliver them so that liability is in conversion rather than contract and B then secures an injunction requiring A to return the goods, would it be morally repugnant for B to offer to give up the injunction in return for a payment that exceeds compensation? Courts would not hesitate to enjoin conversion because it is viewed as morally repugnant. Why not view breach of contract the same way?

2. Professor Edward Yorio has argued that the appropriate response to damages being undercompensatory is to change the measure of damages to make them fully compensatory rather than grant specific performance. Edward Yorio, In Defense of Money Damages for Breach of Contract, 82 Colum.L.Rev. 1365, 1367–70 (1982). He also argues that specific performance is far less flexible about the measure of relief than monetary relief is so that damages can be adjusted to take account of a wide variety of circumstances. Edward Yorio, A Defense of Equitable Defenses, 51 Ohio St.L.J. 1201 (1990).

Professor Schwartz does not evaluate the issue of whether the law should be dedicated to complete compensation. Should it? See Jeffrey Standen, The Fallacy of Full Compensation, 73 Wash.U.L.Q. 145 (1995).

3. Even if compensatory damages are undercompensatory, they may provide a more efficient remedy than specific performance if the new buyer, C, still values the goods more than the contract buyer, B. But, if C really values the widgets more than B, wouldn't C make B an offer for the widgets that B would accept, thereby achieving an efficient outcome? After all, the difference between the values that B and C place on the widgets are potential gains of trade. Similarly, A could pay B for the right to deliver the widgets to C.

Judge Richard Posner asserts that "the seller [A] can always pay the buyer [B] to surrender the right of specific performance and presumably will do so if a substitute transfer [to C] would yield a higher price. But the additional negotiation will not be costless." Richard Posner, Economic Analysis of Law 131 (4th ed.1992). "Transaction costs" include the costs of identifying those with whom one needs to bargain, getting together with them, bargaining with them, and enforcing the bargain. Judge Posner's point is that specific performance generates two bargains—one between A and B to terminate B's right to specific performance and another between A and C to sell the widgets. In contrast, the damage remedy requires only one bargain—between A and C.

Professor Schwartz responds, in a portion of the article not included above, that there are other factors to consider. Alan Schwartz, 89 Yale L.J. at 284–291. If A has to deliver to B, then B could sell the widgets to C, which would mean only one bargain. Or A could deliver to B and then still sell to C by buying substitute goods in the market, just as B would have had to do if relegated to a damage remedy. It would be harder for A to buy substitute goods where there is no smoothly functioning market, but those are precisely the cases where courts are most likely to grant specific performance. Moreover, under the damage remedy, B would have to take A to court to get the damages or else they would have to settle the suit, another bargain, but either would result in transaction costs. So which remedy yields lower transaction costs? If the damage remedy yields lower transaction costs, are they low enough to offset the effects of undercompensatory damages? Many scholars have joined the debate on whether specific performance or damages is more efficient. See Jeffrey Standen, The Fallacy of Full Compensation, 73 Wash.U.L.Q. 145, 146 n.5 (1995).

### *Note on Constitutional and Statutory Variations on the Inadequacy Requirement*

Constitutions sometimes dictate the choice between injunctive and legal relief. For example, by permitting the taking of property for a public use through the payment of compensation, the fifth amendment denies the property owner injunctive relief. See U.S.Const.amend. V; Hawaii Housing Authority v. Midkiff, 467 U.S. 229, 104 S.Ct. 2321, 81 L.Ed.2d 186 (1984). For another example, the prior restraint doctrine makes it much more difficult to enjoin speech than to punish it after the fact. New York Times Co. v. United States, 403 U.S. 713, 91 S.Ct. 2140, 29 L.Ed.2d 822 (1971).

Statutes sometimes enlarge or set aside the inadequate remedy at law rule. For example, the Tax Injunction Act provides that "the district courts shall not enjoin, suspend or restrain the assessment, levy or collection of any tax under State law where a plain, speedy and efficient remedy may be had in the courts of such State." 28 U.S.C. § 1341. Where the only state remedy to overassessment of a tax is to pay the tax and seek a refund, the denial of a federal injunction in effect relegates the taxpayer to a remedy at law. While the Tax Injunction Act makes federal injunctions available in terms that parallel the traditional formulation of the inadequacy rule, federal courts construe the statute more strictly than the inadequacy rule. Compare Rosewell v. LaSalle Nat. Bank, 450 U.S. 503, 101 S.Ct. 1221, 67 L.Ed.2d 464 (1981)(denying injunctive relief against state tax overassessment although state remedy requires two years to get a refund and denies interest on the refund) and National Private Truck Council, Inc., v. Oklahoma Tax Commission, ___ U.S. ___, 115 S.Ct. 2351, 132 L.Ed.2d 509 (1995)(denying both injunctive relief and declaratory judgments when a tax refund, an adequate remedy at law, is available) with Bowen v. Massachusetts, 487 U.S. 879, 108 S.Ct. 2722, 101 L.Ed.2d 749 (1988)(approving injunction against federal withholding of grant on basis that remedy at law would take several years, thereby creating uncertainty). Perhaps the outcomes differ because the Tax Injunction Act has purposes that differ from the inadequacy rule—to protect state sovereignty and the fiscal stability of state and local governments. See also, e.g., 28 U.S.C. § 1342 (limiting injunctions against administrative decisions affecting utility rates); Norris–LaGuardia Act, 29 U.S.C. §§ 101–115 (barring injunctions against peaceful conduct arising out of labor disputes).

Legislatures sometimes provide that courts should grant injunctions without regard to the inadequacy rule. E.g., Cal.Water Code § 13361(c) ("it shall not be necessary to allege or prove * * * that the remedy at law is inadequate"); Cal.Civil Code § 3387 ("[i]t is to be presumed that the breach of an agreement to transfer real property cannot be adequately relieved by pecuniary compensation"). Courts have interpreted some statutes that do not explicitly set aside the inadequacy rule as implicitly doing so. Courts reason that the legislature presumed any violation of the statute would cause irreparable injury (e.g., People ex rel. Edgar v. Miller, 110 Ill.App.3d 264, 65 Ill.Dec. 814, 441 N.E.2d 1328, 1331 (1982)) or that there is inherent judicial power to enforce legislative policy (e.g., Blim v. Western Electric Co. Inc., 731 F.2d 1473, 1478 (10th Cir.), cert. denied, 469 U.S. 874, 105 S.Ct. 233, 83 L.Ed.2d 161 (1984)). How does this claim of inherent judicial power square with the cases in chapter 1(B)?

Finally, a statute may provide that equitable doctrines, such as the inadequacy rule, shall apply. For a very important instance, the Administrative Procedure Act states that "[n]othing herein * * * affects * * * the power or duty of the court to * * * deny relief on any other appropriate legal or equitable ground * * * ". 5 U.S.C. § 702(1).

Analogously to the inadequacy doctrine, the statute governing clean up of toxic waste bars courts from considering most challenges to EPA clean-up actions or administrative orders to clean up except after the fact, by which time the relief is substitutionary or penal rather than specific. Comprehensive Environmental Response, Compensation, and Liability Act, 42 U.S.C. § 9613. The statute opts for after the fact review, even though it often is not fully adequate to protect the challenger's rightful position, in order to avoid litigation delays in clean ups. For another analogy, consider the exhaustion of administrative remedies doctrine that requires courts to deny relief if plaintiff has an adequate administrative remedy. E.g., McKart v. United States, 395 U.S. 185, 89 S.Ct. 1657, 23 L.Ed.2d 194 (1969).

## 3. PRACTICALITY OF ENFORCEMENT

"It has long been settled that a court shall not issue an injunction that would be inconvenient or inefficient to administer." Bray v. Safeway Stores, 392 F.Supp. 851, 868 (N.D.Cal.1975). This statement, like many maxims of equity, sacrifices accuracy in describing what courts actually do for the thrill of sounding really decisive.

There is an element of truth in the statement. Concerns about difficulty of enforcement lead to the denial of specific relief of some contracts, particularly personal service or construction contracts where enforcement could involve ongoing monitoring and subjective evaluations of the quality of work. On the other hand, courts often grant injunctions where enforcement will be onerous. Enforcement problems are especially serious in many civil rights and regulatory cases. Indeed, more than 40 years after Brown v. Board of Education was decided, the effort to desegregate the schools of the lead defendant continues. Brown v. Board of Education, 978 F.2d 585 (10th Cir.1992), cert. denied, ___ U.S. ___, 113 S.Ct. 2994, 125 L.Ed.2d 688 (1993). Outside of contract cases, injunctions are so rarely denied because of burdens of supervision that the opinions only infrequently even mention the issue. On the other hand, in Joyce v. City and County of San Francisco, 846 F.Supp. 843 (1994), the court refused to grant a preliminary injunction barring the police from enforcing against the homeless statutes or ordinances prohibiting "life-sustaining" activities in public places. The court was concerned that uncertainty about who is homeless on any particular night and what is a "life-sustaining" activity would create enforcement problems.

A variety of factors help to explain why burdens of supervision are of little import beyond contract cases. First, an often used technique for reducing the burden of supervision—the prophylactic order—is of limited help in personal service or construction contract cases. The prophylactic order (considered in section D(2) of this chapter) avoids difficulties in ensuring that defendant is taking actions precisely attuned to putting plaintiff in his rightful position by requiring defendant to take actions that give plaintiff more than his rightful position but which are easier to supervise. So, if Country Lodge's rightful position is that Miller refrain from putting enough apple mash in the river to be visible and it is hard to know how much apple mash that is or just how much Miller is really putting in the river, a prophylactic order might prohibit all pollution or even close down Miller's operations. While prophylactic orders are sometimes helpful in contract cases, often they are not. For example, the burdens of supervising an order to perform under a contract to build a house of average quality are not eased by ordering the defendant to build a house of superior quality.

Second, the principle does not direct courts to deny specific relief simply because of difficulty of supervision, but only if the "burdens * * * are disproportionate to the advantages to be gained from enforcement and to the harm to be suffered by its denial." Restatement (Second) of Contracts § 366 (1981). Courts generally place a higher value on constitutional, statutory, and common law property rights than they do on enforcement of commercial promises, or at least see compensatory damages as less inadequate in the case of commercial promises. In the rare modern case outside the contract area where the burden of supervision is cited as a reason for denying an injunction, other factors help to explain the outcome. For example, in Joyce v. City and County of San Francisco, 846 F.Supp. 843 (1994), the court was probably more concerned about whether plaintiffs were correct on the merits.

Ramirez de Arellano v. Weinberger, 724 F.2d 143 (D.C.Cir.1983), vacated, 745 F.2d 1500 (D.C.Cir. en banc 1984), nicely illustrates both how judges' policy priorities can affect the treatment of the supervision issue and clashing judicial attitudes about the supervision issue. Plaintiffs sought an injunction against trespasses on their land in Honduras by United States military forces. Judge Scalia, writing for the panel, expressed concern about supervising a decree that would involve ongoing disputes as to conduct in a foreign land. 724 F.2d at 148. Nonetheless, he questioned whether the burden of supervision could justify dismissing the claim for relief except when combined with other problems that he saw in the claim, such as interfering with the President's exercise of his foreign affairs and military powers in the context of the various wars in Central America. Writing for a divided court, en banc, Judge Wilkey termed concerns about supervision "wild speculation":

> It must be presumed that the defendants, all officials of the United States government present in Washington, D.C., will obey an order of the district court. Furthermore, there is simply no factual basis * * * for concluding that an equitable decree would involve this court in numerous or even any monitoring problems. Courts do not monitor compliance with decrees by personal, on-site inspections. Even if the alleged violations were occurring in the corridors of the Pentagon instead of in Honduras, the district court would not monitor its decree by personally inspecting the affected area. If a dispute arises over compliance with any remedial decree, the parties can introduce evidence in the district court to establish whether a violation in fact has occurred. * * * It is absurd to suggest on the basis of plaintiffs' complaint that judicial monitoring of relief would be so problematic that adjudication of the plaintiffs' constitutional claims is barred.

745 F.2d at 1531–32.

This passage reflects a growing willingness to grant the relief first and worry about the problems of supervision if and when they arise. Of equal import, the passage reflects a willingness to look at enforcement as a problem of proof for the plaintiffs rather than a problem of minimizing the risk that the court will look ineffectual. Courts never refrain from issuing money judgments because the plaintiff will not be able to collect or because plaintiff's collection efforts may take up the court's time. Should courts treat injunctions any differently? See Dan B. Dobbs, Law of Remedies §§ 2.8(3), 12.19(3)(2d ed.1993).

Practicality of enforcement comprehends not only the burdens of supervising compliance but also impediments to punishing contempt of an order. Courts traditionally hesitate to grant an injunction against out-of-state activity by a non-resident because the defendant might violate the order yet escape punishment. In contrast, courts do not hesitate to issue money judgments against defendants who reside and have their assets out-of-state. The explanation for the difference lies partly in ensuring that court orders are obeyed and partly in the operation of the full faith and credit clause of the United States Constitution. Art. IV, § 1. Although the clause requires the courts of one state give full faith and credit to "judicial proceedings" of other states, courts have interpreted the clause to require enforcement of money judgments but not injunctions because, traditionally, the issuance of an injunction was regarded as discretionary. Restatement (Second) of Conflict of Laws § 102 comment *c* (1971). However, the Supreme Court has never ruled squarely on this issue and commentators have criticized courts' assertion of discretion to deny an injunction simply because it is an equitable remedy. As matters now stand, a court may enjoin out-of-state activity (id. at § 53) and the court of another state might enforce the injunction (id. at § 102). Even if the decree is not enforced, the sister state will give the findings necessary to the decree preclusive effect so that the plaintiff might get a decree there. Or, the defendant might comply voluntarily or the defendant or some of his assets might be caught in the original jurisdiction.[b] In any event, "the sky will not fall in if the defendant is successful in flouting the decree." Dan B. Dobbs, Handbook of the Law of Remedies at 64 (1973).

## D. GRANTING LESS OR MORE THAN PLAINTIFF'S RIGHTFUL POSITION

### 1. GRANTING LESS THAN PLAINTIFF'S RIGHTFUL POSITION: BALANCING THE EQUITIES

#### *Problem: Country Lodge v. Miller (Reprised) Balancing the Equities*

Recall that Miller set up her apple press to dump waste mash into the river in order to save $20,000 a year. Suppose that Country Lodge has satisfied all the prerequisites for injunctive relief. Miller asks the court to award damages rather than grant an injunction on the ground that the cost to her of complying is greater than the benefit that Country Lodge would derive from the injunction.

(a) What result if compliance would cost Miller no more now than when she built the press and it generates sufficient profits to pay that cost?

(b) What result if compliance would cost Miller not only $20,000 a year, but also an additional one time expenditure of $50,000 to retrofit the plant, which would have been unnecessary if she had built the mill to avoid discharging effluent into the river in the first place? If these retrofit costs were $1,000,000? If these retrofit costs would put her out of the business? Should the judge postpone the effective date of the injunctive relief a month if doing so would reduce the retrofit cost from $50,000 to $5,000?

(c) Should the court refuse to listen to Miller's claim of undue hardship if she had promised Country Lodge that there would be no nuisance? If she knew her planned conduct would be illegal?

(d) Should the court be more likely to deny an injunction on the grounds of undue hardship if Country Lodge knew that Miller's operation would create a nuisance but did not try to prevent it before Miller began to build her press?

(e) Should Miller be able to claim undue hardship if liability arises from her building the press on Country Lodge's land rather than creating a nuisance in the river? If liability arises from a contract to supply cider?

**b.** Courts hesitate to enjoin out of state activity for a reason distinct from practicality of enforcement—that the injunction may interfere with the policies and prerogatives of the sister state. See Restatement (Second) of Conflict of Laws § 53 comments c, d (1971); *Ramirez de Arellano*, 745 F.2d at 1529–30 and 1563 (Scalia dissenting opinion).

(f) In deciding whether a hardship is undue, should the court consider the benefit to nonparties of stopping the pollution?

(g) Should the court refuse to listen to Miller's claim of undue hardship if her liability arises from a constitutional prohibition instead of common law nuisance? From a statutory prohibition?

---

Balancing the equities is a process that allows a judge to withhold injunctive relief altogether or to issue an injunction that stops short of fully achieving plaintiff's rightful position because of undue hardship or unfairness to the defendant, even when plaintiff's remedies at law are inadequate. This section considers what might justify the court's power to compromise plaintiff's rightful position, the limits on this power, and whether it undercuts the goals that the common law, constitutions, or statutes seek to achieve.

Professor Douglas Laycock suggests the following black letter rule for balancing the equities:

> A court should deny permanent specific relief if:
>
> (a) the relief would impose hardship on defendant, and
>
> (b) that hardship is substantially disproportionate to the disadvantage to plaintiff of receiving only substitutionary relief.
>
> In balancing the interests, a court should consider the relative fault of each litigant.

Douglas Laycock, The Death of The Irreparable Injury Rule, 103 Harv. L.Rev. 688, 749–50 (1990). This formulation suggests that the court does not simply balance the injunction's advantages to the plaintiff against the burden on the defendant but instead balances the advantage to the plaintiff of specific rather than substitutionary relief against the disadvantage to the defendant of specific rather than substitutionary relief.

### *Note on When Injunctions are Efficient*

As balancing the equities seeks in part (but only in part) to avoid issuing injunctions that result in inefficiency, it is useful to consider when an injunction will lead to inefficiency. Suppose that the cost to Miller of complying with an injunction to stop the nuisance is $20,000 a year or more and the benefit to Country Lodge is $10,000 a year or more. If the court does not know how much more for each party, then it cannot know whether implementing the injunction would be efficient. After all, if implementation would cost Miller $1,000,000 to retrofit her operation plus $20,000 a year in added operating expenses and all that Country Lodge loses is $10,000 a year in profits, then the injunction is grossly inefficient. But so would be failing to grant an injunction if complying with it involves no retrofit costs for Miller but Country Lodge's owners have an aesthetic attachment to an unspoiled view of the river, which they value at $100,000 a year. In addition to these two extreme possibilities, there are a host of intermediate ones.

Inefficiency is not a problem for the court if it can be confident that the parties will bargain to reach an efficient result. If the court grants an injunction when Miller's cost to stop the pollution is $20,000 and Country Lodge's benefit is $10,000, they both can gain from a deal in which Miller pays something more than $10,000 but less than $20,000 in return for Country Lodge giving up the injunction. Similarly, if the court fails to grant an injunction when Miller's cost is $20,000 but Country Lodge's benefit is $100,000, they both can gain if Country Lodge agrees to pay Miller something more than $20,000 but less than $100,000 to stop polluting. The size of the payment within these ranges depends upon their bargaining positions and tactics. Whether they actually strike a deal depends upon what economists call "transaction costs." Transactions costs include the time spent bargaining and attorney fees. If the transaction costs are zero, then by definition the parties will bargain to achieve an efficient outcome regardless of whether the remedy is an injunction or compensatory damages or even if Miller is held not liable so that no relief is granted. In Judge Calabresi and Mr. Melamed's terminology (reread the passage supra at p. 33), the law's choice of entitlements and whether to back them up with a property rule or a liability rule matters to the distribution of income, but not to efficiency.

Suppose, however, that the transaction costs are sufficiently high that the parties cannot bargain to an outcome different from the one that the court decrees. If the court knows the real stakes for the parties, then it can achieve efficiency by issuing an injunction if and only if the costs of the pollution exceeded the costs of its abatement. But, the court will often have trouble determining the true stakes for the parties because the stakes are often subjective or difficult for outsiders to estimate and each party has a reason to exaggerate.

If the court does not know the costs of abatement, but does know the real costs of the pollution to Country Lodge, it can still ensure an efficient outcome by using a damage remedy because Miller would still abate the pollution if the costs of pollution exceed the costs of abatement. Similarly, if the court does not know the real costs of the pollution to Country Lodge, but does know the costs of abatement, it could grant Country Lodge an injunction but require it pay Miller for the costs of its implementation. This would force Country Lodge's owners to put their money where their mouths are as to the real worth to them of stopping the pollution, but would be unfair because Miller is the one at fault.

The court has a number of other ways to deal with uncertainty about the stakes to the parties, none of them wholly satisfactory. It could estimate the costs of pollution and the costs of abatement and act as if the estimates are accurate, but this course may well lead to inefficiency. Perhaps in part to safeguard plaintiffs from this danger, courts usually require defendants to show that their hardship to them is not just greater, but much greater than the benefit of granting an injunction. The court could also grant Country Lodge an injunction on the theory that the barriers to efficiency posed by transaction costs are less important than the barriers to efficiency posed by the errors that the court could make in assessing the real costs to the parties.

This final alternative makes it important to consider when transactions costs are likely to be high or low. In the case of Country Lodge and Miller, the time and costs are likely to be small relative to the large monetary stakes because only two parties need to bargain and each knows with whom to do so. But transaction costs can include more than time and costs. Country Lodge and Miller may engage in "strategic bargaining." If Miller knows that Country Lodge would prefer to receive any payment more than $10,000 to an injunction and Country Lodge knows that Miller would prefer to make any payment less than $50,000 to an injunction, Country Lodge may hold out for a payment close to $50,000 while Miller may hold out for a payment close to $10,000. The upshot could be stalemate.

There is potential for such strategic bargaining when there is a "bilateral monopoly." Country Lodge and Miller are both monopolists with respect to the subject of their bargaining—Country Lodge's right under the injunction to stop Miller from committing the nuisance—because Miller is the only one who would want to pay Country Lodge to forgo the injunction and Country Lodge is the only one who can sell it. (Does an order requiring specific performance of a contract create a bilateral monopoly and thereby the risk of strategic bargaining?)

Transaction costs can also be high if there are many potential plaintiffs. Suppose that there are 1000 Country Lodges, each damaged $10 a year by Miller's nuisance so that the total harm done by the nuisance is $10,000 a year. Here, transaction costs would prevent bargaining to a more efficient result. (The class action device can sometimes reduce some of these transaction costs.) If any plaintiff can get an injunction as of right, Miller must make a deal with each or risk wasting its payments. The transaction costs include tracking down and reaching agreement with all the plaintiffs, a time consuming and expensive undertaking. Some plaintiffs probably could not be found or would refuse to make a deal. Other plaintiffs may insist on more than their fair share of the payment so that disputes among the plaintiffs are likely to arise. Nuisance cases are more likely than trespass cases to have many potential plaintiffs because a trespass typically injures only one property while a nuisance typically injures many. However, simulations suggest that when potential plaintiffs number a few dozen or so, they bargain cooperatively and that strategic bargaining would not block efficient bargains. See, e.g., Elizabeth Hoffman & Matthew L. Spitzer, Experimental Law and Economics: An Introduction, 85 Colum.L.Rev. 991, 1009–13 (1985); Mark Kelman, Comment on Hoffman and Spitzer's Experimental Law and Economics, 85 Colum.L.Rev. 1037 (1985).

Judge Calabresi and Mr. Melamed conclude that the courts are being efficient in routinely granting injunctions in trespass cases because, in them, transaction costs are unlikely to prevent the parties from bargaining to an efficient outcome. Guido Calabresi & Douglas Melamed, Property Rules, Liability Rules, and Inalienability: One View of the Cathedral, 85 Harv.L.Rev. 1089, 1124–27 (1972). If Miller wants to put a store on Country Lodge's property and that is worth more to Miller than the detriment to Country Lodge, transaction costs are unlikely to stand in the way of a deal. Even if Country Lodge has an injunction against Miller's erecting a store on its property, there is no bilateral monopoly because Miller could buy land from some other neighbor and Country Lodge could sell the right to use its property to someone other than Miller. Moreover, it takes only two parties to make this bargain. Judge Calabresi and Mr. Melamed argue that a court should grant an injunction if the transaction costs of avoiding it are low because the court thereby avoids the risk of misjudging the parties' costs.

As noted in section C(2) of this chapter, the fifth amendment allows takings of property for a public use if "just compensation" is paid. In Judge Calabresi and Mr. Melamed's terms, the amendment allows the government to convert a property owner's entitlement protected by a property rule (an injunction) into an entitlement protected by a liability rule (compensatory damages). Is that efficient? Is it fair to give the government all the gains of trade? Should Miller be able to take Country Lodge's entitlement against nuisances by paying just compensation? Or is Country Lodge's getting an injunction and then selling it to Miller in excess of the real costs of pollution extortion?

For further reading on the efficiency of injunctions, see A. Mitchell Polinsky, An Introduction to Law and Economics 11–26 (2d ed.1989).

## SMITH v. STASO MILLING CO.

United States Court of Appeals, Second Circuit, 1927.
18 F.2d 736.

Appeal from a decree of the District Court of Vermont enjoining the defendant from polluting with slate dust a brook running through the plaintiff's premises, from similarly polluting the air, and from jarring his dwelling house by blasting, and awarding plaintiff judgment in the sum of ten thousand dollars for past damages.

The plaintiff is the owner of a summer residence in the town of Castleton, Vermont, something less than a mile distant from the defendant's crushing mill. This residence he occupied in substantially unchanged form at the time the defendant bought its land and before it put up its mill. The defendant blasts slate rock upon its premises, which it crushes, and makes from the product ground slate roofing material. The grinding creates clouds of dust, part of which, when the wind is in the right direction, is carried over to the plaintiff's premises, which it covers with pulverized dust. This is one grievance.

In the defendant's process of manufacture there are waste products which it puts upon a dump by a belt conveyor. Through the conveyor streams of water are run from driven wells, and the thin, muddy or plastic mass flows out into the first of three settling ponds, the overflow from which passes into a second, and so to a third, the three being together designed to retain all the waste. During heavy rains these ponds become filled with water and carry off through the sluices quantities of the sludge or mud, which the defendant has deposited in them. The last of these empties into a brook which runs through the premises of both parties, and on such occasions quantities of the muddy slate reach the plaintiff's land and leave a sediment upon it. He uses the brook for part of his domestic water supply, and the sludge or silt fills his reservoirs and otherwise interferes with his enjoyment of the premises. This is another and more important grievance.

* * * After the defendant had purchased the land, but before it had put up the plant, the plaintiff wrote, calling attention to the brook which flowed through both premises, advising it that its continued purity was a valuable asset to him, and protesting against any pollution or interference with its flow. The defendant's superintendent called upon him, assured him that there was no danger, because the proposed system of filters and settling basins would prevent any such possibility. The assurance was several times repeated. After the erection of the mill the defendant again assured the plaintiff more than once that the trouble had been in management of the settling ponds.

The defendant has installed dust arresters which are rated to stop 99 per cent of the dust which is produced. It has invested about $1,000,000 altogether in the plant, employs between 125 and 200 men, and its monthly pay roll is between $25,000 and $40,000.

The plaintiff valued his premises at $40,000, though it cost in all less than $30,000 * * *.

The District Judge on conflicting evidence found for the plaintiff on all the questions of fact involved, and absolutely enjoined the activities complained of. * * * The defendant appealed.

LEARNED HAND, Circuit Judge (after stating the facts as above). * * *

The defendant, not arguing that the facts justify no relief, insists that no injunction should go, because of the disastrous effect upon his crushing mill, which must stop its operation if enjoined. We are not satisfied that this must be the consequence, but we are content so to assume. The plaintiff argues that those cases in which such considerations have prevailed, do not represent the law of Vermont, which have never balanced the comparative hardships of the continued wrong and the injunction, when the plaintiff's right is substantial and clear. While we agree that with [a] possible exception [citation omitted], no decision of that state has actually turned upon the doctrine, it appears to us to have had so much recognition in the decisions of its highest court as to be certainly a part of its jurisprudence, at least until we are authoritatively advised to the contrary. * * *

Assuming that the doctrine is not fixed in the law of Vermont, we think that it is as matter of principle a reasonable one. The very right on which the injured party stands in such cases is a quantitative compromise between two conflicting interests. What may be an entirely tolerable adjustment, when the result is only to award damages for the injury done, may become no better than a means of extortion if the result is absolutely to curtail the defendant's enjoyment of his land. Even though the defendant has no power to condemn, at times it may be proper to require of him no more than to make good the whole injury once and for all. If the writ went as of course, we should have no option. Notoriously it * * * is discretionary if any is. To say that whenever an injured party can show that he could recover damages, he has only in addition to prove that the tort will be repeated, appears to us to ignore the substance of the situation in the interest of any apocryphal consistency. Where we are not bound by the local law, we decline to adopt so rigid a canon.

Nevertheless, so far as concerns the pollution of the stream, we think that the injury is so substantial and the wrong so deliberate, that we ought to impose upon the defendant the peril of any failure successfully to avoid it. * * * In the case at bar not only did the defendant have the most explicit warning from the plaintiff, but it gave an equally explicit assurance that it could avoid defiling the brook. It has several times repeated that assurance after occasional overflows. If the plaintiff had filed his bill before the mill was built, the balance of convenience would have been different, and we should not have hesitated to stop what as yet remained only a project. Whether the assurances in fact determined his inaction we need not say; he has shown himself pertinacious, though forbearing, and the chances are that they did. Even if not, these preliminary negotiations seem to us enough absolutely to impose upon the defendant the execution of what it promised. As respects the pollution of the stream, we therefore think that the injunction should remain absolute, and that the defendant must find some way to avoid further injury, or make its peace with the plaintiff as best it can.

As regards the dust the facts are different. True, it is equally a tort so to defile the air. But the injury is less oppressive, and neither the plaintiff's original protest, nor the defendant's promise, covered it. We are not prepared in such a situation to say that, if the defendant cannot by the best known methods arrest all the dust which it emits, it must shut down its mill. The record shows that it has installed arresters which are designed to stop all but one per cent. of the dust, and apparently do so. Yet that which escapes is still enough to affect the plaintiff's enjoyment, and the record does not show beyond question that the defendant cannot prevent it. The best disposition of the case is to affirm the injunction as it stands, but to give leave to the defendant to apply at the foot of the decree for relief upon showing there are no better arresters extant, that it operates those it has at maximum efficiency, that it is theretofore impossible further to reduce the dust, and that if the injunction continues it has no alternative but to stop operation. If that be proved to the satisfaction of the District Judge the injunction should be modified so as merely to limit the dust to that which will escape the arresters now in use. * * *

[The court went on to modify the award of damages.]

### *Notes*

1. *Factors not reflected in the law of liability.* The court holds that Staso Milling's air pollution wrongs Smith and does not hold that the wrong could be repaired by compensatory damages. Nonetheless, the court refuses to enjoin this wrong, which means that it is not putting Smith in his rightful position. Are the decisions on liability and injunctive relief consistent? The standard of liability in nuisance is whether the interference with plaintiff's land use is "substantial and unreasonable, and as such would be offensive or inconvenient to the normal person." William L. Prosser & W. Page Keeton, The Law of Torts § 87 (5th ed.1984). A land use that would be illegal under this standard does not become less so after it begins. So defendant's expenditure or the reliance of its employees on their jobs ought not to affect liability. However, these factors are relevant to the remedy. Therefore, the remedy question may involve factors not reflected in the law of liability.

What result if Smith sought an injunction prior to the construction of the plant? Was the decision to grant injunctive relief against the water pollution consistent with its decision to deny such relief against the air pollution?

2. *The goals of the law of liability.* While it is possible to distinguish the decisions on liability, injunctive relief for the air pollution, and injunctive relief for water pollution, should those distinctions make a difference? Suppose that Staso Milling were liable not for nuisance but for breaching a contract that promised that no air pollution would be emitted. Should the court enjoin the air pollution? Professor Frederic Maitland writes: "When a man has definitely contracted not to do a certain thing, it is not for him to say that it will be greatly to his convenience, and not much to the inconvenience of the other party, that he should be allowed to do it." Equity 327–28 (Alfred H. Chaytor & William J. Whittaker rev. 2d ed.1947). What does this suggest about the goals of the law of contract?

Suppose that Staso Milling was liable for an intentional trespass, such as placing part of its factory on Smith's land. Judge Hand probably would not have balanced the equities to allow the trespass to continue because, as he explains it, the goals of nuisance law themselves balance the competing interests of neighbors. In contrast, the goals of trespass law emphasize the owner's right to prevent intentional physical invasions. But even the goals of trespass law are not absolute; courts will balance the equities in the case of unintentional trespasses that cause little harm to plaintiff. For instance, where someone inadvertently erects a building that encroaches slightly on a neighbors' land, the victim of the trespass will ordinarily be relegated to a damage remedy. But if the encroachment is intentional, an injunction will issue regardless of the relative hardships of the parties.

As *Staso* indicates, state courts were split in their willingness to balance the equities in nuisance cases. In a portion of the opinion that is deleted, Judge Hand cites Whalen v. Union Bag & Paper Co., 208 N.Y. 1, 5, 101 N.E. 805, 806 (1913), which held that balancing the equities cannot justify failing to issue an injunction to halt a nuisance that causes more than slight harm because otherwise balancing "would deprive the poor litigant of his little property by giving it to those already rich." Judge Hand seems to disagree: "[e]ven though the defendant has no power to condemn, at times it may be proper to require of him no more than to make good the whole injury once and for all." But doesn't balancing the equities tend to give rich nuisance makers the power to condemn their neighbors' property?

Reflecting a national trend towards balancing the equities in nuisance cases, the New York Court of Appeals overruled *Whalen* in Boomer v. Atlantic Cement Co., 26 N.Y.2d 219, 309 N.Y.S.2d 312, 257 N.E.2d 870 (1970). While the *Whalen* court emphasized that the defendant there should have known that its conduct infringed plaintiff's rights, *Boomer* was decided more than a half century later in a more industrialized society, in which reciprocal interference between adjacent landowners has become routine. Indeed, Whalen was a farmer while the Boomers operated a junk yard. Daniel A. Farber, Reassessing *Boomer:* Justice, Efficiency, and Nuisance Law, in Property Law and Legal Education: Essays in Honor of John E. Cribbet 9 (Peter Hay & Michael H. Hoeflich eds. 1988). This change in interaction between adjacent landowners makes Judge Hand's view of nuisance law as a balancing of the competing interests particularly apt.

*Boomer* was distinguished in Walgreen Co. v. Sara Creek Property Co., 966 F.2d 273 (7th Cir.1992), which affirmed an injunction against the defendant-landlord breaching a lease clause giving the tenant-plaintiff the right to be the only pharmacy in the shopping center. In comparing the pros and cons of damage and injunctive relief, Judge Richard Posner expressed concern that damages would be difficult to calculate and, if too small, could lead to an inefficient breach of the lease clause. He thought that the parties could do a better job than the court of determining the impact upon themselves. At the same time, he expressed concern that an injunction might prove inefficient—that is, that having a second pharmacy in the center might be worth more to the landlord than it cost the tenant, yet the parties might nonetheless be unable to strike a bargain to get rid of it. However, he decided to affirm because the risk of such a failure in negotiations was much smaller than in *Boomer*. Negotiations may fail to get rid of an inefficient injunction because of the more "subtle cost" of the "bilateral monopoly" created by the injunction. Id. at 275. Judge Posner reasoned that the risk from strategic bargaining was much larger in a case like *Boomer*. There, the bargaining range was huge (the damages to plaintiffs were supposedly a few hundred thousand dollars while an injunction would shut down a factory worth $45 million) while in *Walgreen* the bargaining range was far smaller. The bargaining range is apt to be large in just those cases when the defendant can point to an undue hardship.

3. *Balancing the equities.* Professor Chayes, in the article excerpted in chapter 1, views balancing the equities as giving the trial judge wide-ranging discretion to decree what seems sensible, whether that is more than, less than, or the same as plaintiff's rightful position. The polar opposite to

Professor Chayes' approach would be to deny the judge discretion and require that the decree order defendant to achieve plaintiff's rightful position exactly. Professor Schoenbrod has proposed a middle ground in which the judge has discretion, but it is limited by the following principle:

> The injunction should require the defendant to achieve the plaintiff's rightful position unless (a) different relief is consistent with the goals of the violated rule and (b) the case involves a factor justifying departure from the rule that was not reflected in its formulation, but the injunction may never aim to achieve more than the plaintiff's rightful position.

David Schoenbrod, The Measure of An Injunction: A Principle to Replace Balancing the Equities and Tailoring the Remedy, 72 Minn.L.Rev. 627, 664 (1988).

4. *Efficiency and fairness.* Balancing the equities also goes under the names "undue hardship," "the balance of convenience" and "balancing equities and hardships." *Staso* considers hardship/convenience and equities—in other words, efficiency and fairness. Efficiency and fairness are also the chief concerns of the law of nuisance. The gist of the decision on air pollution in *Staso* is that it is efficient to let it continue, should controlling the emissions be impracticable, but unfair to Smith. An award of damages would then provide some recompense for the unfairness. As to the water pollution, the court decides in essence that it would be unfair to take account of the hardship on Staso Milling so that considerations of fairness override considerations of efficiency. In contrast, if the wrong is both unfair and inefficient, the court would readily grant an injunction.

We have so far identified three possible outcomes in nuisance cases: (1) no relief, (2) damages to the party injured by the nuisance, and (3) an injunction stopping the nuisance. Scholars have identified a fourth and fifth possibility. As a fourth possibility, a court could enjoin the nuisance but make the victim of the nuisance pay damages to the party enjoined. Such an outcome might make sense when it is efficient to stop the nuisance, but unfair. Furthermore, requiring the victim to pay ensures that stopping the nuisance is truly efficient. However, apparently only one court has issued such a compensated injunction. Spur Industries v. Del E. Webb Development Co., 108 Ariz. 178, 494 P.2d 700 (1972). In that case, Del Webb established a large subdivision near Spur's smelly feedlot and sold lots to the public. Keeping the feedlot open was probably inefficient given the harm to many homeowners relative to the cost of moving the feedlot. Yet, it was fair to put the cost on Webb rather than Spur because Webb had, in essence, come to the nuisance. Should Webb have gotten an injunction if he had not yet sold any lots? If the city rather than Webb had sought the injunction, should it have been granted without requiring compensation to Spur? Would you advise a developer similarly situated to Webb to bring a suit to close down the nuisance?

Professor Farber, supra at p. 97, offers a fifth possibility. Where it would be highly inefficient to stop the nuisance, but the nuisance is egregious, he would deny an injunction but set damages based not on the harm to plaintiff, but rather on what it would have cost defendant to have purchased the right to make the nuisance if it had sought to do so before building its factory. In essence, Farber's proposal is that damages be geared to defendant's rightful position rather than plaintiff's. For Farber, ordinary compensatory damages are inadequate because they give all the gains from trade to the defendant and therefore reward defendant's egregious taking of plaintiff's rights. Do you agree with his proposal? How would the court apply his measure of damages in *Staso?* Should his proposal be applied to intentional breaches of contracts?

5. *Impact on the public.* Notice that *Staso* weighs the hardship from an injunction on the defendant and the public (Staso's employees) on one side of the balance and the benefits from an injunction to the plaintiff on the other. So the court considers the detriments to the public but not the benefits. *Boomer,* which also considered the impact on the public in the same one-sided way, offered the following explanation:

> The public concern with air pollution arising from many sources in industry and in transportation is currently accorded ever wider recognition accompanied by a growing sense of responsibility in State and Federal Governments to control it. * * *
>
> But there is now before the court private litigation in which individual property owners have sought specific relief from a single plant operation. The threshold question raised by the division of view on this appeal is whether the court should resolve the litigation between the parties now before it as equitably as seems possible; or whether, seeking promotion of the general public welfare, it should channel private litigation into broad public objectives.
>
> A court performs its essential function when it decides the rights of parties before it. Its decision of private controversies may sometimes greatly affect public issues. Large questions of law are often resolved by the manner in which private litigation is decided. But this is normally an incident to the court's main function to settle controversy. It is a rare exercise of judicial power to use a decision in private litigation as a purposeful mechanism to achieve direct public objectives greatly beyond the rights and interests before the court.
>
> Effective control of air pollution is a problem presently far from solution even with the full public and financial powers of government. In large measure adequate technical procedures are yet to be developed and some that appear possible may be economically impracticable.
>
> It seems apparent that the amelioration of air pollution will depend on technical research in great depth; on a carefully balanced consideration of the economic impact of close regulation; and of the actual effect on public health. It is likely to require massive public expenditure and to demand more than any local community can accomplish and to depend on regional and interstate controls.
>
> A court should not try to do this on its own as a by-product of private litigation and it seems manifest that the judicial establishment is neither equipped in the limited nature of any judgment it can pronounce nor prepared to lay down and implement an effective policy for the elimination of air pollution. This is an area beyond the circumference of one private lawsuit. It is a direct responsibility for government and should not thus be undertaken as an incident to solving a dispute

between property owners and a single cement plant—one of many—in the Hudson River valley.

26 N.Y.2d at 222–23, 309 N.Y.S.2d at 314–15, 257 N.E.2d at 871. Are you convinced?

Compare the dictum in Sierra Club v. Morton, 405 U.S. 727, 740 n. 15, 92 S.Ct. 1361, 1369 n. 15, 31 L.Ed.2d 636 (1972)("Once this standing is established, the party may assert the interests of the general public in support of his claims for equitable relief.").

## BROWN v. BOARD OF EDUCATION (*BROWN II*)

Supreme Court of the United States, 1955.
349 U.S. 294, 75 S.Ct. 753, 99 L.Ed. 1083.

MR. CHIEF JUSTICE WARREN delivered the opinion of the Court.

These cases were decided on May 17, 1954. The opinions of that date,[1] declaring the fundamental principle that racial discrimination in public education is unconstitutional, are incorporated herein by reference. All provisions of federal, state, or local law requiring or permitting such discrimination must yield to this principle. There remains for consideration the manner in which relief is to be accorded.

Because these cases arose under different local conditions and their disposition will involve a variety of local problems, we requested further argument on the question of relief.[2] In view of the nationwide importance of the decision, we invited the Attorney General of the United States and the Attorneys General of all states requiring or permitting racial discrimination in public education to present their views on that question. The parties, the United States, and the States of Florida, North Carolina, Arkansas, Oklahoma, Maryland, and Texas filed briefs and participated in the oral argument.

1. 347 U.S. 483, 74 S.Ct. 686, 98 L.Ed. 873 [*Brown I*]. 347 U.S. 497, 74 S.Ct. 693, 98 L.Ed. 884 [*Bolling v. Sharpe*].

2. Further argument was requested on the following questions, 347 U.S. 483, 495–496, note 13, 74 S.Ct. 686, 692, 98 L.Ed. 873, previously propounded by the Court:

"4. Assuming it is decided that segregation in public schools violates the Fourteenth Amendment

"(a) would a decree necessarily follow providing that, within the limits set by normal geographic school districting, Negro children should forthwith be admitted to schools of their choice, or

"(b) may this Court, in the exercise of its equity powers, permit an effective gradual adjustment to be brought about from existing segregated systems to a system not based on color distinctions?

"5. On the assumption on which questions 4(a) and (b) are based, and assuming further that this Court will exercise its equity powers to the end described in question 4(b),

"(a) should this Court formulate detailed decrees in these cases;

"(b) if so, what specific issues should the decrees reach;

"(c) should this Court appoint a special master to hear evidence with a view to recommending specific terms for such decrees;

"(d) should this Court remand to the courts of first instance with directions to frame decrees in these cases, and if so what general directions should the decrees of this Court include and what procedures should the courts of first instance follow in arriving at the specific terms of more detailed decrees?"

These presentations were informative and helpful to the Court in its consideration of the complexities arising from the transition to a system of public education freed of racial discrimination. The presentations also demonstrated that substantial steps to eliminate racial discrimination in public schools have already been taken, not only in some of the communities in which these cases arose, but in some of the states appearing as amici curiae, and in other states as well. Substantial progress has been made in the District of Columbia and in the communities in Kansas and Delaware involved in this litigation. The defendants in the cases coming to us from South Carolina and Virginia are awaiting the decision of this Court concerning relief.

Full implementation of these constitutional principles may require solution of varied local school problems. School authorities have the primary responsibility for elucidating, assessing, and solving these problems; courts will have to consider whether the action of school authorities constitutes good faith implementation of the governing constitutional principles. Because of their proximity to local conditions and the possible need for further hearings, the courts which originally heard these cases can best perform this judicial appraisal. Accordingly, we believe it appropriate to remand the cases to those courts.

In fashioning and effectuating the decrees, the courts will be guided by equitable principles. Traditionally, equity has been characterized by a practical flexibility in shaping its remedies and by a facility for adjusting and reconciling public and private needs.[5] These cases call for the exercise of these traditional attributes of equity power. At stake is the personal interest of the plaintiffs in admission to public schools as soon as practicable on a nondiscriminatory basis. To effectuate this interest may call for elimination of a variety of obstacles in making the transition to school systems operated in accordance with the constitutional principles set forth in our May 17, 1954, decision. Courts of equity may properly take into account the public interest in the elimination of such obstacles in a systematic and effective manner. But it should go without saying that the vitality of these constitutional principles cannot be allowed to yield simply because of disagreement with them.

While giving weight to these public and private considerations, the courts will require that the defendants make a prompt and reasonable start toward full compliance with our May 17, 1954, ruling. Once such a start has been made, the courts may find that additional time is necessary to carry out the ruling in an effective manner. The burden rests upon the defendants to establish that such time is necessary in the public interest and is consistent with good faith compliance at the earliest practicable date. To that end, the courts may consider problems related to administration, arising from the physical condition of the

5. See Hecht Co. v. Bowles, 321 U.S. 321, 329–330, 64 S.Ct. 587, 591, 592, 88 L.Ed. 754.

school plant, the school transportation system, personnel, revision of school districts and attendance areas into compact units to achieve a system of determining admission to the public schools on a nonracial basis, and revision of local laws and regulations which may be necessary in solving the foregoing problems. They will also consider the adequacy of any plans the defendants may propose to meet these problems and to effectuate a transition to a racially nondiscriminatory school system. During this period of transition, the courts will retain jurisdiction of these cases.

The judgments below, except that in the Delaware case, are accordingly reversed and the cases are remanded to the District Courts to take such proceedings and enter such orders and decrees consistent with this opinion as are necessary and proper to admit to public schools on a racially nondiscriminatory basis with all deliberate speed the parties to these cases. The judgment in the Delaware case—ordering the immediate admission of the plaintiffs to schools previously attended only by white children—is affirmed on the basis of the principles stated in our May 17, 1954, opinion, but the case is remanded to the Supreme Court of Delaware for such further proceedings as that Court may deem necessary in light of this opinion.

### *Notes*

1. The Tenth Circuit recently ruled that the plaintiffs in *Brown*, the school desegregation case from Topeka, Kansas, have yet to be restored fully to their rightful position. See Brown v. Board of Education, 978 F.2d 585 (10th Cir.1992), cert. denied ___ U.S. ___, 113 S.Ct. 2994, 125 L.Ed.2d 688 (1993). Such is "deliberate speed." But, what the rightful position entails is controversial, as the next section and chapter 3(B) will show.

2. However the plaintiffs' rightful position is defined, what justification, if any, can there be for failing to grant plaintiffs their rightful position forthwith in any constitutional case, let alone a case with the importance of *Brown*? Dean Peter Shane writes:

> In some cases, a court may defend remedial delay (rightly or wrongly) as necessary for the maximum vindication of right—because the maximum vindication of right cannot be accomplished without remedial steps that require planning, review, and staged implementation. In some cases, however, such a justification for delay is not available. A pointed example occurs in prisoners' "conditions of confinement" suits. A violation of the constitutional right to freedom from cruel and unusual punishment may be maximally protected by immediate release. While the threat of release is often used to induce state authorities to correct unconstitutional conditions, release is never the remedy of first resort. This can only be because courts recognize a proper place in the remedial process for balancing remedial interests against other legitimate social concerns. Yet, what these concerns comprise and the weight they should enjoy are notably discretionary decisions.

Peter M. Shane, Rights, Remedies, and Restraint, 64 Chi.-Kent L.Rev. 531, 557 (1988). Dean Shane builds upon Professor Paul Gewirtz's thoughtful analysis of *Brown II*. Paul Gewirtz, Remedies and Resistance, 92 Yale L.J. 585 (1983).

3. *Brown II* states that "it should go without saying that the vitality of these constitutional principles cannot be allowed to yield simply because of disagreement with them." Does the Court really mean this or is it just striking an attractive pose?

4. Is *Brown II* consistent with Professor Schoenbrod's principle quoted at page 98?

5. Note that the Supreme Court, in remanding to the lower courts, instructs them to give the defendant school boards a substantial role in formulating the remedy. In essence, the matters are remanded to the defendants, although with close judicial supervision. What could justify giving defendants who had fought desegregation tooth and nail any role in implementing the remedy?

Professor Paul R. Dimond argues that *Brown II* is a great victory precisely because its strategy of giving the political branches the lead in determining the scope, pace, and design of the remedy left the Supreme Court free to identify the wrong in unstinting terms. He argues that because of the limits on the courts in exercising their countermajoritarian powers:

> We should concede that the more massive and entrenched the wrong of discrimination, the more important it is for the courts to declare the full extent of that wrong. The courts must also permit the ultimate remedy to be worked out in a political process in which those who are aggrieved will at least have a continuing claim that the declared wrong cannot be remedied in the courts alone.

Paul R. Dimond, *Brown* and the Transformation of the Constitution: Concluding Remarks, 61 Fordham L.Rev. 63, 65–66 (1992). Do you agree? An example of Professor Dimond's approach is McDuffy v. Secretary of Education, 415 Mass. 545, 615 N.E.2d 516, 555–56 (1993). After the Massachusetts high court declared that the legislators and executives of the Commonwealth and its local governments had violated an enforceable provision of the state constitution requiring them to provide an adequate education, it left those officials "to define the precise nature of the task which they face in fulfilling their constitutional duty" and provided no judicial remedy other than that the trial court have the discretion to retain jurisdiction to determine whether "within a reasonable time, appropriate legislative action has been taken."

6. Whether *Brown II* went as far as it should have, make no mistake that it continues to have a huge impact on how schools and other institutions are operated. United States v. Fordice, 505 U.S. 717, 112 S.Ct. 2727, 120 L.Ed.2d 575 (1992)(establishing criteria for desegregation in the state university system). Moreover, Professor Owen M. Fiss in The Civil Rights Injunction (1978) argues that *Brown II* reshaped the law of remedies. Previously, injunctions were the remedies of last resort both because of the inadequate remedy at law rule and the suspicion of injunctions generated by injunctions against strikes in the early days of the union movement. After

*Brown II*, the injunction was the remedy of choice for constitutional violations.

7. The Supreme Court sometimes decides that courts should deny redress for past violations when the claim for relief rests on new constitutional doctrines. It is then said that the new doctrine has only "prospective" effect, which suggests that the new law of liability applies only to future cases. But Professors Richard H. Fallon, Jr. and Daniel J. Meltzer argue that these decisions are best understood as applications of traditional remedial principles, such as avoiding undue hardship caused by reasonable reliance on the old doctrine. Richard H. Fallon, Jr. & Daniel J. Meltzer, New Law, Non–Retroactivity, and Constitutional Remedies, 104 Harv.L.Rev. 1733 (1991). However, denying retrospective application of a new constitutional interpretation raises concerns that the Court is making it too easy to overrule precedent and is not being even handed. In James B. Beam Distilling Co. v. Georgia, 501 U.S. 529, 111 S.Ct. 2439, 115 L.Ed.2d 481 (1991), six members of the Court held that once it gives retroactive application to a new constitutional interpretation in a civil case, it must be given retroactive application in all cases. In Harper v. Virginia Department of Taxation, 509 U.S. 86, 113 S.Ct. 2510, 125 L.Ed.2d 74 (1993), which applied *Beam*, five justices intimated that denying retroactive effect in any civil case might be improper and four others disagreed. The *Harper* majority relied upon Griffith v. Kentucky, 479 U.S. 314, 322–23, 107 S.Ct. 708, 713, 93 L.Ed.2d 649, 658 (1987), which required, henceforth, that in criminal cases all new constitutional interpretations must be applied to all cases on direct appeal.

---

The courts balanced the equities in *Staso,* a common law case, and *Brown II,* a constitutional case. The next question is whether they may balance the equities to allow statutory violations to continue. Professor Zygmunt Plater, who represented the plaintiffs in the following case, later wrote that his clients "made the 'conservative' argument that courts should not be activist but rather should follow the dictates of the words of the statutes before them." Zygmunt Plater, In the Wake of the Snail Darter: An Environmental Law Paradigm and Its Consequences, 19 Mich.J.L. Reform 805, 834 (1986).

## TENNESSEE VALLEY AUTHORITY v. HILL

Supreme Court of the United States, 1978.
437 U.S. 153, 98 S.Ct. 2279, 57 L.Ed.2d 117.

MR. CHIEF JUSTICE BURGER delivered the opinion of the Court.

The questions presented in this case are (a) whether the Endangered Species Act of 1973 requires a court to enjoin the operation of a virtually completed federal dam—which had been authorized prior to 1973—when, pursuant to authority vested in him by Congress, the Secretary of the Interior has determined that operation of the dam would eradicate an endangered species; and (b) whether continued congressional appropriations for the dam after 1973 constituted an implied repeal of the Endangered Species Act, at least as to the particular dam.

I

The Little Tennessee River originates in the mountains of northern Georgia and flows through the national forest lands of North Carolina into Tennessee, where it converges with the Big Tennessee River near Knoxville. The lower 33 miles of the Little Tennessee takes the river's clear, free-flowing waters through an area of great natural beauty. * * * Considerable historical importance attaches to the areas immediately adjacent * * *.

In this area of the Little Tennessee River the Tennessee Valley Authority, a wholly owned public corporation of the United States, began constructing the Tellico Dam and Reservoir Project in 1967, shortly after Congress appropriated initial funds for its development. Tellico is a multipurpose regional development project designed principally to stimulate shoreline development, generate sufficient electric current to heat 20,000 homes, and provide flatwater recreation and flood control, as well as improve economic conditions in "an area characterized by underutilization of human resources and outmigration of young people." Of particular relevance to this case is one aspect of the project, a dam which TVA determined to place on the Little Tennessee, a short distance from where the river's waters meet with the Big Tennessee. When fully operational, the dam would impound water covering some 16,500 acres—much of which represents valuable and productive farmland—thereby converting the river's shallow, fast-flowing waters into a deep reservoir over 30 miles in length.

[The Court describes how litigation under statutes other than the Endangered Species Act slowed and sometimes enjoined the dam's completion. After these efforts to halt the dam had failed and just when the dam was about to go into operation,] a discovery was made in the waters of the Little Tennessee which would profoundly affect the Tellico Project. Exploring the area around Coytee Springs, which is about seven miles from the mouth of the river, a University of Tennessee ichthyologist, Dr. David A. Etnier, found a previously unknown species of perch, the snail darter, or Percina (Imostoma) tanasi. This three-inch, tannish-colored fish, whose numbers are estimated to be in the range of 10,000 to 15,000, would soon engage the attention of environmentalists, the TVA, the Department of the Interior, the Congress of the United States, and ultimately the federal courts, as a new and additional basis to halt construction of the dam.

Until recently the finding of a new species of animal life would hardly generate a cause celebre. This is particularly so in the case of darters, of which there are approximately 130 known species, 8 to 10 of these having been identified only in the last five years. The moving force behind the snail darter's sudden fame came some four months after its discovery, when the Congress passed the Endangered Species Act of

1973 (Act), 87 Stat. 884, 16 U.S.C. § 1531 et seq. (1976 ed.). This legislation, among other things, authorizes the Secretary of the Interior to declare species of animal life "endangered" and to identify the "critical habitat" of these creatures. When a species or its habitat is so listed, the following portion of the Act—relevant here—becomes effective:

> " * * * Federal departments and agencies shall * * * utilize their authorities in furtherance of the purposes of this chapter by carrying out programs for the conservation of endangered species * * * listed pursuant to section 1533 of this title and *by taking such action necessary to insure that actions authorized, funded, or carried out by them do not jeopardize the continued existence of such endangered species * * * or result in the destruction or modification of habitat of such species* which is determined by the Secretary * * * to be critical." 16 U.S.C. § 1536 (emphasis added).

In January 1975, the respondents in this case[10] and others petitioned the Secretary of the Interior to list the snail darter as an endangered species. * * * [T]he Secretary formally listed the snail darter as an endangered species on October 8, 1975. * * * [T]he Secretary determined that the snail darter apparently lives only in that portion of the Little Tennessee River which would be completely inundated by the reservoir created as a consequence of the Tellico Dam's completion. The Secretary went on to explain the significance of the dam to the habitat of the snail darter:

> "[T]he snail darter occurs only in the swifter portions of shoals over clean gravel substrate in cool, low-turbidity water. Food of the snail darter is almost exclusively snails which require a clean gravel substrate for their survival. *The proposed impoundment of water behind the proposed Tellico Dam would result in total destruction of the snail darter's habitat.*" (Emphasis added).

Subsequent to this determination, the Secretary declared the area of the Little Tennessee which would be affected by the Tellico Dam to be the "critical habitat" of the snail darter. Using these determinations as a predicate, and notwithstanding the near completion of the dam, the Secretary declared that pursuant to § 7 of the Act, "all Federal agencies must take such action as is necessary to insure that actions authorized, funded, or carried out by them do not result in the destruction or modification of this critical habitat area." This notice, of course, was pointedly directed at TVA and clearly aimed at halting completion or operation of the dam.

* * * In February 1976, pursuant to § 11(g) of the Endangered Species Act, 16 U.S.C. § 1540(g), respondents filed the case now under review, seeking to enjoin completion of the dam and impoundment of the

10. Respondents are a regional association of biological scientists, a Tennessee conservation group, and individuals who are citizens or users of the Little Tennessee Valley Area which would be affected by the Tellico Project.

reservoir on the ground that those actions would violate the Act by directly causing the extinction of the species *Percina (Imostoma) tanasi.*

* * * [T]he court entered its memorandum opinion and order denying respondents their requested relief and dismissing the complaint. The District Court found that closure of the dam and the consequent impoundment of the reservoir would "result in the adverse modification, if not complete destruction, of the snail darter's critical habitat," making it "highly probable" that "the continued existence of the snail darter" would be "jeopardize[d]." Despite these findings, the District Court declined to embrace the plaintiffs' position on the merits: that once a federal project was shown to jeopardize an endangered species, a court of equity is compelled to issue an injunction restraining violation of the Endangered Species Act.

In reaching this result, the District Court stressed that the entire project was then about 80% complete and, based on available evidence, "there [were] no alternatives to impoundment of the reservoir, short of scrapping the entire project." The District Court also found that if the Tellico Project was permanently enjoined, "[s]ome $53 million would be lost in nonrecoverable obligations," meaning that a large portion of the $78 million already expended would be wasted. The court also noted that the Endangered Species Act of 1973 was passed some seven years after construction on the dam commenced and that Congress had continued appropriations for Tellico, with full awareness of the snail darter problem. Assessing these various factors, the District Court concluded:

> "At some point in time a federal project becomes so near completion and so incapable of modification that a court of equity should not apply a statute enacted long after inception of the project to produce an unreasonable result. * * * Where there has been an irreversible and irretrievable commitment of resources by Congress to a project over a span of almost a decade, the Court should proceed with a great deal of circumspection." * * *

Thereafter, in the Court of Appeals, respondents argued that the District Court had abused its discretion by not issuing an injunction in the face of "a blatant statutory violation." The Court of Appeals agreed, and on January 31, 1977, it reversed, remanding "with instructions that a permanent injunction issue halting all activities incident to the Tellico Project which may destroy or modify the critical habitat of the snail darter." * * *

II * * *

[T]wo questions are presented: (a) Would TVA be in violation of the Act if it completed and operated the Tellico Dam as planned? (b) If TVA's actions would offend the Act, is an injunction the appropriate remedy for the violation? For the reasons stated hereinafter, we hold that both questions must be answered in the affirmative.

(A)

It may seem curious to some that the survival of a relatively small number of three-inch fish among all the countless millions of species extant would require the permanent halting of a virtually completed dam for which Congress has expended more than $100 million. The paradox is not minimized by the fact that Congress continued to appropriate large sums of public money for the project, even after congressional Appropriations Committees were apprised of its apparent impact upon the survival of the snail darter. We conclude, however, that the explicit provisions of the Endangered Species Act require precisely that result.

One would be hard pressed to find a statutory provision whose terms were any plainer than those in § 7 of the Endangered Species Act. Its very words affirmatively command all federal agencies "to *insure* that actions *authorized, funded,* or *carried out* by them do not *jeopardize* the continued existence" of an endangered species or "*result* in the destruction or modification of habitat of such species * * *." 16 U.S.C. § 1536. (Emphasis added.) This language admits of no exception. Nonetheless, petitioner urges, as do the dissenters, that the Act cannot reasonably be interpreted as applying to a federal project which was well under way when Congress passed the Endangered Species Act of 1973. [The Court rejects this argument.] * * *

Concededly, this view of the Act will produce results requiring the sacrifice of the anticipated benefits of the project and of many millions of dollars in public funds. But examination of the language, history, and structure of the legislation under review here indicates beyond doubt that Congress intended endangered species to be afforded the highest of priorities.

* * * [T]he legislative history undergirding § 7 reveals an explicit congressional decision to require agencies to afford first priority to the declared national policy of saving endangered species. The pointed omission of the type of qualifying language previously included in endangered species legislation reveals a conscious decision by Congress to give endangered species priority over the "primary missions" of federal agencies.

* * * One might * * * [argue] that in this case the burden on the public through the loss of millions of unrecoverable dollars would greatly outweigh the loss of the snail darter. But neither the Endangered Species Act nor Art. III of the Constitution provides federal courts with authority to make such fine utilitarian calculations. On the contrary, the plain language of the Act, buttressed by its legislative history, shows clearly that Congress viewed the value of endangered species as "incalculable." Quite obviously, it would be difficult for a court to balance the loss of a sum certain—even $100 million—against a congressionally declared "incalculable" value, even assuming we had the power to engage in such a weighing process, which we emphatically do not.

In passing the Endangered Species Act of 1973, Congress was also aware of certain instances in which exceptions to the statute's broad sweep would be necessary. Thus, § 10, 16 U.S.C. § 1539 (1976 ed.), creates a number of limited "hardship exemptions," none of which would even remotely apply to the Tellico Project. In fact, there are no exemptions in the Endangered Species Act for federal agencies, meaning that under the maxim *expressio unius est exclusio alterius* [the expression of one thing implies the exclusion of the other], we must presume that these were the only "hardship cases" Congress intended to exempt.

* * * [W]e are urged to find that the continuing appropriations for Tellico Dam constitute an implied repeal of the 1973 Act, at least insofar as it applies to the Tellico Project. In support of this view, TVA points to the statements found in various House and Senate Appropriations Committees' Reports; those Reports generally reflected the attitude of the Committees either that the Act did not apply to Tellico or that the dam should be completed regardless of the provisions of the Act. Since we are unwilling to assume that these latter Committee statements constituted advice to ignore the provisions of a duly enacted law, we assume that these Committees believed that the Act simply was not applicable in this situation. But even under this interpretation of the Committees' actions, we are unable to conclude that the Act has been in any respect amended or repealed. * * *

(B)

Having determined that there is an irreconcilable conflict between operation of the Tellico Dam and the explicit provisions of § 7 of the Endangered Species Act, we must now consider what remedy, if any, is appropriate. It is correct, of course, that a federal judge sitting as a chancellor is not mechanically obligated to grant an injunction for every violation of law. This Court made plain in Hecht Co. v. Bowles, 321 U.S. 321, 329, 64 S.Ct. 587, 591, 88 L.Ed. 754 (1944), that "[a] grant of jurisdiction to issue compliance orders hardly suggests an absolute duty to do so under any and all circumstances." As a general matter it may be said that "[s]ince all or almost all equitable remedies are discretionary, the balancing of equities and hardships is appropriate in almost any case as a guide to the chancellor's discretion." D. Dobbs, Remedies 52 (1973). Thus, in *Hecht Co.* the Court refused to grant an injunction when it appeared from the District Court findings that "the issuance of an injunction would have 'no effect by way of insuring better compliance in the future' and would [have been] 'unjust' to [the] petitioner and not 'in the public interest.' " 321 U.S., at 326, 64 S.Ct., at 590.

But these principles take a court only so far. Our system of government is, after all, a tripartite one, with each branch having certain defined functions delegated to it by the Constitution. While "[i]t is emphatically the province and duty of the judicial department to say what the law is," Marbury v. Madison, 1 Cranch 137, 177, 2 L.Ed. 60 (1803), it is equally—and emphatically—the exclusive province of the Congress not only to formulate legislative policies and mandate programs and projects, but also to establish their relative priority for the Nation. Once Congress, exercising its delegated powers, has decided the order of priorities in a given area, it is for the Executive to administer the laws and for the courts to enforce them when enforcement is sought.

Here we are urged to view the Endangered Species Act "reasonably," and hence shape a remedy "that accords with some modicum of common sense and the public weal." But is that our function? We have no expert knowledge on the subject of endangered species, much less do we have a mandate from the people to strike a balance of equities on the side of the Tellico Dam. Congress has spoken in the plainest of words, making it abundantly clear that the balance has been struck in favor of affording endangered species the highest of priorities, thereby adopting a policy which it described as "institutionalized caution."

Our individual appraisal of the wisdom or unwisdom of a particular course consciously selected by the Congress is to be put aside in the process of interpreting a statute. Once the meaning of an enactment is discerned and its constitutionality determined, the judicial process comes to an end. We do not sit as a committee of review, nor are we vested with the power of veto. The lines ascribed to Sir Thomas More by Robert Bolt are not without relevance here:

> "The law, Roper, the law. I know what's legal, not what's right. And I'll stick to what's legal.... I'm not God. The currents and eddies of right and wrong, which you find such plain-sailing, I can't navigate, I'm no voyager. But in the thickets of the law, oh there I'm a forester.... What would you do? Cut a great road through the law to get after the Devil? ... And when the last law was down, and the Devil turned round on you—where would you hide, Roper, the laws all being flat? ... This country's planted thick with laws from coast to coast—Man's laws, not God's—and if you cut them down ... d'you really think you could stand upright in the winds that would blow them? ... Yes, I'd give the Devil benefit of law, for my own safety's sake." R. Bolt, A Man for All Seasons, Act I, p. 147 (Three Plays, Heinemann ed. 1967).

We agree with the Court of Appeals that in our constitutional system the commitment to the separation of powers is too fundamental for us to pre-empt congressional action by judicially decreeing what accords with "common sense and the public weal." Our Constitution vests such responsibilities in the political branches.

Affirmed.

MR. JUSTICE POWELL, with whom MR. JUSTICE BLACKMUN joins, dissenting.

[Justice Powell's opinion took issue with the majority's conclusion as to liability.]

MR. JUSTICE REHNQUIST, dissenting.

In the light of my Brother Powell's dissenting opinion, I am far less convinced than is the Court that the Endangered Species Act of 1973 was intended to prohibit the completion of the Tellico Dam. But the very difficulty and doubtfulness of the correct answer to this legal question convinces me that the Act did not prohibit the District Court from refusing, in the exercise of its traditional equitable powers, to enjoin petitioner from completing the Dam. * * *

This Court had occasion in Hecht Co. v. Bowles, 321 U.S. 321, 64 S.Ct. 587, 88 L.Ed. 754 (1944), to construe language in an Act of Congress that lent far greater support to a conclusion that Congress intended an injunction to issue as a matter of right than does the language just quoted. * * *

I choose to adhere to *Hecht Co.'s* teaching:

> "[A] grant of jurisdiction to issue compliance orders hardly suggests an absolute duty to do so under any and all circumstances. We cannot but think that if Congress had intended to make such a drastic departure from the traditions of equity practice, an unequivocal statement of its purpose would have been made." 321 U.S., at 329, 64 S.Ct., at 591.

Since the District Court possessed discretion to refuse injunctive relief even though it had found a violation of the Act, the only remaining question is whether this discretion was abused in denying respondents' prayer for an injunction. The District Court denied respondents injunctive relief because of the significant public and social harms that would flow from such relief and because of the demonstrated good faith of petitioner. * * *

### *Notes*

1. Consider three possible readings of TVA v. Hill: (1) equitable discretion may never be used to allow a statutory violation to continue, (2) equitable discretion may in general be so used, but that the Endangered Species Act prohibited balancing in cases arising under it, or (3) equitable discretion may be so used and the Act does not forbid balancing, but that the balancing in this case came out in favor of the snail darters. Assuming that balancing is permissible in the context of the Endangered Species Act, do the equities compel the issuance of the injunction? Would your answers change if scientists agreed that the snail darter could survive and flourish if relocated to another habitat? Would your answer change if the scientists so agreed and TVA knew, before building the dam, that a critical habitat of an endangered species would be destroyed?

2. Which of these three readings best fits the Court's opinion?

3. American and Russian health agencies, which hold the last known stocks of smallpox virus in liquid nitrogen freezers in Atlanta and Moscow, had agreed to destroy them at the end of 1993, reasoning that the danger posed by release through accident or sabotage is greater than any benefit of keeping them intact. The destruction was postponed. If the federal agency decides to go ahead with making this species extinct, must a court enjoin the destruction? (In considering this question, disregard the fact that Congress amended the Endangered Species Act after *Hill* to create a committee—dubbed the "God Committee"—that can permit species to be wiped out. 16

U.S.C. § 1536(e) and (h)(1988)). The Act also creates a hardship exception that allows extinction of harmful insects.

4. *After the case was over.* Snail darters were discovered in many other habitats. Those who want to develop a listed habitat now hire consultants who will search out unknown habitats of endangered species. Congress eventually enacted legislation that authorized putting the dam into operation although a cost-benefit analysis concluded that, even not counting the money already spent to build the dam, the additional costs of putting it into operation—such as submerging land—would outweigh the benefits.

## WEINBERGER v. ROMERO–BARCELO

Supreme Court of the United States, 1982.
456 U.S. 305, 102 S.Ct. 1798, 72 L.Ed.2d 91.

JUSTICE WHITE delivered the opinion of the Court.

The issue in this case is whether the Federal Water Pollution Control Act (FWPCA or Act), 86 Stat. 816, as amended, 33 U.S.C. § 1251 et seq. (1976 ed. and Supp. IV), requires a district court to enjoin immediately all discharges of pollutants that do not comply with the Act's permit requirements or whether the district court retains discretion to order other relief to achieve compliance. The Court of Appeals for the First Circuit held that the Act withdrew the courts' equitable discretion. We reverse.

I

For many years, the Navy has used Vieques Island, a small island off the Puerto Rico coast, for weapons training. * * * During air-to-ground training, however, pilots sometimes miss land-based targets, and ordnance falls into the sea. That is, accidental bombings of the navigable waters and, occasionally, intentional bombings of water targets occur. The District Court found that these discharges have not harmed the quality of the water.

In 1978, respondents, who include the Governor of Puerto Rico and residents of the island, sued to enjoin the Navy's operations on the island. * * * After an extensive hearing, the District Court found that under the explicit terms of the Act, the Navy had violated the Act by discharging ordnance into the waters surrounding the island without first obtaining a permit from the Environmental Protection Agency (EPA). [The Navy had contended that no permit was required.]

Under the FWPCA, the "discharge of any pollutant" requires a National Pollutant Discharge Elimination System (NPDES) permit. 33 U.S.C. §§ 1311(a), 1323(a). * * *

As the District Court construed the FWPCA, the release of ordnance from aircraft or from ships into navigable waters is a discharge of pollutants, even though the EPA, which administers the Act, had not promulgated any regulations setting effluent levels or providing for the issuance of an NPDES permit for this category of pollutants. Recognizing that violations of the Act "must be cured," the District Court ordered the Navy to apply for an NPDES permit. It refused, however, to enjoin Navy operations pending consideration of the permit application. It explained that the Navy's "technical violations" were not causing any "appreciable harm" to the environment.[4] Moreover, because of the importance of the island as a training center, "the granting of the injunctive relief sought would cause grievous, and perhaps irreparable harm, not only to Defendant Navy, but to the general welfare of this Nation."[5] The District Court concluded that an injunction was not necessary to ensure suitably prompt compliance by the Navy. To support this conclusion, it emphasized an equity court's traditionally broad discretion in deciding appropriate relief and quoted from the classic description of injunctive relief in Hecht Co. v. Bowles, 321 U.S. 321, 329–330, 64 S.Ct. 587, 591–592, 88 L.Ed. 754 (1944): "The historic injunctive process was designed to deter, not to punish."

The Court of Appeals for the First Circuit vacated the District Court's order and remanded with instructions that the court order the Navy to cease the violation until it obtained a permit. Relying on *TVA v. Hill,* * * * the Court of Appeals concluded that the District Court erred in undertaking a traditional balancing of the parties' competing interests. "Whether or not the Navy's activities in fact harm the coastal waters, it has an absolute statutory obligation to stop any discharges of pollutants until the permit procedure has been followed and the Administrator of the Environmental Protection Agency, upon review of the evidence, has granted a permit." The court suggested that if the order would interfere significantly with military preparedness, the Navy should request that the President grant it an exemption from the requirements "in the interest of national security." [6]

* * * We now reverse.

II

* * * Where plaintiff and defendant present competing claims of injury, the traditional function of equity has been to arrive at a "nice adjustment and reconciliation" between the competing claims, *Hecht Co. v. Bowles.* In such cases, the court "balances the conveniences of the parties and possible injuries to them according as they may be affected

4. The District Court wrote:

"In fact, if anything, these waters are as aesthetically acceptable as any to be found anywhere, and Plaintiff's witnesses unanimously testified as to their being the best fishing grounds in Vieques." "[I]f the truth be said, the control of large areas of Vieques [by the Navy] probably constitutes a positive factor in its over all ecology. The very fact that there are in the Navy zones modest numbers of various marine species which are practically nonexistent in the civilian sector of Vieques or in the main island of Puerto Rico, is an eloquent example of res ipsa loquitur."

5. The District Court also took into consideration the delay by plaintiffs in asserting their claims. It concluded that although laches should not totally bar the claims, it did strongly militate against the granting of injunctive relief.

6. Title 33 U.S.C. § 1323(a)(1976) ed., Supp. IV, provides, in relevant part:

"The President may exempt any effluent source of any department, agency, or instrumentality in the executive branch from compliance with any such a requirement if he determines it to be in the paramount interest of the United States to do so.... * * *."

by the granting or withholding of the injunction." Yakus v. United States, 321 U.S. 414, 440, 64 S.Ct. 660, 675, 88 L.Ed. 834 (1944). * * *

In exercising their sound discretion, courts of equity should pay particular regard for the public consequences in employing the extraordinary remedy of injunction. * * * The grant of jurisdiction to ensure compliance with a statute hardly suggests an absolute duty to do so under any and all circumstances, and a federal judge sitting as chancellor is not mechanically obligated to grant an injunction for every violation of law. *TVA v. Hill; Hecht Co. v. Bowles.*

These commonplace considerations applicable to cases in which injunctions are sought in the federal courts reflect a "practice with a background of several hundred years of history," *Hecht Co. v. Bowles*, a practice of which Congress is assuredly well aware. Of course, Congress may intervene and guide or control the exercise of the courts' discretion, but we do not lightly assume that Congress has intended to depart from established principles. *Hecht Co. v. Bowles.* As the Court said in Porter v. Warner Holding Co., 328 U.S. 395, 398, 66 S.Ct. 1086, 1089, 90 L.Ed. 1332 (1946):

> "Moreover, the comprehensiveness of this equitable jurisdiction is not to be denied or limited in the absence of a clear and valid legislative command. Unless a statute in so many words, or by a necessary and inescapable inference, restricts the court's jurisdiction in equity, the full scope of that jurisdiction is to be recognized and applied. 'The great principles of equity, securing complete justice, should not be yielded to light inferences, or doubtful construction.' Brown v. Swann, 10 Pet. 497, 503 [9 L.Ed. 508] . . ."

In *TVA v. Hill,* we held that Congress had foreclosed the exercise of the usual discretion possessed by a court of equity. There, we thought that "[o]ne would be hard pressed to find a statutory provision whose terms were any plainer" than that before us. * * * The purpose and language of the statute under consideration in *Hill,* not the bare fact of a statutory violation, compelled that conclusion. * * *

The purpose and language of the statute limited the remedies available to the District Court; only an injunction could vindicate the objectives of the Act.

That is not the case here. An injunction is not the only means of ensuring compliance. The FWPCA itself, for example, provides for fines and criminal penalties. 33 U.S.C. §§ 1319(c) and (d). Respondents suggest that failure to enjoin the Navy will undermine the integrity of the permit process by allowing the statutory violation to continue. The integrity of the Nation's waters, however, not the permit process, is the purpose of the FWPCA.[7] * * *

7. The objective of this statute is in some respects similar to that sought in nuisance suits, where courts have fully exercised their equitable discretion and ingenuity in ordering remedies. E.g., Spur Industries, Inc. v. Del E. Webb Development Co., 108 Ariz. 178, 494 P.2d 700 (1972); . Boomer v. Atlantic Cement Co., 26 N.Y.2d

This purpose is to be achieved by compliance with the Act, including compliance with the permit requirements. Here, however, the discharge of ordnance had not polluted the waters, and, although the District Court declined to enjoin the discharges, it neither ignored the statutory violation nor undercut the purpose and function of the permit system. The court ordered the Navy to apply for a permit. It temporarily, not permanently, allowed the Navy to continue its activities without a permit.

In *Hill,* we also noted that none of the limited "hardship exemptions" of the Endangered Species Act would "even remotely apply to the Tellico Project." The prohibition of the FWPCA against discharge of pollutants, in contrast, can be overcome by the very permit the Navy was ordered to seek. The Senate Report to the 1972 Amendments explains that the permit program would be enacted because "the Committee recognizes the impracticality of any effort to halt all pollution immediately." S.Rep. No. 92–414, p. 43 (1971), U.S.Code Cong. & Admin.News 1972, p. 3709. That the scheme as a whole contemplates the exercise of discretion and balancing of equities militates against the conclusion that Congress intended to deny courts their traditional equitable discretion in enforcing the statute.

Other aspects of the statutory scheme also suggest that Congress did not intend to deny courts the discretion to rely on remedies other than an immediate prohibitory injunction. Although the ultimate objective of the FWPCA is to eliminate all discharges of pollutants into the navigable waters by 1985, the statute sets forth a scheme of phased compliance. * * * This scheme of phased compliance further suggests that this is a statute in which Congress envisioned, rather than curtailed, the exercise of discretion.

The FWPCA directs the Administrator of the EPA to seek an injunction to restrain immediately discharges of pollutants he finds to be presenting "an imminent and substantial endangerment to the health of persons or to the welfare of persons." 33 U.S.C. § 1364(a). This rule of immediate cessation, however, is limited to the indicated class of violations. For other kinds of violations, the FWPCA authorizes the Administrator of the EPA "to commence a civil action for appropriate relief, including a permanent or temporary injunction, for any violation for which he is authorized to issue a compliance order * * *." 33 U.S.C. § 1319(b). The provision makes clear that Congress did not anticipate that all discharges would be immediately enjoined. Consistent with this view, the administrative practice has not been to request immediate cessation orders. * * *

Both the Court of Appeals and respondents attach particular weight to the provision of the FWPCA permitting the President to exempt federal facilities from compliance with the permit requirements. 33 U.S.C. § 1323(a). They suggest that this provision indicates congressional intent to limit the court's discretion. According to respondents,

219, 309 N.Y.S.2d 312, 257 N.E.2d 870 (1970).

the exemption provision evidences Congress' determination that only paramount national interests justify failure to comply and that only the President should make this judgment.

We do not construe the provision so broadly. We read the FWPCA as permitting the exercise of a court's equitable discretion, whether the source of pollution is a private party or a federal agency, to order relief that will achieve compliance with the Act. The exemption serves a different and complementary purpose, that of permitting noncompliance by federal agencies in extraordinary circumstances. * * *

Should the Navy receive a permit here, there would be no need to invoke the machinery of the Presidential exemption. If not, this course remains open. The exemption provision would enable the President, believing paramount national interests so require, to authorize discharges which the District Court has enjoined. Reading the statute to permit the exercise of a court's equitable discretion in no way eliminates the role of the exemption provision in the statutory scheme. * * *

III * * *

The District Court did not face a situation in which a permit would very likely not issue, and the requirements and objective of the statute could therefore not be vindicated if discharges were permitted to continue. Should it become clear that no permit will be issued and that compliance with the FWPCA will not be forthcoming, the statutory scheme and purpose would require the court to reconsider the balance it has struck.

Because Congress, in enacting the FWPCA, has not foreclosed the exercise of equitable discretion, the proper standard for appellate review is whether the District Court abused its discretion in denying an immediate cessation order while the Navy applied for a permit. We reverse and remand to the Court of Appeals for proceedings consistent with this opinion. * * *

JUSTICE POWELL, concurring. [Opinion omitted.]

JUSTICE STEVENS, dissenting.

The appropriate remedy for the violation of a federal statute depends primarily on the terms of the statute and the character of the violation. Unless Congress specifically commands a particular form of relief, the question of remedy remains subject to a court's equitable discretion. Because the Federal Water Pollution Control Act does not specifically command the federal courts to issue an injunction every time an unpermitted discharge of a pollutant occurs, the Court today is obviously correct in asserting that such injunctions should not issue "automatically" or "mechanically" in every case. It is nevertheless equally clear that by enacting the 1972 Amendments to the FWPCA Congress channeled the discretion of the federal judiciary much more narrowly than the Court's rather glib opinion suggests. Indeed, although there may well be situations in which the failure to obtain an NPDES permit would not require immediate cessation of all discharges,

I am convinced that Congress has circumscribed the district courts' discretion on the question of remedy so narrowly that a general rule of immediate cessation must be applied in all but a narrow category of cases. The Court of Appeals was quite correct in holding that this case does not present the kind of exceptional situation that justifies a departure from the general rule.

* * * [T]he Court's opinion grants an open-ended license to federal judges to carve gaping holes in a reticulated statutory scheme designed by Congress to protect a precious natural resource from the consequences of ad hoc judgments about specific discharges of pollutants.

I

Contrary to the impression created by the Court's opinion, * * * [t]he Court of Appeals did not hold that the District Court had no discretion in formulating remedies for statutory violations. It merely "conclude[d] that the district court erred in undertaking a traditional balancing of the parties' competing interests." The District Court was not free to disregard the "congressional ordering of priorities" and "the judiciary's 'responsibility to protect the integrity of the ... process mandated by Congress.'" The Court of Appeals distinguished a statutory violation that could be deemed merely "technical" from the Navy's "[utter disregard of] the statutory mandate." It then pointed out that an order prohibiting any discharge of ordnance into the coastal waters off Vieques until an NPDES permit was obtained would not significantly affect the Navy's training operations because most, if not all, of the Navy's targets were land-based. Finally, it noted that the statute authorized the Navy to obtain an exemption from the President if an injunction would have a significant effect on national security.

Under these circumstances—the statutory violation is blatant and not merely technical, and the Navy's predicament was foreseen and accommodated by Congress—the Court of Appeals essentially held that the District Court retained no discretion to deny an injunction. The discretion exercised by the District Court in this case was wholly at odds with the intent of Congress in enacting the FWPCA. In essence, the District Court's remedy was a judicial permit exempting the Navy's operations in Vieques from the statute until such time as it could obtain a permit from the Environmental Protection Agency or a statutory exemption from the President. The two principal bases for the temporary judicial permit were matters that Congress did not commit to judicial discretion. First, the District Court was persuaded that the pollution was not harming the quality of the coastal waters, and second, the court was concerned that compliance with the Act might adversely affect national security. The Court of Appeals correctly noted that the first consideration is the business of the EPA and the second is the business of the President. * * *

II * * *

The Court cites no precedent for its holding that an ongoing deliberate violation of a federal statute should be treated like any garden-variety private nuisance action in which the chancellor has the widest discretion in fashioning relief.[9]

Our prior cases involving the appropriate remedy for an ongoing violation of federal law establish a much more stringent test than the Court applies today. * * *

In Albemarle Paper Co. v. Moody, 422 U.S. 405, 95 S.Ct. 2362, 45 L.Ed.2d 280, the Court plainly stated that an equitable remedy for the violation of a federal statute was neither automatic on the one hand, nor simply a matter of balancing the equities on the other. *Albemarle* holds that the district court's remedial decision must be measured against the purposes that inform the Act of Congress that has been violated.

III * * *

It is true that in *TVA v. Hill* there was no room for compromise between the federal project and the statutory objective to preserve the endangered species; either the snail darter or the completion of the Tellico Dam had to be sacrificed. In the FWPCA, the Court tells us, the congressional objective is to protect the integrity of the Nation's waters, not to protect the integrity of the permit process. Therefore, the Court continues, a federal court may compromise the process chosen by Congress to protect our waters as long as the court is content that the waters are not actually being harmed by the particular discharge of pollutants.

On analysis, however, this reasoning does not distinguish the two cases. Courts are in no better position to decide whether the permit process is necessary to achieve the objectives of the FWPCA than they are to decide whether the destruction of the snail darter is an acceptable cost of completing the Tellico Dam. Congress has made both decisions, and there is nothing in the respective statutes or legislative histories to suggest that Congress invited the federal courts to second-guess the former decision any more than the latter. * * *

IV

The decision in *TVA v. Hill* did not depend on any peculiar or unique statutory language. Nor did it rest on any special interest in snail darters. The decision reflected a profound respect for the law and the proper allocation of lawmaking responsibilities in our Government. There we refused to sit as a committee of review. Today the Court authorizes free-thinking federal judges to do just that. Instead of requiring adherence to carefully integrated statutory procedures that assign to nonjudicial decision makers the responsibilities for evaluating potential harm to our water supply as well as potential harm to our national security, the Court unnecessarily and casually substitutes the chancellor's clumsy foot for the rule of law. * * *

9. Indeed, I am unaware of any case in which the Court has permitted a statutory violation to continue.

## *Notes*

1. *Goals and factors.* In considering whether *Weinberger* is consistent with *Hill*, recall the three proposed readings of *Hill* in note 1 to that case (supra at p. 111). None of the opinions in *Weinberger* embraces the first of those readings—that equitable discretion may never be used to allow a statutory violation to continue. But, all concede that the statute in question affects how the equities are balanced. In particular, the opinions are concerned with the goals of the Federal Water Pollution Control Act and the factors that Congress considered in enacting it.

(a) *The statutory goals.* How do the majority and dissent view the goals of the statute? Whose view is most plausible? Is that view consistent with giving the Navy time to apply for a permit?

(b) *Factors that Congress considered.* Justice Stevens' dissent argues that the absence of harm to water quality cannot be the basis for allowing the violation to continue because Congress required all sources to get permits regardless of harmfulness. He also argues that national security cannot be the basis because Congress created presidential exemptions to deal with national security. If neither lack of harmfulness nor national security alone is sufficient to allow a violation to continue, might they still be weighed in the balance if the case presents some other factor that Congress did not take into account?

Does *Weinberger* mean that polluters can safely wait until a judgment of liability is entered against them before applying for a permit? Suppose, for example, that the defendant was not the United States Navy but a privately owned factory discharging some harmless liquid into a stream, that the factory would have to close down if it could not discharge while its permit application were pending, and it had not applied for a permit before litigation began because it was unaware that the FWPCA applied to it. Should the courts allow the violation to continue pending a permit application? See David Schoenbrod, The Measure of An Injunction: A Principle to Replace Balancing the Equities and Tailoring the Remedy, 72 Minn.L.Rev. 627, 650–651 (1988).

If you think that the violation can continue in this first hypo, should the result be any different if the defendant was aware of plaintiff's contention that the FWPCA applied, but believed the plaintiff to be wrong? Id. In City of Los Angeles v. Manhart, 435 U.S. 702, 720, 98 S.Ct. 1370, 1381, 55 L.Ed.2d 657, 672 (1978), the Court balanced the equities in defendants' favor in part because they, not having "the benefit of the extensive briefs and arguments presented to us, may well have assumed that a program like [theirs] was entirely lawful. The courts had been silent on the question, and the administrative agencies had conflicting views."

Should it make any difference if the factory is federally owned but has nothing to do with national security?

Is the Navy's case distinguishable from the previous hypo? A possible distinction is that the Navy did not believe in good faith that it was not liable, but rather used litigation to stall for time. Courts, however, usually feel impelled to assume that coordinate branches of government operate in good faith unless that assumption is demonstrably wrong. But once a court thinks that a defendant is gaming the process, that defendant gets little sympathy. For example, a court enjoined a builder to remove the top twelve floors of a New York City skyscraper. The court found that the builder should have known that the building was taller than was permitted. Parkview Associates v. City of New York, 71 N.Y.2d 274, 525 N.Y.S.2d 176, 519 N.E.2d 1372 (1988). Moreover, once the violation became an issue, the developer rushed to finish the upper floors. Andrew Maykuth, 12 Floors Falling to a Zoning Law: New York Skyscraper Knocked Down to Size, Philadelphia Inquirer, Feb. 22, 1993 at 1.

For an analysis that shows how the goals and structure of another statute affects the balancing of the equities, see Note, Injunctions for NEPA Violations: Balancing the Equities, 59 U.Chi.L.Rev. 1263 (1992).

2. *Statutory interpretation*. Professor Plater argued, in an article made available to the Court while *Weinberger* was under consideration, that balancing the equities to allow statutory violations to continue is never permissible unless the legislature explicitly permits it. Zygmunt Plater, Statutory Violations and Equitable Discretion, 70 Calif.L.Rev. 524 (1982). Professor Plater's canon of statutory construction is precisely opposite to that in *Hecht*, which states in essence that courts have the power to balance unless the legislature explicitly denies it. How the courts approach this question of statutory interpretation is usually decisive because legislatures hardly ever speak explicitly to what discretion courts should have in issuing injunctions. Is Professor Dobbs correct in saying the "Schoenbrod principle" is "a good guide to the construction of statutes"? Dan B. Dobbs, Law of Remedies § 2.10 at 181 (2d ed.1993). Which approach is more likely to reflect what legislators assume about the enforcement of statutes that they enact?

3. *The role of judges*. Is legislative intent the issue here or is it instead the appropriate role for judges? Recall that Justice Harlan, in suggesting in *Bivens* that courts should have power to create remedies where a statute does not explicitly deny that power, showed no concern with legislative intent and much concern with what judges ought to have the power to do. Professor Chayes' article on the role of the judge in public law litigation argues that judges should have broad discretion to balance the equities; Professor Plater argues that judges should have no discretion in statutory cases; Professor Schoenbrod argues for a middle ground. Which position is most compatible with the role of judges in our governmental system? Justice Stevens in *Weinberger* argues that "[c]ourts are in no better position to decide whether the permit process is necessary to achieve the objectives of the FWPCA than they are to decide whether the destruction of the snail darter is an acceptable cost of completing the Tellico Dam." Does balancing put a district court judge in an untenable position? Would the lack of power to balance put a district court judge in an untenable position?

## DAVID SCHOENBROD, THE MEASURE OF AN INJUNCTION: A PRINCIPLE TO REPLACE BALANCING THE EQUITIES AND TAILORING THE REMEDY

72 Minn.L.Rev. 627, 654–57, 664–66 (1988).

* * * In determining liability, the judge decides only whether the elements of the violation are present, whereas in balancing the equities when fashioning a remedy, the judge also considers whether there are factors that make it unfair to order the defendant to stop the violation immediately. For instance, if the defendant builds a structure that violates the setback requirements of the local zoning ordinance, that is the beginning and end of the question of liability. If the plaintiff wants the violation enjoined, however, the judge will want to know whether the defendant encroached intentionally or recklessly, the cost to defendant of removing the encroachment, whether removing the encroachment will harm innocent third parties, the importance to the plaintiff of having the encroachment removed, and so on. Courts make this broader inquiry at the remedial stage primarily because granting an injunction rather than damages presents a greater threat of gross inefficiency.

Consequently, equity introduces flexibility into the cold enforcement of law to address the inefficiencies associated with injunctive relief. This flexibility is justified because the judicial process in cases that seek remedies at law has sources of flexibility not available in cases that seek equitable relief. In suits for damages, much of what goes into balancing the equities in injunction cases gets reflected in jury nullification, the determination of the amount of compensatory or punitive damages, limits on garnishment and execution designed to avoid severe hardship, and sometimes a kind of balancing of the equities in the damage context itself. Moreover, criminal actions involve flexibility in prosecutorial discretion, jury nullification, and sentencing judgment. Thus, a suit for an injunction without balancing the equities would present a rare instance of the judicial process without a safety valve.

Although Plater claims that judges should not balance the equities in statutory cases and should apply statutory rules strictly, the reasons for balancing in nonstatutory cases apply fully to statutory cases. In nonstatutory cases, courts balance the equities because injunctive enforcement of a rule of liability that is fair and efficient in general may be unfair or inefficient in a particular context. In formulating statutory rules, legislatures can rarely confine statutory definitions of violations to instances in which enjoining them would invariably be fair and efficient. Judges need the kind of flexibility that they have in nonstatutory cases to act as a safety valve to prevent unfair and inefficient application of a statutory rule. Plater argues that legislative relief, not balancing the equities, provides the appropriate safety valve in statutory cases. That safety valve, however, is available only in extraordinary cases that get priority on the legislative agenda, such as *TVA v. Hill,* not in garden variety cases. The proposed principle provides a safety valve for all statutory cases by giving judges the flexibility necessary, but in a way that restrains judges' discretion, forcing them to honor the choices that the legislature did make.

Moreover, both Plater's and Chayes's approaches would put the judge in a difficult personal position. The judge in street clothes is in principle an equal of the parties. What justifies the power of the judge in robes is that the judge speaks the law. Regarding findings of liability, judges can readily respond to a defendant's rebuke "how dare you find me liable," with "the law made you liable." This answer is inadequate, however, when the defendant challenges the judge's authority to issue an injunction because the judge must exercise discretion in shaping the injunction to fit the case.[138] Relative to the finding of liability, the injunction therefore looks more like personal opinion than impersonal law. By requiring the judge to end the statutory violation regardless of the consequences, Plater's approach would subject the judge to personal criticism by taking away the judge's flexibility to mitigate the consequences. Similarly, by turning the judge into a policy maker, Chayes's approach fails to offer constraints to both legitimate the exercise of equitable discretion and allow the judge to cast at least some of the blame for the injunction's consequences onto the law. * * *

Plater [attempts] to justify permitting broad discretion to grant injunctions in constitutional and common law cases while denying it in statutory cases on the basis that constitutions and the common law provide rules of liability in terms more open textured than do statutory rules of liability. Plater argues that because judges have more discretion in determining the scope of liability in constitutional and common law cases than in statutory cases, they should similarly have more freedom in fashioning injunctive relief in such cases. In determining liability under statutes, common law, and constitutions, however, Professor Ronald Dworkin asserts that judges should interpret the law rather than make policy decisions. As a result, liability in those cases arguably is not a product of discretion, and therefore there is no discretion in determining liability to independently justify discretion in fashioning relief.

If judges disagree with Dworkin and believe that they should make policy decisions in constitutional and common law cases, judges should nevertheless apply the proposed principle to guide the exercise of that discretion in formulating relief. There is no persuasive reason to use different standards when the relevant authority controlling liability is statutory as opposed to case law. If precedent—constitutional or common law—controls the liability decision in the case at hand, the judge's attitude toward that precedent in formulating relief should be just as respectful as it would be toward a controlling statute. As Professors Owen Fiss and Doug Rendleman suggest, it would be bizarre if judges

138. Even if the judge decides that the violation must end, the injunction will have to state the terms on which this will happen.

had more freedom to undercut constitutional rights than statutory rights through remedial discretion.

Even when precedent does not directly control the judge's liability decision and the judge can base the decision upon policy, the proposed principle should still apply at the remedy stage because it legitimates the judge's exercise of discretion by providing articulated limits. After fixing the rule of liability, the judge may still not want to grant an injunction that achieves the plaintiff's rightful position. The proposed principle would justify such a result if a remedy less than the plaintiff's rightful position does not conflict with the goals of the rule of liability created by the judge and the case involves a factor not reflected in that rule. If these requirements are not met and the judge denies full injunctive relief, the judge's decision ignores the policy concerns underlying the judge's own rule of liability. Candor as well as giving the public and the bar fair notice of the law's practical impact should compel the judge to restate the rule of liability based on an appropriate policy rationale rather than to grant relief contrary to the spirit of the judge's own rule of liability. * * *

### *Note on Balancing in Administrative Enforcement*

Statutes frequently authorize administrative agencies to issue orders against violations of prohibitions in statutes or in agency-promulgated regulations. Unless the statute explicitly directs otherwise, the agencies usually do not take this authorization as a command to order the cessation of all violations forthwith, but rather exercise discretion to allow violations to continue in particular cases for reasons analogous to balancing the equities in the judicial sphere. See Alfred C. Aman, Jr., Administrative Equity: An Analysis of Exceptions to Administrative Rules, 1982 Duke L.J. 277. Closely related to such administrative balancing the equities is the power to grant variances. Zoning ordinances and other legislation sometimes grant administrators the power to permit exceptions to broadly applicable rules of conduct when strict application of the rule would create hardship incommensurate with the public interest.

Instead of allowing violations to continue on a case-by-case basis, can an agency issue a regulation that allows a whole category of violations of a statute to continue on the basis of "equity"?

> Certain limited grounds for the creation of exemptions are inherent in the administrative process, and their unavailability under a statutory scheme should not be presumed, save in the face of the most unambiguous demonstration of congressional intent to foreclose them. But there exists no general administrative power to create exemptions to statutory requirements based upon the agency's perception of costs and benefits.

Alabama Power Co. v. Costle, 636 F.2d 323, 357 (D.C.Cir.1979)(recognizing inherent power to grant categorical exemptions based upon administrative necessity and de minimis harm). But an agency's decision to create a de minimus exception is subject to review. Natural Resources Defense Council v. EPA, 966 F.2d 1292 (9th Cir.1992).

## 2. GRANTING MORE THAN PLAINTIFF'S RIGHTFUL POSITION: PROPHYLAXIS AND IMPOSSIBILITY

### *Problem: Country Lodge v. Miller (Reprised)* *Prophylactic Orders*

Suppose that Country Lodge's rightful position is that Miller put no more than 50 pounds of waste into the river per week. Country Lodge asks that she be enjoined from putting any apple mash in the river on the grounds that Country Lodge does not know how much is going out the pipe and into the river. Miller objects that she will then have to cart away not only the mash, at a cost of $20,000 per year, but also the water used to clean the cider press at an additional cost of $30,000 per year. Should the court grant Country Lodge's request?

---

An injunction whose terms are geared precisely to plaintiff's rightful position (e.g., "Miller shall discharge no more than 50 pounds of waste per year") may fail to achieve plaintiff's rightful position if the defendant can disobey the order without being detected. When the threat of such harm is large enough, courts can hold the defendant to a more readily enforceable standard even though it exceeds plaintiff's rightful position (e.g., "Miller shall discharge nothing"). The court still *aims* for plaintiff's rightful position, but the *terms* of the injunction go beyond that position as prophylaxis against falling short of it. In contrast, balancing the equities may lead to an injunction that aims to achieve less than plaintiff's rightful position.

One example of a prophylactic order is Paramount Pictures v. Davis, 228 Cal.App.2d 827, 39 Cal.Rptr. 791 (1964). Bette Davis had entered a contract that required her to work exclusively for Paramount on "Where Love Has Gone" for a certain period and thereafter to help finish the film on a nonexclusive basis. Davis honored the contract during the exclusive period but violated it by failing to cooperate on scheduling thereafter. The court prohibited her from working for anyone but Paramount until she completed her role. Paramount got her exclusive services for a longer period than specified in the contract (more than its rightful position), but only for the purpose of ensuring that she honor her commitment to finish the film (part of its rightful position). Ordering her not to work for anyone else gives the studio the upper hand in negotiating a filming schedule, but Davis' prior behavior gave grounds for suspicion that she would take advantage of the flexibility inherent in an order that instructed her to complete her obligations on a reasonable basis. A blanket prohibition against working for others is easier for the court to write than an order that specifies a filming schedule.

Hutto v. Finney, 437 U.S. 678, 98 S.Ct. 2565, 57 L.Ed.2d 522 (1978), is another instance of an injunction that went beyond plaintiff's rightful position for prophylactic purposes. There, the district court had found that punitive isolation for longer than 30 days was not in itself cruel and unusual punishment but was so in combination with the terrible conditions in Arkansas's punitive isolation cells. The district court enjoined punitive isolation for longer than 30 days and the Supreme Court affirmed:

> In fashioning a remedy, the District Court had ample authority to go beyond earlier orders and to address each element contributing to the violation. The District Court had given the Department repeated opportunities to remedy the cruel and unusual conditions in the isolation cells. If petitioners had fully complied with the court's earlier orders, the present time limit [on time spent in isolation, which was not in itself a violation, but was so in combination with poor conditions] might well have been unnecessary. But taking the long and unhappy history of the litigation into account, the court was justified in entering a comprehensive order to insure against the risk of inadequate compliance.

437 U.S. at 687, 98 S.Ct. at 2572, 57 L.Ed.2d at 532. *Hutto* suggests that injunctions that go beyond plaintiffs' rightful position require a demonstrated risk that defendants would not comply with a narrower order. Such a requirement parallels the requirement of showing a threat of harm to plaintiff's rightful position as a prerequisite to the issuance of any injunction. See § (C)(1) of this chapter.

Prophylactic orders are also common in enforcement of regulatory statutes. For example, after finding a violation of the securities laws, courts sometimes not only enjoin future violations but also ensure that they do not recur by prohibiting the violator from participating as an officer of any public company, imposing reporting requirements in addition to those in the securities laws, or appointing an independent majority on the violator's board of directors, a receiver, or "special professionals" to ensure compliance. George W. Dent Jr., Ancillary Relief in Federal Securities Law: A Study in Federal Remedies, 67 Minn.L.Rev. 865 (1983).

Courts issue orders that achieve more than plaintiff's rightful position for a second reason—because it is impossible to achieve plaintiff's rightful position precisely, even if the defendant cooperates. In McCarthy v. Briscoe, 429 U.S. 1317, 97 S.Ct. 10, 50 L.Ed.2d 49 (1976), Eugene McCarthy, a former senator, sought the Democratic Party nomination for president and lost. McCarthy then sought to run as an independent, but Texas enacted a statute forbidding independents to appear on the ballot if they had lost a bid for the nomination of a party. McCarthy succeeded in having the statute struck down as unconstitutional just weeks before the general election. Under Texas law, independents need a large number of petition signatures to appear on the ballot, a requirement that is, itself, constitutional. McCarthy had no way of meeting this requirement in the time remaining. His rightful position was to have an opportunity to gather the petition signatures unimpeded by the unconstitutional prohibition on his appearing on the ballot in the general election. Because the court could not recreate his rightful position, it gave him something better—the opportunity to appear on the ballot without any petition signatures.

For another example of an injunction that grants more than plaintiff's rightful position because achieving it precisely is impossible, consider how the National Labor Relations Board responds to unfair labor practices by employers seeking to prevent their employees from voting to make a union their bargaining agent. The traditional remedy, which puts the employees in their rightful position, is for the NLRB to order that the violations cease and the election be held. But when the violations make a fair election impossible and employee sentiment previously expressed through petitioning for an election suggests that the union would have won the election, the NLRB may make the union the exclusive bargaining agent without an election. NLRB v. Gissel Packing Co., 395 U.S. 575, 89 S.Ct. 1918, 23 L.Ed.2d 547 (1969).

With impossibility, as with prophylaxis, courts look carefully to consider whether it is really necessary to grant an injunction that goes beyond plaintiff's rightful position. In Montgomery Ward & Co. v. National Labor Relations Board, 904 F.2d 1156 (7th Cir.1990), the employer had engaged in violations sufficiently severe for the board to make the union the bargaining agent without an election, but eight years elapsed before the NLRB issued such an order. The court remanded it for the NLRB to consider whether the passage of time and the accompanying large turnover of both employees and supervisory staff might make it possible to hold a fair election now.

Deciding whether to issue an injunction that grants more than plaintiff's rightful position, like deciding whether to issue an injunction that grants less, involves balancing. See David Schoenbrod, The Measure of an Injunction: A Principle to Replace Balancing the Equities and Tailoring the Remedy, 72 Minn.L.Rev. 627, 633–34 & nn. 20–23, 636–37 & nn. 41–48. There are interesting differences and similarities in how the balancing is done. To get an injunction that grants less, the defendant must justify that result through a factor not reflected in the law of liability (a "hardship"). To get an injunction that grants more, plaintiff must justify the result through a factor not reflected in the law of liability (the difficulty of supervising a resistant defendant or the impossibility of precisely recreating plaintiff's rightful position). The defendant must show that the hardship outweighs the plaintiff's interest in getting specific rather than substitutionary relief. The plaintiff must show that the threat to its rightful position from a narrower injunction outweighs the harm to defendant from the injunction going beyond plaintiff's rightful position. We have seen that, in balancing claims of hardship, the courts take account of the respective faults of the parties and the goals of the law of liability. In balancing claims of prophylaxis or impossibility, they do the same. The degree of defendant's culpability in violating plaintiff's rights or an earlier injunction counts against the defendant. The injunction may not grant more than the rightful position if that conflicts with the law's goals. For example, in H.K. Porter Co. v. NLRB, 397 U.S. 99, 107–08, 90 S.Ct. 821, 825–26, 25 L.Ed.2d 146, 153 (1970), the Supreme Court struck down an order that an employer accede to the union's position because, even though the employer had violated a statutory requirement and a previous order to bargain in good faith, the goal of the statute was to make private bargaining the means to settle labor disputes.

In deciding whether an injunction should grant more than plaintiff's rightful position, constitutional interests are at stake—liberty or property when the addressee of the injunction is a private person and separation of powers or federalism when the addressee is a governmental institution. When, as in the following case, the injunction allegedly violates first amendment rights, the constitutional issue gets heightened scrutiny. In reading the case, consider not just how courts should scrutinize injunctions that assertedly violate the first amendment but also any injunction that intrudes on the liberty or property interests of a private defendant.

### *(a) The Abortion Protest Example*

## MADSEN v. WOMEN'S HEALTH CENTER, INC.

Supreme Court of the United States, 1994.
512 U.S. ___, 114 S.Ct. 2516, 129 L.Ed.2d 593.

Chief Justice Rehnquist delivered the opinion of the Court.

Petitioners challenge the constitutionality of an injunction entered by a Florida state court which prohibits antiabortion protestors from demonstrating in certain places and in various ways outside of a health clinic that performs abortions. We hold that the establishment of a 36–foot buffer zone on a public street from which demonstrators are excluded passes muster under the First Amendment, but that several other provisions of the injunction do not.

I

Respondents operate abortion clinics throughout central Florida. Petitioners and other groups and individuals are engaged in activities near the site of one such clinic in Melbourne, Florida. They picketed and demonstrated where the public street gives access to the clinic. In September 1992, a Florida state court permanently enjoined petitioners from blocking or interfering with public access to the clinic, and from physically abusing persons entering or leaving the clinic. Six months later, respondents sought to broaden the injunction, complaining that access to the clinic was still impeded by petitioners' activities and that such activities had also discouraged some potential patients from entering the clinic, and had deleterious physical effects on others. The trial court thereupon issued a broader injunction, which is challenged here.

The court found that, despite the initial injunction, protesters continued to impede access to the clinic by congregating on the paved portion of the street—Dixie Way—leading up to the clinic, and by marching in front of the clinic's driveways. It found that as vehicles heading toward the clinic slowed to allow the protesters to move out of the way, "sidewalk counselors" would approach and attempt to give the vehicle's occupants antiabortion literature. The number of people congregating varied from a handful to 400, and the noise varied from singing and chanting to the use of loudspeakers and bullhorns.

The protests, the court found, took their toll on the clinic's patients. A clinic doctor testified that, as a result of having to run such a gauntlet to enter the clinic, the patients "manifested a higher level of anxiety and hypertension causing those patients to need a higher level of sedation to undergo the surgical procedures, thereby increasing the risk associated with such procedures." The noise produced by the protestors could be heard within the clinic, causing stress in the patients both during surgical procedures and while recuperating in the recovery rooms. And those patients who turned away because of the crowd to return at a later date, the doctor testified, increased their health risks by reason of the delay.

Doctors and clinic workers, in turn, were not immune even in their homes. Petitioners picketed in front of clinic employees' residences; shouted at passersby; rang the doorbells of neighbors and provided literature identifying the particular clinic employee as a "baby killer." Occasionally, the protestors would confront minor children of clinic employees who were home alone.

This and similar testimony led the state court to conclude that its original injunction had proved insufficient "to protect the health, safety and rights of women in Brevard and Seminole County, Florida, and surrounding counties seeking access to [medical and counseling] services." The state court therefore amended its prior order, enjoining a broader array of activities. The amended injunction prohibits petitioners[1] from engaging in the following acts:

> (1) * * * entering the * * * property of the Aware Woman Center for Choice [the Melbourne clinic]. . . .
>
> (2) * * * obstructing * * * access to * * * the Clinic.
>
> (3) * * * entering * * * within [36] feet of the property line of the Clinic. . . . [There are exceptions: petitioners may come within 5 feet of the Clinic's east line and owners of property adjacent to the Clinic and their invitees may use their property within the buffer zone.]

1. In addition to petitioners, the state court's order was directed at "Operation Rescue * * * and all persons acting in concert or participation with them, or on their behalf."

(4) During the hours of 7:30 a.m. through noon, on Mondays through Saturdays, during surgical procedures and recovery periods, from singing, * * *, shouting, * * *, use of bullhorns, * * * or other sounds or images observable to or within earshot of the patients inside the Clinic.

(5) * * * in an area within [300] feet of the Clinic, from physically approaching any person seeking the services of the Clinic unless such person indicates a desire to communicate by approaching or by inquiring of the [petitioners]....

(6) * * * from approaching * * * within [300] feet of the residence of any of the [respondents'] employees * * * or blocking * * * the entrances * * * of [their] residences * * *

(7) * * * from physically abusing, grabbing, intimidating, harassing, touching, pushing, shoving, crowding or assaulting persons entering or leaving, working at or using services at the [respondents'] Clinic or trying to gain access to, or leave, any of the homes of owners, staff or patients of the Clinic.

(8) * * * from harassing, intimidating or physically abusing, assaulting or threatening any present or former * * * employee or volunteer who assists in providing services at the [respondents'] Clinic.

(9) * * * from encouraging, inciting, or securing other persons to commit any of the prohibited acts listed herein.

The Florida Supreme Court upheld the constitutionality of the trial court's amended injunction. * * *

* * * [T]he United States Court of Appeals for the Eleventh Circuit heard a separate challenge to the same injunction. [It] struck down the injunction, characterizing the dispute as a clash "between an actual prohibition of speech and a potential hinderance to the free exercise of abortion rights." It stated that the asserted interests in public safety and order were already protected by other applicable laws and that these interests could be protected adequately without infringing upon the First Amendment rights of others. * * * We granted certiorari to resolve the conflict between the Florida Supreme Court and the Court of Appeals * * *

## II

We begin by addressing petitioners' contention that the state court's order, because it is an injunction that restricts only the speech of antiabortion protesters, is necessarily content or viewpoint based. Accordingly, they argue, we should examine the entire injunction under the strictest standard of scrutiny. See Perry Education Association v. Perry Local Educators' Association, 460 U.S. 37 (1983). We disagree. To accept petitioners' claim would be to classify virtually every injunction as content or viewpoint based. An injunction, by its very nature, applies only to a particular group (or individuals) and regulates the activities, and perhaps the speech, of that group. It does so, however, because of the group's past actions in the context of a specific dispute between real parties. The parties seeking the injunction assert a violation of their rights; the court hearing the action is charged with fashioning a remedy for a specific deprivation, not with the drafting of a statute addressed to the general public.

The fact that the injunction in the present case did not prohibit activities of those demonstrating in favor of abortion is justly attributable to the lack of any similar demonstrations by those in favor of abortion, and of any consequent request that their demonstrations be regulated by injunction. There is no suggestion in this record that Florida law would not equally restrain similar conduct directed at a target having nothing to do with abortion; none of the restrictions imposed by the court were directed at the contents of petitioner's message.

Our principal inquiry in determining content neutrality is whether the government has adopted a regulation of speech "without reference to the content of the regulated speech" * * *. We thus look to the government's purpose as the threshold consideration. Here, the state court imposed restrictions on petitioners incidental to their antiabortion message because they repeatedly violated the court's original order. That petitioners all share the same viewpoint regarding abortion does not in itself demonstrate that some invidious content or viewpoint-based purpose motivated the issuance of the order. It suggests only that those in the group *whose conduct* violated the court's order happen to share the same opinion regarding abortions being performed at the clinic. * * *[2] Accordingly, the injunction issued in this case does not demand the level of heightened scrutiny set forth in *Perry Education Assn.* And we proceed to discuss the standard which does govern.

## III

If this were a content-neutral, generally applicable statute, instead of an injunctive order, its constitutionality would be assessed under the standard set forth in Ward v. Rock Against Racism, 491 U.S. 781 (1989), and similar cases. Given that the forum around the clinic is a traditional public forum, we would determine whether the time, place, and manner regulations were "narrowly tailored to serve a significant governmental interest."

There are obvious differences, however, between an injunction and a generally applicable ordinance. Ordinances represent a legislative choice

2. We also decline to adopt the prior restraint analysis urged by petitioners. Prior restraints do often take the form of injunctions. See, *e.g.*, New York Times Co. v. United States, 403 U.S. 713 (1971) (refusing to enjoin publications of the "Pentagon Papers"); . * * *. Not all injunctions which may incidentally affect expression, however, are "prior restraints" in the sense that term was used in *New York Times Co.* * * * Here petitioners are not prevented from expressing their message in any one of several different ways; they are simply prohibited from expressing it within the 36–foot buffer zone. Moreover, the injunction was issued not because of the content of petitioners' expression, as was the case in *New York Times Co.* * * * but because of their prior unlawful conduct.

regarding the promotion of particular societal interests. Injunctions, by contrast, are remedies imposed for violations (or threatened violations) of a legislative or judicial decree. See United States v. W. T. Grant Co., 345 U.S. 629, 632–633 (1953). Injunctions also carry greater risks of censorship and discriminatory application than do general ordinances. "[T]here is no more effective practical guaranty against arbitrary and unreasonable government than to require that the principles of law which officials would impose upon a minority must be imposed generally." Injunctions, of course, have some advantages over generally applicable statutes in that they can be tailored by a trial judge to afford more precise relief than a statute where a violation of the law has already occurred.

We believe that these differences require a somewhat more stringent application of general First Amendment principles in this context. In past cases evaluating injunctions restricting speech, see, e.g., NAACP v. Claiborne Hardware Co., 458 U.S. 886 (1982), Milk Wagon Drivers v. Meadowmoor Dairies, Inc., 312 U.S. 287 (1941), we have relied upon such general principles while also seeking to ensure that the injunction was no broader than necessary to achieve its desired goals. See Carroll v. President and Comm'rs of Princess Anne, 393 U.S. 175 (1968); *Claiborne Hardware*. Our close attention to the fit between the objectives of an injunction and the restrictions it imposes on speech is consistent with the general rule, quite apart from First Amendment considerations, "that injunctive relief should be no more burdensome to the defendants than necessary to provide complete relief to the plaintiffs." Accordingly, when evaluating a content-neutral injunction, we think that our standard time, place, and manner analysis is not sufficiently rigorous. We must ask instead whether the challenged provisions of the injunction burden no more speech than necessary to serve a significant government interest. See, e.g., *Claiborne Hardware* (when sanctionable "conduct occurs in the context of constitutionally protected activity ... 'precision of regulation' is demanded"); *Carroll*. * * *

The Florida Supreme Court concluded that numerous significant government interests are protected by the injunction. It noted that the State has a strong interest in protecting a woman's freedom to seek lawful medical or counseling services in connection with her pregnancy. See Roe v. Wade, 410 U.S. 113 (1973). The State also has a strong interest in ensuring the public safety and order, in promoting the free flow of traffic on public streets and sidewalks, and in protecting the property rights of all its citizens. In addition, the court believed that the State's strong interest in residential privacy, acknowledged in Frisby v. Schultz, 487 U.S. 474 (1988), applied by analogy to medical privacy. The court observed that while targeted picketing of the home threatens the psychological well-being of the "captive" resident, targeted picketing of a hospital or clinic threatens not only the psychological, but the physical well-being of the patient held "captive" by medical circumstance. We agree with the Supreme Court of Florida that the combination of these governmental interests is quite sufficient to justify an appropriately tailored injunction to protect them. We now examine each contested provision of the injunction to see if it burdens more speech than necessary to accomplish its goal.

A

*1*

We begin with the 36–foot buffer zone. The state court prohibited petitioners from "congregating, picketing, patrolling, demonstrating or entering" any portion of the public right-of-way or private property within 36 feet of the property line of the clinic as a way of ensuring access to the clinic. This speech-free buffer zone requires that petitioners move to the other side of Dixie Way and away from the driveway of the clinic, where the state court found that they repeatedly had interfered with the free access of patients and staff. * * *

We have noted a distinction between the type of focused picketing banned from the buffer zone and the type of generally disseminated communication that cannot be completely banned in public places, such as handbilling and solicitation. See *Frisby* 487 U.S. at 486. * * *

The 36–foot buffer zone protecting the entrances to the clinic and the parking lot is a means of protecting unfettered ingress to and egress from the clinic, and ensuring that petitioners do not block traffic on Dixie Way. The state court seems to have had few other options to protect access given the narrow confines around the clinic. As the Florida Supreme Court noted, Dixie Way is only 21 feet wide in the area of the clinic. The state court was convinced that allowing the petitioners to remain on the clinic's sidewalk and driveway was not a viable option in view of the failure of the first injunction to protect access. And allowing the petitioners to stand in the middle of Dixie Way would obviously block vehicular traffic.

The need for a complete buffer zone near the clinic entrances and driveway may be debatable, but some deference must be given to the state court's familiarity with the facts and the background of the dispute between the parties even under our heightened review. Moreover, one of petitioners' witnesses during the evidentiary hearing before the state court conceded that the buffer zone was narrow enough to place petitioners at a distance of no greater than 10 to 12 feet from cars approaching and leaving the clinic. Protesters standing across the narrow street from the clinic can still be seen and heard from the clinic parking lots. We also bear in mind the fact that the state court originally issued a much narrower injunction, providing no buffer zone, and that this order did not succeed in protecting access to the clinic. The failure of the first order to accomplish its purpose may be taken into consideration in evaluating the constitutionality of the broader order. On balance, we hold that the 36–foot buffer zone around the clinic entrances and driveway burdens no more speech than necessary to accomplish the governmental interest at stake.

Justice Scalia's dissent argues that a videotape made of demonstrations at the clinic represents "what one must presume to be the worst of the activity justifying the injunction." This seems to us a gratuitous assumption [because there was other testimony during the three day evidentiary hearing and, before the Supreme Court, petitioners limited their attack on the injunction to a question of constitutional law to the exclusion of issues of fact.] * * * We must therefore judge this case on the assumption that the evidence and testimony presented to the state court supported its findings that the presence of protesters standing, marching, and demonstrating near the clinic's entrance interfered with ingress to and egress from the clinic despite the issuance of the earlier injunction.

*2*

The inclusion of private property on the back and side of the clinic in the 36–foot buffer zone raises different concerns. * * * Patients and staff wishing to reach the clinic do not have to cross the private property abutting the clinic property * * * and nothing in the record indicates that petitioners' activities on the private property have obstructed access to the clinic. * * * We hold that on the record before us the 36–foot buffer zone as applied to the private property to the north and west of the clinic burdens more speech than necessary to protect access to the clinic.

B

In response to high noise levels outside the clinic, the state court restrained the petitioners from "singing, chanting, whistling, shouting, yelling, use of bullhorns, auto horns, sound amplification equipment or other sounds or images observable to or within earshot of the patients inside the [c]linic" during the hours of 7:30 a.m. through noon on Mondays through Saturdays. * * * Noise control is particularly important around hospitals and medical facilities during surgery and recovery periods * * *

We hold that the limited noise restrictions imposed by the state court order burden no more speech than necessary to ensure the health and well-being of the patients at the clinic. * * *

C

The same, however, cannot be said for the "images observable" provision of the state court's order. Clearly, threats to patients or their families, however communicated, are proscribable under the First Amendment. But rather than prohibiting the display of signs that could be interpreted as threats or veiled threats, the state court issued a blanket ban on all "images observable." This broad prohibition on all "images observable" burdens more speech than necessary to achieve the purpose of limiting threats to clinic patients or their families. Similarly, if the blanket ban on "images observable" was intended to reduce the level of anxiety and hypertension suffered by the patients inside the clinic, it would still fail. * * * [I]t is much easier for the clinic to pull its curtains than for a patient to stop up her ears * * *

D

The state court ordered that petitioners refrain from physically approaching any person seeking services of the clinic "unless such person indicates a desire to communicate" in an area within 300 feet of the clinic. The state court was attempting to prevent clinic patients and staff from being "stalked" or "shadowed" by the petitioners as they approached the clinic.

But it is difficult, indeed, to justify a prohibition on *all* uninvited approaches of persons seeking the services of the clinic, regardless of how peaceful the contact may be, without burdening more speech than necessary to prevent intimidation and to ensure access to the clinic. Absent evidence that the protesters' speech is independently proscribable (i.e., "fighting words" or threats), or is so infused with violence as to be indistinguishable from a threat of physical harm, this provision cannot stand. "As a general matter, we have indicated that in public debate our own citizens must tolerate insulting, and even outrageous, speech in order to provide adequate breathing space to the freedoms protected by the First Amendment." The "consent" requirement alone invalidates this provision; it burdens more speech than is necessary to prevent intimidation and to ensure access to the clinic.

E

The final substantive regulation challenged by petitioners relates to a prohibition against picketing, demonstrating, or using sound amplification equipment within 300 feet of the residences of clinic staff. The prohibition also covers impeding access to streets that provide the sole access to streets on which those residences are located. The same analysis applies to the use of sound amplification equipment here as that discussed above: the government may simply demand that petitioners turn down the volume if the protests overwhelm the neighborhood.

As for the picketing, our prior decision upholding a law banning targeted residential picketing remarked on the unique nature of the home, as "the last citadel of the tired, the weary, and the sick." *Frisby.*

But the 300–foot zone around the residences in this case is much larger than the zone provided for in the ordinance which we approved in *Frisby*. The ordinance at issue there made it "unlawful for any person to engage in picketing before or about the residence or dwelling of any individual." The prohibition was limited to "focused picketing taking place solely in front of a particular residence." By contrast, the 300–foot zone would ban "[g]eneral marching through residential neighborhoods, or even walking a route in front of an entire block of houses." The record before us does not contain sufficient justification for this broad a ban on picketing; it appears that a limitation on the time, duration of picketing, and number of pickets outside a smaller zone could have accomplished the desired result.

IV

Petitioners also * * * object to the portion of the injunction making it applicable to those acting "in concert" with the named parties. But petitioners themselves are named parties in the order, and they therefore lack standing to challenge a portion of the order applying to persons who are not parties. * * *

Petitioners also contend that the "in concert" provision of the injunction impermissibly limits their freedom of association guaranteed by the First Amendment.[a] But petitioners are not enjoined from associating with others or from joining with them to express a particular viewpoint. The freedom of association protected by the First Amendment does not extend to joining with others for the purpose of depriving third parties of their lawful rights. * * *

JUSTICE SOUTER, concurring.

I join the Court's opinion and write separately only to clarify two matters in the record. First, the trial judge made reasonably clear that the issue of who was acting "in concert" with the named defendants was a matter to be taken up in individual cases, and not to be decided on the basis of protesters' viewpoints. Second, petitioners themselves acknowledge that the governmental interests in protection of public safety and order, of the free flow of traffic, and of property rights are reflected in Florida law. [Citations to Florida statutes concerning public peace and obstruction of public streets.]

JUSTICE STEVENS, concurring in part and dissenting in part.* * *

I

Unlike the Court, * * * I believe that injunctive relief should be judged by a more lenient standard than legislation. As the Court notes, legislation is imposed on an entire community, regardless of individual culpability. By contrast, injunctions apply solely to an individual or a limited group of individuals who, by engaging in illegal conduct, have been judicially deprived of some liberty-the normal consequence of illegal activity.[2] Given this distinction, a statute prohibiting demonstrations within 36 feet of an abortion clinic would probably violate the First Amendment, but an injunction directed at a limited group of persons who have engaged in unlawful conduct in a similar zone might well be constitutional.

The standard governing injunctions has two obvious dimensions. On the one hand, the injunction should be no more burdensome than necessary to provide complete relief. In a First Amendment context, as in any other, the propriety of the remedy depends almost entirely on the

a. Binding nonparties acting "in concert" with defendants is considered in chapter 3(C)(4) infra.

2. Contrary to Justice Scalia's assumption, the deprivation of liberty caused by an injunction is not a form of punishment. Moreover, there is nothing unusual about injunctive relief that includes some restriction on speech as a remedy for prior misconduct. National Society of Professional Engineers v. United States, 435 U.S. 679, 697–698 (1978).

character of the violation and the likelihood of its recurrence. For this reason, standards fashioned to determine the constitutionality of statutes should not be used to evaluate injunctions.

On the other hand, even when an injunction impinges on constitutional rights, more than "a simple proscription against the precise conduct previously pursued" may be required; the remedy must include appropriate restraints on "future activities both to avoid a recurrence of the violation and to eliminate its consequences." Moreover, "[t]he judicial remedy for a proven violation of law will often include commands that the law does not impose on the community at large." As such, repeated violations may justify sanctions that might be invalid if applied to a first offender or if enacted by the legislature.

In this case, the trial judge heard three days of testimony and found that petitioners not only had engaged in tortious conduct, but also had repeatedly violated an earlier injunction. The injunction is thus twice removed from a legislative proscription applicable to the general public and should be judged by a standard that gives appropriate deference to the judge's unique familiarity with the facts.

II * * *

[As to the 300–foot buffer zone around the clinic, petitioners'] argument and the Court's conclusion * * * are based on a misreading of the injunction.

[The relevant language in the injunction] does not purport to prohibit speech; it prohibits a species of conduct. * * *

The "physically approaching" prohibition entered by the trial court is no broader than the protection necessary to provide relief for the violations it found. The trial judge entered this portion of the injunction only after concluding that the injunction was necessary to protect the clinic's patients and staff from "uninvited contacts, shadowing and stalking" by petitioners. The protection is especially appropriate for the clinic patients given that the trial judge found that petitioners' prior conduct caused higher levels of "anxiety and hypertension" in the patients, increasing the risks associated with the procedures that the patients seek. Whatever the proper limits on a court's power to restrict a speaker's ability to physically approach or follow an unwilling listener, surely the First Amendment does not prevent a trial court from imposing such a restriction given the unchallenged findings in this case.

The Florida Supreme Court correctly concluded:

> "While the First Amendment confers on each citizen a powerful right to express oneself, it gives the picketer no boon to jeopardize the health, safety, and rights of others. No citizen has a right to insert a foot in the hospital or clinic door and insist on being heard-while purposefully blocking the door to those in genuine need of medical services. No picketer can force speech into the captive ear of the unwilling and disabled."

I thus conclude that, under the circumstances of this case, the prohibition against "physically approaching" in the 300–foot zone around the clinic withstands petitioners' First Amendment challenge. I therefore dissent from Part III–D.

III

Because I have joined Parts I, II, III–E, and IV of the Court's opinion and have dissented as to Part III–D after concluding that the 300–foot zone around the clinic is a reasonable time, place, and manner restriction, no further discussion is necessary. The Court, however, proceeds to address challenges to the injunction that, although arguably raised by petitioners' briefs, are not properly before the Court. [Justice Stevens dissents from the remaining portions of the opinion.]

JUSTICE SCALIA, with whom JUSTICE KENNEDY and JUSTICE THOMAS join, concurring in the judgment in part and dissenting in part.

The judgment in today's case has an appearance of moderation and Solomonic wisdom, upholding as it does some portions of the injunction while disallowing others. That appearance is deceptive. The entire injunction in this case departs so far from the established course of our jurisprudence that in any other context it would have been regarded as a candidate for summary reversal.

But the context here is abortion. * * *

Because I believe that the judicial creation of a 36–foot zone in which only a particular group, which had broken no law, cannot exercise its rights of speech, assembly, and association, and the judicial enactment of a noise prohibition, applicable to that group and that group alone, are profoundly at odds with our First Amendment precedents and traditions, I dissent.

I

The record of this case contains a videotape * * * displaying what one must presume to be the worst of the activity justifying the injunction * * *. The tape was shot by employees of, or volunteers at, the Aware Woman Clinic on three Saturdays in February and March 1993; * * * The tape was edited down (from approximately 6 to 8 hours of footage to ½ hour) * * * by the Feminist Majority Foundation.

Anyone seriously interested in what this case was about must view that tape. And anyone doing so who is familiar with run-of-the-mine labor picketing, not to mention some other social protests, will be aghast at what it shows we have today permitted an individual judge to do. I will do my best to describe it. [Justice Scalia's description is omitted.]

The videotape and the rest of the record, including the trial court's findings, show that a great many forms of expression and conduct [by demonstrators from both sides] occurred in the vicinity of the clinic. These include singing, chanting, praying, shouting, the playing of music both from the clinic and from handheld boom boxes, speeches, peaceful picketing, communication of familiar political messages, handbilling, persuasive speech directed at opposing groups on the issue of abortion, efforts to persuade individuals not to have abortions, personal testimony, interviews with the press, and media efforts to report on the protest. What the videotape, the rest of the record, and the trial court's findings do not contain is any suggestion of violence near the clinic, nor do they establish any attempt to prevent entry or exit.

II

A

Under this Court's jurisprudence, there is no question that this public sidewalk area is a "public forum," where citizens generally have a First Amendment right to speak. The parties to this case invited the Court to employ one or the other of the two well established standards applied to restrictions upon this First Amendment right. Petitioners claimed the benefit of so-called "strict scrutiny," the standard applied to content-based restrictions: the restriction must be "necessary to serve a compelling state interest and ... narrowly drawn to achieve that end." Perry Education Assn. v. Perry Local Educators' Assn., 460 U.S. 37, 45 (1983). Respondents, on the other hand, contended for what has come to be known as "intermediate scrutiny" (midway between the "strict scrutiny" demanded for content-based regulation of speech, and the "rational basis" standard that is applied-under the Equal Protection Clause-to government regulation of non-speech activities). That standard, applicable to so-called "time, place and manner regulations" of speech, provides that the regulations are permissible so long as they "are content-neutral, are narrowly tailored to serve a significant government interest, and leave open ample alternative channels of communication." *Perry*. The Court adopts neither of these, but creates, brand-new for this abortion-related case, an additional standard that is (supposedly) "somewhat more stringent" than intermediate scrutiny, yet not as "rigorous" as strict scrutiny. The Court does not give this new standard a name, but perhaps we could call it intermediate-intermediate scrutiny. The difference between it and intermediate scrutiny (which the Court acknowledges is inappropriate for injunctive restrictions on speech) is frankly too subtle for me to describe, so I must simply recite it: "whereas intermediate scrutiny requires that the restriction be "narrowly tailored to serve a significant government interest," the new standard requires that the restriction "burden no more speech than necessary to serve a significant government interest."

* * * [A] restriction upon speech imposed by injunction (whether nominally content based or nominally content neutral) is *at least* as deserving of strict scrutiny as a statutory, content-based restriction.

That is so for several reasons: The danger of content-based statutory restrictions upon speech is that they may be designed and used precisely to suppress the ideas in question rather than to achieve any other proper governmental aim. But that same danger exists with injunctions. Although a speech-restricting injunction may not attack content *as content* (in the present case, as I shall discuss, even that is not true), it lends itself just as readily to the targeted suppression of particular ideas. When a judge, on the motion of an employer, enjoins picketing at the site of a labor dispute, he enjoins (and he *knows* he is enjoining) the expression of pro-union views. Such targeting of one or the other side of an ideological dispute cannot readily be achieved in speech-restricting general legislation except by making content the basis of the restriction; it is achieved in speech-restricting injunctions almost invariably. The proceedings before us here illustrate well enough what I mean. The injunction was sought against a single-issue advocacy group by persons and organizations with a business or social interest in suppressing that group's point of view.

The second reason speech-restricting injunctions are at least as deserving of strict scrutiny is obvious enough: they are the product of individual judges rather than of legislatures—and often of judges who have been chagrined by prior disobedience of their orders. The right to free speech should not lightly be placed within the control of a single man or woman. And the third reason is that the injunction is a much more powerful weapon than a statute, and so should be subjected to greater safeguards. Normally, when injunctions are enforced through contempt proceedings, only the defense of factual innocence is available. The collateral bar rule of Walker v. Birmingham, 388 U.S. 307 (1967), eliminates the defense that the injunction itself was unconstitutional.[b] Thus, persons subject to a speech-restricting injunction who have not the money or not the time to lodge an immediate appeal face a Hobson's choice: they must remain silent, since if they speak their First Amendment rights are no defense in subsequent contempt proceedings. This is good reason to require the strictest standard for issuance of such orders.[1] * * *

Finally, though I believe speech-restricting injunctions are dangerous enough to warrant strict scrutiny even when they are not technically content based, I think the injunction in the present case was content based (indeed, viewpoint based) to boot. The Court claims that it was directed, not at those who *spoke* certain things (anti-abortion sentiments), but at those who *did* certain things (violated the earlier injunction). If that were true, then the injunction's residual coverage of "all persons acting in concert or participation with [the named individuals and organizations], or on their behalf" would not include those who

**b.** The collateral bar rule is discussed in chapter 3(C)(3) of the casebook.

**1.** Justice Stevens believes that speech-restricting injunctions "should be judged by a more lenient standard than legislation" because "injunctions apply solely to [those] who, by engaging in illegal conduct, have been judicially deprived of some liberty." Punishing unlawful action by judicial abridgment of First Amendment rights is an interesting concept; perhaps Eighth Amendment rights could be next. I know of no authority for the proposition that restriction of speech, rather than fines or imprisonment, should be the sanction for misconduct. The supposed prior violation of a judicial order was the only thing that rendered petitioners *subject* to a personally tailored restriction on speech in the first place—not in order to punish them, but to protect the public order. To say that their prior violation not only subjects them to being singled out in this fashion, but also loosens the standards for protecting the public order through speech restrictions, is double counting.

merely entertained the same beliefs and wished to express the same views as the named defendants. But the construction given to the injunction by the issuing judge, which is entitled to great weight, is to the contrary: all those who wish to express the same views as the named defendants are deemed to be "acting in concert or participation." Following issuance of the amended injunction, a number of persons were arrested for walking within the 36–foot speech-free zone. At an April 12, 1993, hearing before the trial judge who issued the injunction, the following exchanges occurred:

> Mr. Lacy: "I was wondering how we can—why we were arrested and confined as being in concert with these people that we don't know, when other people weren't, that were in that same buffer zone, and it was kind of selective as to who was picked and who was arrested and who was obtained for the same buffer zone in the same public injunction."
>
> The Court: "Mr. Lacy, I understand that those on the other side of the issue [abortion-rights supporters] were also in the area. If you are referring to them, the Injunction did not pertain to those on the other side of the issue, because *the word in concert with means in concert with those who had taken a certain position in respect to the clinic, adverse to the clinic. If you are saying that is the selective basis that the pro-choice were not arrested when pro-life was arrested, that's the basis of the selection* . . ." (emphasis added).

* * * [Several other colloquys are omitted.] These colloquys leave no doubt that the revised injunction here is tailored to restrain persons distinguished, not by proscribable *conduct*, but by proscribable *views.*

B

I have discussed, in the prior subsection, the policy reasons for giving speech-restricting injunctions, even content-neutral ones, strict scrutiny. There are reasons of precedent as well, which are essentially ignored by the Court.

To begin with, an injunction against speech is the very prototype of the greatest threat to First Amendment values, the prior restraint. As the Chief Justice wrote for the Court last Term: "The term prior restraint is used 'to describe administrative and judicial orders *forbidding* certain communications when issued in advance of the time that such communications are to occur.' . . . [P]ermanent injunctions, *i.e.,*—court orders that actually forbid speech activities—are classic examples of prior restraints."[3] We have said that a "prior restraint on expression comes to this Court with a 'heavy presumption' against its constitutional validity" and have repeatedly struck down speech-restricting injunctions.

3. This statement should be compared with today's opinion, which says that injunctions are not prior restraints (or at least not the nasty kind) if they only restrain speech in a certain area, or if the basis for their issuance is not content but prior unlawful conduct. This distinction has no antecedent in our cases.

At oral argument neither respondents nor the Solicitor General, appearing as *amicus* for respondents, could identify a single speech-injunction case applying mere intermediate scrutiny (which differs little if at all from the Court's intermediate-intermediate scrutiny). We have, in our speech-injunction cases, affirmed both requirements that characterize strict scrutiny: compelling public need and surgical precision of restraint. Even when (unlike in the present case) the First Amendment activity is intermixed with *violent* conduct, " 'precision of regulation' is demanded." NAACP v. Claiborne Hardware Co., 458 U.S. 886, 916 (1982). In Milk Wagon Drivers v. Meadowmoor Dairies, Inc., 312 U.S. 287 (1941), we upheld an injunction prohibiting peaceful picketing, but only because the picketing had been accompanied by 50 instances of window smashing, bombings, stench bombings, destruction of trucks, beatings of drivers, arson, and armed violence. We noted that the "picketing . . . was set in a background of violence" which was "neither episodic nor isolated" and we allowed the ban on picketing "to prevent future coercion," as part of a state court's power "to deal with coercion due to extensive violence." We expressly distinguished the case from those in which there was no "[e]ntanglement with violence" * * *

The utter lack of support for the Court's test in our jurisprudence is demonstrated by the two cases the opinion relies upon. For the proposition that a speech restriction is valid when it "burden[s] no more speech than necessary to accomplish a significant government interest," the Court cites *Claiborne Hardware Co.* and *Carroll*. But as I shall demonstrate in some detail below, *Claiborne* applied a much more stringent test; and the very text of *Carroll* contradicts the Court. In the passage cited, *Carroll* says this: "An order issued in the area of First Amendment rights must be couched in the narrowest terms that will accomplish the pin-pointed objective permitted by constitutional mandate and the essential needs of the public order." That, of course, is strict scrutiny; and it does not remotely resemble the Court's new proposal, for which it is cited as precedential support. "Significant government interest[s]" (referred to in the Court's test) are general, innumerable, and omnipresent-at least one of them will be implicated by any activity set in a public forum. "Essential needs of the public order," on the other hand, are factors of *exceptional* application. And that an injunction "burden no more than necessary" is not nearly as demanding as the requirement that it be couched in the "narrowest terms that will accomplish [a] pin-pointed objective." That the Court should cite this case as its principal authority is an admission that what it announces rests upon no precedent at all.

### III

### A

I turn now from the Court's selection of a constitutional test to its actual application of that test to the facts of the present case. Before doing that, however, it will be helpful—in order to demonstrate how far the Court has departed from past practice—to consider how we proceeded in a relatively recent case that did not involve the disfavored class of abortion protesters. *Claiborne Hardware* involved, like this case, protest demonstrations against private citizens mingling political speech with (what I will assume for the time being existed here) significant illegal behavior.

Writing for the Court, Justice Stevens summarized the events giving rise to the *Claiborne Hardware* litigation: A local chapter of the NAACP, rebuffed by public officials of Port Gibson and Claiborne County in its request for redress of various forms of racial discrimination, began a boycott of local businesses. During the boycott, a young black man was shot and killed in an encounter with Port Gibson police and "sporadic acts of violence ensued." The following day, boycott leader Charles Evers told a group that boycott violators would be disciplined by their own people and warned that the Sheriff "could not sleep with boycott violators at night." He stated at a second gathering that "If we catch any of you going in any of them racist stores, we're gonna break your damn neck." In connection with the boycott, there were marches and picketing (often by small children). "Store watchers" were posted outside boycotted stores to identify those who traded, and their names were read aloud at meetings of the Claiborne County NAACP and published in a mimeographed paper. The chancellor found that those persons were branded traitors, called demeaning names, and socially ostracized. Some had shots fired at their houses, a brick was thrown through a windshield and a garden damaged. Other evidence showed that persons refusing to observe the boycott were beaten, robbed and publicly humiliated (by spanking).

The merchants brought suit against two groups involved in organizing the boycott and numerous individuals. The trial court found tort violations. * * * It issued a broad permanent injunction against the boycotters, enjoining them from stationing "store watchers" at the plaintiffs' business premises; from persuading any person to withhold patronage; from using demeaning and obscene language to or about any person because of his patronage; from picketing or patrolling the premises of any of the respondents; and from using violence against any person or inflicting damage upon any real or personal property. The Mississippi Supreme Court upheld the assessment of liability and the injunction. * * *

Because we recognized that the boycott involved elements of protected First Amendment speech and other elements not so protected, we took upon ourselves a highly particularized burden of review, recognizing a "special obligation on this Court to examine critically the basis on which liability was imposed." "The First Amendment," we noted, "does not protect violence," but when conduct sanctionable by tort liability "occurs in the context of constitutionally protected activity . . . 'precision of regulation' is demanded." Then, criticizing the Mississippi Supreme Court for "broadly assert[ing]—without differentiation—that intimidation, threats, social ostracism, vilification, and traduction were devices used by the defendants to effectuate the boycott," we carefully examined the record for factual support of the findings of liability. While affirming that a "judgment tailored to the consequences of [individuals'] unlawful conduct may be sustained," we said that "mere association with [a] group-absent a specific intent to further an unlawful aim embraced by that group-is an insufficient predicate for liability." We said in conclusion that any characterization of a political protest movement as a violent conspiracy "must be supported by findings that adequately disclose the evidentiary basis for concluding that specific parties agreed to use unlawful means, that carefully identify the impact of such unlawful conduct, and that recognize the importance of avoiding the imposition of punishment for constitutionally protected activity." Because this careful procedure had not been followed by the Mississippi courts, we set aside the entire judgment, including the injunction.

B

I turn now to the Court's performance in the present case. I am content to evaluate it under the lax (intermediate-intermediate scrutiny) standard that the Court has adopted, because even by that distorted light it is inadequate.

The first step under the Court's standard would be, one should think, to identify the "significant government interest" that justifies the portions of the injunction it upheld * * *.

Assuming then that the "significant interests" the Court mentioned must in fact be significant enough to be protected by state law (a concept that includes a prior court order), which law has been, or is about to be, violated, the question arises: what state law is involved here? The only one even mentioned is the original September 30, 1992, injunction,[5] which had been issued (quite rightly, in my judgment) in response to threats by the originally named parties (including petitioners here) that they would " '[p]hysically close down abortion mills,' " "bloc[k] access to clinics," "ignore the law of the State," and "shut down a clinic." * * *

According to the Court, the state court imposed the later injunction's "restrictions on petitioner[s'] ... antiabortion message because they repeatedly violated the court's original order." Surprisingly, the Court accepts this reason as valid, without asking whether the court's findings of fact support it—whether, that is, the acts of which the petitioners stood convicted *were* violations of the original injunction. * * *

[The] only findings and conclusions of the court that could conceivably be considered to relate to a violation of the original injunction * * * all concern behavior by the protestors causing traffic on the street in front of the abortion clinic to slow down, and causing vehicles crossing

5. Justice Souter points out that "petitioners themselves acknowledge that the governmental interests in protection of public safety and order, of the free flow of traffic, and of property rights are reflected in Florida law." This is true but quite irrelevant. As the preceding sentence of text shows, we are concerned here not with state laws in general, but with state laws that these respondents had been found to have violated. There is *no* finding of violation of any of these cited Florida statutes.

the pedestrian right-of-way, between the street and the clinic's parking lot, to slow down or even, occasionally, to stop momentarily while pedestrians got out of the way. As far as appears from the court's findings, all of these results were produced, not by anyone intentionally seeking to block oncoming traffic, but as the incidental effect of persons engaged in the activities of walking a picket line and leafletting on public property in front of the clinic. There is no factual finding that petitioners engaged in any intentional or purposeful obstruction.

Now let us compare these activities with the earlier injunction, violation of which is the asserted justification for the speech-free zone. Walking the return leg of the picket line on the paved portion of Dixie Way (instead of on the sidewalk), and congregating on the unpaved portion of that street, may, for all we know, violate some municipal ordinance (though that was not alleged, and the municipal police evidently did not seek to prevent it); but it assuredly did not violate the earlier injunction, which made no mention of such a prohibition. Causing the traffic along Dixie Way to slow down "in response to the congestion" is also irrelevant; the injunction said nothing about slowing down traffic on public rights of way. It prohibited the doing (or urging) of *only three things:* 1) "physically abusing persons entering, leaving, working or using any services" of the abortion clinic (there is no allegation of that); 2) "trespassing on [or] sitting in" the abortion clinic (there is no allegation of that); and 3) "blocking, impeding or obstructing ingress into or egress from" the abortion clinic.

Only the last of these has any conceivable application here, and it seems to me that it must reasonably be read to refer to *intentionally* blocking, impeding or obstructing, and *not* to such temporary obstruction as may be the normal and incidental consequence of other protest activity. That is obvious, first of all, from the context in which the original injunction was issued-as a response to the petitioners' threatened actions of trespass and blockade, i.e., the physical shutting down of the local clinics. Secondly, if that narrow meaning of intentional blockade, impediment or obstruction was not intended, and if it covered everything up to and including the incidental and "momentary" stopping of entering vehicles by persons leafletting and picketing, the original injunction would have failed the axiomatic requirement that its terms be drawn with precision * * *. And finally, if the original injunction did not have that narrow meaning it would assuredly have been unconstitutional, since it would have prevented speech-related activities that were, insofar as this record shows, neither criminally or civilly unlawful nor inextricably intertwined with unlawful conduct. See *Milk Wagon Drivers*; *Carroll*.

If the original injunction is read as it must be, there is nothing in the trial court's findings to suggest that it was violated. The Court today speaks of "the failure of the first injunction to protect access." But the first injunction did not broadly "protect access." It forbade particular acts that impeded access, to-wit, intentionally "blocking, impeding or obstructing." The trial court's findings identify none of these acts, but only a mild interference with access that is the incidental by-product of leafletting and picketing. There was no sitting down, no linking of arms, no packing en masse in the driveway; the most that can be alleged (and the trial court did not even make this a finding) is that on one occasion protestors "took their time to get out of the way." If that is enough to support this one-man proscription of free speech, the First Amendment is in grave peril.

I almost forgot to address the facts showing prior violation of law (including judicial order) with respect to the other portion of the injunction the Court upholds: the no-noise-within-earshot-of-patients provision. That is perhaps because, amazingly, neither the Florida courts *nor this Court* makes the slightest attempt to link that provision to prior violations of law. The relevant portion of the Court's opinion, Part II–B, simply reasons that hospital patients should not have to be bothered with noise, from political protests or anything else (which is certainly true), and that therefore the noise restrictions could be imposed *by injunction* (which is certainly false). Since such a law is reasonable, in other words, it can be enacted by a single man to bind only a single class of social protesters. The pro-abortion demonstrators who were often making (if respondents' videotape is accurate) more noise than the petitioners, can continue to shout their chants at their opponents exiled across the street to their hearts' content. [When the Court has upheld an injunction restricting noise, it enforced] an *ordinance* not an *injunction*; it applied to *everyone*. * * *

Perhaps there is a local ordinance in Melbourne, Florida, prohibiting loud noise in the vicinity of hospitals and abortion clinics. Or perhaps even a Florida common-law prohibition applies, rendering such noise-making tortious. But the record in this case shows (and, alas, the Court's opinion today demands) neither indication of the existence of any such law nor a finding that it had been violated. The fact that such a law would be reasonable is enough, according to the Court, to justify a single judge in imposing it upon these protesters alone. The First Amendment (and even the common law of injunctions) reels in disbelief.

The Court does not even attempt a response to the point I have made in this section, insofar as the injunction against noise is concerned. * * * With respect to the 36–foot speech-free zone, the Court attempts a response, which displays either a misunderstanding of the point I have made or an effort to recast it into an answerable one. My point does not rely, as the Court's response suggests upon my earlier description of the videotape. That was set forth just for context, to show the reader what suppression of normal and peaceful social protest is afoot here. Nor is it relevant to my point that "petitioners themselves studiously refrained from challenging the factual basis for the injunction." I accept the facts as the Florida court found them; I deny that those facts support its conclusion (set forth as such in a separate portion of its opinion * * *) that the original injunction had been violated. * * *

To sum up: The interests assertedly protected by the supplementary injunction did not include any interest whose impairment was a violation of Florida law or of a Florida-court injunction. Unless the Court intends today to overturn long-settled jurisprudence, that means that the interests cannot possibly qualify as "significant interests" under the Court's new standard.

C

Finally, I turn to the Court's application of the second part of its test: whether the provisions of the injunction "burden no more speech than necessary" to serve the significant interest protected.

This test seems to me amply and obviously satisfied with regard to the noise restriction that the Court approves: it is only such noise as would reach the patients in the abortion clinic that is forbidden—and not even at all times, but only during certain fixed hours and "during surgical procedures and recovery periods." (The latter limitation may raise vagueness and notice problems, but that does not concern us here. * * *)[c] With regard to the 36–foot speech-free zone, however, it seems to me just as obvious that the test which the Court sets for itself has not been met.

Assuming a "significant state interest" of the sort cognizable for injunction purposes (i.e., one protected by a law that has been or is threatened to be violated) in both (1) keeping pedestrians off the paved portion of Dixie Way, and (2) enabling cars to cross the public sidewalk at the clinic's driveways without having to slow down or come to even a "momentary" stop, there are surely a number of ways to protect those interests short of banishing the entire protest demonstration from the 36–foot zone. For starters, the Court could have (for the first time) ordered the demonstrators to stay out of the street (the original injunction did not remotely require that). It could have limited the number of demonstrators permitted on the clinic side of Dixie Way. And it could have forbidden the pickets to walk on the driveways. The Court's only response to these options is that "[t]he state court was convinced that [they would not work] in view of the failure of the first injunction to protect access." But must we accept that conclusion as valid—when the original injunction contained no command (or at the very least no *clear* command) that had been disobeyed, and contained nothing even *related* to staying out of the street? If the "burden no more speech than necessary" requirement can be avoided by merely opining that (for some reason) no lesser restriction than *this* one will be obeyed, it is not much of a requirement at all.

But I need not engage in such precise analysis, since the Court itself admits that the requirement is not to be taken seriously. "The need for a complete buffer zone," it says, "*may be debatable,* but some deference must be given to the state court's familiarity with the facts and the background of the dispute between the parties even under our height-

**c.** How specific an injunction must be is considered in the casebook in chapter 3(B).

ened review." (emphasis added). In application, in other words, the "burden no more speech than is necessary" test has become an "arguably burden no more speech than is necessary" test. This renders the Court's intermediate-intermediate scrutiny not only no *more* stringent than plain old intermediate scrutiny, but considerably *less* stringent. * * *

In his dissent in Korematsu v. United States, 323 U.S. 214 (1944), the case in which this Court permitted the wartime military internment of Japanese–Americans, Justice Jackson wrote the following:

> "A military order, however unconstitutional, is not apt to last longer than the military emergency.... But once a judicial opinion ... rationalizes the Constitution to show that the Constitution sanctions such an order, the Court for all time has validated the principle of racial discrimination in criminal procedure and of transplanting American citizens. The principle then lies about like a loaded weapon ready for the hand of any authority that can bring forward a plausible claim of an urgent need."

What was true of a misguided military order is true of a misguided trial-court injunction. And the Court has left a powerful loaded weapon lying about today.

What we have decided seems to be, and will be reported by the media as, an abortion case. But it will go down in the lawbooks, it will be cited, as a free-speech injunction case—and the damage its novel principles produce will be considerable. The proposition that injunctions against speech are subject to a standard indistinguishable from (unless perhaps more lenient in its application than) the "intermediate scrutiny" standard we have used for "time, place, and manner" legislative restrictions; the notion that injunctions against speech need not be closely tied to any violation of law, but may simply implement sound social policy; and the practice of accepting trial-court conclusions permitting injunctions without considering whether those conclusions are supported by any findings of fact—these latest by-products of our abortion jurisprudence ought to give all friends of liberty great concern. * * *

## *Notes*

1. *The rightful position.* Do the justices agree on the respondents' (clinic's) rightful position? Do the justices agree that the injunction grants more than respondents' rightful position?

2. *The facts.* Assuming Chief Justice Rehnquist's test is appropriate, who best applies it to the 36 foot buffer zone?

3. Is the injunction content based? Is the injunction a prior restraint? Note that the prior restraint doctrine, like the inadequate remedy at law doctrine, sometimes tells would-be plaintiffs that they cannot prevent a violation for which they can get a remedy—through damages or sanctions—after the fact.

4. Assuming that the injunction is neither content based nor a prior restraint, should courts apply a slightly higher level of scrutiny to an injunction that allegedly violates first amendment rights than to a similar statute (as Chief Justice Rehnquist argues), a much higher standard (as Justice Scalia argues), or a lower standard (as Justice Stevens argues)? Writing before the Court decided *Madsen*, one scholar expressed concern about "the injunction's unique concentration of power [in the judge] with its dual potential for articulating public, particularly constitutional, values and for threatening individual liberty." Doug Rendleman, Irreparability Irreparably Damaged, 90 Mich. L. Rev. 1642, 1671 (1992).

5. Unlike the injunction in *Madsen*, most prophylactic injunctions do not raise first amendment issues, but they do impinge on liberty or property. Should courts apply a higher or lower level of scrutiny to an injunction that allegedly unnecessarily impinges on defendants' liberty (but not first amendment rights) than to a similar statute? Suppose, for example, that parents are worried about someone with a record of sex offenses against children who now frequents the neighborhood playground and seek an injunction enjoining that person to stay away from the playground. Should the court evaluate this request against the standard that it would apply to a statute that bars convicted sex offenders from playgrounds?

6. Does *Madsen* require that a prophylactic injunction in an abortion protest case be preceded by the violation of a narrower injunction? Compare NOW v. Operation Rescue, 37 F.3d 646, 649 (D.C.Cir.1994)(holding that a prior violation is needed) with Pro–Choice Network v. Schenck, 67 F.3d 377 (2d Cir. en banc 1995)(violations of a narrower injunction are not a prerequisite for prophylactic relief).

7. Congress has enacted a Freedom of Access to Clinic Entrances Act, which makes it a federal crime to block access to a reproductive health facility or use force or threats against people using the facility. The statute has been upheld, generally on the basis of *Madsen*. See, e.g., American Life League, Inc. v. Reno, 47 F.3d 642, 649 (4th Cir.), cert. denied, ___ U.S. ___, 116 S.Ct. 55, 133 L.Ed.2d 19 (1995).

### *(b) The School Desegregation Example*

The Supreme Court's 1955 order in *Brown II* (supra at p. 100) mandated (1) the dismantling of dual school systems and (2) the admission of all children to unitary schools on a racially nondiscriminatory basis. After over a decade of foot dragging by school boards, the Supreme Court finally demanded prompt action: "the burden on a school board today is to come forward with a plan that promises realistically to work, and promises realistically to work *now*." Green v. School Board of New Kent County, 391 U.S. 430, 439, 88 S.Ct. 1689, 1694, 20 L.Ed.2d 716, 724 (1968). *Green* struck down a desegregation plan that complied only superficially with *Brown II* 's mandate. The school board in *Green* had adopted a "freedom of choice" plan, under which school children could choose which of the county's two schools (the formerly white school or the formerly African–American school) to attend. All the white children chose to attend the previously white school, and 85% of the African–American children chose the African–

American school. A unanimous Court held that the freedom of choice plan perpetuated the racial identification of each school and therefore failed *Brown II*'s first criteria:

> The New Kent School Board's "freedom of choice" plan cannot be accepted as a sufficient step to "effectuate a transition" to a unitary system. * * * [T]he school system remains a dual system. Rather than further the dismantling of the dual system, the plan has operated simply to burden children and their parents with a responsibility which *Brown II* placed squarely on the School Board.

391 U.S. at 441–42, 88 S.Ct. at 1696, 20 L.Ed.2d at 725–26. Did the plan also fail to satisfy the second criteria of *Brown II*'s order—to admit children to unitary schools on a racially nondiscriminatory basis?

Pupil assignments could achieve racially mixed schools relatively quickly and easily in *Green*. There, half the population was African–American, the other half white, all living in racially integrated neighborhoods. An injunction requiring the school board to assign pupils to the nearest school would integrate the schools with little or no busing.

Subsequent cases presented the courts with tougher logistic and conceptual problems. Where neighborhoods are not racially mixed, a school policy that assigns each child to the nearest school will often produce schools that are not racially mixed. In considering whether the school district has a responsibility to achieve integration, courts distinguish between segregation due to official acts or policies, which is called *de jure* segregation, and segregation due to other factors, which is called *de facto* segregation. In *Green,* the two schools in the County had been segregated due to official acts of the school board, in assigning all African–American children to one school and all white children to the other. However, residential segregation, and therefore the school segregation that results from neighborhood pupil assignment, may have many different causes: (a) past de jure discrimination by the school board; (b) past de jure discrimination by other governments, such as the state or the municipality, if it is distinct from the school board; (c) private discrimination by real estate agents, landlords, and sellers of real estate; and (d) African–Americans' own preferences and their lower average income. These factors, in turn, have previous causes—some rooted in private actions, some rooted in public actions.

There was a dispute as to whether de facto as well as de jure segregation is unconstitutional and gives rise to liability. If so, plaintiffs' rightful position is to attend an *integrated* school rather than a school that is *not segregated due to official action*. If not, could a court allow a school that had engaged previously in de jure segregation to adopt a desegregation plan that assigned children to schools on a nondiscriminatory basis, yet still did not produce tangible integration? Or could the court require a desegregation plan that produced integrated schools out of segregated residential patterns, even though plaintiffs have no right, per se, to integrated schools?

## SWANN v. CHARLOTTE–MECKLENBURG BOARD OF EDUCATION

Supreme Court of the United States, 1971.
402 U.S. 1, 91 S.Ct. 1267, 28 L.Ed.2d 554.

MR. CHIEF JUSTICE BURGER delivered the opinion of the Court.

* * * This case and those argued with it arose in States having a long history of maintaining two sets of schools in a single school system deliberately operated to carry out a governmental policy to separate pupils in schools solely on the basis of race. That was what *Brown v. Board of Education* was all about. These cases present us with the problem of defining in more precise terms than heretofore the scope of the duty of school authorities and district courts in implementing *Brown I* and the mandate to eliminate dual systems and establish unitary systems at once. * * *

I

The Charlotte–Mecklenburg school system, the 43d largest in the Nation, encompasses the city of Charlotte and surrounding Mecklenburg County, North Carolina. The area is large * * * spanning roughly 22 miles east-west and 36 miles north-south. During the 1968–1969 school year the system served more than 84,000 pupils in 107 schools. Approximately 71% of the pupils were found to be white and 29% Negro. [Most of the] Negro students attended * * * schools which were either totally Negro or more than 99% Negro.

This situation came about under a desegregation plan approved by the District Court at the commencement of the present litigation in 1965, based upon geographic zoning with a free-transfer provision. The present proceedings were initiated in September 1968 by petitioner Swann's motion for further relief based on *Green v. County School Board*. All parties now agree that in 1969 the system fell short of achieving the unitary school system that [*Green* requires].

The District Court * * * found that residential patterns in the city and county resulted in part from federal, state, and local government action other than school board decisions. School board action based on these patterns, for example, by locating schools in Negro residential areas and fixing the size of the schools to accommodate the needs of immediate neighborhoods, resulted in segregated education. These findings were subsequently accepted by the Court of Appeals.

* * * [T]he District Court was presented with two alternative pupil assignment plans—the finalized "board plan" and the "Finger plan."

*The Board Plan.* * * * The board plan proposed substantial assignment of Negroes to nine of the system's 10 high schools, producing 17% to 36% Negro population in each. The projected Negro attendance at the 10th school, Independence, was 2%. The proposed attendance zones for the high schools were typically shaped like wedges of a pie, extending outward from the center of the city to the suburban and rural areas of the county in order to afford residents of the center city area [which had the largest minority concentration] access to outlying schools.

As for junior high schools, the board plan rezoned the 21 school areas so that in 20 the Negro attendance would range from 0% to 38%. The other school, located in the heart of the Negro residential area, was left with an enrollment of 90% Negro.

The board plan with respect to elementary schools relied entirely upon gerrymandering of geographic zones. More than half of the Negro elementary pupils were left in nine schools that were 86% to 100% Negro; approximately half of the white elementary pupils were assigned to schools 86% to 100% white.

*The Finger Plan.* The plan submitted by the court-appointed expert, Dr. Finger, adopted the school board zoning plan for senior high schools with one modification: it required that an additional 300 Negro students be transported from the Negro residential area of the city to the nearly all-white Independence High School. [The Finger plan also achieved greater integration of the junior high schools and elementary schools through busing. The District Court adopted the Finger plan.] * * *

On appeal the Court of Appeals affirmed the District Court's order as to * * * the secondary school plans, but vacated the order respecting elementary schools. While agreeing that the District Court properly disapproved the board plan concerning these schools, the Court of Appeals feared that the [busing of elementary school students] would place an unreasonable burden on the board and the system's pupils. * * *

II * * *

Over the 16 years since *Brown II,* many difficulties were encountered in implementation of the basic constitutional requirement that the State not discriminate between public school children on the basis of their race. Nothing in our national experience prior to 1955 prepared anyone for dealing with changes and adjustments of the magnitude and complexity encountered since then. Deliberate resistance of some to the Court's mandates has impeded the good-faith efforts of others to bring school systems into compliance. * * *

III

The objective today remains to eliminate from the public schools all vestiges of state-imposed segregation. * * *

If school authorities fail in their affirmative obligations under these holdings, judicial authority may be invoked. Once a right and a violation have been shown, the scope of a district court's equitable powers to remedy past wrongs is broad, for breadth and flexibility are inherent in equitable remedies. * * * Hecht Co. v. Bowles, 321 U.S. 321, 329–330, 64 S.Ct. 587, 592, 88 L.Ed. 754 (1944).

* * * [A] school desegregation case does not differ fundamentally from other cases involving the framing of equitable remedies to repair the denial of a constitutional right. The task is to correct, by a balancing of the individual and collective interests, the condition that offends the Constitution.

In seeking to define even in broad and general terms how far this remedial power extends it is important to remember that judicial powers may be exercised only on the basis of a constitutional violation. Remedial judicial authority does not put judges automatically in the shoes of school authorities whose powers are plenary. Judicial authority enters only when local authority defaults.

School authorities are traditionally charged with broad power to formulate and implement educational policy and might well conclude, for example, that in order to prepare students to live in a pluralistic society each school should have a prescribed ratio of Negro to white students reflecting the proportion for the district as a whole. To do this as an educational policy is within the broad discretionary powers of school authorities; absent a finding of a constitutional violation, however, that would not be within the authority of a federal court. As with any equity case, the nature of the violation determines the scope of the remedy. In default by the school authorities of their obligation to proffer acceptable remedies, a district court has broad power to fashion a remedy that will assure a unitary school system. * * *

IV * * *

The construction of new schools and the closing of old ones are two of the most important functions of local school authorities and also two of the most complex. * * * The result * * *, when combined with one technique or another of student assignment, will determine the racial composition of the student body in each school in the system. Over the long run, the consequences of the choices will be far reaching. People gravitate toward school facilities, just as schools are located in response to the needs of people. The location of schools may thus influence the patterns of residential development of a metropolitan area and have important impact on composition of inner-city neighborhoods.

In the past, choices in this respect have been used as a potent weapon for creating or maintaining a state-segregated school system. In addition to the classic pattern of building schools specifically intended for Negro or white students, school authorities have sometimes, since *Brown*, closed schools which appeared likely to become racially mixed through changes in neighborhood residential patterns. This was sometimes accompanied by building new schools in the areas of white suburban expansion farthest from Negro population centers in order to maintain the separation of the races with a minimum departure from the formal principles of "neighborhood zoning." Such a policy does more than simply influence the short-run composition of the student body of a new school. It may well promote segregated residential patterns which, when combined with "neighborhood zoning," further lock the school system into the mold of separation of the races. Upon a proper showing a district court may consider this in fashioning a remedy. * * *

V

The central issue in this case is that of student assignment, and there are essentially four problem areas: * * *

(1) *Racial Balances or Racial Quotas.* * * * If we were to read the holding of the District Court to require, as a matter of substantive constitutional right, any particular degree of racial balance or mixing, that approach would be disapproved and we would be obliged to reverse. The constitutional command to desegregate schools does not mean that every school in every community must always reflect the racial composition of the school system as a whole. * * *

(2) *One-race Schools.* The record in this case reveals the familiar phenomenon that in metropolitan areas minority groups are often found concentrated in one part of the city. In some circumstances certain schools may remain all or largely of one race until new schools can be provided or neighborhood patterns change. Schools all or predominantly of one race in a district of mixed population will require close scrutiny to determine that school assignments are not part of state-enforced segregation.

In light of the above, it should be clear that the existence of some small number of one-race, or virtually one-race, schools within a district is not in and of itself the mark of a system that still practices segregation by law. The district judge or school authorities should make every effort to achieve the greatest possible degree of actual desegregation and will thus necessarily be concerned with the elimination of one-race schools. No per se rule can adequately embrace all the difficulties of reconciling the competing interests involved; but in a system with a history of segregation the need for remedial criteria of sufficient specificity to assure a school authority's compliance with its constitutional duty warrants a presumption against schools that are substantially disproportionate in their racial composition. Where the school authority's proposed plan for conversion from a dual to a unitary system contemplates the continued existence of some schools that are all or predominantly of one race, * * * [t]he court should scrutinize such schools, and the burden upon the school authorities will be to satisfy the court that their racial composition is not the result of present or past discriminatory action on their part. * * *

(3) *Remedial Altering of Attendance Zones.* The maps submitted in these cases graphically demonstrate that one of the principal tools employed by school planners and by courts to break up the dual school system has been a frank—and sometimes drastic—gerrymandering of school districts and attendance zones. An additional step was [assigning students to a school not only from its neighborhood but also from a distant neighborhood] to accomplish the transfer of Negro students out of formerly segregated Negro schools and transfer of white students to

formerly all-Negro schools. * * * As an interim corrective measure, this cannot be said to be beyond the broad remedial powers of a court.

Absent a constitutional violation there would be no basis for judicially ordering assignment of students on a racial basis. All things being equal, with no history of discrimination, it might well be desirable to assign pupils to schools nearest their homes. But all things are not equal in a system that has been deliberately constructed and maintained to enforce racial segregation. * * *

In this area, we must of necessity rely to a large extent, as this Court has for more than 16 years, on the informed judgment of the district courts in the first instance and on courts of appeals. * * *

(4) *Transportation of Students.* The scope of permissible transportation of students as an implement of a remedial decree has never been defined by this Court and by the very nature of the problem it cannot be defined with precision. * * * Bus transportation has been an integral part of the public education system for years, and was perhaps the single most important factor in the transition from the one-room schoolhouse to the consolidated school. * * *

[The amount of busing under the District Court's plan] compares favorably with the transportation plan previously operated in Charlotte * * *.

An objection to transportation of students may have validity when the time or distance of travel is so great as to either risk the health of the children or significantly impinge on the educational process. District courts must weigh the soundness of any transportation plan in light of what is said in subdivisions (1), (2), and (3) above. It hardly needs stating that the limits on time of travel will vary with many factors, but probably with none more than the age of the students. The reconciliation of competing values in a desegregation case is, of course, a difficult task with many sensitive facets but fundamentally no more so than remedial measures courts of equity have traditionally employed.

VI

The Court of Appeals, searching for a term to define the equitable remedial power of the district courts, used the term "reasonableness." In *Green,* this Court used the term "feasible" and by implication, "workable," "effective," and "realistic" in the mandate to develop "a plan that promises realistically to work, and ... to work *now.*" On the facts of this case, we are unable to conclude that the order of the District Court is not reasonable, feasible and workable. However, in seeking to define the scope of remedial power or the limits on remedial power of courts in an area as sensitive as we deal with here, words are poor instruments to convey the sense of basic fairness inherent in equity. Substance, not semantics, must govern, and we have sought to suggest the nature of limitations without frustrating the appropriate scope of equity. * * *

The order of the District Court * * * is * * * affirmed. * * *

## *Notes*

1. The Court in *Swann* held that only de jure segregation gives rise to liability, but called for "the greatest possible degree of actual desegregation"—which would surely be an appropriate remedy if de facto segregation were the standard of liability. The challenge of *Swann* is to explain this seeming disparity. With the standard of liability being de jure and not de facto, what is the appropriate remedy against school authorities on the facts of *Swann*?

a. *Make the school board assign students to schools on a color-blind basis.* This remedy permits pupil assignment based upon principles such as minimizing pupils travel time. Due to housing patterns, such assignments could lead to one race schools.

b. *Make the schools admit students on a color-blind basis, but nonetheless require color-conscious action to correct for residential segregation caused by past school segregation.* This remedy allows color-conscious action to repair racial imbalances traceable to past violations by the defendants. Such a remedy would be far more limited than that in *Swann*. According to Dean Peter Shane, *Swann*

> clearly did more than restore the pattern of school attendance that would have prevailed but for the school authorities' racially segregative acts. * * * Although the school board's school site location decisions undoubtedly exacerbated the perpetuation of racial imbalance in the public schools after 1954, Charlotte–Mecklenburg was an urban school district with significant residential segregation that neither the district court nor the court of appeals attributed entirely to school board action. Although the precise contribution of state-required segregation to the pattern of school attendance in 1971 might have been impossible to prove, it is unlikely that the schools would all have been racially balanced, even without official segregation.

Peter M. Shane, School Desegregation Remedies and the Fair Governance of Schools, 132 U.Pa.L.Rev. 1041, 1065–66 (1984).

c. *Make the schools admit students on a color-blind basis, but nonetheless require color-conscious action to correct for residential segregation caused by any governmental unit, whether the school board or any other entity.* Rizzo v. Goode held that a defendant that is not a proven violator cannot be made responsible for correcting the violations of others. A possible corollary is that a proven violator cannot be made responsible for correcting the separate violations of others. A series of recent school desegregation cases tend to suggest that a school board will be held responsible only for correcting its own violations and not actions of other public or private actors. E.g., Freeman v. Pitts, 503 U.S. 467, 112 S.Ct. 1430, 118 L.Ed.2d 108 (1992) (reproduced infra at p. 256), Missouri v. Jenkins (*Jenkins III* ), 515 U.S. ___, 115 S.Ct. 2038, 132 L.Ed.2d 63 (1995) (reproduced infra at p. 157).

d. *Make defendants achieve racial balance within the school district.* Dean Shane contends that the Court has never clearly explained why its remedy seems broader than the right that it has identified. He suggests an explanation:

> Where minority students are systematically vulnerable to hostile or insensitive treatment, the racial separation of schools effectively subjugates minority students in the competition for educational resources and deprives them of any basis for reasonable confidence in the evenhanded administration of their schools.

132 U.Pa.L.Rev. at 1043. On this basis, the breadth of the remedy is prophylactic. There are hints of such prophylactic thinking in *Swann*. For example, the Court states that "in a system with a history of segregation the need for remedial criteria of sufficient specificity to assure a school authority's compliance with its constitutional duty warrants a presumption against schools that are substantially disproportionate in their racial composition." Swann v. Charlotte–Mecklenburg Board of Education, 402 U.S. 1, 26, 91 S.Ct. 1267, 1281, 28 L.Ed.2d 554 (1971). The prophylactic rationale does not necessarily mean that the broader remedy is appropriate indefinitely. See also Board of Education v. Dowell, 498 U.S. 237, 111 S.Ct. 630, 112 L.Ed.2d 715 (1991).

e. *Make defendants achieve racial balance throughout the metropolitan area.* This possibility is discussed in Missouri v. Jenkins (Jenkins III), reproduced infra.

Can you think of any other rationale for the breadth of the remedy in *Swann*?

For an excellent discussion of these possibilities, see Mark G. Yudof, School Desegregation: Legal Realism, Reasoned Elaboration, and Social Science Research in the Supreme Court, 42 L. & Contemp.Probs. 57 (Autumn 1978).

2. In comparison to these various approaches to *Swann*, consider the following approaches to a case in which an employee who is contractually obligated to keep secret an employer's client information, quits, takes a job with a rival, and divulges information about one client:

(a) Order the former employee not to divulge further client information.

(b) Order the employee not to divulge further client information and the rival not to go after that one client.

(c) Order the employee not to work for the rival.

E.g., PepsiCo. v. Redmond, 54 F.3d 1262 (7th Cir.1995)(former employee ordered not to work for rival because of likelihood that trade secrets would be revealed).

3. The preceding notes dealt with ways in which the remedy might have given plaintiffs more than their rightful position in terms of substance. Plaintiffs certainly got more than their rightful position in terms of procedure in that *Swann* does not remand the design of the desegregation plan to the school board, although plaintiffs rightful position is to have the school board treat them in a way that complies with the fourteenth amendment. Is supplanting the school board consistent with the rightful position concept? Professor William Fletcher argues that courts are supposed to supplant state

and local government only to the extent that those governments have demonstrated that they cannot be trusted to remedy the wrong. William A. Fletcher, The Discretionary Constitution: Institutional Remedies and Judicial Legitimacy, 91 Yale L.J. 635, 649–650 (1982).

4. *Swann* says that how far beyond the rightful position the injunction may take plaintiffs and push defendants is a question without a specific answer. However, its references to balancing and citation to *Hecht* suggest that the analysis should be similar to that done when considering when relief may achieve less than plaintiff's rightful position. The Court shows much more solicitude to the non violator school children than the violator school board.

---

*Swann*, which was decided during an era of evident resistance to the commands of *Brown*, focused on thwarting that resistance by making clear that the school boards had to take real action. *Missouri v. Jenkins*, decided during an era of concern about the scope of judicial authority, focused on defining the outer limits of the duty to desegregate.

## MISSOURI v. JENKINS (*JENKINS III*)

Supreme Court of the United States, 1995.
515 U.S. ___, 115 S.Ct. 2038, 132 L.Ed.2d 63.

CHIEF JUSTICE REHNQUIST delivered the opinion of the Court. * * *

I * * *

This case has been before the same United States District Judge since 1977. Missouri v. Jenkins, 491 U.S. 274, 276, 109 S.Ct. 2463, 105 L.Ed.2d 229 (1989)(*Jenkins I*). In that year, the Kansas City, Missouri, School District (KCMSD), the school board, and the children of two school board members brought suit against the State and other defendants. Plaintiffs alleged that the State, the surrounding suburban school districts (SSD's), and various federal agencies had caused and perpetuated a system of racial segregation in the schools of the Kansas City metropolitan area. The District Court realigned the KCMSD as a nominal defendant and certified as a class, present and future KCMSD students. The KCMSD brought a cross-claim against the State for its failure to eliminate the vestiges of its prior dual school system.

After a trial that lasted 7 ½ months, the District Court dismissed the case against the federal defendants and the SSD's, but determined that the State and the KCMSD were liable for an intradistrict violation, i.e., they had operated a segregated school system within the KCMSD. The District Court determined that prior to 1954 "Missouri mandated segregated schools for black and white children." * * *

The District Court determined that "[s]egregation ha[d] caused a system wide *reduction* in student achievement in the schools of the KCMSD." The District Court made no particularized findings regarding the extent that student achievement had been reduced or what portion of that reduction was attributable to segregation. The District Court also identified 25 schools within the KCMSD that had enrollments of 90% or more black students.

The District Court, pursuant to plans submitted by the KCMSD and the State, ordered a wide range of quality education programs for all students attending the KCMSD. * * * [Under these programs, all schools in the district would get reduced class size, full-day kindergarten, expanded summer school, before- and after-school tutoring, an early childhood development program, and substantial yearly cash grants.] The total cost for these quality education programs has exceeded $220 million.

The District Court also set out to desegregate the KCMSD but believed that "[t]o accomplish desegregation within the boundary lines of a school district whose enrollment remains 68.3% black is a difficult task." Because it had found no interdistrict violation, the District Court could not order mandatory interdistrict redistribution of students between the KCMSD and the surrounding SSD's. * * * Milliken v. Bradley, 418 U.S. 717 (1974)(*Milliken I*). The District Court refused to order additional mandatory student reassignments because they would "increase the instability of the KCMSD and reduce the potential for desegregation." * * *

In November 1986, the District Court approved a comprehensive magnet school and capital improvements plan and held the State and the KCMSD jointly and severally liable for its funding. Under the District Court's plan, every senior high school, every middle school, and one-half of the elementary schools were converted into magnet schools. The District Court adopted the magnet-school program to "provide a greater educational opportunity to *all* KCMSD students," and because it believed "that the proposed magnet plan [was] so attractive that it would draw non-minority students from the private schools who have abandoned or avoided the KCMSD, and draw in additional non-minority students from the suburbs." * * * Since its inception, the magnet school program has operated at a cost, including magnet transportation, in excess of $448 million. In April 1993, the District Court considered, but ultimately rejected, the plaintiffs' and the KCMSD's proposal seeking approval of a long-range magnet renewal program that included a 10–year budget of well over $500 million, funded by the State and the KCMSD on a joint-and-several basis.

In June 1985, the District Court ordered substantial capital improvements to combat the deterioration of the KCMSD's facilities. In formulating its capital-improvements plan, the District Court dismissed as "irrelevant" the "State's argument that the present condition of the facilities [was] not traceable to unlawful segregation." Instead, the District Court focused on its responsibility to "remed[y] the vestiges of segregation" and to "implemen[t] a desegregation plan which w[ould] maintain and attract non-minority members." [The total cost of the program was over $540 million.]

As part of its desegregation plan, the District Court has ordered salary assistance to the KCMSD. * * *[T]he District Court has ordered salary assistance to all but three of the approximately 5,000 KCMSD employees. The total cost of this component of the desegregation remedy since 1987 is over $200 million.

The District Court's desegregation plan has been described as the most ambitious and expensive remedial program in the history of school desegregation. The annual cost per pupil at the KCMSD far exceeds that of the neighboring SSD's or of any school district in Missouri. * * * These massive expenditures have financed

> "high schools in which every classroom will have air conditioning, an alarm system, and 15 microcomputers; a 2,000–square-foot planetarium; green houses and vivariums; a 25–acre farm with an air-conditioned meeting room for 104 people; a Model United Nations wired for language translation; broadcast capable radio and television studios with an editing and animation lab; a temperature controlled art gallery; movie editing and screening rooms; a 3,500–square-foot dust-free diesel mechanics room; 1,875–square-foot elementary school animal rooms for use in a zoo project; swimming pools; and numerous other facilities."

Missouri v. Jenkins (*Jenkins II*), 495 U.S. 33, 77, 110 S.Ct. 1651, 1676–77, 109 L.Ed.2d 31 (1990)(Kennedy, J., concurrence). Not surprisingly, the cost of this remedial plan has "far exceeded KCMSD's budget, or for that matter, its authority to tax." The State, through the operation of joint-and-several liability, has borne the brunt of these costs. The District Court candidly has acknowledged that it has "allowed the District planners to dream" and "provided the mechanism for th[ose] dreams to be realized." * * *

II

With this background, we turn to the present controversy. First, the State has challenged the District Court's requirement that it fund salary increases for KCMSD instructional and noninstructional staff. The State claimed that funding for salaries was beyond the scope of the District Court's remedial authority. Second, the State has challenged the District Court's order requiring it to continue to fund the remedial quality education programs for the 1992–1993 school year. The State contended that under Freeman v. Pitts, 503 U.S. 467 (1992), it had achieved partial unitary status with respect to the quality education programs already in place.[a] * * * [The District Court and Court of Appeals rejected the state's claims. The Court of Appeals] found significant the District Court's determination that although "there had been a trend of improvement in academic achievement, ... the school district

a. *Freeman* is reproduced infra at p. 256.

was far from reaching its maximum potential because KCMSD is still at or below national norms at many grade levels." * * *

The Court of Appeals denied rehearing en banc, with five judges dissenting. * * *

Because of the importance of the issues, we granted certiorari to consider the following: (1) whether the District Court exceeded its constitutional authority when it granted salary increases to virtually all instructional and noninstructional employees of the KCMSD, and (2) whether the District Court properly relied upon the fact that student achievement test scores had failed to rise to some unspecified level when it declined to find that the State had achieved partial unitary status as to the quality education programs.

III

Respondents argue that the State may no longer challenge the District Court's remedy, and in any event, the propriety of the remedy is not before the Court. We disagree on both counts. In *Jenkins II*, we granted certiorari to review the manner in which the District Court had funded this desegregation remedy. [*Jenkins II* is reproduced in chapter 3(C)(5).] Because we had denied certiorari on the State's challenge to review the scope of the remedial order, we resisted the State's efforts to challenge the scope of the remedy. Thus, we neither "approv[ed]" nor "disapprov[ed], the Court of Appeals' conclusion that the District Court's remedy was proper."

* * * An analysis of the permissible scope of the District Court's remedial authority is necessary for a proper determination of whether the order of salary increases is beyond the District Court's remedial authority, and thus, it is an issue subsidiary to our ultimate inquiry. * * *

Almost 25 years ago, in Swann v. Charlotte–Mecklenburg Bd. of Ed., 402 U.S. 1 (1971), * * * [a]lthough recognizing the discretion that must necessarily adhere in a district court in fashioning a remedy [in a school desegregation case], we also recognized the limits on such remedial power * * *

Three years later, in [Milliken v. Bradley, 418 U.S. 717 (1974) (*Milliken I*)], we held that a District Court had exceeded its authority in fashioning interdistrict relief where the surrounding school districts had not themselves been guilty of any constitutional violation. We said that a desegregation remedy "is necessarily designed, as all remedies are, to restore the victims of discriminatory conduct to the position they would have occupied in the absence of such conduct." "[W]ithout an interdistrict violation and interdistrict effect, there is no constitutional wrong calling for an interdistrict remedy." We also rejected "[t]he suggestion ... that schools which have a majority of Negro students are not 'desegregated,' whatever the makeup of the school district's population and however neutrally the district lines have been drawn and administered."

Three years later, in Milliken v. Bradley, 433 U.S. 267 (1977)(*Milliken II*), we articulated a three-part framework derived from our prior cases to guide district courts in the exercise of their remedial authority.

> In the first place, like other equitable remedies, the nature of the desegregation remedy is to be determined by the nature and scope of the constitutional violation. *Swann.* The remedy must therefore be related to 'the condition alleged to offend the Constitution.... ' *Milliken I.* Second, the decree must indeed be *remedial* in nature, that is, it must be designed as nearly as possible 'to restore the victims of discriminatory conduct to the position they would have occupied in the absence of such conduct.' *Milliken I.* Third, the federal courts in devising a remedy must take into account the interests of state and local authorities in managing their own affairs, consistent with the Constitution.

We added that the "principle that the nature and scope of the remedy are to be determined by the violation means simply that federal-court decrees must directly address and relate to the constitutional violation itself." * * *

Proper analysis of the District Court's orders challenged here, then, must rest upon their serving as proper means to the end of restoring the victims of discriminatory conduct to the position they would have occupied in the absence of that conduct and their eventual restoration of "state and local authorities to the control of a school system that is operating in compliance with the Constitution." We turn to that analysis.

The State argues that the order approving salary increases is beyond the District Court's authority because it was crafted to serve an "interdistrict goal," in spite of the fact that the constitutional violation in this case is "intradistrict" in nature. * * *

Here, the District Court has found, and the Court of Appeals has affirmed, that this case involved no interdistrict constitutional violation that would support interdistrict relief. Thus, the proper response by the District Court should have been to eliminate to the extent practicable the vestiges of prior de jure segregation within the KCMSD: a system-wide reduction in student achievement and the existence of 25 racially identifiable schools with a population of over 90% black students.

The District Court and Court of Appeals, however, have felt that because the KCMSD's enrollment remained 68.3% black, a purely intra district remedy would be insufficient. * * *

Instead of seeking to remove the racial identity of the various schools within the KCMSD, the District Court has set out on a program to create a school district that was equal to or superior to the surrounding SSD's. * * * The District Court's remedial order has all but made the KCMSD itself into a magnet district.

We previously have approved of intradistrict desegregation remedies involving magnet schools. *Milliken II.* * * *

The District Court's remedial plan in this case * * * [seeks] to attract nonminority students from outside the KCMSD schools. But this *inter*district goal is beyond the scope of the *intra*district violation identified by the District Court. In effect, the District Court has devised a remedy to accomplish indirectly what it admittedly lacks the remedial authority to mandate directly: the interdistrict transfer of students. * * *

[In *Milliken I*, Justice Stewart, who provided the Court's fifth vote,] wrote separately to underscore his understanding of that decision. In describing the requirements for imposing an "interdistrict" remedy, Justice Stewart stated: "Were it to be shown, for example, that state officials had contributed to the separation of the races by drawing or redrawing school district lines; by transfer of school units between districts; or by purposeful, racially discriminatory use of state housing or zoning laws, then a decree calling for the transfer of pupils across district lines or for restructuring of district lines might well be appropriate. In this case, however, no such interdistrict violation was shown." Justice Stewart concluded that the Court properly rejected the District Court's interdistrict remedy because "[t]here were no findings that the differing racial composition between schools in the city and in the outlying suburbs was caused by official activity of any sort."

* * * Nothing in *Milliken I* suggests that the District Court in that case could have circumvented the limits on its remedial authority by requiring the State of Michigan, a constitutional violator, to implement a magnet program designed to achieve the same interdistrict transfer of students that we held was beyond its remedial authority. Here, the District Court has done just that. * * *

Respondents argue that the District Court's reliance upon desegregative attractiveness is justified in light of the District Court's statement that segregation has "led to white flight from the KCMSD to suburban districts." The lower courts' "findings" as to "white flight" are both inconsistent internally[7], and inconsistent with the typical supposition, bolstered here by the record evidence, that "white flight" may result from desegregation, not *de jure* segregation.[8] The United States, as *amicus curiae*, argues that the District Court's finding that "de jure segregation in the KCMSD caused white students to leave the system . . . is not inconsistent with the district court's earlier conclusion that the suburban districts did nothing to cause this white flight and therefore could not be included in a mandatory interdistrict remedy." But the

**7.** Compare * * * Jenkins, 807 F.2d, at 662 ("[N]one of the alleged discriminatory actions committed by the State or the federal defendants ha[s] caused any significant current interdistrict segregation"), with Jenkins v. Missouri, 855 F.2d 1295, 1302 (C.A.8 1988)("These holdings are bolstered by the district court's findings that the preponderance of black students in the district was due to the State and KCMSD's constitutional violations, which caused white flight").

**8.** "During the hearing on the liability issue in this case there was an abundance of evidence that many residents of the KCMSD left the district and moved to the suburbs because of the district's efforts to integrate its schools."

District Court's earlier findings, affirmed by the Court of Appeals, were not so limited:

> [C]ontrary to the argument of [plaintiffs] that the [district court] looked only to the culpability of the SSDs, the scope of the order is far broader.... It noted that only the schools in one district were affected and that the remedy must be limited to that system. In examining the cause and effect issue, the court noted that "not only is plaintiff's evidence here blurred as to cause and effect, there is no 'careful delineation of the extent of the effect.' " ... The district court thus dealt not only with the issue whether the SSDs were constitutional violators but also whether there were significant interdistrict segregative effects.... When it did so, it made specific findings that negate current significant interdistrict effects, and concluded that the requirements of *Milliken* had not been met.

Jenkins v. Missouri, 807 F.2d 657, 672 (C.A.8 1986)(affirming, by an equally divided court, the District Court's findings and conclusion that there was no interdistrict violation or interdistrict effect)(en banc).[9]

In *Freeman*, we stated that "[t]he vestiges of segregation that are the concern of the law in a school case may be subtle and intangible but nonetheless they must be so real that they have a causal link to the *de jure* violation being remedied." The record here does not support the District Court's reliance on "white flight" as a justification for a permissible expansion of its intradistrict remedial authority through its pursuit of desegregative attractiveness. See *Milliken I*; see also Dayton Bd. of Ed. v. Brinkman, 433 U.S. 406, 417 (1977)(*Dayton I*).

Justice Souter claims that our holding effectively overrules Hills v. Gautreaux, 425 U.S. 284 (1976). In *Gautreaux*, the Federal Department of Housing and Urban Development (HUD) was found to have participated, along with a local housing agency, in establishing and maintaining a racially segregated public housing program. After the Court of Appeals ordered " 'the adoption of a comprehensive metropolitan area plan,' " we granted certiorari to consider the "permissibility in the light of [*Milliken I*] of 'inter-district relief for discrimination in public housing in the absence of a finding of an inter-district violation.' " Because the "relevant geographic area for the purposes of the [plaintiffs'] housing options [was] the Chicago housing market, not the Chicago city limits," we concluded that "a metropolitan area remedy ... [was] not impermissible as a matter of law." 425 U.S. at 298, n.13 (distinguishing *Milliken I*, in part, because prior cases had established that racial segregation in

9. Justice Souter construes the Court of Appeals' determination to mean that the violations by the State and the KCMSD did not cause segregation within the limits of each of the SSD's. But the Court of Appeals would not have decided this question at the behest of these plaintiffs-present and future KCMSD students-who have no standing to challenge segregation within the confines of the SSD's. Ergo, the Court of Appeals meant exactly what it said: the requirements of *Milliken I* had not been met because the District Court's specific findings "negate current significant interdistrict effects."

schools is "to be dealt with in terms of 'an established geographic and administrative school system' ").

In *Gautreaux*, we did not obligate the District Court to "subjec[t] HUD to measures going beyond the geographical or political boundaries of its violation." Instead, we cautioned that our holding "should not be interpreted as requiring a metropolitan area order." We reversed appellate factfinding by the Court of Appeals that would have mandated a metropolitan-area remedy, and remanded the case back to the District Court " 'for additional evidence and for further consideration of the issue of metropolitan area relief.' "

Our decision today is fully consistent with *Gautreaux*. A district court seeking to remedy an *intra*district violation that has not "directly caused" significant interdistrict effects, *Milliken I*, exceeds its remedial authority if it orders a remedy with an interdistrict purpose. This conclusion follows directly from *Milliken II*, decided one year after *Gautreaux*, where we reaffirmed the bedrock principle that "federal-court decrees exceed appropriate limits if they are aimed at eliminating a condition that does not violate the Constitution or does not flow from such a violation." In *Milliken II*, we also emphasized that "federal courts in devising a remedy must take into account the interests of state and local authorities in managing their own affairs, consistent with the Constitution." *Gautreaux*, however, involved the imposition of a remedy upon a federal agency. Thus, it did not raise the same federalism concerns that are implicated when a federal court issues a remedial order against a State.

The District Court's pursuit of "desegregative attractiveness" cannot be reconciled with our cases placing limitations on a district court's remedial authority. It is certainly theoretically possible that the greater the expenditure per pupil within the KCMSD, the more likely it is that some unknowable number of nonminority students not presently attending schools in the KCMSD will choose to enroll in those schools. Under this reasoning, however, every increased expenditure, whether it be for teachers, noninstructional employees, books, or buildings, will make the KCMSD in some way more attractive, and thereby perhaps induce nonminority students to enroll in its schools. But this rationale is not susceptible to any objective limitation. This case provides numerous examples demonstrating the limitless authority of the District Court operating under this rationale. In short, desegregative attractiveness has been used "as the hook on which to hang numerous policy choices about improving the quality of education in general within the KCMSD."

Nor are there limits to the duration of the District Court's involvement. The expenditures per pupil in the KCMSD currently far exceed those in the neighboring SSD's. Sixteen years after this litigation began, the District Court recognized that the KCMSD has yet to offer a viable method of financing the "wonderful school system being built." Each additional program ordered by the District Court—and financed by the State—to increase the "desegregative attractiveness" of the school district makes the KCMSD more and more dependent on additional funding from the State; in turn, the greater the KCMSD's dependence on state funding, the greater its reliance on continued supervision by the District Court. But our cases recognize that local autonomy of school districts is a vital national tradition, and that a district court must strive to restore state and local authorities to the control of a school system operating in compliance with the Constitution. See *Freeman*; *Dowell*.

The District Court's pursuit of the goal of "desegregative attractiveness" results in so many imponderables and is so far removed from the task of eliminating the racial identifiability of the schools within the KCMSD that we believe it is beyond the admittedly broad discretion of the District Court. In this posture, we conclude that the District Court's order of salary increases, which was "grounded in remedying the vestiges of segregation by improving the desegregative attractiveness of the KCMSD," is simply too far removed from an acceptable implementation of a permissible means to remedy previous legally mandated segregation.

Similar considerations lead us to conclude that the District Court's order requiring the State to continue to fund the quality education programs because student achievement levels were still "at or below national norms at many grade levels" cannot be sustained. The State does not seek from this Court a declaration of partial unitary status with respect to the quality education programs. It challenges the requirement of indefinite funding of a quality education program until national norms are met, based on the assumption that while a mandate for significant educational improvement, both in teaching and in facilities, may have been justified originally, its indefinite extension is not. * * *

[Whether students in the KCMSD perform below national norms] clearly is not the appropriate test to be applied in deciding whether a previously segregated district has achieved partially unitary status. The basic task of the District Court is to decide whether the reduction in achievement by minority students attributable to prior de jure segregation has been remedied to the extent practicable. Under our precedents, the State and the KCMSD are "entitled to a rather precise statement of [their] obligations under a desegregation decree." Although the District Court has determined that "[s]egregation has caused a system wide *reduction* in achievement in the schools of the KCMSD," it never has identified the incremental effect that segregation has had on minority student achievement or the specific goals of the quality education programs. Cf. *Dayton I*.

In reconsidering this order, the District Court should * * * consider that the State's role with respect to the quality education programs has been limited to the funding, not the implementation, of those programs. As all the parties agree that improved achievement on test scores is not necessarily required for the State to achieve partial unitary status as to the quality education programs, the District Court should sharply limit, if not dispense with, its reliance on this factor. * * * Insistence upon academic goals unrelated to the effects of legal segregation unwarrantably postpones the day when the KCMSD will be able to operate on its own.

The District Court also should consider that many goals of its quality education plan already have been attained: the KCMSD now is equipped with "facilities and opportunities not available anywhere else in the country." KCMSD schools received AAA rating [the state's highest rating] eight years ago, and the present remedial programs have been in place for seven years. It may be that in education, just as it may be in economics, a "rising tide lifts all boats," but the remedial quality education program should be tailored to remedy the injuries suffered by the victims of prior *de jure* segregation. Minority students in kindergarten through grade 7 in the KCMSD always have attended AAA-rated schools; minority students in the KCMSD that previously attended schools rated below AAA have since received remedial education programs for a period of up to seven years.

On remand, the District Court must bear in mind that its end purpose is not only "to remedy the violation" to the extent practicable, but also "to restore state and local authorities to the control of a school system that is operating in compliance with the Constitution." *Freeman*.

The judgment of the Court of Appeals is reversed.

JUSTICE O'CONNOR, concurring. * * *

What the District Court did in this case, * * * and how it transgressed the constitutional bounds of its remedial powers, is to make desegregative attractiveness the underlying goal of its remedy for the specific purpose of reversing the trend of white flight. However troubling that trend may be, remedying it is within the District Court's authority only if it is "directly caused by the constitutional violation." The Court and the dissent attempt to reconcile the different statements by the lower courts as to whether white flight was caused by segregation or desegregation. One fact, however, is uncontroverted. When the District Court found that KCMSD was racially segregated, the constitutional violation from which all remedies flow in this case, it also found that there was neither an interdistrict violation nor significant interdistrict segregative effects. Whether the white exodus that has resulted in a school district that is 68% black was caused by the District Court's remedial orders or by natural, if unfortunate, demographic forces, we have it directly from the District Court that the segregative effects of KCMSD's constitutional violation did not transcend its geographical boundaries. In light of that finding, the District Court cannot order remedies seeking to rectify regional demographic trends that go beyond the nature and scope of the constitutional violation.

This case, like other school desegregation litigation, is concerned with "the elimination of the discrimination inherent in the dual school systems, not with myriad factors of human existence which can cause discrimination in a multitude of ways on racial, religious, or ethnic grounds." Swann v. Charlotte–Mecklenburg Bd. of Ed., 402 U.S. 1, 22

(1971). Those myriad factors are not readily corrected by judicial intervention, but are best addressed by the representative branches; time and again, we have recognized the ample authority legislatures possess to combat racial injustice. * * *

JUSTICE THOMAS, concurring.

It never ceases to amaze me that the courts are so willing to assume that anything that is predominantly black must be inferior. Instead of focusing on remedying the harm done to those black schoolchildren injured by segregation, the District Court here sought to convert the Kansas City, Missouri, School District (KCMSD) into a "magnet district" that would reverse the "white flight" caused by de segregation. * * *

"Racial isolation" itself is not a harm; only state-enforced segregation is. After all, if separation itself is a harm, and if integration therefore is the only way that blacks can receive a proper education, then there must be something inferior about blacks. Under this theory, segregation injures blacks because blacks, when left on their own, cannot achieve. To my way of thinking, that conclusion is the result of a jurisprudence based upon a theory of black inferiority. * * *

II * * *

A * * *

Our impatience with the pace of desegregation and with the lack of a good-faith effort on the part of school boards led us to approve * * * extraordinary remedial measures. But such powers should have been temporary and used only to overcome the widespread resistance to the dictates of the Constitution. The judicial overreaching we see before us today perhaps is the price we now pay for our approval of such extraordinary remedies in the past. * * *

Our willingness to unleash the federal equitable power has reached areas beyond school desegregation * * * [to include] the reconstruction of entire institutions and bureaucracies * * *

B * * *

Anticipating the growth of our modern doctrine, the Anti–Federalists criticized the Constitution because it might be read to grant broad equitable powers to the federal courts. In response, the defenders of the Constitution "sold" the new framework of government to the public by espousing a narrower interpretation of the equity power. * * * [T]he appropriate conclusion is that the drafters and ratifiers of the Constitution approved the more limited construction offered in response. * * *

In light of this historical evidence, it should come as no surprise that there is no early record of the exercise of broad remedial powers. * * *

D * * *

Contrary to the dissent's conclusion, the District Court's remedial orders are in tension with two common-sense principles. First, the District Court retained jurisdiction over the implementation and modification of the remedial decree, instead of terminating its involvement after issuing its remedy. Although briefly mentioned in *Brown II* as a temporary measure to overcome local resistance to desegregation, 349 U.S., at 301 ("[d]uring this period of transition, the courts will retain jurisdiction"), this concept of continuing judicial involvement has permitted the District Courts to revise their remedies constantly in order to reach some broad, abstract, and often elusive goal. Not only does this approach deprive the parties of finality and a clear understanding of their responsibilities, but it also tends to inject the judiciary into the day-to-day management of institutions and local policies-a function that lies outside of our Article III competence. * * *

Second, the District Court failed to target its equitable remedies in this case specifically to cure the harm suffered by the victims of segregation. Of course, the initial and most important aspect of any remedy will be to eliminate any invidious racial distinctions in matters such as student assignments, transportation, staff, resource allocation, and activities. This element of most desegregation decrees is fairly straightforward and has not produced many examples of overreaching by the district courts. It is the "compensatory" ingredient in many desegregation plans that has produced many of the difficulties in the case before us.

* * * In the absence of special circumstances, the remedy for de jure segregation ordinarily should not include educational programs for students who were not in school (or were even alive) during the period of segregation. * * *

JUSTICE SOUTER, with whom JUSTICE STEVENS, JUSTICE GINSBURG, and JUSTICE BREYER join, dissenting. * * *

II

A

* * * [N]one of the District Court's or Court of Appeals's opinions or orders requires a certain level of test scores before unitary status can be found, or indicates that test scores are the only thing standing between the State and a finding of unitary status as to the KCMSD's Milliken II programs. * * *

* * * The Court of Appeals refused to order the District Court to enter a finding of partial unitary status as to the KCMSD's *Milliken II* programs (and apparently, the District Court did not speak to the issue itself) simply because the State did not attempt to make the showing required for that relief. * * *

In the development of a proper unitary status record, test scores will undoubtedly play a role. It is true, as the Court recognizes, that all parties to this case agree that it would be error to require that the students in a school district attain the national average test score as a prerequisite to a finding of partial unitary status, if only because all sorts of causes independent of the vestiges of past school segregation might stand in the way of the goal. That said, test scores will clearly be relevant in determining whether the improvement programs have cured a deficiency in student achievement to the practicable extent.* * *

B

The other question properly before us has to do with the propriety of the District Court's recent salary orders. While the Court suggests otherwise, the District Court did not ground its orders of salary increases solely on the goal of attracting students back to the KCMSD. From the start, the District Court has consistently treated salary increases as an important element in remedying the systemwide reduction in student achievement resulting from segregation in the KCSMD. * * *

III * * *

[T]he District Court did not mean by an "intradistrict violation" what the Court apparently means by it today. The District Court meant that the violation within the KCMSD had not led to segregation outside of it, and that no other school districts had played a part in the violation. * * *

[The District Court's finding that segregation caused white flight is not contradicted, as the majority asserts, by the Court of Appeals's conclusion that the District Court " 'made specific findings that negate current significant interdistrict effects.... ' " because the Court of Appeals meant interdistrict *segregative* effects.]

Without the contradiction, the Court has nothing to justify its rejection of the District Court's finding that segregation caused white flight but its supposition that flight results from integration, not segregation. The supposition, and the distinction on which it rests, are untenable. At the more obvious level, there is in fact no break in the chain of causation linking the effects of desegregation with those of segregation. There would be no desegregation orders and no remedial plans without prior unconstitutional segregation as the occasion for issuing and adopting them, and an adverse reaction to a desegregation order is traceable in fact to the segregation that is subject to the remedy. When the Court quotes the District Court's reference to abundant evidence that integration caused flight to the suburbs, then, it quotes nothing inconsistent with the District Court's other findings that segregation had caused the flight. The only difference between the statements lies in the point to which the District Court happened to trace the causal sequence.

* * * [For example, property tax-paying] parents of white children, seeing the handwriting on the wall in 1985, could well have decided that the inevitable cost of clean-up would produce an intolerable tax rate and could have moved to escape it. The District Court's remedial orders had not yet been put in place. Was the white flight caused by segregation or desegregation? The distinction has no significance. * * *

B * * *

We are not dealing here with an interdistrict remedy in the sense that *Milliken I* used the term. In the *Milliken I* litigation, the District

Court had ordered 53 surrounding school districts to be consolidated with the Detroit school system, and mandatory busing to be started within the enlarged district, even though the court had not found that any of the suburban districts had acted in violation of the Constitution. * * *

[In *Gautreaux*,] HUD argued that the case should turn on the same principles governing school desegregation orders and that, under *Milliken I*, the District Court's order could not look beyond Chicago's city limits, because it was only within those limits that the constitutional violation had been committed. We agreed with HUD that the principles of *Milliken* apply outside of the school desegregation context, but squarely rejected its restricted interpretation of those principles and its view of limited equitable authority to remedy segregation. We held that a district court may indeed subject a governmental perpetrator of segregative practices to an order for relief with intended consequences beyond the perpetrator's own subdivision, even in the absence of effects outside that subdivision, so long as the decree does not bind the authorities of other governmental units that are free of violations and segregative effects:

> [*Milliken I*'s] holding that there had to be an interdistrict violation or effect before a federal court could order the crossing of district boundary lines reflected the substantive impact of a consolidation remedy on separate and independent school districts. The District Court's desegregation order in *Milliken* was held to be an impermissible remedy not because it envisioned relief against a wrongdoer extending beyond the city in which the violation occurred but because it contemplated a judicial decree restructuring the operation of local governmental entities that were not implicated in any constitutional violation."

Id., at 296 (footnote omitted).

In the face of *Gautreaux*'s language, the Court claims that it was only because the " 'relevant geographic area for the purposes of the [plaintiffs'] housing options [was] the Chicago housing market, not the Chicago city limits,' " that we held that " 'a metropolitan area remedy [was] not impermissible as a matter of law,' " quoting *Gautreaux*. But that was only half the explanation. Requiring a remedy outside the city in the wider metropolitan area was permissible not only because that was the area of the housing market even for people who lived within the city (thus relating the scope of the remedy to the violation suffered by the victims) but also because the trial court could order a remedy in that market without binding a governmental unit innocent of the violation and free of its effects. In "reject[ing] the contention that, since HUD's constitutional and statutory violations were committed in Chicago, *Milliken* precludes an order against HUD that will affect its conduct in the greater metropolitan area," we stated plainly that "[t]he critical distinction between HUD and the suburban school districts in *Milliken* is that HUD has been found to have violated the Constitution. * * *

JUSTICE GINSBURG, dissenting. [omitted]

### *Notes*

1. The district court's remedy in *Jenkins* sought to integrate within the school district, as the remedy in *Swann* did, and to provide compensatory education to make up for the educational deficits caused by segregation, as the remedy in *Milliken II* did. What was new about the remedy in *Jenkins* was the scope of the compensatory education program, the effort to attract white students from private schools and the suburbs, and the attendant costs. The question is whether the scope of the remedy is appropriate.

2. One justification for the scope of the remedy in *Swann* was to integrate the schools to shield African-American students from covert discrimination by the school board. Does that rationale justify the increased scope of the remedy in *Jenkins*?

3. Another justification for the scope of the remedy in *Swann* was to repair the damage that segregation did to the dignity of plaintiffs. Does that rationale justify the increased scope of the remedy?

4. Is attracting white students into the KCMSD necessary to put plaintiffs in their rightful position?

5. In Sterling Drug Co. v. Bayer AG, 14 F.3d 733 (2d Cir.1994), Sterling Drug, which owned the "Bayer" name within United States, got an injunction against Bayer AG, which owns it in most of the rest of the world, barring Bayer AG from using "Bayer" not only within the United States but also in foreign publications and products likely to find there way into the United States. The appeals court affirmed in part, remanding with instructions that the district court narrow the decree's extraterritorial application to uses of the name likely to cause significant confusion among U.S. consumers. For a useful discussion of when a state court should enjoin out of state activity, see David S. Welkowitz, Preemption, Extraterritoriality, and the Problem of State Antidilution Laws, 67 Tulane L.Rev. 1, 70 (1992)("An extraterritorial injunction is presumed improper absent a waiver [by the other states in which it would apply] or a showing that it regulates [matters internal to the state issuing the injunction].").

6. The reparative aspects of school desegregation remedies, such as the remedial education approved in *Milliken II*, benefit students who were not in school when the constitutional violations took place and whose parents may have come from other locales in which constitutional violations did not take place. Has *Jenkins III* implicitly overruled *Milliken II*?

7. *Jenkins III* seems to require more precision in justifying the remedy than did *Madsen* and *Swann*. Justice Thomas argues that such precision is harder to achieve with reparative than preventive remedies. It is easier to be precise in justifying a remedy to repair the damage done by an individual defendant to an individual plaintiff than a remedy to repair the damage done by society to a group. Does the difficulty of achieving much precision mean that society should let bygones be bygones, or that judgments about when and how to repair such damage are so steeped in policy that courts should leave them to legislatures? An article written years before Clarence Thomas

became a Supreme Court Justice helps to understand why he favors letting bygones be:

> Thomas told me a story from his boyhood to illustrate what fairness means to him. He was on the back porch, playing blackjack for pennies with other boys. As the game went on, one boy kept winning. Thomas finally saw how: the cards were marked. The game was stopped. There were angry words. * * * From all sides fast fists snatched back lost money. There could be no equitable redistribution of the pot. The strongest, fastest hands, including those of the boy who had been cheating, got most of the pile of pennies. * * * But no one really wanted to fight—they wanted to keep playing cards. So a different deck was brought out and shuffled, and the game resumed with a simple promise of no more cheating.
>
> That story, Thomas said, is a lot like the story of race relations in America. Whites had an unfair advantage. But in 1964, with the passage of the Civil Rights Act, the government stopped the cheating. The question now is, Should the government return the ill-gotten gains to the losers? * * *
>
> Thomas believes that government simply cannot make amends, and therefore should not try. The best it can do is deal a clean deck and let the game resume, enforcing the rules as they have now come to be understood. * * * Thomas said, "* * * Use what was used to get others into the economy. Show us the precedent for all this experimentation on our race."
>
> * * * "I would be lying to you if I said that I didn't want sometimes to be able to cheat in favor of those of us who were cheated. But you have to ask yourself, in doing that, you do violence to the safe harbor, and that is the Constitution, which says you are to protect an individual's rights no matter what."

Juan Williams, A Question of Fairness, Atlantic Monthly, Feb., 1987 at 70, 78–79.

7. As *Madsen* suggests, remedies that go beyond plaintiffs' rightful position get closer scrutiny when they threaten specially protected rights. In a decision handed down the same day as *Jenkins III*, Adarand Constructors, Inc. v. Pena, ___ U.S. ___, 115 S.Ct. 2097, 132 L.Ed.2d 158 (1995), held that the federal government cannot discriminate in favor of minorities except when narrowly tailored to serve a compelling governmental interest. Such an interest could include remedying past discrimination. The government program at issue in *Adarand* was voluntarily adopted rather than judicially imposed, but the court seemed to think that similar principles would govern the remedy if it were judicially imposed. *Adarand* relied upon City of Richmond v. J.A. Croson Co., 488 U.S. 469, 491, 109 S.Ct. 706, 721, 102 L.Ed.2d 854 (1989), which stated that "[a]bsent searching judicial inquiry into the justification for such race-based measures, there is simply no way of determining what classifications are 'benign' or 'remedial' and what classifications are in fact motivated by illegitimate notions of racial inferiority or simple racial politics." Two weeks after *Adarand* and *Jenkins III* were announced, Miller v. Johnson, ___ U.S. ___, 115 S.Ct. 2475, 132 L.Ed.2d 762 (1995), applied strict scrutiny to racial gerrymandering of

congressional districts to maximize African-American representation, although the gerrymandering was pursuant to a statute enacted under Congress's power to implement the fourteenth amendment. Given the degree of precision required by *Jenkins III* and given that *Madsen* threatened first amendment interests, shouldn't *Madsen* have come out the other way, except if, as Justice Scalia charges, there is a double standard for abortion cases?

*Jenkins III* scrutinizes the scope of the remedy far more closely than does *Swann*. The closer scrutiny in *Jenkins III* might be explained on the basis of the changing composition of the Court. But, there are other possible explanations. *Swann* was decided during an era of footdragging by school board defendants, while the KCMSD could not have been more enthusiastic about the remedy. The remedy in *Jenkins III* was far more aggressive than that in other school desegregation cases, both in terms of costs and its efforts to attract students from the suburbs.

8. Consider the following from Judge Frank H. Easterbrook, Civil Rights and Remedies, 14 Harv.J.L. & Pub.Pol'y 103, 103–04 (1991):

> When we hear an objection to the remedy, it is almost always a disguised objection to the definition of what is due, and not to the methods used to apply the balm. * * *
>
> Because this point is *so* obvious that almost everyone will deny it, I will proceed by example through some contemporary remedial questions. In thinking about each subject, it will help to consider three questions. First, who holds the "rights": individual persons or groups of persons? Second, what does "equality" mean: equal treatment or equal outcomes? Third, what do we expect the government to teach us: the importance of disregarding the characteristics that often are chosen as a basis of private discrimination, or the worth of a society in which persons of diverse backgrounds appear side by side? * * *
>
> There are systematic differences in emphasis between those who think on the one hand that rights are personal, that the government should assure equal treatment, and that it should teach people the irrelevance of race (for example), and, on the other, those who believe that rights belong to groups, that equality of outcomes is most important, and that the government should assure diversity in many walks of life. * * * [T]he conclusions we reach on these questions govern the choice of remedy.

## E. SPECIFIC REMEDIES OTHER THAN INJUNCTIONS

*Specific performance.* The contract remedy of specific performance is an order to perform under a contract. Like an injunction, specific performance is a specific, coercive, equitable remedy, enforced through the contempt power. In essence, specific performance is an injunction to perform under a contract. However, specific performance has some special requirements.

The Restatement (Second) of Contracts, § 362 (1981) states that "specific performance or an injunction will not be granted unless the terms of the contract are sufficiently certain to provide a basis for an appropriate order." Under this *certainty* requirement, a court could find that the parties had an understanding that was certain enough to be a contract and to lead to damages, but not certain enough to lead to specific performance. Although courts often recite this rule, certainty that is sufficient for liability is usually sufficient for specific performance so long as the court is certain enough of the bargain to formulate a workable decree. E.g., Naylor v. Hall, 201 Mont. 59, 67–68, 651 P.2d 1010, 1015 (1982)(absolute certainty in every detail is not a prerequisite for specific performance).

Courts will not direct specific performance of *personal service* contracts. E.g., Pierce v. Douglas School Dist. No. 4, 297 Or. 363, 686 P.2d 332, 337 (1984)(teacher may not be compelled to perform employment contract). Specific enforcement of such contracts would impose difficult burdens of supervision on the court (see section (B)(2) of the next chapter) and raise issues of involuntary servitude. Courts sometimes avoid these problems by forbidding the employee to work for others rather than compelling performance. E.g., Lumley v. Wagner, 42 Eng. Rep. 687 (1852) (forbidding opera singer to perform at theatres other than the one where she had contracted to perform).

The doctrine of *mutuality of remedy* requires that one party be denied specific performance of a contract if the other party would be barred from that remedy. Some jurisdictions have explicitly revoked the rule. Other jurisdictions consider mutuality a relevant, but not controlling, factor in granting specific relief. Still others continue to cite the rule while recognizing broad exceptions to it. As Judge Cardozo put it:

> If there ever was a rule [of] mutuality of remedy * * *, it has been so qualified by exceptions that, viewed as a precept of general validity, it has ceased to be a rule to-day. What equity exacts today as a condition of relief is the assurance that the decree, if rendered, will operate without injustice or oppression either to plaintiff or to defendant.

Epstein v. Gluckin, 233 N.Y. 490, 493–94, 135 N.E. 861, 862 (1922). So, for instance, if there is a substantial risk that a plaintiff seeking specific performance might not perform later duties under the contract, a court might deny specific performance or condition it in such a way that the plaintiff would have to perform.

Some jurisdictions will deny specific performance because of *inadequacy of consideration*. Other jurisdictions allow this defense only upon an additional showing of fraud or unfairness.

*Writs of mandamus, prohibition, and habeas corpus.* A writ of mandamus is an order to a public or corporate officer to perform a ministerial duty. A writ of prohibition is an order to a judge to refrain from unwarranted conduct. A writ of habeas corpus is an order to someone who detains another person to bring that person to court and justify the detention or relinquish it. Like injunctions, these writs are specific and coercive remedies, enforced through the contempt power.

Indeed, these writs can be conceived as special types of injunctions, available against certain defendants for certain purposes.

Nonetheless, the courts usually do not see these writs as the equivalent of injunctions. The most obvious but least important difference is that, unlike injunctions, they are classified as legal remedies because they were originally issued from the courts of law rather than the courts of equity. This might suggest that the writs are free from the requirement that there be no adequate remedy at law. Yet, mandamus and prohibition, but not habeas corpus, are said to be available only where there is no other adequate remedy at law. In addition, courts view mandamus and prohibition as extraordinary and accordingly set up other prerequisites to limit their availability. These prerequisites vary with both the writ and the jurisdiction, and result from both historical anachronisms and modern needs so that it is difficult to generalize about each one's availability and how it may affect the availability of other writs or an injunction to accomplish the same objective.

The writ of mandamus is available only if the plaintiff has a clear right to relief and the defendant has a clear duty to act. However, if an unclear statute, once interpreted, creates a clear duty for the officer to act, the mandamus action will lie. American Cetacean Society v. Baldrige, 768 F.2d 426, 433 (D.C.Cir.1985), rev'd on other grounds sub nom., Japan Whaling Ass'n v. American Cetacean Society, 478 U.S. 221, 106 S.Ct. 2860, 92 L.Ed.2d 166 (1986). "[C]ourts sometimes analogize between a request for mandatory injunction and a writ of mandamus, thereby triggering all of the hypertechnicalities that govern that largely outmoded remedy.... Whenever possible a petitioner should avoid requesting relief using the terms 'mandamus' or 'mandatory injunction.'" Kenneth C. Davis & Richard J. Pierce, Jr., 3 Administrative Law Treatise 180–81 (3d ed.1994). Professor Howard Brill argues that the mandamus should remain as a separate remedy, but acknowledges that courts have increasingly tended to treat it as a species of injunction. Howard Brill, The Citizen's Relief Against Inactive Federal Officials: Case Studies in Mandamus, Action In the Nature of Mandamus, and Mandatory Injunctions, 16 Akron L.Rev. 339 (1983).

The writ of prohibition is available to redress judicial "usurpation of power." Will v. United States, 389 U.S. 90, 95, 88 S.Ct. 269, 273, 19 L.Ed.2d 305, 310 (1967). Because prohibition is essentially an interlocutory appeal, various limits on its availability vindicate the final judgment rule. In most jurisdictions, prohibition gets far less use than mandamus or habeas corpus.

Habeas corpus has a place in the Bill of Rights, U.S. Const. Amend. VI, because it prevents imprisonment without judicial process. Habeas corpus also provides review of criminal convictions in the judicial process supplemental to ordinary appeals and can sometimes be used in military service, immigration, and child custody cases.

*Ejectment and replevin.* Ejectment is an order to the sheriff to put the plaintiff in possession of real estate by, if necessary, ejecting current possessors and removing any physical obstacles. Replevin is an order to the sheriff to put the plaintiff in possession of chattels. Although the characteristics of these actions and their names sometimes vary from jurisdiction to jurisdiction, the essential point is that ejectment and replevin are specific and coercive remedies, but they are not orders to the defendant and so the defendant's failure to help put the plaintiff in possession is not contempt. Restatement (Second) of Torts § 945, Comment on Clause (a) § (a), § 946 Comment on Clause (a) § (a) (1979). However, in ejectment, resisting the sheriff or reentry after ejectment is contempt and, in replevin, active concealment may be contempt. Moreover, injunctions may be used to supplement these remedies at law, such as by ordering the defendant to turn over a unique chattel. N.Y.Civ. Prac.L. & R. § 7109 (McKinney 1980). Ejectment and replevin are remedies at law and the inadequacy rule does not apply to them.

*Declaratory judgment.* Declaratory judgment (covered in chapter 4) is, as the name suggests, not a coercive remedy at all, but rather a declaration of liability or non-liability. Nonetheless, declaratory judgments often function as specific relief for reasons that you will see.

*Statutory remedies for illegal administrative action.* Judicial review and supervision of administrative action, an important part of modern practice, combines common law and new remedies. Milton M. Carrow, Types of Judicial Relief From Administrative Action, 58 Colum.L.Rev. 1 (1958). Where there is no exclusive statutory remedy to review administrative action, a plaintiff may ordinarily seek an injunction, a declaratory judgment, or a writ of mandamus, prohibition, or habeas corpus. Kenneth Culp Davis and Richard J. Pierce, Jr., Administrative Law Treatise ch. 18 (3d ed. 1994). Normally, however, the statutes that authorize administrative action provide for its judicial review. The court may "affirm"—which is in essence a declaration that it is lawful. If not, there are a number of remedial possibilities. The court may "compel agency action unlawfully withheld or unreasonably delayed." 5 U.S.C. § 706(1), which is analogous to an injunction or mandamus. Or the court may "hold unlawful and set aside" the agency action. 5 U.S.C. § 706(2). "[H]old unlawful" is in essence a declaratory judgment. "[S]et aside" goes beyond a declaration because, in their orders, courts will themselves "vacate" agency actions. Finally, if the court decides to neither affirm nor vacate the agency's action, it may "remand" the matter to the agency with directions to the agency to reconsider in light of the court's opinion.

# Chapter 3

# PROCEDURES FOR FORMULATING, ADMINISTERING, AND ENFORCING THE INJUNCTION

## A. PROCEDURES FOR OBTAINING INJUNCTIVE RELIEF

### 1. TYPES OF INJUNCTIONS

As you know, the normal process for seeking a remedy from a court is to file a complaint which includes a prayer for relief specifying the remedies the plaintiff is requesting. The remedies may include one or more of the types of relief studied in this course, including damages or the specific relief a court may afford through an injunction. Sometimes, however, the plaintiff cannot wait for the wheels of justice to turn completely. The plaintiff may need some additional relief immediately. For example, suppose that the plaintiff and the defendant are having a dispute about who owns Blackacre and the defendant is about to tear down an old house on Blackacre that the plaintiff loves. Unless the court intervenes immediately, the plaintiff's loss due to the destruction of the beloved old house could be replaced neither by an injunction issued after a final determination on the merits nor by damages. It makes sense for the court to have the power to act quickly in such a case. In this example, the court probably would order the defendant not to dismantle the house until it had decided who owned Blackacre. (If the defendant won on the merits, and was awarded title to Blackacre, she could then dismantle the house.)

Such an order is called "temporary" or "preliminary" because it lasts only long enough to give the court time to deliberate further on the merits. In contrast, an injunction issued after a final determination is called a "permanent injunction." The word "permanent" signifies not the injunction's duration but rather that it is not contingent upon some further finding on the merits. A permanent injunction continues to apply unless it expires by its own terms or is later modified or dissolved by a court of competent jurisdiction. For example, the court may find that the plaintiff did have a possessory interest in Blackacre, but that it would last for only one year; in that case, the court would issue a "permanent" injunction directing the defendant to keep off Blackacre for that year.

F.R.Civ.P. 65 (reproduced in the Appendix at p. 886), for example, distinguishes among temporary restraining orders ("TROs"), preliminary injunctions and permanent injunctions, but not because their purposes differ (all three command that a defendant do or not do some act). Instead they are distinguished by their different procedures and durations.

A TRO is an emergency order, which can be granted if, but only if, immediate and irreparable harm will result before a hearing can be held; as a result, it can be granted ex parte (i.e., without any notice to the defendant).[a] Usually, the judge issues the TRO on the basis of affidavits or a verified complaint rather than on the basis of live testimony. Because this drastic emergency procedure is subject to abuse, especially when it is used without notice to the adverse party, there are several built-in safeguards. For example, F.R.Civ.P. 65(b) requires that a TRO may be granted without notice to the adverse party only if: (1) it clearly appears from specific facts set forth in an affidavit or verified complaint that there is immediate need for an order before the adverse party can be heard and (2) the attorney of the party seeking the TRO has certified in writing what efforts were made to give notice (formal or informal, such as by telephone or fax) to the adverse party and has provided the reasons supporting the claim that notice should not be required. (If, for example, there were a specific concern that the defendant might take some destructive action between the time notice would be given and the TRO was issued and served.) (3) F.R.Civ.P. 65(c) requires that the TRO applicant must post security for the costs and damages that may be incurred if it is later determined that the TRO wrongfully enjoined another party. (4) A TRO issued without notice is valid for a very limited time—the ten day limit (which can be extended once) established in F.R.Civ.P. 65(b) is a common pattern. The enjoined party may move for the dissolution of the TRO on two days notice or fewer. (5) The defendant is not bound by the restraining order until notified that it exists and what its terms are (see F.R.Civ.P. 65(d)).

A preliminary injunction is another mechanism for granting relief before the court can conduct a full hearing on the merits; often, the preliminary injunction is granted after the TRO has expired. In con-

**a.** The Supreme Court has acknowledged that "There is a place in our jurisprudence for *ex parte* issuance, without notice, of temporary restraining orders of short duration." Carroll v. President & Commissioners of Princess Anne, 393 U.S. 175, 180, 89 S.Ct. 347, 351, 21 L.Ed.2d 325, 330–331 (1968). However, the Court also observed that "there is no place within the area of basic freedoms guaranteed by the First Amendment for such orders where no showing is made that it is impossible to serve or notify the opposing parties and to give them an opportunity to participate." Id. Accordingly, it found unconstitutional a ten day TRO that a state trial court issued prohibiting a public rally because the order was granted ex parte and without any notice.

trast to the TRO, there must be both notice to the defendant (see, e.g., F.R.Civ.P. 65(a)(1)) and a hearing (however informal) on the motion for a preliminary injunction. The procedural safeguards are parallel to those required for a TRO. (1) Specific facts demonstrating the need for the preliminary injunction must be established under oath; if the facts are in dispute, live testimony is often used. (2) The applicant must post security. (3) The preliminary injunction is valid for an indefinite period of time, but until the court conducts a full trial on the merits.

A permanent injunction cannot issue until there has been a full opportunity to hear from both sides, at a hearing or on a motion for summary judgment. Because it is issued only after the parties have had a complete opportunity to be heard, the special safeguards listed above are not applicable.

A final and important safeguard is appellate review. Despite the final judgment rule, courts have interpreted federal (and most state) statutory law to permit an exception for interlocutory appeal from the trial court's decision on the motion to issue a permanent or a preliminary injunction only. E.g., Overton v. City of Austin, 748 F.2d 941 (5th Cir.1984). Generally, there is no interlocutory appeal from decisions regarding a TRO, because of its extremely short duration, unless denial of review amounts to a denial of all relief for the applicant. See, e.g., Rose v. Giamatti, 1989 WL 111451 (Ohio App.1989)(no power to review appeal from a TRO under Ohio statute). In some jurisdictions, the appeal will act as an automatic stay of the injunction until the appeal is resolved. In others, a stay must be obtained from the trial or appellate court. If there is no stay, the injunction must be obeyed pending the outcome of the appeal. See John Y. Gotanda, The Emerging Standards for Issuing Appellate Stays, 45 Baylor L.Rev. 809 (1993). The standard of review is abuse of discretion, which usually means the trial court is given substantial deference in view of the haste with which the judge acts "in the hectic atmosphere of a preliminary-injunction proceeding." American Hospital Supply Corp. v. Hospital Products Ltd., 780 F.2d 589, 595 (7th Cir.1986).

### *Problem: Unauthorized Merchants*

Many "rock n' roll" stars feel plagued by entrepreneurs who show up at their live concerts and sell merchandise, especially T-shirts, to fans outside of the hall. The unauthorized merchants cut into the revenues that would be generated through the sale of souvenirs by authorized vendors inside the hall. No one connected with the rock bands knows the identities of the unauthorized merchants. Can a TRO be granted? Compare Billy Joel v. Various John Does, 499 F.Supp. 791 (E.D.Wis.1980)(granted) with Rock Tours, Ltd. v. Various John Does, 507 F.Supp. 63 (N.D.Ala.1981)(denied). Could the stars keep legal expenses down by seeking a single TRO that prohibits such unauthorized selling in all cities to be visited on a national tour? The same court that had given Billy Joel an injunction denied The Who a TRO that would apply nationally. Brockum Intern. v. Various John Does, 551 F.Supp. 1054 (E.D.Wis.1982). Is this just a matter of the court's taste in music?

## 2. STANDARDS FOR GRANTING PRELIMINARY RELIEF

Appellate courts typically state that the granting of a preliminary injunction or a TRO is within the discretion of the trial court; they also note that such preliminary relief is an extraordinary and drastic remedy that should issue only if the plaintiff makes a clear showing.

> Although these short-hand formulations aptly express the courts' general reluctance to impose an interim restraint on defendant before the parties' rights have been adjudicated, they do not take the place of a sound evaluation of the factors relevant to granting relief * * * [of which] the four most important factors are:
>
> (1) the significance of the threat of irreparable harm to plaintiff if the injunction is not granted;
>
> (2) the state of the balance between this harm and the injury that granting the injunction will inflict on defendant;
>
> (3) the probability that plaintiff will succeed on the merits; and
>
> (4) the public interest.

11A Charles Alan Wright, Arthur Miller & Mary Kay Kane, Federal Practice and Procedure § 2948 at 429–431 (2d ed. 1995). Various courts also state that a preliminary injunction may issue only if necessary to preserve the court's power to decide the merits or only to preserve the status quo. The following materials examine some of these formulations and additional factors that some courts consider.

## CHALK v. UNITED STATES DISTRICT COURT

United States Court of Appeals, Ninth Circuit, 1988.
840 F.2d 701.

POOLE, CIRCUIT JUDGE:

* * * Petitioner [Vincent L.] Chalk has been teaching hearing-impaired students in the Orange County schools for approximately six years. In February 1987, Chalk * * * was diagnosed as having AIDS. On April 20, after eight weeks of treatment and recuperation, he was found fit for duty and released to return to work by his personal physician, Dr. Andrew Siskind. The [Orange County Department of Education], however, placed him on administrative leave pending the opinion of Dr. Thomas J. Prendergast, the Director of Epidemiology and Disease Control for the Orange County Health Care Agency. On May 22, Dr. Prendergast informed the Department that "[n]othing in his [Chalk's] role as a teacher should place his students or others in the school at any risk of acquiring HIV infection."

Chalk agreed to remain on administrative leave through the end of the school year in June. On August 5, Chalk and representatives of the

Department met to discuss his return to the classroom. The Department offered Chalk an administrative position at the same rate of pay and benefits, with the option of working either at the Department's offices or at his home * * *. Chalk refused the offer. On August 6, * * * Chalk filed this action in the district court seeking a preliminary and permanent injunction barring the Department from excluding him from classroom duties. * * *

On August 18, Chalk moved for a preliminary injunction ordering the Department to reinstate him to his classroom duties pending trial. At a hearing on September 8, the district court denied the motion. Following the ruling, the Department reassigned Chalk to an administrative position coordinating grant applications and educational materials for the hearing-impaired program. A panel of this court denied Chalk's emergency petition for a writ of mandamus, but granted his alternative motion for an expedited appeal. Chalk then filed an emergency motion for an injunction pending appeal. We heard oral argument on November 10, and on November 18 we issued an order reversing the district court with this fuller statement of our reasons to follow.

### Standard of Review

The grant or denial of a motion for a preliminary injunction lies within the discretion of the district court, and its order will be reversed only if the court relied on an erroneous legal premise or otherwise abused its discretion. To determine whether there has been an abuse of discretion, the reviewing court must consider "whether the decision was based on a consideration of the relevant factors and whether there has been a clear error of judgment." Citizens to Preserve Overton Park, Inc. v. Volpe, 401 U.S. 402, 416, 91 S.Ct. 814, 824, 28 L.Ed.2d 136 (1971). An order is reversible for legal error if the court did not apply the correct preliminary injunction standard, or if the court misapprehended the law with respect to the underlying issues in the litigation. An abuse of discretion may also occur when the district court rests its conclusions on clearly erroneous findings of fact. A finding of fact is clearly erroneous when "the reviewing court on the entire evidence is left with the definite and firm conviction that a mistake has been committed." United States v. United States Gypsum Co., 333 U.S. 364, 395, 68 S.Ct. 525, 542, 92 L.Ed. 746 (1948).

### Application of the Preliminary Injunction Standard

The basic function of a preliminary injunction is to preserve the *status quo* pending a determination of the action on the merits. The moving party may meet its burden by demonstrating either (1) a combination of probable success on the merits and the possibility of irreparable injury, or (2) that serious questions are raised and the balance of hardships tips sharply in its favor. "These are not separate tests, but the outer reaches 'of a single continuum.' " We will examine each of the elements in turn.

### 1. *Probable Success on the Merits*

[The court concluded that Chalk had a strong probability of success on the merits. It decided provisionally that, within the meaning of the federal statute prohibiting discrimination against otherwise qualified handicapped persons, § 504 of the Rehabilitation Act of 1973, 29 U.S.C. § 794, he is handicapped and that handicap is not a disqualification because authoritative medical experts have concluded that there is a strong likelihood that AIDS is not communicable in the classroom setting.] * * *

### 2. *Irreparable Injury*

Having demonstrated a strong probability of success on the merits, Chalk next had to demonstrate that he was threatened with the possibility of irreparable injury. The district court held that Chalk's proof on this element was insufficient:

> I cannot conclude that there is any irreparable injury to plaintiff if he must wait pending trial. He has a job offered and he can do that job until we can determine by medical testimony the extent of the risk and whether or not it's justified for the court to order the school board to put this man back in the classroom. But I cannot—I simply cannot do it on the basis of the present record.

We believe this determination was clearly erroneous. In making its finding, the court focused on the monetary loss to Chalk and concluded that he was no worse off than before the reassignment. This approach failed to consider the nature of the alternative work offered Chalk. Chalk's original employment was teaching hearing-impaired children in a small-classroom setting, a job for which he developed special skills beyond those normally required to become a teacher. His closeness to his students and his participation in their lives is a source of tremendous personal satisfaction and joy to him and of benefit to them. The alternative work to which he is now assigned is preparing grant proposals. This job is "distasteful" to Chalk, involves no student contact, and does not utilize his skills, training or experience. Such non-monetary deprivation is a substantial injury which the court was required to consider. See Finot v. Pasadena City Bd. of Educ., 250 Cal.App.2d 189, 202–03, 58 Cal.Rptr. 520, 529 (1967)(teacher's reassignment from classroom duty to home teaching, imposed in retaliation for an exercise of first amendment rights, was a "legally remediable detriment").

Several cases support petitioner's claim that his non-monetary deprivation is irreparable. The most striking parallel is E.E.O.C. v. Chrysler Corp., 546 F.Supp. 54 (E.D.Mich.1982), aff'd, 733 F.2d 1183 (6th Cir.1984), where the court granted a preliminary injunction ordering reinstatement of employees terminated in violation of the Age Discrimination in Employment Act. The court acknowledged that the loss of income and its effects were compensable after trial and did not constitute irreparable harm. Nonetheless, irreparable injury was found in the consequent emotional stress, depression and reduced sense of well-being, which constituted "psychological and physiological distress . . . the very type of injury Congress sought to avert." * * *

An additional factor favoring a preliminary injunction here arises from the very nature of Chalk's affliction. Studies and statistics of etiology and terminus of AIDS show that although the time during which such a person may be quick and productive varies, the virus is fatal in all recorded cases. Presently Chalk is fully qualified and able to return to work; but his ability to do so will surely be affected in time. A delay, even if only a few months, pending trial represents precious, productive time irretrievably lost to him.

We therefore conclude that the district court's finding that Chalk had not demonstrated any possibility of irreparable injury was clearly erroneous and must be reversed.

### 3. *The Balance of Hardships*

Having demonstrated a strong probability of success on the merits and the possibility of irreparable injury, Chalk has shown all that is necessary for a preliminary injunction to issue. Nonetheless, we will also briefly address the claimed injury on the part of the Department, since "at least a minimal tip in the balance of hardships must be found even when the strongest showing on the merits is made."

Even under the balance of hardships standard, plaintiff's injury outweighs any harm to the defendant. Defendant's asserted injury is based entirely on the risk to others posed by plaintiff's return to the classroom. As discussed above, this theoretical risk is insufficient to overcome plaintiff's probability of success on the merits, and it is likewise insufficient to outweigh the injury which plaintiff is likely to suffer.

In denying the preliminary injunction, the district court concluded that Chalk's injury was outweighed by the fear that his presence in the classroom was likely to produce:

> The plaintiff desires to teach despite all these circumstances [i.e., that the results could be "so disastrous if . . . by any chance the risk should prove to have been unjustified"]. Counsel has recognized that he doesn't have a constitutional right to do so. On the other hand, he has a statutory right not to be discriminated against. He has a statutory right to go back to the school if he is otherwise qualified.
>
> But I think I have a right—in fact, an obligation to compare on the one hand the trauma on the plaintiff if he is held out from the school for a period of months until we can have a trial in this action. The trauma on him, on the one hand, with the trauma on the children and parents in being required to submit to what they are likely to conclude is an unacceptable risk.[14]

14. The district court apparently miscalculated the reaction of at least some of Chalk's students and their parents. The mothers of five of Chalk's students joined

We recognize that the public interest is one of the traditional equitable criteria which a court should consider in granting injunctive relief. Here, however, there is no evidence of any significant risk to children or others at the school. To allow the court to base its decision on the fear and apprehension of others would frustrate the goals of section 504. * * *

The Court recognizes the concern and fear which is flowing from this small community, particularly from the parents of school age children * * *. However, the Court *may not* be guided by such community fear, parental pressure, and the possibility of lawsuits. * * *

Nonetheless, we recognize that the parties and the district court will have to deal with the apprehensions of other members of the school community, as well as with the inexorable progress of Chalk's disease. Although the time frame is unpredictable, given the current state of medical knowledge, the course of petitioner's condition is reasonably certain. Chalk's immune system will deteriorate over time, leaving him increasingly susceptible to opportunistic infections. These infections do not cause AIDS, nor do they increase the risk of transmission of the AIDS virus, but some of them may themselves be communicable to others in a classroom setting. The district court is in the best position, guided by qualified medical opinion, to determine what reasonable procedures, such as periodic reports from petitioner's doctors, will best give assurance to the Department, the community and the court that no significant risk of harm will arise in the future from Chalk's continued presence in the classroom.* * *

## *Notes*

1. The circuit court says that the goal of a preliminary injunction must be to maintain the "status quo". What does the court mean by status quo? Is it the situation immediately prior to the filing of the suit? Before the filing of the motion for preliminary injunction? Before the school board reacted to Chalk's diagnosis? Before Chalk got AIDS? If the latter, what would be the outcome if Chalk had been denied employment rather than transferred on account of the disease? Or does the court mean by status quo plaintiff's rightful position? If so, how does the court know what that is in advance of deciding the case on the merits?

2. As *Chalk* illustrates, the court's understanding of the law of liability influences not only the assessment of probability of success on the merits but also the assessment of irreparable harm. Is the irreparable harm to Chalk the loss of job satisfaction for the remainder of his life?

3. In balancing the equities, the circuit court considers the upset that Chalk feels from being transferred but not the upset that some officials and parents feel about Chalk being in the classroom. Is that appropriate in the context of this case? How should courts handle the public interest factor in the traditional test? See Note, "The Wild Card that is the Public Interest":

amicus Disability Rights Education and Defense Fund in support of Chalk's appeal, and Chalk was greeted with hugs and homemade gifts upon his return to work following our order of November 18.

Putting a New Face on the Fourth Preliminary Injunction Factor, 72 Tex.L.Rev. 849 (1994)(contending that courts should use the factor to weigh particular harm which will be suffered as a direct consequence of the granting or denying of a particular preliminary injunction).

4. Suppose that the statute upon which Chalk relies provided that an administrative agency could order reinstatement after a finding of discrimination and that a victim could get injunctive relief from a federal district court only after exhausting administrative remedies. Could Chalk get preliminary relief from the federal court? See Wagner v. Taylor, 836 F.2d 566 (D.C.Cir.1987).

5. Note that Chalk was seeking equitable relief, an order returning him to the classroom. The general rule is that a court may grant interim relief only where the relief the plaintiff ultimately seeks is equitable and not legal. The modern authority for this rule is Judge Learned Hand. In Sims v. Stuart, 291 Fed. 707, 707–08 (S.D.N.Y.1922), he said: "It is, of course, true that equity will at times affirmatively restore the status quo ante pending the suit. But never, so far as I know, will it take jurisdiction over a legal claim merely to hurry it along by granting final relief at the outset of a cause." With rare exception, courts continue to follow this rule. E.g., Rosen v. Cascade International, Inc., 21 F.3d 1520 (11th Cir.1994). But see Friends for All Children, Inc. v. Lockheed Aircraft Corp., 746 F.2d 816, 828–31 (D.C.Cir.1984) (reviewing cases, but creating special exception where liability had been determined through partial summary judgment, only the exact amount remained at issue, and any further delay in paying damages would result in irreparable harm to the plaintiffs, who were orphans in need of diagnostic medical care); Rhonda Wasserman, Equity Transformed: Preliminary Injunctions to Require the Payment of Money, 70 B.U.L.Rev. 623 (1990). The major exception to the general rule, pre-judgment attachment of assets, is considered in chapter 8.

6. Shortly after the Ninth Circuit decided his case, Chalk settled with the school board for $35,000 in addition to returning to his position. He died in 1990. Los Angeles Times, August 3, 1990.

## AMERICAN HOSPITAL SUPPLY CORP. v. HOSPITAL PRODUCTS LTD.

United States Court of Appeals, Seventh Circuit, 1986.
780 F.2d 589.

POSNER, CIRCUIT JUDGE.

* * * A district judge asked to decide whether to grant or deny a preliminary injunction must choose the course of action that will minimize the costs of being mistaken. Because he is forced to act on an incomplete record, the danger of a mistake is substantial. And a mistake can be costly. If the judge grants the preliminary injunction to a plaintiff who it later turns out is not entitled to any judicial relief—whose legal rights have not been violated—the judge commits a mistake whose gravity is measured by the irreparable harm, if any, that the injunction causes to the defendant while it is in effect. If the judge

denies the preliminary injunction to a plaintiff who it later turns out is entitled to judicial relief, the judge commits a mistake whose gravity is measured by the irreparable harm, if any, that the denial of the preliminary injunction does to the plaintiff.

These mistakes can be compared, and the one likely to be less costly can be selected, with the help of a simple formula: grant the preliminary injunction if but only if $P \times Hp > (1-P) \times Hd$, or, in words, only if the harm to the plaintiff if the injunction is denied, multiplied by the probability that the denial would be an error (that the plaintiff, in other words, will win at trial), exceeds the harm to the defendant if the injunction is granted, multiplied by the probability that granting the injunction would be an error. That probability is simply one minus the probability that the plaintiff will win at trial; for if the plaintiff has, say, a 40 percent chance of winning, the defendant must have a 60 percent chance of winning $(1.00-.40 = .60)$. The left-hand side of the formula is simply the probability of an erroneous denial weighted by the cost of denial to the plaintiff, and the right-hand side simply the probability of an erroneous grant weighted by the cost of grant to the defendant.

This formula, a procedural counterpart to Judge Learned Hand's famous negligence formula, see United States v. Carroll Towing Co., 159 F.2d 169, 173 (2d Cir.1947), is not offered as a new legal standard; it is intended not to force analysis into a quantitative straitjacket but to assist analysis by presenting succinctly the factors that the court must consider in making its decision and by articulating the relationship among the factors. It is actually just a distillation of the familiar four (sometimes five) factor test that courts use in deciding whether to grant a preliminary injunction. The court asks whether the plaintiff will be irreparably harmed if the preliminary injunction is denied (sometimes also whether the plaintiff has an adequate remedy at law), whether the harm to the plaintiff if the preliminary injunction is denied will exceed the harm to the defendant if it is granted, whether the plaintiff is reasonably likely to prevail at trial, and whether the public interest will be affected by granting or denying the injunction (i.e., whether third parties will be harmed—and these harms can then be added to Hp or Hd as the case may be). The court undertakes these inquiries to help it figure out whether granting the injunction would be the error-minimizing course of action, which depends on the probability that the plaintiff is in the right and on the costs to the plaintiff, the defendant, or others of granting or denying the injunction. All this is explained at length in Roland Machinery Co. v. Dresser Industries, Inc., 749 F.2d 380, 382–88 (7th Cir.1984), where a panel of this court applied the verbal counterpart to our algebraic formula, as did a different panel in Maxim's Ltd. v. Badonsky, 772 F.2d 388, 391 (7th Cir.1985). See also Leubsdorf, The Standard for Preliminary Injunctions, 91 Harv.L.Rev. 525 (1978). The formula is new; the analysis it capsulizes is standard. * * *

SWYGERT, SENIOR CIRCUIT JUDGE, dissenting.

The court today continues what it began in Roland Machinery v. Dresser Industries, 749 F.2d 380 (7th Cir.1984): a wholesale revision of the law of preliminary injunctions. * * *

I would have preferred to avoid commenting on the majority's attempt to reduce the well-developed and complex law of preliminary injunctions to a "simple" mathematical formula. But because of the potentially far-reaching and baneful consequences of today's decision, I must regretfully voice my concerns.

Henceforth, the district courts of this circuit should grant a preliminary injunction if, "but only if," $P \times Hp > (1-P) \times Hd$ * * *.

The majority describes its formula as a procedural counterpart to Judge Hand's negligence formula first appearing in United States v. Carroll Towing, 159 F.2d 169, 173 (2d Cir.1947). *Carroll Towing* was an admiralty case in which a shipowner's duty to provide against injuries resulting from the breaking of a vessel's moorings was expressed in algebraic terms. In Hand's formula the liability of the shipowner depends on whether $B<PL$, where P is the probability that the ship will break away; where L is the gravity of the resulting injury if she does; and where B is the burden of adequate precautions. Various attempts have been made to apply the Hand formula, or some derivation of it, to areas other than negligence. * * * Most courts, however, have continued to view the *Carroll Towing* opinion as a negligence formula. * * * My quarrel, however, is not with *Carroll Towing* but rather with the majority's attempt today to create its equitable analogue. A quantitative approach may be an appropriate and useful heuristic device in determining negligence in tort cases, but it has limited value in determining whether a preliminary injunction should issue. Proceedings in equity and cases sounding in tort demand entirely different responses of a district judge. The judgment of the district judge in a tort case must be definite; the judgment of the district judge in an injunction proceeding cannot, by its very nature, be as definite. The judgment of a district judge in an injunction proceeding must be flexible and discretionary—within the bounds of the now settled four-prong test.

I question the necessity and the wisdom of the court's adoption of a mathematical formula as the governing law of preliminary injunctions. The majority claims that its formula is merely a distillation of the traditional four-prong test. But if nothing is added to the substantive law, why bother? The standard four-prong test for determining whether a preliminary injunction should issue has survived for so many years because it has proven to be a workable summation of the myriad factors a district court must consider in deciding whether to grant an injunction. The test * * * may not exhibit the "precision" the majority seems to demand, but such "precision" is antithetical to the underlying principles of injunctive relief. Equity, as the majority concedes, involves the assessment of factors that cannot be quantified. A district court faced with the task of deciding whether to issue a preliminary injunction must to some extent, the majority concedes, rely on the "feel" of the case.

The majority's formula will not assist the district courts in their assessment of this aspect of the decision to grant a preliminary injunction. The traditional element of discretion residing in the decision of a trial court to grant a preliminary injunction has been all but eliminated by today's decision.

Ironically, the majority never attempts to assign a numerical value to the variables of its own formula. We are never told how to measure P or Hp or Hd. I believe, and the majority appears to concede, that a numerical value could never be assigned to these variables. Who can say, for instance, what *exactly* the probability is that the granting of the injunction was an error? How then will the majority's formula ease in a meaningful way the responsibilities of the district courts? Judges asked to issue a preliminary injunction must, in large part, rely on their own judgment, not on mathematical quanta.

We must, of course, be mindful not to vest too much imprecision in the preliminary injunction standard, for law implies a system of known and generally applicable rules. The existing four-prong test, however, represents the historical balance struck by the courts between the rigidity of law and the flexibility of equity. * * *

## *Notes*

1. Does Judge Posner's approach change the traditional test as expressed on page 180, supra, and as applied in *Chalk?* If so, is the formula an improvement? If not, is it useful nevertheless? Compare, e.g., Linda J. Silberman, Injunctions by the Numbers: Less Than the Sum of Its Parts, 63 Chi–Kent L.Rev. 279, 282 (1987)(the formula "does not clarify the standard and emerges as a disguised effort to extend the heavy hand of appellate review.") with Linz Audain, Of Posner, and Newton, and Twenty–First Century Law: An Economic and Statistical Analysis of the Posner Rule for Granting Preliminary Injunctions, 23 Loy.L.A.L.Rev. 1215, 1218 (1990)(comparing Judge Posner's insight favorably with Sir Isaac Newton's contributions). Citations to other commentators are collected in Douglas Laycock, The Death of the Irreparable Injury Rule 131 n. 44 (1991).

2. There may be less to the formula than meets the eye. In another Seventh Circuit case decided soon after *American Hospital,* Judge Eschbach (who was not a member of that panel) wrote:

> *American Hospital* does not set forth a new standard for granting preliminary injunctions. * * *
>
> As a distillation, the formula admirably reflects the balancing of irreparable harms inherent in the traditional test. However, a formula, of necessity cannot incorporate all of the elements of the traditional test. We note, therefore, that before the district court balances the irreparable harms suffered by the parties, the plaintiff still must establish the other prerequisites to the issuance of a preliminary injunction—namely, that the plaintiff has no adequate remedy at law; that it has a reasonable likelihood of prevailing on the merits; and that an injunction would not harm the public interest.

Brunswick Corp. v. Jones, 784 F.2d 271, 274 n.1 (7th Cir.1986). With this "clarification", is the test in the Seventh Circuit any different from the traditional test?

3. In developing the formula in *American Hospital*, the court was influenced strongly by a law review article, John Leubsdorf, The Standard for Preliminary Injunctions, 91 Harv.L.Rev. 525 (1978):

> Although reducing this model to hard figures is usually impractical, an example that does so will clarify its implications. Suppose the plaintiff is an indigent who claims additional welfare payments of $20 per month. With these payments, he could buy food in bulk at reduced rates, increasing his purchasing power by $32 per month. If five months will elapse before final judgment, the defendant agency has $100 at stake and the plaintiff $160. Although calculable, these potential losses are irreparable because the plaintiff is judgment-proof and the defendant has sovereign immunity from a judgment for payments due in previous months. The judge also estimates that the plaintiff's claim has a 40% chance of success at trial. On these assumptions, the judge can calculate the probable irreparable loss of rights resulting from the grant or denial of preliminary relief. If the defendant must pay the plaintiff's claim during the litigation, it will spend $100 with a 60% chance that the payments will be found legally unnecessary. Therefore, the defendant's probable irreparable loss of rights from the grant of relief is $60. The plaintiff's probable irreparable loss from the denial of relief, based on a similar calculation, is 40% of $160, or $64. Since the estimated $64 loss from denying relief exceeds the estimated $60 loss from granting it, the judge should grant a preliminary injunction.
>
> This result is not trivial. A judge proceeding intuitively might well conclude that the greater potential injury to the plaintiff from the denial of interim relief does not outweigh the defendant's greater probability of success on the merits. Indeed, formulations requiring plaintiffs to show a probability of success in order to secure relief would foreclose an injunction. The intuitive approach also might encourage a judge to rely on vague generalizations about the impact of deprivations on the poor or the need to protect the public from bogus claimants.
>
> The figures presented in the example as the probable irreparable losses of the parties are in a sense statistical myths. The defendant will not actually lose $60 no matter what happens. If the injunction issues it will pay out $100, which will turn out to be either the amount legally due the plaintiff or $100 too much. The $60 probable loss of rights can best be understood as a prediction of the average loss of rights that the defendant would sustain if similar cases were decided many times without reference to each other. Such mathematical expectations of profit or loss are familiar tools in decisionmaking theory. Judges as well as private decisionmakers often weigh alternative courses of action by considering the possible outcomes in light of their probability of occurrence.

91 Harv.L.Rev. at 542–43.

Professor Leubsdorf also addressed the question of whose interests should be weighed when applying his preliminary injunction model:

In recent years, federal courts have given increasing attention to the effect of preliminary relief on the public interest. No doubt this reflects the flowering of broad injunctive relief which affects many persons and the judicial recognition of public interest plaintiffs. On a deeper level, it shows increasing judicial concern with the impact of legal decisions on society, as opposed to their adequacy as remedies for past misconduct.[124]

It does not follow, however, that the interests of everyone affected by the grant or denial of preliminary relief should figure in the interlocutory hearing. The court must determine whose interests it should consider by reference to the substantive law that will apply when the case goes to trial on the merits. An interlocutory decision about specific performance of a contract to make parts for a power plant should turn on the applicable contract law, not the plant's environmental impact. To consider interests irrelevant to the final decision at the preliminary stage will only increase the cost of the litigation and undermine the substantive law. Those whom the law excludes from protection at the final hearing have no greater claim to be taken into account earlier. This is implicit in the basic perception that preliminary relief guards against irreparable loss of rights, not against *damnum absque injuria.*

The substantive law does not always specify the objects of its protection. So long as a party with standing is present, courts granting final relief can limit their inquiry to what the law forbids. The balancing test for preliminary relief, by contrast, calls for difficult judgments about who—parties, neighbors, future generations, and so forth—have interests deserving consideration. These judgments have to be made quickly, and the law of standing provides only a partial guide. Not surprisingly, some courts avoid the problem by invoking generalizations about the public interest.

Id. at 549–50.

## *Problems*

1. How should *Chalk* come out under the *American Hospital* formula? Should it make any difference that: (a) the parents who fear contagion from Vincent Chalk are rich and would pay handsomely to safeguard their children from the perceived risk of contracting AIDS; or (b) the parents are poor but Chalk would give his entire life savings to keep on teaching until he dies?

2. Paula and Donald, who are siblings of deceased parents, each claim the title to Blackacre, which is a vacation home. Should Paula get a preliminary injunction against Donald's entry onto Blackacre, under *Chalk* or *American Hospital*, in the following situations?

(a) Paula, a wealthy law student who does nothing but study, has a small chance of success on the merits of who has title to Blackacre;

124. See Chayes, The Role of the Judge in Public Law Litigation, 89 Harv.L.Rev. 1281 (1976).

Donald holds wild parties that would probably damage the interior, if not destroy Blackacre entirely.

(b) Take the facts as in (a) but assume that Paula is not wealthy.

(c) Assume now that Paula has a strong probability of success on the merits and neither Paula nor Donald would use Blackacre for destructive parties, but Paula, who is a practitioner of primal scream therapy, intends to use Blackacre to treat patients. The neighbors write letters to the court urging that she be kept out.

## 3. THE SECURITY REQUIREMENT

Even if the trial court is convinced that the plaintiff is entitled to preliminary or temporary injunctive relief, it must decide to what degree the defendant deserves protection in the event that the initial decision proves to be incorrect. In particular, the court must decide the amount of security to be imposed on the plaintiff as a prerequisite to obtaining a TRO or a preliminary injunction.

### *(a) The Amount of Security*

Rule 65(c) of the Federal Rules of Civil Procedure provides that "[n]o restraining order or preliminary injunction shall issue except upon the giving of security by the applicant * * *." Although phrased in mandatory terms, the remaining portion of the first sentence of F.R.Civ.P. 65(c) provides that the security required shall be "in such sum as the court deems proper." This language has led some courts to conclude that the decision is discretionary, so long as the district court actually considers the question. See Coquina Oil Corp. v. Transwestern Pipeline Co., 825 F.2d 1461 (10th Cir.1987)(dismissing appeal for want of jurisdiction because of trial court's failure to consider whether to impose a bond to secure a preliminary injunction). The issue then becomes whether the court in exercising its discretion can waive the security requirement altogether or set the amount of the bond at a level below the estimated costs and damages that the enjoined party may actually suffer if the order is granted improperly.

While there are cases where the failure to require the posting of any bond has been considered reversible error, e.g., Maryland Department of Human Resources v. U.S. Department of Agriculture, 976 F.2d 1462 (4th Cir.1992), some courts have avoided this result by requiring a bond set at a nominal face value. This is a particularly common practice in suits to enforce important federal rights or public interests. E.g., Natural Resources Defense Council, Inc. v. Morton, 337 F.Supp. 167, 168–69 (D.D.C.1971), aff'd on other grounds, 458 F.2d 827 (D.C.Cir.1972); 11A Charles Alan Wright, Arthur R. Miller & Mary Kay Kane, Federal Practice and Procedure: Civil § 2954 at 300 (2d ed. 1995). Thus when three nonprofit environmental groups sought to prevent leasing of the Outer Continental Shelf, the district court in *NRDC* granted a preliminary injunction secured entirely by a bond of $100 instead of $750,000 for the first month and $2,500,000 for each month thereafter as requested by the government. The court noted that "the requirement of more than a nominal amount as security would * * * stifle the intent of the [1969 National Environmental Policy] Act since these three 'concerned private organizations' would be precluded from obtaining judicial review of the defendant's actions." 337 F.Supp. at 169.

Appellate courts usually state that trial courts should take the following factors into account when determining whether to waive the bond requirement or to require the posting of a bond set at a nominal sum: the possible harm to the enjoined party if the order is unlawful, the likelihood of the applicant's success on the merits, the applicant's ability to post a substantial bond or surety, and the possible adverse impact that requiring substantial security might have on the enforcement of rights created by remedial legislation. E.g., Continuum Co. v. Incepts, Inc., 873 F.2d 801 (5th Cir.1989).

Aside from the terms of F.R.Civ.P. 65(c), is it appropriate for the district court to give a plaintiff a "free ride" in seeking a preliminary injunction or a TRO? Why not estimate the cost of error realistically and force the plaintiff to decide if it is "worth it" in order to obtain preliminary relief? For discussion of the policy considerations regarding a mandatory security requirement, see James T. Carney, Rule 65 and Judicial Abuse of Power: A Modest Proposal for Reform, 19 Am.J.Tr.Advoc. 87 (1995); Note, Security for Interlocutory Injunctions Under Rule 65(c): Exceptions to the Rule Gone Awry, 46 Hastings L.J. 1863 (1995).

### *(b) Collecting on the Security*

F.R.Civ.P. 65.1 (reproduced in the Appendix infra at p. 887) "permits the liability of a surety to be enforced through an expeditious, summary procedure without the necessity of an independent action." 11A Charles Alan Wright, Arthur R. Miller & Mary Kay Kane, Federal Practice and Procedure: Civil § 2972 at 454 (2d ed. 1995). "In the case of an injunction bond, the claim against the surety does not accrue until it is finally determined that plaintiff was not entitled to the restraining order or injunction * * *. A final determination may take the form of a decree dismissing the suit, total or partial dissolution of the injunction, or the failure to carry the burden of proof at the hearing on the preliminary injunction." Id. at 458–60.

While F.R.Civ.P. 65.1 creates a procedure for collecting damages on a bond posted in a federal court action, the rule does not address the extent of a surety's liability on the bond. See, e.g., Alabama ex rel. Siegelman v. EPA, 925 F.2d 385 (11th Cir.1991) (discussing widely differing standards courts use to determine whether prevailing defendant is entitled to damages on a bond). The question becomes particularly important if no bond is required or if the bond is set at a nominal sum, because a subsequent determination that the defendant was wrongfully enjoined is meaningless if the defendant's recovery of costs and damages is limited to the face value of the bond. E.g., International Association of Machinists v. Eastern Airlines, Inc., 925 F.2d 6 (1st Cir.1991)(federal practice limits recovery to amount of bond). See also Note, Recovery for Wrongful Interlocutory Injunctions Under Rule 65(c), 99 Harv.L.Rev. 828 (1986).

Finally, federal practice under F.R.Civ.P. 65.1 may conflict with the law of the forum state in two important aspects: first, the determination of what constitutes "costs and damages" payable on the bond; and second, the availability of a comparable summary procedure. 11A Charles Alan Wright, Arthur R. Miller & Mary Kay Kane, supra, § 2974 at 469. We will leave the interesting *Erie* problems that result to your civil procedure and conflicts of law classes.

## B. FORMULATING AND ADMINISTERING THE INJUNCTION

### *Problem: Country Lodge v. Miller (Reprised) Drafting and Administering an Injunction*

Assume that the trial court has found that Miller created a nuisance to Country Lodge by dumping too much of the unsightly apple mash waste into the Rural River. The court also finds that because Country Lodge does not have an adequate remedy at law, an injunction is the appropriate relief. According to the court, the test of a violation is whether apple mash is visible in the river as it flows past the Country Lodge property.

The following facts have been established at trial. Miller employs 18 people. Miller and her employees usually dump apple mash into the river through a pipe leading from the apple press; occasionally they find it easier to use wheel barrows to dump excess apple mash into the river. During times of ordinary water flow, if Miller and her employees dump more than 50 pounds of apple mash per hour into the river, it is visible as the water passes by Country Lodge. However, the water flow varies greatly with the seasons and weather conditions, so there are times when just one pound of apple mash per hour is visible at Country Lodge and others when even 100 pounds per hour are not visible. There is equipment available at a cost of $8000 which can meter the flow of apple mash through pipe. In a prior case a few years ago, Miller was held in contempt of court for willfully violating an injunction, which was unrelated to water pollution.

(a) Who should draft the injunction? (b) What should be the precise terms of an injunction that would restore and protect Country Lodge's rightful position under these circumstances? (Try to draft the injunction). (c) How will the injunction be administered; in particular, how will the court know if Miller is violating the injunction?

## 1. DRAFTING THE INJUNCTION

### PORTLAND FEMINIST WOMEN'S HEALTH CENTER v. ADVOCATES FOR LIFE, INC.

United States Court of Appeals, Ninth Circuit, 1988.
859 F.2d 681.

HUG, CIRCUIT JUDGE:

* * * FACTS

* * * The clinic brought an action against [certain right to life] advocates that was based on several spirited demonstrations in front of the clinic's building. * * * The clinic moved for a preliminary injunction, and the motion was brought before a magistrate for an evidentiary hearing.

The magistrate recommended to the district court that a preliminary injunction be issued based on his findings of fact. * * *

The district court adopted the findings in their entirety and issued the following injunction:

> IT IS HEREBY ORDERED that defendants, their agents, servants, employees, and all persons, groups, and organizations acting in concert with one or more of the defendants are enjoined from committing any of the following acts:
>
> 1. obstructing the free and direct passage of any person in or out of the Portland Feminist Women's Health Center (the Center);
>
> 2. demonstrating or distributing literature on the Foster Road sidewalk in front of the Center in a rectangular zone that extends from the Center's front door to the curb and twelve and one-half feet on either side of a line from the middle of the Center's door to the curb;
>
> 3. shouting, screaming, chanting, or yelling during on-site demonstrations;
>
> 4. producing noise by any other means which substantially interferes with the provision of medical services within the Center, including counseling;
>
> 5. trespassing on Center property;
>
> 6. damaging the property of the Center, its employees or clients; and
>
> 7. interfering with the Center's receipt of public utility services.
>
> This Order shall remain in effect until further order of the court.

After the injunction was issued, the demonstrations continued, and at a hearing the district court found several of the individual advocates in contempt. We are asked to determine the validity of both the injunction and the contempt citations.

ANALYSIS

* * * Appellants do not seriously challenge the magistrate's findings of fact or his determination under the preliminary injunction standard. He explicitly found that the defendants engaged in the offending conduct. We proceed in our analysis on the basis that the findings of fact are not clearly erroneous, and the preliminary injunction standard was satisfied.

Appellants challenge the injunction's content with arguments asserting impermissible vagueness for failure to set forth an objective decibel level for prohibited shouting, yelling, chanting, and noise making. They argue that this purported vagueness has a chilling effect on protected activities and places demonstrators at the mercy of the appellees' subjective standards. Because we are dealing with an injunction, the vagueness issue is controlled by Fed.R.Civ.P. 65(d).

Rule 65(d) requires that injunctions "shall be specific in terms; [and] shall describe in reasonable detail . . . the act or acts sought to be restrained." The Supreme Court has indicated that the policy behind the rule is "to prevent uncertainty and confusion on the part of those faced with injunctive orders, and to avoid the possible founding of a contempt citation on a decree too vague to be understood." Schmidt v. Lessard, 414 U.S. 473, 476, 94 S.Ct. 713, 715, 38 L.Ed.2d 661 (1974). We have interpreted the rule and its policy to require that "the language of injunctions . . . be reasonably clear so that ordinary persons will know precisely what action is proscribed." While ambiguities in an injunction are construed in favor of the enjoined party, nonetheless "[i]njunctions are not set aside under Rule 65(d) . . . unless they are so vague that they have no reasonably specific meaning."

We do not find the injunction here in dispute impermissibly vague under the applicable standards. The language that the advocates attack enjoins "shouting, screaming, chanting, or yelling during on-site demonstrations; [and] . . . [p]roducing noise by any other means which substantially interferes with the provision of medical services within the Center, including counseling. . . ." They argue that without a specific decibel level or other objective standard they cannot know whether their conduct violates the injunction. They argue further that without such a standard, the imposition of contempt sanctions under the injunction will be based on the biased and subjective interpretation of the clinic. While an enumerated decibel level certainly would provide a more specific definition of the enjoined conduct than the injunction now provides, we do not believe that such specificity is required. The terms of the injunction place the enjoined parties on fair notice of the actions that are prohibited in language that is reasonably understandable. Greater particularity, while it may be desirable, is not required under Rule 65(d).
* * *

The advocates' strongest challenge to the preliminary injunction is against the third and fourth paragraphs, which prohibit shouting, screaming, chanting, yelling, and producing noise. Whether these provisions are tailored narrowly enough is a close question. The district court found that chanting, shouting, and screaming during demonstrations were audible on the second floor, where medical procedures are performed. Chanting, shouting, screaming, or yelling may be an expressive, albeit unpleasant, form of behavior. If it causes no disruption of clinic operations, such expression would not materially affect the interest at stake here. On the other hand, if the conduct rises to a volume that obstructs the provision of services in the Center, it may be enjoined. Accordingly, we modify the injunction by combining its paragraphs numbered 3 and 4 in the following fashion:

> 3. shouting, screaming, chanting, yelling, or producing noise by any other means, in a volume that substantially interferes with the provision of medical services within the Center, including counseling; . . . .

The remainder of the preliminary injunction is not contested. We see no problem with the prohibition against trespassing, damaging property, and interfering with utility services. * * *

Appellants also challenge the injunction as constitutionally void for vagueness. However, that doctrine does not affect our decision. The vagueness doctrine is based on due process principles that require fair notice and warning. It also incorporates a requirement that specificity be sufficient to avoid arbitrary and discriminatory enforcement. The doctrine's goal is to avoid "allow[ing] policemen, prosecutors, and juries to pursue their personal predilection," by requiring legislators to promulgate specific standards in criminal statutes. These concerns arise in a different context here, where enforcement lies entirely in judicial hands. So viewed, the injunction is not unconstitutionally vague, for reasons we have already set forth. * * *

## *Notes*

1. Even as modified, will the right to life advocates know what is permissible conduct? For example, since they are enjoined from trespassing, how will they be able to tell whether their noise "substantially interferes with the provision of medical services" on the second floor of the clinic?

In this regard, consider McComb v. Jacksonville Paper Co., 336 U.S. 187, 69 S.Ct. 497, 93 L.Ed. 599 (1949). In *McComb*, the Supreme Court, contrary to the findings of the district and circuit courts below, found defendant in contempt of an order which directed it to obey the provisions of the Fair Labor Standards Act dealing with minimum wages, overtime, and the keeping of records. The Court noted that "By its terms it enjoined any practices which were violations of those statutory provisions. Decrees of that generality are often necessary to prevent further violations where a proclivity for unlawful conduct has been shown." 336 U.S. at 192, 69 S.Ct. at 499, 93 L.Ed. at 604.

Justices Frankfurter and Jackson dissented. They noted:

> Obedience must of course be secured for the command of a court. To secure such obedience is the function of a proceeding for contempt. But courts should be explicit and precise in their commands and should only then be strict in exacting compliance. To be both strict and indefinite is a kind of judicial tyranny.
>
> * * * It is for such reasons that this Court has indicated again and again that a statute cannot properly be made the basis of contempt proceedings merely by incorporating a reference to its broad terms into a court order. These considerations become increasingly important as there is increasing use of injunctions for the enforcement of administrative orders and statutory duties.
>
> These are general principles but their application governed the decisions of the District Court and of the Circuit Court of Appeals; they should control the decision here. The two lower courts found that while the practices now complained of by the Administrator of the Wage and Hour Division of the Department of Labor constituted violations of the Fair Labor Standards Act, they were not on any fair consideration covered by the injunction, contempt of which is now charged. The injunction underlying this proceeding takes eight pages of a printed record and particularizes in great detail the violations which were enjoined. It also contains omnibus clauses prohibiting violations of the Fair Labor Standards Act. * * * In short, both courts found no contempt. They did so because there was lacking that clearness of command in the court's order which warranted a finding of its disobedience, if due regard were paid to the proper construction of the injunction as the starting point of the contempt proceedings. * * *
>
> One of the grievances which led to the Norris–LaGuardia Act, 29 U.S.C.A. § 101 et seq., was the generality of the terms of labor injunctions. Ambiguity lurks in generality and may thus become an instrument of severity. Behind the vague inclusiveness of an injunction like the one before us is the hazard of retrospective interpretation as the basis of punishment through contempt proceedings. The two lower courts, in finding that generally to enjoin obedience to a law is too vague a foundation for proceedings in contempt, were avoiding the very evil with which labor injunctions were justly charged. And of course it is not to be assumed that the allowable vagueness of an injunction varies with the use to which the injunction is put. This Court ought not to encourage injunctions couched in such indefinite terms by setting aside the findings of the courts below that the injunction did not forbid with explicitness sufficient to justify a finding of contempt.

336 U.S. at 195–97, 69 S.Ct. at 501–02, 93 L.Ed. at 606–07.

2. One of the other important ways in which Rule 65(d) protects enjoined parties is the requirement that the order "describe in reasonable detail, and not by reference to the complaint or other document, the act or acts sought to be restrained." Usually the court can accommodate this requirement without difficulty. However, the requirement can pose some problems. For example, in a controversy involving the allocation of fishing rights between Indian and non-Indian fishers in the State of Washington

(about which see infra p. 324), the State was required to inform non-Indians of where they could and could not fish at different times. The district court's injunction prohibited non-Indians from fishing for salmon in certain watersheds and marine waters, "unless such person has first ascertained from the Washington Department of Fisheries telephone 'hot-line' * * * that the area to be fished is open for fishing by non-treaty fishermen at the time the individual intends to fish." In United States v. Olander, 584 F.2d 876, 880–81 (9th Cir.1978), vacated on other grounds sub nom., Dolman v. United States, 443 U.S. 914, 99 S.Ct. 3104, 61 L.Ed.2d 878 (1979), the Ninth Circuit rejected a challenge to this provision:

> All that the injunction requires a fisherman to do is to call the hot-line before going fishing, and then to refrain from fishing in any area which the hot-line tells him is closed. * * * The injunction is as specific as the nature of the subject matter regulation of fishing in Puget Sound permits.

Did the district court's order make reference to some "other document?" If so, what else could the district court have done?

3. In the run of the mine case, where the requested relief is fairly apparent, the plaintiff drafts a proposed order and the defendant gets to approve it as to form before the trial court signs it. In many courts, the plaintiff is required to submit a proposed order with the moving papers. E.g., McKinney's New York Rules of Court, Rules of the United States District Court for the Northern District of New York, General Rule 10(d). This simple procedure forces the plaintiff to draft an order that is fairly specific (and therefore enforceable) and is not overreaching in scope. See, e.g., Developments in the Law—Injunctions, 78 Harv. L. Rev. 994, 1064 (1967)("Specificity has long been the hallmark of a well-drafted injunctive decree."). If the proposed order would impose broader relief than the plaintiff is entitled to on the basis of the moving papers, the defendant can object before it is signed and entered by the court.

4. There are cases, however, where the task of drafting the injunction is not so simple and the appropriate scope of injunctive relief is not so clearcut. In those cases, who gets to decide exactly what burdens the decree will impose on the defendants? How is the simultaneously technical and policy-making job of drafting the decree to be accomplished? Thinking back to chapter 2, may the parties agree to write a decree that provides for more than the plaintiff's rightful position? How can the drafting process take account of the fact that events occurring after entry of the injunction may prompt one or more of the parties to seek its modification? For one answer, see Special Project—The Remedial Process in Institutional Reform Litigation, 78 Colum.L.Rev. 784 (1978). That Special Project concludes:

> The court supervising an institutional reform case must organize remedy formulation to attain two primary goals. The formulation process must produce a viable plan, and the plan must be chosen and implemented as rapidly as possible. Speedy production of an adequate and viable plan is most likely when the court maximizes the parties' participation in devising the remedy. Of course, the greater the parties' participation, the larger the amount of factual and interpretive information the court obtains from them.

Although increasing party participation might be thought to slow the remedy formulation process, it frequently has the opposite effect. By provoking simultaneously the efforts of several participants a court protects itself against the failure of any one participant to produce an adequate remedy, and may goad one or more of the others to an at least minimally acceptable effort. Indeed, delay may be avoided by simultaneous, rather than sequential, adoption of a variety of formulation techniques.

The infinite variety of factual circumstances in which federal district courts take responsibility for fashioning institutional relief precludes the academic prescription of any one technique of remedy formulation, or even a comparative evaluation of the alternatives. Different situations will, of course, require different approaches. Observation suggests, however, that there are two important procedural steps courts should consider when formulating remedies. One is to involve all the parties in remedy development. The other is to obtain by the appointment of a special master a neutral source of expert information and a knowledgeable delegate who will push for a prompt and adequate remedial decree.

78 Colum. L. Rev. at 812–13.

The Columbia Special Project strongly advocated the use of a special master (see F.R.Civ.P. 53, Appendix, infra at p. 879) to aid the court in the formulation of an injunction (or decree) in complex cases. Special masters have undertaken the task in many cases, and have taken on many different roles. For a review of the roles played by masters in several different school desegregation cases, see D. Bruce LaPierre, Voluntary Interdistrict School Desegregation in St. Louis: The Special Master's Tale, 1987 Wis.L.Rev. 971; David L. Kirp & Gary Babcock, Judge and Company: Court–Appointed Masters, School Desegregation, and Institutional Reform, 32 Ala.L.Rev. 313 (1981); Curtis J. Berger, Away From the Courthouse and Into the Field: The Odyssey of a Special Master, 78 Colum.L.Rev. 707 (1978).

5. Should affected nonparties and members of the public have an opportunity to comment on proposed decrees that may affect them? See, e.g., Tunney Act, 15 U.S.C. § 16(b)(1981) and Consent Judgments in Actions to Enjoin Discharges of Pollutants, 28 C.F.R. § 50.7(b) (requiring, respectively, time for public comment on antitrust and pollution discharge consent decrees).

Should there be any limits to such participation? In Bustop v. Superior Court, 69 Cal.App.3d 66, 137 Cal.Rptr. 793 (1977), the trial court was ordered to permit a citizen's group to intervene in the remedial phase of the Los Angeles school desegregation suit, after the California Supreme Court had affirmed that the school board had engaged in unlawful segregation. Both the African–American plaintiffs and the defendant school board opposed the intervention of Bustop, whose "prime objective [was] the prevention of mandatory reassignment of students to schools other than those which they now attend or choose to attend." Id. at 69. After *Bustop* was decided, the trial judge permitted intervention by yet another citizen's group, BEST (Better Education for Students Today). BEST "frankly disavowed any knowledge of or position toward *any* integration plan, but asserted that its members were well-intentioned citizens who would certainly have developed positions on the issues by the time they got to court." Stephen C. Yeazell, Intervention and the Idea of Litigation: A Commentary on the Los Angeles School Case, 25 U.C.L.A.L.Rev. 244, 259 (1977). However, if nonparties are not formally bound by the terms of the injunction, see Martin v. Wilks, 490 U.S. 755, 109 S.Ct. 2180, 104 L.Ed.2d 835 (1989), infra at 329, why should they have any role in the process?

6. How active a role may the judge play? In United States v. Microsoft Corp., 56 F.3d 1448 (D.C.Cir.1995), the court of appeals found that the district court had exceeded its authority under the Tunney Act in refusing to enter a proposed antitrust consent decree the Department of Justice had negotiated with the computer software behemoth. The district court concluded that the decree was not in the public interest because the decree did not address certain anticompetitive practices beyond those violations alleged in the original complaint. (The judge happened to have read a book putting Microsoft's practices in a very unfavorable light.) The court of appeals saw the district court as usurping the role of the Attorney General rather than reviewing the decree itself. The appellate court even took the rare step of ordering the case remanded to a different judge, who then approved the settlement. 1995–2 Trade Cases ¶ 71,096 (D.D.C.1995). See generally Marc Galanter & Mia Cahill, "Most Cases Settle": Judicial Promotion and Regulation of Settlements, 46 Stan.L.Rev.1339 (1994).

## 2. ADMINISTERING THE INJUNCTION

### *Problem: Country Lodge v. Miller (Reprised) Determining Compliance With an Injunction*

Suppose that the court prohibits Miller from dumping more than 500 pounds of apple mash waste into the river every week. In the alternative, suppose that the court permits Miller to dump apple mash into the river so long as it is not visible from the Country Lodge property. How can the court determine whether Miller is in compliance with either of these injunctions?

---

With the average "plain vanilla" injunction, it is the plaintiff's responsibility to monitor the defendant's compliance with the terms of the injunction. If the plaintiff detects a violation, she should file for an Order to Show Cause with the court—an order directing the defendant to show cause why he should not be held in contempt of court for violating the injunction. In most cases, this monitoring system works reasonably well. It does not work so well whenever it is difficult to determine whether the defendant—be it a public entity or private corporation—is in compliance with the injunction. Other than relying entirely upon the defendant's good faith, the court needs some mechanism to help it determine whether its orders are being obeyed.

It is usually impractical for the injunction to describe precisely all that must happen to cure the violation. All of the activities of a major government department or enterprise cannot be described in any one document. Moreover, the method of administering the injunction cannot simply funnel all the conceivably relevant bits of information to the court nor should it be permitted to consume overwhelming amounts of time of the parties and counsel. If it does, the substantive progress that the court intends to achieve through the injunction will be thwarted. However, the injunction must be clear enough so that it is evident when the defendants violate its terms. Thus, the court must simultaneously avoid the twin evils of issuing an injunction that is so open ended that it is nothing more than aspirational platitudes on the one hand and so detailed as to tie everyone up in nothing but counterproductive paper work on the other. See Michael G. Starr, Accommodation and Accountability: A Strategy for Judicial Enforcement of Institutional Reform Decrees, 32 Ala.L.Rev. 399 (1981). As the next reading indicates, an injunction must be specific for other reasons as well.

## JAMES A. HENDERSON, JR. & RICHARD A. PEARSON, IMPLEMENTING FEDERAL ENVIRONMENTAL POLICIES: THE LIMITS OF ASPIRATIONAL COMMANDS

78 Colum.L.Rev. 1429, 1430–36 (1978).

"Aspiration," as that concept will be employed in the following analysis, refers to the state of mind with which an actor performs a task. An actor performs "aspirationally" when he aims at accomplishing as best he can the task's underlying objectives as he perceives them. Since the objectives of many tasks are generally understood to carry limitations upon the commitment of resources, the phrase "as best he can" does not require a single-minded, "drop everything else" approach to performing the task. Instead, aspiration requires that, within these limitations, an actor will perform to the best of his ability. Nor need the task be described explicitly in aspirational terms to be aspirational. "Do your best" may accompany a request that an actor perform a given task; but even without such words the actor will be aware of the general nature of the task's purpose and will understand that he is to act in a way to achieve that purpose. * * *

### A. Aspirational Commands and the Legal System

From the very beginnings of our jurisprudence, common-law judges recognized that only essentially nonaspirational patterns of conduct may effectively be compelled by threats of legal sanctions. Thus, criminal law has traditionally consisted almost entirely of commands which are negative, specific, and nonaspirational. Tort law, although vaguer in some respects, is also predominantly negative and nonaspirational. Courts have generally refused to rely upon affirmative, aspirational commands even when they are confronted with specific contexts in which such commands might have appeared to be especially desirable—where, for example, a helpless person could be rescued by the active intervention of another. This same reluctance is reflected in the traditional refusal of courts to order specific performance of personal service contracts, and in the concern in administrative law with constraining, rather than compelling, the exercise of administrative discretion. It is no less clearly reflected in the restraint with which federal lawmakers in the American system have approached the delicate task of attempting to direct the conduct of the states.

This does not mean that the American legal system is indifferent to the importance to society of aspirational conduct. However, it operates to encourage such conduct indirectly, rather than to compel it directly. The major legal institutions which the American system has traditionally relied upon to maintain sufficient levels of individual incentive have been property and contract. Together, they provide the basic common-law framework for an economic marketplace in which decisions affecting resource allocations are made by means of contract bargaining. Bargaining is a voluntary process in which each participant seeks to maximize the benefits to himself which flow from exchange transactions. The benefits which a participant derives from this process are then generally protected by the law of property. As a result, individuals are encouraged to use best efforts in their own self-interest. * * *

Nevertheless, there have been times when lawmakers have overcome their traditional reluctance to rely upon aspirational commands. * * *

### B. The Difficulty of Enforcing Aspirational Commands

It is important to distinguish the difficulties inherent in the enforcement of aspirational commands from the problems involved in the enforcement of law generally. Even nonaspirational commands will be difficult to enforce if the resources devoted to law enforcement are inadequate to the task, or if there is a general disrespect for the source of the law. Aspirational commands present problems of a different order, however. These difficulties stem from the divergence of values between addressor and addressee, a condition which is likely to occur when a lawmaker relies upon threats of sanctions. Thus, when the addressee of an aspirational command is indifferent to, or hostile toward, the values and objectives reflected in an assigned task, aspiration of the sort desired by the addressor will typically be absent. Instead of seeking to maximize the accomplishment of the addressor's values, such an addressee may be expected to respond by either secretly resolving not to aspire in the performance of the task, masking his unwillingness with feigned sincerity, or by honestly misperceiving the addressor's objectives, which typically will only be vaguely described in an aspirational command, and consequently aspiring to perform in a manner which is only marginally useful to the addressor. Indeed, these responses have been characteristic of the experience in civil rights cases.

It must be emphasized that the addressor's problems are not ameliorated by threats of sanctions. The addressor cannot determine, with sufficient accuracy to support a consistent application of sanctions, whether the addressee has secretly refused to aspire. Furthermore, he cannot reduce the risk of the addressee's misinterpretation of his intent because generally he must keep his instructions vague if he is to leave the addressee free to aspire. Of course, both risks could be reduced by telling the addressee specifically what to do. If the addressor could have been specific, however, there would have been no need to rely upon an aspirational command. Thus, there are two basic and unavoidable problems with employing sanction-backed aspirational commands. These are, first, the problem of nonverifiability, inhering in the addressor's inability to determine whether the addressee has actually aspired in performing an assigned task; and second, the problem of vagueness, inhering in the characteristic openendedness of aspirational commands.

1. *Nonverifiability.* The problem of nonverifiability in connection with legal commands to aspire is especially acute because it threatens one of the conditions necessary to the efficacy of a system of sanction-backed legal commands—the requirement that sanctions generally be imposed in response, and only in response, to nonconforming behavior. To be sure, the addressor will be able to detect egregious instances of noncooperation—open defiance by the addressee, for example, will not pass unnoticed. However, there will usually be a range of responses available to the addressee that fall short of obvious bad faith, but that also fall considerably short of aspiration. Even assuming that the sanction is sufficient to discourage obvious bad faith responses, the addressor of a command to aspire will nevertheless be unable generally to determine whether the addressee has responded aspirationally. In a substantial majority of instances, the addressee will plausibly be able to assert that he has done his best under the circumstances, and the addressor will be unable to establish the contrary. * * *

2. *Vagueness.* The nonverifiability problem is starkest in the relatively rare instance in which there is a direct command to aspire in the performance of a simple and concretely defined task. In connection with most aspirational commands, however, the addressor will be unable to describe the task specifically, and accordingly will deliberately allow the addressee substantial discretion in the choice of how to perform. Although the problem of nonverifiability will still be present in such circumstances, vagueness adds another dimension to the addressor's problems in relying upon aspirational commands. In exercising his discretion in choosing among the alternative methods of performance, the addressee will tend to select alternatives consistent with his own values. It follows that in ways important to the addressor, the objectives sought by him will not be accomplished. This will generally occur even though the addressee honestly maintains that he is aspiring in the performance of the assigned task. The addressee may make a conscious effort to substitute the addressor's values for his own, but the more complicated the task to which he is assigned, the less likely he is to succeed with such a substitution, and the less likely it is that the performance will meet the addressor's own objectives. Nevertheless, in these circumstances the addressor could not fairly impose a sanction, although the addressee's performance departs substantially from what the addressor desired. * * *

### *Notes*

1. Imagine that a state agency was not enforcing its own regulations in a complex area such as pollution of underground water sources. How would you draft an unvague injunction to require enforcement of the state regulations? That is not overbroad? That is neither vague nor overbroad?

2. *The prevalence of the problem.* The problem of enforcing injunctions that cannot be implemented easily without the good faith efforts of the defendant is widespread. Suppose for example that a statute requires an administrative agency to promulgate pollution control regulations for a given industry, taking into account both the pollution's consequences to health and the economic cost of its abatement. Assume that in litigation it is proved that in promulgating the regulation the agency studied only the feasibility of pollution control and not the health consequences of the pollution and the court held that as a result, the agency has violated the statute and ordered it to reconsider the regulations. Suppose that on remand to the agency for reconsideration (the customary initial remedy) the agency issued exactly the same standards as before, stating that this time the standards were based on considerations of both health *and* economics. The agency may in fact have taken account of the health consequences or it may have only gone through the motions. The court will have trouble verifying the agency's claim that it has complied with its order.

This problem is by no means limited to environmental law but rather is endemic to judicial review of administrative agencies of all sorts. Statutes that empower agencies typically demand action in light of multiple and conflicting goals. Should the agency be caught failing to consider one of these goals or in considering an illegitimate goal, it is often easy for the agency on remand to repeat its violation while feigning compliance.

The requirement under the National Labor Relations Act that employers and unions bargain in good faith, 29 U.S.C. § 158(d)(1982), is another area where this problem is encountered. Should an employer illegally refuse to bargain, the usual remedy is an order requiring the employer to bargain. This does not mean that the employer must accede to the union's position, only that the two sides attempt in good faith to reach an agreement. The employer can often feign bargaining by making offers that it believes the union will reject.

3. *One way to deal with the problem: prophylactic orders.* One way of dealing with the problem of injunctions that require good faith performance is to order the defendant to do something that cannot be feigned, even if it would put the plaintiff in something more than the rightful position. For instance, when the EPA failed for four years to meet its statutory obligation to consider a state-proposed revision of a Clean Air regulation, the court barred the agency from collecting fines for noncompliance with the existing regulation until the agency responded to the proposal. American Cyanamid v. EPA, 810 F.2d 493 (5th Cir.1987). However, the Supreme Court later rejected this approach, but only because it had not been authorized in the legislation. General Motors Corp. v. United States, 496 U.S. 530, 110 S.Ct. 2528, 110 L.Ed.2d 480 (1990). In effect, the Supreme Court concluded that the prophylactic approach clashed with congressional policy goals under the particular statute in question. See generally William A. Fletcher, The

Discretionary Constitution: Institutional Remedies and Judicial Legitimacy, 91 Yale L.J. 635, 695–696 (1982).

---

Given the practical and legal limitations on "overbroad" injunctions discussed supra, courts often are forced to address the problem of administering injunctions using other techniques, as the following materials illustrate.

## SPECIAL PROJECT—THE REMEDIAL PROCESS IN INSTITUTIONAL REFORM LITIGATION

78 Colum.L.Rev. 784, 821–836 (1978).

Implementation of the decree involves more than judicial retention of jurisdiction and the revision of the substantive aspects of the decree that retention of jurisdiction makes possible. Additionally, there remain problems of resolving disputes, monitoring compliance, and supervising the defendant's actions. The court's response to these problems requires the choice, and sometimes the modification, of a technique of administration. Retention of jurisdiction acknowledges the necessity for judicial involvement during implementation of the remedy but does not in itself constitute a choice of administrative technique.

A wide variety of techniques are available. Traditionally, administration is party oriented, depending on adversarial interplay. However, some judges supplement this by court oriented administration, in which the court acts on its own initiative. A court acting in this latter mode may delegate to court-appointed officers some or most of the necessary functions of administration. The available techniques of judicial administration fall along a continuum between party oriented and court oriented views of implementation. * * *

1. *Party-Centered Administration.* When courts rely on the parties, implementation occurs in the traditional adversarial mode. The court assumes a passive role, playing no part in implementation unless solicited by one of the parties. This judicial passivity places a considerable burden on the plaintiff, particularly when relief is gradual or implementation is drawn out. Overseeing implementation requires a cohesive plaintiff with considerable resources, and courts sometimes act to strengthen a weak plaintiff. As a variant of this practice, with a similar effect, courts sometimes request the participation of the United States as amicus curiae.

The common requirement that the defendant submit compliance reports eases the plaintiff's burden only slightly. Since defendants are unlikely to report noncompliance frankly, the plaintiff's monitoring task remains both crucial and burdensome. * * *

2. *Administrative Techniques with Reduced Reliance on Parties.* * * *

a. *Direct Judicial Initiative as an Administrative Technique.* When courts give themselves a supervisory role, in which they will act without further stimulus by the parties, they have taken a step beyond their traditional passivity. On their own initiative, courts frequently set hearing dates to consider compliance reports and take any necessary action. In addition, a vigorous judge may resort to various informal methods to further implementation.

Yet such court-ordered hearings, once begun, will remain adversarial in nature, with the customary reliance on the parties, and active judicial involvement in remedy administration will be constrained by the limited expertise and time of federal judges. Direct judicial initiative can only provide a limited supplement to party-centered administration. When the latter proves inadequate, the court must often not merely assume a more active role in implementation but also delegate administrative functions to an individual or group whose duties are primarily to the court, rather than to the parties.

b. *Use of Court Appointed Agents to Administer the Remedy.* These court appointed agents are identified by a confusing plethora of titles. * * *

In this discussion, the terms used by the courts will be replaced by terms based on the officer's principal function. The terms that will be used are master, monitor, mediator, administrator, and receiver. This function-based vocabulary provides a consistent basis for discussing the various court-appointed agents.

*Masters.* The master's role is to gather information and make recommendations. He reports to the court and, if required, makes findings of facts and conclusions of law. In the remedial phase of litigation, the master's principal role is to assist the court in formulating the substantive remedy, rather than in implementing it. However, masters sometimes continue to participate in the litigation, assuming implementation functions without change of title. Furthermore, because the remedy formulation and implementation phases of the lawsuit are often simultaneous, an administrator with extensive supervisory power over the defendant's activities may at the same time act as a master and be charged with developing a further plan.

*Monitors.* The monitor's role is to report on the defendant's compliance with the decree and on the achievement of the decree's goals. * * *

Monitors are appropriate if the remedy is complex, if compliance is difficult to measure, or if observation of the defendant's conduct is restricted. If the remedy is complex or covers many institutions, measuring compliance may be a task beyond the plaintiff's resources. If standards of compliance are not evident from the decree, a monitor can help formulate them. When the defendant is a closed institution, such as a prison or mental hospital, observing compliance may be difficult, and then monitors will be appropriate. * * *

*Mediators.* While the monitor's task is only to measure compliance, other court appointees play a more direct role in implementation. A mediator is a delegate whose primary responsibility is handling disputes over the decree's meaning, compliance standards, and the pace of compliance. In addition, a mediator must resolve individual grievances that arise during the remedial regime. Although retention of jurisdiction facilitates bringing such problems into court, doing so is time consuming, expensive, and strains judicial resources, even if the judicial role is informal and the procedural safeguards of a full dress evidentiary hearing are not invoked. * * *

*Administrators.* The administrator is the most innovative and unusual of the devices utilized by the courts for remedy implementation. The administrator's role extends beyond that of the master, monitor, or mediator but, unlike a receiver, the administrator supplements, and does not replace, the normal management of the institutional defendant. The administrator acts at his own instance to implement the remedy and has an executive role.

The authority to appoint an administrator is best grounded in the inherent power of courts "to provide themselves with appropriate instruments required for the performance of their duties" and the Supreme Court's directive that the courts make full use of their equitable powers in civil rights cases. Some courts rest the appointment of an administrator on rule 53, but this is an overly expansive reading of the role of masters under the federal rules. Rule 53 is largely concerned with the master as a fact finder, and though it permits masters to perform certain specific executive tasks, nothing in the rule or the earlier use of masters by the federal courts justifies the extensive and continuing administrative tasks assigned to "masters" in some recent cases.

Appointment of an administrator is most appropriate if implementation is complex and difficult to supervise. In title VII pattern and practice suits, for instance, compliance requires nondiscriminatory handling of hundreds or thousands of individual cases, a task that no judge can supervise. The complex actions required to implement comprehensive prison and mental hospital decrees are also appropriate occasions for the appointment of an administrator. An administrator may also be called for as a reaction to noncompliance with the court's orders.

The reluctance of the courts to use administrators in areas where they would be effective is probably due to considerations of equity and federalism, as the appointment of an administrator is an intrusive technique of remedy implementation. * * *

An administrator's powers normally include monitoring and mediation, but are more extensive. The variety of its functions is often obscured by the variety in terminology used, the variety of tasks a single agency sometimes performs, and the casualness with which the reported opinions describe these tasks. However, the administrator normally is given powers to supervise, coordinate, approve, or even command actions of the defendant to implement the remedy. This involves a substantial delegation of power, either with consent of the parties or imposed by the court.

The scope of this delegation varies. Some administrators are given very specific tasks, while others are granted broad and undefined power to secure implementation. * * *

*Receivers.* While an administrator's power derogates from the authority of the defendant's officers, these officers retain their posts. Administrators, like masters, monitors, and mediators, can only be effective if some cooperation is forthcoming from the defendant. When this is not forthcoming, a receivership may be appropriate. In a receivership, a court-appointed officer replaces the defendant's officers either completely or temporarily and for limited purposes. Imposition of a receivership is consequently a more drastic means of implementation than the appointment of an administrator or any lesser administrative agent. It is the most dramatic assertion of federal equitable power possible and courts have so regarded it. Obviously, removing state political officials from authority is more drastic than merely forcing them to act constitutionally. Receivership remains a device of last resort, used only when less intrusive devices have failed to achieve compliance, although the traditional strict restrictions on its use have been shed. * * *

### *Notes*

1. For further analysis of the authority to use court appointed agents to oversee the implementation of a judicial injunction, see David I. Levine, The Authority for the Appointment of Remedial Special Masters in Federal Institutional Reform Litigation: The History Reconsidered, 17 U.C.Davis L.Rev. 753 (1984); Vincent M. Nathan, The Use of Masters in Institutional Reform Litigation, 10 U.Tol.L.Rev. 419 (1979)(for different reasons, both articles contend that despite the fairly narrow language of F.R.Civ.P. 53, there is sufficient authority to make such appointments). As an alternative approach to the use of *ad hoc* agents, Joanna Kudisch Weinberg, The Judicial Adjunct and Public Law Remedies, 1 Yale L. & Pol'y Rev. 367 (1983), suggests that courts set up permanent offices of judicial adjuncts to handle such assignments. See also Linda J. Silberman, Judicial Adjuncts Revisited: The Proliferation of Ad Hoc Procedure, 137 U.Pa.L.Rev. 2131 (1989).

2. For discussion of the payment of special masters and other court appointed agents, see David I. Levine, Calculating Fees of Special Masters, 37 Hastings L.J. 141 (1985). No governmental entity—even the United States—is immune from paying for the cost of a remedial special master, as it is part of the costs of the litigation. E.g., NORML v. Mullen, 828 F.2d 536 (9th Cir.1987)(affirming the appointment of a master to monitor compliance with an injunction limiting the scope of the activities of a joint state and federal Campaign Against Marijuana Planting).

3. As the Special Project mentions, another equitable tool, receivership, is available if the conditions precedent are present. Most commonly, a court will appoint a receiver to manage the defendant's property (such as a

business in economic distress) on a temporary basis only if there is a danger that the defendant is or will become insolvent or the property at issue will be removed from the jurisdiction of the court, injured or destroyed before the merits of the dispute are decided. F.R.Civ.P. 66 (Appendix, infra p. 888); 12 Charles Alan Wright & Arthur Miller, Federal Practice and Procedure: Civil §§ 2981–86 (1973). Sometimes, courts have used receivers to enforce compliance with the law. E.g., United States v. American Tobacco Co., 221 U.S. 106, 31 S.Ct. 632, 55 L.Ed. 663 (1911)(indicating that receiver might take charge of a company to enforce compliance with antitrust laws); Morgan v. McDonough, 540 F.2d 527 (1st Cir.1976), cert. denied, 429 U.S. 1042, 97 S.Ct. 743, 50 L.Ed.2d 755 (1977)(approving appointment of receiver to ensure compliance with orders to desegregate a high school); United States v. Local 560, International Brotherhood of Teamsters, 780 F.2d 267 (3d Cir.1985) (affirming removal of union's Executive Board and appointment of temporary trustee where Board was part of a racketeering enterprise under RICO), cert. denied, 476 U.S. 1140, 106 S.Ct. 2247, 90 L.Ed.2d 693 (1986). See generally Comment, Union Receiverships Under RICO: A Union Democracy Perspective, 137 U.Pa.L.Rev. 929 (1989); Comment, Equitable Remedies: An Analysis of Judicial Utilization of Neoreceiverships to Implement Large Scale Institutional Change, 1976 Wis.L.Rev. 1161 (reviewing traditional and modern uses of receivers).

4. An injunction might specify only the goals which the defendants must achieve (e.g., provide only so many square feet per prisoner) or it may go on to indicate the milestones according to which progress toward the goals shall proceed (e.g., let the contract to build a new prison facility by a certain date and complete construction by another date). Although milestones do make the injunction somewhat more complicated to write, if the defendants are dilatory, they will be in violation of the court's order at a much earlier stage. This may open the way for increased judicial intervention, in particular under F.R.Civ.P. 70 (Appendix, infra p. 889). See Hansford v. Maplewood Station Business Park, 621 N.E.2d 347 (Ind.App.1993)(applying Indiana's version of Rule 70); David I. Levine, The Authority for the Appointment of Remedial Special Masters in Federal Institutional Reform Litigation: The History Reconsidered, 17 U.C.Davis L.Rev. 753, 796–98 (1984)(discussing application of Rule 70)(both compare appointment under Rule 70 with use of masters under Rule 53).

---

The following is not a written opinion but a transcript of some candid remarks from the bench. The statute in question, designed to curb the dumping of toxic wastes, imposed an absolute duty upon the Environmental Protection Agency.

## ILLINOIS v. COSTLE

United States District Court for the District of Columbia, 1979.
12 Env't Rep.Cas. (B.N.A.) 1597.

GESSELL, D.J.:

As I indicated after the discussion and argument yesterday, in view of the urgency of this matter, the Court is going today to give its ruling orally. * * *

These four proceedings are proceedings to enforce the Resource Conservation and Recovery Act of 1976, 42 U.S.C. § 9601.

The Court has previously found that the Environmental Protection Agency is in default of deadlines which were set by the Congress for the promulgation of various regulations implementing the provisions of the Act relating to hazardous and solid wastes. * * *

Plaintiffs in various forms and manner ask the Court now to establish a specific schedule for the promulgation of some ten regulations which are necessary to implement the provisions of the Act the Court has just referred to.

In response to the Court's request, EPA has submitted a proposed schedule which has been the focus of these decree proceedings.

There is no question that EPA has a duty to promulgate hazardous and solid waste regulations; and I think there is agreement that duty is to promulgate those regulations as quickly as reasonably possible.

The proposed schedule which EPA has submitted is challenged; and it is for the Court to determine whether that schedule or some other schedule is more appropriate.

Of course, the Court cannot appropriate funds; it cannot let out consulting contracts to develop the necessary technical information; it cannot hire personnel; and it cannot manage the agency's effort.

The most the Court can do is to use its influence to assure that everything reasonable is being done to carry out the obvious desire of Congress that there be prompt action to abate the hazards to our environment which the Act addresses. * * *

The agency, itself, recognizes that the estimates are nothing more than estimates; that they are subject to change; and that they are optimistic. * * *

All of the past experience indicates that it is difficult and hazardous to attempt to estimate the time required in meeting these more or less arbitrary deadlines which Congress has set in various EPA matters.

The Court cannot and should not ignore the fact that not only does EPA have other responsibilities in the regulatory area, but that it is presently under very exacting demands in other proceedings to accomplish its regulatory functions.

The Court, accordingly, has determined that it must for the time being accept the position of the agency with respect to the schedule. It appears to the Court that it is a good faith schedule which on the basis of present knowledge is in the public interest.

On the other hand, the Court has taken note and accepted the view of the Environmental Defense Fund and other Plaintiffs here that if a definite schedule is ordered by the Court, it is more likely in some vague and undefinable way that schedule will be achieved. * * *

With these considerations in mind, the Court has fashioned an order directing that the regulations be promulgated on the final dates set in the schedule submitted to the Court. The order goes further and requires that EPA shall, at the end of each quarter, commencing March 31, 1979, file with the Court in affidavit form over the signature of Mr. Costle [the EPA Administrator] a statement indicating any departures from the detailed implementing schedules that the EPA proposed on December 4, with a statement of reason or reasons therefor, together with an updated current estimate of the final promulgation date of each regulation.

The Court is also directing that whenever it appears to EPA that a date set by the Court as the outside date for promulgation of these regulations cannot be met, it shall immediately—and I emphasize, immediately—file an affidavit with the Court over the signature of the Administrator, explaining the facts and circumstances why it does not appear feasible to meet the date as ordered.

The Court is also directing that all of these filings not only, of course, be served on the parties but is directing that copies of the filings be furnished to the appropriate Oversight Committees of the Senate and the House of Representatives. * * *

Now, all of you, I think, are aware of the Court's concerns in this case but I don't want to terminate these proceedings without making it perfectly clear that in acceding to this schedule temporarily, as the Court has done, the Court is not in any respect discounting the position of the Plaintiffs, particularly of the Environmental Defense Fund, that this is a matter that can properly be labeled one approaching crisis proportions.

Well-meaning statutes are not self-implementing. We need a national will to protect the environment from the threatening health and pollution hazards which this Act addresses. There is need of a massive commitment of funds, talent and purpose to these objectives.

If the Court could do anything about it, the Court would; but these are not matters within the reach of the chancellor's foot. There is little a court of equity can do.

These are matters of national policy, political priorities; and I would urge upon the parties with everything at my command that they consider the appropriateness of continuing to rely on courts to accomplish objectives which can only be effectively accomplished in a democracy by resort to the polls, resort to the political processes which the Constitution preserves.

There is little I can do. I have done the most I can. But there are other forums where these issues could be far more properly and effectively ventilated. * * *

I will await with interest the reports from the agency pursuant to the order which I am now handing to the Deputy Clerk. * * *

### Notes

1. Plaintiffs did not even challenge the EPA's good faith even though they would not have brought and continued the suit if they had confidence that the agency was doing the best that it could. Professors Henderson and Pearson, supra at p. 201, showed the problem of proving bad faith. In a portion of their article not reproduced here, they argue that it is somewhat easier to show the absence of good faith when the defendant is a large organization since it is hard to pass the word through an organization to obstruct a court order without the word getting out. Yet, the word may be passed by innuendo and, besides, bureaucratic inertia alone is likely to sabotage a court order that requires action unless the leaders of the organization vigorously promote the action. The absence of good faith is particularly difficult to show when the defendant is a government agency or official because most standards for review of official action put a heavy burden on the plaintiff. For example, the Administrative Procedure Act states that a judge may not overturn administrative action merely because the judge sees it as wrong-headed; it must be so wrong-headed as to be "arbitrary or capricious." 5 U.S.C. § 706(2)(A)(1982).

2. Would an injunction that granted more than the rightful position or the appointment of a receiver have been viable approaches in Illinois v. Costle?

3. Judge Gessell says that he will deal with the problem of getting the agency to act by using the court's "influence." What are the obstacles to agency action? How does he use his influence to deal with them? What else could he have done?

4. Note that this suit could be brought because Congress had imposed a categorical mandate on the EPA, ostensibly depriving the agency of all discretion. Where Congress merely exorts the agency to issue regulations "promptly", citizen's suits are not permitted. Defenders of Wildlife v. Browner, 888 F.Supp. 1005 (D.Ariz.1995).

---

The following article discusses an example of a fairly successful judicial intervention. What factors led to this success?

## MURRAY LEVINE, CHARLES P. EWING & DAVID I. LEVINE, THE USE OF LAW FOR PREVENTION IN THE PUBLIC INTEREST

5 Prevention in Human Services 241, 265–271 (1987).

* * * WUORI v. ZITNAY: SUCCESSFUL IMPLEMENTATION OF A CONSENT DECREE

*Wuori v. Zitnay* (No. 75–80, D.Me.1975) is one of the most successful of the institutional reform cases. The case is unusual because the court gave up active supervision within a relatively few years. The defendants achieved substantial, if not full, compliance with an extensive consent decree which committed the state to improve an institution for the retarded and to create new community facilities as well.

The case was brought in 1975 by Neville Woodruff, an attorney who headed the Legal Services Corporation office in Portland, Maine. In the course of visiting the Pineland Center, an institution that at its peak had housed nearly 1500 mentally retarded individuals, Woodruff received information and documents from some employees who were frustrated by their inability to provide decent care. The institution was overcrowded and in poor condition. The residents had inadequate clothing. Their personal hygiene was poor. Residents were in restraints for unconscionable periods and were overmedicated. There was a lack of both programming and professional services. Dentists were pulling teeth from some residents to prevent self-abuse or harm to others. Moreover, many who had been released to the community as part of an earlier deinstitutionalization thrust were living in inadequate homes and were not receiving adequate habilitation services.

The suit, alleging violations of the Eighth Amendment right to be free of cruel and unusual punishment, or to be free from harm at the hands of the state, was brought in 1975 on behalf of a class of all residents in the institution and all residents who had been conditionally discharged but were still under the supervision of Pineland Center. Shortly after the suit was initiated, George Zitnay was hired by the state of Maine to become Director of Pineland Center. Zitnay, an experienced and gifted institutional administrator, immediately recognized the opportunity the suit presented to gain resources and leverage to improve Pineland. When he was deposed * * * he told the full truth about the institution. Zitnay's testimony, along with the plaintiffs' fully documented case, convinced the state that it could not win. Moreover, state officials would be subject to highly adverse publicity as long as the case was in court. The state agreed to settle out of court.

For the next two years, the plaintiffs' attorney negotiated with the state to develop a satisfactory plan for correcting deficiencies. Meanwhile, Zitnay was promoted from Superintendent of Pineland to State Commissioner of Mental Health and Corrections. The then Governor, the late James B. Longley, under whom Zitnay served, sincerely supported substantial improvement in the care of the mentally retarded. Zitnay was also very able in winning support from parents' groups as well as influential private citizens throughout the state of Maine. Despite such support, progress was slow in arriving at a satisfactory plan to remedy Pineland's deficiencies.

In 1978, the plaintiff's attorney called for assistance from the Mental Health Law Project, a Washington, D.C. public interest law firm with a great deal of experience in this type of litigation. The Mental Health Law Project assisted in developing an extensive, highly detailed plan for institutional reform covering both the Pineland Center and especially community residences and programs. The plan called for the appointment of a special master to oversee implementation. Zitnay and Kevin Concannon, then Director of the Bureau of Mental Retardation, recommended that the State of Maine accept the settlement, for both men understood it could be used as a blueprint and as leverage for modernizing and improving the entire system of care for the mentally retarded throughout Maine. The State's Attorney General, Joseph Brennan, who was later to succeed Longley as governor, accepted their recommendation.

### Implementation Under a Special Master

In July, 1978, United States District Court Judge Edward T. Gignoux, a highly respected jurist, entered the consent decree, based on the plan developed by the parties with the assistance of the Mental Health Law Project, as the judgment of the court. After a search, the judge appointed David Gregory, a University of Maine law professor, as special master for a period of two years. The participants believed the decree would be fully implemented by that time.

The special master began with two assumptions. The first was that the state would not have agreed to anything it did not intend to do. The second was that the limit of what he had to know was what was in the court order. He believed at the time that the total job was one of looking at what the decree required, looking at what was going on in the institution, and then reporting on the differences. As he became aware of institutional dynamics and of the organizational and political complexities of introducing change in public agencies, he soon realized that both assumptions were incorrect.

After the first six months of educating himself about the problems of mental retardation, the culture of the institution, and interagency issues, Gregory took a more active role. He not only gathered information about the state of compliance with the decree, but he began educating the heads of other agencies as to how their actions were affecting implementation of the decree. In effect, he became an advocate for the decree. He worked closely with Zitnay, who was the named defendant, and with Concannon on the task of implementation. He came to understand that although Zitnay was commissioner, he had little direct control over Pineland Center itself and no power over state agencies on the same organizational level as his department (e.g., the state personnel department, the Commissioner of Finance, and the Commissioner of Human Services, basically responsible for Medicaid and other welfare programs). As a consequence of that decision, he tended to confront some department heads vigorously, strongly intimating that he expected their cooperation. For instance, he once had a difficult confrontation with Governor Brennan (Governor Longley's successor) who, as Attorney General, had consented to the decree. Governor Brennan objected strongly to the critical tone of Gregory's reports. Gregory also worked with operators of group homes around the state to encourage them to organize politically to obtain changes in state regulations that limited their ability to program effectively. That activity, too, led to friction between Gregory and some state officials.

During this period, Zitnay and Concannon worked through the state's governmental structure to gain resources to modernize services for the retarded. They kept Gregory fully informed about barriers to implementation and other institutional problems. Gregory conducted his own investigations as to the state of compliance with the decree. He continued to receive information from some employees about deficiencies in programming or about abuses. (Other employees viewed his activities less benignly.) His reports to the court depicted the shortcomings and remaining problems in the institutions. Zitnay and Concannon could make bold requests for resources to correct deficiencies and point to the special master's reports to bolster their requests. In effect, the "blame" for the necessary large budget increases and other legislative changes could be placed on the special master. * * *

As the two year period of court supervision ended, Gregory's reports were still highly critical of the limited progress. He recommended extending the period of the court's supervision until compliance had been achieved. The plaintiffs and defendants resumed negotiations arriving at a stipulation * * * as to what further needed to be done to satisfy the terms of the decree. The state defendants agreed to the continuation of the special master's office, but in view of the friction between Gregory and the defendants, they insisted that Gregory be replaced. The change may have been at the insistence of the Governor.

In retrospect, all parties agreed that Gregory had done a superb job as special master. Although some questioned whether his reports too greatly emphasized the negatives of the defendant's actions, all agreed that had he not adopted an aggressive stance, there would have been much less progress in implementing the decree. * * *

THE NEXT PHASE

The new master was Lincoln Clark, the head of the state court mediation service. An experienced executive and a highly skilled mediator, Clark was a close friend of Judge Gignoux. He knew the major figures in state government and in the legislature. All of the major actors agreed to his appointment. Judge Gignoux appointed Clark to replace Gregory.

With a new governor taking office, Zitnay resigned as commissioner, returned to Pineland Center as superintendent, and was replaced by Kevin Concannon. Clark decided to focus first on Pineland rather than the community facilities, because it had moved far along the road to compliance under Zitnay. The most difficult part of the task was to establish criteria for deciding when the defendant had finally brought Pineland into compliance with the consent decree. Issues such as the number of beds in a room were easy to decide. Issues such as "adequate programming" required a great deal of subjective judgment.

Clark held a great many negotiating sessions among Zitnay, Concannon, and the plaintiffs' attorneys to agree to standards for compliance. Once the parties agreed, Clark brought in an outside consultant to review Pineland against the standards that had been agreed to, and to offer an opinion as to whether its programs met the standards. On the basis of an extensive review, the consultant concluded that Pineland Center was in substantial compliance with the institutional provisions of the consent decree. Clark therefore recommended that Pineland be discharged from the court's active supervision. In September, 1981, Judge Gignoux formally discharged the center from the court's direct supervision through Clark's office. Although this was an important milestone, Clark still faced correcting the remaining deficiencies in the community based treatment system, such as substandard housing, poor programming, and an insufficient number of community residences. Concannon, as Director of the Bureau of Mental Retardation, and later as Commissioner, had made progress in opening new group homes. However, persons seeking to develop group homes were faced with conflicting regulations and fiscal controls that led to great delays in opening new facilities.

In a spirit of negotiation and cooperation, Clark and the plaintiff's attorneys were willing to accept as substantial compliance the establishment of organizational means of accomplishing solutions, even if the precise program for each class member had not yet been achieved. While Clark effectively employed the skills of a mediator, he was well aware that his effectiveness depended upon the coercive power of the court. Clark also used the threat of adverse publicity, as did Gregory before him, to move matters along when progress seemed to be blocked.

Clark's reports to the court assisted the defendants' attempts to augment their budgets. Clark mailed his reports to all of the state legislators, to state officials, and to advocacy organizations. He also spoke informally with the chairman of the health committee of the state legislature, a person he knew well. Commissioner Concannon worked skillfully with the legislature as well to gain new resources and other legislation to assist the development of programs in the community.

Two years after Judge Gignoux had discharged Pineland Center from the court's active supervision, Clark believed that sufficient progress had been made in implementing the community portion of the decree. In the summer of 1983, Clark contracted with outside consultants to determine whether the defendants' claims of progress were warranted. One consultant concluded that not all of the requirements of the consent decree had been met, but that enough had been put into place that the defendants would be able to come into full compliance. Another consultant studied the lives of those class members who left Pineland Center and were living in the community. On the basis of interviews with a randomly selected sample of clients and staff, she concluded that the living, working, and learning experiences of the class members substantially adhered to the standards involved in the two major themes of the consent decree—normalization and habilitation.

An obvious concern was whether the improvements and the progress would survive if the court were to give up jurisdiction and cease supervising the programs. Two methods were developed to continue to monitor the system. A Consumer Advisory Board, created earlier as part of the consent decree, was now given greater monitoring responsibilities. The Board began developing a network of "correspondents"—

people to act as next friends to those who have no families or have been abandoned by their families and to help in monitoring conditions in the many group homes scattered throughout the state. The defendants also agreed to undertake an annual, independent and public review of compliance with standards for institutional and community care incorporated into the consent decree and to publish a plan to remedy any identified deficiencies.

Clark's report, finding compliance with the terms of the consent decree as interpreted through the various stipulations, was submitted to the court in October, 1983. Shortly afterwards Judge Gignoux accepted the findings, discharged the special master, and relinquished active supervision of the case. It was one of the first cases of its kind to come to this degree of successful completion. In August, 1985, M. Levine visited Pineland Center and conducted interviews with important participants. Maine has developed a very good system of care for class members and has improved the system of care for all. Undoubtedly, one could find gaps in the provision of care, and some problems are relatively intractable, but the worst abuses have certainly been curbed, and for most, humane care at the state of the art is being provided. The state continues to identify problems in the system of care, and officials are making efforts to plan for the future. The goal of prevention is being met. * * *

### *Notes*

1. What are the advantages and disadvantages of the roles played respectively by Professor Gregory and Mr. Clark in *Wuori*?

2. After a long period of quiescence, there has been some litigation regarding the matters addressed in *Wuori*. In October 1991, the Consumer Advisory Board that had been established in the consent decree brought an action seeking enforcement of the rights established in the 1978 consent decree. The Board's primary concerns were that the defendants had stopped making appropriate annual assessments of the medical, educational and training needs of the Pineland Center residents and outpatients, that the defendants had failed to create sufficient new community placements for residents and that basic safety at Pineland had been neglected. After some skirmishing over whether Judge Gignoux (who died in the interim) had intended to terminate jurisdiction over the case by 1986, Consumer Advisory Board v. Glover, 989 F.2d 65 (1st Cir.1993)(no such intent expressed), the district court denied the defendants' motions to dissolve the injunction and terminate the decree, 151 F.R.D. 496 (D.Me.1993), and to dismiss the Board's complaint, 151 F.R.D. 490 (D.Me.1993).

3. For a more detailed description of the implementation of the injunction in *Wuori,* see Murray Levine, The Role of Special Master in Institutional Reform Litigation: A Case Study, 8 Law & Policy 275 (1986). For another example of successful implementation of a detailed decree, see Judy Scales-Trent, A Judge Shapes and Manages Institutional Reform: School Desegregation in Buffalo, 17 N.Y.U.Rev. L. & Soc.Change 119 (1989–90)(showing

how district court skillfully used decree implementation process to turn the Buffalo, N.Y. public schools into a "national model of integration").

---

One attorney with extensive experience litigating institutional reform cases has specified the elements he believes are needed for any effective compliance mechanism. Considering what we have examined so far in this course, what would constrain a judge from doing all that the author recommends?

## MICHAEL S. LOTTMAN, ENFORCING JUDICIAL DECREES: NOW COMES THE HARD PART

Mental Disability L.Rep. 69, 74–75 (July–August 1976).

a. An effective compliance mechanism must be established, first of all, in the context of an order, based upon a factual record, which binds the necessary officials and fixes specific responsibility on one or more of such officials for implementation of particular standards or requirements.

b. The order should be as precise and quantitative as possible, and should set forth clearly measurable, objective standards (including deadlines), so that compliance can be monitored accurately and, as far as possible, by clerical or mechanical means.

c. The order should provide for financing of required staff, physical plant improvements, development of community facilities, and other such items, and fix the responsibility for obtaining the necessary funds on the proper defendants.

d. The court should retain jurisdiction over the action.

e. If reporting requirements are included, they should serve as a starting point for compliance activity, not as an exclusive fact-gathering device. The court order, or the monitoring body, should prescribe with great specificity the format, contents, and timing of any required reports, and should structure such reports to elicit factual information rather than opinions. The reporting document should be directly related to specific provisions of the order. If feasible, such reports should be required to be verified under oath or otherwise designated as admissible in evidence, without more, in any proceeding for enforcement or contempt.

f. The monitoring body, whatever its specific form, must be on the premises of the defendant institution or otherwise in contact with the defendants on a full-time, daily basis, and must have access to all relevant records or documents and to residents or patients, defendants' employees, and other persons affected by or involved in the implementation of the order. The monitoring body must be independent of the person or agency whose conduct it is monitoring, and must owe its first allegiance to the court.

g. The monitoring body must be provided with sufficient full-time staff to monitor the defendants' operations on a daily basis, develop required plans or reports, respond to inquiries and complaints, and carry out other functions as assigned by the court. The monitoring body must also have access to professional and legal experts, either on a full-time or consulting basis.

h. While enforcement of court orders should not be made to depend solely on the efforts of attorneys for the plaintiffs, no enforcement mechanism should operate so as to interfere in any way with such attorneys' continuing duty to represent their clients. Counsel for all parties should be served with copies of any communication between the monitoring body and the court.

i. To the extent possible, monitoring bodies should not also be charged with responsibility for developing the plans and designing the requirements whose implementation they must then oversee. This "legislative-executive" role mixture is likely to dilute the effectiveness of the monitoring body.

j. Monitoring bodies should be empowered to do more than merely mediate disputes or make reports to the court; they should, at least, have the authority to make recommendations in regard to implementation of the order which must be followed unless an objection thereto is upheld by the court. The order should spell out in detail the procedure to be followed when the monitoring body identifies a violation of the order or a related problem, and the procedure for making, objecting to, and enforcing the monitoring body's recommendations—in other words, an implementation structure. The monitoring body should be given the procedural and technical weapons necessary to enable it to investigate violations and formulate recommendations.

k. Finally, the court should make it clear from the start that noncompliance with its order will be dealt with by measures of whatever severity is necessary, up to and including proceedings for contempt of court. * * *

### *Problems*

Which techniques should a court select to administer an injunction in a case where:

(a) a local government has violated emission limits for its incinerator and the plaintiff wants the government to install pollution control equipment?

(b) a large private corporation has engaged in employment discrimination?

(c) a federal agency has failed to provide a set of documents under the Freedom of Information Act?

## 3. ACCOMMODATING CHANGING CIRCUMSTANCES: INTERPRETATION AND MODIFICATION OF THE DECREE

As you learned in your first year of law school, there are sound policy reasons for valuing the finality of judgments. Thus, it is fairly difficult to modify a final judgment of a court. See F.R.Civ.P. 60(b) (relief may be granted only upon a showing of limited conditions, such as mistake or fraud, and generally only within a limited period of time, usually one year). Similarly, the doctrine of res judicata applies even where the law which a court relied upon to render the original judgment is later changed by a higher court. E.g., Federated Department Stores Inc. v. Moitie, 452 U.S. 394, 101 S.Ct. 2424, 69 L.Ed.2d 103 (1981). The law also values finality in private negotiations. Thus, you probably read cases in contracts that required a party to continue to perform under long-term or indefinite contracts even though economic conditions had changed and the contract was no longer economically advantageous to one party. E.g., Parev Products v. I Rokeach, 124 F.2d 147 (2d Cir. 1941)(court refused to modify a 25 year contract after 15 years of performance). Tort law also has a strong element of finality. A judgment rendered in a tort case is designed to compensate for all injury—past, present and future. A later change of circumstance (for example, after judgment, the plaintiff actually lives longer than the life expectancy assumed at trial) is not permitted to be the basis for reopening of the litigation or for a modification of the judgment to change the amount awarded originally at trial. See, e.g., Pretre v. United States, 531 F.Supp. 931 (E.D.Mo.1981). As the materials in this section demonstrate, however, at times the finality of an injunction (and its close cousin, the consent decree), has been treated somewhat differently.

### TIMOTHY S. JOST, FROM *SWIFT* TO *STOTTS* AND BEYOND: MODIFICATION OF INJUNCTIONS IN THE FEDERAL COURTS

64 Tex.L.Rev. 1101 (1986).

* * * The injunction is peculiarly a prospective remedy; it is a prediction based on a prediction. It is based on a prediction that unless the court intervenes the obligor will continue to violate the rights of the beneficiary. It is also itself a prediction in that it projects the power of the court into the future, promising that violation of the terms of the injunction will elicit a punitive or coercive response from the court.

Several circumstances, however, impede the court's attempt at prophecy. First, a court can only predict the obligor's future conduct based on its understanding of the obligor's present and past conduct. Even this understanding is necessarily flawed. Limited access to information, which often can be improved only at a considerable cost, and the constraints of bounded rationality hamper the court. But when the court turns from its understanding of the past or present and attempts to envision the future, it encounters even more baffling perplexities. The parties act within a dynamic socioeconomic context in which their behavior and relationship are subject to constant change. The court's vision rapidly blurs as it attempts to peer into the mists of the future and discern evolving factual developments. Moreover, not even the legal context in which the court must operate is static—new statutes and regulations constantly emerge and judicial precedents are expanded, contracted, reinterpreted, and overruled. Yet, trial courts entering injunctions are, by and large, obligated to take as given the state of the law in effect at the time the decree is entered; they have little freedom to predict the future contours of the law. Thus, the court's assumptions about the future almost inevitably fail as the law changes. Finally, in formulating its decree the court is trammeled by the mundane limitations of drafting and by its perception of the practical and political constraints that hedge its power.

Injunctions entered by consent create further complexities. The pervasive use of consent decrees to resolve contemporary equitable litigation is striking. From 1975 through 1981, over seventy percent of Justice Department Antitrust Division case terminations were by consent decree. The [Securities and Exchange Commission] resolves about ninety percent of its cases by consent. Even when the substantive issues in a case are fully litigated to judgment by the court, the remedial resolution frequently results from negotiations by the parties based on the court's substantive decision. Relatively few complex injunctions wholly lack an element of consent.

Consent decrees are not only judicial decrees, but also long-term contracts, the products of bargaining between the parties. This bargaining process could potentially improve the predictive power of the decree. The parties presumably have better access than the court to information about their futures, particularly about their future intentions, and can avail themselves of a greater array of tools for dealing with uncertainty. But insofar as the parties have unequal power in the bargaining process, unequal access to information, or incentives to place risks and burdens on persons not represented in the negotiations, a consent decree may turn out to be even less durable than a fully litigated order. Moreover, it may be in the immediate interest of parties seeking resolution of a conflict (or their attorneys) to incorporate into a consent decree intentional ambiguity and omission, hazarding future conflict to purchase present peace.

Because the injunction is necessarily a static * * * response to a dynamic evolving problem, over time it almost inevitably becomes less responsive to the problem it addresses. * * * The future tricks the court; the injunction, the court's now outdated prediction, plods off into irrelevancy, leaving the beneficiary bereft of protection or the obligor subject to oppression.

What can the court do to accommodate change? Explicit accommodation often may be unnecessary. As time goes on the parties may themselves adjust to the future without revision of the decree. * * * When, however, an injunction's prediction of the future and the unfolding future itself begin to diverge radically, the only solution is modification.

Motions for modification are nominally brought under Federal Rule of Civil Procedure 60(b)(5), which provides that "the court may relieve a party ... from a final judgment, order, or proceeding ... [if] a prior judgment upon which it is based has been reversed or otherwise vacated, or it is no longer equitable that the judgment should have prospective application." The rule, however, merely codifies preexisting law, recognizing the inherent power of a court sitting in equity to modify its decrees prospectively to achieve equality. * * *

### *Note on Interpretation and Modification of a Decree*

Sometimes the court can assist the parties and avoid modification by simply interpreting the injunction or consent decree. "To interpret is to explain and elucidate, not to add or subtract from the text." 2 Milton Handler, Twenty-Five Years of Antitrust 952 (1973). As the Supreme Court has explained:

> [c]onsent decrees are entered into by parties to a case after careful negotiation has produced agreement on their precise terms. The parties waive their right to litigate the issues involved in the case and thus save themselves the time, expense, and inevitable risk of litigation. Naturally, the agreement reached normally embodies a compromise; in exchange for the saving of cost and elimination of risk, the parties each give up something they might have won had they proceeded with the litigation. Thus the decree itself cannot be said to have a purpose; rather the parties have purposes, generally opposed to each other, and the resultant decree embodies as much of those opposing purposes as the respective parties have the bargaining power and skill to achieve. For these reasons, the scope of a consent decree must be discerned within its four corners, and not by reference to what might satisfy the purposes of one of the parties to it.

United States v. Armour & Co., 402 U.S. 673, 681–82, 91 S.Ct. 1752, 1757, 29 L.Ed.2d 256 (1971). See also Huguley v. General Motors Corp., 67 F.3d 129 (6th Cir.1995)(district court's proper role "was to ascertain the intent of the parties at the time of settlement," and not to try to "effectuate what it considered to be the 'goals' of the decree").

If interpretation will not suffice and modification is necessary, how easy should it be to modify a permanent injunction or a consent decree? Should it matter if the plaintiff or the defendant seeks the modification? Should it matter if the decree was imposed by the court in the form of a permanent injunction after a full hearing on the merits or in the form of a consent decree entered after protracted settlement negotiations? Should the law's general interest in valuing finality overcome the desire to do equity? Does it matter if the context is the changing circumstances of public policy involved in a large scale public law case?

The Supreme Court's apparent stated position for many years was that it should be difficult to obtain a modification. In United States v. Swift & Co., 286 U.S. 106, 52 S.Ct. 460, 76 L.Ed. 999 (1932), the Supreme Court reversed a lower court's modification of a consent decree entered over ten years earlier in an antitrust case against the five largest meat packers in the country. Although the trial court had the power to modify consent decrees because they were judicial acts, and not private contracts, Justice Cardozo's opinion seemed to demand that the power to modify was to be used rarely. "Nothing less than a clear showing of grievous wrong evoked by new and unforeseen conditions should lead us to change what was decreed after years of litigation with the consent of all concerned." 286 U.S. at 119, 52 S.Ct. at 464. In another famous phrase from the opinion, Justice Cardozo said that there should be no modification from changed conditions unless the original dangers that were the reason for the decree originally, "once substantial, have become attenuated to a shadow." Id. The meat packer decree was not finally dissolved until 1981. United States v. Swift & Co., 1982–1 Trade Cases (CCH) ¶ 64,464 (N.D.Ill.1981).

However, in 1968, the Court appeared to relax *Swift's* "grievous wrong" standard. In United States v. United Shoe Machinery Corp., 391 U.S. 244, 88 S.Ct. 1496, 20 L.Ed.2d 562 (1968), the trial court had entered a permanent injunction designed to restore competition to the market of the manufacture of shoe machinery. Several years later, the government petitioned the trial court for further relief on the grounds that the defendant continued to dominate the market. The district court refused to grant the requested relief on the strength of *Swift.* The Supreme Court reversed, holding that the "grievous wrong" standard applied only to modifications requested by defendants seeking to avoid the responsibilities imposed by an order.

The uncertainty of when to apply the rigid standard from *Swift* to modifications of injunctions and consent decrees and when a more flexible standard is appropriate has continued. See, e.g., Thomas M. Mengler, Consent Decree Paradigms: Models Without Meaning, 29 B.C.L.Rev. 291 (1988); Marc J. Steinberg, SEC and Other Permanent Injunctions—Standards for Their Imposition, Modification and Dissolution, 66 Cornell L.Rev. 27 (1980). The two cases following the problems represent the Supreme Court's latest efforts to clarify the standards for interpretation and modification of decrees.

### *Problems*

How should a court rule on the following petitions?

1. Employees at a state university seek to modify a consent decree provision, which placed a $6000 cap on legal expenses that the defendant university would pay for the prosecution of successful sex discrimination suits against it, after the plaintiff-employees find that they cannot retain

counsel who are willing to accept cases for that fee alone. See Rajender v. University of Minnesota, 730 F.2d 1110 (8th Cir.1984). Should it matter if the $6000 figure was arrived at by hard bargaining? May the decree be modified because the average cost of legal services in the locality has gone up substantially since the decree was entered?

2. A consent decree, which reflected the then-effective labor statutes, enjoined a railroad and its unions from requiring that all employees be members of a union. One of the union defendants later seeks to modify the decree after Congress amended the law to permit all-union worksites in railroads. See Railway Employees v. Wright, 364 U.S. 642, 81 S.Ct. 368, 5 L.Ed.2d 349 (1961). Should it matter that when it amended the law, Congress did not choose to ban rules prohibiting all-union worksites? Does it make a difference whether the original order was imposed by a consent decree or through an injunction after a trial on the merits?

3. A class of African–American plaintiffs seeks interpretation or modification of a consent decree creating an affirmative action plan for the hiring of firefighters in order to protect newly hired African–Americans from the effects of layoffs caused by unexpectedly severe budgetary constraints. See the next case.

## FIREFIGHTERS LOCAL UNION NO. 1784 v. STOTTS

Supreme Court of the United States, 1984.
467 U.S. 561, 104 S.Ct. 2576, 81 L.Ed.2d 483.

JUSTICE WHITE delivered the opinion of the Court.

Petitioners challenge the Court of Appeals' approval of an order enjoining the City of Memphis from following its seniority system in determining who must be laid off as a result of a budgetary shortfall. Respondents contend that the injunction was necessary to effectuate the terms of a Title VII consent decree in which the City agreed to undertake certain obligations in order to remedy past hiring and promotional practices. Because we conclude that the order cannot be justified, either as an effort to enforce the consent decree or as a valid modification, we reverse.

### I

In 1977 respondent Carl Stotts, a black holding the position of fire-fighting captain in the Memphis, Tennessee, Fire Department, filed a class action complaint in the United States District Court for the Western District of Tennessee. The complaint charged that the Memphis Fire Department and certain city officials were engaged in a pattern or practice of making hiring and promotion decisions on the basis of race in violation of Title VII of the Civil Rights Act of 1964, 42 U.S.C. § 2000e *et seq.*, as well as 42 U.S.C. §§ 1981 and 1983. The District Court certified the case as a class action and consolidated it with an individual action subsequently filed by respondent Fred Jones, a black fire-fighting private in the Department, who claimed that he had been denied a promotion because of his race. Discovery proceeded, settlement negotiations ensued, and in due course, a consent decree was approved and entered by the District Court on April 25, 1980.

The stated purpose of the decree was to remedy the hiring and promotion practices "of the ... Department with respect to blacks." Accordingly, the City agreed to promote 13 named individuals and to provide backpay to 81 employees of the Fire Department. It also adopted the long-term goal of increasing the proportion of minority representation in each job classification in the Fire Department to approximately the proportion of blacks in the labor force in Shelby County, Tennessee. However, the City did not, by agreeing to the decree, admit "any violations of law, rule or regulation with respect to the allegations" in the complaint. The plaintiffs waived any further relief save to enforce the decree, and the District Court retained jurisdiction "for such further orders as may be necessary or appropriate to effectuate the purposes of this decree."

The long-term hiring goal outlined in the decree paralleled the provisions of a 1974 consent decree, which settled a case brought against the City by the United States and which applied citywide. Like the 1974 decree, the 1980 decree also established an interim hiring goal of filling on an annual basis 50 percent of the job vacancies in the Department with qualified black applicants. The 1980 decree contained an additional goal with respect to promotions: the Department was to attempt to ensure that 20 percent of the promotions in each job classification be given to blacks. Neither decree contained provisions for layoffs or reductions in rank, and neither awarded any competitive seniority. The 1974 decree did require that for purposes of promotion, transfer, and assignment, seniority was to be computed "as the total seniority of that person with the City."

In early May, 1981, the City announced that projected budget deficits required a reduction of non-essential personnel throughout the City Government. Layoffs were to be based on the "last hired, first fired" rule under which city-wide seniority, determined by each employee's length of continuous service from the latest date of permanent employment, was the basis for deciding who would be laid off. If a senior employee's position were abolished or eliminated, the employee could "bump down" to a lower ranking position rather than be laid off. As the Court of Appeals later noted, this layoff policy was adopted pursuant to the seniority system "mentioned in the 1974 decree and ... incorporated in the City's memorandum of understanding with the Union."

On May 4, at respondents' request, the District Court entered a temporary restraining order forbidding the layoff of any black employee. The Union, which previously had not been a party to either of these cases, was permitted to intervene. At the preliminary injunction hearing, it appeared that 55 then-filled positions in the Department were to be eliminated and that 39 of these positions were filled with employees having "bumping" rights. It was estimated that 40 least-senior employees in the fire-fighting bureau of the Department would be laid off and that of these 25 were white and 15 black. It also appeared that 56 percent of the employees hired in the Department since 1974 had been black and that the percentage of black employees had increased from approximately 3 or 4 percent in 1974 to 11½ percent in 1980.

On May 18, the District Court entered an order granting an injunction. The Court found that the consent decree "did not contemplate the method to be used for reduction in rank or lay-off," and that the layoff policy was in accordance with the City's seniority system and was not adopted with any intent to discriminate. Nonetheless, concluding that the proposed layoffs would have a racially discriminatory effect and that the seniority system was not a bona fide one, the District Court ordered that the City "not apply the seniority policy proposed insofar as it will decrease the percentage of black lieutenants, drivers, inspectors and privates that are presently employed...." On June 23, the District Court broadened its order to include three additional classifications. A modified layoff plan, aimed at protecting black employees in the seven classifications so as to comply with the court's order, was presented and approved. Layoffs pursuant to the modified plan were then carried out. In certain instances, to comply with the injunction, non-minority employees with more seniority than minority employees were laid off or demoted in rank.[2] * * *

III

The issue at the heart of this case is whether the District Court exceeded its powers in entering an injunction requiring white employees to be laid off, when the otherwise applicable seniority system would have called for the layoff of black employees with less seniority. We are convinced that the Court of Appeals erred in resolving this issue and in affirming the District Court.

A

The Court of Appeals first held that the injunction did no more than enforce the terms of the consent decree. This specific-performance approach rests on the notion that because the City was under a general obligation to use its best efforts to increase the proportion of blacks on the force, it breached the decree by attempting to effectuate a layoff policy reducing the percentage of black employees in the Department even though such a policy was mandated by the seniority system adopted by the City and the Union. A variation of this argument is that since the decree permitted the District Court to enter any later orders that "may be necessary or appropriate to effectuate the purposes of this decree," the City had agreed in advance to an injunction against layoffs that would reduce the proportion of black employees. We are convinced,

2. The City ultimately laid off 24 privates, 3 of whom were black. Had the seniority system been followed, 6 blacks would have been among the 24 privates laid off. Thus, three white employees were laid off as a direct result of the District Court's order. The number of whites demoted as a result of the order is not clear from the record before us.

however, that both of these are improvident constructions of the consent decree.

It is to be recalled that the "scope of a consent decree must be discerned within its four corners, and not by reference to what might satisfy the purposes of one of the parties to it" or by what "might have been written had the plaintiff established his factual claims and legal theories in litigation." United States v. Armour & Co., 402 U.S. 673, 681–682, 91 S.Ct. 1752, 1757, 29 L.Ed.2d 256 (1971). Here, as the District Court recognized, there is no mention of layoffs or demotions within the four corners of the decree; nor is there any suggestion of an intention to depart from the existing seniority system or from the City's arrangements with the Union. We cannot believe that the parties to the decree thought that the City would simply disregard its arrangements with the Union and the seniority system it was then following. Had there been any intention to depart from the seniority plan in the event of layoffs or demotions, it is much more reasonable to believe that there would have been an express provision to that effect. This is particularly true since the decree stated that it was not "intended to conflict with any provisions" of the 1974 decree, and since the latter decree expressly anticipated that the City would recognize seniority. It is thus not surprising that when the City anticipated layoffs and demotions, it in the first instance faithfully followed its preexisting seniority system, plainly having no thought that it had already agreed to depart from it. It therefore cannot be said that the express terms of the decree contemplated that such an injunction would be entered.

The argument that the injunction was proper because it carried out the purposes of the decree is equally unconvincing. The decree announced that its purpose was "to remedy past hiring and promotion practices" of the Department, and to settle the dispute as to the "appropriate and valid procedures for hiring and promotion." The decree went on to provide the agreed-upon remedy, but as we have indicated, that remedy did not include the displacement of white employees with seniority over blacks. Furthermore, it is reasonable to believe that the "remedy", which it was the purpose of the decree to provide, would not exceed the bounds of the remedies that are appropriate under Title VII, at least absent some express provision to that effect. As our cases have made clear, however, and as will be reemphasized below, Title VII protects bona fide seniority systems, and it is inappropriate to deny an innocent employee the benefits of his seniority in order to provide a remedy in a pattern-or-practice suit such as this. We thus have no doubt that the City considered its system to be valid and that it had no intention of departing from it when it agreed to the 1980 decree.

Finally, it must be remembered that neither the Union nor the non minority employees were parties to the suit when the 1980 decree was entered. Hence the entry of that decree cannot be said to indicate any agreement by them to any of its terms. Absent the presence of the Union or the non-minority employees and an opportunity for them to agree or disagree with any provisions of the decree that might encroach on their rights, it seems highly unlikely that the City would purport to bargain away non-minority rights under the then-existing seniority system. We therefore conclude that the injunction does not merely enforce the agreement of the parties as reflected in the consent decree. If the injunction is to stand, it must be justified on some other basis.

B

The Court of Appeals held that even if the injunction is not viewed as compelling compliance with the terms of the decree, it was still properly entered because the District Court had inherent authority to modify the decree when an economic crisis unexpectedly required layoffs which, if carried out as the City proposed, would undermine the affirmative action outlined in the decree and impose an undue hardship on respondents. This was true, the court held, even though the modification conflicted with a bona fide seniority system adopted by the City. The Court of Appeals erred in reaching this conclusion.[9]

Section 703(h) of Title VII provides that it is not an unlawful employment practice to apply different standards of compensation, or different terms, conditions, or privileges of employment pursuant to a bona fide seniority system, provided that such differences ar not the result of an intention to discriminate because of race.[10] It is clear that the City had a seniority system, that its proposed layoff plan conformed to that system, and that in making the settlement the City had not agreed to award competitive seniority to any minority employee whom the City proposed to lay off. The District Court held that the City could

9. The dissent seems to suggest and Justice Stevens expressly states, that Title VII is irrelevant in determining whether the District Court acted properly in modifying the consent decree. However, this was Title VII litigation, and in affirming modifications of the decree, the Court of Appeals relied extensively on what it considered to be its authority under Title VII. That is the posture in which the cases come to us. Furthermore, the District Court's authority to impose a modification of a decree is not wholly dependent on the decree. "[T]he District's Court's authority to adopt a consent decree comes only from the statute which the decree is intended to enforce," not from the parties' consent to the decree. System Federation No. 91 v. Wright, 364 U.S. 642, 651, 81 S.Ct. 368, 373, 5 L.Ed.2d 349 (1961). In recognition of this principle, this Court in *Wright* held that when a change in the law brought the terms of a decree into conflict with the statute pursuant to which the decree was entered, the decree should be modified over the objections of one of the parties bound by the decree. By the same token, and for the same reason, a district court cannot enter a disputed modification of a consent decree in Title VII litigation if the resulting order is inconsistent with that statute. Thus, Title VII necessarily acted as a limit on the District Court's authority to modify the decree over the objections of the City; the issue cannot be resolved solely by reference to the terms of the decree and notions of equity. Since * * * Title VII precludes a district court from displacing a non-minority employee with seniority under the contractually established seniority system absent either a finding that the seniority system was adopted with discriminatory intent or a determination that such a remedy was necessary to make whole a proven victim of discrimination, the District Court was precluded from granting such relief over the City's objection in these cases.

10. Section 703(h) provides that "it shall not be an unlawful employment practice for an employer to apply different standards of compensation, or different terms, conditions, or privileges of employment pursuant to a bona fide seniority or merit system ... provided that such differences are not the result of an intention to discriminate because of race, color, religion, sex, or national origin...." 42 U.S.C. § 2000e–2(h).

not follow its seniority system in making its proposed layoffs because its proposal was discriminatory in effect and hence not a bona fide plan. Section 703(h), however, permits the routine application of a seniority system absent proof of an intention to discriminate. Teamsters v. United States, 431 U.S. 324, 352, 97 S.Ct. 1843, 1863, 52 L.Ed.2d 396 (1977). Here, the District Court itself found that the layoff proposal was not adopted with the purpose or intent to discriminate on the basis of race. Nor had the City in agreeing to the decree admitted in any way that it had engaged in intentional discrimination. The Court of Appeals was therefore correct in disagreeing with the District Court's holding that the layoff plan was not a bona fide application of the seniority system, and it would appear that the City could not be faulted for following the seniority plan expressed in its agreement with the Union. The Court of Appeals nevertheless held that the injunction was proper even though it conflicted with the seniority system. This was error. * * *

A second ground advanced by the Court of Appeals in support of the conclusion that the injunction could be entered notwithstanding its conflict with the seniority system was the assertion that "[i]t would be incongruous to hold that the use of the preferred means of resolving an employment discrimination action decreases the power of a court to order relief which vindicates the policies embodied within Title VII, and 42 U.S.C. §§ 1981 and 1983." The court concluded that if the allegations in the complaint had been proved, the District Court could have entered an order overriding the seniority provisions. Therefore, the court reasoned, "[t]he trial court had the authority to override the Firefighter's Union seniority provisions to effectuate the purpose of the 1980 Decree."

The difficulty with this approach is that it overstates the authority of the trial court to disregard a seniority system in fashioning a remedy after a plaintiff has successfully proved that an employer has followed a pattern or practice having a discriminatory effect on black applicants or employees. If individual members of a plaintiff class demonstrate that they have been actual victims of the discriminatory practice, they may be awarded competitive seniority and given their rightful place on the seniority roster. This much is clear from Franks v. Bowman Transportation Co., 424 U.S. 747, 96 S.Ct. 1251, 47 L.Ed.2d 444 (1976) and Teamsters v. United States, 431 U.S. 324, 97 S.Ct. 1843, 52 L.Ed.2d 396 (1977). *Teamsters,* however, also made clear that mere membership in the disadvantaged class is insufficient to warrant a seniority award; each individual must prove that the discriminatory practice had an impact on him. Even when an individual shows that the discriminatory practice has had an impact on him, he is not automatically entitled to have a non-minority employee laid off to make room for him. He may have to wait until a vacancy occurs, and if there are non-minority employees on layoff, the Court must balance the equities in determining who is entitled to the job. Here, there was no finding that any of the blacks protected from layoff had been a victim of discrimination and no award of competitive seniority to any of them. Nor had the parties in formulating the consent decree purported to identify any specific employee entitled to particular relief other than those listed in the exhibits attached to the decree. It therefore seems to us that in light of *Teamsters,* the Court of Appeals imposed on the parties as an adjunct of settlement something that could not have been ordered had the case gone to trial and the plaintiffs proved that a pattern or practice of discrimination existed. * * *

Finally, the Court of Appeals was of the view that the District Court ordered no more than that which the City unilaterally could have done by way of adopting an affirmative action program. Whether the City, a public employer, could have taken this course without violating the law is an issue we need not decide. The fact is that in these cases the City took no such action and that the modification of the decree was imposed over its objection.[17]

We thus are unable to agree either that the order entered by the District Court was a justifiable effort to enforce the terms of the decree to which the City had agreed or that it was a legitimate modification of the decree that could be imposed on the City without its consent. Accordingly, the judgment of the Court of Appeals is reversed. * * *

JUSTICE O'CONNOR, concurring. [omitted]

JUSTICE STEVENS, concurring in the judgment. [omitted]

JUSTICE BLACKMUN, with whom JUSTICE BRENNAN and JUSTICE MARSHALL join, dissenting.

* * * III

* * * In affirming the District Court, the Court of Appeals suggested at least two grounds on which respondents might have prevailed on the merits.

A

The first of these derives from the contractual characteristics of a consent decree. Because a consent decree "is to be construed for enforcement purposes essentially as a contract," United States v. ITT Continental Baking Co., 420 U.S. 223, 238, 95 S.Ct. 926, 935, 43 L.Ed.2d 148 (1975), respondents had the right to specific performance of the terms of the decree. If the proposed layoffs violated those terms, the District Court could issue an injunction requiring compliance with them. Alternatively, the Court of Appeals noted that a court of equity has inherent power to modify a consent decree in light of changed circumstances. Thus, if respondents could show that changed circumstances justified modification of the decree, the District Court would have authority to make such a change. * * *

17. The Court of Appeals also suggested that under United States v. Swift & Co., 286 U.S. 106, 114–115, 52 S.Ct. 460, 462, 76 L.Ed. 999 (1932), the decree properly was modified pursuant to the District Court's equity jurisdiction. But *Swift* cannot be read as authorizing a court to impose a modification of a decree that runs counter to statutory policy, see n. 9, supra, here §§ 703(h) and 706(g) of Title VII.

The Court rejects the argument that the injunctive relief was a proper exercise of the power to enforce the purposes of the decree principally on the ground that the remedy agreed upon in the consent decree did not specifically mention layoffs. This treatment of the issue is inadequate. The power of the District Court to enter further orders to effectuate the purposes of the decree was a part of the agreed remedy. The parties negotiated for this, and it is the obligation of the courts to give it meaning. In an ideal world, a well-drafted consent decree requiring structural change might succeed in providing explicit directions for all future contingencies. But particularly in civil rights litigation in which implementation of a consent decree often takes years, such foresight is unattainable. Accordingly, parties to a consent decree typically agree to confer upon supervising courts the authority to ensure that the purposes of a decree are not frustrated by unforeseen circumstances. The scope of such authority in an individual case depends principally upon the intent of the parties. Viewed in this light, recourse to such broad notions as the "purposes" of a decree is not a rewriting of the parties' agreement, but rather a part of the attempt to implement the written terms. The District Judge in these cases, who presided over the negotiation of the consent decree, is in a unique position to determine the nature of the parties' original intent, and he has a distinctive familiarity with the circumstances that shaped the decree and defined its purposes. Accordingly, he should be given special deference to interpret the general and any ambiguous terms in the decree. It simply is not a sufficient response to conclude, as the Court does, that the District Court could not enjoin the proposed layoff plan merely because layoffs were not specifically mentioned in the consent decree.

In this regard, it is useful to note the limited nature of the injunctive relief ordered by the District Court. The preliminary injunction did not embody a conclusion that the city could never conduct layoffs in accordance with its seniority policy. Rather, the District Court preliminarily enjoined a particular application of the seniority system as a basis for a particular set of layoffs. Whether the District Court would enjoin a future layoff presumably would depend on the factual circumstances of that situation. * * * There is no way of knowing whether the District Court would conclude that a future layoff conducted on the basis of seniority would frustrate the purposes of the decree sufficiently to justify an injunction. * * *

B

The Court of Appeals also suggested that respondents could have prevailed on the merits because the 1981 layoffs may have justified a modification of the consent decree. This Court frequently has recognized the inherent "power of a court of equity to modify an injunction in adaptation to changed conditions though it was entered by consent." United States v. Swift & Co., 286 U.S. 106, 114, 52 S.Ct. 460, 462, 76 L.Ed. 999 (1932); *accord,* Pasadena City Board of Education v. Spangler, 427 U.S. 424, 437, 96 S.Ct. 2697, 2705, 49 L.Ed.2d 599 (1976); United States v. United Shoe Machinery Corp., 391 U.S. 244, 251, 88 S.Ct. 1496,

1500, 20 L.Ed.2d 562 (1968). "The source of the power to modify is of course the fact that an injunction often requires continuing supervision by the issuing court and always a continuing willingness to apply its powers and processes on behalf of the party who obtained that equitable relief." The test for ruling on a plaintiff's request for a modification of a consent decree is "whether the change serve[s] to effectuate ... the basic purpose of the original consent decree."

The Court rejects this ground for affirming the preliminary injunction, not by examining the purposes of the *consent decree* and whether the proposed layoffs justified a modification of the decree, but rather by reference to Title VII. The Court concludes that the preliminary injunction was improper because it "imposed on the parties as an adjunct of settlement something that could not have been ordered had the case gone to trial and the plaintiffs proved that a pattern or practice of discrimination existed." Thus, the Court has chosen to evaluate the propriety of the preliminary injunction by asking what type of relief the District Court could have awarded had respondents litigated their Title VII claim and prevailed on the merits. Although it is far from clear whether that is the right question,[9] it is clear that the Court has given the wrong answer. * * *

In the instant cases, respondents' request for a preliminary injunction did not include a request for individual awards of retroactive seniority—and, contrary to the implication of the Court's opinion, the District Court did not make any such awards. Rather, the District Court order required the city to conduct its layoffs in a race-conscious manner; specifically, the preliminary injunction prohibited the city from conducting layoffs that would "decrease the percentage of black[s]" in certain job categories. The city remained free to lay off any individual black so long as the percentage of black representation was maintained.

Because these cases arise out of a consent decree, and a trial on the merits has never taken place, it is of course impossible for the Court to know the extent and nature of any past discrimination by the city. For this reason, to the extent that the scope of appropriate relief would depend upon the facts found at trial, it is impossible to determine whether the relief provided by the preliminary injunction would have been appropriate following a trial on the merits. Nevertheless, the Court says that the preliminary injunction was inappropriate because, it

**9.** The Court's analysis seems to be premised on the view that a consent decree cannot provide relief that could not be obtained at trial. In addressing the Court's analysis, I do not mean to imply that I accept its premise as correct. In Steelworkers v. Weber, 443 U.S. 193, 99 S.Ct. 2721, 61 L.Ed.2d 480 (1979), this Court considered whether an affirmative action plan adopted voluntarily by an employer violated Title VII because it discriminated against whites. In holding that the plan was lawful, the Court stressed that the voluntariness of the plan informed the nature of its inquiry. Because a consent decree is an agreement that is enforceable in court, it has qualities of both voluntariness and compulsion. The Court has explained that Congress intended to encourage voluntary settlement of Title VII suits, and cooperative private efforts to eliminate the lingering effects of past discrimination. It is by no means clear, therefore, that the permissible scope of relief available under a consent decree is the same as could be ordered by a court after a finding of liability at trial.

concludes, respondents could not have obtained similar relief had their cases been litigated instead of settled by a consent decree. * * *

For reasons never explained, the Court's opinion has focused entirely on what respondents have actually shown, instead of what they might have shown had trial ensued. It is improper and unfair to fault respondents for failing to show "that any of the blacks protected from layoff had been a victim of discrimination," for the simple reason that the claims on which such a showing would have been made never went to trial. The whole point of the consent decree in these cases—and indeed the point of most Title VII consent decrees—is for both parties to avoid the time and expense of litigating the question of liability and identifying the victims of discrimination. In the instant consent decree, the city expressly denied having engaged in any discrimination at all. Nevertheless, the consent decree in this case provided several persons with both promotions and backpay. By definition, all such relief went to persons never determined to be victims of discrimination, and the Court does not indicate that it means to suggest that the original consent decree in these cases was invalid. Any suggestion that a consent decree can provide relief only if a defendant concedes liability would drastically reduce, of course, the incentives for entering into consent decrees. Such a result would be incongruous, given the Court's past statements that "Congress expressed a strong preference for encouraging voluntary settlement of employment discrimination claims." * * *

### *Notes*

1. Justice Blackmun's dissent points out that the Court is reviewing the district court's decision to grant a preliminary injunction. Does the majority apply the correct standard of review? I.e., how would *Stotts* have come out under the tests applied in *Chalk* and *American Hospital*?

2. The Supreme Court has held that a district court may enter a consent decree that benefits individuals who are not actual victims of an employer's discriminatory practices despite an apparent limitation in Title VII prohibiting relief to such persons because a consent decree is not an "order" within the meaning of the enforcement provisions of Title VII. Writing for the Court, Justice Brennan distinguished those situations where a district court would be barred by Title VII from providing such relief "after a trial or, as in *Stotts,* in disputed proceedings to modify a decree entered upon consent." Local 93 v. City of Cleveland, 478 U.S. 501, 528, 106 S.Ct. 3063, 3078, 92 L.Ed.2d 405 (1986). The Court majority acted over a dissent written by Justice Rehnquist charging that it was ignoring well-considered observations in *Stotts* that were "inconsistent with the result which the Court is apparently determined to reach in this case." Id. at 540. *Stotts* and *Local 93* are reviewed in George M. Sullivan & William A. Nowlin, The Clarification of Firefighters v. Stotts, 37 Lab.L.J. 788 (1986).

3. The facts of *Local 93* also raises a related problem: Under the facts of that case, the defendant city was sued by an organization of African–American and Latino firefighters, alleging that promotion practices in the fire department discriminated against minorities. The city and the plaintiffs

negotiated a settlement, which provided for racial quotas on promotions, without the real participation of the largely white labor union. If the white union later seeks modification, should a trial court use a rigid or flexible standard? See Douglas Laycock, Consent Decrees Without Consent: The Rights of Nonconsenting Third Parties, 1987 U.Chi.Legal F. 103. See also Martin v. Wilks, 490 U.S. 755, 109 S.Ct. 2180, 104 L.Ed.2d 835 (1989), infra at p. 329.

## RUFO v. INMATES OF SUFFOLK COUNTY JAIL

Supreme Court of the United States, 1992.
502 U.S. 367, 112 S.Ct. 748, 116 L.Ed.2d 867.

JUSTICE WHITE delivered the opinion of the Court.

* * * I

This litigation began in 1971 when inmates sued the Suffolk County Sheriff, the Commissioner of Correction for the State of Massachusetts, the Mayor of Boston, and nine city councilors, claiming that inmates not yet convicted of the crimes charged against them were being held under unconstitutional conditions at what was then the Suffolk County Jail. The facility, known as the Charles Street Jail, had been constructed in 1848 with large tiers of barred cells. * * * The court held that conditions at the jail were constitutionally deficient:

> "As a facility for the pretrial detention of presumptively innocent citizens, Charles Street Jail unnecessarily and unreasonably infringes upon their most basic liberties, among them the rights to reasonable freedom of motion, personal cleanliness, and personal privacy. The court finds and rules that the quality of incarceration at Charles Street is 'punishment' of such a nature and degree that it cannot be justified by the state's interest in holding defendants for trial; and therefore it violates the due process clause of the Fourteenth Amendment."

The Court permanently enjoined the government defendants: "(a) from housing at the Charles Street Jail after November 30, 1973 in a cell with another inmate, any inmate who is awaiting trial and (b) from housing at the Charles Street Jail after June 30, 1976 any inmate who is awaiting trial." The defendants did not appeal.

In 1977, with the problems of the Charles Street Jail still unresolved, the District Court ordered defendants, including the Boston City Council, to take such steps and expend the funds reasonably necessary to renovate another existing facility as a substitute detention center. * * * The Court of Appeals [subsequently] ordered that the Charles Street Jail be closed on October 2, 1978, unless a plan was presented to create a constitutionally adequate facility for pretrial detainees in Suffolk County.

Four days before the deadline, the plan that formed the basis for the consent decree now before this Court was submitted to the District Court. * * *

Seven months later, the Court entered a formal consent decree in which the government defendants expressed their "desire . . . to provide, maintain and operate as applicable a suitable and constitutional jail for Suffolk County pretrial detainees." The decree specifically incorporated the provisions of the Suffolk County Detention Center, Charles Street Facility, Architectural Program, which—in the words of the consent decree—"sets forth a program which is both constitutionally adequate and constitutionally required."

Under the terms of the Architectural Program, the new jail was designed to include a total of 309 "[s]ingle occupancy rooms" of 70 square feet arranged in modular units that included a kitchenette and recreation area, inmate laundry room, education units, and indoor and outdoor exercise areas. The size of the jail was based on a projected decline in inmate population, from 245 male prisoners in 1979 to 226 at present.

Although the Architectural Program projected that construction of the new jail would be completed by 1983, work on the new facility had not been started by 1984. During the intervening years, the inmate population outpaced population projections. Litigation in the state courts ensued, and defendants were ordered to build a larger jail. Thereupon, plaintiff prisoners, with the support of the sheriff, moved the District Court to modify the decree to provide a facility with 435 cells. Citing "the unanticipated increase in jail population and the delay in completing the jail," the District Court modified the decree to permit the capacity of the new jail to be increased in any amount, provided that:

> "(a) single-cell occupancy is maintained under the design for the facility; * * *

The number of cells was later increased to 453. Construction started in 1987.

In July 1989, while the new jail was still under construction, the sheriff moved to modify the consent decree to allow the double bunking of male detainees in 197 cells, thereby raising the capacity of the new jail to 610 male detainees. The sheriff argued that changes in law and in fact required the modification. The asserted change in law was this Court's 1979 decision in Bell v. Wolfish, 441 U.S. 520 (1979), handed down one week after the consent decree was approved by the District Court. The asserted change in fact was the increase in the population of pretrial detainees.

The District Court refused to grant the requested modification, holding that the sheriff had failed to meet the standard of United States v. Swift & Co., 286 U.S. 106, 119 (1932):

> "Nothing less than a clear showing of grievous wrong evoked by new and unforeseen conditions should lead us to change what was decreed after years of litigation with the consent of all concerned."

The court rejected the argument that *Bell* required modification of the decree because the decision "did not directly overrule any legal interpretation on which the 1979 consent decree was based, and in these circumstances it is inappropriate to invoke Rule 60(b)(5) to modify a consent decree." The court refused to order modification because of the increased pretrial detainee population, finding that the problem was "neither new nor unforeseen."

The District Court briefly stated that, even under the flexible modification standard adopted by other Courts of Appeals, the sheriff would not be entitled to relief because "[a] separate cell for each detainee has always been an important element of the relief sought in this litigation-perhaps even the most important element." Finally, the court rejected the argument that the decree should be modified because the proposal complied with constitutional standards, reasoning that such a rule "would undermine and discourage settlement efforts in institutional cases." The District Court never decided whether the sheriff's proposal for double celling at the new jail would be constitutionally permissible.

The new Suffolk County Jail opened shortly thereafter.

The Court of Appeals affirmed * * * . We granted certiorari.

II

In moving for modification of the decree, the sheriff relied on Federal Rule of Civil Procedure 60(b)[(5) & (6)] * * *.

There is no suggestion in these cases that a consent decree is not subject to Rule 60(b). A consent decree no doubt embodies an agreement of the parties and thus in some respects is contractual in nature. But it is an agreement that the parties desire and expect will be reflected in and be enforceable as a judicial decree that is subject to the rules generally applicable to other judgments and decrees. Railway Employees v. Wright, 364 U.S. 642, 650–651 (1961). The District Court recognized as much but held that Rule 60(b)(5) codified the "grievous wrong" standard of United States v. Swift, that a case for modification under this standard had not been made, and that resort to Rule 60(b)(6) was also unavailing. This construction of Rule 60(b) was error.

*Swift* was the product of a prolonged antitrust battle between the Government and the meat-packing industry. In 1920, the defendants agreed to a consent decree that enjoined them from manipulating the meat-packing industry and banned them from engaging in the manufacture, sale, or transportation of other foodstuffs. In 1930, several meatpackers petitioned for modification of the decree, arguing that conditions in the meat-packing and grocery industries had changed. The Court rejected their claim, finding that the meatpackers were positioned to manipulate transportation costs and fix grocery prices in 1930, just as they had been in 1920. It was in this context that Justice Cardozo, for the Court, set forth the much-quoted *Swift* standard, requiring "[n]othing less than a clear showing of grievous wrong evoked by new and unforeseen conditions" as a predicate to modification of the meatpackers' consent decree.

Read out of context, this language suggests a "hardening" of the traditional flexible standard for modification of consent decrees. New York State Assn. for Retarded Children, Inc. v. Carey, 706 F.2d 956, 968 (CA2), cert. denied, 464 U.S. 915 (1983). But that conclusion does not follow when the standard is read in context. The *Swift* opinion pointedly distinguished the facts of that case from one in which genuine changes required modification of a consent decree, stating that:

> "The distinction is between restraints that give protection to rights fully accrued upon facts so nearly permanent as to be substantially impervious to change, and those that involve the supervision of changing conduct or conditions and are thus provisional and tentative.... The consent is to be read as directed toward events as they then were. It was not an abandonment of the right to exact revision in the future, if revision should become necessary in adaptation to events to be."

Our decisions since *Swift* reinforce the conclusion that the "grievous wrong" language of *Swift* was not intended to take on a talismanic quality, warding off virtually all efforts to modify consent decrees. *Railway Employees* emphasized the need for flexibility in administering consent decrees, stating: "There is ... no dispute but that a sound judicial discretion may call for the modification of the terms of an injunctive decree if the circumstances, whether of law or fact, obtaining at the time of its issuance have changed, or new ones have since arisen."

The same theme was repeated in our decision last term in Board of Education of Oklahoma City Public Schools v. Dowell, 498 U.S. 237 (1991), in which we rejected the rigid use of the *Swift* "grievous wrong" language as a barrier to a motion to dissolve a desegregation decree.

There is thus little basis for concluding that Rule 60(b) misread the *Swift* opinion and intended that modifications of consent decrees in all cases were to be governed by the standard actually applied in *Swift*. That Rule, in providing that, on such terms as are just, a party may be relieved from a final judgement or decree where it is no longer equitable that the judgment have prospective application, permits a less stringent, more flexible standard.

The upsurge in institutional reform litigation since Brown v. Board of Education, 347 U.S. 483 (1954), has made the ability of a district court to modify a decree in response to changed circumstances all the more important. Because such decrees often remain in place for extended periods of time, the likelihood of significant changes occurring during the life of the decree is increased. * * *

The government petitioners * * * assert that modification would actually improve conditions for some pretrial detainees, who now cannot be housed in the Suffolk County Jail and therefore are transferred to other facilities, farther from family members and legal counsel. In these transfer facilities, the petitioners assert that detainees may be double celled under less desirable conditions than those that would exist if double celling were allowed at the new Suffolk County Jail. The government petitioners also contend that the public interest is implicated here because crowding at the new facility has necessitated the release of some pretrial detainees and the transfer of others to halfway houses, from which many escape.

For the District Court, these points were insufficient reason to modify under Rule 60(b)(5) because its "authority [was] limited by the established legal requirements for modification...." * * * None of the changed circumstances warranted modification because it would violate one of the primary purposes of the decree which was to provide for "[a] separate cell for each detainee [which] has always been an important element of the relief sought in this litigation-perhaps even the most important element." For reasons appearing later in this opinion, this was not an adequate basis for denying the requested modification. The District Court also held that Rule 60(b)(6) provided no more basis for relief. The District Court, and the Court of Appeals as well, failed to recognize that such rigidity is neither required by *Swift* nor appropriate in the context of institutional reform litigation.

It is urged that any rule other than the *Swift* "grievous wrong" standard would deter parties to litigation such as this from negotiating settlements and hence destroy the utility of consent decrees. Obviously that would not be the case insofar as the state or local government officials are concerned. As for the plaintiffs in such cases, they know that if they litigate to conclusion and win, the resulting judgment or decree will give them what is constitutionally adequate at that time but perhaps less than they hoped for. They also know that the prospective effect of such a judgment or decree will be open to modification where deemed equitable under Rule 60(b). Whether or not they bargain for more than what they might get after trial, they will be in no worse position if they settle and have the consent decree entered. At least they will avoid further litigation and perhaps will negotiate a decree providing more than what would have been ordered without the local government's consent. And, of course, if they litigate, they may lose.

III

Although we hold that a district court should exercise flexibility in considering requests for modification of an institutional reform consent decree, it does not follow that a modification will be warranted in all circumstances. Rule 60(b)(5) provides that a party may obtain relief from a court order when "it is no longer equitable that the judgment should have prospective application," not when it is no longer convenient to live with the terms of a consent decree. Accordingly, a party seeking modification of a consent decree bears the burden of establishing that a significant change in circumstances warrants revision of the decree. If the moving party meets this standard, the court should consider whether the proposed modification is suitably tailored to the changed circumstance.[7]

7. The standard we set forth applies when a party seeks modification of a term of a consent decree that arguably relates to the vindication of a constitutional right.

A

A party seeking modification of a consent decree may meet its initial burden by showing either a significant change in factual conditions or in law.

*1*

Modification of a consent decree may be warranted when changed factual conditions make compliance with the decree substantially more onerous. Such a modification was approved by the District Court in this litigation in 1985 when it became apparent that plans for the new jail did not provide sufficient cell space. Modification is also appropriate when a decree proves to be unworkable because of unforeseen obstacles, New York State Assn. for Retarded Children, Inc. v. Carey, 706 F.2d at 969 (modification allowed where State could not find appropriate housing facilities for transfer patients); Philadelphia Welfare Rights Organization v. Shapp, 602 F.2d at 1120–1121 (modification allowed where State could not find sufficient clients to meet decree targets); or when enforcement of the decree without modification would be detrimental to the public interest, Duran v. Elrod, 760 F.2d 756, 759–761 (C.A.7 1985) (modification allowed to avoid pretrial release of accused violent felons).

Respondents urge that modification should be allowed only when a change in facts is both "unforeseen and unforeseeable." Such a standard would provide even less flexibility than the exacting *Swift* test; we decline to adopt it. Litigants are not required to anticipate every exigency that could conceivably arise during the life of a consent decree.

Ordinarily, however, modification should not be granted where a party relies upon events that actually were anticipated at the time it entered into a decree. If it is clear that a party anticipated changing conditions that would make performance of the decree more onerous but nevertheless agreed to the decree, that party would have to satisfy a heavy burden to convince a court that it agreed to the decree in good faith, made a reasonable effort to comply with the decree, and should be relieved of the undertaking under Rule 60(b).

Accordingly, on remand the District Court should consider whether the upsurge in the Suffolk County inmate population was foreseen by the petitioners. * * *

Such a showing is not necessary to implement minor changes in extraneous details that may have been included in a decree (*e.g.*, paint color or design of a building's facade) but are unrelated to remedying the underlying constitutional violation. Ordinarily, the parties should consent to modifying a decree to allow such changes. If a party refuses to consent and the moving party has a reasonable basis for its request, the court should modify the decree. In this case the entire architectural plan became part of the decree binding on the local authorities. Hence, any change in the plan technically required a change in the decree, absent a provision in the plan exempting certain changes. Such a provision was furnished by the 1985 modification of the decree. Of course, the necessity of changing a decree to allow insignificant changes could be avoided by not entering an overly detailed decree.

Even if the decree is construed as an undertaking by petitioners to provide single cells for pretrial detainees, to relieve petitioners from that promise based on changed conditions does not necessarily violate the basic purpose of the decree. That purpose was to provide a remedy for what had been found, based on a variety of factors, including double celling, to be unconstitutional conditions obtaining in the Charles Street Jail. If modification of one term of a consent decree defeats the purpose of the decree, obviously modification would be all but impossible. That cannot be the rule. The District Court was thus in error in holding that even under a more flexible standard than its version of *Swift* required, modification of the single cell requirement was necessarily forbidden.

*2*

A consent decree must of course be modified if, as it later turns out, one or more of the obligations placed upon the parties has become impermissible under federal law. But modification of a consent decree may be warranted when the statutory or decisional law has changed to make legal what the decree was designed to prevent.

This was the case in Railway Employees v. Wright, 364 U.S. 642 (1961). A railroad and its unions were sued for violating the Railway Labor Act, 45 U.S.C. § 151 et seq., which banned discrimination against nonunion employees, and the parties entered a consent decree that prohibited such discrimination. Later, the Railway Labor Act was amended to allow union shops, and the union sought a modification of the decree. Although the amendment did not require but purposely permitted union shops, this Court held that the union was entitled to the modification because the parties had recognized correctly that what the consent decree prohibited was illegal under the Railway Act as it then read and because a "court must be free to continue to further the objectives of th[e] Act when its provisions are amended."

Petitioner Rapone urges that, without more, our 1979 decision in Bell v. Wolfish, 441 U.S. 520 (1979), was a change in law requiring modification of the decree governing construction of the Suffolk County Jail. We disagree. *Bell* made clear what the Court had not before announced: that double celling is not in all cases unconstitutional. But it surely did not cast doubt on the legality of single celling, and petitioners were undoubtedly aware that *Bell* was pending when they signed the decree. Thus, the case must be judged on the basis that it was immaterial to petitioners that double celling might be ruled constitutional, i.e., they preferred even in that event to agree to a decree which called for providing only single cells in the jail to be built.

Neither *Bell* nor the Federal Constitution forbade this course of conduct. Federal courts may not order States or local governments, over their objection, to undertake a course of conduct not tailored to curing a constitutional violation that has been adjudicated. See Milliken v. Bradley (Milliken II), 433 U.S. 267, 281 (1977). But we have no doubt that, to "save themselves the time, expense, and inevitable risk of litigation," United States v. Armour & Co., 402 U.S. 673, 681 (1971), petitioners could settle the dispute over the proper remedy for the constitutional violations that had been found by undertaking to do more than the Constitution itself requires (almost any affirmative decree beyond a directive to obey the Constitution necessarily does that), but also more than what a court would have ordered absent the settlement. Accordingly, the District Court did not abuse its discretion in entering the agreed upon decree, which clearly was related to the conditions found to offend the Constitution.[12]

To hold that a clarification in the law automatically opens the door for relitigation of the merits of every affected consent decree would undermine the finality of such agreements and could serve as a disincentive to negotiation of settlements in institutional reform litigation. * * *

While a decision that clarifies the law will not, in and of itself, provide a basis for modifying a decree, it could constitute a change in circumstances that would support modification if the parties had based their agreement on a misunderstanding of the governing law. For instance, in Pasadena City Board of Education v. Spangler, 427 U.S. 424, 437–438 (1976), we held that a modification should have been ordered when the parties had interpreted an ambiguous equitable decree in a manner contrary to the District Court's ultimate interpretation and the District Court's interpretation was contrary to intervening decisional law. And in Nelson v. Collins, 659 F.2d 420, 428–429 (C.A.4 1981)(en banc), the Fourth Circuit vacated an equitable order that was based on the assumption that double bunking of prisoners was *per se* unconstitutional.

Thus, if the Sheriff and Commissioner could establish on remand that the parties to the consent decree believed that single celling of pretrial detainees was mandated by the Constitution, this misunderstanding of the law could form a basis for modification. In this connection, we note again that the decree itself recited that it "sets forth a program which is both constitutionally adequate and constitutionally *required.*" (Emphasis added).

B

Once a moving party has met its burden of establishing either a change in fact or in law warranting modification of a consent decree, the District Court should determine whether the proposed modification is suitably tailored to the changed circumstance. In evaluating a proposed modification, three matters should be clear.

**12.** Petitioner Rapone contends that the District Court was required to modify the consent decree because "the constitutional violation underlying the decree has disappeared and will not recur" and that "no constitutional violation [is] even alleged" at the new jail, "so there is no constitutional violation to serve as a predicate for the federal court's continued exercise of its equitable power." His argument is not well taken. The District Court did not make findings on these issues, and even if it had ruled that double celling at the new jail is constitutional and that the modification should be granted, we do not have before us the question whether the entire decree should be vacated.

Of course, a modification must not create or perpetuate a constitutional violation. Petitioners contend that double celling inmates at the Suffolk County Jail would be constitutional under *Bell*. Respondents counter that *Bell* is factually distinguishable and that double celling at the new jail would violate the constitutional rights of pretrial detainees. If this is the case—the District Court did not decide this issue—modification should not be granted.

A proposed modification should not strive to rewrite a consent decree so that it conforms to the constitutional floor. Once a court has determined that changed circumstances warrant a modification in a consent decree, the focus should be on whether the proposed modification is tailored to resolve the problems created by the change in circumstances. A court should do no more, for a consent decree is a final judgment that may be reopened only to the extent that equity requires. The court should not "turn aside to inquire whether some of [the provisions of the decree] upon separate as distinguished from joint action could have been opposed with success if the defendants had offered opposition." *Swift*.

Within these constraints, the public interest and "[c]onsiderations based on the allocation of powers within our federal system," *Dowell*, require that the district court defer to local government administrators, who have the "primary responsibility for elucidating, assessing, and solving" the problems of institutional reform, to resolve the intricacies of implementing a decree modification. Brown v. Board of Education, 349 U.S. at 299. See also Missouri v. Jenkins, 495 U.S. 33 (1990); *Milliken II*.[14] Although state and local officers in charge of institutional litigation may agree to do more than that which is minimally required by the Constitution to settle a case and avoid further litigation, a court should surely keep the public interest in mind in ruling on a request to modify based on a change in conditions making it substantially more onerous to abide by the decree. To refuse modification of a decree is to bind all future officers of the State, regardless of their view of the necessity of relief from one or more provisions of a decree that might not have been entered had the matter been litigated to its conclusion. The District Court seemed to be of the view that the problems of the fiscal officers of the State were only marginally relevant to the request for modification in this case. Financial constraints may not be used to justify the creation or perpetuation of constitutional violations, but they are a legitimate concern of government defendants in institutional reform litigation and therefore are appropriately considered in tailoring a consent decree modification.

**14.** The concurrence mischaracterizes the nature of the deference that we would accord local government administrators. As we have stated, the moving party bears the burden of establishing that a significant change in circumstances warrants modification of a consent decree. No deference is involved in this threshold inquiry. However, once a court has determined that a modification is warranted, we think that principles of federalism and simple common sense require the court to give significant weight to the views of the local government officials who must implement any modification.

IV

To conclude, we hold that the *Swift* "grievous wrong" standard does not apply to requests to modify consent decrees stemming from institutional reform litigation. Under the flexible standard we adopt today, a party seeking modification of a consent decree must establish that a significant change in facts or law warrants revision of the decree and that the proposed modification is suitably tailored to the changed circumstance. * * *

JUSTICE THOMAS took no part in the consideration or decision of this case.

JUSTICE O'CONNOR, concurring in the judgment.

* * * I would emphasize that we find fault only with the *method* by which the District Court reached its conclusion. The District Court may well have been justified, for the reasons suggested by Justice Stevens, in refusing to modify the decree, and the court is free, when fully exercising its discretion, to reach the same result on remand. This is a case with no satisfactory outcome. The new jail is simply too small. Someone has to suffer, and it is not likely to be the government officials responsible for underestimating the inmate population and delaying the construction of the jail. Instead, it is likely to be either the inmates of Suffolk County, who will be double celled in an institution designed for single celling; the inmates in counties not yet subject to court supervision, who will be double celled with the inmates transferred from Suffolk County; or members of the public, who may be the victims of crimes committed by the inmates the county is forced to release in order to comply with the consent decree. The District Court has an extraordinarily difficult decision to make. We should not be inclined to second-guess the court's sound judgment in deciding who will bear this burden. * * *

JUSTICE STEVENS, with whom JUSTICE BLACKMUN joins, dissenting.

Today the Court endorses the standard for modification of consent decrees articulated by Judge Friendly in New York State Association for Retarded Children, Inc. v. Carey, 706 F.2d 956 (CA2), cert. denied, 464 U.S. 915 (1983). I agree with that endorsement, but under that standard I believe the findings of the District Court in this action require affirmance of its order refusing to modify this consent decree. * * *

III

It is the terms of the 1979 consent decree, as modified and reaffirmed in 1985, that petitioners now seek to modify. The 1979 decree was negotiated against a background in which certain important propositions had already been settled. First, the litigation had established the existence of a serious constitutional violation. Second, for a period of almost five years after the entry of the 1973 injunction—which was unquestionably valid and which petitioners had waived any right to challenge—the petitioners were still violating the Constitution as well as the injunction. Third, although respondents had already prevailed, they were willing to agree to another postponement of the closing of the

Charles Street Jail if petitioners submitted, and the court approved, an adequate plan for a new facility.

Obviously any plan would have to satisfy constitutional standards. It was equally obvious that a number of features of the plan, such as the site of the new facility or its particular architectural design, would not be constitutionally mandated. In order to discharge their duty to provide an adequate facility, and also to avoid the risk of stern sanctions for years of noncompliance with an outstanding court order, it would be entirely appropriate for petitioners to propose a remedy that exceeded the bare minimum mandated by the Constitution. Indeed, terms such as "minimum" or "floor" are not particularly helpful in this context. The remedy is constrained by the requirement that it not perpetuate a constitutional violation, and in this sense the Constitution does provide a "floor." Beyond that constraint, however, the remedy's attempt to give expression to the underlying constitutional value does not lend itself to quantitative evaluation. In view of the complexity of the institutions involved and the necessity of affording effective relief, the remedial decree will often contain many, highly detailed commands. It might well be that the failure to fulfill any one of these specific requirements would not have constituted an independent constitutional violation, nor would the absence of any one element render the decree necessarily ineffective. The duty of the District Court is not to formulate the decree with the fewest provisions, but to consider the various interests involved and, in the sound exercise of its discretion, to fashion the remedy that it believes to be best.[2] Similarly, a consent decree reflects the parties' understanding of the best remedy, and, subject to judicial approval, the parties to a consent decree enjoy at least as broad discretion as the District Court in formulating the remedial decree. Cf. Firefighters v. Cleveland, 478 U.S. 501, 525–526 (1986). * * *

## IV

The motion to modify that ultimately led to our grant of certiorari was filed on July 17, 1989. As I view these cases, the proponents of that motion had the burden of demonstrating that changed conditions be-

2. It is the difficulty in determining prospectively which remedy is best that justifies a flexible standard of modification. This relationship between the characteristics of a remedial decree in structural reform litigation and the flexible standard of modification is explained in the passage that Judge Friendly found to be the best statement of the applicable legal standard:

> "'The judge must search for the "best" remedy, but since his judgment must incorporate such open-ended considerations as effectiveness and fairness, and since the threat and constitutional value that occasions the intervention can never be defined with great precision, the intervention can never be defended with any certitude. It must always be open to revisions, even without the strong showing traditionally required for modification of a decree, namely, that the first choice is causing grievous hardship. A revision is justified if the remedy is not working effectively or is unnecessarily burdensome.'"

New York State Association for Retarded Children, Inc. v. Carey, 706 F.2d 956, 970 (C.A.2 1983)(quoting Fiss, The Supreme Court–1978 Term–Foreword: The Forms of Justice, 93 Harv.L.Rev. 1, 49 (1979)). The justification for modifying a consent decree is not that the decree did "too much," but that in light of later circumstances, a modified remedy would better achieve the decree's original goals.

tween 1985 and 1989 justified a further modification of the consent decree. The changes that occurred between 1979 and 1985 were already reflected in the 1985 modification. Since petitioners acquiesced in that modification, they cannot now be heard to argue that pre–1985 developments—either in the law or in the facts—provide a basis for modifying the 1985 order. It is that order that defined petitioners' obligation to construct and to operate an adequate facility.

Petitioners' reliance on Bell v. Wolfish, 441 U.S. 520 (1979), as constituting a relevant change in the law is plainly misplaced * * * [I]t was well-known to all parties when the decree was modified in 1985. It does not qualify as a changed circumstance.[5]

The increase in the average number of pretrial detainees is, of course, a change of fact. Because the size of that increase had not been anticipated in 1979, it was appropriate to modify the decree in 1985. But in 1985, the steady progression in the detainee population surely made it foreseeable that this growth would continue. The District Court's finding that "the overcrowding problem faced by the Sheriff is neither new nor unforeseen," is amply supported by the record.

Even if the continuing increase in inmate population had not actually been foreseen, it was reasonably foreseeable. Mere foreseeability in the sense that it was an event that "could conceivably arise" during the life of the consent decree should not, of course, disqualify an unanticipated development from justifying a modification. But the parties should be charged with notice of those events that reasonably prudent litigants would contemplate when negotiating a settlement. Given the realities of today's society, it is not surprising that the District Court found a continued growth in inmate population to be within petitioners' contemplation.

Other important concerns counsel against modification of this consent decree. Petitioners' history of noncompliance after the 1973 injunction provides an added reason for insisting that they honor their most recent commitments. Petitioners' current claims of fiscal limitation are hardly new. These pleas reflect a continuation of petitioners' previous reluctance to budget funds adequate to avoid the initial constitutional violation or to avoid prolonged noncompliance with the terms of the

**5.** As the Court agrees that *Bell v. Wolfish* did not constitute a change in law requiring modification of the decree, the Court does not define further the kind of changes in law that may merit modification. In particular, the Court has no occasion to draw a distinction between the type of change in law recognized in System Federation v. Wright, 364 U.S. 642 (1961), and the change in law that petitioners assert was effected by *Bell*. The distinction is nevertheless significant and deserves mention. In *Wright*, the plaintiffs originally brought suit alleging that a railroad and its unions discriminated against nonunion employees, a practice prohibited by the Railway Labor Act. The defendants entered into a consent decree, promising to refrain from such discrimination. When Congress subsequently amended the Act to permit union shops, the Court concluded that a modification allowing union shops should be granted so as to further the statutory purpose. In contrast to the situation presented in *Wright*, it cannot be contended that *Bell* expressed a policy preference in favor of double celling. * * *

original decree. The continued claims of financial constraint should not provide support for petitioners' modification requests.

The strong public interest in protecting the finality of court decrees always counsels against modifications. In the context of a consent decree, this interest is reinforced by the policy favoring the settlement of protracted litigation. To the extent that litigants are allowed to avoid their solemn commitments, the motivation for particular settlements will be compromised, and the reliability of the entire process will suffer.

It is particularly important to apply a strict standard when considering modification requests that undermine the central purpose of a consent decree. * * * In this action, the entire history of the litigation demonstrates that the prohibition against double celling was a central purpose of the relief ordered by the District Court in 1973, of the bargain negotiated in 1979 and embodied in the original consent decree, and of the order entered in 1985 that petitioners now seek to modify. Moreover, as the District Court found, during the history of the litigation petitioners have been able to resort to various measures such as "transfers to state prisons, bail reviews by the Superior Court, and a pretrial controlled release program" to respond to the overcrowding problem. The fact that double celling affords petitioners the easiest and least expensive method of responding to a reasonably foreseeable problem is not an adequate justification for compromising a central purpose of the decree. In this regard, the Court misses the point in its observation that "[i]f modification of one term of a consent decree defeats the purpose of the decree, obviously modification would be all but impossible." It is certainly true that modification of a consent decree would be impossible if the modification of *any* one term were deemed to defeat the purpose of the decree. However, to recognize that *some* terms are so critical that their modification would thwart the central purpose of the decree does not render the decree immutable, but rather assures that a modification will frustrate neither the legitimate expectations of the parties nor the core remedial goals of the decree. * * *

### *Notes*

1. On remand, the district court found that although some increase was reasonably foreseeable, the specific and sustained rise in the inmate population was not actually foreseen by the parties either when the decree was originally entered in 1979 or was modified in 1985. However, the court also found that single-bunking was "at the least among the most significant objectives of the consent decree" and that the plaintiffs would not have consented to the decree without the provision for single-bunking. Moreover, double-bunking would increase the risk of violence and the risk of transmission of tuberculosis among the inmates. As a result, although the increased inmate population qualified as a change of factual circumstances, the court found that the Sheriff's proposed solution—double-bunking in 197 of the 322 cells in the jail—was not narrowly tailored to those circumstances. The court invited the Sheriff to submit a new proposal that met the objectives of the decree. The district court also denied a motion brought by the Commis-

sioner of Correction for the Commonwealth to entirely vacate the decree. Inmates of Suffolk County Jail v. Rufo, 148 F.R.D. 14 (D.Mass.1993). The First Circuit turned away an appeal by the Commissioner. 12 F.3d 286 (1st Cir.1993). On the Sheriff's revised motion to modify, the district court granted permission to alter up to 100 cells to permit double-bunking, and stated its intent to close the case after an additional five-year monitoring period. 844 F.Supp. 31 (D.Mass.1994).

2. In *Rufo*, Justice White's opinion for the majority relied heavily on the need for flexibility in modifying decrees in institutional reform decrees. However, in *Stotts*, it was the dissent which took that position while Justice White's opinion for the majority took a more rigid approach. What accounts for his change of heart? Is it that "the new rule is that a *plaintiff* seeking modification has to meet an onerous burden while a *defendant* enjoys the benefits of a flexible standard"? David I. Levine, The Modification of Equitable Decrees in Institutional Reform Litigation: A Commentary on the Supreme Court's Adoption of the Second Circuit's Flexible Test, 58 Brook. L.Rev. 1239, 1267 (1993). Or is the *Rufo* Court simply returning the law of modification to a flexible standard with an ancient lineage? See Sweeton v. Brown, 27 F.3d 1162 (6th Cir.en banc 1994)(tracing flexible standard back to Sir Francis Bacon's Ordinances in Equity, written in 1618), cert. denied, ___ U.S. ___, 115 S.Ct. 1118, 130 L.Ed.2d 1082 (1995).

3. *Rufo* has encouraged defendants to seek a re-examination of many consent decrees. See, e.g., Ensley Branch, NAACP v. Seibels, 31 F.3d 1548 (11th Cir.1994)(ordering modifications to the consent decree issued in the litigation leading to Martin v. Wilks, 490 U.S. 755, 109 S.Ct. 2180, 104 L.Ed.2d 835 (1989)(infra at 329)); United States v. Eastman Kodak Co., 63 F.3d 95 (2d Cir.1995)(lifting antitrust decrees entered in 1921 and 1954).

4. The reach of the standards announced in *Rufo* is unsettled. Some courts have held that *Rufo* applies to institutional reform cases only, e.g., W.L. Gore & Associates, Inc. v. C.R. Bard, Inc., 977 F.2d 558 (Fed.Cir.1992)(refusing to apply *Rufo* to patent case), while others have held that it even applies to decrees binding private parties. E.g., Patterson v. Newspaper & Mail Deliverers' Union, 13 F.3d 33 (2d Cir.1993), cert. denied, ___ U.S. ___, 115 S.Ct. 58, 130 L.Ed.2d 16 (1994) ("If a decree seeks pervasive change in long-established practices affecting a large number of people, and the changes are sought to vindicate significant rights of a public nature [here, to redress racial discrimination], it is appropriate to apply a flexible standard * * *".).

5. Sheriff Rufo never personally agreed to the consent decree; his predecessor, Sheriff Kearney did. Can Rufo contend that he should not be bound by that earlier decision? See, e.g., Benjamin v. Malcolm, 156 F.R.D. 561 (S.D.N.Y.1994)(rejecting argument that city should be allowed to modify consent decree approved in previous mayor's administration).

The City of Chicago made such an argument in a successful challenge to a consent decree in which the city had agreed to pay large court judgments more promptly. Later developments clarified that the city had had no legal obligation to change its method of choosing when to pay court judgments. In Evans v. City of Chicago, 10 F.3d 474, 478–79 (7th Cir.en banc 1993), cert. denied, ___ U.S. ___, 114 S.Ct. 1831, 128 L.Ed.2d 460 (1994), the majority released the city from the obligations it had agreed to incur in the consent decree, reasoning:

> "Chicago" did not reach a settlement with the plaintiffs. The consent decree was entered in 1984. Negotiations were conducted on Chicago's behalf by its corporation counsel, who we may suppose acted with the approval of Harold Washington, then Chicago's mayor. Although the decree purports to last for all time—and the district court's decision refusing to vacate the decree * * * reflects a belief that the commitments ought to run perpetually—democracy does not permit public officials to bind the polity forever. What one City Council enacts, another may repeal; what one mayor decrees during his four-year term, another may revoke. Today's lawmakers have just as much power to set public policy as did their predecessors. "Chicago" speaks through its elected representatives, and the people are free to upset even the most enlightened policies of earlier times. The current mayor wants to be free of his predecessor's commitment, concluding that more flexibility over budgets will promote the public welfare. People of good will could be on either side of this disagreement; each mayor may have correctly perceived the needs of the moment.
>
> Governments are in this respect unlike corporations or other contracting parties. A corporate board of directors may enter into commitments that continue after new directors take office; a legislature may not. True, governments may form contracts (for example, to build a new road or repay a loan) and must keep these commitments by virtue of the contract clause of the Constitution, Art. I, § 10, cl. 1. But temporary officeholders may not contract away the basic powers of government to enact laws—or in this case to adopt budgets—in the same way natural persons may make enduring promises about their own future behavior. Why then should things differ if the parties choose not the device of a seal (or even of a statute) but the imprimatur of a district judge?
>
> Consent alone is insufficient to support a commitment by a public official that ties the hands of his successor. * * * Thus the answer to the question "why should consent decrees be enforced when contracts out of court are not?" must concentrate on legal rules that shape the parties' agreement. * * *
>
> It depends on rules of law that govern the public official's conduct. " '[T]he District Court's authority to adopt a consent decree comes only from the statute which the decree is intended to enforce,' not from the parties' consent to the decree." Firefighters v. Stotts, 467 U.S. 561, 576 n. 9, 104 S.Ct. 2576, 2586 n. 9, 81 L.Ed.2d 483 (1984). A state official's promise to follow a rule of federal law retains its force because of the continuing effect of the law, which the state cannot alter. And a settlement of a dispute about the meaning of that law may be enforced if the agreement compromises genuine uncertainties, for then the public official actually may be enhancing or preserving the powers of the democratic branch (by avoiding a worse outcome after trial) rather than ceding the powers of the government.

This method of justifying the implementation of consent decrees implies, however, that the court must ensure that there is a substantial federal claim, not only when the decree is entered but also when it is enforced, and that the obligations imposed by the decree rest on this rule of federal law rather than the bare consent of the officeholder. When making these inquiries, courts are bound by principles of federalism (and by the fundamental differences between judicial and political branches of government) to preserve the maximum leeway for democratic governance. Over the last decade a series of decisions in this circuit has emphasized the district court's responsibility to identify the rule of federal law supporting a consent decree binding the political arms of government, and the corresponding obligation to permit new public officials to set their own policy within the limits established by federal law. * * *

## 4. RETAINING AND CLOSING A CASE

### *Problem: Country Lodge v. Miller (Reprised)*
### *Obtaining Release From an Injunction*

For six months, Miller has obeyed the terms of a permanent injunction, which ordered her to conduct an expensive clean-up and banned any further dumping of apple mash waste in the river. Miller now seeks termination of the injunction. Country Lodge opposes the motion. What result? If the injunction is vacated and Country Lodge subsequently finds a small amount of apple mash in the river (but not as much as before the court issued the injunction originally), may the court sanction Miller for violating the injunction?

---

In typical private law cases, such as a simple trespass action, an injunction preventing further harm (i.e., an order not to trespass) would be imposed in perpetuity. Although any reparative aspect of the order would expire of its own terms (e.g., an order to clean-up whatever damage was caused by the trespass), the court usually would retain jurisdiction to enforce the injunction at any time in the future. Without more, it would be rare to have the defendant in such a case return to court to seek dismissal of the injunction and even more unusual for the court to grant such relief.

The court certainly has the power to grant such a motion for relief. For example, F.R.Civ.P. 60(b)(5) specifically grants a court power to relieve a party from a final judgment if "it is no longer equitable that the judgment should have prospective application." A typical defendant will want to be released as promptly as possible from the court's jurisdiction for several reasons. Once released, the defendant will once again have the ability to take action (and in more complex private and public law cases, make policy decisions) without judicial scrutiny or fear of judicial sanctions. Moreover, the defendant will not have to comply with monitoring rules, such as the necessity to file regular reports. Unless the conduct is independently prohibited by law (such as a statute), the defendant will be under no obligation to continue to avoid the conduct which had been proscribed by the injunction. Lloyd C. Anderson, Release and Resumption of Jurisdiction Over Consent Decrees in Structural Reform Litigation, 42 Miami L.Rev. 401, 413 (1987); Hugh J. Beard, The Role of Res Judicata in Recognizing Unitary Status and Terminating Desegregation Litigation: A Response to the Structural Injunction, 49 La.L.Rev. 1239 (1989). If the trial court is convinced that the defendants are substantially in compliance with its orders, should it release them from the terms of the injunction and from the court's jurisdiction? In certain cases, must the court release the defendant? In reading the next cases, you should also have in mind the cases from chapter 2 in which the courts decided whether it was necessary to issue an injunction against a defendant who had violated the law; in effect, the decision to release a defendant from an injunction is the reverse of the decision to impose an injunction in the first place.

## BOARD OF EDUCATION OF OKLAHOMA CITY PUBLIC SCHOOLS v. DOWELL

Supreme Court of the United States, 1991.
498 U.S. 237, 111 S.Ct. 630, 112 L.Ed.2d 715.

Chief Justice Rehnquist delivered the opinion of the Court.

* * * I

This school desegregation litigation began almost 30 years ago. [The Court reviewed the prolonged history of the case from its inception in 1961.] * * * In 1972, finding that previous efforts had not been successful at eliminating state-imposed segregation, the District Court ordered the Board [of Education of Oklahoma City, Oklahoma] to adopt the "Finger Plan," under which kindergartners would be assigned to neighborhood schools unless their parents opted otherwise; children in grades 1–4 would attend formerly all white schools, and thus black children would be bused to those schools; children in grade 5 would attend formerly all black schools, and thus white children would be bused to those schools; students in the upper grades would be bused to various areas in order to maintain integrated schools; and in integrated neighborhoods there would be stand-alone schools for all grades.

In 1977, after complying with the desegregation decree for five years, the Board made a "Motion to Close Case." The District Court held in its "Order Terminating Case":

> "The Court has concluded that [the Finger Plan] worked and that substantial compliance with the constitutional requirements has been achieved. * * *
>
> "... The School Board, as now constituted, has manifested the desire and intent to follow the law. The court believes that the present members and their successors on the Board will now and in

the future continue to follow the constitutional desegregation requirements. * * *

"... Jurisdiction in this case is terminated ipso facto subject only to final disposition of any case now pending on appeal."

This unpublished order was not appealed.

In 1984, the School Board faced demographic changes that led to greater burdens on young black children. As more and more neighborhoods became integrated, more stand-alone schools were established, and young black students had to be bused farther from their inner-city homes to outlying white areas. In an effort to alleviate this burden and to increase parental involvement, the Board adopted the Student Reassignment Plan (SRP), which relied on neighborhood assignments for students in grades K–4 beginning in the 1985–1986 school year. Busing continued for students in grades 5–12. Any student could transfer from a school where he or she was in the majority to a school where he or she would be in the minority. Faculty and staff integration was retained, and an "equity officer" was appointed.

In 1985, respondents filed a "Motion to Reopen the Case," contending that the School District had not achieved "unitary" status and that the SRP was a return to segregation. Under the SRP, 11 of 64 elementary schools would be greater than 90% black, 22 would be greater than 90% white plus other minorities, and 31 would be racially mixed. The District Court refused to reopen the case, holding that its 1977 finding of unitariness was res judicata as to those who were then parties to the action, and that the district remained unitary. * * * Because unitariness had been achieved, the District Court concluded that court-ordered desegregation must end.

The Court of Appeals for the Tenth Circuit reversed. It held that, while the 1977 order finding the district unitary was binding on the parties, nothing in that order indicated that the 1972 injunction itself was terminated. The court reasoned that the finding that the system was unitary merely ended the District Court's active supervision of the case, and because the school district was still subject to the desegregation decree, respondents could challenge the SRP. The case was remanded to determine whether the decree should be lifted or modified.

On remand, the District Court found that demographic changes made the Finger Plan unworkable, that the Board had done nothing for 25 years to promote residential segregation, and that the school district had bused students for more than a decade in good-faith compliance with the court's orders. The District Court found that present residential segregation was the result of private decisionmaking and economics, and that it was too attenuated to be a vestige of former school segregation. It also found that the district had maintained its unitary status, and that the neighborhood assignment plan was not designed with discriminatory intent. The court concluded that the previous injunctive decree should be vacated and the school district returned to local control.

The Court of Appeals again reversed, holding that " 'an injunction takes on a life of its own and becomes an edict quite independent of the law it is meant to effectuate.' " That court approached the case "not so much as one dealing with desegregation, but as one dealing with the proper application of the federal law on injunctive remedies." Relying on United States v. Swift & Co., 286 U.S. 106, 52 S.Ct. 460, 76 L.Ed. 999 (1932), it held that a desegregation decree remains in effect until a school district can show "grievous wrong evoked by new and unforeseen conditions," and "dramatic changes in conditions unforeseen at the time of the decree that ... impose extreme and unexpectedly oppressive hardships on the obligor," (quoting Jost, From *Swift* to *Stotts* and Beyond: Modification of Injunctions in the Federal Courts, 64 Tex. L.Rev. 1101, 1110 (1986)). Given that a number of schools would return to being primarily one-race schools under the SRP, circumstances in Oklahoma City had not changed enough to justify modification of the decree. * * *

We now reverse the Court of Appeals. * * *

III

The Court of Appeals relied upon language from this Court's decision in *United States v. Swift and Co.* * * *. We hold that its reliance was mistaken. * * *

United States v. United Shoe Machinery Corp., 391 U.S. 244, 88 S.Ct. 1496, 20 L.Ed.2d 562 (1968), explained that the language used in *Swift* must be read in the context of the continuing danger of unlawful restraints on trade which the Court had found still existed. * * * In the present case, a finding by the District Court that the Oklahoma City School District was being operated in compliance with the commands of the Equal Protection Clause of the Fourteenth Amendment, and that it was unlikely that the school board would return to its former ways, would be a finding that the purposes of the desegregation litigation had been fully achieved. No additional showing of "grievous wrong evoked by new and unforeseen conditions" is required of the Board. * * *

Considerations based on the allocation of powers within our federal system, we think, support our view that * * * *Swift* does not provide the proper standard to apply to injunctions entered in school desegregation cases. Such decrees, unlike the one in *Swift*, are not intended to operate in perpetuity. * * * The legal justification for displacement of local authority by an injunctive decree in a school desegregation case is a violation of the Constitution by the local authorities. Dissolving a desegregation decree after the local authorities have operated in compliance with it for a reasonable period of time properly recognizes that "necessary concern for the important values of local control of public school systems dictates that a federal court's regulatory control of such systems not extend beyond the time required to remedy the effects of past intentional discrimination."

The Court of Appeals * * * relied for its statement that "compliance alone cannot become the basis for modifying or dissolving an injunction" on our decision in United States v. W.T. Grant Co., 345 U.S. [629] at 633, 73 S.Ct. [894] at 897, [97 L.Ed. 1303 (1953)]. That case, however, did not involve the dissolution of an injunction, but the question of whether an injunction should be issued in the first place. This Court observed that a promise to comply with the law on the part of a wrongdoer did not divest a district court of its power to enjoin the wrongful conduct in which the defendant had previously engaged.

A district court need not accept at face value the profession of a school board which has intentionally discriminated that it will cease to do so in the future. But in deciding whether to modify or dissolve a desegregation decree, a school board's compliance with previous court orders is obviously relevant. * * * The test espoused by the Court of Appeals would condemn a school district, once governed by a board which intentionally discriminated, to judicial tutelage for the indefinite future. Neither the principles governing the entry and dissolution of injunctive decrees, nor the commands of the Equal Protection Clause of the Fourteenth Amendment, require any such Draconian result.

Petitioner urges that we reinstate the decision of the District Court terminating the injunction, but we think that the preferable course is to remand the case to that court so that it may decide, in accordance with this opinion, whether the Board made a sufficient showing of constitutional compliance as of 1985, when the SRP was adopted, to allow the injunction to be dissolved. The District Court should address itself to whether the Board had complied in good faith with the desegregation decree since it was entered, and whether the vestiges of past discrimination had been eliminated to the extent practicable.

In considering whether the vestiges of *de jure* segregation had been eliminated to the extent practicable, the District Court should look not only at student assignments, but "to every facet of school operations—faculty, staff, transportation, extra-curricular activities and facilities." Green [v. New Kent County School Board, 391 U.S. 430, 88 S.Ct. 1689, 20 L.Ed.2d 716 (1968)]. * * *

After the District Court decides whether the Board was entitled to have the decree terminated, it should proceed to decide respondent's challenge to the SRP. A school district which has been released from an injunction imposing a desegregation plan no longer requires court authorization for the promulgation of policies and rules regulating matters such as assignment of students and the like, but it of course remains subject to the mandate of the Equal Protection Clause of the Fourteenth Amendment. If the Board was entitled to have the decree terminated as of 1985, the District Court should then evaluate the Board's decision to implement the SRP under appropriate equal protection principles. * * *

JUSTICE SOUTER took no part in the consideration or decision of this case.

JUSTICE MARSHALL, with whom JUSTICE BLACKMUN and JUSTICE STEVENS join, dissenting.

* * * [Justice Marshall began by reviewing Oklahoma's record of segregation since the state's admission to the Union in 1907. Turning to the *Dowell* litigation, Justice Marshall found that its] history reveals nearly unflagging resistance by the Board to judicial efforts to dismantle the city's dual education system. * * *

II

I agree with the majority that the proper standard for determining whether a school desegregation decree should be dissolved is whether the purposes of the desegregation litigation, as incorporated in the decree, have been fully achieved. * * * I strongly disagree with the majority, however, on what must be shown to demonstrate that a decree's purposes have been fully realized. In my view, a standard for dissolution of a desegregation decree must take into account the unique harm associated with a system of racially identifiable schools and must expressly demand the elimination of such schools.

A

Our pointed focus in *Brown I* upon the stigmatic injury caused by segregated schools explains our unflagging insistence that formerly *de jure* segregated school districts extinguish all vestiges of school segregation. The concept of stigma also gives us guidance as to what conditions must be eliminated before a decree can be deemed to have served its purpose. * * *

Just as it is central to the standard for evaluating the formation of a desegregation decree, so should the stigmatic injury associated with segregated schools be central to the standard for dissolving a decree. The Court has indicated that "the ultimate end to be brought about" by a desegregation remedy is "a unitary, nonracial system of public education." *Green*. * * * Although the Court has never explicitly defined what constitutes a "vestige" of state-enforced segregation, the function that this concept has performed in our jurisprudence suggests that it extends to any condition that is likely to convey the message of inferiority implicit in a policy of segregation. So long as such conditions persist, the purposes of the decree cannot be deemed to have been achieved.

B

The majority suggests a more vague and, I fear, milder standard. * * *

By focusing heavily on present and future compliance with the Equal Protection Clause, the majority's standard ignores how the stigmatic harm identified in *Brown I* can persist even after the State ceases actively to enforce segregation.[6] * * * [O]ur school-desegregation jurisprudence establishes that the *effects* of past discrimination remain

6. Faithful compliance with the decree admittedly is relevant to the standard for dissolution. The standard for dissolution should require that the school district have exhibited faithful compliance with the decree for a period sufficient to assure the District Court that the school district is committed to the ideal of integrated system. * * *

chargeable to the school district regardless of its lack of continued enforcement of segregation, and the remedial decree is required until those effects have been finally eliminated.

III

Applying the standard I have outlined, I would affirm the Court of Appeals' decision ordering the District Court to restore the desegregation decree. For it is clear on this record that removal of the decree will result in a significant number of racially identifiable schools that could be eliminated. * * *

It is undisputed that replacing the Finger Plan with a system of neighborhood school assignments for grades K–4 resulted in a system of racially identifiable schools. * * * Because this principal vestige of *de jure* segregation persists, lifting the decree would clearly be premature at this point. * * *

In its concern to spare local school boards the "Draconian" fate of "indefinite" "judicial tutelage," the majority risks subordination of the constitutional rights of Afro–American children to the interest of school board autonomy. The courts must consider the value of local control, but that factor primarily relates to the feasibility of a remedial measure, see *Milliken II*, not whether the constitutional violation has been remedied. *Swann* establishes that if further desegregation is "reasonable, feasible, and workable," then it must be undertaken. * * * The School Board does not argue that further desegregation of the one-race schools in its system is unworkable * * *.

We should keep in mind that the court's active supervision of the desegregation process ceased in 1977. Retaining the decree does not require a return to active supervision. It may be that a modification of the decree which will improve its effectiveness and give the school district more flexibility in minimizing busing is appropriate in this case. But retaining the decree seems a slight burden on the school district compared with the risk of not delivering a full remedy to the Afro–American children in the school system. * * *

### *Notes*

1. Would it have made any difference to the Court's analysis if the Finger Plan had been adopted as part of a consent decree rather than as a result of complying with judicially-mandated relief? Cf. Firefighters Local Union No. 1784 v. Stotts, 467 U.S. 561, 104 S.Ct. 2576, 81 L.Ed.2d 483 (1984).

2. The majority notes that on remand the district court first needs to decide "whether the Board made a sufficient showing of constitutional compliance as of 1985, when the SRP was adopted, to allow the injunction to be dissolved." The Supreme Court then instructs the district court that if it decides that the decree should have been terminated by 1985, the lower court "should then evaluate the Board's decision to implement the SRP under appropriate equal protection principles." What is the legal standard to be used in this portion of the proceeding? Who bears the burden of proof?

For example, must the school board show that its decision to implement the SRP will not have a segregative effect? Must the plaintiffs demonstrate that the Board's decision was made with intent to re-segregate the Oklahoma City schools? See Dowell v. Board of Education of Oklahoma City Public Schools, 8 F.3d 1501 (10th Cir.1993)(affirming district court's decisions in defendants' favor on remand).

In this second portion of the proceeding on remand, may the plaintiffs rely on the history of segregation in Oklahoma that Justice Marshall reviewed and the prior "unflagging resistance by the Board to judicial efforts to dismantle the City's dual education system"? See Price v. Austin Independent School District, 945 F.2d 1307 (5th Cir.1991).

3. Suppose on remand that the district court finds that there are no vestiges of de jure segregation with respect to student assignments to schools, but there are some vestiges with respect to other facets of school operations, such as faculty or staff assignments, transportation, extra-curricular activities or facilities. What should the court do? See Freeman v. Pitts, infra.

## FREEMAN v. PITTS

Supreme Court of the United States, 1992.
503 U.S. 467, 112 S.Ct. 1430, 118 L.Ed.2d 108.

JUSTICE KENNEDY delivered the opinion of the Court.

DeKalb County, Georgia, is a major suburban area of Atlanta. This case involves a court-ordered desegregation decree for the DeKalb County School System (DCSS). DCSS now serves some 73,000 students in kindergarten through high school and is the 32d largest elementary and secondary school system in the Nation.

DCSS has been subject to the supervision and jurisdiction of the United States District Court for the Northern District of Georgia since 1969, when it was ordered to dismantle its dual school system. In 1986, petitioners filed a motion for final dismissal. The District Court ruled that DCSS had not achieved unitary status in all respects but had done so in student attendance and three other categories. In its order the District Court relinquished remedial control as to those aspects of the system in which unitary status had been achieved, and retained supervisory authority only for those aspects of the school system in which the district was not in full compliance. The Court of Appeals for the Eleventh Circuit reversed, holding that a district court should retain full remedial authority over a school system until it achieves unitary status in six categories at the same time for several years. We now reverse the judgment of the Court of Appeals and remand * * * .

### I

### A

For decades before our decision in Brown v. Board of Education, 347 U.S. 483 (1954)(*Brown I*), and our mandate in Brown v. Board of Education, 349 U.S. 294, 301 (1955)(*Brown II*), which ordered school districts to desegregate with "all deliberate speed," DCSS was segregated by law. DCSS's initial response to the mandate of *Brown II* was an all too familiar one. Interpreting "all deliberate speed" as giving latitude to delay steps to desegregate, DCSS took no positive action toward desegregation until the 1966–1967 school year, when it did nothing more than adopt a freedom of choice transfer plan. Some black students chose to attend former *de jure* white schools, but the plan had no significant effect on the former *de jure* black schools.

In 1968 we decided Green v. School Bd. of New Kent County, 391 U.S. 430 (1968). We held that adoption of a freedom of choice plan does not, by itself, satisfy a school district's mandatory responsibility to eliminate all vestiges of a dual system. *Green* was a turning point in our law in a further respect. Concerned by more than a decade of inaction, we stated that " '[t]he time for mere "deliberate speed" has run out.' " We said that the obligation of school districts once segregated by law was to come forward with a plan that "promises realistically to work, and promises realistically to work *now*." (emphasis in original). The case before us requires an understanding and assessment of how DCSS responded to the directives set forth in *Green*.

Within two months of our ruling in *Green*, respondents, who are black school children and their parents, instituted this class action in the United States District Court for the Northern District of Georgia. After the suit was filed, DCSS voluntarily began working with the Department of Health, Education and Welfare to devise a comprehensive and final plan of desegregation. The District Court in June 1969 entered a consent order approving the proposed plan, which was to be implemented in the 1969–1970 school year. The order abolished the freedom of choice plan and adopted a neighborhood school attendance plan that had been proposed by the DCSS and accepted by the Department of Health, Education and Welfare subject to a minor modification. Under the plan all of the former *de jure* black schools were closed and their students were reassigned among the remaining neighborhood schools. The District Court retained jurisdiction.

Between 1969 and 1986 respondents sought only infrequent and limited judicial intervention into the affairs of DCSS. They did not request significant changes in student attendance zones or student assignment policies. * * *

In 1986 petitioners filed a motion for final dismissal of the litigation. They sought a declaration that DCSS had satisfied its duty to eliminate the dual education system, that is to say a declaration that the school system had achieved unitary status. The District Court approached the question whether DCSS had achieved unitary status by asking whether DCSS was unitary with respect to each of the factors identified in *Green*. The court considered an additional factor that is not named in *Green*: the quality of education being offered to the white and black student populations.

The District Court found DCSS to be "an innovative school system that has travelled the often long road to unitary status almost to its end," noting that "the court has continually been impressed by the successes of the DCSS and its dedication to providing a quality education for all students within that system." It found that DCSS is a unitary system with regard to student assignments, transportation, physical facilities, and extracurricular activities, and ruled that it would order no further relief in those areas. The District Court stopped short of dismissing the case, however, because it found that DCSS was not unitary in every respect. The court said that vestiges of the dual system remain in the areas of teacher and principal assignments, resource allocation, and quality of education. DCSS was ordered to take measures to address the remaining problems.

B * * *

In the extensive record that comprises this case, one fact predominates: Remarkable changes in the racial composition of the county presented DCSS and the District Court with a student population in 1986 far different from the one they set out to integrate in 1969. Between 1950 and 1985, DeKalb County grew from 70,000 to 450,000 in total population, but most of the gross increase in student enrollment had occurred by 1969, the relevant starting date for our purposes. Although the public school population experienced only modest changes between 1969 and 1986 (remaining in the low 70,000's), a striking change occurred in the racial proportions of the student population. The school system that the District Court ordered desegregated in 1969 had 5.6% black students; by 1986 the percentage of black students was 47%.

To compound the difficulty of working with these radical demographic changes, the northern and southern parts of the county experienced much different growth patterns. The District Court found that "[a]s the result of these demographic shifts, the population of the northern half of DeKalb County is now predominantly white and the southern half of DeKalb County is predominantly black." * * *

The District Court made these findings:

> "[The actions of DCSS] achieved maximum practical desegregation from 1969 to 1986. The rapid population shifts in DeKalb County were not caused by any action on the part of the DCSS. These demographic shifts were inevitable as the result of suburbanization, that is, work opportunities arising in DeKalb County as well as the City of Atlanta, which attracted blacks to DeKalb; the decline in the number of children born to white families during this period while the number of children born to black families did not decrease; blockbusting of formerly white neighborhoods leading to selling and buying of real estate in the DeKalb area on a highly dynamic basis; and the completion of Interstate 20, which made access from DeKalb County into the City of Atlanta much easier.... There is no evidence that the school system's previous unconstitutional conduct

may have contributed to this segregation. This court is convinced that any further actions taken by defendants, while the actions might have made marginal adjustments in the population trends, would not have offset the factors that were described above and the same racial segregation would have occurred at approximately the same speed."

* * * In accordance with its factfinding, the District Court held that it would order no further relief in the areas of student assignment, transportation, physical facilities and extracurricular activities. The District Court, however, did order DCSS to establish a system to balance teacher and principal assignments and to equalize per pupil expenditures throughout DCSS. Having found that blacks were represented on the school board and throughout DCSS administration, the District Court abolished [a] biracial [review] committee as no longer necessary.

Both parties appealed to the United States Court of Appeals for the Eleventh Circuit. The Court of Appeals affirmed the District Court's ultimate conclusion that DCSS has not yet achieved unitary status, but reversed the District Court's ruling that DCSS has no further duties in the area of student assignment. The Court of Appeals held that the District Court erred by considering the six *Green* factors as separate categories. The Court of Appeals rejected the District Court's incremental approach, an approach that has also been adopted by the Court of Appeals for the First Circuit, Morgan v. Nucci, 831 F.2d 313, 318–319 (1987), and held that a school system achieves unitary status only after it has satisfied all six factors at the same time for several years. Because, under this test, DCSS had not achieved unitary status at any time, the Court of Appeals held that DCSS could "not shirk its constitutional duties by pointing to demographic shifts occurring prior to unitary status." The Court of Appeals held that petitioners bore the responsibility for the racial imbalance, and in order to correct that imbalance would have to take actions that "may be administratively awkward, inconvenient, and even bizarre in some situations," Swann v. Charlotte–Mecklenburg Bd. of Education, 402 U.S. 1, 28 (1971), such as pairing and clustering of schools, drastic gerrymandering of school zones, grade reorganization, and busing. We granted certiorari.

II

Two principal questions are presented. The first is whether a district court may relinquish its supervision and control over those aspects of a school system in which there has been compliance with a desegregation decree if other aspects of the system remain in noncompliance. As we answer this question in the affirmative, the second question is whether the Court of Appeals erred in reversing the District Court's order providing for incremental withdrawal of supervision in all the circumstances of this case.

A

The duty and responsibility of a school district once segregated by law is to take all steps necessary to eliminate the vestiges of the unconstitutional *de jure* system. This is required in order to ensure that the principal wrong of the *de jure* system, the injuries and stigma inflicted upon the race disfavored by the violation, is no longer present. This was the rationale and the objective of *Brown I* and *Brown II*. * * *

The objective of *Brown I* was made more specific by our holding in *Green* that the duty of a former *de jure* district is to "take whatever steps might be necessary to convert to a unitary system in which racial discrimination would be eliminated root and branch." We also identified various parts of the school system which, in addition to student attendance patterns, must be free from racial discrimination before the mandate of *Brown* is met: faculty, staff, transportation, extracurricular activities and facilities. The *Green* factors are a measure of the racial identifiability of schools in a system that is not in compliance with *Brown*, and we instructed the District Courts to fashion remedies that address all these components of elementary and secondary school systems.

The concept of unitariness has been a helpful one in defining the scope of the district courts' authority, for it conveys the central idea that a school district that was once a dual system must be examined in all of its facets, both when a remedy is ordered and in the later phases of desegregation when the question is whether the district courts' remedial control ought to be modified, lessened, or withdrawn. But, as we explained last term in *Board of Education of Oklahoma City v. Dowell*, the term "unitary" is not a precise concept:

> "[I]t is a mistake to treat words such as 'dual' and 'unitary' as if they were actually found in the Constitution.... Courts have used the term 'dual' to denote a school system which has engaged in intentional segregation of students by race, and 'unitary' to describe a school system which has been brought into compliance with the command of the Constitution. We are not sure how useful it is to define these terms more precisely, or to create subclasses within them."

It follows that we must be cautious not to attribute to the term a utility it does not have. The term "unitary" does not confine the discretion and authority of the District Court in a way that departs from traditional equitable principles.

That the term "unitary" does not have fixed meaning or content is not inconsistent with the principles that control the exercise of equitable power. The essence of a court's equity power lies in its inherent capacity to adjust remedies in a feasible and practical way to eliminate the conditions or redress the injuries caused by unlawful action. Equitable remedies must be flexible if these underlying principles are to be enforced with fairness and precision. * * * The requirement of a unitary school system must be implemented according to this prescription.

Our application of these guiding principles in Pasadena City Bd. of Education v. Spangler, 427 U.S. 424 (1976), is instructive. There we held that a District Court exceeded its remedial authority in requiring annual readjustment of school attendance zones in the Pasadena school district when changes in the racial makeup of the schools were caused by demographic shifts "not attributed to any segregative acts on the part of the [school district]." * * *

Today, we make explicit the rationale that was central in *Spangler*. A federal court in a school desegregation case has the discretion to order an incremental or partial withdrawal of its supervision and control. This discretion derives both from the constitutional authority which justified its intervention in the first instance and its ultimate objectives in formulating the decree. The authority of the court is invoked at the outset to remedy particular constitutional violations. In construing the remedial authority of the district courts, we have been guided by the principles that "judicial powers may be exercised only on the basis of a constitutional violation," and that "the nature of the violation determines the scope of the remedy." A remedy is justifiable only insofar as it advances the ultimate objective of alleviating the initial constitutional violation.

We have said that the court's end purpose must be to remedy the violation and, in addition, to restore state and local authorities to the control of a school system that is operating in compliance with the Constitution. * * * Partial relinquishment of judicial control, where justified by the facts of the case, can be an important and significant step in fulfilling the district court's duty to return the operations and control of schools to local authorities. In *Dowell*, we emphasized that federal judicial supervision of local school systems was intended as a "temporary measure." Although this temporary measure has lasted decades, the ultimate objective has not changed—to return school districts to the control of local authorities. Just as a court has the obligation at the outset of a desegregation decree to structure a plan so that all available resources of the court are directed to comprehensive supervision of its decree, so too must a court provide an orderly means for withdrawing from control when it is shown that the school district has attained the requisite degree of compliance. A transition phase in which control is relinquished in a gradual way is an appropriate means to this end. * * *

We hold that, in the course of supervising desegregation plans, federal courts have the authority to relinquish supervision and control of school districts in incremental stages, before full compliance has been achieved in every area of school operations. While retaining jurisdiction over the case, the court may determine that it will not order further remedies in areas where the school district is in compliance with the decree. That is to say, upon a finding that a school system subject to a court-supervised desegregation plan is in compliance in some but not all areas, the court in appropriate cases may return control to the school system in those areas where compliance has been achieved, limiting further judicial supervision to operations that are not yet in full compliance with the court decree. In particular, the district court may determine that it will not order further remedies in the area of student assignments where racial imbalance is not traceable, in a proximate way, to constitutional violations.

A court's discretion to order the incremental withdrawal of its supervision in a school desegregation case must be exercised in a manner consistent with the purposes and objectives of its equitable power. Among the factors which must inform the sound discretion of the court in ordering partial withdrawal are the following: whether there has been full and satisfactory compliance with the decree in those aspects of the system where supervision is to be withdrawn; whether retention of judicial control is necessary or practicable to achieve compliance with the decree in other facets of the school system; and whether the school district has demonstrated, to the public and to the parents and students of the once disfavored race, its good-faith commitment to the whole of the court's decree and to those provisions of the law and the Constitution that were the predicate for judicial intervention in the first instance.

In considering these factors a court should give particular attention to the school system's record of compliance. A school system is better positioned to demonstrate its good faith commitment to a constitutional course of action when its policies form a consistent pattern of lawful conduct directed to eliminating earlier violations. And, with the passage of time, the degree to which racial imbalances continue to represent vestiges of a constitutional violation may diminish, and the practicability and efficacy of various remedies can be evaluated with more precision. * * *

B

We reach now the question whether the Court of Appeals erred in prohibiting the District Court from returning to DCSS partial control over some of its affairs. * * *

It was an appropriate exercise of its discretion for the District Court to address the elements of a unitary system discussed in *Green*, to inquire whether other elements ought to be identified, and to determine whether minority students were being disadvantaged in ways that required the formulation of new and further remedies to insure full compliance with the court's decree. * * * The District Court's approach illustrates that the *Green* factors need not be a rigid framework. It illustrates also the uses of equitable discretion. By withdrawing control over areas where judicial supervision is no longer needed, a district court can concentrate both its own resources and those of the school district on the areas where the effects of *de jure* discrimination have not been eliminated and further action is necessary in order to provide real and tangible relief to minority students.

The Court of Appeals' rejection of the District Court's order rests on related premises: first, that given noncompliance in some discrete categories, there can be no partial withdrawal of judicial control; and second, until there is full compliance, heroic measures must be taken to ensure racial balance in student assignments systemwide. Under our analysis and our precedents, neither premise is correct. * * *

The desegregation decree was designed to achieve maximum practicable desegregation. Its central remedy was the closing of black schools and the reassignment of pupils to neighborhood schools, with attendance zones that achieved racial balance. The plan accomplished its objective in the first year of operation, before dramatic demographic changes altered residential patterns. For the entire 17–year period the respondents raised no substantial objection to the basic student assignment system, as the parties and the District Court concentrated on other mechanisms to eliminate the *de jure* taint.

That there was racial imbalance in student attendance zones was not tantamount to a showing that the school district was in noncompliance with the decree or with its duties under the law. Racial balance is not to be achieved for its own sake. It is to be pursued when racial imbalance has been caused by a constitutional violation. Once the racial imbalance due to the *de jure* violation has been remedied, the school district is under no duty to remedy imbalance that is caused by demographic factors. * * * If the unlawful *de jure* policy of a school system has been the cause of the racial imbalance in student attendance, that condition must be remedied. The school district bears the burden of showing that any current imbalance is not traceable, in a proximate way, to the prior violation. * * *

In one sense of the term, vestiges of past segregation by state decree do remain in our society and in our schools. Past wrongs to the black race, wrongs committed by the State and in its name, are a stubborn fact of history. And stubborn facts of history linger and persist. But though we cannot escape our history, neither must we overstate its consequences in fixing legal responsibilities. The vestiges of segregation that are the concern of the law in a school case may be subtle and intangible but nonetheless they must be so real that they have a causal link to the *de jure* violation being remedied. It is simply not always the case that demographic forces causing population change bear any real and substantial relation to a *de jure* violation. And the law need not proceed on that premise.

As the *de jure* violation becomes more remote in time and these demographic changes intervene, it becomes less likely that a current racial imbalance in a school district is a vestige of the prior *de jure* system. * * * It was appropriate for the District Court to examine the reasons for the racial imbalance before ordering an impractical, and no doubt massive, expenditure of funds to achieve racial balance after 17 years of efforts to implement the comprehensive plan in a district where there were fundamental changes in demographics, changes not attributable to the former *de jure* regime or any later actions by school officials. The District Court's determination to order instead the expenditure of scarce resources in areas such as the quality of education, where full compliance had not yet been achieved, underscores the uses of discretion in framing equitable remedies.

To say, as did the Court of Appeals, that a school district must meet all six *Green* factors before the trial court can declare the system unitary and relinquish its control over school attendance zones, and to hold further that racial balancing by all necessary means is required in the interim, is simply to vindicate a legal phrase. The law is not so formalistic. A proper rule must be based on the necessity to find a feasible remedy that insures systemwide compliance with the court decree and that is directed to curing the effects of the specific violation.

We next consider whether retention of judicial control over student attendance is necessary or practicable to achieve compliance in other facets of the school system. Racial balancing in elementary and secondary school student assignments may be a legitimate remedial device to correct other fundamental inequities that were themselves caused by the constitutional violation. * * * As a consequence, a continuing violation in one area may need to be addressed by remedies in another. * * *

There was no showing that racial balancing was an appropriate mechanism to cure other deficiencies in this case. * * * The District Court, not having our analysis before it, did not have the opportunity to make specific findings and conclusions on this aspect of the case, however. Further proceedings are appropriate for this purpose.

The requirement that the school district show its good faith commitment to the entirety of a desegregation plan so that parents, students and the public have assurance against further injuries or stigma also should be a subject for more specific findings. We stated in *Dowell* that the good faith compliance of the district with the court order over a reasonable period of time is a factor to be considered in deciding whether or not jurisdiction could be relinquished. * * * A history of good-faith compliance is evidence that any current racial imbalance is not the product of a new *de jure* violation, and enables the district court to accept the school board's representation that it has accepted the principle of racial equality and will not suffer intentional discrimination in the future. See Morgan v. Nucci, 831 F.2d at 321 ("A finding of good faith ... reduces the possibility that a school system's compliance with court orders is but a temporary constitutional ritual").

When a school district has not demonstrated good faith under a comprehensive plan to remedy ongoing violations, we have without hesitation approved comprehensive and continued district court supervision. * * *

With respect to those areas where compliance had not been achieved, the District Court did not find that DCSS had acted in bad faith or engaged in further acts of discrimination since the desegregation plan went into effect. This, though, may not be the equivalent of a finding that the school district has an affirmative commitment to comply in good faith with the entirety of a desegregation plan, and further proceedings are appropriate for this purpose as well. * * *

JUSTICE THOMAS took no part in the consideration or decision of this case.

JUSTICE SCALIA, concurring.

* * * Our decision will be of great assistance to the citizens of DeKalb County, who for the first time since 1969 will be able to run their own public schools, at least so far as student assignments are concerned. It will have little effect, however, upon the many other school districts throughout the country that are still being supervised by federal judges, since it turns upon the extraordinarily rare circumstance of a *finding* that no portion of the current racial imbalance is a remnant of prior *de jure* discrimination. While it is perfectly appropriate for the Court to decide this case on that narrow basis, we must resolve—if not today, then soon—what is to be done in the vast majority of other districts, where, though our cases continue to profess that judicial oversight of school operations is a temporary expedient, democratic processes remain suspended, with no prospect of restoration, 38 years after Brown v. Board of Education, 347 U.S. 483 (1954)(*Brown I*).

Almost a quarter-century ago, in Green v. School Bd., New Kent County, 391 U.S. 430, 437–438 (1968), this Court held that school systems which had been enforcing *de jure* segregation at the time of *Brown I* had not merely an obligation to assign students and resources on a race-neutral basis but also an "affirmative duty" to "desegregate," that is, to achieve insofar as practicable racial balance in their schools. This holding has become such a part of our legal fabric that there is a tendency, reflected in the Court of Appeals opinion in this case, to speak as though the Constitution requires such racial balancing. Of course it does not: The Equal Protection Clause reaches only those racial imbalances shown to be intentionally caused by the State. * * * For all our talk about "unitary status," "release from judicial supervision," and "affirmative duty to desegregate," the sole question in school desegregation cases (absent an allegation that current policies are intentionally discriminatory) is one of remedies for past violations. * * *

In the context of elementary and secondary education, the presumption was extraordinary in law but not unreasonable in fact. * * * The extent and recency of the prior discrimination, and the improbability that young children (or their parents) would use "freedom of choice" plans to disrupt existing patterns "warrant[ed] a presumption [that] schools that are substantially disproportionate in their racial composition" were remnants of the *de jure* system.

But granting the merits of this approach at the time of *Green*, it is now 25 years later. * * *

At some time, we must acknowledge that it has become absurd to assume, without any further proof, that violations of the Constitution dating from the days when Lyndon Johnson was President, or earlier, continue to have an appreciable effect upon current operation of schools. We are close to that time. While we must continue to prohibit, without qualification, all racial discrimination in the operation of public schools, and to afford remedies that eliminate not only the discrimination but its identified consequences, we should consider laying aside the extraordinary, and increasingly counterfactual, presumption of *Green*. We must soon revert to the ordinary principles of our law, of our democratic heritage, and of our educational tradition: that plaintiffs alleging equal protection violations must prove intent and causation and not merely the existence of racial disparity; that public schooling, even in the South, should be controlled by locally elected authorities acting in conjunction with parents; and that it is "desirable" to permit pupils to attend "schools nearest their homes".

JUSTICE SOUTER, concurring.

I join the Court's opinion holding that where there are vestiges of a dual system in some of a judicially supervised school system's aspects, or *Green*-type factors, a district court will retain jurisdiction over the system, but need not maintain constant supervision or control over factors as to which compliance has been achieved. I write separately only to explain my understanding of the enquiry required by a district court applying the principle we set out today.

We recognize that although demographic changes influencing the composition of a school's student population may well have no causal link to prior *de jure* segregation, judicial control of student assignments may still be necessary to remedy persisting vestiges of the unconstitutional dual system, such as remaining imbalance in faculty assignments. This is, however, only one of several possible causal relationships between or among unconstitutional acts of school segregation and various *Green*-type factors. I think it is worth mentioning at least two others: the dual school system itself as a cause of the demographic shifts with which the district court is faced when considering a partial relinquishment of supervision, and a *Green*-type factor other than student assignments as a possible cause of imbalanced student assignment patterns in the future.

The first would occur when demographic change toward segregated residential patterns is itself caused by past school segregation and the patterns of thinking that segregation creates. Such demographic change is not an independent, supervening cause of racial imbalance in the student body, and we have said before that when demographic change is not independent of efforts to segregate, the causal relationship may be considered in fashioning a school desegregation remedy. Racial imbalance in student assignments caused by demographic change is not insulated from federal judicial oversight where the demographic change is itself caused in this way, and before deciding to relinquish supervision and control over student assignments, a district court should make findings on the presence or absence of this relationship.

The second and related causal relationship would occur after the district court has relinquished supervision over a remedied aspect of the school system, when future imbalance in that remedied *Green*-type factor (here, student assignments) would be caused by remaining vestiges of the dual system. Even after attaining compliance as to student composition, other factors such as racial composition of the faculty, quality of the physical plant, or per-pupil expenditures may leave schools racially identifiable. (In this very case, for example, there is a correlation in particular schools of over representation of black principals and administrators, lower per pupil expenditures, and high percentages of black students. Moreover, the schools in the predominantly black southern section of the school district are the only ones that use "portable classrooms," i.e., trailers.) If such other factors leave a school identifiable as "black," as soon as the district court stops supervising student assignments, nearby white parents may move in the direction of racially identifiable "white" schools, or may simply move their children into these schools. In such a case, the vestige of discrimination in one factor will act as an incubator for resegregation in others. Before a district court ends its supervision of student assignments, then, it should make a finding that there is no immediate threat of unremedied *Green*-type factors causing population or student enrollment changes that in turn may imbalance student composition in this way. And, because the district court retains jurisdiction over the case, it should of course reassert control over student assignments if it finds that this does happen.

JUSTICE BLACKMUN, with whom JUSTICE STEVENS and JUSTICE O'CONNOR join, concurring in the judgment.

It is almost 38 years since this Court decided Brown v. Board of Education, 347 U.S. 483 (1954). In those 38 years the students in DeKalb County, Ga., never have attended a desegregated school system even for one day. The majority of "black" students never have attended a school that was not disproportionately black. Ignoring this glaring dual character of the DeKalb County School System (DCSS), part "white" and part "black," the District Court relinquished control over student assignments, finding that the school district had achieved "unitary status" in that aspect of the system. No doubt frustrated by the continued existence of duality, the Court of Appeals ordered the school district to take extraordinary measures to correct all manifestations of this racial imbalance. Both decisions, in my view, were in error, and I therefore concur in the Court's decision to vacate the judgment and remand the case. * * *

I

Beginning with *Brown*, and continuing through the Court's most recent school-desegregation decision in Board of Education of Oklahoma City v. Dowell, 498 U.S. (1991), this Court has recognized that when the local government has been running *de jure* segregated schools, it is the operation of a racially segregated school system that must be remedied, not discriminatory policy in some discrete subpart of that system. Consequently, the Court in the past has required and decides again today that even if the school system ceases to discriminate with respect to one of the *Green*-type factors, "the [district] court should retain jurisdiction until it is clear that state-imposed segregation has been *completely removed.*" * * *

The obligations of a district court and a school district under its jurisdiction have been clearly articulated in the Court's many desegregation cases. Until the desegregation decree is dissolved under the standards set forth in *Dowell*, the school board continues to have "the affirmative duty to take whatever steps might be necessary to convert to a unitary system in which racial discrimination would be eliminated root and branch." The duty remains enforceable by the district court without any new proof of a constitutional violation, and the school district has the burden of proving that its actions are eradicating the effects of the former *de jure* regime.

Contrary to the Court of Appeals' conclusion, however, retaining jurisdiction does not obligate the district court in all circumstances to maintain active supervision and control, continually ordering reassignment of students. * * *

Whether a district court must maintain active supervision over student assignment, and order new remedial actions depends on two factors. As the Court discusses, the district court must order changes in student assignment if it "is necessary or practicable to achieve compliance in other facets of the school system." The district court also must order affirmative action in school attendance if the school district's conduct was a "contributing cause" of the racially identifiable schools. * * *

II * * *

DCSS claims that it need not remedy the segregation in DeKalb County schools because it was caused by demographic changes for which DCSS has no responsibility. It is not enough, however, for DCSS to establish that demographics exacerbated the problem; it must prove that its own policies did not contribute. Such contribution can occur in at least two ways: DCSS may have contributed to the demographic changes themselves, or it may have contributed directly to the racial imbalance in the schools. * * *

Although respondents challenged the District Court's causation conclusions in the Court of Appeals, that court did not reach the issue. Accordingly, in addition to the issues the Court suggests be considered in further proceedings, I would remand for the Court of Appeals to review, under the foregoing principles, the District Court's finding that DCSS has met its burden of proving the racially identifiable schools are in no way the result of past segregative action.

## *Notes*

1. An opinion in Brown v. Board of Education, 978 F.2d 585 (10th Cir.1992), cert. denied, ___ U.S. ___, 113 S.Ct. 2994, 125 L.Ed.2d 688 (1993), was one of the first occasions for a lower federal court to evaluate *Dowell* and *Freeman* together. A panel majority held that the intentional discrimination first documented in the original *Brown* decision still had not dissipat-

ed sufficiently to declare Topeka's schools unitary. The majority acted over a dissent taking the position that:

> [A] federal court may withdraw from supervision of a school district in increments as the district achieves unitary status over each facet of its operations. [Citing *Freeman*.] Once a school district has achieved unitary status, actions concerning student assignment, even if they result in racial imbalance, must be evaluated under traditional equal protection principles, which require a showing of intentional discrimination. [Citing *Dowell*.]

978 F.2d at 594. Is this a correct reading of the interaction between the two cases? See David I. Levine, The Latter Stages of Enforcement of Equitable Decrees: The Course of Institutional Reform Cases After Dowell, Rufo and Freeman, 20 Hastings Const.L.Q. 579, 632–37 (1993)(suggesting that it is not quite correct).

2. Suppose that the plaintiffs in *Freeman* had initiated their suit at a time when the schools were in the condition of partial desegregation described in the majority opinion. At that point, would the district court have granted an injunction to the plaintiffs? What would its scope be? Would the scope be any different than the injunction remaining in *Freeman* after partial release from judicial supervision?

3. In effect, the defendants in *Freeman* were seeking modification or termination, under F.R.Civ.P. 60(b)(5), of the district court's order to dismantle its dual school system. Surprisingly, *Freeman* does not discuss *Rufo*, which was decided just a few months earlier. Would the result or the analysis in *Freeman* have come out any differently had the Court applied the *Rufo* standards for modification?

## C. RESISTANCE TO THE DECREE

The contempt power is the court's ultimate weapon to deter, overcome, or punish disobedience of an injunction. Because contempt is a powerful weapon, it may harm defendant more than it helps plaintiff and can require a heavy expenditure of judicial time and credibility. So, when a plaintiff complains that a defendant has violated an injunction, courts will often explore less intrusive techniques to prompt compliance, such as "clarifying" the original injunction or issuing a more prophylactic one, instead of initiating contempt proceedings. Such techniques, although nonpunitive in theory, can be quite painful to the defendant.

Just as the likelihood that defendant will violate plaintiff's rights helps determine whether a court will issue an injunction and its scope, so the likelihood that defendant will continue to resist compliance with an injunction helps determine how a court will respond to allegations that defendant has violated it in the past. Professor Robert Goldstein suggests one possible "scenario of escalating intrusiveness" in an institutional reform case:

1. Declaratory judgment with or without guidelines for compliance;
2. Time for good faith compliance;

3. A hearing on the reasons for failure to comply;

4. Plaintiff request for supplemental relief;

5. An order for defendant to submit a detailed remedial plan;

6. An order to plaintiff to submit a plan or to plaintiff and defendant to negotiate a plan;

7. Hearings on a court-ordered plan and/or the appointment of a master to formulate a plan;

8. The remedial order;

9. Appointment of a master or oversight committee with power to gather data and review and guide decree implementation;

10. Time for good faith compliance;

11. Receivership, annulment of state laws slowing relief, closing of institutions, replacement of state officials, reordering of governmental budgets, and other intrusive actions;

12. Contempt.

Robert Goldstein, A *Swann* Song for Remedies: Equitable Relief in the Burger Court, 13 Harv.C.R.-C.L.L.Rev. 1, 65–68 (1978).

This section will look first at contempt's elements, sanctions, and procedures. It will then turn to the when parties are bound, limits on enforcing decrees against persons who are not parties, and special problems in enforcing decrees against governmental defendants.

## 1. THE CONTEMPT POWER

### *Problem: Country Lodge v. Miller (Reprised)* *Civil or Criminal Contempt*

Miller is enjoined from putting anything in the river under a statute that prohibits discharges into the waters of the state without a permit. The court holds Miller in contempt for violating the order. Would it be improper for the court to sentence Miller to 5 days in prison after finding her guilty of contempt by clear and convincing evidence?

---

The contempt power used to deal with violations of injunctions and other court orders is the same power used to deal with disruptive conduct in the court room, the intimidation of jurors, and other obstructions of the judicial process. As explained at the beginning of chapter 2 (p. 33), the contempt power takes three forms: criminal contempt, coercive civil contempt, and compensatory civil contempt.

Contempt proceedings are usually triggered by the plaintiff bringing the violation of the order to the court's attention. Because criminal contempt is brought in the name of the public, the judge and not the plaintiff gets to decide whether to initiate a prosecution for criminal contempt. Indeed the court may initiate such a prosecution without any prompting from the plaintiff or continue it even if plaintiff beseeches the court to stop the prosecution. If the court does decide to commence criminal contempt proceedings, it will generally ask the prosecutor of the jurisdiction to press the charges, but may appoint any member of the bar as a special prosecutor. The Supreme Court has invoked its supervisory powers over federal courts to require that judges may not appoint a special prosecutor unless the United States Attorney has declined the case and that, in any event, may not appoint the plaintiff's attorney as the special prosecutor because of conflicts of interest. Young v. United States ex rel. Vuitton et Fils, S.A. 481 U.S. 787, 107 S.Ct. 2124, 95 L.Ed.2d 740 (1987). In compensatory or coercive civil contempt, plaintiff usually presses the charges.

A single proceeding may result in criminal, compensatory, and coercive sanctions. As Justice Rutledge stated:

> [i]n any other context than one of contempt, the idea that a criminal prosecution and a civil suit for damages or equitable relief could be hashed together in a single criminal-civil hodgepodge would be shocking to every American lawyer and to most citizens.

United States v. United Mine Workers, 330 U.S. 258, 364, 67 S.Ct. 677, 730, 91 L.Ed. 884, 949–50 (1947)(dissenting). Why do you suppose that courts allow civil and criminal contempt to be "hashed"? Moreover, "no judicial opinion or statute has ever required the judge at the initiation of contempt proceedings to determine the type of sanction [criminal or civil] that may be imposed." Robert J. Martineau, Contempt of Court: Eliminating the Confusion Between Civil and Criminal Contempt, 50 U.Cin.L.Rev. 677, 684 (1981)(discussing with approval a new Wisconsin statute that requires such a determination). Nor can the alleged contemnor necessarily tell whether the proceedings are civil or criminal by the identity of the attorney bringing the charges. When the plaintiff is a government, the government's attorney may be competent to bring either kind of charge. Even when the plaintiff is not a government, the identity of the attorney bringing the charge may not be dispositive. For example, in the following case, Hicks, the district attorney, claims to be representing a private plaintiff in a civil contempt proceeding.

## HICKS ON BEHALF OF FEIOCK v. FEIOCK

Supreme Court of the United States, 1988.
485 U.S. 624, 108 S.Ct. 1423, 99 L.Ed.2d 721.

JUSTICE WHITE delivered the opinion of the Court. * * *

I

On January 19, 1976, a California state court entered an order requiring respondent, Phillip Feiock, to begin making monthly payments to his ex-wife for the support of their three children. Over the next six years, respondent only sporadically complied with the order, and by December 1982 he had discontinued paying child support altogether.

His ex-wife sought to enforce the support orders. On June 22, 1984, a hearing was held in California state court on her petition for ongoing support payments and for payment of the arrearage due her. The court examined respondent's financial situation and ordered him to begin paying $150 per month commencing on July 1, 1984. The court reserved jurisdiction over the matter for the purpose of determining the arrearages and reviewing respondent's financial condition.

Respondent apparently made two monthly payments but paid nothing for the next nine months. He was then served with an order to show cause why he should not be held in contempt on nine counts of failure to make the monthly payments ordered by the court. At a hearing on August 9, 1985, petitioner made out a prima facie case of contempt against respondent by establishing the existence of a valid court order, respondent's knowledge of the order, and respondent's failure to comply with the order. Respondent defended by arguing that he was unable to pay support during the months in question. This argument was partially successful, but respondent was adjudged to be in contempt on five of the nine counts. He was sentenced to five days in jail on each count, to be served consecutively, for a total of 25 days. This sentence was suspended, however, and respondent was placed on probation for three years. As one of the conditions of his probation, he was ordered once again to make support payments of $150 per month. As another condition of his probation, he was ordered, starting the following month, to begin repaying $50 per month on his accumulated arrearage, which was determined to total $1650.

At the hearing, respondent had objected to the application of Cal. Civ.Proc.Code Ann. § 1209.5 (1982) against him, claiming that it was unconstitutional under the Due Process Clause of the Federal Constitution because it shifts to the defendant the burden of proving inability to comply with the order, which is an element of the crime of contempt.[1] This objection was rejected, and he renewed it on appeal. The intermediate state appellate court agreed with respondent and annulled the contempt order, ruling that the state statute purports to impose "a mandatory presumption compelling a conclusion of guilt without independent proof of an ability to pay," and is therefore unconstitutional because "the mandatory nature of the presumption lessens the prosecution's burden of proof." In light of its holding that the statute as previously interpreted was unconstitutional, the court went on to adopt a different interpretation of that statute to govern future proceedings: "For future guidance, however, we determine the statute in question should be construed as authorizing a permissive inference, but not a mandatory presumption." The court explicitly considered this reinterpretation of the statute to be an exercise of its "obligation to interpret

1. California Civ.Proc.Code Ann. § 1209.5 (1982) states that "[w]hen a court of competent jurisdiction makes an order compelling a parent to furnish support ... for his child, proof that ... the parent was present in court at the time the order was pronounced and proof of noncompliance therewith shall be prima facie evidence of a contempt of court."

the statute to preserve its constitutionality whenever possible." The California Supreme Court denied review, but we granted certiorari.

II

Three issues must be decided to resolve this case. First is whether the ability to comply with a court order constitutes an element of the offense of contempt or, instead, inability to comply is an affirmative defense to that charge. Second is whether § 1209.5 requires the alleged contemnor to shoulder the burden of persuasion or merely the burden of production in attempting to establish his inability to comply with the order. Third is whether this contempt proceeding was a criminal proceeding or a civil proceeding, i.e., whether the relief imposed upon respondent was criminal or civil in nature.

Petitioner argues that the state appellate court erred in its determinations on the first two points of state law. The court ruled that whether the individual is able to comply with a court order is an element of the offense of contempt rather than an affirmative defense to the charge, and that § 1209.5 shifts to the alleged contemnor the burden of persuasion rather than simply the burden of production in showing inability to comply. We are not at liberty to depart from the state appellate court's resolution of these issues of state law. * * *

The third issue, however, is a different matter: the argument is not merely that the state court misapplied state law, but that the characterization of this proceeding and the relief given as civil or criminal in nature, for purposes of determining the proper applicability of federal constitutional protections, raises a question of federal law rather than state law. This proposition is correct as stated. The fact that this proceeding and the resultant relief were judged to be criminal in nature as a matter of state law is thus not determinative of this issue, and the state appellate court erred insofar as it sustained respondent's challenge to the statute under the Due Process Clause simply because it concluded that this contempt proceeding is "quasi-criminal" as a matter of California law.

III

A

The question of how a court determines whether to classify the relief imposed in a given proceeding as civil or criminal in nature, for the purposes of applying the Due Process Clause and other provisions of the Constitution, is one of long standing, and its principles have been settled at least in their broad outlines for many decades. When a State's proceedings are involved, state law provides strong guidance about whether or not the State is exercising its authority "in a non-punitive, non-criminal manner," and one who challenges the State's classification of the relief imposed as "civil" or "criminal" may be required to show "the clearest proof" that it is not correct as a matter of federal law. Nonetheless, if such a challenge is substantiated, then the labels affixed either to the proceeding or to the relief imposed under state law are not controlling and will not be allowed to defeat the applicable protections of federal constitutional law. This is particularly so in the codified laws of contempt, where the "civil" and "criminal" labels of the law have become increasingly blurred.[4]

Instead, the critical features are the substance of the proceeding and the character of the relief that the proceeding will afford. "If it is for civil contempt the punishment is remedial, and for the benefit of the complainant. But if it is for criminal contempt the sentence is punitive, to vindicate the authority of the court." Gompers v. Bucks Stove & Range Co., 221 U.S. 418, 441, 31 S.Ct. 492, 498, 55 L.Ed. 797 (1911). The character of the relief imposed is thus ascertainable by applying a few straightforward rules. If the relief provided is a sentence of imprisonment, it is remedial if "the defendant stands committed unless and until he performs the affirmative act required by the court's order," and is punitive if "the sentence is limited to imprisonment for a definite period." If the relief provided is a fine, it is remedial when it is paid to the complainant, and punitive when it is paid to the court, though a fine that would be payable to the court is also remedial when the defendant can avoid paying the fine simply by performing the affirmative act required by the court's order. These distinctions lead up to the fundamental proposition that criminal penalties may not be imposed on someone who has not been afforded the protections that the Constitution requires of such criminal proceedings, including the requirement that the offense be proved beyond a reasonable doubt.[5]

The Court has consistently applied these principles. In *Gompers,* decided early in this century, three men were found guilty of contempt and were sentenced to serve 6, 9, and 12 months respectively. The Court found this relief to be criminal in nature because the sentence was determinate and unconditional. "The distinction between refusing to do an act commanded,—remedied by imprisonment until the party performs the required act; and doing an act forbidden,—punished by imprisonment for a definite term; is sound in principle, and generally, if not universally, affords a test by which to determine the character of the punishment." In the former instance, the conditional nature of the punishment renders the relief civil in nature because the contemnor "can end the sentence and discharge himself at any moment by doing what he had previously refused to do." In the latter instance, the unconditional nature of the punishment renders the relief criminal in nature because the relief "cannot undo or remedy what has been done

**4.** California is a good example of this modern development, for although it defines civil and criminal contempts in separate statutes, compare Cal.Civ.Proc.Code Ann. § 1209 (Supp.1988) with Cal.Penal Code Ann. § 166 (1970), it has merged the two kinds of proceedings under the same procedural rules. See Cal.Civ.Proc.Code Ann. §§ 1209–1222 (1982 and Supp.1988).

**5.** We have recognized that certain specific constitutional protections, such as the right to trial by jury, are not applicable to those criminal contempts that can be classified as petty offenses, as is true of other petty crimes as well. This is not true, however, of the proposition that guilt must be proved beyond a reasonable doubt.

nor afford any compensation" and the contemnor "cannot shorten the term by promising not to repeat the offense." * * *

B

In repeatedly stating and following the rules set out above, the Court has eschewed any alternative formulation that would make the classification of the relief imposed in a State's proceedings turn simply on what their underlying purposes are perceived to be. Although the purposes that lie behind particular kinds of relief are germane to understanding their character, this Court has never undertaken to psychoanalyze the subjective intent of a State's laws and its courts, not only because that effort would be unseemly and improper, but also because it would be misguided. In contempt cases, both civil and criminal relief have aspects that can be seen as either remedial or punitive or both * * * As was noted in *Gompers:*

> "It is true that either form of [punishment] has also an incidental effect. For if the case is civil and the punishment is purely remedial, there is also a vindication of the court's authority. On the other hand, if the proceeding is for criminal contempt and the [punishment] is solely punitive, to vindicate the authority of the law, the complainant may also derive some incidental benefit from the fact that such punishment tends to prevent a repetition of the disobedience. But such indirect consequences will not change [punishment] which is merely coercive and remedial, into that which is solely punitive in character, or *vice versa.*" * * *

IV

The proper classification of the relief imposed in respondent's contempt proceeding is dispositive of this case. As interpreted by the state court here, § 1209.5 requires respondent to carry the burden of persuasion on an element of the offense, by showing his inability to comply with the court's order to make the required payments. If applied in a *criminal* proceeding, such a statute would violate the Due Process Clause because it would undercut the State's burden to prove guilt beyond a reasonable doubt. If applied in a civil proceeding, however, this particular statute would be constitutionally valid, Maggio v. Zeitz, 333 U.S. 56, 75–76, 68 S.Ct. 401, 411–412, 92 L.Ed. 476 (1948) * * * [9]

The state court found the contempt proceeding to be "quasi-criminal" in nature without discussing the point. There were strong indications that the proceeding was intended to be criminal in nature, such as the notice sent to respondent, which clearly labeled the proceeding as "criminal in nature," and the participation of the District Attorney in the case. Though significant, these facts are not dispositive of the issue before us, for if the trial court had imposed only civil coercive remedies, as surely it was authorized to do, then it would be improper to invalidate

9. Our precedents are clear, however, that punishment may not be imposed in a civil contempt proceeding when it is clearly established that the alleged contemnor is unable to comply with the terms of the order.

that result merely because the Due Process Clause, as applied in criminal proceedings, was not satisfied.[10] It also bears emphasis that the purposes underlying this proceeding were wholly ambiguous. Respondent was charged with violating nine discrete prior court orders, and the proceeding may have been intended primarily to vindicate the court's authority in the face of his defiance. On the other hand, as often is true when court orders are violated, these charges were part of an ongoing battle to force respondent to conform his conduct to the terms of those orders, and of future orders as well.

Applying the traditional rules for classifying the relief imposed in a given proceeding requires the further resolution of one factual question about the nature of the relief in this case. Respondent * * * was sentenced to five days in jail on each of the five counts, for a total of 25 days, but his jail sentence was suspended and he was placed on probation for three years. If this were all, then the relief afforded would be criminal in nature.[11] But this is not all. One of the conditions of respondent's probation was that he begin making payments on his accumulated arrearage, and that he continue making these payments at the rate of $50 per month. At that rate, all of the arrearage would be paid before respondent completed his probation period. Not only did the order therefore contemplate that respondent would be required to purge himself of his past violations, but it expressly states that "[i]f any two payments are missed, whether consecutive or not, the entire balance shall become due and payable." What is unclear is whether the ultimate satisfaction of these accumulated prior payments would have purged the determinate sentence imposed on respondent. * * * [N]either party was able to offer a satisfactory explanation of this point at argument.[12] If the

**10.** This can also be seen by considering the notice given to the alleged contemnor. This Court has stated that one who is charged with a crime is "entitled to be informed of the nature of the charge against him but to know that it is a charge and not a suit." Gompers v. Bucks Stove & Range Co., 221 U.S. 418, 446, 31 S.Ct. 492, 500, 55 L.Ed. 797 (1911). Yet if the relief ultimately given in such a proceeding is wholly civil in nature, then this requirement would not be applicable. It is also true, of course, that if *both* civil and criminal relief are imposed in the same proceeding, then the " 'criminal feature of the order is dominant and fixes its character for purposes of review.' "

**11.** That a determinate sentence is suspended and the contemnor put on probation does not make the remedy civil in nature, for a suspended sentence, without more, remains a determinate sentence, and a fixed term of probation is itself a punishment that is criminal in nature. A suspended sentence with a term of probation is not equivalent to a conditional sentence that would allow the contemnor to avoid or purge these sanctions. A determinate term of probation puts the contemnor under numerous disabilities that he cannot escape by complying with the dictates of the prior orders, such as: any conditions of probation that the court judges to be reasonable and necessary may be imposed; the term of probation may be revoked and the original sentence (including incarceration) may be reimposed at any time for a variety of reasons without all the safeguards that are ordinarily afforded in criminal proceedings; and the contemnor's probationary status could affect other proceedings against him that may arise in the future (for example,this fact might influence the sentencing determination made in a criminal prosecution for some wholly independent offense).

**12.** It is also perhaps of some significance, though not binding upon us, that the parties reinforce the ambiguity on this point by entitling this contempt order, in the Joint Appendix, as "Order of the Superior Court of the State of California, County of Orange, to Purge Arrearage and Judgment of Contempt."

relief imposed here is in fact a determinate sentence with a purge clause, then it is civil in nature.

* * * [T]he Due Process Clause does not necessarily prohibit the State from employing this presumption [of ability to pay] as it was construed by the state court, *if* respondent would purge his contempt judgment by paying off his arrearage. In these circumstances, the proper course for this Court is to vacate the judgment below and remand for further consideration of § 1209.5 free from the compulsion of an erroneous view of federal law. If on remand it is found that respondent would purge his sentence by paying his arrearage, then this proceeding is civil in nature and there was no need for the state court to reinterpret its statute to avoid conflict with the Due Process Clause. * * *

JUSTICE KENNEDY took no part in the consideration or decision of this case.

JUSTICE O'CONNOR, with whom THE CHIEF JUSTICE and JUSTICE SCALIA join, dissenting. * * *

"* * * In 1983, only half of custodial parents received the full amount of child support ordered; approximately 26% received some lesser amount, and 24% received nothing at all." Brief for Women's Legal Defense Fund et al. as Amici Curiae 26. * * *

Contempt proceedings often will be useless if the parent seeking enforcement of valid support orders must prove that the obligor can comply with the court order. The custodial parent will typically lack access to the financial and employment records needed to sustain the burden imposed by the decision below, especially where the noncustodial parent is self-employed, as is the case here. Serious consequences follow from the California Court of Appeal's decision to invalidate California's statutory presumption that a parent continues to be able to pay the child support previously determined to be within his or her means.

* * * [T]he substance of the proceeding below and the conditions on which the sentence was suspended reveal that the proceeding was civil in nature. Mrs. Feiock initiated the underlying action in order to obtain enforcement of the child support order for the benefit of the Feiock children. The California District Attorney conducted the case under a provision of the [Uniform Reciprocal Enforcement of Support Act (URESA)] that authorizes him to act on Mrs. Feiock's behalf. As the very caption of the case in this Court indicates, the District Attorney is acting on behalf of Mrs. Feiock, not as the representative of the State of California in a criminal prosecution. Both of the provisions of California's enactment of the URESA that authorize contempt proceedings appear in a chapter of the Code of Civil Procedure entitled "Civil Enforcement." It appears that most States enforce child and spousal support orders through civil proceedings like this one, in which the burden of persuasion is shifted to the defendant to show inability to comply. * * *

It is true that the order imposing the sentence does not expressly provide that, *if* respondent is someday incarcerated and *if* he subsequently complies, he will be released immediately. The parties disagree about what will happen if this contingency arises, and there is no need to address today the question of whether the failure to grant immediate release would render the sanction criminal. In the case before us respondent carries something even better than the "keys to the prison" in his own pocket: as long as he meets the conditions of his informal probation, he will never enter the jail.

It is critical that the only conditions placed on respondent's probation, apart from the requirement that he conduct himself generally in accordance with the law, are that he cure his past failures to comply with the support order and that he continue to comply in the future.* The sanction imposed on respondent is unlike ordinary criminal probation because it is collateral to a civil proceeding initiated by a private party, and respondent's sentence is suspended on the condition that he comply with a court order entered for the benefit of that party. This distinguishes respondent's sentence from suspended criminal sentences imposed outside the contempt context.

This Court traditionally has inquired into the substance of contempt proceedings to determine whether they are civil or criminal, paying particular attention to whether the sanction imposed will benefit another party to the proceeding. In this case, the California Superior Court suspended respondent's sentence on the condition that he bring himself into compliance with a court order providing support for his children, represented in the proceeding by petitioner. I conclude that the proceeding in this case should be characterized as one for civil contempt, and I would reverse the judgment below.

### *Notes on In Personam Versus In Rem Enforcement*

1. Enforcing money judgments differs fundamentally from enforcing court orders. A money judgment is not an order of the court and therefore failure to satisfy it is not disobedience of the court. Rather, unless satisfied, the judgment authorizes the sheriff to seize defendant's property, sell it, and pay the plaintiff from the proceeds. (See chapter 8.) So a money judgment is directed against defendant's property rather than defendant's person. It is in rem rather than in personam. In contrast, injunctions and other court orders are generally orders to the defendant personally. This is the origin of the maxim that "equity acts in personam." But equity sometimes acts in rem. Should a defendant resist an order to convey title to real estate, the court may simply decree

* Unlike the Court, I find no ambiguity in the court's sentencing order that hints that respondent can purge his jail sentence by paying off the arrearage alone. The sentencing order suspends execution of the jail sentence and places respondent on probation on the conditions that he *both* make future support payments at $150 per month *and* pay $50 per month on the arrearage. If respondent pays off the arrearage before the end of his probation period, but then fails to make a current support payment, the suspension will be revoked and he will go to jail.

that plaintiff has title. The court may also appoint a receiver to do what the injunction requires of defendant, as was seen at p. 208 of this chapter. Would an in rem order help Ms. Feiock?

2. Although most awards of money are by money judgments, courts do sometimes *order* the payment of money. E.g. Bowen v. Massachusetts, 487 U.S. 879, 108 S.Ct. 2722, 101 L.Ed.2d 749 (1988). But an order to pay money is enforced as a money judgment because society does not want to jail debtors, as chapter 8 will show. An exception is made for failure to pay alimony or child support, as in *Hicks*. The point of the case is, however, not whether failure to pay alimony should be treated as contempt, but how courts should deal with alleged contempts.

### *Notes on the Classification of Contempt Proceedings*

1. *Hicks* holds that a jail sentence for contempt, suspended upon condition of future compliance with a court order in a civil case, is criminal unless the contemnor can purge the contempt. The dissent disagrees. Which side has the better argument?

2. *Hicks* also holds that a suspended jail sentence for contempt is civil if it can be purged. The majority remands for a determination of whether paying off the $1650 of arrearages would effect a purge. One way he might pay off the arrearages is to make the required payments of $50 a month. But that would take 33 months of the 36 months of his probation. Another way he might purge is if he fails to make 2 payments, which would result in his being jailed and the entire balance being due immediately, and then pays off the balance. But, it seems implausible that he could come up with that much money when in jail if he could not come up with the smaller sums needed to avoid jail. No wonder the trial court did not bother to explain in advance whether paying the arrearages would purge the contempt. On the other hand, can you think of another black letter test to determine whether the suspended sentence was imposed to punish past violations or to coerce future compliance?

3. After *Hicks*, can states use civil contempt to coerce the payment of alimony and child support? On remand, the state appellate court held that the California statute at issue in *Hicks* was "unmistakably criminal in nature." However, the court also held that the statute merely made ability to pay an affirmative defense in contempt proceedings. In re Feiock, 215 Cal.App.3d 141, 263 Cal.Rptr. 437 (1989). The court majority explained that once the alleged contemnor raises the affirmative defense by making a prima facie showing of inability to pay, the party seeking criminal contempt has the burden of proving all elements beyond a reasonable doubt, including ability to pay. The dissent charged that the majority had changed its position from its original opinion and now had unconstitutionally imposed on the alleged contemnor a burden that was an element of the offense.

4. Coercive civil contempt usually requires three steps: (1) the issuance of an injunction; (2) a determination of contempt and the imposition of sanctions subject to the condition that defendant can purge; and (3) a finding as to whether defendant has purged. *Hicks* decided that this second step can be taken civilly. Can this third step be also be taken civilly? For example, suppose that Mr. Feiock receives a purgeable suspended sentence, fails to pay, is jailed, and then claims he has no money with which to purge. Should that claim be decided criminally or civilly?

## UNITED MINE WORKERS v. BAGWELL

Supreme Court of the United States, 1994.
512 U.S. ___, 114 S.Ct. 2552, 129 L.Ed.2d 642.

JUSTICE BLACKMUN delivered the opinion of the Court.

We are called upon once again to consider the distinction between civil and criminal contempt. Specifically, we address whether contempt fines levied against a union for violations of a labor injunction are coercive civil fines, or are criminal fines that constitutionally could be imposed only through a jury trial. We conclude that the fines are criminal and, accordingly, we reverse the judgment of the Supreme Court of Virginia.

### I

Petitioners, the International Union, United Mine Workers of America and United Mine Workers of America, District 28 (collectively, the union) engaged in a protracted labor dispute with the Clinchfield Coal Company and Sea "B" Mining Company (collectively, the companies) over alleged unfair labor practices. In April 1989, the companies filed suit in the Circuit Court of Russell County, Virginia, to enjoin the union from conducting unlawful strike-related activities. The trial court entered an injunction which, as later amended, prohibited the union and its members from, among other things, obstructing ingress and egress to company facilities, throwing objects at and physically threatening company employees, placing tire-damaging "jackrocks" on roads used by company vehicles, and picketing with more than a specified number of people at designated sites. The court additionally ordered the union to take all steps necessary to ensure compliance with the injunction, to place supervisors at picket sites, and to report all violations to the court.

On May 16, 1989, the trial court held a contempt hearing and found that petitioners had committed 72 violations of the injunction. After fining the union $642,000 for its disobedience,[1] the court announced that it would fine the union $100,000 for any future violent breach of the injunction and $20,000 for any future nonviolent infraction, "such as exceeding picket numbers, [or] blocking entrances or exits." The Court

1. A portion of these fines was suspended conditioned on the union's future compliance. The court later vacated these fines, concluding that they were "criminal in nature."

early stated that its purpose was to "impos[e] prospective civil fines[,] the payment of which would only be required if it were shown the defendants disobeyed the Court's orders."

In seven subsequent contempt hearings held between June and December 1989, the court found the union in contempt for more than 400 separate violations of the injunction, many of them violent. Based on the court's stated "intention that these fines are civil and coercive," each contempt hearing was conducted as a civil proceeding before the trial judge, in which the parties conducted discovery, introduced evidence, and called and cross-examined witnesses. The trial court required that contumacious acts be proved beyond a reasonable doubt, but did not afford the union a right to jury trial.

As a result of these contempt proceedings, the court levied over $64,000,000 in fines against the union, approximately $12,000,000 of which was ordered payable to the companies. Because the union objected to payment of any fines to the companies and in light of the law enforcement burdens posed by the strike, the court ordered that the remaining roughly $52,000,000 in fines be paid to the Commonwealth of Virginia and Russell and Dickenson Counties, "the two counties most heavily affected by the unlawful activity."

While appeals from the contempt orders were pending, the union and the companies settled the underlying labor dispute, agreed to vacate the contempt fines, and jointly moved to dismiss the case. A special mediator representing the Secretary of Labor, and the governments of Russell and Dickenson Counties, supported the parties' motion to vacate the outstanding fines. The trial court granted the motion to dismiss, dissolved the injunction, and vacated the $12,000,000 in fines payable to the companies. After reiterating its belief that the remaining $52,000,000 owed to the counties and the Commonwealth were coercive, civil fines, the trial court refused to vacate these fines, concluding they were "payable in effect to the public."

The companies withdrew as parties in light of the settlement and declined to seek further enforcement of the outstanding contempt fines. Because the Commonwealth Attorneys of Russell and Dickenson Counties also had asked to be disqualified from the case, the court appointed respondent John L. Bagwell to act as Special Commissioner to collect the unpaid contempt fines on behalf of the counties and the Commonwealth.

The Court of Appeals of Virginia reversed and ordered that the contempt fines be vacated pursuant to the settlement agreement. Assuming for the purposes of argument that the fines were civil, the court concluded "that civil contempt fines imposed during or as a part of a civil proceeding between private parties are settled when the underlying litigation is settled by the parties and the court is without discretion to refuse to vacate such fines."

On consolidated appeals, the Supreme Court of Virginia reversed. The court held that whether coercive, civil contempt sanctions could be settled by private parties was a question of state law, and that Virginia public policy disfavored such a rule, "if the dignity of the law and public respect for the judiciary are to be maintained." The court also rejected petitioners' contention that the outstanding fines were criminal and could not be imposed absent a criminal trial. Because the trial court's prospective fine schedule was intended to coerce compliance with the injunction and the union could avoid the fines through obedience, the court reasoned, the fines were civil and coercive and properly imposed in civil proceedings * * *

II

A

"Criminal contempt is a crime in the ordinary sense," Bloom v. Illinois, 391 U.S. 194, 201 (1968), and "criminal penalties may not be imposed on someone who has not been afforded the protections that the Constitution requires of such criminal proceedings." Hicks v. Feiock, 485 U.S. 624, 632 (1988). See In re Bradley, 318 U.S. 50 (1943)(double jeopardy); Cooke v. United States, 267 U.S. 517, 537 (1925)(rights to notice of charges, assistance of counsel, summary process, and to present a defense); Gompers v. Bucks Stove & Range Co., 221 U.S. 418, 444 (1911) (privilege against self-incrimination, right to proof beyond a reasonable doubt). For "serious" criminal contempts involving imprisonment of more than six months, these protections include the right to jury trial. *Bloom*. In contrast, civil contempt sanctions, or those penalties designed to compel future compliance with a court order, are considered to be coercive and avoidable through obedience, and thus may be imposed in an ordinary civil proceeding upon notice and an opportunity to be heard. Neither a jury trial nor proof beyond a reasonable doubt is required.[2]

Although the procedural contours of the two forms of contempt are well established, the distinguishing characteristics of civil versus criminal contempts are somewhat less clear.[3] In the leading early case addressing this issue in the context of imprisonment, *Gompers v. Bucks Stove & Range Co.,* the Court emphasized that whether a contempt is civil or criminal turns on the "character and purpose" of the sanction involved. * * *

The paradigmatic coercive, civil contempt sanction, as set forth in *Gompers*, involves confining a contemnor indefinitely until he complies with an affirmative command such as an order "to pay alimony, or to surrender property ordered to be turned over to a receiver, or to make a conveyance." Imprisonment for a fixed term similarly is coercive when

2. We address only the procedures required for adjudication of indirect contempts, i.e., those occurring out of court. Direct contempts that occur in the court's presence may be immediately adjudged and sanctioned summarily, and, except for serious criminal contempts in which a jury trial is required, the traditional distinction between civil and criminal contempt proceedings does not pertain.

3. Numerous scholars have criticized as unworkable the traditional distinction between civil and criminal contempt. See, e.g., Dudley, Getting Beyond the Civil/Criminal Distinction: A New Approach to Regulation of Indirect Contempts, 79 Va. L. Rev. 1025, 1033 (1993) (describing the distinction between civil and criminal contempt as "conceptually unclear and exceedingly difficult to apply").

the contemnor is given the option of earlier release if he complies. In these circumstances, the contemnor is able to purge the contempt and obtain his release by committing an affirmative act, and thus "carries the keys of his prison in his own pocket." *Gompers*.

By contrast, a fixed sentence of imprisonment is punitive and criminal if it is imposed retrospectively for a "completed act of disobedience," *Gompers*, such that the contemnor cannot avoid or abbreviate the confinement through later compliance. * * * When a contempt involves the prior conduct of an isolated, prohibited act, the resulting sanction has no coercive effect. "[T]he defendant is furnished no key, and he cannot shorten the term by promising not to repeat the offense."

This dichotomy between coercive and punitive imprisonment has been extended to the fine context. A contempt fine accordingly is considered civil and remedial if it either "coerce[s] the defendant into compliance with the court's order, [or] ... compensate[s] the complainant for losses sustained." United States v. United Mine Workers of America, 330 U.S. 258, 303–304 (1947). Where a fine is not compensatory, it is civil only if the contemnor is afforded an opportunity to purge. See Penfield Co. v. SEC, 330 U.S. 585, 590 (1947). Thus, a "flat, unconditional fine" totalling even as little as $50 announced after a finding of contempt is criminal if the contemnor has no subsequent opportunity to reduce or avoid the fine through compliance.

A close analogy to coercive imprisonment is a per diem fine imposed for each day a contemnor fails to comply with an affirmative court order. Like civil imprisonment, such fines exert a constant coercive pressure, and once the jural command is obeyed, the future, indefinite, daily fines are purged. Less comfortable is the analogy between coercive imprisonment and suspended, determinate fines. In this Court's sole prior decision squarely addressing the judicial power to impose coercive civil contempt fines, *United Mine Workers,* it held that fixed fines also may be considered purgeable and civil when imposed and suspended pending future compliance. See also *Penfield* ("One who is fined, unless by a day certain he [complies] ..., has it in his power to avoid any penalty"); but see *Hicks*, (suspended or probationary sentence is criminal). *United Mine Workers* involved a $3,500,000 fine imposed against the union for nationwide post-World War II strike activities. Finding that the determinate fine was both criminal and excessive, the Court reduced the sanction to a flat criminal fine of $700,000. The Court then imposed and suspended the remaining $2,800,000 as a coercive civil fine, conditioned on the union's ability to purge the fine through full, timely compliance with the trial court's order. * * * [4] The Court concluded, in light of this purge clause, that the civil fine operated as "a coercive

4. Although the size of the fine was substantial, the conduct required of the union to purge the suspended fine was relatively discrete. According to the Court, purgation consisted of (1) withdrawal of the union's notice terminating the Krug–Lewis labor agreement; (2) notifying the union members of this withdrawal; and (3) withdrawing and notifying the union members of the withdrawal of any other notice questioning the ongoing effectiveness of the Krug–Lewis agreement.

imposition upon the defendant union to compel obedience with the court's outstanding order."

This Court has not revisited the issue of coercive civil contempt fines addressed in *United Mine Workers*. Since that decision, the Court has erected substantial procedural protections in other areas of contempt law, such as criminal contempts and summary contempts. Lower federal courts and state courts such as the trial court here nevertheless have relied on *United Mine Workers* to authorize a relatively unlimited judicial power to impose noncompensatory civil contempt fines.

B

Underlying the somewhat elusive distinction between civil and criminal contempt fines, and the ultimate question posed in this case, is what procedural protections are due before any particular contempt penalty may be imposed. Because civil contempt sanctions are viewed as nonpunitive and avoidable, fewer procedural protections for such sanctions have been required. To the extent that such contempts take on a punitive character, however, and are not justified by other considerations central to the contempt power, criminal procedural protections may be in order.

The traditional justification for the relative breadth of the contempt power has been necessity: Courts independently must be vested with "power to impose silence, respect, and decorum, in their presence, and submission to their lawful mandates, and ... to preserve themselves and their officers from the approach and insults of pollution." Courts thus have embraced an inherent contempt authority, as a power "necessary to the exercise of all others."

But the contempt power also uniquely is "liable to abuse." Unlike most areas of law, where a legislature defines both the sanctionable conduct and the penalty to be imposed, civil contempt proceedings leave the offended judge solely responsible for identifying, prosecuting, adjudicating, and sanctioning the contumacious conduct. Contumacy "often strikes at the most vulnerable and human qualities of a judge's temperament," and its fusion of legislative, executive, and judicial powers "summons forth ... the prospect of 'the most tyrannical licentiousness.'" Accordingly, "in [criminal] contempt cases an even more compelling argument can be made [than in ordinary criminal cases] for providing a right to jury trial as a protection against the arbitrary exercise of official power."

Our jurisprudence in the contempt area has attempted to balance the competing concerns of necessity and potential arbitrariness by allowing a relatively unencumbered contempt power when its exercise is most essential, and requiring progressively greater procedural protections when other considerations come into play. The necessity justification for the contempt authority is at its pinnacle, of course, where contumacious conduct threatens a court's immediate ability to conduct its proceedings, such as where a witness refuses to testify, or a party disrupts the court. Thus, petty, direct contempts in the presence of the court traditionally have been subject to summary adjudication, "to maintain order in the courtroom and the integrity of the trial process in the face of an 'actual obstruction of justice.'" In light of the court's substantial interest in rapidly coercing compliance and restoring order, and because the contempt's occurrence before the court reduces the need for extensive factfinding and the likelihood of an erroneous deprivation, summary proceedings have been tolerated.

Summary adjudication becomes less justifiable once a court leaves the realm of immediately sanctioned, petty direct contempts. If a court delays punishing a direct contempt until the completion of trial, for example, due process requires that the contemnor's rights to notice and a hearing be respected. There "it is much more difficult to argue that action without notice or hearing of any kind is necessary to preserve order and enable [the court] to proceed with its business." Direct contempts also cannot be punished with serious criminal penalties absent the full protections of a criminal jury trial. * * *

Still further procedural protections are afforded for contempts occurring out of court, where the considerations justifying expedited procedures do not pertain. Summary adjudication of indirect contempts is prohibited, and criminal contempt sanctions are entitled to full criminal process. Certain indirect contempts nevertheless are appropriate for imposition through civil proceedings. Contempts such as failure to comply with document discovery, for example, while occurring outside the court's presence, impede the court's ability to adjudicate the proceedings before it and thus touch upon the core justification for the contempt power. Courts traditionally have broad authority through means other than contempt-such as by striking pleadings, assessing costs, excluding evidence, and entering default judgment-to penalize a party's failure to comply with the rules of conduct governing the litigation process. See, e.g., Fed. Rule Civ. Proc. 11, 37. Such judicial sanctions never have been considered criminal, and the imposition of civil, coercive fines to police the litigation process appears consistent with this authority. Similarly, indirect contempts involving discrete, readily ascertainable acts, such as turning over a key or payment of a judgment, properly may be adjudicated through civil proceedings since the need for extensive, impartial factfinding is less pressing.

For a discrete category of indirect contempts, however, civil procedural protections may be insufficient. Contempts involving out-of-court disobedience to complex injunctions often require elaborate and reliable factfinding. Such contempts do not obstruct the court's ability to adjudicate the proceedings before it, and the risk of erroneous deprivation from the lack of a neutral factfinder may be substantial. Under these circumstances, criminal procedural protections such as the rights to counsel and proof beyond a reasonable doubt are both necessary and appropriate to protect the due process rights of parties and prevent the arbitrary exercise of judicial power.

C

In the instant case, neither any party nor any court of the Commonwealth has suggested that the challenged fines are compensatory. * * * The issue before us accordingly is limited to whether these fines, despite their noncompensatory character, are coercive civil or criminal sanctions.

The parties propose two independent tests for determining whether the fines are civil or criminal. Petitioners argue that because the injunction primarily prohibited certain conduct rather than mandated affirmative acts, the sanctions are criminal. Respondent in turn urges that because the trial court established a prospective fine schedule that the union could avoid through compliance, the fines are civil in character.

Neither theory satisfactorily identifies those contempt fines that are criminal and thus must be imposed through the criminal process. Petitioners correctly note that *Gompers* suggests a possible dichotomy "between refusing to do an act commanded,—remedied by imprisonment until the party performs the required act; and doing an act forbidden,—punished by imprisonment for a definite term." The distinction between mandatory and prohibitory orders is easily applied in the classic contempt scenario, where contempt sanctions are used to enforce orders compelling or forbidding a single, discrete act. In such cases, orders commanding an affirmative act simply designate those actions that are capable of being coerced.

But the distinction between coercion of affirmative acts and punishment of prohibited conduct is difficult to apply when conduct that can recur is involved, or when an injunction contains both mandatory and prohibitory provisions. Moreover, in borderline cases injunctive provisions containing essentially the same command can be phrased either in mandatory or prohibitory terms. Under a literal application of petitioners' theory, an injunction ordering the union: "Do not strike," would appear to be prohibitory and criminal, while an injunction ordering the union: "Continue working," would be mandatory and civil. In enforcing the present injunction, the trial court imposed fines without regard to the mandatory or prohibitory nature of the clause violated. Accordingly, even though a parsing of the injunction's various provisions might support the classification of contempts such as rock-throwing and placing tire-damaging "jackrocks" on roads as criminal and the refusal to place supervisors at picket sites as civil, the parties have not asked us to review the order in that manner. In a case like this involving an injunction that prescribes a detailed code of conduct, it is more appropriate to identify the character of the entire decree.

Despite respondent's urging, we also are not persuaded that dispositive significance should be accorded to the fact that the trial court prospectively announced the sanctions it would impose. Had the trial court simply levied the fines after finding the union guilty of contempt, the resulting "determinate and unconditional" fines would be considered "solely and exclusively punitive." Respondent nevertheless contends that the trial court's announcement of a prospective fine schedule allowed the union to "avoid paying the fine[s] simply by performing the ... act required by the court's order," *Hicks*, and thus transformed these fines into coercive, civil ones. Respondent maintains here, as the Virginia Supreme Court held below, that the trial court could have imposed a daily civil fine to coerce the union into compliance, and that a prospective fine schedule is indistinguishable from such a sanction.

Respondent's argument highlights the difficulties encountered in parsing coercive civil and criminal contempt fines. The fines imposed here concededly are difficult to distinguish either from determinate, punitive fines or from initially suspended, civil fines. Ultimately, however, the fact that the trial court announced the fines before the contumacy, rather than after the fact, does not in itself justify respondent's conclusion that the fines are civil or meaningfully distinguish these penalties from the ordinary criminal law. Due process traditionally requires that criminal laws provide prior notice both of the conduct to be prohibited and of the sanction to be imposed. The trial court here simply announced the penalty—determinate fines of $20,000 or $100,000 per violation—that would be imposed for future contempts. The union's ability to avoid the contempt fines was indistinguishable from the ability of any ordinary citizen to avoid a criminal sanction by conforming his behavior to the law. The fines are not coercive day fines, or even suspended fines, but are more closely analogous to fixed, determinate, retrospective criminal fines which petitioners had no opportunity to purge once imposed. We therefore decline to conclude that the mere fact that the sanctions were announced in advance rendered them coercive and civil as a matter of constitutional law.

Other considerations convince us that the fines challenged here are criminal. The union's sanctionable conduct did not occur in the court's presence or otherwise implicate the court's ability to maintain order and adjudicate the proceedings before it. Nor did the union's contumacy involve simple, affirmative acts, such as the paradigmatic civil contempts examined in *Gompers*. Instead, the Virginia trial court levied contempt fines for widespread, ongoing, out-of-court violations of a complex injunction. In so doing, the court effectively policed petitioners' compliance with an entire code of conduct that the court itself had imposed. The union's contumacy lasted many months and spanned a substantial portion of the State. The fines assessed were serious, totalling over $52,000,000.[5] Under such circumstances, disinterested factfinding and

**5.** "Petty contempt like other petty criminal offenses may be tried without a jury," and the imposition only of serious criminal contempt fines triggers the right to jury trial. *Bloom*. The Court to date has not specified what magnitude of contempt fine may constitute a serious criminal sanction, although it has held that a fine of $10,000 imposed on a union was insufficient to trigger the Sixth Amendment right to jury trial. See Muniz v. Hoffman, 422 U.S. 454, 477 (1975); . see also 18 U.S.C. § 1(3)(defining petty offenses as crimes "the penalty for which ... does not exceed imprisonment for a period of six months or a fine of not more than $5,000 for an individual and $10,000 for a person other than an individual, or both"). We need not answer today the difficult question where the line between petty and serious contempt fines should be drawn, since a

even-handed adjudication were essential, and petitioners were entitled to a criminal jury trial.

In reaching this conclusion, we recognize that this Court generally has deferred to a legislature's determination whether a sanction is civil or criminal, and that "[w]hen a State's proceedings are involved, state law provides strong guidance about whether or not the State is exercising its authority 'in a nonpunitive, noncriminal manner.' " *Hicks.* We do not deviate from either tradition today. Where a single judge, rather than a legislature, declares a particular sanction to be civil or criminal, such deference is less appropriate. Cf. Madsen v. Women's Health Center, Inc., 512 U.S. ___, ___ (1994). Moreover, this Court has recognized that even for state proceedings, the label affixed to a contempt ultimately "will not be allowed to defeat the applicable protections of federal constitutional law." *Hicks.* We conclude that the serious contempt fines imposed here were criminal and constitutionally could not be imposed absent a jury trial.

III

Our decision concededly imposes some procedural burdens on courts' ability to sanction widespread, indirect contempts of complex injunctions through noncompensatory fines. Our holding, however, leaves unaltered the longstanding authority of judges to adjudicate direct contempts summarily, and to enter broad compensatory awards for all contempts through civil proceedings. Because the right to trial by jury applies only to serious criminal sanctions, courts still may impose noncompensatory, petty fines for contempts such as the present ones without conducting a jury trial. We also do not disturb a court's ability to levy, albeit through the criminal contempt process, serious fines like those in this case.

Ultimately, whatever slight burden our holding may impose on the judicial contempt power cannot be controlling. The Court recognized more than a quarter-century ago:

"We cannot say that the need to further respect for judges and courts is entitled to more consideration than the interest of the individual not be subjected to serious criminal punishment without the benefit of all the procedural protections worked out carefully over the years and deemed fundamental to our system of justice. Genuine respect, which alone can lend true dignity to our judicial establishment, will be engendered, not by the fear of unlimited authority, but by the firm administration of the law through those institutionalized procedures which have been worked out over the centuries." *Bloom.* Where, as here, "a serious contempt is at issue, considerations of efficiency must give way to the more fundamental interest of ensuring the even-handed exercise of judicial power." * * *

JUSTICE SCALIA, concurring.

$52,000,000 fine unquestionably is a serious contempt sanction.

I join the Court's opinion classifying the $52,000,000 in contempt fines levied against petitioners as criminal. As the Court's opinion demonstrates, our cases have employed a variety of not easily reconcilable tests for differentiating between civil and criminal contempts. Since all of those tests would yield the same result here, there is no need to decide which is the correct one—and a case so extreme on its facts is not the best case in which to make that decision. I wish to suggest, however, that when we come to making it, a careful examination of historical practice will ultimately yield the answer. * * *

[At common law,] incarceration until compliance was a distinctive sanction, and sheds light upon the nature of the decrees enforced by civil contempt. That sanction makes sense only if the order requires performance of an identifiable act (or perhaps cessation of continuing performance of an identifiable act). A general prohibition for the future does not lend itself to enforcement through conditional incarceration, since no single act (or the cessation of no single act) can demonstrate compliance and justify release. * * *

As one would expect from this, the orders that underlay civil contempt fines or incarceration were usually mandatory rather than prohibitory, directing litigants to perform acts that would further the litigation (for example, turning over a document), or give effect to the court's judgment (for example, executing a deed of conveyance). * * * The mandatory injunctions issued upon termination of litigation usually required "a single simple act." H. McClintock, Principles of Equity § 15, pp. 32–33 (2d ed. 1948). * * * And where specific performance of contracts was sought, it was the categorical rule that no decree would issue that required ongoing supervision. Compliance with these "single act" mandates could, in addition to being simple, be quick; and once it was achieved the contemnor's relationship with the court came to an end, at least insofar as the subject of the order was concerned. * * *

Even equitable decrees that were prohibitory rather than mandatory were, in earlier times, much less sweeping than their modern counterparts. Prior to the labor injunctions of the late 1800's, injunctions were issued primarily in relatively narrow disputes over property.

Contemporary courts have abandoned these earlier limitations upon the scope of their mandatory and injunctive decrees. They routinely issue complex decrees which involve them in extended disputes and place them in continuing supervisory roles over parties and institutions. See, e.g., Missouri v. Jenkins, 495 U.S. 33, 56–58 (1990); Swann v. Charlotte–Mecklenburg Bd. of Ed., 402 U.S. 1, 16 (1971). Professor Chayes has described the extent of the transformation:

> [The modern decree] differs in almost every relevant characteristic from relief in the traditional model of adjudication, not the least in that it is the centerpiece.... It provides for a complex, on-going regime of performance rather than a simple, one-shot, one-way transfer. Finally, it prolongs and deepens, rather than terminates, the court's involvement with the dispute.

Chayes, The Role of the Judge in Public Law Litigation, 89 Harv. L. Rev. 1281, 1298 (1976).

The consequences of this change for the point under discussion here are obvious: When an order governs many aspects of a litigant's activities, rather than just a discrete act, determining compliance becomes much more difficult. Credibility issues arise, for which the factfinding protections of the criminal law (including jury trial) become much more important. And when continuing prohibitions or obligations are imposed, the order cannot be complied with (and the contempt "purged") in a single act; it continues to govern the party's behavior, on pain of punishment-not unlike the criminal law.

The order at issue here provides a relatively tame example of the modern, complex decree. The amended injunction prohibited, inter alia, rock-throwing, the puncturing of tires, threatening, following or interfering with respondents' employees, placing pickets in other than specified locations, and roving picketing; and it required, inter alia, that petitioners provide a list of names of designated supervisors. Although it would seem quite in accord with historical practice to enforce, by conditional incarceration or per diem fines, compliance with the last provision-a discrete command, observance of which is readily ascertained-using that same means to enforce the remainder of the order would be a novelty. * * *

As the scope of injunctions has expanded, they have lost some of the distinctive features that made enforcement through civil process acceptable. It is not that the times, or our perceptions of fairness, have changed (that is in my view no basis for either tightening or relaxing the traditional demands of due process); but rather that the modern judicial order is in its relevant essentials not the same device that in former times could always be enforced by civil contempt. So adjustments will have to be made. We will have to decide at some point which modern injunctions sufficiently resemble their historical namesakes to warrant the same extraordinary means of enforcement. We need not draw that line in the present case, and so I am content to join the opinion of the Court.

JUSTICE GINSBERG, with whom THE CHIEF JUSTICE joins, concurring in part and concurring in the judgment. * * *

Two considerations persuade me that the contempt proceedings in this case should be classified as "criminal" rather than "civil." First, were we to accept the logic of Bagwell's argument that the fines here were civil, because "conditional" and "coercive," no fine would elude that categorization. The fines in this case were "conditional," Bagwell says, because they would not have been imposed if the unions had complied with the injunction. The fines would have been "conditional" in this sense, however, even if the court had not supplemented the injunction with its fines schedule; indeed, any fine is "conditional" upon compliance or noncompliance before its imposition.†

Second, the Virginia courts' refusal to vacate the fines, despite the parties' settlement and joint motion is characteristic of criminal, not civil proceedings. In explaining why the fines outlived the underlying civil dispute, the Supreme Court of Virginia stated: "Courts of the Commonwealth must have the authority to enforce their orders by employing coercive, civil sanctions if the dignity of the law and public respect for the judiciary are to be maintained." The Virginia court's references to upholding public authority and maintaining "the dignity of the law" reflect the very purposes *Gompers* ranked on the criminal contempt side. * * *

Concluding that the fines at issue "are more closely analogous to ... criminal fines" than to civil fines, I join the Court's judgment and all but Part II–B of its opinion.

### *More Notes on the Classification of Contempt Proceedings*

1. Has the holding in *Hicks* on the classification of suspended sentences been overruled? Professor Earl C. Dudley's article, cited prominently in *Bagwell*, Getting Beyond the Civil/Criminal Distinction: A New Approach to The Regulation of Indirect Contempts, 79 Va.L.Rev. 959, 1051 (1993), argues that *Hicks'* distinction between a suspended sentence with a period of probation and a determinate sentence with a purge clause "does not hold up," chiefly because courts "never impose a jail term and suspend it unconditionally in favor of a probationary period."

2. Has the *Hicks* test for distinguishing coercive civil contempt from criminal contempt been overruled? If so, what is the new test? In NOW v. Operation Rescue, 37 F.3d 646, 659 (D.C.Cir.1994), the court read *Bagwell* to hold that the classification of prospective fixed fines as criminal or civil should turns on "what procedural protections are due before any particular contempt penalty may be imposed, in light of the 'competing concerns' of protecting the judicial process and preventing arbitrary exercises of the contempt power." In striking that balance, courts should consider such factors as (1) whether the contempts go to the core justification of protecting the court's ability to adjudicate the proceedings before it; (2) whether the contempts consist of discrete, readily ascertainable acts so that the factfinding is less troublesome; and, (3) the characterization by the district court, however, the appeals court is not bound by the district courts characterization or the prospective nature of the fine. Harris v. City of Philadelphia, 47 F.3d 1311 (3d

† Bagwell further likens the prospective fines schedule to the civil contempt fine imposed in United States v. Mine Workers, 330 U.S. 258 (1947). In that case, however, the contemnor union was given an opportunity, after the fine was imposed, to avoid the fine by "effect[ing] full compliance" with the injunction. As the Court explains, for purposes of allowing the union to avoid the fine, "full compliance" with the broad no-strike injunction, was reduced to the performance of three affirmative acts. This opportunity to purge, consistent with the civil contempt scenario described in *Gompers*, was unavailable to the unions in this case.

Cir.1995) read *Bagwell* to hold that the fine is not criminal if the the contemnor can purge through an affirmative act. Reich v. Sea Sprite Boat Co., 50 F.3d 413 (7th Cir.1995), cites *Bagwell* for the proposition that sanctions for completed acts are presumptively criminal sanctions. Both Doe v. Maywood Housing Authority, 1994 WL 521050 (N.D.Ill. 1994), and Department of Housing Preservation & Development v. Deka Realty Corp., 208 A.D.2d 37, 620 N.Y.S.2d 837 (N.Y.App.Div.1995), read *Bagwell* to hold that conditional contempt fines are not criminal if they are not "serious," but to leave open the question of what constitutes a serious fine. Conceivably, the test for a serious fine may not be the same as the test for a nonpetty crime.

3. Professor Dudley concludes that "we should abandon the civil/criminal distinction and instead allocate procedural protections in contempt in accord with a less complicated due process model that takes account of both the contempt process' peculiar dangers and the costs of affording those protections." 79 Va.L.Rev. at 1033. He suggests that such a model might well lead to requiring courts contemplating imposing nonpetty sanctions, whether denominated civil or criminal, to accord alleged contemnors with almost all the protections given to defendants charged with crimes. For example, he would provide appointed counsel and jury trial, but not a grand jury. To what extent has Professor Dudley convinced the Court?

4. Do you agree with the Court that there would be little lost by giving most of the criminal procedure protections to alleged contemnors subject to nonpetty sanctions? How likely is it that a jury would have convicted the union in *Bagwell* or would convict the abortion protestors if they defied the second injunction in Madsen v. Women's Health Center, Inc., 512 U.S. ___, 114 S.Ct. 2516, 129 L.Ed.2d 593 (1994)? (reproduced in chapter 2). In *Bagwell*, the union argued at the contempt hearing that it had not violated the injunction because the alleged violations were not instigated by it, but rather were caused by outsiders who were sympathetic with the goals of the strike. Some of the abortion protesters who were charged with violating the injunction in *Madsen* contended that they were independent of the named defendants.

### *Notes on the Elements of Contempt*

1. The majority in *Hicks* states that a prima facie case of contempt is made out by showing a court order, of which defendant had notice, and which defendant violated. On the grounds that contempt requires violation of a court order, the Supreme Court held that a federal district court, which had dismissed a suit pursuant to a stipulation and dismissal order, lacks jurisdiction to enforce the underlying settlement agreement. Breach of the settlement agreement did not violate the only order in the case, which was the one dismissing it. Kokkonen v. Guardian Life Ins. Co. ___ U.S. ___, 114 S.Ct. 1673, 128 L.Ed.2d 391 (1994).

2. *Willfulness.* There is an additional element for criminal contempt—willfulness. Punishment and deterrence, which are the purposes

of criminal contempt, are inappropriate when the contempt was not willful. Should, however, "willfulness" mean that defendant intended to do the acts that violated the order or that defendant intended to do them knowing that they were contemptuous? In United States v. United Mine Workers, 330 U.S. 258, 67 S.Ct. 677, 91 L.Ed. 884 (1947), the government had taken over the mines, which were then as vital to the economy as the petroleum industry is today, to avert a strike. The government subsequently secured a temporary restraining order against a strike. The union and its colorful leader, John L. Lewis, conducted a strike that gripped the nation's attention. They pled that striking was not contempt because counsel had advised them that the court lacked jurisdiction to issue the order so that they intended no contempt. The trial court imposed a $10,000 fine on Lewis and a $3,500,000 fine on the union without indicating whether the fines were criminal or coercive. The Supreme Court upheld the order and the finding of criminal contempt; it provided, however, that $2,800,000 of the fine against the union was to be remitted if the strike ceased, but that the remainder of the fine against the union and the entire fine against Lewis were valid criminal sanctions. Justice Black, concurring in part and dissenting in part, wrote that:

> It is plain that the defendants acted willfuly for they knew that they were disobeying the court's order. But they appear to have believed in good faith, though erroneously, that they were acting within their legal rights. Many lawyers would have so advised them. This does not excuse their conduct; the whole situation emphasizes the duty of testing the restraining order by orderly appeal instead of disobedience and open defiance. However, * * * "the intention with which acts of contempt have been committed must necessarily and properly have an important bearing on the degree of guilt and the penalty which should be imposed." * * *
>
> We should modify the District Court's decrees by making the entire amount of the fines payable conditionally.

330 U.S. at 333–34, 67 S.Ct. at 715, 91 L.Ed. at 933–34.

3. *Burdens.* Due process requires that the elements of criminal contempt be shown beyond a reasonable doubt. For civil contempt, the federal courts and many states require that the elements must be shown by "clear and convincing" evidence, a higher standard than a preponderance of the evidence. Many other states require only a preponderance of the evidence. California, for one, requires proof beyond a reasonable doubt for both compensatory and coercive civil contempt. Which approach is most fitting? See, e.g., Doug Rendleman, Compensatory Contempt: Plaintiff's Remedy When a Defendant Violates An Injunction, 1980 U.Ill.L.F. 971, 980; Maggio v. Zeitz, 333 U.S. 56, 79, 68 S.Ct. 401, 413, 92 L.Ed. 476, 493 (1948)(Black, J., dissenting)("All court proceedings, whether designated as civil or criminal contempt of court or given some other name, which may result in fine, prison sentences, or both,

should in my judgment require the same measure of proof, and that measure should be proof beyond a reasonable doubt.").

4. *Impossibility.* In the federal system and most states, impossibility is a defense as to which the defendant has the burden of production and persuasion for both civil and criminal contempt. If the court erroneously concludes that the contemnor can purge and has not done so, then it has functionally imposed a determinate, nonpurgeable sentence through a civil process. The burden as to impossibility is critical in a case like *Hicks* where the defendant has unique access to the pertinent information. Who should have the burden? In *Hicks,* the state appellate court first held that impossibility was an element of the crime rather than a defense but that, under the statute, violation of a child support order permits but does not mandate a rebuttable presumption that compliance was possible. If the court so presumes, the burden of production would be on the alleged contemnor, but the burden of persuasion would remain on the prosecutor. On remand, the state appellate court reached a somewhat different result by treating impossibility as an affirmative defense.

### *Notes on Sanctions*

1. *Criminal Contempt.* The majority in *United Mine Workers* stated that:

> In imposing a fine for criminal contempt, the trial judge may properly take into consideration the extent of the willful and deliberate defiance of the court's order, the seriousness of the consequences of the contumacious behavior, the necessity of effectively terminating the defendant's defiance as required by the public interest, and the importance of deterring such acts in the future. Because of the nature of these standards, great reliance must be placed upon the discretion of the trial judge.

330 U.S. at 303, 67 S.Ct. at 701, 91 L.Ed. at 918.

The contumacious behavior in *United Mine Workers* was a violation of the War Labor Disputes Act, which provided for a maximum penalty of either a year in jail or a $5000 fine or both. Nonetheless, the fines allowed by the Supreme Court exceeded those in the Act. Was that appropriate?

In some jurisdictions, statutes severely limit sanctions for criminal contempt. In a 1987 case, the New York Court of Appeals determined that the maximum sanction that could be imposed on a large utility for burning coal in defiance of a court order was $250 because of a statutory limit on criminal contempt fines that was last amended in 1981. Department of Environmental Protection v. Department of Environmental Conservation, 70 N.Y.2d 233, 519 N.Y.S.2d 539, 513 N.E.2d 706 (1987). The utility's officers might have been imprisoned, but the Court of Appeals upheld the lower court's decision not to pursue charges against them. In 1993, the statutory limit was increased to $1000. New York, Judiciary Law § 751(1).

2. *Compensatory Civil Contempt.* The measure of the fine in compensatory contempt is ordinarily plaintiff's rightful position—the measure of compensatory damages. So, in the *Country Lodge* problem, plaintiff would receive damages that would include, chiefly, its lost profits. But what if defendant's gain is greater than plaintiff's loss? Restitution—which will be covered in chapter 7—sometimes makes the measure of relief defendant's rightful position in order to deprive defendant of its "unjust enrichment." Because the court, in granting an injunction, denies defendant the option of violating plaintiff's rights for the payment of compensatory damages, isn't the excess of defendant's gain over plaintiff's loss unjust enrichment, especially if defendant's violation of the injunction was willful? Some courts allow a fine pegged to unjust enrichment, some do not. See Dan B. Dobbs, Law of Remedies § 2.8(2) n.23 (2d ed.1993); Dan B. Dobbs, Contempt of Court: A Survey, 56 Cornell L.Rev. 183, 276–78 (1971).

3. *Coercive Civil Contempt.* The basic rule is that the court may never apply more than "the least possible power adequate to the end proposed." Anderson v. Dunn, 19 U.S. (6 Wheat.) 204, 231, 5 L.Ed. 242 (1821). In other words, the sanction must be for coercive rather than punitive purposes. Sometimes, however, what it takes to coerce determined opposition can be awesome or even infinite, as where witnesses subpoenaed to testify against organized crime fear for their lives. There are occasionally statutory limits on coercive civil contempt sanctions. For instance, in federal court, a witness that disobeys an order to testify cannot be held for more than eighteen months. 28 U.S.C. § 1826 (1982).

In the absence of statutory limits, coercive civil contempt sanctions can exceed sanctions for the same conduct punished as criminal contempt or as an ordinary crime. For an extreme example, when a husband refused to obey an Israeli rabbinical court's order to grant his wife a divorce by saying, as is necessary under Jewish law, "I am willing," the court ordered him held in jail until he obeyed. He died in jail 32 years later. Married to Principles, San Francisco Chronicle, Dec. 6, 1994 at A7.

The case of Dr. Elizabeth Morgan also illustrates the potential severity of coercive civil sanctions. Dr. Morgan, then a prominent Washington, D.C. surgeon, sought to deny her former husband, Dr. Eric Foretich who was an oral surgeon, unsupervised visits with their six year old daughter. Dr. Morgan believed that Dr. Foretich had sexually abused the child. After extensive hearings that produced sharply clashing testimony, the trial court ordered Dr. Morgan to produce the child for unsupervised visits with Dr. Foretich. Dr. Morgan instead hid the child. The trial court held Dr. Morgan in civil contempt and, in August, 1987, incarcerated her until she produced the child. In the summer of 1989, Dr. Morgan, who by then had the most seniority among the inmates of the D.C. House of Detention, testified that she would stay in jail until the child turned 18 and would be free of the court's directives. Should the trial court free her from incarceration for civil contempt? See, e.g., Morgan v. Foretich, 564 A.2d 1 (D.C.App.1989)(en banc)(appellate court directs Dr. Morgan be freed because incarceration no longer serves coercive purpose). Before the court could act, Charles Colson (the convicted Watergate-conspirator and born-again Christian), the National Organization of Women, Ross Perot, and others successfully lobbied Congress for legislation that would forbid District of Columbia courts from incarcerating anyone for civil contempt longer than one year in a custody case. The contemnor could be held longer only after being convicted of criminal contempt before a different judge, with the right to a jury and bail. District of Columbia Civil Contempt Imprisonment Limitation Act of 1989, P.L. 101–97. Is this legislation appropriate?

How should courts handle confrontations with stubborn contemnors? See Doug Rendleman, Disobedience and Coercive Contempt Confinement: The Terminally Stubborn Contemnor, 48 Wash. & Lee L.Rev. 185 (1991); Linda S. Beres, Civil Contempt and the Rational Contemnor, 69 Ind.L.J. 723 (1994).

4. *Other responses to violations of court orders.* Other responses to violations include requiring the contemnor to pay the attorney's fees caused by the violation or, particularly in the case of violations of discovery orders, cutting off the contemnor's right to litigate issues connected with the violation. E.g., Fed.R.Civ.P. 37(b)(2).

### *Notes on Procedures*

1. *Criminal contempt.* As pointed out in *Hicks* and *Bagwell,* criminal contempt requires many of the same procedural safeguards as an ordinary criminal prosecution. In particular, the United States Constitution requires that alleged contemnors in state or federal court are entitled to a jury trial unless the offense is petty. The offense is not petty if the contumacious behavior is a crime that carries a maximum sentence of six months or more. If the contumacious behavior is not otherwise a crime, it is not petty if the actual sentence is of six months or more. Codispoti v. Pennsylvania, 418 U.S. 506, 94 S.Ct. 2687, 41 L.Ed.2d 912 (1974). Consecutive sentences, each less than six months, that add up to more than six months constitute an actual sentence of more than six months if the sentences are simultaneously imposed and grow out of the same proceeding. United States v. Pina, 844 F.2d 1 (1st Cir.1988). Judges' desire to avoid the expense and delay of a jury trial are an impetus to make the sentence less than six months.

A sufficiently large fine also can make a contempt not petty, but how large depends on the nature and means of the defendant. In 1966, the Supreme Court said that the rule of thumb is that a $500 fine against an individual is not petty, Cheff v. Schnackenberg, 384 U.S. 373, 375, 86 S.Ct. 1523, 1523, 16 L.Ed.2d 629 (1966), but the thumb may have swollen along with inflation. As to organizational defendants,

Muniz v. Hoffman, 422 U.S. 454, 95 S.Ct. 2178, 45 L.Ed.2d 319 (1975), held that a fine of $10,000 was "petty" in light of defendant union's ability to collect dues from 13,000 members. The Second Circuit has held that a $100,000 fine against a large corporation was not petty, even though it represented less than one percent of its net earnings in one year. United States v. Twentieth Century Fox Film Corp., 882 F.2d 656 (2d Cir.1989), cert. denied, 493 U.S. 1021, 110 S.Ct. 722, 107 L.Ed.2d 741 (1990).

2. *Civil contempt.* A small number of states, most notably California, do not allow compensatory civil contempt, apparently on the theory that compensation is really "damages" so that "the defendant ought to have a trial 'at law' with a jury * * *. On the other hand, that equity took the case in the first place is an indication that the jury trial was a secondary value in the case * * *." Dan B. Dobbs, Handbook on the Law of Remedies 100 (1973). See Doug Rendleman, Compensatory Contempt: Plaintiff's Remedy When a Defendant Violates an Injunction, 1980 U.Ill.L.F. 971, 982–83. In any event, the plaintiff may well prefer to seek compensation in an action for damages rather than in contempt in order to have a jury and to avoid the clear and convincing evidence standard.

## 2. WHEN ARE PARTIES BOUND?

### *Problem: Country Lodge v. Miller (Reprised)* *Violating an Anticipated Order*

In the early fall, the trial court denies an injunction against Miller discharging waste into the river. Country Lodge appeals. While the appeal is pending, Miller discharges waste into the river during the busy apple harvesting season. In the winter, the appellate court directs the trial court to grant the injunction. Is Miller in contempt?

## GRIFFIN v. COUNTY SCHOOL BOARD OF PRINCE EDWARD COUNTY

United States Court of Appeals, Fourth Circuit, en banc, 1966.
363 F.2d 206, cert. denied, 385 U.S. 960, 87 S.Ct. 395, 17 L.Ed.2d 305.

BRYAN, CIRCUIT JUDGE:

[The School Board of Prince Edward County, Virginia, one of the defendants in *Brown,* reacted to the command to desegregate its public schools by closing them and making tuition grants to the Prince Edward County Educational Foundation, a private corporation conducting school for white children only. In 1962, the district court ordered the public schools reopened and enjoined the payment of tuition grants until such re-opening. In 1964, the Supreme Court affirmed. In the early summer of 1964, the board announced that the public schools were no longer closed, that classes would commence in the fall, and that it would resume making tuition grants. On June 29, 1964 the plaintiffs moved the district court to enjoin the processing of tuition grants on the theory that they drained money from the public schools to perpetuate segregation. The district court refused to enjoin tuition grants for the 1964–1965 school year and plaintiffs appealed on July 17, 1964. On July 28, 1964 the plaintiffs moved the court of appeals to accelerate the appeal.]

* * *

As we were then not in session, Chief Judge [Soboloff] requested the Clerk to ask the Board of Supervisors to stipulate that no tuition grants would be paid pending the appeal. On August 4, 1964 the Clerk transmitted this message to the office of the Attorney General of Virginia. In reply the Clerk was told "during the late evening of August 4", that the Board would not make the stipulation. The next morning the Clerk explained that a satisfactory stipulation would be an agreement that the grants would not be paid before the normal time for processing and paying grants, that is not until after the private schools opened in September 1964.

Meanwhile, during the night of August 4 and early morning of August 5, 1964 the Board met and decided to enlarge substantially the tuition grants for the session 1964–65, and ordered that payment of one-half of the total grants be made before September 1, 1964. That night white parents were notified of the Board's action. Checks totalling about $180,000 were distributed before 9 o'clock A.M. and most of them cashed at that hour, August 5, 1964.

On August 13, 1964 in their appeal, the appellants moved to cite the Board for contempt of this court and for an order restoring the moneys distributed during the night and morning of August 4–5, 1964. After argument of the appeal in regular course, the District Court was directed to enjoin the Board from paying any tuition grants to send children to private schools so long as these schools remained segregated.

Our decision did not pass upon the contempt motion, but remanded it to the District Court for "further inquiries into the facts surrounding the payments". [The district court found that the plan to pay the tuition grants was triggered by the Chief Judge's request for a stipulation and that the effort to receive and process 1217 applications for tuition grants required the all-night efforts of some 20 volunteers and the sale of bonds overnight, but concluded that there was no contempt.]

* * *

That these acts of the Board of Supervisors constituted a contempt of this court is beyond cavil. The Board undertook to put the money then available for tuition grants—and then wholly subject to its orders—beyond its control as well as that of the court. In doing so the Board took upon itself to decide its right to exercise, in favor of the private school, the Board's general power to appropriate public funds. This use of power was, as the Board was acutely aware, an arrogation of this court's responsibility. Obviously, the aim was to thwart the impact of any adverse decree which might ultimately be forthcoming on the appeal. In effect it was a "resistance to its [this court's] lawful writ, process, order, rule, decree, or command." 18 U.S.C. § 401(3). The authorities are quite clear on the point.

The Board would escape the judgment of contempt on the argument that the statute limits the power of the court to punish violations of orders or decrees then extant. But precedent does not so contract the statute or constrict its intent. Although this court had not issued an injunction against the appropriation of the moneys to tuition grants, the Board knew that if the plaintiffs succeeded this would be its ultimate decree, as in fact it became. That potential decree was thus then within the statute. Furthermore, the appeal was itself a "process" which was alive at the time of the disbursement and was resisted by the disbursement.

In Merrimack River Savings Bank v. Clay Center, 219 U.S. 527, 31 S.Ct. 295, 55 L.Ed. 320 (1911), a temporary injunction had been issued by a Federal District Court to prevent the destruction by a municipality of a public utility's poles and wires, located in the city streets under an authorized franchise. The suit was dismissed on jurisdictional grounds. However, for and during an appeal to the Supreme Court, the injunction was continued in force. On this review the dismissal was upheld. But before the mandate of dismissal had been issued or could issue, and in the period allowed for presenting an application for a rehearing, the city cut down the poles, destroyed a large section of the wires and thus put the utility out of business. This conduct was declared to be contempt of the Supreme Court, Justice Lurton saying at 535–536, 31 S.Ct. at 296:

> It does not necessarily follow that disobedience of such an injunction, intended only to preserve the status quo pending an appeal, may not be regarded as a contempt of the appellate jurisdiction of this court, which might be rendered nugatory by conduct calculated to remove the subject-matter of the appeal beyond its control, or by its destruction. This we need not decide, since *irrespective of any such injunction actually issued the wilful removal beyond the reach of the court of the subject-matter of the litigation . . . (on) appeal . . . is, in and of itself, a contempt of the appellate jurisdiction of this court. . . .* Unless this be so, a reversal of the decree would be but a barren victory, since the very result would have been brought about by the lawless act of the defendants which it was the object of the suit to prevent. (Accent added.)

The contempt power declared in the *Merrimack* case was not suggested to be rooted in the inherent power of the Supreme Court rather than in the statute now embodied in 18 U.S.C. 401(3). * * * But *Merrimack* is not now cited to power. It is cited as warranting our finding that the putting of the subject-matter of this litigation beyond our reach was a defiance of this court, an anticipatory resistance to its ultimate orders or process. * * *

The present case is quite different factually from Berry v. Midtown Service Corp., 104 F.2d 107 (2d Cir.1939), relied upon by the Board. There the subject-matter disposed of pending appeal was the leviable assets of the judgment debtor-appellant. The Court distinguished that case from ours when it said that the appeal was not "defeated or impaired" by the defendant's assignment. Further distinction is found in its observation that the suit "was not concerned with any specific property," the judgment on appeal merely establishing a general, personal, financial liability.

In our case the disbursement of the moneys seriously impaired the appeal. The suit and the appeal were directed to a specific subject, the Board's right to apply to a certain purpose money within its power. The Board assumed the right in utter and wilful disregard of this court's views. As was said in *Merrimack* * * * such conduct constituted contempt although not formally and explicitly under injunction.

We find the Board of Supervisors and its members guilty of civil contempt. Accordingly, the Board and its constituent individuals, namely, W.W. Vaughan, C.W. Gates, H.M. Jenkins, Charles B. Pickett, John C. Steck and H.E. Carwile, Jr., personally and in their own right, will be ordered jointly and severally to restore to the County Treasurer of Prince Edward County, through recapture or otherwise, an amount equal to the disbursements authorized and made by their resolutions of August 4–5, 1964. This cause will be continued for a period of 90 days from this date for report by the Board and its members of what has been done towards compliance with this order, as well as for the passage of such further orders as may appear proper. * * *

HAYNSWORTH, CHIEF JUDGE, with whom BOREMAN, CIRCUIT JUDGE, joins (dissenting):

* * * I am not in disagreement that the conduct of the Supervisors was unconscionable. However, I must disagree with the majority in their interpretation of the power of this Court to adjudge parties in contempt.

It is clear that this Court has an inherent power to punish contempts. It was originally defined by the seventeenth section of the Judiciary Act of 1789 as the power to punish by fine or imprisonment all contempts of authority in any cause or hearing before the Court. But the power has since been limited and redefined by the Act of Congress of March 2, 1831, now 18 U.S.C. § 401. The statute prescribes:

> A court of the United States shall have power to punish by fine or imprisonment, at its discretion, such contempt of its authority, and none other, as:
>
> (1) Misbehavior of any person in its presence or so near thereto as to obstruct the administration of justice;
>
> (2) Misbehavior of any of its officers in their official transactions;
>
> (3) Disobedience or resistance to its lawful writ, process, order, rule, decree, or command.

Considerable doubt was expressed in Ex parte Robinson, 19 Wall. 505, 86 U.S. 505, as to whether this statute could limit the contempt power of the Supreme Court, which derives its existence and powers from the Constitution, and it is obvious from *Merrimack* that the Court has since gone beyond the statute. But *Robinson* made it clear that there can be no question about the limiting effect the statute has upon the courts of appeals and the district courts. As courts created, not by the Constitution, but, through the power that document vested in Congress, exercise of their inherent contempt powers must be confined to the bounds that Congress has fixed.

Measuring the facts in the present case by the word of Congress, I am unable to find a basis in the statute for a contempt citation here. Phrases (1) and (2) of the statute are not applicable here. The majority finds, under phrase (3), that there was disobedience or resistance to a lawful writ, process, order, rule, decree, or command of this Court. Yet none in fact existed to be disobeyed or resisted. The plaintiff's sought no temporary restraining order or injunction, and none was issued preventing the action taken by the Supervisors. The stipulation requested of the defendants by this court cannot be expanded to fit into any of the things specified in § 401(3).

The word "process," as used in the statute in its context of writs, orders and decrees, obviously means more than the pendency of an appeal or of some other relevant judicial proceeding. It has been traditionally used to encompass such things as a summons, a subpoena, an attachment, a warrant, a mandate, a levy and, generically, other writs and orders. In the context of other orders and writs, "process" can reasonably be understood to mean no more than the sum of more explicit terms, such as "original process," "summary process," "mesne process" and "final process," all of which clearly refer to papers issuing from the court and embodying its commands or judgments, or notice of them. Construed so expansively as the majority's suggestion of equivalence with the pendency of any relevant judicial proceeding, it would entirely contravene the clearly limiting purpose of the congressional act.

Since the suggested construction of the word "process," as used in the statute, is original with the majority, it has never been treated in any reported opinion. The suggestion is inconsistent with the substantially uniform course of decision, however, while the primary theory of the majority is explicitly at odds with the precedents in this and other courts.

This court declared itself in Ex parte Buskirk, 4 Cir., 72 F. 14. There it was held not only that an anticipatory, partial avoidance of a potential decree was not a punishable contempt within the confines of the limiting statute; violation of a stipulation made in open court, without which mesne process might, and probably would, have issued, was held not to be. Implicit in the decision is a narrow, literal reading of the word "process."

Buskirk was a party in a judicial proceeding in a district court for a determination of the ownership of a tract of timber. In open court, he entered into a stipulation that none of the timber would be cut until the court had decided the question of ownership. Nevertheless, pending the court's decision, he began cutting the timber and intentionally removed it beyond the reach of the court. This court held because of the statute, "[h]owever reprehensible such conduct ... may have been ... it nevertheless did not constitute a contempt to the court or its orders."

My brothers now overrule *Buskirk* without deigning to mention it.

Our own decision in *Buskirk* is not an aberration. It is the exemplar of uniform decision. Four of our sister circuits have embraced the same construction of the statute, and have done so in no uncertain terms. No court of appeals, until now, has toyed with any other reading. * * *

I would not quibble with the majority's finding of fact that the conduct of the Supervisors was contemptible, but I do dissent from their conclusion that it was contemptuous and punishable as such, when the conclusion is dependent upon a reading of the statute which relegates it to meaninglessness. Such an unsympathetic construction is particularly inappropriate when the statute was clearly intended to inhibit our authority, has been declared by the Supreme Court to have that effect and has been uniformly construed by the courts of appeals in accordance with that evident intention. Such a statute limiting the jurisdiction of the federal courts is largely enforceable only by the limited courts, themselves. Above all other statutory commands, courts should be scrupulous to conform themselves to jurisdictional statutes, so that they do not appropriate to themselves powers which have been constitutionally withdrawn from them. * * *

### *Notes on Getting Tricky With a Court*

1. Paying the tuition grants was illegal as part of a scheme to perpetuate state sponsored segregation. As such, plaintiffs could have gotten an injunction requiring the school board to recover the grants. The question for the court of appeals was not whether the grants were illegal but whether they were also contempt of court. A finding of contempt offered plaintiffs several advantages over an injunction. First, the contempt sanction provided that the individual board members had to compensate the board to the extent that they could not recover grants from parents. An injunction probably could not impose such personal liability on nonparties (for reasons that will be discussed infra at p. 314) and so would have given the board members no incentive to recoup the grants any more aggressively than necessary to avoid being held in contempt. Second, contempt makes the contemnor potentially liable for the other party's attorneys' fees caused by the contempt and the court of appeals awarded plaintiffs such fees in *Griffin*. Third, contempt connotes guilt—a word usually reserved for the criminal context—even

when the contempt is civil. Note that the court finds defendants "guilty of civil contempt." Such a tinge of guilt is likely to affect the adjudication of future issues in the case. As such, contempt often boosts the plaintiffs' morale and depresses the defendants. Morale can be an important consideration in protracted litigations, which are frequently wars of attrition.

2. In considering whether defendants were properly held in contempt, it is useful to set out some propositions with which most attorneys would agree.

(a) Contempt includes but is not limited to violation of a valid court order. Did defendants violate any such order?

(b) Committing an illegal act—such as breaching a contract or segregating a school—is not in itself contempt although it may give rise to ordinary civil or even criminal liability. Otherwise, all illegal acts would be contempt of court.

(c) The illegal act is not made contemptuous by a court previously declaring that it would be illegal. As you will learn in chapter 4, a declaratory judgment is not a court order, but its issuance may enhance the civil or criminal liability by making clear that the illegal act was done knowingly.

(d) The illegal act is not made contemptuous by the violator promising in a stipulation not to do it. The stipulation is not a court order but rather a contract between the parties to it and may itself give rise to liability as well as preclude the adjudication of the issues resolved in the stipulation.

(e) An illegal act that violates a stipulation that the court approves as part of the settlement of a case, without entering it as a court order, is also not contempt because the stipulation is still not a court order. H.K. Porter Co. v. Nat'l Friction Products Corp., 568 F.2d 24, 25–27 (7th Cir.1977). For this reason, settlements that the parties intend to have enforced through the contempt power are usually styled something like "STIPULATION AND ORDER" and usually conclude with language in which the court orders the parties to abide by their stipulation. Should a party to a stipulation that is not an order violate it, the other party might, amongst other remedies, seek an injunction that the stipulation be obeyed.

3. Plaintiffs could have asked the district court for a stay of the payment of the tuition grants pending appeal and, if denied, could have sought the same relief from the court of appeals. Fed.R.App.P. 8. A stay is to an appeal what an preliminary injunction is to a complaint—an injunction designed to prevent harm pending the court's determination of the merits of the appeal or of the complaint. The standards for the issuance of a stay are similar to those for the issuance of a preliminary injunction—probability of success on the merits, potential harm to plaintiffs if a stay is not issued, potential harm to defendants if a stay is issued, and so on. Should a stay have been issued? Absent a stay, a

defendant that succeeds in the trial court is not under court order. Why did plaintiffs' attorneys not move for a stay? Why did Chief Judge Soboloff not issue a stay sua sponte?

4. The *Griffin* majority concluded that trying to put the money beyond the court's easy reach frustrated the appeal and thereby constituted "[d]isobedience or resistance to its lawful * * * process * * *."

(a) Under this reasoning, would it have been contempt for defendants to have paid the money before the court clerk asked them to stipulate that they would not?

(b) Under this reasoning, would it have been contempt for defendants to have paid the money as soon as plaintiffs moved the district court to enjoin the payments since a motion is also a process?

(c) Does *Merrimack* support the court of appeal's theory?

5. The dissent thinks that the court may well have had an inherent power to punish the defendants until Congress set out to limit that inherent power in 18 U.S.C. § 401 (1982). That section was enacted a century and a half ago after a judge used the contempt power to punish the publication of newspaper reports that criticized him. It is unclear whether the statute applies to just criminal contempts or to civil contempts as well. The Eleventh Circuit held that as to attorneys appearing before the court the "trial judge possesses the inherent power to discipline counsel for misconduct * * * without resort[ing] to the powers of civil or criminal contempt." Kleiner v. First Nat. Bank, 751 F.2d 1193, 1209 (11th Cir.1985).

6. So was *Griffin* rightly decided? Even on its awful facts, two of the five judges would have found no contempt. Scholars have criticized its reasoning, although not its result. E.g., Doug Rendleman, Compensatory Contempt to Collect Money, 41 Ohio State L.J. 625, 633–35 (1980). Shepardizing *Griffin* reveals no cases in which a court rested a finding of contempt upon the violation of an anticipated court order. Courts do, however, claim inherent judicial authority to punish bad faith litigation tactics and conduct like that in *Griffin* should qualify as such. E.g., Kleiner v. First National Bank, 751 F.2d 1193 (11th Cir.1985). But, allowing judges to punish bad faith tactics gives them wider latitude, and the targets of the punishment less notice, than contemplated by 18 U.S.C. § 401. Why did *Griffin* come out as it did?

## 3. THE COLLATERAL BAR RULE

### *Problem: Country Lodge v. Miller (Reprised)*<br>*The Collateral Bar Rule*

In the early fall, the trial court enjoins Miller from discharging waste into the river. Miller continues to discharge waste while she appeals. In the winter, the appellate court overturns the injunction. Is Miller guilty of criminal contempt for violating the injunction prior to the appellate court's action?

# IN RE PROVIDENCE JOURNAL CO.

United States Court of Appeals, First Circuit, 1987.
820 F.2d 1342, 820 F.2d 1354, cert. dismissed, 485 U.S. 693, 108 S.Ct. 1502, 99 L.Ed.2d 785 (1988).[c]

WISDOM, CIRCUIT JUDGE.

This appeal presents an apparent conflict between two fundamental legal principles: the hallowed First Amendment principle that the press shall not be subjected to prior restraints; the other, the sine qua non of orderly government, that, until modified or vacated, a court order must be obeyed. The district court adjudged the defendants/appellants, the Providence Journal Company and its executive editor, Charles M. Hauser, (collectively referred to as the "Journal") guilty of criminal contempt. The Journal admits that it violated the order but argues that the order was a prior restraint and that the unconstitutionality of the order is a defense in the contempt proceeding. We agree. A party subject to an order that constitutes a transparently invalid prior restraint on pure speech may challenge the order by violating it.

FACTS

From 1962 to 1965, the Federal Bureau of Investigation conducted electronic surveillance of Raymond L.S. Patriarca, reputedly a prominent figure in organized crime. The FBI conducted this surveillance without a warrant in violation of his Fourth Amendment rights. The FBI later destroyed all tape recordings relating to this surveillance but retained the logs and memoranda compiled from the recordings. In 1976, the Journal requested the logs and memoranda from the FBI under the Freedom of Information Act ("FOIA"). The FBI refused this request on the ground that disclosure would be an unwarranted invasion of personal privacy. * * *

In the spring of 1985, after the death of Raymond L.S. Patriarca, the Journal renewed its FOIA request to the FBI for the logs and memoranda. The FBI assented to this request and furnished the materials not only to the Journal, but also to WJAR Television Ten and other news media. On November 8, 1985, Raymond J. Patriarca ("Patriarca"), Raymond L.S. Patriarca's son, filed a summons and complaint against the FBI, WJAR, and the Journal * * * [for an injunction preventing the defendants from publishing the released material.]

On November 12, 1985, the summons, complaint, and motion were served on the Journal. One day later, the district court held a conference concerning the request for a temporary restraining order. Counsel for the Journal argued that any restraining order would constitute a

c. Certiorari was dismissed because it was filed by a special prosecutor appointed by the district court while 28 U.S.C. § 518(a) provides that only the Attorney General or the Solicitor General can conduct or argue suits "in which the United States is interested" in the Supreme Court. It was such a suit because it involved a crime against the United States, criminal contempt.

prior restraint forbidden by the First Amendment. Over the objections of counsel for the Journal and the government, the court entered a temporary restraining order barring publication of the logs and memoranda by the Journal and WJAR. The district court set a hearing for November 15, 1985, at which time it would decide whether to vacate the order. The district court later vacated the order and denied preliminary injunctive relief against the Journal and WJAR.

On November 14, 1985, the day after the district court issued the order, and while that order was still in effect, the Journal published an article on the deceased Patriarca that included information taken from the logs and memoranda. The son filed a motion to judge the Journal in contempt. When he declined to prosecute the criminal contempt motion, the district court invoked Fed.R.Crim.P. 42(b) and appointed a special prosecutor. Following a hearing, the district court found the Journal guilty of criminal contempt. Subsequent to a sentencing hearing, the court imposed an 18–month jail term on Hauser, which was suspended, ordered Hauser to perform 200 hours of public service, and fined the Journal $100,000. The Journal appealed.

Discussion

This appeal propounds a question that admits of no easy answer. Each party stands on what each regards as an unassailable legal principle. The special prosecutor relies on the bedrock principle that court orders, even those that are later ruled unconstitutional, must be complied with until amended or vacated.[9] This principle is often referred to as the "collateral bar" rule. The Journal relies on the bedrock principle that prior restraints against speech are prohibited by the First Amendment. In this opinion we endeavor to avoid deciding which principle should take precedence by reaching a result consistent with both principles. * * *

If a publisher is to print a libelous, defamatory, or injurious story, an appropriate remedy, though not always totally effective, lies not in an injunction against that publication but in a damages or criminal action after publication. Although the threat of damages or criminal action may chill speech, a prior restraint "freezes" speech before the audience has the opportunity to hear the message. Additionally, a court asked to issue a prior restraint must judge the challenged speech in the abstract. And, as was true in the instant case, a court may issue a prior restraint in the form of a temporary restraining order or preliminary injunction without a full hearing; a judgment for damages or a criminal sanction may be imposed only after a full hearing with all the attendant procedural protections.

Equally well-established is the requirement of any civilized government that a party subject to a court order must abide by its terms or face criminal contempt. Even if the order is later declared improper or

9. See Walker v. City of Birmingham, 388 U.S. 307, 87 S.Ct. 1824, 18 L.Ed.2d 1210 (1967); United States v. United Mine Workers, 330 U.S. 258, 67 S.Ct. 677, 91 L.Ed. 884 (1947).

unconstitutional, it must be followed until vacated or modified. As a general rule, a party may not violate an order and raise the issue of its unconstitutionality collaterally as a defense in the criminal contempt proceeding. Rather, the appropriate method to challenge a court order is to petition to have the order vacated or amended.

In *Walker v. City of Birmingham,* the Supreme Court upheld contempt citations against Dr. Martin Luther King, Jr. and other civil rights protestors enjoined from parading without a permit. The protestors argued that the order and the ordinance upon which it was based were unconstitutional because they constituted impermissible prior restraints upon the right to free speech and assembly. The Court noted that the ordinance "unquestionably raise[d] substantial constitutional issues" and that "[t]he breadth and vagueness of the injunction itself would also unquestionably be subject to substantial constitutional question". Nonetheless, the Court ruled that the protestors could not raise those constitutional issues collaterally in the contempt proceedings. As the Supreme Court noted in *United States v. United Mine Workers,* so long as the court has jurisdiction over the parties and the subject matter of the controversy, an order it issues must be obeyed.

The *Walker* Court found it significant that the contemnors had not sought to appeal the order they violated. The Court declared: "This case would arise in quite a different constitutional posture if the petitioners, before disobeying the injunction, had challenged it in the Alabama courts, and had been met with delay or frustration of their constitutional claims." The *Walker* Court concluded by noting that "no man can be judge in his own case, however exalted his station, however righteous his motives, and irrespective of his race, color, politics, or religion".

At first glance, *Walker* would appear to control the instant case. There, as here, a party chose to violate an arguably unconstitutional prior restraint rather than to comply with the orderly process of law by seeking relief from an appellate court. *Walker* declares that the contemnors are collaterally barred from challenging the constitutionality of the order forming the basis of the contempt citation. The *Walker* Court was, however, careful to point out that the order issued by the Alabama court was not "transparently invalid". The Court specifically noted that "this is not a case where the injunction was *transparently invalid* or had only a frivolous pretense to validity". The unmistakable import of this language is that a transparently invalid order cannot form the basis for a contempt citation.

Court orders are accorded a special status in American jurisprudence. While one may violate a statute and raise as a defense the statute's unconstitutionality, such is not generally the case with a court order. Nonetheless, court orders are not sacrosanct.[28] An order entered

**28.** See Cobbledick v. United States, 309 U.S. 323, 60 S.Ct. 540, 84 L.Ed. 783 (1940). In *Cobbledick,* the Supreme Court ruled that when a motion to quash a subpoena is denied, the movant may either obey its commands or violate them, and, if cited for

by a court clearly without jurisdiction over the contemnors or the subject matter is not protected by the collateral bar rule.[29] Were this not the case, a court could wield power over parties or matters obviously not within its authority—a concept inconsistent with the notion that the judiciary may exercise only those powers entrusted to it by law.

The same principle supports an exception to the collateral bar rule for transparently invalid court orders. Requiring a party subject to such an order to obey or face contempt would give the courts powers far in excess of any authorized by the Constitution or Congress. Recognizing an exception to the collateral bar rule for transparently invalid orders does not violate the principle that "no man can be judge in his own case" anymore than does recognizing such an exception for jurisdictional defects. The key to both exceptions is the notion that although a court order—even an arguably incorrect court order—demands respect, so does the right of the citizen to be free of clearly improper exercises of judicial authority.

Although an exception to the collateral bar rule is appropriate for transparently void orders, it is inappropriate for arguably proper orders. This distinction is necessary both to protect the authority of the courts when they address close questions and to create a strong incentive for parties to follow the orderly process of law. No such protection or incentive is needed when the order is transparently invalid because in that instance the court is acting so far in excess of its authority that it has no right to expect compliance and no interest is protected by requiring compliance.

The line between a transparently invalid order and one that is merely invalid is, of course, not always distinct. As a general rule, if the court reviewing the order finds the order to have had any pretence to validity at the time it was issued, the reviewing court should enforce the collateral bar rule. Such a heavy presumption in favor of validity is necessary to protect the rightful power of the courts. Nonetheless, there are instances where an order will be so patently unconstitutional that it will be excepted from the collateral bar rule. We now turn to consider whether the order issued by the district court on November 13, 1985, was, as the Journal contends, transparently invalid.

[The court concludes that the Supreme Court has never upheld a prior restraint on publication of news, but that it has implied that such a restraint might be appropriate in certain extreme cases.]

The special prosecutor argues, however, that the order was to last only a short period and merely preserved the status quo while allowing the court a full opportunity to assess the issues. We are sympathetic with the district court on this score. This matter came before the district court on an emergency basis. The court was forced to drop its other duties and immediately address this issue. Counsel for the Journal had received the papers less than 24 hours before they presented

contempt, properly contest its validity in the contempt proceeding. * * *

**29.** United Mine Workers, 330 U.S. at 293, 67 S.Ct. at 695.

their arguments to the district court. Based on counsel's hastily prepared authority and without the opportunity for cool reflection, the district court was forced to make a decision. The court's natural instinct was to delay the matter temporarily so that a careful, thoughtful answer could be crafted. This approach is proper in most instances, and indeed to follow any other course of action would often be irresponsible. But, absent the most compelling circumstances, when that approach results in a prior restraint on pure speech by the press it is not allowed.

It must be said, it is misleading in the context of daily newspaper publishing to argue that a temporary restraining order merely preserves the status quo. The status quo of daily newspapers is to publish news promptly that editors decide to publish. A restraining order disturbs the status quo and impinges on the exercise of editorial discretion. News is a constantly changing and dynamic quantity. Today's news will often be tomorrow's history. This is especially true in the case of news concerning an imminent event such as an election. A restraining order lasting only hours can effectively prevent publication of news that will have an impact on that event and on those that the event affects.

Although there is no question that the Patriarca story was not news concerning an imminent event, extraneous factors required its reasonably prompt publication. The Journal had promised its readers that the Patriarca story would be forthcoming. Moreover, other media not subject to the court order had the same logs and memoranda. Were they to disseminate this information while the Journal remained silent, some readers of the Journal might lose confidence in that paper's editorial competence.[65] * * *

Although the Journal arguably had avenues of appellate relief immediately available to it,[70] we decline to invoke the collateral bar rule because of the Journal's failure to avail itself of these opportunities. When, as here, the court order is a transparently invalid prior restraint on pure speech, the delay and expense of an appeal is unnecessary. Indeed, the delay caused by an appellate review requirement could, in the case of a prior restraint involving news concerning an imminent event, cause the restrained information to lose its value. The absence of such a requirement will not, however, lead to wide-spread disregard of court orders. Rarely will a party be subject to a transparently invalid court order. Prior restraints on pure speech represent an unusual class of orders because they are presumptively unconstitutional. And even

**65.** In United States v. Dickinson, 465 F.2d 496 (5th Cir.1972), the Court of Appeals for the Fifth Circuit applied the collateral bar rule in a contempt proceeding involving a gag order against a newspaper. We decline to follow *Dickinson* for two reasons. First, *Dickinson* involved an order issued to protect a defendant's Sixth Amendment right to a fair trial, while the order in the instant matter was issued merely to protect an individual's interest in privacy. Second, *Dickinson* was decided before [the Supreme Court handed down a case that announced a particularly strict test for prior restraints.]

**70.** Arguably, the Journal could have immediately appealed the order to this Court under 28 U.S.C. § 1292(a)(1). And, although difficult to obtain, the Journal might have sought a writ of mandamus. 28 U.S.C. § 1651(a).

when a party believes it is subject to a transparently invalid order, seeking review in an appellate court is a far safer means of testing the order. For if the party chooses to violate the order and the order turns out not to be transparently invalid, the party must suffer the consequences of a contempt citation.

CONCLUSION

We conclude that the district court's order of November 13, 1985, was transparently invalid. * * *

Because the order was transparently invalid, the appellants should have been allowed to challenge its constitutionality at the contempt proceedings.[74] A fortiori, the order cannot serve as the basis for a contempt citation. The order of the district court finding the Providence Journal Company and its executive editor, Charles M. Hauser, in criminal contempt is therefore reversed.[75]

ORDER

We hereby grant petitioner's suggestion for rehearing en banc. We do not, however, vacate the panel's opinion and order. Rather, we issue the attached en banc opinion as an addendum to, and modification of, said panel opinion; and as so modified said panel opinion and order may stand as reflecting the opinion of the en banc court. * * *

OPINION ON REHEARING

PER CURIAM.

In reflecting en banc upon the conflicting principles of "collateral bar" and "no prior restraint against pure speech," the court recognizes, with the panel, the difficulties of imposing upon a publisher the requirement of pursuing the normal appeal process. Not only would such entail time and expense, but the right sought to be vindicated could be forfeited or the value of the embargoed information considerably cheapened. Nevertheless, it seems to us that some finer tuning is available to

**74.** [In Thomas v. Collins, 323 U.S. 516, 65 S.Ct. 315, 89 L.Ed. 430 (1945) ], a labor organization was enjoined from soliciting union memberships. The organizer violated the order and subsequently challenged its constitutionality arguing that the temporary restraining order constituted a prior restraint on pure speech. The Supreme Court allowed this challenge and reversed the contempt citation.

The Journal argues that *Thomas* stands for the proposition that the collateral bar rule does not apply to prior restraints on pure speech. Because the order of November 13, 1985, was transparently invalid, however, we need not address this issue. We note, however, that *Thomas* does provide support for our holding. *Thomas* held that any prior restraint on pure speech was invalid absent clear and present danger of immediate and irreparable injury to the public welfare. Moreover, *Thomas* establishes that the collateral bar rule is not impregnable in cases involving prior restraints on pure speech.

**75.** In reversing the contempt citation against the Journal and its executive editor, we in no way condone their conduct. From all appearances, the Journal used the presence of the court order to bolster the importance of the Patriarca story. On November 14, 1985, the day before the scheduled hearing on whether to vacate the Court order of November 13, the Journal's front page headline read: "Court restricts media use of FBI tapes on Patriarca; Journal decides to print". * * * [I]t appears to this court that the Journal published the story concerning the court order more for its publicity value than for its news value. * * *

minimize the disharmony between respect for court orders and respect for free speech.

It is not asking much, beyond some additional expense and time, to require a publisher, even when it thinks it is the subject of a transparently unconstitutional order of prior restraint, to make a good faith effort to seek emergency relief from the appellate court. If timely access to the appellate court is not available or if timely decision is not forthcoming, the publisher may then proceed to publish and challenge the constitutionality of the order in the contempt proceedings. In such event whatever added expense and time are involved, such a price does not seem disproportionate to the respect owing court processes; and there is no prolongation of any prior restraint. On the other hand, should the appellate court grant the requested relief, the conflict between principles has been resolved and the expense and time involved have vastly been offset by aborting any contempt proceedings.

We realize that our ruling means that a publisher seeking to challenge an order it deems transparently unconstitutional must concern itself with establishing a record of its good faith effort. But that is a price we should pay for the preference of court over party determination of invalidity. In the instant case, assertions have been made that some eight-and-one-half hours elapsed between the issuance of the order by the district court and the deadline for publication. Not only are we left without a clear conviction that timely emergency relief was available within the restraints governing the publisher's decision making, but we would deem it unfair to subject the publisher to the very substantial sanctions imposed by the district court because of its failure to follow the procedure we have just announced. We recognize that our announcement is technically dictum, but are confident that its stature as a deliberate position taken by us in this en banc consideration will serve its purpose.

### *Notes on the Collateral Bar Rule*

1. *Does the rule make sense? Providence Journal* develops an exception to the collateral bar rule, but does not question the rule itself. Unless one of the exceptions to the rule applies—more about them later—someone who violates an injunction is barred from defending a prosecution for criminal contempt by asserting that the order was invalid. In other words, one may attack the order's validity by direct appeal, but not collaterally in a criminal contempt proceeding. For example, in *Walker v. City of Birmingham,* Dr. King could not attack the validity of an injunction enforcing a constitutionally suspect anti-parade ordinance and so went to jail. (There he wrote the famous "Letter from Birmingham Jail." See David Benjamin Oppenheimer, Martin Luther King, Walker v. City of Birmingham, and the Letter from Birmingham Jail, 26 U.C.Davis L. Rev. 791 (1993).) Some of Dr. King's colleagues who were not named in the injunction were charged with violating the ordinance. They, of course, were not collaterally barred from attacking

its validity, which they successfully did. Shuttlesworth v. City of Birmingham, 394 U.S. 147, 89 S.Ct. 935, 22 L.Ed.2d 162 (1969). Does the general rule against collateral attacks on injunctions make sense? Consider whether the collateral bar rule minimizes the irreparable injury that would be caused by wrongly failing to stop defendant if the injunction should have been issued or wrongly stopping defendant if the injunction should not have been issued. Recall that Justice Scalia's dissent in *Madsen* (reproduced in chapter 2) argued that the collateral bar rule is one reason that injunctions should be scrutinized more closely than statutes.

2. *Exceptions to the collateral bar rule.*

(a) *No direct appeal available.* Footnote 28 in Providence Journal shows that the collateral bar rule does not apply to certain discovery orders for which no direct appeal is available. The court also notes a passage in *Walker* that indicates that the collateral bar rule would not apply if the demonstrators had appealed but had been given the run around. As the court acknowledges, it is difficult to appeal temporary restraining orders. Should the collateral bar rule apply to such orders? Professor Rendleman argues that the collateral bar rule should not apply to ex parte orders. Doug Rendleman, More on Void Orders, 7 Ga.L.Rev. 246 (1973).

(b) *The court lacks jurisdiction.* The collateral bar rule, in effect, puts the burden on the defendant of either obeying the order or going to the trouble of getting it overturned on appeal. The justification for this burden is that the order did not come from just anyone but rather from a judge. However, if the judge is from a low level tribunal that lacks jurisdiction to issue the injunction—say traffic court or small claims court—then putting the burden on defendant loses plausibility. This is the rationale for the lack of jurisdiction exception. However, the most powerful trial courts sometimes may lack jurisdiction for reasons that are quite complex and difficult to evaluate. For instance, the Supreme Court in *United Mine Workers* split 5–4 in holding that the federal district court had jurisdiction to enjoin a strike against the government. Moreover, there is an exception to the no-jurisdiction-exception. Five justices in *United Mine Workers* held that even if the district court ultimately lacked jurisdiction, it had jurisdiction to issue a temporary restraining order to gain the time to determine whether it had jurisdiction. What result if the court failed to consider the jurisdictional issue at all but rather issued the temporary restraining order without mentioning it? See United States Catholic Conference v. Abortion Rights Mobilization, 487 U.S. 72, 79–80, 108 S.Ct. 2268, 2272, 101 L.Ed.2d 69 (1988).

(c) *Transparent invalidity. Walker* suggested transparent invalidity as an exception, but not until *Providence Journal* did a federal court base a holding on this theory. Why hadn't a case gone off on transparent invalidity in the two decades since *Walker*? Should there be a transparent invalidity exception? Should it require, as the *en banc* decision says, an effort to appeal? The Second Circuit Court of Appeals, in United States v. Terry, 17 F.3d 575, 579 (2d Cir.), cert. denied, ___ U.S. ___, 115 S.Ct. 355, 130 L.Ed.2d 310 (1994), joined the First Circuit in finding that a party seeking to invoke the transparent invalidity exception must make a "good faith effort to seek emergency relief from the appellate court."

(d) *Prior restraints.* *Thomas,* discussed in footnote 74, involved a union official found in contempt of an order not to violate a statute that forbade soliciting union membership. The Court struck down the statute on the grounds of prior restraint and freed the official without mention of the collateral bar rule. So *Thomas* is not square support for an exception to the collateral bar rule for prior restraints. Courts in a few states have considered whether there should be such an exception, with mixed results. Richard E. Labunski, The "Collateral Bar" Rule and The First Amendment: The Constitutionality of Enforcing Unconstitutional Orders, 37 Am.U.L.Rev. 323, 328 n.17, 348–63 (1988). Should there be such an exception? See Martin H. Redish, The Proper Role of the Prior Restraint Doctrine in First Amendment Theory, 70 Va.L.Rev. 53, 94 (1984). See also McGraw–Hill Co. v. Procter & Gamble Co., ___ U.S. ___, 116 S.Ct. 6, 132 L.Ed.2d 892 (1995)(Memorandum of Justice Stevens)(refusing to lift a prior restraint because McGraw–Hill did not seek trial court review before seeking an appeal).

3. *A cautionary tale.* When Cable Network News got recordings made by prison officials of conversations between General Manuel Noriega and the attorneys defending him against drug charges, the criminal trial court issued a preliminary injunction barring CNN from broadcasting the tapes for ten days or such lesser time as needed for the court to review the tapes and determine whether a restraint was warranted. To that end, the court also ordered CNN to turn over copies of the tapes. United States v. Noriega, 752 F.Supp. 1032 (S.D.Fla.1990). CNN appealed, but also broadcast portions of the tapes. The order was upheld on appeal. 917 F.2d 1543 (11th Cir.), cert. denied, 498 U.S. 976, 111 S.Ct. 451, 112 L.Ed.2d 432 (1990). After CNN finally gave the trial court copies of the tapes, the judge ruled that their contents did not justify the restraint, but that it was correct to restrain CNN because of its initial refusal to supply the tapes. 752 F.Supp. 1045 (S.D.Fla.1990). Four years later, CNN was found guilty of criminal contempt and directed to pay a fine covering the government's legal fees incurred during the contempt prosecution and to broadcast an apology or, in alternative, pay an additional punitive fine. United States v. CNN, Inc., 865 F.Supp. 1549 (S.D.Fla.1994). CNN apologized.

4. *The attorney's liability.* The ABA Model Code of Professional Responsibility EC 7–22 (1980) states that "[r]espect for judicial rulings is essential to the proper administration of justice; however, a litigant or his lawyer may, in good faith and within the framework of the law, take steps to test the correctness of a ruling of a tribunal." If one of the exceptions to the collateral bar rule is not available, "then counsel may give his opinion that an order is no good, or he may outline to his client

the boundaries of that order and what conduct is and is not included. Except for these limited situations, it is otherwise the duty of the attorney to urge his client to comply with all orders * * * " Denise A. Lier, Liability of the Attorney Who Advises Disobedience, 6 J.Legal Prof. 333, 345 (1981).

## 4. WHO IS BOUND?

### *Problem: Country Lodge v. Miller (Reprised)*
### *Injunctions That Coerce Persons Who Are Not Parties*

Assume that a court has enjoined Miller to stop discharging apple mash.

(a) Would it be proper to enforce the injunction against Miller's employees, who are not parties, if they help her continue to discharge?

(b) Is Jones, who buys Miller's cider mill, bound by the injunction that the court had issued against Miller?

(c) Suppose that the defendant is the Miller County Sewage District, a municipal corporation that operates a sewage treatment plant. Miller's discharge into the river illegally contains toxic chemicals because some users of the sewage system flush them down the drain and the treatment plant presently has no way of removing them. The culprits are probably a small number of the many thousand factories and commercial buildings in the district. Their identity is, so far, unknown. The court decides not to enjoin all discharge from the treatment plant because this would make the county uninhabitable. Instead, it enjoins anyone from putting the toxic chemicals into the sewage system and warns that it will impose heavy sanctions on any person found to violate this order. Newspapers and radio and television stations prominently report the story and a copy of the injunction is mailed to every postal address in the district. Is the injunction binding against anyone other than Miller?

---

## STATE UNIVERSITY OF NEW YORK v. DENTON

New York State Appellate Division, Fourth Department, 1970.
35 A.D.2d 176, 316 N.Y.S.2d 297.

FRANK DEL VECCHIO, JUSTICE PRESIDING:

Appellants, 45 members of the faculty of the State University of New York at Buffalo, appeal from a judgment adjudging them guilty of criminal contempt for violating a preliminary injunction issued by Supreme Court, Erie County. Execution of the 30-day jail sentence has been stayed pending determination of the appeal.

In the course of student disturbances and disorders on the University campus in late February 1970 the administration requested the aid of the Buffalo city police. As a consequence, a sizable number of the public police force moved onto the campus where clashes with students ensued. Members of the University administration were barred from campus offices and a basketball game was disrupted by students demanding the removal of the police officers. The State concedes that the appellants here, as distinguished from the students, "were not party to the violent and disruptive actions leading to the injunction."

In an attempt to prevent further acts of violence, the University on February 27 * * * commenced an action against 13 named students and John Doe and Jane Doe for a permanent injunction. * * * [N]o appearance was made on behalf of the students, and an order was made enjoining the students "and all other persons receiving notice of this preliminary injunction, whether acting individually or in concert" * * * from acting within * * * plaintiff's buildings in such unlawful manner as to disrupt or interfere with plaintiff's lawful and normal operations * * *.

The preliminary injunction was served by posting copies at various locations on the campus.

* * * The judgment we are reviewing found appellants faculty members guilty of willfully violating the provisions of the preliminary injunction of March 5 in that on March 15, acting individually and in concert with each other and in concert with others with notice of the preliminary injunction, they entered the office of the president of the University located on the campus and unlawfully refused to leave the office when asked to do so. Appellants were not among the named defendants in the injunction action, were not parties to the application for the temporary injunction and were never personally served with the order of March 5.

The threshold question to be considered, therefore, is whether appellants were bound by the order of March 5, which was addressed to the named student defendants and "all persons having knowledge" of the order, and whether accordingly appellants may be found guilty of criminal contempt for its violation. Well settled principles of law require a negative answer to the inquiry. * * *

[T]he frequently cited opinion of Judge Learned Hand in Alemite Mfg. Corp. v. Staff, 2 Cir., 42 F.2d 832, [states]:

> . . . (N)o court can make a decree which will bind any one but a party; a court of equity is as much so limited as a court of law; it cannot lawfully enjoin the world at large, no matter how broadly it words its decree. If it assumes to do so, the decree is *pro tanto brutum fulmen* [to that extent, harmless thunder], and the persons enjoined are free to ignore it. It is not vested with sovereign powers to declare conduct unlawful; its jurisdiction is limited to those over whom it gets personal service, and who therefore can have their day in court. Thus, the only occasion when a person not a party may be punished, is when he has helped to bring about, not merely what the decree has forbidden, because it may have gone too far, but what it

has power to forbid, an act of a party. This means that the respondent must either abet the defendant, or must be legally identified with him.

Measured by these criteria, the appellants were not made subject to the preliminary injunction by the language "all persons receiving notice of this preliminary injunction." There is no basis on the facts presented for the conclusion that appellants, who had no opportunity to be heard in the injunction proceedings, were subject to punishment for violation of the order of March 5. "The courts ... may not grant an enforcement order or injunction so broad as to make punishable the conduct of persons who act independently and whose rights have not been adjudged according to law." Regal Knitwear Co. v. National Labor Relations Board, 324 U.S. 9, 13, 65 S.Ct. 478, 481, 89 L.Ed. 661.

We need not reach the question whether there was an adequate showing to justify Special Term's conclusion that appellants had knowledge of the preliminary injunction because we conclude that knowledge of a non-party alone is not sufficient without proof of agency or collusion with the named defendants to impose liability for a violation. * * * We would point out, however, that in our view there is a serious question whether posting alone, without personal service or reading aloud the provisions of the temporary injunction, was sufficient to subject appellants to the prohibition of the mandate and to make them liable to criminal contempt conviction for its violation.

The record in the instant case is devoid of any proof that the students violated the injunction and the evidence is legally insufficient to establish that the faculty members either were agents of or acted in collusion with them. The injunction was specifically aimed at the conduct of the students. The faculty members were not parties to the disruptive actions which led to the injunction nor were they charged with acting in concert with or as agents of the students. Consequently, even if they had knowledge of its provisions, they could not be held in contempt for their independent action in disobeying the injunction.

Plaintiff offered proof that after the faculty members entered the president's office one of the group handed to a University staff member a paper which stated that the group would remain until the police were removed from the campus and that they were in sympathy with the general purposes of the strike. Plaintiff argues that this established that appellants acted in concert and/or collusion with the named defendants as aiders and abettors. The concession that appellants were not parties to the disruptive actions leading to the injunction is a clear indication that they were not acting in concert and/or collusion with the students and, since there was no proof that the students themselves violated the injunction, it cannot be said that appellants aided and abetted them. The mere fact that an actor may be sympathetic to the desires of one properly bound by an injunction, or that by his conduct the former accomplishes what the party enjoined wants accomplished, is not sufficient to establish beyond a reasonable doubt that the conduct was carried out in combination or collusion with the named enjoinee. We conclude therefore that appellants were not bound by the injunction and that the application to punish appellants for contempt of court arising out of a violation of the order of March 5 should have been denied. * * *

## UNITED STATES v. HALL

United States Court of Appeals, Fifth Circuit, 1972.
472 F.2d 261.

WISDOM, CIRCUIT JUDGE:

This case presents the question whether a district court has power to punish for criminal contempt a person who, though neither a party nor bearing any legal relationship to a party, violates a court order designed to protect the court's judgment in a school desegregation case. We uphold the District Court's conclusion that in the circumstances of this case it had this power, and affirm the defendant's conviction for contempt.

On June 23, 1971, the district court entered a "Memorandum Opinion and Final Judgment" in the case of *Mims v. Duval County School Board.* The court required The Duval County [Jacksonville], Florida School Board to complete its desegregation of Duval County Schools * * *

Among the schools marked for desegregation under the plan approved by the district court was Ribault Senior High School, a predominantly white school. * * * After the desegregation order was put into effect racial unrest and violence developed at Ribault, necessitating on one occasion the temporary closing of the school. On March 5, 1972, the superintendent of schools and the sheriff of Jacksonville filed a petition for injunctive relief in the *Mims* case with the district court. This petition alleged that certain black adult "outsiders" had caused or abetted the unrest and violence by their activities both on and off the Ribault campus. The petition identified the appellant Eric Hall, allegedly a member of a militant organization known as the "Black Front", as one of several such outsiders who, in combination with black students and parents, were attempting to prevent the normal operation of Ribault through student boycotts and other activities. As relief the petitioners requested an order "restraining all Ribault Senior High School students and any person acting independently or in concert with them from interfering with the orderly operation of the school and the Duval County School System, and for such other relief as the court may deem just and proper."

At an ex parte session on March 5, 1972, the district court entered an order [providing, inter alia, that no one may go upon the school grounds except enumerated categories of persons, such as students, faculty, and administrators.]

The order went on to provide that "[a]nyone having notice of this order who violates any of the terms thereof shall be subject to arrest, prosecution and punishment by imprisonment or fine, or both, for criminal contempt under the laws of the United States of America.... " The court ordered the sheriff to serve copies of the order on seven named persons, *including Eric Hall.* Hall was neither a party plaintiff nor a party defendant in the *Mims* litigation, and in issuing this order the court did not join Hall or any of the other persons named in the order as parties.

On March 9, 1972, four days after the court issued its order, Hall violated that portion of the order restricting access to Ribault High School by appearing on the Ribault campus. When questioned by a Deputy United States Marshal as to the reasons for his presence, Hall replied that he was on the grounds of Ribault for the purpose of violating the March 5 order. The marshal then arrested Hall and took him into custody. After a non-jury trial, the district court found Hall guilty of the charge of criminal contempt and sentenced him to sixty days' imprisonment.

On this appeal Hall raises two related contentions. Both contentions depend on the fact that Hall was not a party to the *Mims* litigation and the fact that, in violating the court's order, he was apparently acting independently of the *Mims* parties. He first points to the common law rule that a nonparty who violates an injunction solely in pursuit of his own interests cannot be held in contempt. Not having been before the court as a party or as the surrogate of a party, he argues that in accordance with this common law rule he was not bound by the court's order. Second, he contends that Rule 65(d) of the Federal Rules of Civil Procedure prevents the court's order from binding him, since Rule 65(d) limits the binding effect of injunctive orders to "parties to the action, their officers, agents, servants, employees, and attorneys, and ... those persons in active concert or participation with them who receive actual notice of the order by personal service or otherwise." We reject both contentions.

I.

For his first contention, that a court of equity has no power to punish for contempt a nonparty acting solely in pursuit of his own interests, the appellant relies heavily on the two leading cases of Alemite Manufacturing Corp. v. Staff, 2 Cir.1930, 42 F.2d 832, and Chase National Bank v. City of Norwalk, 1934, 291 U.S. 431, 54 S.Ct. 475, 78 L.Ed. 894. In *Alemite* the district court had issued an injunction restraining the defendant and his agents, employees, associates, and confederates from infringing the plaintiff's patent. Subsequently a third person, not a party to the original suit and acting entirely on his own initiative, began infringing the plaintiff's patent and was held in contempt by the district court. The Second Circuit reversed in an opinion by Judge Learned Hand, stating that "it is not the act described which the decree may forbid, but only that act when the defendant does it."

42 F.2d at 833. In *Chase National Bank* the plaintiff brought suit against the city of Norwalk to obtain an injunction forbidding the removal of poles, wires, and other electrical equipment belonging to the plaintiff. The district court issued a decree enjoining the city, its officers, agents, and employees, "and all persons whomsoever to whom notice of this order shall come" from removing the equipment or otherwise interfering with the operation of the plaintiff's power plant. The Supreme Court held that the district court had violated "established principles of equity jurisdiction and procedure" insofar as its order applied to persons who were not parties, associates, or confederates of parties, but who merely had notice of the order. See also Regal Knitwear Co. v. NLRB, 1945, 324 U.S. 9, 13, 65 S.Ct. 478, 89 L.Ed. 661.

This case is different. In *Alemite* and *Chase National Bank* the activities of third parties, however harmful they might have been to the plaintiffs' interests, would not have disturbed in any way the adjudication of rights and obligations as between the original plaintiffs and defendants. Infringement of the *Alemite* plaintiff's patent by a third party would not have upset the defendant's duty to refrain from infringing or rendered it more difficult for the defendant to perform that duty. Similarly, the defendant's duty in *Chase National Bank* to refrain from removing the plaintiff's equipment would remain undisturbed regardless of the activities of third parties, as would the plaintiff's right not to have its equipment removed by the defendant. The activities of Hall, however, threatened both the plaintiffs' right and the defendant's duty as adjudicated in the *Mims* litigation. In *Mims* the plaintiffs were found to have a constitutional right to attend an integrated school. The defendant school board had a corresponding constitutional obligation to provide them with integrated schools and a right to be free from interference with the performance of that duty. Disruption of the orderly operation of the school system, in the form of a racial dispute, would thus negate the plaintiffs' constitutional right and the defendant's constitutional duty. In short, the activities of persons contributing to racial disorder at Ribault imperiled the court's fundamental power to make a binding adjudication between the parties properly before it.

Courts of equity have inherent jurisdiction to preserve their ability to render judgment in a case such as this. This was the import of the holding in United States v. United Mine Workers of America, 1947, 330 U.S. 258, 67 S.Ct. 677, 91 L.Ed. 884. * * * As an alternative holding the court stated that the contempt conviction would have been upheld even if the district court had ultimately been found to be without jurisdiction. This holding affirmed the power of a court of equity to issue an order to preserve the status quo in order to protect its ability to render judgment in a case over which it might have jurisdiction.

The integrity of a court's power to render a binding judgment in a case over which it has jurisdiction is at stake in the present case. In *Mine Workers* disruptive conduct prior to the court's decision could have destroyed the court's power to settle a controversy at least potentially within its jurisdiction. Here the conduct of Hall and others, if unrestrained, could have upset the court's ability to bind the parties in *Mims,* a case in which it unquestionably had jurisdiction. Moreover, the court retained jurisdiction in *Mims* to enter such further orders as might be necessary to effectuate its judgment. Thus disruptive conduct would not only jeopardize the effect of the court's judgment already entered but would also undercut its power to enter binding desegregation orders in the future.

The principle that courts have jurisdiction to punish for contempt in order to protect their ability to render judgment is also found in the use of in rem injunctions. Federal courts have issued injunctions binding on all persons, regardless of notice, who come into contact with property which is the subject of a judicial decree. A court entering a decree binding on a particular piece of property is necessarily faced with the danger that its judgment may be disrupted in the future by members of an undefinable class—those who may come into contact with the property. The in rem injunction protects the court's judgment. The district court here faced an analogous problem. The judgment in a school case, as in other civil rights actions, inures to the benefit of a large class of persons, regardless of whether the original action is cast in the form of a class action. At the same time court orders in school cases, affecting as they do large numbers of people, necessarily depend on the cooperation of the entire community for their implementation. * * *

II.

The appellant also asserts that Rule 65(d) of the Federal Rules of Civil Procedure prevents the court's order from binding him. He points out that he was not a party to the original action, nor an officer, agent, servant, employee, or attorney of a party, and denies that he was acting in "active concert or participation" with any party to the original action.

In examining this contention we start with the proposition that Rule 65 was intended to embody "the common-law doctrine that a decree of injunction not only binds the parties defendant but also those identified with them in interest, in 'privity' with them, represented by them or subject to their control." Regal Knitwear Co. v. NLRB, 1945, 324 U.S. 9, 14, 65 S.Ct. 478, 481, 89 L.Ed. 661. Literally read, Rule 65(d) would forbid the issuance of in rem injunctions. But courts have continued to issue in rem injunctions notwithstanding Rule 65(d), since they possessed the power to do so at common law and since Rule 65(d) was intended to embody rather than to limit their common law powers.

Similarly, we conclude that Rule 65(d), as a codification rather than a limitation of courts' common-law powers, cannot be read to restrict the inherent power of a court to protect its ability to render a binding judgment. We hold that Hall's relationship to the *Mims* case fell within that contemplated by Rule 65(d). By deciding *Mims* and retaining jurisdiction the district court had, in effect, adjudicated the rights of the entire community with respect to the racial controversy surrounding the school system. Moreover, as we have noted, in the circumstances of this case third parties such as Hall were in a position to upset the court's adjudication. This was not a situation which could have been anticipated by the draftsmen of procedural rules. In meeting the situation as it did, the district court did not overstep its powers.

We do not hold that courts are free to issue permanent injunctions against all the world in school cases. Hall had notice of the court's order. Rather than challenge it by the orderly processes of law, he resorted to conscious, willful defiance. See Walker v. Birmingham, 1967, 388 U.S. 307, 87 S.Ct. 1824, 18 L.Ed.2d 1210.

* * * We hold, then, that the district court had the inherent power to protect its ability to render a binding judgment between the original parties to the *Mims* litigation by issuing an interim ex parte order against an undefinable class of persons. We further hold that willful violation of that order by one having notice of it constitutes criminal contempt. The judgment of the district court is affirmed.

### *Notes on Injunctions Against Nonparties*

1. In keeping with *SUNY,* Fed.R.Civ.P. 65(d)(see Appendix, infra at p. 887), literally read, allows courts to bind only "parties to actions, their officers, agents, servants, employees, and attorneys" and "those persons in active concert or participation with them." The rationale is due process. See, e.g., Doug Rendleman, Beyond Contempt: Obligors to Injunctions, 53 Tex.L.Rev. 873 (1975). As a corollary, those who have not had due process are not barred from collaterally attacking the order for improperly purporting to bind them. *Hall*, in contrast, allows orders to bind a wider group and, correspondingly, requires them to challenge the order in court.

2. Suppose that the thirteen named defendants in *SUNY* were the officers of the student organization that organized the protests. Are members of the organization bound if they act at the behest of the officers? And, if so, are the officers in contempt for what the members do? See Roe v. Operation Rescue, 54 F.3d 133 (3d Cir.1995)(leader of abortion protest organization held in contempt for urging others to commit acts from which he was enjoined). Are the members bound if they act on their own initiative? In In re Lennon, 166 U.S. 548, 17 S.Ct. 658, 41 L.Ed. 1110 (1897), a court ordered Lennon's employer, a union railroad, not to boycott the cars of a nonunion railroad. Lennon was held in contempt for failing to obey the injunction against his employer, even though his employer was unlikely to share his pro-union sympathies. In *Alemite Mfg. v. Staff*, the alleged contemnor was originally bound as an employee of the defendant, but went into business for himself, and was held not to be bound because he was motivated by his own interests. One of the issues in *Madsen* (reproduced in chapter 2) was whether nonparties who sympathize with the abortion protestors would be bound.

3. The *Hall* court attempts to distinguish *Alemite* and *Chase National Bank* on the basis that in those cases the injunction against the

nonparty was not needed to protect plaintiff's rights or to allow performance of defendants' duties. Is Hall bound but not a nonparty who tears down the utility poles in *Chase National Bank* because (a) plaintiffs in *Hall* had constitutional rights and the plaintiff in *Chase National Bank* had property rights? (b) plaintiffs in *Hall* had rights against all the world to attend an integrated school while the plaintiff in *Chase National Bank* had rights to its property only against defendants? (c) defendants in *Hall* had an affirmative duty to repair past segregation by setting up an integrated school system while the injunction in *Chase National Bank* was solely preventive?

4. Does *Hall* adequately address the due process concerns of Rule 65(d)? *Hall*'s discussion of *United Mine Workers* is misleading. There, the district court had subject matter jurisdiction to issue a temporary restraining order to keep the peace while it determined if it had subject matter jurisdiction over the case. In *Hall,* the court argues that it has personal jurisdiction over Hall so that it can make the defendants over whom it has personal jurisdiction perform their duties. That *Hall* involves personal rather than subject matter jurisdiction raises due process problems that were not present in *United Mine Workers.* A portion of *Hall,* which was deleted, arguably limits its "broad sweep by noting that, since the contempt occurred within 10 days of the order's issuance, the order could be regarded as an *ex parte* temporary restraining order, valid under Fed.R.Civ.P. 65(b) * * * ." James M. Hirschhorn, Where the Money Is: Remedies to Finance Compliance with Strict Structural Injunctions, 82 Mich.L.Rev. 1815, 1832 n.101 (1984). But, the district court did not limit the order's duration to 10 days and no effort was made to serve Hall before issuing the order. (Recall the discussion of Carroll v. President of Princess Anne County at page 178.)

5. What makes *Hall* a hard case is that keeping outsiders off school grounds probably is necessary to fulfill plaintiffs' rights and prevent serious injuries. Courts, however, have a variety of techniques for controlling nonparties who may interfere with successful implementation of an injunction. Some are listed below. Would any of them have been practical in *SUNY*, *Hall*, or part (c) of Country Lodge v. Miller?

(a) 18 U.S.C. § 1509 makes it a crime to obstruct by threats or force the performance of duties under a federal court order.

(b) Fed.R.Civ.P. 19(a)(1) allows the joinder of a party if "in his absence, complete relief cannot be accorded among those already parties."

(c) Fed.R.Civ.P. 23 allows defendant class actions. Professor Dobbyn evaluated their feasibility to stop outsiders such as Hall:

> What makes the class action inappropriate in this type of situation is that fact that under Rule 23 of the Federal Rules of Civil Procedure the court is required to find that "the representative parties share a common interest with the class and will adequately represent the individual class members * * *" before allowing a class action. That would pose an almost insurmountable problem

here, since the broad spectrum of interests that might become involved * * * from teachers, parents, students, to simple racists, each with his own peculiar reason for opposing some phase of the plan, would be nearly impossible to lump into one "class" homogeneous enough to pass the rigid test of rule 23.

John F. Dobbyn, Contempt Power of the Equity Court Over Outside Agitators, 8 St. Mary's L.J. 1, 7 (1976). Other factors to be considered under Rule 23 are whether the members of the proposed class are so numerous that it would be impractical to join them individually and whether the claims and defenses of the class representative would be typical of those of the rest of the class. Would a defendant class action be more fitting in *Hall* or *SUNY*?

In Planned Parenthood Association v. Project Jericho, No., 1989 WL 9312 (Ohio App.1989), appeal dismissed 44 Ohio St.3d 703, 541 N.E.2d 622, reh'g granted 45 Ohio St.3d 704, 543 N.E.2d 811 (1989), the trial court granted an abortion clinic an injunction against, inter alia, more than four persons picketing in front of the clinic. The trial court made the injunction binding on certain named defendants, the members of a defendant class defined as all persons picketing in a defined area in front of the clinic, and those acting in privity with them. Subsequently, twenty-three people, some named defendants and some not, were found guilty of criminal contempt for violating the order. The appellate court struck down the class certification for the kind of reasons identified by Professor Dobbyn. However, the court affirmed the convictions on the basis that the named defendants were bound apart from the class certification and the other individuals thwarted the injunction, presumably by acting in concert with the named defendants, as discussed in notes 1 and 2. This rationale could conceivably bind the alleged contemnors in *SUNY* if one of the named defendants was present at the demonstration.

6. *Successors to public office.* Fed.R.Civ.P. 25(d) establishes a special rule for successors to public office. It provides that "[w]hen a public officer is a party to an action in his official capacity and during its pendency * * * ceases to hold office, the action does not abate and his successor is automatically substituted as a party." Suppose that the Supervisor of the Miller County Sewage District is defeated at the polls by a candidate who runs on a platform of protecting the river. Should the successor be bound? See Statement of Douglas, J., 368 U.S. at 1012–14, 81 S.Ct. at 24–25 (dissenting from promulgation of the rule).

7. *Successors in ownership.* In part (b) of the reprise of Country Lodge v. Miller (at p. 314), is Jones bound as Miller's successor in ownership? Compare Golden State Bottling Co. Inc. v. NLRB, 414 U.S. 168, 177, 94 S.Ct. 414, 421, 38 L.Ed.2d 388 (1973)(NLRB order against corporation also binding on another corporation that buys the business after a due process hearing on whether the second corporation is a successor) with Travelhost, Inc. v. Blandford, 68 F.3d 958 (5th Cir.1995) (subsequent purchaser of assets of plaintiff's competitor not automatical-

ly bound by injunction issued against former owners of competitor). Fed.R.Civ.P. 65(d) does not explicitly mention successors. In reprise (c) of Country Lodge v. Miller (at p. 314), are users of the sewage system bound because they got their right to discharge from the Miller County Sewage District and are, in that sense, successors to it? See Puget Sound Gillnetters v. United States District Court, 573 F.2d 1123 (9th Cir.1978), judgment vacated by Washington v. Washington State Commercial Passenger Fishing Vessel Assoc., 443 U.S. 658, 99 S.Ct. 3055, 61 L.Ed.2d 823 (1979). To what extent *should* successors be bound? Professor Dobbs has stated:

> It is perfectly appropriate to bind successors in interest by earlier judicial decisions affecting the state of title or incumbrances, and both the law of res judicata and the recording statutes may do this. But an injunction with respect to property does more than adjudge title; it regulates *conduct.* Furthermore, the penalties for failing to observe the state of title and the penalties for conducting oneself in violation of an injunction aimed at another are vastly different.

Dan B. Dobbs, Contempt of Court: A Survey, 56 Cornell L.Rev. 183, 256 (1971).

8. *In rem injunctions. Hall* relies on in rem injunctions, which are orders directed against the whole world with respect to some property within the court's power. For example, the filing of a bankruptcy petition automatically results in the stay of any efforts to collect debts from the debtor except in bankruptcy court. 11 U.S.C. § 362. Such stays do not offend the due process concerns behind Fed.R.Civ.P. 65(d) because they do not deny creditors their day in court but determine that the day shall be spent in bankruptcy court.

Another kind of in rem decree adjudicates title. This practice was extended to regulate conduct in cases dealing with property used for illicit purposes, where injunctions sometimes enjoined the present owner and any succeeding owner from continuing the illicit use. Professor Dan Dobbs objects to these cases on the same grounds as he objects to the successor cases. Dan B. Dobbs, Contempt of Court: A Survey, 56 Cornell L.Rev. 183, 257–58 (1971). Do these in rem cases support the result in *Hall*? See James F. Dobbyn, Contempt Power of the Equity Court Over Outside Agitators, 8 St. Mary's L.J. 1, 9 (1976).

### *Note on Washington v. Washington State Commercial Passenger Fishing Vessel Assoc., 443 U.S. 658, 99 S.Ct. 3055, 61 L.Ed.2d 823 (1979)*

In the 19th century, Native American tribes and the United States entered into a treaty that provided that tribal members could continue to take salmon from the rivers in what is now Washington State. The modern litigation arose because the state allowed non-tribal fishers to take so many salmon that the tribe's catch was endangered. The district court found the state liable. But the problem arose not from the state catching fish, but from many private persons doing so. The court enjoined any non-tribal fisher with notice of the injunction from taking fish except in accord with the injunction. The United States Supreme Court discussed several issues in the case at some length, but devoted only the following footnote to the propriety of enjoining nonparties:

> The associations [object] that the District Court had no power to enjoin individual nontreaty fishermen, who were not parties to its decisions, from violating the allocations that it has ordered. The reason this issue has arisen is that state officials were either unwilling or unable to enforce the District Court's orders against nontreaty fishermen by way of state regulations and state law enforcement efforts. Accordingly, nontreaty fishermen were openly violating Indian fishing rights, and, in order to give federal law enforcement officials the power via contempt to end those violations, the District Court was forced to enjoin them. The commercial fishing organizations, on behalf of their individual members, argue that they should not be bound by these orders because they were not parties to (although the associations all did participate as *amici curiae* in) the proceedings that led to their issuance. * * *
>
> In our view, the commercial fishing associations and their members are probably subject to injunction under either the rule that nonparties who interfere with the implementation of court orders establishing public rights may be enjoined, e.g., United States v. Hall, 472 F.2d 261 (C.A.5 1972), cited approvingly in Golden State Bottling Co. v. NLRB, 414 U.S. 168, 180, 94 S.Ct. 414, 423, 38 L.Ed.2d 388, or the rule that a court possessed of the res in a proceeding *in rem,* such as one to apportion a fishery, may enjoin those who would interfere with that custody. But in any case, these individuals and groups are citizens of the State of Washington, which was a party to the relevant proceedings, and "they, in their common public rights as citizens of the State, were represented by the State in those proceedings, and, like it, were bound by the judgment." Tacoma v. Taxpayers, 357 U.S. 320, 340–41, 78 S.Ct. 1209, 1221, 2 L.Ed.2d 1345 (1958). Moreover, a court clearly may order them to obey that judgment.

443 U.S. 658, 693 n.32, 99 S.Ct. 3055, 3078 n.32, 61 L.Ed.2d 823 (1979). For a history of the fishing rights controversy, see Shannon Bentley, Indians' Right to Fish: The Background, Impact, and Legacy of *United States v. Washington*, 17 Amer.Indian L.Rev. 1 (1992).

If the non-tribal fishers in *Washington* fall within the rule that "nonparties who interfere with the implementation of court orders establishing public rights may be enjoined," why not the faculty in *SUNY* ? Or is the difference between the cases that non-tribal fishers really got their day in court?

If the state had not been a party but the fishing associations were parties, would their members be bound too?

So, now, what's the answer to problem (c) (p. 314)?

### *Note on Notice*

An injunction binds neither party nor nonparty unless there is notice. Notice is obviously no problem when the alleged contemnor admits to having known of the order. Where the alleged contemnor denies notice or remains mum on that point, notice must be shown. Recall that the *SUNY* court prefers, as a means of giving notice, having the injunction read rather than posting it. If the injunction is only posted, many persons may not have read it so that it is difficult to infer notice, especially in a case of criminal contempt where the elements must be shown beyond a reasonable doubt. When, however, the notice is read, all those who can hear will have notice. The alleged contemnors may, of course, contend that they did not hear clearly enough to understand.

The party bringing the contempt action bears the burden of establishing actual knowledge of the injunction, and, at least in criminal contempt proceedings, this must be shown beyond a reasonable doubt. United States v. Baker, 641 F.2d 1311, 1317 (9th Cir.1981). The more indirect the form of communication, the harder it is to show notice. Most courts are reluctant to hold that reporting of the court order in a newspaper constitutes valid notice, unless perhaps it can be shown that the defendant read or subscribed to the publication. United States v. Gedraitis, 520 F.Supp. 84, 88 (E.D.Pa.1981), aff'd, 690 F.2d 351 (3d Cir.1982); Joint School District No. 1 v. Wisconsin Rapids Education Association, 70 Wis.2d 292, 234 N.W.2d 289, 303 (1975). In United States v. Baker, 641 F.2d 1311, 1317 n.8 (9th Cir.1981), which grew out of the same controversy as *Washington*, the court suggested that the government consider "publication of notices of the injunctions in shore locations frequented by fishers, such as hiring halls, marinas, packing plants, post offices, and meeting halls for fishers' associations; and publication in local newspapers."

### *Problem: Country Lodge v. Miller (Reprised)*
### *Injunctions That Harm Persons Who Are Not Proven Violators*

(a) Would it be improper to issue an injunction against Miller's employees, requiring them to clean up the mess on their own time?

(b) Would it be improper to issue an injunction that, in effect, puts Miller out of business because it would harm Wholesaler, who has a long term contract to buy cider from Miller?

### *Note on Non-Violators*

The judgment that defendant wronged plaintiff legitimates the harm that coercive relief does to the defendant. But, to put plaintiff in the rightful position, it may be useful to issue an injunction that harms persons who have not violated plaintiff's rights. Such persons may already been made parties by, for example, joinder or intervention. Fed.R.Civ.P. 19 & 24 (see Appendix, infra at p. 877).

*Injunctions that coerce non-violators. Rizzo v. Goode* (reproduced in chapter 2) held that it was improper for a district court to order the mayor and the police chief to institute a complaint process, which would have helped protect plaintiffs' rights, because the mayor and police were not liable. General Building Contractors Ass'n v. Pennsylvania, 458 U.S. 375, 102 S.Ct. 3141, 73 L.Ed.2d 835 (1982), held that it was improper for a district court to order building contractors to join with a union to establish and fund a training program and to attain minority membership goals in the union because it had not been found that the contractors were participants in the union's discriminatory practices. The Supreme Court struck down the injunction because it treated the building contractors:

> as if they had been properly found liable for the Union's discrimination. A decree containing such provisions, we hold, is beyond the traditional equitable limitations upon the authority of a federal court to formulate such decrees.
>
> Nor does the All Writs Act, 28 U.S.C. § 1651(a), support the extensive liability imposed upon petitioners by the District Court. The District Court did not rely upon this Act, and we think it completely wide of the mark in justifying the relief granted by the District Court. That Act was most recently considered by this Court in United States v. New York Telephone Co., 434 U.S. 159, 98 S.Ct. 364, 54 L.Ed.2d 376 (1977), where we said: "This Court has repeatedly recognized the power of a federal court to issue such commands under the All Writs Act as may be necessary or appropriate to effectuate and prevent the frustration of orders it has previously issued in its exercise of jurisdiction otherwise obtained * * * ." Id., at 172, 98 S.Ct., at 372. In *New York Telephone,* we held that the All Writs Act was available to require a third party to assist in the carrying out of a District Court order pertaining to the installation of [surveillance devices], and in doing so we noted that "(t)he order provided that the Company be fully reimbursed at prevailing rates, and compliance with it required minimal effort on the part of the Company and no disruption to its operations." Id. at 175, 98 S.Ct. at 373.

458 U.S. at 400–01, 102 S.Ct. at 3155–56, 73 L.Ed.2d at 856. At the same time, the Court upheld provisions of the decree that required the building contractors to submit reports to the district court as a means of checking on the union's compliance. It termed such requirements "minor and ancillary." The "minor and ancillary" provisions of the decree are analogous to a subpoena, which is after all a coercive order that one obeys because of civic duty rather than proven wrongdoing. If the building contractors were not already parties, they could have been

joined because "in the person's absence complete relief cannot be accorded among those already parties." Fed.R.Civ.P. 19(a)(1).

*Injunctions that do not coerce but do harm non-violators.* Harm to non-violators, as opposed to coercion of them, is permitted, but is weighed in the balance of equities as cases such as *Staso* and *Brown II* teach. How that harm is weighed will depend on a variety of factors. Franks v. Bowman Transportation Co., 424 U.S. 747, 96 S.Ct. 1251, 47 L.Ed.2d 444 (1976), held that an injunction to remedy employment discrimination could include, in addition to requiring priority hiring of minority job applicants, that those hired be granted retroactive seniority. Faced with the contention that retroactive seniority would disadvantage some current employees, who had not been shown to have violated the statute, the majority stated:

> Without an award of seniority dating from the time when he was discriminatorily refused employment, an individual who applies for and obtains employment * * * pursuant to the District Court's order will never obtain his rightful place in the hierarchy of seniority according to which those various employment benefits are distributed. He will perpetually remain subordinate to persons who, but for the illegal discrimination, would have been in respect to entitlement to these benefits his inferiors.

Id. at 767–768, 96 S.Ct. at 1266, 47 L.Ed.2d at 463.

International Brotherhood of Teamsters v. United States, 431 U.S. 324, 97 S.Ct. 1843, 52 L.Ed.2d 396 (1977), held that where the employer has discriminated an award of retroactive seniority is appropriate even though the union has not illegally discriminated and the retroactive seniority would affect innocent employees under the collective bargaining agreement that the union had negotiated. The Court did not however invalidate the seniority provisions themselves, which provided that a senior employee could not bump a junior employee from an existing job assignment. The upshot was that innocent employees were safe in their existing positions but could not get better positions until members of the plaintiff class with more seniority under the decree had their pick.

What justifies keeping the innocent employees in their present positions—by no means a "minor and ancillary" harm—is that they might not have been ahead of plaintiffs in seniority but for the defendant's violations. Contrast the outcome in *Teamsters* with that in City of Los Angeles v. Manhart, 435 U.S. 702, 98 S.Ct. 1370, 55 L.Ed.2d 657 (1978), brought under the same statute. There, employers were found to have engaged in illegal gender discrimination by requiring higher contributions from female employees for their pensions because of actuarial findings that females lived longer and therefore would receive a pension for a longer period of time. The Court held that the remedy could not be retroactive because that would harm both the defendants and male employees, both of whom had well established expectations under prior law that differential pension contributions were proper.

### *Problem: Country Lodge v. Miller (Reprised) Injunctions That Harm Persons Who Are Not Proven Violators and Are Not Parties*

Country Lodge and Miller propose a consent decree that specifies a program to end Miller's pollution. The proposed consent decree states that it would "constitute a full and complete adjudication and settlement * * * and binds all parties or potential parties who had notice of the instant claims and this Consent Decree." A copy is served upon the state Environmental Protection Agency. It decides not to intervene. After the court enters the consent decree, the state EPA sues Miller, alleging the same facts and legal theories upon which Country Lodge sued. Does the consent decree preclude the second suit?

### *Note on Martin v. Wilks, 490 U.S. 755, 109 S.Ct. 2180, 104 L.Ed.2d 835 (1989)*

"Bound" by a decree might have at least four different meanings: (1) coerced to obey it; (2) precluded, by res judicata or collateral estoppel from attacking it; (3) the loss of rights because the decree is a defense to otherwise illegal conduct; or (4) harmed in some more indirect way. We have dealt so far with first and fourth possibilities, and you probably studied the second category in civil procedure class. We now come to the third possibility. In *Martin v. Wilks,* a group of white firefighters brought an action alleging that the City of Birmingham and related governmental employers violated their rights by giving racially based preferences in promotions to African Americans. The employers' defense was that their promotions policy was dictated by consent decrees entered in a previous case brought by African Americans who claimed that they were the victims of racial discrimination. The Supreme Court had earlier decided that voluntary affirmative action plans do not illegally discriminate *if* they are designed to remedy past discrimination. United Steel Workers of America v. Weber, 443 U.S. 193, 99 S.Ct. 2721, 61 L.Ed.2d 480 (1979); City of Richmond v. J.A. Croson Co., 488 U.S. 469, 109 S.Ct. 706, 102 L.Ed.2d 854 (1989). The plaintiffs in *Martin v. Wilks* denied that the consent decrees were so justified. The district court held that, even if the decrees were not so justified, the government employers had a defense to the charge of racial discrimination because they could show that their hiring policy was compelled by the consent decrees and so they did not have the requisite intent to discriminate. This argument is problematic in that it would shield the employers' conduct even after a showing that the racial preferences were not justified. In a five to four decision, the Supreme Court reversed: "we think this holding contravenes the general rule that a person cannot be deprived of his legal rights in a proceeding to which he is not a party." 490 U.S. 755, 759, 109 S.Ct. 2180, 2183, 104 L.Ed.2d 835 (1989).

The majority focused on whether, under the Federal Rules of Civil Procedure, the justification for the consent decrees could be examined in the new case. The majority took the position that persons affected by a decree, such as the white firefighters are free to attack it collaterally unless they had been joined under Fed.R.Civ.P. 19. The dissent argued that such persons cannot attack the decree except by intervening in the case in which it is entered under Fed.R.Civ.P. 24. The parties to an employment discrimination case would have grave problems joining everyone whose rights might be affected because that group includes future job applicants, some of whom do not presently live in the area. But, putting the burden on members of this group to intervene also presents grave problems because some will be unaware of the case and others may not even know that they will move to the area.

One way out of this dilemma is to count upon parties to the suit to represent the interests of nonparties whose rights might be affected. The employer cannot be counted upon to represent their interests because it often tries to minimize its exposure to damages by offering greater preferences in future hiring and promotion to members of the plaintiff class. The employer in effect saves money at the expense of nonparties. The union, which represents present employees, may not adequately represent the interests of future job applicants. On the other hand, if there is no way to cut off collateral attacks on consent decrees, employers would resist settling such cases.

In *Martin v. Wilks* itself, there were indications in the record that the City agreed to more racial preferences in the future in order to radically reduce its immediate liability for money damages. On the other hand, the interests of the white firefighters who brought the *Martin* case had, in effect, been represented by the Birmingham Firefighters Association, which, as an amicus curiae in the previous case, had raised objections to the decrees. The Association also sought to intervene, but the district court denied the motion as untimely and entered the consent decrees. The court of appeals affirmed the consent decrees in part because the firefighters could "institute an independent Title VII suit, asserting the specific violations of their rights." United States v. Jefferson County, 720 F.2d 1511, 1518 (11th Cir.1983). The majority in *Martin v. Wilks* did not address whether the white firefighters had been adequately represented in the previous case, but rather decided that, under the Federal Rules of Civil Procedure, as now written, they could not be bound unless they were joined.

The Civil Rights Act of 1991 partially reverses *Martin v. Wilks* by barring collateral objections to decrees in employment discrimination suits from persons who: (1) have actual notice of the proposed judgment and a reasonable opportunity to present objections or (2) whose interests were represented by parties. Persons satisfying these conditions are barred from later objecting to the judgment, except if there is fraud, collusion, or lack of jurisdiction. Pub. L. No. 102–166, § 108, 105 Stat. 1076 (1991) (amending 42 U.S.C. § 2000e–2(n)). *Martin v. Wilks* continues to govern decrees in other fields. See, e.g., Landgraf v. U.S.I. Film Products, 511 U.S. ___, 114 S.Ct. 1483, 128 L.Ed.2d 229 (1994).

The Civil Rights Act of 1991 has not proven to be a complete bar to collateral objections to decrees even in employment discrimination suits. On appeal after remand in *Martin*, the Eleventh Circuit upheld the district court's determination that the plaintiffs could attack the decree because, even if the new statutory bar on collateral attacks were retroactive, the conditions for its application were not present. In re Birmingham Reverse Discrimination Employment Litigation, 20 F.3d 1525, 1530 n.1 (11th Cir.1994), cert. denied, ___ U.S. ___, 115 S.Ct. 1695, 131 L.Ed.2d 558 (1995). The Eleventh Circuit held that the plaintiffs in the *Martin* reverse discrimination suit showed that the racial quotas on promotion of firefighters illegally discriminated because they were not tailored narrowly to remedy the wrong. 20 F.3d at 1543. In a subsequent opinion regarding the modification of the decrees the Eleventh Circuit ordered that the decrees' race-based and gender-based preferences be rewritten to be, respectively, narrowly tailored and substantially related to the objective of ending discrimination. The district court was ordered to establish a schedule for attaining neutral selection procedures within "reasonably prompt deadlines" noting that the district court could maintain affirmative action measures if it believed the action was necessary to remedy the lingering effects of discrimination. The court also remanded the determination of whether race-based affirmative action was necessary on departments other than the police and fire departments. Ensley Branch, NAACP v. Seibels, 31 F.3d 1548 (11th Cir.1994).

## 5. ENFORCEMENT AGAINST THE GOVERNMENT

### *Problem: Country Lodge v. Miller (Reprised)*
### *Injunctions That Require the Cooperation of Public Officials*

Suppose the court decides that the best of way of preventing nonparties from putting toxics in the sewage system is to make the Miller County Sewage District stop them.

(a) If the district has regulations forbidding such disposal but is not enforcing them, can the court compel it to enforce its regulations?

(b) If the state's highest court rules that the district lacks the authority, under state law, to promulgate the regulations and the state legislature refuses to grant the authority, can a federal court compel the district to promulgate the regulations, compel the state legislature to grant the district authority to promulgate the regulations, or itself promulgate regulations for the district?

---

Section B of this chapter considered the problems in enforcement arising from difficulties in determining what defendant can do, stating what defendant should do in enforceable terms, and keeping track of what defendant has done in fact. These problems can occur whether the defendant is a private person or governmental entity, as Illinois v. Costle illustrates. This section considers problems that are special to enforcement against governmental defendants.

One such problem is that sanctions against governmental defendants may harm innocent citizens. If Miller, as the private operator of an apple press, willfully violates an injunction, the court would have no compunction about fining Miller for criminal contempt because she brought the harm upon herself. But if the Miller County Sewage District violated an injunction, the fine against it would come out of the pockets of taxpayers rather than the responsible public officials. The court could theoretically jail the officials for criminal contempt, but James Hirschhorn reported that he was "aware of no federal case decided within the past twenty-five years in which a public official has been imprisoned for civil or criminal contempt for violating an injunction." James M. Hirshhorn, Where the Money Is: Remedies to Finance Compliance With Strict Structural Injunctions, 82 Mich.L.Rev. 1815, 1841 (1984). *Spallone v. United States* (reproduced at page 361) is a subsequent example that underlines judicial reluctance to jail officials. Jailing officials is rare partly because the conflict over the jailing could well divert energies and attention from complying with the injunction. In Palmigiano v. Garrahy, 448 F.Supp. 659 (D.R.I.1978), the court responded to contempt by threatening coercive civil fines against the state rather than punishing the officials through criminal contempt. The court emphasized that the violations arose from mismanagement and that the officials could avoid wasting the taxpayers' money on fines by obeying promptly. In this way, the judge used the threat of coercive sanctions against the state to apply political pressure on the officials, while punishing the officials could have created political and practical problems for the judge.

Another problem special to enforcement against government is judicial reluctance to exercise powers assigned to other branches or levels of government. A narrow preventive injunction, by doing no more than stopping a governmental defendant from interfering with plaintiff's rightful position, does not exercise the power of another branch of government but rather keeps that defendant from exceeding its powers. But, reparative injunctions as well as many of the devices for dealing with the difficulties in enforcing injunctions—such as prophylactic orders, monitors, and receivers—go beyond simply preventing future violations. Such devices, by intruding on a governmental defendant's power, raise separation of powers or federalism issues. See Gerald E. Frug, The Judicial Power of the Purse, 126 U.Pa.L.Rev. 715 (1978). If the case involves a federal court and a federal agency or a state court and a state agency, the case would raise separation of powers issues. If it involves a federal court and a state agency, it would raise federalism issues. Robert F. Nagel, Separation of Powers and the Scope of Federal Equitable Remedies, 30 Stan.L.Rev. 661 (1978).

Judges worry about separation of powers and federalism for diverse reasons. Judicial intrusion on the powers of governmental defendants shifts power from electorally accountable to unaccountable hands. Moreover, a judge who strays from public expectations of the judicial role endangers the presumptive legitimacy that public opinion gives to court orders. See Colin S. Diver, The Judge as Political Powerbroker: Superintending Structural Change in Public Institutions, 65 Va.L.Rev. 43 (1979). Furthermore, the judge may not feel competent to make the necessary administrative or political decisions, either because of limited expertise or because the court lacks the fact-finding or outreach capacity of a legislature or an agency. A judge that takes over a governmental agency must conjure with the probability of disaster striking, such as a guard getting killed by a prisoner while the prison is under judicial supervision. See Geoffrey P. Alpert, Ben M. Crouch and C. Ronald Huff, Prison Reform by Judicial Decree: The Unintended Consequences of Ruiz v. Estelle, 9 Justice Sys.J. 291 (1984)(detailing rise in violence in prisons under court supervision). Although such a disaster may well have occurred anyway, the public may place the blame on the court, which would further undermine its legitimacy.

Despite separation of powers and federalism, courts still do issue reparative and prophylactic orders in cases involving governmental defendants. However, sensitivity to separation of powers and federalism issues—which sometimes is called "comity"—weighs in favor of less intrusive action. Milliken v. Bradley [*Milliken II* ], 433 U.S. 267, 280, 97 S.Ct. 2749, 2757, 53 L.Ed.2d 745, 755–56 (1977). A court will intrude only after concluding that the intrusion is necessary to protect plaintiff's rightful position and the harm to governmental structure is less important than vindicating plaintiff's rights. When official incompetence or resistance has gone so far that judges appoint a receiver despite comity, they tend to appoint officials already connected with the governmental defendant. E.g., United States v. Bowers, 828 F.2d 1169 (6th Cir.1987)(mayor appointed as receiver to replace commissioners), cert. denied, 486 U.S. 1006, 108 S.Ct. 1731, 100 L.Ed.2d 195 (1988); Morgan v. McDonough, 540 F.2d 527 (1st Cir.1976)(school superintendent appointed as receiver to replace board of education), cert. denied, 429 U.S. 1042, 97 S.Ct. 743, 50 L.Ed.2d 755 (1977). In such cases, the judge is not so much taking over a political branch of government as cutting the most resistant defendants out of the chain of command.

Comity affects enforcement in decisions far less dramatic than whether to appoint a receiver. Courts defer to governmental defendants in drafting injunctions and judging compliance with them. For example, the court in *Illinois v. Costle* accepted EPA's largely untested claim that it could not promulgate the mandated regulations quickly. Judges do not always accept what governmental defendants say, but a substantial burden of persuasion usually rests upon those who dispute the official pronouncement. This deference accords with the general principle of the Administrative Procedure Act that a judge should not overturn agency action simply because the judge disagrees with it; it must be so wrong as to be "arbitrary [or] capricious." 5 U.S.C. § 706(2)(A)(1988).

We now turn to two thornier problems of enforcement against governmental defendants: (1) political or bureaucratic resistance to compliance and (2) the immunity to suit of officials or institutions essential to compliance.

### *Note on How Politics Complicates Enforcement*

The injunction must overcome the political motives or bureaucratic inertia that led the governmental defendants to violate plaintiff's rights in the first place. The injunction in *Illinois v. Costle* (reproduced supra at p. 209) is a classic example of a judge trying to change the political and bureaucratic milieu to motivate the defendants. EPA failed to meet the statutory deadlines for promulgating the regulations because of a lack of resources and bureaucratic inertia. To grapple with these root sources of the violation, Judge Gesell took what steps he could. He required the agency to report any further slippage to the court and he required that such reports, as well as the regular reports to the court, be signed by the EPA Administrator. He also required that all such reports be sent to the congressional oversight committees. Since the EPA Administrator would be reluctant to report bad news to Congress and more reluctant still to have to testify before Congress or the court about such failures, the decree changed the course of least resistance at EPA from letting the regulations come out when they will to getting them out on the schedule in the decree. Also, by putting the congressional committees on notice, the decree might prompt them to pressure EPA to act more quickly. Finally, by blaming Congress for some of the delay, Judge Gesell was trying to prompt plaintiffs to get Congress to give the agency resources commensurate with the deadlines that it had imposed upon it.

More troublesome are cases when enough voters positively oppose compliance that the legislators or other politically accountable officials refuse to take necessary action. For example, the state legislature might refuse to grant a local government the authority to promulgate regulations required by an injunction or refuse to grant state officials the authority needed to raise and spend money needed to comply.

Virginia v. West Virginia, 246 U.S. 565, 38 S.Ct. 400, 59 L.Ed. 1272 (1918) is an old and striking illustration of the problems that such resistance can pose for the courts. When Virginia decided in 1861 to secede from the Union, the people living in the northwestern part of the state decided to secede from the state and form a new state, West Virginia, which would join the Union. West Virginia's constitution guaranteed to reimburse Virginia for the repayment of a share of Virginia's public debt outstanding on January 1, 1861. Congress consented in 1862 to the formation of this new state. Virginia and West Virginia failed, despite prolonged efforts, to reach agreement on West Virginia's share of the Virginia public debt. In 1906, Virginia invoked the original jurisdiction of the United States Supreme Court to sue West Virginia for reimbursement. In 1915, Virginia obtained a judgment of

$12,393,929.50. However, the West Virginia legislature failed to appropriate funds to satisfy the judgment.

Money judgments are not court orders and the failure to satisfy one is not contempt. Rather, in the ordinary case, the sheriff is authorized to sell the debtor's property and use the proceeds to pay plaintiff. (See chapter 8(B).) Virginia did not attempt to have West Virginia's property seized because, as the parties agreed, it was all devoted to governmental purposes and such property might well be held immune from sale. Instead Virginia asked the Supreme Court to order the West Virginia legislature to levy a tax to raise funds to pay the judgment.

A unanimous opinion for the Court by Chief Justice White rejected West Virginia's contention that federalism was an insurmountable barrier to the Court's power to coerce a state. It reasoned that such a barrier would undercut the purpose of its original jurisdiction over suits between states, which is to provide an effective means of resolving such disputes. The opinion went on to say that, whatever the Court might do, Congress could enact a statute requiring West Virginia to pay. Virginia had not asked for this advisory opinion.

As for judicial action against West Virginia, the Court decided not to decide, at least for a while. The opinion noted that ordering the legislature to levy a tax was not the only means to raise money to satisfy the judgment. For instance, the Court could itself levy a tax or seize the funds of the state. But the opinion stopped short of endorsing any particular action. Rather it suggested that the rejection of West Virginia's contention that the Court may not coerce a state did not dispose of all of the possible objections to the Court's taking any one of these particular actions, such as the "discretion in the legislature of West Virginia as to taxation." Ordering the legislature to levy a tax to be used to pay Virginia would do more than decide *whether* Virginia should be put in its rightful position, but also would decide *how* the political branches of West Virginia should do so. The Court decided not to decide what judicial action, if any, should be taken, but instead set this question down for argument at the next term.

> We say this because, impelled now by the consideration of the character of the parties which has controlled us during the whole course of the litigation, the right judicially to enforce by appropriate proceedings as against a State and its governmental agencies having been determined, and the constitutional power of Congress to legislate * * * having also been pointed out, we are fain to believe that, if we refrain now from passing upon the questions stated, we may be spared in the future the necessity of exerting compulsory power against one of the States of the Union to compel it to discharge a plain duty resting upon it under the Constitution. * * * [W]e should further reserve action in order that full opportunity may be afforded to Congress to exercise the power which it undoubtedly possesses. * * *

The pretentiousness of this language may be in part to camouflage the Court's unwillingness to decide fully the issue that had been briefed and argued and to give the plaintiff prompt relief. (The opinion originated the phrase "deliberate speed," later made famous in *Brown II*, reproduced in chapter 2.) As the Court was undoubtedly aware, while the case was pending, the West Virginia Senate enacted a resolution requesting the Governor to convene a special session when the opinion came down. Shortly after the opinion issued, with the opinion itself providing some political cover, the legislature of West Virginia enacted the legislation necessary for compliance.

If the defendant in *Virginia v. West Virginia* had been a private corporation whose "board of directors" refused to authorize the payment of a judgment, the courts would not have hesitated for so long to override the board by allowing the seizure of its property, the garnishment of its income, or putting the corporation in the hands of a receiver to operate it for the benefit of creditors. Why did the Supreme Court hesitate to override West Virginia's board of directors—its legislature—by (a) ordering the seizure and sale of public land not used for governmental purposes; (b) ordering the seizure and sale of public land used for governmental purposes; (c) ordering the seizure of state bank accounts; (d) ordering the state legislature to levy a tax; or (e) itself levying a tax? Consider what would happen in each instance if state officials and/or citizens resisted the Court's direct orders.

Should the court be any more willing to act if the defendant were a city rather than a state? The opinion in *Virginia v. West Virginia* noted "the many decided cases holding that where a municipality is empowered to levy specified taxation to pay a particular debt, the judicial power may enforce the levy of the tax to meet a judgment rendered in consequence of a default in paying the indebtedness." 246 U.S. at 594, 38 S.Ct. at 403, 62 L.Ed. at 888. Note the qualification that the municipality have the power to levy the tax. In the years following the Civil War, some municipalities attempted to defeat creditors by having the state legislature limit their power to tax. The Supreme Court approved orders to municipal officials, backed by the contempt power, to levy the necessary taxes, nonetheless. However, federal cases have not gone so far in recent decades. See James M. Hirschhorn, Where the Money Is: Remedies to Finance Compliance With Strict Structural Injunctions, 82 Mich.L.Rev. 1815, 1872–74 (1984). Compare City of Vernon v. Superior Court, 38 Cal.2d 509, 241 P.2d 243 (1952)(city council members held in contempt for refusing to levy tax to pay for sewage disposal facilities). In modern times, state constitutions and city charters make it easier for municipalities to borrow by guaranteeing that they will have the power to levy taxes to the extent necessary to pay off general obligation bonds in order to make the bonds marketable. The West Virginia legislature clearly has the power under the state constitution to levy the necessary taxes. Why does the Supreme Court treat it any differently than a municipality that has an unpaid judgment against it and the power to levy the taxes to pay it?

Even though the Supreme Court was not forceful in dealing with the West Virginia legislature's failure to pay the debt, overriding the legislature there would have been easier than in the typical case against a governmental defendant in which implementation requires an appropriation of funds or other legislative authorization. First, there was no substantial question about liability. The same was usually true in the municipal bond cases. In contrast, liability in cases arising under the equal protection clause or a regulatory statute often depends upon judicial construction of terse, vague language and disputed facts. Second, in *Virginia v. West Virginia,* the plaintiff was a state, thereby counter-balancing the political might of the defendant. In contrast, in the typical case, private persons are taking on "city hall" or the state. Third, in *Virginia v. West Virginia,* nine justices could have shared responsibility for the order to levy taxes and those who would have been adversely affected by the order lived far away. In contrast, in the typical case, the district court judge acts alone and often knows and lives among the defendant officials and citizens who would be affected by the order. Finally, there was no immunity problem in *Virginia v. West Virginia.*

### *Note on How Immunity Complicates Enforcement*

Resistance by governmental defendants is also complicated by the immunity of some governments to suit. Sovereign immunity bars suits against a state in its own courts, or suits against the federal government in a federal or a state court. The eleventh amendment has been read to bar suits by private persons against states in federal courts. Hans v. Louisiana, 134 U.S. 1, 10 S.Ct. 504, 33 L.Ed. 842 (1890). See generally Vicki C. Jackson, The Supreme Court, The Eleventh Amendment, and State Sovereign Immunity, 98 Yale L.J. 1 (1988).

Given sovereign immunity, how is it that governmental actions can get challenged in court? For starters, the eleventh amendment does not bar suits brought by the United States or other states, which explains *Virginia v. West Virginia,* for example. Second, local governments are not considered sovereigns under the eleventh amendment and so are amenable to suit in federal court, which explains *Brown v. Board of Education,* for example. See Lincoln County v. Luning, 133 U.S. 529, 10 S.Ct. 363, 33 L.Ed. 766 (1890). However, the courts of some states treat local governments as sovereigns. Third, Congress has the power to abrogate the states' eleventh amendment immunity. Fitzpatrick v. Bitzer, 427 U.S. 445, 96 S.Ct. 2666, 49 L.Ed.2d 614 (1976). Fourth, sovereigns can waive their immunity, although statutes that allegedly waive immunity are strictly construed. See, e.g., United States v. Nordic Village, Inc., 503 U.S. 30, 34, 112 S.Ct. 1011, 1014, 117 L.Ed.2d 181, 187–88 (1992). Governments are more likely to consent to suit over contracts, accidents, or specified types of administrative actions than over broader policy choices.

Fifth, and finally, the plaintiff can sometimes dispense with suing an immune government by suing governmental officials instead. Officials themselves often have some sort of immunity against suits in damages on the theory that the prospect of personal financial liability for official acts would dissuade them from taking office, or, once in office, acting decisively. (Official immunity from damages is discussed in chapter 6). But, official immunity generally does not stop suits for injunctive relief. In the landmark case of Ex parte Young 209 U.S. 123, 28 S.Ct. 441, 52 L.Ed. 714 (1908), the Court allowed a private plaintiff to seek an injunction against the enforcement of an allegedly unconstitutional state statute. Although the suit challenged a state statute, the Court reasoned that the suit was not against the state because an official enforcing an unconstitutional statute acts *ultra vires*. See Joint Anti–Fascist Refugee Committee v. McGrath, 341 U.S. 123, 71 S.Ct 624, 95 L.Ed. 817 (1951)(applying *Ex Parte Young's* reasoning in a suit against a federal official).

The key question under *Ex parte Young* is whether the relief sought is against the state and so barred by the eleventh amendment even though the state is not the defendant. In Edelman v. Jordan, 415 U.S. 651, 94 S.Ct. 1347, 39 L.Ed.2d 662 (1974) and Quern v. Jordan, 440 U.S. 332, 99 S.Ct. 1139, 59 L.Ed.2d 358 (1979) the Court decided that prospective relief, such as an injunction concerning future behavior, is permitted, while retrospective relief, such as an injunction that effectively awards compensation for past wrongdoing, is not because the money would come from the state treasury. Nonetheless, subsequent cases have allowed prospective relief that imposes large costs on the state. See Milliken v. Bradley, 433 U.S. 267, 97 S.Ct. 2749, 53 L.Ed.2d 745 (1977)(affirming injunction requiring state officers to provide remedial education as part of reparative injunctive relief in school segregation case). Hutto v. Finney, 437 U.S. 678, 98 S.Ct. 2565, 57 L.Ed.2d 522 (1978) affirmed attorney's fees awards against state officers as "ancillary" to the prospective relief ordered. So, if a sewage plant is run by a state agency rather than a local government and state law commands its officials to discharge pollution into the river but a federal regulation prohibits the same conduct, a federal court could entertain a suit by Country Lodge to enjoin those officials and would hold that the state law gives them no authority to pollute. In contrast, the court would not entertain an action by Country Lodge for damages even if captioned as against the officials because, as a practical matter, the money to pay the judgment would come from the state treasury.

Although the rule is that prospective relief against state officials is permitted, that rule has its limits. In Kelley v. Metropolitan County Board of Education, 836 F.2d 986 (6th Cir.1987), cert. denied, 487 U.S. 1206, 108 S.Ct. 2848, 101 L.Ed.2d 885 (1988), private plaintiffs got an injunction against the school board to remedy school segregation. Twenty-six years later, the school board filed a third-party complaint against the state and various state officials alleging that the state had participated in the initial wrong-doing and seeking an injunction requiring the state to bear a share of the cost of implementing the remedy. The court of appeals ordered the complaint against the state defendants dismissed on the basis, inter alia, that its purpose was to get state funds rather than put plaintiffs in their rightful position. The court distinguished *Milliken II* on the basis that state officials there were brought into the case at the outset and by the plaintiffs.

This thumbnail sketch of black letter immunity law (which is a core topic in the federal courts course) makes it evident that immunity law influences remedies. Immunity often makes it harder to attack government action through damages than through injunctive relief. Moreover, immunity can complicate successful injunctive relief against state action. Suppose that compliance with the injunction would cost money, say, to repair the state run sewage treatment plant. If the state officials have a repair fund appropriated by the state legislature, then the federal court may make the state officials use those state funds to do the necessary repairs. But, suppose the legislature has not appropriated any money that could be used for repair of the sewage treatment plant and refuses to do so. In that context, being able to seize state assets would be useful, but the state is immune. *Newman v. Alabama* (reproduced in chapter 2) illustrates the quandry. In that case, as in many others, the state did not bother to get itself dismissed as a party defendant. After all, the suit was also against state officials who can be sued for injunctive relief. But, when the judge later began to talk of seizing state assets, the state was allowed to get itself belatedly dismissed. Alabama v. Pugh, 438 U.S. 781, 782, 98 S.Ct. 3057, 3058, 57 L.Ed.2d 1114, 1115–16 (1978) (in a suit against state officials and the state, the state "has an interest in being dismissed from th[e] action in order to eliminate the danger of being held in contempt should it fail to comply with the mandatory injunction.").

*This then is the ultimate problem: putting plaintiff in the rightful position requires action from defendant officials that lack power to take under state law and the legislature refuses to authorize the action.* A court could conceivably react in a number of quite different ways.

1. *The court could postpone responding to the violation of its injunction in the hope that the legislature will grant the authority, the parties will settle, or Congress will act.* This was the Supreme Court's tactic in *Virginia v. West Virginia*, and it worked. But, when patience seems unlikely to pay off, a judge who delays action may well feel that the court is failing the plaintiff.

2. *The court could hold the defendant officials in contempt of court.* But, if the state law that denies the officials power to act is valid and binding, they can successfully argue that obedience is impossible. In New York State Ass'n for Retarded Children, Inc. v. Carey, 631 F.2d 162 (2d Cir.1980), implementation of an injunction by the governor of New York required funds that the legislature refused to appropriate despite his requests. The district court held the governor in contempt but the court of appeals reversed on the basis that compliance was impossible without violating provisions of the state constitution that prohibit spending public funds except pursuant to a valid appropriation. In another

case, state officials were held in contempt because they had helped to create the impossibility by urging the state legislature to deny them the necessary funds. Halderman v. Pennhurst State School & Hospital, 533 F.Supp. 631 (E.D.Pa.1981), aff'd, 673 F.2d 628 (3d Cir.1982), cert. denied, 465 U.S. 1038, 104 S.Ct. 1315, 79 L.Ed.2d 712 (1984).

3. *The court could strike down whatever state law denies defendant officials the necessary authority.* That is easy if the state law is invalid quite apart from the injunction whose implementation it frustrates, as when the state law is unconstitutional or conflicts with a federal statute. For example, a state law that ordered officials to put toxic chemicals in the river, although a federal statute prohibited this, would be invalid even if no federal court had enjoined their discharge. The state statute would also be invalid if its purpose was to countermand a federal court injunction. For example, North Carolina State Board of Education v. Swann, 402 U.S. 43, 45, 91 S.Ct. 1284, 1285–86, 28 L.Ed.2d 586, 589 (1971), invalidated a state statute that prohibited busing of school children in order to frustrate school desegregation injunctions. However, in the more typical case, the state statute is neither invalid apart from the injunction nor designed to frustrate it. When the state legislature has failed to appropriate funds needed to fix the sewage discharge plant, the state law that frustrates compliance with the injunction would be the provision typically found in state constitution that prohibits spending state funds except when the legislature has appropriated them. Or in part (b) of the *Country Lodge* problem at page 331, the state law frustrating compliance would be state constitutional or statutory provisions that limit to varying degrees the authority of local governments to promulgate regulations. Missouri v. Jenkins (*Jenkins II*), 495 U.S. 33, 110 S.Ct. 1651, 109 L.Ed.2d 31 (1990)(reproduced infra at p. 343), is one of the rare examples of a case that puts aside state law of general applicability because it frustrates implementation of a federal court injunction.

4. *The court could order state officials to disregard state law.* Griffin v. School Board, 377 U.S. 218, 233, 84 S.Ct. 1226, 1234, 12 L.Ed.2d 256, 266 (1964), said that a district court could order local officials to use the "power that is theirs" under state law to raise and spend money. The hard question arises when the power is not theirs. Federal cases have sometimes ordered state officials to disregard state law where doing so would not jeopardize the purposes of the state law. For example, in McCarthy v. Briscoe, 429 U.S. 1317, 97 S.Ct. 10, 50 L.Ed.2d 49 (1976)(see supra at p. 125), after striking down as unconstitutional a state statute that would have kept plaintiff off the ballot, the court required state officials to put a candidate on the ballot, although plaintiff did not have a nominating petition required by a still valid state statute. The Court reasoned that the purpose of the petition requirement was served where the candidate was well known.

Federal cases have also collected attorney's fees from states even though the legislature has appropriated no funds for this purpose. Gates v. Collier, 616 F.2d 1268 (5th Cir.1980), dealt with a state's refusal to appropriate funds to pay for an award of attorney fees under an attorney fees statute. "[W]here a state expresses its unwillingness to comply with a valid judgment of a federal district court, the court may use any of the weapons generally at its disposal to ensure compliance. * * * If statutory authority is needed for the court's actions, it may be found in Fed.R.Civ.P. 70." 616 F.2d at 1271. Rule 70, reproduced in the Appendix, infra at p. 889, allows the seizure of the assets of a recalcitrant judgment debtor. *Gates* is impressive because it countermands state law. But, it would be a more useful precedent for plaintiffs if it had not involved a statute that had already stripped the state of its eleventh amendment protection and dealt with something other than attorney's fees. Fees, unlike the much larger sums usually needed to comply with injunctions, do not impact the state's budget choices in a major way. Moreover, fees are often considered a part of court costs, from which the eleventh amendment does not protect states. Hutto v. Finney, 437 U.S. 678, 695–96 nn. 24–26, 98 S.Ct. 2565, 2576 nn. 24–26, 57 L.Ed.2d 522, 537–38 nn. 24–26 (1978). Accord, Hook v. Arizona Department of Corrections, 907 F.Supp. 1326 (D.Ariz.)(ordering payment of special master's fees despite state legislation purporting to preclude payment without specific appropriation), affirmed, 73 F.3d 369 (9th Cir.1995).

Only a few cases have faced the question of whether a federal court may make state officials spend money despite the lack of appropriations. The most typical reaction is to avoid giving an answer. In Welsch v. Likins, 550 F.2d 1122 (8th Cir.1977), the district court had found that unconstitutional conditions existed at a state institution for the mentally retarded and entered an injunction requiring state officials to upgrade the facility. When the state legislature failed to provide necessary funds, the district court enjoined the state commissioner of finance from complying with provisions of the state constitution forbidding expenditure of state funds without an appropriation by the state legislature. The court of appeals vacated the order in the hope that the state legislature would do better next time:

> We do not know why the Legislature that met in 1975 failed to respond more positively to the 1974 requirements of the district court. It is possible that the then Governor and the Legislature did not fully appreciate the force of those requirements; or the Governor and the Legislature may have thought that there was a better way to reach the objectives that the district court thought must be achieved.
>
> In any event, we desire to make it clear to the present Governor and the current Legislature that the [orders to improve the facility] that we uphold today are positive, constitutional requirements, and cannot be ignored. We will not presume that they will be ignored. On the contrary, we think that experience has shown that when governors and state legislatures see clearly what their constitutional duty is with respect to state institutions and realize that the duty

> must be discharged, they are willing to take necessary steps, including the appropriation of necessary funds.

Id. at 1132. So, as in *Virginia v. West Virginia,* the court presumes that the legislature will provide the money now that a high court has made clear that lack of appropriation does not justify the continuance of the violation. See also Robinson v. Cahill, 69 N.J. 449, 355 A.2d 129 (1976) and Abbott v. Burke, 100 N.J. 269, 495 A.2d 376 (1985), both leaving the remedy up to the legislature in the first instance. Is there any tactical advantage in avoiding the question? The court explained its reluctance to tackle the question as follows: "we are dealing with the right of a sovereign state to manage and control its own financial affairs. * * * [N]eedless direct confrontations between a federal court and a state should be avoided, particularly in a field as delicate as the one here involved." Id. at 1131–32. See also Wyatt v. Aderholt, 503 F.2d 1305, 1318 (5th Cir.1974)("The serious constitutional questions presented by federal judicial action ordering the sale of state lands, or altering the state budget * * * should not be adjudicated unnecessarily and prematurely.")

The next principal case, *Jenkins II,* speaks to the propriety of directly coercing state officials to spend unappropriated funds after many attempts to solve the problem through ordinary political channels.

5. *The court could use indirect means to pressure the legislature to grant the necessary authority.* The court of appeals in *Welsch v. Likins* also displayed concern for plaintiffs' rightful position: "The obligation of the defendants to eliminate existing unconstitutionalities does not depend upon what the Legislature may do, or upon what the Governor may do * * *. [I]f Minnesota is going to operate institutions like Cambridge, their operation is going to have to be consistent with the Constitution of the United States." 550 F.2d at 1132.

The court went on to try to reconcile its concern for federalism and plaintiffs' rights by suggesting that the district court could order the closing of the state facilities for the mentally retarded unless the legislature provided the necessary funds. The result in *Welsch v. Likins* can be explained entirely by the rightful position concept: plaintiffs have a constitutional right against being held in a poor facility, but no constitutional right to being kept in a good facility. Yet, in a broader sense, the court is not out to close down state facilities for the mentally retarded. Rather it is dealing with legislative resistance indirectly rather than directly. Instead of affirmatively ordering the state to spend money that the legislature will not appropriate, the court is threatening to issue an order to prevent the state from doing something that it wants to—provide facilities for the mentally retarded. This judicial tactic is sometimes called a "negative order." The negative order circumvents the federalism problem because it leaves "the question of the expenditure of state funds in the hands of citizens of the state, not in the hands of federal judges." New York Ass'n for Retarded Children, Inc. v. Carey, 631 F.2d 162, 165 (2d Cir.1980). The negative order cases, like the personal service contract cases, do not require performance but do enjoin the defendant from performing except to put plaintiffs in their rightful position (see supra at p. 124).

The negative order is like coercive civil contempt in its reliance on coercion. However, the negative order tactic differs in some crucial respects. A finding of contempt is not a prerequisite. The basis for the negative order, as with any other injunction, must be to put the plaintiff in the rightful position rather than, as with criminal or coercive civil contempt, to seek to punish noncompliance. In Country Lodge v. Miller, could the court coerce the legislature to authorize the regulations by enjoining it from passing any other legislation until it provides the necessary authority? By enjoining the issuance of permits to construct any new facility in Miller County that might use toxic chemicals? See Gautreaux v. Romney, 457 F.2d 124, 128 (7th Cir.1972).

To get the attention of defendant officials, negative orders must, if carried out, have severe adverse consequences on the public. For that same reason, judges are anxious to avoid having to carry them out. So they tend to threaten where the threat is enough to bring compliance—typically where the executive and a significant minority in the legislative support providing the necessary authority. See, e.g., Robinson v. Cahill, 69 N.J. 449, 355 A.2d 129 (1976)(court enjoins schools from opening in fall until state legislature provides funds to equalize educational opportunity where governor and a bit less than half of the state legislators favor enacting a state income tax to finance this program; after the threat the legislation is enacted). The negative order makes it easier for the swing votes to change by refocusing attention from the unpopular affirmative action to the still more unpopular consequences of the negative order.

## MISSOURI v. JENKINS (*JENKINS II*)

Supreme Court of the United States, 1990.
495 U.S. 33, 110 S.Ct. 1651, 109 L.Ed.2d 31.

[This opinion deals with questions concerning how to finance the implementation of the school desegregation injunction described in *Jenkins III*, reproduced in chapter 2. The injunction made the Kansas City Missouri School District (KCMSD) and the state jointly and severally liable for the cost of the injunction's implementation. State law limits the power of the KCMSD and other school boards to tax and borrow and gives voters a role in decisions to increase property tax rates above certain levels and to borrow. Voters had rejected all of the KCMSD's many proposals to increase taxes and sell bonds since 1969. Faced with these limits on the KCMSD's ability to raise funds, the district court itself increased the property tax rate and imposed a surcharge on the state income tax to fund implementation of the decree. The court of appeals affirmed the increase in the property tax rate for the previous year, but held that in the future the district court should not itself levy the tax, but rather should have set the KCMSD free from the state law limits on its ability to raise property tax rates. The court of appeals set aside the income tax, pointing out that the KCMSD had no power to tax income.]

JUSTICE WHITE delivered the opinion of the Court. * * *

The State's petition [for certiorari] argued that the remedies imposed by the District Court were excessive in scope and that the property tax increase violated Article III, the Tenth Amendment, principles of federal/state comity. We granted the State's petition, limited to the question of the property tax increase. * * *

III * * *

The State urges us to hold that the tax increase violated Article III, the Tenth Amendment, and principles of federal/state comity. We find it unnecessary to reach the difficult constitutional issues, for we agree with the State that the tax increase contravened the principles of comity that must govern the exercise of the District Court's equitable discretion in this area.

It is accepted by all the parties, as it was by the courts below, that the imposition of a tax increase by a federal court was an extraordinary event. In assuming for itself the fundamental and delicate power of taxation the District Court not only intruded on local authority but circumvented it altogether. Before taking such a drastic step the District Court was obliged to assure itself that no permissible alternative would have accomplished the required task. We have emphasized that although the "remedial powers of an equity court must be adequate to the task, * * * they are not unlimited," and one of the most important considerations governing the exercise of equitable power is a proper respect for the integrity and function of local government institutions. Especially is this true where, as here, those institutions are ready, willing, and—but for the operation of state law curtailing their powers—able to remedy the deprivation of constitutional rights themselves.

The District Court believed that it had no alternative to imposing a tax increase. But there was an alternative, the very one outlined by the Court of Appeals: it could have authorized or required KCMSD to levy property taxes at a rate adequate to fund the desegregation remedy and could have enjoined the operation of state laws that would have prevented KCMSD from exercising this power. The difference between the two approaches is far more than a matter of form. Authorizing and directing local government institutions to devise and implement remedies not only protects the function of those institutions but, to the extent possible, also places the responsibility for solutions to the problems of segregation upon those who have themselves created the problems.

As Brown v. Board of Education, 349 U.S. 294, 299, 75 S.Ct. 753, 755, 99 L.Ed. 1083 (1955), observed, local authorities have the "primary responsibility for elucidating, assessing, and solving" the problems of desegregation. This is true as well of the problems of financing desegregation, for no matter has been more consistently placed upon the shoulders of local government than that of financing public schools. * * *

The District Court therefore abused its discretion in imposing the tax itself. * * *

IV

We stand on different ground when we review the modifications to the District Court's order made by the Court of Appeals. * * *

The State argues that the funding ordered by the District Court violates principles of equity and comity because the remedial order itself was excessive. As the State puts it, "the only reason that the court below needed to consider an unprecedented tax increase was the equally unprecedented cost of its remedial programs." We think this argument aims at the scope of the remedy rather than the manner in which the remedy is to be funded and thus falls outside our limited grant of certiorari in this case. * * * We accept, without approving or disapproving, the Court of Appeals' conclusion that the District Court's remedy was proper.

The State has argued here that the District Court, having found the State and KCMSD jointly and severally liable, should have allowed any monetary obligations that KCMSD could not meet to fall on the State rather than interfere with state law to permit KCMSD to meet them.[19] Under the circumstances of this case, we cannot say it was an abuse of discretion for the District Court to rule that KCMSD should be responsible for funding its share of the remedy. The State strenuously opposed efforts by respondents to make it responsible for the cost of implementing the order and had secured a reversal of the District Court's earlier decision placing on it all of the cost of substantial portions of the order. The District Court declined to require the State to pay for KCMSD's obligations because it believed that the Court of Appeals had ordered it to allocate the costs between the two governmental entities. Furthermore, if the District Court had chosen the route now suggested by the State, implementation of the remedial order might have been delayed if the State resisted efforts by KCMSD to obtain contribution.

* * * We turn to the constitutional issues. The modifications ordered by the Court of Appeals cannot be assailed as invalid under the Tenth Amendment. "The Tenth Amendment's reservation of nondelegated powers to the States is not implicated by a federal-court judgment enforcing the express prohibitions of unlawful state conduct enacted by the Fourteenth Amendment." "The Fourteenth Amendment ... was avowedly directed against the power of the States," and so permits a federal court to disestablish local government institutions that interfere with its commands.

**19.** This suggestion was also made by the judge dissenting below [Chief Judge Lay].

Finally, the State argues that an order to increase taxes cannot be sustained under the judicial power of Article III. Whatever the merits of this argument when applied to the District Court's own order increasing taxes, a point we have not reached, a court order directing a local government body to levy its own taxes is plainly a judicial act within the power of a federal court. We held as much in *Griffin v. Prince Edward County School Bd.*, [ 377 U.S. 218, 233, 84 S.Ct. 1226, 1234, 12 L.Ed.2d 256 (1964)], where we stated that a District Court, faced with a county's attempt to avoid desegregation of the public schools by refusing to operate those schools, could "require the county Supervisors to exercise the power that is theirs to levy taxes to raise funds adequate to reopen, operate, and maintain without racial discrimination a public school system * * *." *Griffin* followed a long and venerable line of cases in which this Court held that federal courts could issue the writ of mandamus to compel local governmental bodies to levy taxes adequate to satisfy their debt obligations.[20]

The State maintains, however, that even under these cases, the federal judicial power can go no further than to require local governments to levy taxes as *authorized under state law*. In other words, the State argues that federal courts cannot set aside state-imposed limitations on local taxing authority because to do so is to do more than to require the local government "to exercise the power *that is theirs*." We disagree. This argument was rejected as early as *Von Hoffman v. City of Quincy*[, 4 Wall. 535, 18 L.Ed. 403 (1867)]. There the holder of bonds issued by the City sought a writ of mandamus against the City requiring it to levy taxes sufficient to pay interest coupons then due. The City defended based on a state statute that limited its power of taxation, and the Circuit Court refused to mandamus the City. This Court reversed, observing that the statute relied on by the City was passed after the bonds were issued and holding that because the City had ample authority to levy taxes to pay its bonds when they were issued, the statute impaired the contractual entitlements of the bondholders, contrary to Art. I, § 10, cl. 1 of the Constitution, under which a State may not pass

**20.** The old cases recognized two exceptions to this rule, neither of which is relevant here. First, it was held that federal courts could not by writ of mandamus compel state officers to release funds in the state treasury sufficient to satisfy state bond obligations. The Court viewed this attempt to employ the writ of mandamus as a ruse to avoid the Eleventh Amendment's bar against exercising federal jurisdiction over the State. See Louisiana v. Jumel, 107 U.S. (17 Otto) 711, 720–721, 2 S.Ct. 128, 135–136, 27 L.Ed. 448 (1883). This holding has no application to this case, for the Eleventh Amendment does not bar federal courts from imposing on the States the costs of securing prospective compliance with a desegregation order. Milliken v. Bradley, 433 U.S. 267, 290, 97 S.Ct. 2749, 2762, 53 L.Ed.2d 745 (1977), and does not afford local school boards like KCMSD immunity from suit, Mt. Healthy City School Dist. Bd. of Education v. Doyle, 429 U.S. 274, 280–281, 97 S.Ct. 568, 572–573, 50 L.Ed.2d 471 (1977). Second, it was held that the writ of mandamus would not lie to compel the collection of taxes when there was no person against whom the writ could operate. This exception also has no application to this case, where there are state and local officials invested with authority to collect and disburse the property tax and where, as matters now stand, the District Court need only prevent those officials from applying state law that would interfere with the willing levy of property taxes by KCMSD.

any law impairing the obligation of contracts. The statutory limitation, therefore, could be disregarded and the City ordered to levy the necessary taxes to pay its bonds.

It is therefore clear that a local government with taxing authority may be ordered to levy taxes in excess of the limit set by state statute where there is reason based in the Constitution for not observing the statutory limitation. In *Von Hoffman*, the limitation was disregarded because of the Contract Clause. Here the KCMSD may be ordered to levy taxes despite the statutory limitations on its authority in order to compel the discharge of an obligation imposed on KCMSD by the Fourteenth Amendment. To hold otherwise would fail to take account of the obligations of local governments, under the Supremacy Clause, to fulfill the requirements that the Constitution imposes on them. However wide the discretion of local authorities in fashioning desegregation remedies may be, "if a state-imposed limitation on a school authority's discretion operates to inhibit or obstruct the operation of a unitary school system or impede the disestablishing of a dual school system, it must fall; state policy must give way when it operates to hinder vindication of federal constitutional guarantees." North Carolina State Bd. of Education v. Swann, 402 U.S. 43, 45, 91 S.Ct. 1284, 1286, 28 L.Ed.2d 586 (1971). Even though a particular remedy may not be required in every case to vindicate constitutional guarantees, where (as here) it has been found that a particular remedy is required, the State cannot hinder the process by preventing a local government from implementing that remedy.[21] * * *

JUSTICE KENNEDY, with whom THE CHIEF JUSTICE, JUSTICE O'CONNOR, and JUSTICE SCALIA join, concurring in part and concurring in the judgment.

* * * Today's casual embrace of taxation imposed by the unelected, life-tenured federal judiciary disregards fundamental precepts for the democratic control of public institutions. * * *

I * * *

The case before us represents the first in which a lower federal court has in fact upheld taxation to fund a remedial decree. * * *

Any purported distinction between direct imposition of a tax by the federal court and an order commanding the school district to impose the tax is but a convenient formalism where the court's action is predicated on elimination of state law limitations on the school district's taxing

**21.** United States v. County of Macon, 99 U.S. (9 Otto) 582, 25 L.Ed. 331 (1879), held that mandamus would not lie to force a local government to levy taxes in excess of the limits contained in a statute in effect at the time the City incurred its bonded indebtedness, for the explicit limitation in the taxing power became part of the contract, the bondholders had notice of the limitation and were deemed to have consented to it, and hence no contractual remedy was unconstitutionally impaired by observing the statute. *County of Macon* has little relevance to the present case, for KCMSD's obligation to fund the desegregation remedy arises from its operation of a segregated school system in violation of the Constitution, not from a contract between KCMSD and respondents.

authority. As the Court describes it, the local KCMSD possesses plenary taxing powers, which allow it to impose any tax it chooses if not "hindered" by the Missouri Constitution and state statutes. This puts the conclusion before the premise. Local government bodies in Missouri, as elsewhere, must derive their power from a sovereign, and that sovereign is the State of Missouri. See Mo. Const., Art. X, § 1 (political subdivisions may exercise only "that power granted to them" by Missouri General Assembly). Under Missouri law, the KCMSD has power to impose a limited property tax levy up to $1.25 per $100 of assessed value. The power to exact a higher rate of property tax remains with the people. * * *

Whatever taxing power the KCMSD may exercise outside the boundaries of state law would derive from the federal court. The Court never confronts the judicial authority to issue an order for this purpose. Absent a change in state law, the tax is imposed by federal authority under a federal decree. The question is whether a district court possesses a power to tax under federal law, either directly or through delegation to the KCMSD.

II

Article III of the Constitution states that "the judicial Power of the United States, shall be vested in one supreme Court, and in such inferior Courts as the Congress may from time to time ordain and establish." The description of the judicial power nowhere includes the word "tax" or anything that resembles it. This reflects the Framers' understanding that taxation was not a proper area for judicial involvement. "The judiciary * * * has no influence over either the sword or the purse, no direction either of the strength or of the wealth of the society, and can take no active resolution whatever." The Federalist No. 78, p. 523 (J. Cooke ed.1961)(A. Hamilton).

Our cases throughout the years leave no doubt that taxation is not a judicial function. Last Term we rejected the invitation to cure an unconstitutional tax scheme by broadening the class of those taxed. We said that such a remedy "could be construed as the direct imposition of a state tax, a remedy beyond the power of a federal court." * * *

The nature of the District Court's order here reveals that it is not a proper exercise of the judicial power. The exercise of judicial power involves adjudication of controversies and imposition of burdens on those who are parties before the Court. The order at issue here is not of this character. It binds the broad class of all KCMSD taxpayers. It has the purpose and direct effect of extracting money from persons who have had no presence or representation in the suit. For this reason, the District Court's direct order imposing a tax was more than an abuse of discretion, for any attempt to collect the taxes from the citizens would have been a blatant denial of due process. * * *

The taxes were imposed by a District Court that was not "representative" in any sense, and the individual citizens of the KCMSD whose property (they later learned) was at stake were neither served with process nor heard in court. The method of taxation endorsed by today's dicta suffers the same flaw, for a district court order that overrides the citizens' state law protection against taxation without referendum approval can in no sense provide representational due process. * * *

A judicial taxation order is but an attempt to exercise a power that always has been thought legislative in nature. * * * Article I, § 1 states that "*all* legislative Powers herein granted shall be vested in a Congress of the United States, which shall consist of a Senate and House of Representatives" (emphasis added). * * *

The confinement of taxation to the legislative branches, both in our Federal and State Governments, was not random. It reflected our ideal that the power of taxation must be under the control of those who are taxed. This truth animated all our colonial and revolutionary history. * * *

* * * [I]mposition of taxes by an authority so insulated from public communication or control can lead to deep feelings of frustration, powerlessness, and anger on the part of taxpaying citizens.

The operation of tax systems is among the most difficult aspects of public administration. It is not a function the judiciary as an institution is designed to exercise. Unlike legislative bodies, which may hold hearings on how best to raise revenues, all subject to the views of constituents to whom the legislature is accountable, the judiciary must grope ahead with only the assistance of the parties, or perhaps random amici curiae. Those hearings would be without principled direction, for there exists no body of juridical axioms by which to guide or review them. On this questionable basis, the Court today would give authority for decisions that affect the life plans of local citizens, the revenue available for competing public needs, and the health of the local economy.

Day-to-day administration of the tax must be accomplished by judicial trial and error, requisitioning the staff of the existing tax authority, or the hiring of a staff under the direction of the judge. The District Court orders in this case suggest the pitfalls of the first course. Forcing citizens to make financial decisions in fear of the fledgling judicial tax collector's next misstep must detract from the dignity and independence of the federal courts.

The function of hiring and supervising a staff for what is essentially a political function has other complications. As part of its remedial order, for example, the District Court ordered the hiring of a "public information specialist," at a cost of $30,000. The purpose of the position was to "solicit community support and involvement" in the District Court's desegregation plan. This type of order raises a substantial question whether a district court may extract taxes from citizens who have no right of representation and then use the funds for expression with which the citizens may disagree.

The Court relies on dicta from Griffin v. School Bd. of Prince Edward County, 377 U.S. 218, 84 S.Ct. 1226, 12 L.Ed.2d 256 (1964) to support its statements on judicial taxation. In *Griffin*, the Court faced an unrepentant and recalcitrant school board that attempted to provide financial support for white schools while refusing to operate schools for black schoolchildren.We stated that the district court could "require the Supervisors to exercise the power *that is theirs* to levy taxes to raise funds adequate to reopen, operate, and maintain without racial discrimination to public school system," for white schools while refusing to operate schools for black schoolchildren. There is no occasion in this case to discuss the full implications of *Griffin's* observation, for it has no application here. *Griffin* endorsed the power of a federal court to order the local authority to exercise *existing* authority to tax.

This case does not involve an order to a local government with plenary taxing power to impose a tax, or an order directed at one whose taxing power has been limited by a state law enacted in order to thwart a federal court order. An order of this type would find support in the *Griffin* dicta, and present a closer question than the one before us. Yet that order might implicate as well the "perversion of the normal legislative process" that we have found troubling in other contexts. See Spallone v. United States, 493 U.S. 265, 110 S.Ct. 625, 107 L.Ed.2d 644 (1990) [reproduced infra at page 361]. A legislative vote taken under judicial compulsion blurs lines of accountability by making it appear that a decision was reached by elected representatives when the reality is otherwise. For this reason, it is difficult to see the difference between an order to tax and direct judicial imposition of a tax.

* * * [T]here was no state authority in this case for the KCMSD to exercise. In this situation, there could be no authority for a judicial order touching on taxation. See United States v. County of Macon, 99 U.S. 582, 591, 25 L.Ed. 331 (1879)(where the statute empowering the corporation to issue bonds contains a limit on the taxing power, federal court has no power of mandamus to compel a levy in excess of that power; "We have no power by mandamus to compel a municipal corporation to levy a tax which the law does not authorize. We cannot create new rights or confer new powers. All we can do is to bring existing powers into operation").

The Court cites a single case, Von Hoffman v. City of Quincy, 4 Wall 535, 18 L.Ed. 403 (1867), for the proposition that a federal court may set aside state taxation limits that interfere with the remedy sought by the district court. But the Court does not heed *Von Hoffman's* holding. There a municipality had authorized a tax levy in support of a specific bond obligation, but later limited the taxation authority in a way that impaired the bond obligation. The Court held the subsequent limitation itself unconstitutional, a violation of the Contracts Clause. Once the limitation was held invalid, the original specific grant of authority remained. There is no allegation here, nor could there be, that the neutral tax limitations imposed by the people of Missouri are unconstitutional. The majority appears to concede that the Missouri tax law does not violate a specific provision of the Constitution, stating instead that state laws may be disregarded on the basis of a vague "reason based in the Constitution." But this broad suggestion does not follow from the holding in *Von Hoffman*.* * *

III * * *

I am required in light of our limited grant of certiorari to assume that the remedy chosen by the District Court was a permissible exercise of its remedial discretion. But it is misleading to suggest that a failure to fund this particular remedy would leave constitutional rights without a remedy. * * * [The opinion argues that the remedy is broader than necessary to cure the violation in terms echoed and adopted five years later in *Jenkins III*.]

The prudence we have required in other areas touching on federal court intrusion in local government, see, e.g., Spallone v. United States, 493 U.S. 265, 110 S.Ct. 625, 107 L.Ed.2d 644 (1990), is missing here. Even on the assumption that a federal court might order taxation in an extreme case, the unique nature of the taxing power would demand that this remedy be used as a last resort. In my view, a taxation order should not even be considered, and this Court need never have addressed the question, unless there has been a finding that without the particular remedy at issue the constitutional violation will go unremedied. * * * There is no showing in this record that, faced with the revenue shortfall, the District Court gave due consideration to the possibility that another remedy among the "wide range of possibilities" would have addressed the constitutional violations without giving rise to a funding crisis. * * *

IV * * *

In pursuing the demand of justice for racial equality, I fear that the Court today loses sight of other basic political liberties guaranteed by our constitutional system, liberties that can coexist with a proper exercise of judicial remedial powers adequate to correct constitutional violations.

### *Notes*

1. As the majority notes, Chief Judge Lay suggested below that the district court should make the state responsible for any shortfall in the funds that could have been provided by the KCMSD. The state could then decide whether to provide the funds itself or to authorize KCMSD to levy higher taxes. Giving the state this option accords with states' power to allocate funds and responsibilities among and between themselves and their subdivisions. Why did the courts take that power away from Missouri? If the district court had put the final responsibility on the state, but the legislature did not provide the necessary funds, how could the district court get the money from the state? Does footnote 20 in the majority opinion mean that the district court could order the state treasurer to disregard prohibitions in the State Constitution on releasing state funds without legislative authorization?

2. Do federal judges have the power under article III of the Constitution to impose taxes to raise money needed to remedy violations of the equal protection clause? This fundamental question puts in conflict the ideal of equal protection and the ideal of "no taxation without representation." The Civil War was fought for one; the Revolutionary War for the other. Does the majority answer this question? The majority distinguishes a judicially imposed tax from instructing the school board to disregard state law limits on its taxing power. Is there substance in this distinction? Is such an instruction more closely analogous to *Von Hoffman*, upon which the majority relies, or *Macon County*, upon which the concurring opinion relies? Does the concurring opinion explain why it is any worse to let the KCMSD disregard state law tax limits than to order an otherwise unwilling school board to tax up to the state law tax limits? See generally D. Bruce LaPierre, Enforcement of Judgments Against State and Local Governments: Judicial Control Over the Power to Tax, 61 Geo.Wash.L.Rev. 299 (1993).

One way out of the possible limits on article III power is for Congress to use its article I powers. To ensure that lack of funds will not frustrate suits brought by the United States against municipalities under the Clean Water Act, which can require them to undertake very expensive projects, the act provides that

> Whenever a municipality is a party to a civil action brought by the United States under this section, the State in which such municipality is located shall be joined as a party. Such a State shall be liable for payment of any judgment, entered against the municipality in such action to the extent that the laws of that State prevent the municipality from raising revenues needed to comply with such judgment.

33 U.S.C. § 1319(e).

3. The concurring opinion argues that the district court should side step the need to confront the limits on KCMSD's taxing power by opting for a less expensive remedy. It is hard to understand why the four votes needed to grant certiorari on the appropriateness of the remedy were not available before *Jenkins III*. Acknowledging that certiorari was denied on this point, the concurring opinion argues that nonetheless comity should have been used to select a less expensive remedy.

4. Would the issue come out differently if presented to today's Supreme Court? Would it make a difference if the defendant was recalcitrant and no less expensive remedy was available?

---

Assuming that the order against the state officials in *Jenkins* passes eleventh amendment muster, what should the district court judge do if there is no state appropriation authorizing the payment of the necessary funds to the Kansas City school system and if such appropriation is necessary under state law? One approach might be to make the members of the state legislature parties to the suit and order them to pass the necessary statute. Consider this approach in light of the following case.

## UNITED STATES v. CITY OF YONKERS

United States Court of Appeals, Second Circuit, 1988.
856 F.2d 444, cert. denied in part, 489 U.S. 1065, 109 S.Ct. 1339, 103 L.Ed.2d 810 (1989) and rev'd in part, sub nom. Spallone v. United States, 493 U.S. 265, 110 S.Ct. 625, 107 L.Ed.2d 644 (1990).

JON O. NEWMAN, CIRCUIT JUDGE:

This appeal presents important issues concerning the enforcement of orders of a United States District Court requiring action by a municipality to remedy violations of the Constitution and statutes of the United States. The principal issues are whether members of the Yonkers City Council may be required to vote to implement remedies contained in a consent judgment agreed to by the City and approved by the City Council, and whether the City, in addition to the council members, may be subjected to the coercive sanctions of civil contempt when the agreed upon legislative action has not been taken. The issues arise on appeals by the City of Yonkers and four members of the Yonkers City Council from orders of the District Court for the Southern District of New York (Leonard B. Sand, Judge) adjudicating the City and the council members in civil contempt and imposing coercive sanctions. We conclude that under the circumstances of this case the recalcitrant council members may be required to vote to implement the consent judgment and that the City, in addition to the council members, may be adjudicated in contempt and subjected to coercive sanctions for failure to abide by the consent judgment and subsequent implementing orders of the District Court. We also conclude that the amount of the monetary sanctions imposed on the City, though properly substantial, should be somewhat reduced. We therefore affirm the order adjudicating the council members in contempt and affirm, as modified, the order adjudicating the City in contempt.

### BACKGROUND

1. The Underlying Lawsuit

The United States filed the underlying lawsuit on December 1, 1980, against the City of Yonkers * * *. The complaint [alleges] that the City * * * had "intentionally ... perpetuated and seriously aggravated residential racial segregation" in violation of the Constitution and Title VIII of the Civil Rights Act of 1968, 42 U.S.C. §§ 3601–3619 (1982) * * *.

The District Court found the City * * * liable * * *.

The Housing Remedy Order [entered on May 28, 1986] included provisions for the construction of 200 units of public housing and for the planning of additional units of subsidized housing. The City had previously agreed to provide acceptable sites for the 200 units of public housing as a condition of receiving its 1983 Community Development Block Grant from the United States Department of Housing and Urban Development (HUD). * * * The City was required to propose sites for

140 units within thirty days and sites for the remaining 60 units within ninety days.

[The Housing Remedy Order also required the City to present a plan for the subsidized housing by November 15, 1986]. * * *

2. Attempts to Implement the Housing Remedy Order

* * * [The City violated the Housing Remedy Order.] The United States and the NAACP [which had intervened] then moved for an adjudication of civil contempt and the imposition of coercive sanctions. Rather than proceed immediately to consideration of contempt sanctions, the District Court patiently endeavored to secure voluntary compliance. * * *

A consent decree was agreed to by the parties [on January 25, 1988], approved by the City Council on January 27, and entered as a consent judgment of the District Court on January 28 ("the Consent Judgment").

With respect to the 200 units of public housing, the Consent Judgment renewed the City's commitment to build the units and identified seven specific sites. * * *

[The Consent Judgment also set 800 units of subsidized housing as "an appropriate target in fulfilling its obligations" under the Housing Remedy Order, required the City to make good-faith efforts to achieve 600 of the units in annual installments of 200 units within each of the next three years. After citizens protested vehemently, the City promptly violated the Consent Decree. The City moved to modify the Consent Decree, offering to return the $30 million federal housing grant. That motion was denied and, on June 13, 1988 after prolonged consultation with the City and other parties, the District Court entered a Long Term Plan Order that specified the terms of the legislation that the City must adopt pursuant to the Consent Decree.]

On June 28 the City Council voted against a resolution "indicating [the Council's] commitment to the implementation of" the Housing Remedy Order, the Consent Judgment, and the Long Term Plan Order.

The following day the District Court directed the plaintiffs to submit an order requiring the City to take "specific implementing action" under a prescribed timetable, violation of which would subject the City to contempt sanctions. In response to the plaintiffs' proposed order setting forth such a timetable, the City argued that the defeat of the resolution on June 28 indicated that the City would not voluntarily adopt legislation contemplated by the Long Term Plan Order and suggested that the Court itself should enter an order adopting the necessary legislation. At a hearing on the proposed timetable on July 12, the District Court invited the parties' comments on the possible creation by the Court of an Affordable Housing Commission to exercise the City Council's functions concerning implementation of the housing remedy orders. The City opposed creation of the Commission because it would divest the Council of its "core legislative as well as executive functions."

3. The Prospect of Contempt * * *

[On July 26 the District Court issued an order that gave the City until August 1 to enact the required legislation called the Affordable Housing Ordinance. If that did not occur, the July 26 Order provided that] the City and the council members were to show cause at 10:00 a.m., August 2, why they should not be adjudged in contempt. If such cause was not shown, each council member failing to vote for such legislation would be fined $500 per day, and, if the legislation was not passed by August 10, such council member would be imprisoned on August 11. The contempt sanction against the City would be daily fines starting at $100 on August 2 and doubling in amount each day of continued noncompliance. The cumulative total of the fines against the City would exceed $10,000 by day 7, exceed $1 million by day 14, exceed $200 million by day 21, and exceed $26 billion by day 28. The order provided that a council member could be purged of contempt by voting in favor of the legislation or by enactment of the legislation. The City could be purged of contempt by enactment of the legislation. The order further provided that all fines would be paid into the Treasury of the United States and would not be refundable, that the Council would meet at least once a week to vote on the legislative package, and that any incarcerated council member would be released to attend such meetings. * * *

[On August 1, the City Council voted four to three not to comply with the July 26 Order.]

4. The Contempt Adjudications * * *

The Court held the City in contempt, imposed the coercive sanctions set forth in the July 26 order, and entered written findings of fact. * * *

[The District Court also held in contempt the four council members who had voted against compliance: Nicholas Longo, Edward Fagan, Peter Chema, and Henry Spallone.]

The District Court denied requests for stays by the City and the four council members. On August 9, after fines for seven days had become due, this Court stayed the contempt sanctions and ordered an expedited appeal. * * *

DISCUSSION

*A. The Council Members* * * *

2. Abuse of Discretion

* * * [T]he council members contend that the District Court exceeded its discretion in adjudicating them in contempt * * * [because] a less confrontational resolution of the matter could have been achieved had the District Court selected the alternatives of either appointing a commission to exercise the Council's housing and related powers or ordering the Affordable Housing Ordinance into effect.

These arguments blend two somewhat different propositions of law, but in the end, both are unavailing. In challenging the District Court's decision to require the Council to enact the Affordable Housing Ordinance, the contemnors are alleging an abuse of discretion in the Court's choice of remedies for the constitutional violations adjudicated in 1986. As the contemnors point out, a District Court, though endowed with broad discretion in fashioning remedies for constitutional violations, see Swann v. Charlotte–Mecklenburg Board of Education, 402 U.S. 1, 91 S.Ct. 1267, 28 L.Ed.2d 554 (1971), must exercise restraint in determining what actions ought to be required of state and local governmental officials. See Rizzo v. Goode, 423 U.S. 362, 380, 96 S.Ct. 598, 608, 46 L.Ed.2d 561 (1976). In challenging the District Court's decision to impose coercive contempt sanctions, the contemnors are alleging an abuse of discretion in the Court's method of enforcing the remedy that had been selected. Though there is no question that courts have authority to enforce their lawful orders through civil contempt, the contemnors properly point out that in selecting contempt sanctions, a court is obliged to use the " 'least possible power adequate to the end proposed.' "

In this case, however, there is a fundamental reason why the choice of implementing legislation as a remedy and the choice of coercive contempt sanctions to enforce compliance with that remedy cannot possibly be an abuse of the District Court's discretion. That reason is the blunt fact that the City agreed in the Consent Judgment to comply with the Housing Remedy Order by the adoption of necessary implementing legislation, specifically including tax abatements and zoning changes. By its approval of the Consent Judgment the City Council itself selected the remedy of implementing legislation and cannot complain that the District Court approved the agreement. Moreover, once committed by its own agreement to adopting implementing legislation, the Council cannot complain that its obligation is enforced by the coercive sanctions of civil contempt. Consent judgments are important devices for resolving difficult controversies. Their effectiveness depends on the ability of all concerned to rely on the enforcement of their terms. In the context of a consent judgment, use of civil contempt sanctions is the "least possible power *adequate* to the end proposed" because faithful performance of the agreement is precisely the end proposed.

To the extent that the council members are contending that the District Court exceeded its discretion in ordering them to adopt the precise terms of the Affordable Housing Ordinance, this argument also is unavailing. * * * The Court proceeded cautiously, according the City a full opportunity to draft the plan and ultimately accepting nearly everything that the City proposed. Similarly, with the specifics of the Affordable Housing Ordinance, the District Court afforded the City the opportunity to have its consultants draft the ordinance and accepted the draft they produced. By ordering passage of the Affordable Housing Ordinance, the District Court was carrying out the terms of the Consent Judgment under which the City agreed to adopt implementing legislation on tax abatements and zoning changes and doing so with details supplied by the City itself. The order of July 26 was well within the discretion of the District Court, as was its decision to enforce that order by civil contempt sanctions. * * *

4. Legislative Immunity

The major defense asserted by the council members is that they are entitled to legislative immunity and that such immunity prohibits a district court from compelling them to vote in favor of a particular ordinance. There is no doubt that state legislators enjoy immunity when engaged "in the sphere of legitimate legislative activity." * * *

Even if we assume for purposes of this appeal that city council members enjoy the same immunity available to state legislators, we would seriously doubt that such immunity insulates them from district court orders requiring them to comply with remedial decrees redressing constitutional violations. The Supreme Court has instructed a district court that, if necessary to secure compliance with a prior federal court remedial decree, it could order county legislators "to exercise the power that is theirs to levy taxes" to reopen the public schools of Prince Edward County, Virginia. Griffin v. County School Board, 377 U.S. 218, 233, 84 S.Ct. 1226, 1234, 12 L.Ed.2d 256 (1964). Though appellants minimize the force of this instruction by calling it dictum, since the need to issue such an order had not then arisen, it is especially forceful dictum when the Supreme Court specifically informs a district court what action it may take in the course of significant litigation. If it had become necessary to order the county legislators to levy taxes, there can be no doubt that the Supreme Court expected the district court to make sure that its order was enforced.

The Supreme Court has also upheld a district court's remedial order that required state and local officials to provide necessary public funds to implement a school desegregation plan. Milliken v. Bradley, 433 U.S. 267, 97 S.Ct. 2749, 53 L.Ed.2d 745 (1977) [*Milliken II*]. In *Milliken* the Court expressly rejected an immunity defense based on Eleventh Amendment sovereign immunity a claim at least as substantial as the immunity defense now asserted by the four council members. The Court pointed out that though a state enjoyed immunity from damage actions, its immunity did not insulate it from a district court judgment requiring prospective action to comply with constitutional requirements, even when compliance would have "a direct and substantial impact on the state treasury." * * *

On this appeal, however, we need not definitively decide whether as a general matter a district court may order city council members to vote in favor of a particular ordinance, even to implement remedies for constitutional violations. This appeal presents the more narrow issue whether such an order may be entered and enforced by contempt sanctions after a city has agreed to entry of a consent judgment committing itself to enact implementing ordinances and a city's legislative body has voted in favor of such a consent decree. On that narrow issue, we have no doubt that federal court authority must prevail. No litigant, least of all public officials sworn to uphold the Constitution of the United States, may be permitted to avoid compliance with solemn commitments they have made in a consent judgment entered by a federal district court to remedy constitutional violations. Without intending to cast doubt on a district court's authority to order legislative action in contested litigation concerning the appropriate choice of remedies for constitutional violations, we note that the Supreme Court has recently observed that consent judgments may contain enforceable obligations that might have been beyond the authority of a district court to enter in contested litigation. See Local No. 93, Int'l Ass'n of Firefighters v. City of Cleveland, 478 U.S. 501, 106 S.Ct. 3063, 92 L.Ed.2d 405 (1986).

Nor is there any merit in appellant Spallone's suggestion that he may not be required to implement the Consent Judgment because he voted against its approval as a member of the City Council. A federal court must be able to rely upon the assurances given by municipalities and their legislative bodies, without regard to the dissenting votes of individual local officials. Once the Yonkers City Council approved the terms of the Consent Judgment, the Council became obligated to carry out its commitments. If a member of the Council is unwilling to abide by such commitments, his option is to decline to serve on the body that is bound, not to act in defiant disregard of the commitments and the federal court judgment that memorializes them.

Whatever the scope of local legislators' immunity, it does not insulate them from compliance with a consent judgment to which their city has agreed and which has been approved by their legislative body.

5. First Amendment

The council members' assertion of a First Amendment defense to the July 26 order and its enforcement requires no extended discussion. Even if we acknowledge that the act of voting has sufficient expressive content to be accorded some First Amendment protection as symbolic speech, the public interest in obtaining compliance with federal court judgments that remedy constitutional violations unquestionably justifies whatever burden on expression has occurred. The council members remain free to express their views on all aspects of housing in Yonkers. But just as the First Amendment would not permit them to incite violation of federal law, it does not permit them to take action in violation of such law.

*B. The City*

To the extent that the City advances the same objections as the council members, particularly the contention that the District Court should have chosen to adopt the Affordable Housing Ordinance itself or to appoint a commission to exercise the City's housing functions, we need not repeat our reasons for rejecting those objections. [Some] contentions, however, require further discussion.

1. Defense of Impossibility

The claim most vigorously pressed by the City is the defense of impossibility. The City contends that enactment of the Affordable Housing Ordinance requires an affirmative vote of a majority of the City Council and that the City, as a corporate entity, is powerless to compel the council members to act. We recognize that civil contempt sanctions may not be imposed upon a person or entity unable to comply with a court's orders. Nevertheless, we conclude that the City's defense of impossibility is unavailing.

Preliminarily, we have some doubt whether the City has done everything it can, apart from securing the favorable votes of a Council majority, to obtain compliance with the orders of the District Court. The City has not requested the Governor of New York to use whatever authority he may have to remove local officials for misconduct, nor has the City requested the New York Emergency Financial Control Board for the City of Yonkers to take whatever action its broad authorizing statute permits it to take under the current circumstances, 1984 N.Y. Laws ch. 103.

More fundamentally, we agree with the position urged by the United States that the City cannot view itself as an entity separate from the City Council for purposes of complying with the Consent Judgment. The City bound itself to take necessary legislative action when it agreed to the Consent Judgment, which explicitly calls for implementing legislation. Having made that commitment, the City may properly be subjected to the coercive force of civil contempt sanctions until compliance with its commitment occurs. The suggestion that the administrative officials of the City are willing to comply but cannot take legislative action conjures up a scheme of separated powers that does not obtain in Yonkers. For purposes of taking official governmental action, the City of Yonkers is the City Council and vice versa. The Council sets municipal policy, it appoints and can replace the city manager, and it is the principal agency of governance for the City. There is not even a separately elected executive authority. The mayor is a council member elected to the Council in a citywide election; the other council members are elected from districts. Under the circumstances of this case, the Council's defiance of the Consent Judgment and the implementing orders of the District Court is the defiance of the City, and the City, along with the defiant council members, may be subject to civil contempt sanctions. As the Supreme Court has observed, "If a state agency refuses to adhere to a court order, a financial penalty may be the most effective means of insuring compliance." Hutto v. Finney, 437 U.S. 678, 691, 98 S.Ct. 2565, 2573, 57 L.Ed.2d 522 (1978). The same may be said of a city.

The City further contends that even if it can legally be held in civil contempt because of the violation of the July 26 order, it was an abuse of discretion to do so under the circumstances here presented, especially since the District Court had available the alternative of ordering the

Affordable Housing Ordinance into effect. We conclude, however, that the District Court neither erred as a matter of law nor exceeded its permissible discretion by using contempt sanctions to coerce the City to fulfill commitments that it had undertaken in the Consent Judgment or by determining that such sanctions were necessary to achieve enactment of the Ordinance. * * *

3. The Amount of the Monetary Sanctions

The City contends that the amount of the coercive fines imposed as a remedial sanction for civil contempt is excessive and a violation of the Due Process Clause of the Fifth Amendment and the Excessive Fines Clause of the Eighth Amendment. [The court concludes that neither the Excessive Fines Clause nor the Cruel and Unusual Punishment Clause of the Eighth Amendment apply to coercive contempt sanctions.[d]]

* * * In any event, the law of contempt itself exerts some outer limits on the normally "wide discretion" of a district court to fashion appropriate remedies to secure compliance with its lawful orders.

The fact that a coercive monetary sanction requires payment of a large daily fine does not necessarily render that sanction beyond the discretion of a district court. The Supreme Court has itself selected as an appropriate sanction a coercive fine of $2,800,000 (in 1947 dollars) to be imposed upon a union if it should fail to comply with a district court order within five days. United States v. United Mine Workers, 330 U.S. 258, 305, 67 S.Ct. 677, 702, 91 L.Ed. 884 (1947). * * *

The City of Yonkers has an annual budget of $337 million. The need for a substantial daily fine to coerce compliance is demonstrated by the City's announcement to the District Court of its willingness to pay $30 million to be relieved of its commitment to build the 200 units of public housing. Obviously, the City believes that there is a price it is willing to pay to avoid compliance with the orders of the District Court. The District Court was entitled to establish a schedule of fines that would secure compliance with its orders, and under the circumstances of this case that schedule would have to reach, without undue delay, a cumulative fine significantly above the price the City was willing to pay for noncompliance. * * * At some point, however, the doubling reaches unreasonable proportions. Under the current schedule the fine for day 25 is more than $1 billion; the fine for day 30 is more than $50 billion.

We believe that the doubling exceeds the bounds of the District Court's discretion when the level of each day's fine exceeds $1 million. The present schedule calls for a fine of more than $800,000 on day 14. We will therefore modify the contempt sanction against the City to provide that the fine shall be $1 million per day on day 15 and $1 million per day for every subsequent day of noncompliance.

CONCLUSION

* * * Unless a stay is granted by the Supreme Court or a Justice thereof, our mandate shall issue seven days from the date of this decision

**d.** But see *Austin v. United States* (reproduced in chapter 5).

and our prior stay of the contempt sanctions shall at that time be vacated. On the date our mandate issues, the fines against each of the four council members shall resume at the level of $500 per day and, if noncompliance continues, each shall be imprisoned, pursuant to paragraph 5 of the Order of July 26, two days after the date our mandate issues. * * *

## SPALLONE v. UNITED STATES

Supreme Court of the United States, 1990.
493 U.S. 265, 110 S.Ct. 625, 107 L.Ed.2d 644.

Chief Justice Rehnquist delivered the opinion of the Court.

* * * Both the city and the councilmembers [who were held in contempt] requested this Court to stay imposition of sanctions pending filing and disposition of petitions for certiorari. We granted a stay as to [the councilmembers (petitioners)], but denied the city's request. 487 U.S. 1251, 109 S.Ct. 14, 101 L.Ed.2d 964 (1988) [Justices Brennan and Marshall dissenting from the grant of the stay]. With the city's daily contempt sanction approaching $1 million per day, the city council finally enacted the Affordable Housing Ordinance on September 9, 1988, by a vote of 5 to 2, petitioners Spallone and Fagan voting no. Because the contempt orders raise important issues about the appropriate exercise of the federal judicial power against individual legislators, we granted certiorari [to the councilmembers but not the city], and now reverse.

II * * *

Petitioners contend that the District Court's orders violate their rights to freedom of speech under the First Amendment, and they also contend that they are entitled as legislators to absolute immunity for actions taken in discharge of their legislative responsibilities. We find it unnecessary to reach either of these questions, because we conclude that the portion of the District Court's order of July 26 imposing contempt sanctions against the petitioners if they failed to vote in favor of the court-proposed ordinance was an abuse of discretion under traditional equitable principles.

* * * [A]s the Court of Appeals recognized, "in selecting contempt sanctions, a court is obliged to use the 'least possible power adequate to the end proposed.' "

Given that the city had entered a consent judgment committing itself to enact legislation implementing the long-term plan, we certainly cannot say it was an abuse of discretion for the District Court to have chosen contempt sanctions against the city, as opposed to petitioners, as a means of ensuring compliance. The city * * * was a party to the action from the beginning, had been found liable for numerous statutory and constitutional violations, and had been subjected to various elaborate remedial decrees which had been upheld on appeal. Petitioners, the individual city councilmen, on the other hand, were not parties to the action, and they had not been found individually liable for any of the violations upon which the remedial decree was based. * * *

It was the city, in fact, which capitulated. * * * While the District Court could not have been sure in late July that this would be the result, the city's arguments against imposing sanctions on it pointed out the sort of pressure that such sanctions would place on the city. * * *

Only eight months earlier, the District Court had secured compliance with an important remedial order through the threat of bankrupting fines against the city alone. After the city had delayed for several months the adoption of a 1987–1988 Housing Assistance Plan (HAP) vital to the public housing required by * * * the remedial order, the court ordered the city to carry out its obligation within two days. The court set a schedule of contempt fines equal to that assessed for violation of the orders in this case, and recognized that the consequence would be imminent bankruptcy for the city. Later the same day, the city council agreed to support a resolution putting in place an effective HAP and reaffirming the commitment of Yonkers to accept funds to build the 200 units of public housing mandated by * * * the remedial order.[4]

The nub of the matter, then, is whether in the light of the reasonable probability that sanctions against the city would accomplish the desired result, it was within the court's discretion to impose sanctions on the petitioners as well under the circumstances of this case.

In Tenney v. Brandhove, 341 U.S. 367, 71 S.Ct. 783, 95 L.Ed. 1019 (1951), we held that state legislators were absolutely privileged in their legislative acts in an action against them for damages. We applied this same doctrine of legislative immunity to regional legislatures in Lake Country Estates, Inc. v. Tahoe Regional Planning Agency, 440 U.S. 391, 404–405, 99 S.Ct. 1171, 1178–1179, 59 L.Ed.2d 401 (1979), and to actions for both damages and injunctive relief in Supreme Court of Virginia v. Consumers Union of United States, Inc., 446 U.S. 719, 731–734, 100 S.Ct. 1967, 1974–1976, 64 L.Ed.2d 641 (1980). The holdings in these cases do not control the question whether local legislators such as practitioners should be immune from contempt sanctions imposed for failure to vote in favor of a particular legislative bill. But some of the same considerations on which the immunity doctrine is based must inform the District Court's exercise of its discretion in a case such as this. "Freedom of speech and action in the legislature," we observed, "was taken as a matter of course by those who severed the Colonies from the Crown and founded our Nation." *Tenney.*

4. The Solicitor General distinguishes the instant sanctions from those threatened in January 1988, because in this case the city and the city council had indicated by the defeat of a resolution proposed by the court that it "Would not 'voluntarily adopt the legislation contemplated by the [court's orders].'" Before the court threatened sanctions for refusal to adopt the 1987–1988 HAP, however, the city council had twice tabled an initiative to enact the HAP and the court previously had been forced to "deem" HAPs to have been submitted for two previous years. Suffice it to say that the council's conduct with regard to the HAP hardly suggested a willingness to comply "voluntarily."

In perhaps the earliest American case to consider the import of the legislative privilege, the Supreme Judicial Court of Massachusetts, interpreting a provision of the Massachusetts Constitution granting the rights of freedom of speech and debate to state legislators, recognized that "the privilege secured by it is not so much the privilege of the house as an organized body, *as of each individual member composing it, who is entitled to this privilege, even against the declared will of the house.* For he does not hold this privilege at the pleasure of the house; but derives it from the will of the people. . . ." Coffin v. Coffin, 4 Mass. 1, 27 (1808). This theme underlies our cases interpreting the Speech or Debate Clause and the federal common law of legislative immunity, where we have emphasized that any restriction on a legislator's freedom undermines the "public good" by interfering with the rights of the people to representation in the democratic process. *Lake Country Estates;* * * * Sanctions directed against the city for failure to take actions such as required by the consent decree coerce the city legislators and, of course, restrict the freedom of those legislators to act in accordance with their current view of the city's best interests. But we believe there are significant differences between the two types of fines. The imposition of sanctions on individual legislators is designed to cause them to vote, not with a view to the interest of their constituents or of the city, but with a view solely to their own personal interests. Even though an individual legislator took the extreme position or felt that his constituents took the extreme position that even a huge fine against the city was preferable to enacting the Affordable Housing Ordinance, monetary sanctions against him individually would motivate him to vote to enact the ordinance simply because he did not want to be out of pocket financially. Such fines thus encourage legislators, in effect, to declare that they favor an ordinance not in order to avoid bankrupting the city for which they legislate, but in order to avoid bankrupting themselves.

This sort of individual sanction effects a much greater perversion of the normal legislative process than does the imposition of sanctions on the city for the failure of these same legislators to enact an ordinance. In that case, the legislator is only encouraged to vote in favor of an ordinance that he would not otherwise favor by reason of the adverse sanctions imposed on the city. A councilman who felt that his constituents would rather have the city enact the Affordable Housing Ordinance than pay a "bankrupting fine" would be motivated to vote in favor of such an ordinance because the sanctions were a threat to the fiscal solvency of the city for whose welfare he was in part responsible. This is the sort of calculus in which legislators engage regularly.

We hold that the District Court, in view of the "extraordinary" nature of the imposition of sanctions against the individual councilmen, should have proceeded with such contempt sanctions first against the city alone in order to secure compliance with the remedial orders. Only if that approach failed to produce compliance within a reasonable time should the question of imposing contempt sanctions against petitioners even have been considered. * * *

JUSTICE BRENNAN, with whom JUSTICE MARSHALL, JUSTICE BLACKMUN, and JUSTICE STEVENS join, dissenting.

I understand and appreciate the Court's concern about the District Court's decision to impose contempt sanctions against local officials acting in a legislative capacity. We must all hope that no court will ever again face the open and sustained official defiance of established constitutional values and valid judicial orders that prompted Judge Sand's invocation of the contempt power in this manner. But I firmly believe that its availability for such use, in extreme circumstances, is essential. As the District Court was aware: "The issues transcend Yonkers. They go to the very foundation of the system of constitutional government. If Yonkers can defy the orders of a federal court in any case, but especially a civil rights case, because compliance is unpopular, and if that situation is tolerated, then our constitutional system of government fails. The issues before the court this morning are no less significant than that." * * *[3]

II * * *

The Court's disfavor of personal sanctions rests on two premises: (1) Judge Sand should have known when he issued the Contempt Order that there was a "reasonable probability that sanctions against the city [alone] would accomplish the desired result,"; and (2) imposing personal fines "effects a much greater perversion of the normal legislative process than does the imposition of sanctions on the city." Because personal fines were both completely superfluous to and more intrusive than sanctions against the city alone, the Court reasons, the personal fines constituted an abuse of discretion. Each of these premises is mistaken.

A

While acknowledging that Judge Sand "could not have been sure in late July that this would be the result," the Court confidently concludes that Judge Sand should have been *sure enough* that fining the city would eventually coerce compliance that he should not have personally fined the councilmembers as well. In light of the information available to Judge Sand in July, the Court's confidence is chimerical. Although the escalating city fines eventually would have seriously disrupted many public services and employment, the Court's failure even to consider the possibility that the councilmembers would maintain their defiant posture

3. While [the vote enacting the Housing Ordinance] vote terminated the contempt sanctions, it by no means heralded a lasting commitment on the part of the city council actually to follow through on the remedial obligations imposed by the Housing Ordinance. Since this date, no new public housing has been built in Yonkers. During the local city council election last November, petitioner Spallone "campaigned [for Mayor] on a pledge to continue the city's resistance to a Federal desegregation order requiring it to build low-income housing in white neighborhoods," N.Y. Times, Nov. 8, 1989, p. 31, col. 5, and Spallone was elected in a "race [that] was widely seen as a referendum on the housing desegregation plan." Petitioners Chema and Fagan were reelected to the council, and the new member filling Spallone's vacated seat also opposes compliance; thus 'candidates opposed to the housing plan appea[r] to hold a majority.' Whether Yonkers officials will *ever* comply with Judge Sand's orders attempting to remedy Yonkers' longstanding racial segregation remains an open question.

despite the threat of fiscal insolvency bespeaks an ignorance of Yonkers' history of entrenched discrimination and an indifference to Yonkers' political reality.

The Court first fails to adhere today to our longstanding recognition that the "district court has firsthand experience with the parties and is best qualified to deal with the 'flinty, intractable realities of day-to-day implementation of constitutional commands.'" Deference to the court's exercise of discretion is particularly appropriate where, as here, the record clearly reveals that the court employed extreme caution before taking the final step of holding the councilmembers personally in contempt. Judge Sand patiently weathered a whirlwind of evasive maneuvers and misrepresentations; considered and rejected alternative means of securing compliance other than contempt sanctions; and carefully considered the ramifications of personal fines. * * *

* * * [T]he Court compounds its error by committing two more. First, the Court turns a blind eye to most of the evidence available to Judge Sand suggesting that, because of the councilmembers' continuing intransigence, sanctions against the city alone might not coerce compliance and that personal sanctions would significantly increase the chance of success. Second, the Court fails to acknowledge that supplementing city sanctions with personal ones likely would secure compliance more promptly, minimizing the overall disruptive effect of the city sanctions on city services generally and long-term compliance with the Consent Decree in particular.

As the events leading up to the Contempt Order make clear, the recalcitrant councilmembers were extremely responsive to the strong segments of their constituencies that were vociferously opposed to racial residential integration. Councilmember Fagan, for example, explained that his vote against the Housing Ordinance required by the Consent Decree "was an act of defiance. The people clearly wanted me to say no to the judge." Councilmember Spallone declared openly that "I will be taking on the judge all the way down the line. I made a commitment to my people and that commitment remains." Moreover, once Yonkers had gained national attention over its refusal to integrate, many residents made it clear to their representatives on the council that they preferred bankrupt martyrdom to integration. As a contemporaneous article observed, "[t]he defiant Councilmen are riding a wave of resentment among their white constituents that is so intense that many insist they are willing to see the city bankrupted...." N.Y.Times, Aug.5, 1988, p.B2, col.4. It thus was not evident that petitioners opposed bankrupting the city; at the very least, capitulation by any individual councilmember was widely perceived as political suicide. As a result, even assuming that each recalcitrant member sought to avoid city bankruptcy, each still had a very strong incentive to play "chicken" with his colleagues by continuing to defy the Contempt Order while secretly hoping that at least one colleague would change his position and suffer the wrath of the electorate. As Judge Sand observed, "[w]hat we have here is competition to see who can attract the greatest notoriety, who will be the political martyr ... *without regard to what is in the best interests of the city of Yonkers.*" (Emphasis added).

Moreover, acutely aware of these political conditions, the city attorney repeatedly warned Judge Sand *not* to assume that the threat of bankruptcy would compel compliance. * * *

The Court's opinion ignores this political reality surrounding the events of July 1988 and instead focuses exclusively on the fact that, eight months earlier, Judge Sand had secured compliance with another remedial order through the threat of city sanctions alone. But this remedial order had required only that the city council adopt a 1987–1988 Housing Assistance Plan, a prerequisite to the city's qualification for federal housing subsidies. In essence, Judge Sand had to threaten the city with contempt fines just to convince the Council to *accept* over $10 million in federal funds. Moreover, the city council capitulated by promising merely to accept the funds any implied suggestion that it ever intended to *use* the money for housing was, of course, proven false by subsequent events. * * *

Moreover, any confidence that city sanctions alone would ever work again was eroded even further by the public outcry against the council's approval of the Consent Decree, which magnified the councilmembers' determination to defy future judicial orders. * * *

The Court, in addition to ignoring all of this evidence before concluding that city sanctions alone would eventually coerce compliance, also inexplicably ignores the fact that imposing personal fines in addition to sanctions against the city would not only help ensure but actually *hasten* compliance. * * * Judge Sand knew that each day the councilmembers remained in contempt, the city would suffer an ever-growing financial drain that threatened not only to disrupt many critical city services but also to frustrate the long-term success of the underlying remedial scheme. * * *

B

The Court purports to bolster its judgment by contending that personal sanctions against city councilmembers effect a greater interference than city sanctions with the " 'interests of ... local authorities in managing their own affairs, consistent with the Constitution.' "

* * * [T]he Court seems to suggest that personal sanctions constitute a "greater perversion of the normal legislative process" merely because they do not replicate that process' familiar mode of decisionmaking.

But the Court has never evinced an overriding concern for replicating the "normal" decisionmaking process when designing coercive sanctions for state and local executive officials who, like legislators, presumably are guided by their sense of public duty rather than private benefit. While recognizing that injunctions against such executive officials occasionally must be enforced by criminal or civil contempt sanctions of fines or imprisonment, see, e.g., Hutto v. Finney, 437 U.S. 678, 690–691, 98

S.Ct. 2565, 2573–2574, 57 L.Ed.2d 522 (1978), we have never held that fining or even jailing these officials for contempt is categorically more intrusive than fining their governmental entity in order to coerce compliance indirectly. * * * But the Court cannot fairly derive this premise from the principle underlying the doctrine of legislative immunity.

The doctrine of legislative immunity recognizes that, when acting collectively to pursue a vision of the public good through legislation, legislators must be free to represent their constituents "without fear of outside interference" that would result from private lawsuits. Supreme Court of Virginia v. Consumers Union of United States, Inc., 446 U.S. 719, 731, 100 S.Ct. 1967, 1974, 64 L.Ed.2d 641 (1980). Of course, legislators are bound to respect the limits placed on their discretion by the Federal Constitution; they are duty-bound not to enact laws they believe to be unconstitutional, and their laws will have no effect to the extent that courts believe them to be unconstitutional. But when acting "in the sphere of legitimate legislative activity," i.e., formulating and expressing their vision of the public good within self-defined constitutional boundaries legislators are to be "immune from deterrents to the uninhibited discharge of their legislative duty." Private lawsuits threaten to chill robust representation by encouraging legislators to avoid controversial issues or stances in order to protect themselves "not only from the consequences of litigation's results but also from the burden of defending themselves." *Supreme Court of Virginia.* To encourage legislators best to represent their constituents' interests, legislators must be afforded immunity from private suit.

But once a federal court has issued a valid order to remedy the effects of a prior, specific constitutional violation, the representatives are no longer "acting in a field where legislators traditionally have power to act."[9] At this point, the Constitution itself imposes an overriding definition of the "public good," and a court's valid command to obey constitutional dictates is not subject to override by any countervailing preferences of the polity, no matter how widely and ardently shared. Local legislators, for example, may not frustrate valid remedial decrees merely because they or their constituents would rather allocate public funds for other uses. More to the point here, legislators certainly may not defy court-ordered remedies for racial discrimination merely because their constituents prefer to maintain segregation: * * * Defiance at this stage results, in essence, in a perpetuation of the very constitutional violation at which the remedy is aimed.[11] Hence, once Judge Sand found

9. I do not mean to suggest that public policy concerns may play no role in designing the scope or content of the underlying remedial order. When each of a variety of different remedial programs would fully remedy the constitutional violation, for example, a district court should take into account relevant and important policy concerns voiced by government defendants in choosing among such remedies. * * *

11. See Columbus Bd. of Education v. Penick, 443 U.S. 449, 459, 99 S.Ct. 2941, 2947, 61 L.Ed.2d 666 (1979)(once court orders desegregation remedy, "[e]ach instance of a failure or refusal to fulfill this affirmative duty continues the violation of the Fourteenth Amendment"). Put another way, remedial defiance by the legislature circumvents the structural protections afforded the citizenry from unconstitutional

that the city (through acts of its council) had engaged in a pattern and practice of racial discrimination in housing and had issued a valid remedial order, the city councilmembers became obliged to respect the limits thereby placed on their legislative independence.

* * * Moreover, even if the Court's characterization of personal fines against legislators as "perverse" were persuasive, it would still represent a myopic view of the relevant remedial inquiry. To the extent that equitable limits on federal courts' remedial power are designed to protect against unnecessary judicial intrusion into state or local affairs, it was obviously appropriate for Judge Sand to have considered the fact that the city's accrual of fines would have quickly disrupted every aspect of the daily operation of local government. Particularly when these broader effects are considered, the Court's pronouncement that fining the city is categorically less intrusive than fining the legislators personally is untenable. * * *

III

The Court's decision today that Judge Sand abused his remedial discretion by imposing personal fines simultaneously with city fines creates no new principle of law; indeed, it invokes no principle of any sort. * * * I worry that the Court's message will have the unintended effect of emboldening recalcitrant officials continually to test the ultimate reach of the remedial authority of the federal courts, thereby postponing the day when all public officers finally accept that "the responsibility of those who exercise power in a democratic government is not to reflect inflamed public feeling but to help form its understanding." Cooper v. Aaron, 358 U.S. 1, 26, 78 S.Ct. 1401, 1413, 3 L.Ed.2d 5 (1958) (Frankfurter, J., concurring).

## *Notes on Tactics to Override Legislative Decisions*

1. *Yonkers* and *Spallone* illustrate a number of tactics to get unwilling governments or government officials to act and their legal and practical limitations.

government behavior by a multi-branch review process, by allowing the legislature de facto to override the court's ruling in a particular case that its behavior violates the Fourteenth Amendment. *Cf.* Cooper v. Aaron, 358 U.S. 1, 18, 78 S.Ct. 1401, 1409, 3 L.Ed.2d 5 (1958)("If the legislatures of the several states may, at will, annul the judgments of the courts of the United States, and destroy the rights acquired under those judgments, the constitution itself becomes a solemn mockery")(quoting United States v. Peters, 5 Cranch 115, 136, 3 L.Ed. 53 (1809)).

Indeed, even were the councilmembers to maintain that the Housing Ordinance they were required to enact itself violated the Constitution, for example, by mandating unjustified racial preferences, the members would nevertheless be bound by a court order considering yet rejecting their constitutional objection. See *Cooper,* supra, at 18, 78 S.Ct. at 1409 ("[F]ederal judiciary is supreme in the exposition of the law of the Constitution" in case adjudication). But in any event, the councilmembers raised no serious substantive objections, constitutional or otherwise, to the Ordinance (which after all was based on the city council-approved Consent Decree).

2. *The court could order the government to act and use the contempt power to make it do so.* The City of Yonkers was ordered to act under a consent decree and was held in contempt for failing to comply.

(a) *The impossibility defense to contempt.* Should the city have been found in contempt if it had a separate legislature and executive and the legislature had not consented to the decree?

Delaware Valley Citizens' Council for Clean Air v. Pennsylvania, 678 F.2d 470 (3d Cir.1982), cert. denied, 459 U.S. 969, 103 S.Ct. 298, 74 L.Ed.2d 280 (*Delaware Valley I*) upheld a finding of contempt against the Commonwealth over its objection that it could not comply with a consent judgment because the legislature had not appropriated the necessary funds. The court reasoned that the Pennsylvania Department of Justice,

> members of which were signatories of this decree, has the exclusive power to compromise and settle lawsuits against the Commonwealth.
>
> * * * Neither can there be any objection to holding the Commonwealth to the terms of the decree based upon the eleventh amendment * * *. That amendment does not apply to suits brought by the United States against a state. Moreover entry of a consent judgment is a waiver of any eleventh amendment immunity that the Commonwealth might have earlier wished to claim.
>
> Because the Commonwealth, including all its branches, is bound by the consent judgment, the argument of inability to comply rings hollow. * * * [T]hose Commonwealth officials sitting in the General Assembly certainly are not incapable of insuring the Commonwealth's compliance.

Subsequently, the Pennsylvania courts held that the state officials lacked authority to enter into the consent decree and enjoined compliance with the federal order. The Third Circuit declared the state court decree of no effect because the federal decision validating the consent decree was res judicata. Delaware Valley Citizens' Council for Clean Air v. Pennsylvania, 755 F.2d 38 (3d Cir.1985), cert. denied, 474 U.S. 819, 106 S.Ct. 67, 88 L.Ed.2d 54 (*Delaware Valley II*). In a concurring opinion, Judge Stern concluded that the state decree was invalid under the Supremacy Clause. See also Badgley v. Santacroce, 800 F.2d 33, 38 (2d Cir.1986), cert. denied, 479 U.S. 1067, 107 S.Ct. 955, 93 L.Ed.2d 1003 (1987)("Even if a state court would hold the defendants in contempt for refusing to house inmates [as ordered] or if compliance would otherwise violate state law, Supremacy Clause considerations require that the judgment of the federal court be respected. * * * In any attempt by a state court to hold defendants in contempt for taking actions required by the judgment of the District Court, that judgment would provide a complete defense.")

(b) *The immunity of the state.* If the defendants are from state rather than city government and the plaintiffs are private persons, then the judge has to consider the eleventh amendment immunity of the state. In this regard, the quote from Hutto v. Finney in the Second Circuit opinion in *Yonkers* is somewhat misleading. *Hutto* did not penalize the state for failing to obey an order directed to it but rather awarded attorney fees that would be paid out of Department of Corrections funds on the grounds that the state officials had litigated in bad faith. The underlying order in the case was directed against state officials rather than the state or one of its agencies. "Even if it might have been better form to omit the reference to the Department of Correction [in the award of fees], the use of that language is surely not reversible error." 437 U.S. at 692–93, 98 S.Ct. at 2574, 57 L.Ed.2d at 535.

(c) *The uncertain effect on recalcitrant officials of holding the government in contempt.* The then-Mayor of Yonkers Nicholas Wasicsko said, before the Supreme Court stayed the contempt sanctions against the Councilmen, that "if anything forces compliance, it will be the Councilmen in the cooler" rather than the fines against the City. New York Times, Aug. 27, 1988 at 1, 28. The sanctions against the government itself may or may not translate into action by the recalcitrant officials.

> YONKERS, Sept. 8—As contempt fines against Yonkers passed $1 million and one-fourth of the city work force faced lay-offs in two days, even steadfast opponents of a court-ordered housing desegregation plan seemed jolted today, and pressure grew for city officials to resolve the crisis. * * *
>
> The People's Union, a citizens' group that has supported the Council's resistance, reversed itself * * *.
>
> A councilman blocking the housing plan, Nicholas V. Longo, said the escalating fines and impending layoffs were prompting more calls for compliance. "Obviously, when the effects of the situation hit people directly, moods change," he said. "I mean the city worker who was employed yesterday, but who might be unemployed Monday has concerns. And I can't say I blame him. The same is true for residents without services."
>
> But at the same time, he added, "there are residents who feel that between the judge and the financial control board, they are being bludgeoned with a baseball bat, and their resolve only gets stronger" to resist the order.

New York Times, Sept. 9, 1988 at A1.

Some citizens will blame hardships not on the recalcitrant officials but on the judge or the plaintiffs. As one Yonkers councilman who resisted compliance said, "[c]learly the blood is on the judge's hands."

Early in the morning of September 9,—although the court was willing to view it as late in the day on September 8 for the purpose of computing contempt fines—Councilmen Chema and Longo changed their votes so that the required legislation was enacted by a vote of 5 to 2.

N.Y. Times, Sept. 10, 1988, at A1; New York Times, Sept. 11, 1988, at A1. The vote took place after the Supreme Court had stayed the contempt sanctions against the councilmembers. In response to the Supreme Court's decision, Mr. Spallone, who had been elected mayor while the case was pending, said that he and his allies on the city council would try to use the decision as a means of opposing implementation of Judge Sand's orders. New York Times, Jan. 11, 1990, at B9. Subsequently, the Spallone-led City Council fired the City's outside law firm, which said the City had no grounds left upon which to fight compliance, and hired new lawyers, including the lawyer for plaintiffs in *Martin v. Wilks* (discussed supra at p. 329) New York Times, March 9, 1990, at B2. Was the *Spallone* majority correct in concluding that Judge Sand should have been reasonably sure that fines against the city alone would eventually bring compliance?

(d) *Collecting sanctions from a government.* Still another Yonkers councilman who resisted compliance said, "I say to [Judge Sand] 'if you want the money, come and get it.'" N.Y. Times, Sept. 10, 1988, at A1. The Yonkers corporation counsel responded that he assumed that the judge "would direct that the check be issued without the Council's OK, or that he could suspend the law making it illegal to transfer funds without the Council's vote—or he could move against the assets of the city." Accord, Hook v. Arizona Department of Corrections, 907 F.Supp. 1326 (D.Ariz.)(state statute blocking payment of special master's fees was unconstitutional under Supremacy Clause), affirmed 73 F.3d 369 (9th Cir.1995).

3. *The court could take the action itself.* In *Yonkers,* this would have meant the court declaring that the legislation was enacted by its fiat, just as the district court in *Jenkins,* in essence, enacted tax and appropriations legislation. Why do the City and Councilmen prefer the court to take the action? Why does the court want them to act? Which is a better approach? Consider what Judge Sand said on this point:

> [T]here does have to come a moment of truth, a moment of reckoning, a moment when the City of Yonkers seeks not to become the national symbol of defiance to civil rights and to heap shame upon shame upon itself, but to recognize its obligation to conform to the laws of the land and not step by step, order by order, but in the way in which any responsible community concerned about the welfare of its citizens functions. That is not going to be accomplished by this court adopting the ordinance.

In contrast to the fierce resistance to the 200 units of housing, Yonkers complied without great fanfare with extensive orders from Judge Sand to desegregate its 20,000 student school system. One explanation for the difference is that the schools are run by officials appointed for five year terms, while action on the housing had to be taken by council members elected for two year terms. Some council members made careers by feeding the flames of resistance, but then found that they could not back down without destroying their political careers. Note, Implementing

Structural Injunctions: Getting a Remedy When Local Officials Resist, 80 Geo.L.J. 2227 (1992), concludes that judges should take direct action. It argues that the alternative of ordering the legislators to act is fraught with first amendment and immunity problems and that the other alternative of sanctioning the government often hurts those who should benefit from the injunction.

4. *Appointing a receiver to take the action.* In *Yonkers,* Judge Sand considered appointing an Affordable Housing Commission, which would, in essence, be a receiver. Why did the city resist this option while wanting the judge to take the action himself? Why did the judge resist this option? After the City Council backed down, Judge Sand did appoint a Fair Housing Opportunity Commission to administer parts of the decree.

5. *The court could order officials to act.* In *Yonkers,* this involved, of course, ordering the council members to vote for the required legislation and holding those who failed to do so in contempt.

(a) *Intrusiveness.* Coercing the officials is more intrusive than coercing the government because the court is requiring not only a change in the city's law but also action on the part of the legislators. Given the admonition that courts should do no more than necessary to put plaintiffs in their rightful position, what, if anything, justifies this extra degree of intrusion?

The majority in *Spallone* found that Judge Sand went further than necessary to put plaintiffs in their rightful position by sanctioning the council members as well as the city. Is sanctioning the councilmembers more intrusive than sanctioning the city alone? If sanctioning the councilmembers was more intrusive, was that intrusiveness justified by the need to avoid a fiscal drain on the city? If Justice Brennan is correct that there is no "independent value" to using the legislative process to implement a decree, why not just have the district court adopt the ordinance for the city, as discussed in note 3? Does *Spallone* mean that, where local executive officials refuse to obey an injunction, a district court must try sanctioning the local government before sanctioning the officials?

*Spallone* raises a number of questions as to how courts should decide when a decree or sanctions enforcing it are too broad. What degree of deference should an appellate court give a trial court's determination that a more intrusive decree is necessary to achieve compliance? If the least intrusive decree is insufficient to bring compliance, in what increments may a trial court become more intrusive? For example, if the least intrusive sanction is to fine Yonkers $100 if the Council does not enact the ordinance, as Judge Sand did, but the City does not respond, should the trial court double the fine each day, as Judge Sand also did? It would be less intrusive, would it not, to increase the fine by smaller amounts or to increase it less frequently?

(b) *First Amendment.* The court of appeals suggests that voting lacks First Amendment significance because it is action rather than speech (are you convinced?) and that, in any event, the first amendment is no excuse for breaking the law. Two cases struck down on first amendment grounds legislation that commanded the members of inferior governmental bodies to vote in a particular way. Clarke v. United States, 886 F.2d 404 (D.C.Cir.1989); Miller v. Town of Hull, 878 F.2d 523 (1st Cir.), cert. denied, 493 U.S. 976, 110 S.Ct. 501, 107 L.Ed.2d 504 (1989). Both reasoned that the legislature could have simply enacted what it wanted rather than commanding others to vote for it. In *Clarke,* Congress enacted legislation that would stop the District of Columbia from spending any money unless the members of the District of Columbia Council voted for a measure that would weaken the District's prohibitions on discrimination against homosexuals. *Clarke* attempts to distinguish *Yonkers* on the basis that, there, "the city's failure to provide the housing was itself an illegal act" while in *Clarke* the refusal of the Council to adopt the measure was not illegal. So would *Clarke* have upheld the statute if Congress had made failure to vote for the measure a felony, rather than crippling the District's government? Justice Brennan argues that there is no First Amendment problem in ordering a legislator to vote because voting pursuant to a decree is purely ministerial. Do you agree?

(c) *Legislative immunity.* The court of appeals suggests that there is no legislative immunity from being ordered to take actions necessary to implement a remedial decree. It invokes *Milliken II*'s holding that, under the eleventh amendment, state officials could be forced to provide funds for prospective action. But the addressees of the *Milliken II* order were not state legislators; the issue was not whether the legislators could be forced to appropriate money but whether executive officials could be forced to use state money to comply. The possibility that the legislature would not appropriate it did not come up. In a broader sense, *Milliken II* stands for the proposition that there are exceptions to eleventh amendment immunity, not that court orders can countermand immunities. The court of appeals held that there was no legislative immunity because the council had voted to bind the city to the consent decree. Should Spallone, who dissented in the original vote, be bound? If not, should the members who changed their votes be bound? For an argument that consent degrees cannot abrogate legislative immunity, see Comment, The Effects of Consent Decrees on Local Legislative Immunity, 56 U.Chi.L.Rev. 1121 (1989).

The *Spallone* majority seems to conclude that state legislators are immune from injunctions when acting in their legislative capacity, while the *Spallone* dissent concludes that neither state nor local legislators should be immune from injunctions on the basis that they have no discretion to violate the Constitution. Should it make any difference that the decree orders the legislators to desist from an unconstitutional act or to take action needed to repair a past violation? Was the violation of Judge Sand's decree also a violation of the Constitution? The Supreme Court has yet to decide whether full legislative immunity extends to local law-making bodies. Lake Country Estates, Inc. v. Tahoe

Regional Planning Agency, 440 U.S. 391, 404 n. 26, 99 S.Ct. 1171, 1178 n. 26, 59 L.Ed.2d 401 (1979). However, several Circuit Courts have held that full immunity attaches to the actions of local legislators. See, e.g., Shoultes v. Laidlaw, 886 F.2d 114, 117 (6th Cir.1989); Rateree v. Rockett, 852 F.2d 946, 949–50 (7th Cir.1988). In addition, the majority of the Circuits have held that local legislators are completely immune from liability under 42 U.S.C. § 1983 (1988). Cases deny legislative immunity to decisions of local governing bodies that dispose of individual cases, such as zoning applications, on the basis that the officials were not acting in a legislative capacity. Note, The Legislative Injunction: A Remedy for Unconstitutional Legislative Inaction, 99 Yale L.J. 231, 241–42 (1989).

6. *Oust the recalcitrant officials.* In *Yonkers,* the judge did not claim judicial power to oust elected officials from office but rather created a situation in which the Governor would have the power to oust them under the terms of special provisions of state law and the city charter.

7. *Toss the defendants a bone.* In *Yonkers,* the councilmen who resisted the decree had vowed to their constituents to never surrender. When some of them began to have second thoughts in the face of the court's contempt power, their previous vows made it embarrassing to back down. So they urged the court to modify the decree in some way favorable to the city so they could claim that they had won something. They were less interested in the substance or size of the court's concession than in its symbolic value. The court refused to toss them a bone, which prolonged the drama and hard feelings. What did the court gain from its unyielding position? What should the court have done?

8. *Update on the Yonkers case.* In December, 1990, a state trial judge ruled that the four council members who voted to defy Judge Sand were liable to the City under a state statute that makes government officials liable for illegal acts that waste public assets. Duffy v. Longo, No. 17423/88 (N.Y. Sup.Ct.), 204 N.Y.L.J. 33 (Dec. 24, 1990). The Appellate Division, however, held that the actions taken by the defendant council members "lack[ed] the necessary element of collusion, fraud, or personal gain," necessary for the attachment of personal liability on the Council members. Duffy v. Longo, 207 A.D.2d 860, 616 N.Y.S.2d 760 (1994). In March 1991, the Court of Appeals rejected the city's challenge to a provision of the consent decree that bars further appeals. United States v. Yonkers Board of Education, 927 F.2d 85 (2d Cir.), cert. denied, 502 U.S. 816, 112 S.Ct. 70, 116 L.Ed.2d 45 (1991).

After the Council backed down, Judge Sand changed the composition of those who would occupy the 200 units of public housing in a direction that existing residents of the neighborhoods would like by giving some preference to current occupants of public housing who have been model tenants. Occupancy began without more high drama, but with some tension. New York Times, June 27, 1993, at 25.

To satisfy the Consent Judgment's requirement for 800 units of private, subsidized low income housing, the city proposed a plan, which Judge Sand criticized for providing too few units, orienting them to face away from the surrounding neighborhoods, and making too many of them owner-occupied. In 1994, Judge Sand rejected another city proposal, imposed an order to build additional units, and appointed a Housing Special Master over the city's objection. The court of appeals affirmed. United States v. Yonkers Board of Education, 29 F.3d 40 (2d Cir.1994), cert. denied, ___ U.S. ___, 115 S.Ct. 2608, 132 L.Ed.2d 853 (1995).

Mayor Nicholas Wasicsko, elected in 1987 at the age of 28 and a former student of one of the casebook authors, was defeated in his bid for reelection in 1989, by Spallone because Wasicsko favored obeying the injunction. In 1991, Spallone was defeated by a candidate supported by Wasicsko and Wasicsko was elected to the City Council. In 1993, he ran for City Council President and lost, which meant he would be out of office again. The following month Wasicsko committed suicide. New York Times, Oct. 31, 1993.

---

*Yonkers* and *Spallone* suggest the fragility of the courts' authority, which is the subject of the following reading.

## ALEXANDER BICKEL, THE LEAST DANGEROUS BRANCH

254–268 (1st ed.1962, 2d ed.1986).

* * * POLITICAL WARFARE AND THE USES OF DECISIONS OF COURTS

The initial reaction to the Court's decision [in *Brown*], both in 1954 and in 1955, when the deliberate-speed decree came down, augured very well indeed for full acceptance, following a period of adjustment that would itself do no violence to principle. As I have indicated, the border states and especially the great border cities, as well as other marginal areas, began immediate compliance, even before issuance of the decree. In the rest of the South, the situation was this. There were some uncompromising, vaguely defiant comments * * * But they were highly exceptional. * * * Senator Russell Long, of Louisiana, while regretting the decision, added: "My oath requires me to accept it as law.... I urge all Southern officials to avoid any sort of rash or hasty action."

* * * [A] turning point came—distinctly and unmistakably, at least in retrospect—on March 11, 1956, with issuance of the Congressional Manifesto of that date by nearly the full membership of the southern delegation. This document was a calculated declaration of political war against the Court's decision. * * *

> We regard the decision of the Supreme Court in the school cases as clear abuse of judicial power. It climaxes a trend in the Federal judiciary undertaking to legislate, in derogation of the authority of

Congress, and to encroach upon the reserved rights of the states and the people. * * *

[The Manifesto] concluded as follows:

> We commend the motives of those states which have declared the intention to resist forced integration by any lawful means. * * *
>
> Even though we constitute a minority in the present Congress, we have full faith that a majority of the American people ... will in time demand that the reserved rights of the states and of the people be made secure against judicial usurpation.
>
> We pledge ourselves to use all lawful means to bring about a reversal of this decision which is contrary to the Constitution and to prevent the use of force in its implementation.
>
> In this trying period, as we all seek to right this wrong, we appeal to our people not to be provoked by the agitators and trouble-makers invading our states and to scrupulously refrain from disorder and lawless acts.

From the stand taken in this document, all else flowed. With few exceptions, moderate positions previously assumed were abandoned throughout the states that had been part of the Confederacy. * * * The southern leaders understood and acted upon an essential truth, which we do not often have occasion to observe and which dawned on the southerners themselves somewhat late; hence the contrast between initial reactions and what followed. The Supreme Court's law, the southern leaders realized, could not in our system prevail—not merely in the very long run, but within the decade—if it ran counter to deeply felt popular needs or convictions, or even if it was opposed by a determined and substantial minority and received with indifference by the rest of the country. This, in the end, is how and why judicial review is consistent with the theory and practice of political democracy. This is why the Supreme Court is a court of last resort presumptively only. No doubt, in the vast majority of instances the Court prevails—not as a result of any sort of tacit referendum; rather, it just prevails, its authority is accepted more or less automatically, and no matter if grudgingly. It takes concerted effort at some risk, and hence not a little daring, to fight back, and then there is no guaranty of victory, as the Progressives and Populists found out. But given passion, vigor, and hard-headedness, it can be done and has been done. * * *

The southern purpose, therefore, was to organize and maintain unbroken the ranks of a determined and politically entrenched minority, and to test the convictions of the rest of the country. In opening this post-judgment colloquy, a colloquy searching not expedients of accommodation and compromise but the validity of the judgment itself, and in attempting this different sort of reprise, the southern leaders applied a lesson that Lincoln had taught. * * *

He and the Republican party, and, as it turned out, a goodly majority of the nation were opposed to the Supreme Court's decision in 1857 in the *Dred Scott Case*. * * * In the debates with Stephen A. Douglas in 1858, Lincoln said that he was against this decision, that he thought it wrong, that he feared its consequences, that he deemed it altogether deplorable. Douglas, on the other hand, without admitting that he necessarily thought the decision right, dwelt heavily on the argument that "whoever resists the final decision of the highest judicial tribunal aims a deadly blow at our whole republican system of government." * * *

Lincoln never advocated disobedience of judicial decrees while they were in force. * * * But he did offer resistance to the principle, in the hope and with the expectation of overturning it. * * *

One need hardly add that all this, summed up in only somewhat milder form in Lincoln's First Inaugural, was heresy against the theoretical basis of *Marbury v. Madison*. Public officers swear to support the Constitution of the United States, and, according to *Marbury v. Madison*, as Douglas was quick to point out, the Constitution is in the Supreme Court's keeping and must be supported as declared by the Court. There can be no pursuit of contrary "political rules" except in contravention of the oath to support the Constitution, meaning the oath to support the Supreme Court's invocations of it. But that is *Marbury v. Madison*; it does not describe the system, as it is or has been. * * * [O]n the supreme occasion, when the system is forced to find ultimate self-consistency, the principle of self-rule must prevail. * * *

[Professor Bickel points out that Presidents Andrew Jackson and Franklin Roosevelt took positions similar to Lincoln's.]

Following the Lincoln–Jackson–Roosevelt tradition, southern politicians were perfectly within their rights in declining to accept the Court's decision in the *School Segregation Cases* as a political rule. They were within their rights in deploring it and arguing against it. They could hope to convert public opinion. They could vote for laws that failed to advance its principle and even failed to concur with it. They could refuse to consider the issue settled and could relitigate it at every opportunity that the judicial process offered, and of course it offers a thousand and one. * * * If they succeeded in turning public opinion, they could realistically look to the day when the principle announced by the Court would be rescinded or allowed to lapse without enforcement. * * *

Success has eluded the southern leaders, but narrowly. For a moment it seemed within reach, while the main body of northern opinion, led by President Eisenhower, mounted no defense. The chief response that was made was in terms of *Marbury v. Madison;* the President sounded almost verbatim like Stephen A. Douglas. This was an argument that could not be won—at the most it could be brought to a standstill. The Court, said the southerners just about unanswerably, had botched the job that Marshall describes in *Marbury v. Madison;*

pretty obviously, the Court had performed some other function, not the one there indicated. But under *Marbury v. Madison,* ran the reply on a parallel rail, the Court is empowered to lay down the law of the land, and citizens must accept it uncritically. Whatever the Court lays down is right, even if wrong, because the Court and only the Court speaks in the name of the Constitution. Its doctrines are not to be questioned; indeed, they are hardly a fit subject for comment. The Court has spoken. The Court must be obeyed. There must be good order and peaceable submission to lawful authority. * * *

The debate was at a standstill. Both sides were right, both sides were wrong, and it didn't matter. The decisive issue, to which the southerners amply devoted their attention, going beyond the fictions of *Marbury v. Madison,* was whether what the Court had done was right or wrong, good or bad. As to this, President Eisenhower had nothing to say, except for one or two very damaging, though sheepish, admissions that he entertained some doubts of his own. And so the real point of the southern attack was missed. At best, the President—and, for its own reasons, also the Congress—politely declined the Court's invitation to join with it in ensuring the success of its now hazardous undertaking. At best, the President made a faint attempt to support the Court by drawing on *its* resources, *its* prestige and mystique, not by bringing to its aid those of the political institutions. This constituted no particular support at all. No wonder the southerners thought for a season that success was within their grasp. No one had joined the decisive issue with them. There was hardly a contest.

Having scented victory, the southern leaders, or at least a sufficient number of them, sought to assure it by turning from litigation and agitation to direct action by the use of mobs. Thus they abandoned the tradition in which they had been acting. For this no support could be found in the position of Lincoln or of those who preceded and followed him. * * * The action at Little Rock * * * raised in much bolder fashion than before the issue of order, the peace of the community as against mob rule, and it caused President Eisenhower to react. Too much cannot be made of this, however. The Executive is obliged to aid in the enforcement of specific judicial decrees that have been flouted. It is a matter of maintaining the peace. But this is an indifferent omen, at best, for the endurance of the Court's principle, if the merits of the decision are not themselves defended as right and good; and Mr. Eisenhower did not so defend them. For enforcement is a crisis of the system, not its norm. When the law summons force to its aid, it demonstrates, not its strength and stability, but its weakness and impermanence. The mob, like revolution, is an ambiguous fact. The mob is bad when it is wrong; it may be heroic when it is right. It is surely a deeply ingrained American belief that mobs of our people do not generally gather to oppose good laws, and the very fact of the mob, therefore, puts the law in question. * * *

But there was another factor in play, and it roused northern opinion, whose latent temper the southern leaders had gravely misestimated. It is this factor that lent decisive consequence to the riots in Little Rock, abetted by [riots and confrontations elsewhere]. Compulsory segregation, like states' rights and like "The Southern Way of Life," is an abstraction and, to a good many people, a neutral or sympathetic one. These riots, which were brought instantly, dramatically, and literally home to the American people, showed what it means concretely. Here were grown men and women furiously confronting their enemy: two, three, a half dozen scrubbed, starched, scared, and incredibly brave colored children. The moral bankruptcy, the shame of the thing, was evident. Television, it should be emphasized, as in the Army–McCarthy hearings, played a most significant role. There was an unforgettable scene, for example, in one CBS newscast from New Orleans, of a white mother fairly foaming at the mouth with the effort to rivet her distracted little boy's attention and teach him how to hate. And repeatedly, the ugly, spitting curse, NIGGER! The effect, achieved on an unprecedented number of people with unprecedented speed, must have been something like what used to happen to individuals (the young Lincoln among them) at the sight of an actual slave auction, or like the slower influence on northern opinion of the fighting in "Bleeding Kansas" in 1854–55.

And so the southern leaders had overplayed their hand. Mob action led to the mobilization of northern opinion in support of the Court's decision—not merely because the mob is disorderly, but because it concretized the abstraction of racism, somewhat in the manner in which the cases and controversies in whose context the Court evolves its principles concretize all abstractions. * * * One of those supreme occasions had been brought about when a decisive reprise is open to the political branches; it was for them to make the Court's decision their rule of political action, or not to do so, and thus to make or break the decision itself. The political branches * * * had independently, on their own responsibility, to speak their moral approval of the Court's decision, to support it by drawing on their own resources, and to act in pursuance of it. This was one time when hiding behind the judges' skirts would not do. The political institutions had a decision of their own to make. * * *

## *Notes*

1. Professor Bickel points out that the courts are vulnerable when the political branches fail to support them on the merits. This can occur not just in the great cases and in the past, but in less spectacular cases and today. In Yonkers in 1988, key opinion leaders did not support the courts on the merits.

> [T]he state's most prominent leaders have been less than outspoken. "I feel all alone," said Mayor Nicholas C. Wasicsko of Yonkers, who supports the [court's] plan but says he does not have enough clout to influence its opponents. "I need someone who has stature or patronage or whatever else it is that would get recalcitrant members [of the City Council, which has blocked implementation] to reconsider."

Mr. Wasicsko says that since the contempt ruling * * * he has heard little from officials, including Andrew P. O'Rourke, the Westchester County Executive; Attorney General Robert Abrams, and Senator Alfonse M. D'Amato. Senator Daniel Patrick Moynihan has said that the court must be obeyed and has offered to help Yonkers, but has not played a prominent role.

Even [New York City Mayor Edward] Koch, who has made headlines with his remarks about foreign countries, has had little to say on the Yonkers case.

[Governor Mario] Cuomo has sent what has been judged—unfairly, he suggests—to have been a mixed message, and so has John Cardinal O'Connor of the Roman Catholic Archdiocese of New York. The Cardinal has both criticized the plan and assailed the situation.

The Governor said yesterday that "the law is the law."

* * * "I am eager to help," Mr. Cuomo said. "But this is before the Court of Appeals."

Then again, Mr. Cuomo did not wait for the resolution of many court actions before taking a position on Shoreham, the nuclear power plant on Long Island that he wants to close. * * *

Joyce Purnick, Little is Said and Less Is Done About Yonkers, New York Times, Aug. 25, 1988 at B1.

2. Professor Bickel's account of the struggle to implement *Brown* divides into three periods: (1) immediately after the *Brown I* and *Brown II* decisions when there was little resistance, (2) the time of growing resistance that followed the Congressional Manifesto, and (3) the backlash against segregation after Little Rock. One might generalize to say enforcement of very controversial court injunctions decisions goes through three periods: (1) presumptive validity, (2) resistance by those opposed, (3) a remand of the merits to the court of public opinion. The first and the third periods are then windows of opportunity to implement the injunction. *Jenkins* and *Yonkers* can be seen as efforts to implement injunctions during the first of these periods—in other words, to trade on the presumptive validity of judicial decisions. *Virginia v. West Virginia* and *Welsch v. Likins* can be seen as efforts to remand to public opinion. Which approach is better? Note, however, that even in *Jenkins* and *Yonkers* the district judges did not go directly from injunction to extremely intrusive action, but, as Professor Goldstein suggests (see supra p. 269), pursued a "scenario of escalating intrusiveness."

In the deliberations leading up to the issuance of the unanimous opinion in *Brown I,* Justice Jackson, who personally opposed segregation, urged an outcome similar to that in *Virginia v. West Virginia*—that the Court state that Congress has the power under section 5 of the fourteenth amendment to outlaw school segregation and declining, in the absence of such legislative action, to hold school segregation an unconstitutional act because the courts lack the administrative machinery to administer a remedy. Richard Kluger, Simple Justice 609–10 (1977). If a judge believes that the courts cannot offer an effective remedy, is it appropriate to decline to reach the issue of liability?

3. Barry Friedman, When Rights Encounter Reality: Enforcing Federal Remedies, 65 S.Cal.L.Rev. 735 (1992), argues that courts often intentionally give the political branches a voice in not only how, but also the extent to which constitutional wrongs are remedied. He cites the role given to Congress in deciding whether there shall be private causes of action for damages and in deciding the scope of governmental and official immunity. He also cites the opportunity that *Spallone* gives legislators to resist injunctions, although at a heavy cost to their constituents. Professor Friedman conceives of constitutional remedies as a dialogue between the courts and the political branches.

Although "dialogue" is an appealing concept, this remedial dialogue might leave voters in the dark as to who is responsible for what government does. For example, some might conclude that the Supreme Court in *Jenkins II* was less than forthright concerning whether the courts get to call the shots on how much school tax is levied, as Professor Friedman points out. Similarly, the Alabama Supreme Court issued an opinion that will confuse voters about who is responsible for school budgets in that state. Opinion of the Justices, 624 So.2d 107 (1993). After a trial court ruled that the state's funding of education produced results that were below state constitutional minima, the state senate asked the state supreme court whether the state legislature was constitutionally required to increase the budget. The court answered yes, which would help to deflect political heat from legislators for the fiscal consequences of increased school spending. The court's answer is curious because the trial court had not yet formulated any remedy and the state legislature was not a defendant. The speaker of the state assembly was a defendant, but he sought to align himself with the plaintiffs.

4. While the "Battle of Little Rock" and cases like *Jenkins II* and *Spallone* are fascinating and useful for exploring the outer limits of the remedial power, they are not typical of injunction cases against governments. According to Ross Sandler & David Schoenbrod, Government by Decree: The High Cost of Letting Judges Make Policy, City Journal 54 (Summer 1994), New York City is the target of many structural injunctions. Most enforce state or federal statutes rather than constitutional rights. The cost of implementing the more important injunctions is equal to a quarter of the city's tax revenues. The impact on the city's truly discretionary spending is even larger because the bulk of the city's budget is made up of such necessities such as interest on the city's debt and the salaries of essential employees. Although the city does not resist compliance in the sense that Yonkers did, it rarely succeeds in fully complying. One reason is that the statutes being enforced cumulatively require the city to do more than its resources allow. A question that such injunctions raise is who gets to make city policy and to whom are they accountable. The statutes are typically unfunded mandates, in which state and federal legislators have made large promises to be fulfilled by local government. The policy choices about the extent to which these promises will be kept, and how, are typically made in consent decrees. Frequently, mayors consent to decrees under which the big expenses come after they are out of office. But even under *Rufo* (reproduced earlier in this chapter), it is difficult for the next mayor to modify the decree. E.g., Benjamin v. Malcolm, 156 F.R.D. 561 (S.D.N.Y.1994)(refusing to allow new mayor to alter predecessor's agreement concerning where meals for pretrial detainees would be cooked).

# Chapter 4

# DECLARATORY JUDGMENT

Declaratory judgment permits a plaintiff to present to a court a controversy which is concrete and adverse but for which the plaintiff does not seek the coercive remedy of damages or an injunction. The declaration of rights or obligations which the court issues is binding upon the parties and, pursuant to the traditional rules of *res judicata* and collateral estoppel, bars further litigation over the disputed issues on which the court has ruled. One corollary of the non-coercive nature of declaratory relief is that such a judgment is not enforceable by contempt.

There are at least four circumstances in which declaratory relief helps to resolve disputes in a fair and efficient manner. First, where the party with the traditional coercive claim elects not to bring a suit, the traditional defendant can use declaratory judgment to resolve the uncertainty as to his legal position. Suppose one party claims that it is owed an unpaid debt by another and has informed a credit rating company of this fact, but has not brought suit to collect the debt. Declaratory judgment provides the alleged debtor a straightforward method of determining whether anything is owed and the opportunity to clear her credit record. Second, declaratory judgment allows the resolution of issues without requiring a party to take steps which might subject him to an adverse coercive decree or sanction. For example, a dispute may arise under a contract containing penalty provisions. Declaratory judgment allows the party with the obligation to perform to resolve the question as to the nature and extent of that duty without risking the penalties and other damage claims under the contract if that party's views as to the interpretation of the contract terms do not prevail. Third, where the parties to a dispute recognize the need for judicial resolution but are sufficiently amicable that they do not wish to seek coercive relief, declaratory judgment allows judicial resolution of the dispute without resort to coercive orders. Finally, declaratory judgment may allow the full resolution of a dispute where parts of the matter are ripe for traditional coercive relief but other parts are not. For example, in a contract dispute if one contract clause has led to a claim for damages but other disputed provisions of the contract remain to be performed it would be efficient to combine a declaratory judgment claim on those provisions with the suit for damages. See Itzhak Zamir, The Declaratory Judgment (2d ed.1993).

Declaratory judgment is the broadest modern form of non-coercive remedy for resolving uncertainty in the legal relations of parties. Numerous older forms provided similar relief in particular types of legal action: bills to quiet or remove a cloud from title; bills for instructions to executors or trustees as to their rights and duties; bills of interpleader to resolve conflicting rights to a fund; applications for judicial declarations of martial status. In many cases, the particular kind of relief was the outgrowth of a repetitive pattern of facts and the courts were not quick to provide analogous relief when some of the facts in the pattern changed. As a result, there were a variety of forms of relief available each with its own prerequisites.

Sharon v. Tucker, 144 U.S. 533, 12 S.Ct. 720, 36 L.Ed. 532 (1892), illustrates this point. Property in the District of Columbia was sold for delinquent taxes in 1837 and eventually passed to plaintiffs who were unable, fifty years later, to obtain an abstract of title acceptable to purchasers because of defects in assessing and advertising the property for sale at the time of the 1837 tax sale. Plaintiffs wanted to obtain clear title to the property so that it could be sold or used to secure a loan. Plaintiffs' effort to obtain a judicial determination of the validity of their title and an injunction against defendants claiming as heirs to the delinquent taxpayer was defeated in the lower courts on the ground that plaintiffs were not in actual possession at the time of commencement of the suit and that it was therefore beyond the power of a court of equity to grant them a bill of peace, one of the specialized causes of action for resolving such disputes. The Supreme Court resolved the matter in plaintiffs' favor, finding that they had obtained title through adverse possession, but in doing so the Court had to distinguish three forms of action which the defendants claimed governed the facts in the case: two types of bills of peace (the first lay to establish a right claimed by plaintiff, but controverted by numerous parties having distinct interests originating in a common source; the second lay where the right of plaintiff to real property had been unsuccessfully assailed in different actions at common law, and the bill is brought to put an end to the controversy) and a bill *quia timet* which is brought to prevent future litigation as to property by removing existing causes of controversy as to its title. In short, determining title to the property was immensely complicated by the question of whether plaintiff had a cause of action entitling him to resolution of the matter.

In many instances, particularized forms for resolving such questions remain, though they have frequently been simplified and modernized; see, e.g., Newman Machine Co., Inc. v. Newman, 275 N.C. 189, 166 S.E.2d 63 (1969), discussing changes in North Carolina law on actions to quiet title. But in the main, declaratory judgment has replaced the old forms of action.

The broadly stated declaratory judgment remedy is comparatively modern. The first effective state declaratory judgment act was passed by New Jersey in 1915. Beginning in 1917, Professors Edwin M. Borchard and Edson R. Sunderland, in numerous articles and books, advocated the passage of statutes establishing the declaratory judgment remedy. Many states passed such statutes over time, but the federal Declaratory Judgment Act was not enacted until 1934, apparently because of congressional concern as to its constitutionality. The Act has been amended, though not in its essential elements, and is now codified at 28 U.S.C. §§ 2201 & 2202.

The Uniform Declaratory Judgment Act is the model on which most state declaratory judgment acts are based. The uniform act is more detailed than its federal counterpart but its central elements are the same: "Courts of record within their respective jurisdictions shall have power to declare rights, status, and other legal relations whether or not further relief is or could be claimed * * *. The declaration may be either affirmative or negative in form and effect; and such declarations shall have the force and effect of a final judgment or decree." U.D.J.A. § 1. The uniform act is more explicit than the federal act in stating that the exercise of jurisdiction by the court is discretionary: "The court may refuse to render or enter a declaratory judgment or decree where such judgment or decree, if rendered or entered, would not terminate the uncertainty or controversy giving rise to the proceeding." U.D.J.A. § 6.

Declaratory judgment is not inherently either an equitable or a legal form of action. It is a form of remedy that is available for claims that would otherwise arise under either law or equity. As a consequence, the right to a jury trial when a plaintiff seeks declaratory relief will depend on whether the parallel coercive claim would be legal or equitable. This is reflected in the language of F.R.Civ.P. 57 (reproduced in the Appendix infra at p. 883). Particularly where there are counterclaims, it may not be easy to ascertain whether the parallel action is legal or equitable. The Supreme Court has put emphasis on preserving the right to jury trial so that competing formulations of the issues in the suit are likely to be resolved in favor of the legal formulation affording jury trial. E.g., Beacon Theatres, Inc. v. Westover, 359 U.S. 500, 79 S.Ct. 948, 3 L.Ed.2d 988 (1959).

The problems most frequently raised by declaratory judgment are whether the remedy is available and appropriate for the resolution of the dispute in question: the courts typically focus on assuring that there is a sufficiently adverse and concrete controversy before the court, or on considering whether other remedies and causes of action are more appropriate to the controversy presented to the court.

## AETNA LIFE INSURANCE CO. v. HAWORTH

Supreme Court of the United States, 1937.
300 U.S. 227, 57 S.Ct. 461, 81 L.Ed. 617.

MR. CHIEF JUSTICE HUGHES delivered the opinion of the Court.

The question presented is whether the District Court had jurisdiction of this suit under the Federal Declaratory Judgment Act.[1] * * *

From the complaint it appears that plaintiff is an insurance company which had issued to the defendant, Edwin P. Haworth, five policies of insurance upon his life, the defendant Cora M. Haworth being named as beneficiary. * * * [T]hey all provided for certain benefits in the event that the insured became totally and permanently disabled. In one policy, for $10,000, issued in 1911, the company agreed, upon receiving the requisite proof of such disability and without further payment of premiums, to pay the sum insured, and dividend additions, in twenty annual installments, or a life annuity as specified, in full settlement. In four other policies issued in 1921, 1928 and 1929, respectively, for amounts aggregating $30,000, plaintiff agreed upon proof of such disability to waive further payment of premiums, promising in one of the policies to pay a specified amount monthly and in the other three to continue the life insurance in force. By these four policies the benefits to be payable at death, and the cash and loan values to be available, were to be the same whether the premiums were paid or were waived by reason of the described disability.

The complaint alleges that in 1930 and 1931 the insured ceased to pay premiums on the four policies last mentioned and claimed the disability benefits as stipulated. He continued to pay premiums on the first mentioned policy until 1934 and then claimed disability benefits. These claims, which were repeatedly renewed, were presented in the form of affidavits accompanied by certificates of physicians. * * *

Plaintiff alleges that consistently and at all times it has refused to recognize these claims of the insured and has insisted that all the policies had lapsed according to their terms by reason of the nonpayment of premiums, the insured not being totally and permanently disabled at any of the times to which his claims referred. Plaintiff further states that taking loans into consideration four of the policies have no value and the remaining policy (the one first mentioned) has a value of only $45 as extended insurance. If, however, the insured has been totally

1. The Act provides:

"(1) In case of actual controversy the courts of the United States shall have power upon petition, declaration, complaint, or other appropriate pleadings to declare rights and other legal relations of any interested party petitioning for such declaration, whether or not further relief is or could be prayed, and such declaration shall have the force and effect of a final judgment or decree and be reviewable as such.

"(2) Further relief based on a declaratory judgment or decree may be granted whenever necessary or proper. The application shall be by petition to a court having jurisdiction to grant the relief. If the application be deemed sufficient, the court shall, on reasonable notice, require any adverse party, whose rights have been adjudicated by the declaration, to show cause why further relief should not be granted forthwith.

"(3) When a declaration of right or the granting of further relief based thereon shall involve the determination of issues of fact triable by a jury, such issues may be submitted to a jury in the form of interrogatories, with proper instructions by the court whether a general verdict be required or not." [Note—the present act, 28 U.S.C. §§ 2201, 2202, is an amended version of the original statute that retains the same essential elements.]

and permanently disabled as he claims, the five policies are in full force, the plaintiff is now obliged to pay the accrued installments of cash disability benefits for which two of the policies provide, and the insured has the right to claim at any time cash surrender values accumulating by reason of the provisions for waiver of premiums, or at his death, Cora M. Haworth, as beneficiary, will be entitled to receive the face of the policies less the loans thereon.

Plaintiff thus contends that there is an actual controversy with defendants as to the existence of the total and permanent disability of the insured and as to the continuance of the obligations asserted despite the nonpayment of premiums. Defendants have not instituted any action wherein the plaintiff would have an opportunity to prove the absence of the alleged disability and plaintiff points to the danger that it may lose the benefit of evidence through disappearance, illness or death of witnesses; and meanwhile, in the absence of a judicial decision with respect to the alleged disability, the plaintiff in relation to these policies will be compelled to maintain reserves in excess of $20,000.

The complaint asks for a decree that the four policies be declared to be null and void by reason of lapse for nonpayment of premiums and that the obligation upon the remaining policy be held to consist solely in the duty to pay the sum of $45 upon the death of the insured, and for such further relief as the exigencies of the case may require.

*First.* The Constitution limits the exercise of the judicial power to "cases" and "controversies." * * * The Declaratory Judgment Act of 1934, in its limitation to "cases of actual controversy," manifestly has regard to the constitutional provision and is operative only in respect to controversies which are such in the constitutional sense. The word "actual" is one of emphasis rather than of definition. Thus the operation of the Declaratory Judgment Act is procedural only. In providing remedies and defining procedure in relation to cases and controversies in the constitutional sense the Congress is acting within its delegated power over the jurisdiction of the federal courts which the Congress is authorized to establish. * * * In dealing with methods within its sphere of remedial action the Congress may create and improve as well as abolish or restrict. The Declaratory Judgment Act must be deemed to fall within this ambit of congressional power, so far as it authorizes relief which is consonant with the exercise of the judicial function in the determination of controversies to which under the Constitution the judicial power extends.

A "controversy" in this sense must be one that is appropriate for judicial determination. A justiciable controversy is thus distinguished from a difference or dispute of a hypothetical or abstract character; from one that is academic or moot. The controversy must be definite and concrete, touching the legal relations of parties having adverse legal interest. It must be a real and substantial controversy admitting of specific relief through a decree of a conclusive character, as distinguished from an opinion advising what the law would be upon a hypothetical state of facts. Where there is such a concrete case admitting of an immediate and definitive determination of the legal rights of the parties in an adversary proceeding upon the facts alleged, the judicial function may be appropriately exercised although the adjudication of the rights of the litigants may not require the award of process or the payment of damages. And as it is not essential to the exercise of the judicial power that an injunction be sought, allegations that irreparable injury is threatened are not required. * * *

*Second.* There is here a dispute between parties who face each other in an adversary proceeding. The dispute relates to legal rights and obligations arising from the contracts of insurance. The dispute is definite and concrete, not hypothetical or abstract. Prior to this suit, the parties had taken adverse positions with respect to their existing obligations. Their contentions concerned the disability benefits which were to be payable upon prescribed conditions. On the one side, the insured claimed that he had become totally and permanently disabled and hence was relieved of the obligation to continue the payment of premiums and was entitled to the stipulated disability benefits and to the continuance of the policies in force. The insured presented this claim formally, as required by the policies. It was a claim of a present, specific right. On the other side, the company made an equally definite claim that the alleged basic fact did not exist, that the insured was not totally and permanently disabled and had not been relieved of the duty to continue the payment of premiums, that in consequence the policies had lapsed, and that the company was thus freed from its obligation either to pay disability benefits or to continue the insurance in force. Such a dispute is manifestly susceptible of judicial determination. It calls, not for an advisory opinion upon a hypothetical basis, but for an adjudication of present right upon established facts.

That the dispute turns upon questions of fact does not withdraw it, as the respondent seems to contend, from judicial cognizance. The legal consequences flow from the facts and it is the province of the courts to ascertain and find the facts in order to determine the legal consequences. That is everyday practice. Equally unavailing is respondent's contention that the dispute relates to the existence of a "mutable fact" and a "changeable condition—the state of the insured's health." The insured asserted a total and permanent disability occurring prior to October, 1930, and continuing thereafter. Upon that ground he ceased to pay premiums. His condition at the time he stopped payment, whether he was then totally and permanently disabled so that the policies did not lapse, is not a "mutable" but a definite fact. It is a controlling fact which can be finally determined and which fixes rights and obligations under the policies. If it were found that the insured was not totally and permanently disabled when he ceased to pay premiums and hence was in default, the effect of that default and the consequent right of the company to treat the policies as lapsed could be definitely and finally adjudicated. If it were found that he was totally and permanently disabled as he claimed, the duty of the company to pay the promised disability benefits and to maintain the policies in force could likewise be adjudicated. There would be no difficulty in either event in passing a conclusive decree applicable to the facts found and to the obligations of the parties corresponding to those facts. If the insured made good his claim, the decree establishing his right to the disability benefits, and to the continuance of the policies in force during the period of the proved disability, would be none the less final and conclusive as to the matters thus determined even though a different situation might later arise in the event of his recovery from that disability and his failure after that recovery to comply with the requirements of the policies. Such a contention would present a distinct subject matter.

If the insured had brought suit to recover the disability benefits currently payable under two of the policies there would have been no question that the controversy was of a justiciable nature, whether or not the amount involved would have permitted its determination in a federal court. Again, on repudiation by the insurer of liability in such a case and insistence by the insured that the repudiation was unjustified because of his disability, the insured would have "such an interest in the preservation of the contracts that he might maintain a suit in equity to declare them still in being." Burnet v. Wells, 289 U.S. 670, 680, 53 S.Ct. 761, 764, 77 L.Ed. 1439. But the character of the controversy and of the issue to be determined is essentially the same whether it is presented by the insured or by the insurer. * * *

Our conclusion is that the complaint presented a controversy to which the judicial power extends and that authority to hear and determine it has been conferred upon the District Court by the Declaratory Judgment Act. * * *

## *Notes*

1. The Supreme Court restated the test for a sufficiently adverse and concrete controversy under the federal Declaratory Judgment Act somewhat more succinctly in Maryland Casualty Co. v. Pacific Coal & Oil Co., 312 U.S. 270, 273, 61 S.Ct. 510, 512, 85 L.Ed. 826 (1941):

> The difference between an abstract question and a "controversy" contemplated by the Declaratory Judgment Act is necessarily one of degree, and it would be difficult, if it would be possible, to fashion a precise test for determining in every case whether there is such a controversy. Basically, the question in each case is whether the facts alleged, under all the circumstances, show that there is a substantial controversy, between parties having adverse legal interests, of sufficient immediacy and reality to warrant the issuance of a declaratory judgment. See Aetna Life Ins. Co. v. Haworth, 300 U.S. 227, 239–242, 57 S.Ct. 461, 463–465, 81 L.Ed. 617. It is immaterial that frequently, in the declaratory judgment suit, the positions of the parties in the conventional suit are reversed; the inquiry is the same in either case.

2. *Maryland Casualty Co.* is also important because it resolved another major issue concerning the use of declaratory judgment actions in insurance disputes; the case permitted a declaratory judgment action by a liability

insurance company against the insured and the person injured as to the scope of coverage, despite the injured person's claim that he had no controversy with the insurance company until he obtained a judgment against the insured and sought payment from the insurer. Following the decisions in *Haworth* and *Maryland Casualty Co.*, the use of declaratory judgment to resolve a wide range of disputes between insurance companies and insureds has become common. E.g., Nationwide Insurance v. Zavalis, 52 F.3d 689 (7th Cir.1995)(federal court may use declaratory relief to determine insurer's duty to defend claim pending in state court). The declaratory judgment action is particularly important in the many states which bar liability insurers who undertake the defense of an insured without a non-waiver agreement from later asserting defenses under the policy such as breach of condition, scope of coverage or continuance of coverage. In such states the declaratory judgment action preceding the liability action allows the liability action to be tried when the insurance carrier has fair knowledge of its legal position. In some states declaratory judgment actions are given preference on trial calendars and the preference is usually of greatest importance in the insurance context. E.g., Cal.Code Civ.Pro. § 1062.3; Fireman's Fund Insurance Co. v. Chasson, 207 Cal.App.2d 801, 24 Cal.Rptr. 726 (1962).

While declaratory judgment is useful to resolve questions between the insurer and the insured, it is not generally appropriate as a mechanism solely to gain a procedural advantage through forum selection in determining the liability of the insured which is the central issue between the injured plaintiff and the insured defendant in the traditional tort action. E.g., Allstate Insurance Co. v. Mercier, 913 F.2d 273 (6th Cir.1990).

3. A declaratory judgment does not necessarily become moot when the dispute between the parties is terminated on appeal. The Supreme Court has ruled that the practice of the Court of Appeals for the Federal Circuit of vacating declaratory judgments concerning patent validity upon a determination of noninfringement of the patent constitutes an abuse of discretion because it "denies the patentee appellate review, prolongs the life of invalid patents, encourages endless litigation (or at least uncertainty) over the validity of outstanding patents, and thereby vitiates the rule announced in Blonder–Tongue Lab., Inc. v. University of Illinois, 402 U.S. 313, 91 S.Ct. 1434, 28 L.Ed.2d 788 (1971) [permitting non-mutual defensive collateral estoppel]". Cardinal Chemical Co. v. Morton International, Inc., 508 U.S. 83, ___, 113 S.Ct. 1967, 1978, 124 L.Ed.2d 1 (1993).

## POE v. ULLMAN

Supreme Court of the United States, 1961.
367 U.S. 497, 81 S.Ct. 1752, 6 L.Ed.2d 989.

MR. JUSTICE FRANKFURTER announced the judgment of the Court and an opinion in which THE CHIEF JUSTICE, MR. JUSTICE CLARK and MR. JUSTICE WHITTAKER join.

These appeals challenge the constitutionality, under the Fourteenth Amendment, of Connecticut statutes which, as authoritatively construed by the Connecticut Supreme Court of Errors, prohibit the use of contraceptive devices and the giving of medical advice in the use of such devices. In proceedings seeking declarations of law, not on review of convictions for violation of the statutes, that court has ruled that these statutes would be applicable in the case of married couples and even under claim that conception would constitute a serious threat to the health or life of the female spouse. * * *

[T]he plaintiffs, Paul and Pauline Poe, are a husband and wife, thirty and twenty-six years old respectively, who live together and have no children. Mrs. Poe has had three consecutive pregnancies terminating in infants with multiple congenital abnormalities from which each died shortly after birth. Plaintiffs have consulted Dr. Buxton, an obstetrician and gynecologist of eminence, and it is Dr. Buxton's opinion that the cause of the infants' abnormalities is genetic, although the underlying "mechanism" is unclear. In view of the great emotional stress already suffered by plaintiffs, the probable consequence of another pregnancy is psychological strain extremely disturbing to the physical and mental health of both husband and wife. Plaintiffs know that it is Dr. Buxton's opinion that the best and safest medical treatment which could be prescribed for their situation is advice in methods of preventing conception. Dr. Buxton knows of drugs, medicinal articles and instruments which can be safely used to effect contraception. Medically, the use of these devices is indicated as the best and safest preventive measure necessary for the protection of plaintiffs' health. Plaintiffs, however, have been unable to obtain this information for the sole reason that its delivery and use may or will be claimed by the defendant State's Attorney (appellee in this Court) to constitute offenses against Connecticut law. The State's Attorney intends to prosecute offenses against the State's laws, and claims that the giving of contraceptive advice and the use of contraceptive devices would be offenses forbidden by Conn.Gen. Stat.Rev.1958, §§ 53–32 and 54–196. * * *

Appellants' complaints in these declaratory judgment proceedings do not clearly, and certainly do not in terms, allege that appellee Ullman threatens to prosecute them for use of, or for giving advice concerning, contraceptive devices. The allegations are merely that, in the course of his public duty, he intends to prosecute any offenses against Connecticut law, and that he claims that use of and advice concerning contraceptives would constitute offenses. The lack of immediacy of the threat described by these allegations might alone raise serious questions of non-justiciability of appellants' claims. But even were we to read the allegations to convey a clear threat of imminent prosecutions, we are not bound to accept as true all that is alleged on the face of the complaint and admitted, technically, by demurrer, any more than the Court is bound by stipulation of the parties. Formal agreement between parties that collides with plausibility is too fragile a foundation for indulging in constitutional adjudication.

The Connecticut law prohibiting the use of contraceptives has been on the State's books since 1879. During the more than three-quarters of a century since its enactment, a prosecution for its violation seems never to have been initiated, save in State v. Nelson, 126 Conn. 412, 11 A.2d

856. The circumstances of that case, decided in 1940, only prove the abstract character of what is before us. There, a test case was brought to determine the constitutionality of the Act as applied against two doctors and a nurse who had allegedly disseminated contraceptive information. After the Supreme Court of Errors sustained the legislation on appeal from a demurrer to the information, the State moved to dismiss the information. Neither counsel nor our own researches have discovered any other attempt to enforce the prohibition of distribution or use of contraceptive devices by criminal process. The unreality of these law suits is illumined by another circumstance. We were advised by counsel for appellants that contraceptives are commonly and notoriously sold in Connecticut drug stores. Yet no prosecutions are recorded; and certainly such ubiquitous, open, public sales would more quickly invite the attention of enforcement officials than the conduct in which the present appellants wish to engage—the giving of private medical advice by a doctor to his individual patients, and their private use of the devices prescribed. The undeviating policy of nullification by Connecticut of its anti-contraceptive laws throughout all the long years that they have been on the statute books bespeaks more than prosecutorial paralysis. What was said in another context is relevant here. "Deeply embedded traditional ways of carrying out state policy * * *"—or not carrying it out—"are often tougher and truer law than the dead words of the written text." Nashville, C. & St. L.R. Co. v. Browning, 310 U.S. 362, 369, 60 S.Ct. 968, 972, 84 L.Ed. 1254.

The restriction of our jurisdiction to cases and controversies within the meaning of Article III of the Constitution is not the sole limitation on the exercise of our appellate powers, especially in cases raising constitutional questions. * * *

The various doctrines of "standing," "ripeness," and "mootness," which this Court has evolved with particular, though not exclusive, reference to such cases are but several manifestations—each having its own "varied application"—of the primary conception that federal judicial power is to be exercised to strike down legislation, whether state or federal, only at the instance of one who is himself immediately harmed, or immediately threatened with harm, by the challenged action. * * *

[J]ust as the declaratory judgment device does not "purport to alter the character of the controversies which are the subject of the judicial power under the Constitution," United States v. State of West Virginia, 295 U.S. 463, 475, 55 S.Ct. 789, 793, 79 L.Ed. 1546, it does not permit litigants to invoke the power of this Court to obtain constitutional rulings in advance of necessity. The Court has been on the alert against use of the declaratory judgment device for avoiding the rigorous insistence on exigent adversity as a condition for evoking Court adjudication. This is as true of state court suits for declaratory judgments as of federal. * * *

Insofar as appellants seek to justify the exercise of our declaratory power by the threat of prosecution, facts which they can no more negative by complaint and demurrer than they could by stipulation preclude our determining their appeals on the merits. It is clear that the mere existence of a state penal statute would constitute insufficient grounds to support a federal court's adjudication of its constitutionality in proceedings brought against the State's prosecuting officials if real threat of enforcement is wanting. If the prosecutor expressly agrees not to prosecute, a suit against him for declaratory and injunctive relief is not such an adversary case as will be reviewed here. Eighty years of Connecticut history demonstrate a similar, albeit tacit agreement. The fact that Connecticut has not chosen to press the enforcement of this statute deprives these controversies of the immediacy which is an indispensable condition of constitutional adjudication. This Court cannot be umpire to debates concerning harmless, empty shadows. To find it necessary to pass on these statutes now, in order to protect appellants from the hazards of prosecution, would be to close our eyes to reality.

Nor does the allegation by the Poes * * * that they are unable to obtain information concerning contraceptive devices from Dr. Buxton, "for the sole reason that the delivery and use of such information and advice may or will be claimed by the defendant State's Attorney to constitute offenses," disclose a necessity for present constitutional decision. It is true that this Court has several times passed upon criminal statutes challenged by persons who claimed that the effects of the statutes were to deter others from maintaining profitable or advantageous relations with the complainants. See, e.g., Truax v. Raich, 239 U.S. 33, 36 S.Ct. 7, 60 L.Ed. 131; Pierce v. Society of Sisters, 268 U.S. 510, 45 S.Ct. 571, 69 L.Ed. 1070. But in these cases the deterrent effect complained of was one which was grounded in a realistic fear of prosecution. We cannot agree that if Dr. Buxton's compliance with these statutes is uncoerced by the risk of their enforcement, his patients are entitled to a declaratory judgment concerning the statutes' validity. And, with due regard to Dr. Buxton's standing as a physician and to his personal sensitiveness, we cannot accept, as the basis of constitutional adjudication, other than as chimerical the fear of enforcement of provisions that have during so many years gone uniformly and without exception unenforced.

Justiciability is of course not a legal concept with a fixed content or susceptible of scientific verification. Its utilization is the resultant of many subtle pressures, including the appropriateness of the issues for decision by this Court and the actual hardship to the litigants of denying them the relief sought. Both these factors justify withholding adjudication of the constitutional issue raised under the circumstances and in the manner in which they are now before the Court.

MR. JUSTICE BRENNAN concurred in the judgment. MR. JUSTICE BLACK, MR. JUSTICE DOUGLAS, MR. JUSTICE HARLAN and MR. JUSTICE STEWART dissented. [opinions omitted]

### *Notes*

1. Given Justice Frankfurter's rationale in Poe v. Ullman, would the plaintiffs have had a basis for seeking a declaration that the Connecticut

statute had fallen into desuetude and was therefore unenforceable? Desuetude, which originated as a doctrine in the civil law, allows the abrogation of a statute by reason of long and continued non-use. E.g., Committee on Legal Ethics v. Printz, 187 W.Va. 182, 416 S.E.2d 720, 726 (W.Va. 1992)("[c]rimes that are malum in se will not lose their criminal character through desuetude, but crimes that are malum prohibitum may"). See generally Corey R. Chivers, Desuetude, Due Process, and the Scarlet Letter Revisited, 1992 Utah L.Rev. 449; Note, Desuetude and Declaratory Judgment: A New Challenge to Obsolete Laws, 76 Va.L.Rev. 1057 (1990) (considers relationship between desuetude and the standing requirements applied in declaratory judgment actions).

2. The other opinions in Poe v. Ullman point out that prior to the decision of the Supreme Court of Errors in the *Nelson* case, there were at least nine birth control clinics in the state, all of which closed following the decision. This suggests that there was a degree of effectiveness to the Connecticut law without any prosecutions.

No opinion mentions that after oral argument, but before the Court announced its decision in *Poe*, the police in North Haven, Connecticut, arrested someone for selling condoms to gasoline station operators. After pleading guilty to violating the aiding and abetting portion of the 1879 statute, the defendant was fined $75; the seized condoms were burned. David J. Garrow, Liberty and Sexuality 178 (1994).

3. Following the Court's decision in Poe v. Ullman, Dr. Buxton served as Medical Director at a center run by the Planned Parenthood League of Connecticut where he provided information and medical advice to married persons on contraception. Dr. Buxton and the Executive Director of the League were found guilty as accessories of violating the Connecticut statutes which were the subject of Poe v. Ullman. Each was fined $100 and appealed. In Griswold v. Connecticut, 381 U.S. 479, 85 S.Ct. 1678, 14 L.Ed.2d 510 (1965), the Supreme Court found the statute unconstitutional. Garrow's book provides a detailed historical account of the development of *Poe* and *Griswold*, including the reactions of the individual justices to the cases.

4. If a state has commenced criminal prosecution while a challenge to the state statute is in its embryonic stages, the federal courts will not enjoin the state court proceedings, Younger v. Harris, 401 U.S. 37, 91 S.Ct. 756, 27 L.Ed.2d 669 (1971), or grant declaratory judgment, Samuels v. Mackell, 401 U.S. 66, 91 S.Ct. 764, 27 L.Ed.2d 688 (1971)(see infra at 395), except in the most exceptional circumstances. Therefore if plaintiffs like the Poes wish to challenge a state statute without risk of having a federal claim for declaratory judgment dismissed in light of a state criminal case, they must not act so that the state is able to return an indictment against them fairly.

5. Another basis on which some courts have refused to grant declaratory relief is the availability of an adequate alternative remedy. If a case could proceed in one of several forms, what are the sound reasons for the plaintiff or the court to prefer one form of relief over the other? See, e.g., Tilcon Minerals, Inc. v. Orange & Rockland Utilities, Inc., 851 F.Supp. 529 (S.D.N.Y.1994)(neither declaratory nor injunctive relief appropriate where

adequate monetary remedies would be available in contract dispute concerning relocation of a rock crushing plant).

### *Note on Jurisdiction Under the Federal Declaratory Judgment Act*

In Skelly Oil Co. v. Phillips Petroleum Co., 339 U.S. 667, 70 S.Ct. 876, 94 L.Ed. 1194 (1950), a case arising under federal question jurisdiction, the Supreme Court stated that the federal Declaratory Judgment Act was not intended to expand the jurisdiction of the federal courts and therefore no case could be brought in the federal courts under the Act that the declaratory judgment *plaintiff* could not have brought had the statute not been enacted. In order to determine whether the federal court had jurisdiction, the court looked to the hypothetical well-pleaded complaint that the plaintiff would have filed for coercive relief for damages or for an injunction.

Despite this instruction, a number of lower federal courts, particularly in declaratory judgment actions brought to resolve a possible claim of patent infringement, looked to the hypothetical well-pleaded complaint that the declaratory judgment *defendant* might have brought and found that federal jurisdiction over that complaint was sufficient for federal jurisdiction in the declaratory judgment action. The coercive complaint of the declaratory judgment defendant in patent infringement is a straightforward one to enjoin infringement and/or for damages for past infringement and is a federal cause of action. The coercive claim of the declaratory judgment plaintiff is not so obvious; it is usually a state common law claim for some form of commercial tort based on the patent holder's threat to interfere with the plaintiff's business, which would not raise a federal question.

In Franchise Tax Board v. Construction Laborers Vacation Trust, 463 U.S. 1, 103 S.Ct. 2841, 77 L.Ed.2d 420 (1983), the Supreme Court followed *Skelly Oil*, holding that federal courts had no jurisdiction over a controversy in which the declaratory judgment plaintiff's coercive complaint did not plead a federal cause of action but in which the defendant's complaint to resolve the same dispute clearly would have raised a federal question. This has left confusion as to the scope of federal court jurisdiction under the Declaratory Judgment Act: is the court to consider only the hypothetical well-pleaded complaint which the plaintiff could bring and thus find no jurisdiction either for cases where the federal issue would be raised by the defendant in its coercive complaint, or for cases where the federal question would arise as a defense or reply to the plaintiff's coercive complaint? Or are the courts to test jurisdiction by whether the nature of the controversy arises under federal law or by whether the defendant's coercive complaint would arise under federal law? The issue has not been fully resolved by the courts. It is explored with an analysis of congressional intent and legislative history in Donald L. Doernberg & Michael B. Mushlin, The Trojan Horse: How the Declaratory Judgment Act Created a Cause of Action and Expanded

Federal Jurisdiction While the Supreme Court Wasn't Looking, 36 U.C.L.A.L.Rev. 529 (1989).

Even if the district court decides that it has subject matter jurisdiction over the controversy, "[s]ince its inception, the Declaratory Judgment Act has been understood to confer on federal courts unique and substantial discretion in deciding whether to declare the rights of litigants." Wilton v. Seven Falls Co., 515 U.S. ___, ___, 115 S.Ct. 2137, 2142, 132 L.Ed.2d 214 (1995). "In the declaratory judgment context, the normal principle that federal courts should adjudicate claims within their jurisdiction yields to considerations of practicality and wise judicial administration." Id., 115 S.Ct. at 2143.

### *Note on the Eleventh Amendment and Declaratory Judgment*

The Supreme Court has refused to grant declaratory relief when it has perceived that such relief would "end run" the constraints of the Eleventh Amendment. In doing so, the Court has provided a useful discussion of when declaratory relief will not be available. In Green v. Mansour, 474 U.S. 64, 106 S.Ct. 423, 88 L.Ed.2d 371 (1985), plaintiffs received benefits under the federal Aid to Families with Dependent Children program and claimed that the defendant Director of the Michigan Department of Social Services had improperly calculated their earned income in violation of applicable federal law. During the course of the litigation Congress amended the statute to conform to the practices of Michigan, rendering prospective relief moot. Plaintiffs could not obtain compensatory relief against the state (see supra at p. 337); they pursued a claim for a declaration that Michigan had not fully compensated them which they could then use against the state in a state court proceeding. The Supreme Court held that the eleventh amendment barred such declaratory relief:

> The propriety of issuing a declaratory judgment may depend upon equitable considerations, see Samuels v. Mackell, 401 U.S. 66, 73, 91 S.Ct. 764, 768, 27 L.Ed.2d 688 (1971), and is also "informed by the teachings and experience concerning the functions and extent of federal judicial power." [Public Service Commission v. Wycoff Co., 344 U.S. 237, 243, 73 S.Ct. 236, 240, 97 L.Ed. 291 (1952)]. Cf. Younger v. Harris, 401 U.S. 37, 44–45, 91 S.Ct. 746, 750–51, 27 L.Ed.2d 669 (1971).
>
> In applying these principles, we have held that a declaratory judgment is not available in a number of instances. In Great Lakes Dredge & Dock Co. v. Huffman, 319 U.S. 293, 63 S.Ct. 1070, 87 L.Ed. 1407 (1943), we held that a declaratory judgment was not available to obtain a determination of the constitutionality of a state tax even though the relevant federal statute prohibited federal courts only from issuing injunctions against the collection of such taxes. We held in *Samuels v. Mackell* that a declaratory judgment declaring a state criminal statute unconstitutional was unavailable where it would have much the same effect as an injunction prohibit-

> ing enforcement of the statute, and the latter was barred by traditional principles of equity, comity, and federalism. In *Wycoff*, we held that it was inappropriate to issue a declaratory judgment deciding whether the plaintiff's business was interstate commerce and therefore potentially immune from state regulation. We reasoned that if the federal judgment were res judicata in subsequent state proceedings, then the federal court will have lifted the case out of the state court before the state agency or court can hear it. On the other hand, if the federal judgment would not have such an effect, then it would "serv[e] no useful purpose as a final determination of rights."
>
> We think that these cases demonstrate the impropriety of the issuance of a declaratory judgment in this case. There is no claimed continuing violation of federal law, and therefore no occasion to issue an injunction. Nor can there be any threat of state officials violating the repealed law in the future. There is a dispute about the lawfulness of respondent's past actions, but the Eleventh Amendment would prohibit the award of money damages or restitution if that dispute were resolved in favor of petitioners. We think that the award of a declaratory judgment in this situation would be useful in resolving the dispute over the past lawfulness of respondent's action only if it might be offered in state court proceedings as res judicata on the issue of liability, leaving to the state courts only a form of accounting proceeding whereby damages or restitution would be computed. But the issuance of a declaratory judgment in these circumstances would have much the same effect as a full-fledged award of damages or restitution by the federal court, the latter kinds of relief being of course prohibited by the Eleventh Amendment.

Green v. Mansour, 474 U.S. 64, 72–73, 106 S.Ct. 423, 427, 88 L.Ed.2d 371 (1985).

### *Problem: Country Lodge v. Miller (Reprised) Declaratory Judgment*

Miller had operated her apple press for three years and disposed of the apple mash into the Rural River. Her downstream neighbor Country Lodge had complained about this practice to the newspaper but had never directly approached Miller about the matter. Miller was contemplating enlarging her operation and investing several thousand dollars in a new apple press which would discharge more mash into the river. She brought an action against Country Lodge seeking a declaration that disposing of apple mash into the Rural River was not a nuisance or an invasion of any right which Country Lodge had as a downstream riparian owner. Should the court rule on this dispute? Would your answer be different if: (a) Country Lodge had never made any complaint to anyone in the past and Miller were not contemplating the installation of a new press; or (b) Country Lodge had threatened Miller with suit each year, telling her that if she put apple mash in the river again it would get an injunction to stop her? On the original set of facts, if Country Lodge sought declaratory judgment that the larger press would create a nuisance, should the court rule on that claim? Should there be a symmetry in the law such that the court would entertain the same claims from Miller and Country Lodge?

## CUNNINGHAM BROTHERS, INC. v. BAIL

United States Court of Appeals, Seventh Circuit, 1969.
407 F.2d 1165, cert. denied, 395 U.S. 959, 89 S.Ct. 2100, 23 L.Ed.2d 745.

CASTLE, CHIEF JUDGE.

Plaintiff brings this appeal from the district court's dismissal of its three-count complaint filed against the individual and corporate defendants under the Declaratory Judgment Act, 28 U.S.C. § 2201. Plaintiff had contracted as general contractor to construct a building for Moore Business Forms, Inc., at Charleston, Illinois. Defendant, Davidson Masonry and Restoration, Inc., was engaged by plaintiff as the masonry subcontractor for the job, and the individual defendants were employees of Davidson who were injured when the platform on which they were standing collapsed.

Defendant Gabel filed a complaint for personal injuries against plaintiff in the district court on October 1, 1967, plaintiff filed its declaratory judgment complaint on November 9, 1967, defendant Katz counterclaimed in the declaratory judgment suit, and at least one of the other individual defendants has since filed suit against plaintiff in a state court. The individual defendants have based their actions on the Illinois Structural Work Act, Ill.Rev.Stat., 1965, Ch. 48, § 60 et seq.

Count I of plaintiff's complaint is directed against the individual defendants only and seeks a declaration that plaintiff did not "have charge of" the work being performed by these defendants at the job site, within the meaning of Illinois Structural Work Act, and that those defendants have no "cause of action" against plaintiff under the Act for any personal injuries they may have sustained on the date of the accident. Counts II & III of the complaint are directed only against Davidson Masonry & Restoration, Inc. Count II seeks a declaration that Davidson, by reason of its contract with plaintiff, is liable to indemnify and hold plaintiff harmless for any amount which may be recovered against plaintiff by the individual defendants. * * *

Plaintiff contends that the district court erred in dismissing the complaint since an action by a potential tort defendant against the potential plaintiffs should fall within the purpose of the Declaratory Judgment Act. Thus, instead of having to wait and be sued in different state and federal forums by the various injured parties, plaintiff argues that it should be allowed to bring them together in one action, along with the alleged indemnitor, and thereby adjudicate the rights of all the parties at one time and place.

We hold that the district court was correct in dismissing the complaint, and accordingly affirm the judgment below.

Regarding the individual defendants, we are of the opinion that to compel potential personal injury plaintiffs to litigate their claims at a time and in a forum chosen by the alleged tortfeasor would be a perversion of the Declaratory Judgment Act. The primary purpose of the Act is "to avoid accrual of avoidable damages to one not certain of his rights and to afford him an early adjudication without waiting until his adversary should see fit to begin suit, after damage had accrued." E. Edelmann & Co. v. Triple–A Specialty Co., 88 F.2d 852, 854 (7th Cir.1937).

Since it is not contended that the present action was brought to avoid damages which would accrue if a certain course of conduct were taken in the future, plaintiff must establish that this suit falls within some other purpose of the Declaratory Judgment Act. Plaintiff attempts to support its action by arguing that the purpose of the Act is not confined solely to settling controversies before they ripen into legal liabilities, but is broad enough to permit the determination of rights which have arisen due to an alleged negligent act which has already occurred. Plaintiff also contends that this action was not brought to determine the issue of negligence, but only to determine the rights of the parties under the contracts between them so as to avoid multiplicity of action.

However, plaintiff has failed to demonstrate how the allowance of the instant declaratory judgment action would "effectuate the purposes of the statute and thereby afford relief from uncertainty and insecurity with respect to rights, status and other legal relations." Sears, Roebuck & Co. v. American Mutual Liability Co., 372 F.2d 435, 438 (7th Cir. 1967); American Auto. Insurance Co. v. Freundt, 103 F.2d 613, 619 (7th Cir.1939); Aetna Casualty & Surety Co. v. Quarles, 92 F.2d 321, 324 (4th Cir.1937). Rather, regarding the individual defendants, plaintiff seems to be attempting to "try issues or determine the validity of defenses in pending cases," as was condemned by *Freundt* and *Quarles*, supra.

Moreover, couching the suit in terms of contract rather than tort does not change the nature of the action. The issue of plaintiff's negligence would necessarily be tried since the individual defendants would be compelled to counterclaim under [F.R.Civ.P.] 13(a). Rules 20(b) and 42(b), regarding separate trials, would be of little value to these defendants, since plaintiff's liability, if any, would be determined in the primary action.

Thus, there is good reason for the noted lack of precedent supporting plaintiff's position. To allow a declaratory judgment action under the facts before us would be to allow a substitute for the traditional procedures for adjudicating negligence cases. We agree with the conclusion reached in Sun Oil Co. v. Transcontinental Gas Pipe Line Corp., 108 F.Supp. 280, 282 (E.D.Pa.1952), aff'd (adopting opinion of district court),

203 F.2d 957 (3d Cir.1953), that "it is not one of the purposes of the declaratory judgment acts to enable a prospective negligence action defendant to obtain a declaration of non-liability."[2]

To so reverse the roles of the parties would affect more than merely the form of action, but would jeopardize those procedures which the law has traditionally provided to injured parties by which to seek judicial relief. Although "[t]he existence of another adequate remedy does not preclude a judgment for declaratory relief in cases where it is appropriate," Rule 57, Fed.Rules Civil Proc., we hold that such relief is inappropriate in the instant case since "more effective relief can and should be obtained by another procedure." Chicago Metallic Mfg. Co. v. Edward Katzinger Co., 123 F.2d 518, 520 (7th Cir.1941).

Although our holding may require the plaintiff here to litigate a number of lawsuits with the injured parties, we feel that this result does not outweigh the right of a personal injury plaintiff to choose the forum and the time, if at all, to assert his claim. We agree with plaintiff that a declaratory judgment action should not be dismissed solely because a more traditional remedy is available. Otherwise, many justiciable declaratory judgment actions would be dismissed on that ground. However, when the traditional remedy provides the parties with the procedural safeguards required by the law to insure the availability of a proper remedy, the courts, in exercising their discretion, may properly dismiss the declaratory judgment action. Since the sustaining of plaintiff's suit in the instant case would force an injured party to litigate a claim which he may not have wanted to litigate at a time which might be inconvenient to him or which might precede his determination of the full extent of his damages, and in a forum chosen by the alleged tortfeasor, we hold that the action was inappropriate for declaratory relief and was therefore properly dismissed against the individual defendants.

There remains the issue of whether plaintiff may seek declaratory relief against the corporate defendant (Davidson), the alleged indemnitor. * * *

"Basically, the question in each case is whether the facts alleged, under all the circumstances, show that there is a substantial controversy, between parties having adverse legal interests, of sufficient immediacy and reality to warrant the issuance of a declaratory judgment." Maryland Casualty Co. v. Pacific Coal & Oil Co., 312 U.S. 270, 273, 61 S.Ct. 510, 512, 85 L.Ed. 826 (1941); See also Aetna Life Ins. Co. v. Haworth, 300 U.S. 227, 239–242, 57 S.Ct. 461, 81 L.Ed. 617 (1937).

It has been held that when an insured is being sued for damages and calls upon his insurer to indemnify and defend the suit, the insurer is "entitled to be advised by a declaratory decree whether it is obligated to defend and indemnify the insured against the claim upon which the suit is brought."

2. Of course, non-liability may be declared in appropriate cases. State Farm Mutual Auto. Ins. Co. v. Mossey, 195 F.2d 56 (7th Cir.1952), cert. den. Du Bois v. Mossey, 344 U.S. 869, 73 S.Ct. 109, 97 L.Ed. 674.

However, in the normal indemnity situation, where, as here, no contractual duty to defend exists, no duty to do anything arises until the alleged indemnitee is adjudged liable. Thus, in the instant case, there is no immediate controversy between the parties since it is not certain that plaintiff will ever be compelled to pay any judgment for which Davidson could be held liable as indemnitor. In these circumstances we hold that the interests of justice would not be served by entertaining a declaratory judgment action at this time. * * *

### *Notes*

1. In light of *Cunningham Brothers,* would it be appropriate for a court to entertain Miller's action for declaratory judgment in any of the fact situations set out in the problem proceeding the case? Should it make a difference that Country Lodge's claim against Miller would arise from Miller's deliberate actions which she believes to be lawful rather than from an accident?

2. The Declaratory Judgment Act does not state that the remedy is unavailable in tort actions. Neither *Cunningham Brothers* nor *Sun Oil Co.,* cited in *Cunningham Brothers*, provides citations to support the conclusion that declaratory judgments are generally unavailable in tort actions. See also Bankers Trust Co. v. Old Republic Insurance Co., 959 F.2d 677, 680 (7th Cir.1992)(describing *Cunningham Brothers* as applying a principle of discretion). Nor does the language of the Act suggest that it is limited in any way to avoiding accrual of avoidable damages to one not certain of his rights. Although Congress took up bills providing for declaratory judgment repeatedly in the 1920's, when the Act was passed in 1934 no debates or hearings were held in either the House or the Senate on the bill; consideration was limited to a brief summary of the bill by its sponsors. Given this limited direct legislative history, how is the court to determine the purposes of the Act? Should it consult the voluminous writings of Professors Borchard and Sunderland? Should it consider the history of declaratory judgment in the states, bearing in mind that the notes of the Advisory Committee to F.R.Civ.P. 57, which addresses declaratory judgments, states that the Uniform Declaratory Judgment Act "affords a guide to the scope and function of the federal act"?

3. In Volkswagenwerk, A.G. v. Watson, 181 Ind.App. 155, 390 N.E.2d 1082 (1979), the Indiana Court of Appeals addressed a case closely parallel to *Cunningham Brothers* in which Volkswagen had been sued on theories of negligence and strict liability in the federal district court and thereafter brought an action in the Indiana state courts seeking a declaration with respect to various tort law questions under Indiana law. The complaint was dismissed in part because Volkswagen was attempting to try issues or determine the validity of defenses in pending cases. The court stated that the determinative factor in whether to allow declaratory judgment was whether the action would result in a just and more expeditious and economical determination of the entire controversy. Under this test how should *Cunningham Brothers* be decided?

4. Consider the weight that should be attached to who commences a lawsuit. In the *Haworth* case, the court of appeals had found that the only

advantage to be derived from a declaratory judgment was the adjudication of Aetna's right of cancellation and the only value of such adjudication was that it settled a defense to a lawsuit the Haworths might bring in the future. Aetna Life Ins. Co. v. Haworth, 84 F.2d 695 (8th Cir.1936), reversed, 300 U.S. 227, 57 S.Ct. 461, 81 L.Ed. 617 (1937). Of course, it is usual and unremarkable that the party who would be a defendant in a suit seeking a coercive remedy will be the plaintiff in a declaratory judgment action—it is frequently the only avenue by which the traditional defendant can force his legal dispute toward resolution. As a result, by using declaratory judgment, the traditional defendant is able to choose his forum for the resolution of the dispute. Is there any reason to disparage this result as the court does in *Cunningham Brothers*? See NUCOR Corp. v. Aceros Y Maquilas de Occidente, 28 F.3d 572, 577 (7th Cir.1994)(courts normally dismiss declaratory judgment actions aimed solely at "wresting the choice of forum from the 'natural' plaintiff").

5. The *Sun Oil Co.* case cited in *Cunningham Brothers* offers another variant. The anchors on Sun Oil's ships had twice damaged Transcontinental's pipeline in the Delaware River near Philadelphia. Sun Oil sued Transcontinental in the Eastern District of Pennsylvania asking for a declaration of non-liability. Shortly thereafter, Transcontinental sued Sun in admiralty in federal court in Texas. The admiralty claims could not be transferred. The federal judge in Pennsylvania stated that most of the witnesses were likely to be near Philadelphia. The unavailability of declaratory judgment for a prospective tort defendant weighed more heavily with the court than economy and efficiency in resolving the dispute or giving consideration to the first plaintiff's choice of forum.

6. The Minnesota Supreme Court reached a different result in Ditzler v. Spee, 288 Minn. 314, 180 N.W.2d 178 (1970). Spee, driving a tractor, allegedly forced a car driven by Mrs. Ditzler off the road injuring Mrs. Ditzler and her minor child. Mrs. Ditzler sued Spee; no suit was brought on behalf of the minor. Spee brought a declaratory judgment action on his liability to the child in the same court in which the tort claim against him was pending and moved to consolidate the cases. The declaratory judgment action was allowed to proceed. The court found that, in these circumstances, the tort plaintiff's choice of forum was not usurped, that the child was not entitled to the advantage of waiting for the outcome of the mother's case before suing and that a multiplicity of suits on the same issues should be avoided unless substantial prejudice could be shown from following that course. The declaratory judgment action would resolve Spee's liability, but, if he were found liable, would not address the child's damage claim.

7. How important is F.R.Civ.P. 13(a) to the result in *Cunningham Brothers* ? The rule states:

> A pleading shall state as a counterclaim any claim which at the time of serving the pleading the pleader has against any opposing party, if it arises out of the transaction or occurrence that is the subject matter of the opposing party's claim and does not require for its adjudication the presence of third parties of whom the court cannot acquire jurisdiction.

Is it unfair to force a tort plaintiff to try damages whenever the tort defendant is ready to try liability? Should Rule 13 be changed?

8. Under the Clean Water Act, the United States may recover the cost of cleaning up spills into navigable waters of oil or hazardous substances from the owner or operator of a facility from which the spill originated. It is not definitively decided whether that action sounds in tort or contract. R.A. Caldwell v. Gurley Refining Co., 755 F.2d 645 (8th Cir.1985). A lessor of a facility from which a spill took place seeks declaratory judgment that the lessee must indemnify him for any claims by the United States seeking to recover the cost of cleaning up the spill. In deciding a motion to dismiss the complaint; does it matter whether the claim of the United States sounds in tort or contract? If it does not matter, why should joint tort defendants be able to resort to declaratory judgment to resolve their disputes as to liability but be unable to bring a declaratory judgment action against the tort plaintiff?

### *Note on Resolving Uncertainty in the Enforcement of Regulations*

The courts have often examined the availability of declaratory judgment for the review of regulations which the government has not yet sought to enforce.

Three decisions of the Supreme Court in 1967 have become the basis on which lower courts address the issue of whether such disputes are "ripe" for judicial resolution. In each case the plaintiffs sought declaratory and injunctive relief against the application to them of actions taken by the Food and Drug Administration. In Abbott Laboratories v. Gardner, 387 U.S. 136, 87 S.Ct. 1507, 18 L.Ed.2d 681 (1967), the FDA had issued an order requiring labels, advertisements, and other printed matter relating to prescription drugs to designate the established name of the particular drug involved every time its trade name was used anywhere in such material. The plaintiff was faced with the choice of complying with this order or risking prosecution for its violation. In Toilet Goods Association, Inc. v. Gardner, 387 U.S. 167, 87 S.Ct. 1530, 18 L.Ed.2d 704 (1967), the FDA had promulgated regulations for the use of color additives which required clearance and certification of each batch of additive; the plaintiff contended that two of the substances included in the regulation fell outside the statutory definition of color additive. Plaintiff had the choice of complying with the FDA's interpretation of the statute or waiting to defend a case brought by the government which might be a criminal prosecution, a seizure action or an injunctive suit. In Toilet Goods Association, Inc. v. Gardner, 387 U.S. 158, 87 S.Ct. 1520, 18 L.Ed.2d 697 (1967), the FDA had promulgated a regulation providing that if a person refused to permit authorized FDA employees access to regulated manufacturing facilities, the FDA might suspend certification service to that person. The plaintiff had the choice of allowing such access or refusing it and perhaps suffering suspension of certification.

In *Abbott Laboratories*, the Court prefaced its analysis of ripeness by discussing review of the actions of governmental agencies and emphasizing the powerful presumption in favor of judicial review of final agency action:

> Early cases in which this type of judicial review was entertained have been reinforced by the enactment of the Administrative Procedure Act, which embodies the basic presumption of judicial review to one "suffering legal wrong because of agency action, or adversely affected or aggrieved by agency action within the meaning of a relevant statute," 5 U.S.C. § 702, so long as no statute precludes such relief or the action is not one committed by law to agency discretion, 5 U.S.C. § 701(a). The Administrative Procedure Act provides specifically not only for review of "[a]gency action made reviewable by statute" but also for review of "final agency action for which there is no other adequate remedy in a court." 5 U.S.C. § 704.

387 U.S. at 140, 87 S.Ct. at 1511, 18 L.Ed.2d 681.

(For an example of a case where the court found that Congress had decided that pre-enforcement review was not to be available, see Lloyd A. Fry Roofing Co. v. U.S. E.P.A., 554 F.2d 885 (8th Cir.1977).)

In each case in the *Abbott Laboratories* trilogy, the FDA had taken final agency action reviewable under the terms of the Administrative Procedure Act. This is important because the United States has not consented to be sued under the Declaratory Judgment Act and therefore, unless an agency's actions are open to judicial review or legal challenge under some other statute, a declaratory judgment suit against the government will be dismissed on the grounds of sovereign immunity. The analysis of what constitutes "final agency action" is a question for administrative law rather than for remedies, but you should know that the issue is often not an easy one to resolve.

Ripeness is a separate question beyond that of whether review of agency action is available. A two pronged test of ripeness emerged out of the *Abbott Laboratories* trilogy: 1) that the issues presented are fit for judicial resolution, and 2) that withholding judicial consideration would result in hardship to the parties. The Court described the basic rationale of the test as being "to prevent the courts, through avoidance of premature adjudication, from entangling themselves in abstract disagreement over administrative policies, and also to protect the agencies from judicial interference until an administrative decision has been formalized and its effects felt in a concrete way by the challenging parties." *Abbott Laboratories*, 387 U.S. at 148–149, 87 S.Ct. at 1515, 18 L.Ed.2d 681 (1967). Consider whether the first prong parallels the issues focused on in *Haworth* and the second some of the issues in *Cunningham Brothers*.

As to the first prong of the test, in *Abbott Laboratories* the issue presented was a purely legal one on which both parties had moved for summary judgment. It should be noted that factual questions are equally fit for judicial resolution in most cases. The Supreme Court made this clear in *Haworth:* "That the dispute turns upon questions of fact does not withdraw it, as respondent seems to contend, from judicial cognizance. The legal consequences flow from the facts and it is the province of the courts to ascertain and find facts in order to determine the legal consequences. That is every day practice." *Aetna Life v. Haworth*, 300 U.S. at 242, 57 S.Ct. at 465, 81 L.Ed. 617. The issue under this prong of the test appears to be whether the factual context of the case has been properly developed: for instance, is there to be further exercise of the agency's discretion which could materially affect the factual context of the controversy.

The second prong of the test requires an immediate impact on the plaintiff rather than a hypothetical or abstract effect. Thus in the *Abbott Laboratories* trilogy, the impact in the first two cases was to require immediate and substantial change in the private party's behavior or risk the possibility of sanctions. Those circumstances were sufficient for the court to hold the controversies ripe for review. In the third case, there was no immediate impact on behavior and the suspension of certification services was not viewed as a substantial sanction with the result that the complaint for declaratory relief was dismissed. The Third Circuit has summarized this result in A.O. Smith Corp. v. F.T.C., 530 F.2d 515, 524 (3d Cir.1976):

> Thus, it appears from the *Abbott Laboratories* trilogy that one seeking discretionary relief may not obtain pre-enforcement judicial review of agency action if there is no immediate threat of sanctions for noncompliance, or if the potential sanction is de minimis. Conversely, the court should find agency action ripe for judicial review if the action is final and clear-cut, and if it puts the complaining party on the horns of a dilemma: if he complies and awaits ultimate judicial determination of the action's validity, he must change his course of day-to-day conduct, for example, by undertaking substantial preliminary paper work, scientific testing and record-keeping, or by destroying stock; alternatively, if he does not comply, he risks sanctions or injuries including, for example, civil and criminal penalties, or loss of public confidence.

In the same case, the Third Circuit pointed out that the irreparable injury standard for injunctive relief is closely akin to but not the same as the hardship to the parties test for ripeness in pre-enforcement review cases.

It is frequently unsatisfactory to wait for a challenge to a regulation to be ripe before resolving uncertainty as to the regulation's meaning. Consequently, Congress frequently provides for the review of regulations in the statute providing authority for promulgation of the regulations. Typically such review must be sought within a limited time in the courts of appeals through a petition to review; the agency decision is reviewable on the administrative record compiled by the agency in making the rule; and such review precludes further challenge to the rule in a civil or criminal enforcement proceeding. E.g., 33 U.S.C. § 1369 (Clean Water Act); 42 U.S.C. § 6976 (Resource Conservation and Recovery Act). The forms and procedure for petitions to review are set out in Fed.R.App.P. 15–20. This exclusive review procedure is effective in resolving certain types of uncertainty. For example, it adequately addresses the question of whether the regulation as written conforms to the language of the statute. But there are a number of circumstances to which such review is not well adapted. First, if a party takes up the regulated activity after the period for review has passed, he will probably be unable to obtain review of the regulation. Second, many regulations are not written with specificity and their meaning only becomes clear through application; review of such regulations prior to application lacks much of the concrete, focused development that we look for in litigation. Procedural regulations are particularly difficult to review in the abstract. Finally, while some exclusive review provisions allow for review on the basis of newly-discovered evidence, such provisions are generally not well suited to judicial reconsideration on the basis of changed circumstances. After the exclusive review period has passed, those seeking regulatory change must generally proceed by petitioning the agency to amend the regulation.

### *Note on Reformation*

Reformation is another remedy which at least in theory is not coercive and deserves a few words of particular emphasis. Reformation is available when a written document, typically a contract or conveyance, does not accurately reflect the intentions of the parties and the court orders the document reformed or corrected to reflect the parties' intentions accurately or the court's opinion simply states the reformed terms of the document making it unnecessary to change the document physically. Suppose Smith agrees to sell 100 widgets to Jones for $10,000 and tells his attorney to draw papers to that effect. Smith's attorney puts in a price of $1,000 by mistake and forwards the paper to Jones who signs it without being aware of the error. Smith has a good cause of action against Jones for reformation. The relief from the judge can take the form of directing the defendant to correct the document in question or to execute a new, correct version, or the judge can simply declare the terms of the contract in her order.

It is important to emphasize, in a reformation action, that the court is not directing the creation of an agreement which is new in substance, only one that is new in form so that the original substance is fairly and properly stated. There is also frequent talk of fraud or misrepresentation in reformation cases; this is fraud or misrepresentation in drawing up the written instrument but not as to the terms of the original agreement. If Smith agrees with a blind man to sell him 100 widgets for $1,000 and then obtains his signature on a contract in which the price is stated as $10,000, there is a good claim for reformation.

If the court is doing no more than assuring the accurate recording of the intentions of the parties, one may question why the parties need to resort to the court at all and whether there is any case or controversy for the court to resolve. Reformation is an important remedy in at least three circumstances. First, if one of the parties is a corporation or a political body, the true controversy may lie not between the individuals who reached agreement but between one of them and the corporate successors of the other. If Smith as President of Widgets, Inc. agrees to supply Jones with 100 widgets for $1,000 but the written document records a $10,000 price and Smith then sells Widgets, Inc. to a third party without discussing the contract with Jones, Jones will have a live controversy with Widgets, Inc. in which Smith would be a central witness for him.

Next, reformation may be an important element of a suit in which the controversy focuses on a part of the agreement which cannot be properly construed without correcting the part subject to reformation. Parties to a contract may dispute whether plaintiff is entitled to liquidated damages and in order to show that his claim is ripe and to collect any judgment, the plaintiff would want reformation of a provision stating that all liquidated damages are due and payable on "January 1, 1999" when the parties had intended to write "January 1, 1989." Another typical form of litigation is a suit for breach of the agreement with a counterclaim for reformation which negates plaintiff's claim.

Finally, the cases involving fraud or misrepresentation in procuring a party's agreement to a written instrument that does not accurately reflect the agreement of the parties will also present matters clearly fit for judicial resolution. There are, of course, cases in which the plaintiff seeking reformation has come to believe that the document does not reflect the agreement of the parties and in which plaintiff claims fraud or misrepresentation in the drawing of the document, but the central question is determining whether the parties reached any agreement on the item in question. A dispute over interpreting an ambiguity on which the parties had no understanding is not appropriately resolved by reformation.

Probably because the plaintiff is asking the court to set aside the plain language of the agreement, the burden of proof in reformation cases is typically one of clear and convincing evidence. In Mississippi, the case for reformation must be proved beyond a reasonable doubt. Neither the statute of frauds nor the parol evidence rule is a bar to the plaintiff presenting his case as to what the actual agreement between the parties was.

Reformation can have collateral consequences of substantial magnitude. In 1986, U.S. Lines, a shipping company, entered into an agreement with Prudential Insurance Co. to reduce a loan secured by some vessels owned by U.S. Lines. The mortgage debt should have been reduced to $92,885,000. By typographical error originating with a secretary in the offices of the lender's attorneys, the documents stated that the loan was reduced to $92,885. U.S. Lines later went into bankruptcy and subordinate mortgage lenders claimed that Prudential's security interest was limited to $92,885. Although not pled as an issue of reformation, the Second Circuit held that the mortgage was good for

$92 million as intended by the parties. Prudential Ins. Co. v. S.S. American Lancer, 870 F.2d 867 (2d Cir.1989).

Prudential then brought an action in state court against the law firm involved with restructuring the loan for negligence, malpractice, and breach of contract, requesting several million dollars in damages. As the basis for damages flowing from the error, Prudential pointed to: (1) the costs of defending the bankruptcy litigation; (2) the payment Prudential made to settle the litigation; (3) the extra dockage and maintenance expenses incurred because of delay in selling the ships; (4) loss of investment or interest income resulting from the delay; and (5) the costs of defending litigation brought by subordinate mortgage holders. Assuming the conceded fact that a secretary in the law firm had made an error which no one noticed thereafter, on what grounds, if any, should Prudential recover? Prudential Insurance Co. v. Dewey Ballantine, Bushby, Palmer & Wood, 170 A.D.2d 108, 573 N.Y.S.2d 981 (1991)(allowing suit against firm representing Prudential), aff'd, 80 N.Y.2d 377, 605 N.E.2d 318, 590 N.Y.S.2d 831 (1992)(no proof of breach of duty of care by borrower's law firm).

# Chapter 5

# CRIMINAL AND CIVIL SANCTIONS

Both the civil and criminal law provide remedies that are not measured solely by plaintiff's or defendant's rightful position. Among these remedies are fines, civil penalties, punitive damages, forfeitures, imprisonment, directions to perform community service and loss of a professional license or status. One typical characteristic of such sanctions is that they are more frequently sought by the government than by a party directly injured by the defendant's actions. Also, the imposition of the sanction does not depend solely on a showing of injury or damage. There are many more convictions for bank robbery than there are for conspiracy to rob a bank where no bank was actually robbed or for attempted bank robbery where no robbery took place; nevertheless, the agreement to rob the bank and the attempt to commit the robbery are both crimes in many jurisdictions. This chapter explores the principles and rules which apply to the imposition of a variety of sanctions and the considerations weighed by judges in exercising their discretion in this area. The focus is on exploring the distinctions between the various forms of sanctions and common concerns which tie many sanction remedies together rather than on providing detailed knowledge of entire complex subjects such as sentencing.

## A. DISTINGUISHING CRIMINAL AND CIVIL SANCTIONS

Where the law gives the court discretion in imposing sanctions, particularly criminal sanctions, judges typically consider the gravity of the offense and the harm or injury it has caused; they also consider the impact of the sanction on the defendant and the community in terms of: (a) deterring the defendant from committing other criminal or civil violations; (b) deterring others who know of the sanction from committing such violations; (c) preventing the defendant through incarceration or supervision on parole or probation from committing such violations; (d) retribution or "just deserts" for committing morally reprehensible acts; and (e) rehabilitating or reforming the personality and character of the defendant so that he will not commit further violations and will lead a useful or socially beneficial life.

In many cases it is difficult to distinguish between sanctions that are remedial in the sense that they return a plaintiff to his rightful position or further a public policy such as safety or preventing fraud, and those remedies that are punitive to the defendant. Frequently a sanction serves both purposes.

It is generally believed that important consequences turn on distinguishing civil from criminal cases. The procedure of the two sorts of cases differs; the burden of proof differs; the available "remedies" may differ. Nevertheless, distinguishing between civil and criminal sanctions involves an element of circularity similar to that in trying to give meaning to the maxim that where there is a right there is a remedy. Certain remedies, primarily the sanction of incarceration and the imposition of penalties not measured by injury or damage to the plaintiff, are usually thought of as criminal sanctions involving punishment. It is a common assumption that courts can only punish a person for the commission of a crime. The issue raised by this section of the chapter is whether that assumption has any validity and, if so, what caveats must be attached to it.

May punishments only be imposed after a criminal proceeding or is punishment defined as the sanctions imposed after a criminal proceeding? Is the legislature free to provide for incarceration or monetary penalties after a criminal or civil proceeding as it chooses? Does historical usage determine when a sanction is civil and when it is criminal? Or is a distinction to be drawn between "remedial" civil sanctions and "punitive" criminal sanctions? If so, how is a court to determine when a case involves one form of sanction rather than another—by considering the legislative history of the statute establishing the sanction or the procedural requirements which must be met before the sanction is imposed or by examining the nature of the sanction itself? If weight is put on the intention of the legislature, what are the constitutional restraints on legislative action?

## KENNEDY v. MENDOZA–MARTINEZ

Supreme Court of the United States, 1963.
372 U.S. 144, 83 S.Ct. 554, 9 L.Ed.2d 644.

MR. JUSTICE GOLDBERG delivered the opinion of the Court.

We are called upon in these two cases to decide the grave and fundamental problem, common to both, of the constitutionality of Acts of Congress which divest an American of his citizenship for "[d]eparting from or remaining outside of the jurisdiction of the United States in time of war or . . . national emergency for the purpose of evading or avoiding training and service" in the Nation's armed forces. * * *

Mendoza–Martinez was born in this country in 1922 and therefore acquired American citizenship by birth. By reason of his parentage, he also, under Mexican law, gained Mexican citizenship, thereby possessing dual nationality. In 1942 he departed from this country and went to Mexico solely, as he admits, for the purpose of evading military service in our armed forces. He concedes that he remained there for that sole purpose until November 1946, when he voluntarily returned to this country. In 1947, in the United States District Court for the Southern District of California, he pleaded guilty to and was convicted of evasion of his service obligations in violation of § 11 of the Selective Training and Service Act of 1940. He served the imposed sentence of a year and a day. For all that appears in the record, he was, upon his release, allowed to reside undisturbed in this country until 1953, when, after a lapse of five years, he was served with a warrant of arrest in deportation proceedings. This was premised on the assertion that, by remaining outside the United States to avoid military service after September 27, 1944, when § 401(j) took effect, he had lost his American citizenship. Following the hearing, the Attorney General's special inquiry officer sustained the warrant and ordered that Mendoza–Martinez be deported as an alien. He appealed to the Board of Immigration Appeals of the Department of Justice, which dismissed his appeal.

Thereafter, Mendoza–Martinez brought a declaratory judgment action in the Federal District Court for the Southern District of California, seeking a declaration of his status as a citizen, of the unconstitutionality of § 401(j), and of the voidness of all orders of deportation directed against him. * * *

The present cases present for decision the constitutionality of * * * § 401(j), added in 1944, and its successor and present counterpart, § 349(a)(10) of the Immigration and Nationality Act of 1952. We have come to the conclusion that there is a basic question in the present cases, the answer to which obviates a choice here between the powers of Congress and the constitutional guarantee of citizenship. That issue is whether the statutes here, which automatically—without prior court or administrative proceedings—impose forfeiture of citizenship, are essentially penal in character, and consequently have deprived the appellees of their citizenship without due process of law and without according them the rights guaranteed by the Fifth and Sixth Amendments, including notice, confrontation, compulsory process for obtaining witnesses, trial by jury, and assistance of counsel. * * *

As the Government concedes, §§ 401(j) and 349(a)(10) automatically strip an American of his citizenship, with concomitant deprivation "of all that makes life worth living," Ng Fung Ho v. White, 259 U.S. 276, 284–285, whenever a citizen departs from or remains outside the jurisdiction of this country for the purpose of evading his military obligations. Conviction for draft evasion * * * is not prerequisite to the operation of this sanction. Independently of prosecution, forfeiture of citizenship attaches when the statutory set of facts develops. It is argued that the availability after the fact of administrative and judicial proceedings * * * to contest the validity of the sanction meets the measure of due process. But the legislative history and judicial expression with respect to every congressional enactment relating to the provisions in question dating back to 1865 establish that forfeiture of citizenship is a penalty for the act of leaving or staying outside the country to avoid the draft. This being so, the Fifth and Sixth Amendments mandate that this punishment cannot be imposed without a prior criminal trial and all its incidents, including indictment, notice, confrontation, jury trial, assistance of counsel, and compulsory process for obtaining witnesses. If the sanction these sections impose is punishment, and it plainly is, the procedural safeguards required as incidents of a criminal prosecution are lacking. We need go no further.

The punitive nature of the sanction here is evident under the tests traditionally applied to determine whether an Act of Congress is penal or regulatory in character, even though in other cases this problem has been extremely difficult and elusive of solution. Whether the sanction involves an affirmative disability or restraint, whether it has historically been regarded as a punishment,[23] whether it comes into play only on a finding of *scienter,* whether its operation will promote the traditional aims of punishment—retribution and deterrence, whether the behavior to which it applies is already a crime, whether an alternative purpose to which it may rationally be connected is assignable for it, and whether it appears excessive in relation to the alternative purpose assigned are all relevant to the inquiry, and may often point in differing directions. Absent conclusive evidence of congressional intent as to the penal nature of a statute, these factors must be considered in relation to the statute on its face. Here, although we are convinced that application of these criteria to the face of the statutes supports the conclusion that they are punitive, a detailed examination along such lines is unnecessary, because the objective manifestations of congressional purpose indicate conclusively that the provisions in question can only be interpreted as punitive. A study of the history of the predecessor of § 401(j), which "is worth a volume of logic," New York Trust Co. v. Eisner, 256 U.S. 345, 349, 41 S.Ct. 506, 507, 65 L.Ed. 963, coupled with a reading of Congress' reasons for enacting § 401(j), compels a conclusion that the statute's primary function is to serve as an additional penalty for a special category of draft evader. * * *

The immediate legislative history of § 401(j) confirms the conclusion, based upon study of the earlier legislative and judicial history, that it is punitive in nature. The language of the section was, to begin with, quite obviously patterned on that of its predecessor, an understandable fact since the draft of the bill was submitted to the Congress by Attorney General Biddle along with a letter to Chairman Russell of the Senate Immigration Committee, in which the Attorney General referred for

**23.** Reference to history here is peculiarly appropriate. Though not determinative, it supports our holding to note that forfeiture of citizenship and the related devices of banishment and exile have throughout history been used as punishment.... Banishment was a weapon in the English legal arsenal for centuries, but it was always "adjudged a harsh punishment even by men who were accustomed to brutality in the administration of criminal justice." Maxey, Loss of Nationality: Individual Choice or Government Fiat? 26 Albany L.Rev. 151, 164 (1962).

precedent to the 1912 reenactment of the 1865 statute. This letter, which was the impetus for the enactment of the bill, was quoted in full text in support of it in both the House and Senate Committee Reports. * * * The letter was couched entirely in terms of an argument that citizens who had left the country in order to escape military service should be dealt with, and that loss of citizenship was a proper way to deal with them. There was no reference to the societal good that would be wrought by the legislation, nor to any improvement in soldier morale or in the conduct of war generally that would be gained by the passage of the statute. The House Committee Report and the sponsors of the bill endorsed it on the same basis. The report referred for support to the fact that the FBI files showed "over 800 draft delinquents" in the El Paso area alone who had crossed to Mexico to evade the draft. The obvious inference to be drawn from the report, the example it contained, and the lack of mention of any broader purpose is that Congress was concerned solely with inflicting effective retribution upon this class of draft evaders and, no doubt, on others similarly situated. Thus, on the floor of the House, Representative Dickstein of New York, the Chairman of the House Committee on Immigration and Naturalization, explained the bill solely as a means of dealing with "draft dodgers who left this country knowing that there was a possibility that they might be drafted in this war and that they might have to serve in the armed forces...." * * * Senator Russell, who was manager of the bill as well as Chairman of the Senate Immigration Committee, explained it in similar terms:

> "Certainly those who, having enjoyed the advantages of living in the United States, were unwilling to serve their country or subject themselves to the Selective Service Act, should be penalized in some measure.... Any American citizen who is convicted of violating the Selective Service Act loses his citizenship. This bill would merely impose a similar penalty on those who are not subject to the jurisdiction of our courts, the penalty being the same as would result in the case of those who are subject to the jurisdiction of our courts." 90 Cong.Rec. 7629 (1944).

The Senate and House debates, together with Attorney General Biddle's letter, brought to light no alternative purpose to differentiate the new statute from its predecessor. Indeed, as indicated, the Attorney General's letter specifically relied on the predecessor statute as precedent for this enactment, and both the letter and the debates, consistent with the character of the predecessor statute, referred to reasons for the enactment of the bill which were fundamentally retributive in nature. When all of these considerations are weighed, as they must be, in the context of the incontestably punitive nature of the predecessor statute, the conclusion that § 401(j) was itself dominantly punitive becomes inescapable. The legislative history of § 349(a)(10) of the Immigration and Nationality Act of 1952, which re-enacted § 401(j), adds nothing to disturb that result. Our conclusion from the legislative and judicial history is, therefore, that Congress in these sections decreed an additional punishment for the crime of draft avoidance in the special category of cases wherein the evader leaves the country. It cannot do this without providing the safeguards which must attend a criminal prosecution. * * *

We conclude, for the reasons stated, that §§ 401(j) and 349(a)(10) are punitive and as such cannot constitutionally stand, lacking as they do the procedural safeguards which the Constitution commands. * * *

MR. JUSTICE DOUGLAS and MR. JUSTICE BLACK, while joining the opinion of the Court, adhere to the views expressed in the dissent of MR. JUSTICE DOUGLAS, in which MR. JUSTICE BLACK joined, in Perez v. Brownell, 356 U.S. 44, 79, 78 S.Ct. 568, 586, 2 L.Ed.2d 603, that Congress has no power to deprive a person of the citizenship granted the native-born by § 1, cl. 1, of the Fourteenth Amendment. * * *

MR. JUSTICE STEWART, with whom MR. JUSTICE WHITE joins, dissenting. * * *

Nearly 50 years ago the Court held that Congress had constitutional power to denationalize a native-born citizen who married a foreigner but continued to reside here. Mackenzie v. Hare, 239 U.S. 299, 36 S.Ct. 106, 60 L.Ed. 297. * * * The power of Congress to denationalize a native-born citizen, without a criminal trial, was reaffirmed in Savorgnan v. United States, 338 U.S. 491, 70 S.Ct. 292, 94 L.Ed. 287. And less than five years ago, in Perez v. Brownell, 356 U.S. 44, 78 S.Ct. 568, 2 L.Ed.2d 603, the Court again upheld this congressional power * * *. In short, it has been established for almost 50 years that Congress under some circumstances may, without providing for a criminal trial, make expatriation the consequence of the voluntary conduct of a United States citizen, irrespective of the citizen's subjective intention to renounce his nationality, and irrespective too of his awareness that denationalization will be the result of his conduct.

The position taken by the Court today is simply that, unlike the statutes involved in *Mackenzie, Savorgnan* and *Perez,* the statutes at issue in the present case employ deprivation of citizenship as a penal sanction. * * *

I cannot find, as the Court does, that § 401(j) was motivated primarily by the desire to wreak vengeance upon those individuals who fled the country to avoid military service. Rather, the statute seems to me precisely the same kind of regulatory measure, rational and efficacious, which this Court upheld against similar objections in *Perez v. Brownell,* supra.[13]

**13.** I cannot suppose that the Court today is saying that Congress can impose denationalization without the safeguards of a criminal trial for conduct which is unexceptionable—like marrying an alien—or relatively innocuous—like voting in a foreign election—but that Congress cannot do so for conduct which is reprehensible.

## UNITED STATES v. HALPER

Supreme Court of the United States, 1989.
490 U.S. 435, 109 S.Ct. 1892, 104 L.Ed.2d 487.

JUSTICE BLACKMUN delivered the opinion of the Court.

In this case, we consider whether and under what circumstances a civil penalty may constitute "punishment" for the purposes of double jeopardy analysis.[1] * * *

I

* * * [Halper, the manager of a laboratory that submitted Medicare claims, was convicted of 65 counts of making false claims under the Medicare program which resulted in a total over-payment to the laboratory of $585. He was sentenced to two years imprisonment and a $5,000 fine. The government then brought this civil action against him under the False Claims Act, 31 U.S.C. §§ 3729–3731, and prevailed on the issue of liability.]

The [district] court then turned its attention to the remedy for Halper's multiple violations. The remedial provision of the Act stated that a person in violation is "liable to the United States Government for a civil penalty of $2,000, an amount equal to 2 times the amount of damages the Government sustains, because of the act of that person, and costs of the civil action." § 3729. Having violated the Act 65 separate times, Halper thus appeared to be subject to a statutory penalty of more than $130,000.

The District Court, however, concluded that in light of Halper's previous criminal punishment, an additional penalty this large would violate the Double Jeopardy Clause. * * *

II

This Court many times has held that the Double Jeopardy Clause protects against three distinct abuses: a second prosecution for the same offense after acquittal; a second prosecution for the same offense after conviction; and multiple punishments for the same offense. The third of these protections—the one at issue here—has deep roots in our history and jurisprudence. * * *

The sole question here is whether the statutory penalty authorized by the civil False Claims Act, under which Halper is subject to liability of $130,000 for false claims amounting to $585, constitutes a second "punishment" for the purpose of double jeopardy analysis.

The Government argues that in three previous cases, Helvering v. Mitchell, 303 U.S. 391, 58 S.Ct. 630, 82 L.Ed. 917 (1938), United States ex rel. Marcus v. Hess, [317 U.S. 537, 63 S.Ct. 379, 87 L.Ed. 443 (1943) ], and Rex Trailer Co. v. United States, 350 U.S. 148, 76 S.Ct. 219, 100 L.Ed. 149 (1956), this Court foreclosed any argument that a penalty assessed in a civil proceeding, and specifically in a civil False Claims Act proceeding, may give rise to double jeopardy. Specifically, the Govern-

1. The Double Jeopardy Clause reads: "[N]or shall any person be subject for the same offence to be twice put in jeopardy of life or limb...." U.S. Const., Amdt. 5.

ment asserts that these cases establish three principles: first, that the Double Jeopardy Clause's prohibition against multiple punishment protects against only a second criminal penalty; second, that criminal penalties are imposed only in criminal proceedings; and, third, that proceedings under, and penalties authorized by, the civil False Claims Act are civil in nature. In addition, the Government argues on the basis of these three cases and others that whether a proceeding or penalty is civil or criminal is a matter of statutory construction, and that Congress clearly intended the proceedings and penalty at issue here to be civil in nature.

The Government, in our view, has misconstrued somewhat the nature of the multiple-punishment inquiry, and, in so doing, has overread the holdings of our precedents. Although, taken together, these cases establish that proceedings and penalties under the civil False Claims Act are indeed civil in nature, and that a civil remedy does not rise to the level of "punishment" merely because Congress provided for civil recovery in excess of the Government's actual damages, they do not foreclose the possibility that in a particular case a civil penalty authorized by the Act may be so extreme and so divorced from the Government's damages and expenses as to constitute punishment.

In *Mitchell,* the Commissioner of Internal Revenue determined that the taxpayer fraudulently had asserted large sums as deductions on his 1929 income tax return. Mitchell was indicted and prosecuted for willful evasion of taxes. At trial, however, he was acquitted. The Government then brought an action to collect a deficiency of $728,709.84 in Mitchell's tax and, as well, a 50% additional amount specified by statute on account of the fraud. Mitchell argued that this second action subjected him to double jeopardy because the 50% addition was intended as punishment, and that the supposedly civil assessment proceeding therefore was actually a second criminal proceeding based on a single course of conduct.

This Court did not agree. The Double Jeopardy Clause, it noted, "prohibits merely punishing twice, or attempting a second time to punish criminally, for the same offense." 303 U.S., at 399, 58 S.Ct., at 633. Because Mitchell was acquitted (and therefore not punished) in his criminal prosecution, the Court was called upon to determine only whether the statute imposed a criminal sanction—in which case the deficiency proceeding would be an unconstitutional second attempt to punish criminally. Whether the statutory sanction was criminal in nature, the Court held, was a question of statutory interpretation; and, applying traditional canons of construction, the Court had little difficulty concluding that Congress intended that the statute impose a civil penalty and that the deficiency sanction was in fact remedial, providing reimbursement to the Government for investigatory and other costs of the taxpayer's fraud. Since "in the civil enforcement of a remedial sanction there can be no double jeopardy," the Court rejected Mitchell's claim.

*Mitchell* at most is of tangential significance for our current inquiry. While the opinion makes clear that the Government may impose both a criminal and a civil sanction with respect to the same act or omission, and that whether a given sanction is criminal is a matter of statutory construction, it simply does not address the question we face today: whether a civil sanction, in application, may be so divorced from any remedial goal that it constitutes "punishment" for the purpose of double jeopardy analysis. * * *

[In *Rex Trailer*], the defendants fraudulently purchased five trucks under the Surplus Property Act of 1944, by claiming veteran priority rights to which they were not entitled. They pleaded *nolo contendere* to criminal charges and paid fines aggregating $25,000. The Government then brought a civil action under the Surplus Property Act of 1944, 58 Stat. 765, which provided three alternative civil remedies: (1) $2,000 for each act plus double damages and costs; (2) recovery "as liquidated damages" of twice the consideration agreed to be given; and (3) recovery of the property plus, "as liquidated damages," retention of the consideration given. The Government sought the first of these remedies which the Court considered "comparable to the recovery under liquidated-damage provisions which fix compensation for anticipated loss." The Court rejected the defendants' claim that the $2,000–per-count penalty constituted a second punishment. Although the Court recognized that the Government's actual loss due to the defendants' fraud was difficult if not impossible to ascertain, it recognized that the Government did sustain injury due to the resultant decrease of motor vehicles available to Government agencies, an increase in undesirable speculation, and damage to its program of promoting bona fide sales to veterans.[6] Since the function of a liquidated damages provision was to provide a measure of recovery where damages are difficult to quantify, the Court found "on the record before it—where the defendants were liable for only $10,000—that they had not been subjected to a "measure of recovery . . . so unreasonable or excessive" as to constitute a second criminal punishment in violation of double jeopardy.

The relevant teaching of these cases is that the Government is entitled to rough remedial justice, that is, it may demand compensation according to somewhat imprecise formulas, such as reasonable liquidated damages or a fixed sum plus double damages, without being deemed to have imposed a second punishment for the purpose of double jeopardy analysis. * * *

III

We turn, finally, to the unresolved question implicit in our cases: whether and under what circumstances a civil penalty may constitute punishment for the purpose of the Double Jeopardy Clause. As noted above, the Government takes the position that punishment in the relevant sense is meted out only in criminal proceedings, and that whether proceedings are criminal or civil is a matter of statutory

6. The Court could have included the Government's investigative and prosecutorial costs. These also must be factored into a determination as to whether the sanction was disproportionate to the Government's loss.

construction. The Government correctly observes that this Court has followed this abstract approach when determining whether the procedural protections of the Sixth Amendment apply to proceedings under a given statute, in affixing the appropriate standard of proof for such proceedings, and in determining whether double jeopardy protections should be applied. But while recourse to statutory language, structure, and intent is appropriate in identifying the inherent nature of a proceeding, or in determining the constitutional safeguards that must accompany those proceedings as a general matter, the approach is not well suited to the context of the "humane interests" safeguarded by the Double Jeopardy Clause's proscription of multiple punishments. This constitutional protection is intrinsically personal. Its violation can be identified only by assessing the character of the actual sanctions imposed on the individual by the machinery of the state.[7]

In making this assessment, the labels "criminal" and "civil" are not of paramount importance. It is commonly understood that civil proceedings may advance punitive as well as remedial goals, and, conversely, that both punitive and remedial goals may be served by criminal penalties.[8] The notion of punishment, as we commonly understand it, cuts across the division between the civil and the criminal law, and for the purposes of assessing whether a given sanction constitutes multiple punishment barred by the Double Jeopardy Clause, we must follow the notion where it leads. Cf. Hicks v. Feiock, 485 U.S. 624, 108 S.Ct. 1423, 99 L.Ed.2d 721 (1988) ("[T]he labels affixed either to the proceeding or to the relief imposed ... are not controlling and will not be allowed to defeat the applicable protections of federal constitutional law"). To that end, the determination whether a given civil sanction constitutes punishment in the relevant sense requires a particularized assessment of the penalty imposed and the purposes that the penalty may fairly be said to serve. Simply put, a civil as well as a criminal sanction constitutes punishment when the sanction as applied in the individual case serves the goals of punishment.

These goals are familiar. We have recognized in other contexts that punishment serves the twin aims of retribution and deterrence. See, e.g., Kennedy v. Mendoza–Martinez, 372 U.S. 144, 168, 83 S.Ct. 554, 567, 9 L.Ed.2d 644 (1963)(these are the "traditional aims of punishment"). Furthermore, "[r]etribution and deterrence are not legitimate nonpunitive governmental objectives." From these premises, it follows that a civil sanction that cannot fairly be said solely to serve a remedial

7. This is not to say that whether a sanction constitutes punishment must be determined from the defendant's perspective. On the contrary, our cases have acknowledged that for the defendant even remedial sanctions carry the sting of punishment. Rather, we hold merely that in determining whether a particular civil sanction constitutes criminal punishment, it is the purposes actually served by the sanction in question, not the underlying nature of the proceeding giving rise to the sanction, that must be evaluated.

8. As the name indicates, punitive damages, available in civil cases, serve punitive goals. By the same token, strict liability crimes are principally directed at social betterment rather than punishment of culpable individuals.

purpose, but rather can only be explained as also serving either retributive or deterrent purposes, is punishment, as we have come to understand the term. * * * We therefore hold that under the Double Jeopardy Clause a defendant who already has been punished in a criminal prosecution may not be subjected to an additional civil sanction to the extent that the second sanction may not fairly be characterized as remedial, but only as a deterrent or retribution.

We acknowledge that this inquiry will not be an exact pursuit. In our decided cases we have noted that the precise amount of the Government's damages and costs may prove to be difficult, if not impossible, to ascertain. Similarly, it would be difficult if not impossible in many cases for a court to determine the precise dollar figure at which a civil sanction has accomplished its remedial purpose of making the Government whole, but beyond which the sanction takes on the quality of punishment. In other words, as we have observed above, the process of affixing a sanction that compensates the Government for all its costs inevitably involves an element of rough justice. Our upholding reasonable liquidated damages clauses reflects this unavoidable imprecision. Similarly, we have recognized that in the ordinary case fixed-penalty-plus-double-damages provisions can be said to do no more than make the Government whole.

We cast no shadow on these time-honored judgments. What we announce now is a rule for the rare case, the case such as the one before us, where a fixed-penalty provision subjects a prolific but small-gauge offender to a sanction overwhelmingly disproportionate to the damages he has caused. The rule is one of reason: Where a defendant previously has sustained a criminal penalty and the civil penalty sought in the subsequent proceeding bears no rational relation to the goal of compensating the Government for its loss, but rather appears to qualify as "punishment" in the plain meaning of the word, then the defendant is entitled to an accounting of the Government's damages and costs to determine if the penalty sought in fact constitutes a second punishment. * * *

We do not consider our ruling far reaching or disruptive of the Government's need to combat fraud. Nothing in today's ruling precludes the Government from seeking the full civil penalty against a defendant who previously has not been punished for the same conduct, even if the civil sanction imposed is punitive. In such a case, the Double Jeopardy Clause simply is not implicated. Nor does the decision prevent the Government from seeking and obtaining both the full civil penalty and the full range of statutorily authorized criminal penalties in the same proceeding. In a single proceeding the multiple punishment issue would be limited to ensuring that the total punishment did not exceed that authorized by the legislature. Finally, nothing in today's opinion precludes a private party from filing a civil suit seeking damages for conduct that previously was the subject of criminal prosecution and punishment. The protections of the Double Jeopardy Clause are not triggered by litigation between private parties. In other words, the only proscription established by our ruling is that the Government may not criminally prosecute a defendant, impose a criminal penalty upon him, and then bring a separate civil action based on the same conduct and receive a judgment that is not rationally related to the goal of making the Government whole. * * *

[JUSTICE KENNEDY filed a concurring opinion.]

## UNITED STATES v. SALERNO

Supreme Court of the United States, 1987.
481 U.S. 739, 107 S.Ct. 2095, 95 L.Ed.2d 697.

CHIEF JUSTICE REHNQUIST delivered the opinion of the Court.

* * * Responding to "the alarming problem of crimes committed by persons on release," S.Rep. No. 98–225, p. 3 (1983), U.S.Code Cong. & Admin.News 1984, pp. 3182, 3185, Congress formulated the Bail Reform Act of 1984, 18 U.S.C. § 3141 *et seq.* (1982 ed., Supp. III), as the solution to a bail crisis in the federal courts. The Act represents the National Legislature's considered response to numerous perceived deficiencies in the federal bail process. By providing for sweeping changes in both the way federal courts consider bail applications and the circumstances under which bail is granted, Congress hoped to "give the courts adequate authority to make release decisions that give appropriate recognition to the danger a person may pose to others if released." S.Rep. No. 98–225, p. 3, U.S.Code Cong. & Admin.News 1984, p. 3185.

To this end, § 3141(a) of the Act requires a judicial officer to determine whether an arrestee shall be detained. Section 3142(e) provides that "[i]f, after a hearing pursuant to the provisions of subsection (f), the judicial officer finds that no condition or combination of conditions will reasonably assure the appearance of the person as required and the safety of any other person and the community, he shall order the detention of the person prior to trial." Section 3142(f) provides the arrestee with a number of procedural safeguards. He may request the presence of counsel at the detention hearing, he may testify and present witnesses in his behalf, as well as proffer evidence, and he may cross-examine other witnesses appearing at the hearing. If the judicial officer finds that no conditions of pretrial release can reasonably assure the safety of other persons and the community, he must state his findings of fact in writing, § 3142(i), and support his conclusion with "clear and convincing evidence," § 3142(f).

The judicial officer is not given unbridled discretion in making the detention determination. Congress has specified the considerations relevant to that decision. These factors include the nature and seriousness of the charges, the substantiality of the Government's evidence against the arrestee, the arrestee's background and characteristics, and the nature and seriousness of the danger posed by the suspect's release. § 3142(g). Should a judicial officer order detention, the detainee is entitled to expedited appellate review of the detention order. §§ 3145(b), (c).

Respondents Anthony Salerno and Vincent Cafaro were arrested on March 21, 1986, after being charged in a 29–count indictment alleging various Racketeer Influenced and Corrupt Organizations Act (RICO) violations, mail and wire fraud offenses, extortion, and various criminal gambling violations. The RICO counts alleged 35 acts of racketeering activity, including fraud, extortion, gambling, and conspiracy to commit murder. At respondents' arraignment, the Government moved to have Salerno and Cafaro detained pursuant to § 3142(e), on the ground that no condition of release would assure the safety of the community or any person. The District Court held a hearing at which the Government made a detailed proffer of evidence. The Government's case showed that Salerno was the "boss" of the Genovese Crime Family of La Cosa Nostra and that Cafaro was a "captain" in the Genovese Family. According to the Government's proffer, based in large part on conversations intercepted by a court-ordered wiretap, the two respondents had participated in wide-ranging conspiracies to aid their illegitimate enterprises through violent means. The Government also offered the testimony of two of its trial witnesses, who would assert that Salerno personally participated in two murder conspiracies. Salerno opposed the motion for detention, challenging the credibility of the Government's witnesses. He offered the testimony of several character witnesses as well as a letter from his doctor stating that he was suffering from a serious medical condition. Cafaro presented no evidence at the hearing, but instead characterized the wiretap conversations as merely "tough talk."

The District Court granted the Government's detention motion, concluding that the Government had established by clear and convincing evidence that no condition or combination of conditions of release would ensure the safety of the community or any person:

> "The activities of a criminal organization such as the Genovese Family do not cease with the arrest of its principals and their release on even the most stringent of bail conditions. The illegal businesses, in place for many years, require constant attention and protection, or they will fail. Under these circumstances, this court recognizes a strong incentive on the part of its leadership to continue business as usual. When business as usual involves threats, beatings, and murder, the present danger such people pose in the community is self-evident." 631 F.Supp. 1364, 1375 (S.D.N.Y.1986).
> * * *

Respondents present two grounds for invalidating the Bail Reform Act's provisions permitting pretrial detention on the basis of future dangerousness. First, they rely upon the Court of Appeals' conclusion that the Act exceeds the limitations placed upon the Federal Government by the Due Process Clause of the Fifth Amendment. Second, they contend that the Act contravenes the Eighth Amendment's proscription against excessive bail. We treat these contentions in turn.

The Due Process Clause of the Fifth Amendment provides that "No person shall ... be deprived of life, liberty, or property, without due process of law...." This Court has held that the Due Process Clause protects individuals against two types of government action. So-called "substantive due process" prevents the government from engaging in conduct that "shocks the conscience," Rochin v. California, 342 U.S. 165, 172, 72 S.Ct. 205, 209, 96 L.Ed. 183 (1952), or interferes with rights "implicit in the concept of ordered liberty," Palko v. Connecticut, 302 U.S. 319, 325–326, 58 S.Ct. 149, 152, 82 L.Ed. 288 (1937). When government action depriving a person of life, liberty, or property survives substantive due process scrutiny, it must still be implemented in a fair manner. This requirement has traditionally been referred to as "procedural" due process.

Respondents first argue that the Act violates substantive due process because the pretrial detention it authorizes constitutes impermissible punishment before trial. * * * The Government, however, has never argued that pretrial detention could be upheld if it were "punishment." The Court of Appeals assumed that pretrial detention under the Bail Reform Act is regulatory, not penal, and we agree that it is.

As an initial matter, the mere fact that a person is detained does not inexorably lead to the conclusion that the government has imposed punishment. To determine whether a restriction on liberty constitutes impermissible punishment or permissible regulation, we first look to legislative intent. Unless Congress expressly intended to impose punitive restrictions, the punitive/regulatory distinction turns on " 'whether an alternative purpose to which [the restriction] may rationally be connected is assignable for it, and whether it appears excessive in relation to the alternative purpose assigned [to it].' "

We conclude that the detention imposed by the Act falls on the regulatory side of the dichotomy. The legislative history of the Bail Reform Act clearly indicates that Congress did not formulate the pretrial detention provisions as punishment for dangerous individuals. See S.Rep. No. 98–225, p. 8. Congress instead perceived pretrial detention as a potential solution to a pressing societal problem. There is no doubt that preventing danger to the community is a legitimate regulatory goal.

Nor are the incidents of pretrial detention excessive in relation to the regulatory goal Congress sought to achieve. The Bail Reform Act carefully limits the circumstances under which detention may be sought to the most serious of crimes. See 18 U.S.C. § 3142(f)(detention hearings available if case involves crimes of violence, offenses for which the sentence is life imprisonment or death, serious drug offenses, or certain repeat offenders). The arrestee is entitled to a prompt detention hearing, and the maximum length of pretrial detention is limited by the stringent time limitations of the Speedy Trial Act. See 18 U.S.C. § 3161 et seq. * * * [T]he statute at issue here requires that detainees be housed in a "facility separate, to the extent practicable, from persons awaiting or serving sentences or being held in custody pending appeal."

18 U.S.C. § 3142(i)(2). We conclude, therefore, that the pretrial detention contemplated by the Bail Reform Act is regulatory in nature, and does not constitute punishment before trial in violation of the Due Process Clause. * * *

We have repeatedly held that the Government's regulatory interest in community safety can, in appropriate circumstances, outweigh an individual's liberty interest. For example, in times of war or insurrection, when society's interest is at its peak, the Government may detain individuals whom the Government believes to be dangerous. See Ludecke v. Watkins, 335 U.S. 160, 68 S.Ct. 1429, 92 L.Ed. 1881 (1948) (approving unreviewable Executive power to detain enemy aliens in time of war); Moyer v. Peabody, 212 U.S. 78, 84–85, 29 S.Ct. 235, 236–237, 53 L.Ed. 410 (1909)(rejecting due process claim of individual jailed without probable cause by Governor in time of insurrection). Even outside the exigencies of war, we have found that sufficiently compelling governmental interests can justify detention of dangerous persons. Thus, we have found no absolute constitutional barrier to detention of potentially dangerous resident aliens pending deportation proceedings. We have also held that the Government may detain mentally unstable individuals who present a danger to the public, and dangerous defendants who become incompetent to stand trial. We have approved of postarrest regulatory detention of juveniles when they present a continuing danger to the community. Even competent adults may face substantial liberty restrictions as a result of the operation of our criminal justice system. If the police suspect an individual of a crime, they may arrest and hold him until a neutral magistrate determines whether probable cause exists. Finally, respondents concede and the Court of Appeals noted that an arrestee may be incarcerated until trial if he presents a risk of flight, or a danger to witnesses.

Respondents characterize all of these cases as exceptions to the "general rule" of substantive due process that the Government may not detain a person prior to a judgment of guilt in a criminal trial. Such a "general rule" may freely be conceded, but we think that these cases show a sufficient number of exceptions to the rule that the congressional action challenged here can hardly be characterized as totally novel. Given the well-established authority of the Government, in special circumstances, to restrain individuals' liberty prior to or even without criminal trial and conviction, we think that the present statute providing for pretrial detention on the basis of dangerousness must be evaluated in precisely the same manner that we evaluated the laws in the cases discussed above.

The Government's interest in preventing crime by arrestees is both legitimate and compelling. * * * [The Bail Reform Act] narrowly focuses on a particularly acute problem in which the Government interests are overwhelming. The Act operates only on individuals who have been arrested for a specific category of extremely serious offenses. Congress specifically found that these individuals are far more likely to be responsible for dangerous acts in the community after arrest. Nor is the Act by any means a scattershot attempt to incapacitate those who are merely suspected of these serious crimes. The Government must first of all demonstrate probable cause to believe that the charged crime has been committed by the arrestee, but that is not enough. In a full-blown adversary hearing, the Government must convince a neutral decision-maker by clear and convincing evidence that no conditions of release can reasonably assure the safety of the community or any person. While the Government's general interest in preventing crime is compelling, even this interest is heightened when the Government musters convincing proof that the arrestee, already indicted or held to answer for a serious crime, presents a demonstrable danger to the community. Under these narrow circumstances, society's interest in crime prevention is at its greatest.

On the other side of the scale, of course, is the individual's strong interest in liberty. We do not minimize the importance and fundamental nature of this right. But, as our cases hold, this right may, in circumstances where the Government's interest is sufficiently weighty, be subordinated to the greater needs of society. We think that Congress' careful delineation of the circumstances under which detention will be permitted satisfies this standard. When the Government proves by clear and convincing evidence that an arrestee presents an identified and articulable threat to an individual or the community, we believe that, consistent with the Due Process Clause, a court may disable the arrestee from executing that threat. * * *

JUSTICE MARSHALL, with whom JUSTICE BRENNAN joins, dissenting.

This case brings before the Court for the first time a statute in which Congress declares that a person innocent of any crime may be jailed indefinitely, pending the trial of allegations which are legally presumed to be untrue, if the Government shows to the satisfaction of a judge that the accused is likely to commit crimes, unrelated to the pending charges, at any time in the future. Such statutes, consistent with the usages of tyranny and the excesses of what bitter experience teaches us to call the police state, have long been thought incompatible with the fundamental human rights protected by our Constitution. Today a majority of this Court holds otherwise. Its decision disregards basic principles of justice established centuries ago and enshrined beyond the reach of governmental interference in the Bill of Rights. * * *

Let us apply the majority's reasoning to a similar, hypothetical case. After investigation, Congress determines (not unrealistically) that a large proportion of violent crime is perpetrated by persons who are unemployed. It also determines, equally reasonably, that much violent crime is committed at night. From amongst the panoply of "potential solutions," Congress chooses a statute which permits, after judicial proceedings, the imposition of a dusk-to-dawn curfew on anyone who is unemployed. Since this is not a measure enacted for the purpose of punishing the unemployed, and since the majority finds that preventing danger to the community is a legitimate regulatory goal, the curfew statute would, according to the majority's analysis, be a mere "regulatory" detention statute, entirely compatible with the substantive components of the Due Process Clause. * * *

The statute now before us declares that persons who have been indicted may be detained if a judicial officer finds clear and convincing evidence that they pose a danger to individuals or to the community. The statute does not authorize the Government to imprison anyone it has evidence is dangerous; indictment is necessary. But let us suppose that a defendant is indicted and the Government shows by clear and convincing evidence that he is dangerous and should be detained pending a trial, at which trial the defendant is acquitted. May the Government continue to hold the defendant in detention based upon its showing that he is dangerous? The answer cannot be yes, for that would allow the Government to imprison someone for uncommitted crimes based upon "proof" not beyond a reasonable doubt. The result must therefore be that once the indictment has failed, detention cannot continue. But our fundamental principles of justice declare that the defendant is as innocent on the day before his trial as he is on the morning after his acquittal. Under this statute an untried indictment somehow acts to permit a detention, based on other charges, which after an acquittal would be unconstitutional. The conclusion is inescapable that the indictment has been turned into evidence, if not that the defendant is guilty of the crime charged, then that left to his own devices he will soon be guilty of something else. * * *

## *Notes*

1. In both *Mendoza–Martinez* and *Salerno,* the Court emphasizes the congressional classification of a sanction as civil or criminal as reflected in the legislative history. Beside the Double Jeopardy Clause, are there other constitutional restraints on the sanctions that Congress may impose as a result of a civil proceeding?

In United States v. Ward, 448 U.S. 242, 100 S.Ct. 2636, 65 L.Ed.2d 742 (1980), the Court stated that the question of whether a statutorily defined penalty is civil or criminal is a matter of statutory construction to be analyzed by addressing two questions: first, did Congress designate the penalty as civil or criminal; second, if the penalty has a civil designation, is it so punitive in purpose or effect as to negate Congress' intention? What is the result of applying that analysis to the civil claims against Halper?

2. In Hicks on behalf of Feiock v. Feiock, 485 U.S. 624, 108 S.Ct. 1423, 99 L.Ed.2d 721 (1988)(reproduced supra at p. 271), addressing the distinction between civil and criminal sanctions in a contempt case, the Court refused to look into the purposes behind the state court's action or behind the state laws. The court found that it was the nature of the remedy that determined whether the contempt proceeding was civil or criminal. Can *Feiock* be reconciled with *Mendoza–Martinez* and *Salerno*?

3. In *Mendoza–Martinez,* the Court concluded that the sanction imposed on the defendant was a punishment so that the defendant was entitled to a criminal trial before the sanction could be imposed. In *Halper,* the

Court concluded that the government could seek the full civil penalty against the defendant even if the civil sanction imposed is punitive. Has *Mendoza–Martinez* been overruled? *Mendoza–Martinez* is cited with apparent approval in both the opinion of the Court and the concurring opinion in *Halper;* if it has not been overruled, how are the two cases to be reconciled?

4. How would you classify the *Salerno* case if you applied the "traditional" tests set out in *Mendoza–Martinez*? See Note, Eighth Amendment—Pretrial Detention: What Will Become of the Innocent?, 78 J.Crim.L. & Criminology 1048 (1988)(comparing *Salerno* and *Mendoza–Martinez*). The "traditional" tests of *Mendoza–Martinez* are frequently referred to as useful tools of analysis. How does one know what relative weight to give each test?

5. A number of statutes provide for both substantial civil penalties and for criminal sanctions, the difference between the two being that scienter is an element of the criminal violation. E.g., Clean Air Act, 42 U.S.C. § 7413(b), (c). Is the government free to proceed against a party both civilly and criminally for the same course of conduct under these statutes? Does it make any difference if the element of scienter which must be shown is one of negligence (as in the Clean Water Act, 33 U.S.C. § 1319(c)(1986)) rather than one of knowing or wilful conduct (as amended, 33 U.S.C. § 1319(c)(1987))?

6. All states have statutes permitting civil commitment of those found to be dangerous to themselves or others because of mental illness. The State of Washington has a separate and different statute addressed to the incarceration of sexually violent predators. Wash.Rev.Code Ann. § 71.09.010. The commitment procedure for sexually violent predators is a sequel to completion of a criminal sentence for a sex offense; the basis for commitment is a showing that the defendant has been convicted or charged with a crime of sexual violence and suffers from a mental abnormality or personality disorder which makes the person likely to engage in predatory acts of sexual violence. Psychiatrists have argued that the "mental abnormality" or "personality disorder" standard is too vague to apply. Although civil in form, the statute requires proof beyond a reasonable doubt. Those who are found to be sexual predators are indefinitely confined in a special commitment center at the state prison. See Predators and Politics: A Symposium on Washington's Sexually Violent Predators Statute, 15 U.Puget Sound L.Rev. 507 (1992). The statute was upheld by the Supreme Court of Washington, In re Personal Restraint of Young, 122 Wash.2d 1, 857 P.2d 989 (1993), but found unconstitutional in a later proceeding in the same case brought in federal court. Young v. Weston, 898 F.Supp. 744 (W.D.Wash. 1995). Which conclusion is correct under *Mendoza–Martinez*, *Halper*, and *Salerno*?

7. In 1987, Montana passed a Dangerous Drug Act, Mont.Code Ann. §§ 15–21–101 et seq., which imposed a large tax on the possession of certain drugs. Taxpayers were not required to file a return or pay any tax until 72 hours after they had been arrested for possession of any of the proscribed drugs. Six members of the Kurth family were arrested for growing and selling marijuana. After pleading guilty, two went to prison and the others received suspended or deferred sentences. In addition, $18,000 was forfeited in an associated civil action. When Montana sought to collect the tax, the

Kurths successfully claimed protection under the double jeopardy clause. Department of Revenue v. Kurth Ranch, ___ U.S. ___, 114 S.Ct. 1937, 128 L.Ed.2d 767 (1994). Although the Supreme Court noted that the high rate of taxation and its deterrent purpose did not alone make the tax a punishment, the additional features of imposing the tax only after commission of the crime and basing the tax on the possession of goods which the Kurths could not lawfully possess were sufficient to make the tax punitive. *Kurth Ranch* expressly extends *Halper* from civil penalties to taxes. Given the different purposes of penalties and taxes, is this extension of *Halper* appropriate? Is Montana free to relabel the tax a mandatory criminal fine and collect it in the initial criminal proceeding?

9. A variety of other civil sanctions may have a punitive aspect. Debarment from eligibility for government contracting and treble damages for false claims to the government are but two examples. A useful survey of these devices in federal and state law is found in David Yellen and Carl V. Mayer, Coordinating Sanctions for Corporate Misconduct: Civil or Criminal Punishment?, 29 Am.Crim.L.Rev. 961 (1992).

### *Notes on Differences Between Civil and Criminal Proceedings*

The cases suggest that whether a remedy in the nature of a sanction is civil or criminal may be determined at least in part by whether the defendant's liability to the sanction is established by a civil or criminal proceeding. There is a basic notion that the more severe the sanction or remedy that can be imposed on a defendant, the more formal, thorough and unassailable in its fact-finding nature the procedure for establishing liability should be. In some regards this is borne out in the way American law operates. Obviously, the proof beyond a reasonable doubt required in a criminal trial puts a greater weight on being sure of the facts before a criminal penalty is imposed than does the proof by preponderance of the evidence that is typical in civil trials. Alternatively, the differences between civil and criminal proceedings may be explained by the greater value our legal system puts on liberty, though this does little to explain the protections afforded a corporation in a criminal trial. Of course, the differences between civil and criminal procedures may be little more than the result of historical practice, particularly insofar as criminal procedure is constrained by the Constitution. Certainly England has been much more willing to reform criminal procedure in the last 200 years than has the United States.

It may be equally accurate to consider criminal and civil procedure as simply different systems for establishing or defeating a claim of liability with a different array of tools provided to the two sides to the dispute.

Without attempting to provide a detailed review of civil or criminal procedure, the following differences between the two systems should be borne in mind, particularly with regard to whether they justify or explain differences in the type of remedy that a judge may impose.

1. *Commencement of the action.* No formal procedure prior to the filing of the complaint is required of the government or a private party in a civil action. F.R.Civ.P. 3. A federal misdemeanor charge, carrying a possible term of imprisonment not in excess of one year, may be brought by the government through an information which requires no pre-charging procedure by the prosecutor. A federal felony charge, carrying a possible term of imprisonment in excess of one year, requires presentation of evidence by the prosecutor to a grand jury consisting of 16 to 23 citizens and the affirmative vote of 12 or more grand jurors as well as the assent of the prosecutor. Fifth Amendment; F.R.Crim.P. 6, 7.

2. *Discovery.* Modern civil discovery is, of course, wide-ranging and is equally available to both plaintiff and defendant. Federal criminal discovery is entirely different. Through the powers of the grand jury, the government has the ability to conduct extensive discovery before returning an indictment. The grand jury has the power to issue both subpoenas for the production of documents and things and for the taking of testimony. There is no territorial limit within the United States on such subpoenas. Under the fifth amendment any one claiming in good faith that his testimony may incriminate him may not be compelled to testify, but the government may obtain from such a party virtually anything relevant to its inquiry other than testimony including documents, blood samples and voice or handwriting exemplars. Schmerber v. California, 384 U.S. 757, 86 S.Ct. 1826, 16 L.Ed.2d 908 (1966); United States v. Dionisio, 410 U.S. 1, 93 S.Ct. 764, 35 L.Ed.2d 67 (1973); United States v. Mara, 410 U.S. 19, 93 S.Ct. 774, 35 L.Ed.2d 99 (1973). Prior to indictment a person who believes or has been informed that he is the target of a grand jury investigation, has no power to conduct discovery against the government or third parties.

Following the return of the indictment, the government can no longer make use of the investigatory power of the grand jury. Discovery by deposition is open to the parties only upon motion to the court and in "exceptional circumstances," such as the reasonable likelihood that a witness will not be able to appear at trial because of illness or death. F.R.Crim.P. 15. Generally, discovery provided for in the rules is limited and, in part, is reciprocal but may be commenced only by the defendant. The defendant may obtain any record of his own statements in the possession of the government and his prior criminal record. F.R.Crim.P. 16. He may also obtain documents and tangible objects in the government's possession which the government intends to offer at trial and reports of examinations or tests, but if he requests such disclosure, he will be subject to reciprocal discovery. The defendant is not entitled to obtain copies of grand jury testimony or exhibits if they do not fall into one of the categories for which discovery is provided. The prior statements and reports of the government's witnesses are not discoverable by the defendant until after the witness has testified, 18 U.S.C. § 3500. But the government must make evidence in its possession which is materially favorable to the accused available to the defendant. Brady v. Maryland, 373 U.S. 83, 83 S.Ct. 1194, 10 L.Ed.2d 215 (1963).

In the real world of criminal trials, less restrictive practice may be followed. In the typical white collar criminal case there is in fact considerable exchange of documents prior to or during trial, but this arises from agreement between the parties or the instructions of judges facing the exigencies of modern trial calendars.

3. *Bail.* Unlike the civil system, a criminal defendant may be required to post bail in an amount or form that will assure his appearance at trial. Failure to post such bail will result in the defendant's pretrial incarceration. 18 U.S.C. § 3141 et seq.; F.R.Crim.P. 46. As *Salerno* shows, in some circumstances a defendant may be detained prior to trial for reasons unrelated to the likelihood of his failure to appear for trial.

4. *Trial.* The government's burden of proof at trial in a criminal case is to prove the defendant committed the crime beyond a reasonable doubt. United States v. Regan, 232 U.S. 37, 34 S.Ct. 213, 58 L.Ed. 494 (1914). But one should note that there is a distinction between the liability phase and the remedy phase of a criminal trial. The government need not prove facts at a sentencing hearing beyond a reasonable doubt and hearsay evidence may be used at a sentencing hearing. McMillan v. Pennsylvania, 477 U.S. 79, 106 S.Ct. 2411, 91 L.Ed.2d 67 (1986); Williams v. New York, 337 U.S. 241, 69 S.Ct. 1079, 93 L.Ed. 1337 (1949). Grand jury proceedings are also not controlled by the rules of evidence; hearsay is routinely used in presentations to the grand jury. A trial before a jury drawn from the district in which the alleged crime was committed is assured by the Sixth Amendment and the defendant may not be compelled to testify nor may the prosecutor draw to the attention of the jury or comment on the defendant's failure to testify. 18 U.S.C. § 3481; Griffin v. California, 380 U.S. 609, 85 S.Ct. 1229, 14 L.Ed.2d 106 (1965). Corporations and other organizations are not protected by the fifth amendment privilege. Bellis v. United States, 417 U.S. 85, 94 S.Ct. 2179, 40 L.Ed.2d 678 (1974).

5. *Effect of conviction.* Remedies following conviction are not limited to fines or imprisonment. Conviction of a felony may carry collateral consequences such as loss of the right to serve on a grand jury, the forfeiture of the instruments or proceeds of a crime, e.g., 18 U.S.C. §§ 3665–3667, 3681, and other disabilities. For example, in 1988, Congress markedly increased the collateral consequences of convictions for distribution or possession of narcotics. 21 U.S.C. § 853(a)(1988). The statute has a graduated scheme of increasing disabilities. After a first conviction for drug possession, the court has discretion to make the defendant ineligible for any or all federal benefits for a year; require that the defendant successfully complete a drug treatment program with periodic testing; and/or require that the defendant perform appropriate community service. A third conviction for drug distribution results in ineligibility for all federal benefits. Federal benefits are defined to

include issuance of a grant, contract, loan, professional license or commercial license by the federal government or by use of federal funds; but federal benefits do not include any retirement, welfare, social security, health, disability or veterans benefit, public housing or any other benefit for which payments or services are required for eligibility.

6. *Administrative proceedings.* Numerous statutes give the government the authority to seek civil penalties not only through proceedings in the district court, but also through administrative proceedings. Often the choice of forum is placed in the hands of the agency. E.g., Resource Conservation and Recovery Act, 42 U.S.C. § 6928 (1983). This choice may carry important procedural consequences: in the administrative forum discovery may be much more limited than in a district court proceeding; cross-examination of witnesses may be limited or prohibited; the opportunity for jury trial is obviously not present; direct evidence may be presented in writing rather than through live witnesses; ultimately, the hearing provided may be of a legislative rather than an adjudicatory type. The courts have also held that sanctions imposed by administrative agencies are reviewable in the courts only on the ground that the agency acted outside its legal authority or abused its discretion. Butz v. Glover Livestock Commission Co., 411 U.S. 182, 93 S.Ct. 1455, 36 L.Ed.2d 142 (1973); Moffer v. Watt, 690 F.2d 1037 (D.C.Cir.1982).

## B. PROPORTIONALITY IN SENTENCING

The Sentencing Reform Act of 1984 fundamentally changed criminal sentencing practices in the federal courts. Prior to the passage of the Act, 18 U.S.C. §§ 3551–3673, 28 U.S.C. §§ 991–998, it was generally accepted that federal district courts had virtually unfettered discretion in imposing criminal sentences which were within the statutory terms established by Congress. Dorszynski v. United States, 418 U.S. 424, 94 S.Ct. 3042, 41 L.Ed.2d 855 (1974). The courts of appeals rarely required the district courts to state reasons for the sentences they imposed. E.g., United States v. Bazzano, 712 F.2d 826 (3d Cir.1983), cert. denied, 465 U.S. 1078, 104 S.Ct. 1439, 79 L.Ed.2d 760 (1984). There were exceptions—one was that the district court was to individualize the sentence rather than mechanically impose sentence based solely on the crime committed. United States v. Barker, 771 F.2d 1362 (9th Cir.1985). The Supreme Court aligned itself with this position many years ago: "The belief no longer prevails that every offense in a like legal category calls for an identical punishment without regard to the past life and habits of a particular offender." Williams v. New York, 337 U.S. 241, 247, 69 S.Ct. 1079, 1083, 93 L.Ed. 1337 (1949).

One result of this system was that reported decisions on sentencing questions were rare, with the consequence that comparatively little could be learned from reported cases about what sanctions judges imposed in criminal cases and why they imposed them.

Not surprisingly, judges differed markedly in their views of what punishment fit the criminal and the crime:

> The region in which the defendant is convicted is likely to change the length of time served from approximately six months more if one is sentenced in the South to twelve months less if one is sentenced in Central California * * *. [F]emale bank robbers are likely to serve six months less than their similarly situated male counterparts * * * [and] black [bank robbery] defendants convicted * * * in the South are likely to actually serve approximately thirteen months longer than similarly situated bank robbers convicted * * * in other regions.

Sentencing Guidelines: Hearings on Sentencing Guidelines Before the Subcomm. on Criminal Justice of the House Comm. on the Judiciary, 100th Cong., 1st Sess. 676–77 (testimony of Commissioner Ilene H. Nagel). Growing dissatisfaction with these disparities and with the federal parole system which significantly influenced the time actually served by federal prisoners led Congress in 1984 to establish the United States Sentencing Commission with the aim of constraining the discretion of district court judges in sentencing.

The Sentencing Reform Act profoundly changed criminal sentencing in the federal courts. The United States Sentencing Commission promulgated guidelines, binding on district court judges, which severely limited the range within which a defendant could be sentenced for a given crime. The guidelines approach was upheld in Mistretta v. United States, 488 U.S. 361, 109 S.Ct. 647, 102 L.Ed.2d 714 (1989). Claims of failure to follow the requirements of the guidelines were reviewable in the courts of appeals. Under the guidelines, perhaps in keeping with changing views of society, the dominant determinant of the sentence for individuals is the crime and not the criminal. The emphasis passed from indefinite sentences aimed at rehabilitation to sentences whose length was fully known at the time of sentence and which were focused on the "just deserts" to which the crime gave rise. Curiously, a different tack was taken with sentences for organizations, including corporations. For corporate defendants, emphasis was put on the past actions of the corporation and probationary sentences designed to reform corporate conduct were given great prominence.

Before the passage of the Act, there were few reported decisions explaining the rationale for sentencing decisions. After the promulgation of the guidelines, the basis for federal sentencing is primarily found in the statements of the Commission while courts have primarily interpreted and analyzed the content of the guidelines.

## UNITED STATES SENTENCING COMMISSION, SENTENCING GUIDELINES FOR UNITED STATES COURTS

52 Fed.Reg. 18046 (May 13, 1987).

### * * * 3. The Basic Approach

To understand these guidelines and the rationale that underlies them, one must begin with the three objectives that Congress, in enacting the new sentencing law, sought to achieve. Its basic objective was to enhance the ability of the criminal justice system to reduce crime through an effective, fair sentencing system. To achieve this objective, Congress first sought honesty in sentencing. It sought to avoid the confusion and implicit deception that arises out of the present sentencing system which requires a judge to impose an indeterminate sentence that is automatically reduced in most cases by "good time" credits. * * *

Second, Congress sought uniformity in sentencing by narrowing the wide disparity in sentences imposed by different federal courts for similar criminal conduct by similar offenders. Third, Congress sought proportionality in sentencing through a system that imposes appropriately different sentences for criminal conduct of different severity.

Honesty is easy to achieve: The abolition of parole makes the sentence imposed by the court the sentence the offender will serve. There is a tension, however, between the mandate of uniformity (treat similar cases alike) and the mandate of proportionality (treat different cases differently) which, like the historical tension between law and equity, makes it difficult to achieve both goals simultaneously. Perfect uniformity—sentencing every offender to five years—destroys proportionality. Having only a few simple categories of crimes would make the guidelines uniform and easy to administer, but might lump together offenses that are different in important respects. For example, a single category for robbery that lumps together armed and unarmed robberies, robberies with and without injuries, robberies of a few dollars and robberies of millions, is far too broad.

At the same time, a sentencing system tailored to fit every conceivable wrinkle of each case can become unworkable and seriously compromise the certainty of punishment and its deterrent effect. A bank robber with (or without) a gun, which the robber kept hidden (or brandished), might have frightened (or merely warned), injured seriously (or less seriously), tied up (or simply pushed) a guard, a teller or a customer, at night (or at noon), for a bad (or arguably less bad) motive, in an effort to obtain money for other crimes (or for other purposes), in the company of a few (or many) other robbers, for the first (or fourth) time that day, while sober (or under the influence of drugs or alcohol), and so forth.

The list of potentially relevant features of criminal behavior is long; the fact that they can occur in multiple combinations means that the list of possible permutations of factors is virtually endless. The appropriate relationships among these different factors are exceedingly difficult to establish, for they are often context specific. Sentencing courts do not treat the occurrence of a simple bruise identically in all cases, irrespective of whether that bruise occurred in the context of a bank robbery or in the context of a breach of peace. This is so, in part, because the risk that such a harm will occur differs depending on the underlying offense with which it is connected (and therefore may already be counted, to a different degree, in the punishment for the underlying offense); and also because, in part, the relationship between punishment and multiple harms is not simply additive. The relation varies, depending on how much other harm has occurred. (Thus, one cannot easily assign points for each kind of harm and simply add them up, irrespective of context and total amounts.)

The larger the number of subcategories, the greater the complexity that is created and the less workable the system. Moreover, the subcategories themselves, sometimes too broad and sometimes too narrow, will apply and interact in unforeseen ways to unforeseen situations, thus failing to cure the unfairness of a simple, broad category system. Finally, and perhaps most importantly, probation officers and courts, in applying a complex system of subcategories, would have to make a host of decisions about whether the underlying facts are sufficient to bring the case within a particular subcategory. The greater the number of decisions required and the greater their complexity, the greater the risk that different judges will apply the guidelines differently to situations that, in fact, are similar, thereby reintroducing the very disparity that the guidelines were designed to eliminate.

In view of the arguments, it is tempting to retreat to the simple, broad-category approach and to grant judges the discretion to select the proper point along a broad sentencing range. Obviously, however, granting such broad discretion risks correspondingly broad disparity in sentencing, for different courts may exercise their discretionary powers in different ways. That is to say, such an approach risks a return to the wide disparity that Congress established the Commission to limit.

In the end, there is no completely satisfying solution to this practical stalemate. * * *

A philosophical problem arose when the Commission attempted to reconcile the differing perceptions of the purposes of criminal punishment. Most observers of the criminal law agree that the ultimate aim of the law itself, and of punishment in particular, is the control of crime. Beyond this point, however, the consensus seems to break down. Some argue that appropriate punishment should be defined primarily on the basis of the moral principle of "just deserts." Under this principle, punishment should be scaled to the offender's culpability and the resulting harms. Thus, if a defendant is less culpable, the defendant deserves less punishment. Others argue that punishment should be imposed primarily on the basis of practical "crime control" considerations. Defendants sentenced under this scheme should receive the punishment that most effectively lessens the likelihood of future crime, either by deterring others or incapacitating the defendant.

Adherents of these points of view have urged the Commission to choose between them, to accord one primacy over the other. Such a choice would be profoundly difficult. The relevant literature is vast, the arguments deep, and each point of view has much to be said in its favor. A clear-cut Commission decision in favor of one of these approaches would diminish the chance that the guidelines would find the widespread acceptance they need for effective implementation. As a practical matter, in most sentencing decisions both philosophies may prove consistent with the same result.

For now, the Commission has sought to solve both the practical and philosophical problems of developing a coherent sentencing system by taking an empirical approach that uses data estimating the existing sentencing system as a starting point. It has analyzed data drawn from 10,000 presentence investigations, crimes as distinguished in substantive criminal statutes, the United States Parole Commission's guidelines and resulting statistics, and data from other relevant sources, in order to determine which distinctions are important in present practice. After examination, the Commission has accepted, modified, or rationalized the more important of these distinctions. * * *

### 4. The Guidelines' Resolution of Major Issues

#### * * * *(a) Real Offense vs. Charge Offense Sentencing*

One of the most important questions for the Commission to decide was whether to base sentences upon the actual conduct in which the defendant engaged regardless of the charges for which he was indicted or convicted ("real offense" sentencing), or upon the conduct that constitutes the elements of the offense with which the defendant was charged and of which he was convicted ("charge offense" sentencing). A bank robber, for example, might have used a gun, frightened bystanders, taken $50,000, injured a teller, refused to stop when ordered, and raced away damaging property during escape. A pure real offense system would sentence on the basis of all identifiable conduct. A pure charge offense system would overlook some of the harms that did not constitute statutory elements of the offenses of which the defendant was convicted.

The Commission initially sought to develop a real offense system. After all, the present sentencing system is, in a sense, a real offense system. The sentencing court (and the parole commission) take account of the conduct in which the defendant actually engaged, as determined in a presentence report, at the sentencing hearing, or before a parole commission hearing officer. The Commission's initial efforts in this direction, carried out in the spring and early summer of 1986, proved unproductive mostly for practical reasons. To make such a system work, even to formalize and rationalize the status quo, would have required the Commission to decide precisely which harms to take into account, how to add them up, and what kinds of procedures the courts should use to determine the presence or absence of disputed factual elements. The Commission found no practical way to combine and account for the large number of diverse harms arising in different circumstances; nor did it find a practical way to reconcile the need for a fair adjudicatory procedure with the need for a speedy sentencing process, given the potential existence of hosts of adjudicated "real harm" facts in many typical cases. The effort proposed as a solution to these problems required the use of, for example, quadratic roots and other mathematical operations that the Commission considered too complex to be workable, and, in the Commission's view, risked return to wide disparity in practice.

The Commission therefore abandoned the effort to devise a "pure" real offense system and instead experimented with a "modified real offense system", which it published for public comment in a September 1986 preliminary draft.

This version also foundered in several major respects on the rock of practicality. It was highly complex and its mechanical rules for adding harms (e.g., bodily injury added the same punishment irrespective of context) threatened to work considerable unfairness. Ultimately, the Commission decided that it could not find a practical or fair and efficient way to implement either a pure or modified real offense system of the sort it originally wanted, and it abandoned that approach.

The Commission, in its January 1987 Revised Draft and the present guidelines, has moved closer to a "charge offense" system. The system is not, however, pure; it has a number of real elements. For one thing, the hundreds of overlapping and duplicative statutory provisions that make up the federal criminal law have forced the Commission to write guidelines that are descriptive of generic conduct rather than tracking purely statutory language. For another, the guidelines, both through specific offense characteristics and adjustments, take account of a number of important, commonly occurring real offense elements such as role in the offense, the presence of a gun, or the amount of money actually taken.

Finally, it is important not to overstate the difference in practice between a real and a charge offense system. The federal criminal system, in practice, deals mostly with drug offenses, bank robberies and white collar crimes (such as fraud, embezzlement, and bribery). For the most part, the conduct that an indictment charges approximates the real and relevant conduct in which the offender actually engaged. * * *

*(b) Departures*

The new sentencing statute permits a court to depart from a guideline-specified sentence only when it finds "an aggravating or mitigating circumstance ... that was not adequately taken into consideration by the Sentencing Commission ...". 18 U.S.C. 3553(b). Thus, in principle, the Commission, by specifying that it had adequately considered a particular factor, could prevent a court from using it as grounds for departure. In this initial set of guidelines, however, the Commission does not so limit the courts' departure powers. The Commission intends the sentencing courts to treat each guideline as carving out a "heartland," a set of typical cases embodying the conduct that each guideline describes. When a court finds an atypical case, one to which a particular guideline linguistically applies but where conduct significantly differs from the norm, the court may consider whether a departure is warranted.

[The following are] a few factors that the court cannot take into account as grounds for departure:

> [§ 5H1.10. Race, Sex, National Origin, Creed, Religion and Socio–Economic Status (Policy Statement). These factors are not relevant in the determination of a sentence. * * * Drug dependence or alcohol abuse is not a reason for imposing a sentence below the guidelines. * * * The Commission considered the relevance of economic hardship and determined that personal financial difficulties and economic pressures upon a trade or business do not warrant a decrease in sentence.] * * *

*(e) Multi–Count Convictions*

The Commission, like other sentencing commissions, has found it particularly difficult to develop rules for sentencing defendants convicted of multiple violations of law, each of which makes up a separate count in an indictment. The reason it is difficult is that when a defendant engages in conduct that causes several harms, each additional harm, even if it increases the extent to which punishment is warranted, does not necessarily warrant a proportionate increase in punishment. A defendant who assaults others during a fight, for example, may warrant more punishment if he injures ten people than if he injures one, but his conduct does not necessarily warrant ten times the punishment. If it did, many of the simplest offenses, for reasons that are often fortuitous, would lead to life sentences of imprisonment—sentences that neither "just deserts" nor "crime control" theories of punishment would find justified.

Several individual guidelines provide special instructions for increasing punishment when the conduct that is the subject of that count involves multiple occurrences or has caused several harms. The guidelines also provide general rules for aggravating punishment in light of multiple harms charged separately in separate counts. These rules may produce occasional anomalies, but normally they will permit an appropriate degree of aggravation of punishment when multiple offenses that are the subjects of separate counts take place.

* * * They essentially provide: (1) When the conduct involves fungible items, e.g., separate drug transactions or thefts of money, the amounts are added and the guidelines apply to the total amount. (2) When nonfungible harms are involved, the offense level for the most serious count is increased (according to a somewhat diminishing scale) to reflect the existence of other counts of conviction.

The rules have been written in order to minimize the possibility that an arbitrary casting of a single transaction into several counts will produce a longer sentence. In addition, the sentencing court will have adequate power to prevent such a result through departures where necessary to produce a mitigated sentence. * * *

### *(g) Sentencing Ranges*

In determining the appropriate sentencing ranges for each offense, the Commission began by estimating the average sentences now being served within each category. It also examined the sentence specified in congressional statutes, in the parole guidelines, and in other relevant, analogous sources.* * *

While the Commission has not considered itself bound by existing sentencing practice, it has not tried to develop an entirely new system of sentencing on the basis of theory alone. Guideline sentences in many instances will approximate existing practice, but adherence to the guidelines will help to eliminate wide disparity. For example, where a high percentage of persons now receive probation, a guideline may include one or more specific offense characteristics in an effort to distinguish those types of defendants who now receive probation from those who receive more severe sentences. In some instances, short sentences of incarceration for all offenders in a category have been substituted for a current sentencing practice of very wide variability in which some defendants receive probation while others receive several years in prison for the same offense. Moreover, insofar as many who currently plead guilty often receive lesser sentences, so the guidelines also provide potential discounts for those defendants who accept responsibility and those who cooperate with the government. * * *

### *Notes*

1. Sentencing proceedings differ markedly in procedure from trials to establish guilt or liability. "[A] sentencing judge 'may appropriately conduct an inquiry broad in scope, largely unlimited either as to the kind of information he may consider, or the source from which it may come.'" Nichols v. United States, ___ U.S. ___, ___, 114 S.Ct. 1921, 1927–28, 128 L.Ed.2d 745 (1994). Thus, the courts rely not only on what was presented at trial or at the taking of a guilty plea but also on the report of the probation office and such presentations as the government and the defendant choose to make. The rules of evidence do not apply to the sentencing proceeding, F.R.Evid. 1101(d)(3); United States v. Jarrett, 705 F.2d 198 (7th Cir.1983), cert. denied, 465 U.S. 1004, 104 S.Ct. 995, 79 L.Ed.2d 228 (1984), the factual allegations need not be open to cross-examination, the courts frequently rely on hearsay, and the burden of proof beyond a reasonable doubt does not apply. E.g., United States v. Tucker, 404 U.S. 443, 92 S.Ct. 589, 30 L.Ed.2d 592 (1972); McMillan v. Pennsylvania, 477 U.S. 79, 106 S.Ct. 2411, 91 L.Ed.2d 67 (1986). The exclusionary rule does not apply to federal sentencing determinations. Evidence gained as a result of a Fourth Amendment violation may be used by a court in calculating the appropriate sentence under the federal Sentencing Guidelines. E.g., United States v. Torres, 926 F.2d 321 (3d Cir.1991); United States v. McCrory, 930 F.2d 63 (D.C.Cir.1991), cert. denied, 502 U.S. 1037, 112 S.Ct. 885, 116 L.Ed.2d 788 (1992).

2. In dissent, Commissioner Paul H. Robinson stated that the Sentencing Commission failed to develop a rational and coherent policy upon which to base the sentencing guidelines; instead the Commission put too much emphasis on developing ranges of acceptable sentences derived from "averaging" past sentences for the same offense. Commissioner Robinson pointed out the pitfalls of such an approach:

> Consider, for example, the case of a young addict who sells drugs to acquaintances to support his own habit. One judge may impose a long term of imprisonment in order to send a strong deterrent message to drug sellers. Another judge may impose a very short term of incarceration followed by supervised release conditioned upon the offender's participation in a community drug treatment program in the belief that curing the offender's addiction is more likely to remove him from the roll of drug dealers.
>
> The guidelines might rationally embody either of such alternative policies. But by adopting no policy, and relying upon a mathematical average of sentences, the guidelines provide "bastardized" sentences that will serve neither of the two purposes. For the young addict, the "averaged" sentence will be too short to send the strong deterrent message, and will not provide the treatment necessary for rehabilitation.

52 Fed.Reg. at 18122.

Is there any impropriety in a criminal sentencing system in which sentences are imposed on the basis of such different views of the purposes of the law as those set out in Commissioner Robinson's hypothetical? The purposes of sentencing have traditionally been held to be just punishment, deterrence, incapacitation of the dangerous, and rehabilitation. Can sentencing based on diverse theories and policies be avoided in cases where the purposes of sentencing may not be congruent?

3. The Sentencing Guidelines for individuals have faced a broad attack in recent years, both from academic analysts and from the sentencing judges. E.g., Jeffrey Standen, Plea Bargaining in the Shadow of the Guidelines, 81 Calif. L. Rev. 1471 (1993); Albert W. Alschuler, The Failure of Sentencing Guidelines: A Plea for Less Aggregation, 58 U.Chi.L.Rev. 901 (1991); David Margolick, "Chorus of Judicial Critics Assail Sentencing Guides," New York Times, April 12, 1992, p.1, col. 1. There have been a number of repeated criticisms of the Sentencing Commission's work:

(a) The guidelines are not based on any well-defined system of guiding principles or goals of punishment. A consequence of this failing is that it is not possible to determine from any basis of principle or theory whether the sentences imposed under the guidelines are appropriate.

(b) The guidelines have produced a shift to sentences based primarily on the harm caused by the offense rather than on the characteristics of the offender. One example is the drug courier who is sentenced on the basis of the amount of drugs carried despite the fact that the courier is frequently a woman traveling with children, selected so as not to match a drug courier profile and whose motive is an economic one driven by the sums offered by a dealer which frequently bear no relation to the amount of drugs carried. A courier with no record, carrying 55 grams of crack is likely to be in a 121–151 month guideline range. Deborah Young, Rethinking the Commission's Drug Guidelines: Courier Cases Where Quantity Overstates Culpability, 3 Fed.Sent.Rptr. 63 (1990). The courts of appeals have not been friendly to departures from the guidelines based on the defendant's personal characteristics. E.g., United States v. Poff, 926 F.2d 588 (7th Cir. en banc), cert. denied, 502 U.S. 827, 112 S.Ct. 96, 116 L.Ed.2d 67 (1991).

(c) Although the guidelines give the impression of less disparity in sentencing, this is largely the result of sentences being placed in the categories which the guidelines have created rather than the result of any detailed analysis showing that comparable facts are being sentenced comparably. One well known example is that possession or sale of crack cocaine is punished much more severely under the guidelines than is possession or sale of equivalent amounts of cocaine in powder form. Congress has rejected a Sentencing Commission recommendation that this problem be solved by easing the penalties regarding crack cocaine, but is considering legislation to increase the penalties regarding powdered cocaine. See "Law Proposed to Level Drug Penalties", Los Angeles Times, Nov. 7, 1995. The Supreme Court has agreed to consider an aspect of the racial disparity in sentencing that has been created by the vast difference in these penalties. United States v. Armstrong, 48 F.3d 1508 (9th Cir.), cert. granted, ___ U.S. ___, 116 S.Ct. 377, 133 L.Ed.2d 301 (1995).

Another extreme example of illusory uniformity is Chapman v. United States, 500 U.S. 453, 111 S.Ct. 1919, 114 L.Ed.2d 524 (1991), in which the Supreme Court upheld a sentence for distributing and selling LSD. The sentence, under both the statute's five year mandatory minimum sentence provision and as the guidelines then provided, was based on the weight of the mixture or substance containing the LSD. The majority opinion set out the following table showing the differences in sentences for 100 doses of LSD depending on which carrier was used:

| *Carrier* | *Weight of 100 doses* | *Guidelines range (months)* |
|---|---|---|
| Sugar Cube | 227 gr. | 188–235 |
| Blotter paper | 1.4 gr. | 63–78 |
| Gelatin Capsule | 225 mg. | 27–33 |
| Pure LSD | 5 mg. | 10–16 |

This sort of result led Judge Easterbrook, writing for the majority when the case was before the Seventh Circuit, to state: "Experience with the guidelines suggests * * * that every attempt to make the system of sentences 'more rational' carries costs and concealed irrationalities, both loopholes and unanticipated severity. Criminals have neither a moral nor a constitutional claim to equal or entirely proportional treatment." United States v. Marshall, 908 F.2d 1312, 1326 (7th Cir.1990)(en banc), aff'd sub nom., Chapman v. United States, 500 U.S. 453, 111 S.Ct. 1919, 114 L.Ed.2d 524 (1991). In response to *Chapman,* the Sentencing Commission has now provided that when applying the guidelines, courts are to give each dose of LSD a presumed weight regardless of the weight of the carrier; however, the actual weight of the LSD/carrier combination still must be used when calculating congressionally-mandated minimum sentences. Neal v. United States, ___ U.S. ___, 116 S.Ct. 763, ___ L.Ed.2d ___ (1996). Whatever the rights of criminals may be, such disparity is probably worse than what one would have found under the former system of discretionary sentencing.

(d) The guidelines have generally produced more stringent sentences than was the case before they were established. Professor Alschuler suggests that this phenomenon is the result both of legislatures intending to increase sentences and the emphasis of sentencing commissions on harm-based rather than individualized offender-based sentencing.

(e) Discretion has not been removed from sentencing—rather the discretion of judges, probation officers, and parole boards has been severely diminished and the power of prosecutors substantially enhanced. A student commentator noted:

> There is every indication that manipulation of the Guidelines occurs through charge and fact bargaining. The overwhelming majority of judges perceive that plea agreements frequently dismiss provable charges and that the parties often negotiate facts relevant to the Guidelines. Although the level of manipulation is impossible to pinpoint, studies indicate that it transpires in every district in at least a significant minority of cases. In the area of departures for substantial assistance, prosecutors sometimes make motions on behalf of defendants regardless of the quality of their assistance in order to induce guilty pleas, benefit defendants they find sympathetic, or mitigate sentences they consider too harsh.

Note, Reestablishing the Federal Judge's Role in Sentencing, 101 Yale L.J. 1109, 1120 (1992).

Suggestions for reform include: panels of sentencing judges instead of guidelines in order to avoid individual idiosyncracies while reducing the present range of prosecutorial discretion and allowing consideration of all the facts and circumstances of a case; focus by sentencing commissions on paradigm cases and sentencing problems with the paradigms working as precedent from which a judge is free to depart when facing different facts in the case before her; and more flexible guidelines allowing judges to take into account more elements of the offense and characteristics of the offender than they are able to do under the present regime. See Symposium, Twenty Years of Sentencing Reform, 78 Judicature 168 (1995).

4. For a more optimistic view of how a sentencing commission may be able effectively to address some of the problems posed by the blurred line between civil and criminal cases, see John C. Coffee, Jr., Does "Unlawful" Mean "Criminal"?: Reflections on the Disappearing Tort/Crime Distinction in American Law, 71 B.U.L.Rev. 193 (1991). For an examination of the state experience with guidelines, see Richard S. Frase, State Sentencing Guidelines: Still Going Strong, 78 Judicature 173 (1995) (discussing guidelines in the 17 states which have adopted them to date).

5. The Sentencing Commission has introduced into sentences for organizations an analysis which reflects the vicarious nature of organizational liability. Simply put, to the extent an organization has taken steps to

prevent and detect violations of law, the organization's sentence will be reduced. The Commission has set out seven benchmarks for evaluating due diligence in the prevention and detection of crime: (1) establishment of compliance standards and procedures for employees that are reasonably capable of reducing the prospect of criminal conduct; (2) assignment of specific high-level personnel to oversee compliance with such standards and procedures; (3) taking due care not to delegate substantial discretionary authority to individuals with a propensity to engage in illegal activities; (4) taking steps to communicate the standards and procedures effectively, e.g., by training or practical publications; (5) taking reasonable steps to achieve compliance with its standards, e.g., by auditing and providing confidential systems to report criminal conduct; (6) enforcement of the standards through an appropriate disciplinary mechanism; and (7) responding appropriately to the discovery of an offense, including modifying the program to prevent and detect violations of law. U.S. Sentencing Commission, Guidelines Manual, Commentary to § 8A1.2. This provision of the Sentencing Guidelines has fostered a substantial growth in corporate compliance and ethics programs.

The theory and development of the organizational guidelines is addressed in Ilene Nagel and Winthrop Swenson, The Federal Sentencing Guidelines for Corporations: Their Development, Theoretical Underpinnings, and Some Thoughts about Their Future, 71 Wash.U.L.Q. 205 (1993). Discussion of corporate compliance programs and the application of the guidelines can be found in Jeffrey M. Kaplan, Joseph E. Murphy and Winthrop M. Swenson, Compliance Programs and the Corporate Sentencing Guidelines: Preventing Criminal and Civil Liability (1995).

6. Just as most civil litigation is settled, most criminal litigation is resolved through plea bargains and guilty pleas. "The Commission's data reveals that a defendant who pled guilty will typically receive a sentence reduced by thirty to forty percent. A Guideline system that reflects actual past practice should provide such a reduction. Yet, to explicitly write a reduction into the Guidelines * * * is to explicitly tell a defendant that a guilty plea means a lower sentence and that insistence upon a jury trial means a higher sentence." Stephen Breyer, The Federal Sentencing Guidelines and the Key Compromises Upon Which They Rest, 17 Hofstra L.Rev. 1, 28 (1988). (Justice Breyer was a commissioner when he was a circuit judge.) Is there a way out of this constitutional conundrum? If sentences in litigated cases are governed by sentencing guidelines, should the court permit prosecutors to enter into plea bargains outside the range of sentences set out in the guidelines? Should the guidelines explicitly provide an incentive for plea bargains? If you do not believe it appropriate for prosecutors to have authority to enter plea bargains outside the range of sentences suggested by the Commission, would you also believe it appropriate for a court or Congress to attempt to constrain the discretion of the prosecutor in deciding to initiate a criminal case and in choosing what crimes to charge in an indictment?

7. When the Sentencing Guidelines first went into effect, there were judges who believed they would relieve the stress of the most humanly taxing part of the judge's job. Judge Weinstein wrote:

> Sentencing under the guideline procedure may reduce internal stress on judges. Most find it extremely difficult to look into the eye of another human being and punish him or her severely, particularly when the family is standing by, about to suffer more than the defendant. The numerical mechanics of the new system avoids emotion. The guidelines encourage a judge to rule under the illusion that he or she is no longer personally responsible for a sentencing decision. Replacing human empathy and judgment with computer-generated calculations cut the sentences loose from the three-dimensional defendant, and promises to reduce the number of sleepless nights and painful choices for judges that the old system fostered.

Jack B. Weinstein, A Trial Judge's First Impression of the Federal Sentencing Guidelines, 52 Alb.L.Rev. 1, 10–11 (1987).

Matters have not worked out that way. A number of judges find themselves fundamentally at odds with the sentences the Guidelines impose. A few have resigned. Some senior judges have refused to accept assignment to criminal cases. Others have found innovative ways to influence the final result. One federal judge, in a case involving a gun possession charge and a charge involving crack, informed the jury that if the defendant were convicted on the crack charge he would, under the Sentencing Guidelines, have to be sentenced to life imprisonment without parole because of two prior convictions. The jury convicted only on the gun charge. Traditionally, informing a jury of the sentencing consequences of its verdict is very unusual and in this case the prosecutor believed the judge had virtually dictated the verdict. N.Y. Times, p. 1, col. 1 (Dec. 29, 1989).

### *Problem: United States v. Miller (Reprised)* *Sentencing Guidelines*

Half a dozen statutes make it a crime to emit or discharge pollutants in quantities greater than allowed by a permit or regulation established by the U.S. Environmental Protection Agency or its state equivalent. A maximum of five years imprisonment is a typical sanction available under the statutes.

Miller was convicted on twenty counts of violating the terms of the water discharge permit for the apple press and the insecticides and anti-bacterial agents she used to clean her facility. Miller was well known in the community for employing people with disabilities. (Miller's daughter had severe physical disabilities and she had for many years championed the fair and generous treatment of people with disabilities.) In 1990, the pollution control equipment failed but Miller continued to operate for six months while the equipment was replaced. During that time there were daily violations of the terms of the water discharge permit. EPA warned Miller that such behavior was illegal but did not take action against her. In 1992, a similar episode took place. EPA brought an administrative action against Miller, who argued that compliance would require shutting the plant, putting the workers with disabilities on the unemployment lines and that the discharge caused no demonstrable harm to the river since the chemicals discharged were only modestly toxic and the water quality standards in the river were not violated. EPA assessed a civil penalty of $75,000. In 1995, through an employee operator error, the equipment broke a third time. Miller was able to get the equipment repaired in three weeks but decided to lie to the EPA when reporting her discharges; she reported no daily violations even though she knew twenty had taken place. An employee turned Miller in to the government and she pled guilty to the ensuing twenty count indictment.

Smith, who was Miller's next door neighbor, was convicted of two counts of discharging pollutants without a permit. Smith ran a small haulage and non-hazardous waste disposal business. Grey Chemical, a specialty chemical manufacturer, was Smith's biggest customer. Grey gave Smith a load of 100 barrels to dispose of. Smith found that no local hazardous waste disposal company would take two of the barrels, which contained highly toxic chemicals. Rather than start a squabble with Grey, Smith heaved the two barrels into a nearby swamp. He had never done anything like that before. Two weeks later, a game warden on regular patrol found the barrels before anything leaked out of them. That was lucky because, if the barrels had corroded and leaked, the chemicals would have spread through the swamp and, if not discovered for a month after leaking, would have cost $1 million to clean up. Smith was remorseful and offered to do 25 weekends of community service at a recycling center, if the charge were dropped. The prosecutor turned the offer down saying the environmental laws were designed to protect against risk and, in that context, Smith had committed a serious crime.

Identify the factors you think the trial court should take into account and the weight that should be given to them so that Miller and Smith would receive fair sentences. The Sentencing Commission typically starts with a base offense level between 1 and 25 and then increases or decreases levels on the basis of the presence or absence of specific offense characteristics relating to the crime and adjustments related to the defendant's role in the offense, criminal history and so on.

## SOLEM v. HELM

Supreme Court of the United States, 1983.
463 U.S. 277, 103 S.Ct. 3001, 77 L.Ed.2d 637.

JUSTICE POWELL delivered the opinion of the Court.

The issue presented is whether the Eighth Amendment proscribes a life sentence without possibility of parole for a seventh nonviolent felony.

I

By 1975 the State of South Dakota had convicted respondent Jerry Helm of six nonviolent felonies. In 1964, 1966, and 1969 Helm was convicted of third-degree burglary. In 1972 he was convicted of obtaining money under false pretenses. In 1973 he was convicted of grand larceny. And in 1975 he was convicted of third-offense driving while intoxicated. The record contains no details about the circumstances of any of these offenses, except, that they were all nonviolent, none was a crime against a person, and alcohol was a contributing factor in each case.

In 1979 Helm was charged with uttering a "no account" check for $100. The only details we have of the crime are those given by Helm to the state trial court:

> " 'I was working in Sioux Falls, and got my check that day, was drinking and I ended up here in Rapid City with more money than I had when I started. I knew I'd done something I didn't know exactly what. If I would have known this, I would have picked the check up. I was drinking and didn't remember, stopped several places.' "

After offering this explanation, Helm pleaded guilty.

Ordinarily the maximum punishment for uttering a "no account" check would have been five years' imprisonment in the state penitentiary and a $5,000 fine. As a result of his criminal record, however, Helm was subject to South Dakota's recidivist statute:

> "When a defendant has been convicted of at least three prior convictions [sic] in addition to the principal felony, the sentence for the principal felony shall be enhanced to the sentence for a Class 1 felony." SD Codified Laws § 22–7–8 (1979)(amended 1981).

The maximum penalty for a "Class 1 felony" was life imprisonment in the state penitentiary and a $25,000 fine. Moreover, South Dakota law explicitly provides that parole is unavailable * * *. The Governor is authorized to pardon prisoners, or to commute their sentences, SD Const., Art IV, § 3, but no other relief from sentence is available even to a rehabilitated prisoner.

Immediately after accepting Helm's guilty plea, the South Dakota Circuit Court sentenced Helm to life imprisonment under § 22–7–8. * * *

[Helm sought habeas relief which was granted by Court of Appeals for the Eighth Circuit.]

## II

The Eighth Amendment declares: "Excessive bail shall not be required, nor excessive fines imposed, nor cruel and unusual punishments inflicted." The final clause prohibits not only barbaric punishments, but also sentences that are disproportionate to the crime committed.

### A

The principle that a punishment should be proportionate to the crime is deeply rooted and frequently repeated in common-law jurisprudence. * * * When prison sentences became the normal criminal sanctions, the common law recognized that these, too, must be proportional.

The English Bill of Rights repeated the principle of proportionality in language that was later adopted in the Eighth Amendment: "excessive Baile ought not to be required nor excessive Fines imposed nor cruell and unusuall Punishments inflicted." 1 Wm. & Mary, sess. 2, ch. 2 (1689). * * *

Although the Framers may have intended the Eighth Amendment to go beyond the scope of its English counterpart, their use of the language of the English Bill of Rights is convincing proof that they intended to provide at least the same protection—including the right to be free from excessive punishments.

B

The constitutional principle of proportionality has been recognized explicitly in this Court for almost a century. In the leading case of Weems v. United States, 217 U.S. 349, 30 S.Ct. 544, 54 L.Ed. 793 (1910), the defendant had been convicted of falsifying a public document and sentenced to 15 years of "*cadena temporal,*" a form of imprisonment that included hard labor in chains and permanent civil disabilities. The Court noted that "it is a precept of justice that punishment for crime should be graduated and proportioned to offense," and held that the sentence violated the Eighth Amendment. The Court endorsed the principle of proportionality as a constitutional standard, and determined that the sentence before it was "cruel in its excess of imprisonment," as well as in its shackles and restrictions.

The Court next applied the principle to invalidate a criminal sentence in Robinson v. California, 370 U.S. 660, 82 S.Ct. 1417, 8 L.Ed.2d 758 (1962). A 90–day sentence was found to be excessive for the crime of being "addicted to the use of narcotics." The Court explained that "imprisonment for ninety days is not, in the abstract, a punishment which is either cruel or unusual." Thus there was no question of an inherently barbaric punishment. "But the question cannot be considered in the abstract. Even one day in prison would be a cruel and unusual punishment for the 'crime' of having a common cold."

Most recently, the Court has applied the principle of proportionality to hold capital punishment excessive in certain circumstances. Enmund v. Florida, 458 U.S. 782, 102 S.Ct. 3368, 73 L.Ed.2d 1140 (1982)(death penalty excessive for felony murder when defendant did not take life, attempt to take life, or intend that a life be taken or that lethal force be used); Coker v. Georgia, 433 U.S. 584, 592, 97 S.Ct. 2861, 2866, 53 L.Ed.2d 982 (1977)(plurality opinion)("sentence of death is grossly disproportionate and excessive punishment for the crime of rape"); *id.,* at 601, 97 S.Ct., at 2870 (Powell, J., concurring in judgment in part and dissenting in part)("ordinarily death is disproportionate punishment for the crime of raping an adult woman"). And the Court has continued to recognize that the Eighth Amendment proscribes grossly disproportionate punishments, even when it has not been necessary to rely on the proscription.

C

* * * We hold as a matter of principle that a criminal sentence must be proportionate to the crime for which the defendant has been convicted. Reviewing courts, of course, should grant substantial deference to the broad authority that legislatures necessarily possess in determining the types and limits of punishments for crimes, as well as to the discretion that trial courts possess in sentencing convicted criminals. But no penalty is *per se* constitutional. * * *

III

A

* * * [A] court's proportionality analysis under the Eighth Amendment should be guided by objective criteria, including (i) the gravity of the offense and the harshness of the penalty; (ii) the sentences imposed on other criminals in the same jurisdiction; and (iii) the sentences imposed for commission of the same crime in other jurisdictions.

B

Application of these factors assumes that courts are competent to judge the gravity of an offense, at least on a relative scale. In a broad sense this assumption is justified, and courts traditionally have made these judgments—just as legislatures must make them in the first instance. Comparisons can be made in light of the harm caused or threatened to the victim or society, and the culpability of the offender. Thus in *Enmund* the Court determined that the petitioner's conduct was not as serious as his accomplices' conduct. Indeed, there are widely shared views as to the relative seriousness of crimes. See Rossi, Waite, Bose, & Berk, The Seriousness of Crimes: Normative Structure and Individual Differences, 39 Am. Sociological Rev. 224, 237 (1974). For example, as the criminal laws make clear, non-violent crimes are less serious than crimes marked by violence or the threat of violence.

There are other accepted principles that courts may apply in measuring the harm caused or threatened to the victim or society. The absolute magnitude of the crime may be relevant. Stealing a million dollars is viewed as more serious than stealing a hundred dollars—a point recognized in statutes distinguishing petty theft from grand theft. Few would dispute that a lesser included offense should not be punished more severely than the greater offense. Thus a court is justified in viewing assault with intent to murder as more serious than simple assault. * * * Similarly, an accessory after the fact should not be subject to a higher penalty than the principal.

Turning to the culpability of the offender, there are again clear distinctions that courts may recognize and apply. In *Enmund* the Court looked at the petitioner's lack of intent to kill in determining that he was less culpable than his accomplices. Most would agree that negligent conduct is less serious than intentional conduct. South Dakota, for example, ranks criminal acts in ascending order of seriousness as follows: negligent acts, reckless acts, knowing acts, intentional acts, and malicious acts. A court, of course, is entitled to look at a defendant's motive in committing a crime. Thus a murder may be viewed as more serious when committed pursuant to a contract.

This list is by no means exhaustive. It simply illustrates that there are generally accepted criteria for comparing the severity of different crimes on a broad scale, despite the difficulties courts face in attempting to draw distinctions between similar crimes. * * *

IV

Helm's crime was "one of the most passive felonies a person could commit." State v. Helm, 287 N.W.2d, at 501 (Henderson, J., dissenting). It involved neither violence nor threat of violence to any person. The $100 face value of Helm's "no account" check was not trivial, but neither was it a large amount. One hundred dollars was less than half the amount South Dakota required for a felonious theft. It is easy to see why such a crime is viewed by society as among the less serious offenses.

Helm, of course, was not charged simply with uttering a "no account" check, but also with being a habitual offender. And a State is justified in punishing a recidivist more severely than it punishes a first offender. Helm's status, however, cannot be considered in the abstract. His prior offenses, although classified as felonies, were all relatively minor.[22] All were nonviolent and none was a crime against a person. * * *

Helm's present sentence is life imprisonment without possibility of parole. Barring executive clemency, Helm will spend the rest of his life in the state penitentiary. This sentence is far more severe than the life sentence we considered in Rummel v. Estelle [, 445 U.S. 263, 100 S.Ct. 1133, 63 L.Ed.2d 382 (1980)]. Rummel was likely to have been eligible for parole within 12 years of his initial confinement, a fact on which the Court relied heavily. Helm's sentence is the most severe punishment that the State could have imposed on any criminal for any crime. Only capital punishment, a penalty not authorized in South Dakota when Helm was sentenced, exceeds it.

We next consider the sentences that could be imposed on other criminals in the same jurisdiction. * * *

In sum, there were a handful of crimes that were necessarily punished by life imprisonment: murder, and, on a second or third offense, treason, first-degree manslaughter, first-degree arson, and kidnaping. There was a larger group for which life imprisonment was authorized in the discretion of the sentencing judge, including: treason, first-degree manslaughter, first-degree arson, and kidnaping; attempted

22. Helm, who was 36 years old when he was sentenced, is not a professional criminal. The record indicates an addiction to alcohol, and a consequent difficulty in holding a job. His record involves no instance of violence of any kind. Incarcerating him for life without possibility of parole is unlikely to advance the goals of our criminal justice system in any substantial way. Neither Helm nor the State will have an incentive to pursue clearly needed treatment for his alcohol problem, or any other program of rehabilitation.

murder, placing an explosive device on an aircraft, and first-degree rape on a second or third offense; and any felony after three prior offenses. Finally, there was a large group of very serious offenses for which life imprisonment was not authorized, including a third offense of heroin dealing or aggravated assault.

Criminals committing any of these offenses ordinarily would be thought more deserving of punishment than one uttering a "no account" check—even when the bad-check writer had already committed six minor felonies. Moreover, there is no indication in the record that any habitual offender other than Helm has ever been given the maximum sentence on the basis of comparable crimes. It is more likely that the possibility of life imprisonment under § 22–7–8 generally is reserved for criminals such as fourth-time heroin dealers, while habitual bad-check writers receive more lenient treatment. In any event, Helm has been treated in the same manner as, or more severely than, criminals who have committed far more serious crimes.

Finally, we compare the sentences imposed for commission of the same crime in other jurisdictions. The Court of Appeals found that "Helm could have received a life sentence without parole for his offense in only one other state, Nevada," 684 F.2d, at 586, and we have no reason to doubt this finding. * * * We are not advised that any defendant such as Helm, whose prior offenses were so minor, actually has received the maximum penalty in Nevada. It appears that Helm was treated more severely than he would have been in any other State.

The State argues that the present case is essentially the same as *Rummel v. Estelle,* for the possibility of parole in that case is matched by the possibility of executive clemency here. The State reasons that the Governor could commute Helm's sentence to a term of years. We conclude, however, that the South Dakota commutation system is fundamentally different from the parole system that was before us in *Rummel.*

As a matter of law, parole and commutation are different concepts, despite some surface similarities. Parole is a regular part of the rehabilitative process. Assuming good behavior, it is the normal expectation in the vast majority of cases. The law generally specifies when a prisoner will be eligible to be considered for parole, and details the standards and procedures applicable at that time. Thus it is possible to predict, at least to some extent, when parole might be granted. Commutation, on the other hand, is an ad hoc exercise of executive clemency. A Governor may commute a sentence at any time for any reason without reference to any standards. * * *

The Texas and South Dakota systems in particular are very different. In *Rummel,* the Court did not rely simply on the existence of some system of parole. Rather it looked to the provisions of the system presented, including the fact that Texas had "a relatively liberal policy of granting 'good time' credits to its prisoners, a policy that historically has allowed a prisoner serving a life sentence to become eligible for parole in as little as 12 years." 445 U.S., at 280, 100 S.Ct., at 1142. * * *

The possibility of commutation is nothing more than a hope for "an *ad hoc* exercise of clemency." It is little different from the possibility of executive clemency that exists in every case in which a defendant challenges his sentence under the Eighth Amendment. Recognition of such a bare possibility would make judicial review under the Eighth Amendment meaningless.

V

The Constitution requires us to examine Helm's sentence to determine if it is proportionate to his crime. Applying objective criteria, we find that Helm has received the penultimate sentence for relatively minor criminal conduct. He has been treated more harshly than other criminals in the State who have committed more serious crimes. He has been treated more harshly than he would have been in any other jurisdiction, with the possible exception of a single State. We conclude that his sentence is significantly disproportionate to his crime, and is therefore prohibited by the Eighth Amendment. * * *

CHIEF JUSTICE BURGER, with whom JUSTICE WHITE, JUSTICE REHNQUIST, and JUSTICE O'CONNOR join, dissenting.

The controlling law governing this case is crystal clear, but today the Court blithely discards any concept of *stare decisis,* trespasses gravely on the authority of the states, and distorts the concept of proportionality of punishment by tearing it from its moorings in capital cases. Only three Terms ago, we held in Rummel v. Estelle, 445 U.S. 263, 100 S.Ct. 1133, 63 L.Ed.2d 382 (1980), that a life sentence imposed after only a *third* nonviolent felony conviction did not constitute cruel and unusual punishment under the Eighth Amendment. Today, the Court ignores its recent precedent and holds that a life sentence imposed after a *seventh* felony conviction constitutes cruel and unusual punishment under the Eighth Amendment. Moreover, I reject the fiction that all Helm's crimes were innocuous or non-violent. Among his felonies were three burglaries and a third conviction for drunken driving. By comparison Rummel was a relatively "model citizen." Although today's holding cannot rationally be reconciled with *Rummel,* the Court does not purport to overrule *Rummel.* I therefore dissent. * * *

The facts in *Rummel* bear repeating. Rummel was convicted in 1964 of fraudulent use of a credit card; in 1969, he was convicted of passing a forged check; finally, in 1973 Rummel was charged with obtaining money by false pretenses, which is also a felony under Texas law. These three offenses were indeed nonviolent. Under Texas' recidivist statute, which provides for a mandatory life sentence upon conviction for a third felony, the trial judge imposed a life sentence as he was obliged to do after the jury returned a verdict of guilty of felony theft.

Rummel, in this Court, advanced precisely the same arguments that respondent advances here; we rejected those arguments notwithstanding that his case was stronger than respondent's. The test in *Rummel* which we rejected would have required us to determine on an abstract moral scale whether Rummel had received his "just deserts" for his crimes. We declined that invitation; today the Court accepts it. * * *

The lesson the *Rummel* Court drew from *Weems* and from the capital punishment cases was that the Eighth Amendment did not authorize courts to review sentences of *imprisonment* to determine whether they were "proportional" to the crime. * * *

> "Given the *unique nature* of the punishments considered in *Weems* and in the death penalty cases, one could argue without fear of contradiction by any decision of this Court that for crimes concededly classified and classifiable as felonies, that is, as punishable by significant terms of imprisonment in a state penitentiary, the *length of the sentence actually imposed is purely a matter of legislative prerogative.*" 445 U.S., at 274, 100 S.Ct., at 1139. (Emphasis added.)

Five Justices joined this clear and precise limiting language. * * *

The *Rummel* Court emphasized, as has every opinion in capital cases in the past decade, that it was possible to draw a "bright line" between "the punishment of death and the various other permutations and commutations of punishment short of that ultimate sanction"; similarly, a line could be drawn between the punishment in *Weems* and "more traditional forms of imprisonment imposed under the Anglo–Saxon system." 445 U.S., at 275, 100 S.Ct., at 1140. However, the *Rummel* Court emphasized that drawing lines between different sentences of imprisonment would thrust the Court inevitably "into the basic line-drawing process that is pre-eminently the province of the legislature" and produce judgments that were no more than the visceral reactions of individual Justices. * * *

## *Notes*

1. In Harmelin v. Michigan, 501 U.S. 957, 111 S.Ct. 2680, 115 L.Ed.2d 836 (1991), the Supreme Court considered the application of the Eighth Amendment's prohibition against cruel and unusual punishment to a first time offender convicted under Michigan law for possession of more than 650 grams of a mixture containing cocaine who received a mandatory term of life in prison without the possibility of parole. Harmelin possessed 672.5 grams of undiluted cocaine and was also found to have marijuana cigarettes, four brass cocaine straws, a cocaine spoon, 12 Percodan tablets, 25 tablets of Phendimetrazine Tartrate, a Motorola beeper, plastic bags containing cocaine, a coded address book, and $3500 in cash. Relevant to sentences imposed in the same jurisdiction, Michigan has no death penalty; life without parole is reserved for three crimes: first-degree murder; manufacture, distribution or possession with intent to manufacture or distribute 650 grams or more of narcotics; and possession of 650 grams or more of narcotics. With regard to sentences for the same crime in other jurisdictions, no other state imposes so severe a penalty. Mandatory life for a first-time drug offender without possibility of parole is imposed only in Alabama and only when the defendant possesses ten kilograms or more of cocaine.

The federal sentencing guidelines would provide a sentence of a little more than ten years.

The Court affirmed the Michigan sentence. Justice Scalia, joined by Chief Justice Rehnquist, would have overruled *Solem* and would hold that the Eighth Amendment does not contain a guarantee of proportionality with regard to prison sentences; they would limit the proportionality analysis to death penalty jurisprudence, making it inapplicable to the Eighth Amendment generally. In addition, Justice Scalia did not require any consideration of mitigating factors such as the first-time offense in this mandatory sentencing case. The heart of the opinion is a lengthy historical account of the origins and application of the cruel and unusual punishment clause.

Justice Kennedy, joined by Justices O'Connor and Souter, concurred in the judgment and in the refusal to require consideration of mitigating factors, but reached this result by reading *Solem* narrowly to require at the outset only consideration of *Solem's* first test: analysis of the gravity of the offense and the harshness of the penalty. Satisfied that Harmelin's sentence did not run afoul of the cruel and unusual punishment clause under that test, these justices went no further because they found the intra- and inter-jurisdictional analysis appropriate only in the rare case where the comparison of the crime committed and the sentence imposed leads to an inference of gross disproportionality.

The remaining four justices (White, Stevens, Blackmun and Marshall) dissented. They would have applied all three *Solem* tests and would have vacated the sentence.

Thus at the present time, there is no single test for applying the cruel and unusual punishment clause to prison sentences which commands support from a majority of the Supreme Court. Regardless of whether the procedure set out by Justice Kennedy or that adopted by the dissenters is pursued, a number of points relevant to the present state of *Solem* should be noted:

(a) Proportionality analysis will be used to invalidate only a few rare sentences. In his dissent, Justice White points out that the parties to *Harmelin* cited only four cases decided in the eight years after *Solem* which reversed sentences on the basis of proportionality analysis.

(b) Justice Kennedy makes the least objective of *Solem's* three tests the centerpiece of his application of the rule. This makes it very hard to predict when the Supreme Court would again reverse a criminal prison sentence on proportionality grounds.

(c) Justice Kennedy points out that "appropriate sentences" are ultimately derived from penological theories and judgments and that the prevailing diversity of views on penology must allow a broad range of sentences. The Eighth Amendment and the Constitution do not adopt any particular penological theory. The state and federal systems have accorded different weight at different times to retribution, deterrence, incapacitation, and rehabilitation. Finally, it is the legislatures, not the courts, that have primacy in setting the sanctions for criminal behavior. Giving appropriate deference to the legislature in an area where there are few agreed-on basic principles will produce a very wide range of acceptable sentencing practices.

(d) The references in the *Harmelin* opinion to the federal sentencing guidelines underscore that while the courts are reluctant to attempt to detail rules to achieve even coarse-grained comparative proportionality between sentences, the Sentencing Commission is struggling toward that end.

In 1992, the Supreme Court of Michigan reviewed the statute mandating life imprisonment for conviction of possession of 650 grams or more of cocaine. Michigan v. Bullock, 440 Mich. 15, 485 N.W.2d 866 (1992). Applying the principles of *Solem*, the court struck down the portion of the statute that denied parole considerations as "an unduly disproportionate response to the serious problems posed by drugs in our society." Id. at 877. It was therefore cruel and unusual punishment, in violation of the Michigan constitution, because it would allow a severe penalty for mere possession without proof that the defendant "committed, aided, intended, or even contemplated" any violent crime. Id. at 876.

2. *Solem* rests much of its analysis on the distinction between violent and non-violent crimes and on the magnitude of harm to the victim of the crime. How can the *Solem* standards be applied to crimes such as consensual sodomy or taking of gratuities by government officials? See Note, Cruel and Unusual Punishment and Sodomy Statutes: The Breakdown of the *Solem v. Helm* Test, 56 U.Chi.L.Rev. 367 (1989).

3. In Ingraham v. Wright, 430 U.S. 651, 664, 97 S.Ct. 1401, 1408, 51 L.Ed.2d 711 (1977), a case addressing the use of corporal punishment in the Florida public schools, the Supreme Court stated: "An examination of the history of the eighth amendment and the decisions of this Court construing the prescriptions against cruel and unusual punishment confirms that it was designed to protect those convicted of crimes. We adhere to this longstanding limitation * * *." Four Justices dissented, taking a broader view of the amendment:

> The Eighth Amendment places a flat prohibition against the infliction of "cruel and unusual punishments." This reflects a societal judgment that there are some punishments that are so barbaric and inhumane that we will not permit them to be imposed on anyone, no matter how opprobrious the offense. * * * If there are some punishments that are so barbaric that they may not be imposed for the commission of crimes, designated by our social system as the most thoroughly reprehensible acts an individual can commit, then, a fortiori, similar punishments may not be imposed on persons for less culpable acts, such as breaches of school discipline. Thus, if it is constitutionally impermissible to cut off someone's ear for the commission of murder, it must be unconstitutional to cut off a child's ear for being late to class. Although there were no ears cut off in this case, the record reveals beatings so severe that if they were inflicted on a hardened criminal for the commission of a serious crime, they might not pass constitutional muster.
>
> Nevertheless, the majority holds that the Eighth Amendment "was designed to protect [only] those convicted of crimes," relying on a vague and inconclusive recitation of the history of the Amendment. Yet the

constitutional prohibition is against cruel and unusual *punishments;* nowhere is that prohibition limited or modified by the language of the Constitution. Certainly, the fact that the Framers did not choose to insert the word "criminal" into the language of the Eighth Amendment is strong evidence that the Amendment was designed to prohibit all inhumane or barbaric punishments, no matter what the nature of the offense for which the punishment is imposed.

No one can deny that spanking of schoolchildren is "punishment" under any reasonable reading of the word, for the similarities between spanking in public schools and other forms of punishment are too obvious to ignore. Like other forms of punishment, spanking of schoolchildren involves an institutionalized response to the violation of some official rule or regulation proscribing certain conduct and is imposed for the purpose of rehabilitating the offender, deterring the offender and others like him from committing the violation in the future, and inflicting some measure of social retribution for the harm that has been done. Id. at 684–685, 97 S.Ct. at 1419–1420 (White, J., dissenting).

How is the reasoning in the first three cases in this chapter likely to influence the Court in deciding later cases involving the question of whether the eighth amendment applies in a context other than a criminal case?

## C. PUNITIVE DAMAGES

Claims for and awards of punitive damages exhibit aspects of both tort and criminal law. Punitive or exemplary damages "are not compensation for injury. Instead, they are private fines levied by civil juries to punish reprehensible conduct and to deter its future occurrence." Gertz v. Robert Welch, Inc., 418 U.S. 323, 350, 94 S.Ct. 2997, 3012, 41 L.Ed.2d 789 (1974). The Restatement (Second) of Torts, § 908, provides a similar definition:

(1) Punitive damages are damages, other than compensatory or nominal damages, awarded against a person to punish him for his outrageous conduct and to deter him and others like him from similar conduct in the future.

(2) Punitive damages may be awarded for conduct that is outrageous, because of the defendant's evil motive or his reckless indifference to the rights of others. In assessing punitive damages, the trier of fact can properly consider the character of the defendant's act, the nature and extent of the harm to the plaintiff that the defendant caused or intended to cause and the wealth of the defendant.

Punishment and deterrence are the most frequently cited purposes of punitive damages, but other related purposes have been identified as well. Exemplary damages may serve a compensatory function where the injury or outrage is palpable but there is no generally agreed on measure of damages and, by covering litigation costs and attorneys' fees, they make the plaintiff whole to an extent not typically provided for in American courts. Punitive damages may serve an educational function, closely related to the deterrence function, of making plain to the public generally the rights of plaintiffs and the liability of defendants. They supplement or, in some cases take the place of, governmental law enforcement effort. Certainly, as a practical matter, the possibility of obtaining punitive or exemplary damages will encourage the development of complex and difficult factual cases for plaintiffs who cannot themselves afford extensive litigation expenses.

Many of the recurring issues raised by punitive damages reflect the unsure marriage of tort and criminal law that fathered this remedy. If the remedy is a punishment of the defendant, how should the trial procedures and the plaintiff's burden of proof differ from the criminal law? Since the punitive award to the plaintiff is generally thought to be over and above what he receives to make himself whole, what facts or conduct concerning the defendant are relevant to determining the amount of damages to be awarded? Is it appropriate for the successful plaintiff to retain all of a punitive award or should some or all of it pass to the government or to some organization devoted to countering the sort of injurious conduct in which the defendant engaged? In a mass tort, are multiple punitive awards against the same defendant for the same course of conduct fair to either the defendant or to a late-arriving plaintiff who finds the defendant insolvent? Is there any practical and realistic mechanism to address this problem?

Punitive damages have been the focus of public debate and extensive legal commentary in recent years. Until the middle of this century, punitive damages were generally restricted to intentional and dignitary torts. Dorsey D. Ellis, Jr., Fairness and Efficiency in the Law of Punitive Damages, 56 S.Cal.L.Rev. 1 (1982). Since 1950, there has been a growth of punitive damage awards in other areas:

> *Contracts.* The black letter rule for 200 years has been that punitive damages are not available for breach of contract. Restatement (Second) of Contracts § 355 (1981). Beginning in the 1960s, courts permitted the award of punitive damages for bad faith breach of insurance contracts. Such awards are now allowed in a majority of jurisdictions. Although a few jurisdictions have permitted a tort action, for which punitive damages may be available, for other forms of breach of contract, the trend now seems to be in the opposite direction. E.g., Freeman & Mills, Inc. v. Belcher Oil Co., 11 Cal.4th 85, 44 Cal.Rptr.2d 420, 900 P.2d 669 (1995)(overruling previous decisions which had permitted tort recovery for certain noninsurance breaches of contract) (reproduced infra at p. 637); Kerry Macintosh, Gilmore Spoke Too Soon: Contract Rises From the Ashes of the Bad Faith Tort, 27 Loyola L.A.L.Rev. 483 (1994).
>
> *Products Liability.* Prior to 1976, there were very few punitive damage awards in product liability cases. There was limited comment on this, but since punishment was traditionally associated with wilful or intentional acts, it may have appeared anomalous to the courts to punish a defendant for negligence or for tortious

conduct for which he was strictly liable. In addition, in Roginsky v. Richardson–Merrell, Inc., 378 F.2d 832 (2d Cir.1967), Judge Friendly raised three other problems as he struck down a punitive damage award: (1) the inequity of punishing shareholders for the misdeeds of low-level employees; (2) the possibility that the defendant would be insured against punitive damage liability; and (3) the risk of excessive punishment through repeated punitive awards involving a single defective product. In 1976, Professor David G. Owen published his massive and seminal article, Punitive Damages in Products Liability Litigation, 74 Mich.L.Rev. 1257 (1976), arguing in favor of punitive damages in appropriate products liability cases. Such cases are no longer unusual. E.g., Grimshaw v. Ford Motor Co., 119 Cal.App.3d 757, 174 Cal.Rptr. 348 (1981) (reproduced infra at p. 455).

*Mass Torts.* The first mass tort action in which punitive damages issues arose was brought in 1961 to challenge the sale of an anti-cholesterol drug. Such cases are now common and focus the issue of multiple punitive damage claims. E.g., Dunn v. HOVIC, 1 F.3d 1371 (3d Cir. en banc), cert. denied, ___ U.S. ___, 114 S.Ct. 650, 126 L.Ed.2d 608 (1993) (reproduced infra at p. 470).

There is limited empirical evidence of the growth of punitive damage awards. One study by the Rand Corporation supports the conventional wisdom of defendants that the number of actions claiming punitive damages and the size of the awards has grown drastically. For instance, Rand analyzed civil jury verdicts for the period 1960–84 in Cook County (Chicago), Illinois and San Francisco County, California in the following categories: business tort and contract cases, intentional tort cases and personal injury cases (both negligence and strict liability). In Cook County in 1960–64, punitive damages were awarded in 0.2% of all cases in which compensatory relief was awarded; in 1980–84, punitive damages were awarded in 3.9% of those cases. In San Francisco for the same period the awards grew from 2% to 13.6% of the cases. Peterson, Sharma & Stanley, Punitive Damages—Empirical Findings (1988).

Other studies support the position that the size and number of punitive damage awards in relation to compensatory awards have not grown dramatically. E.g., Michael Rustad, In Defense of Punitive Damages in Products Liability: Testing Tort Anecdotes with Empirical Data, 78 Iowa L. Rev. 1 (1992); Jerry J. Phillips, Multiple Punitive Damage Awards, 39 Vill.L.Rev. 433, 440–441 (1994). Another recent analysis suggests that over the 25 years from 1965 to 1990, punitive damages were awarded in approximately 2% of the cases with the number trending upward in the 1970s and early '80s but, leaving aside asbestos cases, trending downward in the later years of the period. David G. Owen, A Punitive Damages Overview: Functions, Problems and Reform, 39 Vill.L.Rev. 363, 372–73 (1994). It remains unclear whether the behavior of judges and juries or products manufacturers has changed significantly in recent years in a manner that supports the "reform" of punitive damages.

## GRIMSHAW v. FORD MOTOR CO.

Court of Appeal of California, Fourth District, 1981.
119 Cal.App.3d 757, 174 Cal.Rptr. 348.

TAMURA, ACTING PRESIDING JUSTICE.

A 1972 Ford Pinto hatchback automobile unexpectedly stalled on a freeway, erupting into flames when it was rear ended by a car proceeding in the same direction. Mrs. Lilly Gray, the driver of the Pinto, suffered fatal burns and 13–year-old Richard Grimshaw, a passenger in the Pinto, suffered severe and permanently disfiguring burns on his face and entire body. Grimshaw and the heirs of Mrs. Gray (Grays) sued Ford Motor Company and others. Following a six-month jury trial, verdicts were returned in favor of plaintiffs against Ford Motor Company. Grimshaw was awarded $2,516,000 compensatory damages and $125 million punitive damages; * * * On Ford's motion for a new trial, Grimshaw was required to remit all but $3½ million of the punitive award as a condition of denial of the motion.

Ford appeals from the judgment and from an order denying its motion for a judgment notwithstanding the verdict as to punitive damages. Grimshaw appeals from the order granting the conditional new trial and from the amended judgment entered pursuant to the order. * * *

At the moment of impact, the Pinto caught fire and its interior was engulfed in flames. According to plaintiffs' expert, the impact of the Galaxie had driven the Pinto's gas tank forward and caused it to be punctured by the flange or one of the bolts on the differential housing so that fuel sprayed from the punctured tank and entered the passenger compartment through gaps resulting from the separation of the rear wheel well sections from the floor pan. By the time the Pinto came to rest after the collision, both occupants had sustained serious burns. When they emerged from the vehicle, their clothing was almost completely burned off. Mrs. Gray died a few days later of congestive heart failure as a result of the burns. Grimshaw managed to survive but only through heroic medical measures. He has undergone numerous and extensive surgeries and skin grafts and must undergo additional surgeries over the next 10 years. He lost portions of several fingers on his left hand and portions of his left ear, while his face required many skin grafts from various portions of his body. * * *

In 1968, Ford began designing a new subcompact automobile which ultimately became the Pinto. Mr. Iacocca, then a Ford Vice President, conceived the project and was its moving force. Ford's objective was to build a car at or below 2,000 pounds to sell for no more than $2,000. * * *

It was then the preferred practice in Europe and Japan to locate the gas tank over the rear axle in subcompacts because a small vehicle has less "crush space" between the rear axle and the bumper than larger cars. The Pinto's styling, however, required the tank to be placed behind the rear axle leaving only 9 or 10 inches of "crush space"—far less than in any other American automobile or Ford overseas subcompact. In addition, the Pinto was designed so that its bumper was little more than a chrome strip, less substantial than the bumper of any other American car produced then or later. The Pinto's rear structure also lacked reinforcing members known as "hat sections" (2 longitudinal side members) and horizontal cross-members running between them such as were found in cars of larger unitized construction and in all automobiles produced by Ford's overseas operations. The absence of the reinforcing members rendered the Pinto less crush resistant than other vehicles. Finally, the differential housing selected for the Pinto had an exposed flange and a line of exposed bolt heads. These protrusions were sufficient to puncture a gas tank driven forward against the differential upon rear impact. * * *

During the development of the Pinto, prototypes were built and tested. Some were "mechanical prototypes" which duplicated mechanical features of the design but not its appearance while others, referred to as "engineering prototypes," were true duplicates of the design car. These prototypes as well as two production Pintos were crash tested by Ford to determine, among other things, the integrity of the fuel system in rear-end accidents. Ford also conducted the tests to see if the Pinto as designed would meet a proposed federal regulation requiring all automobiles manufactured in 1972 to be able to withstand a 20–mile-per-hour fixed barrier impact without significant fuel spillage and all automobiles manufactured after January 1, 1973, to withstand a 30–mile-per-hour fixed barrier impact without significant fuel spillage.

The crash tests revealed that the Pinto's fuel system as designed could not meet the 20–mile-per-hour proposed standard. * * *

Ford contends that the court erroneously admitted irrelevant documentary evidence highly prejudicial to Ford. We find the contention to be without merit. * * *

*Exhibit No. 125:*

Exhibit No. 125 was a report presented at a Ford production review meeting in April 1971, recommending action to be taken in anticipation of the promulgation of federal standards on fuel system integrity. The report recommended, *inter alia,* deferral from 1974 to 1976 of the adoption of "flak suits" or "bladders" in all Ford cars, including the Pinto, in order to realize a savings of $20.9 million. The report stated that the cost of the flak suit or bladder would be $4 to $8 per car. The meeting at which the report was presented was chaired by Vice President Harold MacDonald and attended by Vice President Robert Alexander and occurred sometime before the 1972 Pinto was placed on the market. A reasonable inference may be drawn from the evidence that despite management's knowledge that the Pinto's fuel system could be made safe at a cost of but $4 to $8 per car, it decided to defer corrective measures to save money and enhance profits. The evidence was thus highly relevant and properly received. * * *

Ford contends that it was entitled to a judgment notwithstanding the verdict on the issue of punitive damages on two grounds: First, punitive damages are statutorily and constitutionally impermissible in a design defect case; second, there was no evidentiary support for a finding of malice or of corporate responsibility for malice. In any event, Ford maintains that the punitive damage award must be reversed because of erroneous instructions and excessiveness of the award.

*"Malice" Under Civil Code Section 3294:*

The concept of punitive damages is rooted in the English common law and is a settled principle of the common law of this country. (Owen, Punitive Damages in Products Liability Litigation, 74 Mich.L.Rev. 1258, 1262–1263 (hereafter Owen); Mallor & Roberts, Punitive Damages, Towards A Principled Approach, 31 Hastings L.J. 639, 642–643 (hereafter Mallor & Roberts); Note, Exemplary Damages in the Law of Torts, 70 Harv.L.Rev. 517, 518–520.) The doctrine was a part of the common law of this state long before the Civil Code was adopted. When our laws were codified in 1872, the doctrine was incorporated in Civil Code section 3294, which at the time of trial read: "In an action for the breach of an obligation not arising from contract, where the defendant has been guilty of oppression, fraud, or malice, express or implied, the plaintiff, in addition to the actual damages, may recover damages for the sake of example and by way of punishing the defendant."

Ford argues that "malice" as used in section 3294 and as interpreted by our Supreme Court in Davis v. Hearst, 160 Cal. 143, 116 P. 530, requires *animus malus* or evil motive—an intention to injure the person harmed—and that the term is therefore conceptually incompatible with an unintentional tort such as the manufacture and marketing of a defectively designed product. This contention runs counter to our decisional law. As this court recently noted, numerous California cases after *Davis v. Hearst*, supra, have interpreted the term "malice" as used in section 3294 to include, not only a malicious intention to injure the specific person harmed, but conduct evincing "a conscious disregard of the probability that the actor's conduct will result in injury to others."

In Taylor v. Superior Court, 24 Cal.3d 890, 157 Cal.Rptr. 693, 598 P.2d 854, our high court's most recent pronouncement on the subject of punitive damages, the court observed that the availability of punitive damages has not been limited to cases in which there is an actual intent to harm plaintiff or others. The court concurred with the *Searle* (G.D. Searle & Co. v. Superior Court, 49 Cal.App.3d 22, 122 Cal.Rptr. 218) court's suggestion that conscious disregard of the safety of others is an appropriate description of the *animus malus* required by Civil Code section 3294, adding: "In order to justify an award of punitive damages on this basis, the plaintiff must establish that the defendant was aware of the probable dangerous consequences of his conduct, and that he wilfully and deliberately failed to avoid those consequences." * * *

The interpretation of the word "malice" as used in section 3294 to encompass conduct evincing callous and conscious disregard of public safety by those who manufacture and market mass produced articles is consonant with and furthers the objectives of punitive damages. The primary purposes of punitive damages are punishment and deterrence of like conduct by the wrongdoer and others. In the traditional noncommercial intentional tort, compensatory damages alone may serve as an effective deterrent against future wrongful conduct but in commerce-related torts, the manufacturer may find it more profitable to treat compensatory damages as a part of the cost of doing business rather than to remedy the defect. (Owen, supra p. 1291; Note, Mass Liability and Punitive Damages Overkill, 30 Hastings L.J. 1797, 1802.) Deterrence of such "objectionable corporate policies" serves one of the principal purposes of Civil Code section 3294. Governmental safety standards and the criminal law have failed to provide adequate consumer protection against the manufacture and distribution of defective products. Punitive damages thus remain as the most effective remedy for consumer protection against defectively designed mass produced articles. They provide a motive for private individuals to enforce rules of law and enable them to recoup the expenses of doing so which can be considerable and not otherwise recoverable.

We find no statutory impediments to the application of Civil Code section 3294 to a strict products liability case based on design defect. * * *

[Ford's] contention that the potential liability for punitive damages in other cases for the same design defect renders the imposition of such damages violative of Ford's due process rights also lacks merit. Followed to its logical conclusion, it would mean that punitive damages could never be assessed against a manufacturer of a mass produced article. No authorities are cited for such a proposition; indeed, as we have seen, the cases are to the contrary. We recognize the fact that multiplicity of awards may present a problem, but the mere possibility of a future award in a different case is not a ground for setting aside the award in this case, particularly as reduced by the trial judge. If Ford should be confronted with the possibility of an award in another case for the same conduct, it may raise the issue in that case. We add, moreover, that there is no necessary unfairness should the plaintiff in this case be rewarded to a greater extent than later plaintiffs. As Professor Owen has said in response to such a charge of unfairness: "This conception ignores the enormous diligence, imagination, and financial outlay required of initial plaintiffs to uncover and to prove the flagrant misconduct of a product manufacturer. In fact, subsequent plaintiffs will often ride to favorable verdicts and settlements on the coattails of the firstcomers." That observation fits the instant case. * * *

Ford's final contention is that the amount of punitive damages awarded, even as reduced by the trial court, was so excessive that a new trial on that issue must be granted. Ford argues that its conduct was less reprehensible than those for which punitive damages have been awarded in California in the past; that the $3½ million award is many times over the highest award for such damages ever upheld in California; and that the award exceeds maximum civil penalties that may be enforced under federal or state statutes against a manufacturer for marketing a defective automobile. We are unpersuaded.

In determining whether an award of punitive damages is excessive, comparison of the amount awarded with other awards in other cases is not a valid consideration. * * * In deciding whether an award is excessive as a matter of law or was so grossly disproportionate as to raise the presumption that it was the product of passion or prejudice, the following factors should be weighed: The degree of reprehensibility of defendant's conduct, the wealth of the defendant, the amount of compensatory damages, and an amount which would serve as a deterrent effect on like conduct by defendant and others who may be so inclined. Applying the foregoing criteria to the instant case, the punitive damage award as reduced by the trial court was well within reason.[14]

In assessing the propriety of a punitive damage award, as in assessing the propriety of any other judicial ruling based upon factual determinations, the evidence must be viewed in the light most favorable to the judgment. Viewing the record thusly in the instant case, the conduct of Ford's management was reprehensible in the extreme. It exhibited a conscious and callous disregard of public safety in order to maximize corporate profits. Ford's self-evaluation of its conduct is based on a review of the evidence most favorable to it instead of on the basis of the evidence most favorable to the judgment. Unlike malicious conduct directed toward a single specific individual, Ford's tortious conduct endangered the lives of thousands of Pinto purchasers. Weighed against the factor of reprehensibility, the punitive damage award as reduced by the trial judge was not excessive.

Nor was the reduced award excessive taking into account defendant's wealth and the size of the compensatory award. Ford's net worth was 7.7 billion dollars and its income after taxes for 1976 was over 983 million dollars. The punitive award was approximately .005% of Ford's net worth and approximately .03% of its 1976 net income. The ratio of the punitive damages to compensatory damages was approximately 1.4 to one. Significantly, Ford does not quarrel with the amount of the compensatory award to Grimshaw.

**14.** A quantitative formula whereby the amount of punitive damages can be determined in a given case with mathematical certainty is manifestly impossible as well as undesirable. (Mallor & Roberts, *supra,* 31 Hastings L.J. 639, 666–667, 670.) The authors advocate abandonment of the rule that a reasonable relationship must exist between punitive damages and actual damages. They suggest that courts balance society's interest against defendant's interest by focusing on the following factors: . Severity of threatened harm; degree of reprehensibility of defendant's conduct, profitability of the conduct, wealth of defendant, amount of compensatory damages (whether it was high in relation to injury), cost of litigation, potential criminal sanctions and other civil actions against defendant based on same conduct. In the present case, the amount of the award as reduced by the judge was reasonable under the suggested factors, including the factor of any other potential liability, civil or criminal.

Nor was the size of the award excessive in light of its deterrent purpose. An award which is so small that it can be simply written off as a part of the cost of doing business would have no deterrent effect. An award which affects the company's pricing of its product and thereby affects its competitive advantage would serve as a deterrent. The award in question was far from excessive as a deterrent against future wrongful conduct by Ford and others.

Ford complains that the punitive award is far greater than the maximum penalty that may be imposed under California or federal law prohibiting the sale of defective automobiles or other products. For example, Ford notes that California statutes provide a maximum fine of only $50 for the first offense and $100 for a second offense for a dealer who sells an automobile that fails to conform to federal safety laws or is not equipped with required lights or brakes; that a manufacturer who sells brake fluid in this state failing to meet statutory standards is subject to a maximum of only $50; and that the maximum penalty that may be imposed under federal law for violation of automobile safety standards is $1,000 per vehicle up to a maximum of $800,000 for any related series of offenses. It is precisely because monetary penalties under government regulations prescribing business standards or the criminal law are so inadequate and ineffective as deterrents against a manufacturer and distributor of mass produced defective products that punitive damages must be of sufficient amount to discourage such practices. Instead of showing that the punitive damage award was excessive, the comparison between the award and the maximum penalties under state and federal statutes and regulations governing automotive safety demonstrates the propriety of the amount of punitive damages awarded.

### Grimshaw's Appeal

Grimshaw has appealed from the order conditionally granting Ford a new trial on the issue of punitive damages and from the amended judgment entered pursuant to that order.

Grimshaw contends that the new trial order is erroneous because (1) the punitive damages awarded by the jury were not excessive as a matter of law, (2) the specification of reasons was inadequate; and (3) the court abused its discretion in cutting the award so drastically. For reasons to be stated, we have concluded that the contentions lack merit.

The court prefaced its specification of reasons with a recitation of the judicially established guidelines[16] for determining whether a punitive award is excessive. The court then observed that there was evidence in the record (referring to Exhibit 125) which might provide a possible rational basis for the 125 million dollar jury verdict which would dispel

**16.** The court stated that "the principles by which the propriety of the amount of punitive damages awarded will be judged are threefold: . (1) Is the sum so large as to raise a presumption that the award was the result of passion and prejudice and therefore excessive as a matter of law; (2) Does the award bear a reasonable relationship to the net assets of the defendant; and (3) Does the award bear a reasonable relationship to the compensatory damages awarded."

any presumption of passion or prejudice, adding, however, that the court was not suggesting that the amount was warranted "or that the jury did utilize Exhibit 125, or any other exhibits, and if they did, that they were justified in so doing." The court then noted, based on the fact that Ford's net worth was 7.7 billion and its profits during the last quarter of the year referred to in the financial statement introduced into evidence were more than twice the punitive award, that the award was not disproportionate to Ford's net assets or to its profit generating capacity. The court noted, however, that the amount of the punitive award was 44 times the compensatory award, the court stated that while it did not consider that ratio alone to be controlling because aggravating circumstances may justify a ratio as high as the one represented by the jury verdict, it reasoned that the ratio coupled with the amount by which the punitive exceeded the compensatory damages (over 122 million dollars) rendered the jury's punitive award excessive as a matter of law.

Grimshaw contends that the court erred in determining that the ratio of punitive to compensatory damages rendered the punitive excessive as a matter of law. The trial court, however, did not base its decision solely on the ratio of punitive to compensatory. It took into account the ratio, the "aggravating circumstances" (the degree of reprehensibility), the wealth of the defendant and its profit generating capacity, the magnitude of the punitive award, including the amount by which it exceeded the compensatory. Those were proper considerations for determining whether the award was excessive as a matter of law. When a trial court grants a new trial for excessive damages, either conditionally or outright, a presumption of correctness attaches to the order and it will not be reversed unless it plainly appears that the judge abused his discretion. In the case at bench, we find no abuse of discretion. * * *

Finally, Grimshaw contends the court abused its discretion in reducing the award to $3½ million as a condition of its new trial order and urges this court to restore the jury award or at least require a remittitur of substantially less than that required by the trial court. * * *

Here, the judge, exercising his independent judgment on the evidence, determined that a punitive award of $3½ million was "fair and reasonable." Evidence pertaining to Ford's conduct, its wealth and the savings it realized in deferring design modifications in the Pinto's fuel system might have persuaded a different fact finder that a larger award should have been allowed to stand. Our role, however, is limited to determining whether the trial judge's action constituted a manifest and unmistakable abuse of discretion. Here, the judge referred to the evidence bearing on those factors in his new trial order and obviously weighed it in deciding what was a "fair and reasonable" award. We cannot say that the judge abused the discretion vested in him by Code of Civil Procedure section 662.5 or that there is "no substantial basis in the record" for the reasons given for the order. Finally, while the trial judge may not have taken into account Ford's potential liability for punitive damages in other cases involving the same tortious conduct in reducing the award, it is a factor we may consider in passing on the

request to increase the award. Considering such potential liability, we find the amount as reduced by the trial judge to be reasonable and just.
* * *

## PACIFIC MUTUAL LIFE INSURANCE COMPANY v. HASLIP

Supreme Court of the United States, 1991.
499 U.S. 1, 111 S.Ct. 1032, 113 L.Ed.2d 1.

JUSTICE BLACKMUN delivered the opinion of the Court.

This case is yet another that presents a challenge to a punitive damages award.

I.

[Lemmie L. Ruffin, Jr., was an agent for Pacific Mutual Life Insurance Company and for Union Fidelity Life Insurance Company, two unaffiliated companies. Cleopatra Haslip, Cynthia Craig, Alma M. Calhoun, and Eddie Hargrove were employees of Roosevelt City, an Alabama municipality. Ruffin, presenting himself as an agent of Pacific Mutual, sold the city a package combining group health insurance and individual life insurance for its employees. The health insurance was issued by Union Fidelity; the life insurance by Pacific Mutual. This type of package, which was not unusual, tended to boost life insurance sales by minimizing the loss of customers who wished to have both health and life protection.

By arranging for the group health premiums to be sent directly to him, Ruffin was able to misappropriate most of the premiums. Because the notices of lapsed health coverage were also sent in care of Ruffin, the city's employees did not know that their health policies had been canceled. So, when Ms. Haslip was hospitalized, the hospital could not confirm health coverage, and it required Ms. Haslip, upon her discharge, to make a payment upon her bill. Her doctor, when he was not paid, placed her account with a collection agency, which obtained a judgment against her. Haslip and three other employees sued Pacific Mutual and Ruffin (but not Union) for fraud.]

* * * The case against Pacific Mutual was submitted to the jury under a theory of respondeat superior.

Following the trial court's charge on liability, the jury was instructed that if it determined there was liability for fraud, it could award punitive damages. That part of the instructions is set forth in the margin.[1] Pacific Mutual made no objection on the ground of lack of

1. "Now, if you find that fraud was perpetrated then in addition to compensatory damages you may in your discretion, when I use the word discretion, I say you don't have to even find fraud, you wouldn't have to, but you may, the law says you may award an amount of money known as punitive damages.

"This amount of money is awarded to the plaintiff but it is not to compensate the plaintiff for any injury. It is to punish the defendant. Punitive means to punish or it is also called exemplary damages, which

specificity in the instructions and it did not propose a more particularized charge. No evidence was introduced as to Pacific Mutual's financial worth. The jury returned general verdicts for respondents against Pacific Mutual and Ruffin in the following amounts:

| | |
|---|---|
| Haslip: | $1,040,000 [2] |
| Calhoun: | 15,290 |
| Craig: | 12,400 |
| Hargrove: | 10,288 |

Judgments were entered accordingly. * * *

IV

Two preliminary and overlapping due process arguments raised by Pacific Mutual deserve attention before we reach the principal issue in controversy. Did Ruffin act within the scope of his apparent authority as an agent of Pacific Mutual? If so, may Pacific Mutual be held responsible for Ruffin's fraud on a theory of respondeat superior?

Pacific Mutual was held responsible for the acts of Ruffin. The insurer mounts a challenge to this result on substantive due process grounds, arguing that it was not shown that either it or its Birmingham manager was aware that Ruffin was collecting premiums contrary to his contract; that Pacific Mutual had no notice of the actions complained of prior to the filing of the complaint in this litigation; that it did not authorize or ratify Ruffin's conduct; that his contract with the company forbade his collecting any premium other than the initial one submitted with an application; and that Pacific Mutual was held liable and punished for unauthorized actions of its agent for acts performed on behalf of another company. Thus, it is said, when punitive damages were imposed on Pacific Mutual, the focus for determining the amount of those damages shifted from Ruffin, where it belonged, to Pacific Mutual, and obviously and unfairly contributed to the amount of the punitive damages and their disproportionality. Ruffin was acting not to benefit Pacific Mutual but for his own benefit, and to hold Pacific

means to make an example. So, if you feel or not feel, but if you are reasonably satisfied from the evidence that the plaintiff, whatever plaintiff you are talking about, has had a fraud perpetrated upon them and as a direct result they were injured and in addition to compensatory damages you may in your discretion award punitive damages.

"Now, the purpose of awarding punitive or exemplary damages is to allow money recovery to the plaintiffs, it does to the plaintiff, by way of punishment to the defendant and for the added purpose of protecting the public by deterring [sic] the defendant and others from doing such wrong in the future. Imposition of punitive damages is entirely discretionary with the jury, that means you don't have to award it unless this jury feels that you should do so.

"Should you award punitive damages, in fixing the amount, you must take into consideration the character and the degree of the wrong as shown by the evidence and necessity of preventing similar wrong."

2. Although there is controversy about the matter, it is probable that the general verdict for respondent Haslip contained a punitive damages component of not less than $840,000. In Haslip's counsel's argument to the jury, compensatory damages of $200,000 (including out-of-pocket expenditures of less than $4,000) and punitive damages of $3,000,000 were requested. For present purposes, we accept this description of the verdict.

Mutual liable is "beyond the point of fundamental fairness," embodied in due process. It is said that the burden of the liability comes to rest on Pacific Mutual's other policy holders. * * *

[The Court first concludes that Ruffin was acting as Pacific Mutual's agent, and not solely as Union's agent, when he committed the fraud.]

Alabama's common-law rule is that a corporation is liable for both compensatory and punitive damages for fraud of its employee effected within the scope of his employment. We cannot say that this does not rationally advance the State's interest in minimizing fraud. Alabama long has applied this rule in the insurance context, for it has determined that an insurer is more likely to prevent an agent's fraud if given sufficient financial incentive to do so.

Imposing exemplary damages on the corporation when its agent commits intentional fraud creates a strong incentive for vigilance by those in a position "to guard substantially against the evil to be prevented." Louis Pizitz Dry Goods Co. v. Yeldell, 274 U.S. 112, 116 (1927). If an insurer were liable for such damages only upon proof that it was at fault independently, it would have an incentive to minimize oversight of its agents. Imposing liability without independent fault deters fraud more than a less stringent rule. It therefore rationally advances the State's goal. We cannot say this is a violation of Fourteenth Amendment due process. * * *

V

"Punitive damages have long been a part of traditional state tort law." Silkwood v. Kerr–McGee Corp., 464 U.S. 238, 255 (1984). Blackstone appears to have noted their use. See also Wilkes v. Wood, 98 Eng.Rep. 489 (C.P.1763)(The Lord Chief Justice validating exemplary damages as compensation, punishment, and deterrence). Among the first reported American cases are Genay v. Norris, 1 Bay 6 (S.C.1784), and Coryell v. Colbaugh, 1 N.J.L. 77 (1791).

Under the traditional common-law approach, the amount of the punitive award is initially determined by a jury instructed to consider the gravity of the wrong and the need to deter similar wrong conduct. The jury's determination is then reviewed by trial and appellate courts to ensure that it is reasonable.

This Court more than once has approved the common-law method for assessing punitive awards. In Day v. Woodworth, 13 How. 363 (1852), a case decided before the adoption of the Fourteenth Amendment, Justice Grier, writing for a unanimous Court, observed:

> "It is a well-established principle of the common law, that in actions of trespass and all action on the case for torts, a jury may inflict what are called exemplary, punitive, or vindictive damages upon a defendant, having in view the enormity of his offence rather than the measure of compensation to the plaintiff. We are aware that the propriety of this doctrine has been questioned by some writers; but if repeated judicial decisions for more than a century are to be

received as the best exposition of what the law is, the question will not admit of argument. By the common as well as by statute law, men are often punished for aggravated misconduct or lawless acts, by means of a civil action, and the damages, inflicted by way of penalty or punishment, given to the party injured. * * *

"…. This has been always left to the discretion of the jury, as the degree of punishment to be thus inflicted must depend on the peculiar circumstances of each case." * * *

So far as we have been able to determine, every state and federal court that has considered the question has ruled that the common-law method for assessing punitive damages does not in itself violate due process. In view of this consistent history, we cannot say that the common-law method for assessing punitive damages is so inherently unfair as to deny due process and be *per se* unconstitutional. " 'If a thing has been practiced for two hundred years by common consent, it will need a strong case for the Fourteenth Amendment to affect it.' " Sun Oil Co. v. Wortman, 486 U.S. 717, 730 (1988), quoting Jackman v. Rosenbaum Co., 260 U.S. 22, 31 (1922). As the Court in *Day v. Woodworth* made clear, the common-law method for assessing punitive damages was well established before the Fourteenth Amendment was enacted. Nothing in that Amendment's text or history indicates an intention on the part of its drafters to overturn the prevailing method.

This, however, is not the end of the matter. It would be just as inappropriate to say that, because punitive damages have been recognized for so long, their imposition is never unconstitutional. See Williams v. Illinois, 399 U.S. 235, 239 (1970)("[N]either the antiquity of a practice nor the fact of steadfast legislative and judicial adherence to it through the centuries insulates it from constitutional attack …"). We note once again our concern about punitive damages that "run wild." Having said that, we conclude that our task today is to determine whether the Due Process Clause renders the punitive damages award in this case constitutionally unacceptable.

VI

One must concede that unlimited jury discretion—or unlimited judicial discretion for that matter—in the fixing of punitive damages may invite extreme results that jar one's constitutional sensibilities. We need not, and indeed we cannot, draw a mathematical bright line between the constitutionally acceptable and the constitutionally unacceptable that would fit every case. We can say, however, that general concerns of reasonableness and adequate guidance from the court when the case is tried to a jury properly enter into the constitutional calculus. With these concerns in mind, we review the constitutionality of the punitive damages awarded in this case.

We conclude that the punitive damages assessed by the jury against Pacific Mutual were not violative of the Due Process Clause of the Fourteenth Amendment. It is true, of course, that under Alabama law, as under the law of most States, punitive damages are imposed for purposes of retribution and deterrence. They have been described as quasi-criminal. But this in itself does not provide the answer. We move, then, to the points of specific attack.

1. We have carefully reviewed the instructions to the jury. By these instructions, the trial court expressly described for the jury the purpose of punitive damages, namely, "not to compensate the plaintiff for any injury" but "to punish the defendant" and "for the added purpose of protecting the public by [deterring] the defendant and others from doing such wrong in the future." Any evidence of Pacific Mutual's wealth was excluded from the trial in accord with Alabama law.

To be sure, the instructions gave the jury significant discretion in its determination of punitive damages. But that discretion was not unlimited. It was confined to deterrence and retribution, the state policy concerns sought to be advanced. And if punitive damages were to be awarded, the jury "must take into consideration the character and the degree of the wrong as shown by the evidence and necessity of preventing similar wrong." The instructions thus enlightened the jury as to the punitive damages' nature and purpose, identified the damages as punishment for civil wrongdoing of the kind involved, and explained that their imposition was not compulsory.

These instructions, we believe, reasonably accommodated Pacific Mutual's interest in rational decision making and Alabama's interest in meaningful individualized assessment of appropriate deterrence and retribution. The discretion allowed under Alabama law in determining punitive damages is no greater than that pursued in many familiar areas of the law as, for example, deciding "the best interests of the child," or "reasonable care," or "due diligence," or appropriate compensation for pain and suffering or mental anguish. As long as the discretion is exercised within reasonable constraints, due process is satisfied.

2. Before the trial in this case took place, the Supreme Court of Alabama had established post-trial procedures for scrutinizing punitive awards. In Hammond v. City of Gadsden, 493 So.2d 1374 (1986), it stated that trial courts are "to reflect in the record the reasons for interfering with a jury verdict, or refusing to do so, on grounds of excessiveness of the damages." Among the factors deemed "appropriate for the trial court's consideration" are the "culpability of the defendant's conduct," the "desirability of discouraging others from similar conduct," the "impact upon the parties," and "other factors, such as the impact on innocent third parties." The *Hammond* test ensures meaningful and adequate review by the trial court whenever a jury has fixed the punitive damages.

3. By its review of punitive awards, the Alabama Supreme Court provides an additional check on the jury's or trial court's discretion. It first undertakes a comparative analysis. It then applies the detailed substantive standards it has developed for evaluating punitive awards. In particular, it makes its review to ensure that the award does "not exceed an amount that will accomplish society's goals of punishment and

deterrence." Green Oil Co. v. Hornsby, 539 So.2d 218, 222 (1989); Wilson v. Dukona Corp., 547 So.2d 70, 73 (1989). This appellate review makes certain that the punitive damages are reasonable in their amount and rational in light of their purpose to punish what has occurred and to deter its repetition.

Also before its ruling and in the present case, the Supreme Court of Alabama had elaborated and refined the *Hammond* criteria for determining whether a punitive award is reasonably related to the goals of deterrence and retribution. *Hornsby*; *Central Alabama*, 546 So.2d at 376–77. It was announced that the following could be taken into consideration in determining whether the award was excessive or inadequate: (a) whether there is a reasonable relationship between the punitive damages award and the harm likely to result from the defendant's conduct as well as the harm that actually has occurred; (b) the degree of reprehensibility of the defendant's conduct, the duration of that conduct, the defendant's awareness, any concealment, and the existence and frequency of similar past conduct; (c) the profitability to the defendant of the wrongful conduct and the desirability of removing that profit and of having the defendant also sustain a loss; (d) the "financial position" of the defendant; (e) all the costs of litigation; (f) the imposition of criminal sanctions on the defendant for its conduct, these to be taken in mitigation; and (g) the existence of other civil awards against the defendant for the same conduct, these also to be taken in mitigation.

The application of these standards, we conclude, imposes a sufficiently definite and meaningful constraint on the discretion of Alabama fact finders in awarding punitive damages. The Alabama Supreme Court's postverdict review ensures that punitive damages awards are not grossly out of proportion to the severity of the offense and have some understandable relationship to compensatory damages. While punitive damages in Alabama may embrace such factors as the heinousness of the civil wrong, its effect upon the victim, the likelihood of its recurrence, and the extent of defendant's wrongful gain, the fact finder must be guided by more than the defendant's net worth. Alabama plaintiffs do not enjoy a windfall because they have the good fortune to have a defendant with a deep pocket.

These standards have real effect when applied by the Alabama Supreme Court to jury awards. * * * And post-verdict review by the Alabama Supreme Court has resulted in reduction of punitive awards. The standards provide for a rational relationship in determining whether a particular award is greater than reasonably necessary to punish and deter. They surely are as specific as those adopted legislatively in Ohio Rev. Code Ann. § 2307.80(B)(Supp. 1989) and in Mont. Code Ann. § 27–1–221 (1989).[11]

**11.** We have considered the arguments raised by Pacific Mutual and some of its *amici* as to the constitutional necessity of imposing a standard of proof of punitive damages higher than "preponderance of the evidence." There is much to be said in

Pacific Mutual thus had the benefit of the full panoply of Alabama's procedural protections. The jury was adequately instructed. The trial court conducted a post-verdict hearing that conformed with *Hammond*. The trial court specifically found the conduct in question "evidenced intentional malicious, gross, or oppressive fraud," and found the amount of the award to be reasonable in light of the importance of discouraging insurers from similar conduct. Pacific Mutual also received the benefit of appropriate review by the Supreme Court of Alabama. It applied the *Hammond* standards and approved the verdict thereunder. It brought to bear all relevant factors recited in *Hornsby*.

We are aware that the punitive damages award in this case is more than 4 times the amount of compensatory damages, is more than 200 times the out-of-pocket expenses of respondent Haslip, and, of course, is much in excess of the fine that could be imposed for insurance fraud under Ala. Code §§ 13A–5–11 and 13A–5–12(a)(1982), and §§ 27–1–12, 27–12–17, and 27–12–23 (1986). Imprisonment, however, could also be required of an individual in the criminal context. While the monetary comparisons are wide and indeed, may be close to the line, the award here did not lack objective criteria. We conclude, after careful consideration, that in this case it does not cross the line into the area of constitutional impropriety. Accordingly, Pacific Mutual's due process challenge must be, and is, rejected. * * *

JUSTICE SOUTER took no part in the consideration or decision of this case.

JUSTICE SCALIA, concurring in the judgment.

* * * Since it has been the traditional practice of American courts to leave punitive damages (where the evidence satisfies the legal requirements for imposing them) to the discretion of the jury; and since in my view a process that accords with such a tradition and does not violate the Bill of Rights necessarily constitutes "due" process; I would approve the procedure challenged here without further inquiry into its "fairness" or "reasonableness." I therefore concur only in the judgment of the Court. * * *

JUSTICE KENNEDY, concurring in the judgment. [omitted]

JUSTICE O'CONNOR, dissenting. [omitted]

## *Notes*

1. The U.S. Supreme Court revisited its decision in *Haslip* in TXO Production Corp. v. Alliance Resources Corp., 509 U.S. 443, 113 S.Ct. 2711, 125 L.Ed.2d 366 (1993), but left lower courts with even less guidance

favor of a State's requiring, as many do, see, e.g., Ohio Rev. Code Ann. § 2307.80 (1989), a standard of "clear and convincing evidence" or, even, "beyond a reasonable doubt," see Colo. Rev. Stat. § 13–25–127(2)(Supp. 1979), as in the criminal context. We are not persuaded, however, that the Due Process Clause requires that much. We feel that the lesser standard prevailing in Alabama—"reasonably satisfied from the evidence"—when buttressed, as it is, by the procedural and substantive protections outlined above, is constitutionally sufficient.

concerning the constitutional limits of punitive awards. The Court reviewed and upheld a ten million dollar punitive damages award, 526 times the amount of compensatory damages. Alliance Resources persuaded the Court that the jury could have considered potential and "intended" damages as well as actual damages, and in doing so had rationally arrived at the amount of the award. Alliance Resources contended that although the only actual damage in this slander of title action was its $19,000 cost of litigation, the jury could reasonably have concluded that the defendant, TXO, had sought to reduce its royalty payments for oil and gas rights by millions of dollars, thus intending to inflict millions of dollars of damages. Although there was no majority opinion, six justices agreed to uphold the award: Chief Justice Rehnquist, Justices Blackmun and Stevens because the amount was not so "grossly excessive" as to violate due process, Justice Kennedy because he believed that the jury had rationally placed great weight on potential as well as actual damages, and Justices Scalia and Thomas because they believed that there is no "federal constitutional right to a substantively correct 'reasonableness' determination" and that punitive damage awards should be upheld so long as procedural due process has been observed. Justice Stevens' opinion announcing the judgment of the Court reiterated the conclusion in *Haslip* that the Court is unable to draw a mathematical bright line between constitutionally acceptable and unacceptable awards but that review of punitive damages awards should include evaluation for reasonableness. Nevertheless, the Court has apparently left lower courts with more flexibility in deciding when awards are constitutionally acceptable. The only significant requirements seem to be that procedural safeguards such as adequate jury instructions are observed, and that some sort of "reasonableness" review takes place.

2. The requirement that trial and appellate courts review the amount of punitive damage awards was established in Honda Motor Co. Ltd. v. Oberg, ___ U.S. ___, 114 S.Ct. 2331, 129 L.Ed.2d 336 (1994). In that case, the Supreme Court found that the practice under the Oregon Constitution of allowing the courts to vacate a judgment only when there was no evidence to support the jury decision, but not permitting review for excessive awards, was not consistent with the due process standards of *Haslip*.

3. Alabama's treatment of respondent superior is unusual. Typically, a principal is only liable for punitive damages if the tortfeasor is employed in a managerial capacity, if the principal or a managerial agent authorized, ratified or approved the act, or if the principal or a managerial agent recklessly hired the tortfeasor. Restatement of Torts, Second, § 909. Because a principal may incur liability by ratifying its agent's acts, it is critical that defendants identify behavior that may result in punitive damages and respond to it immediately.

4. In *Haslip*, the Court relied on the fact that Alabama courts had the power to review and adjust punitive damage awards as one of the indicia that the *Haslip* award did not violate due process. *Haslip* provides no calculus by which one can judge the appropriateness of a punitive award. At least one post-*Haslip* court has been candid in indicating that it reduced a punitive award from $15 million to $660,000 because it believed that was the just result and it was a fruitless exercise to attempt to justify its result by more fine-grained analysis. State Farm Mutual Auto. Ins. Co. v. Zubiate,

808 S.W.2d 590 (Tex.App.1991). The Fifth Circuit reaffirmed a $500,000 punitive award after a bench trial in a diversity case where $1,000 was awarded in compensatory damages, without expressing a view on whether the award was too large or too small but satisfying itself that that was an issue of state law with which the trial judge was familiar. Eichenseer v. Reserve Life Ins. Co., 934 F.2d 1377 (5th Cir.1991). In terms of setting aside particular monetary awards, does *Haslip* provide guidance beyond the exhortation that at some unidentifiable point punitive awards become excessive? See Hospital Authority of Gwinnett County v. Jones, 261 Ga. 613, 409 S.E.2d 501 (1991), cert. denied, 502 U.S. 1096, 112 S.Ct. 1175, 117 L.Ed.2d 420 (1992)(re-affirming award of $5,001 in "nominal" damages and $1.3 million in punitive damages; since deterrence is not based on actual harm, punitive damages need not bear relationship to actual damages although relationship may be considered if award is challenged as excessive because of undue passion and prejudice).

5. For a time, scholars argued that punitive damages are "fines" that, if excessive, run afoul of the Eighth Amendment's prohibition on excessive fines. Calvin Massey, The Excessive Fines Clause and Punitive Damages: Some Lessons from History, 40 Vanderbilt L. Rev. 1233 (1987); Note, The Constitutionality of Punitive Damages Under the Excessive Fines Clause of the Eighth Amendment, 85 Mich.L.Rev. 1699 (1987). The Court rejected that argument, finding that the amendment does not apply to litigation between private parties. Browning–Ferris Industries of Vermont, Inc. v. Kelco Disposal, Inc., 492 U.S. 257, 109 S.Ct. 2909, 106 L.Ed.2d 219 (1989).

## DUNN v. HOVIC

United States Court of Appeals, Third Circuit, en banc, 1993.
1 F.3d 1371, cert. denied, ___ U.S. ___, 114 S.Ct. 650, 126 L.Ed.2d 608.

SLOVITER, CHIEF JUDGE.

* * * Before us is the appeal of Owens–Corning Fiberglas Corporation (OCF) from the judgment of the district court of the Virgin Islands awarding William Dunn $500,000 in compensatory damages and $2 million in punitive damages. A panel of this court heard argument on OCF's appeal on April 22, 1992 and issued an opinion affirming the compensatory damages award and remitting the punitive damages award to $1 million. Thereafter, the court granted OCF's petition for rehearing in banc, limited to the punitive damages issue. * * *

### I.

### SUFFICIENCY OF THE EVIDENCE FOR A PUNITIVE DAMAGES AWARD

The availability of punitive damages is ordinarily determined by the local law of the relevant jurisdiction, in some instances by statute and in other instances by legal principles developed by courts. Under the Virgin Islands Code:

> The rules of the common law, as expressed in the restatements of the law approved by the American Law Institute and to the extent not so expressed, as generally understood and applied in the United States, shall be the rules of decision in the court of the Virgin

Islands in cases to which they apply, in the absence of local laws to the contrary.

V.I.Code Ann. tit. 1, § 4 (1967). Thus we turn to the Restatement for the prevailing standard.

Section 908(2) of the Restatement (Second) of Torts provides that "[p]unitive damages may be awarded for conduct that is outrageous, because of the defendant's evil motive or his reckless indifference to the rights of others." In applying this section, we have previously stated that such conduct must be shown by clear and convincing evidence. OCF argues that the evidence was insufficient to support the award of punitive damages or, in the alternative, that the verdict went against the clear weight of the evidence, requiring a new trial on whether punitive damages are appropriate.

In support of its argument, OCF points to evidence tending to show that prior to its decision to place warning labels on Kaylo boxes, the prevailing industry belief was that asbestos insulation products were safe. * * *

Nevertheless, we conclude that Dunn presented more than sufficient evidence from which a jury could conclude that OCF acted "with reckless indifference" in failing to place adequate warnings on its Kaylo product. [The court reviewed the evidence in some detail.] * * *

In light of this evidence, we agree with the recent conclusion of the Virginia Supreme Court that "[t]he jury may have concluded ... that Owens–Corning knew that inhalation of dust from its Kaylo product could cause lung disease in humans, that it actively concealed this danger, and it did not warn insulators of this hazard...." Owens–Corning Fiberglas Corp. v. Watson, 243 Va. 128, 413 S.E.2d 630, 642 (1992). The jury could reasonably have found that OCF acted with "reckless indifference to the rights of others" in this case, Restatement (Second) of Torts § 908(2)(1977), and thus, the district court appropriately denied OCF's motion for JNOV and did not abuse its discretion in refusing to grant unconditionally the motion for a new trial. * * *

IV.

EXCESSIVENESS OF THE PUNITIVE DAMAGES AWARDED

OCF's remaining contentions are directed to the allegedly excessive amount of punitive damages awarded. OCF first argues that the jury award was the result of passion, prejudice, or bias, and that the district court should have ordered a new trial unconditionally rather than conditioning the grant of a new trial on Dunn's acceptance of a remitted damages award. Of course, if OCF had shown that the jury verdict resulted from passion or prejudice, a new trial, rather than a remittitur, would have been the proper remedy.

However, we do not accept OCF's argument that in this case the size of the award alone was enough to prove prejudice and passion. Even if there were some level of award that would in itself evidence prejudice and passion, we cannot hold that the $25 million award here, albeit large, necessarily indicates a verdict tainted by prejudice and passion in light of the evidence before the jury concerning OCF's knowledge of the health hazards associated with asbestos, OCF's net after-tax earnings for the three years prior to trial which averaged almost $200 million, and OCF's net worth of approximately $2.2 billion. * * *

A multi-million dollar punitive damages award is not unique in products liability cases. See, e.g., Glasscock v. Armstrong Cork Co., 946 F.2d 1085 (5th Cir.1991)($6.1 million in asbestos case); O'Gilvie v. International Playtex, Inc., 821 F.2d 1438 (10th Cir.1987)($10 million in toxic shock syndrome case), cert. denied, 486 U.S. 1032, 108 S.Ct. 2014, 100 L.Ed.2d 601 (1988); Cathey v. Johns–Manville Sales Corp., 776 F.2d 1565 (6th Cir.1985)($1.5 million in asbestos case), cert. denied, 478 U.S. 1021, 106 S.Ct. 3335, 92 L.Ed.2d 740 (1986); Kociemba v. G.D. Searle & Co., 707 F.Supp. 1517 (D.Minn.1989)($7 million in I.U.D. case); Palmer v. A.H. Robins Co., 684 P.2d 187 (Colo.1984)($6.2 million in Dalkon Shield case).

If an excessive jury determination were per se proof of passion, prejudice, or bias, there would have been no reason for the Supreme Court to have said in *Haslip* that "[t]he Alabama Supreme Court's post-verdict review ensures that punitive damages awards are not grossly out of proportion to the severity of the offense and have some understandable relationship to compensatory damages." We have held that "where no clear judicial error or 'pernicious influence' can be identified but where the verdict is so large as to shock the conscience of the court," the appropriate action for the court is to "order[] plaintiff to remit the portion of the verdict in excess of the maximum amount supportable by the evidence or, if the remittitur [is] refused, to submit to a new trial." * * *

In *Acosta v. Honda Motor Co.*, in considering the issue of punitive damages awards against a manufacturer of a harmful product, we noted that "a jury might decide that a defendant's financial position, as a result of other awards of punitive damages for the same conduct, is so precarious that a sizeable award of punitive damages would be inappropriate." 717 F.2d 828, 839 n. 17 (3d Cir.1983). In this case, OCF made the strategic decision not to introduce into evidence before the jury information concerning other punitive damages awards assessed against it. Had it done so, the jury might have made a smaller award. We thus conclude that OCF has failed to prove that the jury's verdict, admittedly quite large, reflected such passion and prejudice as to mandate a new trial.

OCF contends that when the trial court calculated its remitted punitive damages award, it refused to consider OCF's submission regarding other awards against it because the court believed that evidence should have been presented to the jury. There is nothing in the district court's opinion that supports OCF's contention.

Nor does OCF point to anything in the record to support its contention that the trial court set the remitted damages figure by taking into account OCF's conduct toward persons other than Dunn. * * * In fact, in this case the district court explicitly referred to the amount of the compensatory damages awarded to Dunn when it calculated the amount of the remitted punitive damages award, thus demonstrating that the punitive damages award was intended to represent punishment for OCF's conduct with respect to Dunn. The district court's charge that the jury only award punitive damages if "plaintiff has clearly and convincingly established that *the action of defendant which caused injury to the plaintiff* was wanton and reckless," further reveals the court's awareness that punitive damages were to be assessed only with respect to the harm OCF caused Dunn. * * *

We turn next to our role in the assessment of punitive damages. We cannot leave the amount of punitive damages solely to the trial court because it is evident to us that the Supreme Court in *Haslip* approved review by an appellate court to "determin[e] whether a particular award is greater than reasonably necessary to punish and deter." The principal issue impelling us to take this otherwise routine product liability case in banc is the effect of successive punitive damages awards in mass tort cases arising from the same course of conduct. We, as well as other courts, have expressed concerns in that regard. See In re School Asbestos Litig., 789 F.2d 996, 1005 (3d Cir.)("powerful arguments have been made that, as a matter of constitutional law or of substantive tort law, the courts shoulder some responsibility for preventing repeated awards of punitive damages for the same acts or series of acts"), cert. denied, 479 U.S. 852, 107 S.Ct. 182, 93 L.Ed.2d 117, and cert. denied, 479 U.S. 915, 107 S.Ct. 318, 93 L.Ed.2d 291 (1986); * * *.

Nevertheless, the vast majority of courts that have addressed the issue have declined to strike punitive damages awards merely because they constituted repetitive punishment for the same conduct.

OCF seeks to have this court take the lead and strike the punitive damages award as repetitive, either under Virgin Islands law or on federal due process grounds. It argues that because of the volume of asbestos claims currently before the courts and likely to be filed in the future, the point of "overkill" has been reached with respect to punitive damages in asbestos litigation. OCF claims that asbestos manufacturers have been punished enough, and that the "avalanche" of compensatory claims is more than sufficient to serve the goals of deterrence and punishment. It urges this court, as the "Supreme Court of the Virgin Islands," to strike punitive damages claims in all asbestos cases tried in the territory.

Apparently OCF believes that our function as the highest reviewing court for the Virgin Islands affords us an opportunity that is not available to other federal courts which are constrained by diversity jurisdiction to be circumspect in predicting state tort law. * * * Yet federal courts have not been alone in declining to strike punitive damages awards on the ground that they constitute repetitive punishment for the same conduct. State courts as well have rejected such a contention, both on due process and common law tort grounds. Indeed, OCF has brought no majority opinion from any court to our attention (and our research has not disclosed such a case) which holds that multiple punitive damages claims must be struck on either basis.

In concluding that multiple punitive damages awards are not inconsistent with the due process clause or substantive tort law principles, both state and federal courts have recognized that no single court can fashion an effective response to the national problem flowing from mass exposure to asbestos products. Indeed, these courts have noted the arbitrariness of imposing a cap on punitive damages awards in only a single jurisdiction. As the Supreme Court of Appeals of West Virginia recently stated:

> it seems highly illogical and unfair for courts to determine at what point punitive damage awards should cease. Obviously, those plaintiffs whose cases were heard first would gain the punitive monetary advantage. Certainly, it would be difficult to determine where the cutoff line should be drawn as between the first, tenth, or hundredth punitive damages award. Moreover, because asbestos trials are held nationwide, it is doubtful that one state's ruling would necessarily bind other jurisdictions. * * *

Similar concerns were expressed by the American Law Institute, which in a 1991 Reporters' Study, concluded that even state legislative efforts to limit punitive damages awards were an inappropriate and ineffective means for addressing the multiple punitive damages award problem.

> This kind of single-state action, however, is an ineffectual response to the problem, because one state cannot control what happens in other jurisdictions. In fact, *the state that acts alone may simply provide some relief to out-of-state manufacturers at the expense of its own citizen-victims*, a situation that hardly provides much law reform incentive for state legislators. Moreover, these formulas, which give the lion's share of the punitive award to the first victim able to win a judgment against a particular defendant, are unfair to subsequent plaintiffs and concomitantly risk providing too little deterrence to behavior of this type.

As an alternative to state action, the Study supported a federal legislative solution "to authorize mandatory class actions for multiple punitive damages arising out of large-scale mass torts."

These concerns are equally applicable to our role in reviewing punitive damages awards emanating from the Virgin Islands. Although we do not eschew our role as the final judicial voice on questions of law arising in the Virgin Islands, we are also cognizant that we have not been chosen for that role as directly as have the state supreme courts. This requires that we exercise restraint before imposing novel and/or experimental theories onto that territory's body of law. * * *

We do not disagree with the concerns that have been expressed about punitive damages awards, particularly in the asbestos cases. We differ instead with those who would have the judiciary resolve the conflicting policy arguments. We refrain from adopting such an activist role on what is essentially a policy matter, and believe that insofar as OCF would have us enunciate a prohibition of successive claims of punitive damages in mass tort litigation as a matter of Virgin Islands law, that decision is best left to the United States Congress or the legislature of the Virgin Islands. * * *

In his powerful dissent, Judge Weis has set forth numerous arguments against punitive damages in mass tort cases in general and in asbestos cases in particular. We decline to respond in kind because we do not believe that a judicial opinion of an intermediate appellate court is the appropriate forum for a debate on the policies for and against punitive damages. Indeed, those members of the in banc court supporting the judgment of the court may themselves have differing views on whether and when punitive damages should be awarded.

Judge Weis argues that a "national solution is needed," and would have this court step in because Congress and the Virgin Islands legislature have failed to impose the solution he believes is needed. We believe, to the contrary, that unless a particular defendant has made the showing requisite to a finding of a due process violation as to it, the lower courts have an obligation to follow existing legal principles. * * *

[T]he factual record made by the defendant must, as a prerequisite to relief on due process grounds, include evidence demonstrating the amount of punitive damages it has actually paid in the past. In this case, OCF has simply failed to make such a showing. * * *

In sum, OCF simply has not made a "showing that the total [amount of punitive damages assessed so far] is even close to whatever limit due process might impose on the total punitive damages that may be assessed ... for ... misconduct with respect to asbestos warnings." Nor has OCF shown on this record that it will be unable to satisfy current and future asbestos claims. Although the costs associated with asbestos litigation may have wiped out any profits OCF made from the sale of its Kaylo product, OCF failed to submit any evidence at trial concerning the profitability of its Kaylo product, or concerning the profits of the other manufacturers. In any event, neither Virgin Islands law nor due process requires striking all punitive damages claims simply because the harm caused by a defective product was so severe as to wipe out all profit.

Of course, we do not decide whether another asbestos manufacturer might be able to satisfy this evidentiary hurdle with a different factual record. Nonetheless, we believe that the district courts in this circuit should determine whether a punitive award to a plaintiff in a particular case should be struck by carefully scrutinizing the "punitive damages overkill" evidence submitted to them, both with respect to past awards actually paid by the defendant and the defendant's ability to satisfy future punitive damages awards. These courts should also consider whether the financial status of the defendant is such that future claimants will be unable to collect even compensatory damages because of the limited pool of resources available. It is the defendant's burden to make this evidentiary showing, a burden OCF has not satisfied on the record before us.

Although we reject OCF's due process challenge, we nonetheless agree with OCF that further remittitur of the punitive damage award in this case is appropriate. In reaching this conclusion, we take into consideration all the factors listed in comment e to Restatement of Torts (Second) § 908: the defendant's wealth, its act, the extent of harm, the multiplicity of claims, and, as approved in *Haslip*, the awards of punitive damages in similar cases.

Our review of the list of jury verdicts submitted by OCF to the district court indicates to us that even the $2 million dollar figure greatly exceeds the level of punitive damages awarded in other similar asbestos cases. While we commend the district court's discipline in reducing the punitive damages from $25 million to $2 million, we believe that the district court gave insufficient consideration to the effect of successive punitive awards in asbestos litigation. This factor, above all, leads us to conclude that the maximum amount of punitive damages that could reasonably have been awarded in this case is $1 million.

V.

CONCLUSION * * *

For the foregoing reasons, we will vacate the judgment of punitive damages and remand the case to the district court with instructions to enter a new judgment for punitive damages in the amount of $1,000,000. OCF to bear all costs on appeal.

ALITO, CIRCUIT JUDGE, concurring [Omitted]

WEIS, CIRCUIT JUDGE, dissenting.

I dissent from the judgment of the court permitting punitive damages in this case.

Asbestos litigation is unique. The large number of persons exposed to asbestos has caused a proliferation of claims, the likes of which courts have never seen, causing serious concern that the traditional tort system cannot adequately process the litigation. As this Court said in In re School Asbestos Litigation, 789 F.2d 996, 1000 (3d Cir.1986), asbestos litigation presents "an unparalleled situation in American tort law."

In 1986, an estimated 30,000 personal injury suits had been filed against asbestos manufacturers and producers. That figure has since increased substantially. By 1990, 30,401 asbestos cases were pending in the federal courts alone, with about double that amount in the state courts, for a total of approximately 90,000 cases. A study completed by the National Center for State Courts reports that there may be as many as 129,000 cases pending in state courts alone, making the total of federal and state cases approximately 160,000. Another report estimates that between 1990 and 2049 another 668,363 asbestos-related claims will be filed.

It is not only claims for personal injuries and deaths resulting from asbestos that have inundated the courts. In addition, thousands and thousands of property damage cases further diminish the available pool of resources.

As might be expected, the flood of asbestos cases has taken its toll on the defendant asbestos manufacturers. The Ad Hoc Committee reported that of the twenty-five major asbestos companies, eleven had filed petitions in bankruptcy. Later reports indicate that fifteen or sixteen companies have filed for bankruptcy. Moreover, that "number does not include the numerous smaller distributors that have been targeted in the wake of absent manufacturers and who have in turn become insolvent." Peter H. Schuck, The Worst Should Go First: Deferral Registries in Asbestos Litigation, 15 Harv.J.L. & Pub.Pol'y 541, 555 (1992).

The first of the major asbestos manufacturers to enter bankruptcy was Johns–Manville, which sought to use Chapter 11 essentially as a giant interpleader action. As part of the Manville reorganization, a trust was created to settle pending and future asbestos claims. Although the trust concept had the potential for equitably distributing assets to present and future claimants, the bankruptcy proceeding was itself very expensive and the results ultimately proved to be unsatisfactory. * * *

Subsequent claims and bankruptcy filings have increased the likelihood that future claimants will not be able to recover for their injuries. As the [U.S. Judicial Conference] Ad Hoc Committee said: "[A] large number of individuals have claims ... that are not yet ripe for adjudication. Because many of the defendants in these cases have limited assets that may be called upon to satisfy the judgments obtained under current common tort rules and remedies, there is a 'real and present danger that the available assets will be exhausted before those later victims can seek compensation to which they are entitled.' " * * *

It is within this setting of burgeoning litigation, corporate collapse, and future compensatory inadequacy that the present case involving punitive damages arises. * * *

I propose to meet head-on an issue presented here—that is, whether unfairness to injured persons whose claims will come due after available funds have been exhausted requires a common law bar on continuing punitive awards. I will also review punitive awards in terms of unfairness to asbestos defendants and due process. * * *

I.

COMMON LAW PUNITIVE DAMAGES

The Restatement (Second) of Torts § 908(2) provides that "[p]unitive damages *may* be awarded for conduct that is outrageous, because of the defendant's evil motive or his reckless indifference to the rights of others." (emphasis supplied). Comment a explains that "[t]he purposes of awarding punitive damages ... are to punish the person doing the wrongful act and to discourage him and others from similar conduct in the future."

When considering punitive awards, several basic principles must be emphasized. First, punitive damages are designed for retribution and deterrence. "They are not compensation for injury. Instead, they are private fines levied by civil juries to punish reprehensible conduct and to deter its future occurrence." The fairness inherent in due process requires that punitive assessments not exceed those amounts necessary to inflict retribution and prevent reoccurrence. When retribution and deterrence are accomplished without the imposition of punitive damages, use of that weapon is no longer justified.

Second, punitive damages are a windfall. They do not reimburse losses that plaintiffs have suffered, but provide an amount over and above that necessary for fair compensation.

Third, there is no compelling reason why injured but fully compensated plaintiffs should receive punitive awards. The aims of retribution and deterrence can be accomplished by making punitive damages payable to the state. Indeed, nine states have enacted statutes that designate that a portion of any punitive award goes to the state, ranging from 20% in New York to 75% in Iowa and Georgia.

In the asbestos context, punitive awards are not needed for retribution and deterrence. Actually, there is little conduct to deter because few asbestos-containing products are still manufactured in the United States. Owens–Corning, the defendant in this case, ceased manufacturing asbestos-containing Kaylo in November 1972, more than twenty years ago, and no longer produces or distributes any asbestos-containing products. That being so, this punitive award cannot be justified by a concern that Owens-Corning will continue its challenged practice in the future. * * *

Moreover, the avalanche of compensatory claims against asbestos manufacturers has surely served as more of a punishment and deterrent than individual punitive assessments in isolated cases against manufacturers of other types of products. * * *

That point is illustrated strikingly by Owens–Corning's experience. Compensatory awards have consumed all profits made from the sale of asbestos-containing products. Total gross sales of Kaylo were $142,720,000. As of May 31, 1991, defendant had paid claims for "hundreds of millions of dollars" in 62,588 cases and incurred litigation expenses in excess of $100 million. In 1990 alone, $117 million was paid on 12,300 claims. In addition, 86,192 cases are presently pending with hundreds more being filed each month. In these circumstances, punitive awards are certainly not necessary to provide an effective deterrent. * * *

[P]arochial concerns tend to influence the decision to make punitive damages available in cases of this nature. That approach was apparent, for example, in Fischer v. Johns- Manville Corp., 103 N.J. 643, 512 A.2d 466 (1986). In discussing the suggestion that a limitation on punitive awards be imposed, the *Fischer* Court said: "Such a cap would be ineffective unless applied uniformly. To adopt such a cap in New Jersey would be to deprive our citizens of punitive damages without the concomitant benefit of assuring the availability of compensatory damages for later plaintiffs. This we decline to do." What that opinion failed to acknowledge was that giving windfall punitive awards to early plaintiffs poses the likely prospect that some future New Jersey plaintiffs will be unable to recover compensatory damages for their injuries.

The New Jersey Supreme Court also stated that it failed "to see the distinction, in the case of *Johns-Manville* [before its bankruptcy], between the effect of compensatory damages and that of punitive damages." To some extent, the Court was correct. Every dollar expended on punitive awards, as well as those expended in compensatory damages, will diminish, eventually to the point of exhaustion, resources available for paying future plaintiffs' claims. There is, however, an important distinction. Compensatory damages are a remedy for injuries suffered. Punitive awards are not. A dissenting justice in *Fischer* posed an apt rhetorical question: "But why, for example, should a few Dalkon Shield users receive several millions in punitive-damages awards, while others receive nothing from the bankrupt A.H. Robins Co.?"

Unquestionably, a national solution is needed. Despite the deteriorating situation, Congress has declined to act, and class actions are an inadequate remedy. In the meantime, the drain on available resources continues. It is time—perhaps past due—to stop the hemorrhaging so as to protect future claimants. * * *

I am persuaded that, at this point, the available resources of asbestos manufacturers will be exhausted before all deserving claimants have received compensatory damages. Predictions of future events, of course, always carry some risk of error. In this instance, however, the storm warnings are too foreboding to be brushed aside. Absolute certainty likely will appear only after disaster has struck—when the time for effective anticipatory action has vanished. If there is to be error in forecasting, I would prefer that it be in favor of redress for future claimants, rather than largesse for those who have received adequate relief. * * *

I have no doubt that this Court has the power to prohibit punitive awards in asbestos cases within the Virgin Islands and I am convinced that it has an obligation to do so in order to protect the interests of those whose claims for compensation will be jeopardized.

### Due Process

Some of the same considerations that are important in deciding whether punitive awards are appropriate under local law also play a part in determining whether the assessment of such sums violates due process. * * *

Due process concerns are present in two aspects that have a correlation to the criminal field—proportionality and repetitiveness. The Supreme Court has made it clear that the Excessive Fines Clause of the Eighth Amendment and the Double Jeopardy Clause of the Fifth Amendment are not directly applicable to suits between private litigants. See Browning–Ferris Indus. v. Kelco Disposal, Inc., 492 U.S. 257, 260, 109 S.Ct. 2909, 2912, 106 L.Ed.2d 219 (1989); United States v. Halper, 490 U.S. 435, 451, 109 S.Ct. 1892, 1903, 104 L.Ed.2d 487 (1989). Nevertheless, the analogy between "punishment" in the criminal field and exemplary awards in civil litigation is strong enough that the rationale in the former area is useful in analyzing the scope of the latter. * * *

Although *Halper* found that the "protections of the Double Jeopardy Clause are not triggered by litigation between private parties," that opinion uses language that is quite instructive in a due process analysis. As the Court observed:

> "It is commonly understood that civil proceedings may advance punitive as well as remedial goals, and, conversely, that both punitive and remedial goals may be served by criminal penalties. The notion of punishment, as we commonly understand it, cuts across the division between the civil and the criminal law.... Simply put, a civil as well as a criminal sanction constitutes punishment when the sanction as applied in the individual case serves the goals of punishment."

Those goals are retribution and deterrence. Id. at 448, 109 S.Ct. at 1901; see also Austin v. United States, 509 U.S. ___, 113 S.Ct. 2801, 125 L.Ed.2d 488 (1993)(question is not whether statutory forfeiture is "civil or criminal, but rather whether it is punishment"). * * *

Moreover, unlike the situation in *TXO*, [asbestos] cases do not involve a scenario in which the incumbent corporate officials personally participated in fraudulent and malicious activity. Punitive awards in asbestos cases usually do not punish the individuals who were responsible for the offensive conduct. Thus, in this field, punishment is not only repetitive, but is inflicted on a vicarious basis. Basic notions of due process are offended by punishment that occurs over and over again as has happened in asbestos litigation. * * *

The other phase of substantive due process is proportionality. In its opinion, the *Haslip* majority noted that substantive due process "standards provide for a rational relationship in determining whether a particular award is greater than reasonably necessary to punish and deter." Similarly, in her dissent, Justice O'Connor recognized that whether an award is grossly excessive is an "important substantive due process concern." We may take from *Haslip*, therefore, that a punitive award that is greater than reasonably necessary to punish and deter violates substantive due process. * * *

Having arrived at the principle that at some point further repetitive punitive damages are neither rational nor fair, the difficult question is how to determine when that point has been reached. Some assistance may be found in the approach that courts use to determine whether a traditional punitive award is excessive. Many of the same factors considered in the usual one-on-one case are helpful.

For example, in *Haslip* the Court approved Alabama's judicial review that included such considerations as:

(a) a reasonable relationship between the award and harm from defendant's conduct;

(b) the reprehensibility of defendant's conduct, its duration, defendant's awareness or concealment, and the existence and frequency of past misconduct;

(c) the profitability to defendant of the conduct;

(d) the financial position of defendant;

(e) all the costs of litigation;

(f) the imposition of criminal sanctions; and

(g) the existence of other civil awards against defendant for the same conduct.

In *TXO*, the plurality opinion relied on a general concern of reasonableness. In general, these considerations give the courts some basis on which to decide whether punitive damages should be permitted. However, other matters unique to mass torts—other punitive awards, the effect of those awards on current and future claimants for compensation, and the adverse effect on settlement of pending claims—must also enter into the calculus. After taking all these factors into account to determine that a defendant has been adequately deterred and punished, a court must strike down all subsequent punitive awards in order to preserve due process. * * *

I am persuaded that the punitive damages award against Owens–Corning should be stricken. The amounts awarded in prior litigation have been more than adequate to meet the needs of punishment and deterrence. Thus, permitting an award to the plaintiff serves no rational purpose. * * *

JUDGE GREENBERG, JUDGE HUTCHINSON, and JUDGE SCIRICA join in this dissent.

BECKER, CIRCUIT JUDGE, dissenting. [omitted]

### *Notes*

1. In Punitive Damages in Products Liability Litigation, 74 Mich. L.Rev. 1257 (1976), Professor David Owen suggests that the measure of punitive damages in a products liability case should reflect the following factors:

(1) the amount of the plaintiff's litigation expenses;

(2) the seriousness of the hazard to the public;

(3) the profitability of the marketing misconduct (increased by an appropriate multiple);

(4) the attitude and conduct of the enterprise upon discovery of the misconduct;

(5) the degree of the manufacturer's awareness of the hazard and of its excessiveness;

(6) the number and level of employees involved in causing or covering up the marketing misconduct;

(7) the duration of both the improper marketing behavior and its coverup;

(8) the financial condition of the enterprise and the probable effect thereon of a particular judgment; and

(9) the total punishment the enterprise will probably receive from other sources.

Does the use of such a large number of factors defeat the goal of providing guidelines which a court could use to distinguish permissible from impermissible awards? If the list were to be shortened, which factors would you delete and why?

2. Professor Dan Dobbs has provided a thoughtful analysis of the functions of punitive damages and suggested limiting those functions so that they are better focused and a better system for measuring punitive damages could be achieved. Dobbs identifies just deserts, one of the central aims of criminal sanctions, as the first function of punitive damages and identifies specific deterrence, general deterrence, the financing of litigation and compensation for intangible injury as the others. He argues that just deserts, general deterrence and intangible injury should be dropped from the measure of punitive damages for a variety of reasons: we really have no agreed-on method of measuring damages awarded on those bases; intangible injury is really pain and suffering under a different label, for which compensation rather than punishment is appropriate; the most effective goal for civil litigation is the regulation of conduct through deterrence not the judgment of human worth implicit in these bases of measurement. The measure of damages in these extra-compensatory damage cases would then become the profit or gain derived by the defendant from the activity or plaintiff's reasonable litigation costs. Dan B. Dobbs, Ending Punishment in "Punitive" Damages: Deterrence–Measured Remedies, 40 Ala.L.Rev. 831 (1989). Is Dobbs right that we have no predictable and agreed on method for measuring the "just deserts" of one liable for punitive damages? Is the same true of general deterrence? By suggesting fee-shifting, is Dobbs doing more than urging one arbitrary measure for a damage award in place of others, the only difference being that we have greater ability to measure attorney's fees? Professor Dobbs' article is part of a symposium on punitive damages which provides analyses of a broad range of issues raised by the remedy and serves as a useful source for research and debate. Symposium, Punitive Damages, 40 Ala.L.Rev. 687–1261 (1989).

3. Various statutes, for instance the treble damage provisions of the Sherman Act, provide for awards to plaintiffs well in excess of the damage actually suffered. These statutes serve multiple purposes. They punish a defendant who engages in prohibited activity. They encourage plaintiffs to sue even if damages are small. They encourage plaintiff's counsel to take on complex and time consuming litigation on a contingency basis. They relieve the government of the burden of pursuing cases where the interests of justice may be served by a private suit. Given the difficulty for a court in drawing a bright line between permissible and impermissible punitive damages, should the decision as to what multiple of compensatory damages is acceptable be left to the legislature?

4. The Supreme Court of Alabama introduced two major reforms to Alabama's common law of punitive damages in Life Insurance Company of Georgia v. Johnson, ___ So.2d ___ [1995 WL 683857] (Ala.1995). In this case, Life of Georgia was found to have defrauded an 84 year old woman of low income and little education of $3,132 by selling her a Medicare supplement policy which was worthless because she was covered by Medicaid. The evidence showed that Life of Georgia had engaged in similar conduct in other cases and failed to train its agents appropriately. The jury awarded $250,000 in compensatory damages, including mental anguish, and $15 million in punitive damages. The trial court reduced the punitive award to $12.5 million and the Alabama Supreme Court further reduced it to $5 million. First, the Supreme Court directed that in future punitive damage cases, the trial was to be bifurcated. The jury is first to decide liability and compensatory damages and whether punitive damages should be imposed. If punitive damages are to be imposed, all evidence relevant to the issue of amount would be admissible. This would include evidence on all the questions addressed by Alabama judges in reviewing punitive damage awards under *Hammond* and *Hornsby* (discussed in *Haslip* ), but could include other issues as well. Judges would continue to review the jury awards under *Hammond* and *Hornsby*. This procedural change was made to meet the criticism that juries are given no guidance in determining appropriate punitive damage awards. Second, the Alabama court directed that, after reasonable expenses of litigation, including plaintiff's attorney's fees, had been paid out of the punitive damage judgment, the remainder was to be divided equally between the plaintiff and the State General Fund. This change was made to avoid the windfall effect of punitive damage awards and as a means of strengthening the jury system.

A number of states have made similar changes in procedure or in the disposition of punitive awards. In an asbestos case with the possibility of multiple punitive damage awards against the defendant, the Florida Supreme Court bifurcated the issue of the amount of punitive damages from the trial of other issues. Thus, the defendant can put previous punitive damage awards before the jury and build a record for a due process argument on the cumulative effect of the awards with a reduced risk. W.R. Grace & Co. v. Waters, 638 So.2d 502 (Fla.1994). Several states have adopted statutes requiring a stricter standard of proof for punitive damages and at least eight states have adopted a requirement that trial courts explain their refusal to disturb a jury award of punitive damages. See Transportation Insurance Co. v. Moriel, 879 S.W.2d 10 (Tex.1994).

With some statutory exceptions, no punitive damages are allowed in Nebraska, New Hampshire, and Washington. Connecticut, Missouri, Ohio, Oklahoma, Oregon, and Virginia have statutory measures limiting punitive damages. In Kirk v. Denver Publishing Co., 818 P.2d 262 (Colo.1991), the Colorado Supreme Court found that a state statute that directed one-third of the exemplary damages collected by a plaintiff be paid to the state general fund was an unconstitutional taking of the plaintiff's property, i.e., his judgment against the defendant. In McBride v. General Motors Corp., 737 F.Supp. 1563 (M.D.Ga.1990), the court held unconstitutional, under the excessive fines clause and the double jeopardy clause, a Georgia statute which directed 75% of punitive damage awards in product liability cases to the state. But in Gordon v. State, 608 So.2d 800 (Fla.1992) (per curiam), the Florida Supreme Court upheld a Florida statute, now repealed, under which 60% of the punitive damage award went to the state; the court found that the award accrued directly to the state under the statute and did not become the plaintiff's property. The Iowa Supreme Court reached a similar conclusion in Shepherd Components, Inc. v. Brice Petrides—Donohue & Associates, Inc., 473 N.W.2d 612 (Iowa 1991). Illinois gives the trial court discretion to apportion a punitive damage award between plaintiff, his attorney, and the Illinois Department of Rehabilitation Services. Ill.Rev. Stat.Ch. 100 par. 2–1207 (1986). Kansas limits punitive damage awards in professional liability actions to 25% of the annual gross income of the defendant or $3 million; an award is divided equally between plaintiff and a state fund. Missouri, Mo.Rev.Stat. § 537.675(2), New York, N.Y.Civ.Prac.L. & R. § 8701, Oregon, Or.Rev.Stat. § 18.540(1), and Utah, Utah Code Ann. § 78–18–1(3), also have statutes requiring payment of a portion of a punitive damage award to the state. Another way for the legislature to address this issue would be to tax the awards at a high rate. See James Serven, The Taxation of Punitive Damages: Horton Lays an Egg?, 72 Den.U.L.Rev. 215 (1995) (discussing federal taxation of punitive damage awards).

5. How should a theory of proportionality deal with cases in which the compensatory damages are nominal or negligible? Take account of the fact that two of the leading 18th century English cases which are historical precedents for punitive damages in the United States are illegal search and seizure cases which may well be cases of this sort. Wilkes v. Wood, 98 Eng.Rep. 489 (C.P.1763); Huckle v. Money, 95 Eng.Rep. 768 (C.P.1763). Isn't it likely that many of the dignitary tort cases—e.g., assault and battery, seduction, flagrant cases of trespass and conversion or destruction of property—may be of this sort?

6. Whether insurance is available to cover punitive damage awards turns on a number of issues: the explicit language of the insurance contract, the implicit exceptions to the contract (e.g., one is not insured against intentional acts); the legal standard of liability in a case; the common and statutory law of the jurisdiction in the question. There is great diversity among the courts and the legislatures on this issue. Professor Alan I. Widiss provides an extensive review of the state of the law in Liability Insurance Coverage for Punitive Damages? Discerning Answers to the Conundrum Created by Disputes Involving Conflicting Public Policies, Pragmatic Considerations and Political Actions, 39 Vill.L.Rev. 455 (1994).

7. As a general rule where a statutory scheme does not limit the remedies that a court may impose, punitive or exemplary damages have been found to be available to a plaintiff. E.g., Smith v. Wade, 461 U.S. 30, 103 S.Ct. 1625, 75 L.Ed.2d 632 (1983)(inmate in reformatory for youthful first offenders beaten and sexually assaulted by cellmates; punitive damages available against prison guard in action brought under 42 U.S.C. § 1983); Reich v. Cambridgeport Air Systems, Inc., 26 F.3d 1187 (1st Cir.1994) (Secretary of Labor bringing action under whistleblower provision of Occupational Safety and Health Act on behalf of employee may be awarded exemplary damages). There are exceptions where the award of such damages would be at odds with effectuating the purposes of the statute. International Brotherhood of Electrical Workers v. Foust, 442 U.S. 42, 99 S.Ct. 2121, 60 L.Ed.2d 698 (1979)(punitive damages against union not available under Railway Labor Act for breach of duty of fair representation).

8. States and cities may recover punitive damages under the common law. United States v. Hooker Chemical & Plastics Corp., 748 F.Supp. 67 (W.D.N.Y.1990)(punitive damages available on claim defendant had committed a public nuisance in disposing of toxic waste); City of New York ex rel People v. Taliaferrow, 144 Misc.2d 649, 544 N.Y.S.2d 273 (Sup.Ct.1989), aff'd, 158 A.D.2d 445, 551 N.Y.S.2d 253 (2d Dept.1990) (public nuisance action to stop use of premises for prostitution, $100,000 in punitive damages awarded). On the other hand, punitive damages are generally not available against the government unless authorized by statute. Newport v. Fact Concerts, Inc., 453 U.S. 247, 101 S.Ct. 2748, 69 L.Ed.2d 616 (1981).

## D. CIVIL ECONOMIC SANCTIONS

### WILLIAM DRAYTON, ECONOMIC LAW ENFORCEMENT

4 Harv.Envr.L.Rev. 1, 1–17 (1980).

Regulatory law enforcement, from the time a violation is detected onward, is a mess. If an agency is lucky enough to detect a violation, it is often able to do little more. If jawboning fails to induce compliance, regulators must either give up or litigate, and litigation is uncertain, slow, and costly. Even if the agency does prevail in court, it cannot be sure that the judge, who may be reluctant to impose over-criminalized and standardless penalties, will provide an adequate remedy. As a result, massive delay occurs, public and private resources are wasted, scofflaws are rewarded, and voluntary compliance is undermined.

Breaking this vicious cycle which engenders ever-decreasing voluntary compliance requires a quick, sure, and fair method of ensuring compliance by those violators who have been discovered. The State of Connecticut, with the financial assistance of the Environmental Protection Agency (EPA), has developed and successfully tested such a method. Connecticut's innovation can be adapted to other enforcement programs, including those outside the area of environmental regulation.

Central to the Connecticut approach is an economic standard that recaptures the gains realized from noncompliance by charging violators an amount just sufficient to make compliance as economically attractive as profitable commercial expenditures, thereby denying scofflaws the unfair advantage they would otherwise have over law-abiding competitors. This recapture standard sets a financial charge exactly fitted to the facts of each case, one that varies directly with the value and duration of noncompliance. A simple formula using capital budgeting concepts translates capital costs, operating and maintenance expenditures, taxes, lost profits, and other variables over time into a monthly assessment equal to the average monthly benefits of noncompliance. In a case involving past delinquency, the total benefits of noncompliance, and therefore the assessment, is easily calculated by multiplying this monthly figure times the number of months of delinquency.

Using this recapture standard, a regulatory agency can adopt a host of economic remedies which lie between jawboning, which is often ineffective, and major sanctions, such as permanent injunctions, which are often too expensive and politically unwise. As an upper limit, an administrative agency could impose a civil assessment that would fully recapture the benefits of noncompliance. Less severe impositions, such as surety devices, which would provide for payment of some fraction of the full assessment, could also be based on the recapture standard. The ability to require immediate payment of only part of the full assessment while retaining the option of demanding full payment provides an agency with a flexible range of enforcement responses the agency can adapt to the facts of each negotiating situation. These quick, low-cost, intermediate measures with escalating impact enable an agency to avoid the dilemma of doing all or nothing.

This economic standard makes it reasonable to allow administrative agencies to impose assessments without first going to court. The formula-defined assessments are ministerial and can be reviewed and corrected easily. There is also the safeguard that no firm can ever be charged more than it has saved by ignoring the law. The Connecticut legislature authorized—and the Connecticut business community did not oppose—the delegation of administrative civil penalty powers to the state's environmental agency chiefly because they understood that these safeguards would be effective. By thus removing the chief grounds for fearing such delegation, the Connecticut economic standard opens the way for widespread legislative adoption and judicial acceptance of administrative civil assessments. * * *

## I. Tools of the Connecticut Enforcement Program

### A. *The Recapture Standard*

Most enforcement problems occur because the regulations to be enforced typically require people to do things that are not in their economic interest. In the case of pollution control, for example, a company must make a large investment in equipment which produces no revenue; the company does not recoup its costs, let alone make a profit on this investment. Nearly any other investment would be more profitable, so the incentive to delay or avoid compliance with regulations is great.

The goal of economic remedies, that is, remedies based on the economic standard of recapture, is to make compliance as economically attractive as alternative investment options. The calculations that determine the appropriate remedy are based on the capital budgeting formula that business managers use to evaluate alternative investment opportunities. The costs of the project, such as pollution control equipment, are estimated year by year over the project's life; these estimates are adjusted for taxes and projected inflation; the resulting year-by-year expenditure figures are then brought to a present value; and finally, a flat, monthly rate is determined that will amortize the costs of the project (including lost profits at the industry's average cost of capital rate) over the assessment period.

Economic remedies make compliance a good business investment. An investment in abatement ensures complying companies savings (not having to pay these assessments) as great as the income generated from an equal-cost, profit-generating investment. The larger the benefits of noncompliance are, the larger the assessment will be. Similarly, the longer the delay in coming into compliance, the larger the forfeiture becomes. However, the size of the assessment will not be unfair or excessive, since it will always be *just* large enough to take away the economic benefits of noncompliance and no larger. * * *

Statute books bristle with an impressive array of penalties for environmental infractions. For several reasons, however, they are rarely employed, and then only in a limited and erratic manner. First, available remedies are generally too severe. Injunctions are rare; enforced injunctions are even more so. Administrators, prosecutors, and the courts are reluctant to force polluting plants to close, given the attendant economic losses to the owners, their workers, and the local tax base. Remedies that carry a criminal stigma also seem excessive in most environmental cases; consequently, both prosecutors and courts shy away from their use. Second, the laws that authorize variable penalties almost never provide clear, usable criteria for determining individual assessments. Without such guidance and confronted with unfamiliar, technically complex environmental suits, prosecutors and courts typically shy away from seeking or imposing the stiff remedies necessary to provide adequate incentives for compliance.

Tying assessments to an economic standard should overcome most of these inhibitions. Economic remedies, *just* big enough to ensure achievement of the legislature's regulatory objectives, avoid the massive secondary effects of an injunction, which closes a plant, in whole or in part, until it complies. They merely tax away the benefits noncomplying firms have appropriated by ignoring the law. Removing these benefits has the useful additional effect of protecting complying competitors from being put at an unfair disadvantage. * * *

In addition to being equitable, remedies based on the recapture standard are easy to administer. A state engineer can readily determine the correct economic remedy for a source. This is critical. If the job were too complex or time-consuming, neither enforcement officials nor the courts would use the recapture system, no matter how much confidence they had in the concept. * * *

*B. Graduated Enforcement Response*

When a company falls behind schedule in abating pollution or otherwise breaks the law, enforcement staffs now typically have only two ways of responding. First, they can cajole or attempt to bluff the violator. This jawboning approach generally entails repeatedly excusing past delinquency; if a source has failed to comply with the terms of an order, enforcement staffs can often do little more than trade an extension of the order's deadlines in return for a new promise of good behavior. Alternatively, enforcement staffs can attempt to obtain an injunction and/or a variety of penalties from the courts. This option entails expense, years of additional delay, and a low probability of ultimately obtaining effective relief. Moreover, for the large number of small violations (such as failure to file periodic water pollution monitoring reports), resorting to such an expensive response is unreasonable.

What is needed is a series of intermediate steps. These remedies must have more force than exhortations but be less painful than punitive fines or injunctions. They must be quickly and easily applicable. Such intermediate steps would ensure more rapid and much more uniform compliance—with less effort and costs to the public—than is now the case.

The Connecticut model provides a whole series of such intermediate steps. They are of two types: (1) administratively imposed civil assessments and (2) administratively imposed sureties. Both types are built on the foundation of the recapture standard, a standard particularly suited for such remedies.

1. Economic Civil Assessments

Administratively imposed, economic civil assessments are the first of these intermediate steps. Armed with this authority, an agency can charge a delinquent firm month by month for the benefits it is accruing through its delay.

Economic civil assessments can be used to give companies small warning jabs as well as to charge them for the full benefit of noncompliance. If, as is commonly the case with recalcitrant sources, the company has violated both substantive and procedural requirements of the law, an agency can impose a small civil assessment for the procedural violation while simultaneously warning that failure to come promptly into substantive compliance will lead to much larger economic civil assessments. Alternatively, the agency could impose a full assessment for the source's past substantive violation, but abate the amount actually collected while making clear that future noncompliance will lead to a much larger assessment.

Even if the economic civil assessment is used only rarely, the public's knowledge that it is available gives startling credibility to other, less serious measures. In Connecticut, warning letters sent to notoriously recalcitrant sources mentioning the possibility of such assessments obtained quick, respectful responses. Previous warning letters had been simply ignored.

2. Surety Devices

Surety devices, such as performance bonds and escrows, provide a wide range of additional intermediate steps. By tying them to the recapture standard, sureties can provide a series of finely graduated and economically coherent responses from which an agency can choose depending on the facts of the case before it.

Connecticut's Enforcement Act of 1973 authorizes the Department of Environmental Protection to require such "performance bonds or other security" as may be necessary. Under this broad authorization, the Department selected escrow devices as best suited to administrative environmental regulation. Escrows impose a relatively small cost on a company; they are available to small as well as big businesses; and they impose no additional burdens upon the regulator.

In its basic form, the escrow operates very simply. When the Department becomes concerned about a firm that is not taking steps required for compliance, it requires the source to post cash, government bonds, or other acceptable security. The amount posted is equal to what the estimated economic civil assessment would be for such a source for, say, eighteen months of noncompliance. The security is deposited with an escrow agent, typically a bank. For a small fee the bank will either hold the security until such time as the source comes into compliance and the agent is so notified by the State, or deliver all or part of this security to the State in the event that the source fails to meet future deadlines as agreed. * * *

There is no doubt that imposing such surety liability will have the desired sharp communicative impact. Requiring a source to post a surety virtually ensures extensive high-level management review of the plant manager's actions. The source's lawyers will have to get involved; its managers will have to negotiate and approve an arrangement with an escrow agent; and a significant sum of money must change hands, even if it is not necessarily lost forever. If the root of the problem had been an uncooperative attitude by lower officials, forcing the matter to the attention of higher-level management may well be sufficient to bring about the desired change in the firm's behavior. Moreover, even if the problem reaches higher than local or low-level management, the risk of significant forfeitures can have a dramatic effect on the performance of even the most recalcitrant sources. In Connecticut, for instance, the state required two historically recalcitrant sources of air pollution to post sureties. The firms, which had previously been 66% and 133% behind schedule, respectively, experienced almost no subsequent delay—two and a half percent in the first case, none in the second. Suddenly the managers in these companies treated compliance with the State's orders as urgently as if they were dealing with commercial investment projects. Company officers went as far as to fly to suppliers to ensure on time delivery of necessary equipment. * * * [T]he Connecticut Enforcement Project developed a simple variant of this basic escrow surety device which has virtually the same communicative impact but at a much reduced cost to the firm. This device, the "flexible reserve escrow," is very simple. When an agency first becomes concerned about a company's performance, it will require the company to accept contractual liability for posting the same amount as if the full escrow were imposed. However, the agency could in fact require the firm to post only a small proportion, such as ten percent, of this amount with the agent. * * *

If subsequently the company fell further behind, the regulatory agency could increase the amount required to be held in the flexible reserve escrow account. If the company regained lost time, the agency could reduce the amount of reserve required. Once the source had accepted full liability under the terms of the surety, it would be bound to respond immediately to such subsequent demands by the agency. Because compliance with the terms of the escrow agreement would be a contractual obligation, the source would have no right to demand an administrative hearing or to appeal the agency's actions to the courts. * * *

3. A Progression of Steps

The several surety devices and the economic civil assessments fit together into a coherent progression of steps that an agency can take depending on the degree of cooperation or recalcitrance it faces. The following table illustrates how this progression of steps might be used assuming various degrees of delay.

In the most unlikely event that the last of these steps, the full civil assessment, does not produce compliance, the agency can still take the violator to court to seek even greater penalties and/or an injunction. During such litigation, the violator would continue to be required to pay assessments recapturing the full savings from noncompliance.

The steps in the table are a progression of options, not a rigidly prescribed sequence. Some recalcitrant cases may require the use of relatively drastic steps early in the process. Simple or short cases allow time for only one or two responses. However, having this full range of enforcement options available allows a regulatory agency to select exactly the right combination of responses for each particular enforcement problem.

The intermediate enforcement responses outlined above will allow the regulatory agency (1) to establish its credibility by demonstrating that its promises are backed when necessary by quick and sure responses, (2) to force the upper-level management of noncomplying organizations to focus on the implications of continuing noncompliance, and (3) to do so while imposing only the minimum economic costs necessary on the firm.

### THE PROGRESSION OF ENFORCEMENT OPTIONS

| NUMBER OF MONTHS SOURCE IS BEHIND COMPLIANCE DEADLINE | STEP | COMMENTS |
|---|---|---|
| 1 | Warning letter | Requires quick visible follow-up to be credible. |
| 2 | Warning letter | |
| 3 | Require source to sign acceptance of specific surety liability | Forces top management lawyers to review problem area. |
| 4½ | Require source to post 10% of surety amount in bank | Forces new review by top management, lawyers, and comptroller. |
| 5½ | Increase reserve required in bank to 50% | State can increase and decrease amounts required flexibly. |
| 4½ | Reduce reserve required to 25% | |
| 6 | Partial (50%) forfeiture | Full forfeiture would be at the economic assessment rate that neutralizes the benefits of noncompliance. |
| 7 | Full forfeiture | Forfeitures can go to either a special fund returnable to the source or a general fund. |
| 17 | Civil assessment | At economic civil assessment rate. Begins as soon as surety agreement amount exhausted. |

* * *

## *Notes*

1. In 1977 Congress amended the Clean Air Act and as part of the amendments included a provision directing the Administrator of EPA to establish rules and regulations by which the agency would collect penalties from the owners of facilities which were not in compliance with the requirements of the Act; the penalties are to be equal to the economic value of the

delay in complying with the Act. Clean Air Act, 42 U.S.C. § 7420. The penalty is to be in addition to other remedies available against a violator. The purpose of the provision is easily stated; it seeks to remove all economic incentive for failing to comply with the statute. Thus in a simple hypothetical, if a device costing $50 million should have been installed in a plant by July 1, 1981 in order to reduce the sulphur dioxide emitted from the plant and the device was not installed until July 1, 1984, the penalty would recoup from the plant owner the value of having and using the $50 million over three years and the money saved by not having to operate and maintain the device.

Simple in concept, the program is inevitably complicated in practice. EPA's Federal Register notice setting out and explaining the implementing rules ran to 172 pages. 45 Fed.Reg. 5086–258 (July 28, 1980). The economic analysis needed to determine the value of delayed equipment installation is complex. EPA developed a computer program for calculating this central item which required twelve financial parameters: (1) the firm's projected capital investment schedule, (2) its projected schedule of operation and maintenance expenses; (3) the investment tax credits and (4) depreciation-related tax benefits associated with the installation of pollution controls; (5) the useful life of the control equipment, (6) the firm's marginal income tax rate, (7) an inflation rate, (8) discount rate, (9) interest rate, (10) preferred stock dividend rate, and the portion of the firm's long-term financing provided by (11) equity and (12) preferred shareholders and debt holders. These items are to be run through 56 different formulaic steps.

The calculation is further complicated by the need recognized in the statute to take account of both competing social policies and mitigating circumstances. For instance, exemptions are provided for certain conversions from gas or oil to coal which the government encouraged or required in the 1970s; and delays clearly beyond the control of the facility owner are to be taken into account.

This program raises a number of questions:

A. Two companies may both delay installing a $50 million device for the same period and both pay the same penalty. In one case, this may cause a major violation of a standard devised to protect human health and in the other case only a marginal violation of a regulation designed to protect aesthetic interests. Is this a reasonable result?

B. When one moves beyond installation of large capital items, how effective will this program be? For instance, what is its relevance to (a) failures of equipment which result in short term violations of Clean Air Act requirements; (b) failure to conduct required monitoring of emissions; or (c) negligent failure to report monitoring results accurately? Is it worthwhile for the control of the local dry cleaner who does not operate a business on the scale or with the sophistication of General Motors or Dow Chemical? Does it have any relevance to remedying past violations such as improper disposal of hazardous waste rather than the prevention of future violations which is achieved by installing pollution control equipment?

C. Electric utilities are major emitters of air pollutants. Typically, electric utilities receive a return only on installed equipment so that the utility customers and not the company receive the economic benefit of delayed installation. Should regulated utilities be subject to Section 120 penalties? Does the utility get an economic benefit by attracting customers with low rates? If the penalty is not passed through to customers, is it reasonable for utility stockholders to pay for a benefit they did not receive? If the penalty is passed through, is it reasonable for the customers first to be exposed to the additional pollution and then to pay the government the saving in rates that they obtained? Does the pass through issue raise a question as to how much economic benefit is actually obtained by any company which delays the installation of pollution control equipment?

2. The United States Sentencing Commission addressed criminal sentences for violation of the environmental laws by corporations in its "Discussion Materials on Organizational Sanctions" (July 1988). The Commission proposed that the penalty be derived from analyzing the harm to the victim rather than the benefit to the defendant. In broad outline, the Commission suggested calculating criminal penalties by taking a baseline amount equal to that needed to redress the harm caused by the violation, multiplying the baseline amount by, say, 2.5 to reflect the difficulty of detection and punishment, and adding to that figure the cost of enforcement. The final amount could be mitigated by the amount of any restitution or other compensation made by the defendant. This proposal is directly opposite in concept to that set out in the Drayton article.

3. The EPA has struggled for a number of years in attempting to determine how civil penalties should be assessed for violation of the federal environmental statutes and regulations. Typically the agency has endorsed assessing penalties that are the sum of three factors: first, the economic benefit that the defendant realized by failing to comply with the law; second, an amount which recognizes the gravity of the offense; and third, an amount reflecting the recalcitrance or attitude of the defendant with regard to the offense. This amount is adjusted by mitigating factors such as the factual or legal weakness of the government's case.

The first factor has the obvious advantage that it can be objectively calculated in most cases. It has the equitable attraction that it provides a level playing field between competitors, if everyone in an industry is required to install the same black box for pollution control purposes. It is much less helpful in cases involving record keeping or management practices where the cost of compliance is often very low. Its equitable element is diminished when pollution control is determined by surrounding environmental conditions rather than technological standards.

The gravity of the offense or harm to the environment or risk of harm to the environment, which are variants of the second factor, is typically a subjective matter. The government is rarely able to show actual harm and consequently uses arbitrary surrogates such as pegging a penalty to the percentage amount by which a regulatory standard is exceeded. The third factor, a kind of civil *mens rea*, is equally subjective.

Typically, little attention is paid to remedial costs that do not involve pollution control equipment. Thus, if a defendant paid $500,000 cleaning up waste that was improperly disposed of and which could have been properly disposed of for $500, that additional cost is not treated as a penalty. Nevertheless, clean up costs may be the most compelling deterrent to future violations.

Look back at the problem of Miller and Smith earlier in this chapter. Assume the government proceeded civilly rather than criminally in both cases. What distinctions do you think should be made in determining the factors weighed in reaching a civil penalty rather than a criminal fine or prison sentence? Would the first civil penalty factor described in this note be an appropriate element to consider in criminal sentencing?

4. In Tull v. United States, 481 U.S. 412, 107 S.Ct. 1831, 95 L.Ed.2d 365 (1987), the Supreme Court considered whether the Seventh Amendment provided for jury trial in cases in which the government seeks a civil penalty. On the basis of English practice at the time the Seventh Amendment was adopted, the Court concluded that jury trial was available on the issue of liability. The Court found the amendment silent on the question of whether the jury must also determine the remedy, i.e., the amount of penalty, and that determination of the penalty amount by the judge was permissible since it was not a fundamental part of the system of trial by jury. In the case before it, a claim under Section 309 of the Clean Water Act, 33 U.S.C. § 1319 (1986), the Court concluded that the determination of the penalty should be left to the judge. Justices Scalia and Stevens dissented on whether the penalty could be set by the judge, stating that they could recall no precedent for judgment of civil liability by jury but assessment of amount by the court. The dissent also pointed out that the course followed by the Court was tempting because of the obvious analogy to a judge imposing sentence in a criminal case, but that, if that analogy were followed, the standard of proof at trial should be a showing of guilt beyond a reasonable doubt.

### *Note on Forfeiture*

Civil forfeiture is an ancient form of action which was infrequently used throughout most of the twentieth century except for a few specialized areas such as customs violations. Its use has grown dramatically during the last fifteen years under statutes that provide for the forfeiture of both contraband and the "instrumentalities" of crime. For example, in 1993, the federal government used civil and criminal forfeiture proceedings to seize approximately $1.9 billion of assets. The states have also markedly increased the use of civil forfeiture. The property subject to forfeiture is broadly defined; under the narcotics laws, drugs and drug paraphernalia but also cars, boats, planes and houses used to facilitate violation of the statute are forfeitable.

The common law foundation of civil forfeiture is that the object subject to forfeiture was itself tainted by or guilty of an offense or was contraband and, consequently, should be forfeited to the state. This led to *in rem* proceedings as the procedural form followed in civil forfeiture cases. Thus, federal statutory civil forfeitures are typically governed by the Supplemental Rules for Certain Admiralty and Maritime Claims. See e.g., 21 U.S.C. § 881 (narcotics statute). In other words, the procedural rules of admiralty are the framework for civil forfeiture under many federal statutes.

This procedure differs markedly from a typical civil lawsuit. The complaint is not required to be served on the owner of the property. The complaint is filed with the court and the clerk forthwith issues a summons and warrant for the "arrest" of the property; the property is "arrested" or seized and taken under the control of the marshal and notice of the action and arrest is published in the newspaper. A claimant of the property must file his claim and state the interest in the property on the basis of which he demands restitution and the right to defend the action.

The government's burden is to prove probable cause to believe that the property is subject to forfeiture, e.g., was used in or facilitated narcotics transactions. The rules of evidence do not apply and the government may carry its burden through hearsay testimony. The government may also refuse to identify the basis of hearsay testimony, claiming the informer's privilege.

In response, the claimant seeks to negate the probable cause showing by a preponderance of the evidence, e.g., showing that the property was not used in narcotics transactions. This he must do under the usual rules of evidence and not in reliance on hearsay.

Modern civil forfeiture statutes typically allow an "innocent owner" defense, e.g., 21 U.S.C. § 881(a)(6). The owner can prevail in his claim if he can show that the guilty use of the property was carried out without his knowledge or consent. This defense was not available in civil forfeitures at common law; statutes not providing the defense have withstood constitutional challenge. Neither the Due Process nor the Takings Clause of the Constitution requires an innocent owner defense to civil forfeiture actions. Bennis v. Michigan, ___ U.S. ___, ___ S.Ct. ___, ___ L.Ed.2d ___, 1996 WL 88269 (1996)("long and unbroken line of cases" upholds forfeiture of property used in a crime even if the owner did not know what use was being made of the property).

Congress passed the first federal criminal forfeiture law in 1970 as part of the Racketeer Influenced and Corrupt Organizations Act, 18 U.S.C. § 1961 et seq. Criminal forfeiture is an *in personam* proceeding; the forfeiture turns on whether the defendant is convicted of a crime. The procedural context of criminal forfeiture is the traditional criminal trial and the forfeiture acts as an additional sanction which flows from conviction.

## AUSTIN v. UNITED STATES

Supreme Court of the United States, 1993.
509 U.S. ___, 113 S.Ct. 2801, 125 L.Ed.2d 488.

JUSTICE BLACKMUN delivered the opinion of the Court.

In this case, we are asked to decide whether the Excessive Fines Clause of the Eighth Amendment applies to forfeitures of property under 21 U.S.C. §§ 881(a)(4) and (a)(7). We hold that it does and therefore remand the case for consideration of the question whether the forfeiture at issue here was excessive.

I

On August 2, 1990, petitioner Richard Lyle Austin was indicted on four counts of violating South Dakota's drug laws. Austin ultimately pleaded guilty to one count of possessing cocaine with intent to distribute and was sentenced by the state court to seven years' imprisonment. On September 7, the United States filed an *in rem* action in the United States District Court for the District of South Dakota seeking forfeiture of Austin's mobile home and auto body shop under 21 U.S.C. §§ 881(a)(4) and (a)(7).[1] Austin filed a claim and an answer to the complaint.

On February 4, 1991, the United States made a motion, supported by an affidavit from Sioux Falls Police Officer Donald Satterlee, for summary judgment. According to Satterlee's affidavit, Austin met Keith Engebretson at Austin's body shop on June 13, 1990, and agreed to sell cocaine to Engebretson. Austin left the shop, went to his mobile home, and returned to the shop with two grams of cocaine which he sold to Engebretson. State authorities executed a search warrant on the body shop and mobile home the following day. They discovered small amounts of marijuana and cocaine, a .22 caliber revolver, drug paraphernalia, and approximately $4,700 in cash. In opposing summary judgment, Austin argued that forfeiture of the properties would violate the Eighth Amendment.[2] The District Court rejected this argument and entered summary judgment for the United States.

The United States Court of Appeals for the Eighth Circuit "reluctantly agree[d] with the government" and affirmed. United States v. One Parcel of Property, 964 F.2d 814, 817 (1992). * * *

1. These statutes provide for the forfeiture of:

"(4) All conveyances, including aircraft, vehicles, or vessels, which are used, or are intended for use, to transport, or in any manner to facilitate the transportation, sale, receipt, possession, or concealment of [controlled substances, their raw materials, and equipment used in their manufacture and distribution]. . . . "

"(7) All real property, including any right, title, and interest (including any leasehold interest) in the whole of any lot or tract of land and any appurtenances or improvements, which is used, or intended to be used, in any manner or part, to commit, or to facilitate the commission of, a violation of this subchapter punishable by more than one year's imprisonment. . . . "

Each provision has an "innocent owner" exception. See §§ 881(a)(4)(C) and (a)(7).

2. "Excessive bail shall not be required, nor excessive fines imposed, nor cruel and unusual punishments inflicted." U.S. Const., Amdt. 8.

II

Austin contends that the Eighth Amendment's Excessive Fines Clause applies to *in rem* civil forfeiture proceedings. We have had occasion to consider this Clause only once before. In Browning–Ferris Industries v. Kelco Disposal, Inc., 492 U.S. 257 (1989), * * * [t]he Court concluded that both the Eighth Amendment and § 10 of the English Bill of Rights of 1689, from which it derives, were intended to prevent the government from abusing its power to punish, and therefore "that the Excessive Fines Clause was intended to limit only those fines directly imposed by, and payable to, the government". * * *

Some provisions of the Bill of Rights are expressly limited to criminal cases. * * * The text of the Eighth Amendment includes no similar limitation.

Nor does the history of the Eighth Amendment require such a limitation. * * *

The purpose of the Eighth Amendment, putting the Bail Clause to one side, was to limit the government's power to punish. The Cruel and Unusual Punishments Clause is self-evidently concerned with punishment. The Excessive Fines Clause limits the Government's power to extract payments, whether in cash or in kind, "*as punishment* for some offense." *Browning-Ferris*, 492 U.S. at 265 (emphasis added). "The notion of punishment, as we commonly understand it, cuts across the division between the civil and the criminal law." United States v. Halper, 490 U.S. 435, 447–448 (1989). "It is commonly understood that civil proceedings may advance punitive and remedial goals, and, conversely, that both punitive and remedial goals may be served by criminal penalties." Id., at 447. Thus, the question is not * * * whether forfeiture under §§ 881(a)(4) and (a)(7) is civil or criminal, but rather whether it is punishment.

In considering this question, we are mindful of the fact that sanctions frequently serve more than one purpose. We need not exclude the possibility that a forfeiture serves remedial purposes to conclude that it is subject to the limitations of the Excessive Fines Clause. We, however, must determine that it can only be explained as serving in part to punish. We said in *Halper* that "a civil sanction that cannot fairly be said solely to serve a remedial purpose, but rather can only be explained as also serving either retributive or deterrent purposes, is punishment, as we have come to understand the term." We turn, then, to consider whether, at the time the Eighth Amendment was ratified, forfeiture was understood at least in part as punishment and whether under §§ 881(a)(4) and (a)(7) should be so understood today.

III * * *

Our cases also have recognized that statutory *in rem* forfeitures impose punishment. In Peisch v. Ware, 4 Cranch 347 (1808), for example, the Court held that goods removed from the custody of a revenue officer without the payment of duties, should not be forfeitable for that reason unless they were removed with the consent of the owner or his agent. Chief Justice Marshall delivered the opinion for a unanimous Court:

> "The court is also of the opinion that the removal for which the act punishes the owner with a forfeiture of the goods must be made with his consent or connivance, or with that of some person employed or trusted by him.
>
> "If, by private theft, or open robbery, without any fault on his part, his property should be invaded, while in the custody of the officer of the revenue, the law cannot be understood to punish him with the forfeiture of that property."

Id. at 364.[8]

The same understanding of forfeiture as punishment runs through our cases rejecting the "innocence" of the owner as a common-law defense to forfeiture. See, e.g., Calero–Toledo, 416 U.S., at 683; Goldsmith–Grant Co. v. United States, 254 U.S. 505 (1921); Dobbins's Distillery v. United States, 96 U.S. 395 (1878); United States v. Brig Malek Adhel, 43 U.S. 210 (1844); The Palmyra, 25 U.S. 1 (1827). In these cases, forfeiture has been justified on two theories-that the property itself is "guilty" of the offense, and that the owner may be held accountable for the wrongs of others to whom he entrusts his property. Both theories rest, at bottom, on the notion that the owner has been negligent in allowing his property to be misused and that he is properly punished for that negligence. * * *

In none of these cases did the Court apply the guilty property fiction to justify forfeiture when the owner had done all that reasonably could be expected to prevent the unlawful use of his property. In *The Palmyra*, it did no more than reject the argument that the criminal conviction of the owner was a prerequisite to the forfeiture of his property. In *Brig Malek Adhel*, the owners' claim of "innocence" was limited to the fact that they "never contemplated or authorized the acts complained of." 2 How., at 230. And in *Dobbins' Distillery*, the Court noted that some responsibility on the part of the owner arose "from the fact that he leased the property to the distiller, and suffered it to be occupied and used by the lessee as a distillery." 96 U.S., at 401. The more recent cases have expressly reserved the question whether the fiction could be employed to forfeit the property of a truly innocent owner. If forfeiture had been understood not to punish the owner, there would have been no reason to reserve the case of a truly innocent owner. Indeed, it is only on the assumption that forfeiture serves in part to punish that the Court's past reservation of that question makes sense.

8. In *Peisch*, the removal of the goods from the custody of the revenue officer occurred not by theft or robbery, but pursuant to a writ of replevin issued by a state court. See 4 Cranch at 360. Thus, *Peisch* stands for the general principle that "the law is not understood to forfeit the property of owners or consignees, on account of the misconduct of mere strangers, over whom such owners or consignees could have no control."

The second theory on which the Court has justified the forfeiture of an "innocent" owner's property is that the owner may be held accountable for the wrongs of others to whom he entrusts his property. * * * Like the guilty-property fiction, this theory of vicarious liability is premised on the idea that the owner has been negligent. * * *

In sum, even though this Court has rejected the "innocence" of the owner as a common-law defense to forfeiture, it consistently has recognized that forfeiture serves, at least in part, to punish the owner. * * * We conclude, therefore, that forfeiture generally and statutory *in rem* forfeiture in particular historically have been understood, at least in part, as punishment.

IV

We turn next to consider whether forfeitures under 21 U.S.C. §§ 881(a)(4) and (a)(7) are properly considered punishment today. We find nothing in these provisions or their legislative history to contradict the historical understanding of forfeiture as punishment. Unlike traditional forfeiture statutes, §§ 881(a)(4) and (a)(7) expressly provide an "innocent owner" defense. See §§ 881(a)(4)(C)("no conveyance shall be forfeited under this paragraph to the extent of an interest of an owner, by reason of any act or omission established by that owner to have been committed or omitted without the knowledge, consent, or willful blindness of the owner"); § 881(a)(7)("no property shall be forfeited under this paragraph, to the extent of an interest of an owner, by reason of any act or omission established by that owner to have been committed or omitted without the knowledge or consent of that owner"); These exemptions serve to focus the provisions on the culpability of the owner in a way that makes them look more like punishment, not less. * * * The inclusion of innocent-owner defenses in §§ 881 (a)(4) and (a)(7) reveals a * * * congressional intent to punish only those in drug trafficking. * * *

The legislative history of § 881 confirms the punitive nature of these provisions. When it added subsection (a)(7) to § 881 in 1984, Congress recognized "that the traditional criminal sanctions of fine and imprisonment are inadequate to deter or punish the enormously profitable trade in dangerous drugs." S. Rep. No. 98–225, p. 191 (1983). It characterized the forfeiture of real property as "a powerful deterrent." Id., at 195.

The Government argues that §§ 881 (a)(4) and (a)(7) are not punitive but, rather, should be considered remedial in two respects. First, they remove the "instruments" of the drug trade "thereby protecting the community from the threat of continued drug dealing." Second, the forfeited assets serve to compensate the Government for the expense of law enforcement activity and for its expenditure on societal problems such as urban blight, drug addiction, and other health concerns resulting from the drug trade.

In our view, neither argument withstands scrutiny. Concededly, we have recognized that the forfeiture of contraband itself may be characterized as remedial because it removes dangerous or illegal items from society. The Court, however, previously has rejected government's attempt to extend that reasoning to conveyances used to transport illegal liquor. See One 1958 Plymouth Sedan v. Pennsylvania, 380 U.S. 693, 699 (1965). In that case it noted: "There is nothing even remotely criminal in possessing an automobile." The same, without question, is true of the properties involved here, and the Government's attempt to characterize these properties as "instruments" of the drug trade must meet the same fate as Pennsylvania's effort to characterize the 1958 Plymouth Sedan as "contraband."

The Government's second argument about the remedial nature of this forfeiture is no more persuasive. We previously have upheld the forfeiture of goods involved in customs violations as "a reasonable form of liquidated damages." One Lot Emerald Cut Stones v. United States, 409 U.S. 232, 237 (1972). But the dramatic variations in the value of conveyances and real property forfeitable under §§ 881 (a)(4) and (a)(7) undercut any similar argument with respect to those provisions. * * *

In light of the historical understanding of forfeiture as punishment, the clear focus of §§ 881(a)(4) and (a)(7) on the culpability of the owner, and the evidence that Congress understood those provisions as serving to deter and to punish, we cannot conclude that forfeiture under §§ 881(a)(4) and (a)(7) serves solely a remedial purpose. We therefore conclude that forfeiture under these provisions constitutes "payment to a sovereign as punishment for some offense," *Browning-Ferris*, 492 U.S., at 265, and, as such, is subject to the limitations of the Eighth Amendment's Excessive Fines Clause.

V

Austin asks that we establish a multifactor test for determining whether a forfeiture is constitutionally "excessive." We decline that invitation. * * * Prudence dictates that we allow the lower courts to consider that question in the first instance.[15] * * *

JUSTICE SCALIA, concurring in part and concurring in the judgment.

We recently stated that, at the time the Eighth Amendment was drafted, the term "fine" was "understood to mean a payment to a sovereign as punishment for some offense." Browning–Ferris Industries of Vermont, Inc. v. Kelco Disposal, Inc., 492 U.S. 257, 265 (1989). It seems to me that the Court's opinion obscures this clear statement, and needlessly attempts to derive from our sparse caselaw on the subject of *in rem* forfeiture the questionable proposition that the owner of property taken pursuant to such forfeiture is always blameworthy. I write separately to explain why I consider this forfeiture a fine, and to point

**15.** Justice Scalia suggests that the sole measure of an in rem forfeiture's excessiveness is the relationship between the forfeited property and the offense. We do not rule out the possibility that the connection between the property and the offense may be relevant, but our decision today in no way limits the Court of Appeals from considering other factors in determining whether the forfeiture of Austin's property was excessive.

out that the excessiveness inquiry for statutory *in rem* forfeitures is different from the usual excessiveness inquiry.

I

Whether any sort of forfeiture of property may be covered by the Eighth Amendment is not a difficult question. "Forfeiture" and "fine" each appeared as one of many definitions of the other in various 18th-century dictionaries. * * * Moreover, for the Eighth Amendment to limit cash fines while permitting limitless in-kind assessments would make little sense, altering only the form of the Star Chamber abuses that led to the provisions of the English Bill of Rights, from which our Excessive Fines Clause directly derives. * * *

In order to constitute a fine under the Eighth Amendment, however, the forfeiture must constitute "punishment," and it is a much closer question whether statutory *in rem* forfeitures, as opposed to *in personam* forfeitures, meet this requirement. The latter are assessments, whether monetary or in-kind, to punish the property owner's criminal conduct, while the former are confiscations of property rights based on improper use of the property, regardless of whether the owner has violated the law. * * *

However the theory may be expressed, it seems to me that this taking of lawful property must be considered, in whole or in part, punitive. Its purpose is not compensatory, to make someone whole for injury caused by unlawful use of the property. Punishment is being imposed, whether one quaintly considers its object to be the property itself, or more realistically regards its object to be the property's owner. * * *

The Court apparently believes, however, that only actual culpability of the affected property owner can establish that a forfeiture provision is punitive, and sets out to establish (in Part III) that such culpability exists in the case of *in rem* forfeitures. In my view, however, the caselaw is far more ambiguous than the Court acknowledges. We have never held that the Constitution requires negligence, or any other degree of culpability, to support such forfeitures. * * * If the Court is correct that culpability of the owner is essential, then there is no difference (except perhaps the burden of proof) between the traditional *in rem* forfeiture and the traditional *in personam* forfeiture. Well-established common-law distinctions should not be swept away by reliance on bits of dicta. * * *

*Even if* punishment of personal culpability is necessary for a forfeiture to be a fine; and *even if in rem* forfeitures in general do not punish personal culpability; the *in rem* forfeiture in *this* case is a fine. As the Court discusses in Part IV, this statute, in contrast to the traditional *in rem* forfeiture, *requires* that the owner not be innocent-that he have some degree of culpability for the "guilty" property. Here, the property must "offend" *and* the owner must not be completely without fault. Nor is there any consideration of compensating for loss, since the value of the property is irrelevant to whether it is forfeited. That is enough to satisfy the *Browning-Ferris* standard, and to make the entire discussion in Part III dictum. Statutory forfeitures under §§ 881(a) are certainly *payment* (in kind), to *a sovereign* as *punishment* for an *offense*.

II

That this forfeiture works as a fine raises the excessiveness issue, on which the Court remands. I agree that a remand is in order, but think it worth pointing out that on remand the excessiveness analysis must be different from that applicable to monetary fines and, perhaps, to *in personam* forfeitures. In the case of a monetary fine, the Eighth Amendment's origins in the English Bill of Rights, intended to limit the abusive penalties assessed against the king's opponents, demonstrate that the touchstone is value of the fine in relation to the offense. * * *

Here, however, the offense of which petitioner has been convicted is not relevant to the forfeiture. Section § 881 requires only that the Government show probable cause that the subject property was used for the prohibited purpose. The burden then shifts to the property owner to show, by a preponderance of the evidence, that the use was made without his "knowledge, consent, or willful blindness," 21 U.S.C. §§ 881(a)(4)(C), see also (a)(7), or that the property was not so used. See § 881 (d) (incorporating 19 U.S. C. § 1615). Unlike monetary fines, statutory *in rem* forfeitures have traditionally been fixed, not by determining the appropriate value of the penalty in relation to the committed offense, but by determining what property has been "tainted" by unlawful use, to which issue the value of the property is irrelevant. Scales used to measure out unlawful drug sales, for example, are confiscable whether made of the purest gold or the basest metal. But an *in rem* forfeiture goes beyond the traditional limits that the Eighth Amendment permits if it applies to property that cannot properly be regarded as an instrumentality of the offense-the building, for example, in which an isolated drug sale happens to occur. Such a confiscation would be an excessive fine. The question is not *how much* the confiscated property is worth, but *whether* the confiscated property has a close enough relationship to the offense. * * *

JUSTICE KENNEDY, with whom THE CHIEF JUSTICE and JUSTICE THOMAS join, concurring in part and concurring in the judgment. [omitted]

### *Notes*

1. Before *Austin*, civil forfeiture statutes had routinely been found to be remedial by the courts. After *Austin*, some forfeiture proceedings remain remedial. For instance, the forfeiture of contraband such as narcotics is remedial. The Fifth Circuit has held that the forfeiture of the proceeds of illegal transactions does not constitute punishment. United States v. Arreola–Ramos, 60 F.3d 188 (5th Cir.1995). The Second Circuit found that currency was the instrumentality of the crime of failing to report international currency flow to the U.S. Customs and forfeiture of the money was remedial. United States v. U.S. Currency in the Amount of $145,139, 18 F.3d 73 (2d Cir.), cert. denied, ___ U.S. ___, 115 S.Ct. 72, 130 L.Ed.2d 27

(1994). In Quinones–Ruiz v. United States, 873 F.Supp. 359 (S.D.Cal.1995), the court reached a contrary result, finding that the essence of the crime was lying to the government and that the money was not kept in order to lie about it.

2. The question of whether excessiveness in civil forfeitures is to be measured by an instrumentality test, a proportionality test, or a combination of the two has divided the lower courts. Some courts have set out combined tests. For instance, in United States v. Real Property Located At 6625 Zumirez Drive, 845 F.Supp. 725 (C.D.Cal.1994), the court weighed: (i) the inherent gravity of the offense compared with the harshness of the penalty; (ii) whether the property was an integral part of the commission of the crime; and (iii) whether the criminal activity involving the defendant property was extensive temporally and/or spatially.

The Fourth Circuit adopted an instrumentality test, reasoning that historically in forfeiture the property is the offender and that, in the narcotics statute before it, Congress intended forfeiture to be based on "taint." United States v. Chandler, 36 F.3d 358 (4th Cir.1994), cert. denied, ___ U.S. ___, 115 S.Ct. 1792, 131 L.Ed.2d 721 (1995). The court set up a three part instrumentality test:

> [A court must consider] (1) the nexus between the offense and the property and the extent of the property's role in the offense, (2) the role and culpability of the owner, and (3) the possibility of separating offending property that can readily be separated from the remainder. In measuring the strength and extent of the nexus between the property and the offense, a court may take into account the following factors: (1) whether the use of the property in the offense was deliberate and planned or merely incidental and fortuitous; (2) whether the property was important to the success of the illegal activity; (3) the time during which the property was illegally used and the spacial extent of its use; (4) whether its illegal use was an isolated event or had been repeated; and (5) whether the purpose of acquiring, maintaining or using the property was to carry out the offense. No one factor is dispositive but, to sustain a forfeiture against an Eighth Amendment challenge, the court must be able to conclude, under the totality of circumstances, that the property was a substantial and meaningful instrumentality in the commission of the offense, or would have been, had the offensive conduct been carried out as intended.

In contrast, in addressing an *in personam* criminal forfeiture, the Fourth Circuit applied a proportionality analysis because such forfeiture is a monetary punishment no different from a fine. The Court held that no forfeiture of the proceeds of a crime would be excessive and that for other property the focus should be on the defendant's conduct and the offense committed. United States v. Wild, 47 F.3d 669 (4th Cir.), cert. denied, ___ U.S. ___, 116 S.Ct. 128, 133 L.Ed.2d 77 (1995).

A remaining question is whether the punitive nature of forfeiture makes seizure of property from owners who are innocent or merely negligent an inappropriate remedy. At a minimum, should the threshold of "excessiveness" be lower for such owners?

3. *Austin* follows *Halper* in putting emphasis on punishment rather than on whether a sanction should be labelled civil or criminal. The Supreme Court's determination that civil forfeiture can be punishment has led lower courts to consider whether to apply certain traditionally criminal law doctrines to forfeiture proceedings. See Nancy J. King, Portioning Punishment: Constitutional Limits on Successive and Excessive Penalties, 144 U.Pa.L.Rev. 101 (1995).

Given the procedural advantages of civil forfeiture proceedings, the government has frequently brought both criminal charges and civil forfeiture proceedings against the same defendant addressing the same conduct. Two circuits have found this practice to violate the double jeopardy clause. United States v. $405,089.23 U.S. Currency, 33 F.3d 1210 (9th Cir.1994), cert. granted, ___ U.S. ___, 116 S.Ct. 762, 133 L.Ed.2d 707 (1996); United States v. Ursery, 59 F.3d 568 (6th Cir.1995), cert. granted, ___ U.S. ___, 116 S.Ct. 762, 133 L.Ed.2d 707 (1996). Two other circuits have held that the forfeiture and the criminal action, when closely related in time, were not separate proceedings and so did not violate the double jeopardy clause. United States v. One Single Family Residence, 13 F.2d 1493 (11th Cir.1994); United States v. Millan, 2 F.3d 17 (2d Cir.1993), cert. denied, ___ U.S. ___, 114 S.Ct. 922, 127 L.Ed.2d 215 (1994). The government could avoid the potential double jeopardy problem by prosecuting both the criminal offense and the forfeiture in a single proceeding. In the alternative, as in *Austin,* one sovereign could prosecute the criminal offense and another could bring the forfeiture action.

The exclusionary rule has been applied to a civil forfeiture proceeding to deter violations of the Fourth Amendment by customs officers. United States v. $19,047 in U.S. Currency (Rodriguez), 1994 WL 673704 (S.D.N.Y. 1994). The fugitive disentitlement doctrine has been used to dismiss claims to properties which the government sought to seize through civil forfeiture; the claimant was not entitled to any relief because he had showed disrespect for legal processes by leaving the United States rather than submitting to the court's jurisdiction in the related criminal proceeding for drug smuggling and money laundering. United States v. Real Property Located at Incline Village, 47 F.3d 1511 (9th Cir.1995), cert. granted sub nom. Degen v. United States, ___ U.S. ___, 116 S.Ct. 762, 133 L.Ed.2d 707 (1996).

The Seventh Circuit has held that the due process clause requires the government to participate in a post-seizure adversary hearing on probable cause when the court finds the government has seized through civil forfeiture the assets a criminal defendant needs to obtain counsel. United States v. Michelle's Lounge, 39 F.3d 684 (7th Cir.1994). But forfeiture is not barred because it deprives a criminal defendant of funds to retain counsel. United States v. Monsanto, 491 U.S. 600, 109 S.Ct. 2657, 105 L.Ed.2d 512 (1989)(criminal in personam forfeiture). Nor is it barred when a defendant agrees as part of a plea bargain to give up assets that otherwise would not be subject to forfeiture. Libretti v. United States, ___ U.S. ___, 116 S.Ct. 356, 133 L.Ed.2d 271 (1995).

4. There are a number of federal forfeiture statutes which vary in their scope. Under the customs laws when merchandise is brought into the country without proper payment of duty, the goods may be seized and sold if

a monetary penalty is not timely paid. The monetary penalties vary but in cases of fraud may be as great as the domestic value of the merchandise. 19 U.S.C. § 1592. Any vessel or vehicle used to aid in the illegal entry of goods in the United States may be seized and forfeited to the government. 19 U.S.C. § 1595(a). Under the drug laws, the drugs themselves as well as any aircraft, vehicle or vessel used or intended to be used to facilitate a drug transaction are subject to forfeiture to the United States and no property right exists in such goods; there are exceptions for common carriers and vehicles unlawfully in the possession of the person involved in the drug transaction. 21 U.S.C. § 881.

5. In Alexander v. United States, 509 U.S. ___, 113 S.Ct. 2766, 125 L.Ed.2d 441 (1993), the Court rejected the argument that forfeiture of an entire chain of adult entertainment establishments after the owner was convicted of selling several obscene magazines and tapes, as punishment for RICO violations, violates the First Amendment as a prior restraint on speech. The forfeiture was found not to restrain protected expression, but merely to prevent financing expressive activities with tainted assets. However, the Court did find that the Excessive Fines Clause applied to this *in personam* forfeiture.

6. The aggressive use of forfeiture proceedings in recent years has raised doubts as to their fairness and resulted in calls for reform. Extensive discussion of the entire field is provided in Symposium on Asset Forfeiture Law, 21 J.Legis. 155 (1995); Symposium: What Price Civil Forfeiture? Constitutional Implications and Reform Initiatives, 39 N.Y.L.Sch.L.Rev. 1 (1994). In another critical article, Judge Pratt of the Second Circuit has pointed out the remarkable procedural advantages enjoyed by the government: (a) once the government has demonstrated probable cause for its claim, the claimant of the seized property bears the burden of proving his claim to the property either by showing that there was no ground for the forfeiture or, in the appropriate case, qualifying for an innocent owner defense; (b) probable cause in this context is reduced to reasonable grounds rising above the level of mere suspicion and is less stringent than a preponderance of the evidence test; (c) probable cause may be established by hearsay; (d) the defenses that the property was not used in connection with illegal activity or that the illegal use was without the claimant's knowledge or consent are not easy to prove. George C. Pratt & William B. Peterson, Civil Forfeiture in the Second Circuit, 65 St. John's L.Rev. 653 (1991). The Supreme Court addressed the procedural issue of whether the owner of real property must be given notice and an opportunity to be heard prior to seizure in civil forfeiture cases in United States v. James Daniel Good Real Property, ___ U.S. ___, 114 S.Ct. 492, 126 L.Ed.2d 490 (1993)(reproduced infra at p. 740.)

7. Another civil sanction which resembles those forfeiture provisions which do not allow an innocent owner defense are civil penalties based on strict or absolute liability. The Clean Water Act contains such a provision, 33 U.S.C. § 1321, which allows the imposition of a penalty for the discharge of oil or hazardous substances from a facility regardless of the fault or negligence of the owner or operator. The statute has survived due process challenges to the absolute liability provision, which provides for modest penalties, because it has been justified as a means of funding the administra-

tion and enforcement of the Act. E.g., United States v. Coastal States Crude Gathering Co., 643 F.2d 1125 (5th Cir.), cert. denied, 454 U.S. 835, 102 S.Ct. 136, 70 L.Ed.2d 114 (1981); United States v. Marathon Pipe Line Co., 589 F.2d 1305 (7th Cir.1978).

8. The Clean Water Act contains a provision barring a party from contracting to supply goods or services to the federal government if the contract is to be performed at a facility at which a criminal violation of the Act occurred until the Administrator of EPA certifies that the condition giving rise to the conviction has been corrected. 33 U.S.C. § 1368. Assume two defendants own neighboring facilities manufacturing nails and are convicted of the same Clean Water Act offense and given the same sentence. The first defendant sells nails on the private market, the second sells only to the government. The Act's "listing" provision can have an economic impact on the second defendant that is far greater than the criminal fine. Is listing punishment? Does it or should it make any difference that listing does not require a defendant to pay anything to the government? Is the government as contractor allowed to impose sanctions which it would be barred from imposing as sovereign? Should listing be treated differently from fines under a proportionality or excessiveness analysis?

# Chapter 6

# DAMAGES

---

THE NATURE OF THE SUBJECT

The law of damages consists of the rules, standards, and methods used by the courts for measuring in money the compensation given for losses and injuries. It plays an unusually large part in Anglo–American law because of two distinctive features of the English judicial machinery. First is the presence of the jury, who award the damages under the judge's supervision and control. The rules and formulas used in the exercise of that control make up a substantial part of the law of damages. Second, in dividing jurisdiction between courts of law and courts of equity, the tradition was established that resort must be had to compensation by money damages in preference to specific relief, unless such damages are affirmatively shown to be inadequate for the just protection of the plaintiff's interest. It results from this traditional rule that a judgment for money damages is the normal and preferred remedy in our courts.

Charles McCormick, Handbook on the Law of Damages 1 (1935).

## A. INTRODUCTION

The case that follows introduces and defines the three basic types of damages awards: *nominal damages*, *compensatory damages*, and *punitive damages*. Punitive damages were already discussed in chapter 5. Nominal damages are discussed in a note following the main case. This chapter as a whole focuses on compensatory damages.

As you read the case, think about the justifications for compensatory damages. What purpose does it serve to give people money when their rights are violated? What if the loss they claim is not economic in character? Can all losses be measured in money, or are some things simply beyond price?

# MEMPHIS COMMUNITY SCHOOL DISTRICT v. STACHURA

Supreme Court of the United States, 1986.
477 U.S. 299, 106 S.Ct. 2537, 91 L.Ed.2d 249.

JUSTICE POWELL delivered the opinion of the Court.

This case requires us to decide whether 42 U.S.C. § 1983 authorizes an award of compensatory damages based on the factfinder's assessment of the value or importance of a substantive constitutional right.

I

Respondent Edward Stachura is a tenured teacher in the Memphis, Michigan, public schools. When the events that led to this case occurred, respondent taught seventh-grade life science, using a textbook that had been approved by the school board. The textbook included a chapter on human reproduction. During the 1978–1979 school year, respondent spent six weeks on this chapter. As part of their instruction, students were shown pictures of respondent's wife during her pregnancy. Respondent also showed the students two films concerning human growth and sexuality. These films were provided by the County Health Department, and the Principal of respondent's school had approved their use. Both films had been shown in past school years without incident.

After the showing of the pictures and the films, a number of parents complained to school officials about respondent's teaching methods. These complaints, which appear to have been based largely on inaccurate rumors about the allegedly sexually explicit nature of the pictures and films, were discussed at an open School Board meeting held on April 23, 1979. Following the advice of the School Superintendent, respondent did not attend the meeting, during which a number of parents expressed the view that respondent should not be allowed to teach in the Memphis school system. The day after the meeting, respondent was suspended with pay. The School Board later confirmed the suspension, and notified respondent that an "administration evaluation" of his teaching methods was underway. No such evaluation was ever made. Respondent was reinstated the next fall, after filing this lawsuit.

Respondent sued the School District, the Board of Education, various Board members and school administrators, and two parents who had participated in the April 23 School Board meeting. The complaint alleged that respondent's suspension deprived him of both liberty and property without due process of law and violated his First Amendment right to academic freedom. Respondent sought compensatory and punitive damages under 42 U.S.C. § 1983 for these constitutional violations.

At the close of trial on these claims, the District Court instructed the jury as to the law governing the asserted bases for liability. Turning to damages, the court instructed the jury that on finding liability it should award a sufficient amount to compensate respondent for the injury caused by petitioners' unlawful actions:

"You should consider in this regard any lost earnings; loss of earning capacity; out-of-pocket expenses; and any mental anguish or emotional distress that you find the Plaintiff to have suffered as a result of conduct by the Defendants depriving him of his civil rights."

In addition to this instruction on the standard elements of compensatory damages, the court explained that punitive damages could be awarded, and described the standards governing punitive awards. Finally, at respondent's request and over petitioners' objection, the court charged that damages also could be awarded based on the value or importance of the constitutional rights that were violated:

"If you find that the Plaintiff has been deprived of a Constitutional right, you may award damages to compensate him for the deprivation. Damages for this type of injury are more difficult to measure than damages for a physical injury or injury to one's property. There are no medical bills or other expenses by which you can judge how much compensation is appropriate. In one sense, no monetary value we place upon Constitutional rights can measure their importance in our society or compensate a citizen adequately for their deprivation. However, just because these rights are not capable of precise evaluation does not mean that an appropriate monetary amount should not be awarded. The precise value you place upon any Constitutional right which you find was denied to Plaintiff is within your discretion. You may wish to consider the importance of the right in our system of government, the role which this right has played in the history of our republic, [and] the significance of the right in the context of the activities which the Plaintiff was engaged in at the time of the violation of the right."

The jury found petitioners liable, and awarded a total of $275,000 in compensatory damages and $46,000 in punitive damages. * * *

In an opinion devoted primarily to liability issues, the Court of Appeals for the Sixth Circuit affirmed * * *

We granted certiorari limited to the question whether the Court of Appeals erred in affirming the damages award in the light of the District Court's instructions that authorized not only compensatory and punitive damages, but also damages for the deprivation of "any constitutional right." * * *

III

A

We have repeatedly noted that 42 U.S.C. § 1983[8] creates " 'a species of tort liability' in favor of persons who are deprived of 'rights, privi-

8. Section § 1983 reads:

"Every person who, under color of any statute, ordinance, regulation, custom, or usage, of any State or Territory or the District of Columbia, subjects, or causes to be subjected, any citizen of the United States or other person within the jurisdiction thereof to the deprivation of any rights, privileges, or immunities secured by the Constitution and laws, shall be liable to

leges, or immunities secured' to them by the Constitution." Accordingly, when § 1983 plaintiffs seek damages for violations of constitutional rights, the level of damages is ordinarily determined according to principles derived from the common law of torts.

Punitive damages aside,[9] damages in tort cases are designed to provide "*compensation* for the injury caused to plaintiff by defendant's breach of duty." To that end, compensatory damages may include not only out-of-pocket loss and other monetary harms, but also such injuries as "impairment of reputation . . ., personal humiliation, and mental anguish and suffering." Deterrence is also an important purpose of this system, but it operates through the mechanism of damages that are compensatory—damages grounded in determinations of plaintiffs' actual losses. Congress adopted this common-law system of recovery when it established liability for "constitutional torts." Consequently, "the basic purpose" of § 1983 damages is "to *compensate persons for injuries* that are caused by the deprivation of constitutional rights."

Respondent does not, and could not reasonably, contend that the separate instructions authorizing damages for violation of constitutional rights were equivalent to punitive damages instructions. In these separate instructions, the jury was authorized to find damages for constitutional violations without any finding of malice or ill will. Moreover, the jury instructions separately authorized punitive damages, and the District Court expressly labeled the "constitutional rights" damages compensatory. The instructions concerning damages for constitutional violations are thus impermissible unless they reasonably could be read as authorizing *compensatory* damages.

Carey v. Piphus [435 U.S. 247, 98 S.Ct. 1042, 55 L.Ed.2d 252 (1978)] represents a straightforward application of these principles. *Carey* involved a suit by a high school student suspended for smoking marijuana; the student claimed that he was denied procedural due process because he was suspended without an opportunity to respond to the charges against him. The Court of Appeals for the Seventh Circuit held that even if the suspension was justified, the student could recover substantial compensatory damages simply because of the insufficient procedures used to suspend him from school. We reversed, and held that the student could recover compensatory damages only if he proved actual injury caused by the denial of his constitutional rights. We noted: "[r]ights, constitutional and otherwise, do not exist in a vacuum. Their purpose is to protect persons from injuries to particular interests. . . ."

the party injured in an action at law, suit in equity, or other proper proceeding for redress."

9. The purpose of punitive damages is to punish the defendant for his willful or malicious conduct and to deter others from similar behavior. In Smith v. Wade, 461 U.S. 30, [103 S.Ct. 1625, 75 L.Ed.2d 632] (1983), the Court held that punitive damages may be available in a proper § 1983 case. As the punitive damages instructions used in this case explained, however, such damages are available only on a showing of the requisite intent. App. 94–95 (authorizing punitive damages for acts "maliciously, or wantonly, or oppressively done").

Where no injury was present, no "compensatory" damages could be awarded.

The instructions at issue here cannot be squared with *Carey,* or with the principles of tort damages on which *Carey* and § 1983 are grounded. The jurors in this case were told that, in determining how much was necessary to "compensate [respondent] for the deprivation" of his constitutional rights, they should place a money value on the "rights" themselves by considering such factors as the particular right's "importance ... in our system of government," its role in American history, and its "significance ... in the context of the activities" in which respondent was engaged. These factors focus, not on compensation for provable injury, but on the jury's subjective perception of the importance of constitutional rights as an abstract matter. *Carey* establishes that such an approach is impermissible. The constitutional right transgressed in *Carey*—the right to due process of law—is central to our system of ordered liberty. We nevertheless held that *no* compensatory damages could be awarded for violation of that right absent proof of actual injury. *Carey,* 435 U.S. at 264, 98 S.Ct. at 1052. *Carey* thus makes clear that the abstract value of a constitutional right may not form the basis for § 1983 damages.[11]

Respondent nevertheless argues that *Carey* does not control here, because in this case a *substantive* constitutional right—respondent's First Amendment right to academic freedom—was infringed. The argument misperceives our analysis in *Carey*. That case does not establish a two-tiered system of constitutional rights, with substantive rights afforded greater protection than "mere" procedural safeguards. We did acknowledge in *Carey* that "the elements and prerequisites for recovery of damages" might vary depending on the interests protected by the constitutional right at issue. But we emphasized that, whatever the constitutional basis for § 1983 liability, such damages must always be designed "to *compensate injuries* caused by the [constitutional] deprivation." (emphasis added) That conclusion simply leaves no room for non-compensatory damages measured by the jury's perception of the abstract "importance" of a constitutional right.

Nor do we find such damages necessary to vindicate the constitutional rights that § 1983 protects. See n. 11, *supra.* Section 1983 presupposes that damages that compensate for actual harm ordinarily

**11.** We did approve an award of nominal damages for the deprivation of due process in *Carey*. Our discussion of that issue makes clear that nominal damages, and not damages based on some undefinable "value" of infringed rights, are the appropriate means of "vindicating" rights whose deprivation has not caused actual, provable injury:

"Common-law courts traditionally have vindicated deprivations of certain 'absolute' rights that are not shown to have caused actual injury through the award of a nominal sum of money. By making the deprivation of such rights actionable for nominal damages without proof of actual injury, the law recognizes the importance to organized society that those rights be scrupulously observed; but at the same time, it remains true to the principle that substantial damages should be awarded only to compensate actual injury or, in the case of exemplary or punitive damages, to deter or punish malicious deprivations of rights."

suffice to deter constitutional violations. Moreover, damages based on the "value" of constitutional rights are an unwieldy tool for ensuring compliance with the Constitution. History and tradition do not afford any sound guidance concerning the precise value that juries should place on constitutional protections. Accordingly, were such damages available, juries would be free to award arbitrary amounts without any evidentiary basis, or to use their unbounded discretion to punish unpopular defendants. Such damages would be too uncertain to be of any great value to plaintiffs, and would inject caprice into determinations of damages in § 1983 cases. We therefore hold that damages based on the abstract "value" or "importance" of constitutional rights are not a permissible element of compensatory damages in such cases.

B

Respondent further argues that the challenged instructions authorized a form of "presumed" damages—a remedy that is both compensatory in nature and traditionally part of the range of tort law remedies. * * *

Presumed damages are a *substitute* for ordinary compensatory damages, not a *supplement* for an award that fully compensates the alleged injury. When a plaintiff seeks compensation for an injury that is likely to have occurred but difficult to establish, some form of presumed damages may possibly be appropriate. In those circumstances, presumed damages may roughly approximate the harm that the plaintiff suffered and thereby compensate for harms that may be impossible to measure. As we earlier explained, the instructions at issue in this case did not serve this purpose, but instead called on the jury to measure damages based on a subjective evaluation of the importance of particular constitutional values. Since such damages are wholly divorced from any compensatory purpose, they cannot be justified as presumed damages.[14]

14. For the same reason, Nixon v. Herndon, 273 U.S. 536, 47 S.Ct. 446, 71 L.Ed. 759 (1927), and similar cases do not support the challenged instructions. In *Nixon,* the Court held that a plaintiff who was illegally prevented from voting in a state primary election suffered compensable injury. This holding did not rest on the "value" of the right to vote as an abstract matter; rather, the Court recognized that the plaintiff had suffered a particular injury—his inability to vote in a particular election—that might be compensated through substantial money damages.

*Nixon* followed a long line of cases, going back to Lord Holt's decision in Ashby v. White, 2 Ld.Raym. 938, 92 Eng.Rep. 126 (1703), authorizing substantial money damages as compensation for persons deprived of their right to vote in particular elections. Although these decisions sometimes speak of damages for the value of the right to vote, their analysis shows that they involve nothing more than an award of presumed damages for a nonmonetary harm that cannot easily be quantified:

> "In the eyes of the law th[e] right [to vote] is so valuable that damages are presumed from the wrongful deprivation of it without evidence of actual loss of money, property, or any other valuable thing, and the amount of the damages is a question peculiarly appropriate for the determination of the jury, because each member of the jury has personal knowledge of the value of the right." *Ibid.*

See also Ashby v. White, *supra,* at 955, 92 Eng.Rep., at 137 (Holt, C.J.)("As in an action for slanderous words, though a man does not lose a penny by reason of the speaking [of] them, yet he shall have an action"). The "value of the right" in the context of these decisions is the money value of the particular loss that the plaintiff suffered—a loss of which "each member of

Moreover, no rough substitute for compensatory damages was required in this case, since the jury was fully authorized to compensate respondent for both monetary and nonmonetary harms caused by petitioners' conduct. * * *

IV

The judgment of the Court of Appeals is reversed, and the case is remanded for further proceedings consistent with this opinion.

JUSTICE BRENNAN and JUSTICE STEVENS join the opinion of the Court and also join JUSTICE MARSHALL's opinion concurring in the judgment.

JUSTICE MARSHALL, with whom JUSTICE BRENNAN, JUSTICE BLACKMUN, and JUSTICE STEVENS join, concurring in the judgment.

I agree with the Court that this case must be remanded for a new trial on damages. Certain portions of the Court's opinion, however, can be read to suggest that damages in § 1983 cases are necessarily limited to "out-of-pocket loss," "other monetary harms," and "such injuries as 'impairment of reputation . . ., personal humiliation, and mental anguish and suffering.'" I do not understand the Court so to hold, and I write separately to emphasize that the violation of a constitutional right, in proper cases, may itself constitute a compensable injury. * * *

Following *Carey,* the courts of appeals have recognized that invasions of constitutional rights sometimes cause injuries that cannot be redressed by a wooden application of common-law damages rules. In Hobson v. Wilson, 237 U.S.App.D.C. 219, 275–281, 737 F.2d 1, 57–63 (1984), cert. denied, 470 U.S. 1084, 105 S.Ct. 1843, 85 L.Ed.2d 142 (1985), which the Court cites, plaintiffs claimed that defendant Federal Bureau of Investigation agents had invaded their First Amendment rights to assemble for peaceable political protest, to associate with others to engage in political expression, and to speak on public issues free of unreasonable government interference. The District Court found that the defendants had succeeded in diverting plaintiffs from, and impeding them in, their protest activities. The Court of Appeals for the District of Columbia Circuit held that that injury to a First Amendment—protected interest could itself constitute compensable injury wholly apart from any "emotional distress, humiliation and personal indignity, emotional pain, embarrassment, fear, anxiety and anguish" suffered by plaintiffs. The court warned, however, that that injury could be compensated with substantial damages only to the extent that it was "reasonably quantifiable"; damages should not be based on "the so-called inherent value of the rights violated."

I believe that the *Hobson* court correctly stated the law. When a plaintiff is deprived, for example, of the opportunity to engage in a demonstration to express his political views, "[i]t is facile to suggest that

the jury has personal knowledge." It is *not* the value of the right to vote as a general, abstract matter, based on its role in our history or system of government. Thus, whatever the wisdom of these decisions in the context of the changing scope of compensatory damages over the course of this century, they do not support awards of noncompensatory damages such as those authorized in this case.

no damage is done." Loss of such an opportunity constitutes loss of First Amendment rights " 'in their most pristine and classic form.' " There is no reason why such an injury should not be compensable in damages. At the same time, however, the award must be proportional to the actual loss sustained.

The instructions given the jury in this case were improper because they did not require the jury to focus on the loss actually sustained by respondent. * * *

The Court therefore properly remands for a new trial on damages. I do not understand the Court, however, to hold that deprivations of constitutional rights can never themselves constitute compensable injuries. Such a rule would be inconsistent with the logic of *Carey*, and would defeat the purpose of § 1983 by denying compensation for genuine injuries caused by the deprivation of constitutional rights.

## *Notes*

1. Compensatory damages are usually justified as making good the losses the plaintiff has suffered because of the defendant's wrongful act, or, in other words, as placing the plaintiff in her rightful position. Compensatory damages can be divided into two categories: compensatory damages for pecuniary, or economic losses, and compensatory damages for nonpecuniary losses, such as emotional distress, pain and suffering, loss of consortium, and so on.

Justice Marshall reads the majority's opinion to allow compensatory damages for the deprivation of constitutional rights, provided the jury's award is based on the actual injury the plaintiff suffered, and not on the abstract value of the constitutional right. Indeed, the majority opinion seems to endorse this view, by citing *Hobson* with approval. But, what does it mean to say that a "deprivations of constitutional rights can themselves constitute compensable injuries"?

Doesn't the idea of compensation connote that the thing lost can be replaced by money, that an award of money will make the plaintiff whole again? Does an award of money undo the harm when a person has lost the right to vote in a particular election? If not, what is the point of awarding compensatory damages? Or, is there more to the idea of compensation than making the plaintiff whole?

Professor Radin has argued that two views of the nature of compensatory damages compete within our legal system. Margaret Jane Radin, Compensation and Commensurability, 43 Duke L.J. 56 (1993). One view she characterizes as "commodified." In that view, harm and money are commensurable, and the purpose of awarding damages is to restore the status quo.

In the competing view, harm and money are not commensurable. In that, "noncommodified view", an award of damages serves a different function: It affirms "public respect and public recognition of the transgressor's fault with regard to disrespecting rights." Could one argue that *Stachura* and, particularly, the right to vote cases confirm Professor Radin's perspective?

As you read this chapter, look for other evidence that would support, or challenge, Professor Radin's thesis.

2. What is the relationship between punitive damages and compensatory damages? As the Court noted in a different context, while compensatory damages are not retributive in the sense that punitive damages are, "compensatory damages are quintessentially backward-looking. Compensatory damages may be intended less to sanction wrongdoers than to make victims whole, but they do so by a mechanism that affects the liabilities of defendants." Landgraf v. USI Film Products, ___ U.S. ___, 114 S.Ct. 1483, 128 L.Ed.2d 229 (1994).

3. *Stachura* refers to the right to vote cases as awarding "presumed damages". According to the Court, presumed damages are fundamentally compensatory; they are awarded to compensate the plaintiff for an actual injury. The injury, however, is presumed rather than proven. The jury is allowed to award a substantial amount of money (as opposed to nominal damages) without the plaintiff having produced any evidence of actual loss. The jury determines the amount of the award by inference from the nature of the defendant's wrongdoing.

Presumed damages are most familiar in defamation suits, and in cases of intentional torts like battery and assault. In certain kinds of defamation actions (suits for libel, at least where statement was defamatory on its face, and suits for slander where the words were slanderous *per se* ), juries were allowed to award substantial damages without the plaintiff having shown that his reputation was actually harmed. Harm to the plaintiff's reputation was presumed from the defamatory character of the defendant's remarks; the jury, it was thought, could determine the amount of the harm simply from the nature of the statement. (The availability of presumed damages in defamation cases now, however, is sharply limited by first amendment concerns. Gertz v. Robert Welch, Inc., 418 U.S. 323, 94 S.Ct. 2997, 41 L.Ed.2d 789 (1974); Dun & Bradstreet Inc. v. Greenmoss Builders, Inc., 472 U.S. 749, 105 S.Ct. 2939, 86 L.Ed.2d 593 (1985)). Similarly, in cases of intentional torts like battery or assault, juries have been allowed to presume that the indignity associated with an invasion of one's person caused the plaintiff harm, even though no harm was proven. Thus, the plaintiff simply shows that he was battered, or assaulted, or libeled, and the jury, without more, may award substantial damages if it chooses.

Courts have explained presumed damages in two ways. At times, they have said that such awards are justified because when such valuable, personal rights as the right not to be assaulted or battered or the right to have one's reputation unsullied are violated, some injury certainly must have occurred, even though the plaintiff cannot prove it. Consequently, compensation is in order, even without proof of injury, according to this explanation.

At other times, courts have said simply that "damage flows from the wrongful act, itself injurious to another's right, although no perceptible loss or harm accrues therefrom." Sutherland v. Kroger Co., 144 W.Va. 673, 110 S.E.2d 716 (1959). Thus, an award of substantial damages is necessary in order to vindicate the plaintiff's rights; an award of nominal damages would not suffice, because more than a technical invasion of the plaintiff's rights is at issue. See Restatement (Second) of Torts § 905, comment d.

Which of these two explanations better fits the right to vote cases discussed in *Stachura?* If it is the latter, doesn't it come close to an award based on the "abstract" value of the rights? If "presumed damages" served to vindicate the plaintiff by declaring that his rights are substantial and must be respected, is *Stachura* rightly decided? See Jean C. Love, Damages: A Remedy for the Violation of Constitutional Rights, 67 Calif.L.Rev. 1242 (1979); Christina Whitman, Constitutional Torts, 79 Mich.L.Rev. 5 (1980). What does this add to your understanding of the purpose of compensatory damage awards?

4. *Stachura* has generated some confusion in the courts of appeals. Even in the same circuit, some cases cite *Stachura* for the blanket proposition that "[i]njury must be proved; presumed damages are not available in litigation under § 1983," Turner v. Chicago Housing Authority, 969 F.2d 461 (7th Cir.1992)(Easterbrook, J.), while others view it as authorizing presumed damages whenever a substantive constitutional right is infringed:

> [A]lthough general or, as they are sometimes called, "presumed" damages—compensatory damages awarded without proof of injury—are not recoverable in a constitutional tort suit when the only infringement of constitutional rights is a denial of due process * * * they may be recoverable when substantive constitutional rights, such as the right to freedom of speech or the right to be free from unreasonable searches and seizures are infringed. * * * So if your right to a hearing is taken away but you wouldn't have won your case had you had a hearing, you must, to get more than * * * nominal damages * * * prove some emotional harm or other specific injury * * *. But if your home is illegally invaded or you are illegally prevented from voting or speaking you can seek substantial compensatory damages without laying any proof of injury before the jury, provided that you do not ask for heavy damages on the ground that the constitutional right invaded was "important".

Hessel v. O'Hearn, 977 F.2d 299 (7th Cir.1992)(Posner, J.)

Since *Stachura,* courts have allowed presumed damages for First Amendment and Fourth Amendment violations. See Pembaur v. City of Cincinnati, 882 F.2d 1101 (6th Cir.1989)(trial court erred in awarding only nominal damages for search and seizure conducted in violation of fourth amendment); City of Watseka v. Illinois Public Action Council, 796 F.2d 1547 (7th Cir.1986)(organization unconstitutionally prevented from soliciting could recover damages both for lost revenue and for harm suffered as a result of being prevented from exercising its first amendment rights); Walje v. City of Winchester, 827 F.2d 10 (6th Cir.1987)(firefighter who was suspended for exercising his first amendment rights awarded $5000 in general damages); Piver v. Pender County Board of Education, 835 F.2d 1076, 1082 (4th Cir.1987)(substantial damages may be presumed for a violation of first amendment).

Some courts, however, stake out a middle ground, allowing presumed damages on a case-by-case basis when from the nature of the case, actual injury would be hard to prove, although it most certainly exists, but refusing to allow presumed damages as an additional item of recovery where other damages have been shown, or where, given the nature of the case, actual injury would be easy to prove if it had occurred. Lewis v. Harrison, 805 F.2d 310, 317 (8th Cir.1986)(presumed damages for violation of first amendment freedom of speech are "not for plaintiffs like Lewis, whose damages are readily measurable."); Parrish v. Johnson, 800 F.2d 600, 609 (6th Cir.1986)(general damages may not be presumed whenever the eighth amendment is violated); Gunby v. Pennsylvania Electric Co., 840 F.2d 1108, 1121 (3d Cir.1988)("The justifications that support presumed damages * * * do not apply in section 1981 and Title VII cases. Damages do not follow of course in § 1981 and Title VII cases and are easier to prove when they do.").

### *Note on Nominal Damages*

Nominal damages are a nominal or trivial sum of money (frequently one dollar) awarded to plaintiffs who have established a cause of action, but have not shown an injury for which compensatory damages can be awarded. Nominal damages are not available for every cause of action; some wrongs are not actionable unless actual injury can be proved. For example, actual injury is part of the plaintiff's prima facie case in negligence. There is, thus, no such thing as a nominal damage award in a negligence case; if the plaintiff fails to show an actual injury, she simply loses.

History has played an important role in determining whether nominal damages are available for a particular cause of action. Originally, actions descending from the writ of trespass were actionable without any showing of harm (perhaps because of their quasi-criminal character); those descending from the action on the case required a showing of damages as part of the plaintiff's prima facie case. Now, however, the pattern is considerably more complex. In fact, Professor McCormick has argued that except for negligence, slander, slander of title and perhaps fraud, "in practically all other actions for torts formerly remediable in 'case' the modern decisions seem to adopt the view that, in the absence of actual damage, the defendant's misconduct renders him liable to nominal damages." Certainly it is well-accepted that nominal damages are available where plaintiff proves a breach of contract, and contract is clearly descended from the action on the case. Charles McCormick, Handbook on the Law of Damages 89 (1935). For a thorough discussion, and an attempt to formulate a new rule, see Nappe v. Anschelewitz, Barr, Ansell & Bonello, 97 N.J. 37, 477 A.2d 1224 (1984)(nominal damages are available for all intentional torts, at least where the victim has suffered some injury but cannot prove an entitlement to compensatory damages).

At early common law, wrongs were actionable without any showing of injury because tort law and criminal law overlapped: Sanctioning the defendant's conduct was the primary purpose of the action. Even where the plaintiff had not been injured, the peace had been broken. Nominal damage awards also served a purpose now served by declaratory judgment awards. A plaintiff could sue for nominal damages in order to obtain a definitive adjudication of his rights, which was useful particularly with regard to trespass to land. By suing for trespass, even where no harm had yet occurred, the boundaries of the plaintiff's land could be established, and defendants prevented from acquiring prescriptive rights.

Nominal damages also allowed courts to provide at least some remedy to plaintiffs whose cases failed for a simple lack of proof. If the plaintiff had tried to show damages and failed to persuade the jury, an award of nominal damages allowed the court to require the defendant to pay the plaintiff's costs and, where authorized by statute, plaintiff's attorney fees. Thus, an award of nominal damages also qualifies the plaintiff as a "prevailing party" entitled to attorney fees in cases to which the Civil Rights Attorney's Fees Award Act of 1976, 42 U.S.C. § 1988, applies, although the plaintiff's relative lack of success can be taken into account in determining the amount of the award. Farrar v. Hobby, 506 U.S. 103, 113 S.Ct. 566, 121 L.Ed.2d 494 (1992)(reproduced infra at p. 834). In some courts, an award of nominal damages can serve as the basis for a punitive damage award, although most courts require the plaintiff to show actual injury in order to recover punitive damages. See Nappe v. Anschelewitz, Barr, Ansell & Bonello, 97 N.J. 37, 477 A.2d 1224 (1984).

Thus, the practical significance of nominal damage awards has always been thought to be limited to two sorts of cases: cases where the plaintiff is really after a sort of declaratory judgment, and cases where the plaintiff simply could not persuade the jury to award substantial damages. As for the first category of cases, an action for declaratory judgment now achieves the same purpose. As for the second category, given the crush of litigation that courts (allegedly) now face, isn't it right that a plaintiff who can't prove damages should go away empty-handed? Why not eliminate nominal damage awards altogether?

### *Note on Monetary Relief in Law and Equity*

In the brief quotation at the beginning of this chapter, Professor McCormick describes one of the salient characteristics of the damage award: it is a legal, as opposed to an equitable remedy. As you have seen, the equity courts sought to give a claimant *specific* relief, by undoing the harm that occurred or preventing it from happening in the first place. By contrast, the law courts relied on a *substitutionary* remedy, offering to cure the injury by offering recompense in money.

Of course, the law courts sometimes granted specific relief. Someone whose personal property had been taken, for example, could post a bond and get a writ of replevin from the law courts, which would instruct the person executing the writ to seize the property and return it. The writ of ejectment could give a landowner possession of his property. The writ of habeas corpus could release a party from confinement.

Conversely, equity courts sometimes awarded compensatory, monetary relief. If a claimant sought specific performance of an obligation to pay money, and the legal remedy was inadequate, an equity court would order the money paid. Or, if an injunction had issued, and an additional award of money for past harm could dispose of the case completely, an equity court could order monetary relief under its "clean up jurisdiction." Then, there were cases in which the claimant simply had no cause of action at all in the law courts, such as cases involving trust or mortgages, leaving all remedies up to the equity courts.

In cases like these, whether the relief sought should be characterized as legal or equitable turns on how the court's order would be enforced. Equity courts ordered defendants, personally, to act, and enforced their orders by their contempt power. Law courts relied on separate administrative proceedings to enforce their judgments. Thus, if the defendant failed to pay a money judgment, the plaintiff had to initiate separate proceedings to enforce the judgment, *garnishing* the defendant's wages, or *executing* against her property, for example. Even writs were executed by a sheriff or another administrative officer, who took possession of the property or person in question from the defendant and restored it to the plaintiff. Execution, garnishment, and other post-judgment remedies are considered further in chapter 8.

Although only a few jurisdictions still maintain separate equity or chancery courts, there are reasons why it is still important to understand the circumstances under which equity courts would order "equitable monetary relief." One, discussed in some detail below, is that the right to a jury trial may turn on the characterization of the remedy. Another is Congress's penchant for authorizing courts to grant "appropriate equitable relief" when a statute has been violated. Then, whether courts of equity could award a particular remedy becomes a critical question.

Such an issue surfaced in the Supreme Court's opinion in Mertens v. Hewitt Associates, 508 U.S. 248, 113 S.Ct. 2063, 124 L.Ed.2d 161 (1993). In *Mertens*, beneficiaries of a pension plan alleged that an actuary's wrongdoing caused their pension plan to be underfunded. They sued under a federal statute, the Employee Retirement Income Security Act (ERISA), which provides that a plan beneficiary may bring a civil action:

> "(A) to enjoin any act or practice which violates any provision of [ERISA] or the terms of the plan, or (B) *to obtain other appropriate equitable relief* (i) to redress such violations or (ii) to enforce any provisions of [ERISA] or the terms of the plan. . . ."

§ 502(a)(3), 29 U.S.C. § 1132(a)(3)(emphasis added).

The beneficiaries argued that equity courts routinely awarded compensatory monetary relief against nonfiduciaries who participated in a fiduciary breach; therefore, Congress must have intended to authorize monetary relief against nonfiduciaries when it empowered the courts to award "appropriate equitable relief."

While the Court conceded that equity courts routinely awarded monetary damages in breach of trust cases, the Court held that the phrase "appropriate equitable relief" should be read more narrowly. In other sections of the statute, Congress had authorized courts to award "legal *or* equitable relief"; in § 502(a)(3), Congress authorized only equitable relief. Therefore, the Court reasoned, Congress must have intended to maintain a distinction between actions in which both legal and equitable remedies were to be available, and actions in which only equitable remedies were to be available. To allow damages, the prototypical legal remedy, in an action in which the statute authorized only equitable remedies would obliterate the distinction. Therefore, the Court held, in using the phrase "appropriate equitable relief" Congress must have intended to refer to "those categories of relief that were *typically* available in equity (such as injunction, mandamus, and restitution, but not compensatory damages)." 113 S.Ct. at 2063.

The dispute in *Mertens* came down to semantics: Are compensatory damages to be thought of as a fundamentally legal remedy, even if, historically, equity courts sometimes awarded them? Given the frequency with which Congress has authorized "appropriate equitable relief," the issue is not an isolated one. In other contexts, the Court has taken a fairly expansive view of the equitable power of a court to award monetary relief in order to make the plaintiff whole. See, e.g., School Comm. of Burlington v. Department of Education of Mass., 471 U.S. 359, 369, 105 S.Ct. 1996, 2002, 85 L.Ed.2d 385 (1985)(grant of equitable authority in Individuals with Disabilities Education Act empowers a court to order school authorities to reimburse parents for their expenditures on private special education); Porter v. Warner Holding Co., 328 U.S. 395, 66 S.Ct. 1086, 90 L.Ed. 1332 (1946)(power to order restitution of rents collected in violation of the Emergency Price Control Act is inherent in the court's equitable power); Mitchell v. Robert De Mario Jewelry, Inc., 361 U.S. 288, 80 S.Ct. 332, 4 L.Ed.2d 323 (1960)(power to enjoin discrimination in employment under the Fair Labor Standards Act includes the power to order reimbursement of wages lost because of the discrimination).

Whether an award of money is characterized as damages or as equitable monetary relief can make a difference in other contexts as well. It can determine whether a suit seeking reimbursement of moneys owed under a statute is a claim "seeking relief other than money damages," over which the district courts have jurisdiction. Bowen v. Massachusetts, 487 U.S. 879, 108 S.Ct. 2722, 101 L.Ed.2d 749 (1988). An award of damages may include compensation for emotional distress or punitive damages; equitable monetary relief may be limited to reimbursing actual, monetary losses. Howard v. Lockheed–Georgia Co., 372 F.Supp. 854 (N.D.Ga.1974). And, while an award of damages "flows as a matter of course from a finding of wrongdoing," equitable monetary relief lies in the court's discretion, and can be refused if an award would be inequitable. Thus, where a plaintiff has a choice between pursuing a legal cause of action or an equitable one, the choice may have important consequences.

### *Note on the Right to a Jury Trial*

One of the most important consequences of characterizing a remedy as legal or equitable is that the characterization may determine whether there is a right to a jury trial. The Seventh Amendment preserves the right to a jury trial "[i]n suits at common law, where the value in controversy shall exceed twenty dollars." The right extends beyond the common law forms of action, however; the phrase "suits at common law" includes any suit in which legal, as opposed to equitable, rights are at issue. Parsons v. Bedford, 28 U.S. (3 Pet.) 433, 447, 7 L.Ed. 732 (1830). The right to a jury trial applies even to causes of action created by Congress, if the cause of action is analogous to a suit at common law. Tull v. United States, 481 U.S. 412, 417, 107 S.Ct. 1831, 1835, 95 L.Ed.2d 365 (1987).

There are two questions to be considered in deciding whether there is a right to a jury trial under a particular statute: Are the rights analogous to common law rights, and is the remedy sought legal or equitable in nature? Chauffeurs, Teamsters and Helpers Local No. 391 v. Terry, 494 U.S. 558, 110 S.Ct. 1339, 108 L.Ed.2d 519 (1990). Of the two questions, the nature of the remedy is the more important. Granfinanciera S.A. v. Nordberg, 492 U.S. 33, 109 S.Ct. 2782, 106 L.Ed.2d 26 (1989).

To illustrate the Court's approach to the jury trial question, in *Terry* the question was whether employees suing their union for failing to represent them had a right to a jury trial. The right to representation was a creature of statute, specifically § 301 of the National Labor Relations Act, unknown at common law. The Court struggled in its search for an analogous action. Writing for a plurality, Justice Marshall noted that the duty of fair representation is a fiduciary duty, and that the action was somewhat analogous to an equitable action for breach of trust. Yet, to show that the union had failed in its duty to enforce the labor agreement, the employees would first need to show that the employer had breached it. Therefore, the action was a hybrid, part legal—breach of contract—and part equitable—breach of fiduciary duty—in nature. (Justice Stevens thought the action more comparable to a legal malpractice claim, the three dissenting Justices thought the similarity to the equitable trust action was dispositive, and Justice Brennan thought the analysis should focus exclusively on the nature of the remedy sought, which he thought was legal in this case.)

As for the character of the remedy, Justice Marshall—writing for a majority of the Court on this point—concluded that the remedy sought, back pay and benefits, was essentially equivalent to compensatory damages. Because compensatory damages represented the traditional form of relief offered in courts of law, a jury trial was required. While monetary relief might be characterized as equitable where it is "restitutionary, such as in actions for disgorgement of improper profits," or where it is "incidental to or intertwined with injunctive relief," neither exception was applicable in *Terry*. Therefore, as the issues in the case were neither clearly equitable nor clearly legal, the legal character of the relief sought was controlling, and the plaintiffs had a right to a jury trial.

In passing, the *Terry* Court noted that the circuit courts have agreed that plaintiffs alleging racial or sexual discrimination in employment and seeking backpay under Title VII, however, have no right to a jury trial. The Court pointed out that in Title VII, Congress specifically characterized back pay as equitable relief ("The court may order ... reinstatement ... with or without back pay ..., or any other equitable relief" 42 U.S.C. § 2000e–5(g)), and that in a discrimination case, backpay is generally restitutionary in nature. 110 S.Ct. at 1349. Therefore, the Court felt the remedy sought in *Terry* was "clearly different from backpay sought for violations of Title VII." *Id.* Since the decision in *Terry*, the Civil Rights Act of 1991 has made compensatory damages and punitive damages available in Title VII and ADEA actions, and provides for a jury trial when those damages are sought. 42 U.S.C. §§ 1981a(a),(c).

To test your understanding of all this, suppose an employee argues that she was fired in retaliation for attempting to enforce her right to certain pension benefits, which would violate § 510 of ERISA, and entitle her to a remedy under § 502(a)(3), the provision discussed in *Mertens*, above. Because ERISA has been held to preempt state tort actions for wrongful discharge, she brings her suit in federal court, seeking back pay, reinstatement, and punitive damages. If she proves her case, are these remedies available? She also asks for a jury trial. Should a jury trial be granted? For a discussion of some of the issues involved, see Spinelli v. Gaughan, 12 F.3d 853 (9th Cir.1993).

## B. THE BASIC ISSUES

### CHARLES MCCORMICK, HANDBOOK ON THE LAW OF DAMAGES

2–3 (1935).

What is included in the subject of Damages? In answering this inquiry, it will be helpful to single out certain typical problems arising in a claim for damages,[1] and to consider which of these are embraced in our subject. First, the lawyer to whom is presented such a claim will consider whether the claim is enforceable at all, or, in legal parlance, whether there is a "cause of action." Examples of the matters considered here are such questions as whether an alleged contract is founded on a valid consideration, whether a trespasser on another's land can recover for injuries caused by a dangerous situation there existing, or whether a statute purporting to give a right to sue for losses sustained

1. It is well to notice at the outset that the term "damage" is usually employed by lawyers and judges to mean the loss or injury from which the claim is asserted. "Damages," on the other hand, while sometimes used in the same sense, is more usually and conveniently limited to the meaning of the money award given as compensation for the loss.

by one who has purchased shares of stock is constitutional. Similar in effect are all the questions relating to whether a good defense is available to the whole claim, such as the questions of release, accord and satisfaction, and contributory negligence. Needless to say, all of these matters comprised in our first group, although they determine decisively whether a given claim for damages can be successfully maintained, are outside the subject of Damages itself, as the term is traditionally used to mark off a special subject in the law.

A second inquiry which the lawyer investigating his client's claim for damages would frequently make, is this: What are the *elements* or items of the client's loss, injury, or grievance which will be recognized by the court as grounds of compensation? Will allowance be made, for example, in a contract case for disappointment due to the failure of the bargain; or, in an action for personal injury, can expense of nursing be recovered? Third, and closely allied to the last, is the inquiry: What formula of *measurement* is to be used in fixing compensation for the element or elements of loss which are recognized? The choice here may be between standards of value, e.g., whether the value of some property wrongfully appropriated shall be the market value or the value in use, or the value at the time of taking or the time of trial. Again, the standard may be one of reasonable and necessary expenditure, or the measure may be fixed, as in case of liquidated damages, by agreement of the parties. A fourth avenue of inquiry is the ascertainment of the general rules, standards, and doctrines which place *limits* upon the application of the formulas of compensation to the recognized elements. Chief among these are the requirements of certainty, and of foreseeability either at the time of the making of a contract, or as of the time of the commission of a wrong. Fifth, in examining the claim, the lawyer must inquire into the procedural rules which regulate the manner in which he can best plead and prove the elements of loss or injury, the fashion in which the judge should state the problem of compensation to the jury, and the standards to be used by the trial and appellate judges in reviewing the jury's award.

¶

### Notes

1. *What is the plaintiff's cause of action?* Although Professor McCormick is correct that the existence of a cause of action is outside the subject of damages proper, the plaintiff's cause of action is nonetheless the starting point for determining what damages are available. The purpose of any remedy, after all, is to protect the rightful position, and the rightful position is defined by the substantive law.

In tort cases, the rightful position is usually defined as the *status quo ante,* and the purpose of the damage award is to give the plaintiff a sum of money that will place him in the position he occupied before the tort. In contract cases, the rightful position is usually defined as "the benefit of the bargain", and the damage award aims to place the plaintiff in the position he would have occupied had the contract been performed.

These two goals can be stated in a way that makes them seem perfectly consistent—the plaintiff in either event must be placed in the position he would have occupied had there been no tort/no breach—but there is a tension between them. The tort remedy looks backwards, to the plaintiff's pre-tort position, while the contract remedy looks ahead, and "restores" to the plaintiff a benefit that he expected to get in the future, but never in fact possessed. While in many cases the damages will be the same whether the plaintiff sues in tort or contract, and while in others only one theory may in fact be available, in many cases the plaintiff may have a choice, and that choice may affect the size of the award drastically.

Further, the goal in both tort and contract cases differs from the goal in restitution cases. The goal of the substantive law of restitution is to prevent unjust enrichment by stripping the defendant of unfairly made gains, thereby "restoring" to the plaintiff that which he neither lost nor expected to gain. Again, the size of the plaintiff's recovery may turn on the choice to pursue a cause of action in restitution instead of tort or contract.

Beyond the practical concern of choosing the cause of action that best serves the client's interests, this tension between tort, contract and restitution also raises important normative issues. That is, on particular facts, *should* an injured party be allowed to pursue restitution or compensation, tort compensation or contract compensation? Usually, this normative question is framed as a question of substantive law: Do the facts at hand state a cause of action in tort, in contract, or for restitution? Yet, the decision to allow a cause of action in contract, but not in tort, or for restitution but not for breach of contract, really only matters because it affects the remedy, the amount that can be recovered. Therefore, the remedies course offers the perfect vantage to look back at the substantive law of torts, contracts, and restitution and ask, why one and not the other?

2. *What elements of damages are recoverable?* In speaking of the elements of damage that are recoverable, Professor McCormick had in mind the various elements that make up the compensatory damage award. As a preliminary step, however, the lawyer investigating a damage claim should examine what other kinds of damages are available. If she cannot show actual loss, will nominal damages be recoverable? Are punitive damages a possibility?

Turning to compensatory damages, after the cause of action has been determined, you can begin to zero in on the elements of damages that may be recoverable. For starters, the client usually will have a very clear idea of what losses he wants to recoup. These obvious losses, however, are only a beginning. Think about the client's position. If it is a contract case, how would he have been better off if the contract had been performed? What would he have had then that he does not have now? In a tort case, where would the plaintiff be if the tort had never occurred? What would he have that he does not have now? What injuries would he have avoided? Conversely, what opportunities for gain have his injuries forced him to forgo? If the legal theory is restitution, how has the defendant profited? There is much room for creativity in building the case for damages; frequently, a little thought will reveal losses that were not at first apparent.

The next step is to look to the case law to determine which of these losses are compensable, that is, which is a proper element of damages for the plaintiff's cause of action. Here, an important distinction has developed in the cases between two categories of damages—general damages and special damages. *General damages* are defined as those damages which usually or naturally flow from the defendant's wrongful act. *Special damages,* by contrast, are peculiar to the particular plaintiff's circumstances. For example, if the defendant were held liable for destroying the plaintiff's car, the general damages would be the value of the car: any time property is destroyed, its value is lost. If the plaintiff, however, lost his job because without a car he was late for work, damages to compensate him for the loss of his job would be recoverable only as special damages, if at all. That loss is peculiar to his particular circumstances; it does not "naturally" flow from the destruction of a car.

In many cases, general damages will adequately compensate the plaintiff; after all, general damages evolved because those losses were the ones most frequently experienced. General damages, however, are not always an accurate measure of actual loss. In particular cases, general damages may over- or undercompensate the plaintiff. General damages may overcompensate the plaintiff because they are available automatically, without regard for the plaintiff's actual losses. For example, if defendant reneges on a contract to purchase plaintiff's house, plaintiff is entitled to damages measured by the difference between the contract price and the house's market value, even though the plaintiff has changed her mind and is glad she did not have to sell it.

More frequently, however, general damages will undercompensate the plaintiff, because the plaintiff has suffered losses peculiar to her own circumstances, and thus not included in the general damages. Returning to the example, the plaintiff who has lost her job because her car was destroyed will be undercompensated if she is limited to recovering the market value of the car. Thus, for her, the critical step will be to determine if the loss of her job is compensable as *special damages.* Whether special damages are recoverable turns on the application of the doctrines of foreseeability, certainty, and avoidable consequences, discussed below.

3. *How are the damages to be measured?* Nominal damages, for obvious reasons, do not present much of a measurement problem. As for punitive damages, the standards for measuring them have been discussed in chapter 5.

In measuring compensatory damages, at least where pecuniary losses are concerned, the central concept is that of value. The problem is, value can be measured in many ways. Professor McCormick lists just a few of the possibilities: value may mean market value, or it may mean value in use; it may mean value at the time of trial, or value at the time of the defendant's wrongdoing. The rules that dictate how to measure value, and the policies that explain them, are explored further in the materials that follow.

The concept of value is of no help, however, when compensatory damages are to be awarded for nonpecuniary losses; there is no marketplace to which one can turn to determine the "value" of pain, suffering, humiliation or distress. For this, courts simply turn to the jury, allowing the jury to determine the size of the award based upon evidence of the nature and circumstances of the defendant's wrong and its effect on the plaintiff.

4. *Is the plaintiff's recovery to be limited because his losses were unforeseeable, uncertain, avoidable, offset by benefits, or limited by agreement?*

a. *Was the loss foreseeable?* As we have seen, plaintiffs may be undercompensated if they are limited to general damages and cannot recover their particular, individualized losses as special damages. The most significant barrier to recovering a particular element of loss as special damages is the requirement that damages must be foreseeable before they can be recovered. General damages are foreseeable by definition, because they are naturally expected to flow from the defendant's act. Special damages are another matter. Before any particular element of special damages can be recovered, foreseeability must be established on the facts of the particular case.

b. *Are the plaintiff's losses reasonably certain?* The plaintiff must also prove the amount of her losses with reasonable certainty. The certainty requirement has two aspects. The first overlaps with the substantive law of causation: The plaintiff must show that it is reasonably certain (or probable) that she has suffered a loss because of the defendant's conduct. The second aspect is evidentiary: Once the fact of loss is established, she then must provide the jury with evidence from which the amount of her loss can be established with "reasonable certainty." Courts are wont to say that if the existence of a loss is clearly shown, the plaintiff must merely provide the jury with the best evidence reasonably available of the amount. So long as it is certain that the plaintiff has actually suffered a loss, the certainty rule simply requires her to provide some evidence from which the jury can make a reasonable, non-speculative estimate of the amount of her damages.

c. *Could the plaintiff, by her own actions, reasonably have avoided or limited the loss she suffered?* The plaintiff may not recover damages for any losses that could reasonably have been avoided. This rule requires the plaintiff to mitigate her damages by taking steps to limit the harm she suffers. Thus, if the defendant has wrongfully caused the plaintiff to lose her job, the plaintiff must make a reasonable effort to find other, similar work if she wishes to claim lost wages. If the plaintiff is physically injured, she will not recover damages for any aggravation of the injury that medical care reasonably available to her could have avoided. Although the avoidable consequences rule may often function to limit the plaintiff's recovery, it has a positive aspect as well. Any expenses incurred by the plaintiff in a reasonable attempt to mitigate her losses are recoverable as damages.

d. *Were the plaintiff's losses offset by benefits?* If the defendant's conduct has caused harm to the plaintiff, but at the same time has conferred a benefit on the plaintiff, under appropriate circumstances the plaintiff's recovery must be reduced by the amount of the benefit she has received. Of course, difficult issues can arise as to whether the benefit was really conferred by the defendant's wrongdoing, or whether the plaintiff would have gained the benefit in any event.

e. *Did the plaintiff agree that the defendant's liability would be limited?* Agreements may limit the plaintiff's recovery in a number of ways. In tort cases, the plaintiff may have agreed in advance to waive her right to sue, or to release the defendant from liability, or the plaintiff may have signed a release after the injury occurred. The validity and effect of releases, however, traditionally has been thought of as a matter of substantive law, and left to the torts class. In contract cases, the contract between the parties may include a limitation of liability for consequential damages, or a liquidated damages clause. Ultimately, whether such clauses are enforceable is probably also better thought of as a question of substantive law. It has, however, traditionally been included in the remedies course, so it is discussed in this chapter.

5. *How is the plaintiff's claim to be presented at trial?* One might expect damages to be the one area of the law where something approaching mathematical certainty could be achieved, with each loss tallied up and measured in accordance with generally accepted accounting principles. That expectation could hardly be farther from the truth. As Professor McCormick points out, damages are peculiarly the domain of the jury. The early practice, in fact, was for the jury to hear evidence as to all the items of loss, and simply return a verdict stating the total amount of their judgment, often not even differentiating between compensatory and punitive damages. Even the idea of giving the jury instructions as to the measure of damages is a relatively recent development, dating to the 1850's.

Modern practice at least requires the jury to differentiate between punitive and compensatory damages, and the growing fondness for the special verdict has resulted in the more frequent practice of having juries itemize various elements of the plaintiff's recovery. Still, general verdicts are common, and where damages are unliquidated and disputed, the amount of the award remains the jury's province. Except in rare cases, how the jury calculates any particular item of loss is beyond the ken of all but the jurors themselves.

After the award has been announced, the trial court's review is quite limited. It can act only if an error of law has been committed (as, for example, where the jury has awarded damages for a loss that, as a matter of law, is not compensable) or if the verdict is grossly excessive or inadequate. To reject a jury verdict as excessive, the court must be convinced that the verdict is so large that it must have been the result of passion or prejudice. The standard for review of a verdict for inadequacy is less well established, but an inadequate award can be rejected if the jury's verdict is completely unsupported by the evidence. On appeal, review of the amount of damage awards is even more constrained, if that is possible. An appellate court will act only where the trial court, in rejecting a verdict or in letting it stand, has abused its discretion.

If the trial court is convinced that the jury has erred seriously enough to justify interfering with its traditional prerogative to assess damages, the judge has two options. He can simply order a new trial. Or, he can set the amount of damages himself, giving the parties the option of accepting the new amount or having a new trial. When the judge decides that a verdict is excessive and offers the plaintiff the choice of a lesser amount or a new trial, it is called remittitur. When the verdict is thought inadequate, and the defendant is offered the choice of accepting a larger verdict or a new trial, it is called additur.

Both remittitur and additur threaten the right of the parties to a jury trial, because the risk and expense of a new trial coerce the party into accepting the judge's opinion on damages over the jury's. Remittitur, however, was known at common law, and because the Seventh Amendment guarantees only the right to jury as it existed at common law, the United States Supreme Court has found it constitutional. Additur, however, was unknown at common law, and so in the federal system it has been held unconstitutional. It is still available, though, in many state court systems.

Given the court's limited power over damage awards once the jury has spoken, rules evolved to provide some control over the jury during the trial. Some of these rules, like the rules concerning foreseeability, certainty and avoidability, allow the court to exclude particular items of loss altogether. The rest control the jury by limiting the evidence brought before them through rules of proof and pleading, or by providing the jury with instructions that give the formulae by which losses are to be measured.

The rules of pleading and proof, like the requirements of foreseeability and certainty, favor general damages over special damages. General damages do not need to be alleged in the complaint in order to be recovered. Because general damages "naturally flow" from the defendant's acts, the defendant should be on notice that they will be at issue even if they are not alleged.

So, when a buyer pleads that a seller has breached a contract for the sale of goods, the buyer can recover as general damages the "benefit of the bargain" (the difference between the market value of the goods and the contract price), whether or not that loss is alleged in the complaint. If, however, the plaintiff also wants to recover damages for injury to his business reputation (hoping to persuade the jury that his business reputation was injured by his inability to maintain his inventory), that item of special damages would have to be specifically alleged. Or if the plaintiff alleges that his car has been wrongfully destroyed, he can recover general damages (the value of the car) without alleging it specifically in the complaint. If the lack of a car caused him to miss work, he would have to allege lost wages specifically.

With personal injury cases, the rules of pleading are more complex. First, damages for pain and suffering are general damages, and do not need to be alleged in order to be recovered. Beyond that, whether a particular loss needs to be alleged turns on the extent to which the injury as described in the complaint gives notice of the harm the plaintiff suffered. For example, if the plaintiff alleges that she suffered a blow to the eye, she would no doubt be allowed to prove at trial that her vision was affected, and to recover damages for that injury without having specifically alleged it. If, however, she alleged a blow to the head, and then sought to prove a loss of vision, the evidence might not be admitted on the grounds that the complaint did not give notice that her vision was at issue. In either event, if she sought to recover damages for past or future earnings, because her eyesight was critical to her work, most courts would say this was an item of special damages and needed to be specifically alleged.

Turning to matters of proof, with the exception of two categories of cases, the rules for the proof of general and special damages are the same. The plaintiff bears the burden of proving the amount of her losses with reasonable certainty. The plaintiff who seeks the benefit of her bargain must show the market value of the goods, or land, or services promised to her. The plaintiff who seeks lost earnings must prove what she would have earned had she not been injured.

In two categories of cases, "general damages" has taken on a special meaning, allowing plaintiffs to recover damages without either pleading or proving them. In some cases, general damages are synonymous with presumed damages, and plaintiffs have been allowed to recover substantial sums to compensate them for batteries, assaults and the like, without any proof of loss. Somewhat similarly, in personal injury cases, juries have been allowed to assess pain and suffering damages on the basis of their knowledge of the injury suffered, without any direct evidence of pain and suffering. The plaintiff who suffers a broken arm may recover damages for pain and suffering without either alleging or proving them. The evidence of the broken arm itself gives the jury enough to go on.

The overriding impression left by the cases on pleading and proving damages is that these rules evolved to rescue lawyers who prepared well to prove liability, but gave no thought to damages until the trial of the case was actually underway. The lesson they teach is that a damages case should be carefully planned, beginning even before the complaint is filed. The lawyer who relies on the judge to admit evidence of an injury that was insufficiently alleged, or who allows the jury to award damages without evidence of the size of the loss risks subjecting her client to a lottery (and herself to a malpractice suit). To represent a client's best interest, counsel should plan the damages side of a case from day one. If the client's losses have been itemized, the theory of liability selected with the type of loss in mind, the evidence gathered to substantiate them, and the conduct of the trial planned with an eye toward proving damages, remembering to allege the various elements of loss and to offer proof will be the least of the plaintiff's problems.

Anticipating the damages that will be claimed is also critical for defense counsel. If the plaintiff's damage claims are anticipated, a litigation strategy can be devised to minimize them. Evidence can be gathered to challenge the plaintiff's claims; arguments that the plaintiff's losses were unforeseeable or uncertain can be developed; the lack of attempts to mitigate the loss can be documented. Neither side can afford to make damages an afterthought.

### *Problem: Country Lodge v. Miller (Reprised)* *The Damages Option*

Review the facts in Country Lodge v. Miller, set out in chapter 1. Suppose that when Miller began her operations, the owners of Country Lodge threatened to sue for an injunction prohibiting construction of the cider mill on the grounds that it might pollute the river. The owners of Country Lodge refrained from suing when Miller wrote them a letter that said:

"We do not believe that our cider press will cause any negative environmental impact. Indeed, we share your belief that the river's integrity must be protected. If you allow construction to go forward, we will take whatever steps are reasonably necessary to protect the interest we all share in keeping our river pristine."

Using the five inquiries identified by Professor McCormick, plan litigation strategies to maximize/minimize Country Lodge's damages. If Country Lodge is not successful in obtaining an injunction, but does prove that Miller is liable for the pollution, what damages should Country Lodge recover? If Country Lodge does obtain an injunction, should damages also be awarded?

### *Note on Election of Remedies*

Many remedies may potentially be available when a person is injured, as your analysis of the above variation on the Country Lodge problem probably suggests. Beyond the basic choice between legal and equitable remedies, tort remedies, contract remedies, restitutionary remedies, even statutory remedies may coalesce in a single set of facts.

When multiple remedies are possible, the doctrine of "election of remedies" may come into play. The traditional formulation of the doctrine had two parts: 1) A plaintiff who has two (or more) remedies concurrently available to her must choose between those remedies if they are inconsistent; and 2) Once a plaintiff has clearly elected a remedy, he or she is bound by that choice.

This traditional formulation of the rule could work harsh results. For example, the doctrine of election of remedies could put a plaintiff whose property had been converted to a very difficult choice: He could try to retrieve the property by a writ of replevin, but, having elected his remedy, he might not then be allowed to sue for consequential damages for the loss of his property's use. Or, he could sue for damages, but if the defendant turned out to be have no assets to satisfy the judgment, he might be unable to get his stolen property back, having elected damages as his remedy.

Such a result might have made sense in a legal system that placed a high value on precise pleadings that narrowed the case to a single issue for trial. It seems ludicrous in the modern system of notice pleading, in which multiple causes of action and liberal amendment are commonplace. Thus, modern courts have sharply curtailed and simplified the election of remedies doctrine.

So far as the first prong of the election doctrine is concerned, modern courts have shifted the emphasis from whether the remedies are different in form to asking whether allowing both remedies will result in double recovery, or overcompensation. The cases now recognize that there is no reason not to allow a plaintiff to recover the specific property taken and also to recover damages for loss of the property's use. On the other hand, if allowing two remedies would put the plaintiff in better than the rightful position, clearly a choice must be made. Country Lodge, for example, cannot get both an injunction prohibiting Miller from dumping in the river in the future, and at the same time recover damages based on the harm from future dumping.

The second prong of the traditional doctrine had to do with the timing of the choice. If a plaintiff indicated, by his pleadings or even by his actions, that he intended to pursue a particular remedy, he might be bound by that choice, and precluded from pursuing an alternative, inconsistent remedy. This insistence that a plaintiff had to stick with his first choice of remedy also could work harshly, by forcing plaintiffs to commit themselves to a remedy long before all the facts were in, or by interpreting acts that were not intended as a choice of remedy as manifesting an election.

Again, the modern cases have substantially reinterpreted the rule, this time by emphasizing that the timing of the plaintiff's choice is relevant only to the extent that the choice—or the failure to choose—may harm the defendant. Effectively, this aspect of the doctrine of election of remedies is a variation on the doctrine of estoppel. If the plaintiff indicates that he will pursue one remedy, and it would prejudice the defendant to allow the plaintiff to change his mind, the court may find that the plaintiff has elected his remedy. Or, if the plaintiff has not chosen, and the defendant is prejudiced by the delay, the court may put plaintiff to the choice, or choose for him in a way that will minimize the harm. If there is no harm to the defendant, however, there is no reason not to allow the plaintiff to pursue as many remedies as he wishes, even adding new theories up to the time of trial, so long as the pleading rules allow it.

Finally, the modern cases recognize that rules of res judicata and satisfaction of judgments may be involved in election of remedies cases. Where the plaintiff's case has gone to judgment, and the plaintiff has lost, res judicata usually prevents him from bringing the same suit on a different legal theory, seeking a different remedy. Similarly, if the plaintiff has had a judgment, the rule that a judgment may be satisfied only once prevents him from suing again, on a different legal theory, for a recovery that is essentially duplicative.

On the other hand, suppose the plaintiff has won on the merits, only to discover that the remedy sought is ineffective. To return to an earlier example, suppose he sued for damages for conversion, only to discover the defendant had no assets. Is there any reason he should not be allowed to return to court and seek the return of the specific property taken, if the defendant still has it? Once it is understood that the operation of the election of remedies doctrine on these facts really has to do with preserving the finality of judgments, it becomes apparent that the same rules pertaining to modification of judgments that were studied in chapter 3 ought simply to be applied here.

Election of remedies problems arise most frequently in cases involving deals gone sour, cases in which the plaintiff may have a choice between going ahead with the deal and suing later for damages, or calling the deal off and demanding damages or restitution. Notes following the cases on breach of contract and restitution in chapter 7 explore restitutionary remedies in greater detail. For now, the contours of the modern doctrine of election of remedies can be sketched quickly:

1) So far as pleading goes, a plaintiff may allege as many legal theories and alternative remedies as the facts will support, whether or not they are inconsistent.

2) Most courts now recognize that there is no reason to require a plaintiff to elect among remedies prior to trial, unless failing to elect would harm the defendant.

3) While it is not nearly so important now as it once was that the plaintiff not act in a way that is inconsistent with remedies he may later want to pursue, plaintiffs must still be careful not to indicate that they are pursuing a particular remedy if they might later want to change their minds. If changing their minds prejudices the defendant, they may be stuck with their first choice.

4) Plaintiffs may generally now combine different forms of remedy—legal and equitable, damages and restitution—so long as the combination does not result in double recovery or overcompensation.

5) Once a judgment is entered, rules of res judicata and satisfaction of judgments may preclude seeking additional or alternative remedies, unless changed circumstances justify modifying the judgment.

## C. AN OVERVIEW OF TORT DAMAGES

The case that follows gives an overview of the issues that arise in a tort case where damages are the primary remedy sought. The rest of the cases in this section address those issues in greater detail, and are organized to track the five inquiries identified by Professor McCormick, in section B.

### AYERS v. JACKSON TOWNSHIP

Supreme Court of New Jersey, 1987.
106 N.J. 557, 525 A.2d 287.

STEIN, JUSTICE.

In this case we consider the application of the New Jersey Tort Claims Act (the Act), N.J.S.A. 59:1–1 to 12–3, to the claims asserted by 339 residents of Jackson Township against that municipality.

The litigation involves claims for damages sustained because plaintiffs' well water was contaminated by toxic pollutants leaching into the Cohansey Aquifer from a landfill established and operated by Jackson Township. After an extensive trial, the jury found that the township had created a "nuisance" and a "dangerous condition" by virtue of its operation of the landfill, that its conduct was "palpably unreasonable,"—a prerequisite to recovery under N.J.S.A. 59:4–2—and that it was the proximate cause of the contamination of plaintiffs' water supply. The jury verdict resulted in an aggregate judgment of $15,854,392.78, to be divided among the plaintiffs in varying amounts. The jury returned individual awards for each of the plaintiffs that varied in accordance with such factors as proximity to the landfill, duration and extent of the exposure to contaminants, and the age of the claimant.

The verdict provided compensation for three distinct claims of injury: $2,056,480 was awarded for emotional distress caused by the knowledge that they had ingested water contaminated by toxic chemicals for up to six years; $5,396,940 was awarded for the deterioration of their quality of life during the twenty months when they were deprived of running water; and $8,204,500 was awarded to cover the future cost of annual medical surveillance that plaintiffs' expert testified would be necessary because of plaintiffs' increased susceptibility to cancer and other diseases. * * *

I

* * * A substantial number—more than 150—of the plaintiffs gave testimony with respect to damages, describing in detail the impairment of their quality of life during the period that they were without running water, and the emotional distress they suffered. With regard to the emotional distress claims, the plaintiffs' testimony detailed their emotional reactions to the chemical contamination of their wells and the deprivation of their water supply, as well as their fears for the health of their family members. Expert psychological testimony was offered to document plaintiffs' claims that they had sustained compensable psychological damage as a result of the contamination of their wells.

We now consider each of the plaintiffs' damage claims in the context of the evidence adduced at trial and the legal principles that should inform our application of the Tort Claims Act.

QUALITY OF LIFE

[The court described how, for nearly two years, the plaintiffs' water was provided in 40 gallon, 100 pound barrels, the inconvenience that entailed, and the inevitable discomfort and tension the lack of running water produced among household members.]

The trial court charged the jury that plaintiffs' claim for "quality of life" encompassed "inconveniences, aggravation, and unnecessary expenditure of time and effort related to the use of the water hauled to their homes, as well as to other disruption in their lives, including disharmony in the family unit." The aggregate jury verdict on this claim was $5,396,940. This represented an average award of slightly over $16,000 for each plaintiff; thus, a family unit consisting of four plaintiffs received an average award of approximately $64,000.

[D]efendant argues that this segment of the verdict is barred by the New Jersey Tort Claims Act, which provides:

> No damages shall be awarded against a public entity or public employee for pain and suffering resulting from any injury; provided, however, that this limitation on the recovery of damages for pain and suffering shall not apply in cases of permanent loss of a bodily function, permanent disfigurement or dismemberment where the medical treatment expenses are in excess of $1,000.00.

Defendant contends that the legislative intent in restricting damages for "pain and suffering" was to encompass claims for all "non-objective" injuries, unless the statutory threshold of severity of injury or expense of treatment is met. The township asserts that the inconvenience, aggravation, effort and disruption of the family unit that resulted from the loss of plaintiff's water supply was but a form of "pain and suffering" and therefore uncompensable under the Act.

The Appellate Division rejected the township's contention, concluding that there was a clear distinction between

> the subjectively measured damages for pain and suffering, which are not compensable by the Tort Claims Act, and those which objectively affect quality of life by causing an interference with the use of one's land through inconvenience and the disruption of daily activities.

We agree with the Appellate Division's conclusion. The Tort Claims Act's ban against recovery of damages for "pain and suffering resulting from any injury" is intended to apply to the intangible, subjective feelings of discomfort that are associated with personal injuries. It was not intended to bar claims for inconvenience associated with the invasion of a property interest. * * * [T]he interest invaded here, the right to obtain potable running water from plaintiffs' own wells, is qualitatively different from "pain and suffering" related to a personal injury.

As the Appellate Division acknowledged, plaintiffs' claim for quality of life damages is derived from the law of nuisance. It has long been recognized that damages for inconvenience, annoyance, and discomfort are recoverable in a nuisance action. The Restatement (Second) of Torts section 929 (1977) sets out three distinct categories of compensation with respect to invasions of an interest in land:

> (a) the difference between the value of the land before the harm and the value after the harm, or at [plaintiff's] election in an appropriate case, the cost of restoration that has been or may be reasonably incurred;
>
> (b) the loss of use of the land, and
>
> (c) discomfort and annoyance to him as occupant.

While the first two of these components constitute damages for the interference with plaintiff's use and enjoyment of his land, the third category compensates the plaintiff for his personal losses flowing directly from such an invasion. As such, damages for inconvenience, discomfort, and annoyance constitute "distinct grounds of compensation for which in ordinary cases the person in possession is entitled to recover *in addition to* the harm to his proprietary interests." Restatement Second of Torts section 929 comment e (1977).

Accordingly, we conclude that the quality of life damages represent compensation for losses associated with damage to property, and agree with the Appellate Division that they do not constitute pain and suffering under the Tort Claims Act. We therefore sustain the judgment for quality of life damages.

EMOTIONAL DISTRESS

The jury verdict awarded plaintiffs damages for emotional distress in the aggregate amount of $2,056,480. The individual verdicts ranged from $40 to $14,000.

Many of the plaintiffs testified about their emotional reactions to the knowledge that their well-water was contaminated. * * * [T]he consistent thrust of the testimony offered by numerous witnesses was that they suffered anxiety, stress, fear, and depression, and that these feelings were directly and causally related to the knowledge that they and members of their family had ingested and been exposed to contaminated water for a substantial time period. * * *

[T]he township contended that the jury verdict for emotional distress constituted damages for "pain and suffering resulting from any injury," recovery for which is expressly barred by the Tort Claims Act. The Appellate Division, without deciding the issue of the sufficiency of plaintiffs' proofs, agreed that the verdict for emotional distress was barred by the Act:

> We cannot conceive how plaintiffs' concern that their exposure to toxic wastes might have precipitated a serious illness can be characterized as anything other than pain and suffering. It is a measure of their entirely subjective responses to a situation which, though threatening, never materialized into objective manifestations of injury. Under the circumstances, we conclude that although damages for these intangible harms might be recoverable from a non-governmental entity, as consequential to a nuisance, the language of N.J.S.A. 59:9–2(d), barring damages from a public entity "for pain and suffering resulting from any injury," clearly precludes recovery herein.

[W]e reject plaintiffs' assertion that the Tort Claims Act's limitation against recovery for "pain and suffering resulting from any injury" does not apply to claims based on emotional distress. * * *

Addressing first plaintiffs' contention that emotional distress is not an "injury" as that term is used in the Tort Claims Act, we observe that the Act broadly defines injury to include

> death, injury to a person, damage to or loss of property or any other injury that a person may suffer that would be actionable if inflicted by a private person.

The statutory definition is expansive and unqualified and clearly accommodates "emotional distress" as an injury "that a person may suffer that would be actionable if inflicted by a private person." The term "injury" is also used in N.J.S.A. 59:4–2, which defines the scope of public entity liability. Plainly, if emotional distress did not constitute an injury under this section, plaintiffs could not have asserted a cause of action for emotional distress under the Act. We discern no basis in the legislative history or in the statutory scheme of the Act for assigning a more restrictive meaning to the term "injury" as used in N.J.S.A. 59:9–2(d), the section that limits liability for pain and suffering, than that accorded to the same word in the section of the Act that imposes liability on a public entity. Accordingly, we hold that claims for emotional distress are encompassed by the term "injury" in N.J.S.A. 59:9–2(d).

The term "pain and suffering" is not defined in the Act. The Comment to N.J.S.A. 59:9–2 describes the limitation on damages for pain and suffering as reflecting "the policy judgment that in view of the economic burdens presently facing public entities a claimant should not be reimbursed for non-objective types of damages, such as pain and suffering, except in aggravated circumstances * * *." We are in full accord with the conclusion of the Appellate Division that the subjective symptoms of depression, stress, health concerns, and anxiety described by the plaintiffs and their expert witness constitute "pain and suffering resulting from any injury" as that phrase is used in N.J.S.A. 59:9–2(d). * * *

### Claims for Enhanced Risk and Medical Surveillance

No claims were asserted by plaintiffs seeking recovery for specific illnesses caused by their exposure to chemicals. Rather, they claim damages for the enhanced risk of future illness attributable to such exposure. They also seek to recover the expenses of annual medical examinations to monitor their physical health and detect symptoms of disease at the earliest possible opportunity.

Before trial, the trial court granted defendant's motion for summary judgment dismissing the enhanced risk claim. * * *

With regard to the claims for medical surveillance expenses, the trial court denied defendant's summary judgment motion, and the jury verdict included damages of $8,204,500 for medical surveillance. * * *

1.

Our evaluation of the enhanced risk and medical surveillance claims requires that we focus on a critical issue in the management of toxic tort litigation: at what stage in the evolution of a toxic injury should tort law intercede by requiring the responsible party to pay damages?

[The court first concludes that any plaintiffs who do incur cancer at a later date will be able to sue the Township. The statute of limitations will not have run, because under New Jersey's discovery rule, the cause of action does not accrue until the victim is aware of the injury. Neither will the single controversy rule bar plaintiffs from suing. Usually, the single controversy rule would require the plaintiffs to raise all their claims—property claims and personal injury claims—in the same proceeding. According to the Court, however, the single controversy rule, "cannot sensibly be applied to a toxic-tort claim filed when disease is manifested years after the exposure, merely because the same plaintiff sued previously to recover for property damage or other injuries. In such a case, the rule is literally inapplicable since, as noted, the second cause of action does not accrue until the disease is manifested; hence, it could not have been joined with the earlier claims."] * * *

2.

Much of the same evidence was material to both the enhanced risk and medical surveillance claims. Dr. Joseph Highland, a toxicologist * * * testified concerning the health hazards posed by the chemicals and the exposure levels at which adverse health effects had been experimentally observed. * * *

Dr. Highland testified that the Legler area residents, because of their exposure to toxic chemicals, had an increased risk of cancer; that unborn children and infants were more susceptible to the disease because of their immature biological defense systems; and that the extent of the risk was variable with the degree of exposure to the chemicals. Dr. Highland testified that *he could not quantify the extent of the enhanced risk of cancer* because of the lack of scientific information concerning the effect of the interaction of the various chemicals to which plaintiffs were exposed. However, the jury could reasonably have inferred from his testimony that the risk, although unquantified, was medically significant. * * *

Dr. Highland also testified that the exposure to chemicals had already caused actual physical injury to plaintiffs through its adverse effects on the genetic material within their cells.

Dr. Susan Daum, a physician * * * specializing in the diagnosis and treatment of diseases induced by toxic substances, testified that plaintiffs required a program of regular medical surveillance. Acknowledging her reliance on the report of Dr. Highland, Dr. Daum stated that plaintiffs' exposure to chemicals had produced "a reasonable likelihood that they have now or will develop health consequences from this exposure." * * *

Although both the enhanced risk and medical surveillance claims are based on Dr. Highland's testimony, supplemented by Dr. Daum's testimony in the case of the surveillance claim, these claims seek redress for the invasion of distinct and different interests. The enhanced risk claim seeks a damage award, not because of any expenditure of funds, but because plaintiffs contend that the unquantified injury to their health and life expectancy should be presently compensable, even though no evidence of disease is manifest. Defendant does not dispute the causal relationship between the plaintiffs' exposure to toxic chemicals and the plaintiffs' increased risk of diseases, but contends that the probability that plaintiffs will actually become ill from their exposure to chemicals is too remote to warrant compensation under principles of tort law.

By contrast, the claim for medical surveillance does not seek compensation for an unquantifiable injury, but rather seeks specific monetary damages measured by the cost of periodic medical examinations. The invasion for which redress is sought is the fact that plaintiffs have been advised to spend money for medical tests, a cost they would not have incurred absent their exposure to toxic chemicals. Defendant contends that the claim for medical surveillance damages cannot be sustained, as a matter of law, if the plaintiffs' enhanced risk of injury is not sufficiently probable to be compensable. In our view, however, recognition of the medical surveillance claim is not necessarily dependent on recognition of the enhanced risk claim.

3.

The trial court declined to submit to the jury the issue of defendant's liability for the plaintiffs' increased risk of contracting cancer, kidney or liver damage, or other diseases associated with the chemicals that had migrated from the landfill to their wells. If the issue had not been withheld, the jury could have concluded from the evidence that most or all of the plaintiffs had a significantly but unquantifiably enhanced risk of the identified diseases, and that such enhanced risk was attributable to defendant's conduct. * * *

[N]either the trial court nor the Appellate Division challenged the contention that the enhanced risk of disease was a tortiously-inflicted injury, but both concluded that the proof quantifying the likelihood of disease was insufficient to submit the issue to the jury. As the Appellate Division observed:

> While it is true that damages are recoverable for the prospective consequences of a tortious injury, it must be demonstrated that the apprehended consequences are reasonably probable. * * *

Our disposition of this difficult and important issue requires that we choose between two alternatives, each having a potential for imposing unfair and undesirable consequences on the affected interests. A holding that recognizes a cause of action for unquantified enhanced risk claims exposes the tort system, and the public it serves, to the task of litigating vast numbers of claims for compensation based on threats of injuries that may never occur. It imposes on judges and juries the burden of assessing damages for the risk of potential disease, without clear guidelines to determine what level of compensation may be appropriate. It would undoubtedly increase already escalating insurance rates. It is clear that the recognition of an "enhanced risk" cause of action, particularly when the risk is unquantified, would generate substantial litigation that would be difficult to manage and resolve.

Our dissenting colleague, arguing in favor of recognizing a cause of action based on an unquantified claim of enhanced risk, points out that "courts have not allowed the difficulty of quantifying injury to prevent them from offering compensation for assault, trespass, emotional distress, invasion of privacy or damage to reputation." Although lawsuits grounded in one or more of these causes of action may involve claims for damages that are difficult to quantify, such damages are awarded on the basis of events that have occurred and can be proved at the time of trial. In contrast, the compensability of the enhanced risk claim depends upon the likelihood of an event that has not yet occurred and may never occur—the contracting of one or more diseases the risk of which has been enhanced by defendant's conduct. It is the highly contingent and speculative quality of an unquantified claim based on enhanced risk that renders it novel and difficult to manage and resolve. If such claims were to be litigated, juries would be asked to award damages for the enhanced risk of a disease that may never be contracted, without the benefit of expert testimony sufficient to establish the likelihood that the contingent event will ever occur.

On the other hand, denial of the enhanced-risk cause of action may mean that some of these plaintiffs will be unable to obtain compensation for their injury. Despite the collateral estoppel effect of the jury's finding that defendant's wrongful conduct caused the contamination of plaintiffs' wells, those who contract diseases in the future because of their exposure to chemicals in their well water may be unable to prove a causal relationship between such exposure and their disease. * * * Dismissal of the enhanced risk claims may effectively preclude any recovery for injuries caused by exposure to chemicals in plaintiffs' wells because of the difficulty of proving that injuries manifested in the future were not the product of intervening events or causes. * * *

In deciding between recognition or nonrecognition of plaintiffs' enhanced-risk claim, we feel constrained to choose the alternative that most closely reflects the legislative purpose in enacting the Tort Claims Act. We are conscious of the admonition that in construing the Act courts should "exercise restraint in the acceptance of novel causes of action against public entities." In our view, the speculative nature of an unquantified enhanced risk claim, the difficulties inherent in adjudicating such claims, and the policies underlying the Tort Claims Act argue persuasively against the recognition of this cause of action. Accordingly, we decline to recognize plaintiffs' cause of action for the *unquantified* enhanced risk of disease, and affirm the judgment of the Appellate Division dismissing such claims. We need not and do not decide whether a claim based on enhanced risk of disease that is supported by testimony demonstrating that the onset of the disease is reasonably probable could be maintained under the Tort Claims Act.

4.

The claim for medical surveillance expenses stands on a different footing from the claim based on enhanced risk. It seeks to recover the cost of periodic medical examinations intended to monitor plaintiffs' health and facilitate early diagnosis and treatment of disease caused by plaintiffs' exposure to toxic chemicals. At trial, competent medical testimony was offered to prove that a program of regular medical testing and evaluation was reasonably necessary and consistent with contemporary scientific principles applied by physicians experienced in the diagnosis and treatment of chemically-induced injuries.

The Appellate Division's rejection of the medical surveillance claim is rooted in the premise that even if medical experts testify convincingly that medical surveillance is necessary, the claim for compensation for these costs must fall, as a matter of law, if the risk of injury is not quantified, or, if quantified, is not reasonably probable. This analysis assumes that the reasonableness of medical intervention, and, therefore, its compensability, depends solely on the sufficiency of proof that the occurrence of the disease is probable. We think this formulation unduly impedes the ability of courts to recognize that medical science may necessarily and properly intervene where there is a significant but unquantified risk of serious disease.

This point is well-illustrated by the hypothetical case discussed in the opinion of the Court of Appeals in Friends For All Children v. Lockheed Aircraft Corp., 746 F.2d 816 (D.C.Cir.1984):

> Jones is knocked down by a motorbike when Smith is riding through a red light. Jones lands on his head with some force. Understandably shaken, Jones enters a hospital where doctors recommend that he undergo a battery of tests to determine whether he has suffered any internal head injuries. The tests prove negative, but Jones sues Smith solely for what turns out to be the substantial cost of the diagnostic examinations.
>
> From our example, it is clear that even in the absence of physical injury Jones ought to be able to recover the cost for the various diagnostic examinations proximately caused by Smith's negligent action. A cause of action allowing recovery for the expense of diagnostic examinations recommended by competent physicians will, in theory, deter misconduct, whether it be negligent motorbike riding or negligent aircraft manufacture. The cause of action also accords with commonly shared intuitions of normative justice which underlie the common law of tort. The motorbike rider, through his negligence, caused the plaintiff, in the opinion of medical experts, to need specific medical services—a cost that is neither inconsequential nor of a kind the community generally accepts as part of the wear and tear of daily life. Under these principles of tort law, the motorbiker should pay. * * *

Compensation for reasonable and necessary medical expenses is consistent with well-accepted legal principles. It is also consistent with the important public health interest in fostering access to medical testing for individuals whose exposure to toxic chemicals creates an enhanced risk of disease. The value of early diagnosis and treatment for cancer patients is well-documented.* * *

Accordingly, we hold that the cost of medical surveillance is a compensable item of damages where the proofs demonstrate, through reliable expert testimony predicated upon the significance and extent of exposure to chemicals, the toxicity of the chemicals, the seriousness of the diseases for which individuals are at risk, the relative increase in the chance of onset of disease in those exposed, and the value of early diagnosis, that such surveillance to monitor the effect of exposure to toxic chemicals is reasonable and necessary. In our view, this holding is thoroughly consistent with our rejection of plaintiffs' claim for damages based on their enhanced risk of injury. That claim seeks damages for the impairment of plaintiffs' health, without proof of its likelihood, extent, or monetary value. In contrast, the medical surveillance claim seeks reimbursement for the specific dollar costs of periodic examinations that are medically necessary notwithstanding the fact that the extent of plaintiffs' impaired health is unquantified.

We find that the proofs in this case were sufficient to support the trial court's decision to submit the medical surveillance issue to the jury, and were sufficient to support the jury's verdict.[13]

5.

The medical surveillance issue was tried as if it were a conventional claim for compensatory damages susceptible to a jury verdict in a lump sum. The jury was so instructed by the trial court, and neither plaintiffs' nor defendant's request to charge on this issue sought a different instruction.

In the Appellate Division, defendant argued for the first time that a lump-sum damage award for medical surveillance was inappropriate. Defendant contended that if the court were to uphold all or any part of the medical surveillance award, it should "create an actuar[i]ally-sound fund, to which the plaintiffs may apply in the future for the cost of medical surveillance upon proof that those costs are not otherwise compensable * * * or after deduction of the amounts so reimbursed," and should leave to the trial court, on remand, the task of establishing "details of the creation and supervision of such a fund." * * *

In our view, the use of a court-supervised fund to administer medical-surveillance payments in mass exposure cases, particularly for claims under the Tort Claims Act, is a highly appropriate exercise of the Court's equitable powers. Such a mechanism offers significant advantages over a lump-sum verdict. For Tort Claims Act cases, it provides a method for offsetting a defendant's liability by payments from collateral sources. Although the parties in this case sharply dispute the availability of insurance coverage for surveillance-type costs, a fund could provide a convenient method for establishing credits in the event insurance benefits were available for some, if not all, of the plaintiffs.

In addition, a fund would serve to limit the liability of defendants to the amount of expenses actually incurred. A lump-sum verdict attempts to estimate future expenses, but cannot predict the amounts that actual-

**13.** The jury award for medical surveillance for each plaintiff averaged approximately $500 per year of life expectancy. * * *

ly will be expended for medical purposes. Although conventional damage awards do not restrict plaintiffs in the use of money paid as compensatory damages, mass-exposure toxic-tort cases involve public interests not present in conventional tort litigation. The public health interest is served by a fund mechanism that encourages regular medical monitoring for victims of toxic exposure. Where public entities are defendants, a limitation of liability to amounts actually expended for medical surveillance tends to reduce insurance costs and taxes, objectives consistent with the legislature's admonition to avoid recognition of novel causes of action. * * *

In litigation involving public-entity defendants, we conclude that the use of a fund to administer medical-surveillance damages should be the general rule, in the absence of factors that render it impractical or inappropriate.

However, we decline to upset the jury verdict awarding medical-surveillance damages in this case. Such a result would be unfair to these plaintiffs, since the medical-surveillance issue was tried conventionally, and neither party requested the trial court to withhold from the jury the power to return a lump-sum verdict for each plaintiff in order that relief by way of a fund could be provided. * * *

HANDLER, J., concurring in part and dissenting in part.

* * * The essence of the claim for damages here is the reality of the physical injury caused by the wrongful exposure to toxic chemicals and the increased peril of cancer and other serious diseases that the residents have incurred. * * *

The Court cannot, and does not, dispute or denigrate the expert testimony presented at trial "that the exposure to chemicals had already caused actual physical injury to plaintiffs through its adverse effects on the genetic material within their cells" and that plaintiffs' exposure to chemicals had produced "a reasonable likelihood that they have now and will develop health consequences from this exposure." Dr. Joseph Highland gave uncontested testimony that plaintiffs had already suffered physical injury from the damage to their cellular and genetic material caused by the chemicals to which they were exposed. These chemicals are mutagenic agents: they destroy parts of the genetic material of cells they contact. This destruction may affect only the function of a few cells or it may lead to the failure of major organs. It may make the cells likely starting points for cancer, and it may lead to mutations in the victims' children.

The majority recognizes that plaintiffs have suffered injury. It is self-evident that exposure to highly toxic chemicals is the "infliction of ... harm," "an invasion of a legally protected interest." Nevertheless, the majority concludes that plaintiffs' injury cannot be redressed. Its reasons for treating their claims different from other injury claims are an unsupported fear of "vast numbers of claims" and a belief that no "clear guidelines [exist] to determine what level of compensation may be appropriate."

These reasons are an evasion of the challenge posed by tortious injury that carries with it an enhanced risk of even greater injury, and the need to provide fair compensation for innocent victims suffering this form of injury. The Court postponed a similar determination in Evers v. Dollinger, 95 N.J. 399, 471 A.2d 405 (1984). There a woman brought suit claiming that her doctor's negligent diagnosis and treatment enhanced the risk that her cancer would recur. While her appeal of the trial court's judgment was pending, she suffered a recurrence of the cancer. The majority decided that it need not decide whether enhanced risk, standing alone, is an actionable element. Nevertheless, the Court held that because the disease had recurred, plaintiff would be allowed to recover damages for enhanced risk.

Allowing recovery for enhanced risk in *Evers* where the plaintiff suffered subsequent harm cannot be reconciled with the denial of recovery for enhanced risk in the present case. The majority professes to deny compensation because it cannot "measure" or "quantify" the enhanced risk of future injury. The fact that the plaintiffs in the present case have not—yet—suffered extreme symptoms is no justification for denying recovery. As in *Evers v. Dollinger,* "[t]he Court is ... troubled by a seeming inability to quantify the risk of future cancer. But, adding the incurrence of future harm as a requirement for the recovery for such increased risk does not resolve the dilemma since the risk still remains unquantified." Id. at 421, 471 A.2d 405 (Handler, J., concurring). When the Court allowed recovery for enhanced risk in *Evers*, it did not in the slightest way insist that the risk be quantified.

The majority reasons that plaintiffs' claim is not cognizable in part because the risk of future disease does not rise to the level of "reasonable probability." Yet the court concedes that the plaintiffs have proven that they have a "significantly ... enhanced risk" of contracting serious diseases. It nowhere explains why a risk that generates the "reasonable probability" of future injury can be compensated while one that "significantly enhances" the likelihood of future injury cannot. * * *

The courts have not allowed the difficulty of quantifying injury to prevent them from offering compensation for assault, trespass, emotional distress, invasion of privacy, or damage to reputation. * * * Where new forms of injury have been put before the courts, the courts have developed procedures, standards, and formulas for determining appropriate compensation. This perception was expressed in Capron, Tort Liability in Genetic Counseling, 79 Colum.L.Rev. 618, 649 (1979):

> [T]he collective wisdom of the community on the proper redress for a particular harm, informed by experience, common sense, and a desire to be fair to the parties, seems an acceptable way of arriving at a damage verdict and probably one that is preferable to a more scientific (and sterile) process that excludes nonquantifiable elements to achieve an aura of objectivity and precision.

The plaintiffs' claim of an unquantified enhanced risk should not be characterized as "depend[ing] upon the likelihood of an event that has not yet occurred and may never occur." The injury involved is an actual event: exposure to toxic chemicals. The tortious contamination, moreover, is an event that has surely occurred; it is not a speculative or remote possible happening. Among the consequences of this unconsented-to invasion are genetic damage and a tangible risk of a major disease, a peril that is real even though it cannot be precisely measured or weighed. The peril, moreover, is unquestionably greater than that experienced by persons not similarly exposed to toxic chemicals. The toxic injury and claim for damages are not attributable only to some possible future event. Like claims based on the doctrines of trespass, assault, invasion of privacy, or defamation, the damages suffered are not solely actual consequential damages, but also the disvalue of being subjected to an intrinsically harmful event. The risk of dreadful disease resulting from toxic exposure and contamination is more frightening and palpable than any deficits we may feel or imagine from many other wrongful transgressions. * * *

In deciding whether to recognize plaintiffs' claims, the majority focuses on the problem of sovereign defendants in tort suits involving the unquantified nature of certain injuries. The majority, however, fails to note the long-term benefits lost when compensation is not allowed for injuries caused. Compensation serves to deter negligent behavior. See, e.g., R. Posner, Economic Analysis of Law 142–43 (2nd ed.1977). We disserve this policy in this case, where the defendant municipality has engaged not simply in negligent conduct, but in "palpably unreasonable" conduct causing real and serious injury to its residents. * * *

"A tortfeasor should not be allowed to escape responsibility for causing an increased risk that would not have existed but for his negligence simply because of the statistical uncertainty of the risk."* * *

The majority speaks of the speculative nature of compensating claims of enhanced risk as if such would be an anomaly in the logical and orderly work of tort law compensation. The truth is to the contrary. There are relatively few injuries that can be easily or logically quantified. It is not merely the relatively new tort claims like "pain and suffering" and "emotional distress" that are difficult to quantify. What is the logical method of evaluation for compensating a claim of trespass on land, the battery of unconsented-to surgery, a violation of personal privacy, or an insult to character? When a jury awards $50,000 for an accident that led to the loss of a limb, how is that $50,000 a logical quantification of that injury?

The severe limitation of damages imposed by the Court in this case is inadequate and unfair. No person in her right mind would trade places with any one of these plaintiffs. Does this not suggest that a person would have to be paid a considerable sum of money, more than that permitted here by the Court, before tolerating the injuries suffered by these plaintiffs? Why should not a jury be permitted to make this determination? * * *

## *Notes*

1. *The Plaintiff's Cause of Action.* Studying remedies as a separate course presumes that it is possible to draw a bright line between right and remedy, that issues bearing on the proper remedy and issues of substantive law are separate and distinct. In fact, the line between remedy and substance is often smudged and gray. For example, is the recoverability of damages for medical surveillance and enhanced risk in *Ayers* a question of remedy or of substantive tort law? The defendant characterized it as a substantive question: Because the plaintiffs had not shown an enhanced risk of cancer with sufficient certainty, they had not shown a personal injury, and could not recover the costs of medical surveillance because they had no cause of action against the defendants in the first place. The court, on the other hand, characterized it as a question of remedy: The plaintiffs were harmed by the exposure to toxic chemicals, thus establishing their cause of action, and the recoverability of particular items of loss was therefore a question of the appropriate remedy.

Generally, whether recovery of a particular item of loss will be treated as a substantive or remedial issue will be determined by whether the plaintiff has also suffered some other, compensable loss. To illustrate: suppose that A was hit by a car and seriously injured. A's spouse, B, who saw the accident, was frightened and horrified. A and C, his business partner, lost a chance to make a very profitable deal because A's injuries incapacitated him. A, B, and C sued the driver of the car. Whether B and C can recover damages for their emotional and economic losses, respectively, will be characterized as questions of substantive law: Does the jurisdiction recognize a cause of action for negligently inflicted emotional distress or economic loss? Conversely, because A was physically injured, he clearly can establish a cause of action for negligence. Whether he can recover damages for his emotional distress or for his share of the lost profits will therefore be treated as a question of the appropriate remedy for one injured by another's negligence. Does it make sense to treat A's economic loss as a question of remedy, and C's as a question of substantive law?

2. *The Purpose of Awarding Damages.* "The rules for determining the measure of damages in tort are based upon the purposes for which actions of tort are maintainable. These purposes are:

(a) to give compensation, indemnity, or restitution for harms;

(b) to determine rights;

(c) to punish wrongdoers and deter wrongful conduct;

(d) to vindicate parties and deter retaliation or violent and unlawful self-help."

Restatement (Second) of Torts § 901. The first purpose is achieved by compensatory damages; the second purpose by nominal damages; the third by punitive damages.[a]

**a.** The standards for an award of nominal damages were discussed in connection with Memphis Community School Dist. v. Stachura in part A of this chapter. The standards that govern an award of punitive damages were discussed in chapter 5.

It is important to recognize that compensatory damages, too, deter wrongful conduct, as the dissent in *Ayers* points out. If an activity must absorb—internalize, in the language of the economists—the costs of the accidents for which it is responsible, the cost of that activity will rise, creating an incentive to find a safer way to undertake it. Guido Calabresi, The Costs of Accidents (1970). Although there is vigorous debate over this insight's implications, it has had a profound impact on current thought about the purposes served by tort law. For a useful summary of the debate, see Gary T. Schwartz, Reality in the Economic Analysis of Tort Law: Does Tort Law Really Deter?, 42 U.C.L.A.L.Rev. 377 (1994).

3. *Elements of the Damage Award.* The plaintiff's rightful position provides the starting point in determining what elements of damages are recoverable. Ask, what items of loss must be replaced to restore the plaintiff to her rightful position? In cases involving pecuniary harm, a sort of balance sheet can be employed:

> In determining the measure of recovery, aside from harm to body, emotions or reputation, a balance sheet is in effect set up by the court in which are stated the items of assets and liabilities that have been affected by the tort, (a) before the tort and (b) as they appear at the time of trial. In this are put on one side such assets of the injured person as have been affected by the tort, including his capacity to make profitable use of his time, and on the other side, the same assets at the time of the trial and any existing or prospective liabilities imposed upon him as a result of the tort. The difference, to the extent that it results from the tort, constitutes the theoretical measure of recovery.

Restatement (Second) of Torts § 906 comment a. While nonpecuniary harms are not susceptible of such precise measurement, the theory remains the same: restore the plaintiff to the pre-tort position.

What elements of loss should be compensated to restore the plaintiffs in *Ayers* to their rightful positions? The plaintiffs identified three sorts of losses for which they sought compensation: harm to the quality of their lives; exposure to suspected and known carcinogens; and the costs of medical surveillance that this exposure necessitated. Could they have been more ambitious? What other sorts of losses might they have claimed?

Wouldn't the *Ayers* plaintiffs be recovering double damages if they were compensated once for injury to quality of life and again for emotional distress?

As explained in part B of this chapter, the elements of damages that are routinely recoverable in particular cases have crystallized into a general measure of damages for each tort. The Restatement section quoted in *Ayers* states the general measure of damages for injury to property; the *Stachura* case, at page 508, and the *Pretre* case, page 586, state the general measure for personal injury cases.

4. *Measuring the Damages.* Once it is clear what losses will be compensated, the next problem is to attach a dollar value to them. For pecuniary losses, the critical concept is "value":

> The * * * value of property or services is the amount of money for which the subject matter could be exchanged or procured if there is a

> market * * * or if no market exists, the amount that could be obtained in the usual course of finding a purchaser or hirer of similar property or services. The rental value of property is the * * * value of the use of the property.

Restatement (Second) of Torts § 911.

Once again, nonpecuniary losses are not capable of such precise valuation:

> *Measure of recovery* [for nonpecuniary loss]: The length of time during which pain or other harm to the feelings has been or probably will be experienced and the intensity of the distress are factors to be considered in assessing the amount of damages. In determining this, all relevant circumstances are considered, including sex, age, condition in life and any other fact indicating the susceptibility of the injured person to this type of harm. * * * [D]amages include an amount for the harm suffered to the time of trial and in some cases for that estimated for the future.

Restatement (Second) of Torts § 905 comment i. How did the *Ayers* court arrive at its figures for injury to quality of life? How much would you have awarded the plaintiffs if they had been allowed to recover damages for their emotional distress?

Very little law exists on the proper measurement of nonpecuniary losses, except to say that the amount of the award is in the fact-finder's discretion. What discussion there is in the cases focuses on the admissibility of evidence and the propriety of various jury arguments. Appellate courts have allowed lawyers a free hand in presenting demonstrative evidence to influence the jury's award. The plaintiff, of course, can testify as to the discomfort, annoyance, and so on that the injury has caused. Family and friends may also testify as to the injury's effects. Simply seeing the plaintiff, who may be disfigured or disabled, provides the jury something to go on. Some plaintiffs' lawyers place great stock in "day in the life" films that show how the plaintiff's daily activities have been affected by the injury.

The use of "day-in-the-life" films can raise a number of discovery and evidentiary issues. For example, must the opposing party be allowed to attend the filming or have access to all unused footage? See, e.g., Cisarik v. Palos Community Hosp., 144 Ill.2d 339, 162 Ill.Dec. 59, 579 N.E.2d 873 (1991)(no). What evidentiary standards must be met for a film to be admissible? See Jones v. City of Los Angeles, 20 Cal.App.4th 436, 24 Cal.Rptr.2d 528 (1993).

As for jury arguments, appeals to the jury's sympathy, and attempts to arouse the jury's passion and prejudice are impermissible. Beyond this vague restriction, the controversy has focused on two very specific types of jury argument. One of these is known as the Golden Rule argument. In a Golden Rule argument, counsel asks the jury to place itself in the shoes of the plaintiff, or defendant, and to ask, were I him, how much would I demand as compensation, or were I sued, how much would I think it fair for me to pay? Golden Rule arguments are generally not permitted.

Opinion is divided as to the other traditional argument, the per diem argument. In a per diem argument, counsel suggests a specific amount of compensation for each day, or hour, or minute that the plaintiff will suffer, and then demonstrates to the jury what the award should be by multiplying that amount by the plaintiff's life expectancy in days, hours, or minutes. With this calculation, a small amount can rapidly inflate into an astronomical award. Some jurisdictions permit the per diem argument, provided that the jury is instructed that the figures used are not evidence, but are simply offered by way of argument and illustration. Other jurisdictions do not allow it, because the technique gives a misleading impression of precision.

5. *Limits on the Award.*

a. *Foreseeability.* The concept of foreseeability permeates tort law. The plaintiff must be foreseeable before the defendant owes her a duty. Some harm must be foreseeable before the defendant's behavior will be labeled negligent. If the injury that results was unforeseeable, the court may declare it too remote to be considered proximately caused by the defendant's conduct. Unsurprisingly, there isn't much left to foreseeability at the remedies stage. If foreseeability is a real issue, it will bear on whether the plaintiff has a cause of action, not on the damages that might be available.

Thus, the general rule in tort cases is that if the type of harm the plaintiff suffered was foreseeable, the extent of the harm need not have been. The classic case is McCahill v. New York Transportation Co., 201 N.Y. 221, 94 N.E. 616 (1911), in which the plaintiff was so weakened by his preexisting alcoholism that he unexpectedly died from the relatively minor injuries the defendant caused. Because of the rule that "you take your plaintiff as you find him" (also known as the "thin skull plaintiff rule"), the defendant was liable for the plaintiff's death, although the death was unforeseeable.

Foreseeability can be an issue, however, when a plaintiff attempts, to recover damages for an injury that is different in kind, not merely in extent, from the injury that gave rise to his cause of action. Take, for example, the *Ayers* plaintiffs' claim for emotional distress damages. The court of appeal assumed that the plaintiff's emotional distress "might be recoverable from a non-governmental entity as consequential to a nuisance", but not everyone would agree: The Restatement (Second) of Torts takes a narrower view, allowing only the person in possession of property, not his household members, to recover damages for bodily harm in a nuisance action. (Of course, if the defendant's behavior was negligent, anyone who suffered a personal injury could simply sue for negligence, rather than for nuisance).

Where plaintiffs have attempted to include emotional distress damages as an element of recovery in a suit for injury to property, the results have been mixed. The majority of courts simply deny recovery. See Dan B. Dobbs, Law of Remedies § 5.15(3) (2d ed.1993). Others allow recovery only where some special circumstances, such as a preexisting relationship between the parties or the personal character of the property, make the harm particularly foreseeable. E.g., Windeler v. Scheers Jewelers, 8 Cal.App.3d 844, 88 Cal.Rptr. 39 (1970). Of course, keep in mind that a court that denies recovery for mental distress as a separate item of damages may turn around and measure the value of the property by its "intrinsic" value to the owner. See text at 577.

Assuming that emotional distress is foreseeable when people are exposed to toxic or carcinogenic substances, there may still be problems with recovering emotional distress damages. Of course, if the plaintiff has suffered a physical injury from the exposure, pain and suffering damages including fear of future consequences are routinely available as parasitic damages. Potter v. Firestone, 6 Cal.4th 965, 25 Cal.Rptr.2d 550, 863 P.2d 795 (1993). Some courts find exposure, in itself, to be an injury. Day v. NLO, 851 F.Supp. 869, (S.D.Ohio 1994), Werlein v. United States, 746 F.Supp. 887 (D.Minn. 1990), while others require more tangible harm. Busfield v. A.C. & S. Inc., 434 Pa.Super. 424, 643 A.2d 1095 (Pa.Super.1994)(pleural thickening caused by asbestos exposure is not a legally cognizable injury; emotional distress damages denied)(McEwen, J. concurring); In re Hawaii Federal Asbestos Cases, 734 F.Supp. 1563 (D.Hawaii 1990); Thomas v. FAG Bearings Corp., Inc., 846 F.Supp. 1400 (W.D.Mo.1994). Yet a third view would simply dispense with the injury requirement. See Ironbound Health Rights Advisory Commission v. Diamond Shamrock Chemicals Co., 243 N.J.Super. 170, 578 A.2d 1248 (N.J.Super.A.D.1990)(either physical injury *or* serious mental illness must be shown).

These questions have come to the fore in litigation over fear of exposure to the human immunodeficiency virus (HIV) which causes AIDS. The trend seems to be to allow plaintiffs who have actually been exposed to the virus to recover damages for the fear they "reasonably" suffer, even if they ultimately test HIV negative. Marriott v. Sedco Forex International Resources, Ltd., 827 F.Supp. 59 (D.Mass.1993); K.A.C. v. Benson, 527 N.W.2d 553 (Minn. 1995).

A difficult question in jurisdictions that allow recovery is whether the plaintiff must show that he or she was in fact exposed to the virus, or if it is enough that he or she reasonably believes exposure took place. For example, suppose the plaintiff was stuck by a negligently discarded needle, and fears she will develop hepatitis or AIDS. The needle, however, has been destroyed or cannot be tested. Thus, the plaintiff cannot show that the particular needle that stuck her was contaminated.

In such a situation, the majority view would deny recovery unless actual exposure is shown. Barrett v. Danbury Hospital, 232 Conn. 242, 654 A.2d 748 (Conn.1995); Brzoska v. Olson, 668 A.2d 1355 (Del.1995); Carroll v. Sisters of Saint Francis Health Services, Inc., 868 S.W.2d 585 (Tenn.1993). A minority have allowed recovery without proof of actual exposure, so long as the fear of AIDS is reasonable. Chizmar v. Mackie, 896 P.2d 196 (Alaska 1995); Howard v. Alexandria Hosp., 245 Va. 346, 429 S.E.2d 22 (Va.1993). See also Marchica v. Long Island Railway, 31 F.3d 1197 (2d Cir.1994), cert. denied, ___ U.S. ___, 115 S.Ct. 727, 130 L.Ed.2d 631 (1995)(FELA case).

Of course, even under this line of cases, the plaintiff's fear must be reasonable, and inability to show exposure may draw reasonableness into doubt. See, e.g., Ordway v. Superior Court, 154 Misc.2d 269, 583 N.Y.S.2d 1014 (Sup.1992)(surgeon who unknowingly operated on AIDS victim could not reasonably fear AIDS without showing some unusual occurrence during the operation making exposure possible). In fact, in most of the cases denying recovery, there have been indications that the plaintiff's fears were simply unfounded, namely, that the plaintiff had repeatedly tested negative over a number of years. See e.g. Lubowitz v. Albert Einstein Medical Center, 424 Pa.Super. 468, 623 A.2d 3 (1993)(two negative tests, 3 and 6 months after exposure). By contrast, the cases allowing recovery have focused on the period between possible exposure and the first reliable negative test results. Faya v. Almaraz, 329 Md. 435, 620 A.2d 327, 337 (1993)(fear becomes unreasonable once reliable negative test results are available).

California courts have taken an unusual position on this issue. In Potter v. Firestone Tire and Rubber Co., 6 Cal.4th 965, 25 Cal.Rptr.2d 550, 863 P.2d 795 (1993), the court held that a plaintiff who has not suffered a physical injury can only recover emotional distress damages for exposure to a harmful substance by showing that it is more likely than not the feared consequence will eventuate. See also Kerins v. Hartley 27 Cal.App.4th, 1062, 33 Cal.Rptr.2d 172 (1994)(applying *Potter* to deny recovery in HIV exposure case). Admitting that it might be both foreseeable and reasonable to fear even uncertain future harm, the *Potter* court felt that it was necessary to limit recovery as a matter of policy.

b. *Certainty.* The plaintiffs in a toxic exposure case like *Ayers* or *Potter* suffer a second injury, beyond their emotional distress, from the chemicals' future, dangerous effects: They are now at risk that they will suffer physically and financially if they do become sick in the future.

The problem, of course, is that not everyone who is exposed to a toxic or carcinogenic substance necessarily gets sick. "[W]hen we refer to radiation as a cause of cancer, we do not mean that every individual exposed to a certain amount of radiation will develop cancer. We simply mean that a population exposed to a certain dose of radiation will show a greater incidence of cancer than that same population would have shown in the absence of the added radiation." J.Gofman, M.D., Radiation and Human Health 54–55 (1981), PX–1046.

For the *Ayers* court, the prospect of future losses attributable to an unquantified risk of future disease was too uncertain to permit recovery. Yet, how certain were the losses for which the court allowed recovery? How certain is it that the amount awarded as quality of life damages was accurate? How about the damages for medical monitoring? Those were based on the plaintiffs' life expectancy: Is it certain that any of the plaintiffs will live exactly that long? Consider the following:

> [I]t seems * * * likely from his remarks that the district judge thought that all probabilities are too uncertain to provide a basis for awarding damages. Yet most knowledge, and almost all legal evidence, is probabilistic. Even the proposition that [the plaintiff] will die some day is merely empirical. It is of course highly probable that he will die but it is not certain in the way it is certain that $10^3$ is 1000 * * *.
>
> All this has long been recognized in personal-injury cases, as it is throughout the law. If a tort victim is seriously injured and will require medical attention for the rest of his life, the court in deciding how much to award him for future medical expenses will have to estimate how long he can be expected to live, and it will make this estimate by consulting a

mortality table, which is to say by looking at a statistical summation of the experience of thousands or millions of people. * * *

DePass v. United States, 721 F.2d 203, 207 (7th Cir.1983)(Posner, J. dissenting).

One way to distinguish between the medical surveillance costs and the risk of future cancer-related expenses in *Ayers* is that with regard to the surveillance costs, it is certain the plaintiffs will incur them, only the amount is uncertain. With regard to the risk of cancer, it is not certain whether a particular plaintiff will suffer any injury at all. Indeed, that is often offered as an explanation of the role of certainty in tort law. Certainty only bars recovery where the existence of the loss is uncertain. Where it is certain that the defendant's conduct caused harm, uncertainty as to amount will not bar recovery. Is that a persuasive explanation of the result in *Ayers?*

The court's solution to the indeterminacy problem in *Ayers* is to require the defendant to pay for the cost of medical surveillance, and preserve the plaintiffs' cause of action should cancer eventually occur. This sort of claim-splitting has gathered significant support. At least in cases involving exposure to asbestos, the majority of jurisdictions now allow plaintiffs to bring a second suit if they later develop a second disease. Note, Claim Preclusion in Modern Latent Disease Cases: a Proposal for Allowing Second Suits, 103 Harv.L.Rev. 1989 (1990).

So, when some of the *Ayers* plaintiffs get sick and sue, what will they have to show to recover? Again, consider: " When we refer to radiation as a cause, we do not mean that it causes every case of cancer or leukemia. Indeed, the evidence we have indicating radiation in the causation of cancer and leukemia shows that not all cases of cancer are caused by radiation. * * * We simply mean that a population exposed to a certain dose of radiation will show a greater incidence of cancer than that same population would have shown in the absence of the added radiation." J. Gofman, M.D., Radiation and Human Health 54–55 (1981), PX–1046.

So, when those plaintiffs who do get cancer or some other disease related to the exposure return to court, how will they show that their illness was caused by the defendant?

McKellips v. Saint Francis Hospital, Inc., 741 P.2d 467 (Okl.1987), may suggest an answer. There, the defendant allegedly negligently misdiagnosed decedent's heart attack. An expert testified that a proper diagnosis would have improved the decedent's chances of survival significantly. The court held that the defendant's negligence was actionable because it deprived the decedent of a chance of survival, but that the decedent's estate's damages would be reduced by the chance that he might not have survived in any event: "[R]ecovery is permitted only for the per cent of chance lost times the total amount of damages which are ordinarily allowed." Id. at 477.

Would this provide a satisfactory solution to the problem in *Ayers*? Are there other sorts of injuries where damages ought to be reduced for uncertainty? See Grayson v. Irvmar, 7 A.D.2d 436, 184 N.Y.S.2d 33 (1959) (damages for injury to plaintiff's inchoate opera career must take into account that artistic success is uncertain); Elmer J. Schaefer, Uncertainty and the Law of Damages, 19 Wm. & Mary L.Rev. 719 (1978).

The "loss of a chance" approach has garnered many commentators' support. See, e.g., Daniel A. Farber, Toxic Causation, 71 Minn.L.Rev. 1219 (1987); Joseph King, Jr., Causation, Valuation and Chance in Personal Injury Torts Involving Preexisting Conditions and Future Consequences, 90 Yale L.J. 1353 (1981). Cf. Comment, Decreasing the Risks Inherent in Claims for Increased Risk of Future Diseases, 43 U.Miami L.Rev. 1081 (1988) (arguing the appropriate remedy for the risk of future disease is health insurance at the defendant's expense).

Courts have not been so receptive. When plaintiffs seek to recover damages now for a loss they may incur in the future, courts have held firm against the "discounting" approach the commentators advocate. While some courts have relaxed the standard of proof slightly, e.g., Hicks v. United States, 368 F.2d 626 (4th Cir.1966)("substantial possibility" of harm is sufficient to allow the jury to find that the defendant caused the ultimate injury), for most, only those future consequences of an injury that are more likely than not to occur will be compensated. Sterling v. Velsicol Chemical Corp., 855 F.2d 1188, 1205 (6th Cir.1988)(under Tennessee law, a 25% or 30% increase in the risk of cancer "does not constitute a reasonable medical certainty, but rather a mere possibility or speculation," and therefore damages for future cancer are not recoverable); In re Paoli RR Yard PCB Litigation, 916 F.2d 829, 851 (3d Cir.1990)(Pa. law), cert. denied, 499 U.S. 961, 111 S.Ct. 1584, 113 L.Ed.2d 649 (1991); Mauro v. Raymark Industries, 116 N.J. 126, 561 A.2d 257 (1989). Of course, once past the barrier of reasonable probability, plaintiffs damages are calculated as if it were certain that the harm will occur. Jackson v. Johns–Manville Sales Corp., 781 F.2d 394, 413 (5th Cir.1986)(under Mississippi law, a plaintiff who adduced evidence that he had a greater than 50% chance of getting cancer because of his exposure to asbestos could recover damages for future illness).

Plaintiffs who sue after the illness or harm has already occurred have a better chance at persuading the court to use a "discounting," or "loss of a chance" approach. A number jurisdictions have recently adopted it in medical malpractice cases, allowing plaintiffs who show that the defendant's negligence caused them to lose a chance of recovery to recover damages, discounted by the probability that the harm would have inevitably occurred. E.g., Delaney v. Cade, 255 Kan. 199, 873 P.2d 175 (Kan.1994); Perez v. Las Vegas Medical Center, 107 Nev. 1, 805 P.2d 589 (1991); Scafidi v. Seiler, 119 N.J. 93, 574 A.2d 398 (1990)(characterizing this view as "the clear majority"); cf. Mayhue v. Sparkman, 653 N.E.2d 1384 (Ind.1995) (applying *Hicks*). Some of these courts have hedged, though, insisting that the chance lost must be "substantial" or "significant" before discounted recovery is allowed. *Delaney*, 873 P.2d at 187 (evidence must show that the patient had a substantial chance of survival or of a better recovery rather than an "appreciable" one); *Perez*, 805 P.2d at 592 (loss of a 10% of survival perhaps not actionable); *Scafidi*, 574 A.2d at 405 (increased risk must be a substantial factor in causing the harm in order to satisfy proximate cause).

Of course, some jurisdictions continue to reject the loss of a chance approach altogether. See Dumas v. Cooney, 235 Cal.App.3d 1593, 1610, 1

Cal.Rptr.2d 584 (1991)(plaintiff alleging negligent diagnosis must show that with a correct diagnosis he would have had a better than 50% chance of survival); Fennell v. Southern Maryland Hosp. Center Inc., 320 Md. 776, 580 A.2d 206 (1990)(same). An extreme example is Duarte v. Zachariah, 22 Cal.App.4th 1652, 28 Cal.Rptr.2d 88 (1994). Duarte was referred to Dr. Zachariah for chemotherapy after she had a mastectomy to remove a breast cancer. Dr. Zachariah negligently prescribed an overdose of a drug which damaged Duarte's bone marrow, making further chemotherapy dangerous to her health. As the court of appeal interpreted the evidence, without chemotherapy, 10% of patients in Duarte's condition suffer a recurrence of cancer. With chemotherapy, only 5% suffer a recurrence. Duarte's cancer recurred, but on this evidence, she could only show that there was a 50% chance that the doctor's negligence caused the recurrence. In other words, it was just as likely that she was in the group that would have had a recurrence despite chemotherapy as it was that she was in the group that would have been benefitted by chemotherapy. Because she could not show that more likely than not chemotherapy would have made a difference, her case failed.

c. *Avoidable Consequences.* According to the unavoidable consequences rule, a tort victim cannot recover damages for any harm that could have been avoided by taking reasonable steps after the tort was committed. In personal injury cases, the rule's main effect is to give the plaintiff an incentive to seek reasonable medical care to limit the consequences of the injury. In cases involving damage to property, the rule requires reasonable steps to repair or replace the damaged property if that will limit the plaintiff's losses.

As *Ayers* neatly demonstrates, the rule has a positive corollary: If reasonable steps are taken to limit losses (here, medical surveillance to detect cancer while it is still treatable), the costs of those steps are recoverable as damages. The trend favors allowing plaintiffs who have been exposed to a hazardous substance that increases the chance of serious disease to recover the costs of medical surveillance, if surveillance is reasonable, necessary, and beneficial. Day v. NLO, 851 F.Supp. 869 (S.D.Ohio 1994); Hansen v. Mountain Fuel Supply Co., 858 P.2d 970 (Utah 1993).

d. *Offset by Benefits.* "When the defendant's tortious conduct * * * has conferred a special benefit to the interest of the plaintiff that was harmed, the value of the benefit conferred is considered in mitigation of damages, to the extent that this is equitable." Restatement (Second) of Torts § 920. For example, if a doctor performs an unauthorized operation that actually improves the plaintiff's health, the amount of damages the plaintiff recovers will be reduced by the amount of benefit conferred. Id. comment a, illustration 1.

So, if the plaintiffs in *Ayers* have health insurance that will pay for the costs of medical monitoring, should the award of damages for medical monitoring be reduced? No, according to the *collateral source rule.* The collateral source rule provides that "[p]ayments made to or benefits conferred on the injured party from other sources are not credited against the tortfeasor's liability, although they cover all or part of the harm for which the tortfeasor is liable." Note, California's Collateral Source Rule and

Plaintiff's Receipt of Uninsured Motorist Benefits, 37 Hastings L.J. 667, 670 (1986). In other words, the amount of the plaintiffs' recovery is not reduced even though the plaintiffs may be compensated for the same loss again through their insurance, or by some other collateral source.

When an injured plaintiff is compensated by a collateral source for injuries the defendant caused, the stage is set for a conflict between two of the purposes of compensatory damages. If the plaintiff is allowed to keep the benefit from the collateral source and to recover again from the defendant, the plaintiff has a windfall. To the extent that compensatory damages are supposed to "make the plaintiff whole," the rule that collateral sources are ignored puts the plaintiff in better than his rightful position.

On the other hand, consider the effect on deterrence if benefits from a collateral source reduce the defendant's obligation to pay. If compensatory damages are intended to deter defendants by making them bear the full cost of the harm they cause, letting them off the hook in cases where the plaintiff was wise enough to insure, or fortunate enough to have friends to help out financially, would result in under deterrence. Further, given the expense of litigation, compensatory damages don't really make the plaintiff whole anyway, and why should the defendant benefit from the insurance premiums the plaintiff wisely invested? After all, people should have an incentive to buy insurance, and a rule that deprived them of its benefits would discourage its purchase. See Helfend v. Southern California Rapid Transit District, 2 Cal.3d 1, 15, 84 Cal.Rptr. 173, 465 P.2d 61 (1970). Finally, many plaintiffs will not be overcompensated, because their insurance policies will have subrogation clauses that allow the insurer to recapture any benefits for which the plaintiff later receives compensation. So, double recovery is less common than the statement of the rule would suggest.

Remember, however, that an insurance company is likely to be on both sides of a personal injury lawsuit. As the rule operates, the plaintiff is likely to be compensated by two insurance companies: his own, and the defendants. Thus, the collateral source rule, which after all evolved before insurance was widely available, is often criticized as contributing to unnecessary increases in the cost of insurance. Note, California's Collateral Source Rule and Plaintiff's Receipt of Uninsured Motorist Benefits, 37 Hastings L.J. 667, 670 (1986).

It should not be surprising that eliminating the collateral source rule is high on the agenda of the current movement for tort reform. Legislation limiting the application of the rule has been enacted in at least ten states. Note, 1986 Tort Reform Legislation: A Systematic Evaluation of Caps on Damages and Limitations on Joint and Several Liability, 73 Cornell L.Rev. 628, 633 (1988). Some of those states (e.g., Minnesota, Colorado) have eliminated the collateral source rule in all civil actions. Other states have been more selective, eliminating it in actions against public entities (Pennsylvania) or in medical malpractice actions (California, Florida, Iowa, Arizona, North Dakota, Kansas). Interestingly, most of these statutes acknowledge the policy of encouraging potential plaintiffs to insure by allowing the plaintiff to recover the premiums paid to the collateral source for one or two years prior to the injury.

Where the collateral source rule is abrogated for a specific category of tort liability, constitutional issues may arise. Several courts have declared statutes abrogating the collateral source rule in medical malpractice cases to be unconstitutional because they treat victims of medical malpractice differently from other tort victims, denying them equal protection of the law. Eastin v. Broomfield, 116 Ariz. 576, 570 P.2d 744 (1977); Thompson v. KFB Insurance Co., 252 Kan. 1010, 850 P.2d 773 (1993); Comment, The Kansas Legislature's Attempt to Abrogate the Collateral Source Rule: Three Strikes and They're Out, 42 Kan.L.Rev. 913 (1994). Other jurisdictions have sustained limitations on the collateral source rule against constitutional attack. Fein v. Permanente Medical Group, 38 Cal.3d 137, 211 Cal.Rptr. 368, 695 P.2d 665 (1985)(medical malpractice); Germantown Savings Bank v. City of Philadelphia, 98 Pa.Cmwlth. 508, 512 A.2d 756 (1986)(actions against political subdivisions).

Thinking about the effect of the collateral source rule on insurance brings up, however, another of compensation's purposes. Often it is said that tort law itself functions as a kind of insurance. When the cost of injuries is included in the price of an activity or a product, the price rises, spreading the cost among participants or consumers. With the collateral source rule in place, are consumers paying for the same insurance twice, once in their insurance premiums, and once in the product's price? Which is the more efficient way to insure? The implications of the idea that compensatory damages are a form of insurance are explored further in the next main case.

e. *Caps on Damage Awards: Balancing the Hardships?* In chapter 2, at page 89, the idea of balancing the hardships—leaving the plaintiff short of the rightful position because of the hardship full relief would cause to the defendant—was characterized as a peculiarly equitable notion. Surely, the note asked, no one would advocate paying the plaintiff less than the damages she was owed because of concerns about the effect on the defendant's wealth. Is the New Jersey Tort Claims Act's prohibition on pain and suffering damages in actions against the state a form of balancing the hardships, insofar as it leaves the plaintiffs short of their rightful position in order to conserve the public's wealth? Do you see a similarity to the trade-off Congress made in the statutory scheme in *Chilicky,* text at p. 21?

Pain and suffering damages are a popular target for those who believe the tort system is in need of reform. Some reform efforts are motivated by a belief that juries are simply overcompensating plaintiffs. For example, many states have enacted caps limiting the amount of pain and suffering damages that can be recovered in medical malpractice actions out of a belief that the size of the award is more the product of the defendant's deep pockets than the severity of the plaintiff's injury. For an empirical challenge to the perception that pain and suffering awards are higher in medical malpractice actions, see Neil Vidmar, Empirical Evidence on the Deep Pockets Hypothesis: Jury Awards for Pain and Suffering in Medical Malpractice Cases, 43 Duke L.J. 217 (1993); Neil Vidmar, The Unfair Criticism of Medical Malpractice Juries, Judicature 118 (Oct.-Nov.1992). Other states have limited nonpecuniary compensation across-the-board. See Greist v. Phillips, 322 Or. 281, 906 P.2d 789 (1995) (statute limiting compensation for nonpecuniary loss to $500,000 is constitutional.)

Other reform efforts are more clearly aimed at preventing hardship to the defendant. Statutes like the New Jersey act, which cap or prohibit pain and suffering damages against public entities, are forthrightly justified as protecting the defendant's budget and thus its ability to provide needed public services. Similarly, the Civil Rights Act of 1991 gives victims of intentional discrimination a right to compensatory damages, including non-pecuniary damages, but limits the amount of the award according to the size of the employer's enterprise, which also can only be explained as protecting defendants with fewer assets from hardship. 42 U.S.C. § 1981a (1995). Is this kind of balancing appropriate?

Whether or not it is wise as a matter of policy, creating classes of defendants who are immune from a particular kind of damage award has constitutional implications. The limitation on pain and suffering damages at issue in *Ayers* was upheld against a constitutional attack in Rivera v. Gerner, 89 N.J. 526, 446 A.2d 508 (1982). On the other hand, in Louisiana, a cap on general damages in actions against public defendants was found to be unconstitutional under a provision of the state constitution forbidding sovereign immunity. Chamberlain v. State, 624 So.2d 874 (La.1993).

Caps on noneconomic losses in medical malpractice cases have also gotten a mixed reception from the courts. Caps have been found constitutional in California (Fein v. Permanente Medical Group, 38 Cal.3d 137, 211 Cal.Rptr. 368, 695 P.2d 665)(1985), Louisiana (Butler v. Flint Goodrich Hospital, 607 So.2d 517 (La.1992), Nebraska (Prendergast v. Nelson, 199 Neb. 97, 256 N.W.2d 657 (1977)), South Dakota (Knowles v. United States, 829 F.Supp. 1147 (W.D.S.D. 1993)), and West Virginia (Robinson v. Charleston Area Medical Center, Inc. 186 W.Va. 720, 414 S.E.2d 877 (1991). Caps have, however, been held to be unconstitutional under state constitutions in Texas (Lucas v. United States, 757 S.W.2d 687 (Tex.1988)(violation of provision guaranteeing "open courts")); Florida (Smith v. Dept. of Insurance, 507 So.2d 1080 (Fla.1987)(same)); Illinois (Wright v. Central Du Page Hosp. Ass'n., 63 Ill.2d 313, 347 N.E.2d 736 (1976)(violation of provision against "special laws")); and New Hampshire (Carson v. Maurer, 120 N.H. 925, 424 A.2d 825 (1980)(violation of state equal protection clause)).

f. *Managing the Damage Award.* Tort damages have traditionally been awarded in a lump sum, for past, present and future losses. The *Ayers* court suggests that were it not for the unfairness of changing the rules at such a late date in the litigation, it would abandon this practice. Instead of awarding a lump sum for medical surveillance, the court would create a fund against which the plaintiffs could make claims as they incur costs.

Tort reformers have found the notion of replacing lump sum awards with judgments that are paid out periodically, over time, to be attractive. That way, the defendant maintains control over the award, and gains the benefit of any expenses that, for one reason or another, do not eventuate. In return, the plaintiff gains a measure of security. If expenses exceed what might have been predicted, there is some protection, and the plaintiff is saved the burden of investing the award against future need. On the other hand, such paternalism may be unjustified, and it is not clear how periodically paid judgments are to accommodate the plaintiff's lawyer's fee, given that contingency fees predominate in personal injury litigation. Nonetheless, some tort reform statutes specifically provide for periodic payment of judgments. For an attempt to work out the problems periodic payment of judgments raises, see the Model Periodic Payment of Judgments Act.

*Ayers* does not present very complicated problems in managing a damage award, compared to cases that may involve thousands or tens of thousands of claims, like asbestos, DES, or Agent Orange litigation. The problems in *Ayers* are sensitive primarily because a public entity is the defendant, and the public fisc can be jealously guarded. Should the rules of damages be responsive to the type of litigation involved? Should there be one set of damage rules when the defendant is a public entity, another for private defendants? Should there be a separate set of rules for mass disasters, toxic torts, and the like? How about for cases in which children too young to manage a lump sum award are involved? See Kush v. Lloyd, 616 So.2d 415 (Fla.1992)(parents who recover future extraordinary expenses for an impaired child must hold the award in segregated trust account).

## 1. ELEMENTS OF THE AWARD: NONPECUNIARY HARMS

The next case introduces two statutory forms of action—wrongful death and survival actions—created to fill an important gap in tort recovery. It also provides an opportunity for you to think further about the purposes compensation serves. One of the characteristics that sets tort damages apart is the availability of monetary recovery for nonmonetary harms. What purpose is served by awarding money damages for harms that money cannot make good?

## BELL v. CITY OF MILWAUKEE

United States Court of Appeals, Seventh Circuit, 1984.
746 F.2d 1205.

CUMMINGS, CHIEF JUDGE. * * *

[Daniel Bell was shot in the back as he fled from a police officer (Grady). His family brought a civil rights action on behalf of his estate and his father's estate to recover damages for the shooting and the subsequent racially motivated cover up, and prevailed. Daniel Bell's estate was awarded $100,000 for compensatory damages for "loss of life," and $25,000 in punitive damages. Bell's father's estate recovered $475,000 for the loss of the son's society and companionship. Bell's siblings were awarded $100,000 for loss of society and companionship. The plaintiffs prevailed. On appeal, the awards were affirmed, except for the award for loss of society and companionship to Bell's siblings. With regard to that award, the court of appeals held that while the fourteenth amendment protected Bell's father's liberty interest in his son's society and companionship, the siblings' interests were not constitutionally protected.]

### V. SECTION 1983 CLAIM OF DANIEL BELL'S ESTATE

The district court allowed the plaintiffs to include a special verdict question regarding the violation of Daniel Bell's constitutional rights. The jury found a violation, and awarded $100,000 in damages to the estate of Daniel Bell for the loss of his life and enjoyment thereof. Defendants contend that Wisconsin law does not permit recovery by the estate for the death of Daniel Bell. The district court in ruling upon defendants' post-verdict motions disagreed, holding without explaining that Wis.Stat. § 895.04 allows the personal representative of Daniel Bell's estate to recover for loss of life for the benefit of the estate. The district court also noted that if the Wisconsin wrongful death statute could not be read as allowing the estate to recover, state law would be inconsistent with the deterrent policies of Section 1983 and therefore could not be applied. While the district court's interpretation of Section 895.04 may be in error, its evaluation of the policies behind Section 1983 in regard to Daniel Bell's estate's claim is correct.

Wisconsin survival statute Section 895.01 provides that wrongful death actions survive the death of the victim (as well as the death of the wrongdoer), and wrongful death statute Section 895.04(1) states that "[a]n action for wrongful death may be brought by the personal representative of the deceased person or by the person to whom the amount recovered belongs." What the district court seemingly overlooked, however, is that Wisconsin law does not allow separate recovery for both the estate and the beneficiaries—the very result obtained below. It is well settled under Sections 895.01 and 895.04, and those Sections' predecessors that recovery in a Wisconsin wrongful death action, even if brought in name by the personal representative, cannot include damages for the loss of life itself. The allowed recovery in Wisconsin compensates for the injury to the beneficiaries, within certain statutory recovery limitations, and not for the loss of life of the victim. * * *

The policy behind this rule is that "the cause of action belongs to the beneficiary * * *." As stated in Prunty v. Schwantes, 40 Wis.2d 418, 424–425, 162 N.W.2d 34, 38–39, "After a person dies, he can no longer be compensated * * * [O]ur legislature has decided that the survivors of the deceased are the ones that have actually been damaged, and they are the ones that should be compensated * * *." The rationale implicit in the Wisconsin rule is that the victim once deceased cannot practicably be compensated for the loss of life to be made whole. Thus if the particular compensation policy embodied in Wisconsin wrongful death law were to be applied, Daniel Bell's estate could not raise a claim for loss of life.

Though damages for loss of life are not recoverable by Daniel Bell's estate under Wisconsin law, Wis.Stat. § 895.01 allows the estate to recover for injuries suffered by Daniel Bell prior to death by virtue of, for example, excessive use of force in the course of arrest. Section 895.01 allows survival of actions for "damage to the person". The jury considered the question, however, and found no deprivation of Daniel Bell's rights occurring prior to death. * * *

In short, the Wisconsin statutory scheme creates a survival action in favor of the estate for pre-death injuries and a wrongful death action in favor of the victim's survivors, and neither type of action traditionally allows recovery of damages for loss of life itself. The district court's apparent misconstruction of Wisconsin law, however, has no practical impact on plaintiffs' claims since the application and policy of this point of Wisconsin law are inconsistent with those of Section 1983 and the Fourteenth Amendment protection of life. Therefore, Wisconsin law cannot be applied to preclude the estate's recovery for loss of life, for the reasons set out below. Where the constitutional deprivation sought to be remedied in a Section 1983 action causes death and the applicable state law would deem the action to survive or would allow recovery for the damage claim at issue, courts generally apply the state law. But the more difficult question, the question presented here and addressed by Section 1988[b] is whether a state law is "inconsistent" with federal civil rights law and therefore does not apply where state law would not allow the estate to recover for the loss of life. * * *

The Supreme Court has yet to decide squarely this issue. * * *

In a case where plaintiff died but not as a result of the putatively unconstitutional act, the Supreme Court has confirmed that restrictive state statutes apply to Section 1983 actions. In Robertson v. Wegmann, 436 U.S. 584, 98 S.Ct. 1991, 56 L.Ed.2d 554, the plaintiff who brought a Section 1983 action for malicious prosecution died while his suit was pending. The Court held that pursuant to Section 1988 the applicable Louisiana law governed the survivability issue. Under the state law, the decedent's action abated because no person with the requisite relationship to him was alive at the time of his death. Concluding that this outcome was not inconsistent with the policies of Section 1983, the Court ruled that the action did not survive but explicitly declined to express any view on the particular issue before us, i.e., whether a cause of action exists in favor of the estate despite state law which precludes such, where the alleged deprivation of constitutional rights caused death. * * *

In a *Bivens* action, i.e., an action brought not against state or local officials under Section 1983 but against federal officials directly under the Constitution, the Supreme Court has allowed recovery by the estate notwithstanding restrictive state law. Carlson v. Green, 446 U.S. 14, 100 S.Ct. 1468, 64 L.Ed.2d 15. *Carlson* involved a *Bivens*-type suit brought by a mother on behalf of the estate of her deceased son, alleging that federal prison officials grossly neglected his asthmatic condition and administered drugs which worsened his condition, with defendants'

**b.** 42 U.S.C.A. § 1988 provides: The jurisdiction in civil and criminal matters conferred on the district courts by the provisions of this Title * * * for the protection of all persons in the United States in their civil rights * * * shall be exercised and enforced in conformity with the laws of the United States, so far as such laws are suitable to carry the same into effect; but in all cases where they are not adapted to the object, or are deficient in the provisions necessary to furnish suitable remedies and punish offenses against law, the common law, as modified and changed by the constitution and statutes of the State wherein the court having jurisdiction of such civil or criminal cause is held, so far as the same is not inconsistent with the Constitution and laws of the United States, shall be extended to and govern the said courts in the trial and disposition of the cause * * *

indifference in part attributable to racial prejudice. Plaintiff argued that defendants' acts and omissions violated the deceased's Eighth and Fourteenth Amendment rights. Under Indiana law no recovery was available where the acts complained of caused the victim's death. * * * Although not explicitly discussing the component of damages for loss of life, the Supreme Court found that a uniform federal rule was necessary to achieve the *Bivens* policies of deterring federal officials from violating federal constitutional rights, and held that whenever a state survival statute would extinguish the action brought against defendants whose conduct results in death, federal law permits survival of the action. The Court distinguished *Robertson* on the rationales that in *Carlson* the plaintiff's death was caused by the defendant's acts upon which the suit was based, and no state interests are implicated by applying purely federal law to federal officials who violate the "federal Constitution". * * *

Supreme Court precedent expressing the policies underlying Section 1983 and the guarantees of the Fourteenth Amendment indicate that allowing the estate of Daniel Bell to recover is the proper result under federal policy, and that restrictive state law at issue in this case is inconsistent with the federal policy.

It is axiomatic that the Fourteenth Amendment protects individuals from deprivation by the state of life without due process. Regarding the egregiousness of Grady's conduct, on the basis of his conviction for reckless homicide and the record in general, Grady was at least grossly reckless in the commission of the killing. Under Parratt v. Taylor, 451 U.S. 527, 531–535, 101 S.Ct. 1908, 1910–1913, 68 L.Ed.2d 420, in which the Supreme Court held that even a negligent deprivation of a constitutional right is sufficient for plaintiff to invoke that right, Grady's recklessness clearly suffices, and Daniel Bell most assuredly was denied due process in the deprivation of his life.

Further, the fundamental policies behind Section 1983 are twofold: compensation for and deterrence of unconstitutional acts committed under state law. One of the primary reasons Section 1983 was enacted was to remedy and deter racial killing and other acts violative of the Fourteenth Amendment. The legislative history behind Section 1983 expresses an unequivocal concern for protecting life. * * * The deterrence objective of Section 1983 was not paramount in *Robertson v. Wegmann* as it is here. In *Robertson* death was an intervening circumstance, and thus the Court did not perceive any significant loss of deterrence if the restrictive Louisiana statute were applied, commenting that:

> In order to find even a marginal influence on behavior as a result of Louisiana's survivorship provisions, one would have to make the rather farfetched assumptions that a state official had both the desire and the ability deliberately to select as victims only those persons who would die before conclusion of the § 1983 suit for

reasons entirely unconnected with the official illegality and who would not be survived by any close relatives.

*Robertson,* 436 U.S. at 592 n. 10, 98 S.Ct. at 1996 n. 10. But since in the instant case the killing is the unconstitutional act, there would result more than a marginal loss of influence on potentially unconstitutional actors and therefore on the ability of Section 1983 to deter official lawlessness if the victim's estate could not bring suit to recover for loss of life. Moreover, if Section 1983 did not allow recovery for loss of life notwithstanding inhospitable state law, deterrence would be further subverted since it would be more advantageous to the unlawful actor to kill rather than injure. As the Supreme Court observed in Carey v. Piphus, 435 U.S. 247, 258, 98 S.Ct. 1042, 1049, 55 L.Ed.2d 252, "[I]t is not clear * * * that common-law tort rules of damages will provide a complete solution to the damages issue in every § 1983 case." Therefore it is appropriate, as the Supreme Court has noted in regard to Section 1983 damage issues, to fashion "a federal rule responsive to the need whenever a federal right is impaired."

In sum, we hold that Wis.Stat. §§ 895.01 and 895.04, along with Wisconsin decisions construing those provisions, which would preclude recovery to Daniel Bell's estate for loss of life, are inconsistent with the deterrent policy of Section 1983[41] and the Fourteenth Amendment's protection of life.[42] The Wisconsin law therefore cannot be applied to preclude the $100,000 damages recovered by Daniel Bell's estate for loss of life. * * *

The above-cited decisions also support plaintiffs' contention that the $25,000 punitive damages awarded against Grady in favor of Daniel Bell's estate should be upheld, even though Wis.Stat. § 895.04 does not allow the victim's estate to recover punitive damages. To disallow punitive damages in Section 1983 actions solely on the basis of restrictive state tort law would seriously hamper the deterrence effect of Section 1983. * * *

## *Notes*

1. *The Plaintiff's Cause of Action: Survival and Wrongful Death Actions.* At English common law, actions for personal injury (and most

**41.** Deterrence of wrongful or negligent conduct is also a policy objective of tort law, but as in Wisconsin, survival and wrongful death statutes generally do not seek to deter wrongful deaths through the imposition of damages for loss of life itself. The rationale is typically the extraordinary difficulty in measuring the value of the loss; . and in the context of a survival action, there is the additional inability to restore a deceased to the state he would have enjoyed but for his death. See R. Posner, Tort Law: Cases and Economic Analysis 121–122 (1982). Yet given the stated tort policy of deterrence and the conceivable reduction of the incidence of tortious conduct created by the threat of substantial damages, these dilemmas amount to less than a compelling argument against awarding any damages at all for loss of life. id.

**42.** Our holding that Daniel Bell's estate may properly raise a Section 1983 claim is based upon the Fourteenth Amendment's protection of life and the deterrence objective underlying Section 1983; . it is unnecessary to address whether Section 1983 compensation policy is necessarily inconsistent with the Wisconsin policy of non-compensation where the victim by virtue of death cannot be made whole.

other torts) terminated if either of the parties to the action died. Further, causing the death of a person did not give rise independently to civil liability. So, at least until the middle of the nineteenth century, neither Daniel Bell's estate nor his family would have had a cause of action in tort. Daniel Bell's action would have terminated with his death, and any injuries his family claimed to have suffered because of his death would not have been actionable. Although there were early decisions in America departing from these rules, generally they were adopted as part of the common law. W. Page Keeton et al., Prosser and Keeton on Torts § 127 at 945 (5th ed.1984).

Then, in 1846, Parliament enacted Lord Campbell's Act, 9 & 10 Vic., c. 93, which established a cause of action against one who wrongfully caused another's death for the benefit of those dependent on the decedent for support. Following this lead, every state now has a statutory remedy for wrongful death. See Stuart M. Speiser et al., Recovery for Wrongful Death and Injury (3d ed.1992).

Wrongful death statutes in this country fall roughly into two categories. The majority follow the pattern set by Lord Campbell's Act: they designate certain beneficiaries, and compensate them for the loss of the decedent's support. In other states, however, the wrongful death action is for the benefit of the decedent's estate, and damages aim at compensating the estate for the amounts the decedent would have saved from his earnings and bequeathed to his heirs had he lived his expected life span. See Theodore A. Smedley, Some Order Out of Chaos in Wrongful Death Law, 37 Vand.L.Rev. 273 (1984); Stuart M. Speiser et al., Recovery for Wrongful Death and Injury (3d ed.1992).

In addition, every state has also changed the common law rule that most tort causes of action do not survive the death of either party by enacting survival statutes. Although what specific causes of action survive varies from state to state, personal injury actions survive in most: They can be maintained by the plaintiff's estate if the plaintiff dies, and against the defendant's estate if he dies.

Where the defendant's wrong caused the plaintiff's death, the survival statute and the wrongful death statute may overlap. Then, generally, as in *Bell,* the decedent's cause of action for damages sustained before his death is prosecuted under the survival statute for the benefit of his estate, and a wrongful death action is maintained for the benefit of his dependents. (Procedurally, many states allow both actions to be prosecuted at the same time by the decedent's personal representative.)

2. *The Purpose of the Damage Award: Making the Case for Compensating Nonpecuniary Losses.* What is the point of awarding damages for "loss of life"? Certainly, the award cannot make the plaintiff whole. Consider:

> [I]t is helpful to distinguish between two types of loss in a death case. The first is the loss to the victim. This consists of the utility or satisfaction that the victim would have derived, net of any disutility, over the remaining course of his life. * * * [This] type of loss cannot, strictly speaking, be compensated. No award of damages will restore a dead person to the state of happiness he would have enjoyed but for his death. This is not a compelling argument against awarding damages, provided the purpose of tort damages is deterrent rather than compen-

satory. The threat of having to pay heavy damages will reduce the incidence of tortious conduct, and so increase social welfare, even though the payment of damages in a case where the victim dies will not compensate him.

Richard A. Posner, Tort Law: Cases and Economic Analysis 121–22 (1982).

Yet, there is a conflict between the deterrence goal and the compensation goal of tort damages in a case like this. As an earlier note suggested, insofar as tort damages serve the goal of compensation, they can be thought of as a form of insurance. Richard A. Epstein, The Legal and Insurance Dynamics of Mass Tort Litigation, 13 J.Legal Stud. 475 (1984). Having to pay damage awards increases the price of goods and services, shifting the losses associated with those goods and services and spreading the cost among all those who consume them. The price the consumer pays, thus, is the price of the product plus the price of the insurance.

But while people often insure against possible economic losses, especially against the losses their death would cause to their dependents, no one would buy insurance against the kind of loss Daniel Bell incurred. That is to say, it would not make sense to buy an insurance policy that, in addition to taking care of the decedent's dependents, paid damages to the deceased. Surely, people would rather save the premiums, and have the money while they are alive, rather than shifting the income to a time when they cannot enjoy it. Following out the implications of this argument, some economists argue that many forms of compensation for nonpecuniary loss have this effect of requiring consumers to purchase an irrational form of insurance. John E. Calfee & Paul H. Rubin, Some Implications of Damage Payments for Nonpecuniary Losses, 21 J.Legal Stud. 371 (1992). Of course, others argue that rational people would sometimes insure against nonpecuniary loss, and that there is in fact evidence that forms of insurance against these kinds of losses exist. Steven P. Croley and Jon D. Hanson, The Nonpecuniary Cost of Accident: Pain-and-Suffering Damages in Tort Law, 108 Harv.L.Rev. 1785 (1995); Mark Geistfeld, Placing a Price on Pain and Suffering: A Method for Helping Juries Determine Tort Damages for Nonmonetary Injuries, 83 Cal.L.Rev. 773 (1995); Ellen Pryor Smith, The Tort Law Debate, Efficiency, and the Kingdom of the Ill: A Critique of the Insurance Theory of Compensation, 79 Va.L.Rev. 91 (1993).

Whichever economists might have the best of this argument, does it make sense to evaluate the practice of awarding damages as a form of insurance? Think about the implications: If one were convinced that compensatory damages were not necessary as a form of deterrent—perhaps because the criminal law and the regulatory process were sufficient to maintain an optimal level of safety—and that more efficient forms of insurance were available, would one simply do away with the practice of awarding compensatory damages?

Or, would you agree with Justice Harlan, concurring in the *Bivens* case (in chapter 1), who wrote, "damages as a traditional form of compensation for invasion of a legally protected interest may be entirely appropriate even if no substantial deterrent effects on future official lawlessness might be thought to result"? Earlier in this chapter, in a note following Memphis Community School District v. Stachura, the idea that compensatory damages might have a purpose beyond either deterrence or compensation was introduced. Does the availability of "loss of life" damages in a case like *Bell* support that view? See Margaret Jane Radin, Compensation and Commensurability, 43 Duke L.J. 56 (1993).

Thinking back to *Stachura,* however, raises an interesting doctrinal question. *Stachura* rejected an award of damages for the abstract value of a constitutional right, finding that under § 1983, compensatory damages must "always be designed to compensate injuries caused by the [constitutional] deprivation, [leaving] no room for non-compensatory damages measured by the jury's perception of the abstract 'importance' of a constitutional right." As for deterrence, punitive damages are available. Otherwise, according to *Stachura,* "§ 1983 presupposes that damages that compensate for actual harm ordinarily suffice to deter constitutional violations." 477 U.S. 299, 309–10, 106 S.Ct. 2537, 2544–45, 91 L.Ed.2d 249. If the award of loss of life damages cannot be justified as a form of compensation, does it then lie outside the scope of § 1983?

In another context, the Supreme Court has recognized a distinction between the kind of deterrence compensatory damages provide, and punitive damages. Molzof v. United States, 502 U.S. 301, 112 S.Ct. 711, 116 L.Ed.2d 731 (1992). In *Molzof*, the United States argued that awarding damages for lost enjoyment of life to a comatose plaintiff, or to the estate in a wrongful death suit, is "punitive" in effect because it bears no relation to compensation, and is therefore barred by the Federal Torts Claims Act (FTCA). According to the Court, the FTCA "bars the recovery only of what are *legally* considered punitive damages under traditional common-law principles," and not awards that are arguably punitive in effect. 112 S.Ct. at 718. (Neither the Supreme Court nor the courts below reached the issue of whether loss of enjoyment of life damages were properly available under Wisconsin law.)

Despite the intervening decision in *Stachura, Bell* continues to be followed. Sherrod v. Berry, 629 F.Supp. 159 (N.D.Ill.1985), rev'd on other grounds, 856 F.2d 802 (7th Cir.1988); Bass v. Wallenstein, 769 F.2d 1173 (7th Cir.1985).

3. *The Elements of Damages in Wrongful Death and Survival Actions.* Many survival statutes limit the damages that can be recovered. Prohibitions on punitive damages, like that in *Bell,* and on pain and suffering damages, for example, are common. See, e.g., Cal.Code Civ.Pro. § 377.34 (pain and suffering damages may not be awarded in an action brought by a decedent's personal representative). As for wrongful death statutes, the damages available depend on the theory of the action. Where the wrongful death action is for the estate's benefit (effectively extending the survival action to include all the damage done to the decedent, not simply the damage up to the time of death), the damages are determined by subtracting the decedent's projected lifetime expenses from his projected lifetime earnings. Dan B. Dobbs, Law of Remedies § 8.3(4)(2d ed.1993).

Wrongful death statutes premised on compensating the decedent's dependents are more complicated. The elements vary widely from jurisdiction to jurisdiction. All, of course, recognize that the financial support the decedent would have provided to his dependents must be replaced. Many jurisdictions have gone beyond this, however, to recognize that the decedent's non-monetary contributions to his family—his society, comfort and support—should also be compensated, although the language of the statutes has sometimes forced courts to rationalize recovery by positing that the deceased's society, comfort and services have a financial value that can be determined. See, e.g. Krouse v. Graham, 19 Cal.3d 59, 137 Cal.Rptr. 863, 562 P.2d 1022 (1977). Very few jurisdictions have taken the next step to award damages for the mental anguish of the survivors, although the number may be increasing. W. Page Keeton et al., Prosser and Keeton on Torts § 127 at 952 (5th ed.1984). Finally, a few jurisdictions have recognized that complete compensation requires that both the estate and the dependents be made whole, allowing the heirs to recover lost inheritance and the dependents to recover lost support. Yowell v. Piper Aircraft, 703 S.W.2d 630 (Tex.1986); Martin v. Atlantic Coast Line R.R., 268 F.2d 397 (5th Cir.1959)(Federal Employees Liability Act).

So far as damages for loss of life are concerned, in England, for a time, it was accepted that damages for loss of life could be recovered in a personal injury case in addition to other elements of pecuniary loss and non-pecuniary loss. Certainly, most American jurisdictions would agree that where the plaintiff survives, an injury that shortens the plaintiff's life expectancy requires compensation. Most, however, insist that the prospect of a shorter life is simply one element to be considered in determining pain and suffering damages, rather than an independent item of damages. Compare McDougald v. Garber, 73 N.Y.2d 246, 538 N.Y.S.2d 937, 536 N.E.2d 372 (1989)(error to instruct jury to make a separate award for loss of enjoyment of life) with Fraysier v. United States, 566 F.Supp. 1085 (S.D.Fla.1983)(separate award proper). See also Downie v. United States Lines Co., 359 F.2d 344 (3d Cir.1966)(injured seaman entitled to compensation "based on life expectancy at the time of injury for the physical and mental effects of his injury on his ability to engage in those activities which normally contribute to the enjoyment of life").

Outside the context of § 1983, a few American jurisdictions have suggested that the loss of the enjoyment of life may be a separate, compensable item of damages. Holston v. Sisters of Third Order of St. Francis, 247 Ill.App.3d 985, 187 Ill.Dec. 743, 618 N.E.2d 334 (Ill.App.1993); Gregory v. Carey, 246 Kan. 504, 791 P.2d 1329 (1990); Katsetos v. Nolan, 170 Conn. 637, 368 A.2d 172 (1976). Other courts have insisted that if the plaintiff is not aware of the loss, there is no compensatory purpose to the award and therefore the award is not proper. Paladino v. Campos, 145 N.J.Super. 555, 368 A.2d 429 (1976); McDougald v. Garber, 73 N.Y.2d 246, 538 N.Y.S.2d 937, 536 N.E.2d 372 (1989). What's more, England has retreated, first by limiting loss of life damages in wrongful death cases to a fixed amount, Gammell v. Wilson [1980] 2 All E.R. 557 (L.1250) and then by eliminating them entirely. Administration of Justice Act of 1982. See Note, Hedonic Damages in § 1983 Actions: A Remedy for the Unconstitutional Deprivation of a Life, 44 Wash. & L.L.Rev. 321 (1987).

*Bell's* use of § 1988 to go beyond the limits of the state's wrongful death statute has been applied to issues other than loss of life damages. See, e.g., Guyton v. Phillips, 532 F.Supp. 1154 (N.D.Cal.1981)(survival statute denying pain and suffering damages to decedent's estate is inconsistent with the purposes of § 1983; loss of life damages also awarded). For a thorough discussion of the interaction of § 1983, § 1988 and state wrongful death and survival statutes, see Steven H. Steinglass, Wrongful Death Actions and § 1983, 60 Ind.L.J. 559 (1985).

4. *Measuring the Damage Award:* Assuming damages for loss of the value of life, or lost enjoyment of life, ought to be awarded, how much should the award be? The next case suggests some of the problems that arise in attaching a monetary value to a nonpecuniary harm.

## 2. MEASURING THE DAMAGES

### *(a) Value*

# OHIO v. DEPARTMENT OF THE INTERIOR

United States Court of Appeals, District of Columbia Circuit, 1989.
880 F.2d 432.

WALD, CHIEF JUDGE, and ROBINSON and MIKVA, CIRCUIT JUDGES.[1]

Petitioners are 10 states, three environmental organizations ("State and Environmental Petitioners"), a chemical industry trade association, a manufacturing company and a utility company ("Industry Petitioners"), who seek review of regulations promulgated by the Department of the Interior ("DOI" or "Interior") pursuant to § 301(c)(1)–(3) of the Comprehensive Environmental Response, Compensation and Liability Act of 1980 ("CERCLA" or the "Act"), as amended, 42 U.S.C. § 9651(c). The regulations govern the recovery of money damages from persons responsible for spills and leaks of oil and hazardous substances, to compensate for injuries such releases inflict on natural resources. Damages may be recovered by state and in some cases the federal governments, as trustees for those natural resources.

Petitioners challenge many aspects of those regulations. State and Environmental Petitioners raise ten issues, all of which essentially focus on the regulations' alleged undervaluation of the damages recoverable from parties responsible for hazardous materials spills that despoil natural resources. Industry Petitioners attack the regulations from a different vantage point, claiming they will permit or encourage overstated damages. * * *

We hold that the regulation limiting damages recoverable by government trustees for harmed natural resources to 'the lesser of' (a) the cost of restoring or replacing the equivalent of an injured resource, or (b) the lost use value of the resource is directly contrary to the clearly expressed intent of Congress and is therefore invalid. We also hold that the regulation prescribing a hierarchy of methodologies by which the lost-use value of natural resources may be measured, which focuses exclusively

1. Parts I, II, III, IV, VII, VIII, IX, X, XI and XII were authored by Judge Wald. Part XIII was authored by Judge Robinson. Parts V and VI were authored by Judge Mikva.

on the market values for such resources when market values are available, is not a reasonable interpretation of the statute. * * *

I. BACKGROUND

* * * The relevant provisions of CERCLA * * * [provide] that responsible parties may be held liable for "damages for injury to, destruction of, or loss of natural resources, including the reasonable costs of assessing such injury, destruction, or loss resulting from such a release." § 107(a)(c), 42 U.S.C. § 9607(a)(C). Liability is to "the United States Government and to any State for natural resources within the State or belonging to, managed by, controlled by, or appertaining to such State." * * *

Congress conferred on the President (who in turn delegated to Interior) the responsibility for promulgating regulations governing the assessment of damages for natural resource injuries resulting from releases of hazardous substances or oil, for the purposes of CERCLA and the Clean Water Act's § 311(f)(4)–(5) oil and hazardous substance natural resource damages provisions. * * * CERCLA as amended provides that any assessment performed in accordance with the prescribed procedure is entitled to a rebuttable presumption of accuracy in a proceeding to recover damages from a responsible party. * * *

II. STANDARD OF REVIEW

In reviewing an agency's interpretation of a statute, we first determine "whether Congress has directly spoken to the precise question at issue." Chevron U.S.A., Inc. v. Natural Resources Defense Council, Inc., 467 U.S. 837, 842 (1984). If so, then both Interior and this court "must give effect to the unambiguously expressed intent of Congress."

If, on the other hand, the statute is ambiguous or is silent on a particular issue, this court must assume that Congress implicitly delegated to the agency the power to make policy choices that " 'represent [ ] a reasonable accommodation of conflicting policies that were committed to the agency's care by the statute.' " *Chevron,* 467 U.S. at 844–45. In that event, the court must defer to the agency's interpretation of the statute so long as it is reasonable and consistent with the statutory purpose. This is "Step Two" of *Chevron* analysis. * * *

III. THE "LESSER-OF" RULE

The most significant issue in this case concerns the validity of the regulation providing that damages for despoilment of natural resources shall be "the *lesser of*: restoration or replacement costs; or diminution of use values." 43 C.F.R. § 11.35(b)(2)(1987)(emphasis added).

State and Environmental Petitioners challenge Interior's "lesser of" rule, insisting that CERCLA requires damages to be at least sufficient to pay the cost in every case of restoring, replacing or acquiring the equivalent of the damaged resource (hereinafter referred to shorthandedly as "restoration"). Because in some—probably a majority of—cases lost-use-value will be lower than the cost of restoration, Interior's rule will result in damages award too small to pay for the costs of restoration. * * *

Although our resolution of the dispute submerges us in the minutiae of CERCLA text and legislative materials, we initially stress the enormous practical significance of the "lesser of" rule. A hypothetical example will illustrate the point: imagine a hazardous substance spill that kills a rookery of fur seals and destroys a habitat for seabirds at a sealife reserve. The lost use value of the seals and seabird habitat would be measured by the market value of the fur seals' pelts (which would be approximately $15 each) plus the selling price per acre of land comparable in value to that on which the spoiled bird habitat was located. Even if, as likely, that use value turns out to be far less than the cost of restoring the rookery and seabird habitat, it would nonetheless be the only measure of damages eligible for the presumption of recoverability under the Interior rule.

After examining the language and purpose of CERCLA, as well as its legislative history, we conclude that Interior's "lesser of" rule is directly contrary to the expressed intent of Congress.

### A. *The Contours of "The Precise Question at Issue"*

Commencing our *Chevron* analysis, we must first decide exactly what "the precise question at issue" is in the present case. * * *

That question is not what measure of damages should apply in any or all cases which are brought under the Act. As to that larger question, Interior is obviously correct in asserting that Congress delegated to it a considerable measure of discretion in formulating a standard. The precise question here is a far more discrete one: whether DOI is entitled to treat use value and restoration cost as having equal presumptive legitimacy as a measure of damages.

Interior's "lesser of" rule operates on the premise that, as the cost of a restoration project goes up relative to the value of the injured resource, at some point it becomes wasteful to require responsible parties to pay the full cost of restoration. The logic behind the rule is the same logic that prevents an individual from paying $8,000 to repair a collision-damaged car that was worth only $5,000 before the collision. Just as a prudent individual would sell the damaged car for scrap and then spend $5,000 on a used car in similar condition, DOI's rule requires a polluter to pay a sum equal to the diminution in the use value of a resource whenever that sum is less than restoration cost. What is significant about Interior's rule is the point at which it deems restoration "inefficient." Interior chose to draw the line not at the point where restoration becomes practically impossible, nor at the point where the cost of restoration becomes grossly disproportionate to the use value of the resource, but rather at the point where restoration cost exceeds—by any amount, however small—the use value of the resource. Thus, while we agree with DOI that CERCLA permits it to establish a rule exempting responsible parties *in some cases* from having to pay the full cost of restoration of natural resources, we also agree with Petitioners that it does not permit Interior to draw the line on an automatic "which costs less" basis. * * *

*B. Text and Structure of CERCLA* * * *

1. Section 107(f)(1) and the Measure of Damages

The strongest linguistic evidence of Congress' intent to establish a distinct preference for restoration costs as the measure of damages is contained in § 107(f)(1) of CERCLA. That section states that natural resource damages recovered by a government trustee are "for use only to restore, replace, or acquire the equivalent of such natural resources." 42 U.S.C. § 9607(f)(1). It goes on to state: "The measure of damages in any action under [§ 107(a)(C)] shall not be limited by the sums which can be used to restore or replace such resources."

a. Limitation on Uses of Recovered Damages

By mandating the use of all damages to restore the injured resources, Congress underscored in § 107(f)(1) its paramount restorative purpose for imposing damages at all. It would be odd indeed for a Congress so insistent that all damages be spent on restoration to allow a "lesser" measure of damages than the cost of restoration in the majority of cases. Only two possible inferences about congressional intent could explain the anomaly: Either Congress intended trustees to commence restoration projects only to abandon them for lack of funds, or Congress expected taxpayers to pick up the rest of the tab. The first theory is contrary to Congress' intent to effect a "make-whole" remedy of complete restoration, and the second is contrary to a basic purpose of the CERCLA natural resource damage provisions—that polluters bear the costs of their polluting activities. It is far more logical to presume that Congress intended responsible parties to be liable for damages in an amount sufficient to accomplish its restorative aims. Interior's rule, on the other hand, assumes that Congress purposely formulated a statutory scheme that would doom to failure its goals of restoration in a majority of cases.

In this connection, it should be noted that Interior makes no claim that a "use value" measure will provide enough money to pay for ANY of the three uses to which all damages must be assigned: restoration, replacement *or acquisition of an equivalent resource.* Nor could Interior make such a claim, because its "lesser of" rule not only calculates use value quite differently from restoration or replacement cost but it also fails to link measurement of use value in any way to the cost of acquiring an equivalent resource. For example, Interior could not possibly maintain that recovering $15 per pelt for the fur seals killed by a hazardous substance release would enable the purchase of an "equivalent" number of fur seals.

b. The "Shall Not Be Limited by" Language

The same section of CERCLA that mandates the expenditures of all damages on restoration (again a shorthand reference to all three listed uses of damages) provides that the measure of damages "shall not be limited by" restoration costs. § 107(f)(1), 42 U.S.C. § 9607(f)(1). This provision obviously reflects Congress' apparent concern that its restorative purpose for imposing damages not be construed as making restoration cost a damages ceiling. But the explicit command that damages "shall not be limited by" restoration costs also carries in it an implicit assumption that restoration cost will serve as the basic measure of damages in many if not most CERCLA cases. It would be markedly inconsistent with the restorative thrust of the whole section to limit restoration-based damages, as Interior's rule does, to a minuscule number of cases where restoration is cheaper than paying for lost use. * * *

*C. Legislative History of CERCLA*

The text and structure of CERCLA indicate clearly to us that Congress intended restoration costs to be the basic measure of recovery for harm to natural resources. We next examine the legislative history of CERCLA to ascertain if there are any countervailing indications to our conclusion. * * *

CERCLA's legislative history * * * shows that Congress soundly rejected the two basic premises underlying Interior's "lesser of" rule—first, that the common-law measure of damages is appropriate in the natural resource context, and second, that it is economically inefficient to restore a resource whose use value is less than the cost of restoration. * * *

Accepting for the sake of argument the contention that the "lesser of" rule reflects the common law,[37] support for the proposition that Congress adopted common-law damage standards wholesale into CERCLA is slim to nonexistent. * * * The legislative history illustrates* * * that a motivating force behind the CERCLA natural resource damage provisions was Congress' dissatisfaction with the common law. Indeed, one wonders why Congress would have passed a new damage provision at all if it were content with the common law. * * *

Alternatively, Interior justifies the "lesser of" rule as being economically efficient. Under DOI's economic efficiency view, making restoration cost the measure of damages would be a waste of money whenever restoration would cost more than the use value of the resource. Its explanation of the proposed rules included the following statement:

> [I]f use value is higher than the cost of restoration or replacement, then it would be more rational for society to be compensated for the cost to restore or replace the lost resource than to be compensated for the lost use. Conversely, if restoration or replacement costs are

37. We note in passing that the "lesser of" standard does not apply in all non-CERCLA contexts. See, e.g., Denoyer v. Lamb, 22 Ohio App.3d 136, 490 N.E.2d 615, 618–19 (1984)(restoration cost is proper measure where property is used for a residence or for recreation, so long as restoration cost is not "grossly disproportionate" to diminution in market value); Heninger v. Dunn, 101 Cal.App.3d 858, 162 Cal.Rptr. 104, 106–09 (1980)(restoration cost is proper measure where owner has a personal reason for restoring land to its original condition, so long as restoration cost is not unreasonably disproportionate to diminution in market value); Restatement (Second) of Torts section 929, comment b (1977).

> higher than the value of uses foregone, it is rational for society to compensate individuals for their lost uses rather than the cost to restore or replace the injured natural resource.

50 Fed.Reg. at 52,141. See also 51 Fed.Reg. at 27,704 ("lesser of" rule "promotes a rational allocation of society's assets").

This is nothing more or less than cost-benefit analysis: Interior's rule attempts to optimize social welfare by restoring an injured resource only when the diminution in the resource's value to society is greater in magnitude than the cost of restoring it. And, acknowledgedly, Congress did intend CERCLA's natural resource provisions to operate efficiently. For one thing, the Act requires that the assessment of damages and the restoration of injured resources take place as cost-effectively as possible. Moreover, as we have indicated, there is some suggestion in the legislative history that Congress intended recovery not to encompass restoration cost where restoration is infeasible or where its cost is grossly disproportionate to use value.

The fatal flaw of Interior's approach, however, is that it assumes that natural resources are fungible goods, just like any other, and that the value to society generated by a particular resource can be accurately measured in every case—assumptions that Congress apparently rejected. As the foregoing examination of CERCLA's text, structure and legislative history illustrates, Congress saw restoration as the presumptively correct remedy for injury to natural resources. To say that Congress placed a thumb on the scales in favor of restoration is not to say that it forswore the goal of efficiency. "Efficiency," standing alone, simply means that the chosen policy will dictate the result that achieves the greatest value to society. Whether the particular choice is efficient depends on *how the various alternatives are valued*. Our reading of CERCLA does not attribute to Congress an irrational dislike of "efficiency"; rather, it suggests that Congress was skeptical of the ability of human beings to measure the true "value" of a natural resource. Indeed, even the common law recognizes that restoration is the proper remedy for injury to property where measurement of damages by some other method will fail to compensate fully for the injury.[41] Congress' refusal to view use value and restoration cost as having equal presumptive legitimacy merely recognizes that natural resources have value that is not readily measured by traditional means. Congress delegated to Interior the job of deciding at what point the presumption of restoration falls away, but its repeated emphasis on the primacy of restoration rejected the underlying premise of Interior's rule, which is that restora-

**41.** See, e.g., Trinity Church v. John Hancock Mut. Life Ins. Co., 399 Mass. 43, 502 N.E.2d 532, 536 (1987)(restoration cost is proper measure where diminution in market value is unsatisfactory or unavailable as a measure of damages, as in the case of structural damage to a church); . Weld County Bd. of Com'rs v. Slovek, 723 P.2d 1309, 1316–17 (Colo.1986) (court may, in its discretion, award restoration cost where award of diminution in market value would not adequately compensate owner for some personal reason, provided that restoration cost is not "wholly unreasonable" in relation to diminution in value); see also supra note 37.

tion is wasteful if its cost exceeds—by even the slightest amount—the diminution in use value of the injured resource. * * *

VI. The Hierarchy of Assessment Methods

The regulations establish a rigid hierarchy of permissible methods for determining "use values," limiting recovery to the price commanded by the resource on the open market, unless the trustee finds that "the market for the resource is not reasonably competitive." If the trustee makes such a finding, it may "appraise" the market value in accordance with the relevant sections of the "Uniform Appraisal Standards for Federal Land Acquisition." Only when neither the market value nor the appraisal method is "appropriate" can other methods of determining use value be employed.

Environmental petitioners maintain that Interior's emphasis on market value is an unreasonable interpretation of the statute, under the so-called "second prong" of Chevron U.S.A., Inc. v. Natural Resources Defense Council, Inc., 467 U.S. 837, 845 (1984), and we agree. While it is not irrational to look to market price as *one* factor in determining the use value of a resource, it is unreasonable to view market price as the *exclusive* factor, or even the predominant one. From the bald eagle to the blue whale and snail darter, natural resources have values that are not fully captured by the market system. * * * Courts have long stressed that market prices are not to be used as surrogates for value "when the market value has been too difficult to find, or when its application would result in manifest injustice to owner or public." We find that DOI erred by establishing "a strong presumption in favor of market price and appraisal methodologies."

We are not satisfied that the problem is solved by the provision* * * permitting nonmarket methodologies to be used when the market for the resource is not "reasonably competitive." There are many resources whose components may be traded in "reasonably competitive" markets, but whose total use values are not fully reflected in the prices they command in those markets. Interior itself provides ample proof of the inadequacy of the "reasonably competitive market" caveat. For example, DOI has noted that "the hierarchy established* * *" would dictate a use value for fur seals of $15 per seal, corresponding to the market price for the seal's pelt. Another example of DOI's erroneous equation of market price with use value is its insistence that the sum of the fees charged by the government for the use of a resource, say, for admission to a national park, constitutes "the value to the public of recreational or other public uses of the resource," because "these fees are what the government has determined to represent the value of the natural resource and represent an offer by a willing seller." This is quite obviously and totally fallacious; there is no necessary connection between the total value to the public of a park and the fees charged as admission, which typically are set not to maximize profits but rather to encourage the public to visit the park. In fact, the decision to set entrance fees far below what the traffic would bear is evidence of

Congress's strong conviction that parks are priceless national treasures and that access to them ought to be as wide as possible, and not, as DOI would have it, a sign that parks are really not so valuable after all. * * *

On remand, DOI should consider a rule that would permit trustees to derive use values for natural resources by summing up all reliably calculated use values, however measured, so long as the trustee does not double count. Market valuation can of course serve as one factor to be considered, but by itself it will necessarily be incomplete. * * *

XIII. CONTINGENT VALUATION

* * * DOI's natural resource damage assessment regulations define "use value" as

> the value to the public of recreational or other public uses of the resource, as measured by changes in consumer surplus, any fees or other payments collectable by the government or Indian tribe for a private party's use of the natural resource, and any economic rent accruing to a private party because the government or Indian tribe does not charge a fee or price for the use of the resource.

The regulations provide several approaches to use valuation. When the injured resource is traded in a market, the lost use value is the diminution in market price. When that is not precisely the case, but similar resources are traded in a market, an appraisal technique may be utilized to determine damages. When, however, neither of these two situations obtains, nonmarketed resource methodologies are available. One of these is "contingent valuation" (CV), the subject of controversy here.

The CV process "includes all techniques that set up hypothetical markets to elicit an individual's economic valuation of a natural resource." CV involves a series of interviews with individuals for the purpose of ascertaining the values they respectively attach to particular changes in particular resources. Among the several formats available to an interviewer in developing the hypothetical scenario embodied in a CV survey are direct questioning, by which the interviewer learns how much the interviewee is willing to pay for the resource; bidding formats, for example, the interviewee is asked whether he or she would pay a given amount for a resource and, depending upon the response, the bid is set higher or lower until a final price is derived; and a "take or leave it" format, in which the interviewee decides whether or not he or she is willing to pay a designated amount of money for the resource. CV methodology thus enables ascertainment of individually-expressed values for different levels of quality of resources, and dollar values of individuals' changes in well-being. * * *

Industry Petitioners point out that at common law there can be no recovery for speculative injuries, and they contend that CV methodology is at odds with that principle. CV methodology, they say, is rife with speculation, amounting to no more than ordinary public opinion polling.

We have already noted our disagreement with the proposition that the strictures of the common law apply to CERCLA. That much of Industry Petitioners' argument to the contrary thus fades away. CERCLA does, however, require utilization of the "best available procedures" for determinations of damages flowing from destruction of or injury to natural resources, and Industry Petitioners insist that CV methodology is too flawed to qualify as such. In their eyes, the CV process is imprecise, is untested, and has a built-in bias and a propensity to produce overestimation. * * *

Industry Petitioners urge* * * that even assuming that questions are artfully drafted and carefully circumscribed, there is such a high degree of variation in size of the groups surveyed, and such a concomitant fluctuation in aggregations of damages, that CV methodology cannot be considered a "best available procedure."[86] We think this attack on CV methodology is insufficient in a facial challenge to invalidate CV as an available assessment technique. The extent of damage to natural resources from releases of oil and hazardous substances varies greatly, and though the impact may be widespread and severe, it is in the mission of CERCLA to assess the public loss.[87] Certainly nothing in CV methodology itself shapes the injury inflicted by an environmental disaster, or influences identification of the population affected thereby. The argument of Industry Petitioners strikes at CERCLA, not CV's implementation, and can appropriately be considered only by Congress.

Similarly, we find wanting Industry Petitioners' protest that CV does not rise to the status of a "best available procedure" because willingness-to-pay—a factor prominent in CV methodology—can lead to overestimates by survey respondents. The premise of this argument is that respondents do not actually pay money, and likely will overstate their willingness-to-pay. One study relied upon by Industry Petitioners hypothesizes that respondents may "respond in ways that are more indicative of what they would like to see done than how they would behave in an actual market," and also observes that the converse is possible. The simple and obvious safeguard against overstatement, however, is more sophisticated questioning. Even as matters now stand, the risk of overestimation has not been shown to produce such egregious results as to justify judicial overruling of DOI's careful estimate of the caliber of worth of CV methodology.

**86.** Industry Petitioners cite a study estimating the combined option and existence values to Texas residents of whooping cranes at $109,000,000 (13.9 million Texas residents × $7.13). The estimate rested upon responses to a survey eliciting the amount an individual would pay for a permit to visit the National Wildlife Refuge where the whooping crane winters. Had the survey been nationwide in scope, the estimate would have been $1.58 billion. Brief for Industry Petitioners at 14 n. 24 (referring to J. Stoll & L. Johnson, Concepts of Value, Nonmarket Valuation, and the Case of the Whooping Crane (Natural Resources Working Paper Series, National Resource Workgroup, Dep't of Agricultural Economics, Texas A & M Univ.)(1984) at 23–24, J.A. 2828–2829).

**87.** Thus, in the whooping crane scenario referred to by industry petitioners the intent of CERCLA would be realized, not contravened, by a more expansive survey and a correspondingly higher assessment of damages if people beyond the borders of Texas were affected.

Industry Petitioners also challenge the use of CV AFTER an oil leak or a hazardous waste release has occurred. They fear that application of CV methodology in those circumstances is fraught with a significant bias leading to overvaluation of the damaged resources. As a practical matter, it would be prohibitively expensive, if not physically impossible, to solicit individual valuations of each and every natural resource, or even a sizeable number thereof, in order to avoid any upward bias in the event that the resource is later damaged. Moreover, in light of CERCLA's preference for restoration, it would be a terrible waste of time and energy to conduct broadscale valuation interviewing beforehand. While, depending on whether interviewing occurs before or after damage, the results may differ somewhat, that alone does not reduce CV methodology to something less than a "best available procedure." We have no cause to overturn DOI's considered judgment that CV methodology, when properly applied, can be structured so as to eliminate undue upward biases.

We sustain DOI in its conclusion that CV methodology is a "best available procedure." As such, its conclusion in the Natural Resource Damage Assessment regulations was entirely proper. * * *

### *Problems*

1. *Country Lodge v. Miller (Reprised)*: Assume that the river into which Miller dumps her mash is a natural resource "belonging* * * or appertaining to the State," and that the apple mash is contaminated with a pesticide that is a "pollutant or contaminant." If the state sues Miller as a "responsible party," how will the damage be valued?

2. Tama's home was badly damaged in a fire for which Paul is legally responsible. The fire also destroyed most of Tama's clothing and furniture, a collection of 1960's acid rock posters from her parents' hippie days, the only manuscript of the novel she has been working on since college, and the diary she used to record the details of her high school trip to Israel.

As for her house, it is an older, single family dwelling in what has become a prized commercial area. If the house were demolished, the land could be sold for more than the pre-fire market value of the house and land together. Tama, however, loves her house, and wants to repair it.

How are her damages to be established?

### *Notes*

1. The Department of the Interior issued new regulations in response to *Ohio*. The new regulations eliminate the "lesser of" rule and the hierarchy of assessment methods criticized in the case, and continue the use of contingent valuation methods. The new regulations state that the damage assessment includes the cost of "restoration, rehabilitation, replacement, and/or acquisition of the equivalent of the injured natural resource," and provide the official charged with assessment with a wide choice of methods, all focused on restoration. 43 C.F.R. § 11.82 et seq. (1994). Another statute relying on a similar approach is the Oil Pollution Act of 1990, § 33

U.S.C. 2701–2719 (1990), whose damage assessment provisions are detailed at 15 C.F.R. § 990 (1994).

For general discussions of the problem of valuing natural resources and critiques of contingent valuation, see Comment, Valuing the Environment: NOAA's New Regulations Under the Oil Pollution Act of 1990, 22 Pepp. L.Rev. 167 (1994); Jerry A. Hausman (ed.), Contingent Valuation: A Critical Assessment (1993); Frank B. Cross, Natural Resource Damage Valuation, 42 Vand.L.Rev. 269 (1989).

2. The problem of measuring damages can be broken down into two issues. The first is, what is the target? Should we even be attempting to measure the nonpecuniary value of a natural resource—or of a life, as in *Bell*, page 557. Once that is decided, there remains the question of method: How exactly, do we measure its value? In court, that often is resolved as a question of the admissibility of evidence and the competence of expert witnesses to opine as to value.

For example, methods similar to contingent valuation could be used to establish the hedonic, or nonpecuniary, value of life. Governmental agencies and private industry conduct cost/benefit studies to determine the impact of safety regulations, and those studies necessarily include estimates of the value of life. By reasoning backward from the willingness of people to invest in safety devices that might save a life, a figure for the value of life can be calculated. Similarly, a figure can be calculated by examining the premium people are paid for engaging in risky occupations. Stan Smith and Michael Brookshire, Economic/Hedonic Damages (1990); T.C. Schelling, The Life You Save May Be Your Own, in Samuel Chase (ed.), Public Expenditure Analysis (Brookings: 1966).

Do these sorts of studies and surveys provide a basis for estimating life's value? In Mercado v. Ahmed, 974 F.2d 863 (7th Cir.1992), a trial court had refused to allow an expert to testify that based on a survey of 75 such studies, a boy's diminished enjoyment of life could be valued at between $2.2 million and $2.7 million. The Seventh Circuit affirmed the trial court's decision:

> A survey of attitudes and views of others as a basis for concluding something is true is not necessarily wrong. * * * what is wrong here is not that the evidence is founded on consensus or agreement, it is that the consensus is that of persons who are no more expert than are jurors on the value of life.

Id. at 869. Because no expert consensus as to the appropriate methodology exists, the expert, who was "no more expert in valuing life than the average person" was properly not permitted to testify. Other courts have agreed, finding government and private industry studies unhelpful in establishing the hedonic value of an individual's life. First, the range of values the studies report—from a low of $450,000 to a high of $9 million—is so wide as to give the jury no helpful guidance. Ayers v. Robinson, 887 F.Supp. 1049 (N.D.Ill.1995). Second, the purpose of the studies—to evaluate regulations or safety devices—is so different from the purpose of individualized damage calculations as to make the studies' relevance suspect. Government agencies frequently do not reveal their methodologies, and the numbers they settle on may be as much the result of political compromise as of science. Id. at 1049 n. 4.

3. In most cases, damages are measured by the value of the thing lost, and value means market value. Market value is "what a willing buyer would pay in cash to a willing seller." United States v. Miller, 317 U.S. 369, 374, 63 S.Ct. 276, 280, 87 L.Ed. 336 (1943). But, problems of valuation are not limited to intangibles like life and natural resources. Suppose a person's clothing and household belongings are destroyed?

> "No general rule can be laid down by which the amount of indemnity can be arrived at infallibly in all cases. [Where] commodities which are bought and sold in the market [are destroyed] * * the market value* * * would seem to furnish the best measure * * *. In such cases market value * * * would enable [the plaintiff] to replace the goods which he had lost, with others equal to them in every respect, and thus restore him to as good a position as he was in before the fire occurred. But market value does not in all cases afford a correct measure of indemnity, and is not therefore "a universal test." In some cases there is no market value, properly speaking, and in others, if there is, it plainly would not of itself afford full indemnity. * * *
>
> "We think that as to the furniture, personal effects, and other personal property, the market value, if there was one, would fail to furnish a satisfactory test of the actual loss. * * * It is true that the defendant offered testimony tending 'to show that secondhand household furniture, effects, and other personal property of the kind destroyed, were at the time of the fire, commonly sold in Boston.' * * * [W]e* * * think that a sum equal to the market value would not indemnify the plaintiff for the loss which she has sustained. Such a value would depend largely on considerations which would have nothing to do with the intrinsic value of the articles, or with their actual worth to the owner. And we think that, being in the plaintiff's possession and used and kept for use by her in her house and about her person, without any intention or expectation on her part of selling them or of offering them for sale, they should be regarded as belonging in a sense to the person of the owner, and that the damages should be assessed according to the actual worth of the articles to her for use in the condition in which they were at the time of the fire, excluding any fanciful or sentimental considerations."

Wall v. Platt, 169 Mass. 398, 406–407, 48 N.E. 270 (1897).

Some courts go even farther:

> Where items have been destroyed that "have their primary value in sentiment", "the most fundamental rule of damages that every wrongful injury* * * should be adequately and reasonably compensated requires the allowance of damages in compensation for the reasonable special value of such articles to their owner taking into consideration the feelings of the owner for such property."

Brown v. Frontier Theatres, Inc., 369 S.W.2d 299, 305 (Tex.1963).

What is "actual worth to the owner"? Intrinsic value? Sentimental value?

4. How does a plaintiff prove a thing's "actual worth"? For that matter, how does one prove something's market value? Few people keep detailed records about their possessions, or schedule their depreciation. Most courts allow a property owner to testify as to the value of her own property, without qualifying herself as an expert. Dan B. Dobbs, Law of Remedies § 3.5 (2d ed.1993).

5. The notes following *Ayers*, p. 549, discuss how some courts have imposed obstacles to recovering damages for fear of cancer when a plaintiff has been exposed to a potentially carcinogenic substance but suffers no immediate effects. In Criscuola v. Power Authority of New York, 81 N.Y.2d 649, 621 N.E.2d 1195, 602 N.Y.S.2d 588 (1993), plaintiffs sought direct and consequential damages when the state power authority acquired an easement to run high voltage power lines over their property. Plaintiffs claimed that the market value of their property had been reduced by "cancerphobia" and the public's perception that the high voltage lines posed a health risk. The power authority claimed that there is no scientifically demonstrable risk associated with the lines, and that the public's fears were unreasonable.

The New York Court of Appeals held that the reasonableness of the public's fear was simply not an issue: "Whether the danger is a scientifically genuine or verifiable fact should be irrelevant to the central issue of its market value impact." "[E]vidence of fear in the marketplace is admissible with respect to the value of property taken without proof of the reasonableness of the fear." 81 N.Y.2d at 652, 621 N.E.2d at 1196, 602 N.Y.S.2d at 589. See also Ryan v. Kansas Power and Light Co., 249 Kan. 1, 7, 815 P.2d 528, 533 (1991).

Courts have divided on this issue, some not admitting evidence of the effect of fear of danger from power lines on market value (the so-called majority view, although the New York court could only find four jurisdictions that follow it); some admitting the evidence routinely, so long as the fear affects market value; and some admitting the evidence only if the fear is shown to be reasonable. Which is the better view? Is this consistent with the way "fear of cancer" is treated in personal injury cases?

6. In the usual case, cost of repair or restoration and loss of market value should amount to just about the same thing. A car otherwise worth $5000 that needs $500 worth of engine work ought to be worth about $4500. Thus, in an ordinary case, where property has been damaged or destroyed, courts have generally treated the cost of repair or replacement and the loss in market value as rough equivalents. See Restatement (Second) of Torts § 928 (Where chattels have been damaged, but not destroyed, the owner can recover "(a) the difference between the value of the chattel before the harm and the value after the harm or, at his election in an appropriate case, the reasonable cost of repair or restoration, with due allowance for any difference between the original value and the value after repairs, and (b) the loss of use.")

7. In some cases, as with natural resources, the cost of repair can exceed the loss in market value. (Can you see why it is not a problem if the loss in market value exceeds the cost of repair? Recall the avoidable consequences rule.) Older decisions viewed the problem as one of waste. To use the *Ohio* court's example, if one were to spend $8,000 repairing a car

that was only worth $5,000 to begin with, $3,000 would be wasted—it would be spent without any corresponding gain in value.

Waste, however, is not really the issue. Even if, in our example, the owner of the car were given $8,000 to repair her car, she would spend the money on the repairs only *if it were worth it to her.* If the car were worth so much to her that she would spend $8,000 to repair it, there is no waste: she will get $8,000 in value for her $8,000. In such a case, if she is limited to recovering $5,000, she will be undercompensated. Or, to put it another way, we will have forced her to accept the market's values instead of her own.

On the other hand, if having her car fixed is not worth $8,000 to her, and we give her the $8,000 anyway, she will not spend the money on repairs. Instead, she will simply buy an equivalent car and pocket the difference. The problem, thus, is not waste, it is the potential for windfall. If the plaintiff is given $8,000 and she does not in fact value the car as highly as she claimed, she has gotten more than she lost (she is in better than her rightful position), and at the defendant's expense.

The tort cases are in some degree of conflict on this issue. Both views were represented in Hewlett v. Barge Bertie, 418 F.2d 654 (4th Cir.1969). In *Hewlett,* two barges collided. Hewlett sued, and recovered nominal damages from the admiralty court. On appeal, the court of appeals reversed, finding that Hewlett should have received the cost of repairing his barge: "If [a ship] is not a complete loss, and repossession or repairs are both physically and economically feasible, then the reasonable cost of recovery, including repairs and an allowance for deprivation of use, is the measure. But if the reclamation expense including repairs exceeds the ship's just value at the time of the casualty, or if repairs are not both physically and economically practicable, then it is a constructive total loss, and the limit of compensation is the value plus interest." 418 F.2d at 657. Because the tortfeasor did not show that the cost of the repairs exceeded the total value of the barge, the cost of repair should have been recoverable.

Chief Judge Haynsworth dissented. Hewlett first acquired this barge by salvaging it after it had sunk and been declared a total loss. He spent about $1300 to make it water-tight, so that he could use it as a pontoon, or, potentially, for carrying cargo on deck. The dent the barge suffered in the collision did not affect its scrap value, nor did it reduce its utility:

> "In this case there is no factual equivalency between diminution in value and cost of repair. The parties and the court are agreed that there was no diminution in the market value of the barge, or in any special value it may have had to the [owner]. * * * [If the owner is awarded damages, he] is unduly enriched. He must hope greatly that another errant navigator will hit his battered barge again, and still another yet again, so that each time he may happily pocket the estimated cost of theoretical repairs which neither he nor anyone else will ever dream of undertaking while retaining all along a barge as seaworthy and useful to him and of undiminished worth if he chooses to sell it."

418 F.2d at 654. Who has the better argument? How does it bear on the problem of Tama's house, above? Should the "lesser-of" rule be applied in tort cases?

8. The discussion so far has focused on restoring the plaintiff to her rightful position. What about the defendant's rightful position? In Molinary v. Powell Mountain Coal Co., 892 F.Supp. 136 (W.D.Va.1995), the defendant surface mined coal from the plaintiff's property without permission. The plaintiff sued under the Surface Mining Control and Reclamation Act and the court ordered the defendant to reclaim the land. The plaintiff also sought damages. Instead of awarding the plaintiff damages based on the loss of the use of the property pending restoration (valued at $500, because the land was virtually worthless), or based on the value of what was taken (the mining rights would have been worth $3,317.63), the court measured the damages by the benefit the defendant realized from its wrongful use, the sale price of the coal removed, or $190,122.46.

To reach this result, the court relied on the traditional rule for measuring damages in severance cases. "Bad faith trespassers who sever minerals or timber from the soil are usually subjected to 'harsh' [sic] measure of damages—the value of the severed article itself, not merely the value of the right to mine or harvest it. This value is figured at some point after the article is severed, perhaps even after it is in some manufactured state and the bad faith trespasser is given little or no credit for costs of mining or transporting or milling the article." This measure is justified as a deterrent, and therefore it is limited to trespassers who act in bad faith.

Measuring damages in this fashion provides what is effectively a restitutionary remedy, insofar as its focus is on requiring the defendant to disgorge the profit his wrongdoing generated. Restitutionary remedies are considered in detail in chapter 7.

### *(b) Time and Value*

## REDEVELOPMENT AGENCY OF THE CITY OF BURBANK v. GILMORE

Supreme Court of California, 1985.
38 Cal.3d 790, 214 Cal.Rptr. 904, 700 P.2d 794.

GRODIN, JUSTICE.

We confront an issue created by the sharp rise in market rates of interest during recent years. When a public agency condemns property and exercises its statutory right to take possession before the condemnation price is set or fully paid, does the "just compensation" which the Constitution requires include interest at prevailing market rates rather than a lower "legal" rate specified in the Eminent Domain Law? We conclude that it does.

FACTS

* * * On November 13, 1980, plaintiff Burbank Redevelopment Agency filed its complaint seeking condemnation of a parcel of real property owned by George Strattan and the Gilmores (parcel 9) and a separate parcel of real property owned by the Hudsons (parcel 11). In both cases, plaintiff invoked the so-called "early possession" or "quick-take" provisions of the Eminent Domain Law. Under that procedure, a

condemning agency may take over condemned property prior to trial and judgment by depositing in court the "probable compensation" as determined by appraisal and obtaining an "order for possession". The condemnee may apply for the right to withdraw the court deposit or any portion thereof.

When the "quick-take" procedure is used, the final award of compensation draws "legal interest," commencing when the agency took possession or when it was authorized to do so, whichever is earlier, and continuing until final payment. However, interest ceases to accrue on any amount previously deposited in court when the condemnee withdraws that amount. In other words, the condemnee receives interest on the difference between the final award and any amount previously deposited and withdrawn.

The legal rate of interest on judgments was 7 percent until July 1, 1983. (Cal. Const., art. XV, § 1.) On that date, as permitted by the Constitution, a statute raising the rate of judgment interest to 10 percent became effective. On December 9, 1980, plaintiff deposited $200,000 toward parcel 9 and $160,000 toward parcel 11; the court thereupon issued orders authorizing plaintiff to take possession of both properties. Each order became effective 90 days after service—March 16, 1981, for parcel 9 and March 18, 1981, for parcel 11. An additional $125,590 was deposited on February 16, 1982, on account of parcel 9. Defendants withdrew the full amounts of their respective deposits.[3]

Later, at trial, the value of parcel 9 was fixed at $500,000. The value of parcel 11 was determined to be $284,000. Both amounts substantially exceeded the deposits previously made for the respective parcels. Defendants urged that they were entitled to market interest on the balances due. They introduced extensive and uncontradicted evidence about prevailing rates, during the period since plaintiff had gained possession of parcels 9 and 11, for mortgages, prime business loans, certificates of deposit, government and utility bonds, and government notes of various terms. All the representative rates were well above the 7 percent "legal" rate then in effect. * * *

On June 30, 1982, an interlocutory judgment was entered as to parcel 11, awarding the Hudsons $124,000—the difference between plaintiff's deposit of $160,000 and the final assessed value of $284,000. Interest on this balance due was to accrue "at the legal rate" from March 18, 1981, the possession date for parcel 11, until final payment. On July 21, 1982, a similar judgment was entered as to parcel 9, awarding Strattan and the Gilmores $173,410—the difference between the two original deposits totalling $326,590 and the final assessed value of $500,000. Any balance due after March 16, 1981, the date of

3. Because defendants withdrew the deposits, this case does not present the issue whether condemnees are limited to the statutory rate of interest on amounts they choose to leave on deposit with the court pending trial and judgment. Therefore, we do not decide that question. * * *

possession for parcel 9, was to accrue interest, again at the "legal" rate of 7 percent, until paid.

DISCUSSION

I.

Defendants renew their argument that when condemned property is taken before payment, interest on the balance due must be computed with reference to the prevailing market rate in order to provide constitutional "just compensation." (See U.S. Const., Amends. V, cl. 4, XIV; Cal. Const., art. I, § 19.) We agree.

The governing principles are well established. In Seaboard Air Line Ry. v. U.S. (1923) 261 U.S. 299, 43 S.Ct. 354, 67 L.Ed. 664, the United States Supreme Court explained that when private property is taken for public use, "[t]he just compensation to which the owner is constitutionally entitled is the *full and perfect* equivalent of the property taken." This "means substantially that *the owner shall be put in as good position pecuniarily as he would have been if his property had not been taken.*"

Therefore, if the government pays for condemned property only after taking and using it, the owners "are entitled to have the *full* equivalent of the value of [its] use at the time of the taking paid contemporaneously with the taking." An award in the nature of interest "at a proper rate" is a "fair and reasonable" reimbursement for the deferred payment. This element of "just compensation" is constitutionally required and "cannot be made to depend upon state statutory provisions." * * *

Plaintiff and its amici point to decisions suggesting that the California statute's provision for interest at the "legal" rate is intended simply as a reasonable measure of *damages* for lost use of the *property* during the period between public possession and final payment, where no other evidence of such damages is introduced. But the Supreme Court's more recent remarks in Kirby [Forest Indus., Inc. v. United States (1984) 104 S.Ct. 2187] make clear that interest is constitutionally compelled as reimbursement for lost use of *money due as compensation for the property,* but not paid contemporaneously with the taking. * * *

Plaintiff and its amici urge that the California statute, unlike the federal, assures "just compensation" in ways other than interest, since it provides for such elements of damage as loss of business goodwill. Again, we do not agree. The Legislature may choose to recompense the owner of property or a business for a variety of losses caused by exercise of the eminent domain power. Its choices, however, are not necessarily the measure of the "just" compensation constitutionally due. A statute's provisions may exceed constitutional requirements in one area while failing to fulfill them in another. Whatever other rights he has or lacks, a landowner is *constitutionally* entitled to compensation reasonable under market conditions for any lost use of money arising from a delay between the taking of his property and full payment.

Plaintiff and its amici complain bitterly of the "unjust" cost to government of market-rate condemnation interest in periods when prevailing rates are high. But the difference between the deposit and the final award is nothing more than an involuntary purchase-money loan from the condemnee to the condemner. We cannot see how justice is served by restricting the condemnee, during times of high interest, to a "legal" rate which may be far below the rate the agency would have to pay in its usual financial markets for the same funds. * * *

II.

We have ruled that the just compensation clause is not necessarily satisfied when a rate of interest set by statute is applied as a ceiling in condemnation cases. We must therefore decide what formulas and procedures courts should apply in determining a constitutional rate of return when, as here, statutory guidelines are inadequate. * * *

The majority of state and federal cases have indicated that, since interest is an element of just compensation, its calculation is a matter for the guided discretion of the trial court, case by case. A test often stated is the rate which would have been earned by "a reasonably prudent person investing funds so as to produce a reasonable return while maintaining safety of principal."

Absent specific statutory guidance, we are persuaded that the "prudent investor" principle is a sound basis for calculation of interest as just compensation. This doctrine seems best suited to give the condemnee the "full and perfect" monetary equivalent of a timely cash payment for his property, thus placing him "in as good a position pecuniarily as he would have occupied if the payment had coincided with the appropriation." * * *

MOSK, JUSTICE, concurring.

* * * Until recent United States Supreme Court decisions discussed in the majority opinion, it was assumed that the legal rate of interest was necessarily just compensation. Now that we are holding the statutory rate is no longer a valid determinant of the value of money, the rule that trial courts must ascertain the actual market value of money applies whether the current interest rate is higher or lower than the statutory figure. In other words, interest travels on a two-way street. Just as the value of the property to be condemned rises or falls in accordance with current economic conditions, so must the rate of interest to which the property owner is entitled.

With that understanding, I concur in the majority opinion.

### *Notes*

1. Courts generally agree that prejudgment interest in condemnation cases must be measured by the market rate. See United States v. 429.59 Acres of Land, 612 F.2d 459 (9th Cir.1980). There is, however, some disagreement over how to establish the market rate, chiefly over whether the market rate should be determined by looking to the rate paid on governmen-

tal obligations, or to the rate paid in the market generally. See, e.g., United States v. Blankinship, 543 F.2d 1272 (9th Cir.1976)(rate on government obligations). Did the *Gilmore* court make the right choice? The Gilmores argued that the rate should be determined by the rate they had to pay to borrow money to replace the taken property. Is there any merit to that argument?

2. Under California law, when a business is condemned, the award in an eminent domain proceeding can include damages for loss of good will. Good will measures the value of a business as a going concern; it is a way of capitalizing a business's prospects. If a condemnee received the market value of his property, damages for lost good will, and prejudgment interest measured at the market rate, would he be overcompensated?

3. Almost all jurisdictions have statutes calling for the award of post-judgment interest when there is a delay between the entry and the satisfaction of the judgment. Cal.Code Civ.Pro. § 685.010. If post-judgment interest were awarded in an eminent domain case, what rate should apply?

## NOTE, INTEREST AS DAMAGES IN CALIFORNIA

5 U.C.L.A.L.Rev. 262, 262–264 (1958).

### Theory of Interest as Damages

Throughout the development of the law of interest damages, the courts have seldom expressed with any degree of clarity the reasons for awarding such damages in the absence of an agreement to pay interest. The underlying purpose of damages in general is *compensation* to the plaintiff for the loss or harm he has sustained because of the defendant's act. But it is a difficult matter to determine the harm caused by the failure to receive a previously withheld sum of money until the date of the verdict. When in the development of legal and economic thought, interest was recognized to be "the natural growth of the money" the courts seized upon interest as a convenient and definite method of measuring this loss. The person deprived of the use of his money is at least denied the opportunity of investing it and receiving the going rate. The legal rate of interest affords a quick approximation of the possible return and has generally been used by the courts in California and other jurisdictions.

As will be seen, however, there developed a drastic limitation upon the number of cases in which such compensation could be made to the plaintiff. Most courts have refused to allow interest in the case of damages which are not liquidated or cannot be determined by computation or reference to market values, because the defendant should not be considered at fault for not paying a sum which he could not have ascertained with any degree of certainty. If this statement of the reason underlying the rule requiring certainty is correct it suggests that the primary concern of the courts has not been compensation for the plaintiff, but rather one or both of two other objectives: *punishment* of the defendant for his fault in failing to pay a sum which was ascertainable, or *protection* of the defendant from liability for withholding payment of an uncertain amount.

More recent authorities outside of California have rejected this traditional viewpoint and have regarded compensation to the plaintiff as the overriding purpose of interest damages. This modern rationale would require interest to be allowed when the plaintiff has suffered a pecuniary or economic loss at the hands of the defendant whether the principal damages are denominated certain or uncertain, and whether the cause of action was based on tort or breach of contract. The theory of this trend seems sound. It recognizes that money, and indirectly all property of value, has the ability to reproduce in the sense of earning interest. The plaintiff whose net worth has been maintained at a reduced level by the defendant's failure to pay just damages until after the lapse of time in litigation, has been deprived of the ability to arrange his economic affairs so as to receive a greater investment return; and this is true whether the amount of the reduction must be determined by a jury or is known to the defendant.

An award of interest should not be made, of course, in those cases in which it would result in a double recovery to the plaintiff, as where his damages have already purported to compensate him for all loss. Under the modern theory, moreover, interest would not be given upon those elements of damages representing an injury to personality or feelings. Even though the jury attempts to measure such injuries in monetary terms, the measurement is only an arbitrary one and the addition of interest would serve little purpose.

### *Notes*

1. In common law cases prejudgment interest has always been simple, not compound, interest at the legal rate. After *Gilmore,* what rate applies?

2. Does the distinction between liquidated and unliquidated damages make sense? Why should a litigant who contests liability when the damages are clear be treated differently than one who litigates uncertain damages when liability is clear? Although commentators fairly universally criticize the rule limiting prejudgment interest to liquidated or ascertainable claims, it has proved to have substantial staying power. See Restatement (Second) of Torts § 913; Restatement (Second) of Contracts § 354. Anthony E. Rothschild, Prejudgment Interest: Survey and Suggestion, 77 N.W.U.L.Rev. 192 (1982).

3. Some jurisdictions give the judge or the jury discretion to award prejudgment interest on unliquidated claims. See, e.g., Cal.Civ.Code § 3288 (tort claims). What factors should guide that discretion? See Restatement (Second) of Torts § 913 comment a. In Milwaukee v. Cement Division, National Gypsum Co., ___ U.S. ___, 115 S.Ct. 2091, 132 L.Ed.2d 148 (1995), a maritime case, the Supreme Court held that the plaintiff's comparative fault in causing the loss was not a factor that justified withholding prejudgment interest. Undue delay by the plaintiff in bringing a case, on the other hand, could justify refusing an award, according to the Court.

4. Compensation is not the only justification for awarding prejudgment interest. The policy of promoting settlements also comes into play. Without an award of prejudgment interest, the defendant has an incentive to drag out the proceedings while earning interest on the amount in dispute. So, some jurisdictions have expanded the availability of prejudgment interest in order to promote settlement. An extreme example is in Ruff v. Weintraub, 105 N.J. 233, 519 A.2d 1384 (1987). There, the court affirmed an award of prejudgment interest in a personal injury case, even though much of the award was for future losses, such as injury to earning capacity. The court recognized that interest could hardly be justified as damages for delay when the loss had not yet occurred, but rule 4:42–11(b) of the New Jersey rules of court provided for prejudgment interest on the entire judgment in all but "exceptional" tort cases. The court rationalized the award as encouraging settlement (and requested the New Jersey Civil Practice Commission to reconsider the rule). To the same effect, see LaPlante v. American Honda Motor Co., 27 F.3d 731 (1st Cir.1994) (Rhode Island law). For a more moderate attempt to use prejudgment interest to promote settlement, see Cal.Civ.Code § 3291 (if plaintiff makes a statutory offer of settlement which the defendant refuses, and plaintiff's recovery at trial exceeds his demand, plaintiff may claim interest on the judgment at 10% from the time of the offer).

### *Problem: Country Lodge v. Miller (Reprised) Prejudgment Interest*

The court has declared Miller's operation a nuisance, and enjoined it. In addition, the court has awarded Country Lodge damages for 1) the cost of restoring the riverfront to its original condition; 2) the profits it lost and 3) the owner's annoyance and discomfort. Should prejudgment interest also be awarded?

## PRETRE v. UNITED STATES

United States District Court, Eastern District of Missouri, 1981.
531 F.Supp. 931.

FILIPPINE, DISTRICT JUDGE.

This matter is before the Court for a determination of the amount of damages recoverable by the plaintiffs. The Court having found that plaintiff Weldon Pretre contracted Guillain–Barre Syndrome (GBS) as a result of his swine flu inoculation, the defendant has conceded causation and liability pursuant to the stipulation of the parties. The present issue, therefore, is the amount of all the damages proximately caused by plaintiff Weldon Pretre's inoculation on December 2, 1976. * * *

During the nearly five-month duration of Mr. Pretre's hospital stay following his inoculation, Mrs. Pretre visited the hospital every day, for about 10 hours daily. She helped care for Mr. Pretre, doing such tasks as helping to feed him, emptying bed pans, and helping with his physical therapy. Following Mr. Pretre's release from the hospital in May, 1977, Mrs. Pretre had to help her husband shower. Mr. Pretre was still reliant upon a walker or a wheelchair at that point. Mrs. Pretre, however, took a job in July of 1977 to help support the family.

Mr. Pretre attended physical therapy after his release from the hospital, initially twice a week. Mr. Pretre no longer needed a walker after approximately August of 1977, although he continued with physical therapy, less frequently, until March of 1978.

Mr. Pretre suffers some permanent effects of his inoculation. The muscle strength in his arms has recovered to the level of an average man's, although not to the level of his own muscle strength before December, 1976. He has less than normal feeling in his fingertips, which causes him to fumble when handling very small objects. He also has less sensation in his feet, especially his toes, than is normal. He has a tic in his lower left eyelid, his right eye tears occasionally, and he experiences occasional numbness of the right upper and lower lip, which may cause him to drool. In sum, Mr. Pretre suffers mild sensory residuals of GBS. These neurological residuals are permanent.

Mr. Pretre's major physical problem, however, is his post-phlebitic syndrome, or bilateral chronic venous insufficiency. This is also a permanent condition, in which his deep venous system is not properly returning the blood to his heart, so that there is a backup of blood in the legs. The result of this condition, in Mr. Pretre's case, is that his legs swell when he has been in a standing or normal sitting position for any length of time. The swelling causes discomfort and pain. It has also resulted in a bronze discoloration of his lower legs. The condition renders him more susceptible to leg ulcers. Mr. Pretre must elevate his legs a minimum of three times daily, up to eight times daily, for at least twenty minutes each period, depending on the extent of the swelling.

Although his gait is normal if he walks slowly, he limps slightly if he walks at normal pace. His legs fatigue more easily, and he may require a cane if he walks a great deal. Mr. Pretre's current practice is to elevate his legs about half of his waking hours. He can drive a car, and he does go to the grocery store, to the post office, and on similar errands, but if he attempts four such errands in a day, he experiences pain and swelling in his legs at night. Although the swelling is somewhat less in the morning than it is at night, he had edema of 2+ on a scale of 0 (no edema) to 4 (most severe edema) at 11:00 a.m. during an examination in June, 1981. Mr. Pretre's exercise is limited to walking, and he will not be able to participate in most of the sports he formerly enjoyed.

Mr. Pretre is being treated with the following medications: coumadin (a blood thinner), tranxene, lasix, dilantin, and elavil. He will continue to have to see his physician every two to three months.

Mr. Pretre began seeing a psychiatrist, Dr. Manglesdorf, in July of 1978. His primary complaint was impotence. Dr. Manglesdorf noted in May of 1979 that whereas the plaintiffs, prior to Mr. Pretre's inoculation, had enjoyed sexual relations about four times a week, they were having relations only twice monthly. Dr. Manglesdorf administered Mr. Pretre a Quick Intelligence Test, and determined that Mr. Pretre's intelligence is in the low normal range. Mr. Pretre's last visit to Dr. Manglesdorf was in May, 1980, just over a year prior to the damages phase of this trial.

Mr. Pretre's outward appearance is not that of a disabled man. Nevertheless, in view of the facts that nearly all of Mr. Pretre's former occupations required hard physical labor, that Mr. Pretre has only an eighth grade education, and that the disabilities described above are of a permanent nature, the Court finds that Mr. Pretre is permanently disabled. The Court's finding in this regard is based on physical disabilities alone, not on any depression Mr. Pretre may be experiencing, which, however real, is not of such a degree that it would interfere with employment. However, the Court finds that the evidence did not show that Mr. Pretre will be unable to do odd jobs around the house, such as auto repair, carpentry, and painting. Mr. Pretre will be able to stop as often as he may need to in the course of these endeavours to elevate his feet.

Missouri law governs the nature of damages recoverable by the plaintiffs, because Mr. Pretre's inoculation occurred in Missouri. * * * In determining the proper amount of damages under Missouri law, the Court may consider such factors as the plaintiff's age and educational level, the nature and permanency of the injuries, diminished working and earning capacity, changing economic factors, and the amount of pain and suffering. Mental anguish attendant upon bodily injuries is a compensable injury. Permanent injury is a factor independent of pain and suffering; however, the permanency of injuries may not be found on the basis of conjecture, likelihood or even probability. Plaintiffs may also recover, of course, for medical and hospital expenses, directly caused by Mr. Pretre's inoculation, which have been incurred and which are reasonably certain to be incurred in the future, to the extent of the reasonable value of such expenses.

Missouri law allows recovery for Mrs. Pretre on her claim of loss of consortium. "Consortium . . . includes in addition to material services, elements of companionship, felicity and sexual intercourse, all welded into a conceptualist unity." The damages suffered by Mrs. Pretre require independent consideration of those suffered by Mr. Pretre.

Turning first to the question of Mr. Pretre's medical and hospital expenses,* * * [t]hese total $32,750.72. The Court finds that these expenses were reasonable, directly caused by Mr. Pretre's inoculation, and recoverable by him.

As for future medical expenses, the Court finds that at current rates they would average $350.00 yearly ($150/year for five visits to Dr. Bonsanti, with necessary tests; $200/year for medicine). The Court does not believe that future psychiatric expenses have been proven. Therefore, the Court will award Mr. Pretre $8,465.45 for his future medical expenses, based on an annual cost increase of 9% and a discount rate of 9.5%, as indicated by the testimony of Dr. Grossman at trial.

Mr. Pretre must also be compensated for his lost wages and diminished working and earning capacity. Mr. Pretre has not returned to work since December 24, 1976. Mr. Pretre's federal income tax returns show that his gross income at Ford was $25,454.88 in 1976; in 1975 it was $22,361.44; in 1974 it was $25,605.51; in 1973 it was $25,249.87; and in 1972, it was $18,025.31. However, a large percentage of that income was overtime income, as Mr. Pretre's personnel file at Ford indicates * * *:

| | Base Salary | Overtime Salary |
|---|---|---|
| 1972 | $14,934.66 | $3,090.65 |
| 1973 | 16,011.85 | 9,238.02 |
| 1974 | 17,413.66 | 8,191.85 |
| 1975 | 19,053.84 | 3,307.60 |
| 1976 | 19,673.41 | 5,781.47 |

In addition, starting with the base salary of April 16, 1972, when Mr. Pretre was promoted to a Grade 7, his percentages of annual increase in yearly base salary were as follows:

Increase from 1972 to 1973—.045
from 1973 to 1974—.087
from 1974 to 1975—.094
from 1975 to 1976—.032

This averages a yearly increase of 6.5%. In light of these figures, the Court must reject Dr. Grossman's estimate of the income lost by plaintiff in the years 1977–1981. That estimate was based on a Wage Index Factor which took 1976 as the year zero and measured the percentage rise in all manufacturing production wages in comparison with that year. The percentage rise ran about 9%. "Trending" of past wage loss is acceptable "when closely based upon plaintiff's prior employment history," and subsequent wage gains for his position. The Wage Index Factor used by Dr. Grossman is not based solely on the automotive industry, is not related to plaintiff's position after 1976, and does not comport with plaintiff's salary levels in years prior to 1977.

The Court finds that, in order to compensate Mr. Pretre for past lost wages, the Court must provide Mr. Pretre an annual base salary increase of 6.5% since 1976, plus overtime at an average of the overtime earned in 1972 through 1976, also increased at 6.5% annually. However, the Court's award of overtime will end in March, 1979, because it was established at trial that overtime has been minute since that time. It would be pure speculation to assume that overtime will resume at some point in the future.

Hence, the Court finds that Mr. Pretre has lost the following wages:

| | Base Salary | Overtime Salary |
|---|---|---|
| 1977 | $ 20,952.18 | $ 6,306.84 |
| 1978 | 22,314.07 | 6,716.78 |
| 1979 | 23,764.48 | 1,788.34 |

| | Base Salary | Overtime Salary |
|---|---|---|
| 1980 | 25,309.18 | |
| 1981 (half of year) | 13,477.13 | |
| | $105,817.04 | $ 14,811.96 |
| | Total: | $120,629.00 |

This total is a pre-tax figure. Consequently, it must be reduced by 20%, which, according to Dr. Grossman, was plaintiff's average annual tax in the years 1972 through 1976. Eighty percent of $120,629.00 is $96,503.20, and the Court will award that sum to Mr. Pretre for lost wages. Although it was established at trial that Mr. Pretre would have been laid off by Ford, due to his seniority date, in May, 1980, when production was halved, the Court finds that the plaintiff would have sought similar work. Mr. Pretre must be compensated for the loss of his earning capacity, not merely for the loss of income from any particular job.

Turning to plaintiff's claim for loss of capacity to earn in the future, the proper measure is "the difference viewed as of the time of trial between the value of the plaintiff's services as they will be in view of the harm and as they would have been had there been no harm." A figure for loss of future wages must be based on substantial evidence and must be established with reasonable certainty. Dr. Grossman's estimates as to plaintiff's future wage loss are based on a "current," i.e., a 1981, gross income of $37,910.00 as deduced from the use of the Wage Index Factor previously mentioned. The Court must reject Dr. Grossman's estimate of future losses not only because it is based on a figure derived from the Wage Index Factor but because it is also derived from Mr. Pretre's total salary in 1976, which included a large amount of overtime salary.

Instead, the Court will award Mr. Pretre the sum of $306,933.80 for the present value of the loss of earning capacity. This figure is derived from the use of a "current", i.e., average of 1981 and 1982, after tax income of $22,264.22 (assuming again a 20% tax rate); an annual increase of 6.5%; a discount rate of 9.5% (the rate for interest [sic] free municipal bonds) and a future earning span of 19.2 years.

Mr. Pretre must be compensated for the pain and suffering, both physical and mental, that he has endured as a result of his inoculation. While GBS itself is not an especially painful disease, it understandably caused Mr. Pretre a great deal of mental suffering and anguish about his health. After he developed thrombophlebitis in February of 1977, he experienced a much greater degree of physical pain. This was the direct result of his inoculation. For the pain and suffering, physical and mental, during the period of his hospitalization, the Court will award Mr. Pretre $15,000.00. For the following three months, when Mr. Pretre was yet dependent on a walker or a wheelchair and struggling to regain his mobility, the Court will award him $3,000.00. For the period between September, 1977 and March, 1978, in which Mr. Pretre continued to require physical therapy about once a month, the Court will award Mr. Pretre $5,250.00.

The Court finds that plaintiff's current condition and disabilities need not be painful for the plaintiff, if he elevates his legs whenever needed, except after unusual exertion, which it is within plaintiff's power to control. Therefore, the Court will award Mr. Pretre the sum of $31,000.00 for pain and suffering in the period from March, 1978, for the remainder of Mr. Pretre's life expectancy of 73.6 years.

Finally, the Court believes that an award of $85,000.00 is necessary to compensate Mr. Pretre for his disabilities and their effects. The disabilities have been shown, with more than reasonable certainty, to be permanent. Mr. Pretre's range of activities has been sharply curtailed. For a man accustomed to enjoying numerous sports, it is undoubtedly very frustrating to be in Mr. Pretre's condition. Mr. Pretre's physical relationship, and to some extent, his emotional relationship with his wife have undergone changes for the worse. Their social life has been restricted in some respects, as they cannot participate in sports together. The Court finds that $85,000.00 is necessary to compensate Mr. Pretre for these unfortunate effects of his permanent physical disabilities, apart from the actual pain his injuries may cause.

The Court turns to a consideration of Mrs. Pretre's claim for loss of society. The Court does not believe that it is appropriate to award Mrs. Pretre pay at the rate prevailing for a nurse's aid during the time she spent with her husband in the hospital. Although she may have done many tasks for her husband, the Court finds that these were done out of the extra measure of devotion that may be expected of a spouse, to provide care beyond the level of adequate nursing care. To award Mrs. Pretre the wages of a nurse's aid for the period she spent in the hospital would amount to a finding that the nursing care provided by St. John's Mercy Medical Center was inadequate, and thus that the rates charged by St. John's were not reasonable.

However, this is not to say that Mrs. Pretre has not been forced to shoulder heavy burdens as a result of Mr. Pretre's illness and physical condition, both during and after his hospitalization. She was totally deprived of his emotional and physical support in their home for five months. She bore the emotional and physical burdens placed upon her by Mr. Pretre's weakness following his discharge from the hospital. She has been forced to return to work. She has lost the degree of physical intimacy with her husband which both enjoyed before December, 1976, and she has had to accept a curtailment in their social activities. Mr. Pretre's physical condition and inability to support his family has added an extra strain to the whole of the plaintiffs' marital relationship. For all of these reasons, the Court finds appropriate an award of $75,000.00 to Mrs. Pretre.

In accordance with the foregoing, the Court will enter judgment for plaintiff Weldon Edward Pretre in the amount of $583,903.17 and for plaintiff Charlotte Pretre in the amount of $75,000.00.

### Notes

1. *Discounting to Present Value.* To avoid overcompensation, awards of damages for future losses must be discounted to present value. The arithmetic of discounting is simple: Present value tables are available which state the present value of $1 for any period at any discount rate. The present value of any sum, then, is simply that sum multiplied by the present value of $1. See Stuart M. Speiser et al., Recovery for Wrongful Death and Injury (3d ed.1992). For the more mathematically inclined, the present value of $1 due in $n$ periods, where the rate of interest is $i$, is $1/(1 + i)^n$. As the table below shows, the choice of a discount rate can affect the plaintiff's award drastically:

Present Value of Lost Earnings of $25,000 a Year, for Various Periods and Discount Rates

| | *Discount Rate* | | | |
|---|---|---|---|---|
| ***Period*** | *2%* | *5%* | *10%* | *12%* |
| 10 years | $224,565 | $193,043 | $153,615 | $141,255 |
| 20 years | 408,785 | 311,555 | 212,840 | 186,735 |
| 30 years | 501,603 | 384,313 | 235,673 | 201,138 |

Richard A. Posner, Economic Analysis of Law 194 (4th ed.1992).

2. *Inflation and Interest Rates.* In an inflation-free economy, discounting to present value would accurately compensate future losses. In Jones & Laughlin Steel Corp. v. Pfeifer, 462 U.S. 523, 103 S.Ct. 2541, 76 L.Ed.2d 768 (1983), the Supreme Court explained why inflation must be taken into account and described the approaches various courts have adopted to do so:

> The first stage of the calculation required an estimate of the shape of the lost stream of future income. For many workers, including respondent, a contractual "cost-of-living adjustment" automatically increases wages each year by the percentage change during the previous year in the consumer price index calculated by the Bureau of Labor Statistics. Such a contract provides a basis for taking into account an additional societal factor—price inflation—in estimating the worker's lost future earnings.
>
> The second stage of the calculation requires the selection of an appropriate discount rate. Price inflation—or more precisely, anticipated price inflation—certainly affects market rates of return. If a lender knows that his loan is to be repaid a year later with dollars that are less valuable than those he has advanced, he will charge an interest rate that is high enough both to compensate him for the temporary use of the loan proceeds and also to make up for their shrinkage in value.
>
> At one time many courts incorporated inflation into only one stage of the calculation of the award for lost earnings. In estimating the lost stream of future earnings, they accepted evidence of both individual and societal factors that would tend to lead to wage increases even in an inflation-free economy, but required the plaintiff to prove that those factors were not influenced by predictions of future price inflation. No increase was allowed for price inflation, on the theory that such predictions were unreliably speculative. In discounting the estimated lost

stream of future income to present value, however, they applied the market interest rate. The effect of these holdings was to deny the plaintiff the benefit of the impact of inflation on his future earnings, while giving the defendant the benefit of inflation's impact on the interest rate that is used to discount those earnings to present value. Although the plaintiff in such a situation could invest the proceeds of the litigation at an "inflated" rate of interest, the stream of income that he received provided him with only enough dollars to maintain his existing nominal income; it did not provide him with a stream comparable to what his lost wages would have been in an inflationary economy. This inequity was assumed to have been minimal because of the relatively low rates of inflation. In recent years, of course, inflation rates have not remained low. There is now a consensus among courts that the prior inequity can no longer be tolerated. There is no consensus at all, however, regarding what form an appropriate response should take.

Our sister common law nations generally continue to adhere to the position that inflation is too speculative to be considered in estimating the lost stream of future earnings; they have sought to counteract the danger of systematically undercompensating plaintiffs by applying a discount rate that is below the current market rate. Nevertheless, they have each chosen different rates, applying slightly different economic theories. * * * [I]n Australia, the High Court has adopted a 2% rate, on the theory that it represents a good approximation of the long-term "real interest rate."

In this country, some courts have taken the same "real interest rate" approach as Australia. They have endorsed the economic theory suggesting that market interest rates include two components—an estimate of anticipated inflation, and a desired "real" rate of return on investment—and that the latter component is essentially constant over time. They have concluded that the inflationary increase in the estimated lost stream of future earnings will therefore be perfectly "offset" by all but the "real" component of the market interest rate.

Still other courts have preferred to continue relying on market interest rates. To avoid undercompensation, they have shown at least tentative willingness to permit evidence of what future price inflation will be in estimating the lost stream of future income.

Finally, some courts have applied a number of techniques that have loosely been termed "total offset" methods. What these methods have in common is that they presume that the ideal discount rate—the after-tax market interest rate on a safe investment—is (to a legally tolerable degree of precision) completely offset by certain elements in the ideal computation of the estimated lost stream of future income. They all assume that the effects of future price inflation on wages are part of what offsets the market interest rate. The methods differ, however, in their assumptions regarding which if any other elements in the first stage of the damages calculation contribute to the offset.

Jones & Laughlin Steel Corp. v. Pfeifer, 462 U.S. 523, 103 S.Ct. 2541, 76 L.Ed.2d 768 (1983). Which approach did the *Pretre* court use? Did it apply that approach correctly?

3. *Taxes.* Section 104(a)(2) of the Internal Revenue Code provides that "the amount of any damages received (whether by suit or agreement and whether as lump sum or periodic payments) on account of personal injuries or sickness" is excluded from gross income. Accordingly, the Pretres will not have to pay taxes on their award, even though a large portion of the award is compensation for otherwise taxable lost wages. Therefore it makes sense to calculate their award based on Mr. Pretre's net expected income after taxes, as the court did.

Perhaps surprisingly, however, the majority of courts do not consider taxes when calculating lost earning capacity. The traditional rule has been that lost earning capacity is based on gross earnings, because evidence as to future tax rates and the plaintiff's future tax status is too speculative. In Norfolk & Western Railway v. Liepelt, 444 U.S. 490, 100 S.Ct. 755, 62 L.Ed.2d 689 (1980), the Supreme Court challenged the traditional rule, and held that in a wrongful death case arising under the Federal Employers' Liability Act (where federal and not state law controls), damages for lost support should be based on net earnings after taxes, to avoid overcompensation. Since *Norfolk,* a few state courts have followed the Supreme Court's lead. See, e.g., Ruff v. Weintraub, 105 N.J. 233, 519 A.2d 1384 (1987). Most, however, continue to exclude evidence that the plaintiff's wages would have been taxed. Johnson v. Manhattan & Bronx Surface Transit Operating Authority, 71 N.Y.2d 198, 524 N.Y.S.2d 415, 519 N.E.2d 326 (1988).

If the jury is not going to hear evidence about the taxes the plaintiff is avoiding, should the jury at least be instructed that the award itself is not taxable, so they won't assume the award will be taxed and inflate it? Again, although *Norfolk* held it was error to refuse to instruct the jury that their award would not be taxed, most courts refuse to do so. See Stover v. Lakeland Square Owners Ass'n, 434 N.W.2d 866 (Iowa 1989) (citing cases). Although *Norfolk* has had some impact, see, e.g. Bussell v. DeWalt Products Corp., 105 N.J. 223, 519 A.2d 1379 (1987), most courts continue to believe that an instruction that awards are not taxable is unnecessary and unwise. It presumes that the jury will not heed its mandate to decide the case only on the evidence before it, opens a "Pandora's box" of possible cautionary instructions, and introduces confusion and speculation.

4. What are "damages received on account of personal injury?" Internal Revenue Service regulations interpreting § 104(a)(2) provide that "the term 'damages received' * * * means an amount received through prosecution of a legal suit or action based upon tort or tort-type rights, or through a settlement agreement entered into in lieu of such prosecution." 26 C.F.R. § 1.104–1(c)(1994). In United States v. Burke, 504 U.S. 229, 112 S.Ct. 1867, 119 L.Ed.2d 34 (1992), the Court held that back pay awards under Title VII are not "damages on account of personal injury" because the Title VII remedy lacks the "hallmarks of traditional tort liability", namely, consequential and nonpecuniary damages. Reasoning backward from the remedy, the Court concluded that a statute "whose sole remedial focus is the award of back wages [does not redress] a tort-like personal injury within the meaning of § 104(a)(2)." Id. at 241.

In Commissioner of Internal Revenue v. Schleier, ___ U.S. ___, 115 S.Ct. 2159, 132 L.Ed.2d 294 (1995), the Court concluded that an award of back pay and liquidated damages under the Age Discrimination in Employment Act was not an award of damages received on account of personal injury and therefore should have been included in the taxpayer's gross income. Justice Stevens, writing for the majority, reasoned:

> Whether one treats respondent's attaining the age of 60 or his being laid off on account of his age as the proximate cause of respondent's loss of income, neither the birthday nor the discharge can fairly be described as a "personal injury" or "sickness." Moreover, though respondent's unlawful termination may have caused some psychological or "personal" injury comparable to the intangible pain and suffering caused by an automobile accident, it is clear that no part of respondent's recovery of back wages is attributable to that injury. Thus, in our automobile hypothetical [the opinion earlier offers the hypothetical case of a surgeon who loses income because his finger is injured in an automobile accident], the accident causes a personal injury which in turn causes a loss of wages. In age discrimination, the discrimination causes both personal injury and loss of wages, but neither is linked to the other. The amount of back wages recovered is completely independent of the existence or extent of any personal injury. In short, § 104(a)(2) does not permit the exclusion of respondent's back wages because the recovery of back wages was not "on account of" any personal injury and because no personal injury affected the amount of back wages recovered.

Although the ADEA's remedies are more "tort-like" than the Title VII remedies at issue in *Burke*, the IRS regulation does not replace the statutory requirement that the damages be "account of personal injury or sickness". Thus, to be excluded from gross income, damages must be both on account of personal injury and based upon tort or tort-like rights. 115 S.Ct. at 2167.

A problem with the majority's analysis is that while the opinion asserts that both tangible and intangible harms can be personal injuries, it does not explain why discrimination is not a personal injury. See *Schleier*, 115 S.Ct. at 2169–70, (O'Connor, J. dissenting). This omission may reopen issues that had been taken to be settled under § 104(a)(2). For example, in Bent v. Internal Revenue Service, 835 F.2d 67 (3d Cir.1987), the Third Circuit held that damages for violation of first amendment rights are "on account of personal injury" and therefore excludable from gross income, because the action was based on "tort or tort-like rights." But, if a person is fired from a state job in retaliation for exercising her first amendment right to comment on matters of public concern, has she lost her wages on account of a personal injury, or on account of her statements? Is being deprived of first amendment rights a "personal injury" if discrimination is not? The same issue may arise when damages are recovered for defamation, or invasion of privacy.

A similar issue will arise under the 1991 amendments to Title VII. The 1991 amendments make compensatory and punitive damages available in cases of intentional discrimination. The Internal Revenue Service had taken the position that these amendments made these Title VII actions "tort or tort-like in character," and that compensatory damages, including back pay, received in disparate treatment cases brought under either § 1981a or under Title VII after the 1991 Act would be excludable from gross income as damages for personal injury. I.R.S.Rev.Rul. 93–88 (Dec.20, 1993). But, if a job lost to discrimination is not lost "on account of a personal injury," this ruling is not correct. See *Schleier*, 115 S.Ct. at 2167 n.8.

In other contexts, how a judgment is characterized for tax purposes depends on what the judgment replaces. See, e.g., Commissioner v. Gillette Motor Transport Co., 364 U.S. 130, 80 S.Ct. 1497, 4 L.Ed.2d 1617 (1960); Gail v. United States, 58 F.3d 580 (10th Cir.1995). For an argument that tax policy would be better served by a rule that simply aims to put plaintiffs in the "same post-tax economic position" as they would have occupied but-for the injury, see Joseph Dodge, Taxes and Torts, 77 Cornell L.Rev. 143 (1992).

5. In 1989, § 104(a) was amended to provide that § 104(a)(2) "shall not apply to any punitive damages in connection with a case not involving physical injury or physical sickness." Does this imply that punitive damages in connection with a case that does involve physical injury or physical sickness are excludable from gross income? The courts of appeal are divided. Compare O'Gilvie v. United States, 66 F.3d 1550 (10th Cir.1995) (becoming the fifth circuit to find punitive damages not excludable) with Horton v. Commissioner, 33 F.3d 625 (6th Cir.1994) (excludable). See also James Serven, The Taxation of Punitive Damages: Horton Lays an Egg?, 72 Den.U.L.Rev. 215 (1995).

6. Suppose a taxpayer settled, for a lump sum, a law suit that involved a number of causes of action, some for personal injuries and some not, as well as allegations that would support an award of punitive damages. How much of the lump sum settlement is taxable? To determine whether any or all of the settlement is "damages on account of personal injury," the Internal Revenue Service will look to the allegations of the complaint, as well as to any allocations made in the settlement agreement itself, among other factors. Insuring a favorable tax treatment can be an important factor in how settlement negotiations should be handled and documented. See, e.g. Comment, How to Avoid Unfavorable Tax Treatment for Personal Injury Client's Settlement or Judgment, 30 Gonzaga L.Rev. 343 (1995).

7. *Future earning capacity.* In *Pretre,* the court could rely on Mr. Pretre's past earnings to project his future earnings. In other cases, where the plaintiff is young or unemployed for example, the court may have to rely on general employment statistics to determine earning capacity. According to those statistics, however, a woman is likely to earn much less money in her lifetime than a man; a person of color less than an American of western European ancestry. Should a court take this into account? See Martha Chamallas, Questioning the Use of Race–Specific and Gender–Specific Economic Data in Tort Litigation: A Constitutional Argument, 63 Fordham L.Rev. 73 (1994).

### *Note on Loss of Consortium*

Loss of consortium is a separate cause of action that can be brought by a person whose spouse has suffered debilitating injuries. The action protects the interest in intimate relationships, and the elements of damages awarded in *Pretre* are typical: loss of the spouse's society and comfort, physical and emotional support, physical intimacy and diminished social activity. While loss of consortium is a separate cause of action, brought by the person whose spouse has been injured, it is characterized as a "derivative" action. Thus, as you will see in the next case, defenses that are good against the physically injured spouse's case will also defeat the action for loss of consortium.

An issue that continues to generate some controversy is whether relationships other than the marital relationship deserve protection. Generally, courts have denied loss of consortium recovery to unmarried cohabitants whose partners suffer injuries that affect the relationship. Dan B. Dobbs, Law of Remedies § 8.1(5)(2d ed.1993). The greatest controversy is over whether harm to the parent-child relationship should give rise to a cause of action for loss of consortium. Compare Gallimore v. Children's Hospital Medical Center, 67 Ohio St.3d 244, 617 N.E.2d 1052 (1993)(parents have a claim for harm to the parental relationship caused by medical negligence that left their child deaf) and United States v. Dempsey, 635 So.2d 961 (Fla.1994)(same) with Guenther v. Stollberg, 242 Neb. 415, 495 N.W.2d 286 (1993)(recovery denied).

### 3. LIMITS ON RECOVERY

## MUNN v. SOUTHERN HEALTH PLAN, INC.

United States District Court, Northern District of Mississippi, 1989.
719 F.Supp. 525, aff'd, 924 F.2d 568 (5th Cir.), cert. denied,
502 U.S. 900, 112 S.Ct. 277, 116 L.Ed.2d 229 (1991).

L.T. Senter, Jr., Chief United States District Judge

This wrongful death case presents some of the most difficult questions which this court has ever been asked to resolve. The case arose from an automobile accident which the defendant admits resulted from her negligence in attempting to pass another vehicle in dense fog. The plaintiff's wife was severely injured as a result of the collision and died approximately two hours after the accident. The problem arises because the plaintiff and his wife, both adherents to the Jehovah's Witness faith, refused on religious grounds to allow the doctors who were treating Mrs. Munn to administer a blood transfusion which the defendant contends would have saved her life.

The defendant seeks summary judgment to the effect that if the jury should find, for whatever reason, that she is not liable for damages for Mrs. Munn's death, then the plaintiff is not entitled to recover for any prospective harm beyond the point of Mrs. Munn's death. Because the answer to this question depends, at least in part, upon the legal doctrine which is to be applied to the facts of this case, the court will begin by attempting to resolve that issue.

The defendant has raised three theories which she insists apply under the facts of this case to bar, at least in part, the plaintiff's recovery. These are contributory negligence, assumption of the risk, and the doctrine of avoidable consequences. Only the latter of these clearly applies to the facts of this case.

The doctrine of avoidable consequences, sometimes referred to as the duty of the plaintiff to mitigate damages, "functions as a negative rule, denying an injured person recovery of damages for any reasonably avoidable consequences of the injury." The basic rule is that the plaintiff may not recover from the defendant for injuries which flow from the defendant's wrongful conduct but which could have been avoided by the plaintiff's availing herself of reasonable measures to limit the harm. Simply stated, once the injury has occurred, the plaintiff may not stand idly by and allow her damages to accumulate when she could take reasonable steps to minimize them. The doctrine of avoidable consequences comes into play only after the defendant has committed the wrongful act, but at a time when the plaintiff still has an opportunity to avoid the consequences in whole or in part. * * *

The doctrine is often referred to as the plaintiff's duty to mitigate damages, but such reference lacks legal precision and can lead to confusion with other concepts in the law of damages. The doctrine of avoidable consequences should not be confused with the doctrine of contributory negligence. The latter focuses on issues of proximate causation of, and ultimate liability for, an accident, whereas the former focuses only on measurement of damages resulting from the injury-producing event.

The distinction noted above makes it clear that the present case is not one where the doctrine of contributory negligence should be applied. There has been no allegation that any action or inaction of Mrs. Munn was causally related to the accident which resulted in her injuries. * * *

The other theory raised by the defendant is that by refusing the transfusion, Mrs. Munn assumed the risk of her own death. The doctrine of assumption of the risk provides that a plaintiff who voluntarily assumes a risk of harm arising from the negligent or reckless conduct of the defendant cannot recover for such harm. * * * [T]he risk that is being assumed is the known risk that the defendant does not intend to act, or has already failed to act, in accordance with a duty imposed on him by law. "The result is that the defendant is relieved of all legal duty to the plaintiff; and being under no duty, he cannot be charged with negligence." Prosser [Handbook of the Law of Torts § 68 (4th ed. 1971) ]at 440. In the instant case, by assuming the risk that she would die if she did not agree to a blood transfusion, Mrs. Munn did not relieve the defendant of any duty because the defendant had no duty in relation to the transfusion. * * *

In an earlier motion for summary judgment, the plaintiff raised two issues in relation to the defense based on the doctrine of avoidable consequences which were not addressed by the court in its order denying the motion. Those issues need to be addressed prior to trial and both are relevant to the issue currently before the court. First, the plaintiff contends that the egg-shell or thin skull rule should be applied in this case. The "rule" is actually an exception to the more general rule that a defendant is liable only for those consequences which were the reasonably foreseeable results of an anticipated action. As stated by Prosser, a "defendant is held liable when his negligence operates upon a concealed *physical* condition, such as pregnancy, or a latent disease, or susceptibility to disease, to produce consequences which he could not reasonably anticipate." Prosser, Handbook of the Law of Torts § 43, p.261 (4th ed.1971)(emphasis added). The statement of the rule in the Restatement is much the same:

> The negligent actor is subject to liability for harm to another although a *physical condition* of the other which is neither known nor should be known to the actor makes the injury greater than that which the actor as a reasonable man should have foreseen as a probable result of his conduct.

Restatement (2d) Torts § 461. (Emphasis added.)

Every authority which this court can find which states the "eggshell skull rule" speaks only of physical conditions which pre-exist the injury for which compensation is sought and lead to unforeseeably severe results. The religious beliefs of the plaintiff simply are not covered by this rule.

The plaintiff also presses a first amendment argument. This argument is not fleshed out and relies entirely on cases where a state attempted to force a Jehovah's Witness to accept a blood transfusion. There is a clear distinction, however, between the overt attempt by a state actor to force an individual to take some action which her religion forbids her to take and the application of a universally applied tort doctrine which leaves the person "free to make [her] choice between the practice of [her] religion and the acceptance of treatment that may be contrary thereto." Martin v. Industrial Accident Commission, 304 P.2d 828, 831 (Cal.1956) (upholding denial of worker's comp. death benefits where death was found to be result of refusal of transfusion on religious grounds). An individual has a right under the first amendment to hold religious beliefs and live by them, but that does not mean that anyone who commits a tort against that individual must suffer the consequences of decisions made by the victim based upon those religious beliefs.

It has been argued that persons who refuse medical treatment on religious grounds should be exempted on first amendment grounds from the operation of the doctrine of avoidable consequences. Comment, Medical Care, Freedom of Religion, and Mitigation of Damages, 87 Yale L.J. 1466 (1978). The author contends that the application of this facially neutral doctrine to a tort victim who refuses medical treatment for religious reasons is a denial of a state benefit on religious grounds. The argument is basically that putting the tort victim to the choice of acting in violation of his religious beliefs or losing the right conferred by state law to obtain complete recovery for all harm which results from the wrongful conduct of another places an undue burden on the victim's free exercise rights. Cited in support of this argument are Sherbert v. Verner, 374 U.S. 398 (1963), and Wisconsin v. Yoder, 406 U.S. 205 (1972). *Sherbert* involved the denial of state unemployment benefits to a woman who refused on religious grounds to accept a job which required her to work on Saturday. The Court held that this was an impermissible burden on her free exercise rights. In *Yoder,* the Court held that a state mandatory school attendance law violated the free exercise rights of people of the Amish faith. Each of these cases involves direct state action. If an exception to the doctrine of avoidable consequences is made for those who refuse medical treatment on religious grounds, payment for the harm which could have been avoided will come from the pockets of the tortfeasor, not from the coffers of the state. To adopt an absolute rule which required one citizen to pay damages for the consequences of another's exercising her religious freedom would favor an establishment of religion in a way which seems constitutionally unsupportable. Additionally, the doctrine of avoidable consequences does not automatically bar the plaintiff from recovering the losses sustained after the refusal of medical treatment; it bars recovery of those losses only when the refusal is found to be unreasonable under all of the circumstances known to the tort victim at the time of the refusal. In what has come to be considered as the leading case on this point, the Connecticut [sic] Supreme Court upheld the lower court's decision to submit the question of the objective reasonableness of the plaintiff's refusal of medical treatment to the jury with the instruction that the jurors were to consider the fact that the refusal was based on religious belief as one of the circumstances. Lange v. Hoyt, 114 Conn. 590, 159 A. 575 (1932). The author of the comment also takes exception to this procedure, arguing that the jury is, in effect, being asked to pass upon the reasonableness of the plaintiff's religious belief. This indeed presents a problem. However, neither of the parties have adequately addressed this issue, so the court will delay any attempt to resolve it until the parties may be heard at the jury instruction conference after the evidence is in.

The court holds that the doctrine of avoidable consequences is the appropriate standard to be applied in this case and that its application does not violate the first amendment.

### Application of the Doctrine of Avoidable Consequences in a Wrongful Death Case

As stated earlier, the doctrine of avoidable consequences prevents the plaintiff from recovering for that part of her injury which could have been avoided by taking reasonable steps after the injury occurred.[2] How does this rule operate when the harm which the defendant contends was avoidable is death?

2. Several courts have expanded the doctrine to include measures which if taken prior to the injury would have lessened the severity of the injury. The most common example is the application of the doctrine in cases where the injury resulting from an auto accident was aggravated by the plaintiff's failure to use a seat belt.

Neither party has presented the court with a single authority on this point, nor has exhaustive research turned up a single case where any court has addressed the issues presented by this case. Simply stated, the question is: if the jury should find that the refusal of the blood transfusion was unreasonable and that Mrs. Munn would have lived had she taken the transfusion, then what damages may the plaintiff recover.

The defendant's argument is that if the jury makes this dual finding, then there is no wrongful death and the plaintiff's cause of action is under the survival statute. From a purely technical standpoint, this is a compelling argument. At common law, "if a tortfeasor killed a man, neither the victim's losses before his death nor the losses to his survivors caused by his death were compensable." Because the statutes which have been passed to abrogate this rule are in derogation of the common law, they must be strictly construed. If recovery is not expressly provided for in either the wrongful death or survival statute, then there can be no recovery for the losses suffered by either the survivors or the estate. Given this backdrop, if Mrs. Munn's refusal to accept the transfusion is seen as cutting off the defendant's liability for her death, then the plaintiff must fall back on the Mississippi Survival Statute, Miss.Code Ann. § 91–7–233 (1972).

Section 91–7–233 provides: Executors, administrators, and temporary administrators may commence and prosecute any personal action whatever, at law or in equity, which the testator or intestate might have commenced and prosecuted. Mrs. Munn could clearly have commenced an action against Ms. Algee to recover for the injuries she sustained as a result of Ms. Algee's wrongful conduct. Included in her recovery, if any, would have been prospective relief for the future effects of the injuries which were received in the accident, such as lost income, future pain and suffering, and future medical expenses. However, in the usual survival action, the calculation of these damages is based, not upon a mortality table, but upon the actual date of the tort victim's death. In survival actions, "damages must of course be based upon the known period of life, and no recovery may be had for any prospective loss of earnings, expenses, or suffering based upon any probable life expectancy of the deceased, such as would be appropriate if the deceased were prosecuting the case in his lifetime." McCormick, Damages, 337–38 (1935). This rule clearly applies where the death results from an intervening cause which is deemed sufficient to break the causal connection between the tort and the death; but it is not so clear that it applies in this case.

In the usual personal injury case, in addition to the action under the survival statute, the plaintiff, as the husband of the decedent, would have a claim for his own losses which were caused by the injury to his wife—i.e., loss of services, loss of consortium, etc. This claim could be brought "at common law without the aid of statute." However, once again, recovery could be had only for the losses incurred by the plaintiff during the time period between the commission of the tort and the death of Mrs. Munn, if the damages resulting from the death are not attributable to the defendant.

The plaintiff counters with the argument that a straightforward application of the doctrine of avoidable consequences would allow him, both on his own behalf and on behalf of the decedent's estate, to recover damages for any harm which could not have been avoided by allowing the transfusion. A perfunctory reading of the rule, as generally stated, supports this argument. Generally, it is said that the plaintiff may recover for the harm which resulted from the defendant's wrongful act and which could not have been avoided by the plaintiff's acting reasonably after the injury has occurred. The plaintiff alleges that his wife suffered severe physical injury, including a broken pelvis, broken ribs, a punctured and collapsed lung, and a severed artery, which would have resulted in long term disability, pain and suffering, and future medical expenses if she had survived. These consequences could not have been avoided by allowing the transfusion and, therefore, should be recoverable. On a purely emotional level, this argument is appealing; however, any attempt to ground such a holding on legal principles is thwarted by the stark reality that these consequences were never actually suffered by the plaintiff's decedent. This court can find no authority for allowing recovery of purely hypothetical losses.

The argument for recovery of damages for injuries to Mr. Munn which were actually suffered as a result of the death, at least to the extent that they would have occurred even if the plaintiff had taken the transfusion and survived, does not share this infirmity. Clearly, given the extent of the decedent's injuries, if she had lived, there would have been some loss of consortium and services to her husband and quite possibly lost earnings which under this argument ought now to be recoverable by her estate. There are serious problems with allowing recovery of damages for these elements of the loss. Whether the problem is addressed in terms of proximate cause or simply in terms of a public policy against allowing recovery from this defendant for consequences which the plaintiff could have avoided matters little. The doctrine of avoidable consequences operates to relieve the defendant of any legal obligation to pay damages for harm which the victim of her wrongful act could have avoided. The damages which the plaintiff seeks to recover did not occur as a result of the personal injuries suffered by the decedent but as a result of Mrs. Munn's death—a death for which the defendant has no legal obligation to pay damages if the jury should find that the death was avoidable and that the refusal of the transfusion was unreasonable.

### Conclusion

The court holds that the doctrine of avoidable consequences is the appropriate standard to be applied in this case and that its application does not violate the plaintiff's first amendment rights. The court further holds that this question should be submitted to the jury through an appropriate instruction telling the jurors that they may consider the fact that it was based on religious belief. The court also holds that the plaintiff may not recover for purely hypothetical injuries which never occurred because of her death if the jury should find that the refusal of the transfusion was unreasonable and that the decedent would have survived had she taken the transfusion; nor may he recover for the harm actually suffered which resulted from his wife's death even though it would have been suffered to some extent even if she had taken the transfusion and lived.

### *Notes*

1. How is the jury to decide whether decedent's refusal was reasonable? In Small v. Combustion Engineering, 209 Mont. 387, 681 P.2d 1081 (1984), the plaintiff had refused low-risk knee surgery that was nearly certain to restore his ability to walk. The plaintiff, who was manic-depressive, considered only the operation's risks and ignored its benefits. The court found his choice objectively unreasonable, but reasonable for the plaintiff personally. The court felt obliged to take the plaintiff's point of view, and allowed him to recover. Is that the right result? The Restatement (Second) of Torts says reasonableness is to be judged by the same reasonable person standard that defines negligence. "Thus [the plaintiff's] physical and mental condition after an injury are considered in determining whether he was unreasonable in failing to take steps to reduce the harm or in refusing aid." § 918 comment c. Yet, when determining whether someone has been negligent, insanity and other mental deficiencies do "not relieve the actor from liability for conduct which does not conform to the standard of a reasonable" person. Restatement (Second) of Torts § 283B. For a thorough discussion of these issues, see Guido Calabresi, Ideals, Beliefs, Attitudes and the Law (1985).

2. Requiring an injured party to take reasonable steps to limit his losses avoids waste. Look again at the notes following Ohio v. Department of Interior, text at p. 575, especially those discussing the *Hewlett v. Barge Bertie* case. If Mrs. Munn valued her religious principles more than her life, wouldn't sacrificing those principles be the greater harm? If she had undergone the transfusion, could she recover for the damage to her principles?

3. If the jury decides Mrs. Munn behaved unreasonably, what damages are recoverable? Normally, one who fails to take reasonable steps to mitigate his losses can nonetheless recover damages for those losses that were unavoidable. Here, however, there is a paradox: Because of the way in which wrongful death damages are calculated, Mrs. Munn's recovery would probably have been greater had she lived. The focus on pecuniary loss and the exclusion of damages for loss of life mean that wrongful death recoveries for injured children or for non-working spouses can be shockingly small.

4. Mr. Munn's claim is also barred by his wife's unreasonable behavior. Loss of consortium is a derivative claim; defenses that prevail against the injured party also bar an action by the spouse. Similarly, wrongful death claims are derivative.

5. Only a minority of jurisdictions follow the seat belt rule adverted to in the main case. In most jurisdictions, the plaintiff's failure to wear a seat belt does not reduce her damages. W. Page Keeton et al., Prosser and Keeton on Torts § 65 at 459 (5th ed.1984).

6. At trial, the jury in *Munn* was instructed, "In determining whether or not Elaine Munn's decision to refuse the blood transfusion was unreasonable, you may consider that the blood transfusions were medically recommended. But, you may also consider her religious beliefs and related teachings, together with the known risks of blood transfusions, if you find that to be a factor in her decision." The jury awarded damages of $241.44 for Mr. Munn's medical expenses, $10,411 for Mrs. Munn's medical expenses, and $10,000 for Mrs. Munn's pain and suffering.

On appeal, the Fifth Circuit affirmed. The trial court had erred by allowing the defendant to question Mr. Munn about religious beliefs and practices completely unrelated to medical treatment (such as Jehovah's Witnesses's refusal to salute the flag or "do service to their country"). Nonetheless, the error was harmless, because the jury was clearly persuaded that Mrs. Munn's objectively unreasonable refusal of treatment caused her death, and because the amount of the jury's award was not, in the court's opinion, influenced by the improperly admitted evidence. Munn v. Algee, 924 F.2d 568 (5th Cir.), cert. denied, 502 U.S. 900, 112 S.Ct. 277, 116 L.Ed.2d 229 (1991).

The court did question the trial court's jury instruction on avoidable consequences, however: "[A] case-by-case approach to religiously motivated refusals to mitigate damages can involve weighing the reasonableness of religious beliefs and thus arguably violate the establishment clause." 924 F.2d at 574–75. Therefore, a purely objective approach—one that avoids any mention of religious beliefs—is preferable. As for the Munns' argument that ignoring religious beliefs entirely impermissibly burdens free exercise rights, "generally applicable rules imposing incidental burdens on particular religions do not violate the free exercise clause." 924 F.2d at 574.

On this last point, what of the trial court's concern with Sherbert v. Verner and Wisconsin v. Yoder (text at p. 600)? On this point, the Court of Appeals' silence speaks loudly. The opinion merely cites two 1961, pre-*Sherbert* cases, and Employment Division, Department of Human Resources v. Smith, 494 U.S. 872, 110 S.Ct. 1595, 108 L.Ed.2d 876 (1990)(free exercise clause does not prohibit application of Oregon Drug laws to ceremonial ingestion of peyote). See David C. Williams and Susan H. Williams, Volitionalism and Religious Liberty, 76 Cornell L.Rev. 769 (1991).

In 1993, however, Congress passed legislation intended to overturn the *Smith* decision. The Religious Freedom Restoration Act of 1993 requires any substantial burden on the exercise of religion to be justified by a compelling governmental interest. In Williams v. Bright, 632 N.Y.S.2d 760 (Sup.1995), a New York trial court held that subjecting a Jehovah's Witness's refusal to have a transfusion to a "reasonableness" test would burden the exercise of her religion and served no compelling governmental interest. Noting that all damage awards are tailored to the injured individual's circumstances, the court concluded:

> [T]he plaintiff's devout belief * * * was as much a part of her as her age, her gender, her physical condition * * *. She may not be penalized for her beliefs, and the defendants are no more unfairly burdened than if the fortuitously injured party had been a brain surgeon, [or] a ballet dancer * * *

7. Is it relevant that while the Munns and many Jehovah's Witnesses are African–Americans, their case was tried before a predominantly white jury? Dissenting, Judge Alvin B. Rubin found it hard to believe that irrelevant evidence about the Jehovah's Witnesses' controversial ideology did not affect the verdict. "I see no way that a reviewing court could be sure—other than by substituting its own views for those of the jury or by inventing some post-hoc rationalization for the verdict—that Algee's appeal to the jury's religious prejudice and nationalism had but slight effect on the verdict." 924 F.2d at 583 (Rubin, J. dissenting).

## 4. MANAGING DAMAGES ACTIONS: THE NEW PUBLIC LAW LITIGATION?

An earlier note, page 555, suggested that the trend toward caps on damages might be seen as a form of balancing the hardships, a way of fine-tuning the remedy to limit its impact, not just on the defendant, but on the public generally. It represents a judgment that fully compensating injured victims is not important enough to justify what the reformers see as a potential harm to the public in terms of higher insurance rates, fewer doctors entering risky specialties, curtailed public services, and so on.

As the Court noted in *Brown II*, page 101, it is equity that traditionally "has been characterized by a * * * facility for adjusting and reconciling public and private needs," and it was this equitable facility to which Chayes drew attention with his argument that a new creation, public law litigation, had arrived on the scene. As legislatures and courts become aware that tort law is indeed public law, are suits for damages taking on some of the characteristics of public law litigation?

## PETER H. SCHUCK, THE ROLE OF JUDGES IN SETTLING COMPLEX CASES: THE AGENT ORANGE EXAMPLE

53 U.Chi.L.Rev. 337, 341–348 (1986).

I.

On May 7, 1984, Chief Judge Jack B. Weinstein of the Eastern District of New York, flanked by his special masters, announced that the Agent Orange class action had been settled only a few hours earlier, just before jury selection was to begin. The settlement of that action, which was then probably the largest single personal injury litigation in history, created a fund that now totals about $200 million and increases by over $40,000 each day. Approximately 250,000 individual and group claims have been lodged against this fund, and in May of 1985 the court established the framework for the complicated administrative apparatus that is to resolve and administer those claims. * * *

The class was defined to include some 2.4 million American veterans exposed to Agent Orange during the war in Vietnam, the wives and children (born and unborn) of those veterans, and exposed Vietnam veterans from Australia and New Zealand. The seven defendants (pared down from an original twenty-four) were the chemical companies that manufactured Agent Orange. The United States, not named by plaintiffs as a defendant, was joined by the defendants on an indemnity-contribution theory. Judge Pratt, who originally presided over the case, dismissed the government as a party in 1980. Although Judge Weinstein brought the government back into the case just before the settlement, he subsequently dismissed the claims against it.

* * * From the moment that Judge Weinstein replaced Judge Pratt on October 21, 1983, the goal of settlement was uppermost in his mind. He believed that toxic tort cases like Agent Orange, involving mass exposures and causal relationships that are extremely difficult and costly to prove, could not be litigated properly or at an acceptable social cost under traditional rules. Absent settlement, he predicted a one-year trial with results that would remain inconclusive for years to come. Although he harbored genuine doubts about the veterans' evidence on causation, he deeply sympathized with their plight. In open court and in his written opinions, he denounced the "injustices" they suffered, believed that "[t]hey and their families should receive recognition, medical treatment and financial support," and shared the now-conventional view that the American people had failed to discharge "the nation's obligations to Vietnam veterans and their families." The prospect of having either to direct a verdict for the chemical companies or to reverse a jury verdict in favor of the veterans could not have been an appealing one. Unquestionably, he was prepared to do his duty if necessary, but a negotiated settlement offered the far more attractive possibility: everyone would gain something, soon, and at an acceptable social cost.

Earlier settlement discussions between the parties had failed. The court, however, had not been involved in those negotiations. And since then, circumstances had changed—most particularly, the identity and judicial style of the presiding judge. Weinstein immediately established a May 7, 1984 trial date—a little more than six months away—and left no doubt of his implacable determination to hold to it. He did this despite—or perhaps because of—the fact that the parties had to that point conducted little discovery except on a single issue, the government contract defense. He dragged the United States back into the case, believing that the government's presence would greatly facilitate settlement. He also indicated that he would submit the issue of government liability to the jury on an "advisory" basis (the Federal Tort Claims Act precluded a binding jury decision). Finally, he revealed to the parties, albeit only as a "tentative," "preliminary," and, as it turned out, non-appealable matter, how he intended to rule on a number of important and complex legal issues, such as choice-of-law and governmental immunity.

In February 1984, Weinstein requested and obtained permission to retain, at the defendants' expense, an unnamed consultant to develop a settlement strategy and plan. That consultant was later revealed to be Ken Feinberg, a lawyer whom Weinstein knew and trusted. Feinberg was not only knowledgeable about toxic tort litigation, but also had a reputation as an effective mover, shaker, and conciliator. By mid-March, he had prepared a settlement plan. It stated no dollar amount but contained three sections: an analysis of the elements for determining the aggregate settlement amount, especially the various sources of uncertainty and the likely number and nature of claims; a discussion of alternative criteria for allocating any liability among the chemical companies; and a discussion of alternative criteria for distributing any settlement fund to claimants. This document, which the judge made available to the lawyers, occasioned considerable disagreement but succeeded in setting the terms for the negotiations that followed.

On April 10, less than three weeks before trial, Weinstein appointed three special masters for settlement. Feinberg and David I. Shapiro, a prominent class action expert and skillful negotiator, would work with the lawyers. Leonard Garment, a Washington political insider, would explore what resources the government might contribute to a settlement. Feinberg and Shapiro immediately identified three major obstacles to settlement: the parties were more than a quarter of a billion dollars apart; each side was deeply divided internally over whether and on what terms to settle (and in defendants' case, how to allocate liability); and the government was manifestly unwilling to contribute toward a settlement fund or even to participate in settlement negotiations.

The judge and special masters decided to convene an around-the-clock negotiating marathon at the courthouse during the weekend before the trial. The lawyers were ordered to appear on Saturday morning, May 5, with their "toothbrushes and full negotiating authority." On that morning, while preliminary jury selection work was proceeding in another room, Weinstein met with the lawyers and gave them a "pep talk" about settlement. Then the special masters undertook a grueling two-day course of shuttle diplomacy, holding separate meetings with each side interspersed with private conferences with Judge Weinstein. On several occasions, the judge met privately with each side.

Several features of the discussion were particularly salient in generating the settlement agreement. First, the court did not permit the two sides to meet face-to-face until the very end, after the terms of the deal had been defined. This strategy preserved the court's control over the negotiations and prevented them from fragmenting. In particular, it stymied the plaintiffs' lawyers in their last-ditch effort to improve on the deal by settling with five of the defendants and isolating Monsanto and Diamond Shamrock, the two companies they thought most vulnerable to liability and punitive damages.

Second, the masters attempted to break log-jams in the negotiations by helping the lawyers to predict the consequences of the various approaches under consideration, and by proposing alternative solutions. * * *

Third, when especially difficult issues arose that threatened to derail the settlement, the parties agreed to be bound by the judge's decision. The most important example of the judge acting as arbitrator involved perhaps the most difficult question facing the defendants—how to allocate liability among themselves. * * *

Fourth, the judge and his special masters, while being careful not to be duplicitous, did emphasize different things to each side. In their discussions with plaintiffs' lawyers, they stressed the weakness of the evidence on causation, the novelty of many questions of law in the case, the consequent risk of reversal on appeal of a favorable verdict, the prospect that they might lose everything if they rejected settlement, and the enormous costs of continued litigation. To the defendants' lawyers, they stressed the presumed pro-plaintiff sympathies of Brooklyn juries, the reputational damage that protracted litigation and unfavorable publicity would cause their clients, and the high costs of the trial and of the inevitable appeals.

Fifth, a common theme in all discussions was the pervasive uncertainty that surrounded the law, the facts, the duration and ultimate outcome of the litigation, and the damages likely to be awarded. By almost all accounts, it was this uncertainty that proved to be the decisive inducement to settlement. On one count, however, Judge Weinstein left little doubt in the lawyers' minds: the court, having crafted and taken responsibility for the settlement, was in a position to make it stick.

Sixth, the imminence and ineluctability of trial "concentrated the minds" of the lawyers as nothing else could have done. This deadline imparted to their deliberations an urgency and a seriousness that swept aside objections that might have undermined negotiations in less compelling circumstances. The lawyers' growing physical and mental exhaustion during that weekend of feverish intensity abetted the conciliatory effect. As one plaintiff's lawyer later complained in his challenge to the validity of the settlement, "the Judge wore us all down with that tactic."

Seventh, the judge and special masters displayed a degree of skill, sophistication, imagination, and artistry in fashioning the settlement that almost all the participants viewed as highly unusual. But even this would not have availed had Judge Weinstein not inspired an extraordinary measure of respect, even awe, in the lawyers, and had the special masters not been viewed as enjoying the authority to speak and make commitments for him.

Eighth, the settlement was negotiated without any agreement (or even any serious discussion) of how the settlement fund would be distributed among the claimants, and without reliable information as to the number of claims that would be filed. The first, of course, was of great interest to the plaintiffs and a matter of indifference to the defendants. The second, however, was significant to both sides. It is not at all certain that settlement could have been reached had the parties been required to resolve these issues in advance. The problem was not simply that preparation of a distribution plan required an immense amount of analysis. A protracted process of political compromise and education was also needed to gain support for the plan, a process whose results even now remain doubtful and perhaps legally vulnerable.

Ninth, the lawyers on the PMC [plaintiffs' management committee] at the time of the settlement possessed very different personalities, ideologies, and incentives than those of the group of lawyers that had launched the case and carried it through its first five years. These differences likely affected the lawyers' disposition to settle. The veterans' passionate desire for vindication at trial, quite apart from their wish for compensation, had strongly driven their chosen lawyer, Victor Yannacone, during the earlier stages of the litigation. Yet the PMC's deliberations concerning the settlement were strongly influenced by lawyers who had only the most attenuated relationship to the veterans. And under the terms of an internal fee-sharing agreement, these lawyers would be secured financially by even a "low" settlement.

Finally, the court was prepared to allocate substantial resources to the quest for a settlement. Judge Weinstein devoted a great deal of his own time to thinking through and implementing a settlement strategy. His three special masters for settlement commanded high compensation and worked long hours. Their billings to the court totaled hundreds of thousands of dollars, even excluding the massive amount of work they later invested in connection with the distribution plan.

[The settlement reached was for $180 million, although, as the article indicates, the fund increased as interest accrued. The distribution plan called for nearly $150 million to be distributed through a payment program that distributed death and disability benefits to individual veterans and family members like an insurance policy but without requiring proof of causation or otherwise adhering to traditional tort principles. Another portion, roughly $45 million, was to be turned over to a class assistance foundation benefitting both veterans and family members.

On appeal, the Second Circuit upheld the plan to distribute funds to individual disabled veterans and families of deceased veterans without requiring a particularized showing of individual causation. In re Agent Orange Litigation, 818 F.2d 179 (2d Cir.1987), cert. denied 487 U.S. 1234, 108 S.Ct. 2899, 101 L.Ed.2d 932 (1988). The court did find it was improper, however, to devote $45 million to the class assistance foundation. Because there would be no assurance that the foundation's self-governing and self-perpetuating board of directors would possess the independent, disinterested judgment required to allocate the funds fairly, the appellate court held that the district court must either directly supervise the class assistance programs, or add the money to the fund for distribution.]

## *Notes*

1. For a more detailed description and analysis of the Agent Orange litigation, see Peter H. Schuck, Agent Orange on Trial: Mass Toxic Disasters in the Courts (1986). Some of the highlights of the litigation are reported

at: 635 F.2d 987 (2d Cir.1980)(state laws apply, and not federal common law); 100 F.R.D. 718 (E.D.N.Y.1983)(certifying the class); 597 F.Supp. 740 (E.D.N.Y.1984)(approving settlement of the class action); 611 F.Supp. 1223 (E.D.N.Y.1985)(granting manufacturers' motion for summary judgment against plaintiffs who had opted out of the class action, because causation had not been established); 611 F.Supp. 1396 (E.D.N.Y.1985)(approving distribution plan); 818 F.2d 145 (2d Cir.1987) (upholding class certification and settlement), cert. denied, 484 U.S. 1004, 108 S.Ct. 695, 98 L.Ed.2d 648 (1988); and 818 F.2d 179 (2d Cir.1987)(upholding distribution plan), cert. denied, 484 U.S. 1004, 108 S.Ct. 695, 98 L.Ed.2d 648 (1988).

2. How does the settlement reached in the *Agent Orange* case compare to the traditional tort remedy? Should settlements be thought of as remedies at all? Does it make a difference that the case is a class action, in which any settlement must be approved by the judge?

## ABRAM CHAYES, THE ROLE OF THE JUDGE IN PUBLIC LAW LITIGATION

89 Harv.L.Rev. 1281 (1976).

Reproduced at pages 5–8.

## RICHARD L. MARCUS, *PUBLIC LAW LITIGATION* AND LEGAL SCHOLARSHIP

21 U.Mich.J.L.Reform 647, 671–81 (1988).

### B. Treating Public Law Litigation Differently: The Link Between Chayes and Current Issues * * *

1. *The tort "crisis"*—Personal injury litigation seems to display few of the features that Chayes found peculiar to public law litigation. The legal rules have evolved over time, but they certainly look different from the high-toned constitutional principles that typify the school desegregation or prison conditions suit. The relief seems to be prototypically private—a single transfer of money from defendant to plaintiff if plaintiff wins.

But tort law has changed. The nineteenth-century individualism that supported doctrines like the fellow-servant rule and made contributory negligence a complete defense has yielded to a different attitude that views tort remedies as ways to shift the costs of accidents. More significantly, products liability, scarcely an important part of the docket fifty years ago, has emerged as the major focus of innovation in tort law. Path-breaking scholars and courts have propelled plaintiffs into new theories not solely to improve the plaintiffs' chances of compensation, but also and explicitly to alter the behavior of providers of goods and services. Thus courts are increasingly willing to entertain the idea of punitive damages in products liability cases, explicitly endorsing relief designed to alter conduct.

These developments have, not surprisingly, provoked spirited opposition. The insurance industry, in particular, has regularly complained that shifts in the law have undermined its ability to make the calculations necessary to set premium levels. A few notable bankruptcies resulting from massive tort litigation (e.g., Manville Corp. and A.H. Robins) seem to lend substance to arguments that tort liability has gotten out of hand. Even the instrumental argument has been turned on its head by those who assert that regulation through jury verdicts is stifling innovation in technology. It is harder to say now than it was in 1976 that "conventional" tort litigation has only private significance; in terms of social importance, it may rival the sort of cases Chayes had in mind. * * * That, in turn, leads judges presiding over all types of litigation to engage in what Chayes observed in public law litigation—managerial judging.

2. *Managerial judging*—There can be little doubt that Chayes was correct in perceiving a great shift in judicial behavior from the classical model in which the judge was a passive arbiter. He saw this change as resulting from the judge's need to fashion a remedy for unconstitutional conditions, a development that made the judge step in and take over matters that formerly would have been left to the parties. Active judicial involvement, then, was a response to necessity.

In retrospect, it seems that Chayes perceived the necessity and the response too narrowly. The features of public law litigation that prompted judicial efforts to control litigation cannot meaningfully be limited to that kind of litigation. As might have been expected, judges promptly applied the lessons they had learned from their public law litigation experiences outside that realm. Having found a significant public interest in most civil litigation, judges reacted by taking charge of ordinary cases in a way somewhat similar to that in which they had taken control of the cases Chayes described. * * *

The obvious result of this protean role for the judge is to expand the judge's control over the development of the case, sometimes including responsibility for the proper preparation of the case. On a much broader scale than Chayes realized, then, modern judging raises problems of legitimacy of the investigating magistrate when measured against the classical model. Ad hoc judicial activity is hard to square with the notion that the Federal Rules of Civil Procedure should be applied in the same manner in all cases; the triumph of equity now seems to mean that the rules are merely guideposts. As a result, there is a troubling possibility that judges may indulge their own preferences about kinds of litigation in expanding or contracting litigation opportunities. The 1983 amendments even provide some support for that by inviting judges to restrict discovery if the expense seems unwarranted by "the importance of the issues at stake in the litigation."

Without seeming to realize it, Chayes hit upon a fundamental shift in judicial behavior. The theoretical ramifications of that shift are increasingly important in the academy, and resolution of these issues turns largely on reassessing the Fulleresque view of litigation, as Chayes suggested.

3. *Adjudication v. mediation*—Another feature of public law litigation that Chayes focused on may be even more fundamental than managerial judging. Chayes noted the tendency of judges to sidestep their responsibility to devise remedies by pressuring the parties to negotiate a consent decree. He properly perceived that this sort of prodding could not easily be fit into the classical image of the judge as a decision maker, not a facilitator.

As with the judicial management phenomenon, the idea of the judge as mediator was gaining popularity at the time Chayes was writing, and it also applied to a much greater range of cases than Chayes appreciated. In part, this was a reaction to the increasing pressures of growing caseloads, but it also represented the feeling of some judges that all or nothing outcomes in court often were inferior as a matter of justice to the negotiated outcomes that could result from mediation. The relation between the flexibility of negotiated outcomes and the incentives to settle litigation was hardly a new insight, but judges did not begin acting on that insight in large numbers until the late 1970's. By 1983 the practice had achieved such acceptance that it was enshrined in the amendments to the federal rules.

Managerial judging was originally designed to speed adjudication, but it lends itself to mediation as well because it provides the judge with much information about the case and many occasions for inviting or persuading the litigants to consider alternatives. But mediation is even more difficult to fit into the classical model of litigation. Thus, for decades after the federal rules were adopted in 1938, many judges felt that judicial involvement in the settlement process was inappropriate. The insight that the all or nothing results dictated by the law often will be less attractive to the parties than a compromise in no way undermines this traditional reluctance. To the contrary, the law's preference for all or nothing results suggests that compromises are to be shunned.

It is not surprising that public law litigation would strain the traditional view, however, because the remedy so often seems detached from the finding of a violation. As a consequence, one could say the all or nothing motif does not apply in such cases because it is so hard to know what the "all" might be, and always possible that the court will fashion something less than "all."

But the ambivalence in public law cases ran deeper; very often the consent decree was a negotiated resolution of *both* violation and remedy. This reality flowed easily from the nature of the problem courts confronted in framing decrees. The remedy problem in a prison conditions case, for example, arises because no single aspect of the prison's operations is necessarily unconstitutional if considered apart from all the others. In *Hutto v. Finney,* for example, the district court found the Arkansas prison system to violate the eighth amendment because it was "a dark and evil world completely alien to the free world." It then tried to prod the defendants to improve conditions. When that failed, the court imposed a specific injunction which, in part, set thirty days as the maximum sentence for confinement in isolation. The problem was that confining inmates in isolation for more than thirty days was not, standing alone, a constitutional violation. The Supreme Court nevertheless upheld the thirty day limitation because "[t]he length of time each inmate spent in isolation was simply one consideration among many" and, "taking the long and unhappy history of the litigation into account, the court was justified in entering a comprehensive order to insure against the risk of inadequate compliance."

If the problem with fashioning a decree is caused by the difficulty of identifying exactly which features of the defendant's conduct constitute a violation, it is a short step to prodding the parties to make a deal on both violation and remedy. In taking that step, the court can build on the long history of consent decrees in antitrust and employment discrimination cases. But once that step is taken, the distinguishing features of public law litigation seem to recede; if hard liability decisions can be avoided in those cases, they can be escaped in others as well. Moreover, to the extent the public law litigation cases take up a lot of judicial time and energy, it is attractive to use mediation to dispose of the other less weighty portion of the docket.

The current tort crisis atmosphere reinforces this trend. Should tort plaintiffs be left to pursue the all or nothing result at trial or encouraged to accept a "fair" settlement? Where the main uncertainty is the proper amount of compensation, the judge can feel relatively comfortable urging acceptance of a fair amount, based on the verdicts obtained in similar cases, whether or not that suggestion can be backed up with punishment for the party who resists the judge's suggestions. But liability is often unclear; in such cases, judges may have more effective tools to capitalize on uncertainty, because liability often depends more on the judge's decisions than does the measure of damages, which is usually left to the jury. By suggesting proplaintiff or prodefendant inclinations on the legal issues, the judge can powerfully affect the settlement atmosphere. Where the judge's influence is greatest, however, there are no referents like jury verdicts in other cases to guide the judge in selecting a settlement figure. What is the right amount to settle a weak case? How does a judge develop rules for that? What will rules regarding "fair" settlements of weak cases do to the substantive law, with its increasingly regulatory impetus, if they dilute the distinction between cases in which there should and should not be liability? * * *

### *Notes*

1. Looking at the traditional model of adjudication and the characteristics of public law litigation identified by Professor Chayes, where does the *Agent Orange* litigation fit? How does it depart from the traditional model? Would you call *Agent Orange* public law litigation?

What other damages actions have you seen that might be characterized as "public law litigation?"

2. Is it a good idea to import the active judicial role and emphasis on settlement that characterize public law litigation into cases like *Agent Orange,* or into ordinary tort or contract cases, for that matter? Professor David Rosenberg has argued that mass exposure cases in fact demand "public law mechanisms":

> Public law mechanisms would accomplish the same general purposes in mass exposure litigation that they achieve in civil rights or consumer fraud cases—regulating institutional policies or systematic practices that violate external substantive norms, and assuring access for the critical mass of claims necessary to generate appropriate levels of deterrence for enhancing the tort system's utilitarian and rights-based objectives. The keystone of the public law process is the class action and the managerial role for the judiciary that class action procedure authorizes. Public law adjudication of mass exposure claims would also entail remedial innovations, such as the use of scheduled or nonindividualized damages and insurance fund judgments. * * * [A]pplying public law process to mass exposure cases would likely enhance the system's functional productivity considerably. By enabling courts to exploit the aggregative nature of mass exposure claims, public law procedures would fulfill not only the utilitarian goals of the tort system, but the system's rights-based objectives as well—for such procedures would afford courts the greatest possible opportunity to remedy and prevent tortiously imposed risks of disease and would thus make the system more, not less, responsive to individual rights.

David Rosenberg, The Causal Connection in Mass Exposure Cases: A "Public Law" Vision of the Tort System, 97 Harv.L.Rev. 851 (1984). Similarly, Judge Weinstein himself has called for reforms to enable courts to cope with this sort of litigation, emphasizing, inter alia, the need for class actions; active, managerial judges; mechanisms to limit the total damages awarded; and distribution systems that provide scheduled recoveries without further adjudication, along the lines of worker's compensation systems. Jack B. Weinstein, Individual Justice in Mass Tort Litigation: The Effect of Class Actions, Consolidations, and Other Multiparty Devices (1995).

3. If tort law is taking on the characteristics of public law litigation, is that a positive or a negative development? On the substantive side, so far as promoting public values goes, critics of the tort system have argued that tort law is ineffective, if not counterproductive, at creating incentives to safety. See Peter W. Huber, Liability: The Legal Revolution and its Consequences (1988); Stephen Sugarman, Doing Away with Personal Injury Litigation (1989). On the procedural side, the managerial role the public law model forces on judges also has its critics. See Judith A. Resnik, Managerial Judging, 96 Harv.L.Rev. 374 (1982), and Stephen H. Subrin, How Equity Conquered Common Law: The Federal Rules of Civil Procedure in Historical Perspective, 135 U.Pa.L.Rev. 909 (1987).

As for the remedy, the strongest similarity between institutional reform cases and cases like *Agent Orange* is the pressure for settlement generated by the complexity, expense, and controversial character of the lawsuit. See Peter H. Schuck, Agent Orange on Trial 340 (1986). As the *Agent Orange* litigation demonstrates, that pressure operates on the judge as well as on the parties. In this, however, public law litigation is not really unique. As the costs of litigation have spiraled upwards, and as dockets have become increasingly crowded, the pressure to settle has come to bear on all kinds of litigation, and the responsibility for promoting settlement has increasingly landed on the judge. See Wayne D. Brazil, Effective Approaches to Settlement: A Handbook for Lawyers and Judges (1988).

Is an active role for judges in settling cases necessarily a good thing, however? In a part of the article that has been omitted, Professor Schuck argues that the judge's active participation in settling cases raise problems, if the judge overreaches his power to coerce settlement, becomes unable to assess the settlement fairly because he is overinvolved, or fails to protect against the risk of procedural unfairness inherent in informal settlement proceedings. Did Judge Weinstein successfully avoid these problems? For example, how did the judge reach the conclusion that $180 million was an appropriate amount for the settlement? At one point in the settlement discussion, one of the masters pressed the judge to urge a $200 million settlement, but the judge refused because the plaintiff's case was so "shaky." Richard L. Marcus, Apocalypse Now? (Book Review: Agent Orange on Trial), 85 Mich.L.Rev. 1267 (1987). Is this troubling?

Professor Marcus is also troubled because the pressure to settle can "blur the distinction between cases in which there should and should not be liability." There are also federalism issues. "Rule 23 is not a warrant for tort reform in federal court in order to cure 'defects' in state tort law." Richard L. Marcus, They Can't Do That Can They? Tort Reform via Rule 23, 80 Cornell L.Rev. 858 (1995). Professor Owen Fiss has also argued that there may be reasons why final adjudication is preferable to settlement. Owen Fiss, Against Settlement, 93 Yale L.J. 1073 (1984). Do you agree?

## D. AN OVERVIEW OF CONTRACT DAMAGES

The next case gives an overview of the issues that arise when damages are sought as the remedy for a breach of contract. Again, the notes that follow the case are organized along the lines suggested by the excerpt from McCormick on Damages at page 522. Contract damages are covered extensively in the first year contracts course; after this overview, our focus is on the gray areas in which tort, contract, and, in the next chapter, restitution overlap.

### 1. THE BASIC RULES

### GREAT AMERICAN MUSIC MACHINE, INC. v. MID–SOUTH RECORD PRESSING CO.

United States District Court, Middle District of Tennessee, 1975.
393 F.Supp. 877.

MORTON, DISTRICT JUDGE.

This suit is brought by plaintiffs Great American Music Machine, Inc. (GrAMM), a Colorado corporation, and Ralph Harrison, a citizen and resident of Colorado, against Mid–South Record Pressing Company, a division of GRT Corporation, with its principal place of business in Davidson County, Tennessee. The complaint seeks monetary damages, based upon breach of contract and implied warranty in connection with some record albums which plaintiffs allege were defectively pressed by Mid–South. The defendant counterclaims on its open account with the plaintiff corporation in the stipulated amount of thirteen thousand and twenty-five dollars and thirty-nine cents ($13,025.39). Jurisdiction of this court is properly invoked under 28 U.S.C. § 1332.

Findings of Fact

In August of 1971, plaintiff Harrison and several of his close friends and business associates formed "Crossroads Limited Partnership," the predecessor to plaintiff corporation. The partnership was formed for the purpose of promoting and exploiting the musical talents of Harrison as a songwriter and singer, although he was then unknown in the entertainment field and had never performed professionally. The business plan of the partnership was to finance the production of a master tape for an album by Ralph Harrison, convert the partnership into a corporation, produce and promote the album and Harrison as an artist, and raise additional capital through a public offering of the stock of the corporation. GrAMM was incorporated by the Crossroads venture in March of 1972, and all the rights of Crossroads were merged into the new corporation.

In the fall of 1971, Harrison went to New York City to produce the master tape for an album featuring himself as the singing artist. The production cost of the master tape was thirty-one thousand and eighty-eight dollars ($31,088.00). The title of the album was to be "Free Spirit Movin'."

In early February of 1972, Harrison and an investor in the venture came to Nashville, Tennessee, to contract for the pressing and packaging of the record album. On behalf of GrAMM, they contracted orally with the defendant, Mid–South Record Pressing Company, for the pressing of forty thousand (40,000) record albums, at a cost of thirteen thousand and twenty-five dollars and thirty-nine cents ($13,025.39). GrAMM received assurances that the records would be of high quality. Although there was some dispute in the testimony at trial, it appears to the satisfaction of this court that there was some discussion with Janet Tabor, manager of defendant company, concerning the overall business plan of GrAMM. It is the finding of this court that GrAMM's plan to offer stock to the public in June of 1972 was mentioned in this discussion.

Under the terms of the oral agreement between the parties, Mid–South was to mail directly to members of ESA, a national sorority, some thirty-two thousand (32,000) copies of the album. (One of Harrison's songs on the record had been adopted by ESA as its theme song.) GrAMM supplied the postage in advance for this mailing. To be enclosed with the albums sent to ESA members was a letter requesting that five dollars ($5.00) be remitted to GrAMM, of which one dollar

($1.00) would be donated to a certain service project of the sorority. The bulk of the remaining 8,000 albums was to be sent to Gambit Records, a Nashville company with whom GrAMM had contracted for nationwide distribution. By mid-February of 1972, a test pressing of good quality had been approved by GrAMM, and Mid–South commenced production of the album. Though there was some dispute in the testimony at trial, the court finds that the contemplated delivery date was the first week of April, 1972.

On April 3, 1972, GrAMM received a shipment of the records at its office in Denver, Colorado. At that time it was discovered by Harrison and others that the records were defective in that they were warped, pitted and blistered, producing excessive surface noises when played. GrAMM immediately sent two representatives to Nashville on April 4, 1972, to investigate the situation. Upon arrival, the GrAMM representatives learned that some eight thousand (8,000) of the records had already been shipped to ESA members; roughly four thousand (4,000) records had been delivered to Gambit, from which an undetermined number had been sent to distributors and disc jockeys around the country.

The court finds as a matter of fact that the first pressing of the record by Mid–South was for the most part commercially unacceptable. Witnesses for both the plaintiff and the defendant testified as to this fact. Gordon Close, one of the GrAMM representatives sent to Nashville in early April, and Janet Tabor of Mid–South both agreed that the larger part of the records still on hand at Mid–South were unusable and that the entire lot should be scrapped and new records pressed. To be included in the new pressing were replacements for the defective albums which had already been shipped out. * * *

Although GrAMM did not complain of the quality of the second pressing nor reject the second batch of albums, it has refused to pay its open account with Mid–South. The amount due on the account is $13,025.39.

In relation to the contemplated stock offering by GrAMM, plaintiff introduced evidence at trial attempting to show that Mr. Mike McBride of Equidyne, Inc., a brokerage firm in Salt Lake City, Utah, had agreed to a firm underwriting of five hundred thousand dollars ($500,000.00) worth of GrAMM securities. * * *

From the evidence developed at trial with regard to the underwriting offer, it is difficult for this court to ascertain exactly why the underwriting did not go through. * * *

### Conclusions of Law

The court finds that the defendant company breached implied warranties of merchantability and fitness for a particular purpose, T.C.A. § 47–2–314 and § 47–2–315, in the first pressing of the record albums. Defendant also breached its express contractual agreement to produce records of high quality. * * *

The court finds as a matter of law that plaintiff justifiably rejected the entire first pressing of the record albums as nonconforming goods. T.C.A. § 47–2–602. This rejection included the 12,000 records which had already been shipped out to ESA members and Gambit. Plaintiff notified the defendant of the defects as soon as it became aware of them, on the day it received initial shipment. The defective records had only negligible value as scrap, and defendant made no request that they be returned to it. The cost of retrieving the records already distributed would have greatly exceeded their value as scrap. Any revenue from the records that were shipped to ESA members appears to have been from the second "replacement" batch of records.

With regard to the second pressing of the record albums, the court finds that plaintiff GrAMM is liable on its open account with defendant in the amount of $13,025.39. Plaintiff's liability is predicated upon the fact that it accepted the repressed records and under T.C.A. § 47–2–607 must pay at the contract rate for goods accepted by it. The fact that plaintiff accepted the second batch of records does not, however, in any way preclude its suit for damages occasioned by the defective pressing of the first batch of records. The delivery of the second batch of records did not constitute a cure within the meaning of T.C.A. § 47–2–508, as the damage had already occurred and the time set for performance had expired.

Having previously determined that defendant Mid–South breached express and implied warranties, we now turn to the question of damages. Plaintiff GrAMM has elected to sue for breach of contract, rather than suing in tort for negligence. The damages recoverable for a breach of contract "... are limited to those reasonably within the contemplation of the defendant when the contract was made, while in a tort action a much broader measure of damages is applied." Prosser, Handbook on the Law of Torts, p. 613.

The standard measure of damages under the Uniform Commercial Code, as adopted in Tennessee, is not particularly helpful under the facts of this case. Under T.C.A. § 47–2–714(2):

> The measure of damages for breach of warranty is the difference at the time and place of acceptance between the value of the goods accepted and the value they would have had if they had been as warranted....

In the instant case, no credible evidence was proffered to the court to reflect the difference between the value that the records would have had if they had been perfectly pressed the first time and delivered on time, as warranted, and the value of the repressed records which were delivered late, after some of the defective records had already been distributed.

Fortunately, the drafters of the Code anticipated such unique factual circumstances and added the following provision to § 47–2–714(2):

> ... unless special circumstances show proximate damages of a different amount.

Additionally, T.C.A. § 47–2–714(3) provides:

> In a proper case any incidental and consequential damages under the next section may also be recovered.

T.C.A. § 47–2–715 explains what may be included as incidental and consequential damages:

> (1) Incidental damages resulting from the seller's breach include expenses reasonably incurred in inspection, receipt, transportation and care and custody of goods rightfully rejected, any commercially reasonable charge, expenses or commissions in connection with effecting cover and *any other reasonable expense incident to the delay or other breach.*
>
> (2) Consequential damages resulting from the seller's breach include
>
> > (a) any loss resulting from general or particular requirements and needs of which the seller at the time of contracting had reason to know and which could not reasonably be prevented by cover or otherwise; and
> >
> > (b) injury to person or property proximately resulting from any breach of warranty. (emphasis added)

According to Comment 4 to the above-quoted section:

> The burden of proving the extent of loss incurred by way of consequential damage is on the buyer, but the section on liberal administration of remedies rejects any doctrine of certainty which requires almost mathematical precision in the proof of loss. *Loss may be determined in any manner which is reasonable under the circumstances.* (emphasis added)

With regard to certainty of proof required on damage questions generally, Tennessee law provides:

> . . . there is a clear distinction between the measure of proof necessary to establish the fact that plaintiff had sustained some damage, and the measure of proof necessary to enable the jury to fix the amount. The rule which precludes the recovery of uncertain damages applies to such damages as are not the certain result of the wrong, not to those damages which are definitely attributable to the wrong and only uncertain in respect of their amount. (citation omitted) Acuff v. Vinsant, 59 Tenn.App. 727, 443 S.W.2d 669 (Tenn. App.1969), at 674.

The question of allowable damages in this case is made more difficult by the speculative nature of the business venture undertaken by GrAMM. It is undisputed that Harrison had not demonstrated that his talents as a songwriter and artist had any appreciable market value prior to the production of the record, "Free Spirit Movin'." The proof clearly indicates the extremely hazardous nature of an undertaking to produce a "hit" record and create a "star" in the entertainment world.

Plaintiff GrAMM contends that the defective first pressing and resultant delay and confusion virtually destroyed the market for the "Free Spirit Movin'" album, and that Mid–South's breach also caused the failure of the firm underwriting of $500,000 by Equidyne. Plaintiff concedes that it is impossible to project with reasonable certainty what the future profits of the new corporation might have been. Instead, plaintiff asks for (1) the cost of laying the ground work for the manufacture and distribution of the album, including production costs of the record, plus advertising and promotional costs; (2) the cost of keeping the corporation going as a business entity from the date of the breach until the date that plaintiff finally had a successful public offering and began producing music for commercial use; (3) the capital lost from the projected underwriting which failed to materialize, less that realized from a subsequent stock offering; and (4) expenses allegedly incurred following the breach in an attempt by GrAMM to rehabilitate the record, including: advertising expenses, promotional salaries, telephone costs, office supplies, payroll taxes, and salaries of management personnel and secretaries.

As previously noted, while the amount of damages may be approximated, the fact of damage attributable to the wrong must be proven with reasonable certainty. The court rejects the first two elements of damages propounded by the plaintiff, for the reason that the plaintiff did not prove to the court's satisfaction that there was ever any appreciable market for the record, nor that any such market was destroyed.

With regard to the existence of any market for the record, it is noteworthy that 32,000 of the 40,000 records pressed were to be shipped to ESA members as a promotional gimmick, with the request that $5.00 be remitted. The ESA members were, of course, under no legal obligation to pay the requested price for this unordered merchandise. 39 U.S.C. § 3010. There was no proof as to what percentage of the ESA members was likely to send in the requested price.

It was shown at trial that the usual practice among unknown artists in the record industry is to first put out a "single" record, as this is less expensive than an album. In this manner, the marketability of the artist can be tested prior to the production of an album. Ralph Harrison had never produced a single record, nor even performed professionally, prior to the production of the "Free Spirit Movin'" album. Therefore, the court must necessarily rely on the proof at trial with regard to the marketability potential of "Free Spirit Movin'."

James Fogelsong, President of Dot Records and an expert in the music field, testified that the lyrics and artist's performance in "Free Spirit Movin'" were not exceptional in any way; that its production was ordinary or worse; and that the musical instruments in the album "were not in time." Paul Perry, a disc jockey for a popular Nashville radio station, testified that he was impressed with the jacket of the album, but not with the ingredients of the record. He testified that he found no fault with the pressing of the album, and that the ingredients on the record couldn't measure up to the programming standards of his station in any event. He further testified that, in his opinion, the album "would not have had any major marketization," even with an initial pressing of highest quality.

Plaintiff offered no credible expert witnesses to refute the testimony of Fogelsong and Perry. No market survey or other reliable evidence with regard to market potential was introduced by plaintiff. Based upon the proof, the court concludes that no appreciable market existed for the "Free Spirit Movin' "album.

Although GrAMM proved the amount of its investment and the cost of operating its business during the period in question, it offered no convincing proof that, with an initial pressing of high quality, it would in all probability have sold a sufficient number of records to recoup its investment. "Ordinarily, damages are said to be speculative when the probability that a circumstance will exist as an element for compensation becomes conjectural." 25 C.J.S. § 2. In the absence of credible proof that the album had a probability of success, the court cannot speculate that this would have been the case. In fact, the proof at trial convinced the court that the album had a far greater chance of failure than of success. * * *

The law is well settled that the injured party is not to be put in a better position by a recovery of damages for breach of contract than he would have been in if there had been full performance. 25 C.J.S. Damages § 3. In this case, to grant plaintiff its entire investment in the album as damages for the breach by defendant would in all probability be to put GrAMM in a far better financial position than it would have been in had there been no breach. This the court will not do. It does not appear that plaintiff would have recouped the investment even if there had been no breach.

The court also rejects plaintiff's damages claim with regard to the failure of the $500,000.00 firm stock underwriting to materialize. First, the proof was not sufficiently clear as to why the underwriting did not go through. In absence of such satisfactory proof, the court cannot hold defendant liable for the failure.

Secondly, the court finds that such damages are too remote to have reasonably been within the contemplation of the parties at the time the contract was made. Although it appears from the proof that some mention was made of the stock offering in the conversation between GrAMM and Mid–South representatives, it does not appear that it was discussed in such detail that defendant would have had any idea that it might be held liable for the failure of the underwriting. As noted by the court in Baker v. Riverside Church of God, 61 Tenn.App. 270, 453 S.W.2d 801 (1970), in quoting from Squire et al. v. Western Union Telegraph Co., 98 Mass. 233 (1867):

> A rule of damages which should embrace within its scope all the consequences which might be shown to have resulted from a failure or omission to perform a stipulated duty or service would be a

serious hindrance to the operations of commerce and to the transaction of the common business life. The effect would often be to impose a liability wholly disproportionate to the nature of the act or service which a party had bound himself to perform and to the compensation paid and received therefore. 453 S.W.2d 801, 810.

In the case currently before the court, plaintiff asks damages in excess of $200,000 for breach of a $13,000 contract. The breach of the contract has not been satisfactorily proven to be the cause of the alleged loss. Certainly, these damages may not be allowed.

Under the circumstances peculiar to this case, the court finds the best measure of allowable damages to be the expenses reasonably incurred by GrAMM in its efforts to rehabilitate the record following the breach.

The court concludes that the following elements may be included in the expenses of rehabilitating the record:

(1) salaries and travel expenses of GrAMM representatives sent to Nashville to negotiate the re-pressing of the record album and act as GrAMM's quality control agents;

(2) salaries of other GrAMM employees for the period in which they were actively engaged in the rehabilitation of the record;

(3) extra mailing and handling costs attributable to the defective first pressing;

(4) reasonable telephone costs;

(5) advertising and promotional expenses reasonably incurred by GrAMM in rehabilitating the record; and

(6) a reasonable amount for office supplies and various other miscellaneous expenses.

* * *

## *Notes*

1. *The Plaintiff's Cause of Action.* Tort law is to some extent an aggregation of many distinct causes of action, each defining distinct legally protected interests and therefore calling for distinct remedies. By contrast, at least since the late 19th century, contract law has been seen as a unified field. Whatever the subject matter of the particular contract, the Law of Contracts governs. The same principles, substantive and remedial, are determinative in all cases, although the application of those principles turns on the contract at hand, of course.

There have always been those who have argued that the unity of the field of contracts is illusory, largely the product of overactive academic imaginations. See, e.g., Grant Gilmore, Death of Contract (1974). Indeed, recent developments provide some support for the argument that there is less a single Law of Contracts than a law of insurance contracts, of employment contracts, of commercial contracts, and so on, with remedies for each.

The codification of the law of sales in article two of the Uniform Commercial Code, the Tennessee version of which governs in *GrAMM*, suggests this diversity by providing a framework of substantive and remedial principles peculiar to contracts for the sale of goods. Paradoxically, however, article two also confirms the universality of contract remedies; its provisions generally mirror the common law of contracts closely enough that a case like *GrAMM* may be used to study those general principles. Still, article two does frequently depart from the general principles of substantive and remedial contract law in order to reflect the demands of the commercial field to which it applies. Where relevant, those departures have been noted, although any detailed treatment of the law of sales perforce is left to the commercial law courses. For detailed discussions of article two, see Ray D. Henson, The Law of Sales (1985); James J. White, Handbook of the Law Under the Uniform Commercial Code (1980).

2. *The Purpose of the Damage Award: Protecting the Expectation, Reliance, and Restitution Interests.* According to the Restatement (Second) of Contracts § 344,

> Judicial remedies under the rules stated in this Restatement serve to protect one or more of the following interests of a promisee:
>
> (a) his "expectation interest," which is his interest in having the benefit of his bargain by being put in as good a position as he would have been in had the contract been performed,
>
> (b) his "reliance interest," which is his interest in being reimbursed for loss caused by reliance on the contract by being put in as good a position as he would have been in had the contract not been made, or
>
> (c) his "restitution interest," which is his interest in having restored to him any benefit that he has conferred on the other party.

The vehicle that promotes these purposes is the compensatory damage award, and that is the primary focus of this section. Nominal damages are available in contract cases, however, when no actual injury to one of these three interests can be shown. Punitive damages are another matter. Any interest in punishing or deterring the breaching party is noticeably absent from the Restatement's summary of the purposes of contract remedies, and traditional wisdom would have it that punitive damages are not available unless the plaintiff can recast his cause of action to sound in tort:

> Punitive damages are not recoverable for a breach of contract unless the conduct constituting the breach is also a tort for which punitive damages are recoverable.

Restatement (Second) of Contracts § 355. Considerable inroads have been made on the traditional rule, as the materials at page 637 discuss.

Focusing for a moment on purposes compensatory damage awards are intended to serve, think about this hypothetical: Suppose you are offered a job in another city, and you must sell your car to cover the moving expenses. You have advertised it in the paper for several days at a price of $800, with no success. Time is short, and realizing your predicament, your roommate offers to buy it from you for $600, which is all she can afford. You agree to sell it to her. Ten minutes later, someone calls, offers to buy it for $800, and when told it has been sold, ups the offer to $900. You agree to sell it to the caller, and immediately inform your roommate. Being a law student, she immediately sues you. Assuming an enforceable contract was formed, what damages should she recover?

As we have seen, contract damages ostensibly protect the promisee's reliance, expectation, and restitution interests, interests that are usually consistent. In fact, the article that first identified how contract damages protect these three interests did so precisely to show that they frequently overlap. Lon Fuller & William Perdue, The Reliance Interest in Contract Damages, 46 Yale L.J. 52 (1936). For example,

> [W]here the reliance interest is conceived to embrace the loss of the opportunity to enter similar contracts with other persons, the reliance and expectation interests will have a tendency to approach one another, the precise degree of their correspondence depending upon the extent to which other opportunities of similar nature were open to the plaintiff when he entered the contract on which suit is brought. The physician who by making one appointment deprives himself of the opportunity of making a precisely similar appointment with another patient presents a case of a complete correspondence between the reliance and expectation interests. The tendency of the expectation and reliance interests to coalesce in cases of this sort has the consequence that the same item of damages may often be classified under either heading. Thus, where the defendant's breach of contract results in the plaintiff's property remaining idle for a period, the courts in awarding the plaintiff the rental value of the premises have sometimes considered that they were granting reimbursement for the loss of the opportunity to employ the property for other purposes (the reliance interest), and sometimes that they were granting compensation for the loss of profits which would have been made had the defendant performed his promise (expectation interest).

Id. at 74–5. Observing this overlap, Professors Fuller and Perdue argued that the express measure of contract damages and the unstated motives of the courts had diverged: Often, though courts measured damages by expectation, what they were actually compensating was the plaintiff's reliance. The expectation measure simply relieved plaintiffs of the burden of *proving* reliance, lost opportunities being inherently difficult to establish.

Thus, Professors Fuller and Perdue argued that the expectation measure of damages was justified because by protecting reliance even where it could not be proved, the expectation measure both served the ends of corrective justice by undoing the harm caused by the breach, and promoted contracting by encouraging reliance. At the same time, however, Professors Fuller and Perdue's thesis posed a substantial challenge to traditional contract doctrine: "It may be said parenthetically that [our] discussion * * *, though directed primarily to the normal measure of recovery where damages are sought, also has relevance to the more general question, why should a promise which has not been relied on ever be enforced at all * * *?" Id. at 57. See also Patrick S. Atiyah, The Rise and Fall of Freedom of Contract (1979)(arguing that expectancies based merely on a promise have little claim to the law's protection, and in fact are rarely enforced).

So, in a case such as that posed at the beginning of this note, where there has been no reliance, should the promisee recover damages? Without reliance, why should we say there is a contract at all? Do promises have some independent moral and legal force that makes them enforceable even without reliance, a force that the expectation measure acknowledges? See Charles Fried, Contract as Promise (1981). Can economics provide an answer? See Avery Katz, Reflections on Fuller and Perdue's The Reliance Interest in Contract Damages: A Positive Economic Framework, 21 U.Mich. J.L.Ref. 541, 542 (1988); Richard A. Epstein, Beyond Foreseeability: Consequential Damages in the Law of Contract, 18 J.Legal Stud. 105, 110 (1989)(contract damages should be determined by the contract's express terms or, if the contract is silent, by choosing the rule the parties would have chosen to maximize their joint gains).

If the answer to Professors Fuller and Perdue is that for moral or economic reasons, contracts must be enforced even where there is no reliance, why stop with expectation damages? If breaching a contract is wrong, and the defendant did it deliberately, shouldn't punitive damages be available? If a promisor earns a profit by breaching a contract, and breaching a contract is wrong, shouldn't the defendant have to give up any profit earned by his wrongdoing? These questions are explored in sections that follow.

3. *Elements of the Damage Award.* Turning to the elements of compensatory damages that may be available when contract damages are sought, the idea of a balance sheet may again be helpful. On one side of the ledger would be the plaintiff's losses: the value of the lost performance, plus any incidental or consequential damages. On the other side of the ledger are the plaintiff's savings. First, the plaintiff may have saved the cost of his own performance when the defendant's breach made it unnecessary for him to perform. Second, the plaintiff may be able to act to avoid some losses; the wrongly fired worker may be able to find another job or the manufacturer whose customer has breached may be able to find a new buyer for his goods. These "losses avoided" must be added to the plaintiff's savings. Then, after the various elements have been identified, the expectation damages may be calculated by subtracting the plaintiff's savings from the plaintiff's losses, or as the Restatement puts it:

> [T]he injured party has a right to damages based on his expectation interest as measured by
>
> (a) the loss in the value to him of the other party's performance caused by its failure or deficiency, plus
>
> (b) any other loss, including incidental or consequential loss, caused by the breach, less
>
> (c) any cost or other loss that he has avoided by not having to perform.

Restatement (Second) of Contracts, § 347.

The Restatement's formula for calculating expectation is universal; it can be applied to any type of contract. In practice, however, more specific formulae have evolved as the measure of damages for specific types of contracts. To borrow an example from Professor E. Allan Farnsworth, when a property owner breaches a construction contract before the work is completed, the Restatement would measure the builder's expectation as the unpaid contract price minus the cost of completing the house (assuming for the sake of simplicity that the builder suffered neither incidental nor consequential damages, and was unable to avoid any losses). Practically speaking, however, it can be very difficult to show the cost of completing a half-built house. It is much easier for the contractor to show how much profit he expected to make when he entered the contract, and how much he has spent on performance so far (his reliance). Therefore, he would prefer to measure his damages by his expected profit plus his costs so far, and indeed, the cases support such a measure. E. Allan Farnsworth, Contracts § 12.10 p. 849 (1982). Because the builder's expected profit is equal to the contract price minus his costs so far minus the cost of completion, the "profits plus reliance" measure is the algebraic equivalent of the Restatement's "loss of value minus costs saved" measure.

The materials in this chapter include the damage measures for most of the basic types of contracts. As you encounter them, it may be helpful to relate each to the Restatement's basic measure of expectation. It is also important to understand that in most cases damages that protect the plaintiff's expectation interest—the "benefit of the bargain,"—simultaneously protect his reliance and restitution interests. For example, if a defendant promises to sell the plaintiff a car worth $6,000 for only $5,000, and then breaches after accepting the plaintiff's deposit of $500, one way to measure the damages would be the value of the car ($6,000) less the cost the plaintiff avoided by not having to pay the balance of the purchase price ($4500), or $1,500. An award of $1,500 protects the plaintiff's expectation by giving him the $1,000 profit he expected; it protects his reliance interest by returning his $500 deposit; and it protects his restitution interest by taking the $500 away from the defendant. In other cases, however, reliance or restitution damages may be alternative remedies for a contract breach; the plaintiff may choose to sue for damages measured by his reliance, or for restitution, instead of seeking expectation damages.

Ignoring limitations like foreseeability, certainty, etc., what would the damages have been in *Great American Music Machine (GrAMM)?* What award would be necessary to protect the plaintiff's expectation interest? His reliance interest? His restitution interest? If the plaintiff is given the "benefit of the bargain," are his reliance and restitutionary interests adequately protected?

4. *Measuring the Damages.* Because non-pecuniary losses are rarely recoverable in contract cases, the primary problem in measuring the damages lies in supplying the values necessary to fill in the relevant general damages formula, and in establishing the amount of whatever special damages have been incurred with reasonable certainty. There are parallels, however, to the sorts of issues discussed under the heading of measuring tort damages, page 546.

a. *Cost of completion or diminution in value?* In Ohio v. Department of the Interior, page 566 and the notes that follow it, the question of whether damages should be measured by cost of repair or diminution in value was examined. In contract cases, the analogous issue arises when the cost of completing the performance called for by a breached contract exceeds the market value to be gained from performance.

Peevyhouse v. Garland Coal & Mining Company, 382 P.2d 109 (Okla. 1962), is one of the classic examples. Garland Coal had leased the Peevyhouses' land for a strip-mining operation. When Garland Coal returned the land to the Peevyhouses after five years, they failed to perform remedial and restorative work the lease called for. The evidence adduced at trial showed that the remedial work would cost $29,000 to perform, but that the land was worth only $300 less because of the failure to do the work. At trial, the jury awarded the Peevyhouses $5,000 in damages.

The Supreme Court of Oklahoma reversed:

> We * * * hold that where, in a coal mining lease, lessee agrees to perform certain remedial work on the premises concerned at the end of the lease period, and thereafter the contract is fully performed by both parties except that the remedial work is not done, the measure of damages in an action by lessor against lessee for damages for breach of contract is ordinarily the reasonable cost of performance of the work; however, where the contract provision breached was merely incidental to the main purpose in view, and where the economic benefit which would result to lessor by full performance of the work is grossly disproportionate to the cost of performance, the damages which lessor may recover are limited to the diminution in value resulting to the premises because of the non-performance. * * *
>
> Under the most liberal view of the evidence herein, the diminution in value resulting to the premises because of non-performance of the remedial work was $300.00. * * * We are of the opinion that the judgment of the trial court for plaintiffs should be, and it is hereby, modified and reduced to the sum of $300.00, and as so modified it is affirmed.

382 P.2d at 114. For a thorough history of the case, see Judith L. Maute, Peevyhouse v. Garland Coal & Mining Co. Revisited: The Ballad of Willie and Lucille, 89 Nw.U.L.Rev. 1341 (1995).

On the other hand, in Groves v. John Wunder Co., 205 Minn. 163, 286 N.W. 235, 236 (1939), a contractor leased the plaintiff's land for a gravel quarry, agreeing to grade the land evenly after removing the gravel. The contractor did not do the grading, and the plaintiff sued. The evidence showed that the cost of the grading would be $60,000, while the total value of the plaintiff's property would be only $12,160 even after the grading was done. Nonetheless, the court found that the proper measure of damages was the cost of performance. Any other rule "handsomely rewards bad faith and deliberate breach of contract."

Which is the better result? Would it matter whether the land were a family farm, or property held by a developer speculating on property values?

Should the same rules apply in contract cases that apply in tort cases? The same sort of issue can arise in eminent domain cases, when the cost of acquiring a substitute for the land taken is greater than the market value of the land. See, e.g., United States v. 50 Acres of Land, 469 U.S. 24, 105 S.Ct. 451, 83 L.Ed.2d 376 (1984). What rules should apply then? For an attempt to explain the choice of a measure by reference to the differing substantive goals in each area, see Robert Cooter, Unity in Tort, Contract and Property: The Model of Precaution, 73 Calif.L.Rev. 1 (1985).

b. *Taxes, Time and Value:* If the award is intended to compensate for future losses, it must be reduced to present value, just as a tort award would be. On the other hand, contract damages are not excluded from gross income by 42 U.S.C. § 104(a)(2), as damages received on account of personal injury are, so they are taxable if they otherwise constitute income. Whether a particular element of damages constitutes a taxable gain, and whether the gain is income or a capital gain, can be difficult to determine. See e.g., Gail v. United States, 58 F.3d 580 (10th Cir.1995).

Prejudgment interest is recoverable in a contract case if the breach "consists of a failure to pay money or to render a performance with fixed or ascertainable monetary value." Restatement (Second) of Contracts § 354. An interesting issue of timing can arise in connection with prejudgment interest. The usual rule is that contract damages are measured as of the time of the breach. In Anchorage Asphalt Paving Co. v. Lewis, 629 P.2d 65 (Alaska 1981), however, the trial court measured damages from breach of a contract to pave a road as the cost of completing the paving as of the time of trial.

The Alaska Supreme Court affirmed, despite the general rule that damages for breach of contract should be determined as of the date of the breach. The court went on to hold that because the damages had been measured as of the time of the trial, to award prejudgment interest would be "an unwarranted and unjustified compounding of damages." Is that the right result?

5. *Limits on the Award.*

a. *Foreseeability.* Consideration of the role of foreseeability in contract damages begins with Hadley v. Baxendale, 156 Eng.Rep. 145 (1854), a fixture of the basic course in contracts. In *Hadley,* the defendant breached a contract to deliver a mill shaft to be repaired. The delay that resulted caused the mill owner to lose profits, because his mill was unable to operate without the shaft. Yet the court denied the mill owner recovery, because the loss of profits was unforeseeable:

> When two parties have made a contract which one of them has broken, the damages which the other party ought to receive in respect of such breach of contract should be such as may fairly and reasonably be considered either arising naturally, i.e., according to usual course of things, from such breach of contract itself, or such as may reasonably be supposed to have been in the contemplation of both parties, at the time they made the contract as the probable result of the breach of it. Now, if the special circumstances under which the contract was actually made were communicated by the plaintiffs to the defendants, and thus known to both parties, the damages resulting from the breach of such a contract, which they would reasonably contemplate, would be the amount of the injury which would ordinarily follow from a breach of contract under these special circumstances so known and communicated.

156 Eng.Rep. at 151.

Because of *Hadley,* the distinction between general and special (or consequential) damages in contract cases takes on added importance. General damages are those that, under the first prong of *Hadley*'s test, arise "naturally" from that breach, and are foreseeable by definition. Special, or consequential, damages fall under *Hadley*'s second prong, and must be proven to have been foreseeable based on special circumstances known to the breaching party at the time the contract was formed.

For a time, the requirement that special damages be shown to be foreseeable was interpreted to require the plaintiff to show that the loss was not merely foreseeable, but that the breaching party, by entering the contract knowing the circumstances, tacitly consented to be liable for that loss in the event of a breach. The tacit agreement variation of the *Hadley* rule, however, has been rejected by virtually every state that has considered it, and by the Restatement of Contracts and the UCC as well. Note, The Tacit Agreement Test—Arkansas Clings to a Dinosaur, 40 Ark.L.Rev. 403, 406 (1986). The Restatement (Second) of Contracts § 351, states the settled rule:

> (2) Loss may be foreseeable as a probable result of a breach because it follows from the breach
>
> (a) in the ordinary course of events
>
> (b) as a result of special circumstances, beyond the ordinary course of events, that the party in breach had reason to know.
>
> (3) A court may limit damages for foreseeable loss by excluding recovery for loss of profits, by allowing recovery only for loss incurred in reliance, or otherwise, if it concludes that in the circumstances justice so requires in order to avoid disproportionate compensation.

The UCC's version of *Hadley* is in § 2–715(2)(a), which is quoted in *GrAMM*. Does it differ from the Restatement's formulation? Was the court in *GrAMM* correct in holding that the damages with regard to the failure of the stock underwriting were too remote, given its finding that the plan to make a public offering of the stock was mentioned in discussions with Mid–South?

One of the challenges of studying remedies is to account for the ways in which the same concept—here, foreseeability—is treated differently in tort and contract suits. For example, Harrison attempted to cast his suit in negligence, but failed because of the statute of limitations. Had he been successful, would it have made any difference? How do the rules governing foreseeability in tort compare to the rule derived from *Hadley?* If Harrison had been allowed to pursue his negligence claim, would damages attributable to the underwriting failure have been recoverable? See *EVRA v. Swiss Bank Corp.*, text at 650.

The comparison of tort and contract remedies is the subject of the next section of this chapter. To give a quick answer, because Harrison's losses were purely economic, most courts would have held that no cause of action in negligence could be stated. That is simply to say, a court would probably decide that contract rules ought to govern this loss. But why?

b. *Certainty.* Damages can be recovered for a particular element of loss "only to the extent that the evidence affords a sufficient basis for estimating their amount in money with reasonable certainty". Restatement (Second) of Contracts § 352. Although both tort and contract damages must be certain, courts may apply the requirement somewhat differently in different contexts. For example, in Evergreen Amusement Corp. v. Milstead, 206 Md. 610, 112 A.2d 901 (1955), a contractor breached an agreement to clear and grade a site for a drive-in movie theater. The property owner sued, seeking damages measured by the profits he lost because the theater's opening was delayed. The court denied recovery of this element of damages. The plaintiff pointed to a number of antitrust cases that seemed to support recovery, and the court responded: "While the opinions do not articulate that the damages were allowed to make effective the civil sanctions of the anti-trust statutes and, indeed, in one case, perhaps self-consciously, suggest that there is no distinction in the rules as to damages between anti-trust cases and others, nevertheless, it seems clear that the courts, in order to lay a basis for punitive triple damages, have relaxed the standards of proof in anti-trust suits to permit the establishment of lost profits as basic damages."

Does it make sense to allow an item of loss in an antitrust or tort case, and deny the same element in a contract case as too uncertain, on basically the same proof? Keep in mind that contract liability is strict, although it can be argued that courts could—and do—use doctrines like foreseeability, certainty and avoidability to respond to different degrees of fault. George M. Cohen, The Fault Line in Contract Damages, 80 Va.L.Rev. 1225 (1994).

How much certainty should be required in a tort case? In Grayson v. Irvmar Realty Corp., 7 A.D.2d 436, 184 N.Y.S.2d 33 (1959), the plaintiff recovered damages for the injury her loss of hearing caused to her career as an opera singer. She was 21, however, and had never actually earned any money singing although she was professionally trained and was preparing for her debut. Were her damages reasonably certain?

The requirement that the amount of the plaintiff's losses be shown with sufficient certainty has always posed particular problems for plaintiffs involved in new or entrepreneurial ventures, as in *Evergreen* or *GrAMM*. In fact, lost profits from a new business have sometimes been considered *per se* uncertain and unrecoverable. This *per se* rule is supported by the notion that while an established business can use its past earning records to show lost profits with reasonable certainty, a new business has no track record and thus cannot provide any non-speculative basis for calculating damages.

Two developments have lead to a relaxation of the certainty requirement. First, according to Professor McCormick, the certainty requirement evolved to control speculation by the jury. Yet, "with increasing confidence in other developing doctrines which are used to control verdicts, such as the doctrines of 'contemplation of the parties' in contract cases and of 'proximate cause' in tort cases, and with increasing flexibility in controlling the size of the verdict on the motion for new trial or on appeal, the judges have come to relax their strict insistence that the jury shall not 'speculate' as to the amount. 'Certainty' becomes 'reasonable certainty' and then 'reasonable probability.' " Charles McCormick, Handbook on the Law of Damages at 118 (1935). See also Note, Averting the New Business' Battle to Prove Lost Profits: A Reintroduction of the Traditional Reasonable Certainty Rule as a Penalty Default, 67 S.Cal.L.Rev. 1573 (1994). Professor McCormick was writing in 1935, however; the advent of cases involving radiation, toxins, and carcinogens has brought certainty back into the spotlight. See Ayers v. Jackson Township, text at p. 532; In re: Agent Orange Litigation, text at p. 605.

Second, as economic forecasting has become more sophisticated—and as courts have become more comfortable with economic experts—the *per se* rule regarding new businesses has declined, and what was a *per se* rule has become a rule of evidence, in most jurisdictions. With regard to losses suffered by a new business, as with any other loss, the plaintiff must simply provide evidence from which the jury may estimate the amount with reasonable certainty, and without speculation. What sort of evidence might the plaintiff in *GrAMM* have produced to persuade the court that recovery was appropriate? How about in *Evergreen?*

When expectation damages are unavailable because they are too uncertain, courts often fall back the concept of general damages. Thus, in *Evergreen*, instead of recovering damages based on his lost profits, the plaintiff recovered general damages for the loss of the use of his land, that is, the land's rental value for the period for time of the delay. Is it clear that the rental value of an unused parcel can be established with any greater certainty than the profits it might generate? After all, what is the rental value if not a projection of the profits that might be available from the various uses to which the land might be put? Professor Dobbs has argued that the certainty rule simply confirms that the law is biased to favor capital investments over entreprenurial ventures. Dan B. Dobbs, Law of Remedies § 3.4 (2d ed.1993).

If even general damages are unavailable or unsatisfactory, as in *GrAMM*, an alternative measure of damages may be available. In contract cases, for example, if expectation damages are too uncertain, the plaintiff may recover damages measured by the plaintiff's reliance, in order at least to protect the plaintiff from losses suffered because he relied on the defendant's promise. In *GrAMM,* the plaintiff relied on the defendant's promise by paying the production, advertising, and promotional costs of the record; by paying the operating costs of the corporation; and by investing capital in the underwriting venture. Yet, the court denies recovery for these losses. Why?

Even the reliance measure is limited by the overall remedial goal of placing the plaintiff in the position he would have occupied if the contract had been performed. Where the plaintiff is involved in a losing deal, reliance damages may overcompensate him; they may leave him in a better position than if the contract had been performed. So, reliance damages are limited in losing contracts:

> Under the rule stated [in section 349], the injured party may, if he chooses, ignore the element of profit and recover as damages his expenditures in reliance. He may choose to do this if he cannot prove his profit with reasonable certainty. He may also choose to do this in the case of a losing contract, one under which he would have had a loss rather than a profit. In that case, however, it is open to the party in breach to prove the amount of the loss, to the extent that he can do so

with reasonable certainty, ... and have it subtracted from the injured party's damages.

Restatement (Second) of Contracts § 349 comment a. Note, however, on whom the Restatement places the burden of showing that a loss was expected, and its amount. In light of this, was *GrAMM* rightly decided?

Another alternative to compensating the plaintiff for his lost expectations is restitution. That alternative is discussed, along with restitution generally, in chapter 7 (although in fact it has never been quite clear whether restitution should be considered an alternative remedy for breach of contract, or a distinct substantive right).

c. *Avoidable Consequences.* The rule regarding avoidable consequences is the same in contract as in tort: If, through reasonable efforts, a loss could have been avoided, damages for that amount cannot be recovered. Restatement (Second) of Contracts § 350; UCC § 2–715(1)(consequential damages which "could not reasonably be avoided by cover or otherwise" may be recovered). The usual effect of the avoidable consequences rule is to promote cover, to give plaintiffs the incentive to continue to pursue their presumably profitable enterprises by obtaining an equivalent performance from someone else.

There are, however, exceptions to the rule. For one, a majority of states continue to adhere to a common law rule that allows landlords to recover damages from a lessee who has abandoned the property even though others stand ready to rent it. See 21 A.L.R.3d 534 for a summary of the jurisdictions that continue to follow this rule.

Again, the rule also has a positive side: reasonable sums expended in attempting to avoid the loss can be recovered. Are there any items of recovery in *GrAMM* that fall into this category?

d. *Offset by benefits.* The offset rule, too, applies in contract cases. Restatement (Second) of Contracts § 347, comment *e*. As the following article demonstrates, the difficulty in applying the offset rule lies in determining whether the benefit was actually the product of the defendant's actions.

## CHARLES J. GOETZ & ROBERT E. SCOTT, MEASURING SELLERS' DAMAGES: THE LOST PROFITS PUZZLE

31 Stanford L.Rev. 323, 323–327 (1979).

A buyer repudiates a fixed-price contract to purchase goods, and the seller sues for damages. How should a court measure the seller's loss? The answer seems simple: The seller should be awarded damages sufficient to place it in the same economic position it would have enjoyed had the buyer performed the contract. But the seductive conceptual simplicity of the compensation principle disguises substantial practical problems in measuring seller's damages.

Contract law has traditionally minimized measurement difficulties by basing damages in most cases on the difference between the contract price and market value of the repudiated goods. The common law courts generally limited the seller to such market damages whenever the seller had a resale market for the contract goods. These courts assumed that combining this damage award with proceeds from a resale would give the seller the profits that performance would have earned it. * * *

But as the Uniform Commercial Code damages scheme supplanted the common law, the notion was advanced that the common law rule erroneously used the contract-market formula to measure loss in several circumstances in which the compensation principle demanded that the seller recover by direct proof the profit lost because of the breach. * * *

The "lost-volume seller" is the second category where market damages are frequently believed to measure true losses inadequately. Market resales do not replace or substitute for the breached contract when such resales would have been made even if the buyer had not breached. The seller may contend that, while it did in fact resell the contract goods, the other buyer would have purchased anyway. Therefore, if the breaching buyer had fully performed the contract, the seller would have realized two profits from two sales. Since selling the goods to the second buyer produced only one profit for the seller, the breaching party ought to pay over the other profit in order to put the seller in the position it would have achieved had the buyer performed. Conventional analysis has assumed that whenever the seller is able to supply all available buyers at the prevailing price, its damages are presumptively equal to the entire expected profit lost on the breached contract. * * *

e. *Limiting damages by agreement.* Parties to a contract have the power to limit liability expressly in the agreement, or to alter the measure of damages the common law would impose. See UCC § 2–719(2). The power, however, is not unlimited. Most jurisdictions have limited the power of the parties to exclude consequential damages, as in the UCC:

> Consequential damages may be limited or excluded unless the limitation or exclusion is unconscionable. Limitation of consequential damages for injury to the person in the case of consumer goods is prima facie unconscionable but limitation of damages where the loss is commercial is not.

UCC § 2–719(3).

Another technique for limiting exposure to damages in the event of breach is the liquidated damages clause. A liquidated damages clause sets a specific amount of damages that will be recoverable in the event of a breach. Not all liquidated damages clauses are enforceable, however:

> Damages for breach by either party may be liquidated in the agreement but only at an amount that is reasonable in the light of the anticipated or actual loss caused by the breach and the difficulties of proof of loss. A term fixing unreasonably large liquidated damages is unenforceable on grounds of public policy as a penalty.

Restatement (Second) of Contracts § 356.

## JUSTIN SWEET, LIQUIDATED DAMAGES IN CALIFORNIA

60 Calif.L.Rev. 84, 85–90 (1972).

* * *

### Policy Considerations and Trends in Party Autonomy

The question of how much autonomy the law should give parties to employ clauses that control the amount of damages recoverable for contract breach is part of the general issue of party autonomy. Even in periods of maximum party autonomy, there have been some controls on contractmaking, such as the Statute of Frauds, capacity requirements, legality requirements, and usury laws. Also, the consideration doctrine limited pure contractual freedom by not enforcing gift promises and by balancing extremely unequal bargaining power through the mutuality concept. Until the 20th century, however, the general norm was party autonomy.

The most important reason for the modern trend away from autonomy is that much of 19th–century contract law was predicated upon the model of a contract between two parties of relatively equal bargaining power who negotiate and conclude a mutually acceptable agreement. Instead, the bulk of contracts today are various forms of adhesion contracts, the mass-produced, nonnegotiated contracts pioneered by the insurance, utilities, and transportation industries. The consent in these adhesion contracts is a fiction. The party handed a form usually has no time to read it, would not understand it if he took the time, would not be able to find anyone with authority to change it if he wished to, and very likely would not be able to make the transaction if he insisted upon a change from the standard form.

Largely because of adhesion contracts, the past 20 years have seen a proliferation of legal controls on contracts. There is more judicial intervention through the back door of interpretation and, increasingly now, direct intervention through refusal to enforce contracts that courts think are unjust.

### *A. Reasons for Liquidated Damages Provisions*

As the norm has changed from negotiated contract to adhesion contract, the reasons for employing liquidated damages clauses have changed, and accompanying this has been a change in judicial attitude toward enforcement. First, consider the use of liquidation clauses in the model of a negotiated contract. Both contracting parties often wish to control their risk exposure, and permitting them to do encourages risk-taking. The performing party may also wish to avoid the feared irrationality of the judicial process in determining actual damages. He may also be fearful that the court will give insufficient consideration to legitimate excuses for nonperformance, that the court may be unduly sympathetic to plaintiff's claim that any loss he incurred should be paid for by the party whose nonperformance caused the loss or that the court may consider contract breach an immoral act.

There are also reasons why the nonperforming party as well may wish to use a liquidated damages clause. Sometimes a breach will cause damage, but the amount of damages cannot be proven under damage rules. For example, in wartime procurement contracts it may be impossible to establish the damages caused by delayed or defective performance by the contractor. Without an enforceable clause purporting to liquidate damages, the nonperforming party may fear that the performing party will have insufficient incentive to perform if the latter realizes that damages he has caused are not sufficiently provable to be collected. Such a clause is a penalty in that its principal function is to coerce performance. Yet if it is reasonable—not disproportionate to actual, although unprovable, damages or to the contract price—it will be enforced. Without a liquidated damages clause there is also a danger that contractor may recover the full contract price despite a breach that caused some unprovable losses. Thus while the nonperforming party may be motivated principally by the penalty aspects of the clause, he may to a lesser degree be motivated by the desire to prevent what appears to him to be unjust enrichment.

Liquidated damages clauses may also be inserted to improve upon what the parties believe to be a deficiency in the litigation process: the cost and difficulty of judicially proving damages. Through a liquidation clause the parties attempt to use contract to settle the amount of damages involved and thus improve the normal rules of damages. Also, when the clause is phrased in such a way as to indicate that the breaching party will pay a specified amount if a particular breach occurs, troublesome problems involved in proving causation and foreseeability may be avoided.

In the adhesion contract situation there are some similarities in objectives; the desire to control the irrationality and expense of the litigation process and the need to know the extent of risk exposure are still involved. There are, however, obvious additional objectives of the stronger party. He can dictate the terms of the contract; if he is the performing party, he is likely to use the contract clause to limit his exposure almost to the vanishing point, and if he is the nonperforming party, he may try to use a penalty clause to coerce performance, or he may try to use a genuine liquidation clause to make vindication of his legal rights as convenient and inexpensive as possible. In the adhesion context, then, the stronger party may try to limit his own liability and to set an agreed amount that is sufficiently high to coerce performance. In the event performance is not rendered, the clause may obtain a settlement or win the case.

### B. *Judicial Responses to Liquidated Damages Provisions*

Moving from the reasons why liquidated damages clauses are used by the parties, let us consider what motivates courts to uphold or reject these clauses. Some courts undoubtedly are persuaded by the argument that the parties have paid their money and taken their chances. Since the parties have assumed certain risks, courts often see no particular reason to relieve them from the risks they have taken. Treating the liquidated damages clauses as any other, such courts uphold the clauses to reward the party who has guessed best on the question of damages. Other courts enforce these clauses because they believe that protecting the reasonable expectations of the contracting parties encourages risk-taking and assists in planning. Still other courts look at the contract as a package and enforce the liquidation clause because they feel that the party attacking the clause has received benefits under the contract. This is especially likely when such a clause is directly related to the contract price. For example, in one important case, a gun manufacturer offered to supply guns at different prices depending upon when delivery had to be made. The government chose the quickest delivery at the highest price. Nonenforcement of the delay-damage liquidation clause in this case would have disturbed the package arrangement and created unjust enrichment.

Courts also enforce these clauses because they believe liquidated damages clauses help the courts achieve just results. Sometimes the computation of damages in litigation is no better than a guess; as long as the amount selected by the parties is within a reasonable range, the courts feel that enforcing the amount selected is likely to be as fair as any amount determined by the court. Furthermore, courts believe that if such agreements are enforced, at least in theory the use of such clauses should expand, resulting in fewer breaches, fewer law suits, fewer or easier trials, and in many cases, at least as just a result.

Finally, courts recognize that enforcement of these clauses can cure defects in the litigation process. For example, the requirements as to certainty may seem too restrictive. A court may enforce a liquidation clause to ensure that a party will get a just recovery that might otherwise be denied him because he cannot establish the loss with sufficient certainty.

Many purported liquidated damages clauses, however, are not enforced. The traditional rationale for nonenforcement is that courts will not aid in coercion, oppression, or unjust enrichment; courts seek only to compensate, and enforcement of penalty clauses is contrary to that purpose. Thus, enforcement of a clause not based upon an estimate of proper compensation would cause an unconscionable result.

Refusal to enforce these clauses may recognize the protection contracting parties need from their own unfortunate optimism and their failure to consider in advance the possibility that subsequent events may affect their performance. Like the doctrines of consideration, frustration, impossibility, and mistake, not enforcing a liquidation clause reflects the idea that the performing party should not be held strictly to his promise. The refusal to enforce a liquidation clause does not preclude the plaintiff from recovering actual damages. This method of relieving a party from his contractual promise gives the judge the comfortable feeling that he is not upsetting traditional law but merely putting the plaintiff to his proof of damages.

Moreover, modern courts are beginning to look at the realities of the contractmaking process. They realize that if the clause is part of an adhesion contract, some of the reasons for permitting and encouraging party autonomy do not apply. When one party is under great compulsion and has no choice, it is not likely that the amount is fair risk assumption. Party autonomy is less attractive in such a context, especially when enforcing the clause would do violence to a damages rule that the court believes to be salutary.

## 2. CONTRACT OR TORT?: THE UNCERTAIN BOUNDARY

### FREEMAN & MILLS, INC. v. BELCHER OIL CO.

Supreme Court of California, 1995.
11 Cal.4th 85, 900 P.2d 669, 44 Cal.Rptr.2d 420.

LUCAS, C.J.

I. FACTS

* * * In June 1987, defendant Belcher Oil Company retained the law firm of Morgan, Lewis & Bockius (Morgan) to defend it in a Florida lawsuit. Pursuant to a letter of understanding * * * Belcher Oil was to pay for costs incurred on its behalf, including fees for accountants. [Morgan] hired plaintiff, the accounting firm of Freeman & Mills, Incorporated, to provide a financial analysis and litigation support for Belcher Oil in the Florida lawsuit.

* * * In April 1988, [Neil] Bowman [Belcher Oil's general counsel] became dissatisfied with Morgan's efforts and the lawyers were discharged. Bowman asked Morgan for a summary of the work performed by Freeman & Mills and, at the same time, directed [Morgan] to have Freeman & Mills stop their work for Belcher Oil. * * * Freeman & Mills's final statement was for $70,042.50 in fees, plus $7,495.63 for costs, a total of $77,538.13.

Freeman & Mills billed Morgan, but no payment was forthcoming. Freeman & Mills then billed Belcher Oil directly and, for about a year, sent monthly statements and regularly called Bowman about the bill, but no payment was forthcoming. In August 1989, [Morgan] finally told Freeman & Mills that Belcher Oil refused to pay their bill. Freeman & Mills then wrote to Bowman asking that the matter be resolved. In September 1989, Bowman responded, complaining that Belcher Oil had not been consulted about the extent of Freeman & Mills's services and suggesting Freeman & Mills should look to Morgan for payment of whatever amounts were claimed due.

Ultimately, Freeman & Mills filed this action against Belcher Oil, alleging * * * causes of action for breach of contract, "bad faith denial of contract," and quantum meruit. Belcher Oil answered and the case was presented to a jury in a bifurcated trial, with punitive damages reserved for the second phase. * * *

The jury returned its first phase verdict. On Freeman & Mills's breach of contract claim, the jury found [that Belcher Oil had breached the contract], and that the amount of damages suffered by Freeman & Mills was $25,000. The jury also [found that] Belcher Oil had denied the existence of the contract and had acted with oppression, fraud, or malice. Thereafter, the jury returned its verdict awarding $477,538.13 in punitive damages and judgment was entered consistent with the jury's verdicts.

[The trial court granted a motion to correct the jury's verdict to give] Freeman & Mills $131,614.93 in compensatory damages (the $25,000 actually awarded by the jury, plus the $77,538.13 included in the punitive damage award, plus $29,076.80 for prejudgment interest), and $400,000 * * * in punitive damages.

Belcher Oil appealed from the "corrected" judgment. * * *

II. The *Seaman's* Decision

The tort of bad faith "denial of contract" was established in a per curiam opinion in *Seaman's* [Direct Buying Service v. Standard Oil Co., 36 Cal.3d 752 (1984)]. These were the facts before the court in that case: In 1971, Seaman's Direct Buying Service, a small marine fueling station in Eureka, wanted to expand its operation by developing a marine fuel dealership in conjunction with a new marina under development by the City of Eureka. When Seaman's approached the city about a long term lease of a large parcel of land in the marina, the city required Seaman's to obtain a binding commitment from an oil supplier. To that end, Seaman's negotiated with several companies and, by 1972, reached a tentative agreement with Standard Oil.

Both Seaman's and Standard Oil signed a letter of intent setting forth the basic terms of their arrangement but that letter was subject to government approval of the contract, continued approval of Seaman's credit status, and future agreement on specific arrangements. Seaman's showed the letter to the city and, shortly thereafter, signed a 40–year lease with the city.

Shortly thereafter, an oil shortage dramatically reduced the available supplies of oil and, in November 1973, Standard Oil told Seaman's that new federal regulations requiring allocation of petroleum products to those that had been customers since 1972 precluded its execution of a new dealership agreement. In response, Seaman's obtained an exemption from the appropriate federal agency. Standard Oil appealed and persuaded the agency to reverse the order, but Seaman's eventually had the exemption reinstated contingent on a court determination that a valid contract existed between the parties.

Seaman's then asked Standard Oil to stipulate to the existence of a contract, stating that a refusal would force it to discontinue operations. Standard Oil's representative refused the request, telling Seaman's, "See you in court." Seaman's business collapsed and it sued Standard Oil for damages on four theories—breach of contract, fraud, breach of the implied covenant of good faith and fair dealing, and interference with Seaman's contractual relationship with the City.

The case was tried to a jury, which returned its verdicts in favor of Seaman's on all theories except fraud, awarding compensatory and punitive damages. Standard Oil appealed. We considered "whether, and under what circumstances, a breach of the implied covenant of good faith and fair dealing in a commercial contract may give rise to an action in tort." For purposes of completeness, we quote from *Seaman's* at some length:

"It is well settled that, in California, the law implies in every contract a covenant of good faith and fair dealing. Broadly stated, that covenant requires that neither party do anything which will deprive the other of the benefits of the agreement. California courts have recognized the existence of this covenant, and enforced it, in cases involving a wide variety of contracts...." In the seminal cases of Comunale v. Traders & General Ins. Co. [ (1958) ]50 Cal.2d 654, and Crisci v. Security Ins. Co. [ (1967) ]66 Cal.2d 425, this court held that a breach of the covenant of good faith and fair dealing by an insurance carrier may give rise to a cause of action in tort as well as in contract.

"While the proposition that the law implies a covenant of good faith and fair dealing in all contracts is well established, the proposition advanced by Seaman's—that breach of the covenant always gives rise to an action in tort—is not so clear. In holding that a tort action is available for breach of the covenant in an insurance contract, we have emphasized the 'special relationship' between insurer and insured, characterized by elements of public interest, adhesion, and fiduciary responsibility. No doubt there are other relationships with similar characteristics and deserving of similar legal treatment.

"When we move from such special relationships to consideration of the tort remedy in the context of the ordinary commercial contract, we move into largely uncharted and potentially dangerous waters. Here, parties of roughly equal bargaining power are free to shape the contours of their agreement and to include provisions for attorney fees and liquidated damages in the event of breach. They may not be permitted to disclaim the covenant of good faith but they are free, within reasonable limits at least, to agree upon the standards by which application of the covenant is to be measured. In such contracts, it may be difficult to distinguish between breach of the covenant and breach of contract, and there is the risk that interjecting tort remedies will intrude upon the expectations of the parties. This is not to say that tort remedies have no place in such a commercial context, but that it is wise to proceed with caution in determining their scope and application.

"For the purposes of this case it is unnecessary to decide the broad question which Seaman's poses. Indeed, it is not even necessary to predicate liability on a breach of the implied covenant. It is sufficient to recognize that a party to a contract may incur tort remedies when, in addition to breaching the contract, it seeks to shield itself from liability by denying, in bad faith and without probable cause, that the contract exists.

"It has been held that a party to a contract may be subject to tort liability, including punitive damages, if he coerces the other party to pay more than is due under the contract terms through the threat of a lawsuit, made ' "without probable cause and with no belief in the existence of the cause of action." ' There is little difference, in principle, between a contracting party obtaining excess payment in such manner, and a contracting party seeking to avoid all liability on a meritorious contract claim by adopting a 'stonewall' position ('see you in court') without probable cause and with no belief in the existence of a defense. Such conduct goes beyond the mere breach of contract. It offends accepted notions of business ethics. Acceptance of tort remedies in such a situation is not likely to intrude upon the bargaining relationship or upset reasonable expectations of the contracting parties."

*Seaman's* concluded that, because a good faith denial of the existence of a binding contract is not a tort, the trial court's failure to instruct the jury on the requirement of bad faith was error, and that error was prejudicial.

### III. Stare Decisis

* * * As we explain below, developments occurring subsequent to the *Seaman's* decision convince us that it was incorrectly decided, that it has generated unnecessary confusion, costly litigation, and inequitable results, and that it will continue to produce such effects unless and until we overrule it.

### IV. Subsequent Developments

A. California Supreme Court Decisions—Subsequent opinions of this court indicate a continuing reluctance, originally reflected in *Seaman's* itself, to authorize tort recovery for noninsurance contract breaches.

In Foley v. Interactive Data Corp. (1988) 47 Cal.3d 654, we * * * refused to afford such remedies for the essentially contractual claim of breach of the implied covenant arising in [the employment] context.

In reaching our conclusion in *Foley,* we relied in part on certain basic principles relevant to contract law, including the need for "predictability about the cost of contractual relationships," and the purpose of contract damages to compensate the injured party rather than punish the breaching party. Focusing on the implied covenant, we observed that, with the exception of insurance contracts, "[b]ecause the covenant is a contract term, ... compensation for its breach has almost always been limited to contract rather than tort remedies." * * *

Most recently, in Applied Equipment Corp. v. Litton Saudi Arabia Ltd. (1994) 7 Cal.4th 503, we held that a contracting party may not be held liable in tort for conspiring with another to interfere with his own contract. * * * We noted that limiting contract breach damages to those within the reasonably foreseeable contemplation of the parties when the contract was formed "serves to encourage contractual relations and commercial activity by enabling parties to estimate in advance the financial risks of their enterprise."

Our decisions in *Foley* * * * and *Applied Equipment* each contain language that strongly suggests courts should limit tort recovery in contract breach situations to the insurance area, at least in the absence of violation of an independent duty arising from principles of tort law other than denial of the existence of, or liability under, the breached contract. * * *

B. Court of Appeal Decisions

* * * Many of the pertinent Court of Appeal decisions recognize compelling policy reasons supporting the preclusion of tort remedies for contractual breaches outside the insurance context. * * * For example, * * * [in] Harris [v. Atlantic Richfield Co. (1993) 14 Cal.App.4th 70], the Court of Appeal denied a tort recovery for bad faith contract breach in violation of public policy. The court elaborated on the applicable policy considerations as follows: "The traditional goal of contract remedies is compensation of the promisee for the loss resulting from the breach, not compulsion of the promisor to perform his promises. Therefore, 'willful' breaches have not been distinguished from other breaches. The restrictions on contract remedies serve purposes not found in tort law. They protect the parties' freedom to bargain over special risks and they promote contract formation by limiting liability to the value of the promise. This encourages efficient breaches, resulting in increased production of goods and services at lower cost to society. * * *

C. Criticism by Courts of Other Jurisdictions

We decided *Seaman's* in 1984. Since then, courts of other jurisdictions have either criticized or declined to follow our *Seaman's* analysis. Of all the states, only Montana has recognized the tort of bad faith in typical arm's length commercial contracts, and recently even that state has qualified the tort by requiring a showing of a special relationship between the contracting parties. (See Story v. Bozeman (Mont.1990) 791 P.2d 767, 776.).

Ninth Circuit Judge Kozinski expressed his candid criticism of *Seaman's* in a concurring opinion in Oki America, Inc. v. Microtech Intern., Inc. (9th Cir.1989) 872 F.2d 312, 314–317. Among other criticism, Judge Kozinski found the *Seaman's* holding unduly imprecise and confusing. As he stated, "It is impossible to draw a principled distinction between a tortious denial of a contract's existence and a permissible denial of liability under the terms of the contract. The test . . . seems to be whether the conduct 'offends accepted notions of business ethics.' This gives judges license to rely on their gut feelings in distinguishing between a squabble and a tort. As a result, both the commercial world and the courts are needlessly burdened . . . . ."

Judge Kozinski also mentioned the substantial costs associated with *Seaman's* litigation, and the resulting interference with contractual relationships. "Perhaps most troubling, the willingness of courts to subordinate voluntary contractual arrangements to their own sense of public policy and proper business decorum deprives individuals of an important measure of freedom. The right to enter into contracts—to adjust one's legal relationships by mutual agreement is too easily smothered by government officers eager to tell us what's best for us." * * *

V. *Seaman's* Should be Overruled

As previously indicated, the *Seaman's* decision has generated uniform confusion and uncertainty regarding its scope and application, and widespread doubt about the necessity or desirability of its holding. * * *

For all the foregoing reasons, we conclude that *Seaman's* should be overruled. We emphasize that nothing in this opinion should be read as affecting the existing precedent governing enforcement of the implied covenant in insurance cases. Further, nothing we say here would prevent the Legislature from creating additional civil remedies for noninsurance contract breach, including such measures as providing litigation costs and attorney fees in certain aggravated cases, or assessing increased compensatory damages covering lost profits and other losses attributable to the breach, as well as restoration of the *Seaman's* holding if the Legislature deems that course appropriate

Concurring and Dissenting Opinion by Mosk, J.:

I concur in the judgment. I disagree, however, with the majority's conclusion that *Seaman's* Direct Buying Service, Inc. v. Standard Oil Co. (1984) 36 Cal.3d 752, was wrongly decided. * * *

I will discuss below the various circumstances under which courts have found or may find a breach of contract to be tortious—circumstances broader than may be suggested by the majority's holding. As I will explain, a tortious breach of contract outside the insurance context may be found when (1) the breach is accompanied by a traditional common law tort, such as fraud or conversion; (2) the means used to breach the contract are tortious, involving deceit or undue coercion or; (3) one party intentionally breaches the contract intending or knowing that such a breach will cause severe, unmitigatable harm in the form of mental anguish, personal hardship, or substantial consequential damages. I will then explain why in my view *Seaman's* was correctly decided. Finally, I will explain why *Seaman's* is distinguishable from the present case.

I.

The notion that a breach of contract might be tortious causes conceptual difficulty because of the fundamental difference between the objectives of contract and tort law. "[Whereas] [c]ontract actions are created to protect the interest in having promises performed," "[t]ort actions are created to protect the interest in freedom from various kinds of harm. The duties of conduct which give rise to them are imposed by law, and are based primarily on social policy, not necessarily based upon the will or intention of the parties.... "

This difference in purpose has its greatest practical significance in the differing types of damages available under the two bodies of law. "Contract damages are generally limited to those within the contemplation of the parties when the contract was entered into or at least reasonably foreseeable by them at that time; consequential damages beyond the expectations of the parties are not recoverable." Damages for emotional distress and mental suffering, as well as punitive damages, are also generally not recoverable. "This limitation on available damages serves to encourage contractual relations and commercial activity by enabling parties to estimate in advance the financial risks of their enterprise." "In contrast, tort damages are awarded to compensate the victim for injury suffered. For the breach of an obligation not arising from contract, the measure of damages ... is the amount which will compensate for all the detriment proximately caused thereby, whether it could have been anticipated or not. (Civ.Code § 3333.)" Both emotional distress damages and punitive damages are, under the proper circumstances, available to the tort victim.

Tort and contract law also differ in the moral significance that each places on intentional injury. Whereas an intentional tort is seen as reprehensible—the deliberate or reckless harming of another—the intentional breach of contract has come to be viewed as a morally neutral act, as exemplified in Justice Holmes's remark that "[t]he duty to keep a contract at common law means a prediction that you must pay damages if you do not keep it—and nothing else." (Holmes, The Path of the Law (1897) 10 Harv.L.Rev. 457,462.) This amoral view is supported by the economic insight that in intentional breach of contract may create a net benefit to society. The efficient breach of contract occurs when gain to the breach party exceeds the loss to the party suffering the breach, allowing the movement of resources to their more optimal use. (See Posner, Economic Analysis of Law (1986) 107–108.) * * *

But while the purposes behind contract and tort law are distinct, the boundary line between the two areas of the law is neither clear not fixed. * * *. The courts "have extended the tort liability for misfeasance to virtually every type of contract where defective performance may injure the promisee. An attorney or abstractor examining a title, a physician treating a patient, a surveyor, an agent collecting a note or lending money or settling a claim, or a liability insurer defending a suit, all have been held liable in tort for their negligence." * * *

Nor are the rules that determine whether the action will sound in tort or contract, or both, clear cut. When the breach of contract also involves physical injury to the promisee, or the destruction of tangible property, as opposed to damage to purely economic interests, then the action will generally sound in tort. Thus, a manufacturer that sells defective automobiles may be liable to an automobile dealer in contract for delivery of nonconforming goods, but will be liable in tort if one of the nonconforming automobiles leads to an accident resulting in physical injury. * * *

It is also true that public policy does not always favor a limitation on damages for intentional breaches of contract. The notion that society gains from an efficient breach must be qualified by the recognition that many intentional breaches are not efficient. As Judge Posner explained in Patton [v. Mid–Continent Systems, Inc. (7th Cir.1988) 841 F.2d 742, 751]: "Not all breaches of contract are involuntary or otherwise efficient. Some are opportunistic; the promisor wants the benefit of the bargain without bearing the agreed-upon costs, and exploits the inadequacies of purely compensatory remedies (the major inadequacies being that pre-and post-judgment interest rates are frequently below market levels when the risk of nonpayment is taken into account and that the winning party cannot recover . . . attorney's fees)." Commentators have also pointed to other "inadequacies of purely compensatory remedies" that encourage inefficient breaches (i.e. breaches that result in greater losses to the promisee than gains for the promisor): the lack of emotional distress damages, even when such damages are the probable result of the breach, and the restriction of consequential damages to those in the contemplation of the parties at the time the contract was formed.

In addition to fully compensating contract plaintiffs and discouraging inefficient breaches, the imposition of tort remedies for certain intentional breaches of contract serves to punish and deter business practices that constitute distinct social wrongs independent of the breach. For example, we permit the plaintiff to recover exemplary damages in cases in which the breached contract was induced through promissory fraud, even though the plaintiff has incurred the same loss whether the contract was fraudulently induced or not. Our determination to allow the plaintiff to sue for fraud and to potentially recover exemplary damages is not justified by the plaintiffs [sic] greater loss, but by the fact that the breach of a fraudulently induced contract is a significantly greater wrong, from society's standpoint, than an ordinary breach. * * *

As the above illustrate, the rationale for limiting actions for intentional breaches of contract to contract remedies—that such limitation promotes commercial stability and predictability and hence advances commerce—is not invariably a compelling one. Breaches accompanied by deception or infliction of intentional harm may be so disruptive of commerce and so reprehensible in themselves that the value of deterring such actions through the tort system outweighs the marginal loss in the predictability of damages that may result. But in imposing tort duties to deter intentionally harmful acts among contracting parties, courts must be cautious not to fashion remedies which overdeter the illegitimate and as a result chill legitimate activities. Thus, courts should be careful to apply tort remedies only when the conduct in question is so clear in its deviation from socially useful business practices that the effect of enforcing such tort duties will be, as in the case of fraud, to aid rather than discourage commerce.

[N]ot all tortious breaches of contract arise from conventional torts. Numerous courts have recognized types of intentionally tortious activity that occur exclusively or distinctively within the context of a contractual relationship. The most familiar type of tortious breach of contract in this state is that of the insurer, whose unreasonable failure to settle or resolve a claim has been held to violate the covenant of good faith and fair dealing. Tort liability is imposed primarily because of the distinctive characteristics of the insurance contract: the fiduciary nature of the relationship, the fact that the insurer offers a type of quasi-public service that provides financial security and peace of mind, and the fact that the insurance contract is generally one of adhesion. In these cases, the special relationship between insurer and insured supports the elevation of the covenant of good faith and fair dealing, a covenant implied by law in every contract and generally used as an aid to contract interpretation, into a tort duty.

Because the good faith covenant is so broad and all-pervasive, this court and others have been reluctant to expand recognition of the action for tortious breach of the covenant beyond the insurance context. Unfortunately, the preoccupation of California courts with limiting the potentially enormous scope of this tort has diverted attention away from the useful task of identifying specific practices employed by contracting parties that merit the imposition of tort remedies. Other jurisdictions not so preoccupied have made greater progress in developing a common law of tortious breach of contract. While the cases are not easily amenable to classification, they appear to fit into two broad categories.

The first category focuses on tortious means used by one contracting party to coerce or deceive another party into foregoing its contractual rights. For example, in Advanced Medical v. Arden Medical Systems (3d Cir.1992) 955 F.2d 188, Advanced Medical, Inc. (Advanced), a distributor of medical products, entered into an agreement with a manufacturer of a high- technology blood analysis device, whereby the former was designated as the latter's exclusive distributor for the mid-Atlantic region. The manufacturing company was eventually acquired by Johnson & Johnson, which disapproved of the exclusive distributorship. Instead of merely breaching the agreement, Johnson & Johnson used a variety of questionable tactics to "drive Advanced out of the contract," including marketing competing products not made available to Advanced, and withholding its support services. The court, applying Pennsylvania law, held that in addition to a breach of contract, there was sufficient evidence to submit the question of punitive damages to a jury on a theory of Johnson & Johnson's "tortious interference" with its own contract. * * *

A second type of tortious intentional breach has been found when the consequences of the breach are especially injurious to the party suffering the breach, and the breaching party intentionally or knowingly inflicts such injury. Cases of this type have generally occurred outside the commercial context, involving manifestly unequal contracting parties and contracts concerning matters of vital personal significance, in which great mental anguish or personal hardship are the probable result of the breach. In these cases, courts have permitted substantial awards of emotional distress damages and/or punitive damages, both as a means of providing extra sanctions for a defendant engaging in intentionally injurious activities against vulnerable parties, and as a way of fully compensating plaintiffs for types of injury that are neither readily amendable to mitigation nor generally recoverable as contract damages. For example, in K–Mart Corp. v. Ponsock (Nev.1987) 732 P.2d 1364, 1370, disapproved on other grounds by Ingersoll–Rand Co. v. McClendon (1990) 498 U.S. 133, 137, the Nevada Supreme Court allowed a $50,000 award of punitive damages to stand when an employer discharged a long-term employee on a fabricated charge for the purpose of defeating the latter's contractual entitlement to retirement benefits. * * *

The principle that certain contractual interests of vulnerable parties deserve greater protection than ordinary contract damages would otherwise provide has led our Legislature to authorize special sanctions for various types of intentional breaches. For example, one who is the victim of an intentional breach of warranty of consumer goods may recover twice the amount of actual damages (Civ.Code, § 1794, subd. (c)) and treble damages may be awarded to a retail seller who is injured by "willful or repeated" warranty violations (id., § 1794.1, subd. (a)). Labor Code section 206 provides for treble damages for the willful failure to pay wages after the Labor Commissioner determines the wages are owing. * * *

II.

* * * [Turning to the *Seaman's* case,] there are some commercial cases in which the harm intentionally inflicted on an enterprise cannot be mitigated, and in which ordinary contract damages are insufficient compensation. *Seaman's* is such a case. In *Seaman's*, because of the unusual combination of market forces and government regulation set in motion by the 1973 oil embargo, Standard's conduct had a significance beyond the ordinary breach: its practical effect was to shut Seaman's out of the oil market entirely, forcing it out of business. In other words, Standard intentionally breached its contract with Seaman's with the knowledge that the breach would result in Seaman's demise. Having thus breached its contract with blithe disregard for the severe and, under these rare circumstances, unmitigatable injury it caused Seaman's, Standard was justly subject to tort damages.

* * * A breach should not be considered tortious if the court determines that it was justified by avoidance of some substantial, unforeseen cost on the part of the breaching party, even if such cost does not excuse that party's nonperformance. Nor should a tortious breach under these circumstances be recognized if it is clear that the party suffering the harm voluntarily accepted that risk under the contract. But the intentional or knowing infliction of severe consequential damages on a business enterprise through the unjustified, bad faith breach of a contract is reprehensible and costly both for the party suffering the

breach and for society as a whole, and is therefore appropriately sanctioned through the tort system.

III.

The present case, on the other hand, is essentially a billing dispute between two commercial entities. Belcher Oil claimed, apparently in bad faith and without probable cause, that it had no contractual agreement with Freeman & Mills. That is, Belcher Oil not only intentionally breached its contract, but then asserted a bad faith defense to its liability. As explained above, the solution which the Legislature has devised for this kind of transgression is the awarding of the other party's attorney fees, and this is precisely what occurred—Freeman & Mills was awarded $212,891 in attorney fees pursuant to Code of Civil Procedure sections 128.5 and 2033, subdivision (c). To permit the award of punitive damages in addition to this sum would upset the legislative balance established in the litigation sanctions statutes and make tortious actions—intentional breach of contract and the assertion of a bad faith defense—which we have consistently held not to be tortious.

On this basis, I concur in the majority's disposition in favor of Belcher Oil on the bad faith denial of contract cause of action.* * *

### *Notes*

1. The exchange between the majority and Justice Mosk thoroughly reviews the differences between tort and contract damages, and suggests some explanations for them. Which of the justifications do you find most persuasive?

2. As Justice Mosk points out, a basic difference between tort and contract remedies is that the fact that contract damages are to the benefit of the bargain may in fact encourage breach under some circumstances. Does it make sense to have a remedy that effectively encourages breach of contract? Consider:

> [I]n some cases a party would be tempted to breach the contract simply because his profit from breach would exceed his expected profits from completion of the contract, and if damages are limited to loss of expected profit, there will be an incentive to commit a breach. There should be. The opportunity cost of completion to the breaching party is the profit that he would make from a breach, and if it is greater than the profits from completion, then completion will involve a loss to him. If this loss is greater than the gain to the other party from completion, breach would be value-maximizing and should be encouraged. And because the victim of the breach is made whole for his loss, he is indifferent; hence encouraging breaches in these circumstances will not deter people from entering into contracts in the future.
>
> An arithmetical illustration may be helpful here. I sign a contract to deliver 100,000 custom-ground widgets at $.10 apiece to A for use in his boiler factory. After I have delivered 10,000, B comes to me, explains that he desperately needs 25,000 custom ground widgets at once since otherwise he will be forced to close his pianola factory at

great cost, and offers me $.15 apiece for 25,000 widgets. I sell him the widgets and as a result do not complete timely delivery to A, who sustains $1,000 in lost profits from my breach. Having obtained an additional profit of $1,250, I am better off even after reimbursing A for his loss. Society is also better off. Since B was willing to pay me $.15 per widget, it must mean that each widget was worth at least $.15 to him. But it was worth only $.14 to A—the $.10 that he paid plus his expected profit of $.04 ($1000 divided by 25,000). Thus the breach resulted in a transfer of the 25,000 widgets from a less to a more valuable use. To be sure, had I refused to sell to B, he could have gone to A and negotiated an assignment of part of A's contract with me to him. But this would have introduced an additional step and so imposed additional transaction costs.

Thus far the emphasis has been on the economic importance of not awarding damages in excess of the lost expectation. It is equally important, however, not to award less than the expectation loss. Suppose A contracts to sell B for $100,000 a machine that is worth $110,000 to B., i.e., that would yield him a profit of $10,000. Before delivery C comes to A and offers him $109,000 for the machine promised B. A would be tempted to breach were he not liable to B for B's loss of expected profit. Given that measure of damages, C will not be able to induce a breach of A's contract with B unless he offers B more than $110,000, thereby indicating that the machine really is worth more to him than to B. The expectation rule thus assures that the machine ends up where it is most valuable.

Richard A. Posner, Economic Analysis of Law 89–90 (2d ed.1977). For basic treatments of economic analysis, see A. Mitchell Polinsky, An Introduction to Law and Economics (2d ed.1989); Louis A. Kornhauser, An Introduction to the Economic Analysis of Contract Remedies, 57 U.Colo.L.Rev. 683 (1986). Although economic explanations of the contract remedy have gained wide acceptance, see Restatement (Second) of Contracts § 344, they are not without their detractors. See, e.g., Ian R. Macneil, Efficient Breach of Contract: Circles in the Sky, 68 Va.L.Rev. 947 (1982); Daniel A. Farber, Reassessing the Economic Efficiency of Compensatory Damages for Breach of Contract, 66 Va.L.Rev. 1443 (1980).

3. For some years, tort law and tort remedies have been expanding into areas formerly dominated by contract. The majority's opinion in *Freeman & Mills* is no doubt intended to signal the end of that expansion.

Yet, the majority does not question the soundness of the cases holding that a breach of the covenant of good faith and fair dealing by an insurer gives rise to tort liability, and tort damages. The majority apparently agrees with Justice Mosk that there is something special about insurance contracts that justifies this treatment.

If compelling performance, other than by compensating the promisee for her lost expectation, is a bad idea, why should insurance contracts be treated any differently? Consider:

What are the features of the insurance contract which distinguish it from the ordinary commercial contract? * * * An obvious difference * * * is a party's motivation for entering the contract. In insurance contracts, a party does not seek "to obtain a commercial advantage but to protect [him or herself] against the risk of accidental losses * * *. Among considerations in purchasing liability insurance, as insurers are well aware, is the peace of mind and security it will provide in the event of an accidental loss * * *".

Another oft repeated difference is that there exists a "great disparity in the economic situations and bargaining abilities of the insurer and the insured." Thus, the normal protections provided a party by the open marketplace are absent in these contracts.

A further very important characteristic of the insurance contract is that ordinary contract damages are inadequate to protect the insured's rights. In the first place, they offer no motivation whatsoever for the insurer *not* to breach. If the only damages an insurer will have to pay upon a judgment of breach are the amounts that it would have owed under the policy plus interest, it has every interest in retaining the money, earning the higher rates of interest on the outside market, and hoping eventually to force the insured into a settlement for less than the policy amount. * * *

Secondly, contract damages do not adequately protect the insured's interest. Unlike a party to an ordinary commercial contract who can turn to the marketplace to replace necessary "widgets" not delivered by a breaching seller, an insured has nowhere to turn to replace monthly disability payments. Money damages paid pursuant to a judgment years after the insurer has initially reneged on payment do not remedy the harm suffered by the insured, namely the immediate inability to support oneself and its attendant horrors.

Wallis v. Superior Court, 160 Cal.App.3d 1109, 1117–1118, 207 Cal.Rptr. 123, 128–129 (1984).

Would Judge Posner agree that insurance contracts should be treated differently? If the problem is that contract damages undercompensate, are punitive damages the right solution? See Michael Traynor, Bad Faith Breach of a Commercial Contract: A Comment on the Seaman's Case, 8 Bus.L.News (1984)(arguing for an expanded definition of foreseeability to forestall bad faith); C. Delos Putz & Nona Klippen, Commercial Bad Faith: Attorney Fees—Not Tort Liability—Is the Remedy for Stonewalling, 21 U.S.F.L.Rev. 419 (1987); Note, Sailing the Uncharted Seas of Bad Faith, 69 Minn.L.Rev. 1161 (1985). These issues are thoroughly reviewed in Symposium, The Law of Bad Faith in Contract and Insurance, 72 Tex.L.Rev. 1203 (1994).

4. Justice Mosk suggests three doctrinal "hooks" for punitive damages in contract cases. First, if "the breach is accompanied by a traditional common law tort, such as fraud or conversion", tort damages may be available. Almost all jurisdictions recognize that if the plaintiff can plead an independent tort for which punitive damages are recoverable in addition to the breach of contract, punitive damages may be recovered. See Restatement (Second) of Contracts § 355. The tort of promissory fraud is particularly powerful, at least if the court is willing to infer from the defendant's nonperformance that he entered the contract without the intent ever to

perform. See Rosener v. Sears, Roebuck & Co., 110 Cal.App.3d 740, 168 Cal.Rptr. 237 (1980).

Second, Justice Mosk suggests, tort recovery may be had where the means used to breach the contract are tortious, involving deceit or undue coercion. That is how he would characterize the insurance cases, and, indeed, many jurisdictions recognize that bad faith breach can give rise to tort liability in insurance cases. John Sebert, Punitive and Nonpecuniary Damages in Actions Based upon Contract: Toward Achieving the Objective of Full Compensation, 33 U.C.L.A.L.Rev. 1565, 1614 n.178 (1986) (15 jurisdictions).

The other cases that Justice Mosk cites do support the notion that there can be tort remedies for kinds of behavior that you won't find listed in the Restatement of Torts. As some jurisdictions have put it, there can be tort liability "where elements of tort mingle with the breach," so long as an award of punitive damages would serve the public interest. Hibschman Pontiac, Inc. v. Batchelor, 266 Ind. 310, 362 N.E.2d 845 (1977). This proposition is not without controversy, however. Doesn't Judge Kozinski have a valid point (at p. 641) when he argues that imposing tort liability for sharp dealing is inappropriate?

Justice Mosk's third category involves cases in which "one party intentionally breaches the contract intending or knowing that such a breach will cause severe, unmitigatable harm in the form of mental anguish, personal hardship, or substantial consequential damages." Do the cases he cites strongly support that proposition? The insurance cases, again, provide some support, especially insofar as the fact that the damage cannot be mitigated motivates the courts to allow tort recovery. Further, there certainly are cases allowing damages for emotional distress when the contract that was breached was of a particularly personal nature. On the other hand, can the result in those cases be explained as perfectly within the scope of contract damages, because the personal nature of the contract makes the distress foreseeable under Hadley v. Baxendale? See, e.g., B & M Homes v. Hogan, 376 So.2d 667 (Ala.1979)(mental distress is foreseeable, recoverable element of contract damages when builder's faulty construction of home results in severe defects).

5. As Justice Mosk notes, another way in which tort law has expanded into contractual relationships is by imposing tort liability when a party to a contract behaves negligently. The next case suggests that there, too, contract law may now be regaining lost ground.

## EVRA CORP. v. SWISS BANK CORP.

United States Court of Appeals, Seventh Circuit, 1982.
673 F.2d 951.

POSNER, CIRCUIT JUDGE.

The question—one of first impression—in this diversity case is the extent of a bank's liability for failure to make a transfer of funds when requested by wire to do so. The essential facts are undisputed. In 1972 Hyman–Michaels Company, a large Chicago dealer in scrap metal, entered into a two-year contract to supply steel scrap to a Brazilian corporation. Hyman–Michaels chartered a ship, the Pandora, to carry the scrap to Brazil. The charter was for one year, with an option to extend the charter for a second year; specified a fixed daily rate of pay for the hire of the ship during both the initial and the option period, payable semi-monthly "in advance"; and provided that if payment was not made on time the Pandora's owner could cancel the charter. Payment was to be made by deposit to the owner's account in the Banque de Paris et des Pays–Bas (Suisse) in Geneva, Switzerland.

The usual method by which Hyman–Michaels, in Chicago, got the payments to the Banque de Paris in Geneva was to request the Continental Illinois National Bank and Trust Company of Chicago, where it had an account, to make a wire transfer of funds. Continental would debit Hyman–Michaels' account by the amount of the payment and then send a telex to its London office for retransmission to its correspondent bank in Geneva—Swiss Bank Corporation—asking Swiss Bank to deposit this amount in the Banque de Paris account of the Pandora's owner. The transaction was completed by the crediting of Swiss Bank's account at Continental by the same amount.

When Hyman–Michaels chartered the Pandora in June 1972, market charter rates were very low, and it was these rates that were fixed in the charter for its entire term—two years if Hyman–Michaels exercised its option. Shortly after the agreement was signed, however, charter rates began to climb and by October 1972 they were much higher than they had been in June. The Pandora's owners were eager to get out of the charter if they could. At the end of October they thought they had found a way, for the payment that was due in the Banque de Paris on October 26 had not arrived by October 30, and on that day the Pandora's owner notified Hyman–Michaels that it was canceling the charter because of the breach of the payment term. Hyman–Michaels had mailed a check for the October 26 installment to the Banque de Paris rather than use the wire-transfer method of payment. It had done this in order to have the use of its money for the period that it would take the check to clear, about two weeks. But the check had not been mailed in Chicago until October 25 and of course did not reach Geneva on the twenty-sixth.

When Hyman–Michaels received notification that the charter was being canceled it immediately wired payment to the Banque de Paris, but the Pandora's owner refused to accept it and insisted that the charter was indeed canceled. The matter was referred to arbitration in accordance with the charter. On December 5, 1972, the arbitration panel ruled in favor of Hyman–Michaels. The panel noted that previous arbitration panels had "shown varying degrees of latitude to Charterers":

> "In all cases, a pattern of obligation on Owners' part to protest, complain, or warn of intended withdrawal was expressed as an essential prerequisite to withdrawal, in spite of the clear wording of

the operative clause. No such advance notice was given by Owners of M/V Pandora."

One of the three members of the panel dissented; he thought the Pandora's owner was entitled to cancel.

Hyman–Michaels went back to making the charter payments by wire transfer. On the morning of April 25, 1973, it telephoned Continental Bank and requested it to transfer $27,000 to the Banque de Paris account of the Pandora's owner in payment for the charter hire period from April 27 to May 11, 1973. Since the charter provided for payment "in advance," this payment arguably was due by the close of business on April 26. The requested telex went out to Continental's London office on the afternoon of April 25, which was nighttime in England. Early the next morning a telex operator in Continental's London office dialed, as Continental's Chicago office had instructed him to do, Swiss Bank's general telex number, which rings in the bank's cable department. But that number was busy, and after trying unsuccessfully for an hour to engage it the Continental telex operator dialed another number, that of a machine in Swiss Bank's foreign exchange department which he had used in the past when the general number was engaged. We know this machine received the telexed message because it signaled the sending machine at both the beginning and end of the transmission that the telex was being received. Yet Swiss Bank failed to comply with the payment order, and no transfer of funds was made to the account of the Pandora's owner in the Banque de Paris.

No one knows exactly what went wrong. One possibility is that the receiving telex machine had simply run out of paper, in which event it would not print the message although it had received it. Another is that whoever took the message out of the machine after it was printed failed to deliver it to the banking department. Unlike the machine in the cable department that the Continental telex operator had originally tried to reach, the machines in the foreign exchange department were operated by junior foreign exchange dealers rather than by professional telex operators, although Swiss Bank knew that messages intended for other departments were sometimes diverted to the telex machines in the foreign exchange department.

At 8:30 a.m. the next day, April 27, Hyman–Michaels in Chicago received a telex from the Pandora's owner stating that the charter was canceled because payment for the April 27–May 11 charter period had not been made. Hyman–Michaels called over to Continental and told them to keep trying to effect payment through Swiss Bank even if the Pandora's owner rejected it. This instruction was confirmed in a letter to Continental dated April 28, in which Hyman–Michaels stated: "please instruct your London branch to advise their correspondents to persist in attempting to make this payment. This should be done even in the face of a rejection on the part of Banque de Paris to receive this payment. It is paramount that in order to strengthen our position in an arbitration that these funds continue to be readily available." Hyman–Michaels did not attempt to wire the money directly to the Banque de Paris as it had done on the occasion of its previous default. Days passed while the missing telex message was hunted unsuccessfully. Finally Swiss Bank suggested to Continental that it retransmit the telex message to the machine in the cable department and this was done on May 1. The next day Swiss Bank attempted to deposit the $27,000 in the account of the Pandora's owner at the Banque de Paris but the payment was refused.

Again the arbitrators were convened and rendered a decision. In it they ruled that Hyman–Michaels had been "blameless" up until the morning of April 27, when it first learned that the Banque de Paris had not received payment on April 26, but that "being faced with this situation," Hyman–Michaels had "failed to do everything in [its] power to remedy it. The action taken was immediate but did not prove to be adequate, in that [Continental] Bank and its correspondent required some 5/6 days to trace and effect the lost instruction to remit. [Hyman–Michaels] could have ordered an immediate duplicate payment—or even sent a Banker's check by hand or special messengers, so that the funds could have reached owner's Bank, not later than April 28th." By failing to do any of these things Hyman–Michaels had "created the opening" that the Pandora's owner was seeking in order to be able to cancel the charter. It had "acted imprudently." The arbitration panel concluded, reluctantly but unanimously, that this time the Pandora's owner was entitled to cancel the agreement. * * *

Hyman–Michaels then brought this diversity action against Swiss Bank, seeking to recover its expenses in the second arbitration proceeding plus the profits that it lost because of the cancellation of the charter. The contract by which Hyman–Michaels had agreed to ship scrap steel to Brazil had been terminated by the buyer in March 1973 and Hyman–Michaels had promptly subchartered the Pandora at market rates, which by April 1973 were double the rates fixed in the charter. Its lost profits are based on the difference between the charter and subcharter rates. * * *

The case was tried to a district judge without a jury. [He ruled that] under Illinois law [Swiss Bank] was liable to Hyman–Michaels for $2.1 million in damages. This figure was made up of about $16,000 in arbitration expenses and the rest in lost profits on the subcharter of the Pandora. * * *

[Under Swiss law, Hyman–Michaels could not have prevailed because it was not in privity with Swiss Bank. Illinois law does not require privity. The court avoided the choice of law problem, however, by concluding that the trial court had erred in allowing Hyman–Michaels to recover even under Illinois law.]

When a bank fails to make a requested transfer of funds, this can cause two kinds of loss. First, the funds themselves or interest on them may be lost, and of course the fee paid for the transfer, having bought nothing, becomes a loss item. These are "direct" (sometimes called "general") damages. Hyman–Michaels is not seeking any direct damages in this case and apparently sustained none. It did not lose any part of the $27,000; although its account with Continental Bank was debited by this amount prematurely, it was not an interest-bearing account so Hyman–Michaels lost no interest; and Hyman–Michaels paid no fee either to Continental or to Swiss Bank for the aborted transfer. A second type of loss, which either the payor or the payee may suffer, is a dislocation in one's business triggered by the failure to pay. Swiss Bank's failure to transfer funds to the Banque de Paris when requested to do so by Continental Bank set off a chain reaction which resulted in an arbitration proceeding that was costly to Hyman–Michaels and in the cancellation of a highly profitable contract. It is those costs and lost profits—"consequential" or, as they are sometimes called, "special" damages—that Hyman–Michaels seeks in this lawsuit, and recovered below. It is conceded that if Hyman–Michaels was entitled to consequential damages, the district court measured them correctly. The only issue is whether it was entitled to consequential damages. * * *

The rule of *Hadley v. Baxendale*—that consequential damages will not be awarded unless the defendant was put on notice of the special circumstances giving rise to them—has been applied in many Illinois cases, and *Hadley* cited approvingly. In Siegel v. Western Union Tel. Co., 312 Ill.App. 86, 92–93, 37 N.E.2d 868, 871 (1941), the plaintiff had delivered $200 to Western Union with instructions to transmit it to a friend of the plaintiff's. The money was to be bet (legally) on a horse, but this was not disclosed in the instructions. Western Union misdirected the money order and it did not reach the friend until several hours after the race had taken place. The horse that the plaintiff had intended to bet on won and would have paid $1650 on the plaintiff's $200 bet if the bet had been placed. He sued Western Union for his $1450 lost profit, but the court held that under the rule of *Hadley v. Baxendale*, Western Union was not liable, because it "had no notice or knowledge of the purpose for which the money was being transmitted."

The present case is similar, though Swiss Bank knew more than Western Union knew in *Siegel;* it knew or should have known, from Continental Bank's previous telexes, that Hyman–Michaels was paying the Pandora Shipping Company for the hire of a motor vessel named Pandora. But it did not know when payment was due, what the terms of the charter were, or that they had turned out to be extremely favorable to Hyman–Michaels. And it did not know that Hyman–Michaels knew the Pandora's owner would try to cancel the charter, and probably would succeed, if Hyman–Michaels was ever again late in making payment, or that despite this peril Hyman–Michaels would not try to pay until the last possible moment and in the event of a delay in transmission would not do everything in its power to minimize the consequences of the delay. Electronic funds transfers are not so unusual as to automatically place a bank on notice of extraordinary consequences if such a transfer goes awry. Swiss Bank did not have enough information to infer that if it lost a $27,000 payment order it would face a liability in excess of $2 million.

It is true that in both *Hadley* and *Siegel* there was a contract between the parties and here there was none. We cannot be certain that the Illinois courts would apply the principles of those cases outside of the contract area. As so often in diversity cases, there is an irreducible amount of speculation involved in attempting to predict the reaction of a state's courts to a new issue. The best we can do is to assume that the Illinois courts would look to the policies underlying cases such as *Hadley* and *Siegel* and, to the extent they found them pertinent, would apply those cases here. We must therefore ask what difference it should make whether the parties are or are not bound to each other by a contract. On the one hand, it seems odd that the absence of a contract would enlarge rather than limit the extent of liability. After all, under Swiss law the absence of a contract would be devastating to Hyman–Michaels' claim. Privity is not a wholly artificial concept. It is one thing to imply a duty to one with whom one has a contract and another to imply it to the entire world.

On the other hand, contract liability is strict. A breach of contract does not connote wrongdoing; it may have been caused by circumstances beyond the promisor's control—a strike, a fire, the failure of a supplier to deliver an essential input. And while such contract doctrines as impossibility, impracticability, and frustration relieve promisors from liability for some failures to perform that are beyond their control, many other such failures are actionable although they could not have been prevented by the exercise of due care. The district judge found that Swiss Bank had been negligent in losing Continental Bank's telex message and it can be argued that Swiss Bank should therefore be liable for a broader set of consequences than if it had only broken a contract. But *Siegel* implicitly rejects this distinction. Western Union had not merely broken its contract to deliver the plaintiff's money order; it had "negligently misdirected" the money order. "The company's negligence is conceded." 312 Ill.App. at 88, 91, 37 N.E.2d at 869, 871. Yet it was not liable for the consequences.

*Siegel,* we conclude, is authority for holding that Swiss Bank is not liable for the consequences of negligently failing to transfer Hyman–Michaels' funds to Banque de Paris; reason for such a holding is found in the animating principle of *Hadley v. Baxendale*, which is that the costs of the untoward consequence of a course of dealings should be borne by that party who was able to avert the consequence at least cost and failed to do so. In *Hadley* the untoward consequence was the shutting down of the mill. The carrier could have avoided it by delivering the engine shaft on time. But the mill owners, as the court noted, could have avoided it simply by having a spare shaft. 9 Ex. at 355–56, 156 Eng.Rep. at 151. Prudence required that they have a spare shaft anyway, since a replacement could not be obtained at once even if there was no undue delay in carting the broken shaft to and the replacement shaft from the manufacturer. The court refused to imply a duty on the part of the carrier to guarantee the mill owners against the consequences of their own lack of prudence, though of course if the parties had stipulated for such a guarantee the court would have enforced it. The notice requirement of *Hadley v. Baxendale* is designed to assure that such an improbable guarantee really is intended.

This case is much the same, though it arises in a tort rather than a contract setting. Hyman–Michaels showed a lack of prudence throughout. It was imprudent for it to mail in Chicago a letter that unless received the next day in Geneva would put Hyman–Michaels in breach of a contract that was very profitable to it and that the other party to the contract had every interest in canceling. It was imprudent thereafter for Hyman–Michaels, having narrowly avoided cancellation and having (in the words of its appeal brief in this court) been "put . . . on notice that the payment provision of the Charter would be strictly enforced thereafter," to wait till [sic] arguably the last day before payment was due to instruct its bank to transfer the necessary funds overseas. And it was imprudent in the last degree for Hyman–Michaels, when it received notice of cancellation on the last possible day payment was due, to fail to pull out all the stops to get payment to the Banque de Paris on that day, and instead to dither while Continental and Swiss Bank wasted five days looking for the lost telex message. Judging from the obvious reluctance with which the arbitration panel finally decided to allow the Pandora's owner to cancel the charter, it might have made all the difference if Hyman–Michaels had gotten payment to the Banque de Paris by April 27 or even by Monday, April 30, rather than allowed things to slide until May 2.

This is not to condone the sloppy handling of incoming telex messages in Swiss Bank's foreign department. But Hyman–Michaels is a sophisticated business enterprise. It knew or should have known that even the Swiss are not infallible; that messages sometimes get lost or delayed in transit among three banks, two of them located 5000 miles apart, even when all the banks are using reasonable care; and that therefore it should take its own precautions against the consequences—best known to itself—of a mishap that might not be due to anyone's negligence.

We are not the first to remark the affinity between the rule of *Hadley v. Baxendale* and the doctrine, which is one of tort as well as contract law and is a settled part of the common law of Illinois, of avoidable consequences. If you are hurt in an automobile accident and unreasonably fail to seek medical treatment, the injurer, even if negligent, will not be held liable for the aggravation of the injury due to your own unreasonable behavior after the accident. If in addition you failed to fasten your seat belt, you may be barred from collecting the tort damages that would have been prevented if you had done so. Hyman–Michaels' behavior in steering close to the wind prior to April 27 was like not fastening one's seat belt; its failure on April 27 to wire a duplicate payment immediately after disaster struck was like refusing to seek medical attention after a serious accident. The seat-belt cases show that the doctrine of avoidable consequences applies whether the tort victim acts imprudently before or after the tort is committed.

The rule of *Hadley v. Baxendale* links up with tort concepts in another way. The rule is sometimes stated in the form that only foreseeable damages are recoverable in a breach of contract action. So expressed, it corresponds to the tort principle that limits liability to the foreseeable consequence of the defendant's carelessness. The amount of care that a person ought to take is a function of the probability and magnitude of the harm that may occur if he does not take care. If he does not know what that probability and magnitude are, he cannot determine how much care to take. That would be Swiss Bank's dilemma if it were liable for consequential damages from failing to carry out payment orders in timely fashion. To estimate the extent of its probable liability in order to know how many and how elaborate fail-safe features to install in its telex rooms or how much insurance to buy against the inevitable failures, Swiss Bank would have to collect reams of information about firms that are not even its regular customers. It had no banking relationship with Hyman–Michaels. It did not know or have reason to know how at once precious and fragile Hyman–Michaels' contract with the Pandora's owner was. These were circumstances too remote from Swiss Bank's practical range of knowledge to have affected its decisions as to who should man the telex machines in the foreign department or whether it should have more intelligent machines or should install more machines in the cable department, any more than the falling of a platform scale because a conductor jostled a passenger who was carrying fireworks was a prospect that could have influenced the amount of care taken by the Long Island Railroad. See Palsgraf v. Long Island R.R., 248 N.Y. 339, 162 N.E. 99 (1928).

In short, Swiss Bank was not required in the absence of a contractual undertaking to take precautions or insure against a harm that it could not measure but that was known with precision to Hyman–Michaels, which could by the exercise of common prudence have averted it completely. As Chief Judge Cardozo (the author of *Palsgraf*) remarked in discussing the application of *Hadley v. Baxendale* to the liability of telegraph companies for errors in transmission, "The sender can protect himself by insurance in one form or another if the risk of nondelivery or error appears to be too great.... The company, if it takes out insurance for itself, can do no more than guess at the loss to be avoided." Kerr S.S. Co. v. Radio Corp. of America, 245 N.Y. 284, 291–92, 157 N.E. 140, 142 (1927). * * *

The legal principles that we have said are applicable to this case were not applied below. Although the district judge's opinion is not entirely clear, he apparently thought the rule of *Hadley v. Baxendale* inapplicable and the imprudence of Hyman–Michaels irrelevant. He did state that the damages to Hyman–Michaels were foreseeable because "a major international bank" should know that a failure to act promptly on a telexed request to transfer funds could cause substantial damage; but *Siegel* * * * make[s] clear that that kind of general foreseeability, which is present in virtually every case, does not justify an award of consequential damages.

We could remand for new findings based on the proper legal standard, but it is unnecessary to do so. The undisputed facts, recited in this opinion, show as a matter of law that Hyman–Michaels is not entitled to recover consequential damages from Swiss Bank. * * *

## *Notes*

1. Both tort and contract rely on foreseeability to limit liability for remote losses. In contract, foreseeability is defined by *Hadley v. Baxendale*: the party charged with liability must be on notice of the special circumstances giving rise to the loss. See also UCC 2–715(2) ("Consequential damages resulting from the seller's breach include, (a) any loss resulting from general or particular requirements and needs of which the seller at the time of contracting had reason to know * * * "). In tort, foreseeability casts its net farther: So long as the type of harm that occurs is foreseeable, the extent of harm or the manner in which it occurs is irrelevant. A defendant whose negligence causes harm will be liable for all the consequences that follow, so long as the damage that occurs is of the same general sort, from the same physical forces as the harm that was foreseeable. See, e.g., Petition of Kinsman Transit Co., 338 F.2d 708 (2d Cir.1964).

If *EVRA* were analyzed as a tort case, what would the outcome be? Keep in mind that remoteness of the loss is not the only question foreseeability bears upon. For example, did Swiss Bank owe Hyman–Michaels, who after all was not its customer, a duty? Foreseeability is one among a number of factors courts examine to determine whether one person owes another a duty to use reasonable care; others important factors are whether the plaintiff's loss was certainly caused by the wrong, whether the causal connection was close, whether the defendant's behavior was morally wrong, the social policy of deterring negligent behavior and the availability of insurance. J'Aire Corp. v. Gregory, 24 Cal.3d 799, 157 Cal.Rptr. 407, 598 P.2d 60 (1979)(one who contracts with the owner of a building to make repairs has a duty to the owner's lessees to use reasonable care to avoid economic loss to their businesses).

There has been a general trend to limit the availability of purely economic damages in both negligence and strict liability actions. The logic has been, basically, that actions for purely economic loss should be brought as contract actions, even if the loss is the result of negligence. At least at the time of EVRA, however, Illinois had apparently not joined that trend, if the trial court was correct in its conclusion that EVRA could sue without establishing privity.

Assuming that the Illinois decisions abolishing the privity requirement establish a duty, was Swiss Bank negligent? Did they fail to act reasonably in light of their customers' foreseeable losses? Was Hyman–Michaels contributorily negligent? Did Hyman–Michaels act reasonably to mitigate its losses?

2. At points, Judge Posner hints at each of the above—duty, due care, contributory negligence, and avoidable consequences—as explaining why Hyman–Michaels cannot recover its special damages. It is not surprising that he believes they overlap; as an advocate of an economic approach to law, Judge Posner believes that all of these doctrines share the same goal—

economic efficiency. Formal distinctions between tort and contract notwithstanding, the goal of each is to insure that the costs of accidents fall on those who most cheaply could have avoided them. See Richard A. Posner, Economic Analysis of Law (4th ed.1992). Thus, the rule in *Hadley v. Baxendale* is "animated" by the principle "that the costs of the untoward consequences of a course of dealings should be borne by that party who was able to avert the consequence at least cost and failed to do so."

But, how does Judge Posner know that the miller was the cheapest cost avoider? How expensive are mill shafts, and how often do they break? How long does it usually take to repair one? Do the repairs always mean lost profits, or are millers sometimes able to defer work until the shaft is repaired, without a loss? Doesn't Judge Posner need more facts before he can conclude that the rule in *Hadley* placed the loss on the cheapest cost avoider? See Richard A. Epstein, Beyond Foreseeability: Consequential Damages in the Law of Contract, 18 J.Legal Stud. 105 (1989).

More importantly, how does Judge Posner know that Hyman–Michaels was the cheapest cost avoider? Is that the kind of decision that can or should be made in the first instance on appeal?

3. Economic explanations of Hadley v. Baxendale usually focus on how the rule promotes efficiency by giving the party who has better information about what is at stake an incentive to share that information. Then, the parties can bargain over who will take precautions against that loss, and at what cost. Knowing what steps to take to avoid a loss, however, requires two sorts of information: information about the size of the loss, and information about how likely the loss is to occur. In most contract contexts, it makes sense to encourage the party in possession of information about the size of the loss to disclose, because few promisors are likely candidly to disclose the probability that they will fail to perform. Robert Cooter, Unity in Tort, Contract and Property, 73 Calif.L.Rev. 1 (1985); cf. Richard Craswell, Performance, Reliance and One–Sided Information, 18 J.Legal Stud. 365 (1989).

In *EVRA*, only Hyman–Michaels knew what was at stake, but only Swiss Bank knew how likely it was that the telex would go astray. Is efficiency better served by a rule that requires all of a bank's customers to inform the bank of the nature of their transactions, or by a rule that would encourage banks to warn of or take steps to prevent unreasonable delays? Is it realistic to expect Hyman–Michaels to notify the bank of what was at stake? See Note, EVRA Corp. v. Swiss Bank Corp.: Consequential Damges for Bank Negligence in Wire Transfers, 9 Rutgers Comp. & Tech.L.J. 369 (1983)(arguing that notice is impractical). If Hyman–Michaels cannot reasonably notify Swiss Bank, how is Hyman–Michaels to know what steps to take to insure against the loss, without knowing how likely the loss is to occur? See Note, An Economic Approach to Hadley v. Baxendale, 62 Neb.L.Rev. 157 (1983)(without information as to the risks, customers are likely to over or under insure).

4. Does *EVRA* suggest that contract law is reclaiming some lost ground from tort law? Arguably, the courts' increasing reluctance to allow plaintiffs to bring tort actions when a defendant's defective product or even negligent behavior causes purely economic harm represents a similar development.

Even the area of professional negligence, identified by Justice Mosk in his concurrence in *Freeman & Mills* as occupying the gray area between tort and contract, is perhaps shifting back toward a contract approach. For example, recent decisions have taken the position that emotional distress damages are not available in legal malpractice actions, unless special circumstances make them particularly foreseeable. E.g., Wehringer v. Powers & Hall, 874 F.Supp. 425 (D.Mass.) (discussing the cases), affirmed, 65 F.3d 160 (1st Cir.1995). See also Kevin Tierney, Contractual Aspects of Malpractice, 19 Wayne St.L.Rev. 1457 (1973).

# Chapter 7

# RESTITUTION AND RESTITUTIONARY REMEDIES

## A. INTRODUCTION

### RESTATEMENT OF RESTITUTION

(1937).

Section One. Unjust Enrichment.

A person who has been unjustly enriched at the expense of another is required to make restitution to the other.

### DOUGLAS LAYCOCK, THE SCOPE AND SIGNIFICANCE OF RESTITUTION

67 Tex.L.Rev. 1277, 1277–1284 (1989).

The law of restitution offers substantive and remedial principles of broad scope and practical significance. In an outline of the sources of civil liability, the principal headings would be tort, contract, and restitution. * * * [Yet] [d]espite its importance, restitution is a relatively neglected and underdeveloped part of the law. In the mental map of most lawyers, restitution consists largely of blank spaces with undefined borders and only scattered patches of familiar ground. * * *

I. THE DEFINING CONCEPTS OF RESTITUTION

*A. An Historical Definition*

The rules of restitution developed much like the rules of equity. Restitution arose to avoid unjust results in specific cases—as a series of innovations to fill gaps in the rest of the law. Consequently, any definition of restitution risks the self-conscious circularity of Maitland's definition of equity[6]: restitution consists of those rules that originated in writs and equitable remedies that lawyers think of as restitutionary.

6. 'Equity is that body of rules which is administered only by those courts which are known as Courts of Equity.' F. Maitland, Equity 1 (2d ed. 1936).

The *Restatement* [of Restitution, published in 1937] attempted to induce a unifying principle and thus to provide a more satisfactory definition. The *Restatement* legitimated three insights: that a seemingly great variety of specific rules serve a common purpose, that these rules can be thought of as a single body of law under the name 'restitution,' and that these rules support a general principle that unjust enrichment must be disgorged. This was a major accomplishment; it created the field.

But the effort succeeded only in part. Drafting decisions that were probably inevitable in 1937 have become increasingly problematic over the years, in part because of the other great legal publication of 1937, the Federal Rules of Civil Procedure. The subtitle of the *Restatement*, and of its two great subdivisions, is 'Quasi Contracts and Constructive Trusts.' These categories depend in part on the separation of law and equity, and even more on a categorization of claims rooted in the forms of action and dependent on fictional pleadings. Yet the Federal Rules merged law and equity, put the last nail in the coffin of the forms of action, and embodied both the realist emphasis on substantial justice and a modern distaste for legal fiction.

The reporters of the *Restatement* were sympathetic to these trends, but they could not yet escape the past. Their work is laden with references to the pre–1937 roots of restitution, and they did not fully avoid the view that restitution is the body of law historically available under the label of quasi-contract or constructive trust. But a definition in terms of common-law writs is little help to modern lawyers. It is also misleading: restitution is both broader and narrower than the historic scope of quasi-contract and constructive trust. The search for definition must be conceptual rather than historical.

### B. *A Conceptual Definition*

Lawyers use the word 'restitution' in at least two senses. 'Restitution' means recovery based on and measured by unjust enrichment. * * * It follows from the focus on enrichment that restitution measures recovery by defendant's gain rather than plaintiff's loss. * * *

'Restitution' also retains its original literal meaning, which is simply restoration of something lost or taken away. Thus, restitution continues to include remedies that restore to plaintiff the specific thing he lost or that undo disrupted transactions and restore both parties to their original positions in kind. The *Restatement* refers to in-kind restoration of specific property as 'specific restitution.' * * *

'Restitution' is sometimes used in a third sense—to restore the value of what plaintiff lost. The Restatement employs the term this way at least occasionally, and the usage is common in the statutes requiring criminals to make restitution to their victims. But restitution of the value of what plaintiff lost is simply compensatory damages. Used in this sense, 'restitution' loses all utility as a means of distinguishing one body of law from another. Restitution must be distinguished from compensation, either by its focus on restoration of the loss in kind or by its focus on defendant's gain as the measure of recovery. * * *

Restitution is also commonly distinguished from injunctions and specific performance, even though these remedies also grant specific relief and are premised on the inadequacy of substitutionary remedies such as damages. An injunction can order defendant to return specific property to plaintiff, and in this simple case, the injunction is a means of achieving specific restitution.

But most injunctive remedies are not restitutionary in this sense. Injunctions prevent future wrongdoing or ameliorate the future consequences of a past wrong by some means more complex than restoring possession of misappropriated property or reversing a transaction. Specific performance decrees award plaintiff something he has never had, because it was promised to him and cannot be obtained elsewhere. Thus, injunctions and specific performance are more often preventive than restorative. They are historically subject to different rules, and they raise different policy considerations. The occasional restitutionary use of injunctions is part of restitution and should be recognized as such, but most of the law of injunctions and specific performance is outside the field.

### II. The Practical Significance of Restitution

Many cases of unjust enrichment are also covered by other principles, including the basic rules of tort and contract. If defendant steals a hundred-dollar bill, he is unjustly enriched in the amount of one hundred dollars. But he has also committed a tort; indeed, it is the tort that makes his enrichment unjust. The tort damages are also one hundred dollars. If defendant is solvent, it will rarely matter whether plaintiff recovers one hundred dollars in damages for the tort or one hundred dollars in restitution of the unjust enrichment.

Because of such overlaps, one gets little sense of the practical significance of restitution by systematically developing all applications of the unjust enrichment and specific restitution principles. It is more enlightening to ask what restitution adds to the other sources of civil liability. The restitutionary claim matters in three sets of cases: (1) when unjust enrichment is the only source of liability; (2) when plaintiff prefers to measure recovery by defendant's gain, either because it exceeds plaintiff's loss or because it is easier to measure; and (3) when plaintiff prefers specific restitution, either because defendant is insolvent, because the thing plaintiff lost has changed in value, or because plaintiff values the thing he lost for nonmarket reasons. * * *

## *Note on Approaching Restitution Cases*

As you read the cases that follow, you may find it helpful to focus on three questions. The first is procedural: Did the plaintiff bring his case in law or in equity, and how did he plead it? The second is substantive: What was the plaintiff required to show in order to establish a right to restitution? The third is remedial: What remedy did the plaintiff get?

*Procedure:* Professor Laycock notes that the Restatement of Restitution is divided into two parts, quasi-contract and constructive trust, corresponding to the two kinds of actions that were most frequently used to bring claims based on a theory of unjust enrichment. In a quasi-contract case, the plaintiff alleged that the defendant had received some benefit—money, goods, services—from the plaintiff, and that defendant had implicitly promised to pay for it. Using quasi-contract, the plaintiff could avoid procedural entanglements that made the common law action on the debt cumbersome, by asking the court to enforce the new, implied promise to pay.

In some cases, this promise was implied (more accurately, inferred) from the parties' own dealings and behavior; it was a contract "implied in fact", no different in legal effect from an express contract. In other cases, the contract was said to be "implied in law". Then, the court imposed an obligation to pay based, essentially, on the notion that unjust enrichment ought to be avoided:

> In quasi contracts the obligation arises, not from consent of the parties, as in the case of contracts, express or implied in fact, but from the law of natural immutable justice and equity. * * * Where a case shows that it is the duty of the defendant to pay, the law imputes to him a promise to fulfill that obligation. The duty, which thus forms the foundation of a quasi-contractual obligation, is frequently based on the doctrine of unjust enrichment.

12 Am.Jur. 502 § 6. Thus, although some of the earliest forms of action in the common law were restitutionary in character (the action of replevin, for example, by which a plaintiff could recover specific property taken from him), it was with quasi-contract that the concept of unjust enrichment as an independent source of a legal obligation entered the common law.

In the equity courts, the constructive trust was the primary vehicle for enforcing the obligation to return benefits unjustly acquired. If an equity court concluded that the defendant was in possession of property that it was unjust for him to retain, it would declare that the property was held in constructive trust for the person to whom it equitably belonged, and order the property returned. The name constructive "trust" is thus somewhat misleading. Just as "implied in law", quasi-contracts did not rest on an actual promise, the obligation to return the property did not arise from a true trust. Rather, it arose from the courts' desire to avoid unjust enrichment.

*Substance.* By now, the *Restatement's* characterization of restitution as constituting—with torts and contracts—the third, main branch of civil liability has gained wide acceptance. See Richard A. Epstein, The Ubiquity of the Benefit Principle, 67 S.Cal.L.Rev. 1369 (1994). Yet, while torts and contracts are mainstays of the first year curriculum, it usually falls to the remedies course to cover the substantive law of restitution.

The law of restitution operates at two extremes. At one extreme are broad principles, such as the principle that restitution will be awarded whenever a defendant is unjustly enriched, or the principle that volunteers and officious intermeddlers may not recover in restitution. Restatement of Restitution §§ 1,2. These broad principles, however, function more to justify results than to decide cases. At the other extreme are narrow rules, adequate to the case before the court, but too narrow to function as rules of decision as new cases arise.

Part of the problem is that the conditions under which restitution has been sought are infinitely variable. Three patterns, however, tend to be repeated. In the first, the plaintiff has conferred a benefit on the defendant that the defendant did not request. In the second pattern, the plaintiff has conferred a benefit on the defendant at the defendant's request—perhaps pursuant to a contract—and, rather than attempting to enforce the contract, the plaintiff prefers to seek the return of his performance or its value. In the third pattern, the defendant has acquired a benefit tortiously or by other wrongdoing. The cases that follow illustrate each of these patterns.

*Remedy*. As with tort and contract remedies, the concept of the rightful position is critical to understanding restitutionary remedies. Instead of aiming at the plaintiff's rightful position, however, restitution aims at the defendant's. Disgorgement is the key concept. By making the defendant disgorge the benefits he cannot justly retain, the law of restitution returns the defendant to the position he should, "in equity and good conscience", have occupied.

As the discussion of procedure, above, makes clear, the law of restitution developed concurrently in the courts of law and equity. With the some exceptions (replevin, again, for example), the remedy in the law courts was a money judgment. Although the parallels are not exact, the inquiries suggested by Professor McCormick that were used to frame the discussion of tort and contract damages—elements, measure, limits, and so on—are also useful here, and the notes following the cases track those inquiries.

This chapter ends with a discussion of the equitable, restitutionary remedies; in particular, the constructive trust. It is important to recognize that the constructive trust cases provide more than just a discussion of an alternative remedy for unjust enrichment. Because the law of restitution evolved concurrently in the law courts and the equity courts, much of the substantive law of restitution developed in the equity courts. Thus, it is important to recognize as you read the constructive trust cases that the cases are defining the terms of the obligation itself.

## B. RESTITUTION AND UNSOLICITED BENEFITS

### *Problem: Country Lodge v. Miller (Reprised)*
### *Restitution for Benefits Conferred*

Suppose that after Country Lodge threatened to sue Miller for polluting the river, Miller built settling ponds downriver from her plant to clear the water. Because the ponds also remove silt from the river, the water flowing past Country Lodge now is even clearer and purer than it was before the apple mill began operation. For the first time in years, Country Lodge's guests are able to enjoy wading and swimming in the water. Can Miller recover in restitution for the benefit she has bestowed on Country Lodge? Can Miller recover in restitution from her property insurer, if the insurer would have been liable for any damages recovered by Country Lodge had the pollution been allowed to continue?

## KOSSIAN v. AMERICAN NATIONAL INSURANCE CO.

Court of Appeal of California, Fifth District, 1967.
254 Cal.App.2d 647, 62 Cal.Rptr. 225.

STONE, ASSOCIATE JUSTICE.

On February 19, 1964, fire destroyed a portion of the Bakersfield Inn, owned by one Reichert. At the time, the property was subject to a first deed of trust in which defendant was the beneficiary. Pursuant to the requirements of the deed of trust, defendant's interest in the property was protected by policies of fire insurance. On March 16, 1964, Reichert, as owner in possession, entered into a written contract with plaintiff whereby plaintiff agreed to clean up and remove the debris from the fire damaged portion of the Inn for the sum of $18,900. Defendant had no knowledge of the execution of the agreement between plaintiff and Reichert.

Plaintiff commenced work in the middle of March 1964, and completed it in early April. During the entire time work was in progress Reichert was in possession of the premises as owner, although defendant caused a notice of Reichert's default under the deed of trust to be filed four days after the contract for demolition was entered into between plaintiff and Reichert. The record does not reflect that plaintiff had actual knowledge of the notice of default until after the work was completed.

Some time after plaintiff had fully performed the contract, Reichert filed a petition in bankruptcy. The trustee in bankruptcy abandoned the premises comprising the Bakersfield Inn, together with any interest in the four fire insurance policies up to the amount of $424,000. Each policy contained a provision insuring against the cost of cleaning up and removing debris caused by fire damage.

Following abandonment of the policies by the trustee in bankruptcy, Reichert and his wife assigned their interest in them to defendant in accordance with the terms of the deed of trust. Defendant submitted proofs of loss, claiming a total of $160,000, including the sum of $18,000 as the estimated cost for removing and cleaning up debris. These claims were rejected by the carriers; negotiations followed; the compromise figure of $135,620 was agreed upon and this amount paid to defendant. We do not have an itemization of the adjusted claims of loss upon which the compromised loss settlement was made, so that the record is not clear as to what part of the $18,900 cost of debris removal defendant received. It is clear, however, that the insurance payment included at least a part of the cost of debris removal and demolition.

Defendant demonstrates, by a careful analysis of the facts, that there was no direct relationship between plaintiff and defendant in regard to either the work performed on the property after the fire or in relation to the fire insurance policies. The contract for debris removal was between plaintiff and Reichert, and defendant did not induce plaintiff, directly or indirectly, to enter into that contract. Plaintiff had no lien against the property resulting from his work, and if he had such a lien it would have been wiped out by defendant's foreclosure of its first deed of trust.

Had the circumstances been simply that defendant, by foreclosure, took the property improved by plaintiff's debris removal, there would be a benefit conferred upon defendant by plaintiff, but no unjust enrichment. It is the additional fact that defendant made a claim to the insurance carriers for the value of work done by plaintiff that is the nub of the case.

Defendant argues that plaintiff was not a party to the insurance contracts, while defendant had a contract right to collect indemnity for losses resulting from the fire, including the debris removal cost. This contract right was embodied in the insurance policies. Defendant relies upon Russell v. Williams, 58 Cal.2d 487 at page 490, 24 Cal.Rptr. 859, at page 861, 374 P.2d 827, at page 829 where it is said:

> "It is a principle of long standing that a policy of fire insurance does not insure the property covered thereby, but is a personal contract indemnifying the insured against loss resulting from the destruction of or damage to his interest in that property. This principle gives rise to the supplemental rule that, in the absence of a special contract, the proceeds of a fire insurance policy are not a substitute for the property the loss of which is the subject of indemnity."

Defendant says it made no agreement, express or implied, with plaintiff that it would pay for the debris removal or that any part of the insurance proceeds would be applied for that purpose. Therefore, concludes defendant, there being no privity of relationship between it and plaintiff, and no fraud or deceit alleged or proved, defendant has the right to the property benefited by plaintiff's work and labor expended in removing the debris and to the insurance payments as well.

Plaintiff makes no claim to the insurance "fund" upon the ground he relied thereon similar to the reliance of a mechanic or materialman that forms the basis of an equitable claim to a building fund. He relies upon the basic premise that defendant should not be allowed to have the fruits of plaintiff's labor and also the money value of that labor. This, of course, is a simplified pronouncement of the doctrine of unjust enrichment, a theory which can, in some instances, have validity without privity of relationship.

The most prevalent implied-in-fact contract recognized under the doctrine of unjust enrichment is predicated upon a relationship between the parties from which the court infers an intent. However, the doctrine also recognizes an obligation *imposed* by law regardless of the intent of the parties. In these instances there need be no relationship that gives substance to an implied intent basic to the "contract" concept, rather the obligation is imposed because good conscience dictates that under the circumstances the person benefited should make reimbursement.

Plaintiff's claim does not rest upon a quasi contract implied in fact but upon an equitable obligation *imposed* by law. It is true that defendant's right to the insurance payment was a contract right embodied in the policies of insurance, as explicated in Russell v. Williams, supra, nevertheless the indemnity payment was based in part upon a claim of loss that did not exist because plaintiff had already remedied the loss by his work for which he was not paid.

We are cited no California cases that are close aboard, and independent research reveals none. Lack of precedent applicable to the facts peculiar to this case is not surprising, however, as the authors of the Restatement recognize that the essential nature of equity cases concerned with problems of restitution makes definitive precedent unlikely. We are guided by the "Underlying Principles" delineated in the Restatement on Restitution: "The rules stated in the Restatement of this subject depend for their validity upon certain basic assumptions in regard to what is required by justice in the various situations. In this Topic, these are stated in the form of principles. They cannot be stated as rules since either they are too indefinite to be of value in a specific case or, for historical or other reasons, they are not universally applied. They are distinguished from rules in that they are intended only as general guides for the conduct of the courts * * *."

The governing principle is expressed in the opening sentence of the Restatement on Restitution, as follows: "The Restatement of this subject deals with situations in which one person is accountable to another on the ground that otherwise he would unjustly benefit or the other would unjustly suffer loss."

The question, simply stated, is whether in a jurisdiction that recognizes the equitable doctrine of unjust enrichment one party should be indemnified twice for the same loss, once in labor and materials and again in money, to the detriment (forfeiture) of the party who furnished the labor and materials. We conclude that the doctrine of unjust enrichment is applicable to the facts of this case, and that plaintiff is entitled to reimbursement out of the insurance proceeds paid defendant for work done by plaintiff.

The facts concerning the amount of insurance recovered by defendant and the percentage of the total proof of loss attributable to plaintiff's work are not altogether clear, probably because this is a proceeding for summary judgment before trial of the action. In any event, it is clear that defendant, in addition to taking over the property which plaintiff cleared of debris, also received indemnity insurance payments covering at least part of the cost for clearing that property of debris. The amount can be made certain by a trial on the merits, and if it develops that defendant recovered only a part of the cost for debris removal, this fact does not preclude a partial recovery by plaintiff. We learn from the Restatement, page 611: "Where a person is entitled to restitution from another because the other, without tortious conduct, has received a benefit, the measure of recovery for the benefit thus received is the value of what was received * * *."

Thus, to the extent defendant received insurance for debris removal performed by plaintiff, plaintiff should recover. If defendant received less than the value of plaintiff's work, as defendant seems to contend, then plaintiff should recover pro tanto.

The judgment is reversed.

## *Notes*

1. In the excerpt that begins this chapter, Professor Laycock identifies three practical advantages to seeking restitution. Which of those three applies here?

2. *On procedure:* Although the courts of law and equity have been merged into a single judicial system in most jurisdictions, the historical distinction between law and equity can still have significant effects, as section A of chapter 6 pointed out. As you may have noticed, the *Kossian* court mixes the language of law and equity fairly indiscriminately. So, is restitution legal or equitable?

The answer is both. An action seeking restitution could be brought in the law courts or in the equity courts, depending on the nature of the case and the remedy sought. *Kossian*, for example, is a legal action, with a legal remedy: a money judgment for the amount of the benefit the defendant unjustly received.

Yet, *Kossian* is not unusual in the way the opinion mixes the language of law and equity. This mixture can seem confusing, until one realizes that the word "equity" can be used in two senses. In one sense, it refers to the historical, courts of equity, as distinguished from the courts of law. In that sense, restitution is not solely equitable in character.

Equity, however, has a broader sense, a sense in which it simply refers to fairness or justice. Restitution, with its focus on *unjust* enrichment, is equitable in character in the sense that both the law courts and the courts of equity focused on considerations of fairness and justice—equity—in order to "do the right thing."

3. *On the substantive law:* The plaintiff in *Kossian* had no claim against the insurance policies themselves, had no express or implied contract with the defendant, and was not defrauded nor deceived by the defendant. Why, then, does he have any right to part of the insurance proceeds?

According to the court, it is because the defendant will be "unjustly enriched," unless he pays part of the insurance proceeds over to the plaintiff. Because the insurance claim was compromised, however, it is almost certain that at trial the plaintiff will receive less than the contract price he agreed on with Reichert, and perhaps even less than it cost him in labor and materials to do the job. Yet, the court indicates that the plaintiff will recover only the insurance proceeds, and intimates that the defendant would not have an obligation to pay the plaintiff for his labor at all if he had not received the insurance proceeds.

Is that the right result? The defendant has received more than just the insurance proceeds; he has the benefit of the plaintiff's labor as well. There is nothing to suggest that the original contract price was out of line, and the defendant's property is certainly worth more as a result of the work that was done. Therefore, shouldn't he have an obligation to pay for the work, regardless of whether he collected on the policy? Would it have mattered if the defendant knew of plaintiff's contract with Reichert at some point after Reichert's default?

4. The difficult substantive question in a restitution case is, is it *unjust* for the defendant to retain the benefit? The rule often stated is that officious intermeddlers and volunteers are not entitled to restitution for the benefits they confer on another. Restatement of Restitution, § 2.

Does the *Kossian* court offer any useful rationale for its decision that restitution is appropriate on these facts? How does one determine whether a benefit has been conferred officiously or voluntarily? The opinions are not much help: it seems to be generally accepted that "intermeddler" and "volunteer" are little more than labels used to justify, rather than to explain, the result in a particular case. Saul Levmore, Explaining Restitution, 71 Va.L.Rev. 65 (1985).

Professor Levmore offers several insights as to why courts may require restitution in some cases of unsolicited benefits and not in others. His premise is that requiring restitution effectively creates a bargain between the parties, by requiring the defendant to pay the plaintiff for the value of the benefit received. Courts may be reluctant to create such a bargain for a number of reasons. It may be difficult for the court to decide on the actual value of the benefit that has been conferred. Further, even if the value of the benefit can be determined, it may not be clear that the recipient desired it or could afford it. Finally, by requiring the provider of services to bargain rather than allowing him to act first and get paid later, the courts support the development of active markets that promote efficient resource allocation.

Would Professor Levmore agree with the result in *Kossian?*

5. Professor Dan Dobbs has suggested a slightly different set of principles to decide these sorts of restitution cases:

> The first principle is that one who has conferred a benefit upon another with an intention to make a gift, has no equitable claim for relief against the recipient of the benefit in the absence of fraud, mistake, duress or undue influence. * * * The second principle is that one who confers a benefit upon another without affording that other the opportunity to reject the benefit, has no equitable claim for relief against the recipient of the benefit in the absence of some special policy that would outweigh the right of free choice in the benefited party.

Dan B. Dobbs, Handbook on the Law of Remedies 229 (1973). Would Professor Dobbs agree with the result in *Kossian?*

6. In *Kossian*, the plaintiff performed his services under a mistaken belief that Reichert, with whom he contracted, still owned the property. Would it have made a difference if the plaintiff had known, before he started work, that Reichert had defaulted and the defendant had taken possession? Should a plaintiff ever get restitution if he knowingly performs services for someone who has not solicited them? According to the Restatement, a person who confers a benefit on another without mistake, coercion or request generally cannot claim restitution, "except where the benefit was necessary for the protection of the interests of the other or third persons." Restatement of Restitution § 112.

In Berry v. Barbour, 279 P.2d 335 (Okla.1954),the defendant hired plaintiff to do some repairs on a building defendant owned. While plaintiff was working, a fire broke out. (The plaintiff was not at fault in any way for the fire.) In extinguishing the blaze, firefighters cut several holes in the building's roof. Plaintiff repaired the holes without contacting defendant, who was in Germany at the time. Should the plaintiff have a valid claim for restitution?

According to the Restatement, a person who preserves the property of another can claim restitution if he was 1) in possession of the property at the time, 2) it was not reasonably possible to communicate with the owner, 3) he had no reason to think that the services were unwanted, 4) he intended to charge for his services or to retain the property if it was not claimed, and the 5) owner accepted possession of the repaired or improved property. Restatement of Restitution, § 117. The Restatement applies a similar rule when unsolicited services are provided to another in order to preserve their life or health: the services must be necessary to prevent serious harm, and the person providing the services must expect compensation, and have no reason to believe the services are unwanted. Restatement of Restitution § 115.

How would the Restatement's principles apply in *Berry*? Would Professors Dobbs and Levmore agree that these factors should determine the result?

7. So far, all of the cases discussed have involved services. Slightly different rules apply when money is paid by mistake. For example, if a person pays money to another in the mistaken belief that he has a duty to do so, he can get restitution. Restatement of Restitution § 15. Why should it be easier to get restitution for money paid by mistake than for services rendered by mistake? Do the principles Professors Levmore and Dobbs advocate suggest an explanation?

8. *On the remedy.* The remedy for unjust enrichment in *Kossian* would be a money judgment. As in the case of compensatory damages, the remedy would be substitutionary in character, giving the plaintiff an award of money as a substitute for the value of the benefit conferred on the defendant.

With restitution, as with compensatory damages, questions of how the benefit to the defendant is to be measured inevitably arise. Here, the court measures the defendant's unjust enrichment by the amount of the insurance proceeds attributable to the cost of cleaning up the property. Is that the proper measure? Why not the price the plaintiff and Reichert had negotiated? Why not the reasonable value of the plaintiff's services?

Think about what the appropriate measure of damages might be in some of the other situations suggested in the notes. If a doctor saves an unconscious person's life, is the measure of restitutionary recovery the value of the doctor's services, or the value of the person's life? Principles that determine the measure of damages are discussed in the next case.

## C. RESTITUTION AND WRONGFULLY ACQUIRED BENEFITS

### *Problem: Country Lodge v. Miller (Reprised) A Restitution Option?*

During the first year of the cider mill's operation, Miller saved $20,000 by dumping her apple mash into the river instead of installing an alternative means of disposal. Assuming that Country Lodge can establish that dumping the apple mash was a nuisance, could Country Lodge seek restitution rather than tort damages? In the language of the case that follows, could Miller "waive" the tort of nuisance and sue Miller in assumpsit? If so, how would the award be measured?

### OLWELL v. NYE & NISSEN

Supreme Court of Washington, 1946.
26 Wash.2d 282, 173 P.2d 652.

MALLERY, JUSTICE.

On May 6, 1940, plaintiff, E.L. Olwell, sold and transferred to the defendant corporation his one-half interest in Puget Sound Egg Packers, a Washington corporation having its principal place of business in Tacoma. By the terms of the agreement, the plaintiff was to retain full ownership in an "Eggsact" egg-washing machine, formerly used by Puget Sound Egg Packers. The defendant promised to make it available for delivery to the plaintiff on or before June 15, 1940. It appears that the plaintiff arranged for and had the machine stored in a space adjacent to the premises occupied by the defendant but not covered by its lease. Due to the scarcity of labor immediately after the outbreak of the war, defendant's treasurer, without the knowledge or consent of the plaintiff, ordered the egg washer taken out of storage. The machine was put into operation by defendant on May 31, 1941, and thereafter for a period of three years was used approximately one day a week in the regular course of the defendant's business. Plaintiff first discovered this use in January or February of 1945 when he happened to be at the plant on business and heard the machine operating. Thereupon plaintiff offered to sell the machine to defendant for $600 or half of its original cost in 1929. A counter offer of $50 was refused and approximately one month later this action was commenced to recover the reasonable value of defendant's use of the machine, and praying for $25 per month from the commencement of the unauthorized use until the time of trial. * * * The court entered judgment for plaintiff in the amount of $10 per week for the period of 156 weeks covered by the statute of limitations, or $1,560, and gave the plaintiff his costs.

The theory of the respondent was that the tort of conversion could be "waived" and suit brought in quasi-contract, upon a contract implied in law, to recover, as restitution, the profits which inured to appellant as a result of its wrongful use of the machine. With this the trial court agreed and in its findings of facts found that the use of the machine "resulted in a benefit to the users, in that said use saves the users approximately $1.43 per hour of use as against the expense which would be incurred were eggs to be washed by hand; that said machine was used by Puget Sound Egg Packers and defendant, on an average of one day per week from May of 1941, until February of 1945 at an average saving of $10.00 per each day of use."

In substance, the argument presented by the assignments of error is that the principle of unjust enrichment, or quasi-contract, is not of universal application, but is imposed only in exceptional cases because of special facts and circumstances and in favor of particular persons; that respondent had an adequate remedy in an action at law for replevin or claim and delivery; that any damages awarded to the plaintiff should be based upon the use or rental value of the machine and should bear some reasonable relation to its market value. * * *

It is uniformly held that in cases where the defendant *tortfeasor* has benefited by his wrong, the plaintiff may elect to "waive the tort" and bring an action in assumpsit for restitution. Such an action arises out of a duty imposed by law devolving upon the defendant to repay an unjust and unmerited enrichment.

It is clear that the saving in labor cost which appellant derived from its use of respondent's machine constituted a benefit.

According to the Restatement of Restitution, § 1(b), p. 12,

> "A person confers a benefit upon another if he gives to the other possession of or some other interest in money, land, chattels, or choses in action, performs services beneficial to or at the request of the other, satisfies a debt or a duty of the other, or in any way adds to the other's security or advantage. *He confers a benefit not only where he adds to the property of another, but also where he* saves the

other from expense or loss. The word 'benefit', therefore denotes any form of advantage." (Italics ours)

It is also necessary to show that while appellant benefited from its use of the egg-washing machine, respondent thereby incurred a loss. It is argued by appellant that since the machine was put into storage by respondent, who had no present use for it, and for a period of almost three years did not know that appellant was operating it and since it was not injured by its operation and the appellant never adversely claimed any title to it, nor contested respondent's right of repossession upon the latter's discovery of the wrongful operation, that the respondent was not damaged because he is as well off as if the machine had not been used by appellant.

The very essence of the nature of property is the right to its exclusive use. Without it, no beneficial right remains. However plausible, the appellant cannot be heard to say that his wrongful invasion of the respondent's property right to exclusive use is not a loss compensable in law. To hold otherwise would be subversive of all property rights since his use was admittedly wrongful and without claim of right. The theory of unjust enrichment is applicable in such a case.

We agree with appellant that respondent could have elected a "common garden variety of action," as he calls it, for the recovery of damages. It is also true that except where provided for by statute, punitive damages are not allowed, the basic measure for the recovery of damages in this state being compensation. If, then, respondent had been *limited* to redress *in tort* for damages, as appellant contends, the court below would be in error in refusing to make a finding as to the value of the machine. In such case the award of damages must bear a reasonable relation to the value of the property.

But respondent here had an election. He chose rather to waive his right of action *in tort* and to sue *in assumpsit* on the implied contract. Having so elected, he is entitled to the measure of restoration which accompanies the remedy.

"Actions for restitution have for their primary purpose taking from the defendant and restoring to the plaintiff something to which the plaintiff is entitled, or if this is not done, causing the defendant to pay the plaintiff an amount which will restore the plaintiff to the position in which he was before the defendant received the benefit. If the value of what was received and what was lost were always equal, there would be no substantial problem as to the amount of recovery, since actions of restitution are not punitive. In fact, however, the plaintiff frequently has lost more than the defendant has gained, and sometimes the defendant has gained more than the plaintiff has lost.

"In such cases the measure of restitution is determined with reference to the tortiousness of the defendant's conduct or the negligence or other fault of one or both of the parties in creating the situation giving rise to the right to restitution. If the defendant was tortious in his acquisition of the benefit he is required to pay for what the other has lost although that is more than the recipient benefited. *If he was consciously tortious in acquiring the benefit, he is also deprived of any profit derived from his subsequent dealing with it.* If he was no more at fault than the claimant, he is not required to pay for losses in excess of benefit received by him and he is permitted to retain gains which result from his dealing with the property." (Italics ours) Restatement of Restitution, pp. 595, 596.

Respondent may recover the profit derived by the appellant from the use of the machine.

[The court then held that the plaintiff could not recover more than he had prayed for in the complaint, and directed the trial court to reduce the judgment to $25.00 per month, or $900].

### *Notes*

1. In the excerpt that begins this chapter, Professor Laycock identifies three practical advantages to seeking restitution. Which of those three applies here?

2. *On procedure.* "Assumpsit" was the common law *form of action* used to bring a quasi-contract claim. As you will remember from your civil procedure class, the forms of action were pleading devices. To bring a case in the law courts, the plaintiff had to fit it to one of the recognized forms, which were often highly technical.

Most jurisdictions have abandoned the forms of action in favor of notice pleading. Under notice pleading, to bring a restitution case, or any other case, it is simply necessary to set forth the facts that entitle the plaintiff to relief. Nonetheless, some understanding of the forms of action is helpful, particularly in reading the older cases.

The form of action of assumpsit required the plaintiff to allege that the defendant had received some benefit from the plaintiff, and (implicitly) promised to pay for it. Assumpsit could be further broken down into what were known as the "common counts" based on the nature of the benefit received: money had and received, goods sold and delivered, quantum meruit (the value of labor done), and so on. Thus, by "waiving" the tort form of action and suing in assumpsit, the plaintiff could base his claim on the benefit the defendant had received rather than on the harm the plaintiff had suffered.

Yet, the phrase "waiving the tort and suing in assumpsit" is potentially misleading, if "waiving" is taken to mean relinquishing a right or claim against the defendant. By choosing to sue in assumpsit for unjust enrichment rather than in tort for the harm caused, the plaintiff is in no sense relinquishing his right to recover from the defendant. Indeed, frequently it is the tortious character of the defendant's actions that makes the enrichment clearly unjust.

The phrase is also troublesome in connection with the notion of election of remedies, which was introduced earlier, text at page 530. Apparently unaware that the "promise to pay" is a fiction forced on plaintiffs by the need to plead in assumpsit, some courts have held that a plaintiff who seeks relief on a quasi-contract theory has "elected" to affirm the transaction, and cannot later change to a tort theory of recovery. The better view would recognize that it is unjust enrichment, not a promise, that justifies restitution, and that so long as there is no double recovery, there is no inconsistency between tort and restitution in this context.

3. *On the substantive law.* Not all torts can be "waived." For example, it is generally agreed that the plaintiff in a defamation suit does not have the option of foregoing damages in order to recover the profits the defendant's publication earned. Hart v. E.P. Dutton & Co., 197 Misc. 274, 93 N.Y.S.2d 871 (1949); Dan B. Dobbs, Law of Remedies § 7.2 (2d ed.1993). How should a court go about deciding what torts can be waived? That is, when can a plaintiff sue in restitution to recover the benefits of defendant's tortious conduct?

According to Professor Palmer, courts are slowly moving away from the notion that assumpsit is only available as an alternative cause of action for a select number of torts, and toward recognizing that an action in restitution should always be available when the defendant has acquired a benefit through tortious wrongdoing. George E. Palmer, Law of Restitution § 2.1 (1978). As this idea becomes more generally accepted, however, courts will need to develop some principle to determine whether the defendant's benefit actually was derived from the invasion of the plaintiff's right. Id.

Professor Daniel Friedmann has attempted to articulate such a principle:

> [R]estitution may be justified on the general principle that a person who obtains—though not necessarily tortiously—a benefit at the expense of another through appropriation of a property or quasi-property interest held by the other person is unjustly enriched and should be liable to the other for any benefit attributable to the appropriation. This principle draws its strength from fundamental concepts of property that prohibit exploitation of another's right—even if the other is unable or unwilling to exploit the right himself—without his consent. But unlike an approach based on traditional property concepts, it permits restitution in cases involving "nonexclusive" interests—quasi-property—and may even be extended * * * to certain kinds of contract rights that may, for purposes of this analysis, be considered to be proprietary. In addition, the principle abandons the waiver-of-tort concept altogether, permitting restitution even if the defendant's act is not a tort or, if prima facie a tort, excused or justified.

Daniel Friedmann, Restitution of Benefits Obtained Through the Appropriation of Property or the Commission of a Wrong, 80 Colum.L.Rev. 504, 509 (1980).

Would Professor Friedmann allow restitution the *Country Lodge* problem? Does the interest in being free from pollution qualify as a "quasi-property" interest?

4. According to the doctrine of balancing the hardships, a court might not order Miller to install pollution control devices that cost $20,000 in order to avoid a $10,000 harm, although it would order her to pay damages to Country Lodge. This result is frequently justified as economically efficient: it would be wasteful to expend $20,000 to avoid the loss of $10,000. If

Country Lodge is granted restitution, won't that undercut the economically efficient result? Does this explain why the tort of nuisance is not "waivable"?

Wouldn't the same argument apply to *Olwell,* however? Isn't using an egg-washing machine more socially valuable than letting it sit in a shed? Shouldn't Puget Sound Egg Packers be encouraged to put this machine to use, contingent on their willingness to pay the plaintiff's damages?

5. Professor Friedmann's principle would allow restitution even where the defendant's act is not wrongful. Does this seem right? Suppose that during a storm a ship owner orders the plaintiff's goods jettisoned in order to save the lives of his crew and passengers. Should he owe restitution to the plaintiff? If he jettisons the plaintiff's goods to save his own? If he jettisons goods that he promised to sell to the plaintiff at the voyage's end?

6. *On the remedy: Measuring the restitutionary recovery.* If the shipowner in note 5 above, or Miller in the *Country Lodge* problem, owes restitution to the plaintiff, how is the recovery to be measured? As *Olwell* notes, there are three possibilities, depending on the facts of the particular case:

*The plaintiff's loss and the defendant's gain may be equal.* In such a case, "There [is] no substantial problem as to the amount of recovery, since actions of restitution are not punitive." Of course, if the plaintiff's loss and the defendant's gain are equal, there is also no immediately apparent reason to sue in restitution: The plaintiff can sue in tort and recover the same amount. In such cases, there may be a conceptual difference between tort and restitution, but there is no practical difference in the amount recovered.

There may, however, be other practical consequences to the choice. Because of quasi-contract's distinct historical roots, some technical distinctions between tort and quasi-contract still exist. Thus, in some states, different rules with regard to the statute of limitations, survivorship, and sovereign immunity may apply depending on the plaintiff's choice of tort or quasi-contract.

*The plaintiff's loss may be greater than the defendant's gain.* Then, "If the defendant was tortious in his acquisition of the benefit he is required to pay for what the other has lost although that is more than the recipient benefited."

If the theory of the plaintiff's case is unjust enrichment, why should his recovery ever exceed the benefit the defendant received? Measuring recovery by the plaintiff's loss, is inconsistent with the conceptual goal of preventing unjust enrichment, to the extent the plaintiff's loss exceeds the plaintiff's gain. Suppose the defendant has converted the plaintiff's property and sold it, foolishly, for far less than it was worth. If the plaintiff sues in assumpsit, should he recover the value of the item, or the amount the defendant actually received? According to *Olwell,* the answer has been the former, but is that really consistent with a theory of preventing unjust enrichment?

Formal pleadings aside, another way to look at the issue would be, where restitution and tort point to inconsistent results, which should predominate? Should the goal of tort law—restoring the plaintiff to his rightful position—be undercut because the plaintiff selected the wrong legal theory? Allowing the plaintiff to recover his losses even when they exceed the defendant's gain effectively means that in cases where both tort and restitution actions are available, at a minimum the tort goal of restoring the plaintiff to his rightful position will be served.

*The defendant's gain may be greater than the plaintiff's loss.* "If [the defendant] was consciously tortious in acquiring the benefit, he is also deprived of any profit derived from his subsequent dealing with it."

Depriving the defendant of his profits is usually justified by invoking the principle that "No one should profit from his own wrongdoing." Restatement of Restitution § 3. But while this principle may justify requiring the defendant to disgorge his profits, does it necessarily justify handing them over to the plaintiff?

Often, awarding the plaintiff the defendant's profits is justified because the defendant has deprived the plaintiff of an opportunity to make a profit himself. Thus, in cases of unfair competition, or interference with contract, where the plaintiff and the defendant are in the same business, awarding the plaintiff the defendant's profits in a way simply acknowledges that if the defendant had not interfered, the plaintiff might have made those profits himself. Similarly, in trademark cases, an award of profits is often justified as compensating the plaintiff for the loss of profits he might have made himself, had the defendant not violated his trademark.

Where an award of profits can be thought of as compensating the plaintiff for the loss of the opportunity to make the same profit himself, justifying restitution is straightforward: as in the first of *Olwell*'s categories, the defendant's gain is equal to the plaintiff's loss. In other cases, however, this justification may not be available. In *Olwell* itself, for example, the plaintiff lacked the capacity to make use of the machine the defendant converted, and so his loss—even in terms of opportunity—was clearly less than the defendant's gain. The only loss Olwell suffered was the loss of the opportunity to rent or sell the machine. Why should he recover more? The defendant may have profited, but not at the plaintiff's expense!

Thus, if the plaintiff has done nothing to earn a profit, didn't expect to earn one, and couldn't have earned it himself had he tried, why should he get a windfall? Consider the following remarks, made in a copyright infringement case:

> It is true that if the infringer makes greater profits than the copyright owner lost, because the infringer is a more efficient producer than the owner or sells in a different market, the owner is allowed to capture the additional profit even though it does not represent a loss to him. It may seem wrong to penalize the infringer for his superior efficiency and give the owner a windfall. But it discourages infringement. By preventing infringers from obtaining any net profit it makes any would-be infringer negotiate directly with the owner of a copyright that he wants to use, rather than bypass the market by stealing the copyright and forcing the owner to seek compensation from the courts for his loss. Since the infringer's gain might exceed the owner's loss, especially as loss is measured by a court, limiting damages to that loss would not effectively deter this kind of forced exchange.

Taylor v. Meirick, 712 F.2d 1112 (7th Cir.1983). Does this justification sound familiar? What is the relationship between disgorgement and punitive damages?

Some conscious tortfeasors, however, are not required to give up their profits. The classic hypothetical exploring the limits of disgorgement runs along these lines: If an artist steals paint, brushes and canvas and creates a masterpiece, can the victim of the theft recover the value of the painting by way of restitution? The answer, of course, is no: The painting's value is the product of the artist's skill, not of his theft. Thus, at some point, it is inappropriate to measure restitution by profits, if the profits are primarily attributable to the defendant's skill and efforts, not to his wrongdoing. The plaintiff's recovery would be limited to the value of the property taken from him.

By this logic, in *Olwell,* the plaintiff would recover the rental value of the egg-washing machine. (Of course, even this award can be conceptualized as restitutionary. The defendant benefited, at a minimum, by not having to rent or buy a machine to wash his eggs. Although the rental value is general damages for a temporary taking of property, on the facts of *Olwell,* rental value exceeds the plaintiff's actual losses, because the plaintiff had no plans to rent the machine. Thus, on the facts of a case like *Olwell,* general damages in tort are actually restitutionary in character). Similarly, in patent cases, recovery is limited by statute to a reasonable royalty or licensing fee, and in trademark cases, the court may, in its discretion, so limit the recovery.

Even if a court decides that disgorgement is appropriate, it may still take the defendant's efforts into account in two ways. First, it may consider the defendant's efforts in choosing how to measure his profits. For example, in *Olwell,* why didn't the court measure the recovery by the percentage of the plant's profits proportionate to the increased production the machine made possible? Wouldn't that be a more accurate measure of the defendant's profits than the labor costs saved? Although the court did not explicitly consider the possibility, profits above the labor expenses saved are more directly attributable to the defendant's skill in marketing than to the egg-washing machine. After all, the defendant could have made those profits without infringing the plaintiff's rights, simply by hiring more workers.

A second way to take the defendant's efforts into account is to apportion the profits between the defendant's efforts and the product of the plaintiff's property. The leading case is Sheldon v. Metro–Goldwyn Pictures Corp., 309 U.S. 390, 60 S.Ct. 681, 84 L.Ed. 825 (1940). Metro–Goldwyn produced a movie that plagiarized plaintiff's play. While Metro–Goldwyn was clearly liable to the plaintiff for the profits attributable to the infringement of plaintiff's copyright, the Court found it necessary to apportion the profits, because, "The testimony showed quite clearly that in the creation of profits from the exhibition of a motion picture, the talent and popularity of the 'motion picture stars' generally constitutes the main drawing power of the picture, and that this is especially true where the title of the picture is not identified with any well-known play or novel." 309 U.S. at 407, 60 S.Ct. at

687. Therefore, the Court affirmed an award of twenty per cent of the net profits to the plaintiffs.

*Olwell* 's assertion that a conscious wrongdoer will always be stripped of his profits is probably over broad. As Professor Palmer has noted, there are "no easy formulas" to determine "whether, or the extent to which, the defendant's gain is the product not solely of the plaintiff's interest but also of contributions made by the defendant. * * * Instead, the court must resort to general considerations of fairness, taking into account the nature of the defendant's wrong, the relative extent of his contribution, and the feasibility of separating this from the contribution traceable to the plaintiff's interest." George E. Palmer, Law of Restitution § 2.12 at 161 (1978).

Thus, despite *Olwell*'s assertions, restitution in quasi-contract for conversion has usually been measured by the value of the chattel. Restatement of Restitution § 151. If the property itself has increased in value, or generated direct profits, those profits may be recovered, but where the defendant has used the property, the recovery has generally been measured by the reasonable value of the property's use. Restatement of Restitution § 157 comment d. Similarly, in patent cases, and at the court's discretion in trademark cases, an infringer's "profits" are measured by a reasonable royalty (the equivalent of rental value) rather than by the infringer's actual profits.

Another alternative to a profit-based measure is to measure recovery by the expenses the defendant saved. An interesting example is City of Chicago v. Roppolo, 113 Ill.App.3d 602, 69 Ill.Dec. 435, 447 N.E.2d 870 (1983). In *Roppolo,* the defendant, a developer, had promised to move and rehabilitate a landmark building in order to get a zoning amendment critical to his project approved. Then, he tore down the building. The court imposed a "constructive trust" on the developer, in the amount of the expenses he saved by not having to move and rehabilitate the building. See also Daniel Farber, Reassessing *Boomer*: Justice, Efficiency, and Nuisance Law, in Property Law and Legal Education: Essays in Honor of John Cribbet (P. Hay & M. Hoeflich, eds. 1988)(damages in nuisance cases should be measured by the amount the defendant would have had to pay to acquire the right to pollute).

Sometimes, however, recovery is measured by the defendant's actual profits. In quasi-contract, the leading example is Edwards v. Lee's Administrator, 265 Ky. 418, 96 S.W.2d 1028 (1936). There, a property owner recovered a part of the profits his neighbor had earned by offering tours of a cave that extended under both parcels. By analogy, there are a number of tort causes of action in which the tort measure of damages arguably allows profits to be recovered, interference with contract and appropriation of the right of publicity being the most common examples. See George E. Palmer, Law of Restitution § 2.9. (1978). And in trademark, copyright, and insider trading cases, profits are frequently recovered. See Douglas Laycock, Modern American Remedies 534 (2d ed.1994).

# D. RESTITUTION AND SOLICITED BENEFITS

## HUTCHISON v. PYBURN

Court of Appeals of Tennessee, 1977.
567 S.W.2d 762.

DROWOTA, JUDGE.

This is a case involving fraud in the sale of realty in which plaintiffs-vendees were awarded both rescission of the deed and punitive damages by the Chancery Court of Davidson County. Since the case is before us without a bill of exceptions, our recitation of the facts follows the allegations of plaintiffs-appellees and the findings of the Chancellor.

In January of 1973, plaintiffs William and Jo Lynn Hutchison purchased a house and lot from defendants Robert and Carol Pyburn for $24,000.00. Of this amount, $23,500.00 represented a loan from Home Federal Savings & Loan Association which was secured by a deed of trust. Defendant Jack Williams built the house and sold the property to the Pyburns, and his brother, defendant John Williams, was real estate agent for the Pyburns in the sale of the property to plaintiffs. In July of 1973, plaintiffs noticed seepage from their sewage disposal system, investigated, and discovered that their property had not been approved as a home site by the Metropolitan Board of Health because it lacked the requisite topsoil to sustain the septic tank and overflow field needed for sewage disposal. Further, the Metropolitan Department of Code Administration had been informed of the problem, and had issued a building permit to defendant Jack Williams only by mistake. Evidently defendant Pyburn had become aware of the sewage problem after purchasing the property from Williams and had prevailed on Williams to release him from his obligation to purchase it, whereupon Pyburn and Williams negotiated the sale to plaintiffs.

Plaintiffs brought suit, alleging that the defendants Pyburn and Williams knew of the property's condition and that there was no practical means of correcting it at the time of the sale. They charged that defendants' failure to inform them of the sewage problem amounted to fraud and deceit, and that the condition of the property represented a breach of the warranties contained in the deed. The Chancellor dismissed the case against defendant John Williams, but entered a decree in favor of plaintiffs against the Pyburns and Jack Williams. The decree allowed plaintiffs rescission of the contract, incidental damages in the form of expenses incurred in connection with the property, moving costs, and attorney's fees, from all of which was deducted the reasonable rental value of the property for the period of plaintiffs' occupancy. In addition to the sum due plaintiffs in incidental damages, which was set at $3,168.94, the Chancellor assessed $5,000.00 in punitive damages against the defendants and made a specific finding that defendants' misrepresentation was fraudulent. * * *

Defendants * * * assert that the trial court erred in awarding punitive damages for misrepresentations incident to a contract when rescission of the contract and deed was also decreed. * * *

In Tennessee it is established that courts of equity are empowered to award punitive damages. * * *

One objection raised to the award of punitive damages in this case is that it is inconsistent with rescission of the deed under the doctrine of election of remedies. That doctrine estops a plaintiff who has clearly chosen to pursue one of two inconsistent and irreconcilable remedies from later resorting to the other. The "essential element" here is "that the remedies be inconsistent." * * * There is no such inconsistency, however, between the remedy of rescission and an award of punitive damages. The latter * * * is designed to penalize and deter, and results from the nature of defendant's conduct rather than from the harm it causes. The character of punitive damages, then, is in no wise inconsistent with rescission and its concomitant remedies of restitution and incidental damages. The latter are all aimed at *redressing* the harm done the plaintiff and, while this means they may be considered inconsistent with a remedy such as compensatory damages, which also aims at redress but by a different method, they may not be so considered with respect to the *deterrent* sanction of punitive damages. Thus, plaintiffs' choice of rescission as a means of redress is not inconsistent with their request for punitive damages and does not estop them from making that request.

Similarly, punitive damages do not conflict with the theoretical aim of equitable rescission, which is to return the parties to the status in which they were prior to the transaction. That aim is simply one approach to redressing the wrong done to plaintiff, an approach that differs from that of compensatory damages, which are intended to redress the wrong by directly compensating the plaintiff for what he has lost. But again, punitive damages are not intended to redress the plaintiff's wrong, but to make an example of the defendant's conduct. Since they thus relate to considerations totally different from those of rescission, punitive damages neither frustrate rescission's redressing of plaintiff's wrong by return of the parties to the *status quo,* nor are they inconsistent with it.

Cases often announce the rule that there must be proof of "actual damages" before punitive damages may be awarded. The cases are unclear, however, as to the meaning of "actual damages" in this context. It has been logically suggested that the phrase should mean no more than that the plaintiff cannot get punitive damages without proving a valid cause of action, that is, without showing that he has been legally injured in some way, which is really a roundabout way of saying that there can be no cause of action for punitive damages alone. * * * That approach, applied broadly, would allow recovery of punitive damages if plaintiff, in addition to showing the requisite degree of bad conduct and intent by defendant, could merely prove his entitlement to injunctive relief or nominal damages. But we need not go so far here in construing "actual damages" not to mean strictly an award of compensatory damages. Returning to the case before us, we hold simply that plaintiffs' proof of their entitlement to rescission of the deed, refund of the purchase price, and incidental damages such as moving expenses, shows sufficient harm and loss to them to satisfy the "actual damages" prerequisite to recovery of punitive damages in Tennessee.

Finally, defendants point to a proposition which we agree is the general rule in Tennessee and elsewhere: punitive damages may not be recovered in an action for breach of contract. This case, however, is not one for breach of contract, for plaintiffs asked that the contract be made a nullity by rescission. Further, the pleadings and memorandum of the trial court indicate that the main thrust of the action is a claim of fraud and misrepresentation against all the defendants, although an additional claim of breach of warranty was asserted against the Pyburns, with whom plaintiffs were in privity. Thus, regardless of any overtones of contract that may appear in this suit, there also clearly exists here a cause of action against all defendants for the sort of tortious misconduct required as a basis for recovery of punitive damages * * *. For this reason, such a recovery cannot be defeated by the rule that punitive damages are unavailable in contract actions. * * *

## *Notes*

1. In the excerpt that begins this chapter, Professor Laycock identifies three practical advantages to seeking restitution. Which of those three applies here?

To understand why a plaintiff might seek restitution instead of damages, some background on the tort of fraud is necessary. In most jurisdictions, the measure of damages for fraud is the difference between the value the plaintiff expected to receive if the defendant's representations had been true, and the value the plaintiff did receive. This "benefit of the bargain" measure would seem to belong more to the law of contracts than to the law of torts. Its adoption by a majority of jurisdictions represents the recognition that fraud in the inducement to a contract lies on the border between tort and contract.

A few jurisdictions, however, keep to a more "tort-like" measure, measuring damages by how much the plaintiff is "out-of-pocket;" that is, by the difference between the value of what the plaintiff had before the tort and the value of what he has after.

Both of these measures, however, require that the misrepresentation affect the value of what the plaintiff bargained for. If that is not the case, perhaps because some other factor intervened to affect the values involved, rescission may offer a better chance at recovery. For example, in Goodwin v. Dick, 220 Mass. 556, 107 N.E. 925 (1915), the plaintiff bought stock on the intentionally false representation that it was treasury stock. The stock was worthless, but it would also have been worthless if it had actually been treasury stock. Under the benefit of the bargain measure, the value of what plaintiff was promised and the value of what he got were the same, so the plaintiff would recover nothing. Under an "out-of-pocket" approach, the result would be the same, because the misrepresentation did not cause the stock to be worthless. Yet, if the plaintiff had sued for rescission, he would have recovered the purchase price. In such a case, so far as the plaintiff is concerned, it is rescission or nothing at all.

In *Hutchison*, of course, causation is not a problem. The misrepresentations clearly affected the value of the property. So, why did they rescind instead of seeking damages?

2. *On procedure.* The remedy of rescission avoids, or cancels, a transaction. Where the transaction is executory, rescission amounts to no more than an announcement that the deal is off. More commonly, rescission is sought when a plaintiff has transferred something of value to a defendant and then wants it, or its equivalent in money, returned. Thus, restitution usually goes hand in hand with rescission, as each party is required to give up the benefits it acquired under the voided transaction in order to return the other to the *status quo ante*.

Although *Hutchison* speaks of rescission as an equitable remedy, rescission was not restricted to the equity courts. At law, rescission was available by an action in quasi-contract. Thus, in *Hutchison,* the plaintiff could have rescinded the contract by offering to return the property, and then sued in quasi-contract for the return of the purchase price. (One of the distinctions between legal and equitable rescission is that, at law, the plaintiff rescinded the contract by tendering restitution to the defendant and then suing. In the equity courts, tender was not required; the plaintiff sued, and the court rescinded the contract if the plaintiff prevailed.)

Depending on the case, there can be advantages to seeking equitable rescission. In a case like *Hutchison*, rescission, or cancellation, of the deed is the type of remedy that would not have been available at law. While the law courts effected restitution by entering a money judgment in the plaintiff's favor, the equity courts could order the defendant to return the specific property he had received. As a result, equitable rescission gave the plaintiff an advantage over the defendant's creditors, if the defendant was insolvent. Indeed, a court of equity could create a lien on the property in order to secure the plaintiff's entitlement to return of the purchase price and incidental damages.

The choice between an equitable and legal remedy raises an issue discussed in chapter 2: In order to have the benefits of equitable rescission, must the plaintiff show that the legal remedy is inadequate? The answer to that question is complex. Certainly, there are cases in which the availability of rescission in equity has turned on the adequacy of the legal remedy. Thus, plaintiffs have been allowed an equitable remedy where they could show that they sought the return of specific, unique property, or that complete relief required cancellation of a document (which could not be accomplished by a law court), or that the defendant was insolvent and only an equitable remedy could guarantee recovery, but denied equitable relief when they simply sought return of the purchase price.

At the same time, however, equitable rescission has been allowed in many cases without any discussion of the inadequacy requirement. In part, this may be because for a time there was no way to rescind a contract for fraud at common law. Thus, equity courts originally took cognizance of claims for rescission based on fraud because there was no equivalent action at law, and never let go, even after the law courts developed one.

If this explanation were completely accurate, however, equitable rescission would always be available for contracts induced by fraud. Oddly, it is not. While almost all courts allow the defrauded purchaser of land to seek rescission in equity, without concern for the adequacy of the legal remedy, many jurisdictions limit the defrauded purchaser of goods to his legal, quasi-contract remedy unless the legal remedy is inadequate. At bottom, the best one can say is that sometimes an adequate legal remedy bars equitable rescission, sometimes it does not, largely without rhyme or reason.

3. *On the substantive law.* Rescission and restitution are potentially available as remedies in a variety of contract cases. As *Hutchison* indicates, a contract can be rescinded for fraud, or, for that matter, for duress or coercion. When a contract is induced by innocent or negligent misrepresentations, rescission and restitution may be the only remedy available, if the jurisdiction does not recognize a tort action for negligent or innocent misrepresentation. Rescission and restitution are also available as remedies for a substantial breach of contract, as discussed in the notes following the next case.

Restitution is also an important remedy in cases of failed contracts. For example, where a plaintiff has conferred a benefit on a defendant pursuant to a contract that turns out to be invalid or unenforceable, restitution may be the only appropriate remedy. Thus, in Pyeatte v. Pyeatte, 135 Ariz. 346, 661 P.2d 196 (Ariz.App.1982), Mr. and Ms Pyeatte agreed that she would support him through law school, and that after he graduated, he would support her further education. One year after Mr. Pyeatte's graduation, however, he and Ms Pyeatte dissolved their marriage. In the dissolution proceeding, the trial court awarded Ms Pyeatte $23,000 in damages for the husband's breach of their oral contract.

On appeal, the court found that the terms of the oral agreement were not sufficiently certain to create a binding contract. Nonetheless, the court remanded the matter to the trial court, holding that Ms Pyeatte stated a cause of action for restitution:

> Appellee * * * argues that appellant's education, which she subsidized and which he obtained through the exhaustion of community assets constitutes a benefit for which he must, in equity, make restitution. * * *
>
> Restitution is available to a party to an agreement where he performs services for the other believing that there is a binding contract. * * *
>
> In Wisner [v. Wisner, 129 Ariz. 333, 631 P.2d 115 (App.1981) ]we observed that "[i]n our opinion, unjust enrichment, as a legal concept, is not properly applied in the setting of a marital relationship." Our observation was directed to the wife's claim in that case for restitution for the value of her *homemaking services* during the couple's 15–year marriage and for the couple's reduced income during the husband's lengthy training period. Where both spouses perform the usual and

incidental activities of the marital relationship, upon dissolution there can be no restitution for performance of these activities. Where, however, the facts demonstrate an agreement between the spouses and an extraordinary or unilateral effort by one spouse which inures solely to the benefit of the other by the time of the dissolution, the remedy of restitution is appropriate.

When a party seeks restitution of benefits conferred under an agreement, the interaction between the law of restitution and the law of contracts can be problematic. In *Pyeatte*, for example, given that the Pyeatte's contract was unenforceably vague, it may seem that requiring Mr. Pyeatte to pay Ms Pyeatte for her services is tantamount to enforcing the contract, therefore violating the rule against enforcing vague agreements.

Where the agreement is unenforceable because it is indefinite, that should not be a concern, however. The policy of the law of contracts is simply not to allow a party to recover the benefit of an indefinite bargain. So long as Ms Pyeatte's recovery is limited to restitution, that policy is not contravened.

In other cases, though, restitution may be inconsistent with the policies that make the underlying contract unenforceable. For example, if the contract is unenforceable because its end is illegal, it may be appropriate also to deny restitution in order to discourage such contracts. For a thorough discussion of whether restitution is available for benefits conferred under unenforceable contracts, see Dan B. Dobbs, Law of Remedies §§ 13.1 to 13.5 (2d ed.1993).

Another complication arises when the party who has breached a contract seeks restitution. For example, a builder may have performed a substantial amount of work on a landowner's property before breaching; or the buyer of goods may have paid part of the purchase price, and then reneged. If the breacher is sued, the value of his part performance is generally offset from the nonbreaching party's damages. But if the nonbreaching party does not sue, and the breacher seeks restitution, the traditional rule denies recovery. The fairness of this result is questionable, and inroads have been made on the traditional rule (as always, with the caveat that restitution must be limited to benefits that nonbreaching party actually received). Thus, the Uniform Commercial Code allows the breaching buyer to recover payments in excess of damages owed to the seller, UCC § 2–718(2), and a number of cases support restitution in favor of the breaching builder, if the landowner is actually enriched. See Dan B. Dobbs, Law of Remedies § 12.24 (2d ed.1993).

4. *On the remedy: The elements of restitutionary recovery.* The plaintiff's award in *Hutchison* can be divided into several components: (1) rescission of the deed, (2) refund of the purchase price, (3) incidental damages, (4) punitive damages and (5) attorney fees. That the defendant should refund the purchase price seems obvious: That is the restitutionary element of the action for rescission and restitution.

But is it so clear that the plaintiff should recover incidental damages, if this is an action for restitution? The court draws a distinction between compensatory damages, which it says would be inconsistent with the restitutionary nature of plaintiff's claim, and incidental damages, which are not.

What is the difference between compensatory damages and incidental damages? Aren't incidental damages a form of compensatory damages? If this is an action for restitution, in which the theory is to avoid unjust enrichment, how was the defendant enriched by the plaintiff's moving expenses? If damages are premised on letting the deal stand while compensating the injured party, while restitution is premised on undoing the deal, is it fair to let the plaintiff seek both in the same action?

Consider the court's response in Utemark v. Samuel, 118 Cal.App.2d 313, 317, 257 P.2d 656, 659 (1953):

> It appears to have been the purpose of the court to place the *defendants* in *status quo* regardless of any loss *plaintiffs* might suffer, but it was the plaintiffs, not the defendants, who were entitled to be restored to their former position. This is the purpose of rescission. Equity is solicitous that the innocent party who rescinds be not made to suffer. It exercises no such solicitude for the wrongdoer who has brought about a situation in which one or the other must lose.

Recall *Olwell's* account of the appropriate measure of damages: Where the plaintiff's loss is greater than the defendant's gain, and the defendant's conduct was tortious, the measure is the plaintiff's loss.

What this means is that the restitutionary goal and the tort goal end up the same: to restore the *status quo ante*. There is, however, an important difference for the Hutchisons. If they sued for tort damages, their award (in a jurisdiction that followed the "out of pocket" rule) would be a money judgement for the difference between what they paid for the land and its value. They would be stuck with the land. A restitutionary remedy returns them the full purchase price, and leaves the defendants holding the bag.

This raises an interesting conceptual problem. Should we conceive of cases where the restitutionary remedy simply gives the plaintiff back what he parted with as restitution cases, or should we reserve the label "restitution" for cases that truly aim at disgorging profits?

5. Suppose, in *Hutchison*, the plaintiffs had planned on operating a business on the property purchased from the defendant and, as a result of the defendant's fraud, they were unable to operate for several months? Following the logic of *Utemark*, should they be able to recover the profits they lost as consequential damages?

While many courts allow plaintiffs to recover incidental damages such as moving expenses, costs incurred in attempting to put the property to use, or consequential damages for harm caused by the misrepresented condition, lost profits have been routinely denied. With regard to contracts for the sale of goods, however, the Uniform Commercial Code, § 2–711, now expressly allows recovery of lost profits in addition to incidental and consequential damages when a buyer rescinds a contract for breach of warranty. When a buyer rescinds because of fraud, lost profits are recoverable under the Code in jurisdictions following the benefit of the bargain rule, but not in jurisdictions where fraud damages are limited to out of pocket losses. See George E. Palmer, Law of Restitution § 3.9 at 280 (1978).

6. The award of attorney's fees to the plaintiffs in *Hutchison* is enigmatic. As chapter 10 discusses, under the American rule, each party is

liable for its own attorney's fees unless one of a limited number of exceptions applies. There is no general exception for restitution cases. Possibly, the Hutchison's contract contained a clause providing for the payment of attorneys' fees to the prevailing party in the event of a dispute. Although courts occasionally deny enforcement of such clauses on the grounds that the contract has been rescinded, most courts recognize that restitution is simply an alternative remedy for the underlying fraud or breach, and that the fiction of rescission does not change the character of the action. Compare Bodenhamer v. Patterson, 278 Or. 367, 563 P.2d 1212 (1977)(denying attorney's fees) with Katz v. Van Der Noord, 546 So.2d 1047 (Fla.1989)(fees awarded).

7. Should punitive damages be recoverable in a restitution case? Courts are divided, according to Professor Dobbs. Dan B. Dobbs, Law of Remedies § 4.5(5)(2d ed.1993). Some see the doctrine of election of remedies as a bar, although the discussion above, at p. 530, should make it clear that it need not be. Others deny recovery because punitive damages cannot be awarded without actual, compensatory damages (see text at p. 518), or because punitive damages were not awarded in equity courts. See Alcorn County, Mississippi v. U.S. Interstate Supplies, Inc. 731 F.2d 1160 (5th Cir.1984). None of these reasons can really withstand critical scrutiny, and the trend is probably to allow punitive damages where fraud, oppression or malice is shown.

## EARTHINFO, INC. v. HYDROSPHERE RESOURCE CONSULTANTS, INC.

Supreme Court of Colorado, 1995.
900 P.2d 113.

JUSTICE SCOTT delivered the Opinion of the Court.

In January 1990, Hydrosphere Resource Consultants, Inc. (Hydrosphere), filed this action against petitioner, EarthInfo, Inc. (EarthInfo), seeking to rescind the parties' software development contracts due to EarthInfo's failure to make royalty payments. The trial court determined that EarthInfo had breached its contracts with Hydrosphere, ordered the contracts rescinded, and ordered that EarthInfo repay to Hydrosphere all the net profits it realized as a result of its breach. The court of appeals affirmed the trial court. * * *

I

Between 1986 and 1988, Hydrosphere entered into several contracts with US West, Inc. (US West) * * * to develop a number of products that employ CD–ROM technology. The products were designed to exploit hydrological and meteorological information collected by government agencies and to make that information available to the general public through Hydrosphere. Under the Contracts, Hydrosphere was to develop the CD–ROM units and create the software that enables end-users to access the otherwise public information on line from the CD–ROM units.

The Contracts vested all rights of ownership, copyrights, and patents in the products to US West. Under the terms of the Contracts, Hydrosphere had an ongoing obligation to provide technical support to end-users of the products, and US West was to create user manuals, and package and market the products. US West was also to pay Hydrosphere a fixed hourly development fee as well as royalties, calculated as a percentage of net sales, for "inventive product ideas." Payments under the Contracts were made on a quarterly basis.

On February 10, 1989, US West assigned its interest in the Contracts to EarthInfo . * * * EarthInfo agreed to pay US West $60,432. EarthInfo also entered into a separate agreement with Hydrosphere in which it agreed to honor US West's obligations under the Contracts, including the continued payment of royalties on the products already developed by Hydrosphere. EarthInfo fulfilled its contractual obligations through June 30, 1990. Hydrosphere then claimed that sales of a new derivative product were subject to royalty payments; EarthInfo claimed that the Contracts did not address derivative products, and therefore objected to increasing its royalty obligation. On October 30, 1990, when the third-quarter royalty payments were due, EarthInfo informed Hydrosphere that it was withholding these payments and any further royalty payments pending clarification of the basis for the royalty payments. EarthInfo continued to make payments of the fixed hourly development fees. A total of $19,000 in fixed fees was paid to Hydrosphere after June 30, 1990. After strained negotiations, Hydrosphere notified EarthInfo by letter on December 12, 1990, that it was rescinding the Contracts.

On January 11, 1991, Hydrosphere filed a breach of contract action against EarthInfo * * *. [After trial], the trial court ruled that EarthInfo did not owe royalties on sales of the derivative product, but the court determined that EarthInfo had breached its Contracts with Hydrosphere when it unilaterally suspended royalty payments on the other products. In a subsequent hearing, both parties sought rescission of the Contracts and restitution as a remedy. The trial court found "the breach was substantial" and that "due to the nature of the contracts between the parties and the depth of their disputes, damages would be inadequate." The trial court determined that the appropriate remedy would be rescission. * * * [The court] set June 30, 1990, the date through which EarthInfo had paid royalties, as the date of rescission.

As restitution between the parties, the court ordered EarthInfo to return to Hydrosphere all tangible property developed under the Contracts. In addition, the court found that "since rescission is an equitable remedy the court has discretion in determining the appropriate relief for the parties," and ordered EarthInfo to return to Hydrosphere all property, promotional materials and proprietary information related to the Hydrodata products. In addition, the court held EarthInfo responsible in equity "for the repayment to Hydrosphere of the net profits realized by EarthInfo" from June 30, 1990, until the date of the order, totaling $265,204.91. The court found Hydrosphere "in equity responsible for the repayment to EarthInfo of amounts paid by EarthInfo" in acquiring the Hydrodata product line from US West, totalling $60,432, and in fixed hourly development fees paid by EarthInfo after June 30, 1990, in the amount of $19,000. The costs incurred by EarthInfo were deducted from the net profits, resulting in a judgment in favor of Hydrosphere in the amount of $185,772.91.

EarthInfo appealed * * *.

II

This case presents a question of first impression for this court: whether a party that breaches a contract can be required to disgorge to the non-breaching party any benefits received as a result of the breach. Because this issue has remained largely unexplored, the rules of application are neither settled nor uniform. The difficulty in resolving this issue stems from a subtle conflict between the law of restitution and the law of contracts. This conflict is well articulated in what has become a leading article on the disgorgement principle:

> It is a principle of the law of restitution that one should not gain by one's own wrong; it is a principle of the law of contracts that damages for breach should be based on the injured party's lost expectation. In many cases, the principles are mutually consistent. If, on breach, the injured party's lost expectation equals or exceeds the gain by the party in breach, then damages based on expectation strip the party in breach of all gain, and make the injured party whole. But if the injured party's lost expectation is less than the gain realized by the party in breach, then damages based on expectation do not strip the party in breach of all gain. This situation brings the two principles into conflict.

E. Allan Farnsworth, Your Loss or My Gain? The Dilemma of the Disgorgement Principle in Breach of Contract, 94 Yale L.J. 1339, 1341 (1985). According to Farnsworth, courts have been reluctant to award profits to a nonbreaching party in a breach of contract action, thus allowing the party in breach to keep part of the gain, since in effect "a 'mere' breach of contract is not a 'wrong.'" Many others, however, have suggested that if the gain realized by the party in breach exceeds the injured party's loss, the measure of damages should strip the party in breach of all gain. We adopt neither approach as a general rule, and hold instead that whether profits are awarded to a nonbreaching party shall be determined within the discretion of the trial court on a case by case basis.

A

Rescission of a contract may be granted if the facts show a substantial breach, that the injury caused by the breach is irreparable, and that damages are inadequate, difficult or impossible to assess. A contract can also be rescinded by the "mutual consent" or "actions" of the parties.

Here, the trial court found not only that EarthInfo's breach was substantial, but that "due to the nature of the contracts between the parties and the depth of their disputes, damages would be inadequate." The trial court also found that although the Contracts "contemplate an ongoing relationship" between the parties, "[i]t is unrealistic to assume that damages could be computed and awarded and that the parties could then resume that relationship in a productive manner." The trial court found further that both parties sought rescission of the Contracts. Thus, the trial court concluded that rescission was necessary.[7] Since evidence in the record supports the trial court's findings, we conclude that rescission of the Contracts was warranted.

Rescission of a contract normally is accompanied by restitution on both sides. The contract is "being unmade, so restoration of benefits received under the contract seems to follow." Restitution measures the remedy by the defendant's gain and seeks to force disgorgement of that gain in order "to prevent the defendant's unjust enrichment." Restitution, which seeks to prevent unjust enrichment of the defendant, differs in principle from damages, which measure the remedy by the plaintiff's loss and seek to provide compensation for that loss. . As a consequence, "in some cases the defendant gains more than the plaintiff loses, so that the two remedies may differ in practice as well as in principle." [9]

A party seeking to rescind a contract must return the opposite party to the status quo ante, or the position in which he or she was prior to entering into the contract. The rule of returning the parties to the status quo ante is equitable and it requires the use of practicality in the readjustment of the parties' rights. Since rescission is an equitable remedy, it is within the trial court's sound discretion to determine the method for accomplishing a return to the status quo ante based upon the facts as determined by the trier of fact. All uncertainties as to the amount of benefit are to be resolved against the party committing the material breach.

The main options for measurement of the benefit conferred on the breaching party are these:

(1) the increased assets in the hands of the defendant from the receipt of property;

7. The trial court held: The court finds not only that the breach was substantial, but that due to the nature of the contracts between the parties and the depth of their disputes, damages would be inadequate. The contracts contemplate an ongoing relationship. It is unrealistic to assume that damages could be computed and awarded and that the parties could then resume that relationship in a productive manner.... Rescission is, therefore, an appropriate remedy. The court explained further that "[a] principal reason why a remedy limited to damages is inappropriate is that it would leave the products developed by Hydrosphere in the hands of a hostile and uncooperative EarthInfo, with the latter under a continuing duty to pay royalties, and also with an interest in promoting its own product line."

9. In the event a defendant's gains in a transaction exceed the plaintiff's losses and the plaintiff recovers the defendant's gains as restitution, the plaintiff will receive a greater reward and will be better off than if he or she were awarded damages for the defendant's breach. Thus, the plaintiff's expectations are exceeded because recovery is not based on the loss in value to the plaintiff, but rather on the benefit to the breaching defendant.

(2) the market value of services or intangibles provided to the defendant, without regard to whether the defendant's assets were actually increased; that is, the amount which it would cost to obtain similar services, whether those services prove to be useful or not;

(3) the use value of any benefits received, as measured by (i) market indicators such as rental value or interest or (ii) actual gains to the defendant from using the benefits, such as the gains identified in item (5) below;

(4) the gains realized by the defendant upon sale or transfer of an asset received from the plaintiff;

(5) collateral or secondary profits earned by the defendant by use of an asset received from the plaintiff, or, what is much the same thing, the savings effected by the use of the asset.

Dan B. Dobbs, Law of Remedies § 4.1(4) at 566–67 (footnote omitted). It is the fifth option, disgorgement of profits, which is principally at issue in this case.

No easy formulas exist for determining when restitution of profits realized by a party is permissible. Instead, the court must resort to general considerations of fairness, taking into account the nature of the defendant's wrong, the relative extent of his or her contribution, and the feasibility of separating this from the contribution traceable to the plaintiff's interest. 1 George E. Palmer, The Law of Restitution § 2.12 at 161 (1978) [hereinafter "Palmer"]. Thus, the more culpable the defendant's behavior, and the more direct the connection between the profits and the wrongdoing, the more likely that the plaintiff can recover all defendant's profits. See, e.g., Douglas Laycock, The Scope and Significance of Restitution, 67 Tex.L.Rev. 1277, 1289 (1989). The trial court must ultimately decide whether the whole circumstances of a case point to the conclusion that the defendant's retention of any profit is unjust.

Generally, the mere breach of a contract will not make the defendant accountable for benefits thereby obtained, whether through dealings with a third person or otherwise. As noted by Dobbs § 4.1(4) at 566–67:

> [t]o require a defendant to give up profits may operate with particular severity because at least some of the profits would almost always be attributable to the defendant's efforts or investment. So the profit recovery as a measure of restitution is extraordinary. In general, the defendant who is not a serious wrongdoer is held only to make restitution measured by actual gains in assets or in gains of services or intangibles which he [or she] in fact sought in the relevant transaction.

Id. If, however, the defendant's wrongdoing is intentional or substantial, or there are no other means of measuring the wrongdoer's enrichment, recovery of profits may be granted. See generally George E. Palmer, Law of Restitution § 2.12 at 164–65.

B

The trial court determined that EarthInfo's breach of the Contracts was substantial, damages were difficult to assess, and the parties mutually consented to rescission. Thus, the trial court required EarthInfo to disgorge all the profits it realized as a result of the breach. The court returned to EarthInfo the consideration it agreed to pay for the Hydrodata product line and also allowed it to retain the profits it earned when it was making the royalty payments. The court held EarthInfo responsible, however, for the repayment to Hydrosphere of the net profits it realized from June 30, 1990 until the date of the order, determining that to be the most equitable treatment of the parties given the nature of the dispute. We agree that EarthInfo must be required to disgorge the profits it accrued as a result of its breach since its breach was conscious and substantial.

The trial court found that the Contracts between EarthInfo and Hydrosphere did not require EarthInfo to pay royalties on sales of the derivative product. EarthInfo was still required, however, to pay royalties on all other products under the written Contracts. The trial court determined that EarthInfo's repudiation of its long-standing royalty obligations to Hydrosphere was a substantial breach of the Hydrodata Contracts. The trial court's factual determinations are supported by the evidence and should not be disturbed on appeal absent a clear showing of abuse of discretion. The trial court's order represents a permissible exercise of its discretion.

Since the record supports the trial court's findings that EarthInfo consciously and substantially breached its Contracts with Hydrosphere, damages were difficult to assess, and the parties mutually agreed to rescission, retention of profits by EarthInfo would be an unjust enrichment. Accordingly, we find that the extraordinary remedy of restitution and disgorgement of profits is justified.

III

The remaining issue then is the determination of the profits to be returned to Hydrosphere. The petitioner contends that the trial court erred in failing to apportion the net profits in a way that reflected the relative contributions to those profits by the parties. We agree.

"Courts have recognized that some apportionment must be made between those profits attributable to the plaintiff's property and those earned by the defendant's efforts and investment, limiting the plaintiff to the profits fairly attributable to his share." "Even the wilful wrongdoer should not be made to give up that which is his [or her] own; the principle is disgorgement, not plunder." The defendant's personal efforts in contributing to profits [sic] must be taken into account, but are often difficult to measure. For example, if the defendant uses the plaintiff's machine in producing goods, which it packages, distributes and sells to retail customers, it may increase its profits, but we are not so sure that the increase has much if any connection with the plaintiff's machine. We can be sure, however, that the defendant's profits relate in part to the defendant's own investments, efforts, or enterprising attitude. [Dobbs § 4.5(3)] at 647.

Dobbs' example of profit-making complexity is similar to the profit-making in the case at hand. EarthInfo used Hydrosphere's software programming in five items produced, packaged, distributed, and sold by EarthInfo. EarthInfo's marketing, packaging and enhancement of the products presumably contributed to the earning of the net profits; that contribution should be accounted for and withheld from the disgorgement of those profits by Hydrosphere.

No single rule governing the burden of proving apportionment is adequate for all cases or all facets of a single case. Profit claims can be calculated first by identifying and deducting legitimate business expenses from gross income. The defendant usually has the best access to this information and may properly be required to prove such expenses. Second, gross income of the defendant is produced at least in part "by investment, enterprise, and management skill of the defendant," and the defendant should receive credit for its own efforts and investments. ... The court must determine which part of the profit results from the defendant's own independent efforts and which part results from the benefits provided by the plaintiff. The court must seek to determine a fair apportionment that will result in a reasonable approximation or informed estimate of the relative contributions of the two parties. The allocation of the burden of establishing such approximation, and degree of specificity of proof required, may be affected by such factors as the seriousness of the defendant's wrongdoing and the extent to which the plaintiff's contribution was at risk in the profit making enterprise. Where the relative contributions of the two parties are inseparable or untraceable, there should be no recovery of profits by the plaintiff unless the defendant is a very serious wrongdoer. In the present case, considering the nature and extent of the breach as well as the other relevant factors, we hold that it is the burden of the plaintiff to establish facts sufficient to permit the trial court to determine the relative contributions of the parties so that profits can be fairly apportioned. * * *

The trial court made no findings with respect to the relative contributions of each party and whether they are inseparable. Thus, this case should be remanded to the trial court for further proceedings so that the court's order that EarthInfo disgorge its profits is limited to those profits attributable to Hydrosphere. Accordingly, we affirm in part, reverse in part, and return this case to the court of appeals with directions that it remand the case to the trial court for recalculation of wrongful profits attributable to Hydrosphere and entry of a new order of restitution.

### *Notes*

1. According to the Restatement (Second) of Contracts, the victim of a serious breach or repudiation of contract is entitled "to restitution for any benefit that he has conferred on the other party by way of part performance or reliance." Restatement (Second) of Contracts § 373(a). The only exception is that there is no right to restitution if the victim has completely

performed and the only obligation owing is the payment of a definite sum of money for the performance. Id. § 373(b). *EarthInfo* simply takes this principle to its logical extreme, by measuring the restitutionary recovery according to principles developed in restitution cases like *Olwell* (text at p. 672).

2. Restitutionary recovery is particularly valuable—and controversial—when a party finds itself in a losing contract. When enmeshed in a losing deal, there is a strong incentive for a party to find a way out, if that can be done without risking liability for damages. Think back, for example, to EVRA Corp. v. Swiss Bank, at p. 650. Once the market rate for charters rose higher than the rate in the long-term charter the parties had agreed to, the ship owner had a strong incentive to insist on strict performance of the charter agreement. If the charterer could be induced to breach, then the ship owner would be free to call off the deal and charter the ship at market rates.

This incentive to induce the other party to breach when you find yourself in a losing contract is exacerbated if the nonbreaching party can also sue for restitution. Suppose a builder agrees to build a house for a contract price of $100,000. When the house is half finished, the builder realizes the construction has cost her $60,000 so far, and it will take another $60,000 in labor and materials to finish the house. She has made a bad deal. If she walks away and is sued for breach, she will have to pay the cost of completing the house, less the unpaid contract price, and she will lose $20,000.

Consider, however, what happens if she can induce the owner to breach. If the owner has made partial payments, and the jurisdiction prohibits restitution in favor of a breaching party, she may come out ahead. Or, she can sue for breach and seek reliance damages, but as we have already seen, her reliance damages will be limited in order to prevent giving her more than the benefit of her bargain.

So, suppose instead of suing for breach of contract damages, she asks for rescission of the contract, and restitution. She escapes from her obligation to complete the performance, and recovers damages based upon the value of the performance she has conferred on the owner. Assuming the value of her labor and materials is closer to the $60,000 it cost her to perform than to the contract price, she walks away without any loss.

Does that seem like the right result? The question is controversial. On the one hand, if recovery is based on unjust enrichment, it seems only logical that the plaintiff should recover the full value of the benefits the defendant received. On the other hand, full restitutionary recovery effectively rewrites the parties' bargain, obliging the defendant to pay full value when he promised—with the plaintiff's consent—to pay less. It invites opportunism, giving the party who made a bad deal a tremendous incentive to induce a breach by the other party. It complicates reaching fair settlements, and is not a remedy either party to a contract would agree to in advance of a breach. Andrew Kull, Restitution as a Remedy for Breach of Contract, 67 S.C.L.Rev. 1465 (1994).

Professor Kull argues that the Restatement's position rests on a misunderstanding of rescission as a remedy for breach. Id. Rescission, properly understood, is a remedy that simply unwinds an agreement that can no longer go forward, and it traditionally was available as a remedy only where the transaction was still capable of being unwound. The early cases thus limited rescission to cases in which 1) the breach was substantial, tantamount to a repudiation of the contract, 2) the transaction could be fully unwound by returning the benefits received, *in specie*, and 3) the performance had not gone so far as to make unwinding the deal impracticable. Id. at 1515–16. While these restrictions may be too strict, Professor Kull urges that limitations along these lines are necessary to avoid inefficiency and inequity. Does he have a point?

3. When a defendant breaches in order to make a profit from the breach, it raises a different question than that addressed by Professor Kull. Then, allowing restitution measured by the defendant's profits-disgorgement-would seem to be at odds with another basic premise of contract damages, the notion of efficient breach. See text at pp. 647–648. Can the result in *EarthInfo* be reconciled with the notion that it is sound policy encourage economically efficient breaches?

While the *EarthInfo* court relies heavily on Professor Palmer's treatise to justify its result, Professor Palmer in fact is skeptical of profit-based restitution as a remedy for breach of contract. According to Professor Palmer, courts have ordered contract breachers to disgorge their profits only in a few situations. When a seller in a land sale agreement breaches in order to sell to a third party at a higher price, for example, many courts allow the original buyer to impose a constructive trust on the profit from the resale. Timko v. Useful Homes Corp., 114 N.J.Eq. 433, 168 A. 824 (1933). (The theory, known as equitable conversion, is that the buyer becomes the equitable owner of the property when the contract is formed). Also, when an employee breaches his contract by revealing trade secrets, or by violating a covenant not to compete, courts sometimes require him to disgorge his profits. See George E. Palmer, Law of Restitution § 4.9 at 488 (1978). Outside of these contexts, Professor Palmer asserts, "there is small likelihood that courts will grant restitution of gains obtained [from third parties] through breach of contract. Certainly the available evidence points to the rejection of any general principle to this effect." Id. at § 4.9(e) at 449.

4. What, though, should be made of the fact that Earthinfo's breach was deliberate and unexcused? After all, Earthinfo had no apparent reason not to pay the royalties it acknowledged were due, except perhaps to exert settlement leverage over Hydrosphere in its dispute over the new products. Without a restitutionary remedy, does the threat of contract damages provide any disincentive to this type of behavior?

There are commentators who believe disgorgement is an appropriate remedy for breach of contract in some cases. Professor E.Allan Farnsworth, for example, has argued that in cases of "abuse of contract," where the defendant's breach has left the plaintiff with no way to obtain a reasonable substitute for the defendant's performance, restitution measured by the defendant's savings from breach should be available, because expectation damages present a significant risk of undercompensation. E. Allan Farnsworth, Your Loss or My Gain? The Dilemma of the Disgorgement Principle in Breach of Contract, 94 Yale L.J. 1339 (1985). Would this be such a case?

Professor Farnsworth's justification for disgorgement is very similar to an explanation sometimes offered for allowing punitive damages for bad faith breach of an insurance contract. See text at p. 648; Richard E. Speidel, The Borderland of Contract, 10 N.Ky.L.Rev. 163, 192–193 (1983)(punitive damages are appropriate "where the breaching party captures an immediate gain under circumstances where the prospect of full compensation to the aggrieved party is low.") Does disgorgement offer an appealing alternative to punitive damages in some of the situations discussed earlier at pp. 649–650?

5. Alternatively, isn't EarthInfo's behavior—using the property without paying for it—almost like a conversion, for which disgorgement is an appropriate remedy? What result would the rule Professor Daniel Friedman advocates, at p. 676 in the text, reach?

6. Could restitution offer a way out of the *Peevyhouse/Groves* dilemma, discussed at p. 627 in the text? Recovery could be measured by the defendant's savings; that is, "the saving of the costs of modification." E. Allan Farnsworth, Your Loss or My Gain? The Dilemma of the Disgorgement Principle in Breach of Contract, 94 Yale L.J. 1339, 1393 (1985). In other words, the plaintiff should be able to recover whatever amount he would have charged had the defendant requested a modification of the contract to conform with his performance. Id. at 1389.

## E. EQUITABLE RESTITUTIONARY REMEDIES

### *Problem: Moore v. Regents of the University of California*

John Moore suffered from hairy cell leukemia. As part of his treatment, a doctor at the University of California's hospital removed Moore's spleen, which had swollen from its normal weight of a few ounces to more than fifteen pounds. Using various bioengineering techniques, the doctor and his research colleagues developed a cell line using Moore's spleen that has extraordinary research and therapeutic potential. It has already been patented and sold to biotech firms, and the cell line's worth is probably measured in the tens, if not hundreds of millions of dollars. Assuming that the doctor violated his fiduciary duty to disclose his research research and economic interests before obtaining Moore's consent to the operation (see Moore v. Regents of University of California, 51 Cal.3d 120, 271 Cal.Rptr. 146, 793 P.2d 479 (1990), cert. denied, 499 U.S. 936, 111 S.Ct. 1388, 113 L.Ed.2d 444 (1991)), what remedies may be available to Moore?

### LATHAM v. FATHER DIVINE

Court of Appeals of New York, 1949.
299 N.Y. 22, 85 N.E.2d 168.

DESMOND, J.

* * * For present purposes, then, we have a case where one possessed of a large property and having already made a will leaving it to certain persons, expressed an intent to make a new testament to contain

legacies to other persons, attempted to carry out that intention by having a new will drawn which contained a large legacy to those others, but was, by means of misrepresentations, undue influence, force, and indeed, murder, prevented, by the beneficiaries named in the existing will, from signing the new one. Plaintiffs say that those facts, if proven, would entitle them to a judicial declaration, which their prayer for judgment demands, that defendants, taking under the already probated will, hold what they have so taken as constructive trustees for plaintiffs, whom decedent wished to, tried to, and was kept from, benefiting.* * *

A constructive trust will be erected whenever necessary to satisfy the demands of justice. Since a constructive trust is merely "the formula through which the conscience of equity finds expression" its applicability is limited only by the inventiveness of men who find new ways to enrich themselves unjustly by grasping what should not belong to them. Nothing short of true and complete justice satisfies equity, and, always assuming these allegations to be true, there seems no way of achieving total justice except [by the imposition of a constructive trust].

## SNEPP v. UNITED STATES

Supreme Court of the United States, 1980.
444 U.S. 507, 100 S.Ct. 763, 62 L.Ed.2d 704.

PER CURIAM. * * *

I

Based on his experiences as a CIA agent, Snepp published a book about certain CIA activities in South Vietnam. Snepp published the account without submitting it to the Agency for prepublication review. As an express condition of his employment with the CIA in 1968, however, Snepp had executed an agreement promising that he would "not . . . publish . . . any information or material relating to the Agency, its activities or intelligence activities generally, either during or after the term of [his] employment . . . without specific prior approval by the Agency." The promise was an integral part of Snepp's concurrent undertaking "not to disclose any classified information relating to the Agency without proper authorization." Thus, Snepp had pledged not to divulge *classified* information and not to publish *any* information without prepublication clearance. The Government brought this suit to enforce Snepp's agreement. It sought a declaration that Snepp had breached the contract, an injunction requiring Snepp to submit future writings for prepublication review, and an order imposing a constructive trust for the Government's benefit on all profits that Snepp might earn from publishing the book in violation of his fiduciary obligations to the Agency.

The District Court found that Snepp had "willfully, deliberately and surreptitiously breached his position of trust with the CIA and the [1968] secrecy agreement" by publishing his book without submitting it for prepublication review. The court also found that Snepp deliberately misled CIA officials into believing that he would submit the book for prepublication clearance. Finally, the court determined as a fact that publication of the book had "caused the United States irreparable harm and loss." The District Court therefore enjoined future breaches of Snepp's agreement and imposed a constructive trust on Snepp's profits.

The Court of Appeals accepted the findings of the District Court and agreed that Snepp had breached a valid contract. It specifically affirmed the finding that Snepp's failure to submit his manuscript for prepublication review had inflicted "irreparable harm" on intelligence activities vital to our national security. Thus, the court upheld the injunction against future violations of Snepp's prepublication obligation. The court, however, concluded that the record did not support imposition of a constructive trust. The conclusion rested on the court's perception that Snepp had a First Amendment right to publish unclassified information and the Government's concession—for the purposes of this litigation—that Snepp's book divulged no classified intelligence. In other words, the court thought that Snepp's fiduciary obligation extended only to preserving the confidentiality of classified material. It therefore limited recovery to nominal damages and to the possibility of punitive damages if the Government—in a jury trial—could prove tortious conduct. * * *

II

Snepp's employment with the CIA involved an extremely high degree of trust. In the opening sentence of the agreement that he signed, Snepp explicitly recognized that he was entering a trust relationship. The trust agreement specifically imposed the obligation not to publish *any* information relating to the Agency without submitting the information for clearance. Snepp stipulated at trial that—after undertaking this obligation—he had been "assigned to various positions of trust" and that he had been granted "frequent access to classified information, including information regarding intelligence sources and methods." Snepp published his book about CIA activities on the basis of this background and exposure. He deliberately and surreptitiously violated his obligation to submit all material for prepublication review. Thus, he exposed the classified information with which he had been entrusted to the risk of disclosure.

Whether Snepp violated his trust does not depend upon whether his book actually contained classified information. The Government does not deny—as a general principle—Snepp's right to publish unclassified information. Nor does it contend—at this stage of the litigation—that Snepp's book contains classified material. The Government simply claims that, in light of the special trust reposed in him and the agreement that he signed, Snepp should have given the CIA an opportunity to determine whether the material he proposed to publish would compromise classified information or sources. Neither of the Government's concessions undercuts its claim that Snepp's failure to submit to prepublication review was a breach of his trust.

Both the District Court and the Court of Appeals found that a former intelligence agent's publication of unreviewed material relating to intelligence activities can be detrimental to vital national interests even if the published information is unclassified. When a former agent relies on his own judgment about what information is detrimental, he may reveal information that the CIA—with its broader understanding of what may expose classified information and confidential sources—could have identified as harmful. In addition to receiving intelligence from domestically based or controlled sources, the CIA obtains information from the intelligence services of friendly nations and from agents operating in foreign countries. The continued availability of these foreign sources depends upon the CIA's ability to guarantee the security of information that might compromise them and even endanger the personal safety of foreign agents.

Undisputed evidence in this case shows that a CIA agent's violation of his obligation to submit writings about the Agency for prepublication review impairs the CIA's ability to perform its statutory duties. Admiral Turner, Director of the CIA, testified without contradiction that Snepp's book and others like it have seriously impaired the effectiveness of American intelligence operations. He said:

> "Over the last six to nine months, we have had a number of sources discontinue work with us. We have had more sources tell us that they are very nervous about continuing work with us. We have had very strong complaints from a number of foreign intelligence services with whom we conduct liaison, who have questioned whether they should continue exchanging information with us, for fear it will not remain secret. I cannot estimate to you how many potential sources or liaison arrangements have never germinated because people were unwilling to enter into business with us."

In view of this and other evidence in the record, both the District Court and the Court of Appeals recognized that Snepp's breach of his explicit obligation to submit his material—classified or not—for prepublication clearance has irreparably harmed the United States Government.

III

The decision of the Court of Appeals denies the Government the most appropriate remedy for Snepp's acknowledged wrong. Indeed, as a practical matter, the decision may well leave the Government with no reliable deterrent against similar breaches of security. No one disputes that the actual damages attributable to a publication such as Snepp's generally are unquantifiable. Nominal damages are a hollow alternative, certain to deter no one. The punitive damages recoverable after a jury trial are speculative and unusual. Even if recovered, they may bear no relation to either the Government's irreparable loss or Snepp's unjust gain.

The Government could not pursue the only remedy that the Court of Appeals left it without losing the benefit of the bargain it seeks to enforce. Proof of the tortious conduct necessary to sustain an award of punitive damages might force the Government to disclose some of the very confidences that Snepp promised to protect. The trial of such a suit, before a jury if the defendant so elects, would subject the CIA and its officials to probing discovery into the Agency's highly confidential affairs. Rarely would the Government run this risk. In a letter introduced at Snepp's trial, former CIA Director Colby noted the analogous problem in criminal cases. Existing law, he stated, "requires the revelation in open court of confirming or additional information of such a nature that the potential damage to the national security precludes prosecution." When the Government cannot secure its remedy without unacceptable risks, it has no remedy at all.

A constructive trust, on the other hand, protects both the Government and the former agent from unwarranted risks. This remedy is the natural and customary consequence of a breach of trust. It deals fairly with both parties by conforming relief to the dimensions of the wrong. If the agent secures prepublication clearance, he can publish with no fear of liability. If the agent publishes unreviewed material in violation of his fiduciary and contractual obligation, the trust remedy simply requires him to disgorge the benefits of his faithlessness. Since the remedy is swift and sure, it is tailored to deter those who would place sensitive information at risk. And since the remedy reaches only funds attributable to the breach, it cannot saddle the former agent with exemplary damages out of all proportion to his gain. The decision of the Court of Appeals would deprive the Government of this equitable and effective means of protecting intelligence that may contribute to national security. We therefore reverse the judgment of the Court of Appeals insofar as it refused to impose a constructive trust on Snepp's profits, and we remand the cases to the Court of Appeals for reinstatement of the full judgment of the District Court.

MR. JUSTICE STEVENS, with whom MR. JUSTICE BRENNAN and MR. JUSTICE MARSHALL join, dissenting.

In 1968, Frank W. Snepp signed an employment agreement with the CIA in which he agreed to submit to the Agency any information he intended to publish about it for prepublication review. The purpose of such an agreement, as the Fourth Circuit held, is not to give the CIA the power to censor its employees' critical speech, but rather to ensure that classified, nonpublic information is not disclosed without the Agency's permission.

In this case Snepp admittedly breached his duty to submit the manuscript of his book, *Decent Interval*, to the CIA for prepublication review. However, the Government has conceded that the book contains no classified, nonpublic material. Thus, by definition, the interest in confidentiality that Snepp's contract was designed to protect has not been compromised. Nevertheless, the Court today grants the Government unprecedented and drastic relief in the form of a constructive trust over the profits derived by Snepp from the sale of the book. Because that remedy is not authorized by any applicable law and because it is most inappropriate for the Court to dispose of this novel issue summarily on the Government's conditional cross-petition for certiorari, I respectfully dissent.

I

The rule of law the Court announces today is not supported by statute, by the contract, or by the common law. Although Congress has enacted a number of criminal statutes punishing the unauthorized dissemination of certain types of classified information, it has not seen fit to authorize the constructive trust remedy the Court creates today. Nor does either of the contracts Snepp signed with the Agency provide for any such remedy in the event of a breach. The Court's *per curiam* opinion seems to suggest that its result is supported by a blend of the law of trusts and the law of contracts. But neither of these branches of the common law supports the imposition of a constructive trust under the circumstances of this case.

Plainly this is not a typical trust situation in which a settlor has conveyed legal title to certain assets to a trustee for the use and benefit of designated beneficiaries. Rather, it is an employment relationship in which the employee possesses fiduciary obligations arising out of his duty of loyalty to his employer. One of those obligations, long recognized by the common law even in the absence of a written employment agreement, is the duty to protect confidential or "classified" information. If Snepp had breached that obligation, the common law would support the implication of a constructive trust upon the benefits derived from his misuse of confidential information.

But Snepp did not breach his duty to protect confidential information. Rather, he breached a contractual duty, imposed in aid of the basic duty to maintain confidentiality, to obtain prepublication clearance. In order to justify the imposition of a constructive trust, the majority attempts to equate this contractual duty with Snepp's duty not to disclose, labeling them both as "fiduciary." I find nothing in the common law to support such an approach. * * *

[E]ven assuming that Snepp's covenant to submit to prepublication review should be enforced, the constructive trust imposed by the Court is not an appropriate remedy. If an employee has used his employer's confidential information for his own personal profit, a constructive trust over those profits is obviously an appropriate remedy because the profits are the direct result of the breach. But Snepp admittedly did not use confidential information in his book; nor were the profits from his book in any sense a product of his failure to submit the book for prepublication review. For, even if Snepp had submitted the book to the Agency for prepublication review, the Government's censorship authority would surely have been limited to the excision of classified material. In this case, then, it would have been obliged to clear the book for publication in precisely the same form as it now stands. Thus, Snepp has not gained any profits as a result of his breach; the Government, rather than Snepp, will be unjustly enriched if he is required to disgorge profits attributable entirely to his own legitimate activity.

Despite the fact that Snepp has not caused the Government the type of harm that would ordinarily be remedied by the imposition of a constructive trust, the Court attempts to justify a constructive trust remedy on the ground that the Government has suffered *some* harm. The Court states that publication of "unreviewed material" by a former CIA agent "can be detrimental to vital national interests even if the published information is unclassified." * * * I do not believe, however, that the Agency has any authority to censor its employees' publication of unclassified information on the basis of its opinion that publication may be "detrimental to vital national interests" or otherwise "identified as harmful." * * *

The Court also relies to some extent on the Government's theory at trial that Snepp caused it harm by flouting his prepublication review obligation and thus making it appear that the CIA was powerless to prevent its agents from publishing any information they chose to publish, whether classified or not. * * *

In any event, to the extent that the Government seeks to punish Snepp for the generalized harm he has caused by failing to submit to prepublication review and to deter others from following in his footsteps, punitive damages is, as the Court of Appeals held, clearly the preferable remedy "since a constructive trust depends on the concept of unjust enrichment rather than deterrence and punishment." * * *

## *Notes*

1. In the excerpt that begins this chapter, Professor Laycock identifies three practical advantages to seeking restitution. Which of those three applies here?

2. *On procedure.* The constructive trust is an equitable remedy. Must there be an independent basis for equitable jurisdiction—an inadequate legal remedy, for example—before a constructive trust can be imposed? Nominally, the answer may be yes, but at least according to Professor Palmer, courts frequently ignore the requirement. See George E. Palmer, Law of Restitution § 1.6 at 36 (1978).

Further, where a case involves wrongdoing by a trustee or other fiduciary, there was no adequate remedy at law. At common law, no form of action existed to enforce a trust. If a grantor conveyed legal title to a grantee, intending the property to be held in trust for some beneficiary, so far as the law courts were concerned the property belonged to the trustee. If the beneficiary wished to compel the trustee to honor the terms of the trust, he had to seek relief in equity, where the beneficiary's "equitable ownership" would be acknowledged. The equity courts, thus, got into the business of supervising trustees to ensure that they observed their fiduciary duties in the handling of funds and property entrusted to them.

Yet, it is important to recognize that the constructive trust and the express trust have little but the name in common. An express trust is a substantive legal arrangement. The establishment of the trust creates property rights in the beneficiary, and imposes substantive duties on the trustee. Does the recognition of a constructive trust similarly impose duties and create rights? Although occasionally courts will talk about the duties of a constructive trustee, it has generally been recognized that with regard to duties, the constructive trust is a remedy, not a substantive legal arrangement. The only "duty" of a constructive trustee is to comply with the court's order to transfer the property to the plaintiff.

3. *On the substantive law.* According to the Restatement of Restitution, § 190, "Where a person in a fiduciary relationship to another acquires property, and the acquisition or retention of the property is in violation of his duty as fiduciary, he holds it upon a constructive trust for the other." On the other hand, a mere breach of contract does not give rise to a constructive trust. Bear Kaufman Realty, Inc. v. Spec Development, Inc., 268 Ill.App.3d 898, 206 Ill.Dec. 239, 645 N.E.2d 244 (Ill.App.1994). According to Professor Palmer, the employer-employee relationship is not enough, standing alone, to impose an obligation to disgorge profits made from breach. George E. Palmer, Law of Restitution § 1.5 at 26 (1978), citing Williams v. Herring, 183 Iowa 127, 165 N.W. 342 (1917). On what basis, then, did the Court find that Snepp was a fiduciary? For a discussion of some of the problems in defining fiduciary relationships, see Deborah DeMott, Beyond Metaphor: An Analysis of Fiduciary Obligation, 1988 Duke L.J. 879.

Employees do stand in a fiduciary relationship to their employers for some purposes. Employers have recovered awards based on the profits former employees garnered by revealing trade secrets or confidential information, or by violating covenants not to compete. (The cases are collected in George E. Palmer, Law of Restitution § 2.8(b)(1978)). The information Snepp revealed, however, was not classified. How did Snepp do anything more than merely breach his contract? Suppose an employee breached his contract by quitting when he had promised to work for a specific period of time. Should his employer be able to assert a constructive trust over the wages he earns at his new job? Is the Court persuasive in its argument that Snepp violated his duty as fiduciary, as opposed to simply breaching his employment contract?

Trustees have a duty not to use a fiduciary position for personal profit. Thus, where trustees abscond with trust property, or use it for their own purposes, the constructive trust recaptures the misappropriated property, along with any profits or income derived from it by the trustee. The information Snepp used in his book, however, was conceded not to be classified or proprietary, so it is not clear that he used his fiduciary position for profit in this sense.

The duties of a fiduciary however, go farther: a fiduciary may not use her position for personal profit even where the profit is not obtained at the principal's expense. Mosser v. Darrow, 341 U.S. 267, 71 S.Ct. 680, 95 L.Ed. 927 (1951). Thus, trustees have been held accountable when they acquire an asset so related to the principal's business as to create a conflict of interest, even though the principal was offered and refused the asset. Pratt v. Shell Petroleum Corp., 100 F.2d 833 (10th Cir.1938). Similarly, fiduciaries who accept secret rewards or commissions have been held to hold them in constructive trust, though clearly the principal could never have received the benefit himself. Even profits obtained by a violation of law have been subject to a constructive trust, as in Diamond v. Oreamuno, 24 N.Y.2d 494, 301 N.Y.S.2d 78, 248 N.E.2d 910 (1969), where a constructive trust was imposed for a corporation's benefit on profits corporate officers realized through insider trading.

Plainly, the rationale of these cases is deterrence. Daniel Friedmann, Restitution of Benefits Obtained Through the Appropriation of Property or the Commission of a Wrong, 80 Colum.L.Rev. 504, 510 (1980). So, essentially, is the rationale of *Snepp*. Fiduciaries must not be allowed to profit from their wrongs, and, if they are to be stripped of their profits, the only logical party to receive the profits is the principal, windfall or no.

Stripping defendants of their profits is a powerful deterrent, attractive to the proponents of many policy goals. Thus, restitutionary remedies have been pressed into the service of crime prevention (see United States v. Banco Cafetero Panama, 797 F.2d 1154 (2d Cir.1986)(text at p. 717)(forfeiture of proceeds of drug transactions)), environmental protection (William Drayton, Economic Law Enforcement, 4 Harv.Envr.L.Rev. 1 (1980)(text at p. 485)(advocating a recapture standard that would measure the penalty for noncompliance with pollution regulations by the profits made by noncompliance), and even architectural preservation (see Jane P. Kourtis, The Constructive Trust: Equity's Answer to the Need for a Strong Deterrent to the Destruction of Historic Landmarks, 16 B.C.Envtl.Aff.L.Rev. 793 (1989)). How does restitution stack up against punitive damages as a deterrent? What are the advantages and disadvantages of each?

One objection to using the constructive trust to cause the defendant to disgorge his profits, however, is that profit-based restitution strikes too broadly, depriving the wrongdoer not only of the profits generated by his wrong, but also of the profits generated by his efforts, skill and talent. Indeed, the remedy has sometimes been denied precisely because sorting out the defendant's own contributions to the profit is impossibly complex. Dan B. Dobbs, Law of Remedies § 4.5(3) (2d ed.1993). Should some effort be made, therefore, to determine what profits Snepp would have made had he submitted the book for review and then published it? As the government conceded that the book contained no classified information, shouldn't it be presumed that the very same book would eventually have been published, only a little later? In some cases, it is possible to argue that it is appropriate to use the constructive trust to strip fiduciaries of their profits, because the principal in fact has a right to the fiduciary's efforts, skill and talent. Does that logic hold for *Snepp?* If so, shouldn't some effort be made to compensate Snepp for the time he spent writing the book?

4. *On the remedy*. The constructive trust imposed on Snepp's royalties strikingly resembles another equitable remedy available to redress unjust enrichment, the equitable accounting. One of the duties equity imposed upon trustees was the duty to account to the beneficiary for the disposition of the trust's property. Equitable accounting enforced that duty, allowing the beneficiary of a trust to hold the trustee to answer for the property entrusted to him; if the property was income-generating, the trustee could be held answerable for the profits through an accounting for profits. Dan B.

Dobbs, Law of Remedies § 4.3(5) (2d ed.1993). The difference between a constructive trust (which, through tracing can also reach profits generated by the property held in trust) and an accounting is that an accounting typically resulted in a money judgment against the trustee personally. Dale Oesterle, Deficiencies of the Restitutionary Right to Trace Misappropriated Property in Equity and in UCC § 9–306, 68 Cornell L.Rev. 172, 173 n. 4 (1983).

From its origins in the law of trusts, the accounting for profits later became available as a remedy whenever a fiduciary profited wrongfully from his position, or whenever profit-generating property was acquired wrongfully and the legal remedy was inadequate, either because tracing was involved or because the accounts involved were so complex that the simple forms of accounting available at law were inadequate. Dale Oesterle, Restitution and Reform, 79 Mich.L.Rev. 336, 351 (1979). For example, accounting for profits became available as a remedy in cases of unfair competition, trademark infringement and copyright infringement, among others. Dan B. Dobbs, Law of Remedies § 4.3 (2d ed.1993).

5. In a footnote, the Court upheld the prepublication agreement at issue against constitutional attack, finding that Snepp's voluntary agreement to submit to prepublication screening obviated any first amendment problems. Could the government require all its employees to sign prepublication agreements? In 1983, the Reagan Administration issued National Security Decision Directive 84, which suggested that anyone with access to sensitive information would have to sign a lifetime prepublication screening agreement. The directive was never implemented because of the controversy it engendered. Would the directive have withstood a first amendment challenge? See United States v. National Treasury Employees Union, ___ U.S. ___, 115 S.Ct. 1003, 130 L.Ed.2d 964 (1995)(ban on federal employees receiving honoraria unconstitutional at least as applied to lower level employees); Lee C. Bollinger, "Government Secrets: The First Amendment Implications of Prepublication Review Agreement," Statement for the Committee on Government Operations, U.S. House of Representatives, Oct. 19, 1983. In Agee v. Central Intelligence Agency, 500 F.Supp. 506 (D.D.C.1980), a constructive trust over the royalties from a book published without prepublication review was denied because the government was enforcing prepublication agreements selectively, demonstrating that the enforcement decision was "clouded by content considerations rather than wholly legitimate concerns for security."

Over half of the states have enacted statutes impressing an "involuntary trust" on any profits generated by novels, movies, plays, etc. written by criminals about their crimes. See, e.g., Cal. Civ. Code § 2225; N.Y. Executive Law § 632–A. These statutes require that the profits be held in trust for a specified number of years for the benefit of victims who may establish damage claims against the criminal. Thus, they are not truly restitutionary; rather, they operate as a form of garnishment. (Garnishment is discussed in chapter 8.)

The New York statute was found unconstitutional by a unanimous Court, however, in Simon and Schuster, Inc. v. Members of the New York State Crime Victims Board, 502 U.S. 105, 112 S.Ct. 501, 116 L.Ed.2d 476

(1991). The first two steps in Justice O'Connor's opinion are straightforward. First, the statute imposed a content-based restriction on speech, which could only be justified by a compelling state interest. Second, while the state has a compelling interest in compensating the victims from the fruit of the crime, it has "little if any interest" in singling out speech as the sole source of compensation.

Therefore, the question becomes, is the statute narrowly tailored to reach the goal of ensuring that victims are compensated from the proceeds of the crime? Justice O'Connor concluded that New York's statute was not. The opinion reviews a list of works from Thoreau's Civil Disobedience to The Confessions of St. Augustine that might have been subject to a trust under the statute's definitions, and concludes that the statute was over inclusive: "The Son of Sam law clearly reaches a wide range of literature that does not enable a criminal to profit from his crime while a victim remains uncompensated." 505 U.S. at 122, 112 S.Ct. at 511. Justice Blackmun concurred, but urged that the Court, in light of the fact that many jurisdictions have similar statutes, should have given the lower courts additional guidance by finding the statute unconstitutionally under inclusive as well. Justice Kennedy concurred, arguing that even a compelling interest cannot justify a direct, content-based burden on speech protected by the first amendment.

## TORRES v. EASTLICK (IN RE NORTH AMERICAN COIN & CURRENCY, LTD)

United States Court of Appeals, Ninth Circuit, 1985.
767 F.2d 1573, cert. denied 475 U.S. 1083, 106 S.Ct. 1462, 89 L.Ed.2d 719 (1986).

CANBY, CIRCUIT JUDGE:

North American Coin and Currency, Ltd. (hereinafter NAC or debtor) was an Arizona corporation in the business of buying and selling precious metals. The appellants are former customers of NAC who placed orders with the company and paid for them during the week of September 13, 1982, immediately before NAC filed for voluntary reorganization under Chapter 11 of the Bankruptcy Code. They brought this class action against the Bankruptcy Trustee, seeking to recover their funds from the bankruptcy estate. They claim that the trustee holds the funds in constructive trust for them because the debtor obtained the money by fraud or misrepresentation. On cross-motions for summary judgment, the bankruptcy court found for the trustee. The district court affirmed. We have jurisdiction over the appeal pursuant to 28 U.S.C. § 1291, and we affirm. * * *

[After discovering that NAC was threatened with insolvency, several people affiliated with NAC ("the principals") decided that they should try to operate the company for one more week until a scheduled board of director's and shareholder's meeting. To keep the company operating, while protecting new customers in case the company did not survive, the principals placed all receipts from new transactions during the week before the shareholder's meeting in a new bank account, labeled "Special Trust Account." If the board of directors voted to keep the company going and the shareholders infused the necessary new capital, the trust account funds were to be used to fill the customers' precious metals orders. If the company failed, the principals anticipated that the customers would get their money back.]

* * * NAC filed a Chapter 11 petition for reorganization on September 23, 1982. The funds in the "Special Trust Account" remain intact. The plaintiffs now assert that the trustee for NAC holds those funds in constructive trust for them.

Property that is truly in trust is not "property of the [trustee's] estate" within the meaning of section 541 of the Bankruptcy Code, 11 U.S.C. § 541. Plaintiffs argue that the same result must follow for property that is subject to a constructive trust. They further contend that, because the existence and nature of the debtor's interests in property are determined by reference to state law, they are entitled to all of the funds in the Special Account if Arizona law would view those funds as subject to a constructive trust.

While we agree that any constructive trust that is given effect must be a creature of Arizona law, we cannot accept the proposition that the bankruptcy estate is automatically deprived of any funds that state law might find subject to a constructive trust. * * * A constructive trust is not the same kind of interest in property as a joint tenancy or a remainder. It is a remedy, flexibly fashioned in equity to provide relief where a balancing of interests in the context of a particular case seems to call for it. Moreover, in the case presented here it is an inchoate remedy; we are not dealing with property that a state court decree has in the past placed under a constructive trust. We necessarily act very cautiously in exercising such a relatively undefined equitable power in favor of one group of potential creditors at the expense of other creditors, for ratable distribution among all creditors is one of the strongest policies behind the bankruptcy laws.

While state law must be applied in a manner consistent with federal bankruptcy law, we do not suggest that it is irrelevant. Arizona law permits the imposition of a constructive trust "whenever title to property has been obtained through actual fraud, misrepresentation, concealment, undue influence, duress, or through any other means which render it unconscionable for the holder of legal title to retain and enjoy its beneficial interest."

In permitting the imposition of a constructive trust for actions amounting to actual fraud, Arizona law is not inconsistent with federal bankruptcy law. Bankruptcy trustees have been held to have no interest in property acquired by fraud of bankrupts, as against the rightful owners of the property. The principle underlying this rule is that the creditors should not benefit from fraud at the expense of those who have been defrauded. * * *

In Arizona, as elsewhere, "actual fraud" is characterized by a willful intent to deceive. The debtor commits fraud, even though he has made no affirmative false representations, if he commits himself to a transaction with no intention of carrying it out. An intention not to carry out the transaction—in other words, a fraudulent intent—may be inferred where the debtor conceals his insolvency knowing that his financial situation is so hopeless that he can never meet the obligation he has acquired. However, the debtor's mere failure to disclose his insolvency, without more, does not constitute a fraud entitling the creditor to rescind the transaction. If the debtor believes in good faith that he will be able to carry out the transaction, he lacks the deceptive intent necessary for a finding of fraud.

We conclude that the evidence on which the plaintiffs rely does not support an inference that NAC intended to defraud them. * * *

Plaintiffs' final contention is that, even if the circumstances do not amount to actual fraud, we should impose a constructive trust on the ground that plaintiffs' funds were obtained by "means which render it unconscionable for the holder of legal title to retain and enjoy its beneficial interest." For reasons of federal bankruptcy policy to which we have already referred, we are reluctant so to exercise a general equitable power in the circumstances here presented. We fully recognize that plaintiffs have sustained substantial losses as a result of the NAC bankruptcy. Plaintiffs, however, comprise only one of several comparable groups of creditors who sustained substantial losses. Plaintiffs happened to place their orders during the week of September 13, with the result that their funds were placed in a "trust" account (even though it was contemplated that the funds might later be removed to complete the transactions). Another group of customers placed their orders shortly before September 13, but sent in their purchase money during the week of September 13. Their funds were not placed in a special account, and they must look to the bankruptcy proceeding for their relief. Other customers both placed their orders and sent in their funds prior to September 13, but their orders had not been executed at the time of the bankruptcy. They, too, are treated as general creditors in the bankruptcy. We fail to discern the equitable principle that requires us to protect the plaintiffs' investments fully, at the expense of these other creditors. Indeed, the equities, as well as the principles underlying the bankruptcy laws, point in the other direction. * * *

### *Notes*

1. In the excerpt that begins this chapter, Professor Laycock identifies three practical advantages to seeking restitution. Which of those three applies here?

2. *On procedure.* Frequently, constructive trusts are asserted against defendants whose obligations exceed their assets, as here. A legal remedy would be inadequate, because a money judgment would be unenforceable, so there is no problem with establishing that an equity court could have taken cognizance of the case.

If the defendant was not insolvent, the Restatement at least made a distinction between a constructive trust arising and a constructive trust being specifically enforceable. While a constructive trust might arise whenever an actor was subject to an equitable duty to convey property to another (see the discussion of the substantive law, below), that trust would only be specifically enforced if the legal remedy was inadequate. See Restatement of Restitution § 160 comment e.

The Restatement took this view because it viewed the constructive trust as a substantive legal arrangement that comes into being when property is wrongfully acquired and that "exists" even if a court of equity would not have taken cognizance of the case. For example, suppose the defendant obtains the plaintiff's car by fraud, and still has it in his possession. If the plaintiff sought specific relief in equity, it is generally accepted that it would not be forthcoming: his legal remedy, replevin, would be adequate. George E. Palmer, Law of Restitution § 1.4 at 18 (1978). According to the Restatement of Restitution, however, the defendant would nonetheless have been a "constructive trustee". Restatement of Restitution § 160 comment e. Thus, the Restatement of Restitution treats the constructive trust as "arising" when the property subject to the trust is acquired by the defendant, even though no court of equity would enforce it specifically. In the Restatement's terms, whether a constructive trust exists and how it will be enforced are two separate questions, and only the latter turns on the existence of a ground for equity jurisdiction.

The difference between calling the constructive trust a remedy (the position Professor Palmer prefers, see George E. Palmer, Law of Restitution § 1.4 at 17 (1978)) and calling it a substantive legal arrangement is largely semantic, if not metaphysical. An occasional case, however, may turn on the difference. Compare United States v. Fontana, 528 F.Supp. 137 (S.D.N.Y. 1981)(if the property in question was acquired by a breach of fiduciary duty, then a constructive trust arose at that time, and the property therefore was not subject to the government's tax lien, even if the beneficiary of the constructive trust did not file suit until after the tax lien was filed) with Taylor Assoc. v. Diamant, 178 B.R. 480 (Bankr.App.9th Cir.1995)(because constructive trust is inchoate remedy until it is imposed by court, property is subject to trustee's strong arm powers and can be recovered for the debtor's estate).

3. *On the substantive law.* Although the constructive trust is often used as a remedy for wrongdoing—fraud, breach of fiduciary duty, and the like—it is not limited to those situations. Unjust enrichment is all that is required: "Where a person holding title to property is subject to an equitable duty to convey it to another on the ground that he would be unjustly enriched if he were permitted to retain it, a constructive trust arises." (Restatement of Restitution § 160 )(1937). A constructive trust can be used to recover benefits conferred by mistake, Citizens Federal Bank v. Cardian Mortgage Corporation, 122 B.R. 255 (Bankr.E.D.Va.1990)(Virginia law)(money credited to account by bookkeeping error), or simply to avoid unfairness, Carr v. Carr, 120 N.J. 336, 576 A.2d 872 (1990)(constructive trust imposed over a portion of decedent's estate in favor of spouse who, because decedent died while their divorce was pending, had no claim under New Jersey statutes.)

On the other hand, the fact that the defendant owes the plaintiff a debt is not, standing alone, sufficient to give rise to a constructive trust. If money were paid or property delivered to another under circumstances that merely gave rise to a debt, the fact that the defendant was insolvent would not make that debt specifically enforceable. Restatement of Restitution § 160 comment f. Thus, the plaintiffs in *North American Coin and Currency* failed because they could not show that the money had been obtained by fraud, and under Arizona law, without fraud, a constructive trust could not arise. They were left with a mere debt.

In refusing to impose a constructive trust, however, is the court applying Arizona law or federal bankruptcy law? See Thomas H. Jackson, Statutory Liens & Constructive Trust in Bankruptcy: Undoing the Confusion, 61 Am. Bankruptcy L.J. 287 (1987). For a time, the Ninth Circuit's opinion in *North American Coin and Currency* generated some confusion on that point. The Ninth Circuit attempted to clarify the situation in Mitsui Manufacturers Bank v. Unicom Computer Corp., 13 F.3d 321 (9th Cir.1994). Holding that under California law a constructive trust could arise when a debtor negligently detained another's property, the court commented: "[W]e reject the [view] that our opinion in *In re North Am. Coin & Currency, Ltd.* created an elaborate, multi-part test to determine whether and under what circumstances a constructive trust may be imposed on property of a debtor * * *. Our decision should not be read as saying more than what it actually says; viz., that while state law must be the starting point in determining whether a constructive trust may arise in a federal bankruptcy case, that law must be applied in a manner not inconsistent with federal bankruptcy law." Is that clear?

4. *On the remedy.* As discussed above, a constructive trust can be specifically enforced, at least when the property in question is unique or the defendant insolvent. Then, it results in an order, directed to the defendant, to turn the wrongfully acquired property over to the plaintiff. Because the constructive trust gives the plaintiff the subject property *in specie,* the plaintiff acquires an advantage over an insolvent defendant's other creditors. Thus, had a constructive trust been imposed in *North American Coin & Currency,* the account in question would simply have been turned over to the plaintiffs. Similarly, the constructive trust can allow a plaintiff to reach property that would otherwise be exempt from a money judgment under a homestead or other exemption.

Without the constructive trust, the account remains in the debtor's estate. The plaintiffs are free to pursue their claim by seeking a money judgment for the amounts they are owed, but that judgment will simply establish them as general creditors, entitled to a share of the debtor's assets.

In order to establish a constructive trust, according to the court, they must show that the money was acquired by fraud. Why should that be the case? If NAC still has the plaintiffs' money, shouldn't NAC return it?

On the other hand, why should the plaintiffs have an advantage over NAC's other creditors, even if they can show fraud? According to the court, property acquired by fraud never becomes part of the bankrupt's estate because, in a sense, it is never his property. Why, though, does the manner in which the property was acquired make a difference? The court says that creditors should not benefit from the debtor's fraud at the expense of the one who was defrauded. Should they benefit from the defendant's breach of contract at the expense of the plaintiff?

## THE CORPORATION OF THE PRESIDENT OF THE CHURCH OF JESUS CHRIST OF LATTER-DAY SAINTS v. JOLLEY

Supreme Court of Utah, 1970.
24 Utah 2d 187, 467 P.2d 984.

CROCKETT, CHIEF JUSTICE.

This appeal challenges a judgment and decree of the district court which impressed against the defendant Vickie C. Jolley a constructive trust upon two new automobiles, a 1968 Pontiac Firebird and a 1968 Chevrolet Corvette which had been given her by one LaMar Kay, who had purchased the cars with money embezzled from the plaintiff church. On appeal defendant makes two contentions: 1) that a constructive trust can be imposed only on a fiduciary or confidant and not upon a third person with respect to whom no such relationship exists; and 2) that even if such a constructive trust could be imposed it should extend only to the amount of funds which were identified as being embezzled from the plaintiff and traced into that property.

Where the evidence is in dispute it is surveyed in the light favorable to the trial court findings. The said LaMar Kay was an accountant employed by the plaintiff church. During 1967 and 1968, by the use of fictitious firm names and pretended payment of claims he was engaged in a scheme of embezzling funds. In April of 1968 he drew from a fictitious account in the name of "Barker and Clayton" in the Murray State Bank a check in the amount of $4,305.57 made payable to Peck and Shaw, automobile dealers, with which he paid $4,224.62 for the Pontiac Firebird in question.

In August, 1968, he drew another check on the same account in the amount of $3,000 with which he purchased a cashier's check payable to Capital Chevrolet; this check was then presented to the latter company as part payment for the 1968 Chevrolet Corvette which had a total purchase price of $5,008.87. The balance on this car was paid by $50 cash on August 26, 1968, and $1,958.87 on August 30, 1968. The latter two cash payments admittedly were not traced directly through the "Barker and Clayton" account of embezzled funds into the Corvette automobile. But the evidence does show that a few days before he made those cash payments on that automobile, LaMar Kay had drawn $2,700 in cash from that account.

Upon completion of the purchases as above stated, the titles to both of these automobiles were transferred to the defendant Vickie C. Jolley; and there is no evidence nor contention made that she gave any legal consideration for them. Inasmuch as she is not a bona fide purchaser for value, her defenses in raising the question as to her lack of knowledge of the source of the funds which purchased the automobiles, and her averment that a constructive trust can only be impressed upon the wrongdoing fiduciary or confidant are of no avail to her. Where one has stolen or embezzled the money or property of another, he obtains no title whatsoever. A constructive trust may be impressed upon it in his hands; and equity may continue the trust effective against any subsequent transferee, unless transferred to a bona fide purchaser and under circumstances where equity would require a different result. The evidence in this case justified the court in its conclusion that the defendant had no better title to these automobiles than LaMar Kay had, and that they were held in constructive trust for the benefit of the plaintiff.

As to the defendant's second contention: that the plaintiff is not entitled to recover an equitable portion of the Corvette represented by the $1,958.87 and $50 cash payments which were not traced directly to the embezzled funds, this is to be said: Such direct tracing of funds is not an indispensable requisite to the conclusion arrived at. In the nature of the function of determining facts it is essential that the court or jury have the prerogative of finding not only facts based upon direct evidence, but also those which may be established from the reasonable inferences that may be deduced therefrom. The circumstances here shown concerning the associations of the defendant with LaMar Kay, including the facts that she went with him on the occasion of the purchase of the automobile; and that a few days previous to making the payments in question he had withdrawn $2,700 from the embezzled funds account, provide a reasonable basis for the trial court to believe that it was paid for entirely by money embezzled from plaintiff.

Affirmed.

HENRIOD, JUSTICE (dissenting).

Without expressing any opinion as to the rest of the main opinion and its conclusion, I dissent from that portion which includes $50 and $1,958.87 cash, in any amount upon which a purported trust could be impressed. The main opinion's own language reflects the weakness of the decision with respect to those amounts, which is compounded by the obvious conjecture indulged by 'guessing' that such amounts must have been a part of a much greater withdrawal. * * *

## *Notes*

1. *Jolley* demonstrates another advantage of the equitable remedies for unjust enrichment: To prevent unjust enrichment, the equity courts would follow, or "trace" the wrongfully held property through changes both in form (from money to car) and in possession (from Kay to Jolley), so long as a bona fide purchase for value did not intervene. The benefits of tracing are obvious: If the property has changed forms, only by tracing can the plaintiff obtain a specific restitutionary remedy and the advantage over general creditors that goes with it. The same is true if the property has changed hands: Tracing allows a specific remedy against the new holder, as to whom there might otherwise be no remedy at all.

Moreover, in the right circumstances, following property into its product can turn a neat profit for the plaintiff. Suppose Kay had bought stock with the church's money, instead of buying the cars. The stock would then be the product of the embezzled funds, and the church would be able to assert a constructive trust over it, profiting from any appreciation in its value. The church would get a windfall, which would be justified by adverting to the maxim that a wrongdoer should not profit from his wrongdoing.

Thus, while a profit-based measure of recovery has been the exception rather than the rule where legal restitution is concerned, equity has always admitted the possibility through the constructive trust. Both the profit-based measure of damages, however, and the capture of profits through the constructive trust have been restricted to cases of conscious wrongdoing. If the defendant acquired the plaintiff's property innocently and exchanged it for more valuable property, a constructive trust would not be enforced over the acquired property. That is, if Jolley, not knowing the cars were bought with embezzled money, had exchanged the cars for stock, and the stock appreciated in value, the church could not enforce a constructive trust over the stock. The church, instead, would be limited to another equitable remedy, the *equitable lien.*

An *equitable lien,* like any lien, is a security interest in another's property; it gives the holder of the lien the right to sell the property and have the proceeds applied to his claim. If the proceeds of the sale exceed the claim, the excess belongs to the property owner (and his creditors). If the proceeds of the sale are insufficient to satisfy the claim, the lienholder may, at least in the case of an equitable lien, have a money judgment for the deficiency.

In some circumstances, as where the innocent recipient of property subject to a constructive trust has exchanged it for more valuable property, an equitable lien may be the only equitable remedy available to a plaintiff. In other cases, however, the plaintiff may actually prefer an equitable lien, even though a constructive trust would also be available. For example, if Kay had used the embezzled funds to purchase stock, and the stock's value had depreciated, should the church seek a constructive trust over the stock, an equitable lien against it, or a money judgment for the amount embezzled?

A third equitable remedy, *subrogation,* may also come into play in cases where property subject to a constructive trust is exchanged. Where property subject to a constructive trust has been used to satisfy a debt, neither the constructive trust nor the equitable lien is available as a remedy, because the property is no longer in the defendant's possession. (Nor would any remedy lie against the creditor whose debt was satisfied, because unless he had notice of the defendant's wrongdoing, he would have given value in exchange for the property and thus would be a bona fide purchaser for value.) In such a case, the only equitable remedy open to the plaintiff is subrogation. Subrogation places the plaintiff in the same position occupied by the creditor whose debt was satisfied, giving the plaintiff the advantage of whatever security or priorities that creditor might have had. For example, if Kay used the embezzled funds to pay off the mortgage on his home, subrogation would place the church in the mortgagee's position, with its claim secured by Kay's home.

2. The right to a constructive trust, an equitable lien, or subrogation turns on the plaintiff's ability to trace the wrongfully acquired property into some property currently in the defendant's possession (or in the case of subrogation, into a discharged debt). As the dissent in *Jolley* points out, if the plaintiff cannot show that the second car was bought with the embezzled funds, it cannot impose a constructive trust on the car. But why should that be the case? Why should it make a difference whether Kay bought the car with his own money, and spent the church's money on fast living, or if he bought the car with the church's money and wasted his own? Consider the following:

> * * * [I]n this case we are asked * * * to hold that, where one's property has been wrongfully applied and dissipated by another, a charge remains upon the estate of the latter for the amount thus wrongfully taken, upon the ground that his estate is thereby so much larger, and that the trust property is really and clearly there, in a substituted form, although it cannot be directly traced. * * * While one who has been wronged may follow and take his own property, or its visible product, it is quite a different thing to say that he may take the property of somebody else. The general property of an insolvent debtor belongs to his creditors, as much as particular trust property belongs to a cestui que trust. * * *
>
> "Suppose that an insolvent debtor, D., has only $1,000 of property, but is indebted to the amount of $2,0C0, one-half of which is due to A., and the other half to B. In this condition of things D.'s property can only pay fifty per cent of his debts. By such distribution A. and B. would each be equitably entitled to $500. Now, suppose D., while in that condition, collects $1,000 for F., but instead of remitting the money, as he should, he uses it in paying his debt in full to A. By doing so, D. has not increased his assets a penny, nor diminished his aggregate indebtedness a penny. The only difference is that he now owes $1,000 each to B. and F., whereas he previously owed $1,000 each to A. and B. Now if F. is to have preference over B., then his claim will absorb the entire amount of D.'s property, leaving nothing whatever for B. In other words, the $500 to which B. was equitably entitled from his insolvent debtor, upon a fair distribution of the estate, has, without any fault of his, been paid to another, merely in consequence of the wrongful act of the debtor." [Francis v. Evans, 69 Wis. 115, 33 N.W. 93 (1887), (Taylor J. dissenting)] * * * The illustration demonstrates that the mere fact that a trustee has used the money does not show that it has gone into his estate. If used to pay debts, he has simply turned it over to a creditor, thereby giving him a preference, while his own estate and indebtedness remains exactly as before. Suppose he had stolen the money, and turned it over to somebody from whom it could not be reclaimed. Can anyone say the owner should have an equitable lien upon the thief's insolvent estate in preference to his creditors? They and the owner are equally innocent, and each must bear his own misfortune.

Slater v. Oriental Mills, 18 R.I. 352, 27 A. 443, 444 (1893). The theory that the plaintiff's assets are "still in" the defendant's estate even if they cannot be traced specifically (the "swollen assets" theory) has generally been rejected. The plaintiff must be able to trace in order to assert a constructive trust or other equitable restitutionary remedy. Only if F. can show that D. used his own money to pay A., and kept F.'s, can F. assert a constructive trust over the remaining $1000.

But should the result really turn on which specific dollar bills D. used to pay A.? Professor Dale Oesterle thinks not:

> Assume that Wrongdoer, with ten dollars in his pocket, steals ten dollars from Owner. Wrongdoer then deposits his ten dollars in an interest-bearing bank account and exchanges Owner's ten dollars for a hat. At the time Owner gets a judgment against Wrongdoer, the bank account has produced one dollar of interest and the hat is worth fifteen dollars. Owner traces into the hat and realizes a profit of five dollars from his stolen money. Tracing conclusively presumes that Wrongdoer's benefit from the conversion is the traceable product—the hat. Wrongdoer argues that his real benefit from the conversion is not fifteen dollars but eleven dollars, for had he not stolen Owner's money, Wrongdoer would have purchased the hat with his ten dollars and foregone the one dollar of interest. His profit from the conversion, Wrongdoer contends, was the money stolen, plus the one dollar of interest that he was able to earn as a result of depositing his own ten dollars with a bank at market rates of interest. * * *
>
> Objectively, the wealth that Wrongdoer gained as the result of the conversion depends on whether he still would have bought the hat had he not taken Owner's money. If so, then the actual benefits arising from the misappropriation are measured more accurately by the difference between Wrongdoer's wealth after the misappropriation and Wrongdoer's wealth had he purchased the misappropriated property with available funds or lines of credit. Wrongdoer's actual benefit arising from the conversion is his ability to forego use of the other available sources of capital to purchase the hat. The four dollar gain, representing what Wrongdoer would have realized if he had acted lawfully in purchasing the hat with his own ten dollars (or with a borrowed ten dollars) is not a benefit derived from the conversion; rather, the benefit is attributable to extraneous factors, such as smart trading, or favorable market conditions. On the other hand, if Wrongdoer would not have bought the hat without Owner's money, then he can be said to have the hat solely as the result of the conversion. * * *

Dale Oesterle, Deficiencies of the Restitutionary Right to Trace Misappropriated Property in Equity and in UCC § 9–306, 68 Corn.L.Rev. 172, 198 (1983). According to Professor Oesterle, if the goal is to prevent unjust enrichment, tracing based on physical exchanges (which dollars were spent for what) is unprincipled. Because tracing ignores causation, it may deprive the defendant of gains that are not "unjust," because they are not the result of the defendant's misappropriation, but rather the result of his efforts, skill or luck. To do so cannot be justified as necessary to prevent unjust enrichment; it is simply punitive.

3. Tracing can also be used to capture profits generated by the misappropriated property itself. Where the misappropriated property has generated dividends, interest, rents, or any other form of income, those profits may

be recovered. Restatement of Restitution §§ 158, 205. If the profits are to some extent attributable to the defendant's efforts, should that be taken into account? See text at pp. 679, 705; Dale Oesterle, Deficiencies of the Restitutionary Right to Trace Misappropriated Property in Equity and in UCC § 9–306, 68 Corn.L.Rev. 172 (1983).

4. In tracing cases, the burden of showing that the defendant exchanged property subject to a constructive trust for other property is on the plaintiff. Was the church's evidence sufficient to establish the right to a constructive trust over Jolley's Corvette? To aid plaintiffs who must trace wrongfully acquired property through various incarnations in order to get some equitable remedy, a number of tracing fictions have evolved. Although the next case is not, strictly speaking, an equitable restitution case, it does demonstrate how the tracing fictions operate.

## UNITED STATES v. BANCO CAFETERO PANAMA

United States Court of Appeals, Second Circuit, 1986.
797 F.2d 1154.

JON O. NEWMAN, CIRCUIT JUDGE:

This appeal concerns the Government's attempt to forfeit approximately $3 million in five bank accounts as "proceeds traceable" to narcotics transactions. * * *

### I. BACKGROUND

The Government alleges that it has probable cause to believe that the funds at issue ultimately derive from the drug dealings of a criminal conspiracy led by Gilberto Rodriguez–Orejuela, President of First Interamericas Bank ("FIB"). The Rodriguez group allegedly operated a massive drug business in the United States and deposited the proceeds of this business in FIB accounts. Between August 1983 and March 1985, when the Panama National Banking Commission closed FIB, some $46 million were transferred by FIB into an account that BC Panama maintained at the Irving Trust Company ("Irving Trust") in New York City. Millions of dollars were subsequently transferred from this BC Panama account into accounts maintained by BC Panama at four other banks and into one account maintained by BC Colon at Irving Trust. * * *

Because one of these accounts has a negative balance, the Government's claim against it has become moot. The Government represents that approximately $3 million remain in the other five accounts. * * *

### II. TRACEABLE PROCEEDS

These forfeiture actions were brought pursuant to 21 U.S.C. § 881, which provides in pertinent part:

> (a) The following shall be subject to forfeiture to the United States and no property right shall exist in them: * * *
>
> (6) All moneys, negotiable instruments, securities, or other things of value furnished or intended to be furnished by any

> person in exchange for a controlled substance in violation of this subchapter, [and] all proceeds traceable to such an exchange, * * * except that no property shall be forfeited under this paragraph, to the extent of the interest of an owner, by reason of any act or omission established by that owner to have been committed or omitted without the knowledge or consent of that owner.

Appellants contend that, even if the Government's factual allegations regarding the Rodriguez conspiracy are true, the five seized accounts may not be considered "proceeds traceable" to narcotics exchanges within the meaning of section 881(a)(6).

Appellants rely on the realities of banking practice and the law that has developed as a result. When a customer deposits funds into a bank account, his bank credits the account in an amount equal to the deposit. At any given moment, the credit balance of an account is the cumulative result of all transactions affecting the account. Banks are not bailees of their depositors' money, and a depositor may not replevy his money as a specific res or follow it into the hands of another bank customer.

Appellants argue that these principles govern the instant controversy and that their bank accounts are therefore insulated from forfeiture. Their argument rests primarily on the fungibility of money and on the burdens of investigation that they claim will be imposed upon banks if the Government's forfeiture theory is deemed legally valid. In considering the Government's claim for forfeiture and the appellants' objections to it, it will be helpful to keep in mind three distinct contexts in which there will arise the question whether a credit balance in a bank account is "proceeds traceable to [a narcotics] exchange" within the meaning of section 881(a)(6).

A. *Account Used Solely for Drug Proceeds.* The first context is the straightforward situation where a seller of narcotics opens a bank account and deposits into the account only money received from drug sales. The deposited money has been exchanged for a credit. This credit is clearly "traceable proceeds" under the forfeiture statute. The statute covers any asset exchanged directly for narcotics, such as a bar of gold or a car. Congress has also made it clear that "traceable proceeds" includes an asset indirectly exchanged for narcotics in one or more "intervening legitimate transactions, or otherwise changed in form...." If the seller of drugs uses the cash he receives to buy a bar of gold or a car, that asset is "traceable proceeds," and so is a credit at a bank. * * *

B. *Account Used for Drug Proceeds and Other Transactions.* The second and more problematic context arises where the account of the narcotics seller is not devoted solely to deposits from drug sales but is a general purpose account into which funds from legitimate transactions are also deposited and from which money is withdrawn. As to this context, appellants contend that the fungibility of money makes it impossible to consider any portion of the depositor's credit balance to be "traceable proceeds" because the credit balance does not represent just the proceeds of drug sales but is instead the net result of various deposits and withdrawals. Though this context presents some accounting choices, shortly to be considered, we think it clear that Congress intended the forfeiture statute to apply to a credit balance reflecting the cumulative results of deposits into and withdrawals from an account into which were deposited proceeds from drug sales. The legislative history that discussed "intervening" transactions explicitly recognized that the forfeiture statute could reach proceeds "commingled" with other assets:

> [I]f such proceeds were, for example, commingled with other assets, involved in intervening legitimate transactions, or otherwise changed in form: they would still be subject to forfeiture, but only to the extent that it could be shown that a traceable connection to an illegal transaction in controlled substances existed.

Explanatory Statement [1978 U.S.Code Cong. & Ad.News 9518] at 9522.

This statement is clear enough about commingling, but it offers no help in determining under what circumstances a "traceable connection" exists between a drug sale and a credit balance of an active account into which some drug sale proceeds were deposited. That problem requires consideration of accounting. Three basic approaches appear to be possible. If $100 from a drug sale is deposited into an active account, one approach is to consider the account to be "traceable proceeds" to the extent of $100 as long as the account balance never falls below that sum.[5] This might be called a "drugs-in, last-out" rule. This approach, more properly called the "lowest intermediate balance" rule, is used to determine the rights of a trust beneficiary to a trustee's bank account in which trust funds and the trustee's personal funds have been commingled. * * * A second approach is to consider "traceable proceeds" to be a pro rata share of any withdrawal from the account or of any asset purchased with such withdrawal, the share determined by the ratio of the $100 tainted deposit to the funds in the account immediately after the deposit. This option of an "averaging" rule, as an alternative to the "lowest intermediate balance" rule, is used to resolve tracing problems where withdrawals are made from an account in which trust and personal funds have been commingled. A third approach is to consider "traceable proceeds" to be any one withdrawal, or any asset purchased with such withdrawal, to the extent of $100. This might be called a "drugs-in, first-out" rule. The Government contends that it is entitled to the benefit, at its option, of either the first or third approach.

We conclude that the Government's position is sufficiently correct to enable it to prevail on this appeal. Where the credit in a depositor's account represents the net results of transactions that include a deposit of drug money, there is a plausible argument to be made *either* that the account contains the "traceable proceeds" of the tainted deposit (so long

5. Under this approach, untainted money added to the account after the balance has fallen below the amount of the tainted proceeds is immune from seizure.

as the balance has not fallen below the amount of the tainted deposit) *or* that any withdrawal (in excess of the tainted deposit) contains the "traceable proceeds" of such a deposit. Which approach reflects reality in any particular case will depend on the precise circumstances. For example, if a depositor placed a $175 check from his automobile insurer in payment of a damage claim into an account that contained $100 from a drug sale and the next day paid a $175 bill for car repairs, a fact-finder would be entitled to conclude that the $175 withdrawal did not contain "traceable proceeds" of the drug transaction but solely the "traceable proceeds" of the insurance payment, with the tainted deposit remaining in the account. Obviously few cases will present facts that neatly match untainted deposits with withdrawals, and the real question therefore becomes which side bears the risk of the inevitable uncertainty that will arise in most cases. Congress has answered that question in the Government's favor by assigning it a lenient burden of proof in obtaining forfeiture of "traceable proceeds" of drug transactions.

To establish a prima facie case for forfeiture of drug proceeds, the Government need only demonstrate probable cause for a forfeiture. To satisfy the probable cause requirement, the Government must have reasonable grounds to believe that certain property is subject to forfeiture. * * * If the Government satisfies the probable cause requirement, the claimant bears the ultimate burden of proving that the factual predicates for forfeiture have not been met.

Congress's allocation of the burden of proof in drug proceeds forfeiture cases persuades us that the Government is correct in its view that it can establish a prima facie case for forfeiture in the context of bank accounts by relying on either the "drugs-in, last-out" approach or the "drugs-in, first-out" approach. In almost all cases, once the Government has shown probable cause to believe that a person has sold drugs and has deposited the proceeds of a drug sale into a bank account, there will be probable cause to believe that the bank account contains "traceable proceeds" of the sale (if the balance has not fallen below the amount of the deposit) *and* probable cause to believe that a withdrawal contains such "traceable proceeds" (if the withdrawal exceeds the deposit). The burden will then be on the claimant to demonstrate that no portions of the account or no portions of the withdrawal, depending on which the Government pursues, are "traceable proceeds" of the drug sale. * * *

C. *Account Funded at Another Bank With Drug Proceeds.* The third context occurs where a bank at which a depositor's credit balance includes "traceable proceeds" of a drug transaction moves funds into its account at a second bank or, as allegedly occurred in this case, into the second bank's account at a third bank. FIB allegedly moved its forfeitable funds into BC Panama's account at Irving Trust. When FIB made these deposits, Irving Trust credited BC Panama's account and BC Panama credited FIB's account.[8] This transaction is functionally identi-

8. In this case, BC Panama's credits to its customers are located in Panama, beyond the *in rem* jurisdiction of United States courts. As a result, the Government

cal to a deposit by FIB into its own account with BC Panama and a transfer by BC Panama into its account at Irving Trust.

We see no reason why the statutory framework, including the burden of proof rules and the innocent owner defense, should apply any differently in this context than in the simpler context of a drug seller making deposits into his account at his own bank. Congress wished to reach proceeds of drug transactions exchanged through a series of "intervening" transactions and "changed in form." When the drug seller's bank receives his cash proceeds from a drug sale in exchange for a credit in favor of the drug seller, the cash received is still "traceable proceeds" of a drug sale, notwithstanding the fact that the drug seller's credit balance in his account is also "traceable proceeds." Without deciding whether the Government is entitled to forfeit both the cash from the bank and the credit balance from the depositor, cf. [United States v. $4,255,625.39, 762 F.2d 895, 903 (11th Cir.1985), cert. denied, 474 U.S. 1056, 106 S.Ct. 795, 88 L.Ed.2d 772 (1986) ](suggesting that cumulative forfeitures are permissible), we agree with the Government that either is vulnerable to forfeiture. The cash in the hands of the bank does not cease to be "traceable proceeds" just because it is commingled with the bank's other cash.[10] * * *

Nothing in the terms or legislative history of the forfeiture statute gives the slightest reason to believe that Congress wished to accord banks any special insulation from vulnerability to forfeiture of assets traceable to drug proceeds. On the contrary, Congressional concern with money laundering points in precisely the opposite direction.

Appellants contend that a broad application of the forfeiture statute to bank accounts will wreak havoc in the banking industry. They argue that banks will accept deposits at their peril, since investigation of the sources of customers' deposits would be costly, time-consuming, and often unilluminating. The risk is vastly overstated. A bank has no duty to investigate the source of its customers' deposits. It acts at its peril only when, as a passive receiver of knowledge, it learns that a deposit is derived from drug profits and nevertheless accepts that deposit. The statute imposes no investigatory costs on the banking system. Moreover, as the Government conceded at argument, the bank's knowledge, for purposes of the innocent owner defense, is not the cumulative knowledge of all the bank's employees. For a bank to be vulnerable to forfeiture of its cash, the fact that particular funds are immediate or traceable drug proceeds and the fact that those funds have been deposited at the bank must be known to the same employee of that bank. As a result, banks need not engage in costly internal control procedures to ensure that one employee does not accept funds for deposit that another employee, who is unaware of the deposit, knows to be tainted. We need

has looked to the accounts of BC Panama and BC Colon in this country to recover the drug proceeds of the Rodriguez group.

10. If the drug seller used $100 from a drug sale to buy a watch from a jeweler who knew the source of the $100, the $100 would not be immune to forfeiture just because it was commingled with other cash in the jeweler's cash register.

not decide on this appeal what level of authority the employee with knowledge of both taint and deposit must occupy to render forfeitable cash or accounts of a bank. Cf. Model Penal Code § 2.07(1)(c), (4)(c)(1974)("high managerial agent").

Applying the statute to the facts alleged in this case, we agree with the District Court that the BC Panama account at Irving Trust is vulnerable to forfeiture, as are the accounts into which funds from that account were transferred. Whether the Government can establish probable cause to believe the accounts are traceable proceeds of narcotics transactions and, if so, whether the claimants can sustain their burden of proof to establish either that the accounts are not forfeitable or that the claimants are entitled to the innocent owner defense are matters to be determined at trial. * * *

### *Notes*

1. Another advantage of tracing is that it can allow a plaintiff to recover misappropriated money that has been commingled with other money. Tracing, however, may be difficult when the commingled account has been subject to multiple deposits and withdrawals. In *Banco Cafetero Panama,* a strong public policy favored a liberal approach to tracing. Should the fictions indulged in to effectuate this strong public policy also be available to private litigants? Generally, they have been; the rules discussed in *Banco Cafetero Panama* are variations on the most widely accepted tracing rules.

2. "Drugs-in, first-out" is a variation on the rule in Clayton's Case, 1 Mer. 572 (1816), a rule more commonly known as "first in, first out" (FIFO). Basically an accounting principle, FIFO posits that withdrawals are made in the same order as deposits, so that the money first deposited is first withdrawn. Suppose Thief steals $100 from Owner, and deposits it in an account, to which he adds $100 of his own. He then withdraws $100, and spends it, leaving $100 in the account. Under FIFO, the $100 remaining in the account belongs to Thief. The first money deposited (Owner's) is presumed to have been the first money withdrawn.

3. Whatever its merits as an accounting principle, FIFO has little to recommend it in restitution cases, if equity and the prevention of unjust enrichment are the goals. In cases involving the commingling of a claimant's and a wrongdoer's funds, it has largely been replaced by the rule in *Hallett's Estate* (Knatchbull v. Hallett, 13 Ch.Div. 356), which makes its appearance in *Banco Cafetero Panama* as the "drugs-in, last-out" rule. According to *Hallett's Estate,* the wrongdoer is presumed to spend his own money first, whatever the order of deposits. Thus, in the above example, Thief would be presumed to have spent his own money first, and the $100 remaining in the account would be presumed to be Owner's.

As the court in *Banco Cafetero Panama* notes, however, the rule in *Hallett's Estate* is qualified by the *lowest intermediate balance* rule. Once all the wrongdoer's money has been withdrawn, subsequent withdrawals can only have been from the misappropriated funds. Even if the balance in the account later increases, the claimant's stake cannot exceed the lowest balance in the account between the time of the original deposit and the present. Subsequent deposits to the account are not treated as restoring the claimant's funds, unless there is specific evidence that they were so intended. Thus, to continue with the example, if Thief withdraws an additional $25 from the account, reducing the balance to $75, the $25 withdrawal must have been Owner's money, as Thief's money has all already been withdrawn. Even if the balance in the account later increases to $100 or more because of subsequent deposits, Owner's claim against the account is limited to $75, the lowest intermediate balance. (It is important to keep in mind, however, that tracing is only required when an equitable remedy is sought. Owner can only impose a constructive trust on $75 in the account. He can, of course, seek a money judgment to compensate him for the additional $25.)

Applying the lowest intermediate balance rule, however, can be complicated. See, e.g., Republic Supply Co. v. Richfield Oil Co., 79 F.2d 375 (9th Cir.1935)(rule is to be applied not by looking at the precise order of deposits and withdrawals, but by the account's daily closing balance). Also, some courts have made it relatively easy to establish that subsequent deposits to an account were intended to restore the trust fund, in which case the lowest intermediate balance rule does not preclude recovery. See, e.g., Mitchell v. Dunn, 211 Cal. 129, 294 P. 386 (1930).

Congress has eliminated the lowest intermediate balance rule in a variety of forfeiture situations by enacting 18 U.S.C. § 984. Under § 984, so long as the forfeiture action is brought within a year, the lowest intermediate balance rule does not apply, and "any identical property found in the same place or account as the property involved in the offense" can be forfeited. Ironically, while *Banco Cafetero's* application of the lowest intermediate balance rule inspired the legislation, the legislation was not made applicable to forfeitures under 18 U.S.C. § 881(a)(6), the provision involved in *Banco Cafetero*, so the decision is still good law. United States v. All Funds, 832 F.Supp. 542 (E.D.N.Y.1993).

4. Thieves are not necessarily wastrels. Suppose Thief's first withdrawal from the account is invested lucratively, rather than wasted. Should it then be presumed that he spent his own money first? In allowing the government the benefit of either the drugs-in, first-out or last-out presumption at its election, the *Banco Cafetero Panama* court is following an approach developed in an English case, *In re: Oatway* (Herstslet v. Oatway [1903] 2 Ch.Div. 356), and followed in many American jurisdictions. The *In re Oatway,* or option, rule allows the claimant of a commingled fund to choose whether to treat any particular withdrawal as his, so long as his money could be traced to the account at the time of the withdrawal, consistent with the lowest intermediate balance rule.

5. The *averaging approach* mentioned by the *Banco Cafetero Panama* court is used when money belonging to two or more claimants is commingled in one account. Suppose Thief embezzles $100 from Owner One and $100 from Owner Two and deposits it all in one account. Then, Thief spends $100 from the account on stock, which has appreciated by the time of trial to a value of $150. Finally, Thief withdraws the remaining $100, and spends it. Under the FIFO approach, the stock (the first withdrawal) would be presumed to have been purchased with Owner One's money (the first deposit). Owner One would have a claim to the stock, and Owner Two

(whose money remained in the account, according to the fiction) would have a money judgment against the presumably insolvent Thief. (The *Hallett's Estate* approach is irrelevant because there is no reason to presume that Thief would spend one claimant's money before another's).

The *averaging,* or *pro rata,* approach attempts to treat all claimants equitably by giving each a proportionate claim against any withdrawal in an amount determined by the claimant's share in the account at the time the withdrawal was made. Thus, since Owner One and Owner Two each had a claim to half of the account at the time of the withdrawal, each would have a claim to half of the stock.

6. Keep in mind that the tracing fictions are equitable devices, and their use may be limited to avoid harm to creditors. See Bank of Alex Brown v. Goldberg, 158 B.R. 188 (Bankr.E.D.Cal.1993)(creditor must show his property was specifically and directly exchanged for the property subject to the trust if defendant is insolvent, unless tracing will not harm other creditors), affirmed, 168 B.R. 382 (9th Cir.BAP 1994).

7. The Restatement of Restitution takes a different approach to tracing. According to the Restatement, when a claimant's money and a wrongdoer's money have been commingled, and then a withdrawal is made, the claimant is entitled to an equitable lien *in the entire amount of his claim* (limited, of course, by the lowest intermediate balance rule) on both the amount withdrawn and its product as well as on the amount remaining in the account. If the wrongdoer is a conscious wrongdoer, the claimant may opt instead for a proportionate share of both what remains in the account and the withdrawn amount (or its product). The Restatement's goal is to simplify and rationalize the law by eliminating the tracing fictions, but its approach is extremely difficult to apply in complex cases, and it has not been well-received by the courts. See George E. Palmer, Law of Restitution § 2.17 at 208 (1978).

## *A Tracing Problem*

Arielle is an accountant who keeps the books for several small businesses. On August 15, she embezzled $10,000 from Grady, one of her clients. She used $4,000 to make the last payment on her car loan, and deposited the remaining $6,000 in her personal checking account. On August 30, she wrote a check to her landlord for $1,000. On September 1, she deposited $2,000 of her own money in the account. On September 17, she bought 30 shares of common stock in Notachance, Inc., for $100 a share, paying for it with money from the account. On September 19, she embezzled $8,000 from a second client, Sarah, and deposited it in the account. On October 1, she deposited $2,000 of her own money in the account. On October 3, she purchased 600 shares of common stock in Quikbux, Inc., for $10 a share.

Grady and Sarah have discovered Arielle's embezzling. Identify the remedies available to them. (Notachance, Inc. is currently selling for $50 a share; Quikbux is going for $20.)

# Chapter 8

# COLLECTION OF MONETARY JUDGMENTS

## A. PROVISIONAL RELIEF

In many instances, a plaintiff cannot wait for the wheels of justice to turn completely. Time may be of the essence. As we have seen in chapter 3, the court has power, in equity, to issue TROs and preliminary injunctions. Where money, rather than equitable relief is at issue, even though the court may not issue an injunction, it does have specialized procedures to make certain that assets do not disappear pending a full consideration on the merits. Because the purpose is to make sure that the defendants will be able to satisfy any money judgment which the court may render, the assets do not even have to be related to the underlying controversy. E.g., Maine R.Civ.Proc. 4A(c)(1993). See also F.R.Civ.P. 64 ("all remedies providing for seizure of person or property for the purpose of securing satisfaction of judgment ultimately to be entered * * * are available * * * in the manner provided by the law of the state in which the district court is held"). If necessary, the court can even appoint a receiver to operate the asset (such as a business) until the right to ownership is decided on the merits. See F.R.Civ.P. 66.

An important concern about provisional legal relief has been that it be fair to both sides in the legal dispute. As the next cases indicate, the Supreme Court of the United States has assessed the constitutionality of many of the most commonly used procedures.

### CONNECTICUT v. DOEHR

Supreme Court of the United States, 1991.
501 U.S. 1, 111 S.Ct. 2105, 115 L.Ed.2d 1.

JUSTICE WHITE delivered an opinion, Parts I, II, and III of which are the opinion of the Court.*

This case requires us to determine whether a state statute that authorizes prejudgment attachment of real estate without prior notice or

* THE CHIEF JUSTICE, JUSTICE BLACKMUN, JUSTICE KENNEDY, and JUSTICE SOUTER join Parts I, II, and III of this opinion, and JUSTICE SCALIA joins Parts I and III.

hearing, without a showing of extraordinary circumstances, and without a requirement that the person seeking the attachment post a bond, satisfies the Due Process Clause of the Fourteenth Amendment. We hold that, as applied to this case, it does not.

I

On March 15, 1988, Petitioner John F. DiGiovanni submitted an application to the Connecticut Superior Court for an attachment in the amount of $75,000 on respondent Brian K. Doehr's home in Meridan, Connecticut. DiGiovanni took this step in conjunction with a civil action for assault and battery that he was seeking to institute against Doehr in the same court. The suit did not involve Doehr's real estate nor did DiGiovanni have any pre-existing interest either in Doehr's home or any of his other property.

Connecticut law authorizes prejudgment attachment of real estate without affording prior notice or the opportunity for a prior hearing to the individual whose property is subject to the attachment. The State's prejudgment remedy statute provides, in relevant part:

> "The court or a judge of the court may allow the prejudgment remedy to be issued by an attorney without hearing * * * upon verification by oath of the plaintiff or of some competent affiant, that there is probable cause to sustain the validity of the plaintiff's claims and (1) that the prejudgment remedy requested is for an attachment of real property.... " Conn.Gen.Stat. § 52–278e (1991).

The statute does not require the plaintiff to post a bond to insure the payment of damages that the defendant may suffer should the attachment prove wrongfully issued or the claim prove unsuccessful.

As required, DiGiovanni submitted an affidavit in support of his application. In five one-sentence paragraphs, DiGiovanni stated that the facts set forth in his previously submitted complaint were true; that "I was willfully, wantonly and maliciously assaulted by the defendant, Brian K. Doehr"; that "[s]aid assault and battery broke my left wrist and further caused an ecchymosis to my right eye, as well as other injuries"; and that "I have further expended sums of money for medical care and treatment." The affidavit concluded with the statement, "In my opinion, the foregoing facts are sufficient to show that there is probable cause that judgment will be rendered for the plaintiff."

On the strength of these submissions the Superior Court judge, by an order dated March 17, found "probable cause to sustain the validity of the plaintiff's claim" and ordered the attachment on Doehr's home "to the value of $75,000." The sheriff attached the property four days later, on March 21. Only after this did Doehr receive notice of the attachment. He also had yet to be served with the complaint, which is ordinarily necessary for an action to commence in Connecticut. As the statute further required, the attachment notice informed Doehr that he had the right to a hearing: (1) to claim that no probable cause existed to sustain the claim; (2) to request that the attachment be vacated, modified, or that a bond be substituted; or (3) to claim that some portion of the property was exempt from execution.

Rather than pursue these options, Doehr filed suit against DiGiovanni in Federal District Court, claiming that § 52–278e(a)(1) was unconstitutional under the Due Process Clause of the Fourteenth Amendment. The District Court upheld the statute and granted summary judgment in favor of DiGiovanni. On appeal, a divided panel of the United States Court of Appeals for the Second Circuit reversed. * * * We granted certiorari * * *.

II

With this case we return to the question of what process must be afforded by a state statute enabling an individual to enlist the aid of the State to deprive another of his or her property by means of the prejudgment attachment or similar procedure. Our cases reflect the numerous variations this type of remedy can entail. In Sniadach v. Family Finance Corp. of Bay View, 395 U.S. 337, 89 S.Ct. 1820, 23 L.Ed.2d 349 (1969), the Court struck down a Wisconsin statute that permitted a creditor to effect prejudgment garnishment of wages without notice and prior hearing to the wage earner. In Fuentes v. Shevin, 407 U.S. 67, 92 S.Ct. 1983, 32 L.Ed.2d 556 (1972), the Court likewise found a Due Process violation in state replevin provisions that permitted vendors to have goods seized through an *ex parte* application to a court clerk and the posting of a bond. Conversely, the Court upheld a Louisiana *ex parte* procedure allowing a lienholder to have disputed goods sequestered in Mitchell v. W.T. Grant Co., 416 U.S. 600, 94 S.Ct. 1895, 40 L.Ed.2d 406 (1974). *Mitchell*, however, carefully noted that *Fuentes* was decided against "a factual and legal background sufficiently different . . . that it does not require the invalidation of the Louisiana sequestration statute." Those differences included Louisiana's provision of an immediate postdeprivation hearing along with the option of damages; the requirement that a judge rather than a clerk determine that there is a clear showing of entitlement to the writ; the necessity for a detailed affidavit; and an emphasis on the lien-holder's interest in preventing waste or alienation of the encumbered property. In North Georgia Finishing, Inc. v. Di–Chem, Inc., 419 U.S. 601, 95 S.Ct. 719, 42 L.Ed.2d 751 (1975), the Court again invalidated an *ex parte* garnishment statute that not only failed to provide for notice and prior hearing but that also failed to require a bond, a detailed affidavit setting out the claim, the determination of a neutral magistrate, or a prompt postdeprivation hearing.

These cases "underscore the truism that '[d]ue process unlike some legal rules, is not a technical conception with a fixed content unrelated to time, place and circumstances.'" Mathews v. Eldridge, 424 U.S. [319] at 334, 96 S.Ct., at 902 [(1976)] (quoting Cafeteria Workers v. McElroy, 367 U.S. 886, 895, 81 S.Ct. 1743, 1748, 6 L.Ed.2d 1230 (1961)). In *Mathews*, we drew upon our prejudgment remedy decisions to determine what process is due when the government itself seeks to effect a deprivation on its own initiative. That analysis resulted in the now familiar threefold inquiry requiring consideration of "the private interest that will be affected by the official action"; "the risk of an erroneous deprivation of such interest through the procedures used, and the probable value, if any, of additional or substitute safeguards"; and lastly "the Government's interest, including the function involved and the fiscal and administrative burdens that the additional or substitute procedural requirement would entail."

Here the inquiry is similar but the focus is different. Prejudgment remedy statutes ordinarily apply to disputes between private parties rather than between an individual and the government. Such enactments are designed to enable one of the parties to "make use of state procedures with the overt, significant assistance of state officials," and they undoubtedly involve state action "substantial enough to implicate the Due Process Clause." Tulsa Professional Collection Services, Inc. v. Pope, 485 U.S. 478, 486, 108 S.Ct. 1340, 1345, 99 L.Ed.2d 565 (1988). Nonetheless, any burden that increasing procedural safeguards entails primarily affects not the government, but the party seeking control of the other's property. For this type of case, therefore, the relevant inquiry requires, as in *Mathews*, first, consideration of the private interest that will be affected by the prejudgment measure; second, an examination of the risk of erroneous deprivation through the procedures under attack and the probable value of additional or alternative safeguards; and third, in contrast to *Mathews*, principal attention to the interest of the party seeking the prejudgment remedy, with, nonetheless, due regard for any ancillary interest the government may have in providing the procedure or forgoing the added burden of providing greater protections.

We now consider the *Mathews* factors in determining the adequacy of the procedures before us, first with regard to the safeguards of notice and a prior hearing, and then in relation to the protection of a bond.

III

We agree with the Court of Appeals that the property interests that attachment affects are significant. For a property owner like Doehr, attachment ordinarily clouds title; impairs the ability to sell or otherwise alienate the property; taints any credit rating; reduces the chance of obtaining a home equity loan or additional mortgage; and can even place an existing mortgage in technical default where there is an insecurity clause. Nor does Connecticut deny that any of these consequences occurs.

Instead, the State correctly points out that these effects do not amount to a complete, physical, or permanent deprivation of real property; their impact is less than the perhaps temporary total deprivation of household goods or wages. But the Court has never held that only such extreme deprivations trigger due process concern. To the contrary, our cases show that even the temporary or partial impairments to property rights that attachments, liens, and similar encumbrances entail are sufficient to merit due process protection. Without doubt, state procedures for creating and enforcing attachments, as with liens, "are subject to the strictures of due process."[4]

We also agree with the Court of Appeals that the risk of erroneous deprivation that the State permits here is substantial. By definition, attachment statutes premise a deprivation of property on one ultimate factual contingency—the award of damages to the plaintiff which the defendant may not be able to satisfy. For attachments before judgment, Connecticut mandates that this determination be made by means of a procedural inquiry that asks whether "there is probable cause to sustain the validity of the plaintiff's claim." Conn.Gen.Stat. § 52–278e(a). The statute elsewhere defines the validity of the claim in terms of the likelihood "that judgment will be rendered in the matter in favor of the plaintiff." Conn.Gen.Stat. § 52–278c(a)(2)(1991). What probable cause means in this context, however, remains obscure. * * *

We need not resolve this confusion since the statute presents too great a risk of erroneous deprivation * * *. If the statute demands inquiry into the sufficiency of the complaint, or, still less, the plaintiff's good-faith belief that the complaint is sufficient, requirement of a complaint and a factual affidavit would permit a court to make these minimal determinations. But neither inquiry adequately reduces the risk of erroneous deprivation. Permitting a court to authorize attachment merely because the plaintiff believes the defendant is liable, or because the plaintiff can make out a facially valid complaint, would permit the deprivation of the defendant's property when the claim would fail to convince a jury, when it rested on factual allegations that were sufficient to state a cause of action but which the defendant would dispute, or in the case of a mere good-faith standard, even when the complaint failed to state a claim upon which relief could be granted. The potential for unwarranted attachment in these situations is self-evident and too great to satisfy the requirements of due process absent any countervailing consideration.

Even if the provision requires the plaintiff to demonstrate, and the judge to find, probable cause to believe that judgment will be rendered in favor of the plaintiff, the risk of error was substantial in this case. As the record shows, and as the State concedes, only a skeletal affidavit need be and was filed. The State urges that the reviewing judge normally reviews the complaint as well, but concedes that the complaint may also be conclusory. It is self-evident that the judge could make no

4. Our summary affirmance in Spielman–Fond, Inc. v. Hanson's Inc., 417 U.S. 901, 94 S.Ct. 2596, 41 L.Ed.2d 208 (1974), does not control. In *Spielman-Fond*, the District Court held that the filing of a mechanic's lien did not amount to the taking of a significant property interest. A summary disposition does not enjoy the full precedential value of a case argued on the merits and disposed of by a written opinion. The facts of *Spielman-Fond* presented an alternative basis for affirmance in any event. Unlike the case before us, the mechanic's lien statute in *Spielman-Fond* required the creditor to have a pre-existing interest in the property at issue. As we explain below, a heightened plaintiff interest in certain circumstances can provide a ground for upholding procedures that are otherwise suspect.

realistic assessment concerning the likelihood of an action's success based upon these one-sided, self-serving, and conclusory submissions. And as the Court of Appeals said, in a case like this involving an alleged assault, even a detailed affidavit would give only the plaintiff's version of the confrontation. Unlike determining the existence of a debt or delinquent payments, the issue does not concern "ordinarily uncomplicated matters that lend themselves to documentary proof." The likelihood of error that results illustrates that "fairness can rarely be obtained by secret, one-sided determination of facts decisive of rights.... [And n]o better instrument has been devised for arriving at truth than to give a person in jeopardy of serious loss notice of the case against him and an opportunity to meet it."

What safeguards the State does afford do not adequately reduce this risk. Connecticut points out that the statute also provides an "expeditiou[s]" postattachment adversary hearing; notice for such a hearing; judicial review of an adverse decision; and a double damages action if the original suit is commenced without probable cause. Similar considerations were present in *Mitchell* where we upheld Louisiana's sequestration statute despite the lack of predeprivation notice and hearing. But in *Mitchell*, the plaintiff had a vendor's lien to protect, the risk of error was minimal because the likelihood of recovery involved uncomplicated matters that lent themselves to documentary proof, and plaintiff was required to put up a bond. None of these factors diminishing the need for a predeprivation hearing is present in this case. It is true that a later hearing might negate the presence of probable cause, but this would not cure the temporary deprivation that an earlier hearing might have prevented. "The Fourteenth Amendment draws no bright lines around three-day, 10–day or 50–day deprivations of property. Any significant taking of property by the State is within the purview of the Due Process Clause." *Fuentes*.

Finally, we conclude that the interests in favor of an *ex parte* attachment, particularly the interests of the plaintiff, are too minimal to supply such a consideration here. Plaintiff had no existing interest in Doehr's real estate when he sought the attachment. His only interest in attaching the property was to ensure the availability of assets to satisfy his judgment if he prevailed on the merits of his action. Yet there was no allegation that Doehr was about to transfer or encumber his real estate or take any other action during the pendency of the action that would render his real estate unavailable to satisfy a judgment. Our cases have recognized such a properly supported claim would be an exigent circumstance permitting postponing any notice or hearing until after the attachment is effected. Absent such allegations, however, the plaintiff's interest in attaching the property does not justify the burdening of Doehr's ownership rights without a hearing to determine the likelihood of recovery.

No interest the government may have affects the analysis. The State's substantive interest in protecting any rights of the plaintiff cannot be any more weighty than those rights themselves. Here the plaintiff's interest is *de minimis*. Moreover, the State cannot seriously plead additional financial or administrative burdens involving predeprivation hearings when it already claims to provide an immediate post-deprivation hearing.

Historical and contemporary practice support our analysis. Prejudgment attachment is a remedy unknown at common law. Instead, "it traces its origin to the Custom of London, under which a creditor might attach money or goods of the defendant either in the plaintiff's own hands or in the custody of a third person, by proceedings in the mayor's court or in the sheriff's court." Generally speaking, attachment measures in both England and this country had several limitations that reduced the risk of erroneous deprivation which Connecticut permits. Although attachments ordinarily did not require prior notice or a hearing, they were usually authorized only where the defendant had taken or threatened to take some action that would place the satisfaction of the plaintiff's potential award in jeopardy. Attachments, moreover, were generally confined to claims by creditors. As we and the Court of Appeals have noted, disputes between debtors and creditors more readily lend themselves to accurate *ex parte* assessments of the merits. Tort actions, like the assault and battery claim at issue here, do not. Finally, as we will discuss below, attachment statutes historically required that the plaintiff post a bond.

Connecticut's statute appears even more suspect in light of current practice. A survey of state attachment provisions reveals that nearly every State requires either a preattachment hearing, a showing of some exigent circumstance, or both, before permitting an attachment to take place. * * *

We do not mean to imply that any given exigency requirement protects an attachment from constitutional attack. Nor do we suggest that the statutory measures we have surveyed are necessarily free of due process problems or other constitutional infirmities in general. We do believe, however, that the procedures of almost all the States confirm our view that the Connecticut provision before us, by failing to provide a preattachment hearing without at least requiring a showing of some exigent circumstance, clearly falls short of the demands of due process.

## IV

### A

Although a majority of the Court does not reach the issue, Justices Marshall, Stevens, O'Connor, and I deem it appropriate to consider whether due process also requires the plaintiff to post a bond or other security in addition to requiring a hearing or showing of some exigency.[7]

7. Ordinarily we will not address a contention advanced by a respondent that would enlarge his or her rights under a judgment, without the respondent filing a cross-petition for certiorari. Here the Court of Appeals rejected Doehr's argument that § 52–278e(a)(1) violates due process in failing to mandate a preattachment bond. Nonetheless, this case involves considerations that in the past have prompted us "to consider the question highlighted by respondent." First, as our cases have

As noted, the impairments to property rights that attachments affect merit due process protection. Several consequences can be severe, such as the default of a homeowner's mortgage. In the present context, it need only be added that we have repeatedly recognized the utility of a bond in protecting property rights affected by the mistaken award of prejudgment remedies.

Without a bond, at the time of attachment, the danger that these property rights may be wrongfully deprived remains unacceptably high even with such safeguards as a hearing or exigency requirement. The need for a bond is especially apparent where extraordinary circumstances justify an attachment with no more than the plaintiff's *ex parte* assertion of a claim. We have already discussed how due process tolerates, and the States generally permit, the otherwise impermissible chance of erroneously depriving the defendant in such situations in light of the heightened interest of the plaintiff. Until a postattachment hearing, however, a defendant has no protection against damages sustained where no extraordinary circumstance in fact existed or the plaintiff's likelihood of recovery was nil. Such protection is what a bond can supply. Both the Court and its individual members have repeatedly found the requirement of a bond to play an essential role in reducing what would have been too great a degree of risk in precisely this type of circumstance.

But the need for a bond does not end here. A defendant's property rights remain at undue risk even when there has been an adversarial hearing to determine the plaintiff's likelihood of recovery. At best, a court's initial assessment of each party's case cannot produce more than an educated prediction as to who will win. This is especially true when, as here, the nature of the claim makes any accurate prediction elusive. In consequence, even a full hearing under a proper probable-cause standard would not prevent many defendants from having title to their homes impaired during the pendency of suits that never result in the contingency that ultimately justifies such impairment, namely, an award to the plaintiff. Attachment measures currently on the books reflect this concern. All but a handful of States require a plaintiff's bond despite also affording a hearing either before, or (for the vast majority, only under extraordinary circumstances) soon after, an attachment takes place. Bonds have been a similarly common feature of other prejudgment remedy procedures that we have considered, whether or not these procedures also included a hearing.

The State stresses its double damages remedy for suits that are commenced without probable cause. This remedy, however, fails to

shown, the notice and hearing question and the bond question are intertwined and can fairly be considered facets of same general issue. Thus, "[w]ithout undue strain, the position taken by respondent before this Court ... might be characterized as an argument in support of the judgment below" insofar as a discussion of notice and a hearing cannot be divorced from consideration of a bond. Second, this aspect of prejudgment attachment "plainly warrants our attention, and with regard to which the lower courts are in need of guidance." Third, "and perhaps most importantly, both parties have briefed and argued the question."

make up for the lack of a bond. As an initial matter, the meaning of "probable cause" in this provision is no more clear here than it was in the attachment provision itself. Should the term mean the plaintiff's good faith or the facial adequacy of the complaint, the remedy is clearly insufficient. A defendant who was deprived where there was little or no likelihood that the plaintiff would obtain a judgment could nonetheless recover only by proving some type of fraud or malice or by showing that the plaintiff had failed to state a claim. Problems persist even if the plaintiff's ultimate failure permits recovery. At best a defendant must await a decision on the merits of the plaintiff's complaint, even assuming that a [statutory] action may be brought as a counterclaim. Settlement, under Connecticut law, precludes seeking the damages remedy, a fact that encourages the use of attachments as a tactical device to pressure an opponent to capitulate. An attorney's advice that there is probable cause to commence an action constitutes a complete defense, even if the advice was unsound or erroneous. Finally, there is no guarantee that the original plaintiff will have adequate assets to satisfy an award that the defendant may win.

Nor is there any appreciable interest against a bond requirement. Section 52–278e(a)(1) does not require a plaintiff to show exigent circumstances nor any pre-existing interest in the property facing attachment. A party must show more than the mere existence of a claim before subjecting an opponent to prejudgment proceedings that carry a significant risk of erroneous deprivation.

B

Our foregoing discussion compels the four of us to consider whether a bond excuses the need for a hearing or other safeguards altogether. If a bond is needed to augment the protections afforded by preattachment and postattachment hearings, it arguably follows that a bond renders these safeguards unnecessary. That conclusion is unconvincing, however, for it ignores certain harms that bonds could not undo but that hearings would prevent. The law concerning attachments has rarely, if ever, required defendants to suffer an encumbered title until the case is concluded without any prior opportunity to show that the attachment was unwarranted. Our cases have repeatedly emphasized the importance of providing a prompt postdeprivation hearing at the very least. Every State but one, moreover, expressly requires a preattachment or postattachment hearing to determine the propriety of an attachment.

The necessity for at least a prompt postattachment hearing is self-evident because the right to be compensated at the end of the case, if the plaintiff loses, for all provable injuries caused by the attachment is inadequate to redress the harm inflicted, harm that could have been avoided had an early hearing been held. An individual with an immediate need or opportunity to sell a property can neither do so, nor otherwise satisfy that need or recreate the opportunity. The same applies to a parent in need of a home equity loan for a child's education, an entrepreneur seeking to start a business on the strength of an otherwise strong credit rating, or simply a homeowner who might face the disruption of having a mortgage placed in technical default. The extent of these harms, moreover, grows with the length of the suit. Here, oral argument indicated that civil suits in Connecticut commonly take up to four to seven years for completion. Many state attachment statutes require that the amount of a bond be anywhere from the equivalent to twice the amount the plaintiff seeks. These amounts bear no relation to the harm the defendant might suffer even assuming that money damages can make up for the foregoing disruptions. It should be clear, however, that such an assumption is fundamentally flawed. Reliance on a bond does not sufficiently account for the harms that flow from an erroneous attachment to excuse a State from reducing that risk by means of a timely hearing.

If a bond cannot serve to dispense with a hearing immediately after attachment, neither is it sufficient basis for not providing a preattachment hearing in the absence of exigent circumstances even if in any event a hearing would be provided a few days later. The reasons are the same: a wrongful attachment can inflict injury that will not fully be redressed by recovery on the bond after a prompt postattachment hearing determines that the attachment was invalid.

Once more, history and contemporary practice support our conclusion. Historically, attachments would not issue without a showing of extraordinary circumstances even though a plaintiff bond was almost invariably required in addition. Likewise, all but eight States currently require the posting of a bond. Out of this 42 State majority, all but one requires a preattachment hearing, a showing of some exigency, or both, and all but one expressly require a postattachment hearing when an attachment has been issue *ex parte*. This testimony underscores the point that neither a hearing nor an extraordinary circumstance limitation eliminates the need for a bond, no more than a bond allows waiver of these other protections. To reconcile the interests of the defendant and the plaintiff accurately, due process generally requires all of the above. * * *

CHIEF JUSTICE REHNQUIST with whom JUSTICE BLACKMUN joins, concurring in part and concurring in the judgment.

I agree with the Court that the Connecticut attachment statute, "as applied in this case," fails to satisfy the Due Process Clause of the Fourteenth Amendment. I therefore join Parts I, II and III of its opinion. Unfortunately, the remainder of the Court's opinion does not confine itself to the facts of this case, but enters upon a lengthy disquisition as to what combination of safeguards are required to satisfy Due Process in hypothetical cases not before the Court. I therefore do not join Part IV.

As the Court's opinion points out, the Connecticut statute allows attachment not merely for a creditor's claim, but for a tort claim of assault and battery; it affords no opportunity for a pre-deprivation hearing; it contains no requirement that there be "exigent circumstances," such as an effort on the part of the defendant to conceal assets; no bond is required from the plaintiff; and the property attached is one in which the plaintiff has no pre-existing interest. The Court's opinion is, in my view, ultimately correct when it bases its holding of unconstitutionality of the Connecticut statute as applied here on our cases of *Sniadach*; *Fuentes*; *Mitchell*; and *North Georgia Finishing*. But I do not believe that the result follows so inexorably as the Court's opinion suggests. All of the cited cases dealt with personalty—bank deposits or chattels—and each involved the physical seizure of the property itself, so that the defendant was deprived of its use. These cases, which represented something of a revolution in the jurisprudence of procedural due process, placed substantial limits on the methods by which creditors could obtain a lien on the assets of a debtor prior to judgment. But in all of them the debtor was deprived of the use and possession of the property. In the present case, on the other hand, Connecticut's prejudgment attachment on real property statute, which secures an incipient lien for the plaintiff, does not deprive the defendant of the use or possession of the property.

The Court's opinion therefore breaks new ground, and I would point out, more emphatically than the Court does, the limits of today's holding. In Spielman–Fond, Inc. v. Hanson's, Inc., 379 F.Supp. 997, 999 (D.Ariz.1973), the District Court held that the filing of a mechanics' lien did not cause the deprivation of a significant property interest of the owner. We summarily affirmed that decision. Other courts have read this summary affirmance to mean that the mere imposition of a lien on real property, which does not disturb the owner's use or enjoyment of the property, is not a deprivation of property calling for procedural due process safeguards. I agree with the Court, however, that upon analysis the deprivation here is a significant one, even though the owner remains in undisturbed possession. "For a property owner like Doehr, attachment ordinarily clouds title; impairs the ability to sell or otherwise alienate the property; taints any credit rating; reduces the chance of obtaining a home equity loan or additional mortgage; and can even place an existing mortgage in technical default when there is an insecurity clause." Given the elaborate system of title records relating to real property which prevails in all of our states, a lienor need not obtain possession or use of real property belonging to a debtor in order to significantly impair its value to him.

But in *Spielman-Fond, Inc.*, there was, as the Court points out in fn. 4, an alternate basis available to this Court for affirmance of that decision. Arizona recognized a pre-existing lien in favor of unpaid mechanics and materialmen who had contributed labor or supplies which were incorporated in improvements to real property. The existence of such a lien upon the very property ultimately posted or noticed distinguishes those cases from the present one, where the plaintiff had no pre-existing interest in the real property which he sought to attach. Materialman's and mechanic's lien statutes award an interest in real property to workers who have contributed their labor, and to suppliers who have furnished material, for the improvement of the real property. Since neither the labor nor the material can be reclaimed once it has become a part of the realty, this is the only method by which workmen or small businessmen who have contributed to the improvement of the property may be given a remedy against a property owner who has defaulted on his promise to pay for the labor and the materials. To require any sort of a contested court hearing or bond before the notice of lien takes effect would largely defeat the purpose of these statutes.

Petitioner in its brief relies in part on our summary affirmance in Bartlett v. Williams, 464 U.S. 801, 104 S.Ct. 46, 78 L.Ed.2d 67 (1983). That case involved a *lis pendens*, in which the question presented to this Court was whether such a procedure could be valid when the only protection afforded to the owner of land affected by the *lis pendens* was a post-sequestration hearing. A notice of *lis pendens* is a well established traditional remedy whereby a plaintiff (usually a judgment creditor) who brings an action to enforce an interest in property to which the defendant has title gives notice of the pendency of such action to third parties; the notice causes the interest which he establishes, if successful, to relate back to the date of the filing of the *lis pendens*. The filing of such notice will have an effect upon the defendant's ability to alienate the property, or to obtain additional security on the basis of title to the property, but the effect of the lis pendens is simply to give notice to the world of the remedy being sought in the lawsuit itself. The *lis pendens* itself creates no additional right in the property on the part of the plaintiff, but simply allows third parties to know that a lawsuit is pending in which the plaintiff is seeking to establish such a right. Here, too, the fact that the plaintiff already claims an interest in the property which he seeks to enforce by a lawsuit distinguishes this class of cases from the Connecticut attachment employed in the present case. * * *

It is both unwise and unnecessary, I believe, for the Court to proceed, as it does in Part IV, from its decision of the case before it to discuss abstract and hypothetical situations not before it. This is especially so where we are dealing with the Due Process Clause which, as the Court recognizes, "unlike some legal rules, is not a technical conception with a fixed content unrelated to time, place and circumstances. And it is even more true in a case involving constitutional limits on the methods by which the states may transfer or create interests in real property; in other areas of the law, dicta may do little damage, but those who insure titles or write title opinions often do not enjoy the luxury of distinguishing between dicta and holding."

The two elements of due process with which the Court concerns itself in Part IV—the requirement of a bond, and of "exigent circumstances"—prove to be upon analysis so vague that the discussion is not only unnecessary, but not particularly useful. Unless one knows what the terms and conditions of a bond are to be, the requirement of a "bond" in the abstract means little. The amount to be secured by the bond and the conditions of the bond are left unaddressed—is there to be liability on the part of a plaintiff if he is ultimately unsuccessful in the underlying lawsuit, or is it instead to be conditioned on some sort of good faith test? The "exigent circumstances" referred to by the Court are admittedly equally vague; nonresidency appears to be enough in some states, an attempt to conceal assets is required in others, an effort to flee the jurisdiction in still others. We should await concrete cases which present questions involving bonds and exigent circumstances before we attempt to decide when and if the Due Process Clause of the Fourteenth Amendment requires them as prerequisites for a lawful attachment.

JUSTICE SCALIA, concurring in part and concurring in the judgment.

Since the manner of attachment here was not a recognized procedure at common law, I agree that its validity under the Due Process Clause should be determined by applying the test we set forth in Mathews v. Eldridge, 424 U.S. 319, 96 S.Ct. 893, 47 L.Ed.2d 18 (1976); and I agree that it fails that test. I join Parts I and III of the Court's opinion, and concur in the judgment of the Court.

### *Notes*

1. What is the holding in *Doehr*? See Note, Connecticut v. Doehr and Procedural Due Process Values: The Sniadach Tetrad Revisited, 79 Cornell L.Rev. 1603 (1994). May Connecticut's *lis pendens* practice still be applied in other circumstances? For example, suppose a Connecticut home owner contracts for her house to be painted for a set price, but then refuses to pay because she is dissatisfied with the quality of the work. The painter files suit for breach of contract and obtains an attachment on the house without hearing or bond. Does the homeowner have a claim under the due process clause? See, e.g., Shaumyan v. O'Neill, 987 F.2d 122 (2d Cir.1993); New Destiny Development Corp. v. Piccione, 802 F.Supp. 692 (D.Conn.1992)(both holding Connecticut's *lis pendens* statute constitutional as applied to different factual circumstances than were present in *Doehr*).

To put an end to such case-by-case litigation, Connecticut amended the statute at issue in *Doehr*. A plaintiff seeking to attach property must now file an affidavit showing facts sufficient to demonstrate probable cause that the plaintiff will obtain a favorable judgment. The affidavit must also show exigent circumstances, such as defendant's likely removal of the property from the state or hiding or disposal of property. Defendant may request that a bond be posted. Conn.Gen.Stat. § 52–278e (1994).

2. The "Denver Boot" is used to immobilize automobiles that the police have determined are owned by people who owe numerous parking tickets. The boot, which is much cheaper to use than a towing service, can't be removed without special equipment. Naturally, it is not removed until the parking tickets are cleared. Is this a violation of due process? See Patterson v. Cronin, 650 P.2d 531 (Colo.1982). What about towing and destroying an apparently abandoned car without pre-seizure notice and hearing? Perry v. Village of Arlington Heights, 905 F.Supp. 465 (N.D.Ill. 1995).

Consider Judge Posner's views:

> Suppose, for example, that the issue is whether the owner of an apparently abandoned car should be notified, and given an opportunity for a hearing, before the car is towed away and sold for scrap. The chance that the car wasn't really abandoned, but broke down or was stolen, is not trivial, and the cost of a hearing is modest relative to the value of the car; * * * But suppose we are speaking of * * * illegally parked cars. Since the cars are not about to be destroyed, the deprivation is much less than in the case of the abandoned car. The probability of error is also much lower, because ordinarily the determination of whether a car is illegally parked is cut and dried. And the cost of a predeprivation hearing is very high; if the owner has to be notified before the car is towed, he'll remove it and the deterrent effect will be eliminated.

Richard Posner, Economic Analysis of Law 550 (4th ed.1992). How might the person who wrote *American Hospital* reduce the question of whether to grant a pre-seizure hearing to another "simple formula"?

3. What is the status of self-help remedies under the line of cases discussed in *Doehr*? For example, section 9–503 of the Uniform Commercial Code provides:

> Unless otherwise agreed a secured party has on default the right to take possession of the collateral. In taking possession a secured party may proceed without judicial process if this can be done without breach of the peace or may proceed by action. If the security agreement so provides the secured party may require the debtor to assemble the collateral and make it available to the secured party at a place to be designated by the secured party which is reasonably convenient to both parties. Without removal a secured party may render equipment unusable, and may dispose of collateral * * *.

Does this provision still pass muster? Compare Flagg Brothers, Inc. v. Brooks, 436 U.S. 149, 98 S.Ct. 1729, 56 L.Ed.2d 185 (1978)(self-help does not invoke any state action) with Lugar v. Edmondson Oil Co., 457 U.S. 922, 102 S.Ct. 2744, 73 L.Ed.2d 482 (1982)(state officers helping private creditor invokes state action). See Louis F. Del Duca, Pre–Notice, Pre–Hearing, Pre–Judgment Seizure of Assets—Self Help Repossession Under UCC § 9–503, Its Antecedents and Future, 79 Dick.L.Rev. 211 (1975); Note, Through the Eyes of the Debtor: Mississippi Reexamines the Breach of the Peace Exception to Uniform Commercial Code Section 9–503, 15 Miss.C.L.Rev. 145 (1994).

4. Many of the cases the Court relied upon in *Doehr* concerned consumer credit transactions. What does the imposition of these requirements do to the cost of credit or goods sold on credit? Is this desirable from the point of view of sellers, such as department stores? From the point of view of those buyers who have every intention of making their installment payments? See Peter V. Letsou, The Political Economy of Consumer Credit Regulation, 44 Emory L.J. 587 (1995)(explaining how coercive remedies enhance lender-borrower relationships). Does it matter that few debtors have a defense on the merits? See James J. White, The Abolition of Self–Help Repossession: The Poor Pay More, 1973 Wis.L.Rev. 503 (estimating that 6 of every 1000 people whose cars are repossessed have a meritorious

defense to non-payment). Or, even if the risk of error is low, is there value in the hearing itself, at least in terms of the dignity of the individual whose property is at risk? See Jerry L. Mashaw, The Supreme Court's Due Process Calculus for Administrative Adjudication in Mathews v. Eldridge: Three Factors in Search of a Theory of Value, 44 U.Chi.L.Rev. 28 (1976).

5. Prejudgment seizure is a powerful tool because it shifts the strategic balance of subsequent litigation: time now becomes the creditor's friend. A debtor who needs the seized property quickly may settle on terms worse than could be achieved through litigation or negotiation with the creditor. A dramatic example of the power of frozen assets to induce a prompt settlement is a case involving an eminent New York law firm. Kaye, Scholer, Fierman, Hays & Handler paid $41 million to settle with the government only six days after the federal Office of Thrift Supervision filed a lawsuit alleging that the firm had withheld information concerning its client, a failed savings and loan association. The key to the huge and quick settlement was the seizure order, which prevented the partners from disposing of law firm or individual assets pending the outcome of the suit. The use of the seizure order was surprising, given the fact that the firm was hardly likely to disappear or to be judgment proof. See Marshall L. Small, Limitations Imposed by the Federal Debt Collection Procedures Act on Use of Pre–Judgment Remedies to Enforce Federal Administrative Agency Claims for Monetary Payments, 49 Bus.Law. 1541 (1994); Stephanie B. Goldberg, Kaye Scholer: The Tremors Continue, 78–Jul. A.B.A.J. 50 (1992).

How might a state limit the grounds for effecting pre-judgment seizure of property to protect abuse? Should the law distinguish between residents and non-residents? Individuals and corporations? Perpetrators of fraud and upstanding citizens? See, e.g., Robert J. Kheel, New York's Amended Attachment Statute: A Prejudgment Remedy in Need of Further Revision, 44 Brook.L.Rev. 199 (1978).

6. As states have changed their prejudgment statutes to conform with the Supreme Court's line of decisions in this area, prejudgment attachment has come to resemble the temporary restraining order (TRO) even more than before. However, the two remedies still retain some differences, which yield advantages to plaintiffs who are able to choose between legal and equitable relief. For example, one difference between prejudgment replevin and a TRO is that a writ of replevin serves as a lien on defendant's property from the time the writ is issued, thus putting plaintiff creditor ahead of other creditors with respect to the replevied property in the event the creditor files for bankruptcy. Furthermore, often a writ of replevin must be served on the holder of defendant's property by a sheriff, or a United States Marshal for federal court cases, while a TRO may be served by anyone. Because of crowded court calendars, it may take a day or longer to find a sheriff or marshal to serve the writ of replevin. Finally, a writ of replevin attaches only to so much property as is actually seized, while, if it is available, preliminary relief may bar the disposition of property simply by serving the person in possession or control. Compare In re Estate of Ferdinand Marcos, 25 F.3d 1467 (9th Cir.1994), cert. denied, ___ U.S. ___, 115 S.Ct. 934, 130 L.Ed.2d 879 (1995)(allowing preliminary injunction under Rule 65 or All Writs Act preventing secreting or dissipating assets while tort claims of families of victims of torture and execution were pending) with

Mitsubishi International Corp. v. Cardinal Textile Sales, Inc. 14 F.3d 1507 (11th Cir.1994), cert. denied, ___ U.S. ___, 115 S.Ct. 1092, 130 L.Ed.2d 1061 (1995)(Rule 65 and All Writs Act do not authorize enjoining defendant from dispersing assets that may be required to satisfy future money judgment).

Are there situations in which a creditor might wish to use both remedies? Should there be any differences or should attachment look exactly like a TRO? Recall Rule 65(b)'s requirement that a TRO without notice may not issue unless it clearly appears from specific sworn facts that immediate, irreparable injury, loss or damage will result to the applicant before the adverse party can be heard in opposition. Also recall that in deciding whether to grant any injunction, a court must balance the hardships to the opposing parties.

7. Abusive use of attachment statutes may subject the abuser to liability. Thus, the Supreme Court unanimously permitted a suit under 42 U.S.C. § 1983 that alleged that the owner and manager of a trailer park conspired with local deputy sheriffs to illegally evict—and thus unreasonably seize—the plaintiffs' trailer home in violation of their constitutional rights under the fourth and fourteenth amendments. The trailer home was badly damaged during the eviction, which the deputy sheriffs knew was illegal because no eviction order had been issued. Soldal v. Cook County, 506 U.S. 56, 113 S.Ct. 538, 121 L.Ed.2d 450 (1992).

In a similar vein, the Court has held that private defendants charged with liability under 42 U.S.C. § 1983 for invoking state replevin, garnishment and attachment statutes later declared unconstitutional are not entitled to the qualified immunity that governmental officials enjoy. Wyatt v. Cole, 504 U.S. 158, 112 S.Ct. 1827, 118 L.Ed.2d 504 (1992). However, one court has held that plaintiffs seeking to hold private actors liable for invoking an unconstitutional state procedure must demonstrate that the defendants failed to act in good faith. Thus, the Fifth Circuit dismissed *Wyatt* on remand because the plaintiffs failed to show that the defendants knew or should have known that the state's replevin statute was unconstitutional prior to its invalidation by a court. Wyatt v. Cole, 994 F.2d 1113 (5th Cir.), cert. denied, ___ U.S. ___, 114 S.Ct. 470, 126 L.Ed.2d 421 (1993).

8. One of the tools that the government has used in the "War on Drugs" has been to seize the assets of those suspected to be drug dealers. If the alleged dealers are found to be not guilty, the assets are returned. The seizures even include the money that would be used to pay for attorneys to represent these alleged dealers in their criminal trials. What form of due process must be included in these seizure statutes to withstand scrutiny? See the next case.

## UNITED STATES v. JAMES DANIEL GOOD REAL PROPERTY

Supreme Court of the United States, 1993.
510 U.S. ___, 114 S.Ct. 492, 126 L.Ed.2d 490.

JUSTICE KENNEDY delivered the opinion of the Court.

The principal question presented is whether, in the absence of exigent circumstances, the Due Process Clause of the Fifth Amendment prohibits the Government in a civil forfeiture case from seizing real property without first affording the owner notice and an opportunity to be heard. We hold that it does. * * *

I

On January 31, 1985, Hawaii police officers executed a search warrant at the home of claimant James Daniel Good. The search uncovered about 89 pounds of marijuana, marijuana seeds, vials containing hashish oil, and drug paraphernalia. About six months later, Good pleaded guilty to promoting a harmful drug in the second degree, in violation of Hawaii law. He was sentenced to one year in jail and five years' probation, and fined $1,000. Good was also required to forfeit to the State $3,187 in cash found on the premises.

On August 8, 1989, four and one-half years after the drugs were found, the United States filed an *in rem* action in the United States District Court for the District of Hawaii, seeking to forfeit Good's house and the four-acre parcel on which it was situated. The United States sought forfeiture under 21 U.S.C. § 881(a)(7), on the ground that the property had been used to commit or facilitate the commission of a federal drug offense.[1]

On August 18, 1989, in an *ex parte* proceeding, a United States Magistrate Judge found that the Government had established probable cause to believe Good's property was subject to forfeiture under § 881(a)(7). A warrant of arrest *in rem* was issued, authorizing seizure of the property. The warrant was based on an affidavit recounting the fact of Good's conviction and the evidence discovered during the January 1985 search of his home by Hawaii police.

The Government seized the property on August 21, 1989, without prior notice to Good or an adversary hearing. At the time of the seizure, Good was renting his home to tenants for $900 per month. The Government permitted the tenants to remain on the premises subject to an occupancy agreement, but directed the payment of future rents to the United States Marshal.

Good filed a claim for the property and an answer to the Government's complaint. He asserted that the seizure deprived him of his property without due process of law and that the forfeiture action was invalid because it had not been timely commenced under the statute.

**1.** Title 21 U.S.C. § 881(a)(7) provides: .
"(a) The following shall be subject to forfeiture to the United States and no property right shall exist in them:

* * *

"(7) All real property, including any right, title, and interest (including any leasehold interest) in the whole of any lot or tract of land and any appurtenances or improvements, which is used, or intended to be used, in any manner or part, to commit, or to facilitate the commission of, a violation of this subchapter punishable by more than one year's imprisonment, except that no property shall be forfeited under this paragraph, to the extent of an interest of an owner, by reason of any act or omission established by that owner to have been committed or omitted without the knowledge or consent of that owner."

The District Court granted the Government's motion for summary judgment and entered an order forfeiting the property.

The Court of Appeals for the Ninth Circuit affirmed in part, reversed in part, and remanded for further proceedings. The court was unanimous in holding that the seizure of Good's property, without prior notice and a hearing, violated the Due Process Clause. * * *

We now affirm the due process ruling * * * .

II

The Due Process Clause of the Fifth Amendment guarantees that "[n]o person shall ... be deprived of life, liberty, or property, without due process of law." Our precedents establish the general rule that individuals must receive notice and an opportunity to be heard before the Government deprives them of property.

The Government does not, and could not, dispute that the seizure of Good's home and four-acre parcel deprived him of property interests protected by the Due Process Clause. By the Government's own submission, the seizure gave it the right to charge rent, to condition occupancy, and even to evict the occupants. Instead, the Government argues that it afforded Good all the process the Constitution requires. The Government makes two separate points in this regard. First, it contends that compliance with the Fourth Amendment suffices when the Government seizes property for purposes of forfeiture. In the alternative, it argues that the seizure of real property under the drug forfeiture laws justifies an exception to the usual due process requirement of preseizure notice and hearing. We turn to these issues.

A

The Government argues that because civil forfeiture serves a "law enforcement purpos[e]," the Government need comply only with the Fourth Amendment when seizing forfeitable property. We disagree. The Fourth Amendment does place restrictions on seizures conducted for purposes of civil forfeiture, One 1958 Plymouth Sedan v. Pennsylvania, 380 U.S. 693, 696, 85 S.Ct. 1246, 1248, 14 L.Ed.2d 170 (1965)(holding that the exclusionary rule applies to civil forfeiture), but it does not follow that the Fourth Amendment is the sole constitutional provision in question when the Government seizes property subject to forfeiture.

We have rejected the view that the applicability of one constitutional amendment pre-empts the guarantees of another. As explained in Soldal v. Cook County, 506 U.S. 56, 70, 113 S.Ct. 538, 548, 121 L.Ed.2d 450 (1992):

> "Certain wrongs affect more than a single right and, accordingly, can implicate more than one of the Constitution's commands. Where such multiple violations are alleged, we are not in the habit of identifying as a preliminary matter the claim's 'dominant' character. Rather, we examine each constitutional provision in turn."

Here, as in *Soldal*, the seizure of property implicates two " 'explicit textual source[s] of constitutional protection,' " the Fourth Amendment and the Fifth. The proper question is not which Amendment controls but whether either Amendment is violated.

Nevertheless, the Government asserts that when property is seized for forfeiture, the Fourth Amendment provides the full measure of process due under the Fifth. The Government relies on Gerstein v. Pugh, 420 U.S. 103, 95 S.Ct. 854, 43 L.Ed.2d 54 (1975), and Graham v. Connor, 490 U.S. 386, 109 S.Ct. 1865, 104 L.Ed.2d 443 (1989), in support of this proposition. That reliance is misplaced. *Gerstein* and *Graham* concerned not the seizure of property but the arrest or detention of criminal suspects, subjects we have considered to be governed by the provisions of the Fourth Amendment without reference to other constitutional guarantees. In addition, also unlike the seizure presented by this case, the arrest or detention of a suspect occurs as part of the regular criminal process, where other safeguards ordinarily ensure compliance with due process.

*Gerstein* held that the Fourth Amendment, rather than the Due Process Clause, determines the requisite post-arrest proceedings when individuals are detained on criminal charges. Exclusive reliance on the Fourth Amendment is appropriate in the arrest context, we explained, because the Amendment was "tailored explicitly for the criminal justice system," and its "balance between individual and public interests always has been thought to define the 'process that is due' for seizures of person or property in criminal cases." Furthermore, we noted that the protections afforded during an arrest and initial detention are "only the *first* stage of an elaborate system, unique in jurisprudence, designed to safeguard the rights of those accused of criminal conduct." (Emphasis in original.)

So too, in *Graham* we held that claims of excessive force in the course of an arrest or investigatory stop should be evaluated under the Fourth Amendment reasonableness standard, not under the "more generalized notion of 'substantive due process.' " Because the degree of force used to effect a seizure is one determinant of its reasonableness, and because the Fourth Amendment guarantees citizens the right "to be secure in their persons . . . against unreasonable . . . seizures," we held that a claim of excessive force in the course of such a seizure is "most properly characterized as one invoking the protections of the Fourth Amendment."

Neither *Gerstein* nor *Graham*, however, provides support for the proposition that the Fourth Amendment is the beginning and end of the constitutional inquiry whenever a seizure occurs. That proposition is inconsistent with the approach we took in Calero–Toledo v. Pearson Yacht Leasing Co., 416 U.S. 663, 94 S.Ct. 2080, 40 L.Ed.2d 452 (1974), which examined the constitutionality of *ex parte* seizures of forfeitable property under general principles of due process, rather than the Fourth Amendment. And it is at odds with our reliance on the Due Process

Clause to analyze prejudgment seizure and sequestration of personal property. See, e.g., Fuentes v. Shevin, 407 U.S. 67, 92 S.Ct. 1983, 32 L.Ed.2d 556 (1972); Mitchell v. W.T. Grant Co., 416 U.S. 600, 94 S.Ct. 1895, 40 L.Ed.2d 406 (1974).

It is true, of course, that the Fourth Amendment applies to searches and seizures in the civil context and may serve to resolve the legality of these governmental actions without reference to other constitutional provisions. * * * But the purpose and effect of the Government's action in the present case go beyond the traditional meaning of search or seizure. Here the Government seized property not to preserve evidence of wrongdoing, but to assert ownership and control over the property itself. Our cases establish that government action of this consequence must comply with the Due Process Clauses of the Fifth and Fourteenth Amendments.

Though the Fourth Amendment places limits on the Government's power to seize property for purposes of forfeiture, it does not provide the sole measure of constitutional protection that must be afforded property owners in forfeiture proceedings. So even assuming that the Fourth Amendment were satisfied in this case, it remains for us to determine whether the seizure complied with our well-settled jurisprudence under the Due Process Clause.

B

Whether *ex parte* seizures of forfeitable property satisfy the Due Process Clause is a question we last confronted in *Calero-Toledo*, which held that the Government could seize a yacht subject to civil forfeiture without affording prior notice or hearing. Central to our analysis in *Calero-Toledo* was the fact that a yacht was the "sort [of property] that could be removed to another jurisdiction, destroyed, or concealed, if advance warning of confiscation were given." The ease with which an owner could frustrate the Government's interests in the forfeitable property created a " 'special need for very prompt action' " that justified the postponement of notice and hearing until after the seizure.

We had no occasion in *Calero-Toledo* to decide whether the same considerations apply to the forfeiture of real property, which, by its very nature, can be neither moved nor concealed. * * *

The right to prior notice and a hearing is central to the Constitution's command of due process. "The purpose of this requirement is not only to ensure abstract fair play to the individual. Its purpose, more particularly, is to protect his use and possession of property from arbitrary encroachment—to minimize substantively unfair or mistaken deprivations of property.... " *Fuentes*.

We tolerate some exceptions to the general rule requiring predeprivation notice and hearing, but only in " 'extraordinary situations where some valid governmental interest is at stake that justifies postponing the hearing until after the event.' " Whether the seizure of real property for purposes of civil forfeiture justifies such an exception requires an examination of the competing interests at stake, along with the promptness and adequacy of later proceedings. The three-part inquiry set forth in Mathews v. Eldridge, 424 U.S. 319, 96 S.Ct. 893, 47 L.Ed.2d 18 (1976), provides guidance in this regard. The *Mathews* analysis requires us to consider the private interest affected by the official action; the risk of an erroneous deprivation of that interest through the procedures used, as well as the probable value of additional safeguards; and the Government's interest, including the administrative burden that additional procedural requirements would impose.

Good's right to maintain control over his home, and to be free from governmental interference, is a private interest of historic and continuing importance. The seizure deprived Good of valuable rights of ownership, including the right of sale, the right of occupancy, the right to unrestricted use and enjoyment, and the right to receive rents. All that the seizure left him, by the Government's own submission, was the right to bring a claim for the return of title at some unscheduled future hearing.

In *Fuentes*, we held that the loss of kitchen appliances and household furniture was significant enough to warrant a predeprivation hearing. And in Connecticut v. Doehr, 501 U.S. 1, 111 S.Ct. 2105, 115 L.Ed.2d 1 (1991), we held that a state statute authorizing prejudgment attachment of real estate without prior notice or hearing was unconstitutional, in the absence of extraordinary circumstances, even though the attachment did not interfere with the owner's use or possession and did not affect, as a general matter, rentals from existing leaseholds.

The seizure of a home produces a far greater deprivation than the loss of furniture, or even attachment. It gives the Government not only the right to prohibit sale, but also the right to evict occupants, to modify the property, to condition occupancy, to receive rents, and to supersede the owner in all rights pertaining to the use, possession, and enjoyment of the property.

The Government makes much of the fact that Good was renting his home to tenants, and contends that the tangible effect of the seizure was limited to taking the $900 a month he was due in rent. But even if this were the only deprivation at issue, it would not render the loss insignificant or unworthy of due process protection. The rent represents a significant portion of the exploitable economic value of Good's home. It cannot be classified as *de minimis* for purposes of procedural due process. In sum, the private interests at stake in the seizure of real property weigh heavily in the *Mathews* balance.

The practice of *ex parte* seizure, moreover, creates an unacceptable risk of error. Although Congress designed the drug forfeiture statute to be a powerful instrument in enforcement of the drug laws, it did not intend to deprive innocent owners of their property. The affirmative defense of innocent ownership is allowed by statute. * * *

The *ex parte* preseizure proceeding affords little or no protection to the innocent owner. In issuing a warrant of seizure, the magistrate judge need determine only that there is probable cause to believe that the real property was "used, or intended to be used, in any manner or part, to commit, or to facilitate the commission of" a felony narcotics offense. The Government is not required to offer any evidence on the question of innocent ownership or other potential defenses a claimant might have. * * *

The purpose of an adversary hearing is to ensure the requisite neutrality that must inform all governmental decisionmaking. That protection is of particular importance here, where the Government has a direct pecuniary interest in the outcome of the proceeding.[2] Moreover, the availability of a postseizure hearing may be no recompense for losses caused by erroneous seizure. Given the congested civil dockets in federal courts, a claimant may not receive an adversary hearing until many months after the seizure. And even if the ultimate judicial decision is that the claimant was an innocent owner, or that the Government lacked probable cause, this determination, coming months after the seizure, "would not cure the temporary deprivation that an earlier hearing might have prevented." *Doehr*.

This brings us to the third consideration under *Mathews*, "the Government's interest, including the function involved and the fiscal and administrative burdens that the additional or substitute procedural requirement would entail." The governmental interest we consider here is not some general interest in forfeiting property but the specific interest in seizing real property before the forfeiture hearing. The question in the civil forfeiture context is whether *ex parte* seizure is justified by a pressing need for prompt action. We find no pressing need here.

This is apparent by comparison to *Calero-Toledo*, where the Government's interest in immediate seizure of a yacht subject to civil forfeiture justified dispensing with the usual requirement of prior notice and hearing. Two essential considerations informed our ruling in that case: first, immediate seizure was necessary to establish the court's jurisdiction over the property, and second, the yacht might have disappeared had the Government given advance warning of the forfeiture action. * * * Neither of these factors is present when the target of forfeiture is real property.

Because real property cannot abscond, the court's jurisdiction can be preserved without prior seizure. * * *

In the case of real property, the res may be brought within the reach of the court simply by posting notice on the property and leaving a copy

2. The extent of the Government's financial stake in drug forfeiture is apparent from a 1990 memo, in which the Attorney General urged United States Attorneys to increase the volume of forfeitures in order to meet the Department of Justice's annual budget target: . "We must significantly increase production to reach our budget target. '... Failure to achieve the $470 million projection would expose the Department's forfeiture program to criticism and undermine confidence in our budget projections. Every effort must be made to increase forfeiture income during the remaining three months of [fiscal year] 1990.' "

of the process with the occupant. In fact, the rules which govern forfeiture proceedings under § 881 already permit process to be executed on real property without physical seizure * * *.

Nor is the *ex parte* seizure of real property necessary to accomplish the statutory purpose of § 881(a)(7). The Government's legitimate interests at the inception of forfeiture proceedings are to ensure that the property not be sold, destroyed, or used for further illegal activity prior to the forfeiture judgment. These legitimate interests can be secured without seizing the subject property.

Sale of the property can be prevented by filing a notice of *lis pendens* as authorized by state law when the forfeiture proceedings commence. If there is evidence, in a particular case, that an owner is likely to destroy his property when advised of the pending action, the Government may obtain an *ex parte* restraining order, or other appropriate relief, upon a proper showing in district court. See Fed.Rule Civ.Proc. 65. The Government's policy of leaving occupants in possession of real property under an occupancy agreement pending the final forfeiture ruling demonstrates that there is no serious concern about destruction in the ordinary case. Finally, the Government can forestall further illegal activity with search and arrest warrants obtained in the ordinary course.

In the usual case, the Government thus has various means, short of seizure, to protect its legitimate interests in forfeitable real property. There is no reason to take the additional step of asserting control over the property without first affording notice and an adversary hearing.

Requiring the Government to postpone seizure until after an adversary hearing creates no significant administrative burden. A claimant is already entitled to an adversary hearing before a final judgment of forfeiture. No extra hearing would be required in the typical case, since the Government can wait until after the forfeiture judgment to seize the property. From an administrative standpoint it makes little difference whether that hearing is held before or after the seizure. And any harm that results from delay is minimal in comparison to the injury occasioned by erroneous seizure.

C

It is true that, in cases decided over a century ago, we permitted the *ex parte* seizure of real property when the Government was collecting debts or revenue. See, e.g., Springer v. United States, 102 U.S. 586, 593–594, 26 L.Ed. 253 (1881); Murray's Lessee v. Hoboken Land & Improvement Co., 18 How. 272, 15 L.Ed. 372 (1856). Without revisiting these cases, it suffices to say that their apparent rationale—like that for allowing summary seizures during wartime, and seizures of contaminated food,—was one of executive urgency. "The prompt payment of taxes," we noted, "may be vital to the existence of a government." *Springer*. See also G.M. Leasing Corp. v. United States, 429 U.S. 338, 352, n. 18, 97 S.Ct. 619, 628, n. 18, 50 L.Ed.2d 530 (1977)("The rationale underlying [the revenue] decisions, of course, is that the very existence of government depends upon the prompt collection of the revenues").

A like rationale justified the *ex parte* seizure of tax-delinquent distilleries in the late nineteenth century, since before passage of the Sixteenth Amendment, the Federal Government relied heavily on liquor, customs, and tobacco taxes to generate operating revenues. In 1902, for example, nearly 75 percent of total federal revenues—$479 million out of a total of $653 million—was raised from taxes on liquor, customs, and tobacco.

The federal income tax code adopted in the first quarter of this century, however, afforded the taxpayer notice and an opportunity to be heard by the Board of Tax Appeals before the Government could seize property for nonpayment of taxes. In Phillips v. Commissioner, 283 U.S. 589, 51 S.Ct. 608, 75 L.Ed. 1289 (1931), the Court relied upon the availability, and adequacy, of these preseizure administrative procedures in holding that no judicial hearing was required prior to the seizure of property. These constraints on the Commissioner could be overridden, but only when the Commissioner made a determination that a jeopardy assessment was necessary. Writing for a unanimous Court, Justice Brandeis explained that under the tax laws "[f]ormal notice of the tax liability is thus given; the Commissioner is required to answer; and there is a complete hearing *de novo*.... These provisions amply protect the [taxpayer] against improper administrative action." * * *

Similar provisions remain in force today. The current Internal Revenue Code prohibits the Government from levying upon a deficient taxpayer's property without first affording the taxpayer notice and an opportunity for a hearing, unless exigent circumstances indicate that delay will jeopardize the collection of taxes due.

Just as the urgencies that justified summary seizure of property in the 19th century had dissipated by the time of *Phillips*, neither is there a plausible claim of urgency today to justify the summary seizure of real property under § 881(a)(7). Although the Government relies to some extent on forfeitures as a means of defraying law enforcement expenses, it does not, and we think could not, justify the prehearing seizure of forfeitable real property as necessary for the protection of its revenues.

D

The constitutional limitations we enforce in this case apply to real property in general, not simply to residences. That said, the case before us well illustrates an essential principle: Individual freedom finds tangible expression in property rights. At stake in this and many other forfeiture cases are the security and privacy of the home and those who take shelter within it.

Finally, the suggestion that this one petitioner must lose because his conviction was known at the time of seizure, and because he raises an as applied challenge to the statute, founders on a bedrock proposition: fair procedures are not confined to the innocent. The question before us is the legality of the seizure, not the strength of the Government's case.

In sum, based upon the importance of the private interests at risk and the absence of countervailing Government needs, we hold that the seizure of real property under § 881(a)(7) is not one of those extraordinary instances that justify the postponement of notice and hearing. Unless exigent circumstances are present, the Due Process Clause requires the Government to afford notice and a meaningful opportunity to be heard before seizing real property subject to civil forfeiture.[3]

To establish exigent circumstances, the Government must show that less restrictive measures—i.e., a *lis pendens*, restraining order, or bond—would not suffice to protect the Government's interests in preventing the sale, destruction, or continued unlawful use of the real property. We agree with the Court of Appeals that no showing of exigent circumstances has been made in this case, and we affirm its ruling that the *ex parte* seizure of Good's real property violated due process.

III

We turn now to the question whether a court must dismiss a forfeiture action that the Government filed within the statute of limitations, but without complying with certain other statutory timing directives. * * *

We hold that courts may not dismiss a forfeiture action filed within the five-year statute of limitations for noncompliance with the internal timing requirements of [the relevant statute]. The Government filed the action in this case within the five-year statute of limitations, and that sufficed to make it timely. We reverse the contrary holding of the Court of Appeals. * * *

CHIEF JUSTICE REHNQUIST, with whom JUSTICE SCALIA joins, and JUSTICE O'CONNOR joins in Parts II and III, concurring in part and dissenting in part.

I concur in Parts I and III of the Court's opinion and dissent with respect to Part II. The Court today departs from longstanding historical precedent and concludes that the *ex parte* warrant requirement under the Fourth Amendment fails to afford adequate due process protection to property owners who have been convicted of a crime that renders their real property susceptible to civil forfeiture under 21 U.S.C. § 881(a)(7). It reaches this conclusion although no such adversary hearing is required to deprive a criminal defendant of his liberty before trial. And its reasoning casts doubt upon long settled law relating to seizure of property to enforce income tax liability. I dissent from this ill-considered and disruptive decision.

3. We do not address what sort of procedures are required for preforfeiture seizures of real property in the context of criminal forfeiture. We note, however, that the federal drug laws now permit seizure before entry of a criminal forfeiture judgment only where the Government persuades a district court that there is probable cause to believe that a protective order "may not be sufficient to assure the availability of the property for forfeiture." 21 U.S.C. § 853(f).

I

The Court applies the three-factor balancing test for evaluating procedural due process claims set out in Mathews v. Eldridge, 424 U.S. 319, 96 S.Ct. 893, 47 L.Ed.2d 18 (1976), to reach its unprecedented holding. I reject the majority's expansive application of *Mathews*. *Mathews* involved a due process challenge to the adequacy of administrative procedures established for the purpose of terminating Social Security disability benefits, and the *Mathews* balancing test was first conceived to address due process claims arising in the context of modern administrative law. No historical practices existed in this context for the Court to consider. The Court has expressly rejected the notion that the *Mathews* balancing test constitutes a "one-size- fits-all" formula for deciding every due process claim that comes before the Court. More importantly, the Court does not work on a clean slate in the civil forfeiture context involved here. It has long sanctioned summary proceedings in civil forfeitures. See, e.g., Dobbins's Distillery v. United States, 96 U.S. 395, 24 L.Ed. 637 (1878)(upholding seizure of a distillery by executive officers based on *ex parte* warrant ); and G.M. Leasing Corp. v. United States, 429 U.S. 338, 97 S.Ct. 619, 50 L.Ed.2d 530 (1977)(upholding warrantless automobile seizures).

A

The Court's fixation on *Mathews* sharply conflicts with both historical practice and the specific textual source of the Fourth Amendment's "reasonableness" inquiry. The Fourth Amendment strikes a balance between the people's security in their persons, houses, papers, and effects and the public interest in effecting searches and seizures for law enforcement purposes. Compliance with the standards and procedures prescribed by the Fourth Amendment constitutes all the "process" that is "due" to respondent Good under the Fifth Amendment in the forfeiture context. We made this very point in *Gerstein* with respect to procedures for detaining a criminal defendant pending trial:

> "The historical basis of the probable cause requirement is quite different from the relatively recent application of variable procedural due process in debtor-creditor disputes and termination of government-created benefits. The Fourth Amendment was tailored explicitly for the criminal justice system, and its balance between individual and public interests always has been thought to define the 'process that is due' for seizures of person *or property* in criminal cases, including the detention of suspects pending trial."

The *Gerstein* Court went on to decide that while there must be a determination of probable cause by a neutral magistrate in order to detain an arrested suspect prior to trial, such a determination could be made in a nonadversarial proceeding, based on hearsay and written testimony. It is paradoxical indeed to hold that a criminal defendant can be temporarily deprived of liberty on the basis of an *ex parte* probable cause determination, yet respondent Good cannot be temporarily deprived of property on the same basis. As we said in United States v.

Monsanto, 491 U.S. 600, 615–616, 109 S.Ct. 2657, 2666–2667, 105 L.Ed.2d 512 (1989):

> "[I]t would be odd to conclude that the Government may not restrain property, such as the home and apartment in respondent's possession, based on a finding of probable cause, when we have held that (under appropriate circumstances), the Government may restrain persons where there is a finding of probable cause to believe that the accused has committed a serious offense."

Similarly, in *Graham* the Court faced the question of what constitutional standard governs a free citizen's claim that law enforcement officials used excessive force in the course of making an arrest, investigatory stop, or other "seizure" of his person. We held that the Fourth Amendment, rather than the Due Process Clause, provides the source of any specific limitations on the use of force in seizing a person: "Because the Fourth Amendment provides an explicit textual source of constitutional protection against this sort of physically intrusive governmental conduct, that Amendment, not the more generalized notion of 'substantive due process' must be the guide for analyzing these claims." The "explicit textual source of constitutional protection" found in the Fourth Amendment should also guide the analysis of respondent Good's claim of a right to additional procedural measures in civil forfeitures.

B

The Court dismisses the holdings of *Gerstein* and *Graham* as inapposite because they concern "the arrest or detention of criminal suspects." But we have never held that the Fourth Amendment is limited only to criminal proceedings. In *Soldal*, we expressly stated that the Fourth Amendment "applies in the civil context as well." Our historical treatment of civil forfeiture procedures underscores the notion that the Fourth Amendment specifically governs the process afforded in the civil forfeiture context, and it is too late in the day to question its exclusive application. As we decided in *Calero-Toledo*, there is no need to look beyond the Fourth Amendment in civil forfeitures proceedings involving the Government because *ex parte* seizures are "too firmly fixed in the punitive and remedial jurisprudence of the country to be now displaced."

The Court acknowledges the long history of *ex parte* seizures of real property through civil forfeiture, and says "[w]ithout revisiting these cases,"—whatever that means—that they appear to depend on the need for prompt payment of taxes. The Court goes on to note that the passage of the Sixteenth Amendment alleviated the Government's reliance on liquor, customs, and tobacco taxes as sources of operating revenue. Whatever the merits of this novel distinction, it fails entirely to distinguish the leading case in the field, *Phillips*, a unanimous opinion authored by Justice Brandeis. That case dealt with the enforcement of income tax liability, which the Court says has replaced earlier forms of taxation as the principle source of governmental revenue. There the Court said:

> "The right of the United States to collect its internal revenue by summary administrative proceedings has long been settled ... [w]here, as here, adequate opportunity is afforded for a later judicial determination of the legal rights, summary proceedings to secure prompt performance of pecuniary obligations to the government have been consistently sustained."

> "Where only property rights are involved, mere postponement of the judicial enquiry is not a denial of due process, if the opportunity given for the ultimate judicial determination of the liability is adequate."

Thus today's decision does not merely discard established precedence regarding excise taxes, but deals at least a glancing blow to the authority of the Government to collect income tax delinquencies by summary proceedings.

II

The Court attempts to justify the result it reaches by expansive readings of *Fuentes* and *Doehr*. In *Fuentes*, the Court struck down state replevin procedures, finding that they served no important state interest that might justify the summary proceedings. Specifically, the Court noted that the tension between the private buyer's use of the property pending final judgment and the private seller's interest in preventing further use and deterioration of his security tipped the balance in favor of a prior hearing in certain replevin situations. "[The provisions] allow summary seizure of a person's possessions when no more than private gain is directly at stake." Cf. Mitchell v. W.T. Grant Co., 416 U.S. 600, 94 S.Ct. 1895, 40 L.Ed.2d 406 (1974)(upholding Louisiana sequestration statute that provided immediate postdeprivation hearing along with the option of damages).

The Court in *Fuentes* also was careful to point out the limited situations in which seizure before hearing was constitutionally permissible, and included among them "summary seizure of property to collect the internal revenue of the United States." Certainly the present seizure is analogous, and it is therefore quite inaccurate to suggest that *Fuentes* is authority for the Court's holding in the present case.

Likewise in *Doehr*, the Court struck down a state statute authorizing prejudgment attachment of real estate without prior notice or hearing due to potential bias of the self-interested private party seeking attachment. The Court noted that the statute enables one of the private parties to "make use of state procedures with the overt, significant assistance of state officials," that involve state action "substantial enough to implicate the Due Process Clause." *Doehr*. The Court concluded that, absent exigent circumstances, the private party's interest in attaching the property did not justify the burdening of the private property owner's rights without a hearing to determine the likelihood of recovery. In the present case, however, it is not a private party but the Government itself which is seizing the property.

The Court's effort to distinguish *Calero-Toledo* is similarly unpersuasive. The Court says that "[c]entral to our analysis in *Calero-Toledo* was the fact that a yacht was the 'sort [of property] that could be removed to another jurisdiction, destroyed, or concealed, if advanced warning of confiscation were given.'" But this is one of the *three* reasons given by the Court for upholding the summary forfeiture in that case: the other two—"fostering the public interest and preventing continued illicit use of the property," and the fact that the "seizure is not initiated by self-interested private parties; rather, Commonwealth officials determine whether seizure is appropriate . . .," are both met in the present case. And while not capable of being moved or concealed, the real property at issue here surely could be destroyed or damaged. Several dwellings are located on the property that was seized from respondent Good, and these buildings could easily be destroyed or damaged to prevent them from falling into the hands of the Government if prior notice were required.

The government interests found decisive in *Calero-Toledo* are equally present here: the seizure of respondent Good's real property serves important governmental purposes in combatting illegal drugs; a preseizure notice might frustrate this statutory purpose by permitting respondent Good to destroy or otherwise damage the buildings on the property; and Government officials made the seizure rather than self-interested private parties seeking to gain from the seizure. * * *

III

This is not to say that the Government's use of civil forfeiture statutes to seize real property in drug cases may not cause hardship to innocent individuals. But I have grave doubts whether the Court's decision in this case will do much to alleviate those hardships, and I am confident that whatever social benefits might flow from the decision are more than offset by the damage to settled principles of constitutional law which are inflicted to secure these perceived social benefits. I would reverse the decision of the Court of Appeals *in toto*.

JUSTICE O'CONNOR, concurring in part and dissenting in part.

JUSTICE THOMAS, concurring in part and dissenting in part.

[opinions omitted]

### *Notes*

1. Does Judge Posner's analysis (supra p. 738) help to decide whether people like Mr. Good should have the preseizure hearing the Court mandates here?

2. *James Daniel Good* concerned real estate. Should the holding be extended to personal property? See, e.g., United States v. Daccarett, 6 F.3d 37 (2d Cir.1993), cert. denied, ___ U.S. ___, 114 S.Ct. 1294, 127 L.Ed.2d 648 (1994)(allowing seizure of bank account due to exigent circumstances). If so, is the dissent correct to charge that the decision deals "at least a glancing

blow to the authority of the Government to collect income tax delinquencies by summary proceedings"?

3. *Another parking problem*. Consider the plight of Ms Ilana Love. She found a parking ticket on her car for parking illegally in a handicapped space. The fine is $275. She cannot obtain an administrative hearing without prepaying the fine. Is this procedure a deprivation of property without due process under *James Daniel Good*? Love v. City of Monterey, 37 Cal.App.4th 562, 43 Cal.Rptr.2d 911 (1995).

4. What should the remedy be for improperly failing to provide a preseizure hearing? Dismissal of the forfeiture action with prejudice? Dismissal, but without prejudice to refile, if the statute of limitations permits? E.g., United States v. 2751 Peyton Woods Trail, 66 F.3d 1164 (11th Cir. 1995). Damages under *Bivens* or § 1983? E.g., Conkey v. Reno, 885 F.Supp. 1389 (D.Nev.1995). The use value of the property seized until a hearing is held? E.g., United States v. All Assets and Equipment of West Side Bldg. Corp., 58 F.3d 1181 (7th Cir.1995), cert. denied, ___ U.S. ___, 116 S.Ct. 698, 133 L.Ed.2d 656 (1996). The exclusion from the forfeiture proceeding of any evidence obtained as a result of the pre-hearing seizure? See, e.g., United States v. 51 Pieces of Real Property, 17 F.3d 1306, 1315 (10th Cir.1994).

## B. POST-JUDGMENT RELIEF

### 1. BASIC COLLECTION STRATEGY

### JAMES J. BROWN, COLLECTING A JUDGMENT

13 Litigation 31 (Fall 1986).

You win the big one: a $5 million judgment. With it comes rave reviews from clients, colleagues, friends, and relatives. You have the judgment framed and hang it on your wall.

But wait a second. "Where's the money?" the managing partner asks. The real world rears its ugly head. It dawns on you that the defendant isn't going to stroll into your office with a certified check for five million bucks.

You close your door, take the judgment off your wall, and replace it with the certificate you got for coaching your daughter's little league team. You stop taking phone calls and start looking for the rules on collecting judgments.

Begin with Federal Rule of Civil Procedure 69 [reproduced in Appendix, infra at p. 889]. It says that procedures for enforcing judgments follow state law, except when a federal statute specifically governs.

Under state law, the first step is to record the judgment in the county where the debtor resides or owns property. A federal judgment may be recorded in the same manner as a state judgment in any locality within the federal district where the judgment was entered. File a certified copy of the judgment in the county land records, usually at the registry of deeds or county recorder's office, and pay the filing fee. The judgment becomes a lien on the debtor's property in the county where you record it. * * *

Say you have a federal judgment from the United States District Court for the District of Maryland at Baltimore. If the debtor owns property in Howard County, Maryland (which does not encompass Baltimore, but is in the same federal district), you would record the judgment by filing a certified copy with the appropriate office of Howard County. The judgment will then be a lien against the debtor's Howard County property.

* * * If you know the debtor has property in other counties in the same state but outside the federal district where the judgment was entered, follow the state procedures for registering the judgment there. Registering the judgment means enrolling it on the court docket. Then record the judgment in the new county so it becomes a lien on any real property the debtor owns there.

Judgments obtained in a federal district court may also be registered in other federal districts once they become final by appeal or otherwise. * * *

So once you register the judgment in another district, you can record it and get the resulting lien against the debtor's property in any county within the registering district. * * *

Now you have liens on the debtor's property in various places. That is a good start, because it will establish your priority interest in that property if you get into a scuffle with creditors who come along later. But how do you get your money?

If the debtor has property in the jurisdiction where the judgment was entered or registered, have the court clerk issue a writ of execution against the property (sometimes called an attachment writ or a garnishment writ). Then present the writ to the U.S. marshal, who will attach the property to satisfy your judgment. * * *

You should describe the property to the marshal as specifically as possible. If there are different kinds of property, request different writs from the clerk. For example, in the federal district courts, there are usually separate forms of writs for: Attachment on Judgment (personal property, goods, chattels); Attachment on Judgment (credits); and Attachment on Judgment (garnishment of wages, earnings, salary, commissions and pensions). Consult the clerk on what writs should be issued.

If the debtor's property is in the hands of a third party such as a bank, proceed in accordance with state law (unless a particular federal statute applies) to attach (or garnish) those credits and have them applied against your judgment. (You should check applicable state and federal law on exemptions, especially when garnishing wages.) Writs of attachment on a judgment may be obtained from each court where your judgment is registered, and the process can be repeated until your judgment is satisfied. * * *

If the debtor owns personal property, recording the judgment in the county courthouse or registry of deeds may not be enough. For example, if the property is an aircraft, the U.S. marshal should attach it in accordance with state law.

* * * Once the marshal has attached and levied on the property, he will auction the property, sell it, and apply the sale proceeds, after expenses, to the judgment. Any excess proceeds are distributed to other lienholders in the order of their priorities, and, if there is anything left, to the debtor. * * *

To find the debtor's assets, you may use the same discovery devices available in prejudgment litigation, and more. * * * Rule 69 entitles a judgment creditor to use the discovery procedures found in Rules 26 through 37. In addition, you may use applicable state discovery procedures and state supplementary proceedings. As usual, the timing and sequence of discovery is your choice. An examination of the judgment debtor in supplementary proceedings is an excellent way to begin post-judgment discovery.

To start the process, file a petition for supplementary proceedings. In that petition, recite the facts concerning your judgment, and include a request to examine the judgment debtor and have him bring documents. * * *

If the debtor is a publicly held company, your request should call for quarterly and annual reports filed with the Securities and Exchange Commission. If the debtor is required to file other disclosure documents with local, state or federal agencies, get those too.

In post-judgment discovery, more than one examination of the debtor is often necessary, and you may have to move for sanctions under Rule 37 to get all the necessary documents from a recalcitrant debtor. You should also go after other sources of information about the debtor and his finances.

If the debtor has an accountant, subpoena the accountant and his records concerning the debtor. * * *

Even if the debtor has "lost" his financial statements or tax returns, you will find them in the accountant's files. If the debtor does not have an accountant, and still has not produced tax returns, move the court for an order requiring the debtor to give you written authorization to obtain copies of his returns from the Internal Revenue Service.

In some cases, you may suspect that the debtor has not produced all his bank records. When that happens, go right to the source. If you know where the debtor banks, subpoena the records from the bank.

* * * Credit card account statements are clues to the debtor's spending patterns, and they can help you trace exactly where he was on a given day. The records might show that the debtor stopped at a

marina for food and gas, using a boat you did not realize that he or his alter ego corporation owned. * * *

During post-judgment litigation, you can often get injunctions or writs to freeze or attach assets that the debtor has transferred to others. This will prevent the assets from being further dissipated while your post-judgment litigation proceeds.

You should consider restraining asset transfers during a post-judgment appeal by invoking Federal Civil Procedure Rule 62 [reproduced in Appendix, infra at p. 884]. If the debtor is unable to post a supersedeas bond, you can move the court to set other conditions for securing the judgment pending appeal. This will make it easier to collect the judgment if the debtor's appeal is unsuccessful. If the debtor does post a bond, the judgment can be satisfied against the bond. * * *

Under certain state and federal laws, receiverships may be established to administer the affairs and conserve the assets of financially troubled companies. More often than not, bankruptcy is the preferred method of administering and reorganizing insolvent companies. In [one] case, we proceeded under federal receivership statutes to give us quick access to the debtor's business and to prevent further dissipation of assets. * * *

The postjudgment litigation may be lengthy and expensive. There is no easy way at the beginning to assure your client that the money he spends in post-judgment discovery and litigation will produce an even bigger recovery. Usually, the preliminary post-judgment discovery, if done properly, will tell you how much of the judgment you can collect. * * *

## *Notes*

1. Collection problems can be quite involved. For example, does the legal definition of "property" include intangible property such as the ownership of securities? If so, how can a creditor collect such intangible property? If the registered holder of stock has sold the certificate representing his shares subsequent to a judgment against him but before collection has been accomplished, can a creditor reach the certificate?

The UCC permits attachment or levy upon a security only if the certificate which represents the debtors' shares is itself seized. This hinders creditors in their efforts at collection, but protects bona fide purchasers of securities and promotes free transferability. However, certain securities fall outside the ambit of the UCC, for example, if they represent shares which are not commonly traded on securities exchanges. In such cases, for example in Arkansas, the law provides that creditors may "seize" the corporate securities merely by having a sheriff leave a writ of execution with the corporation; there is no need to seize the certificates themselves. Thus, in Arkansas at least, a creditor would wish to maintain that securities owned by a debtor are not securities under the terms of the UCC so that even transfers to bona fide purchasers can be thwarted. See Robert Laurence, Enforcing a Money Judgment Against the Defendant's Stocks and Bonds: A

Brief Foray into the Forbidding Realms of Article Eight and the Fourth Amendment, 38 Ark.L.Rev. 561 (1985).

2. In some states, creditors can reach intangible property that otherwise cannot be readily seized through a device known as a "turnover statute." Thus, in Renger Memorial Hospital v. State, 674 S.W.2d 828 (Tex.App.1984), the trial court granted plaintiffs partial satisfaction of a judgment in the form of an order requiring the defendant hospital to turn over a cause of action the hospital owned against its former directors. See generally Bradley J.B. Toben & Keith C. Livesay, Article 3827A and the Maturation of the Creditor's Bill Remedy in Texas, 37 Baylor L.Rev. 587 (1985); Philip K. Maxwell & Tim Labadie, Insurance Law, 48 S.M.U.L.Rev. 1351, 1387–91 (1995)(reviewing requirements for turnover of causes of action).

In a like vein, African–American plaintiffs settled a judgment for $37,500 that was outstanding against the Invisible Empire Knights of the Ku Klux Klan by taking all of the group's tangible and intangible assets, including its name and mailing lists. The plaintiffs intended to destroy the mailing lists, rather than exploit them commercially. Lynne Duke, Klan Unit Gives Up Assets in Rights Suit Settlement, Washington Post, May 20, 1993, at A1.

3. Another consideration is the fact that in most states, a judgment is valid for only a set length of time. For example, Minnesota provides for judgments that are valid for 10 years. Minn.Stat.Ann. 550.01 (1988). Maine, however, provides instead a presumption of payment of a judgment once 20 years have elapsed since it was issued. Me.Rev.Stat.Ann. tit. 14, section 860 (1988). Thus, even if a debtor is paying off a judgment, she may escape paying off some of it if the validity of the judgment ends. On the other hand, even if a debtor is without seizable assets at the time the judgment is rendered, and is apparently "judgment-proof," the debtor may bear watching over the time that the judgment is valid in the event she does acquire some assets that can be seized.

4. Additional practical advice on collection strategy is available in Robert L. Haig & Patricia O. Kahn, Representing the Judgment Creditor, 16 Am.J.Tr.Advoc. 1 (1992). More theoretical material is available in Stephen B. Burbank, Federal Judgments Law: Sources of Authority and Sources of Rules, 70 Tex.L.Rev. 1551 (1992). For advice on collecting judgments in foreign contexts, see Charles Platto & William G. Horton, Enforcement of Foreign Judgments Worldwide (2d ed.1993); James Richardson, Debt Recovery in Europe (1993).

## KAHN v. BERMAN

California Court of Appeal, First District, 1988.
198 Cal.App.3d 1499, 244 Cal.Rptr. 575.

SABRAW, ASSOCIATE JUSTICE.

* * *

### I. THE FACTUAL AND PROCEDURAL HISTORY

William and John Kahn contracted with William Berman, Carl Pecson and Ace Truck & Equipment Rental, Inc., for the purchase of the

Ace rental business in Las Vegas, Nevada. After disputes arose between the parties, litigation ensued in the Nevada state courts. * * *

A money judgment was entered on July 19, 1984, against William and Nana Berman in an amount greater than $1.2 million and against Carl and Shirley Pecson in an amount greater than $900,000. The judgment included significant punitive damages based on the jury's verdict that fraud had been committed. It was appealed on December 17, 1984.

The Kahns recorded the entire Nevada money judgment in the San Mateo County Recorder's Office on July 20, 1984. Five days later, on July 25, 1984, a purported $500,000 first deed of trust was recorded against the Berman's [sic] Hillsborough, California, residence by an entity named "The Berman Corporation." The deed of trust bore a date of December 15, 1983, but the notary's acknowledgement of William and Nana Berman's signatures was dated July 20, 1984, just one day after the Nevada judgment was entered. The address listed for the Berman Corporation on the deed of trust was 585 Remillard Drive, Hillsborough, California, the same property purportedly being encumbered.

On March 6, 1985, the Kahns filed an application in the San Mateo County Superior Court requesting entry of a judgment based on the Nevada judgment. A new California judgment was entered on the sister-state judgment by the clerk of the court on March 13, 1985. Notice of entry of the judgment was served on the Bermans on March 14, 1985. However, the notice contained a typographical error—rather than correctly reflecting that judgment had been entered in the amount of $1,237,433.38, it stated that the judgment was for $123,744.38. On September 5, 1985, the Berman's counsel accepted service of a corrected notice of entry of judgment on the sister-state judgment.

The Kahns had a writ of execution against a dwelling house (the Berman's Hillsborough residence) issued by the San Mateo County Superior Court on February 27, 1986. The writ of execution was levied by the sheriff and recorded on March 7, 1986. Notice of the levy was mailed the same day.

On March 31, 1986, the Kahns applied for an order authorizing the sale of the Berman residence. William Berman recorded a declaration of homestead on his Hillsborough residence on April 18, 1986. An abstract of judgment reflecting the Kahns' new California judgment was recorded in the San Mateo County Recorder's Office on May 1, 1986.

The Bermans opposed the Kahns' application for an order of sale on several grounds. Among other things, they argued that they were entitled to a $55,000 homestead exemption based on the April 18, 1986, declaration of homestead. They took the position that the declaration of homestead was senior to any judgment lien based on the Nevada judgment because no *abstract* of the Nevada judgment had been filed in San Mateo by April 18, 1986. In the event the court rejected their declared homestead argument, the Bermans alternatively asserted that they were entitled to claim the statutory homestead exemption authorized by section 704.720. Finally, they argued that, if an order of sale was granted, the minimum bid was required to be at least $555,644.23 (homestead exemption of $55,000, property taxes of $644.23, and the $500,000 Berman Corporation deed of trust).

On July 24, 1986, following a contested hearing, the Kahns obtained an order for the sale of the Bermans' Hillsborough residence pursuant to Code of Civil Procedure section 704.780. Among other things, the order stated that: (1) the sheriff had completed levy on the Bermans' residence in the form and manner required by law; (2) although the property was a valid homestead, the Kahn's judgment lien had priority because the declaration of homestead was not recorded until April 19, 1986 [sic; April 18, 1986]; (3) the fair market value of the dwelling was $450,000; and (4) the Bermans were not entitled to claim the statutory homestead exemption. * * *

### II. Analysis

#### A. *Recordation in California of a Sister State Judgment Does Not Create a Judgment Lien on Real Property in California*

* * * There is presently no single statute which clearly and explicitly lists those money judgments (i.e., California, sister-state, federal or foreign) that may serve as the basis for creation of a judgment lien by recordation. * * *

Reading all of these statutes together with the statutory history, it is apparent that recordation of a sister state judgment cannot directly give rise to a judgment lien on real property located in California—a sister state money judgment must first be reduced to a California judgment.

In the present case, rather than immediately filing an application for entry of a new California judgment based on the Nevada judgment entered on July 19, 1984, plaintiffs recorded a certified copy of the entire Nevada judgment in San Mateo County. Because plaintiffs did not initially comply with the Sister State Money Judgments Act by obtaining a California judgment, the recordation had no effect.

#### B. *The Full Faith and Credit Clause of the United States Constitution Does Not Require California to Follow Nevada Procedures for Creation of a Judgment Lien*

Anticipating the difficulty presented by their initial failure to have a California judgment entered on the Nevada judgment and to then record an abstract of such a California judgment, the Kahns argue in their cross appeal that requiring them to follow California rather than Nevada procedures for enforcement of the Nevada judgment violates the full faith and credit clause of the United States Constitution. (U.S. Const., art. IV, § 1.) They further assert that recording of a certified copy of the Nevada judgment was sufficient under the law of Nevada to create a judgment lien in California.

Although the Kahns correctly recite Nevada law regarding creation of a judgment lien on real property located in Nevada, we disagree with their constitutional assertion that Nevada procedural law must be followed when enforcing a Nevada judgment in California. The Kahns cite only the bare language of Article IV of the Constitution for the proposition that California is required to follow Nevada procedures for creation of a judgment lien in such a case. They fail to provide any other authority on this point. However, our own research reveals that a contrary interpretation was rendered by the United States Supreme Court in the early days of the Constitution.

In McElmoyle v. Cohen (1839) 38 U.S. (13 Pet.) 312, [10 L.Ed. 177], the Supreme Court held that a South Carolina judgment could not be directly enforced by execution in Georgia. The court explained that "To give it the force of a judgment in another State, it must be made a judgment there, and can only be executed in the latter as its laws may permit. It must be conceded that the judgment of a State court cannot be enforced out of the State by an execution issued within it." (Id. 13 Pet. at p. 325; see also * * * Huntington v. Attrill (1892) 146 U.S. 657, 685, 13 S.Ct. 224, 234, 36 L.Ed. 1123, 1134 [Article IV, section 1, of the Constitution does not "put the judgments of other States upon the footing of domestic judgments, to be enforced by execution; but [it leaves] the manner in which they may be enforced to the law of the State in which they are sued on, pleaded, or offered in evidence"], citing *McElmoyle v. Cohen, supra,* 38 U.S. (13 Pet.) 312, 325 * * *.)

It follows from these authorities that the Kahns' argument must be rejected. The full faith and credit clause is not violated by requiring that a sister-state judgment first be reduced to a California judgment before it may serve as the basis for a judgment lien on real property located in California.

*C. The Order Authorizing the Sale of the Bermans' Residence Was Erroneous*

The traditional method for enforcing a money judgment obtained in a sister state was to institute an independent action on the sister-state judgment in a California court. In 1974 the Sister State Money Judgments Act created a simpler alternative method for registration of such judgments.

Section 1710.15, subdivision (a), provides "A judgment creditor may apply for entry of a judgment based on a sister state judgment by filing an application pursuant to Section 1710.20." Once an application is properly filed in an appropriate venue, the clerk of the court is required to enter California judgment. With certain statutory exceptions, the new judgment has the same effect as an original California money judgment and "may be enforced or satisfied in like manner."

The next step in the process is for notice of entry of the California judgment to be served "promptly" by the judgment creditor upon the judgment debtor in the same manner as provided for service of summons. Within 30 days after service of the notice of entry, the judgment debtor is entitled to make a motion to have the new judgment vacated. The judgment can be vacated "on any ground which would be a defense to an action in this state on the sister state judgment...." In most cases, a judgment creditor cannot have a writ of execution issued until at least 30 days after the judgment creditor has been served with notice of entry of the new judgment.

The Kahns completed the statutory prerequisites for enforcement of the Nevada judgment on September 5, 1985, when notice of entry of their new California judgment was accepted by the Bermans' counsel. Rather than creating a judgment lien by recording an abstract of the new judgment, the Kahns next proceeded with execution against the Bermans' residence.[7]

The first step for execution on a dwelling house is for the judgment creditor to have the superior court issue a writ of execution. The judgment creditor then delivers the writ to the levying officer with instructions for service. Next, the officer levies on the real property. After the levy, the officer is required to promptly serve notice on the judgment creditor that the levy has been made. Within 20 days after the notice is served, the judgment creditor must apply for an order of sale or the property will be released. The application must state whether the dwelling is a homestead and must also state the amount of any liens or encumbrances on the dwelling. If the court thereafter determines that the dwelling is exempt, it must also determine the fair market value and make an order for its sale subject to the homestead exemption.[8] If no bid is received at the sale which exceeds the amount of the homestead exemption plus the amount needed to satisfy all liens and encumbrances, the homestead cannot be sold.[9] Finally if no bid in excess of 90 percent of the fair market value of the dwelling is received, the creditor must return to court and seek an order permitting the sale for the highest bid that exceeds the total amount of the homestead exemption and all liens and encumbrances.

Although portions of the foregoing statutory scheme were followed in this case, the correct result was not reached. The March 7, 1986, levy on the Bermans' residence gave rise to an execution lien (even though no judgment lien had previously been created). The Kahns thereafter applied for an order of sale * * *. The trial court correctly determined

7. Nothing in the statutory scheme requires a judgment creditor to create a judgment lien. The creditor can simply choose to levy execution, thereby creating an execution lien.

8. Section 704.780, subdivision (b) provides: "The court shall determine whether the dwelling is exempt. If the court determines that the dwelling is exempt, the court shall determine the amount of the homestead exemption and the fair market value of the dwelling and shall make an order for sale of the dwelling subject to the homestead exemption. The order for sale of the dwelling subject to the homestead exemption shall specify the amount of the proceeds of the sale that is to be distributed to each person having a lien or encumbrance on the dwelling and shall include the name and address of each such person. * * *

9. Section 704.800, subdivision (a) provides: "(a) If no bid is received at a sale of a homestead pursuant to a court order for sale that exceeds the amount of the homestead exemption plus any additional amount necessary to satisfy all liens and encumbrances on the property, including but not limited to any attachment or judgment lien, the homestead shall not be sold and shall be released and is not hereafter subject to a court order for sale upon subsequent application by the same judgment creditor for a period of one year."

that the Kahns' March 7, 1986, execution lien had priority over the Bermans' April 18, 1986, declaration of homestead. However, in their response to the application for an order of sale, the Bermans had filed a declaration which established that the property in question was a homestead as defined in section 704.710, subdivision (c),[10] because: (1) it was the principal dwelling where they resided on March 7, 1986 (the date the Kahns' execution lien arose); and (2) they had continuously resided there since that time. The declaration also established that the Bermans were over the age of 65. As a result, the trial court erred when it concluded that the Bermans were not entitled to the $55,000 statutory exemption provided by sections 704.720 and 704.730, subdivision (a)(3).

When the court issued its order of sale * * * , it should have first determined that the property was exempt (i.e., subject to a statutory homestead exemption), next determined the fair market value of the property (found to be $450,000) and the amount of the homestead exemption ($55,000), and finally specified the amounts of the proceeds of the sale to be distributed to the lien and encumbrance holders. Thus, the order of sale should have properly listed, inter alia, the $55,000 homestead exemption, the property tax lien of $644.23, and the $500,000 Berman Corporation deed of trust.[11]

It follows that the order of sale must be and is reversed.

## *Notes*

1. *Kahn* covers the basics of the mechanical steps that must be followed in executing upon a judgment. It also indicates that there is a priority list of who would receive the proceedings from any sheriff's sale. First, the costs of the sale itself are deducted. There may be other liens, such as for the payment of back taxes, mechanics' liens, mortgages, or other judgment creditors. As *Kahn* indicates, the court must rank these liens according to their statutory priority and see that they are paid off in full from the proceeds of the sale in order from first to last until the money runs out. If there is any money left after all the expenses and liens are paid, it goes to the debtor. Thus, in a situation where there are many creditors and limited assets, creditors want to get in the queue as close to the front as possible. See David Gray Carlson & Paul M. Shupack, Judicial Lien Priorities under Article 9 of the Uniform Commercial Code: Part I, 5 Cardozo

**10.** Section 704.710, subdivision (c) provides in relevant part: "(c) 'Homestead' means the principal dwelling (1) in which the judgment debtor or the judgment debtor's spouse resided on the date the judgment creditor's lien attached to the dwelling, and (2) in which the judgment debtor or the judgment debtor's spouse resided continuously thereafter until the date of the court determination that the dwelling is a homestead."

**11.** Needless to say, such an order might have prevented the sale of the property. As we have already noted, section 704.800, subdivision (a), prohibits the sale of a homestead unless a minimum bid sufficient to cover all of the liens and encumbrances is received. At the same time, however, we do not intend to pass on the validity or legitimacy of the $500,000 deed of trust recorded by the "Berman Corporation." It is sufficient to say that the circumstances of the recording were suspicious. Finally, the Kahns have access to other statutory remedies for challenging that deed of trust. (Civ.Code, § 3439 *et seq.* [the Uniform Fraudulent Transfer Act].)

L.Rev. 287 (1984). However, a creditor who is relegated to the end of the queue may end up with more money by driving the debtor into bankruptcy court where new liens (less than 90 days old) are not honored and unsecured creditors share on a pro rata basis any funds remaining after the fully secured creditors are reimbursed.

2. Did the Kahns' attorney commit malpractice? Consider how the minutiae of collection law trip up practitioners with alarming frequency. For example, in Republic National Bank v. United States, 506 U.S. 80, 113 S.Ct. 554, 121 L.Ed.2d 474 (1992), the bank failed to perfect its claim on the proceeds of the sale of property that the federal government had seized from its owner, who was alleged to have purchased the property with the proceeds of narcotics sales. The proceeds were deposited in the U.S. Treasury and the U.S. moved to dismiss for lack of subject matter jurisdiction. In a deeply divided decision (there were two majority opinions because of the vote splitting on different aspects of the case), the Supreme Court allowed the lower court to continue to exercise jurisdiction in the *in rem* civil forfeiture after the *res* was removed from the custody of the U.S. Marshal and placed in the U.S. Treasury.

In United States v. McDermott, 507 U.S. 447, 113 S.Ct. 1526, 123 L.Ed.2d 128 (1993), a judgment creditor had filed a state-law judgment lien on the McDermotts' existing and any subsequently acquired property. The Internal Revenue Service then filed a tax lien against all real and personal property owned or subsequently acquired by the McDermotts, and later still the McDermotts acquired a piece of property. The Court held, 6–3, that the tax lien was "first in time" and therefore first in right as to the subsequently acquired property because a judgment lien is perfected only when property is acquired, while, in contrast, a tax lien created under the Tax Lien Act, 26 U.S.C. § 6323, is perfected when filed.

3. In addition to execution, the remedy at issue in *Kahn,* probably the other most commonly used collection device is garnishment. In garnishment, the creditor obtains money that a third party (the garnishee), usually a bank or an employer, owes to the debtor. The garnishee's obligation to the debtor (and the debtor's obligation to the creditor) are satisfied to the extent the garnishee pays the creditor. Usually only a percentage of the garnishee's debt to the debtor may be used at any one time to satisfy the creditor. E.g., Consumer Credit Protection Act, 15 U.S.C. §§ 1671–77 (1982)(limiting garnishment to 25% of take home pay, unless garnishment is for support of a spouse or child where 60% limitation applies).

## 2. EXEMPT PROPERTY

As the *Kahn* opinion indicates, there are certain properties that are exempt (or partially exempt) from legal attachment and sale and which as a result cannot be used to satisfy judgments. Besides the homestead exemption discussed in *Kahn,* the most common exemption is intended partially to protect wages. The concept of exemption is simple enough to understand: although the state wants creditors to be able to collect judgments against debtors, it does not want to permit the debtor to become totally impoverished in the process. However, as the next cases and materials indicate, deciding whether property is exempt is not always as simple as consulting a statute. In this section, we first read an example of a court interpreting an exemption statute. Then we will consider how exemptions are affected by the interaction of the laws of our two complementary legal regimes—the federal and state governments.

## GUTTERMAN v. FIRST NATIONAL BANK OF ANCHORAGE

Supreme Court of Alaska, 1979.
597 P.2d 969.

RABINOWITZ, CHIEF JUSTICE.

The First National Bank of Anchorage obtained a default judgment against Michael Gutterman. That judgment provided that three paintings owned by Gutterman, then in the possession of an art dealer, were to be delivered to the custody of the clerk of the superior court and sold at an execution sale, with the proceeds to be applied toward satisfaction of the judgment.

Prior to the execution sale, Gutterman notified the court of his claim * * * of an exemption from execution in the paintings in the amount of $300. The sale of the paintings was postponed at the Bank's request, and the Bank subsequently filed a motion to disallow the claim of exemption in the superior court.

The relevant statutory section, AS 09.35.080(a)(2), provides:

> *Exemptions* (a) The following property is exempt from execution, except as otherwise specifically provided when selected and reserved by the judgment debtor or his agent at the time of the levy, or as soon after levy and before sale as the existence of the levy becomes known to him:
>
> * * * (2) books, pictures, and musical instruments belonging to the judgment debtor not to exceed $300 in value. . . .

The parties stipulated that each of the paintings in question was worth more than the $300 exemption provided in the statute. The question thus presented to the superior court was whether Gutterman was entitled to the benefit of the exemption provision and to receive $300 from the proceeds of the sale of the paintings. The superior court held that "pictures" exceeding $300 in value are not property exempt from execution by the terms of the statute and that Gutterman therefore had no exemption right in the proceeds of the execution sale.[1] It is from this decision of the superior court that Gutterman brings this appeal.

1. The superior court noted that, unlike the provisions of AS 09.35.090 concerning the residence exemption, AS 09.35.080 contained no express exemption for the proceeds of a sale of "pictures" or other exempt items enumerated therein. The court reasoned that, accordingly, the legislature "apparently intended ... (a) different treatment with respect to categorical exemptions." It concluded that a picture that exceeds $300.00 in value is not exempt. It is the picture, and not the value, to which the exemption is directed.

In order to properly discuss the question raised by Gutterman as to the nature of the exemption granted by AS 09.35.080(a)(2), it is necessary to briefly place exemption laws in their social and historical context. Exemption laws emerged from bankruptcy law policies concerned with both maintaining a certain basic level of economic vitality in individual debtors and reasonably protecting creditors' rights to satisfaction of legally incurred debt.

In order to protect debtors and their families from pauperism and to facilitate rehabilitation, state laws universally provide for the exemption of certain property, or a certain value of property, from seizure for general debts. The laws range in liberality from the most spartan subsistence standard to the extremes reflected in unlimited exemptions for homesteads and life insurance.

A debtor's property which is not exempted from execution in satisfaction of debt by applicable state or federal laws is subject to the rights of creditors.[5]

While the scope of state exemption laws varies considerably among the states, certain categories of debtors' property are provided some degree of exemption in most states. Prominent among state exemptions is the homestead or residence exemption, which exempts the debtor's homestead from execution sale either entirely or to the extent of a certain specified value.[6] Among the other forms of debtors' property provided varying degrees of protection from creditors are life insurance policies and proceeds; earnings and subsistence allowances; and various types of non-wage income, including welfare payments, retirement income, alimony and child support, or other compensation payments. In addition, some states, though not Alaska, provide general dollar amount exemptions, with the particular assets to be included in the dollar amount left to the debtor's choice.[8]

**5.** AS 09.35.070 expresses this principle in the following terms:

> *Property Liable.* All goods, chattels, money, or other property, both real and personal, or an interest in the property of the judgment debtor not exempt by law, and all property and rights of property seized and held under attachment in the action are liable to execution.

The federal law of exemptions has no applicability to this case. The recently revised federal Bankruptcy Act, which takes effect October 1, 1979, contains specific provisions relating to exemptions under bankruptcy law. * * * The historical and revision notes to that section list some of the items that may be exempted under other federal laws. The revised Act specifically provides that a bankrupt debtor retains exemptions allowed under applicable state law. Prior to enactment of the revised Act, the federal Bankruptcy Act contained no uniform scheme of exemptions, but, instead, deferred to other federal and state law as to exemptions.

**6.** Alaska's residence exemption is defined in AS 09.35.090. A homestead exemption is provided by Section 4 of the Uniform Exemptions Act, approved by the National Conference of Commissioners on Uniform State Laws in 1976. Vukovich reports that all but six jurisdictions provide a homestead exemption. [See Vukovich, Debtors' Exemption Rights, 62 Geo.L.J. 779, 797 (1974).]

**8.** Alaska's exemptions provisions contain no such general dollar amount exemptions, but provide value limitations for specific categories of exempt property. Several commentators have recommended that exemption statutes should prescribe a value limitation for personal property to be chosen by the debtor without restriction as to form or kind. However, this approach has been rejected by both the Uniform Exemp-

The exemption which is the subject of this appeal is one of the specific personal property exemptions provided for in AS 09.35.080(a).[9] * * * Alaska's limited value exemption for "pictures" thus represents a legislative judgment that such items are among the amenities of life in which a debtor may preserve at least a limited investment.[11]

Gutterman does not assert a right to preserve the paintings themselves, which have in fact been sold, but argues that he nonetheless should retain the benefit of the $300 exemption granted to debtors owning "pictures." Resolution of this issue rests on an interpretation of the statutory phrase in AS 09.35.080(a)(2) granting an exemption for "pictures ... belonging to the judgment debtor not to exceed $300 in value." As the superior court's order denying an exemption recognized, the meaning of this statutory phrase is neither clear nor unambiguous.[12]

tions Act and the revised federal Bankruptcy Act.

**9.** AS 09.35.080(a) provides:

(a) The following property is exempt from execution, except as otherwise specifically provided when selected and reserved by the judgment debtor or his agent at the time of the levy, or as soon after levy and before sale as the existence of the levy becomes known to him:

* * *

(2) books, pictures, and musical instruments belonging to the judgment debtor not to exceed $300 in value;

(3) necessary wearing apparel belonging to the judgment debtor for the use of himself or his family; watches or jewelry not to exceed $200 in value;

(4) the tools, implements, apparatus, motor vehicles, books, office furniture, business files, animals, laboratory and any other article necessary to enable any person to carry on the trade, occupation, or profession by which that person habitually earns his living to the value of $2,500, including sufficient quantity of foods to support the animals, if any, for six months;

(5) the following property belonging to the judgment debtor and in actual use or kept for use by and for his family: animals, household goods, furniture, and utensils to the value of $1,200, including food sufficient to support the animals, if any, for six months, and provisions actually provided for family use and necessary for the support of that person and family for six months;

(6) all property of a public or municipal corporation;

(7) no article of property mentioned in this section is exempt from execution issued on a judgment recovered for its price, and, in the event the article of property [h]as been sold or exchanged for other property, the proceeds of the sale or the article for which it was exchanged is not exempt from execution.

Personal and household property exemptions such as those provided in AS 09.35.080(a)(2) are designed to ensure that debtors will have necessary items for living in reasonable comfort and for earning a living. The statutes vary as to the types of items that are exempt and as to the amount of their exempt value. * * *

In addition to useful household items, the exemption statutes also commonly apply to more personalized, arguably less necessary, items such as family pictures, Bibles, wedding rings and other jewelry, books, historical and scientific collections, guns, church pews, and cemetery lots. The states also allow debtors and members of their families to keep all of their clothing or such as is necessary.

**11.** Compare AS 09.35.080(a)(2) with Cal.Civ.Proc.Code § 690.1 (West 1955 & Supp.1979)("Works of art shall not be exempt unless of or by the debtor and his resident family") and Or.Rev.Stat. § 23.160(1)(a)(1977) ("pictures ... to the value of $150"). See also Uniform Exemptions Act § 8(a)(3)("family portraits and heirlooms of particular sentimental value to the individual").

**12.** The superior court's order noted that "[a]t first blush, the Court frankly was inclined to [Gutterman's] position."

Faced with a similar question as to the interpretation of a Massachusetts statute granting an exemption for an "automobile ... not exceeding seven hundred dollars in value," a federal district court observed that:

It is an accepted general rule that "exemption laws are remedial in character and should be liberally construed in favor of the debtor." We therefore conclude that the statute should not be interpreted in a way which completely eliminates a debtor's exemption rights in an item of property within an exempt category because that item's value exceeds the statutory allowance. Instead, we agree with the reasoning and conclusion advanced by one commentator on exemption laws:

> The few statutes which regulate the forced sale of exempt personalty worth more than the statutory maximum provide that the exempt amount is to be paid to the debtor from the proceeds of sale prior to any payment to the execution creditor. The exemption clearly should extend to the proceeds of an involuntary sale of personalty. Otherwise, the exemption is meaningless whenever the value of the personalty exceeds the statutory allowance, since the levying creditor immediately could order the sheriff to pay the total amount to him. Moreover, if the sheriff is forced to sell exempt property, it is likely that the debtor has no nonexempt property. This is a situation where the protection of the exemption laws is needed and appropriate. Accordingly, the courts should afford the debtor a reasonable time to purchase other property with the proceeds.

This is the approach adopted by the Uniform Exemptions Act. The comment to that Act's provision defining a debtor's personal property exemptions, Section 8, makes it

> clear that if an item within any of the categories listed has a value exceeding $500, the individual is nonetheless entitled to an exemption in the items to the extent of $500, and the creditor is entitled to levy only on the excess value. * * *

More helpful to the precise question of statutory interpretation presented here is *Levin v. Mauro,* interpreting a Massachusetts exemption statute worded much like AS 09.35.080(a)(2). The Massachusetts statute provided an exemption in an automobile "not exceeding seven hundred dollars in value;" the Alaska statute provides an exemption in pictures "not to exceed $300 in value." The *Levin* court, after noting the ambiguity of this language and the remedial purpose of exemption statutes, concluded that the Massachusetts statute should be construed to allow "a debtor owning a car in excess of the limit ... to turn it over to the trustee for liquidation ... (and) to purchase another vehicle with $700 derived from liquidation proceeds." In reaching this conclusion, the court rejected as "legitimate, but by no means conclusive," the argument that the Massachusetts legislature had expressly provided setoff schemes with regard to other exemptions and that "if the legislature wanted a setoff it knew how to write one." * * *

If nothing else is clear, it is beyond serious dispute that the statutory phrase 'not exceeding seven hundred dollars in value' is ambiguous on its face, at least with respect to the controlling issue in this case.

Levin v. Mauro, 425 F.Supp. 205, 206 (D.Mass.1977).

We find this analysis and authority persuasive and hold that Gutterman should receive the $300 amount of the exemption from the proceeds of the sale of the paintings. A contrary result would be unreasonable because it would provide no exemption for a debtor whose picture has a value of $300.01 and a full exemption for a debtor owning the same type of property worth just one penny less. We think our resolution of this question fairly balances the rights of debtors and creditors, since their respective interests in such exempt categories of property will be uniform and not dependent on very small differences in the value of such items of property.

The $300 exemption benefit provided by AS 09.35.080(a)(2) does not, however, confer an unrestricted right to that portion of the proceeds from the execution sale. The terms of AS 09.35.080(a)(7) provide that "in the event the article of property has been sold or exchanged the proceeds of the sale or the article for which it was exchanged is not exempt from execution." Thus, the $300 in proceeds to which Gutterman is entitled is not in itself exempt and does not assume the generic exemption afforded the "pictures" from which it is derived.

Notwithstanding this principle, as a matter of exemption law a debtor is allowed and encouraged to convert nonexempt property into exempt property and to change the types of exempt property he or she owns without losing the benefit of the relevant exemptions. * * *

Only in cases of actual fraud as to creditors, such as attempting to convert secured collateral to exempt property, is the practice not recognized by law.

Gutterman's interest in these proceeds is identical to that recognized in several jurisdictions for the proceeds from a voluntary sale of exempt property. More than fifty years ago, the Kansas Supreme Court, in the context of such voluntary sales, stated that:

> It is well settled that the proceeds of exempt property are exempt to the debtor for a reasonable time, to enable him ... to invest the money in other exempt property.

Gutterman shall therefore receive the $300 exemption from the sale proceeds and be allowed a reasonable time in which to reinvest those proceeds in other exempt property. * * *

### *Notes*

1. As *Gutterman* indicates, states can and do exempt certain tangible property from seizure by creditors. For example, one of the most "debtor-friendly" states is Texas. Section 42.001 of the Texas Property Code (1991) exempts a homestead and burial lots and exempts the proceeds of sale of a homestead for six months. Section 41.002 defines an urban homestead as not more than one acre of land together with any improvements which is used for a dwelling or for a business. A rural family is entitled to 200 acres, while a single person is entitled to 100. Section 42.001 also exempts from attachment by creditors up to $30,000 of personal property owned by a family (or $15,000 by an individual), and provides a list of eligible property,

which includes the following items, among others: home furnishings including family heirlooms, provisions for consumption, farming implements, tools and equipment, including a boat, used in a trade or profession, clothing, two firearms, athletic and sporting equipment, a car not used for business, "or, whether or not held for the production of income, two of the following categories of means of travel" which include either horses, colts, mules and donkeys or various wheeled vehicles. The statute also exempts household pets and five cows and their calves, a breeding bull, 20 each of hogs, sheep and goats, 50 chickens and 30 each of four types of domestic fowl. Importantly, Texas also exempts current wages for personal service.

Under such a generous statutory scheme, what is the actual dollar value of a judgment issued against an ordinary individual living in that state likely to be? For discussion of the effect of variations in state exemptions on lending practices and the conduct of debtors, see Teresa A. Sullivan, Elizabeth Warren and Jay L. Westbrook, As We Forgive Our Debtors 241 (1989)(empirical studies suggest that there is little effect).

2. Henry W. Farnam, Chapters in the History of Social Legislation in the United States to 1860, 148–52 (1938), provides some interesting history on the development of exemptions and some explanation for why Texas law is particularly generous to debtors. Farnam traces the U.S. exemption system from its origins in Texas, which took the concept from Spanish law. Soon after gaining independence in 1829, Texas used the homestead exemption as a device to attract immigrants, who would be debtors as they got their farms and ranches started. Starting in 1841, other states followed suit. Although Farnam notes that a form of exemption appears in Leviticus, he believes that the system developed in Texas out of reaction to the harsh English law, "rather than a conscious attempt to copy the institutions of the Jews."

3. As the provisions from Texas indicate, exemption statutes tend to reflect a very particular image of the locality. This tends to hold true for even newly revised statutes. For example, when the Vermont Legislature revised its statute in 1988, it retained exemptions that reflect that state's self-image as a land of subsistence farmers. See, e.g., Parrotte v. Sensenich, 22 F.3d 472 (2d Cir.1994)(dairy farmer's bulls used as breeding stock are exempt under Vermont law as "tools of the trade," even though the cows which produce the milk are not exempt under this category); Note, Vermont's New Debtor's Exemption Statute, 13 Vt.L.Rev. 609 (1989)(new statute protects, inter alia, $5000 in growing crops, ten cords of firewood, various animals and feed for the animals to survive through one winter, three swarms of bees, and one yoke of animals used for team work). What other policy considerations might prompt a state to retain these perhaps outdated exemptions? What property exemptions might be suited to a more urbanized setting?

4. Can exemption statutes be written to avoid becoming quaint anachronisms as society changes? Is the only solution to have the legislature revise the list periodically? One potential solution is called the "wild card." It allows a debtor to transfer some or all of the value of certain unclaimed exemptions to other property that otherwise would be unprotected from creditors. Thus, a Vermont debtor who does not happen to own $5000 in

growing crops can transfer that value to some other property. Vt.Stat.Ann. tit. 12, § 2740(7). The federal exemption plan, which is often used in bankruptcy, allows the transfer of an unused homestead exemption. 11 U.S.C. § 522(d)(5). Besides maintaining flexibility, "wild cards" also equalize the treatment of debtors who do and do not happen to own the specific categories of exempted properties.

5. How is a judgment debtor, who may be unsophisticated, to know of the existence of the exemptions available? The Tenth Circuit has held that New Mexico's postjudgment execution statutes violated due process because they did not require the sheriff to inform the debtor, upon seizure of property, that various exemptions exist and that a procedure is available to protect exempt property. Aacen v. San Juan County Sheriff's Department, 944 F.2d 691 (10th Cir.1991). See also Diana Gribbon Motz & Andrew H. Baida, The Due Process Rights of Postjudgment Debtors and Child Support Obligors, 45 Md.L.Rev. 61 (1986).

## IN THE MATTER OF CAROL J. v. WILLIAM J.

Family Court, City of New York, New York County, 1983.
119 Misc.2d 739, 464 N.Y.S.2d 635.

JACK TURRET, JUDGE:

* * * Petitioner, former wife of respondent, is seeking enforcement of respondent's obligation to support their 2 children under a judgment of divorce of the Superior Court, Judicial District of Fairfield, Connecticut, dated June 13, 1979. This judgment obligates respondent to pay $1,740 per month for alimony and child support. * * * Reference was made to the hearing examiner.

On July 29, 1981, an agreement was reached before the hearing examiner that provided for temporary support ($700 per month) and a contingent payroll deduction order. It was subsequently reconfirmed by the respondent on November 24, 1981, January 6, 1982 and March 11, 1982. On June 14, 1982, the hearing examiner issued a report recommending modification of the temporary order to $500 per month and holding arrears in abeyance. Objections were filed and heard by me on July 28, 1982. At which time, * * * respondent asserted orally that 15 U.S.C. § 1673 prohibits entry of any payroll deduction order in excess of 50% of his disposable income.[1] Ruling from the bench, this court declined to vacate the payroll deduction order and ordered a hearing de novo as the record made before the hearing examiner was insufficient. * * *

On November 29, 1982, the hearing examiner rendered her report. Based on the evidence adduced before her, the hearing examiner found: (1) "[r]espondent is attempting to minimize his duty to support by purposefully reducing his stated or actual income"; (2) "[r]espondent

1. The Consumer Credit Protection Act as amended by 15 U.S.C. § 1673(b)(2)(A) is applicable to garnishment for support.

has skills and experience in an area where the earning opportunities for someone of his background are substantially higher"; * * * .

Typical of respondent's actions which led the hearing examiner to make such findings were his selling an antique car for $8,100 without a cent going for child support; his failure to comply with the financial disclosure request made by Corporation Counsel; the fact that respondent holds a job as a stock and commodities broker for Shearson Loeb Rhodes, where from 1979–1980, he was making approximately $45,000 per year, and that after 16 years in the profession, he presently reports an income of $15,000 per year.

The hearing examiner thus recommended: (1) arrears be fixed at $5,054.63 as of December 2, 1982; (2) an order of support for the 2 children of $800 per month plus an additional $50 per month on arrears, payable to the Support Collection Unit, effective December 21, 1982; (3) vacating the payroll deduction order as a replacement; and (4) respondent be directed to submit proof of his compliance with paragraphs 3 and 4 of the divorce decree pertaining to medical insurance coverage. * * *

The court concurs with the hearing examiner's findings and recommendations except as to * * * the payroll deduction order * * * .

### Payroll Deduction Order

Based on the evidence adduced in all proceedings heretofore held, the court confirms the hearing examiner's finding that respondent "is attempting to minimize his duty to support ..." Precisely for this reason, the court rejects the hearing examiner's recommendation that the payroll deduction order in effect be vacated and a contingent one substituted.

It is a well established equitable principle that one should not be permitted to take advantage of his own wrong. On this principle, an individual may be denied use of a statute by his acts. Though not a court of equity, Family Court should strive to do equitable justice.

One who purposefully minimizes his income, may have his duty to support based upon potential not just actual earnings. To afford respondent the relief of the Consumer Credit Protection Act (15 U.S.C. § 1673), would be to allow him to circumvent this legal obligation through his own acts.

The legislative history of the Consumer Credit Protection Act, Title 15 U.S.C. §§ 1671–1677, indicates a dual purpose intended by Congress. On the one hand, Congress wished to protect debtors from unscrupulous creditors, and on the other, to assure that dependent children receive support. Congress had certain types of creditors in mind in enacting this legislation. It did not seek to shackle such legitimate debt collection as child support. "Its purpose is to protect consumers from a host of unfair, harassing and deceptive debt collection practices without imposing unnecessary restraints on ethical debt collectors." Senate Report No. 95–382, 95th Cong. 1st Session, 1977 U.S.Code Cong. & Ad.News 1695, 1696. Protection of debtors was balanced by allowing for a higher percentage of payroll deduction for child support. Under § 1673(b)(2)(A), between 50%–65% of a spouse's disposable income may be garnished, as opposed to only 25% for other creditors. Congress wanted to "assure an effective program of child support." Senate Report No. 93–1356, 93rd Cong. 2d session, 1974 U.S.Code Cong. & Ad.News 8133, 8134.

* * * Congress in passing such legislation was cognizant of the growing number of single mothers with dependent children receiving Aid to Families with Dependent Children [hereinafter, A.F.D.C.]. Of the 11 million recipients who are on A.F.D.C., four out of five are on the rolls because they have been deprived of the support of a parent. Congress did not intend that a debtor-spouse improperly shield himself from a valid child support order by use of § 1673. Rather, Congress intended that child support payments be made without unduly hampering the debtor-spouse's financial base. Respondent will not be allowed to thwart both Federal and New York State policy to assure support of dependents by perverting the Consumer Credit Protection Act. The Payroll Deduction Order in effect should be modified to reflect the final order of support. * * *

### *Notes*

1. Other federal statutes may affect to what extent other assets of debtors are available to creditors for attachment or garnishment. For example, often, a large source of assets held by individuals is rights to their pension benefits. However, the Employee Retirement Income Security Act of 1974 (ERISA), 29 U.S.C. § 1056(d)(1), flatly forbids the assignment or alienation of pension fund benefits. See, e.g., Guidry v. Sheet Metal Workers National Pension Fund, 493 U.S. 365, 376, 110 S.Ct. 680, 687, 107 L.Ed.2d 782, 795 (1990)("Nor do we think it appropriate to approve any generalized equitable exception—either for employee malfeasance or for criminal misconduct—to ERISA's prohibition on the assignment or alienation of pension benefits.").

2. If a debtor were to retire, start to receive some of those accumulated ERISA pension funds, and put them into a separate bank account, should those withdrawn funds still be exempt from garnishment? Compare Trucking Employees v. Colville, 16 F.3d 52 (3d Cir.1994)(no longer protected) with United States v. Smith, 47 F.3d 681 (4th Cir.1995)(still protected) and Guidry v. Sheet Metal Workers National Pension Fund, 39 F.3d 1078 (10th Cir.en banc 1994), cert. denied, ___ U.S. ___, 115 S.Ct. 1691, 131 L.Ed.2d 556 (1995)(no longer protected under federal law, but 75% protected under state law as "disposable earnings"). Cf. Gutterman v. First National Bank of Anchorage, 597 P.2d 969 (Alaska 1979)(court grants debtor time to put proceeds from sale of exempt property into other exempt property). However, a fraudulent transfer of assets into a retirement account may not be protected. See Tompkins County Trust Co. v. Gowin, 163 Misc.2d 418, 621 N.Y.S.2d 476 (Sup.Ct.1994).

3. Should creditors be permitted to garnish students' bank accounts? Accounts whose funds are traceable to federally guaranteed student loans? See Schaerrer v. Westman Commission Company, 769 P.2d 1058 (Colo.1989).

4. In *Carol J.*, the court based the support payment on what the husband should have been earning, rather than what he reported. But what if instead of the suspicion that Mr. J. was fraudulently concealing income, his income dropped because he chose to do more ego-satisfying, but less financially rewarding, work? If Mr. J. decided to leave the stress of the brokerage business (and the $45,000+ per annum) and fulfill his dream to become captain of a sport fishing boat in Florida, where he was happy but made less than half of what he did before, could the court order Mr. J. to get back to selling pork-belly futures at the brokerage? To pay Mrs. J. as if he were still at the brokerage?

At least one court has held that a spouse cannot be forced to work overtime and on weekends to maintain a certain level of spousal and child support. The father had been working 16–hour days as a theatrical stagehand while the couple was still married, but he changed to the shorter hours and lower pay of television work shortly after they were separated and a temporary support order was issued. A unanimous California Supreme Court held that, although it would be appropriate under these suspicious facts to base support on the father's ability to earn rather than his actual income, the support payments had to be based on objectively reasonable hours and not on an extraordinary work regimen. In re Marriage of Simpson, 4 Cal.4th 225, 14 Cal.Rptr.2d 411, 841 P.2d 931 (1992).

Suppose Mrs. J. believes that Mr. J. could earn more money, and pay more support, if he moved from a small town where unemployment is high and wages are low to a large city where prevailing wages are much higher. Can the court base an order on what theoretically he could earn in the city? See Johansen v. State, 491 P.2d 759 (Alaska 1971).

## 3. FORECLOSURE SALES

## GRIGGS v. MILLER

Supreme Court of Missouri, Division No. 2, 1963.
374 S.W.2d 119.

WALTER H. BOHLING, SPECIAL COMMISSIONER.

[The original defendant in this case, W.A. Brookshire, was sued separately by Ray Crouch and by Dorothy Contestible for debts allegedly owed. Plaintiff Crouch won a judgment of nearly $2,000. Contestible's $17,000 judgment was under appeal.

Missouri law provides that winning plaintiffs may immediately "execute" on defendant's property to pay the judgment, unless defendant posts a bond. Missouri law also permits the defendant to choose which property is to be sold at execution sale and to decide the order of sale, with the sale proceeding until the debt is satisfied.

Defendant Brookshire owned a 322 acre farm, more than 200 head of cattle, and corporate stock. Additionally, Brookshire had deposited collateral with an insurance company sufficient to satisfy Crouch's judgment. Sheriff Powell and Crouch knew of defendant's assets and collateral. Furthermore, Crouch had in his possession more than $10,-000 worth of defendant's cattle.

Defendant Brookshire requested the sheriff to sell only one 40 acre section of the farm, which Brookshire contended would satisfy his debts because the entire farm was worth between $50,000 and $90,000. The sheriff, however, held an execution sale for the entire farm. Brookshire warned the participants not to purchase the farm because the judgment was on appeal. He advised them that he had other assets "probably" sufficient to cover the debt, including the collateral and the cattle that Crouch was holding.

Nonetheless, the entire farm was sold to Bill Griggs for $20,600. Defendant withheld possession, and Griggs sued him. The court appointed Miller as trustee to represent Brookshire's interests when Brookshire was confined to state prison and could not defend himself.]
* * *

A sheriff conducting an execution sale is the agent of the property owner and the judgment creditor, and his duty is to protect the interests of both and to see that the property is not sacrificed. We said in Gordon v. Hickman, 96 Mo. 350, 356, 9 S.W. 920, 921, 922: "If the property can be divided without prejudice, and a part will sell for the debt and costs, a part only shall be sold." Forced sales of property usually do not bring full value.

Sheriff Powell's advertisement of the sale of defendant's 322 acre farm was to "sell all of said real estate or as much thereof as *it* be necessary to pay the judgment of $1,966.69," in the Henry County Circuit Court, which, with interest and costs, amounted to $2,308.16 on the day of sale.

Defendant's farm was never advertised for sale under the Audrain County (Contestible) execution. * * *

Sheriff Powell testified he paid out the $20,600.00 purchase money about two hours after the sale. * * *

It is not questioned but that this 322 acre farm, consisting of approximately eight forties, could have been offered for sale in parcels. Rule 76.24 contemplates that the officer "divide such property, if susceptible of division, and sell so much thereof as will be sufficient to satisfy such execution." This was not done, and we hold that it should have been so divided. In Brookshire v. Powell, Mo., 335 S.W.2d 176, 181, the disparity between the market value of this farm and a bid of $2,300 was considered so great as to require setting aside that execution sale and sheriff's deed. In the case at bar the Henry County judgment, interest and costs amounted to $2,308.16; and for that amount under said execution and the constructive levy of the Audrain County execution, but without an advertisement for sale under Rule 76.36, under said Audrain County execution, it is sought to justify this forced sale for $20,600 of property valued at about $46,000. * * *

Defendant is entitled to relief upon doing equity. Accordingly, if defendant will, within thirty days, deposit in this court, for the use and benefit of those entitled thereto, the sum of $20,600 with interest at the rate of 6% per annum from the date of sale until the same is paid, the decree appealed from will be reversed and the cause remanded with directions to cancel the sheriff's sale and the sheriff's deed to plaintiff made pursuant thereto; otherwise the decree will stand affirmed. In either event the costs are assessed against the estate of defendant Brookshire. * * *

### *Notes*

1. Note that the defendant protested that he "probably" had sufficient cattle to satisfy the Crouch judgment. Should the creditors (and their agent, the sheriff) have to satisfy the judgment against property in a particular order, such as personal property before real estate? See, e.g., Matter of Silverman, 6 B.R. 991 (Bankr.D.N.J.1980). For centuries, this has been true. "Bailiffs shall [not] seize any land or rent for any debt, so long as the chattels of the debtor are sufficient to repay the debt * * *." Magna Carta, chapter 9, signed by King John at Runnymede, 1215 A.D.

Feudal England was based on tenure in land. It was viewed as disruptive of society to permit the Crown to repossess land which had been granted to a tenant who later went into debt, where the tenant had other chattels sufficient to satisfy the debt. Thus, the Magna Carta sought to limit the power of creditors to seize land in payment of debt. Other provisions of the Magna Carta sought to prevent abuse by sheriffs, who rented their jurisdictions—bailiwicks—from the Crown and derived income from debt collection. Thus, not unlike the Missouri statute discussed in *Griggs,* Chapter 27 of the Magna Carta prohibited a sheriff from attaching any more of a deceased debtor's chattels than were necessary to satisfy the claims against him, and required the attachment to be done in front of witnesses after showing proper authorization from the Crown. See William F. Swindler, Magna Carta: Legend and Legacy (1965).

Given the structural changes that have occurred in Anglo–American society from the time of King John to the present, what are some arguments for and against retention of the rule that the debtor is permitted to choose which property will be levied upon?

2. Why did it matter to the *Griggs* court whether all of the judgments were advertised before the sale? See, e.g., Ford & Vlahos v. ITT Commercial Finance Corp., 8 Cal.4th 1220, 1233, 885 P.2d 877, 885, 36 Cal.Rptr.2d 464, 472 (1994):

> "In contrast to notice, one purpose of which is to alert the debtor and other secured creditors to take steps to protect their interests, possibly including locating bidders for their collateral, the purpose of requiring adequate advertising of a foreclosure sale is to force the secured party to ensure the auction is well attended by legitimate bidders, so the highest commercially reasonable price for the collateral will be obtained."

Compare Deibler v. Atlantic Properties Group, Inc., 652 A.2d 553 (Del.), cert. denied, ___ U.S. ___, 116 S.Ct. 55, 133 L.Ed.2d 20 (1995)(no due process violation where skeletal requirements of Delaware notice statute were met because debtors themselves could publicize sheriff's sale of stock and provide additional information to entice potential bidders).

3. In Guardian Loan Company v. Early, 47 N.Y.2d 515, 419 N.Y.S.2d 56, 392 N.E.2d 1240 (1979), the New York Court of Appeals refused to set aside a transfer of the debtors' house, which was sold for about 7 percent of its estimated value. The debtors, the Earlys, had obtained postponements of two previous sheriff's sales, but never satisfied the judgment against them. In petitioning the court to revoke the transfer, it was alleged that a flat tire caused the Earlys to be late to the sale, and that the couple had nearly enough cash to satisfy the judgment. The court held that it had broad authority to prevent misuse of sheriff's sales, but it lacked any statutory grounds for setting aside a sale that complied "with the notice, time or manner of such sale."

What factors must a court consider in deciding whether to cancel a deed created by a sheriff's sale of the debtor's property? Apart from statutory considerations, what public policy concerns might a court look to in deciding whether to overturn the results of such sales? Whose interests does the court protect in declining to cancel deed transfers effected by sheriff's sales? For one answer, see Robert R. Wisdom Oil Co. v. Gatewood, 682 S.W.2d 882, 885 (Mo.App.1984):

> Execution sales may be set aside upon motion of parties, not only in cases of fraud or where inadequacy in the sales price is so great as to shock the judicial conscience, but also in cases of irregularity in the conduct of the sale to the prejudice of any party having an interest in the action, or cases of accident or surprise where because of some misunderstanding, mistake, misapprehension or other fortuity, the parties are prevented from being present at the sale to protect their interests. Or stated another way, mere inadequacy of consideration will not justify the setting aside of a judicial sale unless accompanied by some irregularity. Irregularities that have been recognized to fall within this rule include, a mortgagor's mistake as to the date of the sale; a misleading description of the property to be sold; the sale of an excessive portion of real property; a sale made after the sheriff announced sales were concluded; and a sale at an unusual hour.

4. Previously, we noted that a creditor who was last in the queue might find that bankrupting the debtor might net the creditor more money. For a few years in the 1980's and 1990's, another reason to consider bankruptcy was that in some federal circuits, the bankruptcy court could set aside certain sheriff's sales of property if there was reason to believe that the sales price did not reach a set amount (usually 70%) of the fair market value of the property. When the asset was resold by the bankruptcy court, pro rata distribution rules applied. The Supreme Court has now decided (by a 5–4 vote) that a bankruptcy court has no power to set aside a forced sale conducted in accordance with state foreclosure law. According to Justice Scalia's opinion for the majority, the consideration received in a noncollusive and regularly conducted nonjudicial foreclosure sale establishes the "reasonably equivalent value" of property as a matter of law. Justice Souter's dissent would have read a 1984 amendment to the Bankruptcy Code, 11

U.S.C. § 542(a)(2)(A), as specifically authorizing a trustee in bankruptcy to avoid certain pre-bankruptcy transfers, including those on foreclosure sales, that a bankruptcy court determined were not made in exchange for a reasonably equivalent value. BFP v. Resolution Trust Corp., 511 U.S. ___, 114 S.Ct. 1757, 128 L.Ed.2d 556 (1994). For analysis of *BFP*, compare Michael H. Rubin & Stephen P. Stronchein, Security Devices, 55 La.L.Rev. 611 (1995) (generally supportive of decision, but noting questions left unanswered) with William N. Eskridge, Jr. & Philip P. Frickey, The Supreme Court, 1993 Term—Foreword: The Law as Equilibrium, 108 Harv.L.Rev. 26, 83 (1994) (calling *BFP* "an astonishing decision for a textualist").

## 4. BODY EXECUTION

## LANDRIGAN v. MCELROY

Supreme Court of Rhode Island, 1983.
457 A.2d 1056.

WEISBERGER, JUSTICE.

The defendant appeals from a Superior Court order granting the plaintiff's motion for a body execution pursuant to G.L.1956 (1969 Reenactment) § 9–25–15. The defendant contends that the body execution statute contravenes the Fourteenth Amendment to the Constitution of the United States. We agree that a portion of the statute is unconstitutional. Accordingly, we sustain the defendant's appeal, vacate the order that granted the plaintiff's motion for a body execution, and remand the case to the Superior Court.

The facts that led to the issuance of the body execution in this case are undisputed. A civil action for assault and battery in the Superior Court resulted in a jury verdict for plaintiff. Judgment was entered in the amount of $42,029.28 plus interest on December 3, 1976. The trial justice denied defendant's motion for a new trial, and defendant appealed to this court. On February 22, 1979, we summarily denied and dismissed defendant's appeal. The plaintiff then requested that the clerk of the Superior Court prepare an execution on the judgment. During March and April of 1979 two executions were issued, but both were returned unsatisfied.

Thereupon, plaintiff moved pursuant to § 9–25–15 for an execution against the body of defendant.[1] Arguing that the body execution statute was unconstitutional, defendant objected. After a hearing, a Superior Court justice granted plaintiff's motion and on April 29, 1980, ordered that an execution issue against the body of defendant. On the same day, a stay pending appeal to this court was granted.

**1.** General Laws 1956 (1969 Reenactment) § 9–25–15 provides in part: "An execution, original, alias, or pluries, may issue against the body of a defendant not exempt from arrest in an action * * * sounding in tort in which the title to real estate was not in dispute * * * provided, however, that no execution, original, alias or pluries, shall issue against the body of a defendant unless so ordered by a justice of the superior court or a justice of a district court upon the written ex parte motion of a party named in the action."

The arguments of defendant on appeal can be summarized as follows: (1) section 9–25–15 denies defendant the equal protection of the laws by depriving him of his fundamental right to physical liberty without a compelling state interest, [and] (2) the issuance of a body execution without a prior hearing concerning defendant's ability to pay the tort judgment does not comport with the requirements of procedural due process * * *. Before we address the merits of these claims, however, we must discuss the background of the body execution statute.

History of the Body Execution Statute

Imprisonment for debt is an ancient remedy. Note, Body Attachment and Body Execution: Forgotten But Not Gone, 17 Wm. & Mary L.Rev. 543 (1976); see Howe, Studies in the Civil Law 205–06 (2d ed. 1905). Indeed, under Roman law creditors could seize and imprison even insolvent debtors and sell them into slavery; if more than one creditor had a claim against a debtor, they could partition the debtor's body into proportionate shares. At common law, the writs of *capias ad respondendum* and *capias ad satisfaciendum* authorized the arrest of the debtor at the initiation of the lawsuit or after judgment had been rendered respectively. Vestiges of these procedures existed in colonial America and in the United States during the post-Revolutionary War period. In response to abusive utilization of body execution statutes by creditors during the late-eighteenth and nineteenth centuries, state legislatures enacted statutory and constitutional provisions that limited or entirely prohibited imprisonment for debt. See generally, Note, Imprisonment for Debt: In the Military Tradition, 80 Yale L.J. 1679, 1679 n. 1 (1971) (listing statutory and constitutional provisions concerning body execution). The Constitution of the State prohibits, absent a strong presumption of fraud, continued imprisonment of a judgment debtor "after he shall have delivered up his property for the benefit of his creditors * * * ." R.I. Const., art. I, sec. 11. Moreover, once a contract judgment debtor is imprisoned pursuant to a body execution, he or she may obtain release almost immediately by taking the "poor debtor's oath."[3] In addition, the creditor for whose benefit the debtor is imprisoned must pay in advance for the prisoner's board.[4]

Section 9–25–15 must be examined in light of these limitations and its own legislative history. The body execution statute originated in the Court and Practice Act of 1905. * * * In 1961 the Legislature amended the statute to enable judgment creditors to obtain through ex parte motion execution against the bodies of judgment debtors. Clearly, this amendment was intended "to deprive judgment creditors of arbitrary

3. The defendant in this case, however, is a debtor on a tort judgment. He therefore would not be subject to discharge pursuant to the "poor debtor's oath" until six months after imprisonment.

4. In 1975 the Legislature increased the amount that a creditor must pay in advance for the board of a debtor imprisoned pursuant to a body execution from $4.00 per week to $210.00 per week. In our opinion, this evinces a legislative intent to discourage the use of body execution as a means for satisfying judgments. We note further that supplementary proceedings in aid of execution are more readily available to assist judgment creditors in obtaining satisfaction. * * *

power to issue, through their counsel, body executions against judgment debtors and to require submission of the petitions to judicial scrutiny." Martin v. Estrella, 110 R.I. 368, 370, 292 A.2d 884, 886 (1972). We have held, however, that once a judgment creditor sets forth one of the statutory grounds for issuance of a body execution, the trial justice has no choice but to grant the creditor's motion. As will become evident, our decision today overrules *Martin v. Estrella* to the extent that the court's opinion in that case deprives a trial justice of any discretion to deny a motion for a body execution.

THE CONSTITUTIONAL VALIDITY OF § 9–25–15

The defendant bases his equal-protection challenge to § 9–25–15 on the doctrine enunciated by the United States Supreme Court in Williams v. Illinois, 399 U.S. 235, 90 S.Ct. 2018, 26 L.Ed.2d 586 (1970), and Tate v. Short, 401 U.S. 395, 91 S.Ct. 668, 28 L.Ed.2d 130 (1971). In both cases the Court addressed the constitutionality of imprisoning a defendant beyond the statutorily authorized term solely because the defendant was unable to pay a fine that accompanied his sentence. The Court determined that such imprisonment constituted invidious discrimination in violation of the equal-protection clause. These cases make clear that the state cannot imprison an individual solely because of a lack of money.

The defendant points out that a federal district court relied on *Williams* and *Tate* to strike down, as facially repugnant to the equal-protection clause, the body execution statute of another state. In Abbit v. Bernier, 387 F.Supp. 57 (D.Conn.1974), the court found that even though the Connecticut statute did not expressly exclude a preincarceration hearing to determine ability to pay, the state courts implemented the statute without providing for such hearings. Consequently, the court struck down the statute as unconstitutional. Subsequently, a Connecticut state court found that the *Abbit* court erroneously concluded that court practices in the state did not include a hearing to determine the judgment debtor's ability to pay. Palumbo v. Manson, 35 Conn. Supp. 130, 133, 400 A.2d 288, 289–90 (Super.Ct.1979). Accordingly, the state court upheld the body execution statute by interpreting it as requiring such a hearing.[6]

The body execution statute at issue in *Abbit* and *Palumbo* was silent concerning a preincarceration hearing to determine the judgment debtor's ability to pay. The "ex parte" amendment to our statute, on the other hand, implicitly excludes such a hearing. Moreover, this court's interpretation of that amendment in *Martin v. Estrella, supra,* deprives a trial justice of any discretion to deny issuance of a body execution once a creditor sets forth the existence of a statutory ground. We are of the opinion, therefore, that § 9–25–15 is incapable of an interpretation upholding its validity as long as the "ex parte" language is an effective part of the statute.

**6.** Subsequently, the Connecticut Legislature repealed the body execution statute.

* * * By failing to provide for a preincarceration hearing to determine ability to pay, the statute in effect enables only tort judgment debtors who are able to pay to obtain immediate release from imprisonment. These individuals need only comply with the judgments and executions against them. On the other hand, tort judgment debtors who are unable to pay must remain in prison for at least six months.[7] They are, therefore, incarcerated solely because of their lack of money. This disparate treatment is precisely the type of invidious discrimination prohibited by the Court in *Williams* and *Tate*.

Moreover, imprisoning a tortfeasor who is unable to pay a judgment does not implement the governmental interest in enforcing judgments and executions. Supplemental proceedings in aid of execution more effectively further this interest because such proceedings enable a creditor to obtain satisfaction of a judgment on an installment payment basis. In short, imprisoning debtors who are unable to pay judgments against them does not have a rational connection with enforcement of the obligation to pay. This court will not attribute to the Legislature an intent that would result in absurdities or would defeat the underlying purpose of legislation.

We hold that the ex parte hearing provision of the 1961 amendment to § 9–25–15 is unconstitutional as violative of the equal-protection clause. We assume, however, that the Legislature would prefer that this court strike down only the unconstitutional portion if such a construction is reasonably possible. Accordingly, we shall sever the ex parte hearing portion of the 1961 amendment to § 9–25–15 from the rest of the statute, strike down this element as unconstitutional, and interpret the remaining portion of the statute as requiring a hearing to determine the judgment debtor's ability to pay. [The Court then explained the basis for its power to sever the unconstitutional portion of the statute.] * * *

### *Notes*

1. Similarly, the Supreme Court has held that a felon who was fined and placed on probation on the condition that he make restitution to his victim and who did not pay could not be imprisoned for that reason alone. The trial court had to inquire into why the felon had not paid and to determine whether alternative orders, such as extending the time to pay, might be appropriate. Bearden v. Georgia, 461 U.S. 660, 103 S.Ct. 2064, 76 L.Ed.2d 221 (1983). Compare Hicks on Behalf of Feiock v. Feiock, 485 U.S. 624, 108 S.Ct. 1423, 99 L.Ed.2d 721 (1988)(allowing the use of jail as a coercive remedy where a defendant failed to obey a court order requiring the payment of child support).

7. Certain poor debtors may obtain post-body execution release almost immediately by taking the "poor debtor's oath." We do not limit our opinion, however, to the application of the body execution statute only to tort judgment debtors. The requirements of equal protection and due process apply equally to the application of the body execution statute to debtors who are unable to pay nontort judgments.

2. Is a broader attack on body execution statutes appropriate? In Kinsey v. Preeson, 746 P.2d 542 (Colo.1987), the Supreme Court of Colorado struck down that state's body execution statute on the grounds that it failed the rational basis test. The court noted:

> [A]n indigent judgment debtor will suffer imprisonment based solely on an involuntary inability to pay the judgment and still owe the entire amount of the judgment after serving time in jail. Imprisoning an indigent debtor will not serve the coercive purpose of the body execution statute. In fact, jailing the indigent debtor defeats the purpose of obtaining payment for the judgment creditor by precluding gainful employment during the period of incarceration.

746 P.2d at 549. What if the real effect of imprisonment under such statutes is to "set off a family-wide scramble to come up with the money"? Even if effective, is it fair? See Suzanne Daley, Court Tells South Africa to Stop Imprisoning Debtors, New York Times, October 1, 1995 at p. 4; Coetzee v. South Africa, 1995 SA ___ (CC).

3. If body execution is unavailable, what is the court to do to a debtor who is not indigent, but is able to hide assets so that they are not subject to levy or garnishment? If the debtor is determined enough, perhaps not much. E.g., Lepak v. McClain, 844 P.2d 852 (Okla.1992) (Oklahoma Constitution prohibits statute allowing incarceration to be used to enforce money judgments in civil contempt proceedings). But see David L. Chambers, Making Fathers Pay (1979)(value of using vigorous collection methods) and Robert C. Davis & Tanya M. Bannister, Improving Collection of Court–Ordered Restitution, 79 Judicature 30 (1995)(simple reminder letters to convicted offenders improves rate of money collected by crime victims).

# Chapter 9

# CONDUCT OF THE PLAINTIFF: BARS TO OBTAINING RELIEF

In both equity and law there are traditional rules, principles, and maxims which focus on the behavior of the plaintiff and, when applicable, bar the plaintiff from obtaining relief. Ultimately all of the principles and rules that we examine in this chapter involve misconduct by the plaintiff, but the degree and type of misconduct varies and traditionally a number of different maxims or principles have been invoked by the courts to bar a plaintiff from obtaining relief. Stated in their boldest traditional form, these rules and principles bar plaintiff from all relief; in some circumstances they are used to modify or adjust a remedy. Frequently law and equity expressed the same root idea in different terms and applied different tests to the plaintiff's behavior. The categories established by the various principles are frequently not well defined at the margin, so that one category shades imperceptibly into another. For instance, the proposition that in order to obtain relief one must come into a court with "clean hands" is a very broad proposition. It can include the stricture against misleading another party to his detriment, which is found in equitable estoppel, or the prohibition against delaying the commencement of an action while the defendant proceeds with the activity that the plaintiff complains of, which is part of laches. The principles which have been inherited from equity are typically more flexible and less distinct than those which are derived from law.

The group of principles and maxims that we examine in this chapter are typically included in remedies courses, but they are often combined with other principles such as that of undue hardship or *de minimus non curat lex.* They are frequently dealt with in conjunction with undue hardship and similar concepts because a legal procedure that balances the equities between the plaintiff and the defendant requires the examination of the plaintiff's conduct and where that examination results in the plaintiff receiving no relief, the cases become very like those in this chapter. When you have finished this chapter you should re-examine Smith v. Staso Milling Co., 18 F.2d 736 (2d Cir.1927), which is set out at p. 93 and ask yourself how many of the issues in that case could be categorized or argued under the headings of unclean hands, equitable estoppel, or laches. To a large extent, the framing of the issues in dispute determines whether the court "balances the equities" or decides the case under one of the principles examined in this chapter.

The connection to *de minimus* cases lies in the fact that the principles and maxims discussed in this chapter are conceived of as defenses. If a remedies course is organized to focus in one place on defenses, the cases here become naturally grouped with the *de minimus* cases.

We have addressed the cases in this chapter with the emphasis on the plaintiff's conduct for two reasons. First, these cases develop the theme of determining remedies by focusing on what will return the plaintiff to her rightful position by taking up the issue of what sort of conduct by the plaintiff will lead a court to conclude that the plaintiff should obtain nothing from the defendant. Second, some of these cases deal with the conduct of the plaintiff toward the court or third parties so that they do not always fit neatly with cases which focus on the relations between plaintiff and defendant. There are some forms of conduct by which the plaintiff may defeat his claim for relief regardless of the defendant's behavior.

### *Problem: Country Lodge v. Miller (Reprised) Plaintiff's Conduct*

Country Lodge has sued, seeking to enjoin Miller from polluting the Rural River which flows from Miller's property past that of Country Lodge. Country Lodge also claims damages for loss of business, alleging that numerous customers have complained of the unsightly river in the fall when Miller discharges her apple mash. Miller first defends by claiming that Country Lodge has unclean hands since it too is discharging garbage into the river. Should Country Lodge be denied relief in the following circumstances:

a) Country Lodge's discharges are only one-tenth the volume of Miller's?

b) Miller, being upstream, is not affected by Country Lodge's discharges?

Would your answer be different if Country Lodge's discharges were a breeding ground for insects which harmed Miller's apples?

What if Miller had gone to Country Lodge before beginning her discharge, told Country Lodge what she planned to do, and Country Lodge said it had no objection to Miller discharging apple mash?

Assume Country Lodge's owner had read in the newspaper that Miller was about to install a big apple press and discharge mash into the river and that experience in a neighboring county showed that the discharge would be unsightly. If Country Lodge waited to sue until Miller starting discharging the apple mash, should that delay bar Country Lodge from obtaining relief? Should it matter whether the relief sought was damages or an injunction?

On the same set of facts, suppose EPA sued Miller for discharging apple mash without a permit; should EPA be barred from obtaining relief? Would it make a difference to your answer if Miller had applied to EPA for a discharge permit a year before but, despite a statutory requirement that EPA act on all permit applications within six months, EPA had failed to act because it considered other permit applications more important? What if EPA's Director of Water Pollution had erroneously, but in good faith, told Miller that she came within an exception to the statute and did not need a permit for her apple mash discharge?

## A. UNCLEAN HANDS AND IN PARI DELICTO

"He who comes into equity must come with clean hands" is a central maxim of equity with a direct effect on the plaintiff's ability to obtain relief: the court will not provide relief to one who does not come with clean hands. While the metaphor of the maxim is a powerful image, it is, of course, remarkably uninformative as to the legal principle involved. It could be recast to state that courts will not grant relief to plaintiffs who have committed improper conduct with regard to the matter in litigation. This reformulation certainly focuses on the core of the maxim. "The desire to avoid rewarding wrongful conduct forms the basis of the clean hands doctrine." Powell, Inc. v. Abney, 669 F.2d 348, 350 (5th Cir.1982). But this reformulation still leaves a central issue vague: what sorts of conduct are improper? Moreover, it may too narrowly restrict the sweep of the maxim, which has been interpreted elastically when considering how closely the plaintiff's behavior must be connected to the matter in litigation.

"In pari delicto potior est conditio defendentis"—in a case of equal or mutual fault, the position of the defending party is the better one—is the common law parallel to the clean hands doctrine. A plaintiff who is *in pari delicto* with the defendant will receive no relief from the court. *In pari delicto* carries a greater emphasis on equality of fault than does the clean hands defense and involves a mutuality of wrong-doing.

These defenses have important common threads. First, their successful invocation leads to the denial of all relief to the plaintiff. Second, this result is not justified by the defendant's conduct, which may be reprehensible, but by the plaintiff's misconduct. Third, the basis on which the maxims are applied is often not the rights of the litigant to the case but the interests of the public and the protection of the integrity of the court. But it is an open question in many cases whether the decision of the court to accept one of these defenses and leave things as it found them clearly serves the interests of the public. Frequently the court has to rely on long term arguments to the effect that its refusal to grant relief to plaintiffs who behave in an unacceptable manner will discourage others from such behavior in the future. Not only do these arguments look to the long term impacts, they ignore the windfall that defendant obtains. Obviously we would be better off with a system that was simultaneously just to the plaintiff, defendant and the public. You should consider throughout the reading of these cases whether there are other mechanisms that would more fairly adjust the interests of the plaintiff, defendant, and the public.

## KEYSTONE DRILLER CO. v. GENERAL EXCAVATOR CO.

Supreme Court of the United States, 1933.
290 U.S. 240, 54 S.Ct. 146, 78 L.Ed. 293.

MR. JUSTICE BUTLER delivered the opinion of the Court.

The question presented is whether the Circuit Court of Appeals rightly applied the maxim, He who comes into equity must come with clean hands.

Petitioner owns five patents which may be conveniently identified as the Clutter patent and the four Downie patents. They all cover devices constituting parts of a ditching machine operated on the principle of a mechanical hoe or mattock. The Clutter patent is basic and the Downie patents are for claimed improvements.

Prior to the commencement of these suits, the petitioner brought a suit in the Eastern Division of the Northern Ohio District against the Byers Machine Company for infringement of the first three patents. January 31, 1929, the court held them valid and infringed, and granted injunction. Defendant appealed.

[In February 1929 Keystone brought suit against, inter alia, General Excavator alleging infringement of the same three patents.] Plaintiff immediately applied for temporary injunctions to restrain further infringement. The applications were based upon the complaints, supporting affidavits and the pleadings, opinion and decree in the *Byers* Case. The court filed a memorandum in which it is stated that, while plaintiff had sustained its patents as against the defenses of an alleged impecunious infringer, defendants were in good faith pressing new defenses that seemed to have merit enough to prevent the application of the rule permitting a temporary injunction merely because of the prior adjudication. The court denied the injunctions, but upon condition that defendants give bonds to pay the profits or damages that might be decreed against them. * * * November 5, 1930, the Circuit Court of Appeals affirmed the decree in the *Byers* Case. * * * The district court held the Clutter patent and the first and fourth Downie patents valid and infringed, the second Downie not infringed, and the third Downie patent invalid.

At the trial of these cases, defendants introduced evidence that plaintiff did not come into court with clean hands. It was sufficient to sustain findings of fact made by both courts, in substance as follows: June 27, 1921, Downie filed the application on which was issued his first patent. In the preceding winter he had learned of a possible prior use at Joplin, Mo., by Bernard R. Clutter. The latter is a brother of the patentee of the Clutter patent and had then recently been in the service of plaintiff as demonstrator in the use of ditching machinery. Downie made the application and assigned his rights to plaintiff, of which he was secretary and general manager. The patent issued, and plaintiff, contemplating the bringing of an infringement suit thereon against the Byers Machine Company, was advised that the prior use at Joplin was sufficient to cast doubt upon the validity of the patent. Downie then went to Bernard R. Clutter and for valuable considerations * * * obtained from Clutter an affidavit prepared by Downie to the effect that Clutter's use of the device was an abandoned experiment, and also obtained Clutter's agreement to assign plaintiff any rights he might have as inventor, to keep secret the details of the prior use, and, so far as he was able, to suppress the evidence. No proof of such use was produced at the trial of that case. The defendants in these suits took Clutter's deposition early in 1930. He did not then disclose his arrangement with plaintiff for concealment of evidence in the *Byers* Case. Their suspicions being aroused by his testimony, defendants in the latter part of that year again examined him and secured facts upon which they were able to compel the plaintiff to furnish the details of the corrupt transaction.

The district court characterized Downie's conduct as highly reprehensible, and found that his purpose was to keep Clutter silent. But it also found that the plaintiff did nothing to suppress evidence in these cases. It expressed the opinion that matters pertaining to the motion for preliminary injunction had no bearing upon the merits, and that plaintiff's use of the *Byers* decree was not a fraud upon the court. And it ruled the maxim did not apply. The Circuit Court of Appeals held the contrary, reversed the decrees of the District Court, and remanded the cases, with instructions to dismiss the complaints without prejudice.

Plaintiff contends that the maxim does not apply unless the wrongful conduct is directly connected with and material to the matter in litigation, and that, where more than one cause is joined in a bill and plaintiff is shown to have come with unclean hands in respect of only one of them, the others will not be dismissed.

The meaning and proper application of the maxim are to be considered. As authoritatively expounded, the words and the reasons upon which it rests extend to the party seeking relief in equity. "It is one of the fundamental principles upon which equity jurisprudence is founded, that before a complainant can have a standing in court he must first show that not only has he a good and meritorious cause of action, but he must come into court with clean hands. He must be frank and fair with the court, nothing about the case under consideration should be guarded, but everything that tends to a full and fair determination of the matters in controversy should be placed before the court." Story's Equity Jurisprudence (14th Ed.) § 98. * * * This court has declared: "It is a principle in chancery, that he who asks relief must have acted in good faith. The equitable powers of this court can never be exerted in behalf of one who has acted fraudulently, or who by deceit or any unfair means has gained an advantage. To aid a party in such a case would make this court the abetter of iniquity." Bein v. Heath, 6 How. 228, 247, 12 L.Ed. 416. * * *

But courts of equity do not make the quality of suitors the test. They apply the maxim requiring clean hands only where some unconscionable act of one coming for relief has immediate and necessary relation to the equity that he seeks in respect of the matter in litigation. They do not close their doors because of plaintiff's misconduct, whatever its character, that has no relation to anything involved in the suit, but only for such violations of conscience as in some measure affect the equitable relations between the parties in respect of something brought before the court for adjudication. They apply the maxim, not by way of punishment for extraneous transgressions, but upon considerations that make for the advancement of right and justice. They are not bound by formula or restrained by any limitation that tends to trammel the free and just exercise of discretion.

Neither the plaintiff's corruption of Clutter in respect of the first Downie patent nor its use in these cases of the *Byers* decree can fairly be deemed to be unconnected with causes of action based on the other patents.

Its bills show the devices covered by the five patents to be important, if not essential, parts of the same machine. And its claims warrant the inference that each supplements the others. This is made plain by mere reference to the things patented. The Clutter device is for the hoe or mattock arrangement. The first Downie is for an improvement designed, by a drop bottom scoop and other means, to permit more accurate dumping. The second Downie had for its main purpose the elimination of a "blind spot" in the unloading operation. The third Downie makes possible and convenient the use of scoops of different widths upon the same machine. The fourth Downie device consists of detachable rake teeth for a scoop.

Had the corruption of Clutter been disclosed at the trial of the *Byers* Case, the court undoubtedly would have been warranted in holding it sufficient to require dismissal of the cause of action there alleged for the infringement of the Downie patent. Promptly after the decision in that case plaintiff brought these suits and immediately applied for injunctions *pendente lite*. It used the decree of validity there obtained in support, if not indeed as the basis, of its applications. And plaintiff's misconduct in the *Byers* suit remaining undisclosed, that decree was given weight on the motions for preliminary injunctions. As the litigation was to continue for years and the use of the devices in question was essential to the ditching machinery, it is clear that the injunctions would have been a burdensome detriment to defendants. The amounts of the bonds required in lieu of injunctions attest the importance of the advantage obtained by use of the decree. While it is not found, as reasonably it may be inferred from the circumstances, that from the beginning it was plaintiff's intention through suppression of Clutter's evidence to obtain decree in the *Byers* Case for use in subsequent infringement suits against these defendants and others, it does clearly appear that the plaintiff made the *Byers* Case a part of his preparation in these suits. The use actually made of that decree is sufficient to show that plaintiff did not come with clean hands in respect of any cause of action in these cases.

The relation between the device covered by the first Downie patent and those covered by the other patents, taken in connection with the use to which plaintiff put the *Byers* decree, is amply sufficient to bring these cases within the maxim.

Decrees affirmed.

### *Notes*

1. It appears plaintiff had four good patents and one perhaps obtained by misrepresentation. The Court found that the patented devices were each an important, if not essential, part of the same machine. This suggests that if infringement of the four good patents were enjoined, defendant would not be able to manufacture a machine which would be competitive with the plaintiff's. Why should plaintiff's unclean hands with regard to one patent deprive him of the benefit of the other four? Would the result have been different if the suppression of evidence had been brought to light earlier? Namely, if the first Downie patent had been held invalid in the *Byers* case, would an injunction against the infringement of the other four patents have been upheld? Is an obstruction of the processes of the court a greater wrong leading to a correspondingly greater denial of access to relief than fraudulently obtaining a patent?

2. The defense of inequitable conduct by the patent applicant as a bar to enforcement of a patent was recognized by the Supreme Court in Precision Co. v. Automotive Co., 324 U.S. 806, 65 S.Ct. 993, 89 L.Ed. 1381 (1945). The formulation of the defense developed by the courts focuses on the intent of the patentee to mislead or deceive the Patent and Trademark Office and on the materiality of the deceptive act to patent issuance. "Establishing that a patent was procured by fraud or with such egregious conduct as to render it unenforceable requires clear, unequivocal, and convincing evidence of an intentional misrepresentation or withholding of a material fact from the PTO." Orthopedic Equip. Co. v. All Orthopedic Appliances, 707 F.2d 1376, 1383 (Fed.Cir.1983). "In addition to the materiality of the undisclosed information, a challenger of a patent must, to establish that the patentee acted inequitably, demonstrate that the patentee intended to mislead or deceive the PTO." La Bounty Mfg., Inc. v. U.S. International Trade Commission, 958 F.2d 1066 (Fed.Cir.1992). A recent administrative rule defines materiality and indicates how far a patent applicant must go in disclosing information adverse to his application. 37 C.F.R. §§ 1.56(a)-(b)(1992). The rule is stated in general terms and interpretation of "materiality" by the courts will continue. The extensive caselaw on this issue is surveyed and analyzed in Robert J. Goldman, Evolution of the Inequitable Conduct Defense in Patent Litigation, 7 Harv. J.L. & Tech. 37 (1993).

3. It may well be that unsuccessful fraud will not have the serious consequences that plaintiff faced in *Keystone*. In Niner v. Hanson, 217 Md. 298, 142 A.2d 798 (1958), plaintiff had perjured himself in earlier litigation between the same parties but had recanted before the termination of the first proceeding. In rejecting an unclean hands defense, the majority noted: "It has been held in a number of well-considered cases that dismissal is not required even where the complainant was guilty of fraud, perjury or suppression of evidence, where the wrongdoing does not result in benefit to the wrongdoer, or operate as a fraud or imposition upon the court in which relief is sought." The dissent believed the court had misstated the issue: "the question to be resolved in this action is whether the [plaintiff's] wrongful conduct is connected with, or related to, the dispute and not whether the [defendant] has been injured." What interests are served by these differing formulations of the rule?

4. The unclean hands doctrine derives from the maxims of the equity court. If plaintiff in *Keystone* sued for damages rather than for an injunction to prevent further infringement of its patents, would the result in the case be the same? Would it make sense for the court to grant damages but not an injunction?

## CLINTON E. WORDEN & CO. v. CALIFORNIA FIG SYRUP CO.

Supreme Court of the United States, 1903.
187 U.S. 516, 23 S.Ct. 161, 47 L.Ed. 282.

MR. JUSTICE SHIRAS delivered the opinion of the Court.

The courts below concluded, upon the evidence, that the defendants sold a medical preparation named, marked, and packed, in imitation of the complainant's medicine, for the purpose and with the design and intent of deceiving purchasers and inducing them to buy defendant's preparation instead of the complainant's. We see no reason to dissent from that conclusion, and if there were no other questions in the case, we should be ready to affirm the decree, awarding a perpetual injunction and an account of the profits and gains derived from such unfair and dishonest practices.

Another ground, however, is urged against the complainant's right to invoke the aid of a court of equity, in that the California Fig Syrup Company, the complainant, has so fraudulently represented to the public the nature of its medical preparation that it is not entitled to equitable relief.

Some courts have gone so far as to hold that courts of equity will not interfere by injunction in controversies between rival manufacturers and dealers in so-called quack medicines.

It may be said, in support of such a view, that most, if not all, the States of this Union have enactments forbidding and making penal the practice of medicine by persons who have not gone through a course of appropriate study, and obtained a license from a board of examiners; and there is similar legislation in respect to pharmacists. And it would seem to be inconsistent, and to tend to defeat such salutary laws, if medical preparations, often and usually containing powerful and poisonous drugs, are permitted to be widely advertised and sold to all who are willing to purchase. Laws might properly be passed limiting and controlling such traffic by restraining retail dealers from selling such medical preparations, except when prescribed by regular medical practitioners.

But we think that, in the absence of such legislation, courts cannot declare dealing in such preparations to be illegal, nor the articles themselves to be not entitled, as property, to the protection of the law.

We find, however, more solidity in the contention, on behalf of the appellants, that when the owner of a trade-mark applies for an injunction to restrain the defendant from injuring his property by making false representations to the public, it is essential that the plaintiff should not in his trade-mark, or in his advertisements and business, be himself guilty of any false or misleading representation; that if the plaintiff makes any material false statement in connection with the property which he seeks to protect, he loses his right to claim the assistance of a court of equity; that where any symbol or label claimed as a trade-mark is so constructed or worded as to make or contain a distinct assertion which is false, no property can be claimed on it, or, in other words, the right to the exclusive use of it cannot be maintained. * * *

In the Circuit Court of the United States for the Eastern District of Michigan, April 1, 1895, the California Fig Syrup Company filed a bill, seeking to restrain Frederick Stearns & Company from infringing complainant's trade-mark. The court declined to grant an injunction, and dismissed the bill with costs, holding that the words "Syrup of Figs" or "Fig Syrup," if descriptive of a syrup, one of the characteristic ingredients of which is the juice of the fig, cannot be sustained as a valid trademark or trade name, and that, under the facts of the case, the use of the name "Syrup of Figs," in connection with a description of the preparation as a fruit remedy, "nature's pleasant laxative," applied to a compound, whose active ingredient is senna, and containing but a small proportion of fig juice, which has no considerable laxative properties, is deceptive, and deprives one so using it of any claim to equitable relief.

On appeal to the Circuit Court of Appeals of the Sixth Circuit the decree * * * was affirmed. In his opinion Circuit Judge Taft, after stating that the term "Syrup of Figs," if intended to describe the character of the article considered, could not be used as a trade-mark, proceeded to say:

> But the second ground presented, and that upon which the court below rested its decision, prevents the complainant from having any relief at all. That ground is that the complainant has built up its business and made it valuable by an intentional deceit of the public. It has intended the public to understand that the preparation which it sells has, as an important medicinal agent in its composition, the juice of California figs. This has undoubtedly led

the public into the purchase of the preparation. The statement is wholly untrue. Just a suspicion of fig juice has been put into the preparation, not for the purpose of changing its medicinal character, or even its flavor, but merely to give a weak support to the statement that the article sold is syrup of figs. This is a fraud upon the public. It is true it may be a harmless humbug to palm off upon the public as syrup of figs what is syrup of senna, but it is nevertheless of such a character that a court of equity will not encourage it by extending any relief to the person who seeks to protect a business which has grown out of and is dependent upon such deceit. It is well settled that if a person wishes his trade-mark property to be protected by a court of equity, he must come into court with clean hands, and if it appears that the trade-mark for which he seeks protection is itself a misrepresentation to the public, and has acquired a value with the public by fraudulent misrepresentations in advertisements, all relief will be denied to him. This is the doctrine of the highest court of England, and no court has laid it down with any greater stringency than the Supreme Court of the United States. * * *

The argument for complainant is, that because fig juice or syrup has no laxative property everybody ought to understand that when the term is used to designate a laxative medicine it must have only a fanciful meaning. But the fact is admitted that the public believe that fig juice or syrup has laxative medicinal properties. It is to them that the complainant seeks to sell its preparation, and it is with respect to their knowledge and impressions that the character, whether descriptive or fanciful, of the term used, is to be determined.

* * * That the complainant company, years after it had established a popular demand for its product, issued statements in medical journals and newspapers and circulars, that the medical properties of their compound were derived from senna, does not relieve it from the charge of deceit and misrepresentation to the public. Such publications went only to giving information to wholesale dealers. The company by the use of the terms of its so-called trade-mark on its bottles, wrappers, and cartons continued to appeal to the consumers, out of whose credulity came the profits of their business. And, indeed, it was the imitation by the defendants of such false and misleading representations that led to the present suit.

* * * [U]pon the entire evidence in the case, and in the light of the authorities cited by the counsel of the respective parties, our conclusions are that the name "Syrup of Figs" does not, in fact, properly designate or describe the preparation made and sold by the California Fig Syrup Company, so as to be susceptible of appropriation as a trade-mark, and that the marks and names, used upon the bottles containing complainant's preparation, and upon the cartons and wrappers containing the bottles, are so plainly deceptive as to deprive the complainant company of a right to a remedy by way of an injunction by a court of equity. * * *

Mr. Justice McKenna dissented.

## *Notes*

1. There appears to be no claim in this case that the California Fig Syrup Co. acted in any improper manner with regard to the defendant. Is it appropriate for the defendant, in effect, to claim that since both it and plaintiff are defrauding the public, the Court should not restrain its injury to the plaintiff?

2. Since the rationale of the Court's decision rests on the misrepresentation to the public by the plaintiff, would it be improper for the Court to fashion a decree that prohibited both plaintiff and defendant from engaging in misrepresentation? Could a court invite a public authority or a member of the consuming public to intervene in the action and request such relief? If the Court is unable or unwilling to take such action when it has identified misrepresentation to the public as the wrong which controls the case, how has the Court's decision served the interest of equity or justice? If the public authorities or misled consumers do not choose to bring an action against the California Fig Syrup Co., why should the court use this case as a vehicle to protect them? Is the issue of plaintiff's behavior likely to be fully and effectively developed by the litigants in this case? Should standards of standing or justiciability be applied to unclean hands controversies?

3. Assume the *Worden* court had before it a plaintiff who was seeking to recover a debt and the defendant offered persuasive evidence that the money he had borrowed from the plaintiff was the proceeds of an illegal drug transaction. Are the plaintiff's hands sufficiently clean to allow recovery?

4. The Supreme Court addressed an unclean hands defense in the context of a claim based on a statute in McKennon v. Nashville Banner Publishing Co., 513 U.S. ___, 115 S.Ct. 879, 130 L.Ed.2d 852 (1995). Plaintiff alleged that she was fired because of her age in violation of the Age Discrimination in Employment Act of 1967. In her deposition in the case, plaintiff revealed that she had removed confidential financial documents from the employer's premises, which was a basis for discharge. The employer sought summary judgment. The Court found the purpose of the statute to be both to provide compensation to employees who suffered age discrimination and to deter employers from discriminating; in that context the Court rejected the unclean hands defense but held that plaintiff's misconduct was still relevant to the remedy. The Court found that reinstatement or front pay would not be an appropriate remedy in this case, but that backpay was compensation to restore plaintiff to her rightful position absent discrimination and that in fashioning its remedy the district court should start with backpay from the date of firing to discovery of the removal of the documents and then consider extraordinary equitable circumstances in the case.

5. The criminal law has some doctrines that sound analogous to unclean hands. The exclusionary rule that holds evidence obtained in violation of the defendant's Fourth Amendment rights inadmissable is an obvious example. United States v. Tucker, 28 F.3d 1420 (6th Cir.1994), cert. denied, ___ U.S. ___, 115 S.Ct. 1426, 131 L.Ed.2d 308 (1995), explicates the basis and limits of the defense of entrapment, which is another obvious

parallel. The judicially created defense of entrapment focuses on the predisposition of the defendant to commit the crime, not on the overzealous or outrageous nature of the government's conduct; it is rooted in the proposition that Congress could not have intended to punish criminally those who were induced by the government to commit a crime. The entrapment defense differs from the exclusionary rule in that it does not involve violation of an independent constitutional right of the defendant and thus the actions of the government are not the focus of scrutiny. The court rejected arguments that would base the entrapment defense on a due process claim or invocation of the court's supervisory power. The possibility that the Supreme Court would dismiss an indictment on the basis of outrageous government conduct in inducing a crime remains a possibility only in the sense that the Court is reluctant to announce that a remedy will never be available under any circumstances. United States v. Russell, 411 U.S. 423, 93 S.Ct. 1637, 36 L.Ed.2d 366 (1973); Hampton v. United States, 425 U.S. 484, 96 S.Ct. 1646, 48 L.Ed.2d 113 (1976).

## BATEMAN EICHLER, HILL RICHARDS, INC. v. BERNER

Supreme Court of the United States, 1985.
472 U.S. 299, 105 S.Ct. 2622, 86 L.Ed.2d 215.

JUSTICE BRENNAN delivered the opinion of the Court.

The question presented by this case is whether the common-law in pari delicto defense bars a private damages action under the federal securities laws against corporate insiders and broker-dealers who fraudulently induce investors to purchase securities by misrepresenting that they are conveying material nonpublic information about the issuer.

I

The respondent investors filed this action in the United States District Court for the Northern District of California, alleging that they incurred substantial trading losses as a result of a conspiracy between Charles Lazzaro, a registered securities broker employed by the petitioner Bateman Eichler, Hill Richards, Inc. (Bateman Eichler), and Leslie Neadeau, President of T.O.N.M. Oil & Gas Exploration Corporation (TONM), to induce them to purchase large quantities of TONM over-the-counter stock by divulging false and materially incomplete information about the company on the pretext that it was accurate inside information. Specifically, Lazzaro is alleged to have told the respondents that he personally knew TONM insiders and had learned, inter alia, that (a) "[v]ast amounts of gold had been discovered in Surinam, and TONM had options on thousands of acres in gold-producing regions of Surinam"; (b) the discovery was "not publically known, but would subsequently be announced"; (c) TONM was currently engaged in negotiations with other companies to form a joint venture for mining the Surinamese gold; and (d) when this information was made public, "TONM stock, which was then selling from $1.50 to $3.00/share, would increase in value from $10 to $15/share within a short period of time, and ... might increase to $100/share" within a year. Some of the respondents aver that they contacted Neadeau and inquired whether Lazzaro's tips were accurate; Neadeau stated that the information was "not public knowledge" and "would neither confirm nor deny those claims," but allegedly advised that "Lazzaro was a very trustworthy and a good man."

The respondents admitted in their complaint that they purchased TONM stock, much of it through Lazzaro, "on the premise that Lazzaro was privy to certain information not otherwise available to the general public." Their shares initially increased dramatically in price, but ultimately declined to substantially below the purchase price when the joint mining venture fell through.

Lazzaro and Neadeau are alleged to have made the representations set forth above knowing that the representations "were untrue and/or contained only half-truths, material omissions of fact and falsehoods," intending that the respondents would rely thereon, and for the purpose of "influenc[ing] and manipulat[ing] the price of TONM stock" so as "to profit themselves through the taking of commissions and secret profits." The respondents contended that this scheme violated, inter alia, § 10(b) of the Securities Exchange Act of 1934, 48 Stat. 891, 15 U.S.C. § 78j(b),[7] and SEC Rule 10b–5 promulgated thereunder, 17 CFR § 240.10b–5 (1984).[8] They sought capital losses and lost profits, punitive damages, and costs and attorney's fees. * * *

II

The common-law defense at issue in this case derives from the Latin, in pari delicto potior est conditio defendentis: "In a case of equal or mutual fault . . . the position of the [defending] party . . . is the better one." The defense is grounded on two premises: first, that courts should not lend their good offices to mediating disputes among wrongdoers; and second, that denying judicial relief to an admitted wrongdoer is an effective means of deterring illegality. In its classic formulation, the in pari delicto defense was narrowly limited to situations where the plaintiff truly bore at least substantially equal responsibility for his

7. That section provides:

"It shall be unlawful for any person, directly or indirectly, by the use of any means or instrumentality of interstate commerce or of the mails, or of any facility of any national securities exchange—

* * *

"(b) To use or employ, in connection with the purchase or sale of any security registered on a national securities exchange or any security not so registered, any manipulative or deceptive device or contrivance in contravention of such rules and regulations as the Commission may prescribe as necessary or appropriate in the public interest or for the protection of investors."

8. That Rule provides:

"It shall be unlawful for any person, directly or indirectly, by the use of any means or instrumentality of interstate commerce, or of the mails or of any facility of any national securities exchange,

"(a) To employ any device, scheme, or artifice to defraud,

"(b) To make any untrue statement of a material fact or to omit to state a material fact necessary in order to make the statements made, in the light of the circumstances under which they were made, not misleading, or

"(c) To engage in any act, practice, or course of business which operates or would operate as a fraud or deceit upon any person, in connection with the purchase or sale of any security."

injury, because "in cases where both parties are in delicto, concurring in an illegal act, it does not always follow that they stand in pari delicto; for there may be, and often are, very different degrees in their guilt." 1 J. Story, Equity Jurisprudence 304–305 (13th ed.1886)(Story). Thus there might be an "inequality of condition" between the parties, id., at 305, or "a confidential relationship between th[em]" that determined their "relative standing" before a court, 3 J. Pomeroy, Equity Jurisprudence § 942a, p. 741 (5th ed.1941)(Pomeroy). In addition, the public policy considerations that undergirded the in pari delicto defense were frequently construed as precluding the defense even where the plaintiff bore substantial fault for his injury: "there may be on the part of the court itself a necessity of supporting the public interests or public policy in many cases, however reprehensible the acts of the parties may be." 1 Story 305. Notwithstanding these traditional limitations, many courts have given the in pari delicto defense a broad application to bar actions where plaintiffs simply have been involved generally in "the same sort of wrongdoing" as defendants.

In [Perma Life Mufflers, Inc. v. International Parts Corp., 392 U.S. 134, 88 S.Ct. 1981, 20 L.Ed.2d 982 (1968)], we emphasized "the inappropriateness of invoking broad common-law barriers to relief where a private suit serves important public purposes." That case involved a treble-damages action against a Midas Muffler franchisor by several of its dealers, who alleged that the franchise agreement created a conspiracy to restrain trade in violation of the Sherman and Clayton Acts. The lower courts barred the action on the grounds that the dealers, as parties to the agreement, were in pari delicto with the franchisor. In reversing that determination, the opinion for this Court emphasized that there was no indication that Congress had intended to incorporate the defense into the antitrust laws, which "are best served by insuring that the private action will be an ever-present threat to deter anyone contemplating [illegal] business behavior." Accordingly, the opinion concluded that "the doctrine of in pari delicto, with its complex scope, contents, and effects, is not to be recognized as a defense to an antitrust action." The opinion reserved the question whether a plaintiff who engaged in "truly complete involvement and participation in a monopolistic scheme"—one who "aggressively support[ed] and further[ed] the monopolistic scheme as a necessary part and parcel of it"—could be barred from pursuing a damages action, finding that the muffler dealers had relatively little bargaining power and that they had been coerced by the franchisor into agreeing to many of the contract's provisions.

In separate opinions, five Justices agreed that the concept of "equal fault" should be narrowly defined in litigation arising under federal regulatory statutes. "[B]ecause of the strong public interest in eliminating restraints on competition, ... many of the refinements of moral worth demanded of plaintiffs by ... many of the variations of in pari delicto should not be applicable in the antitrust field." Id., at 151, 88 S.Ct., at 1991 (Marshall, J., concurring in result). The five Justices concluded, however, that where a plaintiff truly bore at least substantially equal responsibility for the violation, a defense based on such fault—whether or not denominated in pari delicto—should be recognized in antitrust litigation.[17]

Bateman Eichler argues that *Perma Life*—with its emphasis on the importance of analyzing the effects that fault-based defenses would have on the enforcement of congressional goals—is of only marginal relevance to a private damages action under the federal securities laws. Specifically, Bateman Eichler observes that Congress expressly provided for private antitrust actions—thereby manifesting a "desire to go beyond the common law in the antitrust statute in order to provide substantial encouragement to private enforcement and to help deter anticompetitive conduct"—whereas private rights of action under § 10(b) of the Securities Exchange Act of 1934 are merely implied from that provision—thereby, apparently, supporting a broader application of the in pari delicto defense. * * *

We disagree. Nothing in *Perma Life* suggested that public policy implications should govern only where Congress expressly provides for private remedies; the classic formulation of the in pari delicto doctrine itself required a careful consideration of such implications before allowing the defense. Moreover, we repeatedly have emphasized that implied private actions provide "a most effective weapon in the enforcement" of the securities laws and are "a necessary supplement to Commission action." J.I. Case Co. v. Borak, 377 U.S. 426, 432, 84 S.Ct. 1555, 1560, 12 L.Ed.2d 423 (1964). * * * We therefore conclude that the views expressed in *Perma Life* apply with full force to implied causes of action under the federal securities laws. Accordingly, a private action for damages in these circumstances may be barred on the grounds of the plaintiff's own culpability only where (1) as a direct result of his own actions, the plaintiff bears at least substantially equal responsibility for the violations he seeks to redress, and (2) preclusion of suit would not significantly interfere with the effective enforcement of the securities laws and protection of the investing public.

A

The District Court and Court of Appeals proceeded on the assumption that the respondents had violated § 10(b) and Rule 10b–5, an assumption we accept for purposes of resolving the issue before us. Bateman Eichler contends that the respondents' delictum was substantially par to that of Lazzaro and Neadeau for two reasons. First, whereas many antitrust plaintiffs participate in illegal restraints of trade only "passively" or as the result of economic coercion, as was the case in

**17.** Justice White concluded that "the in pari delicto defense in its historic formulation is not a useful concept" in antitrust law, but emphasized that he "would deny recovery where plaintiff and defendant bear substantially equal responsibility for injury resulting to one of them." The other four Justices would have allowed explicit, though limited, use of the in pari delicto defense itself. Id., at 147, 88 S.Ct., at 1988 (Fortas, J., concurring in result); . id., at 148–149, 88 S.Ct., at 1989 (Marshall, J., concurring in result); id., at 153, 88 S.Ct., at 1991 (Harlan, J., joined by Stewart, J., concurring in part and dissenting in part).

*Perma Life,* the ordinary tippee acts voluntarily in choosing to trade on inside information. Second, § 10(b) and Rule 10b–5 apply literally to "any person" who violates their terms, and do not recognize gradations of culpability.

We agree that the typically voluntary nature of an investor's decision impermissibly to trade on an inside tip renders the investor more blameworthy than someone who is party to a contract solely by virtue of another's overweening bargaining power. We disagree, however, that an investor who engages in such trading is necessarily as blameworthy as a corporate insider or broker-dealer who discloses the information for personal gain. Notwithstanding the broad reach of § 10(b) and Rule 10b–5, there are important distinctions between the relative culpabilities of tippers, securities professionals, and tippees in these circumstances. The Court has made clear in recent Terms that a tippee's use of material nonpublic information does not violate § 10(b) and Rule 10b–5 unless the tippee owes a corresponding duty to disclose the information. * * * In the context of insider trading, we do not believe that a person whose liability is solely derivative can be said to be as culpable as one whose breach of duty gave rise to that liability in the first place.

Moreover, insiders and broker-dealers who selectively disclose material nonpublic information commit a potentially broader range of violations than do tippees who trade on the basis of that information. A tippee trading on inside information will in many circumstances be guilty of fraud against individual shareholders, a violation for which the tipper shares responsibility. But the insider, in disclosing such information, also frequently breaches fiduciary duties toward the issuer itself. And in cases where the tipper intentionally conveys false or materially incomplete information to the tippee, the tipper commits an additional violation: fraud against the tippee. Such conduct is particularly egregious when committed by a securities professional, who owes a duty of honesty and fair dealing toward his clients. * * * Absent other culpable actions by a tippee that can fairly be said to outweigh these violations by insiders and broker-dealers, we do not believe that the tippee properly can be characterized as being of substantially equal culpability as his tippers.

There is certainly no basis for concluding at this stage of this litigation that the respondents were in pari delicto with Lazzaro and Neadeau. The allegations are that Lazzaro and Neadeau masterminded this scheme to manipulate the market in TONM securities for their own personal benefit, and that they used the purchasing respondents as unwitting dupes to inflate the price of TONM stock. The respondents may well have violated the securities laws, and in any event we place no "stamp of approval" on their conduct. But accepting the facts set forth in the complaint as true—as we must in reviewing the District Court's dismissal on the pleadings—Lazzaro and Neadeau "awakened in [the respondents] a desire for wrongful gain that might otherwise have remained dormant, inspired in [their] mind[s] an unfounded idea that [they were] going to secure it, and then by fraud and false pretenses deprived [them] of [their] money," * * * actions that, if they occurred, were far more culpable under any reasonable view than the respondents' alleged conduct.

B

We also believe that denying the in pari delicto defense in such circumstances will best promote the primary objective of the federal securities laws—protection of the investing public and the national economy through the promotion of "a high standard of business ethics ... in every facet of the securities industry." SEC v. Capital Gains Research Bureau, Inc., 375 U.S. 180, 186–187, 84 S.Ct. 275, 280, 11 L.Ed.2d 237 (1963). Although a number of lower courts have reasoned that a broad rule of caveat tippee would better serve this goal, we believe the contrary position adopted by other courts represents the better view.

To begin with, barring private actions in cases such as this would inexorably result in a number of alleged fraudulent practices going undetected by the authorities and unremedied. The Securities and Exchange Commission has advised us that it "does not have the resources to police the industry sufficiently to ensure that false tipping does not occur or is consistently discovered," and that "[w]ithout the tippees' assistance, the Commission could not effectively prosecute false tipping—a difficult practice to detect." * * * Thus it is particularly important to permit "litigation among guilty parties [that will serve] to expose their unlawful conduct and render them more easily subject to appropriate civil, administrative, and criminal penalties." Kuehnert v. Texstar Corp., 412 F.2d 700, 706, n. 3 (C.A.5 1969)(Godbold, J., dissenting). The in pari delicto defense, by denying any incentive to a defrauded tippee to bring suit against his defrauding tipper, would significantly undermine this important goal.[28]

Moreover, we believe that deterrence of insider trading most frequently will be maximized by bringing enforcement pressures to bear on the sources of such information—corporate insiders and broker-dealers.

> "The true insider or the broker-dealer is at the fountainhead of the confidential information.... If the prophylactic purpose of the law is to restrict the use of all material inside information until it is made available to the investing public, then the most effective means of carrying out this policy is to nip in the bud the source of the information, the tipper, by discouraging him from 'making the initial disclosure which is the first step in the chain of dissemina-

**28.** Our analysis is buttressed by reference to § 9(e) of the Securities Exchange Act of 1934, 48 Stat. 890, 15 U.S.C. § 78i(e), which allows co-conspirators a right of contribution against "any person who, if joined in the original suit, would have been liable to make the same payment." This provision overrides the common-law rule against contribution from co-conspirators, which was grounded on the premise that "parties generally in pari delicto should be left where they are found." Texas Industries, Inc. v. Radcliff Materials, Inc., 451 U.S. 630, 635, 101 S.Ct. 2061, 2064, 68 L.Ed.2d 500 (1981). As the Commission observes, "[s]urely, the Congress that provided that a brokerage professional such as Lazzaro could recover from his fellow manipulators should be understood to have also permitted the victims of Lazzaro's manipulative scheme to sue him." Brief for SEC as Amicus Curiae at 26.

tion.' This can most readily be achieved by making unavailable to him the defense of in pari delicto when sued by his tippee upon charges based upon alleged misinformation." Nathanson v. Weis, Voisin, Cannon, Inc., 325 F.Supp. 50, 57–58 (S.D.N.Y.1971).

In addition, corporate insiders and broker-dealers will in many circumstances be more responsive to the deterrent pressure of potential sanctions; they are more likely than ordinary investors to be advised by counsel and thereby to be informed fully of the "allowable limits on their conduct." Kuehnert v. Texstar Corp., supra, at 706 (Godbold, J., dissenting). Although situations might well arise in which the relative culpabilities of the tippee and his insider source merit a different mix of deterrent incentives, we therefore conclude that in tipper-tippee situations such as the one before us the factors discussed above preclude recognition of the in pari delicto defense.

Lower courts reaching a contrary conclusion have typically asserted that, absent a vigorous allowance of the in pari delicto defense, tippees would have, "in effect, an enforceable warranty that secret information is true," id., at 705, and thus no incentive not to trade on that information. These courts have reasoned, in other words, that tippees in such circumstances would be in "the enviable position of 'heads-I-win tails-you-lose,' "—if the tip is correct, the tippee will reap illicit profits, while if the tip fails to yield the expected return, he can sue to recover damages.

We believe the "enforceable warranty" theory is overstated and overlooks significant factors that serve to deter tippee trading irrespective of whether the in pari delicto defense is allowed. First, tippees who bring suit in an attempt to cash in on their "enforceable warranties" expose themselves to the threat of substantial civil and criminal penalties for their own potentially illegal conduct.[32] Second, plaintiffs in litigation under § 10(b) and Rule 10b–5 may only recover against defendants who have acted with scienter. * * * Thus "if the tip merely fails to 'pan out' or if the information itself proves accurate but the stock fails to move in the anticipated direction, the investor stands to lose all of his investment. Only in the situation where the investor has been deliberately defrauded will he be able to maintain a private suit in an attempt to recoup his money."

We therefore conclude that the public interest will most frequently be advanced if defrauded tippees are permitted to bring suit and to expose illegal practices by corporate insiders and broker-dealers to full public view for appropriate sanctions. As the Ninth Circuit emphasized in this case, there is no warrant to giving corporate insiders and broker-dealers "a license to defraud the investing public with little fear of prosecution."

32. In addition to potential liability under § 10(b) and Rule 10b–5, investors also are subject to liability under §§ 2 and 3 of the Insider Trading Sanctions Act of 1984, 98 Stat. 1264–1265, 15 U.S.C.A. §§ 78u(d)(2), 78ff(a)(Supp.1985), which imposes severe civil sanctions on persons who have illegally used inside information, as well as criminal fines of up to $100,000.

THE CHIEF JUSTICE concurs in the judgment.

JUSTICE MARSHALL took no part in the decision of this case.

### *Notes*

1. The Supreme Court addressed the availability of the *in pari delicto* defense under the securities laws a second time in Pinter v. Dahl, 486 U.S. 622, 108 S.Ct. 2063, 100 L.Ed.2d 658 (1988). Dahl had purchased a $310,000 interest in oil and gas leases from Pinter and told various friends and relatives of the venture; they in turn, without meeting or speaking to Pinter, invested $7,500 each in the leases. When the venture failed, Dahl and the other investors sued Pinter for rescission under Section 12(1) of the Securities Act of 1933, 45 U.S.C. § 771(1), for the unlawful sale of unregistered securities. Pinter contended that Dahl's active solicitation of the other investors and his knowledge that the securities were unregistered put him *in pari delicto* and barred recovery. The Court continued its retreat from the expansive language of Justice Black's opinion for the Court in *Perma Life* stating that five Justices in that case recognized that a narrow, traditional formulation of the *in pari delicto* defense was available in private anti-trust actions. The Court found the defense available in *Pinter* as well, after applying the *Bateman Eichler* test. The facts before the Court in *Pinter* were insufficient to determine whether Dahl was at equal fault with Pinter and the case was remanded for further factual development. Thus the Court is clearly holding open the prospect that, in an appropriate case, the *in pari delicto* defense will be available in a private action brought under regulatory statutes such as the securities and anti-trust laws.

2. Equality of fault is never easy to measure. For instance, in a state in which gambling is illegal and the winner of a wager does not obtain legal title to his winnings, should it be a defense to a charge of robbery that the defendant was recouping his own property? The courts have divided on the answer. See People v. Rosen, 11 Cal.2d 147, 78 P.2d 727 (1938).

3. If the plaintiffs in *Bateman Eichler* had been more fortunate and the price of their stock had risen, they might have been sued by the people from whom they bought the stock. If the *Bateman Eichler* plaintiffs then brought an action in contribution against Lazzaro and Neadeau, should that suit be barred by an *in pari delicto* defense? Would it serve the purposes of the securities acts to allow the original tipper to suffer no monetary consequences for providing good tips?

Should it make any difference whether Congress has provided for an action in contribution under the securities laws? In Northwest Airlines, Inc. v. Transport Workers Union of America, AFL–CIO, 451 U.S. 77, 101 S.Ct. 1571, 67 L.Ed.2d 750 (1981), and Texas Industries, Inc. v. Radcliff Materials, Inc., 451 U.S. 630, 101 S.Ct. 2061, 68 L.Ed.2d 500 (1981), the Supreme Court held that where a common law claim to contribution is raised under a federal statute and Congress has neither indicated that such a remedy was to be available nor that courts were to develop substantive law, that the old American common law rule of no right to contribution among joint tortfeasors was to apply.

4. Some courts have suggested that even where a narrow *in pari delicto* defense is made out by a defendant in an insider trading case, the

defense should be rejected if it appears that defendant's unlawful activities were of a sort likely to have a substantial impact on the investing public and the primary legal responsibility for and ability to control that impact is with the defendant. Do you agree?

5. In Mascenic v. Anderson, 53 Ill.App.3d 971, 11 Ill.Dec. 718, 369 N.E.2d 172 (1977), plaintiff placed real property in a land trust of which his paramour, the defendant, was sole beneficiary. This was done solely to prevent plaintiff's wife from obtaining any interest in the property in the event of a divorce. Defendant then conspired with an attorney to defraud plaintiff of his beneficial interest in the property. An unclean hands defense succeeded in the trial court but failed on appeal where the court held that under the defense the conduct of plaintiff must be connected to the transaction complained of and must be directed to the defendant making the contention. Would the court have reached the same result if the defendant had raised an *in pari delicto* defense?

6. If the Court in Worden v. California Fig Syrup Co. had employed the analysis adopted in *Perma Life* and *Bateman Eichler,* which emphasizes promoting the objective of the relevant statute, how would that case have been decided? Are the relevant statutes the trademark laws or the laws regulating the practice of medicine? Would it make any difference if the plaintiff's actions were alleged to be in violation of state law rather than federal law? What if the plaintiff's actions violate common law but not statutory law?

7. In *Perma Life,* Justice Black emphasized that Congress had not adopted the *in pari delicto* defense in passing the anti-trust laws. Would it be a sound approach to recognize none of the defenses which turn on the plaintiff's misconduct in cases under regulatory statutes where Congress has not explicitly adopted the defense?

## B. ESTOPPEL

The definition of equitable estoppel or estoppel in pais varies among the courts. In the case that follows, the Ninth Circuit sets out a four part test. Other courts have expressed closely similar standards in different language. The Fifth Circuit stated the principle in narrative form in Central Bank and Trust Company v. General Finance Corporation, 297 F.2d 126, 129 (5th Cir.1961): "The doctrine of estoppel applies where, by words or conduct, one person wilfully, culpably or negligently causes another to believe in the existence of a state of things by which the other may be induced to act so as to change his previous position to his injury."

Equitable estoppel should be distinguished from the defense of waiver. Waiver is the voluntary and intentional abandonment of a known right by the plaintiff. There are three elements that differ between estoppel and waiver: first, waiver does not require any alteration of position by the defendant to be effective; second, estoppel may typically arise even if plaintiff acted negligently and did not intend to give up his rights; and finally, consideration is generally necessary for a waiver to be effective.

As the following case shows, one should not be misled by the rubric "equitable estoppel" to believe that this defense is limited to cases which arise in equity.

## JOHNSON v. WILLIFORD

United States Court of Appeals, Ninth Circuit, 1982.
682 F.2d 868.

FLETCHER, CIRCUIT JUDGE.

The government appeals from the district court's order granting Johnson's writ of habeas corpus. Johnson was convicted and sentenced under a federal statute requiring a minimum term of ten years, without possibility of parole. Neither the sentencing order nor the initial sentence computation report noted Johnson's ineligibility for parole. After numerous reviews by the Parole Commission and various other federal officers, none of whom uncovered the error, Johnson was released on parole.

Some 15 months later when the error was discovered, he was arrested and his parole revoked. In response, Johnson petitioned for a writ of habeas corpus. The district court ordered his immediate release pending action on the petition. * * *

FACTS

Johnson was convicted in the Northern District of Florida of conspiring to import marijuana, importing marijuana, and engaging in a continuing criminal enterprise in violation of 21 U.S.C. § 848 (1976). On May 25, 1977, he was sentenced to consecutive terms of five, five, and ten years, respectively, for these three convictions. * * *

From August 30, 1977 to September 18, 1978, Johnson was imprisoned at the Federal Correctional Institution (F.C.I.) at McNeil Island, Washington. While there, his sentence computation record was prepared, indicating parole eligibility on September 18, 1980. Johnson was moved to Lompoc F.C.I., and authorities there reviewed his sentence computation on October 11, 1978. On May 17, 1979, the sentence computation was reviewed by the administrative systems manager of the western regional office of the Bureau of Prisons. On July 23, 1979, Johnson's case manager recommended a presumptive parole date of September 18, 1980. This recommendation was reviewed by the unit manager at Terminal Island F.C.I. Copies of the recommendation were supplied to the United States Parole Offices in the Northern District of Florida and the Southern District of California. On September 14, 1979, after a Parole Commission hearing, Johnson's release was continued to the presumptive parole date of September 18, 1980. On February 25, 1980, a case manager at Terminal Island F.C.I. recommended a parole date of September 18, 1980, with prior release to a half-way house. * * * Johnson was released on parole on September 18, 1980, and remained on parole for fifteen months. At the time of his release, Johnson was 39 years old. Aside from the marijuana related offenses for which he was convicted, the record reveals only one prior incident of criminal conduct—a 10 year old drunk driving conviction. The district court found that he had made an "excellent" adjustment to parole, living with his wife and his two teenage children, operating an agricultural business, reporting regularly to his parole officer and keeping his court appearances. In the words of the district court, "[H]is reintegration into society has been good."

ANALYSIS

*I. Violation of 21 U.S.C. § 848 is a Non-Parolable Offense.*

At the time of Johnson's conviction, 21 U.S.C. § 848(c) provided, in pertinent part, that:

> In the case of any sentence imposed under this section, imposition or execution of such sentence shall not be suspended, probation shall not be granted and section 4202 of Title 18 [making parole available] * * * shall not apply. * * *

*II. The Government is Estopped From Enforcing the Non-Parolability Provision of § 848 in This Case.*

A. The Government is not Immune from Estoppel in this Case

In general, equitable estoppel is not available as a defense against the government, especially when the government is acting in its sovereign, as opposed to its proprietary, capacity. Nevertheless, this court has held that "where justice and fair play require it," estoppel will be applied against the government, even when the government acts in its sovereign capacity if the effects of estoppel do not unduly damage the public interest. * * * The Supreme Court has never explicitly endorsed this theory, although "no fewer than eight circuits ... have stated that there are some circumstances in which the Government will be estopped," Hansen v. Harris, 619 F.2d 942, 959 (2d Cir.1980)(Newman, J., concurring) (collecting cases), rev'd per curiam, 450 U.S. 785, 101 S.Ct. 1468, 67 L.Ed.2d 685 (1981), and [Moser v. United States, 341 U.S. 41, 71 S.Ct. 553, 95 L.Ed. 729 (1951)] has been cited as a case wherein the Supreme Court by its holding, in fact, estopped the Government. [United States v.] Lazy FC Ranch, 481 F.2d [985 (9th Cir.1973)] at 989.

In a recent decision, Miranda v. INS, 673 F.2d 1105 (9th Cir.1982), our court reaffirmed the application of equitable estoppel against the government acting in its sovereign capacity. The court, relying on an estoppel theory, had originally reversed a decision of the Board of Immigration Appeals. Miranda v. INS, 638 F.2d 83 (9th Cir.1980). The Supreme Court vacated the panel's original decision and remanded for further consideration in light of *Hansen.* Miranda v. INS, 454 U.S. 808, 102 S.Ct. 81, 70 L.Ed.2d 77 (1981). Upon reconsideration, the *Miranda* panel adhered to its original judgment. It described *Hansen* as a case in which application of estoppel would circumvent "the conditions defined by Congress for charging the public treasury," Miranda, 673 F.2d at 1105–06 (quoting Federal Crop Insurance Corp. v. Merrill, 332 U.S. 380, 385, 68 S.Ct. 1, 3, 92 L.Ed. 10 (1947)), while application of estoppel in

*Miranda* would not create a drain on the public fisc. In this respect, the instant case is indistinguishable from *Miranda.*

We turn now to an examination of whether the threshold requirements for estoppel against the government described in *Lazy FC Ranch* are present here. Under *Lazy FC Ranch,* the government's wrongful conduct must threaten "to work a serious injustice" and the public's interest must not "be unduly damaged by the imposition of estoppel." 481 F.2d at 989. The Parole Commission's deliberate decision to release Johnson on parole, and his subsequent successful reintegration into the community, suggest that his continuation on parole status does not seriously threaten the public interest. The injustice to Johnson if he is reincarcerated is apparent. The government says in its brief, "petitioner's case is in some respects a sympathetic one." We think this is an understatement. The record discloses at least eight separate administrative reviews of Johnson's projected parole date. Each review confirmed that Johnson could be paroled. His expectation of release on parole on September 18, 1980, was raised almost as soon as he began to serve his sentence, and was encouraged and heightened by the successive administrative reviews. The government argues that Johnson has received a windfall, and that while a return to custody would disappoint his expectations, "those expectations were not justified in any event," in light of his conviction and sentencing under § 848. This assertion is plainly incorrect. The progress of Johnson's case through eight administrative reviews culminating in 15 months of parole release surely justified him in expecting to continue, during good behavior, in that status. The frustration of those expectations would be a serious injustice. Even convicted criminals are entitled to be treated by their government in a fair and straightforward manner. We find that under these facts appellee may raise the defense of estoppel against the Government.

B. The Elements of Equitable Estoppel Are Present in This Case

Our inquiry so far has focused on whether this is the kind of case in which estoppel may be asserted against the government. Having concluded that it is, we now turn to an examination of whether the traditional elements giving rise to equitable estoppel are present. The four required elements were described by this court in United States v. Georgia–Pacific Company, 421 F.2d 92, 96 (9th Cir.1970):

(1) The party to be estopped must know the facts;

(2) he must intend that his conduct shall be acted on or must so act that the party asserting the estoppel has a right to believe it is so intended;

(3) the latter must be ignorant of the facts; and

(4) he must rely on the former's conduct to his injury.

The first element is present. Johnson's initial sentence computation report indicates plainly that he was convicted under § 848. The progress reports prepared from time to time all include recitations of his offenses. Prior to Johnson's release, the government had been treating all other prisoners in the same position as Johnson as ineligible for parole. Although there was no case holding that § 848 convictions were non-parolable in the wake of the 1976 Parole Commission and Reorganization Act until United States v. Valenzuela, 646 F.2d 352 (9th Cir. 1980), the government can hardly deny knowledge of what it has always treated as settled law.

The second element is also present. Johnson surely had a right to believe, after his parole computation had passed successfully through as many as eight administrative reviews, culminating in his ultimate release on parole for a period of 15 months, that he would remain on parole during good behavior.

The difficult question concerns the third element. The government argues that the crucial "fact" is simply the proper meaning of § 848, and that Johnson should be charged with constructive knowledge despite the fact that the government, the expert here, has misinterpreted or misapplied the statute in eight separate reviews in this case. In Brandt v. Hickel, 427 F.2d 53, 56 (9th Cir.1970), this court observed that "some forms of erroneous advice are so closely connected to the basic fairness of the administrative decision making process that the government may be estopped from disavowing the misstatement." In the instant case, the Government's active misadvice to Johnson regarding his eligibility for parole prevents us from charging appellee with even constructive knowledge of the proper meaning of section 848. Accordingly, we find the third element of estoppel present.

Finally, there is obvious detrimental reliance in this case. Johnson has been reunited with his family and has left the safe haven of steady employment as a fruit packer in order to start and operate his own fruit packing business. By the time of his rearrest, he had hired five employees, was solely responsible for the business banking accounts, and had been extended credit by local businesses.

In summary, we find that the requisite elements of equitable estoppel are all present and that the government should be estopped. * * *

### *Notes*

1. The Court accurately states that the Supreme Court has not held that the government may be estopped by the actions of its agents. It is an open question whether the Supreme Court is ever likely to find a case in which it would hold the government estopped. This issue was considered in Heckler v. Community Health Services of Crawford County, Inc., 467 U.S. 51, 60–61, 104 S.Ct. 2218, 2224, 81 L.Ed.2d 42 (1984), reh'g denied, 475 U.S. 1061, 106 S.Ct. 1289, 89 L.Ed.2d 596 (1986), in which Justice Stevens wrote for the majority:

> When the Government is unable to enforce the law because the conduct of its agents has given rise to an estoppel, the interest of the citizenry as a whole in obedience to the rule of law is undermined. It is for this reason that it is well settled that the Government may not be estopped on the same terms as any other litigant. Petitioner urges us to expand

this principle into a flat rule that estoppel may not in any circumstances run against the Government. We have left the issue open in the past,[12] and do so again today. Though the arguments the Government advances for the rule are substantial, we are hesitant, when it is unnecessary to decide this case, to say that there are *no cases* in which the public interest in ensuring that the Government can enforce the law free from estoppel might be outweighed by the countervailing interest of citizens in some minimum standard of decency, honor, and reliability in their dealing with their Government.[13]

Justice Rehnquist replied in a concurring opinion:

Sixty-seven years ago, in Utah Power & Light Co. v. United States, 243 U.S. 389, 37 S.Ct. 387, 61 L.Ed. 791 (1917), private parties argued that they had acquired rights in federal lands, contrary to the law, because Government employees had acquiesced in their exercise of those rights. In that case the Court laid down the general principle governing claims of estoppel on behalf of private individuals against the Government:

> As a general rule, laches or neglect of duty on the part of officers of the Government is no defense to a suit by it to enforce a public right or protect a public interest. And, if it be assumed that the rule is subject to exceptions, we find nothing in the cases in hand which fairly can be said to take them out of it as heretofore understood and applied in this court. A suit by the United States to enforce and maintain its policy respecting lands which it holds in trust for all the people stands upon a different plane in this and

**12.** See INS v. Miranda, 459 U.S. 14, 19, 103 S.Ct. 281, 284, 74 L.Ed.2d 12 (1982)(per curiam); . Schweiker v. Hansen, 450 U.S. 785, 788, 101 S.Ct. 1468, 1470, 67 L.Ed.2d 685 (1981)(per curiam); Montana v. Kennedy, 366 U.S. 308, 315, 81 S.Ct. 1336, 1341, 6 L.Ed.2d 313 (1961). In fact, at least two of our cases seem to rest on the premise that when the Government acts in misleading ways, it may not enforce the law if to do so would harm a private party as a result of governmental deception. See United States v. Pennsylvania Industrial Chemical Corp., 411 U.S. 655, 670–675, 93 S.Ct. 1804, 1814–1817, 36 L.Ed.2d 567 (1973)(criminal defendant may assert as a defense that the Government led him to believe that its conduct was legal); Moser v. United States, 341 U.S. 41, 71 S.Ct. 553, 95 L.Ed. 729 (1951)(applicant cannot be deemed to waive right to citizenship on the basis of a form he signed when he was misled as to the effect signing would have on his rights). This principle also underlies the doctrine that an administrative agency may not apply a new rule retroactively when to do so would unduly intrude upon reasonable reliance interests.

**13.** See generally St. Regis Paper Co. v. United States, 368 U.S. 208, 229, 82 S.Ct. 289, 301, 7 L.Ed.2d 240 (1961)(Black, J., dissenting)("Our Government should not by picayunish haggling over the scope of its promise, permit one of its arms to do that which, by any fair construction, the Government has given its word that no arm will do. It is no less good morals and good law that the Government should turn square corners in dealing with the people than that the people should turn square corners in dealing with their government"); Federal Crop Insurance Corporation v. Merrill, 332 U.S. 380, at 387–388, 68 S.Ct. 1, at 4–5, 92 L.Ed. 10 (1947)(Jackson, J., dissenting)("It is very well to say that those who deal with the Government should turn square corners. But there is no reason why the square corners should constitute a one-way street"); Brandt v. Hickel, 427 F.2d 53, 57 ( [9th Cir]. 1970)("To say to these appellants, 'The joke is on you. You shouldn't have trusted us', is hardly worthy of our great government"); Menges v. Dentler, 33 Pa. 495, 500 (1859)("Men naturally trust in their government, and ought to do so, and they ought not to suffer for it").

some other respects from the ordinary private suit to regain the title to real property or to remove a cloud from it.

Since then we have applied that principle in a case where a private party relied on the misrepresentation of a Government agency as to the coverage of a crop insurance policy, a misrepresentation which the Court agreed would have estopped a private insurance carrier. We have applied it in a case where a private party relied on a misrepresentation by a Government employee as to Social Security eligibility, a misrepresentation which resulted in the applicant's losing 12 months of Social Security benefits. And we have applied it on at least three occasions to claims of estoppel in connection with the enforcement of the immigration laws and the denial of citizenship because of the conduct of immigration officials. In none of these cases have we ever held the Government to be estopped by the representations or conduct of its agents. In INS v. Hibi, [414 U.S. 5, 94 S.Ct. 19, 38 L.Ed.2d 7 (1973)(per curiam) ], we noted that it is still an open question whether, in some future case, "affirmative misconduct" on the part of the Government might be grounds for an estoppel.

I agree with the Court that there is no need to decide in this case whether there are circumstances under which the Government may be estopped, but I think that the Court's treatment of that question gives an impression of hospitality towards claims of estoppel against the Government which our decided cases simply do not warrant. In footnote 12, the Court intimates that two of our decisions have allowed the Government to be estopped: United States v. Pennsylvania Industrial Chemical Corp., 411 U.S. 655, 93 S.Ct. 1804, 36 L.Ed.2d 567 (1973), and Moser v. United States, 341 U.S. 41, 71 S.Ct. 553, 95 L.Ed. 729 (1951). But these cases are not traditional equitable estoppel cases. *Pennsylvania Industrial Chemical Corp.* was a criminal prosecution, and we held that "to the extent that [Government regulations] deprived [the defendant] of fair warning as to what conduct the Government intended to make criminal, we think there can be no doubt that traditional notions of fairness inherent in our system of criminal justice prevent the Government from proceeding with the prosecution." And the Court's rather cryptic opinion in *Moser,* holding that an alien who declined to serve in the Armed Forces was not barred from United States citizenship pursuant to a federal statute, expressly rejected any doctrine of estoppel, and rested on the absence of a knowing and intentional waiver of the right to citizenship.

We do not write on a clean slate in this field, and our cases have left open the possibility of estoppel against the Government only in a rather narrow possible range of circumstances. Because I think the Court's opinion, in its efforts to phrase new statements of the circumstances under which the Government may be estopped, casts doubt on these decided cases, I concur only in the judgment.

467 U.S. at 66–68, 104 S.Ct. at 2227–2228, 81 L.Ed.2d 42. See also Office of Personnel Management v. Richmond, 496 U.S. 414, 110 S.Ct. 2465, 110 L.Ed.2d 387 (1990)(holding there can be no estoppel against the government by claimant seeking public funds not otherwise authorized by law).

2. As is apparent from the cases discussed in the preceding note, the courts have found the law governing an agent and principal to be different when the principal is the government rather than a private party. What makes the government different? If it is to protect the government or the public fisc from the negligence or malfeasance of government agents, why shouldn't a corporate treasury have equal protection? Wouldn't the government have an action against its agent in damages if the public was injured monetarily? Why is such a remedy not adequate?

If the central interest is protection of the public from non-monetary injury or assuring that the will of Congress is carried out, isn't Johnson v. Williford wrongly decided?

What interest is served by the result in a case like Schweiker v. Hansen, where a private party loses 12 months of Social Security benefits? What principle justifies the government in benefiting from the negligence or misconduct of its officers and employees?

3. Green v. Christiansen, 732 F.2d 1397 (9th Cir.1984), is another case involving release of a federal prisoner before his sentence was complete. The Ninth Circuit did not find the government estopped from reincarcerating Green because he had no expectation that he should be released and he was not so misled that it would be improper to charge him with constructive knowledge that he had time to serve. How does one establish a reliance interest in his freedom? Given the clarity of the statute in the *Johnson* case, why did Johnson not have constructive knowledge of being liable to reincarceration?

4. The Ninth Circuit returned to the issue of equitable estoppel against the government in Watkins v. United States Army, 875 F.2d 699 (9th Cir. en banc 1989), cert. denied, 498 U.S. 957, 111 S.Ct. 384, 112 L.Ed.2d 395 (1990). Watkins was drafted into the Army in 1967. He re-enlisted in 1970, 1974 and 1979. He was denied re-enlistment in 1982. Watkins was an exemplary soldier. From the time of his pre-induction medical exam, he had routinely informed the Army that he was a homosexual. Throughout the period of his Army service the Army's regulations prohibited the re-enlistment of homosexuals. The 1982 denial of re-enlistment was based solely on Watkins' homosexuality.

In determining whether there was a basis for invoking equitable estoppel against the government, the court posed a two prong test before addressing the traditional elements of estoppel laid out in Johnson v. Williford: first, a party seeking to estop the government must establish affirmative misconduct going beyond mere negligence; and second, estoppel is only available where the government's act will cause serious injustice and the public's interest will not suffer undue damage by the imposition of liability. The majority found that Watkins prevailed on both of these tests as well as on the traditional elements of estoppel and enjoined the Army from relying on its regulation barring homosexuals from re-enlistment as a basis for refusing re-enlistment to Watkins.

In what sense was the Army's prior re-enlistment of Watkins affirmative misconduct? While it may plainly have been misconduct with regard to the regulations, was it misconduct that was harmful to Watkins? Why should a party seeking to bar the government from changing its course of conduct have to show that that course of action was based on affirmative misconduct rather than negligence?

In addressing the fourth element of its traditional estoppel test, Watkins' reliance on the Army's course of action, the court found that Watkins was injured because he developed military rather than civilian skills and had invested fourteen years toward a pension. These injuries could be compensated by providing funds for retraining and quantifying the value of the forfeited pension interest. If the Army's regulation against re-enlisting homosexuals is constitutionally sound, would it be better to give Watkins money damages and not carve out an exception to the regulation? Other homosexuals will not be able to obtain a position in the Army. Why should Watkins get a job in the future rather than damages for the Army's past conduct?

Watkins ultimately settled his case, accepting voluntary retirement with an honorable discharge. He received approximately $135,000 in back pay and full retirement benefits as well as a retroactive promotion to sergeant first class.

### *Note on the Government as Plaintiff*

The Clean Air Act, 42 U.S.C. §§ 7401 et seq. controls air pollution through a division of responsibility between the federal government and the states. The federal EPA sets national standards for permissible concentrations of pollutants in the ambient air and the states develop implementation plans establishing emission limits for particular plants or types of facilities; these state implementation plans ("SIPs") are to assure that the national air standards are met. EPA approves SIPs, which are then enforceable both under state law and by EPA under the Clean Air Act. The states may choose to revise their SIPs to reflect changed circumstances or knowledge and those revisions are submitted to EPA for approval. Courts held that, under the statute, EPA has four months in which to approve or reject a SIP revision. Of course, a SIP revision becomes effective as a matter of state law when it is adopted by the state regardless of EPA's approval or failure to act on the proposed revision; but the revision only becomes effective as a matter of federal law when EPA approves the revision.

EPA has been notoriously slow in acting on proposed SIP revisions, frequently taking much longer than four months. This puts an industrial operator in a difficult position: if it complies with the revised SIP which is state law, it may be subject to an action for penalties or injunctive relief by EPA for violation of federal law during the period in which EPA failed to act on the proposed SIP revision. In these circumstances, if EPA brings an action to enforce the unrevised federal SIP, the agency is enforcing federal law as written against the defendant but, having failed to carry out its statutory duty, which might result in there being no violation of federal law and at a minimum would clarify the applicable regulatory requirement for the defendant, EPA comes into the court with the sort of cloud upon its claim that in a private suit would lead the court to consider whether the agency should obtain the full relief to which it would be entitled in a case where there was simply a violation of a SIP.

The courts of appeals dealt with these circumstances in different ways. The District of Columbia Circuit decided that penalties accrued in the period after the statutory deadline for EPA action had passed but before EPA acted on a SIP revision, should be held in abeyance pending EPA's final action on the proposed SIP revision. If the revision were approved, no penalty would be collected; if it were rejected, penalties for the entire period would be collected. The court reasoned that if the revision were approved, then the post-deadline penalties were the result of EPA's failure to act on time; if the revision were rejected, the defendant would not benefit undeservedly. Duquesne Light Company v. Environmental Protection Agency, 698 F.2d 456, 470–72 (D.C.Cir.1983). The Fifth Circuit, putting particular emphasis on the important role played by the states under the Clean Air Act, ruled that EPA was barred from collecting any penalties for violation of the federal SIP for the period from the four month statutory deadline for acting on SIP revisions to the date on which EPA acted on the proposed revision. The court believed the possibility of collecting penalties might improperly influence EPA to disapprove SIP revisions and found it unacceptable to leave a company, which was complying with state law, open to a penalty because of delays within EPA. American Cyanamid Company v. U.S. Environmental Protection Agency, 810 F.2d 493 (5th Cir.1987); see General Motors Corp. v. Environmental Protection Agency, 871 F.2d 495 (5th Cir.1989)(applying the *American Cyanamid* reasoning to other provisions of the Clean Air Act).

The First Circuit chose a third path, setting out two remedies. First, the affected manufacturer could bring an action under the Clean Air Act to compel EPA to act on the proposed SIP revision. Second, the court considering EPA's enforcement action should take the agency's delay in acting on the proposed SIP revision into account in setting penalties. The court believed this gave EPA the necessary incentive to act without unreasonable delay but protected the interest of the public in enforcing clean air regulations where SIP revisions were rejected after delay by EPA. United States v. General Motors Corporation, 876 F.2d 1060 (1st Cir.1989).

None of these cases speaks in terms of traditional principles or maxims in other areas of public or private law such as unclean hands. Indeed an unclean hands defense is unlikely to succeed: "The general principles of equity are applicable in a suit by the United States to secure the cancellation of a conveyance or the recision of a contract. But they will not be applied to frustrate the purpose of its laws or to thwart public policy." Pan American Petroleum & Transport Co. v. United States, 273 U.S. 456, 506, 47 S.Ct. 416, 424, 71 L.Ed. 734 (1927). Nevertheless, the underlying fact situation is clearly akin to the cases in this chapter: the plaintiff has engaged in misconduct and the question for the court is whether the misconduct is sufficiently extreme or relevant to the dispute before the court so that the plaintiff should be barred from receiving relief.

The First Circuit case went to the Supreme Court, which held that EPA is not required to act on a proposed SIP revision within four months as that requirement refers only to actions required on the original SIP and not on a revision. Moreover, the Court held that even though the Administrative Procedure Act required EPA to conclude matters "within a reasonable time," EPA is not barred from bringing suit to enforce an existing SIP on the ground that it has unreasonably delayed action on a proposed revision. The Court did not reach the issue of remedies. General Motors Corp. v. United States, 496 U.S. 530, 110 S.Ct. 2528, 110 L.Ed.2d 480 (1990). The problem of how to address the errant government plaintiff remains.

## C. LACHES AND STATUTES OF LIMITATIONS

By statutes of limitations, the legislature bars the commencement of lawsuits after a set period of time from the events which give rise to the controversy or from the discovery of facts which provide plaintiff with the factual basis to pursue her claim. For example, the general rule under federal criminal law is that suit is barred if an indictment is not returned within five years after the offense is committed. 18 U.S.C. § 3282. But there are exceptions; for instance, there is no limitation on the bringing of indictments for offenses punishable by death. 18 U.S.C. § 3281. The states typically have limitation periods applicable to different categories of lawsuits: torts, money damages, criminal offenses and so on. The basic rationale of statutes of limitation, is two-fold: with the passage of time evidence becomes less reliable—memories fade, witnesses die, documents no longer can be found—and there is an interest in insuring repose and finality even in potential disputes. In selecting a limitation period, the legislature balances the substantive policies behind the cause of action with the interest in repose. There is, of course, a great deal of dispute over how the limitation periods are to be measured, but these are beyond the scope of this book.

The legislative bars to commencing a lawsuit are paralleled by the equitable defense of laches. As with the other equitable principles explored in this chapter, there are numerous formulations of the principle of laches. Laches is fairly defined as delay by a plaintiff in asserting his rights which is not excusable or reasonable and which works to the prejudice or injury of the defendant. Prejudice comes in a variety of forms; changing one's economic position based on the belief that there is no live controversy with the plaintiff and the routine destruction of documents through a corporate document retention policy are two common examples. Laches bars pursuit of her claim by the plaintiff. Laches obviously differs from a statute of limitation by considering the conduct of the plaintiff and its effect on the defendant rather than simply measuring a period of time. Laches is a defense to equitable actions; some courts following the merger of law and equity will allow the laches defense in legal actions, Borland By and Through Utah State Dept. of Social Services v. Chandler, 733 P.2d 144 (Utah 1987), but generally the defense is limited to equitable actions, e.g., Turner v. Guy, 311 N.E.2d 921, 2 Mass.App.Ct. 343 (1974).

## SAFFRON v. DEPARTMENT OF THE NAVY

United States Court of Appeals, District of Columbia Circuit, 1977.
561 F.2d 938, cert. denied, 434 U.S. 1033, 98 S.Ct. 765, 54 L.Ed.2d 780 (1978).

SPOTTSWOOD W. ROBINSON, III, CIRCUIT JUDGE.

The pivotal question confronting us is whether the six-year limitation imposed generally by 28 U.S.C. § 2401(a) on litigation brought against the United States is applicable to the suit of a discharged federal employee for restoration to his job as well as to his claim therein for damages. We hold that the effort in each respect was an action against the United States within the contemplation of that section and consequently is barred in full.

I

On November 26, 1965, the Department of the Navy terminated appellant's employment as a civilian aircraft engine mechanic. Administrative remedies by which he challenged his dismissal were exhausted on April 26, 1966, when the Board of Appeals and Review of the Civil Service Commission upheld the Navy. On February 4, 1975 more than eight years and nine months later appellant filed in the District Court for the District of Columbia the lawsuit in which this appeal is taken. Appellant sought a judgment setting aside his removal from federal service, reinstating him in his job, and awarding damages, including backpay and other employment benefits.

Appellees, mainly the Department of the Navy, moved to dismiss the suit on the ground that relief was barred by Section 2401(a) and the conventional doctrine of laches. The District Court granted the motion, concluding that monetary recovery was foreclosed by the statute and that job-restoration was precluded by undue prejudicial delay. Appellant argues that during the lengthy interval between the final administrative decision and institution of suit, extensive efforts on his part to obtain remediation tolled the limitation period and negated the defense of laches.

That appellant actively engaged in other endeavors to rectify his situation seems to be conceded. He wrote many letters and made numerous visits to members of the business, governmental and political communities, complaining of his dismissal and soliciting assistance. He also contacted more than a dozen attorneys in efforts to maintain legal representation, often without success. In November, 1967, he brought in the District Court for the District of Rhode Island a suit under the Freedom of Information Act for access to records pertaining to his discharge, and eventually obtained an order that all available data be turned over to him. Appellant states that subsequently he tendered a second complaint, pro se, to that court but that it was "rejected by the clerk, who suggested (that he) file the suit in" this circuit.

On November 24, 1971, appellant applied pro se to the District Court for the District of Columbia for a writ of mandamus to the Secretary of Labor and others, but suffered a dismissal without prejudice. On February 22, 1972, he asked leave to amend his complaint but was refused; continuing pro se, he then opted for summary reversal by this court. That, on June 2, 1972, the court denied, and instead granted the Navy's motion for summary affirmance. As we have stated, the instant litigation was commenced on February 4, 1975, and the appeal contests the District Court's ruling that appellant's claims were time-barred.

II

Congress has not seen fit to enact a comprehensive array of time limitations on the enforcement of federally-created rights. For relatively few, Congress has prescribed limitation periods, and when it has done so its mandate, of course, must be obeyed. When, however, Congress has not spoken, the applicable limitation traditionally has depended upon the nature of the litigation, a treatment inherited from the days when the common law and equity jurisprudence flourished as separate doctrinal systems. For actions at law, congressional silence was accepted as a reflection of federal policy to abide nonfederal statutes of limitation applicable in analogous situations; when, however, the relief sought was purely equitable in character, the doctrine of laches peculiarly a creature of equity measured timeliness of the suit. This distinction has survived four decades of merger of common law and equity procedure in the federal courts.

Suits against the United States, at least some of them however, comprise one of the special categories of litigation for which Congress has erected a time barrier. Section 2401(a) specifies that "(e)very civil action commenced against the United States shall be barred unless a complaint is filed within six years after the right of action first accrues." This mandate is but an exertion of the undoubted congressional power to impose restrictions upon the institution of litigation authorized against the Federal Government. The critical inquiry, then, relates to the extent to which Section 2401(a) impacts either or both of appellant's prayers for relief.

III

Dismissal, on the basis of Section 2401(a), of appellant's claim for a monetary judgment, we are satisfied, was eminently correct. On this branch of the case appellant sought damages, including salary and other financial benefits lost by reason of the termination of his employment. Relief of that character would have been possible only by resort to the federal fisc, and the effort in court to obtain it, nominally against named federal officials, was in every sense a "civil action commenced against the United States." By the terms of the statute, the six-year limitation period began to run from the time the "right of action first accrue(d)" certainly no later than final administrative disposition of appellant's claim on April 26, 1966 and the record does not support an argument that compliance with Section 2401(a) was frustrated by obstructionism on the part of the Navy. The filing of the complaint in the instant litigation on February 4, 1975, came too late for a money award.

Appellant's endeavors to secure reinstatement to his job, however, generates somewhat more difficulty, which the parties' argumentative approach has accentuated. In this court, the briefs on both sides, while postulating monetary recovery as a matter implicating Section 2401(a), have treated reinstatement solely as a problem of laches. Accordingly, the litigants, like the District Court, have focused exclusively on disputes over the reasonableness of the delay in instituting the case before us and resulting prejudice to the Navy. Despite the relevance of those considerations on an issue of laches had appellant's action been brought within the six-year period, no one has satisfactorily explained why Section 2401(a) does not itself bar reinstatement as well as the monetary demand. Our own research which is now to follow has demonstrated that the parties' analysis is faulty; that appellant's reinstatement bid, notwithstanding its equitable nature, is intercepted by Section 2401(a), and consequently also is barred.

IV

Even prior to unification of district-court proceedings in one form of action, it had become well settled that whenever the courts of law and equity possessed concurrent jurisdiction to enforce the claimant's right, statutes of limitation were to be as forcefully applied in equity as at law. A sufficient though perhaps not the sole reason was that, in all such instances, the statute imposed its restraint on the claim in suit, and not merely on the court in which it was asserted. For obviously greater reason, the concurrency rule continues in full vigor after the procedural wedding of law and equity.

We have no doubt but that the rule, independently of any other consideration, governs the case at bar. The one right that appellant presses in this litigation is to freedom from legally unjustified molestation in the job he held as an employee of the Navy. On the premise that the right has been infringed by an unlawful discharge, appellant demands redress in the form of both restoration and damages. While the former undoubtedly partakes of an equitable hue, the latter undeniably is legal relief in an ancient role; and while these complementary remedies are capable of that sort of distinction, "(t)here is in fact but a single right and single default involved. . . ."

This, we find, is the kind of parallelism that demonstrates applicability of the concurrency rule. As we read the Supreme Court's pronouncements on the subject, only when a court is importuned "to enforce rights cognizable only in equity (are) statute(s) barring legal causes of action ... not controlling." Put another way, "(t)he decisive feature ... which gives jurisdiction the flavor of concurrency, is not the narrow question of whether formal relief requested in a particular action is equitable or legal, primary or incidental, but the broader determination of whether the federal right in issue may be judicially enforced in any action by means both legal and equitable." Additionally to the binding effect of the Supreme Court's expositions of federal law, this view is thoroughly consistent with our own rather numerous holdings in the area as well as those of other courts. * * *

The all-important factor from our viewpoint is that despite the historical dissimilarity of the remedies pursued, the right they purportedly would vindicate is single and indivisible. Where that is so, and remediation does not lie exclusively within the domain of equity, the availability of legal relief to enforce the underlying right summons the statute of limitations into play as to the whole. * * *

### *Notes*

1. In 1990, Congress provided a general statute of limitation for civil cases under future federal statutes, 28 U.S.C. § 1658:

> Except as otherwise provided by law, a civil action arising under an Act of Congress enacted after [December 1, 1990] may not be commenced later than 4 years after the cause of action accrues.

In private litigation under a federal statute where no limitation period is provided, it is settled practice to borrow the local time limitation for the parallel state cause of action, if it is not inconsistent with federal law or policy to do so. Wilson v. Garcia, 471 U.S. 261, 105 S.Ct. 1938, 85 L.Ed.2d 254 (1985). The question of characterization of a federal cause of action for limitation borrowing purposes is ultimately a question of federal law. DelCostello v. Teamsters, 462 U.S. 151, 103 S.Ct. 2281, 76 L.Ed.2d 476 (1983)(court borrowed a federal statute of limitation where it appeared to more closely reflect Congressional balance between repose and substantive policies behind claim); Arnold v. Duchesne County, 26 F.3d 982 (10th Cir.1994)(court refused to borrow Utah statute which explicitly established limitation period applicable to 42 U.S.C. § 1983), cert. denied, ___ U.S. ___, 115 S.Ct. 721, 130 L.Ed.2d 626 (1995). In *Wilson v. Garcia,* addressing the federal remedial statute for violations of civil rights under color of state law, 42 U.S.C. § 1983, the Supreme Court decided that practical considerations favored characterizing all claims under § 1983 as falling in one category with one statute of limitation applicable in a given state rather than attempting to parse each particular claim and determine the appropriate state limitation period for that claim.

Limitations taken from state law do not bar suits by the United States when it sues to vindicate a public right or interest, absent a clear showing of Congressional intent to the contrary. United States v. Summerlin, 310 U.S. 414, 416–17, 60 S.Ct. 1019, 1020–21, 84 L.Ed. 1283 (1940). This doctrine has its origins in the common law principle that time does not run against the king. Today it is justified on the ground that public rights and revenues should not be lost due to the negligence of public officials. Guaranty Trust Co. v. United States, 304 U.S. 126, 132, 58 S.Ct. 785, 788–789, 82 L.Ed. 1224 (1938); SEC v. Rind, 991 F.2d 1486, 1491 (9th Cir.), cert. denied, ___ U.S. ___, 114 S.Ct. 439, 126 L.Ed.2d 372 (1993). But the government is subject to applicable federal statutes of limitations and the courts have not been willing to carve out exceptions to the limitation periods on the grounds that it is difficult for government to discover statutory or regulatory violations and bring its claims within the applicable limitation period. 3M Co. v. Browner, 17 F.3d 1453 (D.C.Cir.1994).

2. The Louisiana Supreme Court has held that the bar imposed by a statute of limitation may be overcome by showing that the defendant has acted so as to prevent the plaintiff from bringing his cause of action. This is part of the equitable doctrine of "*contra non valentem agere nulla currit praescriptio*": a prescription or limitation does not run against a party who is unable to act. Wimberly v. Gatch, 635 So.2d 206 (La.1994). A suit against a child molester by the parents of the child was not barred by a limitation period where research showed that the normal reaction of a sexually abused child was secrecy and delayed disclosure. The court viewed the equitable doctrine as an application of the principle that one should not be able to take advantage of one's own wrongful act.

## SHELL v. STRONG

United States Court of Appeals, Tenth Circuit, 1945.
151 F.2d 909.

PHILLIPS, CIRCUIT JUDGE.

On August 1, 1932, Strong and Shell entered into a written contract which recited that Strong had purchased seven quarter sections of land situated in Wichita County, Kansas, and had paid therefor $9,600, and that Shell was desirous of obtaining a one-half interest in the profits that might be derived from the use or sale of such land. It provided that Shell should pay one-half of all taxes on the land becoming due and payable for the year 1932 and succeeding years during the life of the contract; that Shell should have a one-half interest in all the profits realized from the land during the life of the contract, either from crops or from the sale of the land; that Shell should have an option to purchase, for $4,800, a one-half interest in the land at any time during the life of the contract, and that upon the exercise of such option, Strong would convey a one-half interest in the land to Shell, or such person as Shell might designate, by a good and sufficient warranty deed; and that the contract should continue for a period of five years from August 1, 1932.

Shell managed and rented the land and collected the income therefrom from the date of the contract until the year 1936. Thereafter, Strong managed the land. During the term of the contract, each paid one-half of the taxes and one-half of the incidental expenses and received one-half of the net income. On or about August 1, 1934, the parties made a settlement of the interest due from Shell to Strong, and Shell was given credit for the amount of interest which had accrued to that date. Shell made no direct payments of interest after August 1, 1934, but on or about October 15, 1936, Strong received $478.18 as a bonus under an oil and gas mining lease on a portion of the land, and after deducting an expense item of $1.50, credited one-half of the remainder, or $238.34, on interest due from Shell. Shell consented to such application of the bonus money.

On July 31, 1937, Shell tendered to Strong $5,373.87, and demanded a deed to an undivided one-half interest in the land. Strong refused to accept the tender and refused to convey the one-half interest to Shell. The sum tendered included the agreed price of $4,800 and the balance of the interest due from Shell to Strong to July 31, 1937, and other items for which Shell was liable under the contract.

On July 31, 1942, Shell brought this action against Strong seeking specific performance of the contract to convey an undivided one-half interest in the land.

Strong filed an answer in which he set up a number of defenses. At the pretrial conference, all of such defenses were abandoned except laches.

At the trial, evidence was introduced with respect to the value of the land on July 31, 1937, and July 31, 1942, and the intervening period. The trial court found that there was no material difference in the value of the land on July 31, 1937, and July 31, 1942; that there was a decrease in value between July 31, 1937, and the early part of 1939, and that in 1940 the land began to increase in value. The trial court concluded, as a matter of law, that Shell had abandoned the contract and was barred from relief in equity by laches. Shell has appealed.

Lapse of time alone does not constitute laches. Delay will not bar relief where it has not worked injury, prejudice, or disadvantage to the defendant or others adversely interested.

Since laches is an equitable defense, its application is controlled by equitable considerations. It cannot be invoked to defeat justice, and it will be applied only where the enforcement of the right asserted will work injustice.

A court of equity is not bound by the statute of limitations, but, in the absence of extraordinary circumstances, it will usually grant or withhold relief in analogy to the statute of limitations relating to actions at law of like character. Under ordinary circumstances, a suit in equity will not be stayed for laches before, and will be stayed after, the time fixed by the analogous statute, but if unusual conditions or extraordinary circumstances make it inequitable to allow the prosecution of a suit after a briefer, or to forbid its maintenance after a longer, period than that fixed by the analogous statute, a court of equity will not be bound by the statute, but will determine the extraordinary case in accordance with the equities which condition it. When a suit is brought within the time fixed by the analogous statute, the burden is on the defendant to show, either from the face of the complaint or by his answer, that extraordinary circumstances exist which require the application of the doctrine of laches. On the other hand, when the suit is brought after the statutory time has elapsed, the burden is on the complainant to aver and prove circumstances making it inequitable to apply laches to his case.

Shell brought his action within the period of the analogous statute of limitations. The burden was upon Strong to establish such a change in conditions to his prejudice that would make it inequitable to grant Shell relief by way of specific performance. The trial court evidently believed the burden rested on Shell to explain his delay in bringing the suit.

By waiving the other defenses asserted in the answer and urging only laches as a bar to relief, Strong conceded he had no other defense to the action. It is clear, therefore, that in refusing to accept the tender and convey a one-half interest in the land to Shell, Strong breached the contract. Strong stood before the court, admitting that he had breached the contract and asking the court to condone the breach and deny Shell any relief in equity solely because Shell had waited until the last day of the analogous statute of limitations to commence the action and because, although there was no substantial difference in the value of the land on the date of the tender and on the date of the commencement of the action, there had been some fluctuation in value during the intervening period.

Strong did not deny that the contract was valid and enforceable against him. He did not deny his obligation to convey. In that sense, he did not repudiate the contract. He simply refused to accept the tender and make the conveyance.

The record is devoid of any proof that Strong either acted or refrained from acting to his prejudice in reliance upon a belief that Shell would not insist on performance of the contract.

While farmlands in Kansas fluctuate in value, increasing in value during periods of rainfall adequate for the growing of crops, and decreasing in value during periods of drought, such lands are not comparable with undeveloped mining properties, the exploration of which may prove them to be of great value or to be practically worthless, or with other properties highly speculative in character.

It is a general rule that the mere fact that the value of the land, which is the subject of the contract, has increased or diminished since the contract was executed will not warrant a court in refusing to grant a decree of specific performance, in the absence of a showing that the plaintiff in bad faith delayed bringing his action in order to speculate on a change in value to his advantage.

Strong wholly failed to establish any prejudice to him as the result of the delay in the commencement of the action. While the land did fluctuate in value in the interim, since the value of the land at the time of the tender and at the time suit was commenced was substantially the same, Strong suffered no disadvantage from the delay.

We are of the opinion that Strong wholly failed to establish any basis for the application of the doctrine of laches.

The judgment is reversed and the cause remanded with instructions to enter judgment awarding Shell specific performance of the contract.

MURRAH, CIRCUIT JUDGE (dissenting).

I cannot consent to the reversal of judgment of the chancellor in this case. It is a cardinal principle of equitable jurisprudence that one who seeks specific performance of a contract must show that he has been "prompt, ready, able and eager to perform and abide by the same"—equity aids only the diligent, not the ones who slumber on their rights. Furthermore, an action for specific performance appeals largely to the discretion of the trial court, and will not be granted unless it affirmatively appears that it is equitable to do so.

If a party to a contract fails to assert his rights under it for such a length of time as to give the impression that he has waived or abandoned it, or has acquiesced in the other party's repudiation of it, he will be denied specific performance. * * * Thus, it has always been the law in Kansas that "when a contract is repudiated by one of the parties thereto, the other party has a right to take such steps as he may deem necessary to protect himself against loss or damage because of such repudiation. The law imposes on him the duty of acting promptly, and if he does not so act, he can neither have specific performance nor collect damages, but will be held to have acquiesced in the repudiation of the contract." Parks v. Monroe, 99 Kan. 368, 161 P. 638. * * * When on July 31, 1937, appellee refused appellant's tender under the contract, it became the duty of appellant to act with reasonable diligence and promptitude if he was to have the assistance of equity in the enforcement of his rights under the contract. But he did nothing to manifest his interest in the contract or its repudiation—for five years, lacking one day, he wholly ignored the contract and its repudiation. He neither tendered the interest on the unpaid purchase price, nor demanded any of the rents or profits from the land which the contract gave him.

The land in question was leased for oil and gas in 1936—"there was an oil boom in 1937 and royalty could be sold." The trial court found, and it is not disputed, that when on July 31, 1937, the tender was made under the contract, the land was of greater value than the contract price. Shell had the legal right to exercise his option to purchase by appropriate tender at any propitious time during the contractual period, but after the refusal of the tender he could not choose the most advantageous time to enforce his tender in a court of equity. Following the "oil boom" in 1937 there was a "material decrease" in the value of the land, but in 1940 the land began to increase in value and continued to increase because of good crops until the trial date. When in 1942 the land had increased $5,000 in excess of the purchase price the appellant decided to compel performance of the contract, and brought this suit in equity for that purpose just one day less than five years from the date of its repudiation. Based on these undisputed facts the trial court held that the unexplained failure of the appellant to seek relief after repudiation for five years, lacking one day, indicated an abandonment of the contract and his acquiescence in its repudiation by the appellee.

Since specific performance rests largely within the sound discretion of the trial court, we have not the right to override its judgment unless from all the facts we must say that the trial court acted arbitrarily. We should not reverse simply because as the trier we might have appraised the facts differently and drawn different conclusions therefrom. From my own appraisal of the facts, I am unable to say that the trial court arbitrarily closed its doors to one who came with clean hands, was diligent and otherwise without fault.

I would affirm the judgment.

### *Notes*

1. The question of laches arises in *Shell* because the remedy prayed for is specific performance of the contract, namely, conveying a one-half interest in the land to plaintiff. Could plaintiff have obtained relief in the district court equivalent to specific performance if he had prayed for damages? Is there a sound basis for relief that differs widely in its effect on the parties depending on whether specific performance or damages is prayed for? For instance, would the result in *Shell* be different if the defendant had built a house on the land in 1940 at his own expense? Edward Yorio, A Defense of Equitable Defenses, 51 Ohio St.L.J. 1201 (1990), provides an extensive analysis of the flexibility provided to courts in calculating damages or determining relief when equitable defenses come into play.

2. In Environmental Defense Fund, Inc. v. Alexander, 614 F.2d 474 (5th Cir.), cert. denied, 449 U.S. 919, 101 S.Ct. 316, 66 L.Ed.2d 146 (1980), laches was found to be a good defense to a suit by an environmental group seeking to enjoin the Corps of Engineers from proceeding with construction of the Tennessee–Tombigbee Waterway with a 300 foot channel rather than the 170 foot channel authorized by Congress. Plaintiffs' response to the laches claim reduced to the assertion that they did not realize for a long period that it was illegal for the Corps to do what it had done. The court held that laches did not depend on subjective awareness of the legal basis on which a claim could be made.

In examining the prejudicial aspect of laches in the case, the court balanced the equities, weighing the expenditure by defendants against the benefits claimed by plaintiffs. Is such balancing appropriate in all cases where laches is raised as a defense or only in public law cases?

Is there any conflict between this approach to laches in a public law environmental case and the emphasis in *Bateman Eichler* on furthering the intent of Congress? Wouldn't the intent of Congress in the *Environmental Defense Fund* case be furthered by rejecting the laches defense and requiring the Corps to build the channel authorized by Congress?

3. In Fitzgerald v. O'Connell, 120 R.I. 240, 386 A.2d 1384 (1978), a case in which specific performance for the purchase of real estate was prayed for, the court summarized the grounds on which laches is usually found:

> In the past, typical examples of prejudice that have supported the defense of laches have been the loss of evidence, a change of title, or the

death of a key witness. Evidence that a defendant expended sums of money in constructing improvements has also been held to be sufficient prejudice to support a finding of laches. Where the subject matter is speculative and subject to rapid fluctuation in value, such as oil and mining properties, the doctrine of "speculative delay" may bar a claim to ownership if the claimant asserts his interest only after the risk has passed and the value of the property has become apparent.

4. It is a long standing principle that the defense of laches is not available against the government when it acts in its sovereign capacity or where it has a direct pecuniary interest in a matter. Costello v. United States, 365 U.S. 265, 81 S.Ct. 534, 5 L.Ed.2d 551 (1961); United States v. Summerlin, 310 U.S. 414, 60 S.Ct. 1019, 84 L.Ed. 1283 (1940). But the immunity to the defense does not extend to those cases in which a government sues for the use and benefit of an individual or in which a government acts like a business in a commercial transaction or in its proprietary capacity. E.g., Clearfield Trust Co. v. United States, 318 U.S. 363, 63 S.Ct. 573, 87 L.Ed. 838 (1943); La Republique Francaise v. Saratoga Vichy Spring Co., 191 U.S. 427, 24 S.Ct. 145, 48 L.Ed. 247 (1903).

The equitable estoppel cases involving the government do not appear to make these distinctions between the various capacities in which the government acts. Do you perceive a sound reason for recognizing these differences in laches but not in estoppel?

There is at least one lower court case in which laches was applied against the government. Lane v. United States, 639 F.2d 758 (Ct.Cl.1981). The government brought an equitable counterclaim to recoup gratuities from a former employee and the court found the claim delayed, trivial and based on tainted records. The court found that the modern basis for the rule that laches does not apply to the government lay in the interest in protecting public property and public rights and that that rationale permitted an exception in the case before the court.

It is probable that in *EDF v. Alexander,* EDF would claim that it was acting as a private attorney general representing the interests of all citizens in protecting public property and public rights. If the government is not subject to a laches defense when it acts in that capacity, why should the laches defense be applicable to plaintiffs like EDF?

5. Seven Native Americans recently began a trademark cancellation proceeding against a number of trademarks associated with the Washington Redskins football team. The petitioners sought cancellation under Section 2(a) of the Trademark Act, 15 U.S.C. § 1052(a), which bars the registration of marks which consist of scandalous matter or bring persons into contempt or disrepute. The earliest Redskin trademark was issued in 1967. The owner of the trademark, Pro Football, Inc., raised a defense of laches. On a pretrial motion, the Trademark Trial and Appeal Board struck the defense on the ground that there was an interest beyond the personal interest of the petitioners where trial might show that the marks hold a substantial segment of the population up to public ridicule. Harjo v. Pro Football, Inc., 30 USPQ 2d 1828 (PTO TTAB 1994). Is this a variant of the private attorney general theory that EDF might have raised?

6. Despite the broad doctrinal statements that the claims of the government are not barred by laches or statutes of limitation not imposed by Congress, the courts have indicated that in fashioning relief they can and should take into account the passage of time since the events giving rise to the claim and whether the defendant has been prejudiced by the unexcused conduct of the government during that time. Occidental Life Ins. Co. of California v. EEOC, 432 U.S. 355, 373, 97 S.Ct. 2447, 2458, 53 L.Ed.2d 402 (1977); SEC v. Rind, 991 F.2d 1486 (9th Cir.), cert. denied, ___ U.S. ___, 114 S.Ct. 439, 126 L.Ed.2d 372 (1993); SEC v. Willis, 777 F.Supp. 1165, 1174 (S.D.N.Y.1991), reaffirmed, 787 F.Supp. 58 (S.D.N.Y.1992). Does this amount to saying that in theory the government is not barred by laches but in fact the court is free to weigh the elements of a laches defense in order to reach a "just" result?

# Chapter 10

# ATTORNEYS' FEES

Court-awarded attorneys' fees are an important aspect of many types of litigation. Where fees are available, compiling, negotiating and litigating a fee request can take as much as a tenth of the time spent on the case, or more if fees issues are hotly disputed. Most awards are measured in the tens of thousands of dollars, but seven- and eight-figure awards are not unknown in certain areas of the law, such as anti-trust cases.

Attorneys' fees are important for reasons beyond the time and money involved. Just as the availability of damages tends to encourage or discourage particular conduct by would-be plaintiffs and defendants, the possible award of fees affects, and is intended to affect, the behavior of the litigants and their attorneys. Fees can prompt litigation which could not be paid for otherwise or fund the expansion of a private firm or public interest group after a successful suit. The availability of fees for supervising compliance with a decree can radically enlarge the plaintiff's role in decree administration and enforcement. At the same time, the availability of fees to a prevailing defendant, or even the threat of such fees, can discourage suits altogether or prompt plaintiffs to delete from complaints less promising causes of action.

Working on a fee application is a time for retrospection. It forces the attorneys and the judge to think back on a train of events that often goes back years. Since the application should document how each block of hours was used, the process makes one recall events that were so intense when they happened that one would have never believed that they could be forgotten. Moreover, it is now the prevailing attorney who is on trial: did she use her time prudently or could she have conducted the case in a more cost-effective manner? Perhaps it is these elements, as much as the amounts of money involved, that makes the fee application so hotly contested in some cases; the case in chief is over, but the attorneys fight on, reviewing their own behavior in the suit.

Just as the fees stage of the case provides a thoughtful lawyer with a chance to come to terms with the end of a significant involvement, it also should provide students of remedies with a chance to reflect on what they have been studying. Fees litigation, after all, involves the courts self-consciously writing about the entire litigation process and its place in public policy. Moreover, it involves two themes of recurring importance in this book. One theme is equity. When courts determine that they have the power to award fees, their thinking as to who gets them and in what amount represents the height of equitable decision-making. A second theme is the source and limits of remedial powers. What are the appropriate roles of the legislature and the courts in making fees decisions?

Some of the voluminous attorneys' fee literature has been collected in Kathryn M. Christie, Attorney Fee Shifting: A Bibliography, 47 Law & Contemp.Probs. 347 (1984)(103 items cited); Dan B. Dobbs, Awarding Attorney Fees Against Adversaries: Introducing the Problem, 1986 Duke L.J. 435, 436 n.10 (1986). Comprehensive treatment of the topic is available in: Mary F. Derfner & Arthur D. Wolf, Court Awarded Attorneys Fees (1990 and 1995 Supp.)(three volumes); Alba Conte, Attorney Fee Awards (1993 & 1995 Supp.).

## A. THE POWER OF THE COURT TO AWARD ATTORNEYS' FEES

### *Problem: Country Lodge v. Miller (Reprised) Paying the Attorneys*

Assume that Country Lodge prevails in its suit against Miller and wins a judgment for $8500 for lost profits. Country Lodge's attorney submits a bill for 28 hours of work at $100 per hour ($2800). If that bill is paid out of the judgment, has the law restored Country Lodge to its rightful position?

Now assume that Miller prevails because the court determines that she had a legal right to put biodegradable apple mash into the river. Miller's attorneys billed her $2000 to defend her in the suit Country Lodge brought. Should Country Lodge have to reimburse Miller for the cost of the defense?

---

The basic "American Rule" regarding attorneys' fees has long been that each side pays its own unless a court is authorized by a statute or a recognized equitable exception to shift payment of the fees to the opposing party. Arcambel v. Wiseman, 3 U.S. (3 Dall.) 306, 1 L.Ed. 613 (1796), is recognized as the judicial source of the American Rule. In contrast, under the "English Rule," prevailing parties recover fees as a matter of course from the losing party. The English Rule is followed in most common law countries, see Mary F. Derfner, The True "American Rule": Drafting Fee Legislation in the Public Interest, 2 W. New Eng.L.Rev. 251 (1979); and in western Europe, see Werner Pfennigstorf, The European Experience with Attorney Fee Shifting, 47 Law &

Contemp. Probs. 37, 85–124 (1984). Japan is one of the very few other major industrial countries in the world to follow the American Rule. See Kojima & Taniguchi, Access to Justice in Japan: Japanese National Report on Access to Justice, 1 Access to Justice 689, 705 (1978). Alaska is an example of a state where the English Rule has been adopted by statute in a modified form—prevailing parties are compensated only partially, not in full. Alaska Civ.Rule 82 provides successful plaintiffs with fee awards determined by a complicated sliding-scale system. For successful defendants, Rule 82 permits reasonable awards based on equitable considerations and the value of the legal services performed. Note, Rule 82 Revisited: Attorney Fee Shifting in Alaska, 10 Alaska L.Rev. 429 (1993).

The Supreme Court of the United States has offered several reasons for its adherence to the American Rule. These include: 1) to avoid discouraging the poor from bringing a meritorious lawsuit because of the possibility of having to pay the other side's fees; 2) not penalizing any party merely for bringing a suit; and 3) not imposing a great burden on judicial administration due to the inherent difficulty in computing fees. See, e.g., Fleischmann Distilling Corp. v. Maier Brewing Co., 386 U.S. 714, 87 S.Ct. 1404, 18 L.Ed.2d 475 (1967); Oelrichs v. Spain, 82 U.S. (15 Wall.) 211, 21 L.Ed. 43 (1872). The reported cases often reflect tension between the Supreme Court and the lower courts because of the lower courts' desire to restore the parties to their rightful positions by making the prevailing parties whole. The American Rule is frequently criticized because it forces a vindicated party to pay its own fees, which often substantially cut into the award of damages or come directly from the party's pocket when there is no monetary award.

Perhaps because there are situations where the American Rule appears to be unfair, the courts have created and applied certain exceptions to the rule, and thereby have allowed some parties to obtain fees. These equitable exceptions include: (1) *Bad Faith*—where fees are awarded because the losing party has brought the suit in bad faith, vexatiously or for oppressive reasons, see, e.g., Kansas City Southern R. Co. v. Guardian Trust Co., 281 U.S. 1, 50 S.Ct. 194, 74 L.Ed. 659 (1930); (2) *Contempt*—where fees are awarded against a party who willfully disobeys a court order which leads to additional legal expenses for the prevailing party, see, e.g., Trustees v. Greenough, 105 U.S. (15 Otto) 527, 26 L.Ed. 1157 (1881); (3) *Common Fund*—where fees are awarded to a party who preserves or generates a common fund for a class of plaintiffs, see, e.g., Alyeska Pipeline Service Co. v. Wilderness Society, 421 U.S. 240, 95 S.Ct. 1612, 44 L.Ed.2d 141 (1975); and (4) *Substantial Benefit*—where fees are awarded to a prevailing party when the suit has benefitted the defendant, such as in a shareholders' derivative suit, see, e.g., Mills v. Electric Auto–Lite Co., 396 U.S. 375, 90 S.Ct. 616, 24 L.Ed.2d 593 (1970). For discussion of exceptions to the American Rule, see Charles Silver, A Restitutionary Theory of Attorneys' Fees in Class Actions, 76 Cornell L.Rev. 656 (1991).

In Alyeska Pipeline Co. v. Wilderness Society, supra, the Supreme Court held that it must wait for Congress to create further exceptions to the American Rule. Therefore, the Court rejected an opportunity to establish a new exception for federal courts, the "private attorney general" theory, which would shift fees in cases where private citizens brought suits benefitting society as a whole. The Court held that Congress had made specific and explicit provisions for the allowance of attorney's fees under selected statutes granting or protecting various federal rights, and for the Court to make an exception where Congress had not would be improper. The Court believed that this would be an intrusion of the judicial branch of government into the legislature's domain. Justice Marshall's dissent took the position that the private attorney general theory was simply a version of the substantial benefit theory, which the Court had previously recognized.

Congress responded to *Alyeska* by creating a plethora of new fee shifting statutes, including: Civil Rights Attorney's Fees Awards Act of 1976, 42 U.S.C. § 1988, Toxic Substance Control Act, 15 U.S.C. § 2619, Truth in Lending Act, 15 U.S.C. § 1640, and many more. Well over one hundred federal statutes now authorize courts to award attorneys' fees. Federal Statutes Authorizing the Award of Attorney Fees, 9 Attorney Fee Award Rep.No. 5 at 2–3 (October 1986). The bulk of attorneys' fees litigation at the Supreme Court level now consists of interpreting congressional intent in these statutes.

While *Alyeska* means that most fee awards now are by statute, the judge-made exceptions are, of course, of continuing importance. For example, even after *Alyeska,* the Supreme Court has held consistently that the courts have the inherent power to make a lawyer who has litigated in bad faith pay fees. E.g., Chambers v. NASCO, Inc., 501 U.S. 32, 111 S.Ct. 2123, 115 L.Ed.2d 27 (1991)(can use inherent power in diversity case, even where law of the state forbids fee shifting to sanction bad faith litigation); Willy v. Coastal Corp., 503 U.S. 131, 112 S.Ct. 1076, 117 L.Ed.2d 280 (1992)(allowing fees under F.R.Civ.P. 11, even if it is later determined that court did not have subject matter jurisdiction over the action). Moreover, *Alyeska* is a limit on federal courts only; state courts have more freedom to create new equitable exceptions. Thus in Serrano v. Priest, 20 Cal.3d 25, 141 Cal.Rptr. 315, 569 P.2d 1303 (1977), the California Supreme Court adopted the private attorney general theory soon after *Alyeska* rejected it. When should judges, especially in state court, create other exceptions?

## BRANDT v. SUPERIOR COURT

Supreme Court of California, 1985.
37 Cal.3d 813, 210 Cal.Rptr. 211, 693 P.2d 796.

KAUS, JUSTICE.

When an insurer tortiously withholds benefits, are attorney's fees, reasonably incurred to compel payment of the policy benefits, recoverable as an element of the damages resulting from such tortious conduct? We hold that they are and accordingly issue a writ of mandate directing the trial court to reinstate the portion of the complaint seeking attorney's fees as damages.

According to the complaint real party in interest Standard Insurance Company (Standard) issued a group disability income insurance policy to Vicom Associates, petitioner's employer, under which petitioner was insured. Petitioner sustained a loss covered by the policy when he became totally disabled. He made a timely demand on Standard for benefits, which it unreasonably refused to pay. Petitioner therefore filed an action against Standard for (1) breach of contract, (2) breach of the covenant of good faith and fair dealing, and (3) for violation of the statutory prohibitions against unfair claims practices. In his causes of action for breach of the duty of good faith and fair dealing and for the statutory violations, petitioner listed attorney's fees incurred in connection with the contract cause of action as part of the resulting damage. Standard successfully moved to strike the portions of the complaint seeking attorney's fees. Petitioner then filed the present mandate proceeding. * * *

"It is well settled that if an insurer, in discharging its contractual responsibilities, 'fails to deal *fairly and in good faith* with its insured by refusing, without proper cause, to compensate its insured for a loss covered by the policy, such conduct may give rise to a cause of action in tort for breach of an implied covenant of good faith and fair dealing.' When such a breach occurs, the insurer is 'liable for any damages which are the proximate result of that breach.' " (Austero v. Washington National Ins. Co., 132 Cal.App.3d at pp. 419–420, 182 Cal.Rptr. 919 [dis. opn. of Morris, P.J.].)

When an insurer's tortious conduct reasonably compels the insured to retain an attorney to obtain the benefits due under a policy, it follows that the insurer should be liable in a tort action for that expense. The attorney's fees are an economic loss—damages—proximately caused by the tort. These fees must be distinguished from recovery of attorney's fees *qua* attorney's fees, such as those attributable to the bringing of the bad faith action itself. What we consider here is attorney's fees that are recoverable as damages resulting from a tort in the same way that medical fees would be part of the damages in a personal injury action.

"When a pedestrian is struck by a car, he goes to a physician for treatment of his injuries, and the motorist, if liable in tort, must pay the pedestrian's medical fees. Similarly, in the present case, an insurance company's refusal to pay benefits has required the insured to seek the services of an attorney to obtain those benefits, and the insurer, because its conduct was tortious, should pay the insured's legal fees." (*Austero*)

Code of Civil Procedure section 1021 does not preclude an award of attorney's fees under these circumstances. "Section 1021 leaves to the agreement of the parties 'the measure and mode of compensation of attorneys.' However, here, as in the third party tort situation, 'we are not dealing with "the measure and mode of compensation of attorneys" but with damages wrongfully caused by defendant's improper actions.'" (*Austero*) In such cases there is no recovery of attorney's fees *qua* attorney's fees. This is also true in actions for false arrest and malicious prosecution, where damages may include attorney's fees incurred to obtain release from confinement or dismissal of the unjustified charges or to defend the prior suit.

The fact that—here as well as in *Austero*—the fees claimed as damages are incurred in the very lawsuit in which their recovery is sought, does not in itself violate section 1021's general requirement that parties bear their own costs of legal representation, though it may make the identification of allowable fees more sophisticated. If the insured were to recover benefits under the policy in a separate action before suing on the tort, the distinction between fees incurred in the policy action, recoverable as damages, and those incurred in the tort action, nonrecoverable, would be unmistakable. * * *

The fees recoverable, however, may not exceed the amount attributable to the attorney's efforts to obtain the rejected payment due on the insurance contract. Fees attributable to obtaining any portion of the plaintiff's award [such as for emotional distress] which exceeds the amount due under the policy are not recoverable. * * *

MOSK, JUSTICE, concurring.

[omitted]

LUCAS, JUSTICE, dissenting.

I respectfully dissent. In my view, the trial court properly denied petitioner's request for attorney fees.

The American rule has long been that each party to litigation should bear his own attorney fees. The California Legislature first adopted this rule in 1851. * * *

Although this court may have an inherent equitable power to award attorney fees in certain cases, we have "moved cautiously in expanding the nonstatutory bases on which awards of attorney's fees may be predicated." We have acknowledged limited exceptions only "when overriding considerations of justice seemed to compel such a result." "Three of these exceptions, discussed at length in Serrano v. Priest (1977) 20 Cal.3d 25, 34–47 [141 Cal.Rptr. 315, 569 P.2d 1303], base recovery of attorney fees to the prevailing party on the fact that the litigation has conferred benefits on others. Thus, if the litigation has succeeded in creating or preserving a common fund for the benefit of a number of persons, the plaintiff may be awarded attorney fees out of that fund. Likewise, if a judgment confers a substantial benefit on a defendant, such as in a corporate derivative action, the defendant may be required to pay the attorney fees incurred by the plaintiff. Finally, under the 'private attorney general' concept attorney fees may be awarded to those who by litigation secure benefits for a broad class of persons by effectuating a strong public policy." Petitioner does not contend that his request for attorney fees comes within any of these exceptions.

A fourth exception is the "third-party tort" situation. "A person who through the tort of another has been required to act in the protection of his interests by bringing or defending an action *against a third person* is entitled to recover compensation for the reasonably necessary loss of time, attorney's fees, and other expenditures thereby suffered or incurred." (Italics added, Prentice v. North Amer. Title Guar. Corp. (1963) 59 Cal.2d 618, 620, 30 Cal.Rptr. 821, 381 P.2d 645.) Likewise, petitioner does not claim his request for attorney fees comes within this exception.

Petitioner suggests, however, that section 1021 would not preclude recovery of attorney fees *as damages* incurred "independently" of the litigation in which the right to damages is established. According to petitioner, the "third-party tort" exception is only one example of the broader "collateral litigation" exception. Other examples include recovery of attorney fees occasioned by false imprisonment or by malicious prosecution. Thus, petitioner asserts that in general a party should be allowed to recover attorney fees for legal services independently incurred, and that any limitations on this rule are the exceptions.

But in fact section 1021 applies with equal force to collateral litigation. In each of the examples mentioned above, it was not the fact of collateral litigation per se that led to the award. Attorney fees are given in false imprisonment or malicious prosecution suits not because collateral litigation is involved, but as sanctions against the abuse of process those two torts represent. Likewise, in the third party tort exception, it is the presence of the third party, not the existence of collateral litigation, that is the important factor. It is one thing for a tortfeasor to force the victim to sue him; in such a case the victim must bear his own attorney fees. But it is quite another thing for the tortfeasor to inject the victim into litigation with another person. Even so, the tortfeasor is not liable for attorney fees expended in the suit against the third party unless his tort was the proximate cause of the expense. * * *

Furthermore, even if there were some general exception for collateral litigation, the present type of case would not appear to qualify. It is contended that we can find collateral litigation in the fact that the insured has two causes of action against the insurance company: one for breach of contract and one for violation of the duty of good faith and fair dealing. The contract suit is regarded as if it were a prior suit and the tort suit as if it were a later suit; since the insurer's tort is what caused it to deny benefits, the suit to recover benefits was occasioned by the tort and therefore in the tort suit the insured should be allowed to recover the attorney fees he expended in the contract suit.

But this analysis appears to mistake the nature of the bad faith tort. When an insurance company withholds payments in bad faith its actions amount to both a breach of contract and a tort, but two separate breaches of duty are not involved. The single duty breached—the covenant of good faith and fair dealing—"springs from the contractual relationship between the parties." The plaintiff may bring suit on both contract and tort theories, but ultimately he must elect which remedy to pursue. There simply is no collateral suit from which attorney fees may be recovered.

The analysis of the Court of Appeal in Mustachio v. Ohio Farmers Ins. Co. (1975) 44 Cal.App.3d 358, 118 Cal.Rptr. 581, is similarly flawed. Focusing on the fact that the insurer's breach of the duty of good faith constitutes a tort, the court concluded that plaintiff insured was entitled to attorney fees because his employment of an attorney was proximately caused by the insurer's tort. Admittedly, plaintiff's employment of an attorney was a foreseeable consequence of defendant insurer's breach, but this logic would apply to *any* tort suit to which a collateral cause of action is attached, effectively allowing the exception to swallow the American rule on attorney fees.

The *Mustachio* opinion failed to follow the logic of the proposed collateral litigation exception to its end. Rather, the court argued that there is something special about an insurance contract that requires its bad faith breach by an insurer to be treated differently from any other tort suit. The relationship between an insured and his insurer may involve a fiduciary relationship, but we have recently held that tortious breach of such a relationship is not a sufficient basis for creating an exception to section 1021.

The mere fact that an insurance contract is bought to secure peace of mind is not a sufficient reason to create an exception to section 1021. In *Crisci,* we discussed the peace of mind of the insured as a basis for granting the type of damages most appropriate to compensate an insured for the disturbance of his tranquility: damages for emotional distress. (See, Crisci v. Security Ins. Co., 66 Cal.2d 425, at pp. 432–34, 58 Cal.Rptr. 13, 426 P.2d 173 (1967).) Such damages alone should be enough to compensate for an insured's loss of peace of mind.

Even if emotional distress damages are insufficient, an insured may seek numerous additional items of damage in an action for bad faith breach of contract that he could not obtain for simple breach of contract. He may recover for awards against him in excess of the policy limits if the insurer has refused in bad faith to settle within the policy limits. He may recover all economic loss proximately caused. If he can prove oppression, fraud or malice, he may recover punitive damages. Given the numerous types of damages that the plaintiff may recover for a tortious breach of his insurance contract, any or all of which can and often do exceed the policy limits, I can see no persuasive need to create an exception to the general rule that each party must bear his own attorney fees.

The *Mustachio* opinion implies that tortious breach of an insurance contract is such a serious abuse that attorney fees must be awarded as well: "If the insurer, instead of bargaining with the insured in good faith, tortiously violates its covenant of good faith and fair dealing and thereby makes it reasonable for the insured to seek the protection of counsel, plain justice demands that the insurer be financially responsible for an expense which but for its tortious conduct would not have been incurred."

But it must be remembered that an insured need not establish the level of misconduct shown by the insurance company in *Mustachio* in order to recover on a bad faith tort. He must prove only that the insurance company acted negligently, i.e., that a "prudent insurer" would have paid the claim. Mere breach of the duty of good faith is "not meant to connote the absence or presence of positive misconduct of a malicious or immoral nature...." Such negligence on the part of the insurer is enough to warrant an award of damages for emotional distress, economic loss, and the like because of the special nature of the insurance contract, but it is not such an abuse of process as to justify an award of attorney fees. The argument is more convincing when the insurer has acted with malice, but in that case punitive damages may be awarded; when punitive damages are not justified, I can see little reason for an award of attorney fees.

For the reasons stated, I would deny the peremptory writ.

### *Notes*

1. Why does the court majority believe that this type of tort should be treated as an exception to the American Rule? Is this class of cases truly distinguishable from all others? Or is the court majority simply uncomfortable with the fact that the American Rule seems to be undercompensating this plaintiff? See Note, Brandt v. Superior Court: A New Exception to the General Rule Against Recovering Attorney's Fees, 14 W.St.U.L.Rev. 241 (1986).

2. Should the *Brandt* decision have any effect on the availability of punitive damages? Of emotional distress damages? In terms of restoring someone to the rightful position, is it better to compensate for these two non-pecuniary items of damage or for the out of pocket attorneys' fees or for all three?

3. Although California appellate courts continue to follow *Brandt,* the holding has been limited to its facts. See, e.g., Fuhrman v. California Satellite Systems, 179 Cal.App.3d 408, 231 Cal.Rptr. 113 (1986). Colorado and Arizona have adopted the *Brandt* ruling. Bernhard v. Farmers Insurance Exchange, 885 P.2d 265 (Col.App.), Col. cert.granted (1994); Schwartz v. Farmers Insurance Co., 166 Ariz. 33, 800 P.2d 20 (Az.App.1990). Montana has declined to follow *Brandt*. Tynes v. Bankers Life Co., 224 Mont. 350, 730 P.2d 1115 (1986).

4. In a case somewhat analogous to *Brandt*, the Supreme Court has held that attorney's fees and related expenses may not be recovered by a private party under CERCLA as a "response cost." The Court majority concluded that the Act did not clearly provide for the recovery of attorney's fees expended in litigating a cost recovery action. Justice Scalia's dissent (joined by Justices Blackmun and Thomas) contended that it was sufficient

that the Act specifically allowed for the recovery of the costs of "enforcement activities" as part of the definition of the "necessary costs of response" to the release of a hazardous substance. All of the justices agreed that work done by attorneys in identifying other potentially responsible parties was a recoverable response cost because such work could be performed by any number of professionals (such as engineers) and benefitted the cleanup effort rather than just reallocating the costs. Key Tronic Corp. v. United States, ___ U.S. ___, 114 S.Ct. 1960, 128 L.Ed.2d 797 (1994).

5. Sometimes courts do hold that attorney's fees are included within other legislatively-created categories. For example, the Oregon Supreme Court has held that an act limiting the "liability" of a public entity to $100,000 applies to damages, costs and attorney's fees in an employment discrimination action. Griffin v. Tri–County Metropolitan Transportation District, 318 Or. 500, 870 P.2d 808 (1994).

## B. THE PARTIES THAT CONGRESS HAS MADE ELIGIBLE FOR ATTORNEYS' FEES

Congress authorizes the award of fees for a variety of reasons. First, Congress may wish to encourage citizens to bring actions against the government to assure compliance with Congressional directives. Many environmental and civil rights fee awards provisions are designed to foster citizen oversight of government. E.g., Clean Air Act, 42 U.S.C. § 304(a)(2), (d); 42 U.S.C. § 7604(a)(2), (d). Second, Congress sometimes encourages citizens to bring enforcement actions against other private parties because, even though government enforces the law, private attorneys general have the resources, information, or interest needed to get the job done or because the rights involved are sufficiently important that private persons should not have to wait upon government action. E.g., Clayton Act, 15 U.S.C. § 15, False Claims Act, 31 U.S.C. § 3730, Clean Air Act § 304(a)(1), 42 U.S.C. § 7604(a)(1). Third, Congress may want to make justice more accessible to those who are not rich. E.g., Equal Access to Justice Act, 5 U.S.C. § 504, 28 U.S.C. § 2412. Fourth, Congress may want to deter and punish those who abuse the judicial process. E.g., 28 U.S.C. § 1927; cf. F.R.Civ.P. 11, 16(f), 26(g), 37(a)(4), 56(g). Finally, the Constitution may require it, as in providing counsel for indigents prosecuted for crimes. Criminal Justice Act, 18 U.S.C. § 3006A. (The payment of such fees, unlike most other federal statutes affecting attorneys' fees, does not turn on whether the defendant prevails at trial and is not designed to encourage litigation.)

Congress has not seen fit to serve these purposes uniformly. Sometimes statutes that would seem to fit within the pattern of those under which fees are awarded do not authorize fees. E.g., National Environmental Policy Act, 42 U.S.C. § 4331 et seq. It must also be emphasized that statutes that authorize fees do not necessarily allow them for all actions brought under the statute. For instance, fees may be unavailable to certain successful parties. Because there are differences between the fees provisions under many of these statutes, caution must be used in carrying results under one statute over to a case under another. It is necessary to check the specific language, legislative history, and interpretation of each fees provision. It is also important to plead clearly an entitlement to relief on the merits under statutes which provide for an award of fees and to request attorneys fees as a specific item in the prayer for relief.

## FARRAR v. HOBBY

Supreme Court of the United States, 1992.
506 U.S. 103, 113 S.Ct. 566, 121 L.Ed.2d 494.

JUSTICE THOMAS delivered the opinion of the Court.

We decide today whether a civil rights plaintiff who receives a nominal damages award is a "prevailing party" eligible to receive attorney's fees under 42 U.S.C. § 1988. The Court of Appeals for the Fifth Circuit reversed an award of attorney's fees on the ground that a plaintiff receiving only nominal damages is not a prevailing party. Although we hold that such a plaintiff is a prevailing party, we affirm the denial of fees in this case.

I

Joseph Davis Farrar and Dale Lawson Farrar owned and operated Artesia Hall, a school in Liberty County, Texas, for delinquent, disabled, and disturbed teens. After an Artesia Hall student died in 1973, a Liberty County grand jury returned a murder indictment charging Joseph Farrar with willful failure to administer proper medical treatment and failure to provide timely hospitalization. The State of Texas also obtained a temporary injunction that closed Artesia Hall.

Respondent William P. Hobby, Jr., then Lieutenant Governor of Texas, participated in the events leading to the closing of Artesia Hall. After Joseph Farrar was indicted, Hobby issued a press release criticizing the Texas Department of Public Welfare and its licensing procedures. He urged the department's director to investigate Artesia Hall and accompanied Governor Dolph Briscoe on an inspection of the school. Finally, he attended the temporary injunction hearing with Briscoe and spoke to reporters after the hearing.

Joseph Farrar sued Hobby, Judge Clarence D. Cain, County Attorney Arthur J. Hartell III, and the director and two employees of the Department of Public Welfare for monetary and injunctive relief under 42 U.S.C. §§ 1983 and 1985. The complaint alleged deprivation of liberty and property without due process by means of conspiracy and malicious prosecution aimed at closing Artesia Hall. Later amendments to the complaint added Dale Farrar as a plaintiff, dropped the claim for injunctive relief, and increased the request for damages to $17 million. After Joseph Farrar died on February 20, 1983, petitioners Dale Farrar and Pat Smith, coadministrators of his estate, were substituted as plaintiffs.

The case was tried before a jury in the Southern District of Texas on August 15, 1983. Through special interrogatories, the jury found that all of the defendants except Hobby had conspired against the plaintiffs but that this conspiracy was not a proximate cause of any injury suffered by the plaintiffs. The jury also found that Hobby had "committed an act or acts under color of state law that deprived Plaintiff Joseph Davis Farrar of a civil right," but it found that Hobby's conduct was not "a proximate cause of any damages" suffered by Joseph Farrar. The jury made no findings in favor of Dale Farrar. In accordance with the jury's answers to the special interrogatories, the District Court ordered that "Plaintiffs take nothing, that the action be dismissed on the merits, and that the parties bear their own costs."

The Court of Appeals for the Fifth Circuit affirmed in part and reversed in part. The court affirmed the failure to award compensatory or nominal damages against the conspirators because the plaintiffs had not proved an actual deprivation of a constitutional right. Because the jury found that Hobby had deprived Joseph Farrar of a civil right, however, the Fifth Circuit remanded for entry of judgment against Hobby for nominal damages.

The plaintiffs then sought attorney's fees under 42 U.S.C. § 1988. On January 30, 1987, the District Court entered an order awarding the plaintiffs $280,000 in fees, $27,932 in expenses, and $9,730 in prejudgment interest against Hobby. * * *

A divided Fifth Circuit panel reversed the fee award. After reviewing our decisions in Hewitt v. Helms, 482 U.S. 755, 107 S.Ct. 2672, 96 L.Ed.2d 654 (1987), Rhodes v. Stewart, 488 U.S. 1, 109 S.Ct. 202, 102 L.Ed.2d 1 (1988) (per curiam ), and Texas State Teachers Assn. v. Garland Independent School Dist., 489 U.S. 782, 109 S.Ct. 1486, 103 L.Ed.2d 866 (1989), the majority held that the plaintiffs were not prevailing parties and were therefore ineligible for fees under § 1988:

> "The Farrars sued for $17 million in money damages; the jury gave them nothing. No money damages. No declaratory relief. No injunctive relief. Nothing.... [T]he Farrars did succeed in securing a jury-finding that Hobby violated their civil rights and a nominal award of one dollar. However, this finding did not in any meaningful sense 'change the legal relationship' between the Farrars and Hobby. Nor was the result a success for the Farrars on a 'significant issue that achieve[d] some of the benefit the [Farrars] sought in bringing suit.' When the sole relief sought is money damages, we fail to see how a party 'prevails' by winning one dollar out of the $17 million requested."

The majority reasoned that even if an award of nominal damages represented some sort of victory, "surely [the Farrars'] was 'a technical victory ... so insignificant and ... so near the situations addressed in *Hewitt* and *Rhodes*, as to be insufficient to support prevailing party status' "(quoting *Garland*). * * *

II

The Civil Rights Attorney's Fees Award Act of 1976, 90 Stat. 2641, as amended, 42 U.S.C. § 1988, provides in relevant part:

> "In any action or proceeding to enforce a provision of sections 1981, 1982, 1983, 1985, and 1986 of this title, title IX of Public Law 92–318 ..., or title VI of the Civil Rights Act of 1964 ..., the court, in its discretion, may allow the prevailing party, other than the United States, a reasonable attorney's fee as part of the costs."

"Congress intended to permit the ... award of counsel fees only when a party has prevailed on the merits." Hanrahan v. Hampton, 446 U.S. 754, 758, 100 S.Ct. 1987, 1989, 64 L.Ed.2d 670 (1980)(per curiam). Therefore, in order to qualify for attorney's fees under § 1988, a plaintiff must be a "prevailing party." Under our "generous formulation" of the term, " 'plaintiffs may be considered "prevailing parties" for attorney's fees purposes if they succeed on any significant issue in litigation which achieves some of the benefit the parties sought in bringing suit.' " Hensley v. Eckerhart, 461 U.S. 424, 433, 103 S.Ct. 1933, 1939, 76 L.Ed.2d 40 (1983)(quoting Nadeau v. Helgemoe, 581 F.2d 275, 278–279 (C.A.1 1978)). * * *

We have elaborated on the definition of prevailing party in three recent cases. In *Hewitt*, we addressed "the peculiar-sounding question whether a party who litigates to judgment and loses on all of his claims can nonetheless be a 'prevailing party.' " In his § 1983 action against state prison officials for alleged due process violations, respondent Helms obtained no relief. "The most that he obtained was an interlocutory ruling that his complaint should not have been dismissed for failure to state a constitutional claim." Observing that "[r]espect for ordinary language requires that a plaintiff receive at least some relief on the merits of his claim before he can be said to prevail," we held that Helms was not a prevailing party. We required the plaintiff to prove "the settling of some dispute which affects the behavior of the defendant towards the plaintiff."

In *Rhodes*, we reversed an award of attorney's fees premised solely on a declaratory judgment that prison officials had violated the plaintiffs' First and Fourteenth Amendment rights. By the time the District Court entered judgment, "one of the plaintiffs had died and the other was no longer in custody." Under these circumstances, we held, neither plaintiff was a prevailing party. We explained that "nothing in [*Hewitt*] suggested that the entry of [a declaratory] judgment in a party's favor automatically renders that party prevailing under § 1988." We reaffirmed that a judgment—declaratory or otherwise—"will constitute relief, for purposes of § 1988, if, and only if, it affects the behavior of the defendant toward the plaintiff." Whatever "modification of prison policies" the declaratory judgment might have effected "could not in any way have benefitted either plaintiff, one of whom was dead and the other released."[3]

Finally, in *Garland*, we synthesized the teachings of *Hewitt* and *Rhodes*. "[T]o be considered a prevailing party within the meaning of § 1988," we held, "the plaintiff must be able to point to a resolution of the dispute which changes the legal relationship between itself and the defendant." We reemphasized that "[t]he touchstone of the prevailing party inquiry must be the material alteration of the legal relationship of the parties." Under this test, the plaintiffs in *Garland* were prevailing parties because they "obtained a judgment vindicating [their] First Amendment rights [as] public employees" and "materially altered the [defendant] school district's policy limiting the rights of teachers to communicate with each other concerning employee organizations and union activities."

Therefore, to qualify as a prevailing party, a civil rights plaintiff must obtain at least some relief on the merits of his claim. The plaintiff must obtain an enforceable judgment against the defendant from whom fees are sought, *Hewitt*, or comparable relief through a consent decree or settlement, Maher v. Gagne, 448 U.S. 122, 129, 100 S.Ct. 2570, 2574, 65 L.Ed.2d 653 (1980). Whatever relief the plaintiff secures must directly benefit him at the time of the judgment or settlement. Otherwise, the judgment or settlement cannot be said to "affec[t] the behavior of the defendant toward the plaintiff." *Rhodes*. Only under these circumstances can civil rights litigation effect "the material alteration of the legal relationship of the parties" and thereby transform the plaintiff into a prevailing party. *Garland*. In short, a plaintiff "prevails" when actual relief on the merits of his claim materially alters the legal relationship between the parties by modifying the defendant's behavior in a way that directly benefits the plaintiff.

## III

### A

Doubtless "the basic purpose of a § 1983 damages award should be to compensate persons for injuries caused by the deprivation of constitutional rights." Carey v. Piphus, 435 U.S. 247, 254, 98 S.Ct. 1042, 1047, 55 L.Ed.2d 252 (1978). For this reason, no compensatory damages may be awarded in a § 1983 suit absent proof of actual injury. Accord, Memphis Community School Dist. v. Stachura, 477 U.S. 299, 307, 308, n.11, 106 S.Ct. 2537, 2543, 2543–2544, n. 11, 91 L.Ed.2d 249 (1986). We have also held, however, that "the denial of procedural due process should be actionable for nominal damages without proof of actual injury." *Carey*. The awarding of nominal damages for the "absolute" right to procedural due process "recognizes the importance to organized society that [this] righ[t] be scrupulously observed" while "remain[ing] true to the principle that substantial damages should be awarded only to compensate actual injury." Thus, *Carey* obligates a court to award

3. Similarly, the plaintiff in [*Hewitt*]"had long since been released from prison" by the time his failed lawsuit putatively prompted beneficial changes in prison policy. * * *

nominal damages when a plaintiff establishes the violation of his right to procedural due process but cannot prove actual injury.

We therefore hold that a plaintiff who wins nominal damages is a prevailing party under § 1988. When a court awards nominal damages, it neither enters judgment for defendant on the merits nor declares the defendant's legal immunity to suit. To be sure, a judicial pronouncement that the defendant has violated the Constitution, unaccompanied by an enforceable judgment on the merits, does not render the plaintiff a prevailing party. Of itself, "the moral satisfaction [that] results from any favorable statement of law" cannot bestow prevailing party status. *Hewitt.* No material alteration of the legal relationship between the parties occurs until the plaintiff becomes entitled to enforce a judgment, consent decree, or settlement against the defendant. A plaintiff may demand payment for nominal damages no less than he may demand payment for millions of dollars in compensatory damages. A judgment for damages in any amount, whether compensatory or nominal, modifies the defendant's behavior for the plaintiff's benefit by forcing the defendant to pay an amount of money he otherwise would not pay. As a result, the Court of Appeals for the Fifth Circuit erred in holding that petitioners' nominal damages award failed to render them prevailing parties. * * *

B

Although the "technical" nature of a nominal damages award or any other judgment does not affect the prevailing party inquiry, it does bear on the propriety of fees awarded under § 1988. Once civil rights litigation materially alters the legal relationship between the parties, "the degree of the plaintiff's overall success goes to the reasonableness" of a fee award under *Hensley*. Indeed, "the most critical factor" in determining the reasonableness of a fee award "is the degree of success obtained." In this case, petitioners received nominal damages instead of the $17 million in compensatory damages that they sought. This litigation accomplished little beyond giving petitioners "the moral satisfaction of knowing that a federal court concluded that [their] rights had been violated" in some unspecified way. * * *

In some circumstances, even a plaintiff who formally "prevails" under § 1988 should receive no attorney's fees at all. A plaintiff who seeks compensatory damages but receives no more than nominal damages is often such a prevailing party. As we have held, a nominal damages award does render a plaintiff a prevailing party by allowing him to vindicate his "absolute" right to procedural due process through enforcement of a judgment against the defendant. *Carey.* In a civil rights suit for damages, however, the awarding of nominal damages also highlights the plaintiff's failure to prove actual, compensable injury. Whatever the constitutional basis for substantive liability, damages awarded in a § 1983 action "must always be designed 'to *compensate injuries* caused by the [constitutional] deprivation.'" *Stachura* (quoting *Carey*) (emphasis and brackets in original). When a plaintiff recovers only nominal damages because of his failure to prove an essential element of his claim for monetary relief, the only reasonable fee is usually no fee at all. * * *

Although the Court of Appeals erred in failing to recognize that petitioners were prevailing parties, it correctly reversed the District Court's fee award. We accordingly affirm the judgment of the Court of Appeals. * * *

JUSTICE O'CONNOR, concurring.

If ever there was a plaintiff who deserved no attorney's fees at all, that plaintiff is Joseph Farrar. He filed a lawsuit demanding 17 million dollars from six defendants. After 10 years of litigation and two trips to the Court of Appeals, he got one dollar from one defendant. As the Court holds today, that is simply not the type of victory that merits an award of attorney's fees. Accordingly, I join the Court's opinion and concur in its judgment. I write separately only to explain more fully why, in my view, it is appropriate to deny fees in this case. * * *

II

In the context of this litigation, the technical or *de minimis* nature of Joseph Farrar's victory is readily apparent: He asked for a bundle and got a pittance. While we hold today that this pittance is enough to render him a prevailing party, it does not by itself prevent his victory from being purely technical. * * *

The difference between the amount recovered and the damages sought is not the only consideration, however. *Carey* makes clear that an award of nominal damages can represent a victory in the sense of vindicating rights even though no actual damages are proved. Accordingly, the courts also must look to other factors. One is the significance of the legal issue on which the plaintiff claims to have prevailed. *Garland*. Petitioners correctly point out that Joseph Farrar in a sense succeeded on a significant issue—liability. But even on that issue he cannot be said to have achieved a true victory. Respondent was just one of six defendants and the only one not found to have engaged in a conspiracy. If recovering one dollar from the least culpable defendant and nothing from the rest legitimately can be labeled a victory—and I doubt that it can—surely it is a hollow one. Joseph Farrar may have won a point, but the game, set, and match all went to the defendants.

Given that Joseph Farrar got *some* of what he wanted—one seventeen millionth, to be precise—his success might be considered material if it also accomplished some public goal other than occupying the time and energy of counsel, court, and client. Section 1988 is not "a relief Act for lawyers." Riverside v. Rivera, 477 U.S. 561, 588, 106 S.Ct. 2686, 2701, 91 L.Ed.2d 466 (1986)(Rehnquist, J., dissenting). Instead, it is a tool that ensures the vindication of important rights, even when large sums of money are not at stake, by making attorney's fees available under a private attorney general theory. Yet one searches these facts in vain for the public purpose this litigation might have served. The District Court speculated that the judgment, if accompanied by a large fee award, might deter future lawless conduct, but did not identify the kind of lawless conduct that might be prevented. Nor is the conduct to be deterred apparent from the verdict, which even petitioners acknowledge is "regrettably obtuse." Such a judgment cannot deter misconduct any more than a bolt of lightning can; its results might be devastating, but it teaches no valuable lesson because it carries no discernable meaning. * * *

III

In this case, the relevant indicia of success—the extent of relief, the significance of the legal issue on which the plaintiff prevailed, and the public purpose served—all point to a single conclusion: Joseph Farrar achieved only a *de minimis* victory. As the Court correctly holds today, the appropriate fee in such a case is no fee at all. Because the Court of Appeals gave Joseph Farrar everything he deserved—nothing—I join the Court's opinion affirming the judgment below.

JUSTICE WHITE, with whom JUSTICE BLACKMUN, JUSTICE STEVENS, and JUSTICE SOUTER join, concurring in part and dissenting in part.

We granted certiorari in this case to decide whether 42 U.S.C. § 1988 entitles a civil rights plaintiff who recovers nominal damages to reasonable attorney's fees. Following our decisions in *Garland*, *Hewitt*, *Hensley* and *Carey*, the Court holds that it does. With that aspect of today's decision, I agree. * * *

However, I see no reason for the Court to reach out and decide what amount of attorney's fees constitutes a reasonable amount in this instance. That issue was neither presented in the petition for certiorari nor briefed by petitioners. The opinion of the Court of Appeals was grounded exclusively in its determination that Farrar had not met the threshold requirement under § 1988. At no point did it purport to decide what a reasonable award should be if Farrar was a prevailing party.

It may be that the District Court abused its discretion and misapplied our precedents by belittling the significance of the amount of damages awarded in ascertaining petitioners' fees. But it is one thing to say that the court erred as a matter of law in awarding $280,000; quite another to decree, especially without the benefit of petitioners' views or consideration by the Court of Appeals, that the only fair fee was no fee whatsoever.

* * * Estimating what specific amount would be reasonable in this particular situation is not a matter of general importance on which our guidance is needed. Short of holding that recovery of nominal damages *never* can support the award of attorney's fees—which, clearly, the majority does not—the Court should follow its sensible practice and remand the case for reconsideration of the fee amount. * * *

## *Notes*

1. As *Farrar* indicates, the question of who is "prevailing" is fairly easy to decide if the plaintiff secures a judgment of violation. But how does a court decide whether a party has "prevailed" in other situations? In deciding this issue, the courts seem to be asking themselves a series of questions:

(a) Is the plaintiff in a position to benefit from relief from the defendant? See, e.g., Rhodes v. Stewart, 488 U.S. 1, 109 S.Ct. 202, 102 L.Ed.2d 1 (1988)(prisoner-plaintiffs were not prevailing parties because their claims were moot: one plaintiff had died and the other had been released from prison when the case was decided in their favor); Hewitt v. Helms, 482 U.S. 755, 107 S.Ct. 2672, 96 L.Ed.2d 654 (1987) (prisoner-plaintiff not prevailing party despite change in prison rules that may have been catalyzed by his suit, in part because rule change was not made until after prisoner was released).

(b) Has the plaintiff obtained entry of a judgment in court? If so, what degree of success must the plaintiff have met with to be deemed the prevailing party? In Ruckelshaus v. Sierra Club, 463 U.S. 680, 103 S.Ct. 3274, 77 L.Ed.2d 938 (1983), the Supreme Court held that a party is not entitled to attorneys' fees if it does not prevail on the merits of any of its claims, leaving open exactly what degree of success was necessary to constitute a prevailing plaintiff. In Texas State Teachers Ass'n v. Garland Independent School District, 489 U.S. 782, 791, 109 S.Ct. 1486, 1492–93, 103 L.Ed.2d 866 (1989), the Court determined that a prevailing plaintiff merely had to succeed on " 'any significant issue in litigation which achieve[d] some of the benefit the parties sought in bringing the suit.' " Prior to this case, lower courts had grappled with pinpointing the standard, yielding such tests as success on every claim, success on the central issue, substantial success, some success, or merely the existence of a meritorious claim absent any success.

(c) Even if the plaintiff has not obtained entry of a favorable judgment on the basis of a decision rendered by the trier of fact, can the plaintiff nevertheless be a prevailing party if the lawsuit has operated as a catalyst for post-litigation changes in a defendant's conduct? Compare, e.g., S–1 and S–2 v. State Board of Education, 21 F.3d 49 (4th Cir.), cert. denied, ___ U.S. ___, 115 S.Ct. 205, 130 L.Ed.2d 135 (1994)(*Farrar* prohibits catalyst theory) with Baumgartner v. Harrisburg Housing Authority, 21 F.3d 541 (3d Cir.1994)(collecting and following cases holding that *Farrar* does not reject catalyst theory). See also Maher v. Gagne, 448 U.S. 122, 100 S.Ct. 2570, 65 L.Ed.2d 653 (1980)(plaintiff who obtains consent decree is a "prevailing party"); Hanrahan v. Hampton, 446 U.S. 754, 100 S.Ct. 1987, 64 L.Ed.2d 670 (1980) (procedural and evidentiary rulings, which may affect the disposition of the merits, are not themselves matters on which a party may "prevail" for purposes of shifting fees under § 1988).

(d) Some statutes may not require that the court determine whether the plaintiff is a prevailing party. E.g., Sheppard v. Riverview Nursing Centre, Inc., 870 F.Supp. 1369 (D.Md.1994)(allowing fees under Title VII where plaintiff proves that discrimination was a motivating factor for employment decision even though plaintiff does not "prevail" because same employment decision would have been reached anyway).

2. As the post-*Alyeska* decisions repeatedly mention, statutory provisions allowing the court to award fees to the "prevailing party" in its "discretion" have been read to mean that the prevailing plaintiff should ordinarily get fees unless special circumstances would render such an award unjust. E.g., Newman v. Piggie Park Enterprises, Inc., 390 U.S. 400, 88 S.Ct. 964, 19 L.Ed.2d 1263 (1968). What factors should cause a court to *deny* fees to a prevailing party?

(a) Should the prevailing plaintiff get fees even if it is well heeled and can afford an attorney? E.g., Herrington v. County of Sonoma, 883 F.2d 739 (9th Cir.1989)(wealthy land owners who had strong financial incentive to bring suit awarded fees under § 1988); Jones v. Wilkinson, 800 F.2d 989 (10th Cir.1986)(corporate plaintiffs entitled to fees).

(b) Assume that the defendant, a large, private corporation, prevails against a non-profit citizens group. Should the prevailing defendant get fees? Despite statutes that almost invariably refer to "prevailing parties," the usual rule is that the prevailing defendant does not get fees unless the case is "frivolous, unreasonable, or without foundation." Christiansburg Garment Co. v. EEOC, 434 U.S. 412, 98 S.Ct. 694, 54 L.Ed.2d 648 (1978). What arguments other than "deep pocket" theories can you supply in support of this doctrine? What suppositions do your arguments make about the value of public law litigation? For a useful analysis of these issues, see Harold J. Krent, Explaining One–Way Fee Shifting, 79 Va.L.Rev. 2039 (1993).

Under the Copyright Act, however, all "prevailing parties" must be treated alike—i.e., fees are to be awarded to prevailing defendants or prevailing plaintiffs simply as a matter of the court's discretion. Fogerty v. Fantasy, Inc., 510 U.S. ___, 114 S.Ct. 1023, 127 L.Ed.2d 455 (1994). Justice Thomas wrote separately to indicate that while he agreed with the Court's plain language approach in *Fogerty*, he would take the same approach with the virtually identical language contained in Title VII of the Civil Rights Act and, as a result, would reject completely the dual standard created by *Christiansburg Garment.*

(c) What if an entity intervenes in a lawsuit brought under Title VII, challenging the plaintiff's legal positions, but the district court rejects the intervenor's contentions and rules in favor of the plaintiffs on the merits? May the prevailing plaintiffs obtain fees from the unsuccessful intervenor for the costs associated with responding to the intervenors? Independent Federation of Flight Attendants v. Zipes, 491 U.S. 754, 109 S.Ct. 2732, 105 L.Ed.2d 639 (1989).

(d) Should pro se litigants be awarded fees? In Kay v. Ehrler, 499 U.S. 432, 111 S.Ct. 1435, 113 L.Ed.2d 486 (1991), the Supreme Court unanimously held that a victorious pro se litigant who is also an attorney may not be awarded attorneys' fees under 42 U.S.C. § 1988. Although the Court could not find a clear answer to the question in the text or legislative history of the act, the Court created a rule that served the policies underlying § 1988 and that would create an incentive to retain independent counsel in every case. A lawyer acting in a pro se capacity may be at a disadvantage because he or she may not be able to serve as a witness and would be deprived of the independent and detached judgment of a third party. Although not directly at issue in the case, the Court expressed its satisfaction with the unanimous position of the circuits that pro se litigants who are not lawyers are not entitled to attorneys' fees. The decision is criticized in Charles Silver, Incoherence and Irrationality in the Law of Attorneys' Fees, 12 Rev. Litigation 301 (1993).

(e) Suppose a plaintiff's lawyer, sensing that her client's case is weak, asks the jury for just a nominal damage award ostensibly to vindicate principle. Is it an appropriate response for the court or defense counsel to inform the jury that if it does make an award of nominal damages, the plaintiff may be entitled to attorney's fees? See Brooks v. Cook, 938 F.2d 1048 (9th Cir.1991)(not appropriate). But see Romberg v. Nichols, 48 F.3d 453 (9th Cir.1994), cert. denied, ___ U.S. ___, 116 S.Ct. 379, 133 L.Ed.2d 303 (1995) (cannot escape *Farrar* by seeking only nominal damages at close of trial).

3. When the United States is a party, a private party seeking fees has an additional fee statute available. Under the Equal Access to Justice Act, 28 U.S.C. § 2412(d), fees of up to $75 per hour (which may be adjusted for inflation) may be awarded to a party who has prevailed against the United States (either as plaintiff or defendant), "unless the court finds that the position of the United States was substantially justified * * * ."

In Pierce v. Underwood, 487 U.S. 552, 564, 108 S.Ct. 2541, 2550, 101 L.Ed.2d 490 (1988), the Supreme Court interpreted "substantially" to mean "not 'justified to a high degree,' but rather 'justified in substance or in the main'—that is justified to a degree that could satisfy a reasonable person." Three justices, concurring with the majority, disagreed with this definition, arguing that "the Government can avoid fees only where it makes a clear showing that its position had a solid basis (as opposed to a marginal basis or a not unreasonable basis) in both law and fact." Id. at 579, 108 S.Ct. at 2557. See generally Harold J. Krent, Fee-shifting Under the Equal Access to Justice Act—A Qualified Success, 11 Yale L. & Pol'y Rev. 458 (1993); Gregory C. Sisk, The Essentials of the Equal Access to Justice Act: Court Awards of Attorney's Fees for Unreasonable Government Conduct, 55 La. L.Rev. 217 (1994) (Part One), 56 La.L.Rev. 1 (1995) (Part Two).

4. Does the Eleventh Amendment bar the award of attorneys' fees against the states? Hutto v. Finney, 437 U.S. 678, 98 S.Ct. 2565, 57 L.Ed.2d 522 (1978), in a divided opinion held that an award may be made against a state under section 1988 because Congress may qualify the Eleventh Amendment in implementing the Fourteenth Amendment and the fees are awarded as an element of costs, which have long been awarded against the states. In Missouri v. Jenkins (*Jenkins I*), 491 U.S. 274, 109 S.Ct. 2463, 105 L.Ed.2d 229 (1989), the Supreme Court reaffirmed that the Eleventh Amendment has no application to an award of attorney's fees which is ancillary to a grant of prospective relief against a State. Because it went on to hold that the same was true for the calculation of the amount of reasonable attorneys' fees, the Court concluded that an award against a State of a fee could include an enhancement for delay in payment. (Similarly, Congress has authorized

an award against the United States to include an award of interest to compensate for delay in payment. 42 U.S.C. § 2000e–16(d).)

5. May attorneys' fees be awarded against state court judges? Supreme Court of Virginia v. Consumers Union, 446 U.S. 719, 100 S.Ct. 1967, 64 L.Ed.2d 641 (1980), held that state court judges could be liable under section 1988 for attorneys' fees in their capacity as the enforcement mechanism for state professional responsibility rules but not for acts undertaken in their legislative capacity to promulgate rules for attorneys' professional conduct. Thus the Court reversed an award of attorneys' fees against the Virginia Supreme Court and its members which was premised on legislative acts and omissions, specifically the failure to modify a ban on lawyer advertising in the Virginia Code of Professional Responsibility. In Pulliam v. Allen, 466 U.S. 522, 104 S.Ct. 1970, 80 L.Ed.2d 565 (1984), the Court affirmed an attorneys' fee award against a state magistrate who was enjoined from unconstitutionally imposing bail on persons arrested for nonjailable offenses and of incarcerating persons who could not meet the bail. Because congressional intent "could hardly be more plain," the Court rejected the contention that attorneys' fees were the functional equivalent of monetary damages, which were indisputably prohibited by judicial immunity.

## C. THE MEASURE OF THE FEES

Once a court has decided that fees should be awarded in a particular case, it must determine what is a "reasonable" fee under the pertinent statute. Courts have had greater leeway in determining how to calculate fees than even the elastic concept "reasonable" suggests. Prior to the 1970s, many courts awarded attorney's fees as they would a contingency fee, based on a "reasonable" percentage of the recovery. More recently, courts have tended to adopt the "lodestar" formulation, which entails multiplying compensable hours by an hourly rate. In making the calculation, courts have discretion to adjust the lodestar for such factors as risk of losing the case or unusually poor representation by the attorney.

For example, if an attorney spent 2,000 hours on a matter, much of the time may have been spent in administrative proceedings or causes of action that a court would deem uncompensable under a fee statute or insufficiently related to work covered by a fee statute to be reimbursed. Hence, compensable hours might easily be reduced to 500. A court may also exercise wide latitude in calculating the hourly rate. The attorney in this controversy may be ten years out of law school, doing work and carrying responsibilities commensurate to a junior partner at a law firm in a large city who commands $150 per hour, or she may work for a public interest firm where salary plus overhead may amount to only $30 per hour. The higher figures would make the lodestar $300,000 (2000 hours × $150) while the lower would make it $15,000 (500 hours × $30). This variation may be augmented further if the court makes adjustments to the lodestar. If the chance of victory were 1 in 3, the $300,000 lodestar could be increased by a factor of three to $900,000.

Conversely, if the court disregarded the risk of losing the case and instead elected to penalize the attorney for poor performance, the $15,000 lodestar could be halved to $7,500. Bear in mind that, at the beginning of a case, the attorney has no way of knowing what the fee award will be since a court will make an award determination only after the suit has been resolved on the merits.

In many instances, judges do not have the range of discretion that these numbers suggest. In some statutes, the legislature has mandated a specific result. E.g., 42 U.S.C. § 406(b)(1)(setting 25% of recovery as ceiling in social security disability cases). Sometimes, courts have developed structured methods for calculating fees which Congress in turn has incorporated into new fees legislation. See Blanchard v. Bergeron, 489 U.S. 87, 109 S.Ct. 939, 103 L.Ed.2d 67 (1989). Nonetheless, substantial areas for judicial interpretation remain.

## 1. WHAT WORK IS COMPENSABLE?

### SULLIVAN v. HUDSON

Supreme Court of the United States, 1989.
490 U.S. 877, 109 S.Ct. 2248, 104 L.Ed.2d 941.

JUSTICE O'CONNOR delivered the opinion of the Court.

The issue before us in this case is whether a Social Security claimant is entitled to an award of attorney's fees under the Equal Access to Justice Act [28 U.S.C. § 2412] for representation provided during administrative proceedings held pursuant to a district court order remanding the action to the Secretary of Health and Human Services. * * *

II

In 1980, Congress passed the EAJA in response to its concern that persons "may be deterred from seeking review of, or defending against, unreasonable governmental action because of the expense involved in securing the vindication of their rights." * * *

The EAJA was designed to rectify this situation by providing for an award of a reasonable attorney's fee to a "prevailing party" in a "civil action" or "adversary adjudication" unless the position taken by the United States in the proceeding at issue "was substantially justified" or "special circumstances make an award unjust." That portion of the Act applicable to "civil actions" provides, as amended, in relevant part that

> [e]xcept as otherwise specifically provided by statute, a court shall award to a prevailing party other than the United States fees and other expenses ... incurred by that party in any civil action ... including proceedings for judicial review of agency action, brought by or against the United States in any court having jurisdiction of that action, unless the court finds that the position of the United States was substantially justified or that special circumstances make an award unjust.

Application of this provision to respondent's situation here requires brief consideration of the structure of administrative proceedings and judicial review under the Social Security Act. [The Court explained that under this Act, the relationship between the reviewing court and the agency was particularly close.] * * *

The detailed provisions for the transfer of proceedings from the courts to the Secretary and for the filing of the Secretary's subsequent findings with the court suggest a degree of direct interaction between a federal court and an administrative agency alien to traditional review of agency action under the Administrative Procedure Act. As one source puts it:

> The remand power places the courts, not in their accustomed role as external overseers of the administrative process, making sure that it stays within legal bounds, but virtually as coparticipants in the process, exercising ground-level discretion of the same order as that exercised by ALJs and the Appeals Council when they act upon a request to reopen a decision on the basis of new and material evidence.

J. Mashaw [et al.], Social Security Hearings and Appeals 133 (1978).

Where a court finds that the Secretary has committed a legal or factual error in evaluating a particular claim, the district court's remand order will often include detailed instructions concerning the scope of the remand, the evidence to be adduced, and the legal or factual issues to be addressed. * * * Deviation from the court's remand order in the subsequent administrative proceedings is itself legal error, subject to reversal on further judicial review. In many remand situations, the court will retain jurisdiction over the action pending the Secretary's decision and its filing with the court. The court retains the power in such situations to assure that its prior mandate is effectuated.

Two points important to the application of the EAJA emerge from the interaction of the mechanisms for judicial review of Social Security benefits determinations and the EAJA. First, in a case such as this one, where a court's remand to the agency for further administrative proceedings does not necessarily dictate the receipt of benefits, the claimant will not normally attain "prevailing party" status * * * until after the result of the administrative proceedings is known. * * *

Second, the EAJA provides that an application for fees must be filed with the court "within thirty days of final judgment in the action." * * * The Secretary concedes that a remand order from a district court to the agency is not a final determination of the civil action and that the district court "retains jurisdiction to review any determination rendered on remand."

Thus, for purposes of the EAJA, the Social Security claimant's status as a prevailing party and the final judgment in her "civil action . . . for review of agency action" are often completely dependent on the successful completion of the remand proceedings before the Secretary.

Moreover, the remanding court continues to retain jurisdiction over the action within the meaning of the EAJA, and may exercise that jurisdiction to determine if its legal instructions on remand have been followed by the Secretary. Our past decisions interpreting other fee-shifting provisions make clear that where administrative proceedings are intimately tied to the resolution of the judicial action and necessary to the attainment of the results Congress sought to promote by providing for fees, they should be considered part and parcel of the action for which fees may be awarded.

In Pennsylvania v. Delaware Valley Citizens' Council, 478 U.S. 546, 106 S.Ct. 3088, 92 L.Ed.2d 439 (1986), we considered whether the costs of representation before federal and state administrative agencies in defense of the provisions of a consent decree entered under the Clean Air Act were compensable under the fee-shifting provision of that statute. Section 304(d) of the Clean Air Act provides for the award of a reasonable attorney fee in conjunction with "any final order in any action brought pursuant to" certain provisions of the Act. In *Delaware Valley,* we rejected the contention that the word "action" in the fee-shifting provision should be read narrowly to exclude all proceedings which could be plausibly characterized as "non-judicial." We indicated that

> [a]lthough it is true that the proceedings [at issue] were not "judicial" in the sense that they did not occur in a courtroom or involve "traditional" legal work such as examination of witnesses or selection of jurors for trial, the work done by counsel in these two phases was as necessary to the attainment of adequate relief for their client as was all of their earlier work in the courtroom which secured Delaware Valley's initial success in obtaining the consent decree.

Similarly, in New York Gaslight Club, Inc. v. Carey, 447 U.S. 54, 100 S.Ct. 2024, 64 L.Ed.2d 723 (1980), we held that under the fee-shifting provision of Title VII, 42 U.S.C. section 2000e–5(k), a federal court could award attorney's fees for services performed in state administrative and judicial enforcement proceedings. We noted that the words of the statute, authorizing "the court" to award attorney's fees "[i]n any action or proceeding under this title," could be read to include only federal administrative or judicial proceedings. Looking to the entire structure of Title VII, we observed that Congress had mandated initial resort to state and local remedies, and that "Congress viewed proceedings before the EEOC and in federal court as supplements to available state remedies for employment discrimination." Given this interlocking system of judicial and administrative avenues to relief, we concluded that the exclusion of state and local administrative proceedings from the fee provisions would clearly clash with the congressional design behind the statutory scheme whose enforcement the fee-shifting provisions was designed to promote. See also, Webb v. Dyer County Board of Education, 471 U.S. 234, 243, 105 S.Ct. 1923, 1928, 85 L.Ed.2d 233 (1985)(work performed in administrative proceedings that is "both useful and of a type ordinarily necessary to advance civil rights litigation" may be compensable under section 1988).

We think the principles we found persuasive in *Delaware Valley* and *Carey* are controlling here. As in *Delaware Valley,* the administrative proceedings on remand in this case were "crucial to the vindication of [respondent's] rights." *Delaware Valley,* supra, at 561, 106 S.Ct. at 3096. No fee award at all would have been available to respondent absent successful conclusion of the remand proceedings, and the services of an attorney may be necessary both to ensure compliance with the District Court's order in the administrative proceedings themselves, and to prepare for any further proceedings before the district court to verify such compliance. In addition, as we did in *Carey,* we must endeavor to interpret the fee statute in light of the statutory provisions it was designed to effectuate. Given the "mandatory" nature of the administrative proceedings at issue here, and their close relation in law and fact to the issues before the District Court on judicial review, we find it difficult to ascribe to Congress an intent to throw the Social Security claimant a lifeline that it knew was a foot short. Indeed, the incentive which such a system would create for attorneys to abandon claimants after judicial remand runs directly counter to long established ethical canons of the legal profession. See, American Bar Association, Model Rules of Professional Conduct, Rule 1.16, pp. 53–55 (1984). Given the anomalous nature of this result, and its frustration of the very purposes behind the EAJA itself, Congress cannot lightly be assumed to have intended it. Since the judicial review provisions of the Social Security Act contemplate an ongoing civil action of which the remand proceedings are but a part, and the EAJA allows "any court having jurisdiction of that action" to award fees, 28 U.S.C. § 2412(d)(1)(A), we think the statute, read in light of its purpose "to diminish the deterrent effect of seeking review of, or defending against, governmental action," permits a court to award fees for services performed on remand before the Social Security Administration. Where a court finds that the Secretary's position on judicial review was not substantially justified within the meaning of the EAJA, see, Pierce v. Underwood, 487 U.S. 552, 108 S.Ct. 2541, 101 L.Ed.2d 490 (1988), it is within the court's discretion to conclude that representation on remand was necessary to the effectuation of its mandate and to the ultimate vindication of the claimant's rights, and that an award of fees for work performed in the administrative proceedings is therefore proper.

The Secretary mounts two interrelated challenges to this interpretation of section 2412(d)(1)(A). While the Secretary's contentions are not without some force, neither rises to the level necessary to oust what we think is the most reasonable interpretation of the statute in light of its manifest purpose. First, the Secretary argues that plain meaning of the term "civil action" in section 2412(d)(1)(A) excludes any proceedings outside of a court of law. Of course, if the plain language of the EAJA evinced a congressional intent to preclude the interpretation we reach here, that would be the end of the matter. In support of this proposition, the Secretary points out that the " '[t]erm [action] in its usual legal sense means a suit brought in a court; a formal complaint within the jurisdiction of a court of law.' " Second, the Secretary notes that Congress did authorize EAJA fee awards under 5 U.S.C. section 504(a)(1) (1982 ed., Supp. V) where an agency "conducts an adversary adjudication," and that an adversary adjudication is defined in section 504(b)(1)(C)(1982 ed., Supp. V) as "an adjudication ... in which the position of the United States is represented by counsel or otherwise." Under 28 U.S.C. section 2412(d)(3)(1982 ed., Supp. V) a court is empowered to award fees for representation before an agency to a party who prevails in an action for judicial review to "the same extent authorized in [5 U.S.C. section 504(a) ]." Thus, the Secretary concludes that since benefits proceedings before the Secretary and his designates are nonadversarial, and a court is explicitly empowered to award fees for agency proceedings where such proceedings satisfy the requirements of section 504(a)(1), the principle of *expressio unius est exclusio alterius* [the mention of one is the exclusion of another] applies, and a court may never award fees for time spent in nonadversarial administrative proceedings.

We agree with the Secretary that for purposes of the EAJA Social Security benefit proceedings are not "adversarial" within the meaning of section 504(b)(1)(C) either initially or on remand from a court. The plain language of the statute requires that the United States be represented by "counsel or otherwise," and neither is true in this context. Nonetheless, we disagree with the conclusion the Secretary would draw from this fact. First, as *Delaware Valley, Webb,* and *Carey* indicate, administrative proceedings may be so intimately connected with judicial proceedings as to be considered part of the "civil action" for purposes of a fee award. This is particularly so in the Social Security context where "a suit [has been] brought in a court" and "a formal complaint within the jurisdiction of a court of law," remains pending and depends for its resolution upon the outcome of the administrative proceedings. Second, we disagree with the Secretary's submission that a negative implication can be drawn from the power granted a court to award fees based on representation in a prior adversary adjudication before an agency. Section 2412(d)(3) provides that "[i]n awarding fees and other expenses under this subsection to a prevailing party in any action for judicial review of an adversary adjudication" the court may award fees to the same extent that they would have been available before the agency itself under section 504(a)(1). On its face, the provision says nothing about the power of a court to award reasonable fees for representation in a *nonadversarial* adjudication which is wholly ancillary to a civil action for judicial review. That Congress carved the world of EAJA proceedings into "adversary adjudications" and "civil actions" does not necessarily speak to, let alone preclude, a reading of the term "civil action" which includes administrative proceedings necessary to the completion of a civil action.

We conclude that where a court orders a remand to the Secretary in a benefits litigation and retains continuing jurisdiction over the case pending a decision from the Secretary which will determine the claimant's entitlement to benefits, the proceedings on remand are an integral part of the "civil action" for judicial review and thus attorney's fees for representation on remand are available subject to the other limitations in the EAJA. * * *

JUSTICE WHITE, with whom THE CHIEF JUSTICE, JUSTICE SCALIA, and JUSTICE KENNEDY join, dissenting.

* * * [T]he majority looks to § 2412(d)(1)(A), the provision of the EAJA dealing with fees incurred in "civil actions," as the basis for authorizing the award of fees at issue here. The majority reasons that "[s]ince the judicial review provisions of the Social Security Act contemplate an ongoing civil action of which the remand proceedings are but a part, and section 2412(d)(1)(A) of the EAJA allows 'any court having jurisdiction of that action' to award fees, ... the statute ... permits a court to award fees for services performed on remand before the Social Security Administration." In so construing section 2412, however, the majority * * *—in its effort to reach the result it desires, * * * ignores the plain language of the statute it is construing.

Section 2412(d)(1)(A), by its terms, does not authorize the recovery of fees incurred in proceedings on remand before the Social Security Administration. That section provides in relevant part that "a court shall award to a prevailing party other than the United States fees and other expenses ... *incurred by that party in any civil action* ..., including proceedings for judicial review of agency action, brought by or against the United States in any court having jurisdiction of that action" (Emphasis added). The plain meaning of "civil action" is a proceeding in a court, see, Black's Law Dictionary 26, 222 (5th ed. 1979); Fed.Rules Civ.Proc. 2, 3, and any argument to the contrary is foreclosed by the statute itself—the civil action must be one brought "in any court having jurisdiction." Clearly, the Social Security Administration is not a court, see, 28 U.S.C. section 451 (defining "court of the United States"), and so section 2412 does not apply to fees incurred in proceedings before the Social Security Administration. * * *

Section 504, not section 2412, is the provision of the EAJA that governs the recovery of fees in proceedings before administrative agencies; indeed, Congress was careful to place section 504 in Title 5 of the United States Code, which governs procedures before administrative agencies, while placing section 2412 in Title 28, which governs procedures before the courts. The lack of any authorization in section 504(a)(1) for fees under the present circumstances provides further confirmation of the plain meaning of the EAJA. As the majority holds, the fee authorization in section 504(a)(1) is limited to adversary administrative adjudications, which do not include the nonadversary proceedings before the Social Security Administration. Applying the maxim of statutory construction *expressio unius est exclusio alterius,* the express congressional authorization for recovery of fees in adversary agency adjudications coupled with the lack of authorization for recovery of fees in nonadversary adjudications indicates Congress' intent not to authorize recovery of fees in nonadversary agency adjudications.

The majority's dismissal of these arguments misses the mark. First, the majority takes the position that a "civil action" includes remand proceedings before the Social Security Administration because a formal complaint remains pending in court and depends on the outcome of the administrative proceeding for its resolution. But the mere retention of jurisdiction while the case is on remand before the agency does not transform fees incurred before the agency into fees incurred before the court. It was the Social Security Administration that conducted the proceedings on remand and it was the Social Security Administration that ultimately made the award of benefits in this case, not the District Court. All the District Court did was to dismiss respondent's petition for judicial review once the agency had made its award on remand, which surely is not enough to characterize the agency proceedings as part of an ongoing civil action in court.

In this regard, the majority's reliance on [*Delaware Valley*] and [*Carey*] is misplaced. In *Delaware Valley,* we interpreted section 304(d) of the Clean Air Act, 42 U.S.C. section 7604(d), which allows the "court" to award fees "in issuing any final order in any action brought pursuant to" section 304(a) of the Act, as allowing recovery of fees incurred in enforcing a consent decree in administrative proceedings. But that Act applied to fee awards in "any action" brought under the Act, and did not expressly limit the award to fees "incurred ... in any civil action ... brought ... in any court," as the statute does here. Moreover, the legislative history of the Clean Air Act equated "action" with "proceeding," suggesting a broader meaning to the term, and certainly did not expressly reject the construction we gave to the statute. The same is true of *Carey,* in which this Court construed 42 U.S.C. section 2000e–5(k), authorizing "the court" to award fees "[i]n any action or proceeding under this title," as well as Webb v. Dyer County Bd. of Education, 471 U.S. 234, 243, 105 S.Ct. 1923, 1928, 85 L.Ed.2d 233 (1985)(construing 42 U.S.C. section 1988), and North Carolina Dept. of Transportation v. Crest Street Community Council, Inc., 479 U.S. 6, 15, 107 S.Ct. 336, 342, 93 L.Ed.2d 188 (1986)(same) * * * . In short, these decisions have no application to the EAJA because its plain language indicates otherwise * * * .

I find the statutory language plainly and unambiguously to preclude the construction given the EAJA by the majority. But even if the language of the statute might somehow be seen as ambiguous, its legislative history makes unmistakably clear that Congress did not intend fees to be awarded under the EAJA for work done in proceedings on remand before the Social Security Administration.

Little need be said because the legislative history is so straightforward. That history makes clear that in reenacting the EAJA, Congress considered and rejected a provision that would have extended the EAJA to administrative proceedings before the Social Security Administration, including those on remand from district court. * * * Senator Heflin, an active supporter of the provision extending the EAJA to Social Security proceedings, acknowledged that this effort failed because of "institutional opposition." He stated: "While I believe this is an area ripe for protection, political realities dictate otherwise. And this seems to be a fight which will have to be fought another day." 131 Cong.Rec. 20350 (1985).

There is no suggestion in the legislative history that remand proceedings were somehow included elsewhere in the EAJA. To the contrary, the House Report on the 1985 reenactment expressly states that fees cannot be recovered under the EAJA in precisely the situation facing the Court. The House Report reads as follows:

> The court will usually decline to make an award upon the remand decision because the remand order did not yet make the applicant a "prevailing party" and therefore eligible under the EAJA ... [T]he remand decision is not a "final judgment," nor is the agency decision after remand. Instead, the District Court should enter an order affirming, modifying, or reversing the final HHS decision, and this will usually be the final judgment that starts the 30 days running.... As ... courts have found the only fees which will be available will be for those activities *undertaken in connection with the initial proceedings and not those associated with the administrative proceeding.*

H.R.Rep. No. 99–120, pt. 1, p. 19–20 (1985)(emphasis added).

This discussion does not, as respondent asserts, refer only to the initial administrative proceeding and not the proceeding on remand. Instead, this language affirms what the language of the EAJA likewise makes plain: that the EAJA does not authorize recovery of fees incurred in remand proceedings before the Social Security Administration.

Our duty is to apply statutes as they were enacted by Congress, not to take it upon ourselves to overcome the "political realities" that blocked what we might consider to be good legislation. However desirable it might be as a matter of policy for Social Security claimants to be able to recover attorney's fees for proceedings on remand before the agency, that is not the statute that Congress enacted. Therefore, I dissent.

## *Notes*

1. The citizen suit provisions of many statutes allowing fees require that a notice letter be sent so many days in advance of suit warning that the suit will be filed unless the problem is cleared up. Is the time spent in researching and writing that letter compensable? SPIRG of New Jersey v. Anchor Thread, 26 Env't.L.Rep. 20, 665 (D.N.J.1984). See also Tolentino v. Friedman, 46 F.3d 645 (7th Cir.)(allowing fees for letters and notices sent under Fair Debt Collection Practices Act), cert. denied, ___ U.S. ___, 115 S.Ct. 2613, 132 L.Ed.2d 856 (1995).

2. As *Sullivan* indicates, often an aggrieved party will seek redress in an administrative forum before filing suit in a court. Assume that the party obtains relief in that forum. Should a court have the power to award fees for the work done in that forum? Should it make a difference whether the judicial action is filed before or after the administrative proceeding is completed? Compare New York Gaslight Club, Inc. v. Carey, 447 U.S. 54, 100 S.Ct. 2024, 64 L.Ed.2d 723 (1980)(fees awarded where judicial action filed before plaintiff prevailed in administrative proceeding) with North Carolina Department of Transportation v. Crest Street Community Council, Inc., 479 U.S. 6, 107 S.Ct. 336, 93 L.Ed.2d 188 (1986)(fees may not be awarded where judicial action not filed until after plaintiff prevailed in administrative proceeding). Should it make a difference whether aggrieved parties are required to exhaust their administrative remedies before filing a judicial action? Compare New York Gaslight Club, Inc. v. Carey, 447 U.S. 54, 100 S.Ct. 2024, 64 L.Ed.2d 723 (1980)(fees awarded for work performed in administrative forum where administrative remedies had to be exhausted before pursuing judicial remedy) with Webb v. Dyer County Board of Education, 471 U.S. 234, 105 S.Ct. 1923, 85 L.Ed.2d 233 (1985)(no fees awarded for work performed in administrative forum where plaintiff pursued optional administrative remedy before filing in court). For criticism of having the availability of fees turn on these distinctions, see Marjorie A. Silver, Evening the Odds: The Case for Attorneys' Fee Awards for Administrative Resolution of Title VI and Title VII Disputes, 67 N.C.L.Rev. 379 (1989).

3. Small distinctions continue to matter in determining whether fees for legal work performed before administrative agencies will be compensable. In Ardestani v. INS, 502 U.S. 129, 112 S.Ct. 515, 116 L.Ed.2d 496 (1991), the Supreme Court rejected a request for fees under the EAJA. The holding was that fees incurred in INS administrative deportation proceedings were not eligible for reimbursement under the EAJA because the proceedings did not occur "under section 554" of the Administrative Procedure Act, even though that section states that it applies to "every case of adjudication required by statute to be determined on the record after opportunity for an agency hearing." Justice O'Connor's majority opinion took a plain language approach to the statutory interpretation question to decide that the EAJA did not reach the INS proceedings. She ignored a dissent that relied heavily on her majority opinion in *Sullivan v. Hudson*; the dissenters argued that once the trial court determined that the government's position was not substantially justified, the specific legislative history and overall purposes of the EAJA strongly favored the availability of attorney's fees in deportation proceedings.

4. Another series of complications in determining what work is compensable arises when a suit involves more than one claim and:

(a) all the claims have attorney fee shifting provisions, but the plaintiff prevails on only one or a few of them;

(b) only some of the claims litigated provide for counsels' fees, yet the plaintiff prevails on all claims;

(c) only some of the claims allow fee shifting, and the plaintiff prevails only on those claims permitting fee shifting;

(d) only some of the claims allow fee shifting, and the plaintiff prevails only on those claims not permitting fee shifting;

(e) there are multiple claims, some of which authorize fees, yet the court declines to resolve a claim, because it involves constitutional issues or a difficult, novel issue the court prefers to postpone deciding for another time.

Should any fees be awarded in these situations? What work is compensable? For a case sorting out how to award fees in a diversity case involving state law claims, only some of which permit fee-shifting, see Schultz v. Hembree, 975 F.2d 572 (9th Cir.1992). See also Mary F. Derfner & Arthur D. Wolf, 1 Court Awarded Attorney Fees, 12–1—12–30 (1994).

5. Frequently in an institutional reform case, over half the time in a controversy is spent after judgment and relatively little of that time is spent in court or drafting papers for court. Much more time is consumed in determining what defendants can do, helping them to do it and checking that they have done it. What theories can you develop to justify or deny compensation for such time? Assume that the case involves conditions in an institution that will take years or even a decade or more to correct. Does the plaintiff's lawyer have a guarantee of compensation for any time spent watch-dogging that institution as to matters that are somehow connected to the suit? Compare, e.g., Turner v. Orr, 785 F.2d 1498 (11th Cir.1986)(attorneys' fees awarded to plaintiff to cover the cost of monitoring and enforcing defendant's compliance with a consent judgment, and, presumably, such fees were to cover the lifetime of the judgment) with Halderman v. Pennhurst State School & Hospital, 49 F.3d 939 (3d Cir.1995)(no fees for time spent in public relations efforts). Recall the material from chapter 3; must the order or consent decree specifically provide that the plaintiff's attorney will be compensated for this time?

6. Should the time spent preparing and litigating the fee application be compensable? The Supreme Court has held that once a court determines under the Equal Access to Justice Act that the government's position was not substantially justified, a second finding regarding substantial justification is not necessary to award fees for any litigation over the fee award. INS v. Jean, 496 U.S. 154, 110 S.Ct. 2316, 110 L.Ed.2d 134 (1990). However, the Ninth Circuit has approved reducing the "fees-on-fees" in proportion to the amount actually awarded for work on the underlying merits of the case. Thompson v. Gomez, 45 F.3d 1365 (9th Cir.1995)(awarding 87.2% of fees on fees where plaintiffs received 87.2% of fees claimed).

7. Although fee requests need to be filed in a timely manner, it may not be utterly clear when the time begins to run. For example, in a case like *Sullivan v. Hudson*, where there is a remand to an administrative agency, when must the plaintiff file for fees? In Melkonyan v. Sullivan, 501 U.S. 89, 111 S.Ct. 2157, 115 L.Ed.2d 78 (1991), the Supreme Court held that the filing period for an attorney's fee application under the EAJA commences after expiration of the time to appeal a final judgment rendered by a court that terminates the action for which EAJA fees may be received. The time period does not commence until after entry of the administrative agency order following remand from the district court, which may well come after the time to appeal the court's final judgment. In Shalala v. Schaefer, 509

U.S. ___, 113 S.Ct. 2625, 125 L.Ed.2d 239 (1993), the Court reiterated that the 30–day time limit is triggered by the entry of judgment rather than final disposition on remand. The Court also eliminated a source of confusion about the application of this rule under the Social Security Act by requiring district courts to enter a judgment whether or not an order of remand is also issued. See also F.R.Civ.P. 54(d)(2)(1993 amendments establish procedures and deadlines for presenting claims for attorneys' fees).

## 2. THE RATE OF COMPENSATION

Ordinarily less work is compensable than would be billed by an attorney in private practice handling the same matter. In this sense, "reasonable" fees differ from market practices. What about the calculation of the amount of the fees for the work that is compensable? Should the fee be that which an attorney in private practice would bill a prosperous client or what cost the firm actually incurs in providing the legal work? Can the court enhance the award due to factors such as providing an especially high quality of legal work? These questions are vitally important to public interest firms which may have to rely on court-awarded fees for survival; they also have an influence on the willingness of private firms to take on *pro bono* cases.

In Blum v. Stenson, 465 U.S. 886, 104 S.Ct. 1541, 79 L.Ed.2d 891 (1984), the Supreme Court held that enhancements for quality of work should only rarely be made and only where there is specific evidence of exceptional quality. In addition, the court held that the number of people benefitted as a result of the lawsuit was not relevant when the fee was provided for by statute. "Unlike the calculation of attorney's fees under the 'common fund doctrine' where a reasonable fee is based on a percentage of the fund bestowed on the class, a reasonable fee under § 1988 reflects the amount of attorney time reasonably expended on the litigation." See Dan B. Dobbs, Reducing Attorney's Fees for Partial Success: A Comment on *Hensley* and *Blum,* 1986 Wis.L.Rev. 835.

*Blum* also held that the appropriate hourly rate awarded under the Civil Rights Attorney's Fees Awards Act of 1976, 42 U.S.C. § 1988, should be based on prevailing market rates rather than rates commensurate with the actual cost of providing the service and that these rates should apply to all attorneys, whether they work for a private firm or a public interest group. In a similar vein, the Court has held that a "reasonable attorney's fee" may include separate compensation for paralegals, law clerks, and recent law graduates at prevailing market rates, where the practice in the relevant market is to bill for such work separately. Missouri v. Jenkins (*Jenkins I*), 491 U.S. 274, 109 S.Ct. 2463, 105 L.Ed.2d 229 (1989). However, absent specific statutory authorization, the Court has held that the "reasonable attorney's fee" does not include the fees charged by an expert witness either to testify at trial, Crawford Fitting Co. v. J.T. Gibbons, Inc., 482 U.S. 437, 107 S.Ct. 2494, 96 L.Ed.2d 385 (1987), or to help an attorney prepare for trial, West Virginia University Hospitals, Inc. v. Casey, 499 U.S. 83, 111 S.Ct. 1138, 113 L.Ed.2d 68 (1991). (For one example of such authorization in response to these decisions, see The Civil Rights Act of 1991, 42 U.S.C.A. § 1988(c).)

The Supreme Court has frequently addressed the propriety of making other upward or downward adjustments:

### *(a) Superior Performance*

In Pennsylvania v. Delaware Valley Citizens' Council for Clean Air, 478 U.S. 546, 565–566, 106 S.Ct. 3088, 3098, 92 L.Ed.2d 439, 456–457 (1986), the Court refined *Blum's* holding:

> A strong presumption that the lodestar figure—the product of reasonable hours times a reasonable rate—represents a "reasonable" fee is wholly consistent with the rationale behind the usual fee-shifting statute, including the one in the present case. These statutes were not designed as a form of economic relief to improve the financial lot of attorneys, nor were they intended to replicate exactly the fee an attorney could earn through a private fee arrangement with his client. Instead, the aim of such statutes was to enable private parties to obtain legal help in seeking redress for injuries resulting from the actual or threatened violation of specific federal laws. Hence, if plaintiffs, such as Delaware Valley, find it possible to engage a lawyer based on the statutory assurance that he will be paid a "reasonable fee," the purpose behind the fee-shifting statute has been satisfied.
>
> Moreover, when an attorney first accepts a case and agrees to represent the client, he obligates himself to perform to the best of his ability and to produce the best possible results commensurate with his skill and his client's interests. Calculating the fee award in a manner that accounts for these factors, either in determining the reasonable number of hours expended on the litigation or in setting the reasonable hourly rate, thus adequately compensates the attorney, and leaves very little room for enhancing the award based on his post-engagement performance. In short, the lodestar figure includes most, if not all, of the relevant factors comprising a "reasonable" attorney's fee, and it is unnecessary to enhance the fee for superior performance in order to serve the statutory purpose of enabling plaintiffs to secure legal assistance.

### *(b) Risk of Loss Contingency*

In City of Burlington v. Dague, 505 U.S. 557, 112 S.Ct. 2638, 120 L.Ed.2d 449 (1992), the Supreme Court dealt with adjusting the lodestar, under a fee-shifting statute, based on the contingency that there is a risk of losing the case:

> We note at the outset that an enhancement for contingency would likely duplicate in substantial part factors already subsumed in the lodestar. The risk of loss in a particular case (and, therefore, the attorney's contingent risk) is the product of two factors: (1) the legal and factual merits of the claim, and (2) the difficulty of

establishing those merits. The second factor, however, is ordinarily reflected in the lodestar—either in the higher number of hours expended to overcome the difficulty, or in the higher hourly rate of the attorney skilled and experienced enough to do so. Taking account of it again through lodestar enhancement amounts to double-counting.

The first factor (relative merits of the claim) is not reflected in the lodestar, but there are good reasons why it should play no part in the calculation of the award. * * * [T]he consequence of awarding contingency enhancement to take account of this "merits" factor would be to provide attorneys with the same incentive to bring relatively meritless claims as relatively meritorious ones. Assume, for example, two claims, one with underlying merit of 20%, the other of 80%. Absent any contingency enhancement, a contingent-fee attorney would prefer to take the latter, since he is four times more likely to be paid. But with a contingency enhancement, this preference will disappear: the enhancement for the 20% claim would be a multiplier of 5 ($^{100}/_{20}$), which is quadruple the 1.25 multiplier ($^{100}/_{80}$) that would attach to the 80% claim. Thus, enhancement for the contingency risk posed by each case would encourage meritorious claims to be brought, but only at the social cost of indiscriminately encouraging nonmeritorious claims to be brought as well. * * *

[W]e perceive no * * * basis, fairly derivable from the fee-shifting statutes, by which contingency enhancement, if adopted, could be restricted to fewer than all contingent-fee cases. And we see a number of reasons for concluding that no contingency enhancement whatever is compatible with the fee- shifting statutes at issue. First, just as the statutory language limiting fees to prevailing (or substantially prevailing) parties bars a prevailing plaintiff from recovering fees relating to claims on which he lost, so should it bar a prevailing plaintiff from recovering for the risk of loss. An attorney operating on a contingency-fee basis pools the risks presented by his various cases: cases that turn out to be successful pay for the time he gambled on those that did not. To award a contingency enhancement under a fee-shifting statute would in effect pay for the attorney's time (or anticipated time) in cases where his client does not prevail.

Second, * * * "we have generally turned away from the contingent-fee model"—which would make the fee award a percentage of the value of the relief awarded in the primary action—"to the lodestar model." We have done so, it must be noted, even though the lodestar model often (perhaps, generally) results in a larger fee award than the contingent-fee model. * * *

Contingency enhancement is a feature inherent in the contingent-fee model (since attorneys factor in the particular risks of a case in negotiating their fee and in deciding whether to accept the case). To engraft this feature onto the lodestar model would be to concoct a hybrid scheme that resorts to the contingent-fee model to increase a fee award but not to reduce it. Contingency enhancement is therefore not consistent with our general rejection of the contingent-fee model for fee awards, nor is it necessary to the determination of a reasonable fee.

### *(c) Contingency Fee Contract*

In Blanchard v. Bergeron, 489 U.S. 87, 109 S.Ct. 939, 103 L.Ed.2d 67 (1989), the Court was faced with whether an award of attorney's fees under section 1988 was limited to no more than the amount provided in the plaintiff's contingent-fee arrangement with the attorney. In this case, the 40% contingency contract would have yielded a $4,000 fee on a $10,000 recovery; the district court had calculated the reasonable fee to be $7,500 plus costs. The Court unanimously[a] held:

> As we understand § 1988's provision for allowing a "reasonable attorney's fee," it contemplates reasonable compensation, in light of all of the circumstances, for the time and effort expended by the attorney for the prevailing plaintiff, no more and no less. Should a fee agreement provide less than a reasonable fee calculated in this manner, the defendant should nevertheless be required to pay the higher amount. The defendant is not, however, required to pay the amount called for in a contingent fee contract if it is more than a reasonable fee calculated in the usual way. It is true that the purpose of § 1988 was to make sure that competent counsel was available to civil rights plaintiffs, and it is of course arguable that if a plaintiff is able to secure an attorney on the basis of a contingent or other fee agreement, the purpose of the statute is served if the plaintiff is bound by his contract. On that basis, however, the plaintiff should recover nothing from the defendant, which would be plainly contrary to the statute. And Congress implemented its purpose by broadly requiring all defendants to pay a reasonable fee to all prevailing plaintiffs, if ordered to do so by the court. Thus it is that a plaintiff's recovery will not be reduced by what he must pay his counsel. Plaintiffs who can afford to hire their own lawyers, as well as impecunious litigants, may take advantage of this provision. And where there are lawyers or organizations that will take a plaintiff's case without compensation, that fact does not bar the award of a reasonable fee. All of this is consistent with and reflects our decisions in cases involving court-awarded attorney's fees. * * *
>
> If a contingent fee agreement were to govern as a strict limitation on the award of attorney's fees, an undesirable emphasis might be placed on the importance of the recovery of damages in civil rights litigation. The intention of Congress was to encourage successful civil rights litigation, not to create a special incentive to

a. Justice Scalia wrote a separate concurring opinion on a point not relevant here.

prove damages and shortchange efforts to seek effective injunctive or declaratory relief. Affirming the decision below would create an artificial disincentive for an attorney who enters into a contingent fee agreement, unsure of whether his client's claim sounded in state tort law or in federal civil rights, from fully exploring all possible avenues of relief. Section 1988 makes no distinction between actions for damages and suits for equitable relief. Congress has elected to encourage meritorious civil rights claims because of the benefits of such litigation for the named plaintiff and for society at large, irrespective of whether the action seeks monetary damages.

It should also be noted that we have not accepted the contention that fee awards in § 1983 damages cases should be modeled upon the contingent fee arrangements used in personal injury litigation. "[W]e reject the notion that a civil rights action for damages constitutes nothing more than a private tort suit benefiting only the individual plaintiffs whose rights were violated. Unlike most private tort litigants, a civil rights plaintiff seeks to vindicate important civil and constitutional rights that cannot be valued solely in monetary terms." City of Riverside v. Rivera, 477 U.S. 561, 574, 106 S.Ct. 2686, 2694, 91 L.Ed.2d 466 (1986).

Respondent cautions us that refusing to limit recovery to the amount of the contingency agreement will result in a "windfall" to attorneys who accept § 1983 actions. Yet the very nature of recovery under § 1988 is designed to prevent any such "windfall." Fee awards are to be reasonable, reasonable as to billing rates and reasonable as to the number of hours spent in advancing the successful claims. Accordingly, fee awards, properly calculated, by definition will represent the reasonable worth of the services rendered in vindication of a plaintiff's civil rights claim. It is central to the awarding of attorney's fees under § 1988 that the district court judge, in his or her good judgment, make the assessment of what is a reasonable fee under the circumstances of the case. The trial judge should not be limited by the contractual fee agreement between plaintiff and counsel.

489 U.S. at 93–96, 109 S.Ct. at 944–946.

### *Notes*

1. Some lower courts have read *Dague* as requiring the lodestar to be used in all cases completely unadorned with enhancements. E.g., Morris v. American National Can Corp., 988 F.2d 50 (8th Cir.1993). However, Gomez v. Gates, 804 F.Supp. 69 (C.D.Cal.1992), reasoned that *Dague* did not reject all enhancements. It therefore awarded an enhancement to account for the undesirability of the plaintiffs and the case. (The complaint alleged that officers of the Los Angeles Police Department had used deadly force unnecessarily against the plaintiffs, who admitted that they were fleeing from the scene of a robbery they had just committed.) Florin v. Nationsbank of Georgia, 34 F.3d 560 (7th Cir.1994), allowed an enhancement for risk in a common fund case because the fee came from the class of plaintiffs and not

from the defendants. A fee awarded under state law need not follow *Dague*. E.g., Mangold v. California PUC, 67 F.3d 1470 (9th Cir.1995); Rendine v. Pantzer, 276 N.J.Super. 398, 648 A.2d 223 (N.J.Super Ct.1994).

2. For some time, it was unclear whether there was any per se rule that attorney's fees had to be proportionate to the damages recovered. In City of Riverside v. Rivera, 477 U.S. 561, 106 S.Ct. 2686, 91 L.Ed.2d 466 (1986), the Supreme Court affirmed an attorney's fee award of $245,000 where the jury awarded only $33,350 in compensatory and punitive damages. Only a plurality thought that Congress did not intend to adopt a strict proportionality rule. However, *Blanchard*, supra pp. 858–59, which on this issue was a unanimous opinion, cited *Rivera* with approval, suggesting that the plurality result is now the law.

3. In *Blanchard*, the fee the court awarded was $7,500 plus costs, rather than the $4,000 called for under the contingency contract. Suppose instead the jury in *Blanchard* awarded $100,000 in damages, making the contingency fee $40,000, but the court still set the "reasonable" statutory fee at $7500. What amount should the attorney receive in each situation? How much should the client net? See Venegas v. Mitchell, 495 U.S. 82, 110 S.Ct. 1679, 109 L.Ed.2d 74 (1990)(the statutory award does not set a ceiling on the contingency fee; it "controls what the losing defendant must pay, not what the prevailing plaintiff must pay his lawyer.") Should there be outside review of the reasonableness of the contingency fee agreement? See Newton v. Cox, 878 S.W.2d 105 (Tenn.1994) (legislature may set limit on contingency fees in medical malpractice actions). As a practical note, it is well to make written provision between the client and the law firm as to who will receive court-awarded fees. It is also prudent for lawyers to assign in writing any fees coming from their work done for the firm to avoid both disputes and possible tax problems.

4. In reasoning parallel to *Blanchard*, the Federal Circuit has held that a fee award under the EAJA is made to the prevailing party and not to the party's attorney. FDL Technologies, Inc. v. United States, 967 F.2d 1578 (Fed.Cir.1992). It made a difference because the party had filed for bankruptcy; the award became part of the assets available to all creditors. The attorney was just another unsecured creditor of the debtor.

5. Another set of questions concern whether and how a fee award should account for delay in payment. Some courts award fees on the basis of prevailing rates at the time of the award as a means of accounting for delay; others use fees prevailing at the time the work was performed and then add on interest. See, e.g., In re Telesphere International Securities Litigation, 753 F.Supp. 716 (N.D.Ill.1990). In addition, the Eighth Circuit has held that a court also may award post-judgment interest on attorney's fees accruing from the date that the trial court determined that the plaintiff class was entitled to fees, rather than the date when the fees were quantified. Jenkins v. Missouri, 931 F.2d 1273 (8th Cir.), cert. denied, 502 U.S. 925, 112 S.Ct. 338, 116 L.Ed.2d 278 (1991).

# D. CONFLICTS OF INTEREST

## IN RE FINE PAPER ANTITRUST LITIGATION

United States District Court, Eastern District of Pennsylvania, 1983.
98 F.R.D. 48, affirmed in relevant part, 751 F.2d 562 (3d Cir.).

McGLYNN, DISTRICT JUDGE.

[This opinion involves the calculation of attorneys' fees in a series of consolidated private class action anti-trust suits brought against corporations in the "fine paper" industry; the suits resulted in an overall settlement in which the defendants paid $50 million into a common fund for the compensation of the plaintiffs in the nation-wide class.] * * *

II. ORGANIZATIONAL STRUCTURE OF THE PRIVATE PLAINTIFFS' CASE

The lawyers representing the private plaintiffs' class created an organizational structure consisting of tiers of committees and subcommittees with numerous "Chairmen" and scores of "Co-chairmen" for virtually every task in the case. This arrangement succeeded in utilizing the services of over three dozen law firms and state attorneys general and resulted in enormous charges against the fund by lawyers and numerous paralegals. This top-heavy structure was a model of inefficiency and worked to the detriment of thousands of unnamed class members on whose behalf counsel purported to act. For a three-year period, approximately 97,000 hours were billed to the class—70,000 in lawyer hours and over 16,000 in paralegal hours. Most of this time, approximately 85,000 hours, was spent in the two-year period after the initial $30 million in settlements had been obtained. Such billing, most of which was at senior partner rates, resulted in an aggregate proposed lodestar of nearly $8 million and, with the application of the requested multipliers, a total fee request of over $20 million.

*(A) Formation of the Organizational Structure*

On July 18, 1977 Specks & Goldberg, Ltd. filed a complaint in the Northern District of Illinois on behalf of Herst Litho, Inc., a New York based company. * * * On October 11, 1977, Specks & Goldberg, Ltd. filed a second *Fine Paper* case in the District of Connecticut, this time on behalf of Phillip and Ruth Meroney of New Orleans. * * * Each of these actions was brought on behalf of a national class of direct purchasers of fine paper similar to the class eventually certified by the court.

After filing these two complaints, Specks circulated copies of them to several lawyers with whom he had worked in prior class actions * * * . These lawyers in turn filed actions in various United States District Courts. For example, * * * Harold Kohn filed his complaint on behalf of his firm's client in the Southern District of New York in November of 1977. Kohn testified that although his client was a member of the national class sought by Specks in his initial complaint, he decided to file his complaint because Specks "begged" him to "over a period of several months." * * *

[T]wenty-three additional cases had been filed by various lawyers, despite the fact that their clients' interests were already protected by the previously-filed class actions. Indeed, many of these complaints were filed as late as 1979, after the first $30 million of settlements had been obtained and the class already had been certified. As noted by the class objectors, the only logical reason for these new filings was to permit counsel to participate in the case and thereby to obtain attorneys' fees.

*(B) Preorganization Meetings Among Counsel*

As the complaints were being filed, Granvil I. Specks and others began planning for the distribution of patronage, that is, deciding to which firms the work assignments would be allocated. The planning appears to have begun in January 1978 in anticipation of the February 3, 1978 "organizational meeting" in Chicago * * * at which the structure of the case was formally proposed, voted upon and determined by various plaintiffs' counsel. * * *

[T]here was a meeting of plaintiffs' counsel in Atlanta, Georgia where many of the same lawyers were attending a hearing in the *Armored Car Antitrust Litigation.* This meeting was referred to by Aaron M. Fine of Philadelphia, an experienced antitrust lawyer, who wrote to Specks on March 8, 1978 to complain about not being invited to participate in the Atlanta session. Certain documents, including Mr. Fine's letter, are quoted at length because they provide some insight into the workings of the class action bar and help to demonstrate that the polestar of plaintiffs' organizational structure in this case was patronage, not efficiency:

> * * * When I asked you who was going to be on the Executive Committee, you identified lawyers in five Philadelphia firms, including Dave Berger. While I have great respect and admiration for Dave's legal abilities, I questioned you about his inclusion on the Executive Committee when we were to be excluded, in view of the fact that he had not yet to our knowledge filed a fine paper case and that we had not only filed a case, but taken an active part in obtaining the impoundment of the Grand Jury documents and in the transfer hearing before the Multidistrict Panel. You replied that Dave would certainly have to have a case on file to be on the committee and that he was selected to be on the committee because of his "position in the industry." I asked whether you meant his position in the fine paper industry, and you replied that you meant his position in the plaintiffs' antitrust industry, which may, in fact, be an apt description of what is going on. * * *

*(D) The Addition of New Law Firms and the Exclusion of Others*

The number of law firms appearing as counsel for the class continued to grow even after the organizational structure was in place. For example, eight of the petitioning firms did not become involved in the case until well after the first $30 million in settlements were in the bank and the class had been certified. Kohn repeatedly objected to the entry of additional firms, but Specks and other members of the Executive Committee nonetheless assigned work to the newcomers. Incredibly, while new counsel were being invited to participate, other counsel, including some who had been involved from the outset were frozen out of the case. * * *

*(E) The Operation of the Committee System*

It was inevitable that this type of structure would generate wasted hours on useless tasks, propagate duplication and mask outright padding. * * *

IV. The Fee Petitions

* * * The fees and expenses requested range from a low of $16,529, by Litman, Litman, Harris & Specter of Pittsburgh, to a high of $4,397,321 by Specks & Goldberg, Ltd. of Chicago. The petitions totaled $20,220,962 for attorneys' fees and $1,197,151 for expenses. * * *

At the time the fee petitions were filed, Specks and other counsel recognized that some of the fee requests were outrageous. * * * Specks called the fee petition of Saveri & Saveri, which requested fees in excess of 2 million dollars, including $650 per hour for every hour Guido Saveri spent on the case "ridiculous" and thought that the petition should be "substantially reduced and cannot be allowed." Lowell E. Sachnoff, one of the petitioning attorneys here, told Specks that many of the firm's fee petitions had "inflated lodestar time, rates, and multiples" and, accordingly, he urged co-lead counsel to make the "Herculean effort" to "sweep out the Aegean [sic] stables." * * *

IX. Guidelines

When applying the *Lindy* analysis[b] to the fee petitions in the instant case, I have had to make numerous rulings with respect to compensable hours, hourly rates and multipliers which are applicable to most—if not all—of the fee petitions. Before proceeding to a *Lindy* analysis of each individual fee petition, it would seem appropriate to outline in a general way the standards by which I measured the accuracy of the data submitted, the reasonableness of the hours charged and rates sought and the appropriateness of a multiplier for contingency and quality.

*(A) Compensable Hours* * * *

I have disallowed or reduced time for the following tasks:

(a) Pretrial Memorandum

* * * [T]his was one of the major examples of maladministration in this case. No less than 51 plaintiff lawyers devoted a total of over 4,500 hours to this task at a cost (based on the fees requested) of over one million dollars. This was a grossly excessive amount of time to expend on this one brief and accordingly, I have reduced each firm's hours expended on this task by one-half.

**b.** Lindy Brothers Builders, Inc. v. American Radiator & Standard Sanitary Corp., 487 F.2d 161 (3d Cir.1973)(I), appeal following remand, 540 F.2d 102 (3d Cir. 1976)(II), were the Third Circuit's major opinions on calculating fees at that time.

(b) Read and Review Time

* * * [H]undreds of hours have been billed to the class by attorneys for reading and reviewing documents for which the attorneys were not responsible. This time has been disallowed for all attorneys except members of the fourteen member Executive Committee.

(c) Fee Petition Time

In accordance with the rule of *Lindy II,* time involved in the preparation of fee petitions is not compensable as it does not enure to the benefit of the class.

(d) Pretrial Conferences

* * * [C]ounsel billed a total of 1446 hours for the 31 conferences. This large number of hours was primarily due to the attendance of attorneys who contributed nothing to the conferences but were merely there as spectators. The hours billed by these attorneys will not be compensated by the class.

(e) Hours Without Adequate Supporting Data

Hundreds of hours which were described by vague or meaningless terms or insufficiently documented, will not be compensated. "The burden is clearly on counsel to file adequately-documented applications for fees and those who fail to meet that burden do so at their own risk."

(f) Industrial Analysis Committee

Approximately 1800 lawyer and paralegal hours have been billed to the class for work on the Industrial Analysis Committee. * * *

The work of this committee was basically useless. It duplicated the efforts of others and resulted in no appreciable benefit to the class. * * *

*(B) Hourly Rate*

Because of the duplication, waste and inefficiency which resulted from the participation of 41 sets of attorneys and the committee structure established by counsel, "it is only proper that the fee award be adjusted to reflect this." Because of these circumstances, attorneys cannot expect to receive the same hourly rates awarded to them by other courts in class action litigation. The abundance of attorneys representing the class substantially diluted each attorney's role and, therefore, the rates should be reduced accordingly to reflect their diminished contribution. In many instances, adequate representation for the class may result in some degree of duplication but the proliferation of lawyers here cannot be justified on any rational basis.

In this litigation, it was not unusual for senior partners to devote a great deal of time to clerical, administrative and investigative tasks such as document review. Partners will not be compensated at partner-level rates for tasks which are customarily performed by junior associates or paralegals. * * *

*(C) Multipliers*

I will allow, for the contingency factor, a positive multiplier of 1.5 for all compensable time expended prior to the $30 million settlements consummated in January of 1979. Once the initial settlements were approved, there was no risk of non-payment for services or reimbursement of expenses. * * *

No positive quality multiplier will be allowed. Under all the circumstances of the case, I am not persuaded that any counsel demonstrated such an unusually high degree of skill as would warrant compensation beyond that reflected in the hourly rates.

Specks & Goldberg, however, because of its dominant leadership role, must be charged with primary responsibility for all the wasted hours, duplication and gross inefficiency which marked this case from its inception. While I recognize that in a case as large and complex as this, some duplication of effort is inevitable, nevertheless, the court cannot condone the needless proliferation of lawyers, wasted time and unnecessary expenses, all of which were orchestrated by Mr. Specks despite warnings and objections by his co-lead counsel.

Based on the record before me, a good case can be made for denying the Specks & Goldberg petition altogether. But weighing in the balance the positive aspects of the firm's contribution such as the vital role Granvil Specks played in the settlement negotiations and the utilization of his broad experience in class action litigation, I am convinced that something less Draconian is in order.

*Lindy I* and its progeny authorize the application of a negative multiplier as a "penalty" based on "[a]n evaluation of the professional methods utilized in processing the case." This is the course I will follow and, accordingly, I will apply a negative multiplier of .5 to the Specks & Goldberg lodestar. This reflects my considered judgment that effective management could have produced the same results in less than half the time expended. The application of a negative multiplier is necessary in a case of this nature to remind counsel, particularly those in a leadership role, that a class action is something more than a fee-generating device. It is a cause of action belonging to the members of the class to whom counsel owe a duty of fidelity. Their primary job is to create a fund for the class not the lawyers.

*(D) Expenses*

The petitioning attorneys here have asked the court for reimbursement of expenses totaling $1,197,151. * * *

First, where I have disallowed attorney time (e.g., for unnecessary attendance by an attorney at a pretrial conference), I have not permitted reimbursement for any expenses incurred in connection with such time.

Second, I have assumed that the class members "have agreed to pay [only] modest to moderate travel and per diem costs when the trips served their beneficial interests." Accordingly, petitioners have not been reimbursed for "unnecessary or extravagant travel and related expenses."

Finally, I have scrutinized with particular care repeated charges for meals consumed at hometown restaurants and have disallowed those which appeared to have been arranged primarily for the benefit of the lawyer.

### X. The Depth of the Review

In *Lindy II,* the Court of Appeals stated that it "did not ... intend that a district court, in setting an attorney's fee, become enmeshed in a meticulous analysis of every detailed facet of the professional representation," nor "that the inquiry into the adequacy of the fee assume massive proportions, perhaps even dwarfing the case in chief." Unfortunately, the expectations of *Lindy II* cannot be realized in this case. The internecine warfare which broke out among plaintiffs' counsel resulted in charges of gross mismanagement, ethical misconduct, bad faith and overreaching. The eruption from within, in turn, generated an all out assault from without in the form of the class objectors' investigations and report. These circumstances made it imperative for the court to undertake a thorough examination of each of the fee petitions.

I regret to say that my inquiry has given substance to the worst fears of the critics of the class action device—that it is being manipulated by lawyers to generate fees. Some of the petitioners here were reminded on a prior occasion that

> [t]he principal attacks on the [Rule 23] are largely the result of conduct by counsel for plaintiffs in some cases who have acted as though the rule was adopted for their benefit rather than for the multitude of individuals comprising the class or classes whose rights they were presumably vindicating.... It would be ironic indeed if class actions ... were to be restricted or eliminated as a result of the conduct of a very small segment of the bar specializing in plaintiffs' representation.

My rulings with respect to the fees may seem harsh to many, but as long as Rule 23 and *Lindy* and its progeny impose upon the court the duty to protect the class from overreaching by class counsel, I have no alternative. Moreover, the court must take a firm stand if Rule 23 is to retain respectability as a legitimate and effective tool of judicial administration.

### XI. The Individual Fee Petitions

* * * In sum, I have allowed fees totaling $4,343,103 and expenses of $1,121,020. * * *

## *Notes*

1. For another case in a somewhat similar vein, see Grendel's Den, Inc. v. Larkin, 749 F.2d 945 (1st Cir.1984). A prominent law professor requested $176,137.50 in fees (640.5 hours at $275 per hour) for a suit brought on behalf of an establishment which was denied a liquor license because it was

within 500 feet of a church. The complaint alleged that the controlling statute allowing this denial violated the Establishment Clause of the First Amendment. The professor won on the merits in the Supreme Court, but that proved to be just a warm-up for the battle waged over attorney's fees. The district court awarded $159,048 in fees and expenses, even though no contemporaneous time records were maintained. The Court of Appeals reduced the award to $113,640.85, finding the hourly rates charged and the number of hours billed for some of the work excessive. In particular, the Court of Appeals found that with respect to a request for fees for 19 hours of oral argument, there was "no justification for the presence of two top echelon attorneys at each proceeding," and reduced the claim to 8 hours. The court also reduced a claim for hotel expenses from $917.24 to $400, stating that it was unreasonable to have stayed two nights in an expensive three-bedroom hotel suite in order to argue for one hour before the Supreme Court. In addition, the court took a dim view of a $5,500 bill for writing an eighteen line footnote in one of the briefs.

2. What can a court do to avoid *Fine Paper*-like excesses in the future? For some thoughts on the problem, see Third Circuit Task Force, Court Awarded Attorney Fees, 108 F.R.D. 237, 262–63 (1985)(recommending several changes, including: frank discussion of fees at an early judicial status conference, setting a proposed budget for the litigation in advance and establishing a maximum estimated number of hours that will be included in the lodestar).

In In re Continental Illinois Securities Litigation, 572 F.Supp. 931 (N.D.Ill.1983), the court put the plaintiffs on notice at the outset that, should they prevail on the merits and request an award of attorney's fees, it would apply certain standards in reviewing the bills. Work that could be done by junior people, such as basic research and document review, would be compensated at lower rates than work which could only be done with a high level of skill, regardless of who actually did the work.

These warnings and guidelines did not prevent difficulties, however. After the case settled for $45 million in 1989, the judge ended up reviewing a mountain of vague documentation supporting the fee petitions and determined that some of the fee requests had to be cut down substantially. In re Continental Illinois Securities Litigation, 750 F.Supp. 868 (N.D.Ill.1990). However, the Seventh Circuit reversed and directed the trial court to review the fee requests again with a more generous hand. 962 F.2d 566 (7th Cir.1992)(Posner, J.)("[I]t is not the function of judges in fee litigation to determine the equivalent of the medieval just price. It is to determine what the lawyer would receive if he were selling his services in the market rather than being paid by court order.") The circuit court was still not satisfied with the district court's work. 985 F.2d 867 (7th Cir.1993). When last heard from, the trial court and plaintiffs' lawyers were litigating yet another mandamus action to determine whether the circuit ordered (or merely suggested) that the trial court award a fee based on a percentage of the common fund. (The trial court preferred to determine a reasonable fee based on the lodestar method while the plaintiffs' attorneys believed they would do better with a percentage.) 813 F.Supp. 633 and 148 F.R.D. 594 (N.D.Ill.1993).

3. One federal judge trying to keep down litigation costs in a securities case used a novel bidding process to select lead counsel to represent the class of plaintiffs. The judge chose the low-bidding law firm, who promised to do the work for a maximum of $325,000 in expenses plus a low contingency fee based on the amount of recovery. In re Oracle Securities Litigation, 132 F.R.D. 538 (N.D.Cal.1990). One losing bidder, who had estimated the costs alone at $1.3 million, later criticized the cap as unethical, arbitrary and unrealistic. This disappointed bidder charged that the winning firm would have to choose between its ethical duty to represent the class zealously and the financial incentive to avoid incurring nonreimbursable expenses. The trial court rejected these contentions. 136 F.R.D. 639 (N.D.Cal.1991). The case finally settled for $25 million to the plaintiffs, with $5.6 million in fees and expenses for the lead counsel and another $595,000 for other plaintiffs' firms. 852 F.Supp. 1437 (N.D.Cal.1994). See Randall S. Thomas & Robert G. Hansen, Auctioning Class Action and Derivative Lawsuits: A Critical Analysis, 87 Nw.U.L.Rev. 423 (1993).

4. The general dissatisfaction with the complexities of the lodestar approach have caused some courts to return to compensating on the basis of a percentage of the recovery, especially in common fund cases. E.g., In re Thirteen Appeals, 56 F.3d 295 (1st Cir.1995)(joining six other circuits in allowing or requiring percentage method in lieu of cumbersome lodestar method in common fund cases). See also Charles Silver, Unloading the Lodestar: Toward a New Fee Award Procedure, 70 Tex.L.Rev. 865 (1992), which takes aim at the problems of the lodestar approach and suggests replacing it with a contract-based fee award procedure.

5. It is somewhat unsettled who is entitled to challenge a fee award. Compare, e.g., In re Busy Beaver Building Centers, 19 F.3d 833 (3d Cir.1994)(bankruptcy court has power and duty to review fee application even when no interested party objects) with In re First Capital Holdings Corp., 33 F.3d 29 (9th Cir.1994)(class member who received full recovery on claim lacks standing to object to fee award).

---

Negotiations about fees in the context of negotiations about the merits present particular difficulties. It is said that in some class action suits, the first item on the agenda of settlement conferences is the fee for the plaintiffs' attorneys. Is it proper in a public law case for a negotiated settlement on the merits to include a negotiated fee? Is it proper for defendants to offer to settle the case on the merits favorably to plaintiffs only if there is no fee?

## EVANS v. JEFF D.

Supreme Court of the United States, 1986.
475 U.S. 717, 106 S.Ct. 1531, 89 L.Ed.2d 747.

JUSTICE STEVENS delivered the opinion of the Court.

The Civil Rights Attorney's Fees Awards Act of 1976 (Fees Act), provides that "the court, in its discretion, may allow the prevailing party

. . . a reasonable attorney's fee" in enumerated civil rights actions. 42 U.S.C. § 1988. In Maher v. Gagne, 448 U.S. 122, 100 S.Ct. 2570, 65 L.Ed.2d 653 (1980), we held that fees *may* be assessed against state officials after a case has been settled by the entry of a consent decree. In this case, we consider the question whether attorney's fees *must* be assessed when the case has been settled by a consent decree granting prospective relief to the plaintiff class but providing that the defendants shall not pay any part of the prevailing party's fees or costs. We hold that the District Court has the power, in its sound discretion, to refuse to award fees.

I

* * * [The petitioners, state officials in Idaho, were sued by a class of handicapped children because of alleged deficiencies in the educational and health care provided. Respondents were represented by Charles Johnson from the Idaho Legal Aid Society.]

In March 1983, one week before trial, petitioners presented respondents with a new settlement proposal. As respondents themselves characterize it, the proposal "offered virtually all of the injunctive relief [they] had sought in their complaint." The Court of Appeals agreed with this characterization, and further noted that the proposed relief was "more than the district court in earlier hearings had indicated it was willing to grant." 743 F.2d 648, 650 (C.A.9 1984). As was true of the earlier partial settlement, however, petitioners' offer included a provision for a waiver by respondents of any claim to fees or costs. Originally, this waiver was unacceptable to the Idaho Legal Aid Society, which had instructed Johnson to reject any settlement offer conditioned upon a waiver of fees, but Johnson ultimately determined that his ethical obligation to his clients mandated acceptance of the proposal. The parties conditioned the waiver on approval by the District Court.

After the stipulation was signed, Johnson filed a written motion requesting the District Court to approve the settlement "except for the provision on costs and attorney's fees," and to allow the respondents to present a bill of costs and fees for consideration by the court. At the oral argument on that motion, Johnson contended that petitioners' offer had exploited his ethical duty to his clients—that he was "forced," by an offer giving his clients "the best result [they] could have gotten in this court or any other court," to waive his attorney's fees.[6] The District

6. Johnson's oral presentation to the District Court reads in full as follows:

"In other words, an attorney like myself can be put in the position of either negotiating for his client or negotiating for his attorney's fees, and I think that that is pretty much the situation that occurred in this instance.

"I was forced, because of what I perceived to be a result favorable to the plaintiff class, a result that I didn't want to see jeopardized by a trial or by any other possible problems that might have occurred. And the result is the best result I could have gotten in this court or any other court and it is really a fair and just result in any instance and what should have occurred years earlier and which in fact should have been the case all along. That result I didn't want to see disturbed on the basis that my attorney's fees would cause a problem and cause that result to be jeopardized."

Court, however, evaluated the waiver in the context of the entire settlement and rejected the ethical underpinnings of Johnson's argument. Explaining that although petitioners were "not willing to concede that they were obligated to [make the changes in their practices required by the stipulation], ... they were willing to do them as long as their costs were outlined and they didn't face additional costs," it concluded that "it doesn't violate any ethical considerations for an attorney to give up his attorney fees in the interest of getting a better bargain for his client[s]." Accordingly, the District Court approved the settlement and denied the motion to submit a costs bill.

When respondents appealed from the order denying attorney's fees and costs, petitioners filed a motion requesting the District Court to suspend or stay their obligation to comply with the substantive terms of the settlement. Because the District Court regarded the fee waiver as a material term of the complete settlement, it granted the motion.[7] The Court of Appeals, however, granted two emergency motions for stays requiring enforcement of the substantive terms of the consent decree pending the appeal. More dramatically, after ordering preliminary relief, it invalidated the fee waiver and left standing the remainder of the settlement; it then instructed the District Court to "make its own determination of the fees that are reasonable" and remanded for that limited purpose.

In explaining its holding, the Court of Appeals emphasized that Rule 23(e) of the Federal Rules of Civil Procedure gives the court the power to approve the terms of all settlements of class actions,[8] and that the strong federal policy embodied in the Fees Act normally requires an award of fees to prevailing plaintiffs in civil rights actions, including those who have prevailed through settlement. The court added that "[w]hen attorney's fees are negotiated as part of a class action settlement, a conflict frequently exists between the class lawyers' interest in compensation and the class members' interest in relief." "To avoid this conflict," the Court of Appeals relied on Circuit precedent which had "disapproved simultaneous negotiation of settlements and attorney's fees" absent a showing of "unusual circumstances."[10] In this case, the

7. The District Court wrote a letter to respondents' counsel explaining the conditional nature of petitioners' settlement offer: "[T]he defendants' signing of the stipulation was dependent upon the Court's approval of the finding that it was appropriate to accept a stipulation where plaintiffs waived attorneys fees.... The defendants entered into the stipulation only as a compromise matter with the understanding that they would not pay any attorneys fees, and advised the Court that if there were going to be attorneys fees that they wanted to proceed with trial because they did not think they were required to conform to the stipulation legally. * * * [U]ntil the validity of the stipulation is determined, the Court feels it is entirely unfair to enforce it."

8. "Dismissal or Compromise. A class action shall not be dismissed or compromised without the approval of the court, and notice of the proposed dismissal or compromise shall be given to all members of the class in such manner as the court directs." Fed.Rules Civ.Proc. 23(e).

10. [The circuit court cited as precedent, Mendoza v. United States, 623 F.2d 1338 (9th Cir.1980), and Prandini v. National Tea Co., 557 F.2d 1015 (3d Cir.1977). However, in neither case did the courts actually reject a part of a settlement and enforce the remainder.]

Court of Appeals found no such "unusual circumstances" and therefore held that an agreement on fees "should not have been a part of the settlement of the claims of the class." It concluded:

> "The historical background of both Rule 23 and section 1988, as well as our experience since their enactment, compel the conclusion that a stipulated waiver of all attorney's fees obtained solely as a condition for obtaining relief for the class should not be accepted by the court."

The importance of the question decided by the Court of Appeals, together with the conflict between its decision and the decisions of other Courts of Appeals, led us to grant certiorari. We now reverse.

II

The disagreement between the parties and *amici* as to what exactly is at issue in this case makes it appropriate to put certain aspects of the case to one side in order to state precisely the question that the case does present.

To begin with, the Court of Appeals' decision rested on an erroneous view of the District Court's power to approve settlements in class actions. Rule 23(e) wisely requires court approval of the terms of any settlement of a class action, but the power to approve or reject a settlement negotiated by the parties before trial does not authorize the court to require the parties to accept a settlement to which they have not agreed. Although changed circumstances may justify a court-ordered modification of a consent decree over the objections of a party after the decree has been entered, and the District Court might have advised petitioners and respondents that it would not approve their proposal unless one or more of its provisions was deleted or modified, Rule 23(e) does not give the court the power, in advance of trial, to modify a proposed consent decree and order its acceptance over either party's objection. The options available to the District Court were essentially the same as those available to respondents: it could have accepted the proposed settlement; it could have rejected the proposal and postponed the trial to see if a different settlement could be achieved; or it could have decided to try the case. The District Court could not enforce the settlement on the merits and award attorney's fees any more than it could, in a situation in which the attorney had negotiated a large fee at the expense of the plaintiff class, preserve the fee award and order greater relief on the merits. The question we must decide, therefore, is whether the District Court had a duty to reject the proposed settlement because it included a waiver of statutorily authorized attorney's fees.

That duty, whether it takes the form of a general prophylactic rule or arises out of the special circumstances of this case, derives ultimately from the Fees Act rather than from the strictures of professional ethics. Although respondents contend that Johnson, as counsel for the class, was faced with an "ethical dilemma" when petitioners offered him relief greater than that which he could reasonably have expected to obtain for his clients at trial (if only he would stipulate to a waiver of the statutory fee award), and although we recognize Johnson's conflicting interests between pursuing relief for the class and a fee for the Idaho Legal Aid Society, we do not believe that the "dilemma" was an "ethical" one in the sense that Johnson had to choose between conflicting duties under the prevailing norms of professional conduct. Plainly, Johnson had no ethical obligation to seek a statutory fee award. His ethical duty was to serve his clients loyally and competently. Since the proposal to settle the merits was more favorable than the probable outcome of the trial, Johnson's decision to recommend acceptance was consistent with the highest standards of our profession. The District Court, therefore, correctly concluded that approval of the settlement involved no breach of ethics in this case.

The defect, if any, in the negotiated fee waiver must be traced not to the rules of ethics but to the Fees Act. Following this tack, respondents argue that the statute must be construed to forbid a fee waiver that is the product of "coercion." They submit that a "coercive waiver" results when the defendant in a civil rights action (1) offers a settlement on the merits of equal or greater value than that which plaintiffs could reasonably expect to achieve at trial but (2) conditions the offer on a waiver of plaintiffs' statutory eligibility for attorney's fees. Such an offer, they claim, exploits the ethical obligation of plaintiffs' counsel to recommend settlement in order to avoid defendant's statutory liability for its opponents' fees and costs.

The question this case presents, then, is whether the Fees Act requires a district court to disapprove a stipulation seeking to settle a civil rights class action under Rule 23 when the offered relief equals or exceeds the probable outcome at trial but is expressly conditioned on waiver of statutory eligibility for attorney's fees. For reasons set out below, we are not persuaded that Congress has commanded that all such settlements must be rejected by the District Court. Moreover, on the facts of record in this case, we are satisfied that the District Court did not abuse its discretion by approving the fee waiver.

III

The text of the Fees Act provides no support for the proposition that Congress intended to ban all fee waivers offered in connection with substantial relief on the merits. * * *

In fact, we believe that a general proscription against negotiated waiver of attorney's fees in exchange for a settlement on the merits would itself impede vindication of civil rights, at least in some cases, by reducing the attractiveness of settlement. * * *

Most defendants are unlikely to settle unless the cost of the predicted judgment, discounted by its probability, plus the transaction costs of further litigation, are greater than the cost of the settlement package. If fee waivers cannot be negotiated, the settlement package must either contain an attorney's fee component of potentially large and typically uncertain magnitude, or else the parties must agree to have the fee fixed by the court. Although either of these alternatives may well be acceptable in many cases, there surely is a significant number in which neither alternative will be as satisfactory as a decision to try the entire case. * * *

The unpredictability of attorney's fees may be just as important as their magnitude when a defendant is striving to fix its liability. Unlike a determination of costs, which ordinarily involve smaller outlays and are more susceptible of calculation, "[t]here is no precise rule or formula" for determining attorney's fees, Hensley v. Eckerhart, 461 U.S. 424, 436, 103 S.Ct. 1933, 1941, 76 L.Ed.2d 40 (1983). Among other considerations, the district court must determine what hours were reasonably expended on what claims, whether that expenditure was reasonable in light of the success obtained, and what is an appropriate hourly rate for the services rendered. Some District Courts have also considered whether a "multiplier" or other adjustment is appropriate. The consequence of this succession of necessarily judgmental decisions for the ultimate fee award is inescapable: a defendant's liability for his opponent's attorney's fees in a civil rights action cannot be fixed with a sufficient degree of confidence to make defendants indifferent to their exclusion from negotiation. It is therefore not implausible to anticipate that parties to a significant number of civil rights cases will refuse to settle if liability for attorney's fees remains open, thereby forcing more cases to trial, unnecessarily burdening the judicial system, and disserving civil rights litigants. Respondents' own waiver of attorney's fees and costs to obtain settlement of their educational claims is eloquent testimony to the utility of fee waivers in vindicating civil rights claims. We conclude, therefore, that it is not necessary to construe the Fees Act as embodying a general rule prohibiting settlements conditioned on the waiver of fees in order to be faithful to the purposes of that Act.

IV

The question remains whether the District Court abused its discretion in this case by approving a settlement which included a complete fee waiver. As noted earlier, Rule 23(e) wisely requires court approval of the terms of any settlement of a class action. The potential conflict among members of the class—in this case, for example, the possible conflict between children primarily interested in better educational programs and those primarily interested in improved health care—fully justifies the requirement of court approval.

The Court of Appeals, respondents, and various *amici* supporting their position, however, suggest that the court's authority to pass on settlements, typically invoked to ensure fair treatment of class members, must be exercised in accordance with the Fees Act to promote the availability of attorneys in civil rights cases. Specifically, respondents assert that the State of Idaho could not pass a valid statute precluding the payment of attorney's fees in settlements of civil rights cases to which the Fees Act applies. From this they reason that the Fees Act must equally preclude the adoption of a uniform state-wide policy that serves the same end, and accordingly contend that a consistent practice of insisting on a fee waiver as a condition of settlement in civil rights litigation is in conflict with the federal statute authorizing fees for prevailing parties, including those who prevail by way of settlement. Remarkably, there seems little disagreement on these points. Petitioners and the *amici* who support them never suggest that the district court is obligated to place its stamp of approval on every settlement in which the plaintiffs' attorneys have agreed to a fee waiver. The Solicitor General, for example, has suggested that a fee waiver need not be approved when the defendant had "no realistic defense on the merits," or if the waiver was part of a "vindictive effort . . . to teach counsel that they had better not bring such cases."

We find it unnecessary to evaluate this argument, however, because the record in this case does not indicate that Idaho has adopted such a statute, policy, or practice. Nor does the record support the narrower proposition that petitioners' request to waive fees was a vindictive effort to deter attorneys from representing plaintiffs in civil rights suits against Idaho. It is true that a fee waiver was requested and obtained as a part of the early settlement of the education claims, but we do not understand respondents to be challenging that waiver, and they have not offered to prove that the petitioners' tactics in this case merely implemented a routine state policy designed to frustrate the objectives of the Fees Act. Our own examination of the record reveals no such policy.

In light of the record, respondents must—to sustain the judgment in their favor—confront the District Court's finding that the extensive structural relief they obtained constituted an adequate quid pro quo for their waiver of attorney's fees. The Court of Appeals did not overturn this finding. Indeed, even that court did not suggest that the option of rejecting the entire settlement and requiring the parties either to try the case or to attempt to negotiate a different settlement would have served the interests of justice. Only by making the unsupported assumption that the respondent class was entitled to retain the favorable portions of the settlement while rejecting the fee waiver could the Court of Appeals conclude that the District Court had acted unwisely.

What the outcome of this settlement illustrates is that the Fees Act has given the victims of civil rights violations a powerful weapon that improves their ability to employ counsel, to obtain access to the courts, and thereafter to vindicate their rights by means of settlement or trial. For aught that appears, it was the "coercive" effect of respondents' statutory right to seek a fee award that motivated petitioners' exceptionally generous offer. Whether this weapon might be even more powerful if fee waivers were prohibited in cases like this is another question, but it is in any event a question that Congress is best equipped to answer. Thus far, the Legislature has not commanded that fees be paid whenever a case is settled. Unless it issues such a command, we shall rely primarily on the sound discretion of the district courts to appraise the reasonableness of particular class-action settlements on a case-by-case basis, in the light of all the relevant circumstances. In this case, the District Court did not abuse its discretion in upholding a fee waiver which secured broad injunctive relief, relief greater than that which plaintiffs could reasonably have expected to achieve at trial.

The judgment of the Court of Appeals is reversed.

It is so ordered.

JUSTICE BRENNAN, with whom JUSTICE MARSHALL and JUSTICE BLACKMUN join, dissenting.

[omitted]

### *Notes*

1. The Supreme Court's decision has been criticized as creating a chilling effect on public interest litigation. The critics contend that attorneys will have less incentive to accept these cases when there is a strong possibility of being faced with the problem in *Evans*. See, e.g., Note, Waive Goodbye to Law in the Public Interest—The Use of Coercive Fee Waivers in Civil Rights Actions, 19 Ariz.St.L.J. 749 (1987).

One response to *Evans* has been to write ethical rules that would prohibit negotiations as to fees, leaving the award of reasonable fees to the court after the parties reach a settlement on the merits. Note, Fee Waivers and Civil Rights Settlement Offers: State Ethics Prohibitions, 87 Colum.L.Rev. 1214 (1987). This approach has not succeeded everywhere. For example, in 1989, the California Supreme Court rejected a proposed rule, endorsed by the State Bar, which was intended to nullify *Evans*. Proposed Rule of Professional Conduct 2–400, Bar Misc. 6004, read in part, " 'A member shall not make or present a settlement offer in any case involving a request by the opposing party for attorneys fees pursuant to private attorney general statutes which is conditioned on opposing counsel waiving all or substantially all fees.' " See Comment, Simultaneous Negotiation and the Conditioning of Settlement on the Merits Upon Waiver of Statutory Attorney's Fees: An Ethical and Policy Analysis, 29 Ariz.L.Rev. 517, 526 n.88 (1987)(state bars are divided on the permissibility of fee negotiations and waivers: the District of Columbia, Maine, Maryland, and New York severely restrict them; Michigan and George permit simultaneous negotiations).

2. At least two circuit courts have extended *Evans* from class actions to the context of individual civil rights actions and have concluded that the district court should not allow the plaintiff's attorney to intervene to challenge the propriety of a fee waiver. Willard v. City of Los Angeles, 803 F.2d 526 (9th Cir.1986); Panola Land Buying Association v. Clark, 844 F.2d 1506 (11th Cir.1988). These opinions have been criticized as ignoring the fact that *Evans* merely decided whether a district court was required to disapprove a settlement which included a fee waiver and did not decide whether a disapproval was permitted. Note, Fee as the Wind Blows: Waivers of Civil Rights Actions Since Evans v. Jeff D., 102 Harv.L.Rev. 1278 (1989).

3. Another tool that defendants can use to their advantage is F.R.Civ.P. 68, reproduced in the Appendix at p. 888, which provides that "(a)t any time more than 10 days before trial begins, a party defending against a claim may serve upon the adverse party an offer to allow judgment to be taken against him for the money or property or the effect specified in

his offer with costs then accrued." Further, if the offeree declines the offer and "[i]f the judgment finally obtained by the offeree is not more favorable than the offer, the offeree must pay the costs incurred after the making of the offer." Thus, those "costs" accrued after the making and rejection of a valid offer, are shifted to the offeree (who is usually the plaintiff) if the latter recovers less than the offer. However, F.R.Civ.P. 68 nowhere defines the term "costs," and is silent on whether attorneys' fees are "costs." Plainly, the inclusion of statutorily authorized attorney's fees as "costs" under the rule profoundly affects the availability of a fee award to otherwise entitled plaintiffs or prevailing parties.

In Marek v. Chesny, 473 U.S. 1, 105 S.Ct. 3012, 87 L.Ed.2d 1 (1985), the Supreme Court held that absent congressional expression to the contrary, where the underlying fee shifting statute defined "costs" as including attorney's fees, such fees were to be included as "costs" for purposes of Rule 68. The Court majority acted over a bitter dissent by Justice Brennan in which he charged that the Court's reasoning was wholly inconsistent with the history and structure of the Federal Rules, that its application would produce absurd variations in Rule 68's operation based on nothing more than minute differences in statutory language, and that the Court's interpretation would seriously undermine the purposes behind the attorney's fees provisions of the civil rights laws. See also Peter Margulies, After *Marek,* the Deluge: Harmonizing the Interaction Under Rule 68 of Statutes That Do and Do Not Classify Attorneys' Fees as "Costs", 73 Iowa L.Rev. 413 (1988)(risk-averse plaintiffs more likely to accept a low settlement than face paying post-offer costs). Should Rule 68 be amended? If so, how? See, e.g., William W Schwarzer, Fee-shifting Offers of Judgment—An Approach to Reducing the Cost of Litigation, 76 Judicature 147 (1992); David A. Anderson, Improving Settlement Devices: Rule 68 and Beyond, 23 J.Leg.Studies 225 (1994). When the Supreme Court's Advisory Committee on the Civil Rules tried in 1983 and again in 1984, it faced a storm of criticism and abandoned the effort. See Stephen B. Burbank, Proposals to Amend Rule 68—Time to Abandon Ship, 19 Mich.J.L.Reform 425 (1986).

# Appendix

# SELECTED FEDERAL RULES OF CIVIL PROCEDURE

* * *

IV. PARTIES * * *

## Rule 19. Joinder of Persons Needed for Just Adjudication

**(a) Persons to Be Joined if Feasible.** A person who is subject to service of process and whose joinder will not deprive the court of jurisdiction over the subject matter of the action shall be joined as a party in the action if (1) in the person's absence complete relief cannot be accorded among those already parties, or (2) the person claims an interest relating to the subject of the action and is so situated that the disposition of the action in the person's absence may (i) as a practical matter impair or impede the person's ability to protect that interest or (ii) leave any of the persons already parties subject to a substantial risk of incurring double, multiple, or otherwise inconsistent obligations by reason of the claimed interest. If the person has not been so joined, the court shall order that the person be made a party. If the person should join as a plaintiff but refuses to do so, the person may be made a defendant, or, in a proper case, an involuntary plaintiff. If the joined party objects to venue and joinder of that party would render the venue of the action improper, that party shall be dismissed from the action.

**(b) Determination by Court Whenever Joinder not Feasible.** If a person as described in subdivision (a)(1)–(2) hereof cannot be made a party, the court shall determine whether in equity and good conscience the action should proceed among the parties before it, or should be dismissed, the absent person being thus regarded as indispensable. The factors to be considered by the court include: first, to what extent a judgment rendered in the person's absence might be prejudicial to the person or those already parties; second, the extent to which, by protective provisions in the judgment, by the shaping of relief, or other measures, the prejudice can be lessened or avoided; third, whether a judgment rendered in the person's absence will be adequate; fourth, whether the plaintiff will have an adequate remedy if the action is dismissed for nonjoinder.

**(c) Pleading Reasons for Nonjoinder.** A pleading asserting a claim for relief shall state the names, if known to the pleader, of any persons as described in subdivision (a)(1)–(2) hereof who are not joined, and the reasons why they are not joined.

**(d) Exception of Class Actions.** This rule is subject to the provisions of Rule 23.

(As amended Feb. 28, 1966, eff. July 1, 1966; Mar. 2, 1987, eff. Aug. 1, 1987.)

* * *

### Rule 24. Intervention

**(a) Intervention of Right.** Upon timely application anyone shall be permitted to intervene in an action: (1) when a statute of the United States confers an unconditional right to intervene; or (2) when the applicant claims an interest relating to the property or transaction which is the subject of the action and the applicant is so situated that the disposition of the action may as a practical matter impair or impede the applicant's ability to protect that interest, unless the applicant's interest is adequately represented by existing parties.

**(b) Permissive Intervention.** Upon timely application anyone may be permitted to intervene in an action: (1) when a statute of the United States confers a conditional right to intervene; or (2) when an applicant's claim or defense and the main action have a question of law or fact in common. When a party to an action relies for ground of claim or defense upon any statute or executive order administered by a federal or state governmental officer or agency or upon any regulation, order, requirement or agreement issued or made pursuant to the statute or executive order, the officer or agency upon timely application may be permitted to intervene in the action. In exercising its discretion the court shall consider whether the intervention will unduly delay or prejudice the adjudication of the rights of the original parties.

**(c) Procedure.** A person desiring to intervene shall serve a motion to intervene upon the parties as provided in Rule 5. The motion shall state the grounds therefor and shall be accompanied by a pleading setting forth the claim or defense for which intervention is sought. The same procedure shall be followed when a statute of the United States gives a right to intervene. When the constitutionality of an act of Congress affecting the public interest is drawn in question in any action to which the United States or an officer, agency, or employee thereof is not a party, the court shall notify the Attorney General of the United States as provided in Title 28, U.S.C. § 2403. When the constitutionality of any statute of a State affecting the public interest is drawn in question in any action in which that State or any agency, officer, or employee thereof is not a party, the court shall notify the attorney general of the State as provided in Title 28, U.S.C. § 2403. A party challenging the constitutionality of legislation should call the attention of the court to its consequential duty, but failure to do so is not a waiver of any constitutional right otherwise timely asserted.

(As amended Dec. 27, 1946, eff. Mar. 19, 1948; Dec. 29, 1948, eff. Oct. 20, 1949; Jan. 21, 1963, eff. July 1, 1963; Feb. 28, 1966, eff. July 1, 1966; Mar. 2, 1987, eff. Aug. 1, 1987; Apr. 30, 1991, eff. Dec. 1, 1991.)

### Rule 25. Substitution of Parties * * *

**(d) Public Officers; Death or Separation From Office.**

**(1)** When a public officer is a party to an action in an official capacity and during its pendency dies, resigns, or otherwise ceases to hold office, the action does not abate and the officer's successor is automatically substituted as a party. Proceedings following the substitution shall be in the name of the substituted party, but any misnomer not affecting the substantial rights of the parties shall be disregarded. An order of substitution may be entered at any time, but the omission to enter such an order shall not affect the substitution.

**(2)** A public officer who sues or is sued in an official capacity may be described as a party by the officer's official title rather than by name; but the court may require the officer's name to be added.

(As amended Dec. 29, 1948, eff. Oct. 20, 1949; Apr. 17, 1961, eff. July 19, 1961; Jan. 21, 1963, eff. July 1, 1963; Mar. 2, 1987, eff. Aug. 1, 1987.)

* * *

## VI. TRIALS

* * *

### Rule 53. Masters

**(a) Appointment and Compensation.** The court in which any action is pending may appoint a special master therein. As used in these rules the word "master" includes a referee, an auditor, an examiner, and an assessor. The compensation to be allowed to a master shall be fixed by the court, and shall be charged upon such of the parties or paid out of any fund or subject matter of the action, which is in the custody and control of the court as the court may direct; provided that this provision for compensation shall not apply when a United States magistrate judge is designated to serve as a master. The master shall not retain the master's report as security for the master's compensation; but when the party ordered to pay the compensation allowed by the court does not pay it after notice and within the time prescribed by the court, the master is entitled to a writ of execution against the delinquent party.

**(b) Reference.** A reference to a master shall be the exception and not the rule. In actions to be tried by a jury, a reference shall be made only when the issues are complicated; in actions to be tried without a jury, save in matters of account and of difficult computation of damages, a reference shall be made only upon a showing that some exceptional condition requires it. Upon the consent of the parties, a magistrate judge may be designated to serve as a special master without regard to the provisions of this subdivision.

**(c) Powers.** The order of reference to the master may specify or limit the master's powers and may direct the master to report only upon particular issues or to do or perform particular acts or to receive and report evidence only and may fix the time and place for beginning and closing the hearings and for the filing of the master's report. Subject to the specifications and limitations stated in the order, the master has and shall exercise the power to regulate all proceedings in every hearing before the master and to do all acts and take all measures necessary or proper for the efficient performance of the master's duties under the order. The master may require the production before the master of evidence upon all matters embraced in the reference, including the production of all books, papers, vouchers, documents, and writings applicable thereto. The master may rule upon the admissibility of evidence unless otherwise directed by the order of reference and has the authority to put witnesses on oath and may examine them and may call the parties to the action and examine them upon oath. When a party so requests, the master shall make a record of the evidence offered and excluded in the same manner and subject to the same limitations as provided in the Federal Rules of Evidence for a court sitting without a jury.

**(d) Proceedings.**

**(1) *Meetings.*** When a reference is made, the clerk shall forthwith furnish the master with a copy of the order of reference. Upon receipt thereof unless the order of reference otherwise provides, the master shall forthwith set a time and place for the first meeting of the parties or their attorneys to be held within 20 days after the date of the order of reference and shall notify the parties or their attorneys. It is the duty of the master to proceed with all reasonable diligence. Either party, on notice to the parties and master, may apply to the court for an order requiring the master to speed the proceedings and to make the report. If a party fails to appear at the time and place appointed, the master may proceed ex parte or, in the master's discretion, adjourn the proceedings to a future day, giving notice to the absent party of the adjournment.

**(2) *Witnesses.*** The parties may procure the attendance of witnesses before the master by the issuance and service of subpoenas as provided in Rule 45. If without adequate excuse a witness fails to appear or give evidence, the witness may be punished as for a contempt and be subjected to the consequences, penalties, and remedies provided in Rules 37 and 45.

**(3) *Statement of Accounts.*** When matters of accounting are in issue before the master, the master may prescribe the form in which the accounts shall be submitted and in any proper case may require or receive in evidence a statement by a certified public accountant who is called as a witness. Upon objection of a party to any of the items thus submitted or upon a showing that the form of statement is insufficient, the master may require a different form of statement to be furnished, or the accounts or specific items thereof to be proved by oral examination of the accounting parties or upon written interrogatories or in such other manner as the master directs.

**(e) Report.**

**(1)** ***Contents and Filing.*** The master shall prepare a report upon the matters submitted to the master by the order of reference and, if required to make findings of fact and conclusions of law, the master shall set them forth in the report. The master shall file the report with the clerk of the court and serve on all parties notice of the filing. In an action to be tried without a jury, unless otherwise directed by the order of reference, the master shall file with the report a transcript of the proceedings and of the evidence and the original exhibits. Unless otherwise directed by the order of reference, the master shall serve a copy of the report on each party.

**(2)** ***In Non–Jury Actions.*** In an action to be tried without a jury the court shall accept the master's findings of fact unless clearly erroneous. Within 10 days after being served with notice of the filing of the report any party may serve written objections thereto upon the other parties. Application to the court for action upon the report and upon objections thereto shall be by motion and upon notice as prescribed in Rule 6(d). The court after hearing may adopt the report or may modify it or may reject it in whole or in part or may receive further evidence or may recommit it with instructions.

**(3)** ***In Jury Actions.*** In an action to be tried by a jury the master shall not be directed to report the evidence. The master's findings upon the issues submitted to the master are admissible as evidence of the matters found and may be read to the jury, subject to the ruling of the court upon any objections in point of law which may be made to the report.

**(4)** ***Stipulation as to Findings.*** The effect of a master's report is the same whether or not the parties have consented to the reference; but, when the parties stipulate that a master's findings of fact shall be final, only questions of law arising upon the report shall thereafter be considered.

**(5)** ***Draft Report.*** Before filing the master's report a master may submit a draft thereof to counsel for all parties for the purpose of receiving their suggestions.

**(f) Application to Magistrate Judge.** A magistrate judge is subject to this rule only when the order referring a matter to the magistrate judge expressly provides that the reference is made under this Rule.

(As amended Feb. 28, 1966, eff. July 1, 1966; Apr. 28, 1983, eff. Aug. 1, 1983; Mar. 2, 1987, eff. Aug. 1, 1987; Apr. 30, 1991, eff. Dec. 1, 1991; Apr. 22, 1993, eff. Dec. 1, 1993.)

## VII. JUDGMENT

### Rule 54. Judgments; Costs

**(a) Definition; Form.** "Judgment" as used in these rules includes a decree and any order from which an appeal lies. A judgment shall not contain a recital of pleadings, the report of a master, or the record of prior proceedings.

**(b) Judgment Upon Multiple Claims or Involving Multiple Parties.** When more than one claim for relief is presented in an action, whether as a claim, counterclaim, cross-claim, or third-party claim, or when multiple parties are involved, the court may direct the entry of a final judgment as to one or more but fewer than all of the claims or parties only upon an express determination that there is no just reason for delay and upon an express direction for the entry of judgment. In the absence of such determination and direction, any order or other form of decision, however designated, which adjudicates fewer than all the claims or the rights and liabilities of fewer than all the parties shall not terminate the action as to any of the claims or parties, and the order or other form of decision is subject to revision at any time before the entry of judgment adjudicating all the claims and the rights and liabilities of all the parties.

**(c) Demand for Judgment.** A judgment by default shall not be different in kind from or exceed in amount that prayed for in the demand for judgment. Except as to a party against whom a judgment is entered by default, every final judgment shall grant the relief to which the party in whose favor it is rendered is entitled, even if the party has not demanded such relief in the party's pleadings.

**(d) Costs; Attorneys' Fees.**

**(1)** ***Costs Other than Attorneys' Fees.*** Except when express provision therefor is made either in a statute of the United States or in these rules, costs other than attorneys' fees shall be allowed as of course to the prevailing party unless the court otherwise directs; but costs against the United States, its officers, and agencies shall be imposed only to the extent permitted by law. Such costs may be taxed by the clerk on one day's notice. On motion served within 5 days thereafter, the action of the clerk may be reviewed by the court.

**(2)** ***Attorneys' Fees.***

**(A)** Claims for attorneys' fees and related nontaxable expenses shall be made by motion unless the substantive law governing the action provides for the recovery of such fees as an element of damages to be proved at trial.

**(B)** Unless otherwise provided by statute or order of the court, the motion must be filed and served no later than 14 days after entry of judgment; must specify the judgment and the statute, rule, or other grounds entitling the moving party to the award; and must state the amount or provide a fair estimate of the amount sought. If directed by the court, the motion shall also disclose the terms of any agreement with respect to fees to be paid for the services for which claim is made.

**(C)** On request of a party or class member, the court shall afford an opportunity for adversary submissions with respect to the motion in accordance with Rule 43(e) or Rule 78. The court may determine issues of liability for fees before receiving submissions bearing on issues of evaluation of services for which liability is imposed by the court. The court shall find the facts and state its conclusions of law as provided in Rule 52(a), and a judgment shall be set forth in a separate document as provided in Rule 58.

**(D)** By local rule the court may establish special procedures by which issues relating to such fees may be resolved without extensive evidentiary hearings. In addition, the court may refer issues relating to the value of services to a special master under Rule 53 without regard to the provisions of subdivision (b) thereof and may refer a motion for attorneys' fees to a magistrate judge under Rule 72(b) as if it were a dispositive pretrial matter.

**(E)** The provisions of subparagraphs (A) through (D) do not apply to claims for fees and expenses as sanctions for violations of these rules or under 28 U.S.C. § 1927.

(As amended Dec. 27, 1946, eff. Mar. 19, 1948; Apr. 17, 1961, eff. July 19, 1961; Mar. 2, 1987, eff. Aug. 1, 1987; Apr. 22, 1993, eff. Dec. 1, 1993.)

* * *

## Rule 57. Declaratory Judgments

The procedure for obtaining a declaratory judgment pursuant to Title 28 U.S.C. § 2201, shall be in accordance with these rules, and the right to trial by jury may be demanded under the circumstances and in the manner provided in Rules 38 and 39. The existence of another adequate remedy does not preclude a judgment for declaratory relief in cases where it is appropriate. The court may order a speedy hearing of an action for a declaratory judgment and may advance it on the calendar.

(As amended Dec. 29, 1948, eff. Oct. 20, 1949.)

* * *

## Rule 60. Relief From Judgment or Order

**(a) Clerical Mistakes.** Clerical mistakes in judgments, orders or other parts of the record and errors therein arising from oversight or omission may be corrected by the court at any time of its own initiative or on the motion of any party and after such notice, if any, as the court orders. During the pendency of an appeal, such mistakes may be so corrected before the appeal is docketed in the appellate court, and thereafter while the appeal is pending may be so corrected with leave of the appellate court.

**(b) Mistakes; Inadvertence; Excusable Neglect; Newly Discovered Evidence; Fraud, etc.** On motion and upon such terms as are just, the court may relieve a party or a party's legal representative from a final judgment, order, or proceeding for the following reasons: (1) mistake, inadvertence, surprise, or excusable neglect; (2) newly discovered evidence which by due diligence could not have been discovered in time to move for a new trial under Rule 59(b); (3) fraud (whether heretofore denominated intrinsic or extrinsic), misrepresentation, or other misconduct of an adverse party; (4) the judgment is void; (5) the judgment has been satisfied, released, or discharged, or a prior judgment upon which it is based has been reversed or otherwise vacated, or it is no longer equitable that the judgment should have prospective application; or (6) any other reason justifying relief from the operation of the judgment. The motion shall be made within a reasonable time, and for reasons (1), (2), and (3) not more than one year after the judgment, order, or proceeding was entered or taken. A motion under this subdivision (b) does not affect the finality of a judgment or suspend its operation. This rule does not limit the power of a court to entertain an independent action to relieve a party from a judgment, order, or proceeding, or to grant relief to a defendant not actually personally notified as provided in Title 28, U.S.C., § 1655, or to set aside a judgment for fraud upon the court. Writs of coram nobis, coram vobis, audita querela, and bills of review and bills in the nature of a bill of review, are abolished, and the procedure for obtaining any relief from a judgment shall be by motion as prescribed in these rules or by an independent action.

(As amended Dec. 27, 1946, eff. Mar. 19, 1948; Dec. 29, 1948, eff. Oct. 20, 1949; Mar. 2, 1987, eff. Aug. 1, 1987.)

* * *

## Rule 62. Stay of Proceedings to Enforce a Judgment

**(a) Automatic Stay; Exceptions—Injunctions, Receiverships, and Patent Accountings.** Except as stated herein, no execution shall issue upon a judgment nor shall proceedings be taken for its enforcement until the expiration of 10 days after its entry. Unless otherwise ordered by the court, an interlocutory or final judgment in an action for an injunction or in a receivership action, or a judgment or order directing an accounting in an action for infringement of letters patent, shall not be stayed during the period after its entry and until an appeal is taken or during the pendency of an appeal. The provisions of subdivision (c) of this rule govern the suspending, modifying, restoring, or granting of an injunction during the pendency of an appeal.

**(b) Stay on Motion for New Trial or for Judgment.** In its discretion and on such conditions for the security of the adverse party as are proper, the court may stay the execution of or any proceedings to enforce a judgment pending the disposition of a motion for a new trial or to alter or amend a judgment made pursuant to Rule 59, or of a motion for relief from a judgment or order made pursuant to Rule 60, or of a motion for judgment in accordance with a motion for a directed verdict made pursuant to Rule 50, or of a motion for amendment to the findings or for additional findings made pursuant to Rule 52(b).

**(c) Injunction Pending Appeal.** When an appeal is taken from an interlocutory or final judgment granting, dissolving, or denying an injunction, the court in its discretion may suspend, modify, restore, or grant an injunction during the pendency of the appeal upon such terms as to bond or otherwise as it considers proper for the security of the rights of the adverse party. If the judgment appealed from is rendered by a district court of three judges specially constituted pursuant to a statute of the United States, no such order shall be made except (1) by such court sitting in open court or (2) by the assent of all the judges of such court evidenced by their signatures to the order.

**(d) Stay Upon Appeal.** When an appeal is taken the appellant by giving a supersedeas bond may obtain a stay subject to the exceptions contained in subdivision (a) of this rule. The bond may be given at or after the time of filing the notice of appeal or of procuring the order allowing the appeal, as the case may be. The stay is effective when the supersedeas bond is approved by the court.

**(e) Stay in Favor of the United States or Agency Thereof.** When an appeal is taken by the United States or an officer or agency thereof or by direction of any department of the Government of the United States and the operation or enforcement of the judgment is stayed, no bond, obligation, or other security shall be required from the appellant.

**(f) Stay According to State Law.** In any state in which a judgment is a lien upon the property of the judgment debtor and in which the judgment debtor is entitled to a stay of execution, a judgment debtor is entitled, in the district court held therein, to such stay as would be accorded the judgment debtor had the action been maintained in the courts of that state.

**(g) Power of Appellate Court Not Limited.** The provisions in this rule do not limit any power of an appellate court or of a judge or justice thereof to stay proceedings during the pendency of an appeal or to suspend, modify, restore, or grant an injunction during the pendency of an appeal or to make any order appropriate to preserve the status quo or the effectiveness of the judgment subsequently to be entered.

**(h) Stay of Judgment as to Multiple Claims or Multiple Parties.** When a court has ordered a final judgment under the conditions stated in Rule 54(b), the court may stay enforcement of that judgment until the entering of a subsequent judgment or judgments and may prescribe such conditions as are necessary to secure the benefit thereof to the party in whose favor the judgment is entered.

(As amended Dec. 27, 1946, eff. Mar. 19, 1948; Dec. 29, 1948, eff. Oct. 20, 1949; Apr. 17, 1961, eff. July 19, 1961; Mar. 2, 1987, eff. Aug. 1, 1987.)

* * *

## VIII. PROVISIONAL AND FINAL REMEDIES

### Rule 64. Seizure of Person or Property

At the commencement of and during the course of an action, all remedies providing for seizure of person or property for the purpose of securing satisfaction of the judgment ultimately to be entered in the action are available under the circumstances and in the manner provided by the law of the state in which the district court is held, existing at the time the remedy is sought, subject to the following qualifications: (1) any existing statute of the United States governs to the extent to which it is applicable; (2) the action in which any of the foregoing remedies is used shall be commenced and prosecuted or, if removed from a state court, shall be prosecuted after removal, pursuant to these rules. The remedies thus available include arrest, attachment, garnishment, replevin, sequestration, and other corresponding or equivalent remedies, however designated and regardless of whether by state procedure the remedy is ancillary to an action or must be obtained by an independent action.

### Rule 65. Injunctions

**(a) Preliminary Injunction.**

**(1)** ***Notice.*** No preliminary injunction shall be issued without notice to the adverse party.

**(2)** ***Consolidation of Hearing With Trial on Merits.*** Before or after the commencement of the hearing of an application for a preliminary injunction, the court may order the trial of the action on the merits to be advanced and consolidated with the hearing of the application. Even when this consolidation is not ordered, any evidence received upon an application for a preliminary injunction which would be admissible upon the trial on the merits becomes part of the record on the trial and need not be repeated upon the trial. This subdivision (a)(2) shall be so construed and applied as to save to the parties any rights they may have to trial by jury.

**(b) Temporary Restraining Order; Notice; Hearing; Duration.** A temporary restraining order may be granted without written or oral notice to the adverse party or that party's attorney only if (1) it clearly appears from specific facts shown by affidavit or by the verified complaint that immediate and irreparable injury, loss, or damage will result to the applicant before the adverse party or that party's attorney can be heard in opposition, and (2) the applicant's attorney certifies to the court in writing the efforts, if any, which have been made to give the notice and the reasons supporting the claim that notice should not be required. Every temporary restraining order granted without notice shall be indorsed with the date and hour of issuance; shall be filed forthwith in the clerk's office and entered of record; shall define the injury and state why it is irreparable and why the order was granted without notice; and shall expire by its terms within such time after entry, not to exceed 10 days, as the court fixes, unless within the time so fixed the order, for good cause shown, is extended for a like period or unless the party against whom the order is directed consents that it may be extended for a longer period. The reasons for the extension shall be entered of record. In case a temporary restraining order is granted without notice, the motion for a preliminary injunction shall be set down for hearing at the earliest possible time and takes precedence of all matters except older matters of the same character; and when the motion comes on for hearing the party who obtained the temporary restraining order shall proceed with the application for a preliminary injunction and, if the party does not do so, the court shall dissolve the temporary restraining order. On 2 days' notice to the party who obtained the temporary restraining order without notice or on such shorter notice to that party as the court may prescribe, the adverse party may appear and move its dissolution or modification and in that event the court shall proceed to hear and determine such motion as expeditiously as the ends of justice require.

**(c) Security.** No restraining order or preliminary injunction shall issue except upon the giving of security by the applicant, in such sum as the court deems proper, for the payment of such costs and damages as may be incurred or suffered by any party who is found to have been wrongfully enjoined or restrained. No such security shall be required of the United States or of an officer or agency thereof.

The provisions of Rule 65.1 apply to a surety upon a bond or undertaking under this rule.

**(d) Form and Scope of Injunction or Restraining Order.** Every order granting an injunction and every restraining order shall set forth the reasons for its issuance; shall be specific in terms; shall describe in reasonable detail, and not by reference to the complaint or other document, the act or acts sought to be restrained; and is binding only upon the parties to the action, their officers, agents, servants, employees, and attorneys, and upon those persons in active concert or participation with them who receive actual notice of the order by personal service or otherwise.

**(e) Employer and Employee; Interpleader; Constitutional Cases.** These rules do not modify any statute of the United States relating to temporary restraining orders and preliminary injunctions in actions affecting employer and employee; or the provisions of Title 28, U.S.C., § 2361, relating to preliminary injunctions in actions of interpleader or in the nature of interpleader; or Title 28, U.S.C., § 2284, relating to actions required by Act of Congress to be heard and determined by a district court of three judges.

(As amended Dec. 27, 1946, eff. Mar. 19, 1948; Dec. 29, 1948, eff. Oct. 20, 1949; Feb. 28, 1966, eff. July 1, 1966; Mar. 2, 1987, eff. Aug. 1, 1987.)

## Rule 65.1 Security: Proceedings Against Sureties

Whenever these rules, including the Supplemental Rules for Certain Admiralty and Maritime Claims, require or permit the giving of security by a party, and security is given in the form of a bond or stipulation or other undertaking with one or more sureties, each surety submits to the jurisdiction of the court and irrevocably appoints the clerk of the court as the surety's agent upon whom any papers affecting the surety's liability on the bond or undertaking may be served. The surety's liability may be enforced on motion without the necessity of an independent action. The motion and such notice of the motion as the court prescribes may be served on the clerk of the court, who shall forthwith mail copies to the sureties if their addresses are known.

(Added Feb. 28, 1966, eff. July 1, 1966, and amended Mar. 2, 1987, eff. Aug. 1, 1987.)

## Rule 66. Receivers Appointed by Federal Courts

An action wherein a receiver has been appointed shall not be dismissed except by order of the court. The practice in the administration of estates by receivers or by other similar officers appointed by the court shall be in accordance with the practice heretofore followed in the courts of the United States or as provided in rules promulgated by the district courts. In all other respects the action in which the appointment of a receiver is sought or which is brought by or against a receiver is governed by these rules.

(As amended Dec. 27, 1946, eff. Mar. 19, 1948; Dec. 29, 1948, eff. Oct. 20, 1949.)

## Rule 67. Deposit in Court

In an action in which any part of the relief sought is a judgment for a sum of money or the disposition of a sum of money or the disposition of any other thing capable of delivery, a party, upon notice to every other party, and by leave of court, may deposit with the court all or any part of such sum or thing, whether or not that party claims all or any part of the sum or thing. The party making the deposit shall serve the order permitting deposit on the clerk of the court. Money paid into court under this rule shall be deposited and withdrawn in accordance with the provisions of Title 28, U.S.C., §§ 2041, and 2042; the Act of June 26, 1934, c. 756, § 23, as amended (48 Stat. 1236, 58 Stat. 845), U.S.C., Title 31, § 725v; or any like statute. The fund shall be deposited in an interest-bearing account or invested in an interest-bearing instrument approved by the court.

(As amended Dec. 29, 1948, eff. Oct. 20, 1949; Apr. 28, 1983, eff. Aug. 1, 1983.)

## Rule 68. Offer of Judgment

At any time more than 10 days before the trial begins, a party defending against a claim may serve upon the adverse party an offer to allow judgment to be taken against the defending party for the money or property or to the effect specified in the offer, with costs then accrued. If within 10 days after the service of the offer the adverse party serves written notice that the offer is accepted, either party may then file the offer and notice of acceptance together with proof of service thereof and thereupon the clerk shall enter judgment. An offer not accepted shall be deemed withdrawn and evidence thereof is not admissible except in a proceeding to determine costs. If the judgment finally obtained by the offeree is not more favorable than the offer, the offeree must pay the costs incurred after the making of the offer. The fact that an offer is made but not accepted does not preclude a subsequent offer. When the liability of one party to another has been determined by verdict or order or judgment, but the amount or extent of the liability remains to be determined by further proceedings, the party adjudged liable may make an offer of judgment, which shall have the same effect as an offer made before trial if it is served within a reasonable time not less than 10 days prior to the commencement of hearings to determine the amount or extent of liability.

(As amended Dec. 27, 1946, eff. Mar. 19, 1948; Feb. 28, 1966, eff. July 1, 1966; Mar. 2, 1987, eff. Aug. 1, 1987.)

### Rule 69. Execution

**(a) In General.** Process to enforce a judgment for the payment of money shall be a writ of execution, unless the court directs otherwise. The procedure on execution, in proceedings supplementary to and in aid of a judgment, and in proceedings on and in aid of execution shall be in accordance with the practice and procedure of the state in which the district court is held, existing at the time the remedy is sought, except that any statute of the United States governs to the extent that it is applicable. In aid of the judgment or execution, the judgment creditor or a successor in interest when that interest appears of record, may obtain discovery from any person, including the judgment debtor, in the manner provided in these rules or in the manner provided by the practice of the state in which the district court is held.

**(b) Against Certain Public Officers.** When a judgment has been entered against a collector or other officer of revenue under the circumstances stated in Title 28, U.S.C., § 2006, or against an officer of Congress in an action mentioned in the Act of March 3, 1875, ch. 130, § 8 (18 Stat. 401), U.S.C., Title 2, § 118, and when the court has given the certificate of probable cause for the officer's act as provided in those statutes, execution shall not issue against the officer or the officer's property but the final judgment shall be satisfied as provided in such statutes.

(As amended Dec. 29, 1948, eff. Oct. 20, 1949; Mar. 30, 1970, eff. July 1, 1970; Mar. 2, 1987, eff. Aug. 1, 1987.)

### Rule 70. Judgment for Specific Acts; Vesting Title

If a judgment directs a party to execute a conveyance of land or to deliver deeds or other documents or to perform any other specific act and the party fails to comply within the time specified, the court may direct the act to be done at the cost of the disobedient party by some other person appointed by the court and the act when so done has like effect as if done by the party. On application of the party entitled to performance, the clerk shall issue a writ of attachment or sequestration against the property of the disobedient party to compel obedience to the judgment. The court may also in proper cases adjudge the party in contempt. If real or personal property is within the district, the court in lieu of directing a conveyance thereof may enter a judgment divesting the title of any party and vesting it in others and such judgment has the effect of a conveyance executed in due form of law. When any order or judgment is for the delivery of possession, the party in whose favor it is entered is entitled to a writ of execution or assistance upon application to the clerk.

* * *

# Index

References are to Pages

References are to Pages

†

0-314-06778-7

90000

9 780314 067784